"The 2000 presidential election was such a close call— how does that happen? I wonder if it has happened before."

"How am I going to be sure I know all this material for the test? I feel confident now, but..."

"I understand that the Bill of Rights is important, but how is it used in real life?"

mypoliscilab™

Where participation leads to action!

with LongmanParticipate.com 3.0 inside!

This TIMELINE ACTIVITY examines other close-call elections in our history.

PRE-TESTS, POST-TESTS, CHAPTER EXAMS and **STUDY GUIDES** for each chapter of your book help students prepare for exams.

This SIMULATION ACTIVITY helps students judge whether a police officer who is breaking and entering is violating civil rights.

Available in CourseCompass, Web CT, & Blackboard

mypoliscilab™
Where participation leads to action!
with LongmanParticipate.com 3.0 inside!

F rom **simulations** that place students in the role of campaign manager to **timeline activities**, from **pre- and post-chapter tests** to a fully integrated **Ebook**, MyPoliSciLab brings together an amazing collection of resources for both students and instructors. See a demo now at **www.mypoliscilab.com**!

Here's what's in MyPoliSciLab—

Pre-Test, Post Test, and Chapter Exam.
For each chapter of the text, students will navigate through a pre-test, post-test, and a full chapter exam—all fully integrated with the online Ebook so students can assess, review, and improve their understanding of the material in each chapter.

Ebook.
Matching the exact layout of the printed textbook, the Ebook contains multimedia icons in the margins that launch a wealth of exciting resources.

 ### Chapter Review.
For each chapter, students will find additional resources, such as a complete study guide, learning objectives, a summary, and Web explorations.

Research Navigator™.
This database provides thousands of articles from popular periodicals like *Newsweek* and *USA Today* that give students and professors access to topical content from a variety of sources.

New York Times Online Feed & The New York Times Search by Subject™ Archive.
Both provide free access to the full text of *The New York Times* and articles from the world's leading journalists of the *Times*. The online feed provides students with updated headlines and political news on an hourly basis.

LongmanParticipate.com 3.0
Our well-known and highly respected online tool is now fully updated. Students will find over 100 simulations, interactive timelines, comparative exercises and more—all integrated with the online ebook. Available inside MyPoliSciLab or as a website alone.

LongmanParticipate.com 3.0
Inside!

Go to mypoliscilab.com for a free demo.

www.longmanparticipate.com

LongmanParticipate.com version 3.0 inside MyPoliSciLab or as a website alone!

Within the margins of your textbook you will find these icons directing students to the LongmanParticipate.com activities, which will correspond to the chapter content. Now fully updated with brand new activities!

Longman Participate Activities:

SIMULATION. Students are given a role to play —such as Congress member, lobbyist, or police officer—and experience the challenges and excitement of politics firsthand.

VISUAL LITERACY. Students interpret and apply data about intriguing political topics. Each activity begins with an interactive primer on reading graphics.

TIMELINE. With an abundance of media and graphics, students can step through the evolution of an aspect of government.

PARTICIPATION. Bringing the importance of politics home, these activities appear as three types: 1.) Debates, 2.) Surveys, and 3.) Get Involved activities.

COMPARATIVE. Students compare the U.S. political system to that of other countries.

INSTRUCTORS:

Course Management System—

MyPoliSciLab is available in different versions to fit your needs:
- MyPoliSciLab in CourseCompass™
- MyPoliSciLab in Blackboard
- MyPoliSciLab in WebCT

Website alone—
If you do not want a course management system, the LongmanParticipate.com 3.0 activities are available in a website-alone version.

STUDENTS:

If your text did not come with an access code to MyPoliSciLab, you can still get this amazing resource to help you succeed in the course. Just go to www.mypoliscilab.com and click on "How do I get access to mypoliscilab?"

Go to mypoliscilab.com for a free demo.

Where participation leads to action!

American Government

American Government

Continuity and Change

Alternate 2004 Election Update Edition

KAREN O'CONNOR

Professor of Government
American University

LARRY J. SABATO

University Professor
and Robert Kent Gooch Professor of Politics
University of Virginia

PEARSON

Longman

New York San Francisco Boston
London Toronto Sydney Tokyo Singapore Madrid
Mexico City Munich Paris Cape Town Hong Kong Montreal

Vice President/Publisher: Priscilla McGeehon
Executive Editor: Eric Stano
Development Director: Lisa Pinto
Development Editor: Karen Helfrich
Senior Marketing Manager: Megan Galvin-Fak
Media Editor: Patrick McCarthy
Production Manager: Eric Jorgensen
Editorial Assistant: Kara Wylie
Project Coordination, Text Design, Art Studio, and Electronic Page Makeup:
    Electronic Publishing Services Inc., NYC
Project Management for Election Update: Sunflower Publishing Services
Cover Designer/Manager: Nancy Danahy
Cover Images: ©Getty Images Inc.–Stone; Getty Images, Inc.–The Image Bank
Photo Research: Photosearch, Inc.
Senior Manufacturing Buyer: Alfred C. Dorsey
Printer and Binder: RR Donnelley & Sons, Co.
Cover Printer: Phoenix Color Corp.

For permission to use copyrighted material, grateful acknowledgment is made to the copyright holders on the pages where the material appears.

Library of Congress Cataloging-in-Publication Data

O'Connor, Karen, 1952–
    American government: continuity and change / Karen O'Connor, Larry J. Sabato.—2004 alternate election update ed.
        p. cm.
    Includes bibliographical references and index.
    ISBN 0-321-29859-4 (Election Update.)
        1. United States—Politics and government. I. Sabato, Larry. II. Title.
JK276.O23 2003
320.473—dc21

                                2002040568

Visit our Web site at http://www.ablongman.com.

ISBN 0-321-29859-4 (Election Update.)

1 2 3 4 5 6 7 8 9 10—DOW—06 05 04

PEARSON
Longman

To Meghan,
who grew up with this book

Karen O'Connor

To my Introduction to American Politics
students over the years, who all know that
"politics is a good thing"

Larry Sabato

Brief Contents

PART I   FOUNDATIONS OF GOVERNMENT

PART II   INSTITUTIONS OF GOVERNMENT

PART III   POLITICAL BEHAVIOR

APPENDICES

**How it Happened! The 2004 Race for the White House
as reported in the *New York Times* following page 708.**

Detailed Contents

CHAPTER 12   Political Parties   435

CHAPTER 13   Voting and Elections   489

**How it Happened! The 2004 Race for the White House
as reported in the *New York Times* following page 708.**

*I*t has happened again. As we have prepared every new edition of this book over the last decade, we find ourselves unfailingly surprised, challenged, and ultimately riveted by the dramatic changes that continue to take place across our political landscape. In 1992, the year this book first saw print, we experienced the "Year of the Woman" that produced record numbers of women elected to national office. Then, in 1994, we were greeted with the "Year of Angry Male Voter" that produced a Republican revolution in Congress. The editions that followed those years appeared during various phases of the Clinton scandals, including the second impeachment trial of a U.S. President. Then came the 2000 election, when the outcome did not occur until December and appeared to be decided by a single Supreme Court Justice, the terrorist attacks of September 11, 2001, and the history-bucking 2002 midterm elections that returned control of both houses of Congress to the Republicans.

Little did we realize that, not long after those midterm elections, one of the longest, most expensive, divisive, and impassioned campaigns ever for the presidency was about to get underway. The 2004 election was dominated by heated discussion of the preemptive war in Iraq and debates about terrorism, the economy, and social issues like gay marriage. We saw the emergence of so-called 527's as a powerful (and well-financed) political force, unprecedented "get out the vote" efforts by both Republicans and Democrats, and a closely divided and hotly charged electorate that returned George W. Bush to office with a majority of the popular vote and a solid win in the Electoral College.

It can never be said that American politics is boring. For every edition of this text, something unexpected or extraordinarily unusual has occurred, giving question to the old adage, "Politics as usual." At least on the national level, there appears to be little that is usual. Politics and policy form a vital, fascinating process that affects all our daily lives, and we hope that this text reflects that phenomenon and provides you with the tools to understand politics as an evolutionary process where history matters.

In less than a decade, our perceptions of politics, the role of the media, and the utility of voting appear to have undergone tremendous change. Since its inception, this text has tried diligently to reflect those changes and to present information about politics in a manner to engage students actively—many of whom have little interest in politics when they come into the classroom. In this edition, we try to build on a solid, tried-and-true base and at the same time to present information about how politics now seems to be changing at an ever more rapid pace. Thus, we present new information that we hope will whet students' appetites to learn more about politics while providing them with all of the information they need to make informed decisions about their government, politics, and politicians. We very much want our students to make such decisions. We very much want them to *participate*. Our goal with this text is to transmit just this sort of practical, useful information while creating and fostering student interest in American politics despite growing national skepticism about government and government officials at all levels. In fact, we hope that this new edition of our text will explain the national mood about politics and put it in a better context for students to understand their important role in a changing America.

APPROACH

We believe that one cannot fully understand the actions, issues, and policy decisions facing the U.S. government, its constituent states, or "the people" unless these issues are examined from the perspective of how they have evolved over time. Consequently, the title of this book is *American Government: Continuity and Change*. In its pages, we try to examine how the United States is governed today by looking not just at present behavior but also at the Framers' intentions and how they have been implemented and adapted over the years. For example, we believe that it is critical to an understanding of the role of political parties in the United States to understand the Framers' fears of factionalism, how parties evolved, and when and why realignments in party identification occurred.

In addition to questions raised by the Framers, we explore issues that the Framers could never have envisioned, and how the basic institutions of government have changed in responding to these new demands. For instance, no one more than two centuries ago could have foreseen election campaigns in an age when nearly all American homes contain television sets, and the Internet and fax machines allow instant access to information. Moreover, increasing citizen demands and expectations have routinely forced government reforms, making an understanding of the dynamics of change essential for introductory students.

Our overriding concern is that students understand their government as it exists today, so that they may become better citizens and make better choices. We believe that by providing students with information about government, explaining why it is important, and why their participation counts, students will come to see that politics can be a good thing.

To understand their government at all levels, students must understand how it was designed in the Constitution. Each chapter, therefore, approaches its topics from a combination of perspectives, which we believe will facilitate this approach. In writing this book, we chose to put the institutions of government (Part II) before political behavior (Part III). Both sections, however, were written independently, making them easy to switch for those who prefer to teach about the actors in government and elections before discussing its institutions. To test the book, each of us has taught from it in both orders, with no pedagogical problems.

WHAT'S CHANGED IN THIS EDITION?

In this 2004 Election Update Edition of *American Government: Continuity and Change,* we have retained our basic approach to the study of politics as a constantly changing and often unpredictable enterprise. But we also discuss the dizzying array of important events that have taken place since the book last published. Most importantly, we include in-depth coverage of the 2004 campaign for the presidency and its results. We discuss the issues that were paramount during the long election season, including debates over the war in Iraq, leadership and terrorism, the economy, and issues like gay marriage and "moral values." We examine the financing of elections in the wake of campaign finance reform and the emergence of so-called 527 groups, and we include analysis and tallies of both the expenditures and votes for George W. Bush and John Kerry.

Chapter Changes

Many of these changes and others are reflected in this 2004 Election Update. **Chapter 1** contains updated figures on the changing demographics of the United States and new information on voter turnout. **Chapter 2** includes an expanded discussion of the Constitutional Convention debate over the question of slavery. **Chapter 3** discusses the state of state budgets, marriage in the federal system, and the issue of access to abortion. **Chapter 4** includes a new discussion of the growing strength of the Republican Party in state legislatures and governors' offices in the South, and an analysis of the impact of state and local taxes. **Chapter 5** includes a completely revised discussion of obscenity as well as updates on the assault weapon ban, Partial Birth Abortion Ban Act, and the impact of *Lawrence* v. *Texas*. **Chapter 6** has been revised to update coverage of gay rights and affirmative action. **Chapter 7** includes complete coverage of the membership of the 109th Congress, the 2004 elections, a new "Politics Now" box on a minority bill of rights, and judicial nominations. **Chapter 8** begins with a new vignette on Ronald Reagan's funeral and includes updated coverage of the first term of the George W. Bush administration. **Chapter 9** begins with a new vignette on Robert Mueller, John Ashcroft, and homeland security. It also includes updated figures and data on the federal workforce and new coverage of e-government. **Chapter 10** offers updates on the Supreme Court's 2003-04 term, William Rehnquist's illness, judicial appointments, and the characteristics of appointees. **Chapter 11** includes updates on Americans' political knowledge, political behavior in the 2004 election (including exit poll data), tracking polls, exit polling, and the National Election Pool. **Chapter 12** begins with a new vignette on party conventions and contains updated data on party unity, fundraising, identification, and an exploration of "Red and Blue" America. **Chapter 13** features an opening vignette on the 2004 presidential election campaign and contains new data and updated figures on election results, voter turnout, and demographics. **Chapter 14** examines the highly contentious 2004 presidential election, with special attention to new campaign finance regulations and the advertising strategies utilized by both campaigns. **Chapter 15** evaluates the media coverage of major news events in 2004, and also features an updated discussion of how politicians use the media, including a discussion about argumentative news shows like CNN's Crossfire. **Chapter 16** begins with a new vignette on MoveOn.org and Swift Boat Veterans, provides updates on interest group activity in the 2004 election (including the efforts of the Christian Coalition, NRA, and organized labor), and includes new coverage of "Rock the Vote," 527s, and the success of women's PACs in 2004 election.

We have also made a major effort to make certain that this edition contains the most up-to-date scholarship by political scientists, not only on how government works, but what they have said on contemporary debates.

In addition to chapter-by-chapter changes, we developed new features in the 2004 edition designed to enhance student understanding of the political processes, institutions, and policies of American government.

Join the Debate.   To engage students in critical thinking, foster interest in important issues, and help inspire their participation through involvement in decision-making and taking a stand, we developed a *Join the Debate* feature. Included in most chapters, this two-page feature introduces a provocative issue under debate today and explores that issue through a reprinted news article, news commentary, or radio transcript. Topics such as chapter 3's "Should the Federal Government Preempt State Laws?" or chapter 5's "Do 'Three Strikes' Laws Abridge Civil Liberties?" are accompanied by supporting questions and guidance from the authors and are designed to prompt students to examine various arguments in the debate, consider larger context, and take a position on issues that matter in American government today.

Analyzing Visuals.   A feature designed to encourage visual literacy, *Analyzing Visuals* helps students make sense of quantitative and qualitative information presented visually and enables them to get the most out of graphic representations. Building on the popular *Analyzing the Data* feature in the last edition, this new feature examines a greater variety of images, including news photographs and political cartoons, as well as tables, bar graphs, line graphs, maps, and charts. In addition, students are encouraged to analyze and interpret the visual information themselves, using the introductory captions, pointers, and critical thinking questions provided to guide them. A new introductory section, *Analyzing Visuals: A Brief Guide* (see pages xxxviii–xli), offers a foundation for analyzing and interpreting different kinds of visuals that students will encounter in the text. In addition to helping students examine the *Analyzing Visuals* features throughout the book, this introduction offers strategies and suggested questions that can be applied to all the visuals in the text. Topics range from chapter 1's "Changing Age Composition of the United States" to chapter 6's "Police Confront Civil Rights Demonstrators in Birmingham" to chapter 16's "Top Lobbying Expenditures." These visual learning features appear twice per chapter.

FEATURES

The 2004 Election Update Edition has retained the best features and pedagogy from previous editions and added exciting new ones.

Historical Perspective

Every chapter uses history to serve three purposes: first, to show how institutions and processes have evolved to their present states; second, to provide some of the color that makes information memorable; and third, to provide students with a more thorough appreciation that our government was born amid burning issues of representation and power, issues that continue to smolder today. A richer historical texture helps to explain the present.

Comparative Perspective

Changes in Russia, Eastern Europe, North America, South America, and Asia all remind us of the preeminence of democracy, in theory if not always in fact. As new democratic experiments spring up around the globe, it becomes increasingly important for students to understand the rudiments of presidential versus parliamentary government and of multiparty versus two-party systems. To put American government in perspective, we continue to draw comparisons with Great Britain within the text discussion. *Global Politics* boxes compare U.S. politics and institutions with industrialized democracies and non-Western countries such as Russia, Egypt, India, China, and Indonesia.

Enhanced Pedagogy

We have revised and enhanced many pedagogical features to help students become stronger political thinkers and to echo the book's theme of evolving change.

Preview and Review.   To pique students' interest and draw them into each chapter, we begin each chapter with a contemporary vignette. These vignettes, including how eighteen-year-olds acquired the vote, how special interests are lobbying Congress for laws to allow them to go after student debtors, and congressional efforts to deal with violence in public schools in the aftermath of the Columbine shooting, frequently deal with issues of high interest to students, which we hope will whet their appetites to read the rest of the chapter. Each vignette is followed by a bridge paragraph linking the vignette with the chapter's topics and by a roadmap previewing the chapter's major headings. Chapter Summaries restate the major points made under each of these same major headings.

Key Terms.   Glossary definitions are included in the margins of the text for all bold-faced key terms. Key terms are listed once more at the end of each chapter, with page references for review and study.

Special Features.   Each chapter contains several boxed features in keeping with its theme of continuity and change:

- *Global Politics* To put American government in perspective, these boxes compare U.S. politics with that of other nations. Many of these boxes now include comparisons to non-Western nations such as Egypt, India, China, Russia, and Indonesia; some focus on specific issues such as chapter 11's "Public Opinion on Threats to Personal Safety" and chapter 15's "Media Freedom".

- *Politics Now* These extremely contemporary boxes act as a counterpoint to the text's traditional focus on the "roots of government". Based on current clippings, editorials, and moments in time, these boxes are designed to encourage students to think about current issues in the context of the continuing evolution of the American political system. Chapter 5, for example, examines "Civil Liberties and the Bush Administration," and the USA Patriot Act, in particular. Chapter 6 examines the re-introduction of the Equal Rights Amendment in 2002.

- *Continuity & Change* These sections conclude each chapter. They encourage students to think critically and demonstrate with key issues the book's theme of change in America. Many of these sections were revised for the 2004 Edition. Chapter 3, for example, examines the issue of taxation and sales on the Internet. We have retained the popular "Cast Your Vote" student polling questions found at the end of each *Continuity & Change* section.

Selected chapters also have the following special features:

- *Roots of Government* These historical boxes highlight the role that a particular institution, process, or person has played in the course of American politics as it has evolved to the present. Chapter 5, for example, examines the American Civil Liberties Union, while chapter 10 looks at John Marshall's impact on the Supreme Court and the course of U.S. politics.

- *On Campus* These boxes focus in particular on material that we believe will be of great interest to *students*. To that end, this feature examines issues of concern to college campuses, as well as issues, events, or legislation that were initiated on college campuses and that had an impact on the larger arena of American politics. Chapter 5, for example, looks at political speech and mandatory student fees. Chapter 2 describes how one college student's term paper led to the ratification of a constitutional amendment. Chapter 14 examines the role of college campuses in hosting presidential debates.

Web Explorations 🌐

Each chapter contains several links to the World Wide Web through our book-specific Web site. Identified in the margins with an icon, Web Explorations encourage students to learn more and think critically about a specific issue or concept (e.g., "For more about local gun initiatives, go to **www.ablongman.com/oconnor**"). The book Web site also contains a "page search" feature. A student need only enter the page number on which the icon appears to be taken automatically to the appropriate online content.

MyPoliSciLab for *American Government* with Longman Participate.com 3.0 inside!

MyPoliSciLab is a state of the art, interactive online solution for your course. Available in CourseCompass, Blackboard, and WebCT, MyPoliSciLab offers students a wealth of simulations, interactive exercises, and assessment tools—all integrated with an online e-book version of this book. For each chapter, students will navigate through a pre-test, post-test, chapter review, and a full chapter exam, allowing them to review, and improve their understanding of key concepts. In addition to the online chapter content and assessment, students will have access to LongmanParticipate.com (updated 3.0 version), Longman's best-selling interactive online tool, which offers over 100 exercises for students. LongmanParticipate.com (3.0) is also available as a website alone. A free sixth month subscription to MyPoliSciLab or LongmanParticipate.com 3.0 is available when an access card to either site is ordered packaged with this text. To find out more about MyPoliSciLab, visit www.mypoliscilab.com. To find out more about LongmanParticpate.com 3.0, visit www.longmanparticipate.com.

THE ANCILLARY PACKAGE

The ancillary package for *American Government: Continuity and Change, Alternate 2004 Edition*, reflects the pedagogical goals of the text: to provide information in a useful context and with colorful examples. We have tried especially hard to provide materials that are useful for instructors and helpful to students.

Instructor Supplements

Instructor's Manual.   Written by Sue Davis of Denison University. Includes chapter overviews, chapter outlines, learning objectives, key terms, and valuable teaching suggestions for all chapters.

Test Bank.   Written by J. Aaron Knight of Houston Community College. Contains hundreds of challenging and thoroughly revised multiple choice, true-false, and essay questions along with an answer key.

TestGen EQ CD-ROM.   The printed Test Bank is also available through our computerized testing system, TestGen EQ. This fully networkable, user-friendly program enables instructors to view and edit questions, add their own questions, and print tests in a variety of formats.

MyPoliSciLab and LongmanParticipate.com 3.0 Faculty Teaching Guide. Contains chapter-by-chapter detailed summaries for each of the sites' interactive activities, as well as a list of concepts covered, recommendations about how to integrate the sites into coursework, and discussion questions and paper topics for every exercise. Instructors may use the table of contents in the front of the guide to locate information on a given activity icon that appears in the margin of their adopted textbook. This guide also provides faculty with detailed instructions and screen shots showing how to use MyPoliSciLab and LongmanParticipate.com, how to register on the sites, and how to set up and use the administrative features. The introductory chapter describes the numerous additional resources included on the Websites. Written by Scott Furlong of University of Wisconsin.

Digital Media Archive Instructor Presentation CD-Rom for American Government.   A cross-platform CD-ROM that contains electronic images from Longman's American government textbooks, line art, graphics, and audio and video clips that you can easily download into your own electronic presentation program.

PowerPoint® Presentation.   A lecture outline presentation to accompany all the chapters of this new edition along with graphics from the book. See the companion Web site at *www.ablongman.com/oconnor* to download the presentations.

Transparencies.   Full-color acetates of the figures from all chapters of the book.

Interactive American Government Video.   Contains twenty-seven video segments on topics ranging from the term limit debate to Internet pornography to women in the Citadel. Critical thinking questions accompany each clip, encouraging students to "interact" with the videos by analyzing their content and the concepts they address.

Politics in Action Video.   Eleven "lecture-launchers" covering subjects from conducting a campaign to the passage of a bill. Includes narrated videos, interviews, edited documentaries, original footage, and political ads.

American Government Video Program.   Qualified adopters can peruse our list of videos for the American government classroom.

Active Learning Guide for American Government.   This unique guide offers an abundance of innovative suggestions for classroom projects and teaching strategies—including scenarios, role plays, and debates—that will get students actively involved in course material. Written by Richard H. Foster, Mark K. McBeth, Joseph Morris, Sean K. Anderson, and Mark Mussman.

Online Course Management.   Longman offers comprehensive online course management systems such as CourseCompass, WebCT, and BlackBoard in conjunction with this text. These systems provide complete content, class roster, online quizzing and testing, grade administration, and more, over the Internet. Please contact your local Allyn & Bacon/Longman representative for more information.

Student Supplements

MyPoliSciLab for American Government with LongmanParticipate.com 3.0.
MyPoliSciLab is a state of the art, interactive online solution for your course. Available in CourseCompass, Blackboard, and WebCT, MyPoliSciLab offers students a wealth of simulations, interactive exercises, and assessment tools—all integrated with an online e-book version of this book. For each chapter, students will navigate through a pre-test, post-test, chapter review, and a full chapter exam, allowing them to assess, review, and improve their understanding of key concepts. In addition to the online chapter content and assessment, students will have access to LongmanParticipate.com (updated 3.0 version), Longman's best-selling interactive online tool which offers over 100 exercises for students. These exercises include:

- *Simulations* putting students in the role of a political actor.
- *Visual Literacy* exercises getting students interpreting, manipulating, and applying data.
- *Interactive Timelines* enabling students to experience the evolution of an aspect of government.
- *Participation* activities that personalize politics by either getting students involved or exploring their own thoughts and opinions about our system.
- *Comparative* exercises that have students compare aspects of our system to those of other countries.

Students receive feedback at every step, and instructors can track student work through the gradebook feature of their chosen course management system. The activities for the sites were written and revised by **Quentin Kidd,** *Christopher Newport University,* and **William Field,** *Temple University.*

Activities and content for previous versions of the sites were written by: **James Brent,** *San Jose State University;* **Laura Roselle,** *Elon College;* **Denise Scheberle,** *University of Wisconsin;* **B. Thomas Schuman,** *University of New Hampshire;* **Sharon Spray,** *Elon College;* **Cara Strebe,** *San Francisco State University;* **Ruth Ann Strickland,** *Appalachian State University;* **Kaare Strøm,** *University of California, San Diego;* **David Tabb,** *San Francisco State University;* **Paul Benson,** *Tarrant County Community College;* and **Stephen Sandweiss,** *Tacoma Community College.*

LongmanParticipate.com 3.0 is also available as a website alone. A free sixth month subscription to MyPoliSciLab or LongmanParticipate.com 3.0 is available when an access code to either site is ordered packaged with this text. To find out more, visit www.mypoliscilab.com or www.longmanparticipate.com.

Companion Web Site *(www.ablongman.com/oconnor).*

- *Web Explorations*—critical thinking Web exercises (referenced in the text through icons in the margins). The "page search" feature on the site allows students to enter the page number on which they find the icon and be taken right to the content.
- *Practice Tests*—multiple choice, true/false, fill-in-the-blank, and essay questions.
- *Summaries*
- *Online Research and Citation Guide*

Study Guide.   Written by John Ben Sutter of Houston Community College. The printed study guide features chapter outlines, key terms, a variety of practice tests, and critical thinking questions to help students learn.

Study Wizard CD-ROM.   Written by David Dupree of Victor Valley College. This interactive study guide helps students master concepts in the text through practice tests, chapter and topic summaries, and a comprehensive interactive glossary. Students receive immediate feedback on practice tests in the form of answer explanations and page references in the text to go to for extra help. FREE when ordered packaged with the text.

iSearch Guide for Political Science.   This brief yet complete online research guide offers: step-by-step instructions for using the Internet to do research, critical thinking exercises, and information about evaluating sites for academic usefulness. The guide also includes a **FREE access card to the Research Navigator Online Research Database.**

ResearchNavigator.com.   This complete online research resource features: the *New York Times* Search-By-Subject database of articles; ContentSelect, a customized, searchable collection of 25,000+ discipline-specific articles; The *New York Times* "Themes of the Times" collections; Link Library; and more. Access codes come in the iSearch Guide described above.

New York Times Discount Subscription.   A ten-week subscription for only $20! Contact your local Allyn & Bacon/Longman representative for more information.

Culture War? The Myth of a Polarized America.   By Morris P. Fiorina, Stanford University, Samual J. Abrams, Harvard University, and Jeremy C. Pope, Stanford University. The first book in the "Great Questions in Politics" series, *Culture War? The Myth of a Polarized America* combines polling data with a compelling narrative to debunk commonly-believed myths about American politics—particularly the claim that Americans are deeply divided in their fundamental political views.

You Decide! Current Debates in American Politics, 2005 Edition.   Edited by John T. Rourke, University of Connecticut, the new edition of this debate-style reader examines the most current and provocative issues in American politics today. The topics have been selected for their currency, importance, and student interest, and the pieces that argue various sides of a given issue come from recent journals, congressional hearings, think tanks, and periodicals. Free when packaged with this text.

Voices of Dissent: Critical Readings in American Politics, Fifth Edition.   Edited by William F. Grover, St. Michael's College, and Joseph G. Peschek, Hamline University, this collection of critical essays goes beyond the debate between mainstream liberalism and conservatism to fundamentally challenge the status quo. Available at a discount when ordered packaged with the text.

Ten Things That Every American Government Student Should Read.   Edited by Karen O'Connor, American University. We asked American government instructors across the country to vote for ten things beyond the text that they believe every student should read and put them in this brief and useful reader. Free when ordered packaged with the text.

Choices: An American Government Database Reader.   This customizable reader allows instructors to choose from a database of over 300 readings to create a reader that exactly matches their course needs. Go to *www.pearsoncustom.com/database/ choices.html* for more information.

Discount Subscription to Newsweek Magazine.   Students receive twelve issues of *Newsweek* at more than 80% off the regular price. An excellent way for students to keep up with current events.

Penguin–Longman Value Bundles.   Longman offers twenty-five Penguin Putnam titles at more than a 60% discount when packaged with any Longman text. A totally unique offer and a wonderful way to enhance students' understanding of concepts in American Government. Please go to *www.ablongman.com/penguin* for more information.

Writing in Political Science, 3/e.   By Diane Schmidt. Take students step-by-step through all aspects of writing in political science. Available at a discount when ordered packaged with any Longman textbook.

Getting Involved: A Guide to Student Citizenship.   By Mark Kann, Todd Belt, Gabriela Cowperthwaite, and Steven Horn. A unique and practical handbook that guides students through political participation with concrete advice and extensive sample material—letters, telephone scripts, student interviews, and real-life anecdotes—for getting involved and making a difference in their lives and communities.

Texas Politics Supplement, 3/e.   By Debra St. John. A ninety-page primer on state and local government and issues in Texas. Free when shrink-wrapped with the text.

California Politics Supplement, 3/e.   A seventy-page primer on state and local government and issues in California. Free when shrink-wrapped with the text.

Florida Politics Supplement.   By John Bertalan. A fifty-page primer on state and local government and issues in Florida. Free when shrink-wrapped with the text.

ACKNOWLEDGMENTS

Karen O'Connor thanks the thousands of students in her American Government courses at Emory and American University who, over the years, have pushed her to learn more about American government and to have fun in the process. She especially thanks her American University colleagues who offered books and suggestions for this most recent revision—especially Gregg Ivers and David Lublin. Her former professor and longtime friend and co-author, Nancy E. McGlen, has offered support for more than two decades. Her former students, too, have contributed in various ways to this project, especially John R. Hermann, Paul Fabrizio, Bernadette Nye, Sue Davis, Laura van Assendelft, and Sarah Brewer.

For this edition of the book, Ali Yanus, a brilliant undergraduate, offered invaluable assistance. Her fresh perspectives on politics and ideas about things of interest to students, as well as her keen eye for the typo, has greatly benefited the book. Her unbelievably hard work has made this a much better book.

Larry J. Sabato would like to acknowledge the students, past and present in his University of Virginia Introduction to American Politics class, who have offered many valuable suggestions and much thoughtful feedback. He would also like to thank the past and present staff and interns at the UVA Center for Politics—especially communications director Joshua Scott and head teaching assistant Greg Smith, who were truly instrumental in the process of revising this particular edition. Other staff member, interns, and colleagues who helped with this and previous editions of the textbook include, but are not limited to: Jonathan Carr, Howard Ernst, Edwin Fields, Rakesh Gopalan, Jordan Gottfried, Bruce Larson, Matt Smyth, and Matthew Wikswo. Finally, he extends his thanks to the faculty and staff of the Department of Politics at the University of Virginia, especially Debbie Best, Robert Fatton, and Lawrence Schack.

Particular thanks from both of us go to Dennis L. Dresang at the University of Wisconsin–Madison, who co-authored chapter 4 (State and Local Government). We also thank David Potter of Nanzan University, who prepared the Global Politics features, Stefan Haag for his help with many of the Analyzing Visuals features, and Gary Keith for his help with many of the Join the Debate features.

In the now many years we have been writing and rewriting this book, we have been blessed to have been helped by many people at Macmillan, Allyn & Bacon, and now Longman. Eric Stano has been a fantastic editor as well as fun to work with. Our development editor, Karen Helfrich, and our marketing manager, Elizabeth Fogarty, have also done terrific jobs and made this a better book. We would also like to acknowledge the tireless efforts of the Allyn & Bacon/Longman sales force. In the end, we hope that all of these talented people see how much their work and support have helped us to write a better book.

Many of our peers reviewed past editions of the book and earned our gratitude in the process:

Danny Adkison, *Oklahoma State University*

Weston H. Agor, *University of Texas at El Paso*

Victor Aikhionbare, *Salt Lake Community College*

James Anderson, *Texas A&M University*

Judith Baer, *Texas A&M University*

Ruth Bamberger, *Drury College*

Christine Barbour, *Indiana University*

Jon Bond, *Texas A&M University*

Stephen A. Borrelli, *University of Alabama*

Ann Bowman, *University of South Carolina*

Robert C. Bradley, *Illinois State University*

Gary Brown, *Montgomery College*

John Francis Burke, *University of Houston–Downtown*

Greg Caldeira, *Ohio State University*

David E. Camacho, *Northern Arizona University*

Alan R. Carter, *Schenectady County Community College*

Carl D. Cavalli, *North Georgia College and State University*

Steve Chan, *University of Colorado*

Richard Christofferson Sr. *University of Wisconsin–Stevens Point*

David Cingranelli, *State University of New York, Binghamton*

Clarke E. Cochran, *Texas Tech University*

Anne N. Costain, *University of Colorado*

Cary Covington, *University of Iowa*

Stephen C. Craig, *University of Florida*

Lane Crothers, *Illinois State University*

Abraham L. Davis, *Morehouse College*

Robert DiClerico, *West Virginia University*

John Dinan, *Wake Forest University*

John Domino, *Sam Houston State University*

Keith L. Doughtery, *St. Mary's College of Maryland*

David E. Dupree, *Victor Valley College*

Craig F. Emmert, *Texas Tech University*

Walle Engedayehu, *Prairie View A&M University*

Alan S. Engel, *Miami University*

Frank B. Feigert, *University of North Texas*

Evelyn Fink, *University of Nebraska*

Scott R. Furlong, *University of Wisconsin–Green Bay*

James D. Gleason, *Victoria College*

Sheldon Goldman, *University of Massachusetts, Amherst*

Doris Graber, *University of Illinois at Chicago*

Jeffrey D. Green, *University of Montana*

Roger W. Green, *University of North Dakota*

Charles Hadley, *University of New Orleans*

Mel Hailey, *Abilene Christian University*

William K. Hall, *Bradley University*

Robert L. Hardgrave Jr. *University of Texas at Austin*

Chip Hauss, *George Mason University/University of Reading*

Stacia L. Haynie, *Louisiana State University*

John R. Hermann, *Trinity University*

Marjorie Hershey, *Indiana University*

Steven Alan Holmes, *Bakersfield College*

Cornell Hooton, *Emory University*

Jon Hurwitz, *University of Pittsburgh*

Thomas Hyde, *Pfeiffer University*

Joseph Ignagni, *University of Texas at Arlington*

Willoughby Jarrell, *Kennesaw State College*

Susan M. Johnson, *University of Wisconsin–Whitewater*

Dennis Judd, *University of Missouri–St. Louis*

Carol J. Kamper, *Rochester Community College*

Kenneth Kennedy, *College of San Mateo*

Donald F. Kettl, *University of Wisconsin*

Quentin Kidd, *Christopher Newport University*

John Kincaid, *University of North Texas*

Karen M. King, *Bowling Green State University*

Alec Kirby, *University of Wisconsin–Stout*

Jonathan E. Kranz, *John Jay College of Criminal Justice*

John C. Kuzenski, *The Citadel*

Mark Landis, *Hofstra University*

Sue Lee, *North Lake College*

Ted Lewis, *Collin County Community College*

Brad Lockerbie, *University of Georgia*

Cecilia Manrique, *University of Wisconsin–La Crosse*

Larry Martinez, *California State University–Long Beach*

Lynn Mather, *Dartmouth College*

Laurel A. Mayer, *Sinclair Community College*

Steve Mazurana, *University of Northern Colorado*

Clifton McCleskey, *University of Virginia*

James L. McDowell, *Indiana State University*

Carl E. Meacham, *State University of New York, Oneonta*

Stephen S. Meinhold, *University of North Carolina–Wilmington*

Mark C. Miller, *Clark University*

Kenneth F. Mott, *Gettysburg College*

Joseph Nogee, *University of Houston*

Mary Alice Nye, *University of North Texas*

John O'Callaghan, *Suffolk University*

Bruce Oppenheimer, *Vanderbilt University*

Richard Pacelle, *University of Missouri–St. Louis*

Marian Lief Palley, *University of Delaware*

David R. Penna, *Gallaudet University*

Richard M. Pious, *Columbia University*

David H. Provost, *California State University–Fresno*

Lawrence J. Redlinger, *University of Texas at Dallas*

James A. Rhodes, *Luther College*

Leroy N. Rieselbach, *Indiana University*

David Robertson, *Public Policy Research Centers, University of Missouri–St. Louis*

David Robinson, *University of Houston–Downtown*

David W. Rohde, *Michigan State University*

Frank Rourke, *Johns Hopkins University*

Donald Roy, *Ferris State University*

Ronald Rubin, *City University of New York, Borough of Manhattan Community College*

Bruce L. Sanders, *MacComb Community College*

Denise Scheberle, *University of Wisconsin–Green Bay*

Gaye Lynn Scott, *Austin Community College*

Martin P. Sellers, *Campbell University*

Daniel M. Shea, *University of Akron*

John N. Short, *University of Arkansas–Monticello*

Michael Eric Siegel, *American University*

Mark Silverstein, *Boston University*

James R. Simmons, *University of Wisconsin–Oshkosh*

Andrea Simpson, *University of Washington*

Philip M. Simpson, *Cameron University*

Elliott E. Slotnick, *Ohio State University*

Michael W. Sonnleitner, *Portland Community College*

Frank J. Sorauf, *University of Minnesota*

Gerald Stanglin, *Cedar Valley College*

C. S. Tai, *University of Arkansas– Pine Bluff*

Richard J. Timpone, *State University of New York, Stony Brook*

Brian Walsh, *University of Maryland*

Shirley Anne Warshaw, *Gettysburg College*

Matt Wetstein, *San Joaquin Delta College*

Richard Whaley, *Marian College*

Rich Whisonant, *York Technical College*

Martin Wiseman, *Mississippi State University*

Kevan Yenerall, *Bridgewater College*

Finally, we'd also like to thank our peers who reviewed and aided in the development of the current edition:

Kevin Buterbaugh, *Northwest Missouri State University*

Lorrie Clemo, *State University of New York, Oswego*

John Dinan, *Wake Forest University*

Timothy Fackler, *University of Nevada Las Vegas*

Mel Hailey, *Abilene Christian University*

Steven Holmes, *Bakersfield College*

Cecilia Manrique, *University of Wisconsin—La Crosse*

Denise Scheberle, *University of Wisconsin—Green Bay*

Analyzing Visuals: A Brief Guide

The information age requires a new, more expansive definition of literacy. Visual literacy—the ability to analyze, interpret, synthesize, and apply visual information—is essential in today's world. We receive much information from the written and spoken word, but much also comes from visual forms. We are used to thinking about reading written texts critically—for example, reading a textbook carefully for information, sometimes highlighting or underlining as we go along—but we do not always think about "reading" visuals in this way. We should, for images and informational graphics can tell us a lot if we read and consider them carefully. In order to emphasize these skills, this edition of *American Government: Continuity and Change* contains two *Analyzing Visuals* features in each chapter. The features are intended to prompt you to think about the images and informational graphics you will encounter throughout this text, as well as those you see every day in the newspaper, in magazines, on the Web, on television, and in books. We provide critical thinking questions to assist you in learning how to analyze visuals. Though we focus on a couple of visuals in each chapter, we encourage you to examine carefully and ask similar questions of *all* the visuals in this text, and those you encounter elsewhere in your study of and participation in American government.

We look at several types of visuals in the chapters: tables, graphs and charts, maps, news photographs, and political cartoons. This brief guide provides some information about these types of visuals and offers a few questions to guide your analysis of each type.

TABLES

Tables are the least "visual" of the visuals we explore. Tables consist of textual information and/or numerical data arranged in tabular form, in columns and rows. Tables are frequently used when exact information is required and when orderly arrangement is necessary to locate and, in many cases, to compare the information. For example, a table presenting the estimated life expectancy, education levels, earnings, and number of single parents among men and women in 1970 and 2001 would make comparisons of the data visually accessible.

TABLE 1.1   Men and Women in a Changing Society

	1970		2001	
	Men	Women	Men	Women
Estimated life expectancy	67.1	74.1	74.34	80.01
% high school graduates	53	52	84.2	84
% of BAs awarded	56.6	43.4	43.7	56.3
% of MAs awarded	60	40	42.2	57.8
% of PhDs awarded	87	13	58	42
% of JDs awarded	95	5	56	44
Median earnings	$26,760	$14,232	$40,257	$25,551
Single parents	1.2 million	5.6 million	1.78 million	7.57 million

Sources: 1970 data: *1996 Statistical Abstract,* U.S. Department of Commerce, Economics and Statistics Administration, Bureau of the Census. 2001 data: *The World Factbook;* U.S. Census Bureau, *2001 Statistical Abstract of the United States.*

Here are a few questions to guide your analysis:

- What is the purpose of the table? What information does it show? There is usually a title that offers a sense of the table's purpose.

- What information is provided in the column headings (provided in the top row)? How are the rows labeled?

- Is there a time period indicated, such as January to June 2003? Or, are the data as of a specific date, such as June 30, 2003?

- If the table shows numerical data, what do these data represent? In what units? Dollars a special interest lobby provides to a political party? Percentages of men and women responding in a particular way to a poll question about the president's performance? Estimated life expectancy in years?

- What is the source of the information presented in the table?

CHARTS ΛND GRAPHS

Charts and graphs depict numerical data in visual forms. The most common kinds of graphs plot data in two dimensions along horizontal and vertical axes. Examples that you will encounter throughout this text are line graphs, pie charts, and bar graphs. These kinds of visuals emphasize data relationships: at a particular point in time, at regular intervals over a fixed period of time, or, sometimes, as parts of a whole. Line graphs show a progression, usually over time (as in the ideological self-identification of first-year college students). Pie charts (such as the distribution of federal civilian employment) demonstrate how a whole (total federal civilian employment) is divided into its parts (employees in each branch). Bar graphs compare values across categories, showing how proportions are related to each other (as in the numbers of women and minorities in Congress). Bar graphs can present data either horizontally or vertically.

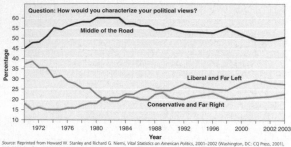

FIGURE 11.2   The Ideological Self-Identification of First-Year College Students
Like the general population, many students who call themselves liberals or conservatives accept only part of the liberal or conservative ideology. During the Ronald Reagan era of the 1980s, the number of people who considered themselves conservative increased. But, by far, most considered their ideology middle of the road. Still, in 2002, more students identified themselves as liberal than had in two decades.

Source: Reprinted from Howard W. Stanley and Richard G. Niemi, *Vital Statistics on American Politics*, 2001–2002 (Washington, DC: CQ Press, 2001), 119. 2001 data from CIRP Press Release: CIRP Freshman Survey (January 28, 2002).

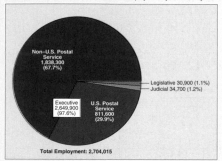

FIGURE 9.1   Distribution of Federal Civilian Employment by Branch, May 2001

Source: Office of Personnel Management, Office of Workplace Information.

Here are a few questions to guide your analysis:

- What is the purpose of the chart or graph? What information does it provide? Or, what is being measured? There is usually a title that indicates the subject and purpose of the figure.

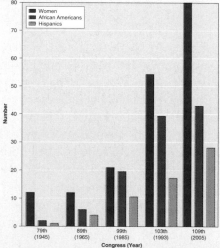

FIGURE 7.1   Numbers of Women and Minorities in Congress

- Is there a time period shown, such as January to June 2003? Or, are the data as of a specific date, such as June 30, 2003? Are the data shown at multiple intervals over a fixed period, or at one particular point in time?

- What do the units represent? Dollars a candidate spends on a campaign? Number of voters versus number of nonvoters in Texas? If there are two or more sets of figures, what are the relationships among them?

- What is the source? Is it government information? Private polling information? A newspaper? A private organization? A corporation? An individual?

- Is the type of chart or graph appropriate for the information that is provided? For example, a line graph assumes a smooth progression from one data point to the next. Is that assumption valid for the data shown?

- Is there distortion in the visual representation of the information? Are the intervals equal? Does the area shown distort the actual amount or the proportion?

MAPS

Maps—of the United States, of particular regions, or of the world—are frequently used in political analysis to illustrate demographic, social, economic, and political issues and trends.

Here are a few questions to guide your analysis:

- Is there a title that identifies the purpose or subject of the map?

- What does the map key/legend show? What are the factors that the map is analyzing?

- What is the region being shown?

- What source is given for the map?

- Maps usually depict a specific point in time. What is the point in time being shown on the map?

FIGURE 4.1   Party of State Governors, 2002
Democrats made gains in the 2002 elections and there is now an even distribution of governors between the two major parties.

Source: http://www.ncsl.org/statevote2002/govParty_post2002.htm.

NEWS PHOTOGRAPHS

If a picture is worth a thousand words, it is no wonder that our newspapers, magazines, and television news broadcasts rely on photographs as well as words to report and analyze the news. Photos can have a dramatic—and often immediate—impact on politics and government. Think about some photos that have political significance. For example, have you seen photos relating to Elian Gonzalez? Do you remember photos from the September 11, 2001, terrorist attack on the World Trade Center? Visual images usually evoke a stronger emotional response from people than do written descriptions. For this reason, individuals and organizations have learned to use photographs as a means to document events, make arguments, offer evidence, and even in some cases to manipulate the viewer into having a particular response.

Here are a few questions to guide your analysis:

- When was the photograph taken? (If there is no date given for the photograph in its credit line or caption, you may be able to approximate the date according to the people or events depicted in the photo. If the photograph appears in a newspaper, you can usually assume that the shot is fairly current with publication.)

- What is the subject of the photograph?

- Why was the photo taken? What appears to be the purpose of the photograph?

- Is it spontaneous or posed? Did the subject know he or she was being photographed?

- Who was responsible for the photo? (An individual, an agency, or organization?) Can you discern the photographer's attitude toward the subject?

- Is there a caption? If so, what kind of information does it provide? Does it identify the subject of the photo? Does it provide an interpretation of the subject?

Thousands of demonstrators took to the streets to protest against the death penalty during the 2000 Republican National Convention in Philadelphia. Earlier that year, Governor George Ryan (R–IL) declared a moratorium on executions because of flaws he found in the justice system after several men on death row were proven innocent.

(Photo courtesy: AFP/Corbis)

POLITICAL CARTOONS

Political cartoons have a long history in America. Some of the most interesting commentary on American politics takes place in the form of political cartoons, which usually exaggerate physical and other qualities of the persons depicted and often rely on a kind of visual short-hand to announce the subject or set the scene—visual cues, clichés, or stereotypes that are instantly recognizable. For example, a greedy corporate executive might be depicted as an individual in professional clothing with paper currency sticking out of his or her pockets. In another cartoon, powdered wigs and quill pens might signal a historical setting. The car-toonist's goal is to comment on and/or criticize political figures, policies, or events. The cartoonist uses several techniques to accomplish this goal, including exaggeration, irony, and juxtaposition. For example, the cartoonist may point out how the results of governmental policies are the opposite of their intended effects (irony). In other cartoons, two people, ideas, or events that don't belong together may be joined to make a point (juxtaposition). Because cartoons comment on political situations and events, you generally need some knowledge of current events to inter-pret political cartoons.

Here are a few questions to guide your analysis:

- Study the cartoon element by element. Political car-toons are often complex. If the cartoon is in strip form, you also need to think about the relationship of the frames in sequence.

- What labels appear on objects or people in the car-toon? Cartoonists will often label some of the ele-ments. For example, a building with columns might be labeled "U.S. Supreme Court." Or, an individual might be labeled "senator" or "Republican."

- Is there a caption or title to the cartoon? If so, what does it contribute to the meaning or impact of the cartoon?

(Photo courtesy: Mike Luckovich and Creators Syndicate, by permission)

- Can you identify any of the people shown? Presi-dents, well-known members of Congress, and world leaders are often shown with specific characteristics that help to identify them. Jimmy Carter was often shown with an exaggerated, toothy smile. George W. Bush is often shown with large ears, small eyes, and bushy eyebrows—sometimes with a "W." or a "43" label.

- Can you identify the event being depicted? Historical events, such as the American Rev-olution, or contemporary events, such as the 2000 presidential election, are often the sub-ject matter for cartoons.

- What are the elements of the cartoon? Objects often represent ideas or events. For exam-ple, a donkey is often used to depict the Democratic Party. Or, an eagle is used to repre-sent the United States.

- How are the characters interacting? What do the speech bubbles contribute to the cartoon?

- What is the overall message of the cartoon? Can you determine what the cartoonist's position is on the subject?

American Government

We the People of the United States, in Order to form a more perfect Union, establish Justice, insure domestic Tranquility, provide for the common defence, promote the general Welfare, and secure the Blessings of Liberty to ourselves and our Posterity, do ordain and establish this Constitution for the United States of America.

The Political Landscape

1

On the facing page, you'll see the words that begin the Preamble to the United States Constitution. Written in 1787 by a group of men we today refer to as the Framers, this document has guided our nation, its government, its politics, its institutions, and its inhabitants for over 200 years.

Back when the Constitution was written, the phrases "We the People" and "ourselves" meant something very different than they do today. After all, voting largely was limited to property-owning white males. Indians, slaves, and women could not vote. Today, through the expansion of the right to vote, the phrase "the People" encompasses men and women of all races, ethnic origins, and social and economic statuses—a variety of peoples and interests. The Framers could not have imagined the variety of people today who are eligible to vote.

In the goals it outlines, the Preamble to the Constitution describes what the people of the United States can expect from their government. In spite of the wave of nationalism that arose in the wake of the September 11, 2001 terrorist attacks, some continue to question how well the U.S. government can deliver on the goals set out in the Preamble. Few Americans today classify the Union as "perfect"; many feel excluded from "Justice" and the "Blessings of Liberty," and even our leaders do not believe that our domestic situation is particularly tranquil, as evidenced by the creation of the Office of Homeland Security. Furthermore, recent poll results and economic statistics indicate that many Americans believe their general welfare is not particularly well promoted by their government. Others simply do not care about government much at all.

Change. If there has been one constant in the life of the United States, it is change. The Framers would be astonished to see the forms and functions that the institutions they so carefully outlined in the Constitution have taken on, and the number of additional political institutions that have arisen to support and fuel the functioning of the national government. The Framers also would be amazed at the array of services and programs the government—especially the national government—provides. They further would be surprised to see how the physical boundaries and the composition of the population have changed over the past 200 plus years. And, they might well wonder, "How did we get here?"

It is part of the American creed that each generation should hand down to the next not only a better America, but an improved economic, educational, and social status. In general, Americans long have been optimistic about our nation, its institutions, and its future. Thomas Jefferson saw the United States as the world's "best hope"; Abraham Lincoln echoed these sentiments when he called it the "last, best hope on earth."[1] But, during the 1990s, for the first time in decades, some of that optimism faded. Many Americans were dismayed by the Clinton/Lewinsky affair, campaign finance abuses, and often even government in general. This disenchantment, some believe, led to the continued low voter turnout in the 2000 election. Still, most Americans continued to report that their lives were better than their parents' and most were optimistic about the future. In the aftermath of the disputed 2000 presidential election, 2001's stock market collapse, terrorist attacks, and the continued economic downswing, however, many are uncertain about what the future holds.

WEB EXPLORATION
To connect with others who are interested in politics, see
www.ablongman.com/oconnor

*I*n this text, we present you with the tools that you need to understand how our political system has evolved, and to prepare you to understand the changes that are yet to come. If you approach the study of American government and politics with an open mind, it should help you become a better citizen. We hope that you learn to ask questions, to understand how various issues have come to be important, and to see why a particular law was enacted and how it was implemented. With such understanding, we further hope that you will learn not to accept at face value everything you see on the television news, hear on the radio, or read in the newspaper. Work to understand your government, and use your vote and other forms of participation to help ensure that your government works for you.

We recognize that the discourse of politics has changed dramatically in just the last few years. The 2000 presidential election and its failure to produce an immediate presidential winner refocused national attention on political participation and the importance of a single vote. Yet, huge efforts to mobilize young voters in 2004 failed to significantly increase their turnout at the polls.

We believe that a thorough understanding of the workings of government will allow you to question and think about the system—the good parts and the bad—and decide for yourself the advantages and disadvantages of possible changes and reforms. Equipped with such an understanding, we hope you will become better informed and more active participants in the political process.

Every long journey begins with a single step. In this chapter, we'll examine the following topics:

- First, we will look at *the roots of American government*. To understand how the U.S. government and our political system work today, it is critical to understand the philosophies that guided the American colonists as they created a system of governance different from those then in existence.

- Second, we will explore *the characteristics of American democracy*. Several enduring characteristics have defined American democracy since its beginning and continue to influence our nation's government and politics today.

- Third, we will explore *the changing political culture and characteristics of the American people*. Because government derives its power from the people, an understanding of who the American people are and how their changing age, racial, and ethnic composition is critical to an understanding of American politics.

- Fourth, we will discuss *political culture and Americans' views about government* and the role that government plays in their lives.

- In highlighting *continuity and change* in our political system, we will examine how the American dream for immigrants has changed over time as the racial and ethnic composition of America also has changed dramatically.

THE ROOTS OF AMERICAN GOVERNMENT: WHERE DID THE IDEAS COME FROM?

The current American political system did not spring into being overnight. It is the result of philosophy, trial and error, and yes, even luck. To begin our examination of why we have the type of government we have today, we look at the theories of government that influenced the Framers who drafted the Constitution and created the United States of America.

From Aristotle to the Enlightenment

Aristotle (384–322 B.C.) and the Greeks were the first to articulate the notion of **natural law,** the doctrine that human affairs should be governed by certain ethical principles. Being nothing more nor less than the nature of things, the principles of natural law can be understood by reason. Later, in the thirteenth century, the Italian priest and philosopher Thomas Aquinas (1225–1274) gave the idea of natural law a new, Christian framework. He argued that natural law and Christianity were compatible because God created the natural law that established individual rights to life and liberty. In contradiction to this view, kings throughout Europe continued to rule as absolute monarchs, claiming their divine right to govern came directly from God. Thus, citizens were bound by the government under which they found themselves, regardless of whether they had a say in its workings: If government reflected God's will, who could argue with it?

In the early sixteenth century, a religious movement to reform the doctrine and institutions of Roman Catholicism began to sweep through Europe. In many cases these efforts at reform resulted in the founding of Protestant churches separate from their Catholic source. During this period, known as the Reformation, the Protestant faith grew as it promoted the belief that people could talk directly to God without the intervention of a priest. The Reformation thus began to alter how people viewed government as they began to believe they should have a say in their own governance.

During the Enlightenment period, the ideas of philosophers and scientists such as Isaac Newton (1642–1727) worked further to affect peoples' views of government. Newton and others argued that the world could be improved through the use of human reason, science, and religious toleration. He and other theorists directly challenged earlier notions that fate alone controlled an individual's destiny and that kings ruled by divine right. Together, the intellectual and religious developments of the Reformation and Enlightenment periods encouraged people to seek alternatives to absolute monarchies and to ponder new methods of governance.

A Growing Idea: Popular Consent

In the late sixteenth century in England, "separatists" split from the Church of England. They believed that their ability to speak one-on-one to God gave them the power to participate directly in the governance of their own local assemblies. They established self-governing congregations and were responsible for the first widespread appearance of self-government in the form of social compacts. When some separatists settled in America during the 1600s, they brought along their beliefs about self-governance. The Mayflower Compact, deemed sufficiently important to be written while that ship was still at sea, reflects this tradition. Although it addressed itself to secular government, the Pilgrims called it a "covenant" and its form was akin to other common religious covenants adopted by Congregationalists, Presbyterians, and Baptists.[2]

Two English theorists of the seventeenth century, Thomas Hobbes (1588–1679) and John Locke (1632–1704), built on conventional notions about the role of government and the relationship of the government to the people in

natural law
A doctrine that society should be governed by certain ethical principles that are part of nature and, as such, can be understood by reason.

WEB EXPLORATION
For more on Aristotle and natural law, see
www.ablongman.com/oconnor

Sir Isaac Newton and other Enlightenment thinkers challenged people's ideas about the nature of government.
(Photo courtesy: SIPA Press)

social contract theory
The belief that people are free and equal by God-given right and that this in turn requires that all people give their consent to be governed; espoused by John Locke and influential in the writing of the Declaration of Independence.

proposing a **social contract theory** of government (see Roots of Government: The Philosophies of Thomas Hobbes and John Locke). They argued that, even before the creation of God-ordained governments theorized by Aquinas, all individuals were free and equal by natural right. This freedom, in turn, required that all men and women give their consent to be governed.

Hobbes and Locke.   In Hobbes's now-classic political treatise, *Leviathan* (1651), he argued for King Charles's restoration to the throne, which finally occurred in 1661. Hobbes argued pessimistically that man's natural state was war. Government, Hobbes theorized, particularly a monarchy, was necessary to restrain man's bestial tendencies because life without government was but a "state of nature." Without written, enforceable rules, people would live like animals—foraging for food, stealing, and killing when necessary. To escape the horrors of the natural state and to protect their lives, Hobbes argued, people must give up certain rights to government.[3] Without government, Hobbes warned, life would basically be "solitary, poor, nasty, brutish, and short"—a constant struggle to survive against the evil of others. For these reasons, governments had to intrude on people's rights and liberties to better control society and to provide the necessary safeguards for property.

Hobbes argued strongly for a single ruler, no matter how evil, to guarantee the rights of the weak against the strong. Leviathan, a biblical sea monster, was his characterization of an all-powerful government. Strict adherence to Leviathan's laws, however encompassing or intrusive on liberty, was but a small price to pay for living in a civilized society, or even for life itself.

In contrast, John Locke, like many other political philosophers of the era, took the basic survival of humanity for granted. He argued that a government's major responsibility was the preservation of private property, an idea that ultimately found its way into the U.S. Constitution. In two of his works (*Essay Concerning Human Understanding* [1690] and *Second Treatise on Civil Government* [1689]), Locke responded to King James II's abuses of power. Locke not only denied the divine right of kings to govern but argued that men were born equal and with natural rights that no king had the power to void. Under what Locke termed social contract theory, the consent of the people is the only true basis of any sovereign's right to rule. According to Locke, people form governments largely to preserve life, liberty, and property, and to assure justice. If governments act improperly, they break their contract with the people and therefore no longer enjoy the consent of the governed. Because he believed that true justice comes from laws, Locke argued that the branch of government that makes laws—as opposed to the one that enforces or interprets laws—should be the most powerful.

Locke believed that having a chief executive to administer laws was important, but that he should necessarily be limited by law or by the social contract with the governed. Locke's writings influenced many

The title page from Thomas Hobbes's *Leviathan* (1651) depicting the people coming together under a single ruler.

(Photo courtesy: Bettmann/Corbis)

Roots of Government

THE PHILOSOPHIES OF THOMAS HOBBES AND JOHN LOCKE

On almost any newspaper or TV news report, on any given day, you can find stories that show Americans grappling with questions about the proper role of government in their lives. These questions are not new. Centuries ago, Thomas Hobbes and John Locke both wrote extensively on these issues. Their ideas, however, differed remarkably. For Hobbes, who viewed humans as basically evil, a government that regulated all kinds of conduct was necessary. Locke, who was more optimistic, saw the need only for more limited government.

Hobbes

Thomas Hobbes was born in 1588 in Gloucestershire, England, and began his formal education at the age of four. By the age of six he was learning Latin and Greek, and by the age of nineteen he had obtained his bachelor's degree from Oxford University. In 1608, Hobbes accepted a position as a family tutor with the earl of Devonshire, a post he retained for the rest of his life.

Hobbes was greatly influenced by the chaos of the English Civil War during the mid-seventeenth century. Its impact is evident in his most famous work, *Leviathan* (1651), a treatise on governmental theory that states his views on man and citizen. *Leviathan* is commonly described as a book about politics, but it also deals with religion and moral philosophy.

Hobbes characterized humans as selfishly individualistic and constantly at war with one another. Thus, he believed that people must surrender themselves to rulers in exchange for protection from their neighbors.

Locke

John Locke, born in England in 1632, was admitted to an outstanding public school at the age of fifteen. It was there that he began to question his upbringing in the Puritan faith. At twenty, he went on to study at Oxford, where he later became a lecturer in Aristotelian philosophy. Soon, however, he found a new interest in medicine and experimental science.

In 1666, Locke met Anthony Ashley Cooper, the first earl of Shaftesbury, a politician who believed in individual rights and parliamentary reform. It was through Cooper that Locke discovered his own talent for philosophy. In 1689, Locke published his most famous work, *Second Treatise on Civil Government*, in which he set forth a theory of natural rights. He used natural rights to support his "social contract [theory]—the view that the consent of the people is the only true basis of any sovereign's right to rule." A government exists, he argued, because individuals agree, through a contract, to form a government to protect their rights under natural law. By agreeing to be governed, individuals agree to abide by decisions made by majority vote in the resolution of disputes.

Both men, as you can see, relied on wealthy royal patrons to allow them the time to work on their philosophies of government. While Hobbes and Locke agreed that government was a social contract between the people and their rulers, they differed significantly about the proper scope of government. Which man's views about government (and people) reflect your views?

American colonists, especially Thomas Jefferson, whose original draft of the Declaration of Independence noted the rights to "life, liberty, and property" as key reasons to split from England.[4] This document was "pure Locke" because it based the justification for the split with England on the English government's violation of the social contract with the American colonists.

WEB EXPLORATION For more on Thomas Hobbes and John Locke, see www.ablongman.com/oconnor

Devising a National Government

Although social contract theorists agreed on the need for government, they did not necessarily agree on the form that a government should take. Thomas Hobbes argued for a single leader; John Locke and Jean-Jacques Rousseau, a French philosopher (1712–1778), saw the need for less centralized power.

The colonists rejected a system with a strong ruler like the British **monarchy** as soon as they declared their independence. Most European monarchical systems gave

monarchy
A form of government in which power is vested in hereditary kings and queens.

hereditary rulers absolute power over all forms of activity. Many of the colonists had fled Great Britain to avoid religious persecution and other harsh manifestations of power wielded by King George II, whom they viewed as a malevolent despot. They naturally were reluctant to put themselves in the same position in their new nation.

While some colonies, such as Massachusetts, originally established theocracies in which religious leaders eventually ruled claiming divine guidance, they later looked to more secular forms of governance. Colonists also did not want to create an **oligarchy,** or "rule by the few or an elite," in which the right to participate is conditioned on the possession of wealth, property, social status, military position, or achievement. Aristotle defined this form of government as a perversion of an **aristocracy,** or "rule of the highest." Again, the colonists were fearful of replicating the landed and titled system of the British aristocracy, and viewed the formation of a representative form of government as far more in keeping with the ideas of social contract theorists. But, the **democracy** in which we live, as settled on by the Framers, is difficult to define. Nowhere is the word mentioned in the Declaration of Independence or the U.S. Constitution. The term comes from two Greek words: *demos* (the people) and *kratia* (power or authority). Thus, democracy, which today enjoys increasing popularity around the world, can be interpreted as a form of government that gives power to the people. The question, then, is how and to which people is this power given?

The Theory of Democratic Government

As evidenced by the creation in 1619 of the Virginia House of Burgesses as the first representative assembly in North America, and its objections to "taxation without representation," the colonists were quick to create participatory forms of government in which most men were allowed to take part. The New England town meeting, where all citizens gather to discuss and decide issues facing the town, today stands as a surviving example of a **direct democracy,** such as was used in ancient Greece when all free, male citizens came together periodically to pass laws and "elect" leaders by lot (see Politics Now: The Internet and Our Changing Society).

Direct democracies, in which the people rather than their elected representatives make political decisions, soon proved unworkable in the colonies. But, as more and more settlers came to the New World, many town meetings were replaced by a system called an **indirect democracy** (this is also called *representative democracy*). This system of government, in which representatives of the people are chosen by ballot, was considered undemocratic by ancient Greeks, who believed that all citizens must have a direct say in their governance.[5] Later, in the 1760s, Jean-Jacques Rousseau also would argue that true democracy is impossible unless all citizens participate in governmental decision making. Nevertheless, indirect democracy was the form of government opted for throughout most of the colonies.

Representative or indirect democracies, which call for the election of representatives to a governmental decision-making body, were formed first in the colonies and then in the new union. Many citizens were uncomfortable with the term "democracy" and used the term "republic" to avoid any confusion between the system adopted and direct democracy. Historically, the term **republic** implied a system of government in which the interests of the people were represented by more educated or wealthier citizens who were responsible to those who elected them. Today, representative democracies are more commonly called "republics," and the words "democracy" and "republic" often are used interchangeably.

Why a Capitalist System?

In addition to fashioning a democratic form of government, the colonists also were confronted with the dilemma of what kind of role the government should play in the economy. Concerns with liberty, both personal and economic, were always at the forefront

oligarchy
A form of government in which the right to participate is always conditioned on the possession of wealth, social status, military position, or achievement.

aristocracy
A system of government in which control is based on rule of the highest.

democracy
A system of government that gives power to the people, whether directly or through their elected representatives.

direct democracy
A system of government in which members of the polity meet to discuss all policy decisions and then agree to abide by majority rule.

indirect (representative) democracy
A system of government that gives citizens the opportunity to vote for representatives who will work on their behalf.

Participation
Democracy and the Internet

republic
A government rooted in the consent of the governed; a representative or indirect democracy.

THE INTERNET AND OUR CHANGING SOCIETY

It is hard to believe that the Internet as we know it was not around when the first edition of this text was published in 1993. What began in 1969 as ARPANET, a communications network developed by the U.S. Department of Defense for its employees to maintain contact with defense contractors and universities in the case of a nuclear attack, has revolutionized how students write papers, people seek information, and even how some individuals date. The Internet is now a vast resource for those interested in politics and may have enormous consequences in the near future as it becomes as critical a part of our daily lives as televisions and telephones.

For the first decade of its existence, the Internet was largely used for e-mail and access to distant data bases, and to facilitate communication among governmental agencies, corporations, and universities.[a] During the early 1980s, all of the interrelated research networks converted to a new protocol that allowed for easy back-and-forth transfer of information; ARPANET became the backbone of the new system, facilitating by 1983 the birth of the Internet we know today.

Only a decade ago, HTML, a hypertext Internet protocol that allowed graphic information to be transmitted over the Internet, was devised. This allowed for the creation of graphic pages—called Web sites—which then became "part of a huge, virtual hypertext network called the World Wide Web."[b] This new, improved Internet was then christened the Web.

By 2000, over 64 percent of all adult Americans reported that they had used the Internet. Almost all schools have Internet access. By 2001, over 50 million households were online. In 2000, female Internet usage surpassed male usage for the first time. Usage by teenage girls soared 126 percent in just four years.[c]

Thus, given estimates that computer ownership and Web access are increasing at remarkable rates, the Web's impact on democracy must be considered.

Near-universal usage of home telephones, for example, changed the way that public opinion was measured, and television eventually changed the way that candidates and their supporters reached potential voters. Most candidates for major office have Web pages and use the Internet to raise campaign funds. More and more Americans look to the Web as a major source of information about politics, and the political parties and interest groups are aware of this fact.

This has brought about increased reliance on candidate and party Web sites to raise money and supporters, a more informed electorate given easier access to information about candidates and issues, and a more effective grassroots mechanism for citizens to contact officials, policy makers, and large corporations. It is hoped that the Internet will enhance voter turnout.

---

[a]"Internet History," http://www.tdi.uregina.ca/~ursc/internet/history.html
[b]"Internet History."
[c]Leslie Walker, "Teen Girls Help Create Female Majority Online," *Washington Post* (August 20, 2000): E3.

---

of their actions and decisions in creating a new government. They were well aware of the need for a well-functioning economy and saw that government had a key role in maintaining one. What a malfunction in the economy is, however, and what steps the government should take to remedy it, were questions that dogged the Framers and continue to puzzle politicians and theorists today.

The American economy is characterized by: (1) the private ownership of property; and, (2) a **free market economy**—two key tenets of **capitalism,** an economic system that favors private control of business and minimal governmental regulation of private industry. In capitalist systems, the laws of supply and demand, interacting freely in the marketplace, set prices of goods and drive production. Under capitalism, sales occur for the profit of the individual. Capitalists believe that both national and individual production is greatest when individuals are free to do with their property or goods as they wish. The government, however, plays an indispensable role in creating and enforcing the rules of the game.

In 1776, the year the Declaration of Independence was signed, Adam Smith (1723–1790) argued that free trade would result in full production and economic health. These ideas were greeted with great enthusiasm in the colonies as independence was proclaimed. Colonists no longer wanted to participate in the mercantile system of Great Britain and other Western European nations. **Mercantile systems** bound trade and its administration to national governments. Smith and his supporters saw free trade as "the

free market economy
The economic system in which the "invisible hand" of the market regulates prices, wages, product mix, and so on.

capitalism
The economic system that favors private control of business and minimal governmental regulation of private industry.

mercantile system
A system that binds trade and its administration to the national government.

Here, the sameness of the track homes of Levittown, New York, the site of afford-able housing for World War II veterans and their families, is clearly shown. Federally guaranteed G.I. low-interest loans made home ownership a possibility for many Americans for the first time in history.

(Photo courtesy: Hulton Archive/Getty Images)

invisible hand" that produced the wealth of nations. This wealth, in turn, became the inspiration and justification for capitalism.

From the mid- to late-eighteenth century, and through the mid-1930s in the United States and in much of the Western world, the idea of *laissez-faire* economics (from the French, "to leave alone") enjoyed considerable popularity. While most states regulated and intervened heavily in their economies well into the nineteenth century, the U.S. national government routinely followed a "hands-off" economic policy. By the late 1800s, however, the national government felt increasing pressure to regulate some aspects of the economy (often, in part, because of the difficulties states faced in regulating large, multistate industries such as the railroads, and from industry's desire to override the patchwork regulatory scheme produced by the states). Thereafter, the Great Depression of the 1930s forced the national government to take a much larger role in the economy. Afterward, any pretense that the United States was a purely capitalist system was abandoned. The worldwide extent of this trend, however, varied by country and over time. In post–World War II Britain, for example, the extent of government economic regulation of industry and social welfare was much greater than that attempted by American policy makers in the same period.

For most of U.S. history, capitalism and the American dream have been alive and well. Hard work has been rewarded with steady jobs and increased earning power and wages, and Americans have expected to hand down improved economic, social, and educational status to their children. In many ways World War II ushered in the era of the American dream. Men returned from the war and went to college, and their tuition was paid for by the G.I. Bill. Prior to the war, a college education was mainly the preserve of the rich; the G.I. Bill made it available to men from all walks of life. Many men got the education they needed to succeed and do much better than their parents had before them. In addition, low-interest-rate mortgages were made available through the Veterans Administration, and the American dream of owning a home became a reality for millions. Capitalism worked and made the efforts to preserve it worthwhile.

Other Economic Systems

Capitalism is just one type of economic system. Others include socialism, communism, and totalitarianism.

Socialism.   **Socialism** is a philosophy that advocates collective ownership and control of the means of economic production. Socialists call for governmental, rather than private, ownership of all land, property, and industry and, in turn, an equitable distribution of the income from those holdings. In addition, socialism seeks to replace the profit motive and competition with cooperation and social responsibility.

Some Socialists actually tolerate capitalism as long as the government maintains some kind of control over the economy. Others reject capitalism outright and insist on the abolition of all private enterprise.

socialism
An economic system that advocates for collective ownership and control of the means of production.

Some Socialists, especially in Western Europe, argue that socialism can evolve through democratic processes. Thus, in nations such as Great Britain, certain critical industries or services including health care and the coal industry have been nationalized, or taken over by the state, to provide for more efficient supervision and to avoid the major concentrations of wealth that occur when individuals privately own key industries.

Communism.   The German philosopher Karl Marx argued that government was simply a manifestation of underlying economic forces and could be understood according to types of economic production. In *Das Kapital* (1867), Marx argued that capitalism would always be replaced by socialist states in which the working class would own the means of production and distribution and be able to redistribute the wealth to meet its needs.

Marx believed that it was inevitable for each society to pass through the stages of history: feudalism, capitalism, socialism, and then **communism**. When society reached communism, Marx theorized, all class differences would be abolished and government would become unnecessary. A system of common ownership of the means of sustenance and production would lead to greater social justice. In practice, most notably in Russia under Vladimir Lenin, and the Soviet dictator, Joseph Stalin, many of the tenets of Marxism were changed or modified.

Marx saw the change coming first in highly industrialized countries such as Britain and Germany, where a fully mature capitalism would pave the way for a socialist revolution. But, Lenin and the Bolshevik Party wanted to have such a revolution in underdeveloped Russia. So, instead of relying on the historical inevitability of the communist future (as Marx envisioned), they advocated forcing that change. Lenin argued that by establishing an elite vanguard party of permanent revolutionaries and a dictatorship of the proletariat (working class), they could achieve socialism and communism without waiting for the historical forces to work. In the 1940s, led by Mao Zedong, China followed the Leninist path.

In practice, the communist states rejected free markets as a capitalist and exploitative way of organizing production and turned instead to planning and state regulation. In capitalist economies, the market sets prices, wages, and product mix. In a planned economy, government makes conscious choices to determine prices, wages, and product mix.

The events leading to the fall of the Berlin Wall dividing free and communist Berlin, in 1989 reflected the increasing inability of communist governments to address economic and political demands of modern society. When the Soviet Union fragmented into fifteen separate countries in 1992, state communism ceased to be an international model for economic and political development. With only a few notable exceptions, such as Cuba and North Korea, most countries, political leaders, and political groups abandoned the rhetoric and policies of communism for market economics and democracy.[6] By 2002, even the Chinese Communist Party, while keeping tight control on political power, had overseen twenty years of market-oriented economic reforms.[7] In Eastern Europe, the discredited Communists generally reinvented themselves as Social Democrats focused on the needs of those unable or unwilling to benefit from the market economy. In some instances, this conversion resulted in election victories and a return to political power. The Russian Communist Party, in contrast, remained generally unrepentant, and its appeal continues to diminish. At the same time, several of the other countries that emerged from the breakup of the Soviet Union have dispensed with communist ideology but have retained many political and economic characteristics of Soviet-style communism.[8]

Totalitarianism.   A totalitarian system is basically a modern form of extreme authoritarian rule. In contrast to governments based on democratic beliefs, totalitarian governments have total authority over their people and their economic system. The tools of **totalitarianism** are secret police, terror, propaganda, and an almost total prohibition on civil rights and liberties. These systems also tend to be ruled in the name of a particular

communism
An economic system in which workers own the means of production and control the distribution of resources.

totalitarianism
An economic system in which the government has total control over the economy.

The horrors of the Taliban regime in Afghanistan are revealed vividly as the cloaked man is shot at close range by the brother of the man he murdered. These public executions were commonplace under the Taliban's version of Islamic justice.

(Photo courtesy: Zaheer Uddin/Webista/Corbis Sygma)

religion or orthodoxy, an ideology, or a personality cult organized around a supreme leader. The reign of the Taliban in Afghanistan came close to the total control of forms of production, the airwaves, education, the arts, and even sports implied by totalitarianism.

CHARACTERISTICS OF AMERICAN DEMOCRACY

As earlier noted, the United States is an indirect democracy. It has several underlying concepts and distinguishing characteristics, including its political culture, which continually affect the citizenry's ideas about government. Many of these characteristics are often in conflict. The political system, for example, is based on an underlying notion of the importance of balance among the legislative, executive, and judicial branches, between the state and federal governments, between the wants of the majority and the minority, and between the rights of the individual and the best interests of the nation as a whole. The Framers built the system on the idea that there would be statesmen who would act for the good of the system. Without such statespersons, the system necessitates constant vigilance to keep a balance as the pendulum swings back and forth between various desires, demands, and responsibilities. To some, government may be a necessary evil, but a good government is less evil if it can keep things in balance as it operates in various spheres. The ideas of balance permeate many of the concepts and characteristics of American democracy presented below.

Simulation

What Are American Civic Values?

Popular Consent

popular consent
The idea that governments must draw their powers from the consent of the governed.

Popular consent, the idea that governments must draw their powers from the consent of the governed, is one distinguishing characteristic of American democracy. Derived from Locke's social contract theory, the notion of popular consent was central to the Declaration of Independence. A citizen's willingness to vote represents his or her consent to be governed and is thus an essential premise of democracy. Growing numbers of nonvoters can threaten the operation and legitimacy of a truly democratic system. So, too, can voting systems where certain kinds of ballots or voting machines, such as many of those used in recent elections, appeared not to count many of the votes cast.

Popular Sovereignty

popular sovereignty
The right of the majority to govern themselves.

The notion of **popular sovereignty,** the right of the majority to govern themselves, has its basis in natural law. Ultimately, political authority rests with the people, who can

10

create, abolish, or alter their governments. The idea that all governments derive their power from the people is found in the Declaration of Independence and the U.S. Constitution, but the term itself did not come into wide use until pre–Civil War debates over slavery. At that time, supporters of popular sovereignty argued that the citizens of new states seeking admission to the Union should be able to decide whether or not their states would allow slavery within their borders. Today, public opinion polls are often used as instantaneous measures of the popular will.

Majority Rule

Majority rule, another basic democratic principle, means that the majority (normally 50 percent of the total votes cast plus one) of citizens in any political unit should elect officials and determine policies. This principle holds for both voters and their elected representatives. Yet, the American system also stresses the need to preserve minority rights, as evidenced by the myriad protections of individual rights and liberties found in the Bill of Rights.

majority rule
The central premise of direct democracy in which only policies that collectively garner the support of a majority of voters will be made into law.

The concept of the preservation of minority rights has changed dramatically in the United States. It wasn't until after the Civil War that slaves were freed and African Americans began to enjoy minimal citizenship rights. By the 1960s, however, rage at America's failure to guarantee minority rights in all sections of the nation fueled the civil rights movement. This ultimately led to congressional passage of the Civil Rights Act of 1964 and the Voting Rights Act of 1965, both designed to further minority rights. Attacks on affirmative action often are fueled by cries that majority rights are being trampled.

Concepts of majority rule today are threatened by a tradition of political apathy that has emerged slowly over time within the American electorate. Since 1972, the percentage of eligible voters who have cast ballots generally has continued to decline. While 63 percent voted in 1972, just under 60 percent of eligible voters voted in 2004. Off-year, nonpresidential elections suffer the lowest rates; in 1998 only 36 percent of those eligible to vote did so. In some states, fewer than 25 percent of those eligible to vote cast a ballot. Although one in five of those who did not vote said they didn't do so because they were "too busy,"[9] 8 percent reported that they stayed home because they didn't like the candidates or issues.[10] Ten percent reported that they were out of town, and 12 percent said they simply were uninterested.[11] Whatever reasons are offered for nonvoting, however, it is an important phenomenon to keep in mind when we talk about majority rule. Most discussions of elections as the voice of the majority really are better cast as discussions of the wishes of the majority who voted.

Individualism

Tremendous value is placed on the individual in American democracy and culture. All individuals are deemed rational and fair, and endowed, as Thomas Jefferson proclaimed in the Declaration of Independence, "with certain unalienable rights." Even today, many view individualism, which holds that the primary function of government is to enable the individual to achieve his or her highest level of development, as a mixed blessing. It is also a concept whose meaning has changed over time. The rugged individualism of the western frontier, for example, was altered as more citizens moved westward, cities developed, and demands for government services increased.

Equality

Another key characteristic of our democracy is the emphasis on political equality, the definition of which has varied considerably over time (as discussed in chapter 6). The importance of political equality is another reflection of Americans' stress on the importance of the individual. Although some individuals clearly wield more political clout than others, the adage "one person, one vote" implies a sense of political equality for all.

Personal Liberty

Personal liberty is perhaps the single most important characteristic of American democracy. The Constitution itself was written to assure "life" and "liberty." Over the years, however, our concepts of liberty have changed and evolved from "freedom *from*" to "freedom *to*." The Framers intended Americans to be free from governmental infringements on freedom of religion and speech, from unreasonable search and seizure, and so on (see chapter 5). The addition of the Fourteenth Amendment to the Constitution and its emphasis on equal protection of the laws and subsequent passage of laws guaranteeing civil rights, however, expanded Americans' concept of liberty to include demands for "freedom to" work or to go to school free from discrimination. Debates over how much the government should do to guarantee these rights or liberties illustrate the conflicts that continue to occur in our democratic system.

Civil Society

Many of these hallmarks of democracy also are fundamentals of what many now term **civil society**. This term is used to describe the "nongovernmental, not-for profit, independent nature" of people and groups who can express their views publicly and engage in an open debate about public policy.[12] With the collapse of the Soviet Union, the U.S. government has used a variety of initiatives to train people how to act in a new democratic system. Independent and politically active citizens are key to the success of any democracy, yet people who have not lived in democratic systems often are unschooled, reluctant, or afraid to participate after years in communist or totalitarian systems. The U.S. government routinely makes grants to nongovernmental organizations, professional associations, civic education groups, and women's groups to encourage the kind of participation in the political system that Americans often take for granted. The fall of the Soviet Union "accelerated the global trend toward democracy... which pushed democracy to the top of the political agenda."[13] U.S. efforts to assist Afghanistan, for example, include not only public works projects but also development of the new democratic government.

THE CHANGING POLITICAL CULTURE AND CHARACTERISTICS OF THE AMERICAN PEOPLE

Political culture has been defined as the "attitudes toward the political system and its various parts, and attitudes toward the role of the self in the system."[14] It is a set of orientations toward a special set of social objects and processes. Where you live, how you were raised, and even your age or age cohort can affect how you view the government or a governmental program.

Americans are very divided on some issues; politicians, media commentators, and even the citizenry itself also tend to focus on how different Americans are. But, before we explore some of those differences, which have profound implications on policy and individual preferences, we must note the similarities of Americans. Most Americans share a common language—English—and have similar aspirations for themselves and their families. Most agree that they would rather live in the United States than anywhere else and that democracy, with all of its warts, is still the best system for most. Most Americans highly value education and want to send their children to the best schools possible, viewing an education as the key to success.

Still, at the heart of the American political system is change, be it in population, demographics, or interest in politics. But, while it is true that America and its population are undergoing rapid change, this is not necessarily a new phenomenon. It is simply new to most of us. In the pages that follow, we take a look at some of the characteristics of the American populace and its political culture. Because the people of the United States are the basis of political power and authority, their characteristics and attitudes have important implications for how America is governed and how and what policies are made.

Changing Size and Population

One year after the Constitution was ratified, less than 4 million Americans lived in the thirteen states. They were united by a single language and opposition to the king. Most shared a similar Protestant-Christian heritage, and those who voted were white male property owners. The Constitution mandated that each of the sixty-five members of the original House of Representatives should represent 30,000 citizens. However, due to rapid growth, that number often was much higher. Anti-Federalists, who opposed a strong national government during the founding period, at least took solace in the fact that members of the House of Representatives, who generally represented far fewer people than senators, would be more in touch with "the People."

As revealed in Figure 1.1, as the nation grew as new states were added, the population also grew. Although the physical size of the United States has remained stable since the addition of Alaska and Hawaii in 1959, there are now more than 286 million Americans. In 2005, a single member of the House of Representatives from Montana represented more than 900,000 people.

WEB EXPLORATION
To get a minute-by-minute update on U.S. population, see
www.ablongman.com/oconnor

Visual Literacy
Understanding
Who We Are

FIGURE 1.1   U.S. Population, 1790–2050
Since around 1890, when more and more immigrants came to America, the population of the United States, although largely fueled by new births and increased longevity, has continued to rise.

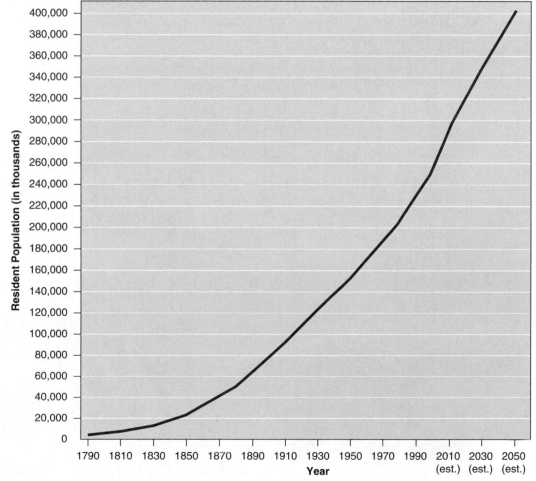

Source: U.S. Census Bureau, *2001 Statistical Abstract of the United States.*

As a result of this growth, most citizens today feel far removed from the national government and their elected representatives. Members of Congress, too, feel this change. Often they represent diverse constituencies with a variety of needs, concerns, and expectations, and they can meet only a relative few of these people in face-to-face electioneering.

Changing Demographics of the U.S. Population

As the physical size and population of the United States have changed, so have many of the assumptions on which it was founded. Some of the dynamism of the American system actually stems from the racial and ethnic changes that have taken place throughout our history, a notion that often gets lost in debates about immigration policy. Moreover, for the first time, the U.S. population is getting much older. This "graying" of America also will lead assuredly to changes in our expectations of government and in our public policy demands. The debate that took place in 2003 over Medicare prescription drug coverage illustrates this phenomenon. Below, we look at some demographic facts (that is, information on characteristics of America's population) and then discuss some implications of these changes for how our nation is governed and what policy issues might arise.

Changes in Racial and Ethnic Composition.   From the start, the population of America has been changed constantly by the arrival of various kinds of immigrants to its shores—Western Europeans fleeing religious persecution in the 1600s to early 1700s, Irish Catholics escaping the potato famine in the 1850s, Chinese laborers arriving to work on the railroads, Northern and Eastern Europeans from the 1880s to 1910s, and most recently, Southeast Asians, Cubans, Mexicans, among others.

Immigration to the United States peaked in the first decade of the 1900s, when nearly 9 million people, many of them from Eastern Europe, entered the

Elian Gonzalez holds American and Cuban flags as a crowd of supporters grows outside his uncle's Miami home. The large Cuban community is a powerful force in Miami politics and objected strenuously to Elian's return to Cuba in 2000.

(Photo courtesy: AFP/Corbis)

Concern over immigration is not a new phenomenon, as this cartoon from the early 1900s depicts.

(Photo courtesy: New York Public Library)

country. The United States did not see another major wave of immigration until the late 1980s, when nearly 2 million immigrants were admitted in one year. Unlike the arrivals in other periods of high immigration, however, these "new" Americans were often "nonwhite"; many were Southeast Asians or Latin Americans. In fact, in 1997, a poll commissioned by PBS revealed that 45 percent of Americans polled thought "too many" immigrants were entering the United States from Latin American countries.[15]

While immigration has been a continual source of changing demographics in America, race has also played a major role in the development and course of politics in the United States. As revealed in Figure 1.2, the racial balance in America is changing

Participation

The Debate Over Immigration

FIGURE 1.2   Race and Ethnicity in America: 2000 and Beyond

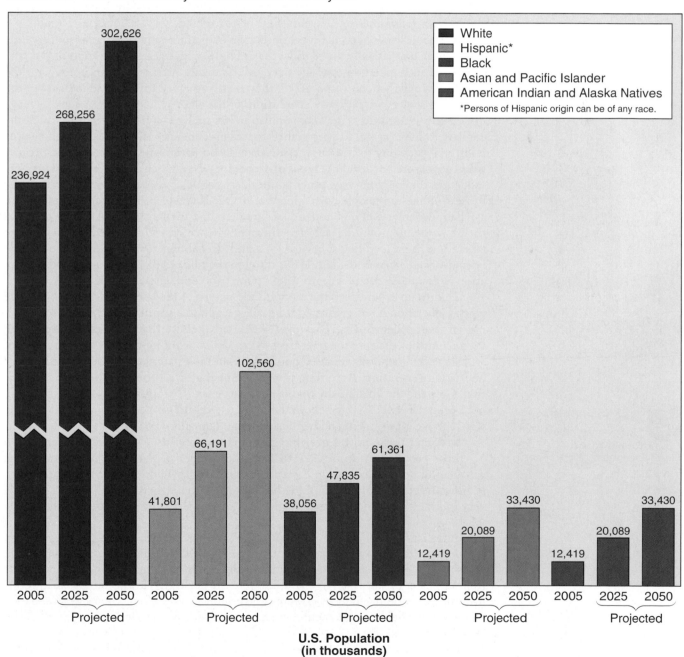

Source: U.S. Census Bureau, *2002 Statistical Abstract of the United States*. Data for 2000 from Census 2000 Summary Table 1.

dramatically. In 2000, for example, whites made up 75.1 percent of the U.S. population, African Americans 12.3 percent, and Hispanics 12.5 percent, surpassing the number of African Americans in the United States for the first time. Originally, demographers did not anticipate Hispanics would surpass African Americans until 2050. In some states, the Hispanic population is rivaling white, non-Hispanic populations.

Changes in Age Cohort Composition.   Just as the racial and ethnic composition of the American population is changing, so too is the average age of the population as is revealed in Analyzing Visuals: Changing Age Composition of the United States. "For decades, the U.S. was described as a nation of the young because the number of persons under the age of twenty greatly outnumber[ed] those sixty-five and older,"[16] but this is no longer the case. Due to changes in patterns of fertility, life expectancy, and immigration, the nation's age profile has changed drastically.[17] When the United States was founded, the average life expectancy was thirty-five years; by 2002, it was nearly eighty years for women and seventy-four years for men.

As people live longer, the types of services and policies they demand from government differ dramatically. In Florida, for example, which leads the nation in the percentage of its population over age sixty-five,[18] citizens are far less concerned with the quality of public schools (especially if they are being taxed for those schools) than the citizens in states with far lower proportions of the elderly.

As the age profile of the U.S. population has changed, political scientists and others have found it useful to assign labels to various generations. Such labels can be useful in understanding the various pressures put on our nation and its government, because when people are born and the kinds of events they experience can have important consequences on how they view other political, economic, and social events. For example, those 76.8 million people born after World War II (1946–1964) often are referred to as "Baby Boomers." These individuals grew up in a very different America than did their parents and now are reaching retirement age, which will put a major strain on the already overburdened Social Security system.[19] In contrast, their children, the 50 million who were born in the late 1960s through the mid-1970s, often are called Generation X-ers, the name of an early 1980s punk band and, later, a novel.[20]

This group experienced the economic downturn of the late 1980s. Jobs were scarce when Generation X-ers graduated from college, and many initially had a hard time paying off their college loans. They overwhelmingly believe that political leaders ignore them, and they distrust the political process. X-ers work longer, are better educated, and are more grassroots oriented politically than their parents.[21] Moreover, it is a very libertarian generation. According to one commentator, a difference between Generation X-ers and the liberal Baby Boomers is that X-ers "see capitalism as something that's not necessarily evil." X-ers believe they "can use capitalism for social change. It's one way to make government and big business stand up and take notice."[22]

In contrast, the fastest-growing group under age sixty-five is called "Generation Y," those people born from 1977 to 1994 (26 percent of the U.S. population). This group, unlike their Generation X predecessors, "has grown up in good times and [they, at least until recently,] have nothing but optimism about their future."[23] This group is very Internet savvy and much more globally focused than any generation before it.

Changes in Family and Family Size.   Family size and household arrangements, which also affect views on government, can be affected by several factors, including age at first marriage, divorce rates, economic conditions, longevity rates, and improvements in health care. In the past, large families were the norm (in part because so many children died early) and gender roles were clearly defined. Women did housework and men worked in the fields. Large families were imperative; children were the source of cheap farm labor.

Industrialization and knowledge of birth control methods, no matter how primitive, began to put a dent in the size of American families by the early 1900s. No longer

Simulation
How to Satisfy
Aunt Martha

WEB EXPLORATION
For more detail on population projections, see
www.ablongman.com/oconnor

WEB EXPLORATION
To learn more about
Generation Y, see
www.ablongman.com/oconnor

ANALYZING VISUALS

Changing Age Composition of the United States

Between 1990 and 2000, the elderly (age sixty-five and older) increased at a rate similar to those people under eighteen years old because of increased life expectancy, immigration, and advanced medical technologies. By 2040, the elderly will comprise nearly the same percentage of the U.S. population as young people. This is a dramatic increase from 1900, when the elderly constituted only 4 percent of the population, and the young were 40 percent of the population. After viewing the bar graph below, answer the critical thinking questions presented in the pointer bubbles, using information provided in this chapter. See Analyzing Visuals: A Brief Guide for additional guidance in analyzing graphs.

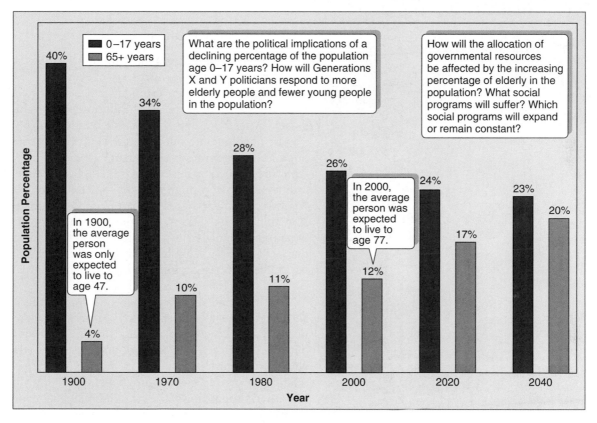

Sources: 1900–1980 data from Susan A. MacManus, *Young v. Old: Generational Combat in the 21st Century.* © 1995 by Westview Press, Inc. Reprinted by permission of Westview Press, a member of Perseus Books, L.L.C. 2000 data from Julie Meyer, "Age: 2000," U.S. Census Bureau, C2KBR/01–12, October 2001. Accessed June 30, 2002, http://www.census.gov/population/www/cen2000/briefs.html. 2020–2040 data from U.S. Census Bureau, National Population Projections, Detailed Files, revised November 2, 2000. Accessed June 30, 2002, http://www.census.gov/population/www/projections/natdet-D1A.html.

needing children to work for the survival of the household unit on the farm, couples began to limit the sizes of their families.

By 1949, 49 percent of those polled thought that four or more children was the "ideal" family size; in 1997, only 8 percent favored large families, and 54 percent responded that no children to two children were the "best."[24] As chronicled in the popular press as well as by the U.S. Department of Commerce, the American family no longer looks like *The Cosby Show* or even *The Brady Bunch*. While the actual number of households in the United States grew from 93.3 million in 1970 to 103 million in 2000, what those households looked like has changed dramatically. In 1940, nine out of ten households were "traditional" family households; by 2000, only 55.6 percent were two-parent family households, 14.9 percent of all households were headed by a single parent, and nearly 30 percent of all households consisted of a single person. Fewer than

WEB EXPLORATION
For more information on families and household composition, see www.ablongman.com/oconnor

one-half of the family households had children under the age of eighteen, and the average U.S. household had 2.62 people.

Since 1970, the number of female-headed households has increased dramatically from 5.5 million to 12.8 million—a whopping 133 percent increase. These changes in composition of households, lower birthrates, and prevalence of single-parent families, especially single female-headed families, affect the kinds of demands people place on government as well as their perceptions of the role that government should play in their lives.

Implications of These Changes

The varied races, ethnic origins, sizes of the various age cohorts, family types, and even gender roles of Americans have important implications for government and politics. Today, a few Americans, including the 2000 Reform Party presidential candidate Patrick Buchanan, believe that immigrants (legal and illegal) are flooding onto our shores with disastrous consequences. Such anti-immigration sentiments are hardly new—in fact, American history is replete with examples of "Americans" set against any new immigration. In the 1840s, for example, the Know Nothing Party arose in part to oppose immigration from Roman Catholic nations, charging that the pope was going to organize the slaughter of all Protestants in the United States. In the 1920s, the Ku Klux Klan, which had over 5 million members, called for barring immigration to stem the tide of Roman Catholics and Jews into the nation.

In the presidential campaign of 1996, immigration (legal and illegal) was a big issue. Many Americans believed (erroneously, for the most part) that floods of immigrants were putting Americans out of work and putting a strain on our already overburdened state and federal resources, especially school systems and welfare programs. In 1998, California voters passed Proposition 227 abolishing bilingual education programs in public elementary and secondary schools, a measure many viewed as anti-immigrant. In 2001, after the attacks on the World Trade Center and the Pentagon, 83 percent of those polled answered yes to the question, "Do you think U.S. immigration laws should be tightened to restrict the number of immigrants from Arab or Muslim countries into the United States?"[25]

The Osbournes are not the Cosbys or the Bradys. Still, in spite of their unconventional ways, to some they exhibit the caring and closeness many see as hallmarks of an American family.

(Photo courtesy: Getty Images)

Changing racial, ethnic, and even age and family demographics also seem to intensify—at least for some—an "us" versus "them" attitude. For example, government affirmative action programs, which were created in the 1960s to redress decades of overt racial discrimination, now have been largely abolished because some people and a majority of the U.S. Supreme Court believe that they give minorities and women unfair advantages in the job market, as well as in access to higher education. As more and more women graduated from college and entered the workforce, for example, some men criticized efforts to widen opportunities for women, while many women complained that a "glass ceiling" barred their advancement to the highest levels in most occupations. Dramatic changes in educational and employment opportunities for women, revealed in Table 1.1, also underscore these changes.

Sociologist James Davison Hunter defines the culture conflict that is the result of changing demographics as "political and social hostility rooted in very different systems of moral understanding."[26] These different worldviews—worker versus CEO, educated

TABLE 1.1	Men and Women in a Changing Society			
	1970		*2001*	
	Men	*Women*	*Men*	*Women*
Estimated life expectancy	67.1	74.1	74.34	80.01
% high school graduates	53	52	84.2	84
% of BAs awarded	56.6	43.4	43.7	56.3
% of MAs awarded	60	40	42.2	57.8
% of PhDs awarded	87	13	58	42
% of JDs awarded	95	5	56	44
Median earnings	$26,760	$14,232	$40,257	$25,551
Single parents	1.2 million	5.6 million	1.78 million	7.57 million

Sources: 1970 data: U.S. Census Bureau, *1996 Statistical Abstract of the United States.* U.S. Department of Commerce, Economics and Statistics Administration, Bureau of the Census. 2001 data: *The World Factbook;* U.S. Census Bureau, *2001 Statistical Abstract of the United States.*

versus uneducated, young versus old, white versus black, male versus female, native-born versus immigrant—can create deep cleavages in society, as exemplified by the "polarizing impulses or tendencies" in American society.[27] Just as the two parties at times seem to be pushed to take extreme positions on many issues, so are many of those who speak out on those issues.

Demographics also affect politics and government because an individual's perspective often influences how he or she hears the debate on various issues. Thus, many African Americans viewed O.J. Simpson's acquittal as vindication for decades of unjust treatment experienced by blacks in the criminal justice system and the poor and working class view corporate collapses such as Enron quite differently than do many richer executives.

These cleavages and the emphasis many politicians put on our demographic differences play out in many ways in American politics. Baby Boomers and the elderly object to any changes in Social Security or Medicare, while those in Generation X vote for politicians

With the slowing of the U.S. economy after several years of economic growth, anti-immigration sentiment is surfacing once again, although immigration, especially from Mexico, is down dramatically post 9/11.

(Photo courtesy: Essdras Suarez/Liaison Agency/Getty Images)

Join the Debate

HOW DOES AMERICA'S PLURALISM AFFECT OUR CORE VALUES?

On September 11, 2002, former New York City Mayor Rudy Giuliani and others commemorated the September 11, 2001, attack on the World Trade Center by reading the names of 2,801 people who were killed there. The names were clearly representative of a wide array of nationalities from around the world and demonstrated in a very real way that modern America includes peoples from all over the globe. The increasingly multicultural nature of life in the United States often stirs debate over the potential effects of such pluralism on American cultural and political values.

Are core American values secure, or are they endangered when America changes? Some Americans worry that the changing demographics of our population will inevitably supplant long-established values with those of peoples socialized in other cultures. They argue that demographic diversity does occasionally have the potential to undermine American liberal democratic values, since some cultures hold different views about women's rights, church-state relations, political competition, and so forth. Others argue that the pluralistic nature of American society enriches social and civic life and enhances core American values.

George Washington University sociologist Amitai Etzioni explores these issues in the following op-ed piece, arguing for the positive effects of pluralism. As you may know, articles on the "op-ed" page of a newspaper (which as the name suggests, usually appears opposite the editorial page) present the perspectives of guest columnists, and, unlike more "objective" news reports, usually put forth an argument on a particular topic. Read the following op-ed article with an eye toward determining whether or not increasing demographic diversity is undermining American liberal democratic values. Are there any beliefs or practices of other cultures that you believe might have that potential? What traditions should a majority be able to insist on preserving in the face of different traditions practiced by a minority? Join the debate over pluralism, American values, and majority/minority dynamics by considering the debating points and questions posed at the end of this feature, and sharpen your own arguments for the position you find most viable.

Our Monochrome Values

By Amitai Etzioni

"What is going to happen to 'white' values?" Dale Hurd repeatedly asked while interviewing me for a TV program for the Christian Broadcasting Network. His concern was aroused by the detailed data about the racial makeup of American society...

Although the precise breakdowns by 63 racial categories (including racial combinations) are not yet known, figures depicting the basic changes in America's demography have been issued. US census data already available are often said to point to a rise of a "majority of minorities" (beginning in California, next in Texas, and thereafter all over the United States). But it is far from obvious what these figures mean, let alone that they entail a decline of European values, those of the founders.

I told Mr. Hurd that American core values—respect for life, liberty, and the pursuit of happiness (as well as the communitarian quest for a more perfect union), the democratic way of life, and the bill of rights—either deserve our commitment because we find them compelling or they should be rejected. The race of whoever first articulated them matters not. Imagine discovering that the ancient Greeks really got their ideas from Egypt or Libya, as some claim. Would they be less valid? What if we learned that John Locke was a Moor?

Also, the fact is that most Americans from all social groups want the same basic things ... prosperity and peace, a brilliant future for themselves and their kids, safe streets and honest government, among other things. (Next time you read about racial discrepancies found in opinion polls, note that the differences played up often amount to less than 20 percent, which means that the

similarities, usually not referred to, amount to more than 80 percent.)

Granted, there are differences on select issues, especially when they directly concern racial relations, for instance between the views of African-Americans and others on the outcome of the O.J. Simpson trial. But these are exceptions, not the rule.

The very notion that there are two American camps, the majority and "the minorities," is a dubious construction. Not only do most minority members agree with the majority on most issues, but on those issues where they differ with the majority, they also disagree with one another. The two major nonwhite groups, Asian Americans and African-Americans, are particularly disparate, with the first much more conservative than the latter....

Furthermore, the very notion that there are monolithic "minorities," a term bandied about daily, ignores the fact that differences within each minority often exceed differences among them. Many Cuban Americans' attitudes are closer to Asian Americans' than those of Puerto Rican Americans, whose viewpoints are closer to African-Americans. Japanese Americans share little with Filipino Americans, and so on. Among those surveyed in the National Latino Political Survey, approximately three-quarters of Puerto Ricans and two-thirds of Cuban Americans and Mexican Americans chose to be labeled by their place of birth, as opposed to "pan-ethnic" terms such as "Hispanic" or "Latino."

Last but not least, Americans of different backgrounds intermarry, and they do so at an ever-rising rate, especially the young, who own the future. Before too long, the majority of Americans will not be minorities or the majority, but people whose parents, in-laws, uncles, and cousins are like those of Tiger Woods: Americans of all kinds. These mul-tiracial and multiethnic Americans will blur the sharp edges now attributed to the various social groups, moving America ever closer to a monochrome society—although its appearance will be more akin to chocolate milk than to that of palefaced Americans.

The importance of all this is that if people were to stop looking at pigmentation and other factors that are skin deep, jumping to the conclusion that there is a close relationship between race and the way one thinks and behaves, they would see that America is much less diverse than racial statistics are often said to imply.

Does all this mean that American society will remain basically unchanged? Certainly not. It has been the genius of America from its inception as a society of immigrants that it both incorporates newcomers and adapts, growing richer by absorbing some of their unique features.

Thus, the US may well become more focused on nations south of its border and on the Pacific Rim than on Europe, but this will entail few basic substantive changes in American foreign policy. We shall still favor free trade, oppose nuclear proliferation, support human rights, and so on. And teaching children more about cultures other than Western ones will add to the broadening of our educational horizons rather than to abandonment of the "classics."

Will we be a society free from racial and ethnic conflict? America never has been. However, we learned long ago to resolve, in peaceful ways, most of these conflicts most of the time. We have nothing to fear but those who try to promote fear.

Source: Amitai Etzioni, *Christian Science Monitor*, June 4, 2001, Vol. 93, Issue 132, page 9. Reprinted by permission of the author.

JOIN THE DEBATE!

CHECK YOUR UNDERSTANDING: Make sure you understand the following key points from the article; go back and review it if you missed any of them:

- Census data trends show a proportionally larger increase of groups that now constitute a minority of the population.
- Intermarrying among the sixty-three racial groups in the population is increasing.
- There are measurable differences of opinion within the same groups in American society.
- The differences of opinion between groups are usually smaller than the degree of agreement.

ADDITIONAL INFORMATION: News articles and op-ed pieces don't provide all the information an informed citizen needs to know about an issue under debate. Here are some questions the article does not answer that you may need to consider in order to join the debate:

- What might be defined as core values?
- Does polling data demonstrate any significant differences among groups on core value issues?
- How have the events of September 11, 2001, affected attitudes about "minority" groups and their contributions to society?

What other information might you want to know? Where might you gather this information? How might you evaluate the credibility of the information you gather? Is the information from a reliable source? Can you identify any potential biases?

IDENTIFYING THE ARGUMENTS: Now that you have some information on the issue, and have thought about what else you need to know, see whether you can present the arguments on both sides of the debate. Here are some ideas to get you started. We've provided one example each of "pro" and "con" arguments, but you should be able to offer others:

PRO: Pluralism enhances core democratic values. Here's why:

- Tolerance for differences is essential in democracy, and exposure to a broad spectrum of influences increases tolerance.

CON: Increasing levels of pluralism has a great potential for undermining core democratic values. Here's why:

- Liberal democratic values of openness and political competition are not as strong in many cultures, and immigrants from those cultures understandably bring with them their own values, some of which are anti-democratic.

TAKING A POSITION AND SUPPORTING IT: After thinking about the information in the op-ed piece on the increasingly pluralistic nature of American society, placing it in the broader context of core American values, and articulating the arguments in the debate, what position would you take? What information supports your position? What arguments would you use to persuade others to your side of the debate? How would you counter arguments on the other side?

who support change, if they vote at all. Many policies are targeted at one group or the other, further exacerbating differences—real or imagined—and lawmakers often find themselves the target of many different factions. All of this can make it difficult to devise coherent policies to "promote the general welfare," as promised in the Constitution.

The Ideology of the American Public

Political ideology

An individual's coherent set of values and beliefs about the purpose and scope of government.

Political ideology is a term used by political scientists to refer to the more or less consistent set of values that historically have been reflected in the political system, economic order, social goals, and moral values of any given society. "It is the means by which the basic values held by a party, class, group or individual are articulated."[28] Most Americans espouse liberalism or conservatism, although a growing number call themselves libertarians, who do not place themselves on traditional liberal/conservative continuums used by political scientists (see Figure 1.3).

You probably already have a good idea of what the terms liberal and conservative mean, but you may not be aware that the meaning of these terms has changed dramatically over time. During the nineteenth century, for example, conservatives supported governmental power and favored a role for religion in public life; in contrast, liberals supported freedom from undue governmental control. (See Table 1.2 for additional information about these terms.) In general, your ideology often is a good predictor of where you stand on a variety of issues (see Table 1.2) as well as how you view the proper role of government.

conservative

One thought to believe that a government is best that governs least and that big government can only infringe on individual, personal, and economic rights.

Conservativism.   According to William Safire's *New Political Dictionary*, a **conservative** "is a defender of the status quo who, when change becomes necessary in tested institutions or practices, prefers that it come slowly, and in moderation."[29] Conservatives are thought to believe that a government is best that governs least, and that big government can only infringe on individual, personal, and economic rights. They want less government, especially in terms of regulation of the economy. Conservatives favor local and state action over federal action, and emphasize fiscal responsibility, most notably in the form of balanced budgets. Conservatives are likely to support smaller, less activist governments and believe that domestic problems like homelessness, poverty, and discrimination are better dealt with by the private sector than by the government. Less rigid conservatives see the need for governmental action in some fields and for steady change in many areas. They seek to achieve such change within the framework of existing institutions, occasionally changing the institutions when they show a need for it.

WEB EXPLORATION
For more information on conservatives, see
www.ablongman.com/oconnor

FIGURE 1.3 Self-Identification as Liberal, Moderate, or Conservative, 1974–2004

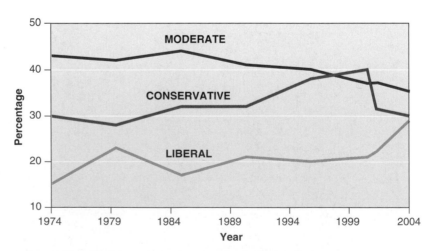

Note: "Liberal" equals the combined percentages of those identifying themselves as extremely liberal, liberal, or slightly liberal; "conservative" equals the combined percentages of those identifying themselves as extremely conservative, conservative, or slightly conservative.

Source: Roper Center at the University of Connecticut, *Public Opinion Online.*

TABLE 1.2	Liberal? Conservative? Libertarian? Chart Your Views on These Issues				
	Abortion Rights	Environmental Regulation	Gun Control Laws	Government Support of:	
				Poor	School Vouchers
Conservative	Oppose	Oppose	Oppose	Oppose	Favor
Liberal	Favor	Favor	Favor	Favor	Oppose
Libertarian	Favor	Oppose	Oppose	Oppose	Oppose

Liberalism.   Liberalism is a political view held by those who "seek to change the political, economic, or social status quo to foster the development and well-being of the individual."[30] Safire defines a **liberal** as "currently one who believes in more government action to meet individual needs, originally one who resisted government encroachments on individual liberties."[31] Liberals now are considered to favor a big government that plays an active role in the economy. They also stress the need for the government to provide for the poor and homeless, to provide a wide array of other social services, and to take an activist role in protecting the rights of women, the elderly, minorities, and the environment. It is a political philosophy that has roots in the American Revolution and eighteenth-century liberalism. Today, many of its supporters refer to it as the "modern revival of classical liberalism."[32]

Libertarianism.   Libertarianism is a political philosophy based largely on individual freedom and the curtailment of state power. **Libertarians** have long believed in the evils of big government and stress that government should not involve itself in the plight of the people or attempt to remedy any social ills. Basically, libertarians, although a very diverse lot, favor a free market economy and an end to governmental intrusion in the area of personal liberties. Generation X-ers are more libertarian in political philosophy than any other age cohort and were credited with the election of Governor Jesse Ventura of Minnesota in 1999. He ran as the Reform Party candidate, became an Independent after election, and now claims to be a libertarian. Liberals criticize libertarian calls for elimination of all government sponsored welfare and public works programs; conservatives bemoan libertarian calls for reductions in the defense budget and elimination of federal agencies such as the Central Intelligence Agency and the Federal Bureau of Investigation.

Problems with Political Labels

When considering what it means when someone identifies himself or herself as a conservative, liberal, libertarian, or some other political philosophy, it is important to

liberal
One considered to favor extensive governmental involvement in the economy and the provision of social services and to take an activist role in protecting the rights of women, the elderly, minorities, and the environment.

WEB EXPLORATION
For more information on liberals, see
www.ablongman.com/oconnor

libertarian
One who favors a free market economy and no governmental interference in personal liberties.

WEB EXPLORATION
For more information on libertarians, see
www.ablongman.com/oconnor

During the 107th Congress, Dick Armey (R–TX), then the House majority leader and chair of the House Select Committee on Homeland Security, talks to then House Democratic Whip Nancy Pelosi (D–CA) as the committee began debate on legislation creating a department of homeland security. In the House, they stand at opposite ends of the liberal (Pelosi) and conservative (Armey) spectrum. Pelosi was elected minority leader in 2002.
(Photo courtesy: Dennis Cook/AP/Wide World Photos)

WEB EXPLORATION
To find out your ideological
stance, go to
www.ablongman.com/oconnor

remember that the labels can be quite misleading and do not necessarily allow us to predict political opinions. In a perfect world, liberals would be liberal and conservatives would be conservative. Studies reveal, however, that many people who call themselves conservative actually take fairly liberal positions on many policy issues. In fact, anywhere from 20 percent to 60 percent will take a traditionally "conservative" position on one issue and a traditionally "liberal" position on another.[33] People who take conservative stances against "big government," for example, often support increases in spending for the elderly, education, or health care. It is also not unusual to encounter a person who could be considered liberal on social issues such as abortion and civil rights but conservative on economic or "pocketbook" issues. Moreover, libertarians, for example, often are against any governmental restrictions on abortion (a liberal view) but against any kind of welfare spending (a conservative view). Today, like libertarians, most Americans' positions on specific issues cut across liberal/conservative ideological boundaries to such a degree that new, more varied ideological categories may soon be needed to capture division within American political thought. (See Table 1.2 to gauge where your political views place you.)

POLITICAL CULTURE AND VIEWS OF GOVERNMENT

Americans' views about and expectations of government and democracy affect the political system at all levels. It has now become part of our political culture to expect negative campaigns, dishonest politicians, and political pundits who make their living bashing politicians and the political process. How Americans view politics, the economy, and their ability to achieve the American dream also is influenced by their political ideology as well as by their social, economic, educational, and personal circumstances.

Since the early 1990s, the major sources of most individuals' on-the-air news—the four major networks (ABC, CBS, FOX, and NBC) along with CNN and C-SPAN—have been supplemented dramatically as the number of news and quasi-news outlets have multiplied like rabbits. First there were weekly programs such as *Dateline* on the regular networks. Then came the rapid expansion of cable programming beginning with CNN and C-SPAN, then the new FOX cable channel, MSNBC, and CNBC—all competing for similar audiences. By Election Night 2000, most people turned to a cable news program to learn who won, never suspecting that the results weren't to be final for five more weeks. These networks' news programming also has been supplemented by the phenomenal development of the Internet as an instantaneous source of news as well as rumor about politics. One online newsletter, the *Drudge Report*, was actually the first to break the story about President Bill Clinton and Monica Lewinsky.

As more and more news programs developed, the pressure on each network or news program to be "the first" with the news—often whether it actually is verifiable or not—multiplied exponentially, as was illustrated on Election Night 2000 when all rushed to "call" states for a particular candidate and to be the first to predict the overall winner. Their focus on political scandals also increased, be it President Bill Clinton's relationship with Monica Lewinsky or Congressman Gary Condit's relationship with Chandra Levy, which made him a suspect in her disappearance. For seven months the nation got a daily diet of speculation and conjecture about "Bill and Monica" until the president finally admitted to an "improper relationship." Chandra Levy's body was found in spring 2002, after Condit was defeated in his Democratic primary.

The competition for news stories, as well as the instantaneous nature of these communications, often highlights the negative, the sensational, the sound bite, and usually the extremes. It's hard to remain upbeat about America or politics amidst the media's focus on personality and scandal. It's hard to remain positive about the fate of Americans and their families if you listen to talk radio or watch talk shows like *Jerry Springer* or *Ricki Lake*. It was far easier for the press to focus on the Clinton/Lewinsky matter

During the 2000 presidential campaign, George W. Bush appeared on informal talk shows like *Oprah Winfrey* and *Live with Regis* in an effort to appeal to women voters.

(Photo courtesy: Tannen Maury/Image Works)

than to devote time and space to a story of a teenage mother who, aided by government programs, went to college, got a job, and became an involved parent and citizen. Those kinds of success stories are generally showcased only in State of the Union Addresses or at presidential nominating conventions.

High Expectations

In roughly the first 150 years of our nation's history, the federal government had few responsibilities, and its citizens had few expectations of it beyond national defense, printing money, collecting tariffs and taxes, and so on. The state governments were generally far more powerful than the federal government in matters affecting the everyday lives of Americans (see chapters 3 and 4).

As the nation and its economy grew in size and complexity, the federal government took on more responsibilities such as regulating some businesses, providing poverty relief, and inspecting food. Then, in the 1930s, in response to the Great Depression, President Franklin D. Roosevelt's New Deal government programs proliferated in almost every area of American life (job creation, income security, aid to the poor, and so on). Since then, many Americans have looked to the government for solutions to all kinds of problems.

Politicians, too, have often contributed to rising public expectations by promising far more than they or government could deliver. Although President Bill Clinton's vow to end "welfare as we know it" was realized by the end of his first term, his ambitious promises to overhaul the health care system went nowhere.

As voters look to governments to solve a variety of problems from education to anthrax, their expectations are not always met. Unmet expectations have led to cynicism about government and apathy, as evidenced in low voter turnout. It may be that Americans have come to expect too much from the national government and must simply readjust their expectations. Nevertheless, Table 1.3 reveals increased confidence in most institutions.

TABLE 1.3   Faith in Institutions

*PERCENTAGE OF AMERICANS DECLARING THEY HAD A "GREAT DEAL"
OF CONFIDENCE IN THE INSTITUTION*

	1966	1975	1986	1996	2002	2004
Congress	42%	13%	16%	8%	19%	8%
Executive branch	41	13	21	10	35	25
The press	29	26	18	11	16	9
Business & industry	55	19	24	23	12	19
Medicine	73	51	46	45	29	19

Sources: Newsweek (January 8, 1996): 32; Public Perspective 8 (February/March 1994): 4. Data for 2002: Public Opinion Online.

A Missing Appreciation of the Good

During the Revolutionary period, average citizens were passionate about politics because the stakes—the very survival of the new nation—were so high. Until September 11, 2001, the stakes weren't readily apparent to many people. If you don't have faith in America, its institutions, or symbols (and Table 1.3 shows that many of us don't), it becomes even easier to blame the government for all kinds of woes—personal as well as societal—or to fail to credit governments for the things governments do well. Many Americans, for example, enjoy a remarkably high standard of living, and much of it is due to governmental programs, practices, and protections from food safety to national security. (See Table 1.4 for quality of life measures.)

Even in the short time between when you get up in the morning and when you leave for classes or work, the government—or its rulings or regulations—pervades your life. The national or state governments, for example, set the standards for whether you wake up on Eastern, Central, Mountain, or Pacific Standard Time. The national government regulates the airwaves and licenses the radio or television broadcasts you might listen to or glance at as you eat and get dressed. States, too, regulate and tax telecommunications. Whether or not the water you use as you brush your teeth contains fluoride is a state or local governmental issue. The federal Food and Drug Administration inspects your breakfast meat and sets standards for the advertising on your cereal box, orange juice carton, and other food packaging. States set standards for food labeling. Are they really "lite," "high in fiber," or "fresh squeezed"? Usually, one or more levels of government is authorized to decide these matters.

TABLE 1.4   How Americans Really Are Doing

	1945	1970	2002
Population	132 million	203 million	285 million
Life expectancy	65.9	70.8	75.4
Per capita income (1999 constant dollars)	$6,367	$12,816	$21,181[c]
Adults who are high school grads	25%[a]	52.3%	84.1%[d]
Adults who are college grads	5%[a]	10.7%	25.6%[d]
Households with phones	46%	87%	94.2%[c]
Households with televisions	0%	95%	98.2%[c]
Households with cable TV	0%	4%	67.5%[c]
Households with computers	n/a	n/a	51%[d]
Women in labor force	29%	38%	60%[d]
Own their own home	46%	63%	66.9%[e]
Annual airline passengers	7 million	170 million	635.4 million[c]
Below poverty rate	39.7%[b]	12.6%	11.8%[c]
Divorce rate (per 1,000 people)	3.5	3.5	4.2[e]
Children born out of wedlock	3.9%	16.7%	33%[c]

[a]1940 figure.   [b]1949 figure.   [c]1999 figure.   [d]2000 figure.   [e]1998 figure.

Source: U.S. Census Bureau, 2001 Statistical Abstract of the United States.

Although all governments have problems, it is important to stress the good they can do. In the aftermath of the Great Depression in the United States, for example, the government created the Social Security program, which dramatically decreased poverty among the elderly. Our contract laws and judicial system provide an efficient framework for business, assuring people that they have a recourse in the courts should someone fail to deliver as promised. Government-guaranteed student loan programs make it possible for many students to attend college. Even something as seemingly mundane as our uniform bankruptcy laws help protect both a business enterprise and its creditors when the enterprise collapses.

Mistrust of Politicians

It's not difficult to see why Americans might be distrustful of politicians. In August 1998, after President Bill Clinton announced to the American public that he had misled them concerning his relationship with Monica Lewinsky, 45 percent said they were disgusted, 33 percent were angry, but only 18 percent were surprised, according to a poll conducted by the *Washington Post*.[34]

President Bill Clinton wasn't the only politician to incur the public's distrust. One 1998 poll conducted by the Pew Charitable Trusts found that 40 percent of those polled thought that most politicians were "crooks."[35] These perceptions are reinforced when politicians such as James A. Traficant, a Democratic representative from Ohio, are tried and convicted of tax evasion and racketeering. Later, he was ousted from the House with only Representative Gary Condit (D-CA) voting against his expulsion.

Voter Apathy

"Campaigns are the conversation of democracy," an observer once said.[36] But, a Gallup poll conducted after the 1988 presidential contest between George Bush and Michael Dukakis found that 30 percent of those who voted would have preferred to check off a "no confidence in either" box had they been given the choice.

Americans, unlike voters in most other societies, get an opportunity to vote on a host of candidates and issues, but some say those choices may just be too numbing. Responsible voters may simply opt not to go to the polls, fearing that they lack sufficient information of the vast array of candidates and issues facing them.

Doris "Granny D" Haddock, who completed a fourteen-month, 3,200-mile trek across America to agitate for campaign finance reform, is an activist voter as opposed to an apathetic voter.

(Photo courtesy: Reuters/Jamal Wilson/Archive Photos)

James A. Traficant (D–OH), who was expelled by the House after his conviction for tax evasion and racketeering, is just one of the most colorful representatives who did not return for the 108th Congress. Also missing were Representatives Gary Condit (D–CA), Bob Barr (R–GA), who led the battle to impeach President Clinton, and Cynthia McKinney (D–GA), who accused the Bush family of profiting from 9/11.

(Photo courtesy: Dennis Cook/AP/Wide World Photos)

THE UNITED STATES IN COMPARATIVE CONTEXT

Two scholars of American politics recently published books examining their field of study in comparative context. The title of one, *America the Unusual*, speaks volumes about how Americans perceive their national politics. The other, *Only in America?*, wonders whether the political differences make that much difference.[a] Do political institutions and practices in the United States truly differ from politics elsewhere?

To give you a sense of how different, and in many cases how similar, politics in this country is to politics in other countries, each chapter of this book includes a Global Politics box that compares some aspect of American politics with that in other countries. One line of comparison will be with Canada, France, Germany, Italy, Japan, the United Kingdom, and the United States (known as the G-7), which represent a variety of experiences within a common framework. They are all industrial democracies, holding among the highest gross national products (GNPs) in the world and enjoying a comparatively high standard of living. The group has become known as the G-8 by the addition of the Russian president to the annual summit. In this book, we continue the G-7 shorthand to stand for a set of advanced capitalist industrial democracies. Even though Russia is now officially a member of this "leadership club," its situation as a country making the transition to capitalism and parliamentary democracy from a socialist economy and political system makes its recent political experience qualitatively different from that of the original G-7 members.

There is, however, variation among the G-7 on specific indicators. The United States, for example, is far larger than any of its counterparts except Canada. It has more than twice the population of Japan. The United States also has a low unemployment rate, especially compared to the European countries. Thus, the industrial democracies provide a pool of good cases for comparison of politics.

Industrial democracies, however, do not represent the majority of political systems in the world. Of the other 190 or so nation-states in existence today, we will consider China, Egypt, India, Indonesia, Mexico, and Russia as representative examples. The first five are typically classified as developing countries. Egypt, India, and Mexico are often characterized as semidemocracies, meaning that they have some democratic features (such as holding regular elections for public offices) but also apply significant constraints on free public participation in politics. Indonesia and Russia have begun the transition to democracy only recently. In one way or another, these representative nations demonstrate the problems many countries face in achieving democracy. China is a communist country, and as such differs from the G-7 even as to basic definitions of democracy. Russia, as discussed above, is classified as a transitional democracy, attempting to move from the socialist political and economic pattern of the former Soviet Union to parliamentary democracy and a capitalist economy.

---

[a]John W. Kingdom, *America the Unusual* (New York: Worth Publishers, 1999). Graham K. Wilson, *Only in America* (Chatham, NJ: Chatham House, 1998).

Vital Statistics of Selected Countries

Country	Population (million, 2000)	Area (1,000 km²)	GDP/ Capita ($ 2000)	Life Expectancy	Form of Government	Labor Force Participation (ratio female to male)
Canada	31.1	9,971	24,800	78.9	federal republic	0.8
China	1,284.9	9,597	3,600	68.6	communist	0.8
Egypt	69.53	1,001	3,600	63.7	republic	0.4
France	59	552	24,400	77.9	unitary republic	0.8
Germany	82	357	23,400	76.5	federal republic	0.7
India	1,029	3,287	2,200	62.9	federal republic	0.5
Indonesia	212.1	1,905	2,900	62.7	unitary republic	0.7
Italy	57.2	301	22,100	78.1	unitary republic	0.6
Japan	126.7	378	24,900	80.5	constitutional monarchy	0.7
Mexico	98.8	1,958	9,100	71.5	federal republic	0.5
Russia	146.9	17,075	7,700	64.9	federation	1.0
United Kingdom	58.8	243	22,800	76.8	constitutional monarchy	0.8
United States	**278.3**	**9,364**	**36,200**	**76.1**	**federal republic**	**0.8**

Sources: United Nations Statistics Division online, http://www.un.org/Depts/unsd/social/. CIA World Factbook 2001 online, http://www.odci.gov/cia/publications/factbook/. World Bank, World Development Indicators 2001.

A Census Bureau report examining the reasons given by the millions of eligible voters who stayed home from the polls on Election Day in 2002 showed that being too busy was the single biggest reason Americans gave for not voting. The head of the Committee for the Study of the American Electorate thinks that time is just an excuse.[37] Instead, he believes many Americans don't vote because they lack real choices. Why vote, if your vote won't make much difference? In fact, unsuccessful presidential candidate Ralph Nader tried to run as an alternative to the two major parties in 2000 and 2004, arguing that there was little difference between Republicans and Democrats.

Some commentators even noted that nonvoting may even be a sign of contentment. If things are good, or you perceive that there is no need for change, why vote?

Whatever the reason, declining voter participation is cause for concern. If information is truly a problem, it may be that the Internet, access to information, and new ways to vote may change the course of elections in the future. The aftermath of the 2000 election, when it first became clear to many Americans that absentee ballots are not always counted and that some kinds of ballots produce large numbers of unreadable ballots, may only serve to exacerbate that problem at worst, or, for the best, lead to reforms.

The 2004 elections saw many jurisdictions adopting touch screen voting machines, early voting, and an increase in absentee and provisional ballots. These changes, along with massive registration and get out the vote drives, hopefully revised this trend as a record number of Americans turned out to vote.

Redefining Our Expectations

Just as it is important to recognize that governments serve many important purposes, it is also important to recognize that government and **politics**—the process by which policy decisions are made—are not static. Politics, moreover, involves conflicts over different and sometimes opposing ideologies, and these ideologies are very much influenced by one's racial, economic, and historical experiences. These divisions are real and affect the political process at all levels. It is clear to most Americans today that politics and government no longer can be counted on to cure all of America's ills. Government, however, will always play a major role. True political leaders will need to help Americans come to terms with America as it is today—not as it was in the past—real or imaginary. Perhaps a discussion on how "community" is necessary for everybody to get along (and necessary for democracy) is in order. Some democratic theorists suggest that the citizen-activist must be ultimately responsible for the resolution of these divisions.

The current frustration and dissatisfaction about politics and government may be just another phase, as the changing American body politic seeks to redefine its ideas about government. This process is one that is likely to define politics well into the future, but the individualistic nature of the American system will have long-lasting consequences on how it can be accomplished. Americans want less government, but as they get older, they don't want less Social Security. They want lower taxes and better roads, but they don't want to pay for toll roads. They want better education for their children but lower expenditures on schools. They want greater security at airports but low fares and quick boarding. Some clearly want less for others but not themselves, which puts politicians in the position of nearly always disappointing voters. This inability to please voters and find a middle ground undoubtedly led to the unprecedented retirements of members of Congress in 1994 and 1996.

Politicians, as well as their constituents, are looking for ways to redefine the role of government, much in the same way that the Framers did when they met in Philadelphia to forge a solution between Americans' quest for liberty and freedom tempered by order and governmental authority. While citizens charge that it is still government as usual, a change is taking place in Washington, D.C. Sacrosanct programs such as Social Security and welfare continually are being reexamined, and some powers and responsibilities are slowly being returned to the states. Thus, the times may be different, but the questions about government and its role in our lives remain the same.

politics
The process by which policy decisions are made.

Comparing Political Landscapes

ANALYZING VISUALS

Voter Turnout: A Generally Apathetic Electorate?

In 2004, a record number of Americans went to the polls—approximately 117 million or nearly 60 percent of the eligible voters. This is the highest turnout since 1968 and about 10 percent above 2000. Nevertheless, because declining voter participation is a cause for concern in a democracy, political scientists have tried to understand why such a small percentage of age-eligible citizens are voting. The Charles Barsotti cartoon below, which originally appeared in *The New Yorker* magazine, offers one possible explanation for low voter turnout. After examining the cartoon, answer the following critical thinking questions: Of the possible causes mentioned in this chapter's material on voter apathy, which cause is the cartoonist depicting? What elements in the cartoon indicate that the person depicted in the cartoon would be a likely voter? What do you perceive to be the cartoonist's purpose in drawing the cartoon? How does the cartoon achieve that purpose? See Analyzing Visuals: A Brief Guide for additional guidance in analyzing political cartoons.

"I'm undecided, but that doesn't mean I'm apathetic or uninformed."

(Photo courtesy: ©The New Yorker Collection 1980 Charles Barsotti from cartoonbank.com. All Rights Reserved.)

Although the Civil War and other national crises such as the Great Depression, the September 11 terrorist attacks, and the anthrax scares created major turmoil, they demonstrated that our system can survive and even change in the face of enormous political, societal, and institutional pressures. Often, these crises have produced considerable reforms. The Civil War led to the dismantling of the slavery system and to the passage of the Thirteenth, Fourteenth, and Fifteenth Amendments (see chapter 6), which led to the seeds of recognition of African Americans as American citizens. The Great Depression led to the New Deal and the creation of a government more actively involved in economic and social regulation. In the 1970s, the Watergate scandal and resignation of President Richard M. Nixon resulted in stricter ethics laws that have led to the resignation or removal of many unethical elected officials.

Elections themselves, which often seem chaotic, help generation after generation remake the political landscape as new representatives seek to shake up the established order. Thus, while elections can seem like chaos, from this chaos comes order and often the explosive productivity of a democratic society.

Continuity & Change

The Face of America

When the original settlers came to what is now the United States, they did so for a variety of reasons. Still, they recognized the critical role that government could play for them in the New World. So, even though the colonists considered themselves British subjects, they knew the importance of fashioning some form of governance, as illustrated by their signatures of agreement on the Mayflower Compact. Those who signed that historic document were largely British, male, and Caucasian. They expected the government to be best that governed least, but they also recognized the importance of order and protection of property and were willing to give up some rights in return for government preservation of those ideals.

Over time, young men in a variety of large and not so large wars fought for what they believed was the American ideal. At the same time, women often left their homes to work in hospitals or factories to help the war effort, generally forgoing their personal goals. Immigrants and native-born citizens alike all shared the American dream.

Today, the American dream is more difficult to see. A new wave of immigrants in the 1980s has changed the composition of many U.S. cities and states, often straining scarce resources such as access to quality public education, which has always been at the forefront of the American political socialization process. Several states, especially California, recently have attempted to restrict the rights and privileges of aliens in unprecedented ways. It is a system of majority rule, where the rights of those newest to our borders often lose out.

As illustrated by Figure 1.2, however, the ethnic "look" of America is changing, and in some places such as California, Texas, and Florida it is changing especially quickly. These changes prompt several questions.

1. What challenges do you believe national and state governments will face as the racial and ethnic composition of their citizenry changes dramatically?
2. In the wake of the 2000 Census that found Hispanics now to be the largest U.S. minority group, do you foresee any changes in how minorities, especially Hispanics, will be treated?

CAST YOUR VOTE What other challenges do you think national and state governments will face in the twenty-first century? To cast your vote, go to www.ablongman.com/oconnor

SUMMARY

In this chapter, we have made the following points:

1. **The Roots of American Government: Where Did the Ideas Come From?**
   The American political system was based on several notions that have their roots in classical Greek ideas, including natural law, the doctrine that human affairs should be governed by certain ethical principles that can be understood by reason. The ideas of social contract theorists John Locke and Thomas Hobbes, who held the belief that people are free and equal by God-given right, have continuing implications for our ideas of the proper role of government in our indirect democracy.

2. **Characteristics of American Democracy**
   Key characteristics of this democracy established by the Framers are popular consent, popular sovereignty, majority rule and the preservation of minority rights, equality, individualism, and personal liberty, as is the Framers' option for a capitalistic system.

3. **The Changing Political Culture and Characteristics of the American People**
   Several characteristics of the American electorate can help us understand how the system continues to evolve and change. Chief among these are changes in size and population, demographics, racial and ethnic makeup, family and family size, age patterns, and ideological beliefs.

4. **Political Culture and Views of Government**
   Americans have high and often unrealistic expectations of government. At the same time, they often fail to appreciate how much their government actually does for them. Some of this failure may be due to Americans' general mistrust of politicians, which may explain some of the apathy evidenced in the electorate.

KEY TERMS

aristocracy, p. 6
capitalism, p. 7
civil society, p. 12
communism, p. 9
conservative, p. 22
democracy, p. 6
direct democracy, p. 6
free market economy, p. 7
indirect (representative) democracy, p. 6
liberal, p. 23
libertarian, p. 23
majority rule, p. 11
mercantile system, p. 7
monarchy, p. 5
natural law, p. 3
oligarchy, p. 6
personal liberty, p. 12
political culture, p. 12
political ideology, p. 22
politics, p. 29
popular consent, p. 10
popular sovereignty, p. 10
republic, p. 6
social contract theory, p. 4
socialism, p. 8
totalitarianism, p. 10

SELECTED READINGS

Almond, Gabriel A., and Sidney Verba. *Civic Culture: Political Attitudes and Democracy in Five Nations*. Princeton, NJ: Princeton University Press, 1963.

Craig, Stephen C., and Stephen Earl Bennett, eds. *After the Boom: The Politics of Generation X*. Lanham, MD: Rowman and Littlefield, 1997.

Dahl, Robert A. *Polyarchy: Participation and Opposition*. New Haven, CT: Yale University Press, 1971.

Elshstain, Jean Bethke. *Democracy on Trial*. New York: Basic Books, 1995.

Glendon, Mary Ann. *Rights Talk: The Impoverishment of Political Discourse*. New York: Free Press, 1991.

Grossman, Lawrence K. *The Electronic Republic: Reshaping Democracy in the Information Age*. New York: Viking, 1995.

Hobbes, Thomas. *Leviathan*. Richard Tuck, ed. New York: Cambridge University Press, 1996.

Hochschild, Jennifer L. *Facing Up to the American Dream: Race, Class, and the Soul of the Nation*. Princeton, NJ: Princeton University Press, 1995.

Hunter, James Davison. *Culture Wars: The Struggle to Define America*. New York: Basic Books, 1991.

Jamieson, Kathleen Hall. *Dirty Politics: Deception, Distraction, and Democracy*. New York: Oxford University Press, 1992.

Locke, John. *Two Treatises of Government*. Peter Lasleti, ed. New York: Cambridge University Press, 1988.

Putnam, Robert D. *Bowling Alone: Collapse and Revival of the American Community*. New York: Simon and Schuster, 2000.

Skocpol, Theda, and Morris Fiorina, eds. *Civic Engagement in American Democracy*. Washington, DC: Brookings Institution Press, 1999.

Verba, Sidney, Kay Schlozman, and Henry Brady. *Voice and Equality: Civic Volunteerism in American Politics*. Cambridge, MA: Harvard University Press, 1995.

NOTES

1. Thomas Byrne Edsall, "The Era of Bad Feelings," *Civilization* (March/April 1996): 37.

2. The English and Scots often signed covenants with their churches in a pledge to defend and further their religion. In the Bible, covenants were solemn promises made to humanity by God. In the colonial context, then, covenants were formal agreements sworn to a new government to abide by its terms.

3. The term "men" is used here because only males were considered fit to vote.

4. Jack C. Plano and Milton Greenberg, *The American Political Dictionary*, 6th ed. (New York: Holt, Rinehart and Winston, 1982).

5. Frank Michelman, "The Republican Civic Tradition," *Yale Law Journal* 97 (1988): 1503.

6. Herbert Kitschelt, Zdenka Mansfeldova, Radoslaw Markowski, and Gabor Toka, *Post-Communist Party Systems: Competition, Representation and Inter-Party Cooperation* (New York: Cambridge University Press, 1999).

7. Merle Goldman and Roderick MacFarquhar, eds., *The Paradox of China's Post-Mao Reforms*, Harvard Contemporary China Series, 12 (Cambridge, MA: Harvard University Press, 1999).

8. Anna Gryzmala-Busse, "The Programmatic Turnaround of Communist Successor Parties in East Central Europe, 1989–1998," *Communist and Post-Communist Studies* 35 (March 2002): 51–66.

9. Lynne Casper and Loretta Bass, "Hectic Lifestyles Make for Record-Low Election Turnout, Census Bureau Reports," *U.S. Census Bureau News* (August 17, 1998).

10. http://www.census.gov/population/socdemo/voting/p20-542/tab12.txt.

11. Ibid.

12. The United States Agency for International Development, "Agency Objectives: Civil Society."

13. Thomas Carothers, "Democracy Promotion: A Key Focus in a New World Order," *Issues of Democracy* (May 2000): online.

14. Gabriel A. Almond and Sidney Verba, *The Civic Culture: Political Attitudes and Democracy in Five Nations* (Princeton, NJ: Princeton University Press, 1963), 4.

15. "The USA's New Immigrants," *USA Today* (October 13, 1997): 11A.

16. Susan A. MacManus, *Young v. Old: Generational Combat in the 21st Century* (Boulder, CO: Westview Press, 1995), 3.

17. MacManus, *Young v. Old*, 4.

18. "Sixty-Five Plus in the United States," http://www.census.gov/socdemo/www/agebrief.html.

19. See William Strauss and Neil Howe, *Generations: The History of America's Future, 1984–2069* (New York: William Morrow, 1991), and Fernando Torres-Gil, *The New Aging: Politics and Generational Change in America* (New York: Auburn House, 1992).

20. William R. Buck and Tracey Rembert, "Not Just Doing It: Generation X Proves That Actions Speak Louder than Words," *Earth Action Network* (September 19, 1997): 28.

21. Ibid.

22. Ibid.

23. Teresa Gubbins, "Teens Push Aside the Boomers, Emerge as New Kings of Cool," *Times-Picayune* (April 11, 1999): B3.

24. Kavita Varma, "Family Values," *USA Today* (March 11, 1997): 6D.

25. *Public Opinion Online*, Question Number 27, Sept. 15–17, 2001.

26. James Davison Hunter. *Culture Wars: The Struggle to Define America* (New York: Basic Books, 1991), 42.

27. Ibid.

28. Plano and Greenberg, *The American Political Dictionary*, 10.

29. William Safire, *Safire's New Political Dictionary* (New York: Random House, 1993), 144–45.

30. Jack C. Plano and Milton Greenberg, *The American Political Dictionary*, 9th ed. (Fort Worth, TX: Harcourt Brace, 1993), 16.

31. Safire, *Safire's New Political Dictionary*.

32. Plano and Greenberg, *The American Political Dictionary*, 16.

33. Philip E. Converse, "The Nature of Belief Systems in Mass Publics," in David E. Apter, ed., *Ideology and Discontent* (New York: Free Press, 1964), 206–21.

34. David Broder and Richard Morin, "Americans See 2 Distinct Bill Clintons," *Washington Post* (August 23, 1998): A10.

35. Howard Wilkinson and Patrick Crowly, "Campaign '98: Races Offer Definite Choices." *Cincinnati Enquirer* (September 7, 1998): B1.

36. "Apathetic Voters? No, Disgusted," *Ledger* (July 12, 1998): A14.

37. Scott Shepard, "Non-voters Too Busy or Apathetic?" *Palm Beach Post* (August 1998): 6A.

The Constitution

At age eighteen, all American citizens today are eligible to vote in state and national elections. This has not always been the case. It took an amendment to the U.S. Constitution—one of only seventeen that have been added since the Bill of Rights was ratified in 1791—to guarantee the franchise to those under twenty-one years of age.

In 1942, during World War II, Representative Jennings Randolph (D–WV) proposed that the voting age be lowered to eighteen, believing that since young men were old enough to be drafted to fight and die for their country, they also should be allowed to vote. He continued to reintroduce his proposal during every session of Congress, and in 1954 President Dwight D. Eisenhower endorsed the idea in his State of the Union message. Presidents Lyndon B. Johnson and Richard M. Nixon—both men who called upon the nation's young men to fight on foreign shores—also echoed his appeal.[1]

By the 1960s, the campaign to lower the voting age took on a new sense of urgency as hundreds of thousands of young men were drafted to fight in Vietnam and thousands were killed in action. "Old Enough to Fight, Old Enough to Vote," was one popular slogan of the day. By 1970, four states—who under the U.S. Constitution are allowed to set the eligibility requirements for their voters—had lowered their voting ages to eighteen, and under considerable pressure from Baby Boomers, Congress passed legislation lowering the voting age in national, state, and local elections to eighteen.

The state of Oregon, however, challenged the constitutionality of the law in court, arguing that Congress had not been given the authority to establish a uniform voting age in state and local government under the Constitution. The U.S. Supreme Court agreed.[2] The decision from the sharply divided Court meant that those under age twenty-one could vote in national elections but that the states were free to prohibit them from voting in state and local elections. The decision presented the states with a logistical nightmare in keeping two sets of registration books—one for those twenty-one and over, and one for those who were not.

Jennings Randolph, by then a senator from West Virginia, reintroduced his proposed amendment to lower the national voting age to eighteen.[3] Within three months of the Supreme Court's decision, Congress sent the proposed Twenty-Sixth Amendment to the states for their ratification. The required three-fourths of the states ratified the amendment within three months—making its adoption, on June 30, 1971, the quickest in the history of the constitutional amending process.

In spite of winning the right to vote through a change in the U.S. Constitution, young people never have voted in large numbers. In spite of issues of concern to those under the age of twenty-five, including Internet privacy, reproductive rights, credit card and cell phone rules and regulations, and the continuance of student loan programs, this group has very low voter turnout rates. In 2004, while more young people went to the polls, their percentage of the electorate remained the same as in 2000.

*T*he Constitution intentionally was written to forestall the need for amendment, and the process by which it could be changed or amended was made time-consuming and difficult. Over the years, thousands of amendments—including those to prohibit child labor, provide equal rights for women, grant statehood to the District of Columbia, and balance the budget—have been debated or sent to the states for their approval, only to die slow deaths. Only twenty-seven amendments have successfully made their way into the Constitution. What the Framers came up with in Philadelphia has continued to work, in spite of continually increasing demands on and dissatisfaction with our national government. Perhaps Americans are happier with the system of government created by the Framers than they realize.

The ideas that went into the making of the Constitution and how the Constitution has evolved to address the problems of a growing and ever-changing nation are at the core of our discussion in this chapter.

- First, we will examine *the origins of the new nation* and the circumstances surrounding the break with Great Britain.
- Second, we will discuss *the Declaration of Independence* and the ideas that lay at its core.
- Third, we will discuss *the first attempts at American government* created by the *Articles of Confederation*.
- Fourth, we will examine the circumstances surrounding the drafting of a *new Constitution* in Philadelphia.
- Fifth, we will review the results of the Framers' efforts—*the U.S. Constitution*.
- Sixth, we will present *the drive for ratification* of the new government.
- Seventh, we will address *the formal methods of amending the Constitution*.
- Eighth, we will explore *the informal methods of amending the Constitution*.
- In highlighting the *continuity and change* inherent in the American political system, we will examine the continuity created by the decennial U.S. Census as well as the change it regularly brings about in how states are represented in Congress.

THE ORIGINS OF A NEW NATION

Starting in the early seventeenth century, colonists came to the New World for a variety of reasons. Often it was to escape religious persecution. Others came seeking a new start on a continent where land was plentiful. The independence and diversity of the settlers in the New World made the question of how best to rule the new colonies a tricky one. More than merely an ocean separated England from the colonies; the colonists were independent people, and it soon became clear that the Crown could not govern the colonies with the same close rein used at home. King James I thus allowed some local participation in decision making through arrangements such as the first elected colonial assembly, the Virginia House of Burgesses, and the elected General Court that governed the Massachusetts Bay colony after 1629. Almost all the colonists agreed that the king ruled by divine right, but English monarchs allowed the colonists significant liberties in terms of self-government, religious practices, and economic organization. For 140 years, this system worked fairly well.[4]

By the early 1760s, however, a century and a half of physical separation, colonial development, and the relative self-governance of the colonies had led to weakening ties with—and loyalties to—the Crown. By this time, each of the thirteen colonies had drafted its own written constitution, which provided the fundamental rules or laws for each colony. Moreover, many of the most oppressive British traditions—feudalism, a rigid class system, and the absolute authority of church and king—were absent in the New World. Land was abundant. The restrictive guild and craft systems that severely limited entry into many skilled professions in England did not exist in the colonies. Although the role of religion was central to the lives of most colonists, there was no single state church, and the British practice of compulsory tithing (giving a fixed percentage of one's earnings to the state-sanctioned and supported church) was nonexistent.

Trade and Taxation

Mercantilism, an economic theory based on the belief that a nation's wealth is measured by the amount of gold and silver in its treasury, justified Britain's maintenance of strict import/export controls on the colonies. After 1650, for example, Parliament passed a series of navigation acts to prevent its chief rival, Holland, from trading with the English colonies. From 1650 until well into the 1700s, England tried to regulate colonial imports and exports, believing that it was critical to export more goods than it imported as a way of increasing the gold and silver in its treasury. These policies, however, were difficult to enforce and were widely ignored by the colonists, who saw little self-benefit in them. Thus, for years, an unwritten agreement existed. The colonists relinquished to the Crown and the British Parliament the authority to regulate trade and conduct international affairs, but they retained the right to levy their own taxes.

This fragile agreement was soon put to the test. The French and Indian War, fought from 1756 to 1763 on the "western frontier" of the colonies and in Canada, was part of a global war initiated by the British. The American phase of the Seven Years' War was fought between England and France with its Indian allies. In North America, its immediate cause was the rival claims of those two European nations for the lands between the Allegheny Mountains and the Mississippi River. The Treaty of Paris (signed in 1763) signaled the end of the war. The colonists expected that with the "Indian problem" on the western frontier now "under control," westward migration and settlement could begin in earnest. In 1763, they were shocked when the Crown decreed that there was to be no further westward movement by British subjects. Parliament believed that expansion into Indian territory would lead to new expenditures for the defense of the settlers, draining the British treasury, which had yet to recover from the high cost of waging the war.

To raise money to pay for the war as well as the expenses of administering the colonies, Parliament enacted the Sugar Act in 1764, which placed taxes on sugar, wine, coffee, and other products commonly exported to the colonies. A postwar colonial depression heightened resentment of the tax. Around the colonies, the political cry "No taxation without representation" was heard. Major protest, however, failed to materialize until imposition of the Stamp Act by the British Parliament in 1765. This law required the colonists to purchase stamps for all documents, including newspapers, magazines, and commercial papers. To add insult to injury, in 1765, Parliament passed the Mutiny, or Quartering Act, which required the colonists to furnish barracks or provide living quarters within their own homes for British troops.

Most colonists, especially those in New England, where these acts hit hardest, were outraged. Men throughout the colonies organized the Sons of Liberty, under the leadership of Samuel Adams and Patrick Henry. Whereas the Sugar

Today, Samuel Adams (1722–1803), shown here in a painting by John Singleton Copley, is well known for the beer that bears his name. His original claim to fame was as a leader against the British and loyalist oppressors (although he did bankrupt his family's brewery business). As a member of the Massachusetts legislature, he advocated defiance of the Stamp Act. With the passage of the Townshend Acts in 1767, he organized a letter-writing campaign urging other colonies to join in resistance. Later, in 1772, he founded the Committees of Correspondence to unite the colonies.

Act was a tax on trade—still viewed as being within the legitimate authority of the Crown the Stamp Act was a direct tax on many items not traditionally under the control of the king. Protests against it were violent and loud. Riots, often led by the Sons of Liberty, broke out. They were especially violent in Boston, where the colonial governor's home was burned by an angry mob, and British stamp agents charged with collecting the tax were threatened. A boycott of goods needing the stamps as well as British imports also was organized.

First Steps Toward Independence

Stamp Act Congress
Meeting of representatives of nine of the thirteen colonies held in New York City in 1765, during which representatives drafted a document to send to the king listing how their rights had been violated.

In 1765, the colonists called for the **Stamp Act Congress,** the first official meeting of the colonies and the first step toward a unified nation. Nine of the thirteen colonies sent representatives to a meeting in New York City, where a detailed list of Crown violations of the colonists fundamental rights was drawn up. Attendees defined what they thought to be the proper relationship between the various colonial governments and the British Parliament; they ardently believed that Parliament had no authority to tax them without colonial representation in the British Parliament. In contrast, the British believed that direct representation of the colonists was impractical and that members of Parliament represented the best interests of all the English, including the colonists.

The Stamp Act Congress and its petitions to the Crown did little to stop the onslaught of taxing measures. Parliament did, however, repeal the Stamp Act and revise the Sugar Act in 1766, largely because of the uproar made by British merchants who were losing large sums of money as a result of the boycotts. Rather than appeasing the colonists, however, these actions emboldened them to increase their resistance. In 1767, Parliament enacted the Townshend Acts, which imposed duties on all kinds of colonial imports, including tea. Response from the Sons of Liberty was immediate. Another boycott was announced, and almost all colonists gave up their favorite drink in a united show of resistance to the tax and British authority.[5] Tensions continued to run high, especially after the British sent 4,000 troops to Boston. On March 5, 1770, English troops opened fire on a mob that included disgruntled dock workers, whose jobs had been taken by British soldiers, and members of the Sons of Liberty, who were taunting the soldiers in front of the Boston Customs House. Five colonists were killed in what became known as the Boston Massacre. Following this confrontation, all duties except those on tea were lifted. The tea tax, however, continued to be a symbolic irritant. In 1772, at the suggestion of Samuel Adams, Boston and other towns around Massachusetts set up **Committees of Correspondence** to articulate ideas and keep communications open around the colony. By 1774, twelve colonies had formed committees to maintain a flow of information among like-minded colonists.

Committees of Correspondence
Organizations in each of the American colonies created to keep colonists abreast of developments with the British; served as powerful molders of public opinion against the British.

Meanwhile, despite dissent in England over the treatment of the colonies, Parliament passed another tea tax designed to shore up the sagging sales of the East India Company, a British exporter of tea. The colonists' boycott had left that British trading house with more than 18 million pounds of tea in its warehouses. To rescue British merchants from disaster, in 1773, Parliament passed the Tea Act, granting a monopoly to the financially strapped East India Company to sell the tea imported from Britain. The company was allowed to funnel business to American merchants loyal to the Crown, thereby undercutting colonial merchants, who could sell only tea imported from other nations. The effect was to drive down the price of tea and to hurt colonial merchants, who were forced to buy tea at the higher prices from other sources.

When the next shipment of tea arrived in Boston from Great Britain, the colonists responded by throwing the Boston Tea Party. Similar "tea parties" were held in other colonies. When the news of these actions reached King George, he flew into a rage against the actions of his disloyal subjects. "The die is now cast," the king told his prime minister. "The colonies must either submit or triumph."

His first act was to persuade Parliament to pass the Coercive Acts in 1774. Known in the colonies as the Intolerable Acts, they contained a key provision calling for a total blockade of Boston Harbor until restitution was made for the tea. Another provision reinforced the Quartering Act. It gave royal governors the authority to house British soldiers in the homes of private citizens, allowing Britain to send an additional 4,000 soldiers to patrol Boston.

The First Continental Congress

The British could never have guessed how the cumulative impact of these actions would unite the colonists. Samuel Adams's Committees of Correspondence spread the word, and food and money were sent to the people of Boston from all over the thirteen colonies. The tax itself was no longer the key issue; now the extent of British authority over the colonies was the far more important question. At the request of the colonial assemblies of Massachusetts and Virginia, all but one colonial assembly agreed to select a group of delegates to attend a continental congress authorized to communicate with the king on behalf of the now-united colonies.

The **First Continental Congress** met in Philadelphia from September 5 to October 26, 1774. It was made up of fifty-six delegates from every colony except Georgia. The colonists had yet to think of breaking with Great Britain; at this point, they simply wanted to iron out their differences with the king. By October, they had agreed on a series of resolutions to oppose the Coercive Acts and to establish a formal organization to boycott British goods. The Congress also drafted a Declaration of Rights and Resolves, which called for colonial rights of petition and assembly, trial by peers, freedom from a standing army, and the selection of representative councils to levy taxes. The Congress further agreed that if the king did not capitulate to their demands, they would meet again in Philadelphia in May 1775.

Paul Revere's engraving of the Boston Massacre was potent propaganda. Five men were killed, not seven, as the legend states, and the rioters in front of the State House (left) were scarcely as docile as Revere portrayed them.

(Photo courtesy: Collection of the New York Historical Society, negative no. 29405)

First Continental Congress
Meeting held in Philadelphia from September 5 to October 26, 1774, in which fifty-six delegates (from every colony except Georgia) adopted a resolution in opposition to the Coercive Acts.

WEB EXPLORATION
For more information on the work of the Continental Congress, see www.ablongman.com/oconnor

Second Continental Congress
Meeting that convened in Philadelphia on May 10, 1775, at which it was decided that an army should be raised and George Washington of Virginia was named commander in chief.

The Second Continental Congress

King George refused to yield, tensions continued to rise, and a **Second Continental Congress** was called. Before it could meet, fighting broke out early in the morning of April 19, 1775, at Lexington and Concord, Massachusetts, with what Ralph Waldo Emerson called "the shot heard round the world." Eight colonial soldiers, called Minutemen, were killed, and 16,000 British troops besieged Boston.

When the Second Continental Congress convened in Philadelphia on May 10, 1775, delegates were united by their increased hostility to Great Britain. The bloodshed at Lexington left no other course but war. To solidify colonial support, a Southerner, George Washington of Virginia, was selected as the commander of the new Continental Army, since to that time, British oppression had been felt most keenly in the Northeast. That task complete, the Congress then sent envoys to France to ask its assistance against France's perennial enemy. In a final attempt to avert conflict, the Second Continental Congress adopted the Olive Branch Petition on July 5, 1775, asking

After the success of *Common Sense*, Thomas Paine wrote a series of essays collectively entitled *The Crisis* to arouse colonists' support for the Revolutionary War. The first *Crisis* papers contain the famous words "These are the times that try men's souls."

(Photo courtesy: Stock Montage, Inc.)

confederation
Type of government in which the national government derives its powers from the states; a league of independent states.

Declaration of Independence
Document drafted by Thomas Jefferson in 1776 that proclaimed the right of the American colonies to separate from Great Britain.

the king to end hostilities. King George rejected the petition and sent an additional 20,000 troops to quell the rebellion. The stage was set for war.

In January 1776, Thomas Paine, with the support and encouragement of Benjamin Franklin, issued (at first anonymously) *Common Sense*, a pamphlet forcefully arguing for independence from Great Britain. In frank, easy-to-understand language, Paine denounced the corrupt British monarchy and offered reasons to break with Great Britain. "The blood of the slain, the weeping voice of nature cries 'Tis Time to Part,' " wrote Paine. *Common Sense*, widely read throughout the colonies, was instrumental in changing minds in a very short time. In its first three months of publication, the forty-seven-page *Common Sense* sold 120,000 copies, the equivalent of approximately 18.75 million books today (given the U.S. population today). One copy of *Common Sense* was in distribution for every thirteen people in the colonies—a truly astonishing number, given the low literacy rate.

THE DECLARATION OF INDEPENDENCE

Common Sense galvanized the American public against reconciliation with England. As the mood in the colonies changed, so did that of the Second Continental Congress. On May 15, 1776, Virginia became the first colony to call for independence, instructing one of its delegates to the Second Continental Congress to introduce a resolution to that effect. On June 7, 1776, Richard Henry Lee of Virginia rose to move "that these United Colonies are, and of right ought to be, free and independent States, and that all connection between them and the State of Great Britain is, and ought to be, dissolved." His three-part resolution—which called for independence, the formation of foreign alliances, and preparation of a plan of **confederation**—triggered hot debate among the delegates. A proclamation of independence from Great Britain was treason, a crime punishable by death. Although six of the thirteen colonies had already instructed their delegates to vote for independence, the Second Continental Congress was suspended to allow its delegates to return home to their respective colonial legislatures for final instructions. Independence was not a move to be taken lightly.

At the same time, committees were set up to consider each point of Lee's proposal. A committee of five was selected to begin work on a **Declaration of Independence.** The Congress selected Benjamin Franklin, John Adams, Robert Livingston, and Roger Sherman as members. Adams lobbied hard for a Southerner to add balance. Thus, owing to his southern origin as well as his "peculiar felicity of expression," Thomas Jefferson was selected as chair.

On July 2, 1776, twelve of the thirteen colonies (with New York abstaining) voted for independence. Two days later, the Second Continental Congress voted to adopt the Declaration of Independence penned by Thomas Jefferson. On July 9, 1776, the Declaration, now with the approval of New York, was read aloud in Philadelphia.[6]

A Theoretical Basis for a New Government

In simple but eloquent language, Jefferson set out the reasons for the colonies' separation from Great Britain. Most of his stirring rhetoric drew heavily on the works of seventeenth- and eighteenth-century political philosophers, particularly the English philosopher John Locke (see Roots of Government: Hobbes and Locke in chapter 1), who had written South Carolina's first constitution, a colonial charter drawn up in 1663 when South Carolina was formed by King Charles II and mercantile houses in England. In fact, many of the words in the opening of the Declaration of Independence closely resemble passages from Locke's *Two Treatises of Government*.

American Renaissance man Thomas Jefferson (1743–1826)—author of the Declaration of Independence and the third president of the United States—voiced the aspirations of a new America as no other individual of his era. In the wake of scientific evidence appearing to prove he fathered at least one child by his slave Sally Hemmings, historians are now reassessing his writings and political thought. Some of her descendants gather at Monticello, Jefferson's home.

(Photo courtesy: Raab Shanna/Corbis Sygma)

Locke was a proponent of social contract theory, a philosophy of government that held that governments exist based on the consent of the governed. According to Locke, people leave the state of nature and agree to set up a government largely for the protection of property. In colonial times, "property" did not mean just land. Locke's notion of property rights included life, liberty, and material possessions. Furthermore, argued Locke, individuals who give their consent to be governed have the right to resist or remove rulers who deviate from those purposes. Such a government exists for the good of its subjects and not for the benefit of those who govern. Thus, rebellion was the ultimate sanction against a government that violated the rights of its citizens.

It is easy to see the colonists' debt to John Locke. In ringing language, the Declaration of Independence proclaims:

> We hold these truths to be self-evident, that all men are created equal, that they are endowed by their Creator with certain unalienable Rights, that among these are Life, Liberty and the pursuit of Happiness.

Jefferson and others in attendance at the Second Continental Congress wanted to have a document that would stand for all time, justifying their break with the Crown and clarifying their notions of the proper form of government. So, Jefferson continued:

> That to secure these rights, Governments are instituted among Men, deriving their just powers from the consent of the governed. That whenever any Form of Government becomes destructive of these ends, it is the Right of the People to alter or abolish it, and to institute new Government, laying its foundation on such Principles and organizing its Powers in such form, as to them shall seem most likely to effect their Safety and Happiness.

After this stirring preamble, the Declaration went on to enumerate the wrongs that the colonists had suffered under British rule. All pertained to the denial of personal rights and liberties, many of which would later be guaranteed by the U.S. Constitution through the Bill of Rights.

After the Declaration was signed and transmitted to the king, the Revolutionary War was fought with a greater vengeance. At a September 1776 peace conference on

Staten Island (New York), British General William Howe demanded revocation of the Declaration of Independence. The Americans refused, and the war raged on while the Congress attempted to fashion a new united government.

THE FIRST ATTEMPT AT GOVERNMENT: THE ARTICLES OF CONFEDERATION

As noted earlier, the British had no written constitution. The colonists in the Second Continental Congress were attempting to codify arrangements that had never before been put into legal terminology. To make things more complicated, the delegates had to arrive at these decisions in a wartime atmosphere. Nevertheless, in late 1777, the **Articles of Confederation,** creating a loose "league of friendship" between the thirteen sovereign or independent states, were passed by the Congress and presented to the states for their ratification.

The Articles created a type of government called a confederation or confederacy. Unlike Great Britain's unitary system of government, wherein all of the powers of the government reside in the national government, the national government in a confederation derives all of its powers directly from the states. Thus, the national government in a confederacy is weaker than the sum of its parts, and the states often consider themselves independent nation-states linked together only for limited purposes such as national defense. Key provisions in the Articles that created the confederacy included:

- A national government with a Congress empowered to make peace, coin money, appoint officers for an army, control the post office, and negotiate with Indian tribes.
- Each state's retention of its independence and sovereignty, or ultimate authority to govern within its territories.
- One vote in the Continental Congress for each state, regardless of size.
- The vote of nine states to pass any measure (a unanimous vote for any amendment).
- The selection and payment of delegates to the Congress by their respective state legislatures.

Thus, the Articles, finally ratified by all thirteen states in March 1781, fashioned a government well reflective of the political philosophy of the times.[7] Although it had its flaws, the government under the Articles of Confederation saw the nation through the Revolutionary War. However, once the British surrendered in 1781, and the new nation found itself no longer united by the war effort, the government quickly fell into chaos.

Problems Under the Articles of Confederation

In today's America, we ship goods, travel by car and airplane across state lines, make interstate phone calls, and more. Over 250 years ago, Americans had great loyalties to their states and often did not even think of themselves as Americans. This lack of national sentiment or loyalty in the absence of a war to unite the citizenry fostered a reluctance to give any power to the national government. Thus, by 1784, just one year after the Revolutionary Army was disbanded, governing the new nation under the Articles of Confederation proved unworkable.[8] In fact, historians refer to the chaotic period from 1781 to 1789 when the former colonies were governed under the Articles of Confederation as the "critical period." Congress rarely could assemble the required quorum of nine states to conduct business. Even when it could, there was little agreement among the states on any policies. To raise revenue to pay off war debts and run the government, various land, poll, and liquor taxes were proposed. But, since Congress had no specific power to tax, all these

Articles of Confederation
The compact among the thirteen original states that was the basis of their government. Written in 1776, the Articles were not ratified by all the states until 1781.

WEB EXPLORATION
For a full text of the Articles of Confederation, see
www.ablongman.com/oconnor

proposals were rejected. At one point, Congress was even driven out of Philadelphia (then the capital of the new national government) by its own unpaid army.

Although the national government could coin money, it had no resources to back up the value of its currency. Continental dollars were worth little, and trade between states became chaotic as some states began to coin their own money. Another weakness of the Articles of Confederation was its failure to allow Congress to regulate commerce among the states and with foreign nations. As a result, individual states attempted to enter into agreements with other countries, and foreign nations were suspicious of trade agreements made with the Congress of the Confederation, as the new government under the Articles was called. In 1785, for example, Massachusetts banned the export of goods in British ships, and Pennsylvania levied heavy duties on ships of nations that had no treaties with the U.S. government.

Fearful of a chief executive who would rule tyrannically, moreover, the draftees of the Articles had made no provision for an executive branch of government that would be responsible for executing, or implementing, laws passed by the legislative branch. Instead, the "president" was merely the presiding officer at meetings. John Hanson, a former member of the Maryland House of Delegates and of the First Continental Congress, was the first person to preside over the Congress of the Confederation. Therefore, he is often referred to as the first president of the United States.

In addition, the Articles of Confederation had no provision for a judicial system to handle the growing number of economic conflicts and boundary disputes among the individual states. Several states claimed the same lands to the west; Pennsylvania and Virginia went to war with each other; Vermont threatened to annex itself to Canada.

The Articles' greatest weakness, however, was the lack of creation of a strong central government. While states had operated independently before the war, during the war they acceded to the national government's authority to wage armed conflict. Once the war was over, however, each state resumed its sovereign status and was unwilling to give up rights, such as the power to tax, to an untested national government. Consequently, the government was unable to force the states to abide by the provisions of the Treaty of Paris, signed in 1783, which officially ended the war. For example, states passed laws to stay the bills of debtors who owed money to Great Britain. They also failed to restore property to many who had remained loyal to Britain during the war. Both actions were in violation of the treaty.

The crumbling economy and a series of bad harvests that failed to produce cash crops, making it difficult for farmers to get out of debt quickly, took their toll on the new nation. George Washington and Alexander Hamilton, both interested in the questions of trade and frontier expansion, soon saw the need for a stronger national government with the authority to act to solve some of these problems. They were not alone. In 1785 and 1786, some state governments began to discuss ways to strengthen the national government. Finally, several states joined together to call for a convention in Philadelphia in 1787.

Before that meeting could take place, however, new unrest broke out in America. In 1780, Massachusetts adopted a constitution that appeared to favor the interests of the wealthy. Property-owning requirements barred the lower and middle classes from voting and office holding. And, as the economy of Massachusetts worsened, banks foreclosed on the farms of many Massachusetts Continental Army veterans who were waiting for promised bonuses that the national government had no funds to pay. The last straw came in 1786, when the Massachusetts legislature enacted a new law requiring the payment of all debts in cash. Frustration and outrage at the new law caused Daniel Shays, a former Revolutionary War army captain, and 1,500 armed, disgruntled, and angry farmers to march to Springfield, Massachusetts. This group forcibly restrained the state court located there from foreclosing on the mortgages on their farms.

The Congress immediately authorized the secretary of war to call for a new national militia. A $530,000 appropriation was made for this purpose, but every state except Virginia refused Congress's request for money. The governor of Massachusetts then

With Daniel Shays in the lead, a group of farmers and Revolutionary War veterans marched on the courthouse in Springfield, Massachusetts, to stop the state court from foreclosing on farmers' mortgages.

(Photo courtesy: Bettmann/Corbis)

Shays's Rebellion
A 1786 rebellion in which an army of 1,500 disgruntled and angry farmers led by Daniel Shays marched to Springfield, Massachusetts, and forcibly restrained the state court from foreclosing mortgages on their farms.

WEB EXPLORATION
For demographic background on the Framers, see
www.ablongman.com/oconnor

tried to raise a state militia, but because of the poor economy, the state treasury lacked the necessary funds to support his action. Frantic attempts to collect private financial support were made, and a militia finally was assembled. By February 4, 1787, this privately paid force put a stop to what was called **Shays's Rebellion.** The failure of the Congress to muster an army to put down the rebellion provided a dramatic example of the weaknesses inherent in the Articles of Confederation and shocked the nation's leaders into recognizing the new government's overwhelming inadequacies.

THE MIRACLE AT PHILADELPHIA: WRITING A CONSTITUTION

On February 21, 1787, in the throes of economic turmoil and with domestic tranquility gone haywire, the Congress passed an official resolution. It called for a Constitutional Convention in Philadelphia for "the sole and express purpose of revising the Articles of Confederation." All states but Rhode Island sent delegates.

Twenty-nine individuals met in sweltering Philadelphia on May 14. Many at that initial meeting were intellectuals, others were shrewd farmers or businessmen, and still others were astute politicians. All recognized that what they were doing could be considered treasonous. Revising the Articles of Confederation was one thing; to call for an entirely new government, as suggested by the Virginia delegation, was another. So, they took their work quite seriously, even to the point of adopting a pledge of secrecy. George Washington, who was unanimously elected the convention's presiding officer, warned:

> Nothing spoken or written can be revealed to anyone—not even your family—until we have adjourned permanently. Gossip or misunderstanding can easily ruin all the hard work we shall have to do this summer.[9]

So concerned about leaks were those in attendance that the delegates agreed to accompany Benjamin Franklin to all of his meals. They feared that the normally gregarious gentleman might get carried away with the mood or by liquor and inadvertently let news of the proceedings slip from his tongue.

The Framers

Fifty-five out of the seventy-four delegates ultimately chosen by their state legislatures to attend the Constitutional Convention labored long and hard that hot summer behind closed doors in Philadelphia. All of them were men; hence they are often referred to as the "Founding Fathers." Most of them, however, were quite young; many were in their twenties and thirties, and only one—Benjamin Franklin, at eighty-one—was very old. Several owned slaves. (See Analyzing Visuals: Who Were the Framers?) Here we generally refer to those delegates as Framers because their work provided the framework for our new government. The Framers brought with them a vast amount of political, educational, legal, and business experience. Although some scholarly debate continues concerning the motives of the Framers for shaping the new national government, it is clear that they were an exceptional lot who ultimately produced a brilliant document reflecting the best efforts of all present.

Motives of the Framers.   Debate about the Framers' motives filled the air during the ratification struggle and has provided grist for the mill of historians and political scientists over the years. Anti-Federalists, who opposed the new Constitution, charged that Federalist supporters of the Constitution were a self-serving, landed, and propertied elite with a vested interest in the capitalistic system that had evolved in the colonies. Federalists countered that they were simply trying to preserve the nation.

In his *Economic Interpretation of the Constitution of the United States* (1913), Charles A. Beard argued that the 1780s were a critical period not for the nation as a whole, but rather for businessmen.[10] These men feared that a weak, decentralized government could harm their economic interests. Beard argued that the merchants wanted a strong national government to promote industry and trade, to protect private property, and most importantly, to ensure payment of the public debt—much of which was owed to them. Therefore, according to Beard, the Constitution represents "an economic document drawn with superb skill by men whose property interests were immediately at stake."[11]

By the 1950s, this view had fallen into disfavor when other historians were unable to find direct links between wealth and the Framers' motives for establishing the Constitution.[12] Robert Brown, for example, faulted Beard's economic approach and his failure to consider the impact of religion and individual views about government.[13] In the 1960s, however, another group of historians began to argue that social and economic factors were, in fact, important motives for supporting the Constitution. In *The Anti-Federalists* (1961), Jackson Turner Main posited that while the Constitution's supporters might not have been the united group of creditors suggested by Beard, they were wealthier, came from higher social strata, and had greater concern for maintaining the prevailing social order than the general public.[14]

In 1969, Gordon S. Wood's *The Creation of the American Republic* resurrected this debate. Wood de-emphasized economics to argue that major social divisions explained different groups' support for (or opposition to) the new Constitution. He concluded that the Framers were representatives of a class that favored order and stability over some of the more radical ideas that had inspired the American Revolutionary War and break with Britain.[15]

July 4th celebration at Independence Hall in Philadelphia, Pennsylvania, where the Declaration was first read aloud.

(Photo courtesy: William Thomas Cain/Getty Images)

The Virginia and New Jersey Plans

The less populous states were concerned with being lost in any new system of government where states were not treated as equals regardless of population. It is not surprising that a large state and then a small one, Virginia and New Jersey, respectively weighed in with ideas about how the new government should operate.

The **Virginia Plan** called for a national system based heavily on the European nation-state model, wherein the national government derives its powers from the people and not from the member states.

Its key features included:

- Creation of a powerful central government with three branches—the legislative, executive, and judicial.
- A two-house legislature with one house elected directly by the people, the other chosen from among persons nominated by the state legislatures.
- The legislature with the power to select the executive and the judiciary.

Virginia Plan
The first general plan for the Constitution, proposed by James Madison. Its key points were a bicameral legislature, an executive chosen by the legislature, and a judiciary also named by the legislature.

ANALYZING VISUALS

Who Were the Framers?

Who were the Framers of the U.S. Constitution? Of the fifty-five delegates who attended some portion of the Philadelphia meetings, seventeen were slaveholders who owned approximately 1,400 slaves. (Washington, Mason, and Rutledge held the greatest number of slaves at the time of the Philadelphia convention.) In terms of education, thirty-one went to college; twenty-four did not. Most of those who did not were trained as business, legal, and printing apprentices, Seven delegates signed both the U.S. Constitution and the Declaration of Independence. After studying the graph below and the material on writing and signing the Constitution in this chapter, answer the follow-

ing critical thinking questions: What is the relationship, if any, between the number of a state's delegates who served in the Continental Congresses and the number of the state's signers of the Constitution? What is the relationship, if any, between a state's population (shown in parentheses below) and the number of the state's signers of the U.S. Constitution? What does that suggest about the conflict between the large states and small states? What is the relationship, if any, between the number of a state's delegates who were slaveholders and the number of the state's signers of the U.S. Constitution? What does that suggest about the conflicts over slavery at the convention?

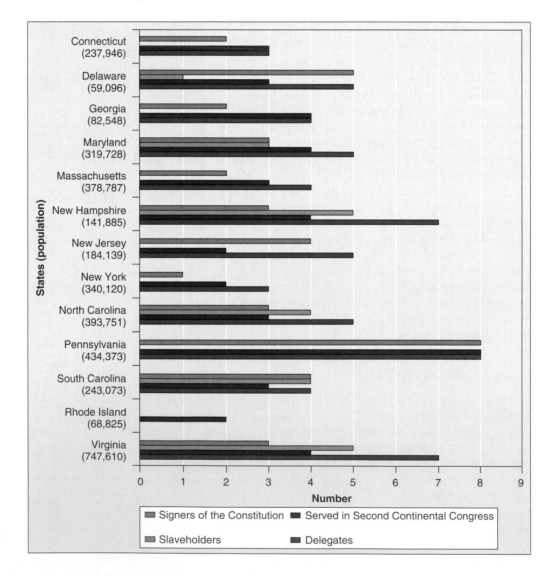

Sources: Clinton Rossiter, *The Grand Convention* (New York: Macmillan, 1966); National Archives and Records Administration, "The Founding Fathers: A Brief Overview," http://www.archives.gov/exhibit_hall/charters_of_freedom/constitution/founding_fathers_overview.html.

In general, smaller states felt comfortable with the arrangements under the Articles of Confederation. These states offered another model of government, the **New Jersey Plan.** Its key features included:

- Strengthening the Articles, not replacing them.
- Creating a one-house legislature with one vote for each state with representatives chosen by state legislatures.
- Giving the Congress the power to raise revenue from duties and postal service.
- Creating a Supreme Court appointed for life by the executive officers.

New Jersey Plan
A framework for the Constitution proposed by a group of small states; its key points were a one-house legislature with one vote for each state, a multiperson "executive," the establishment of the acts of Congress as the "supreme law" of the land, and a supreme judiciary with limited power.

Constitutional Compromises

The most serious disagreement between the Virginia and New Jersey plans concerned state representation in Congress and the North/South division over how slaves were to be counted for purposes of representation and taxation. When a deadlock loomed, Connecticut offered its own compromise. Each state would have an equal vote in the Senate. Again, there was a stalemate. As Benjamin Franklin put it:

> The diversity of opinions turns on two points. If a proportional representation takes place, the small states contend that their liberties will be in danger. If an equality of votes is to be put in its place, large states say that their money will be in danger.... When a broad table is to be made and the edges of a plank do not fit, the artist takes a little from both sides and makes a good joint. In like manner, both sides must part with some of their demands, in order that they both join in some accommodating position.[16]

A committee to work out an agreement soon reported back what became known as the **Great Compromise.** Taking ideas from both the Virginia and New Jersey plans, it recommended:

Great Compromise
A decision made during the Philadelphia Convention to give each state the same number of representatives in the Senate regardless of size; representation in the House was determined by population.

1. In one house of the legislature (later called the House of Representatives), there should be fifty-six representatives—one representative for every 40,000 inhabitants. Representatives were to be elected directly by the people.
2. That house should have the power to originate all bills for raising and spending money.
3. In the second house of the legislature (later called the Senate), each state should have an equal vote, and representatives would be selected by the state legislatures.[17]
4. In dividing power between the national and state governments, national power was declared supreme.

The Great Compromise ultimately met with the approval of all states in attendance. The smaller states were pleased because they got equal representation in the Senate; the larger states were satisfied with the proportional representation in the House of Representatives. The small states then would dominate the Senate while the large states, such as Virginia and Pennsylvania, would control the House. But, because both houses had to pass any legislation, neither body could dominate the other.

The Great Compromise dealt with one major concern of the Framers—how best to treat the differences in large and small states—but other problems stemming largely from regional differences remained. Slavery was one of the thorniest. Southerners feared that the new national government would interfere with its lucrative cotton trade as well as slavery. Thus, when a tax on the importation of slaves was proposed, the convention turned to the larger question of slavery, which divided the northern and southern states. Consequently, in exchange for northern support of continuing the slave trade for twenty more years and for a twenty-year ban on taxing exports to protect the cotton trade, Southerners consented to a provision requiring only a majority vote on navigation laws, the national government was given the authority to regulate foreign commerce, and the Senate was required to cast a two-thirds vote to pass treaties. The southern states, which made up more than one-third of the new union at that time, would be able to check the Senate's power, and it was believed that there would be an adequate supply of slaves by 1808.

Another sticking point concerning slavery remained: how to determine state population for purposes of representation in the House of Representatives. Slaves could not vote, but the southern states wanted them included for purposes of determining population. After considerable dissension, it was decided that population for purposes of representation and the apportionment of direct taxes would be calculated by adding the "whole Number of Free Persons" to "three-fifths of all other Persons." "All other Persons" was the delegates' "tactful" way of referring to slaves. Known as the **Three-Fifths Compromise,** this highly political deal assured that the South would hold 47 percent of the House—enough to prevent attacks on slavery but not so much as to foster the spread of slavery northward.

Unfinished Business

The Framers next turned to fashioning an executive branch. While they agreed on the idea of a one-person executive, they could not settle on the length of the term of office, nor on how the chief executive should be selected. With Shays's Rebellion still fresh in their minds, the delegates feared putting too much power, including selection of a president, into the hands of the lower classes. At the same time, representatives from the smaller states feared that the selection of the chief executive by the legislature would put additional power into the hands of the large states.

Amid these fears, the Committee on Unfinished Portions, whose sole responsibility was to iron out problems and disagreements concerning the office of chief executive, conducted its work. The committee recommended that the presidential term of office be fixed at four years instead of seven, as had earlier been proposed. By choosing not to mention a period of time within which the chief executive would be eligible for reelection, they made it possible for a president to serve more than one term.

The Framers also created the electoral college and drafted rules concerning removal of a sitting president. The electoral college system gave individual states a key role, because each state would select electors equal to the number of representatives it had in the House and Senate. It was a vague compromise that removed election of the president and vice president from both the Congress and the people and put it in the hands of electors whose method of selection would be left to the states. As Alexander Hamilton noted in *Federalist No. 68*, the electoral college was fashioned to avoid the "tumult and disorder" that the Framers feared could result if the "masses" were allowed to vote directly for president. Instead, the selection of the president was left to a small number of men (the electoral college) who "possess[ed] the information and discernment requisite" to decide, in Hamilton's words, the "complicated" business of selecting the president. (See Politics Now: Abolishing the Electoral College?).

In drafting the new Constitution, the Framers also were careful to include a provision for removal of the chief executive. The House of Representatives was given the sole responsibility of investigating and charging a president or vice president with "Treason, Bribery, or other high Crimes and Misdemeanors." A majority vote would then result in issuing articles of impeachment against the president. In turn, the Senate was given sole responsibility to try the chief executive on the charges issued by the House. A two-thirds vote of the Senate was required to convict and remove the president from office. The chief justice of the United States was to preside over the Senate proceedings in place of the vice president (that body's usual leader) to prevent any appearance of impropriety on the vice president's part.

Three-Fifths Compromise
Agreement reached at the Constitutional Convention stipulating that each slave was to be counted as three-fifths of a person for purposes of determining population for representation in the U.S. House of Representatives.

Politics Now

ABOLISHING THE ELECTORAL COLLEGE?

Time after time, controversial Supreme Court decisions or congressional or presidential actions generate calls to amend the Constitution. Nary a session of Congress goes by without some member introducing a proposal for a constitutional amendment.

Vice President Al Gore received more votes for president in the 2000 election than the ultimate victor, George W. Bush. Had Gore won his home state, he would have won the popular and a majority of the electoral college votes. But, that was not the case. In the wake of that hotly contested election, and the Supreme Court's decision in *Bush* v. *Gore* (2000),[a] which effectively stopped the Florida recount and gave Florida's Electoral College votes to Bush, many members of Congress, the media, and academia were clamoring for changes in, or the end of, the electoral college. Others called for amendments to limit Supreme Court justices to eighteen-year terms and to establish a nationwide standard for types of voting mechanisms, from voting machines to absentee ballots.

Among the proposed changes to the Electoral College—most of which would require a constitutional amendment—were the following:

1. Direct Election Plan: Abolish the Electoral College, and elect the president and vice president by popular vote. A CNN/Gallup/*USA Today* poll found that 61 percent of the public agreed with this just one week after the 2000 election—one month before the process ended.[b]
2. Electoral College Reform: There are several plans. The proportional plan would alter the Electoral College to encourage the states to distribute their electors in proportion to the popular state vote for each candidate. Maine and Nebraska already do this. An effort by Colorado to do the same was rejected by voters there in 2004.[c]

[a]513 U.S. 98 (2000).

[b]William Wichterman, "No Small Matter," *Sunday Gazette Mail* (December 10, 2000): 1C.

[c]For more detail on these plans, see L. Paige Whitaker and Thomas H. Neale, "RL30804: The Electoral College: An Overview and Analysis of Reform Proposals," *CRS Report for Congress*, January 16, 2001.

THE U.S. CONSTITUTION

After the compromise on the presidency, work proceeded quickly on the remaining resolutions of the Constitution. The Preamble to the Constitution, the last section to be drafted, contains exceptionally powerful language that forms the bedrock of American political tradition. Its opening line, "We the People of the United States," boldly proclaimed that a loose confederation of independent states no longer existed. Instead, there was but one American people and nation. The original version of the Preamble opened with:

> We the people of the States of New Hampshire, Massachusetts, Rhode Island and the Providence Plantations, Connecticut, New Jersey, New York, Pennsylvania, Delaware, Maryland, Virginia, North Carolina, South Carolina and Georgia, do ordain, declare and establish the following Constitution for the government of ourselves and our Posterity.

The simple phrase "We the People" ended, at least for the time being, the question of whence the government derived its power: It came directly from the people, not from the states. The next phrase of the Constitution explained the need for the new outline of government. "[I]n Order to form a more perfect Union" indirectly acknowledged the weaknesses of the Articles of Confederation in governing a growing nation. Next, the optimistic goals of the Framers for the new nation were set out: to "establish Justice, insure domestic Tranquility, provide for the common defence, promote the general Welfare, and secure the Blessings of Liberty to ourselves and our Posterity"; followed by the formal creation of a new government: "do ordain and establish this Constitution for the United States of America."

On September 17, 1787, the Constitution was approved by the delegates from all twelve states in attendance. While the completed document did not satisfy all the delegates, of the forty-one in attendance, thirty-nine ultimately signed it. The sentiments uttered by Benjamin Franklin probably well reflected those of many others: "Thus, I consent, Sir, to this Constitution because I expect no better, and because I am not sure that it is not the best."[18]

The Basic Principles of the Constitution

The ideas of political philosophers, especially two political philosophers, the French Montesquieu (1689–1755) and the English John Locke (see Roots of Government: Hobbes and Locke in chapter 1), heavily influenced the shape and nature of the government proposed by the Framers. Montesquieu, who actually drew many of his ideas about government from the works of Greek political philosopher Aristotle, was heavily quoted during the Constitutional Convention.

The proposed structure of the new national government owed much to the writings of Montesquieu, who advocated distinct functions for each branch of government, called **separation of powers,** with a system of **checks and balances** between each branch. The Constitution's concern with the distribution of power between states and the national government also reveals the heavy influence of political philosophers, as well as the colonists' experience under the Articles of Confederation.[19]

Federalism.   Today, in spite of current calls for the national government to return power to the states, the question before and during the Convention was how much power states would give up to the national government. Given the nation's experiences under the Articles of Confederation, the Framers believed that a strong national government was necessary for the new nation's survival. However, they were reluctant to create a powerful government after the model of Britain, the country from which they had just won their independence. Its unitary system was not even considered by the colonists. Instead, they fashioned a system now known as the **federal system,** which divides the power of government between a strong national government and the individual states. This system, as the Supreme Court reaffirmed in 1995 in considering term limits, was based on the principle that the federal, or national, government derived its power from the citizens, not the states, as the national government had done under the Articles of Confederation.[20]

Opponents of this system feared that a strong national government would infringe on their liberty. But, James Madison argued that a strong national government with distinct state governments could, if properly directed by constitutional arrangements, actually be a source of expanded liberties and national unity. The Framers viewed the division of governmental authority between the national government and the states as a means of checking power with power, and providing the people with "double security" against governmental tyranny. Later, the passage of the Tenth Amendment, which stated that powers not given to the national government were reserved by the states or the people, further clarified the federal structure (see chapter 3).

Separation of Powers.   Madison and many of the Framers clearly feared putting too much power into the hands of any one individual or branch of government. His famous words, "Ambition must be made to counteract ambition," were widely believed at the Philadelphia convention.

Separation of powers is simply a way of parceling out power among the three branches of government. Its three key features are:

1. Three distinct branches of government: the legislative, the executive, and the judicial.

2. Three separately staffed branches of government to exercise these functions.

3. Constitutional equality and independence of each branch.

separation of powers
A way of dividing power among three branches of government in which members of the House of Representatives, members of the Senate, the president, and the federal courts are selected by and responsible to different constituencies.

checks and balances
A governmental structure that gives each of the three branches of government some degree of oversight and control over the actions of the others.

federal system
Plan of government created in the U.S. Constitution in which power is divided between the national government and the state governments and in which independent states are bound together under one national government.

FIGURE 2.1   Separation of Powers and Checks and Balances Illustrated

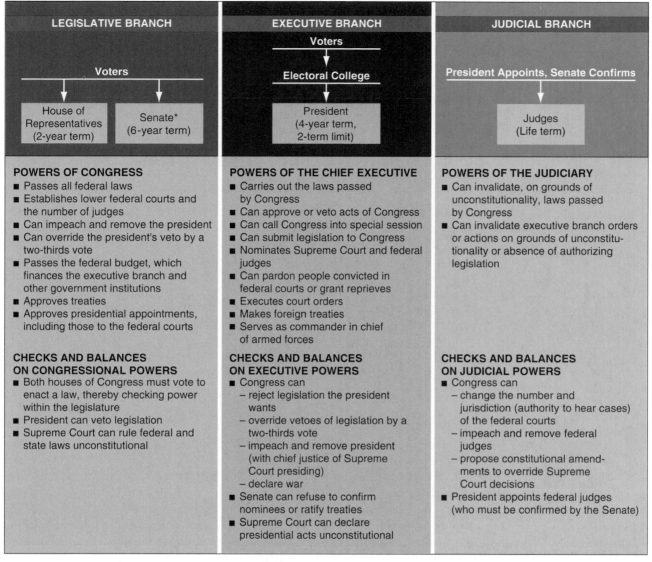

LEGISLATIVE BRANCH	EXECUTIVE BRANCH	JUDICIAL BRANCH
Voters	Voters → Electoral College	President Appoints, Senate Confirms
House of Representatives (2-year term) Senate* (6-year term)	President (4-year term, 2-term limit)	Judges (Life term)

POWERS OF CONGRESS
- Passes all federal laws
- Establishes lower federal courts and the number of judges
- Can impeach and remove the president
- Can override the president's veto by a two-thirds vote
- Passes the federal budget, which finances the executive branch and other government institutions
- Approves treaties
- Approves presidential appointments, including those to the federal courts

CHECKS AND BALANCES ON CONGRESSIONAL POWERS
- Both houses of Congress must vote to enact a law, thereby checking power within the legislature
- President can veto legislation
- Supreme Court can rule federal and state laws unconstitutional

POWERS OF THE CHIEF EXECUTIVE
- Carries out the laws passed by Congress
- Can approve or veto acts of Congress
- Can call Congress into special session
- Can submit legislation to Congress
- Nominates Supreme Court and federal judges
- Can pardon people convicted in federal courts or grant reprieves
- Executes court orders
- Makes foreign treaties
- Serves as commander in chief of armed forces

CHECKS AND BALANCES ON EXECUTIVE POWERS
- Congress can
  - reject legislation the president wants
  - override vetoes of legislation by a two-thirds vote
  - impeach and remove president (with chief justice of Supreme Court presiding)
  - declare war
- Senate can refuse to confirm nominees or ratify treaties
- Supreme Court can declare presidential acts unconstitutional

POWERS OF THE JUDICIARY
- Can invalidate, on grounds of unconstitutionality, laws passed by Congress
- Can invalidate executive branch orders or actions on grounds of unconstitutionality or absence of authorizing legislation

CHECKS AND BALANCES ON JUDICIAL POWERS
- Congress can
  - change the number and jurisdiction (authority to hear cases) of the federal courts
  - impeach and remove federal judges
  - propose constitutional amendments to override Supreme Court decisions
- President appoints federal judges (who must be confirmed by the Senate)

*Prior to 1913, senators were selected by state legislatures.

As illustrated in Figure 2.1, the Framers were careful to create a system in which law-making, law-enforcing, and law-interpreting functions were assigned to independent branches of government. On the national level (and in most states), only the legislature has the authority to make laws; the chief executive enforces laws; and the judiciary interprets them. Moreover, initially, members of the House of Representatives, members of the Senate, the president, and members of the federal courts were selected by and were therefore responsible to different constituencies. Madison believed that the scheme devised by the Framers would divide the offices of the new government and their methods of selection among many individuals, providing each office holder with the "necessary means and personal motives to resist encroachment" on his or her power. The original Constitution placed the selection of senators directly with state legislators, making them more accountable to the states. The Seventeenth Amendment, ratified in 1913, however, called for direct election of senators by the voters, making them directly accountable to the people, thereby making the system more democratic.

The Framers could not have foreseen the intermingling of governmental functions that has since evolved. Locke, in fact, cautioned against giving a legislature the ability to delegate its powers. In Article I of the Constitution, the legislative power is vested in the Congress. But, the president is also given legislative powers via his ability to veto legislation, although his veto can be overridden by a two-thirds vote in Congress. Judicial interpretation then helps to clarify the implementation of legislation enacted through this process.

So, instead of a pure system of separation of powers, a symbiotic, or interdependent, relationship among the three branches of government has existed from the beginning. Or, as one scholar has explained, there are "separated institutions sharing powers."[21] While Congress still is entrusted with making the laws, most proposals for legislation originate with the president. And, although the Supreme Court's major function is to interpret the law, its involvement in areas such as criminal procedure, abortion, and other issues has led many to charge that it has surpassed its constitutional authority and become, in effect, a law-making body.

Checks and Balances.   The separation of powers among the three branches of the national government is not complete. According to Montesquieu and the Framers, the powers of each branch (as well as the two houses of the national legislature and between the states and the national government) could be used to check the powers of the other two branches of government. The power of each branch of government is checked, or limited, and balanced because the legislative, executive, and judicial branches share some authority and no branch has exclusive domain over any single activity. The creation of this system allowed the Framers to minimize the threat of tyranny from any one branch. Thus, for almost every power granted to one branch, an equal control was established in the other two branches. The Congress could "check" the power of the president, the Supreme Court, and so on, carefully creating "balance" among the three branches.

The American System of Checks and Balances

The Articles of the Constitution

The document finally signed by the Framers condensed numerous resolutions into a Preamble and seven separate articles. The first three articles established the three branches of government, defined their internal operations, and clarified their relationships with one another. All branches of government were technically considered equal, yet some initially appeared more "equal" than others. The order of the articles, and the detail contained in the first three, reflects the Framers' concern that these branches of government might abuse their powers. The four remaining articles define the relationships among the states, declare national law to be supreme, and set out methods of amending the Constitution.

Article I: The Legislative Branch.   Article I vests all legislative powers in the Congress and establishes a bicameral legislature, consisting of the Senate and the House of Representatives. It also sets out the qualifications for holding office in each house, the terms of office, methods of selection of representatives and senators, and the system of apportionment among the states to determine membership in the House of Representatives. Article I, section 2, specifies that an "enumeration" of the citizenry must take place every ten years in a manner to be directed by the U.S. Congress. Continuity & Change: Counting Americans reveals how complex and partisan that task has become. Operating procedures and the formal officers of each house also are described in Article I.

One of the most important sections of Article I is section 8. It carefully lists the powers the Framers wished the new Congress to possess. These specified or **enumerated powers** contain many key provisions that had been denied to the Continental Congress under the Articles of Confederation. For example, one of the major weaknesses of the Articles was Congress's lack of authority to deal with trade wars. The Constitution remedied this problem by authorizing Congress to "regulate Commerce with for-

enumerated powers
Seventeen specific powers granted to Congress under Article 1, section 8, of the U.S. Constitution; these powers include taxation, coinage of money, regulation of commerce, and the authority to provide for a national defense.

eign Nations, and among the several States." Congress was also given the authority to coin money.

Today, Congress often enacts legislation that no specific clause of Article 1, section 8, appears to authorize. Laws dealing with the environment, welfare, education, and communications, among others, are often justified by reference to a particular power plus the necessary and proper clause. After careful enumeration of seventeen powers of Congress in Article 1, section 8, a final, general clause authorizing Congress to "make all Laws which shall be necessary and proper for carrying into Execution the foregoing Powers" was added to Article I. Often referred to as the elastic clause, the **necessary and proper clause** has been a source of tremendous congressional activity never anticipated by the Framers, as definitions of "necessary" and "proper" have been stretched to accommodate changing needs and times. The clause is the basis for Congress's **implied powers** that it uses to execute its other powers. The Supreme Court, for example, has coupled Congress's authority to regulate commerce coupled with the necessary and proper clause to allow Congress to ban prostitution (where travel across state lines is involved), regulate trains and planes, establish uniform federal minimum-wage and maximum-hour laws, and mandate drug testing for certain workers.

Article II: The Executive Branch.

Article II vests the executive power, that is, the authority to execute the laws of the nation, in a president of the United States. Section 1 sets the president's term of office at four years and explains the electoral college. It also states the qualifications for office and describes a mechanism to replace the president in case of death, disability, or removal.

The powers and duties of the president are set out in section 3. Among the most important of these are the president's role as commander in chief of the armed forces, the authority to make treaties with the consent of the Senate, and the authority to "appoint Ambassadors, other public Ministers and Consuls, the Judges of the supreme Court, and all other Officers of the United States." Other sections of Article II instruct the president to report directly to Congress "from time to time," in what has come to be known as the State of the Union Address, and to "take Care that the Laws be faithfully executed." Section 4 provides the mechanism for removal of the president, vice

necessary and proper clause
The final paragraph of Article I, section 8, of the U.S. Constitution, which gives Congress the authority to pass all laws "necessary and proper" to carry out the enumerated powers specified in the Constitution; also called the "elastic" clause.

implied power
A power derived from an enumerated power and the necessary and proper clause. These powers are not stated specifically but are considered to be reasonably implied through the exercise of delegated powers.

President George W. Bush delivers his 2002 State of the Union Address to Congress as millions across the nation watch in their homes. Behind him is Vice President Dick Cheney and the Speaker of the House, Dennis Hastert.

(Photo courtesy: Mark Wilson/Getty Images)

president, and other officers of the United States for "Treason, Bribery, or other high Crimes and Misdemeanors" (see chapter 8).

Article III: The Judicial Branch.

Article III establishes a Supreme Court and defines its jurisdiction. During the Philadelphia meeting, the small and large states differed significantly as to the desirability of an independent judiciary and on the role of state courts in the national court system. The smaller states feared that a strong unelected judiciary would trample on their liberties. In compromise, Congress was permitted, but not required, to establish lower national courts. Thus, state courts and the national court system would exist side by side with distinct areas of authority. Federal courts were given authority to decide cases arising under federal law. The Supreme Court was also given the power to settle disputes between states, or between a state and the national government. Ultimately, it was up to the Supreme Court to determine what any provisions of the Constitution actually meant.

Although some delegates to the convention had urged that the president be allowed to remove federal judges, ultimately judges were given appointments for life, presuming "good behavior." And, like the president's, their salaries cannot be lowered while they hold office. This provision was adopted to ensure that the legislature did not attempt to punish the Supreme Court or any other judges for unpopular decisions.

Articles IV Through VII.

The remainder of the Articles attempted to anticipate problems that might occur in the operation of the new national government as well as its relations to the states. Article IV begins with what is called the full faith and credit clause, which mandates that states honor the laws and judicial proceedings of the other states. In 1996, when it appeared that Hawaii might legalize same-sex marriages, the U.S. Congress passed the Defense of Marriage Act to allow states to disregard gay marriages even if they are legal in other states. Vermont recognized the legality of same-sex partnerships in 2000, and Massachusetts began to allow same sex partners to marry in May 2004 prompting efforts in Congress to amend the Constitution. The constitutionality of this act has not been challenged in the federal courts. But, since the full faith and credit clause mandates that states recognize the laws of other states, some question about the legality of the federal law remains. Article IV also includes the mechanisms for admitting new states to the Union.

Article V (discussed in greater detail on p. 59) specifies how amendments can be added to the Constitution. The Bill of Rights, which added ten amendments to the Constitution in 1791, was one of the first items of business when the First Congress met in 1789. Since then, only seventeen additional amendments have been ratified.

supremacy clause
Portion of Article VI of the U.S. Constitution that mandates that national law is supreme to (that is, supersedes) all other laws passed by the states or by any other subdivision of government.

Article VI contains the supremacy clause, which asserts the basic primacy of the Constitution and national law over state laws and constitutions. The **supremacy clause** provides that the "Constitution, and the laws of the United States" as well as all treaties are to be the supreme law of the land. All national and state officers and judges are bound by national law and take oaths to support the federal Constitution above any state law or constitution. Because of the supremacy clause, any legitimate exercise of national power supersedes any state laws or action, in a process that is called preemption. Without the supremacy clause and the federal court's ability to invoke it, the national government would have little actual enforceable power; thus, many commentators call the supremacy clause the linchpin of the entire federal system.

Mindful of the potential problems that could occur if church and state were too enmeshed, Article VI also specifies that no religious test shall be required for holding any office. This mandate strengthens the separation of church and state guarantee that was quickly added to the Constitution when the First Amendment was ratified.

The seventh and final article of the Constitution concerns the procedures for ratification of the new Constitution: Nine of the thirteen states would have to agree to, or ratify, its new provisions before it would become the supreme law of the land.

THE DRIVE FOR RATIFICATION

While delegates to the Constitutional Convention labored in Philadelphia, the Congress of the Confederation continued to govern the former colonies under the Articles of Confederation. The day after the Constitution was signed, William Jackson, the secretary of the Constitutional Convention, left for New York City, by then the nation's capital, to deliver the official copy of the document to the Congress. He also took with him a resolution of the delegates calling upon each of the states to vote on the new Constitution. Anticipating resistance from the representatives in the state legislatures, however, the Framers required the states to call special ratifying conventions to consider the proposed Constitution.

Jackson carried a letter from General George Washington with the proposed Constitution. In a few eloquent words, Washington summed up the sentiments of the Framers and the spirit of compromise that had permeated the long weeks in Philadelphia:

> That it will meet the full and entire approbation of every state is not perhaps to be expected, but each [state] will doubtless consider, that had her interest alone been consulted, the consequences might have been particularly disagreeable or injurious to others; that it is liable to as few exceptions as could reasonably have been expected, we hope and believe; that it may promote lasting welfare of that country so dear to us all, and secure her freedom and happiness is our ardent wish.[22]

The Second Continental Congress immediately accepted the work of the convention and forwarded the proposed Constitution to the states for their vote. It was by no means certain, however, that the new Constitution would be adopted. From the fall of 1787 to the summer of 1788, the proposed Constitution was debated hotly around the nation. State politicians understandably feared a strong central government. Farmers and other working-class people were fearful of a distant national government. Those who had accrued substantial debts during the economic chaos following the Revolutionary War feared that a new government with a new financial policy would plunge them into even greater debt. The public in general was very leery of taxes—these were the same people who had revolted against the king's taxes. At the heart of many of their concerns was an underlying fear of the massive changes that would be brought about by a new system. Favoring the Constitution were wealthy merchants, lawyers, bankers, and those who believed that the new nation could not continue to exist under the Articles of Confederation. For them, it all boiled down to one simple question offered by Madison: "Whether or not the Union shall or shall not be continued."

Federalists Versus Anti-Federalists

Almost as soon as the ink was dry on the last signature to the Constitution, those who favored the new strong national government chose to call themselves **Federalists.** They were well aware that many still generally opposed the notion of a strong national government. Thus, they did not want to risk being labeled "nationalists," so they tried to get the upper hand in the debate by nicknaming their opponents **Anti-Federalists.** Those put in the latter category insisted that they were instead "Federal Republicans" who believed in a federal system. As noted in Table 2.1, Anti-Federalists argued that they simply wanted to protect state governments from the tyranny of a too-powerful national government.[23]

Federalists and Anti-Federalists participated in the mass meetings that were held in state legislatures to discuss the pros and cons of the new plan. Tempers ran high at public meetings, where differences between the opposing groups were highlighted. Fervent debates were published in newspapers. Indeed, newspapers played a powerful role in the adoption process. The entire Constitution, in fact, was printed in the

Federalists
Those who favored a stronger national government and supported the proposed U.S. Constitution; later became the first U.S. political party.

Anti-Federalists
Those who favored strong state governments and a weak national government; opposed the ratification of the U.S. Constitution.

TABLE 2.1   Federalists and Anti-Federalists Compared

	Federalists	Anti-Federalists
Who were they?	Property owners, landed rich, merchants of Northeast and Middle Atlantic states	Small farmers, shopkeepers, laborers
Political philosophy	Elitist: saw themselves and those of their class as most fit to govern (others were to be governed)	Believed in the decency of the common man and in participatory democracy; viewed elites as corrupt; sought greater protection of individual rights
Type of government favored	Powerful central government; two-house legislature; upper house (six-year term) further removed from the people, whom they distrusted	Wanted stronger state governments (closer to the people) at the expense of the powers of the national government; sought smaller electoral districts, frequent elections, referendum and recall, and a large unicameral legislature to provide for greater class and occupational representation
Alliances	Pro-British Anti-French	Anti-British Pro-French

The Federalist Papers
A series of eighty-five political papers written by John Jay, Alexander Hamilton, and James Madison in support of ratification of the U.S. Constitution.

WEB EXPLORATION
To compare *The Federalist Papers* with *The Anti-Federalist Papers*, see www.ablongman.com/oconnor

Pennsylvania Packet just two days after the convention's end. Other major papers quickly followed suit. Soon, opinion pieces on both sides of the adoption issue began to appear around the nation, often written under pseudonyms such as "Caesar" or "Constant Reader," as was the custom of the day.

One name stood out from all the rest: "Publius" (Latin for "the people"). Between October 1787 and May 1788, eighty-five articles written under that pen name routinely appeared in newspapers in New York, a state where ratification was in doubt. Most were written by Alexander Hamilton and James Madison. Hamilton, a young, fiery New Yorker born in the British West Indies, wrote fifty-one, Madison wrote twenty-six, and jointly they penned another three. John Jay, also of New York, and later the first chief justice of the United States, wrote five of the pieces. These eighty-five essays became known as ***The Federalist Papers.***

Today, *The Federalist Papers* are considered masterful explanations of the Framers' intentions as they drafted the new Constitution. At the time, although they were reprinted widely, they were far too theoretical to have much impact on those who would ultimately vote on the proposed Constitution. Dry and scholarly, they lacked the fervor of much of the political rhetoric that was then in use. *The Federalist Papers* did, however, highlight the reasons for the structure of the new government and its benefits. According to *Federalist No. 10*, for example, the new Constitution was called "a republican remedy for the disease incident to republican government." Moreover, these musings of Madison, Hamilton, and Jay continue to be the best single source of the political theories and philosophies that lay at the heart of our Constitution.

Forced on the defensive, the Anti-Federalists responded with their own series of "letters" written by Anti-Federalists adopting the pen names of "Brutus" and "Cato," two ancient Romans famous for their intolerance of tyranny. These "letters" (actually essays) undertook a line-by-line critique of the Constitution and were designed to counteract *The Federalist Papers*.

Anti-Federalists argued that a strong central government would render the states powerless.[24] They stressed the strengths the government had been granted under the Articles of Confederation, and argued that these Articles, not the proposed Constitution, created a true federal system. Moreover, they argued that the strong national government would tax heavily, that the Supreme Court would overwhelm the states by invalidating state laws, and that the president eventually would have too much power, as commander in chief of a large and powerful army.[25]

In particular, the Anti-Federalists feared the power of the national government to run roughshod over the liberties of the people. They proposed that the taxing power of Congress be limited, that the executive be curbed by a council, that the military consist of state militias rather than a national force, and that the jurisdiction of the Supreme

Alexander Hamilton (left), James Madison (center), and John Jay (right) were important early Federalist leaders. Jay wrote five of *The Federalist Papers* and Madison and Hamilton wrote the rest. Madison served in the House of Representatives (1789–1797) and as secretary of state in the Jefferson administration (1801–1808). In 1808, he was elected fourth president of the United States and served two terms (1809–1817). Hamilton became the first secretary of the treasury (1789–1795). He was killed in 1804 in a duel with Vice President Aaron Burr, who was angered by Hamilton's negative comments about his character. Jay became the first chief justice of the United States (1789–1795) and negotiated the Jay Treaty with Great Britain in 1794. He then served as governor of New York from 1795 to 1801.

(Photos courtesy: left, The Metropolitan Museum of Art, Gift of Henry G. Marquand; 1881 (81.11) copyright © 1987 The Metropolitan Museum of Art; center, Colonial Williamsburg Foundation; right, Bettmann/Corbis)

Court be limited to prevent it from reviewing and potentially overturning the decisions of state courts. But, their most effective argument concerned the absence of a bill of rights in the Constitution. James Madison answered these criticisms in *Federalist Nos. 10* and *51*. (The texts of these two essays are printed in Appendices III and IV.) In *Federalist No. 10*, he pointed out that the voters would not always succeed in electing "enlightened statesmen" as their representatives. The greatest threat to individual liberties would therefore come from factions within the government, who might place narrow interests above broader national interests and the rights of citizens. While recognizing that no form of government could protect the country from unscrupulous politicians, Madison argued that the organization of the new government would minimize the effects of political factions. The great advantage of a federal system, Madison maintained, was that it created the "happy combination" of a national government too large to be controlled by any single faction, and several state governments that would be smaller and more responsive to local needs. Moreover, he argued in *Federalist No. 51* that the proposed federal government's separation of powers would prohibit any one branch from either dominating the national government or violating the rights of citizens.

Debate continued in the thirteen states as votes were taken from December 1787 to June 1788, in accordance with the ratifying process laid out in Article VII of the proposed Constitution. Three states acted quickly to ratify the new Constitution. Two small states, Delaware and New Jersey, voted to ratify before the large states could rethink the notion of equal representation of the states in the Senate. Pennsylvania, where Federalists were well organized, was one of the first three states to ratify. Massachusetts assented to the new government but tempered its support by calling for an immediate addition of amendments including one protecting personal rights. New Hampshire became the crucial ninth state to ratify on June 21, 1788. This action completed the ratification process outlined in Article VII of the Constitution and marked the beginning of a new nation. But, New York and Virginia, which between them by then accounted for more

Simulation

You Are James Madison

than 40 percent of the new nation's population, had not yet ratified the Constitution. Thus, the practical future of the new nation remained in doubt.

Hamilton in New York and Madison in Virginia worked feverishly to convince delegates to their state conventions to vote for the new government. In New York, sentiment against it was high. In Albany, fighting, resulting in injuries and death, broke out over the proposed Constitution. When news of Virginia's acceptance of the Constitution reached the New York convention, Hamilton finally was able to convince a majority of those present to follow suit by a narrow margin of three votes. Both states also recommended the addition of a series of structural amendments, and a bill of rights.

Two of the original states—North Carolina and Rhode Island—continued to hold out against ratification. Both had recently printed new currencies and feared that values would plummet in a federal system where the Congress was authorized to coin money. On August 2, 1788, North Carolina became the first state to reject the Constitution on the grounds that no Anti-Federalist amendments were included. Soon after, owing much to the Anti-Federalist pressure for additional protections from the national government, Congress submitted a **Bill of Rights** to the states for their ratification in September 1789. North Carolina then ratified the Constitution by a vote of 194–77. Rhode Island, the only state that had not sent representatives to Philadelphia, remained out of the Union until 1790. Finally, under threats from its largest cities to secede from the state, the legislature called a convention that ratified the Constitution by only two votes (34–32)—one year after George Washington became the first president of the United States.

Bill of Rights
The first ten amendments to the U.S. Constitution.

FORMAL METHODS OF AMENDING THE CONSTITUTION

Once the Constitution was ratified, elections were held. When Congress convened, it immediately sent a set of amendments to the states for their ratification. An amendment authorizing the enlargement of the House of Representatives and another to prevent members of the House from raising their own salaries failed to garner favorable votes in the necessary three-fourths of the states. (See On Campus: A Student's Revenge: The Twenty-Seventh [Madison] Amendment.) The remaining ten amendments, known as the Bill of Rights, were ratified by 1791 in accordance with the procedures set out in the Constitution. Sought by Anti-Federalists as a protection for individual liberties, they offered numerous specific limitations on the national govern-

Timeline

The History of Constitutional Amendments

A STUDENT'S REVENGE: THE TWENTY-SEVENTH (MADISON) AMENDMENT

On June 8, 1789, in a speech before the House of Representatives, James Madison stated:

> [T]here is seeming impropriety in leaving any set of men

without controul [sic] to put their hand into the public coffers, to take out money to put into their pockets…. I have gone therefore so far as to fix it, that no law, varying the compensation, shall operate until there is a change in the legislation.

When Madison spoke these words about his proposal, now known as the Twenty-Seventh Amendment, he had no way of knowing that more than two centuries would pass before it would become an official part of the Constitution. In fact, Madison deemed it worthy of addition only because the conventions of three states (Virginia, New York, and North Carolina) demanded that it be included.

By 1791, when the Bill of Rights was added to the Constitution, only six states had ratified Madison's amendment, and it seemed destined to fade into obscurity. In 1982, however, Gregory Watson, a sophomore majoring in economics at the University of Texas–Austin, discovered the unratified compensation amendment while looking for a paper topic for an American government class. Intrigued, Watson wrote a paper arguing that the proposed amendment was still viable because it had no internal time limit and, therefore, should still be ratified. Watson received a C on the paper.

Despite his grade, Watson began a ten-year, $6,000 self-financed crusade to renew interest in the compensation amendment. Watson and his allies reasoned that the amendment should be revived because of the public's growing anger with the fact that members of Congress had sought to raise their salaries without going on the record as having done so. Watson's perseverance paid off.

Gregory Watson with a document that contains the first ten amendments to the Constitution, as well as the compensation amendment ("Article the second: No law varying the compensation for the services of the Senators and Representatives shall take effect until an election of Representatives shall have intervened"), which finally was ratified in 1992 as the Twenty-Seventh Amendment.

(Photo courtesy: Ziggy Kaluzny/People Magazine Syndication)

On May 7, 1992, the amendment was ratified by the requisite thirty-eight states. On May 18, the United States Archivist certified that the amendment was part of the Constitution, a decision that was overwhelmingly confirmed by the House of Representatives on May 19 and by the Senate on May 20. At the same time that the Senate approved the Twenty-Seventh Amendment, it also took action to ensure that a similar situation would never occur by declaring "dead" four other amendments.

Source: Fordham Law Review (December 1992): 497–539, and Anne Marie Kilday, "Amendment Expert Agrees with Congressional Pay Ruling," *Dallas Morning News* (February 14, 1993): 13A.

ment's ability to interfere with a wide variety of personal liberties, some of which were already guaranteed by many state constitutions (see chapters 5 and 6).

The Bill of Rights includes numerous specific protections of personal rights. Freedom of expression, speech, press, religion, and assembly are guaranteed by the First Amendment. The Bill of Rights also contains numerous safeguards for those accused of crimes.

In addition to guaranteeing these important rights, two of the amendments of the Bill of Rights were reactions to British rule—the right to bear arms (Second Amendment) and the right not to have soldiers quartered in private homes (Third Amendment). More general rights are also included in the Bill of Rights. The Ninth Amendment notes that these enumerated rights are not inclusive, meaning they are not the only rights to be enjoyed by the people, and the Tenth Amendment states that powers not given to the national government are reserved by the states or the people.

The Amendment Process

Article V of the Constitution creates a two-stage amendment process: proposal and ratification.[26] The Constitution specifies two ways to accomplish each stage. As illustrated in Figure 2.2, amendments to the Constitution can be proposed by: (1) a vote of two-thirds of the members in both houses of Congress; or, (2) a vote of two-thirds of the state legislatures specifically requesting Congress to call a national convention to propose amendments.

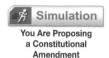

Simulation

You Are Proposing a Constitutional Amendment

The second method has never been used. Historically, it has served as a fairly effective threat, forcing Congress to consider amendments that might otherwise never have been debated. In the 1980s, for example, several states called on Congress to enact a balanced-budget amendment. To forestall the need for a special constitutional convention, in 1985, Congress enacted the Gramm-Rudman-Hollings Act, which called for a balanced budget by the 1991 fiscal year. But, Congress could not meet that target. The act was amended repeatedly until 1993, when Congress postponed the call for a balanced budget, the need for which faded in light of surpluses that occurred during the Clinton administration. The act also was ruled unconstitutional by a three-judge district court that declared the law violated separation of powers principles.

Of the more than 10,000 amendments that have been introduced on one or both floors of the Congress through 2004, only thirty-three mustered the two-thirds vote required for them to be sent to the states for debate and ratification. Only six proposed amendments sent to the states failed to be ratified.

WEB EXPLORATION

For the text of these failed amendments, see www.ablongman.com/oconnor

The ratification process is fairly straightforward. When Congress votes to propose an amendment, the Constitution specifies that the ratification process must occur in one of two ways: (1) a favorable vote in three-fourths of the state legislatures; or, (2) a favorable vote in specially called ratifying conventions in three-fourths of the states.

The Constitution itself was ratified by the favorable vote of nine states in specially called ratifying conventions. The Framers feared that the power of special interests in state legislatures would prevent a positive vote on the new Constitution. Since ratification of the Constitution, however, only one ratifying convention has been called. The Eighteenth Amendment, which caused the Prohibition era by outlawing nationwide the sale of alcoholic beverages, was ratified by the first method—a vote in state legislatures. Millions broke the law, others died from drinking homemade liquor, and still others made their fortunes selling bootleg or illegal liquor. After a decade of these problems, Congress decided to act. An additional amendment—the Twenty-First—was proposed to repeal the Eighteenth Amendment. It was sent to the states for ratification, but with a call for ratifying conventions, not a vote in the state legislatures.[27] Members of Congress correctly predicted that the move to repeal the Eighteenth Amendment would encounter opposition in the statehouses, which were largely controlled by conservative rural interests. Thus, Congress's decision to use the convention method led to quick approval of the Twenty-First Amendment.

FIGURE 2.2   Methods of Amending the Constitution

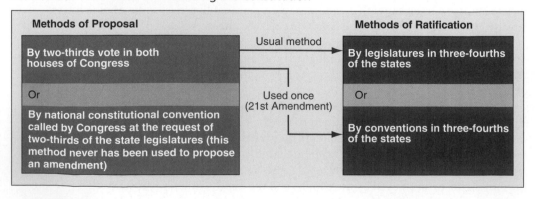

The intensity of efforts to amend the Constitution has varied considerably, depending on the nature of the change proposed. Whereas the Twenty-First Amendment took only ten months to ratify, an equal rights amendment (ERA) was introduced in every session of Congress from 1923 until 1972, when Congress finally voted favorably for it. Even then, years of lobbying by women's groups were insufficient to garner necessary state support. By 1982, the congressionally mandated date for ratification, only thirty-five states—three short of the number required—had voted favorably on the amendment.[28] There is a move afoot in Congress, however, to revive the ERA. In 2002, over 200 House members signed onto a proposed bill to reintroduce the amendment. See chapter 6 for more on the ERA.

Congress also has made several attempts to pass an amendment to ban flag burning, prompted by a Supreme Court decision protecting such actions as free speech. Many were outraged by the Court's 5–4 decision in *Texas* v. *Johnson* (1989) but have been unable to muster the two-thirds vote necessary to send the proposed amendment to the states.[29] Of late, senators introduced proposed amendments to protect victims' rights, as well as to ban gay marriages. If the history of the failed ERA is any indication, chances are slim that either amendment will be ratified.

For all its moral foundation in groups such as the Women's Christian Temperance Union (WCTU), whose members invaded bars to protest the sale of alcoholic beverages, the Eighteenth (Prohibition) Amendment was a disaster. Among its side effects were the rise of powerful crime organizations responsible for illegal sales of alcoholic beverages. Once proposed, it took only ten months to ratify the Twenty-First Amendment, which repealed the Prohibition Amendment.

(Photo courtesy: Hulton Archive/Getty Images)

INFORMAL METHODS OF AMENDING THE CONSTITUTION

The Framers did not want to fashion a government that could respond to the whims of the people. The separation of powers and the checks and balances systems are just two indications of the Framers' recognition of the importance of deliberation and thought as a check against both government tyranny and the rash judgments of intemperate majorities. James Madison, in particular, wanted to draft a system of government that would pit faction against faction, and ambition against ambition, to design a system of representation and policy making that would strengthen minority factions against possible encroachments by majority factions. Although it took a long time, the Constitution eventually was amended to protect the rights of African Americans through the addition of the Thirteenth, Fourteenth, and Fifteenth Amendments.

The Framers also made the formal amendment process a slow one to ensure that amendments were not added lightly to the Constitution. But, the formal amendment process is not the only way that the Constitution has been changed over time. Judicial interpretation and cultural and social change also have had a major impact on the way the Constitution has evolved.

Judicial Interpretation

As early as 1803, under the leadership of Chief Justice John Marshall, in *Marbury* v. *Madison* the Supreme Court declared that the federal courts had the power to nullify acts of the nation's government when they were found to be in conflict with the Constitution.[30] Over the years, this check on the other branches of government and on the states has increased the authority of the Court and significantly has altered the meaning of various provisions of the Constitution, a fact that prompted Woodrow Wilson to call the Supreme Court "a constitutional convention in continuous session." (More detail on the Supreme Court's role in interpreting the Constitution is found in chapters 5, 6, and 10 especially, as well as in other chapters in the book.)

COMPARING CONSTITUTIONS

Americans are accustomed to the idea of a durable written constitution. The U.S. Constitution stands out not only for being the first written constitution in the modern world (Poland followed soon after, in 1790), but because it remains the Constitution of the United States today. In fact, the American case is rather anomalous, both in the number of constitutions it has had (two, if we count the Articles of Confederation) and in the continuity of the basic political rules it outlined. Among the countries surveyed here, only Canada and the United Kingdom have had similar experience with a single constitution. Yet, Canada's constitutional history is nearly a century shorter than that of the United States. Britain's single constitution is unwritten and has evolved over centuries (parts of it date to the Middle Ages), rendering it difficult to compare with a written constitution. More typically, the European countries and Japan have had multiple constitutions. France is the extreme example, with fifteen constitutional regimes since 1789 (five in the first decade after the French Revolution). External events such as World War II, independence in Asia and Africa, and the collapse of the Soviet Union have had significant effects on constitution building around the world.

These constitutions have established a wide range of political systems. Since 1789, France has had monarchies, republics, a commune, and a dictatorship in collaboration with a foreign occupier. The first constitutions in Germany, Italy, and Japan were within anti-democratic monarchies. Italy and Germany had fascist constitutional systems in the 1930s and early 1940s. In Germany and Japan, postwar occupations by outside powers led to new constitutions. Germany, moreover, had two competing constitutional systems during the Cold War, with a parliamentary democracy in West Germany and a Soviet-style socialist political system in East Germany.

Constitutional amendment practices vary as well. Unlike the Framers' desire to make constitutional change difficult, the

Constitutions in Selected Countries		
Country	Number of Constitutions	Year Current Constitution Established
Canada	1	1867
China	4	1982
Egypt	4	1971
France	15	1958
Germany	5	1949
India	1	1950
Indonesia	2	1945
Italy	3	1945
Japan	2	1947
Mexico	5	1917
Russia	5	1993
United Kingdom	n/a	n/a
United States	**2**	**1789**

European parliamentary systems have rather simple amendment procedures: Passage by both houses of the legislature is typically sufficient to add amendments. The Russian and French presidents have the option to submit an amendment to referendum by the public (both countries' current constitutions were ratified in this manner); French President Chirac exercised the option in 2000. Informal, extra-constitutional methods have tended to prevail in nondemocratic settings. Indonesia's 1945 constitution was restored in 1959 amidst civil disorder, and the reality of political power over the next forty years was increasingly remote from constitutional intent. China's three constitutions since 1949 have been largely modifications of their predecessors. In sum, the United States' constitutional history is rather remarkable for its continuity under a single written document.

Comparative

Comparing Constitutions

Today, some argue that the original intent of the Framers, as evidenced in *The Federalist Papers*, as well as in private notes taken by James Madison at the Constitutional Convention, should govern judicial interpretation of the Constitution.[31] Others argue that the Framers knew that a changing society needed an elastic, flexible document that could conform to the ages.[32] In all likelihood, the vagueness of the document was purposeful. Those in attendance in Philadelphia recognized that they could not agree on everything and that it was wiser to leave interpretation to those who would follow them.

Recently, law professor Mark V. Tushnet has offered a particularly stinging criticism of any kind of judicial review and exclusive reliance on the courts to say what the Constitution means.[33] He believes that we must create a "populist" constitutional law

ANALYZING VISUALS

Why Did the Framers Write the Constitution as They Did?

The U.S. Constitution contains many phrases that are open to several interpretations. There are also omissions that raise questions about the democratic nature of the Constitution. The lingering question of how to interpret the Constitution still sparks debates among scholars and citizens. In the cartoon below, Garry Trudeau depicts a conversation between two Framers of the Constitution. Analyze the cartoon by answering the following questions: Who were Pinckney and Rutledge, mentioned in the first frame? To what does the representation compromise refer? Which position on the interpretation of the Constitution does the cartoonist appear to take? Which effect is the cartoonist trying to achieve: exaggeration, irony, or juxtaposition? Does the cartoon achieve its desired effect?

(Photo courtesy: DOONESBURY © G. B. Trudeau. Reprinted with permission of UNIVERSAL PRESS SYNDICATE. All rights reserved.)

that allows people to believe that they have the right to enforce the Constitution and not leave it up to the courts. To give this power to the courts, says Tushnet, necessarily means that "We the People," envisioned by the Framers lose sight of the true meaning of the Constitution.

Social, Cultural, and Legal Change

Even the most far-sighted of those in attendance at the Constitutional Convention could not have anticipated the vast changes that have occurred in the United States. For example, although many were uncomfortable with the Three-Fifths Compromise and others hoped for the abolition of slavery, none could have imagined the status of African Americans today, or that Colin Powell would serve as the U.S. secretary of state and be frequently mentioned as a viable candidate for president or vice president. Likewise, few of the Framers could have anticipated the diverse roles that women would play in American society. The Constitution often has been bent to accommodate such social and cultural changes. Thus, although there is no specific amendment guaranteeing women equal protection of the law, the federal courts have interpreted the

Constitution to prohibit many forms of gender discrimination, thereby recognizing cultural and societal change.

Social change has also caused changes in the way institutions of government act. Thus, as problems such as the Great Depression appeared national in scope, Congress took on more and more power at the expense of the states to solve the economic and social crisis. In fact, Yale law professor Bruce Ackerman argues that on certain occasions, extraordinary times call for extraordinary measures such as the New Deal that, in effect, amend the Constitution. Thus, congressional passage (and the Supreme Court's eventual acceptance) of sweeping New Deal legislation that altered the balance of power between the national government and the states, truly changed the Constitution without benefit of amendment.[34] Today, however, Congress is moving to return much of that power to the states. The actions of the 104th and 105th Congresses to return powers and responsibilities to the states, for example, may be viewed as an informal attempt not necessarily to amend the Constitution but to return the balance of power between the national and state government to that which the Framers intended. Again, within the parameters of its constitutional powers, the Congress acted as the Framers intended without changing the document itself.

Advances in technology have also brought about constitutional change. Wiretapping and other forms of electronic surveillance, for example, now are regulated by the First and Fourth Amendments. Similarly, HIV testing must be balanced against constitutional protections, and all kinds of new constitutional questions are posed in the wake of congressional efforts to regulate what kinds of information can be disseminated on the Internet. Still, in spite of these massive changes, the Constitution survives, changed and ever changing after more than 200 years.

Continuity & Change

Counting Americans

The U.S. Constitution specifically requires that "representatives and direct Taxes shall be apportioned among the several States ... according to their respective numbers.... The actual Enumeration shall be made within three Years after the first Meeting of the Congress of the United States, and within every subsequent Term of ten Years in such a Manner as they shall by Law direct." In response to this, the first U.S. Census was taken in 1790.[35] But, the process was very crude. U.S. marshals and their assistants, providing their own paper, took eighteen months to collect all of the data. And, unlike today, when all personal census survey data are confidential, law required that all local reports be posted in at least two public places.

For years, census data were tabulated by hand. In 1890, a punch card tabulating system was created, revolutionizing the process and allowing for quicker tabulation of data. Over time, the compiling of the U.S. Census has become more and more complex in response to changing governmental needs and well as changing technology. And, as the national government has grown, so have the kinds of data collected by the Census Bureau.

By 1990, the nation had grown so large that even the Census Bureau admitted that, for the first time, its report was more inaccurate than the one before it.[36] Millions of people, especially the poor, homeless, and minorities, were undercounted. Because the allocation of federal dollars, as well as congressional representation, is based on the results of the decennial Census, urban centers and the Democratic Party cried foul, arguing that they were the most hurt by the undercounting of as many as 5.3 million people. Even before the 1990 Census, lawsuits were filed challenging its methods, and in 1991, Congress passed legislation to compel the Census Bureau to contract with the nonpartisan National Academy of Sciences to study more accurate means for the 2000 Census. One of the means suggested was to sample the population. Actually, the Census Bureau began to use sampling in 1940, asking only every fourth household some more detailed questions.

But, this is not the kind of sampling that was suggested by the Clinton administration and subsequently rejected by the Supreme Court in 1999.[37] The administration wanted to be able to adjust the count to include people that the cur-

This ad for U.S. Census 2000, which targets the Native American community, was among the many aimed at groups the Census traditionally had difficulty tracking.

(Photo courtesy: United States Census 2000, G & G Advertising)

rent system was likely to miss. The Court, however, ruled that sampling could not be used to count citizens for the purposes of reallocating congressional seats among the states, although it didn't prohibit the use of sampling-adjusted numbers when states draw their own congressional and legislative district lines.

The 2000 Census was one of the most unique on record. To get Americans enthused about filling out their forms, a lavish campaign and outreach to minorities and immigrants were augmented with a variety of clever television advertisement throughout the nation, publicizing the importance of an accurate count to the distribution of federal dollars to states and local governments. This enormously expensive campaign worked: Early reports revealed that more Americans filled out their forms than in 1980 or 1990. Sixty-seven percent of all households filled out and returned their questionnaires. Response in the Hispanic community was, to some, surprisingly strong as Hispanics became the largest minority in the United States.

In spite of these higher returns, the Clinton administration, to the outrage of Republicans in the Congress, also used sampling to revise the Census count to add millions more people, particularly minorities. The Court's 1999 decision made it clear that sampling could not be used to apportion congressional seats, but it did leave the door open to the use of sampling to redraw legislative boundaries within a state as well as to distribute federal dollars.[38]

The Census has far more political overtones than the Framers envisioned. Sampling is a well-recognized statistical technique, yet its use to "remedy" undercounting is highly contentious. In the future, the Census Bureau will continue to be challenged to come up with more accurate measures to count the population. With increasing use of multiple data bases, one might envision some sort of super-data base that could be combined and refigured to enhance the chances that everyone gets counted.

1. What kind of process might be developed to make sure that undercounting, particularly of certain populations with discrete interests, does not occur in the future?
2. How critical do you believe a totally accurate U.S. Census is to the government's ability to maintain a representative democracy?

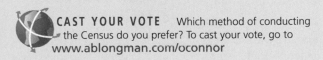

CAST YOUR VOTE   Which method of conducting the Census do you prefer? To cast your vote, go to www.ablongman.com/oconnor

SUMMARY

The U.S. Constitution has proven to be a remarkably enduring document. In explaining how and why the Constitution came into being, this chapter has covered the following points:

1. **The Origins of a New Nation**
   While settlers came to the New World for a variety of reasons, most remained loyal to Great Britain and considered themselves subjects of the king. Over the years, as new generations of Americans were born on colonial soil, those ties weakened. A series of taxes levied by the Crown ultimately led the colonists to convene a Continental Congress and to declare their independence.

2. **The Declaration of Independence**
   The Declaration of Independence (1776), which drew heavily on the writings of John Locke, carefully enumerated the wrongs of the Crown and galvanized public resentment and willingness to take up arms against Great Britain in the Revolutionary War (1775–1782).

3. **The First Attempt at Government: The Articles of Confederation**
   The Articles of Confederation (1781) created a loose league of friendship between the new national government and the states. Numerous weaknesses in the new government became apparent by 1784. Among the major flaws were Congress's inability to tax or regulate commerce, the absence of an executive to administer the government, and a weak central government.

4. **The Miracle at Philadelphia: Writing a Constitution**
   When the weaknesses under the Articles of Confederation became apparent, the states called for a meeting to reform them. The Constitutional Convention (1787) quickly threw out the Articles of Confederation and fashioned a new, more workable form of government. The Constitution was the result of a series of compromises, including those over representation, questions involving large and small states, and over how to determine population. Compromises were also made about how members of each branch of government were to be selected. The electoral college was created to give states a key role in the selection of the president.

5. **The U.S. Constitution**
   The proposed U.S. Constitution created a federal system that drew heavily on Montesquieu's ideas about separation of powers. These ideas concerned a way of parceling out power among the three branches of government, and checks and balances to prevent any one branch from having too much power.

6. **The Drive for Ratification**
   The drive for ratification became a fierce fight between Federalists and Anti-Federalists. Federalists lobbied for the strong national government created by the Constitution; Anti-Federalists favored greater state power.

7. **Formal Methods of Amending the Constitution**
   The Framers created a formal two-stage amendment process to include the Congress and the states. Amendments could be proposed by a two-thirds vote in Congress or of state legislatures requesting that Congress call a national convention to propose amendments. Amendments could be ratified by a positive vote of three-fourths of the state legislatures or specially called state ratifying conventions.

8. **Informal Methods of Amending the Constitution**
   The formal amendment process is not the only way that the Constitution can be changed. Judicial interpretation and social, cultural, and legal changes have also produced constitutional change.

KEY TERMS

Anti-Federalists, p. 55
Articles of Confederation, p. 42
Bill of Rights, p. 58
checks and balances, p. 50
Committees of Correspondence, p. 38
confederation, p. 40
Declaration of Independence, p. 40
enumerated powers, p. 52
federal system, p. 50
The Federalist Papers, p. 56
Federalists, p. 55
First Continental Congress, p. 39
Great Compromise, p. 47
implied powers, p. 53
necessary and proper clause, p. 53
New Jersey Plan, p. 47
Second Continental Congress, p. 39
separation of powers, p. 50
Shays's Rebellion, p. 44
Stamp Act Congress, p. 38
supremacy clause, p. 54
Three-Fifths Compromise, p. 48
Virginia Plan, p. 45

SELECTED READINGS

Ackerman, Bruce. *We the People.* Cambridge, MA: Belknap Press, 1991.

Bailyn, Bernard. *The Ideological Origins of the American Revolution.* Cambridge, MA: Belknap Press, 1967.

Beard, Charles A. *An Economic Interpretation of the Constitution of the United States* (reissue edition). New York: Free Press, 1996.

Bernstein, Richard B., with Jerome Agel. *Amending America.* Lawrence: University Press of Kansas, 1995 (reissue edition).

Bowen, Catherine Drinker. *Miracle at Philadelphia.* Boston: Little, Brown, 1986.

Brinkley, Alan, Nelson W. Polsby, and Kathleen M. Sullivan. *New Federalist Papers: Essays in Defense of the Constitution.* New York: Norton, 1997.

Dahl, Robert A. *How Democratic Is the American Constitution?* New Haven, CT: Yale University Press, 2002.

Hamilton, Alexander, James Madison, and John Jay. *The Federalist Papers.* New York: Bantam Books, 1989 (first published in 1788).

Ketchman, Ralph, ed. *The Anti-Federalist Papers and the Constitutional Convention Debated.* New York: Mentor Books, 1996.

Kyvig, David E. *Explicit and Authentic Acts: Amending the U.S. Constitution, 1776–1995.* Lawrence: University Press of Kansas, 1996.

Levy, Leonard W., ed. *Essays on the Making of the Constitution*, 2nd ed. New York: Oxford University Press, 1987.

Main, Jackson Turner. *The Social Structure of Revolutionary America.* Princeton, NJ: Princeton University Press, 1965.

Rossiter, Clinton. *1787: Grand Convention* (reissue edition). New York: Norton, 1987.

Stoner, James R., Jr. *Common Law and Liberal Theory.* Lawrence: University Press of Kansas, 1992.

Storing, Herbert J. *What the Anti-Federalists Were For.* Chicago: University of Chicago Press, 1981.

Sunstein, Cass R. *Designing Democracy: What Constitutions Do.* New York: Oxford University Press, 2001.

Vile, John R. *Encyclopedia of Constitutional Amendments, and Amending Issues, 1789–1995.* Santa Barbara, CA: ABC-CLIO, 1996.

Wood, Gordon S. *The Creation of the American Republic, 1776–1787* (reissue edition). New York: Norton, 1993.

NOTES

1. See Richard B. Bernstein with Jerome Agel, *Amending America* (New York: New York Times Books, 1993), 138–40.
2. *Oregon v. Mitchell*, 400 U.S. 112 (1970).
3. Bernstein with Agel, *Amending America*, 139.
4. For an account of the early development of the colonies, see D. W. Meining, *The Shaping of America*, vol. 1: *Atlantic America, 1492–1800* (New Haven, CT: Yale University Press, 1986).
5. For an excellent chronology of the events leading up to the writing of the Declaration of Independence and the colonists' break with Great Britain, see Calvin D. Lonton, ed., *The Bicentennial Almanac* (Nashville, TN: Thomas Nelson, 1975).
6. See Gary Wills, *Inventing America: Jefferson's Declaration of Independence* (New York: Random House, 1978). Wills argues that the Declaration was signed solely to secure foreign aid for the ongoing war effort.
7. See Gordon S. Wood, *The Creation of the American Republic, 1776–1787* (reissue edition) (New York: Norton, 1993).
8. For more about the Articles of Confederation, see Merrill Jensen, *The Articles of Confederation* (Madison: University of Wisconsin Press, 1940).
9. Quoted in Selma R. Williams, *Fifty-Five Fathers: The Story of the Constitutional Convention* (New York: Dodd, Mead, 1970), 10.
10. Charles A. Beard, *An Economic Interpretation of the Constitution of the United States* (reissue edition) (New York: Free Press, 1996).
11. Quoted in Richard N. Current, et al., *American History: A Survey*, 6th ed. (New York: Knopf, 1983), 170.
12. John Patrick Diggins, "Power and Authority in American History: The Case of Charles A. Beard and His Critics," *American Historical Review* 86 (October 1981): 701–30.
13. Robert Brown, *Charles Beard and the Constitution: A Critical Analysis of "An Economic Interpretation of the Constitution"* (Princeton, NJ: Princeton University Press, 1956).
14. Jackson Turner Main, *The Anti-Federalists* (Chapel Hill: University of North Carolina, 1961).
15. Wood, *Creation of the American Republic.*
16. Quoted in Doris Faber and Harold Faber, *We the People* (New York: Charles Scribner's Sons, 1987), 31.
17. For more on the political nature of compromise at the convention, see Calvin C. Jillson, *Constitution Making: Conflict and Consensus in the Federal Constitution of 1787* (New York: Agathon, 1988).
18. Quoted in Current, et al., *American History*, 168.
19. Bernard Bailyn, *The Ideological Origins of the American Revolution* (Cambridge, MA: Belknap Press, 1967).
20. *U.S. Term Limits* v. *Thornton*, 514 U.S. 779 (1995).
21. Richard E. Neustadt, *Presidential Power: The Politics of Leadership from FDR to Carter* (New York: Macmillan, 1980), 26.
22. Quoted in Faber and Faber, *We the People*, 51–52.
23. Federal Republicans favored a republican or representative form of government (do not confuse this term with the modern Republican Party, which came into being in 1854; see chapter 12). Ultimately, the word federal came to mean the form of government embodied in the new Constitution, just as confederation meant the "league of states" under the Articles, and later came to mean the "Confederacy" of 1861–65.
24. See Ralph Ketcham, ed., *The Anti-Federalist Papers and the Constitutional Debates* (New York: New American Library, 1986).
25. See Herbert J. Storing, *What the Anti-Federalists Were For* (Chicago: University of Chicago Press, 1981), for a fuller discussion of Anti-Federalist views.
26. See Alan P. Grimes, *Democracy and the Amendments to the Constitution* (Lexington, MA: Lexington Books, 1978).
27. David E. Kyvig, *Repealing National Prohibition* (Chicago: University of Chicago Press, 1978).
28. See Jane J. Mansbridge, *Why We Lost the ERA* (Chicago: University of Chicago Press, 1986).
29. Molly Peterson, "Senate Panel Approves Constitutional Ban on Flag Desecration," LEGI-SLATE, http://www.legislate.com/xp/p-daily/i-19990422101/a-924733492/article.view.
30. 5 U.S. 137 (1803).
31. Speech by Attorney General Edwin Meese III before the American Bar Association, July 9, 1985, Washington, DC. See also Antonin Scalia and Amy Gutman, eds. *A Matter of Interpretation: Federal Courts and the Law* (Princeton, NJ: Princeton University Press, 1998).
32. Speech by William J. Brennan Jr. at Georgetown University, Text and Teaching Symposium, October 10, 1985, Washington, DC.
33. Mark V. Tushnet, *Taking the Constitution Away from the Courts* (Princeton, NJ: Princeton University Press, 1999).
34. Bruce Ackerman, *We the People: Foundations* (Cambridge, MA: Belknap Press, 1991).
35. This box draws heavily on information provided by the U.S. Department of Commerce. See U.S. Census Bureau, "History and Organization," May 1988. Mimeo.
36. *Wisconsin v. City of New York*, 517 U.S. 1 (1996), and Sheldon T. Bradshaw, Note, "Death, Taxes, and Census Litigation: Do the Equal Protection and Apportionment Clauses Guarantee a Constitutional Right to Census Accuracy?" *George Washington University Law Review* 64 (January 1996): 379–413.
37. *DOC* v. *U.S. House of Representatives*, 525 U.S. 314 (1999).
38. D'Vera Cohn, "Clinton to Keep Political Appointees Out of Decision on Census," *Washington Post* (June 14, 2000): A21.

Federalism

3

For decades, candidates running for president have railed against the size of the federal government and promised to downsize it. They assert that the federal government has grown at the expense of powers that the Framers of the Constitution intended the states to enjoy. Not only have most presidents of late tried to shrink the size of the federal government and their own staffs, but Republican presidents and many Republican leaders in Congress have pledged to return authority and power to the states. They argue that over the years, the federal government has acquired vast authority in a host of areas never envisioned by the Framers to be within the realm of the federal government.

But, two events, the terrorist attacks on the World Trade Center and the Pentagon and the economic downturn they exacerbated, "are prompting the biggest expansion in federal powers and the most free-handed new spending of federal dollars in decades,"[1] according to one commentator. In the weeks immediately following September 11, 2001, the president created a Cabinet-level Office of Homeland Security, which later became an official Cabinet department. Security at airports around the nation was federalized, and a new federal agency, the Transportation Security Agency, was created (which later was subsumed into the new Department of Homeland Security). A number of immigrants were detained, and national law enforcement efforts were stepped up. At the 2002 Winter Olympics, for example, nearly one-fourth of the FBI's agents were on hand to ensure the safety of the participants and spectators. With the states' ability to provide for public safety in doubt, federal law enforcement officials were called on to direct security at the international event.

"There has been a searching reassessment [of] what is the role of the federal government now in the globalized society after the Cold War," said former President Bill Clinton.[2] Among some of the major expansions of federal power are the setting of federal standards for airport security personnel, the use of federal workers as airport security screeners, and increased federal police powers to investigate money laundering and to control U.S. borders. Blips in federal power often occur after national emergencies but rarely return immediately to the status quo.

WEB EXPLORATION
For a directory of federalism links, see
www.ablongman.com/oconnor

WEB EXPLORATION
For more on your state and local governments, see
www.ablongman.com/oconnor

he Framers were mindful of the need for government as well as one unifying body of law, and that was the U.S. Constitution. Thus, over 87,900 different state and local governments are ultimately bound by its provisions (see Figure 3.1). Still, many believe that the federal, or national, government is too powerful. In fact, many citizens and their elected representatives have been working through legal channels to divest the national government of some of the enormous powers it has amassed over the years since the states initially ratified the Constitution.

In a 1999 poll conducted by Princeton Survey Research Associates, 74 percent of those who responded agreed that "The federal government should run only those things that cannot be run at the local level."[3] Many, however, probably have not considered all of the ramifications of such a devolution. What happens if one state allows companies to pollute waterways that flow into adjoining states? Are state governments and state bureaucracies better equipped to handle welfare, medical care, job training, or other problems associated with poverty? And, with more responsibilities comes the need for more funds. Will states begin to raise taxes? It's unlikely. With states taking on more responsibilities but having less money to execute them, everyone may have to make do with fewer governmental programs, no matter how beneficial or laudatory their goals.

From its very beginning, the challenge for the United States of America was to preserve the traditional independence and rights of the states while establishing an effective national government. In *Federalist No. 51*, James Madison highlighted the unique structure of governmental powers created by the Framers:

> The power surrendered by the people is first divided between two distinct governments, and then ... subdivided among distinct and separate departments. Hence, a double security arises to the rights of the people.

The Framers, fearing tyranny, divided powers between the state and the national governments. At each level, moreover, powers were divided among executive, legislative, and judicial branches.

Although most of the delegates to the Constitutional Convention favored a strong federal government, they knew that some compromise about the distribution of powers would be necessary. Some of the Framers wanted to continue with the confederate form of government defined in the Articles of Confederation; others wanted a more centralized system, similar to that of Great Britain. Their solution was to create the world's first federal system, in which the thirteen sovereign or independent states were bound together under one national government. The result was a system of government that was "neither wholly national nor wholly federal," as Madison explained in *The Federalist Papers*.

The nature of the federal relationship between the national government and the states, including their respective duties, obligations, and powers, is outlined in the U.S. Constitution, although the word "federal" does not appear in that document. Throughout history, however, this system and the rules that guide it have been continually stretched, reshaped, and reinterpreted by crises, historical evolution, public expectations, and judicial interpretation. All these forces have had tremendous influence on who makes policy decisions and how these decisions get made.

Issues involving the distribution of power between the national government and the states affect you on a daily basis. You do not, for example, need a passport to go from Texas to Oklahoma. There is but one national currency and a national minimum wage. But, many differences exist

FIGURE 3.1 Number of Governments in the United States

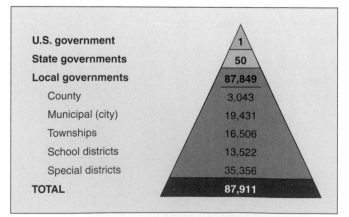

U.S. government	1
State governments	50
Local governments	87,849
County	3,043
Municipal (city)	19,431
Townships	16,506
School districts	13,522
Special districts	35,356
TOTAL	87,911

Source: U.S. Census Bureau, http://www.census.gov/govs/www/gid.html

among the laws of the various states. The age at which you may marry is a state issue, as are laws governing divorce, child custody, and most criminal laws, including how (or if) the death penalty is implemented.

Although some policies or programs are under the authority of the state or local government, others, such as air traffic regulation, are solely within the province of the national government.[4] In many areas, however, the national and state governments work together cooperatively in a system of shared powers. The national government, for example, provides significant assistance to states to improve local schools in a variety of ways from subsidized breakfasts and lunches for students to support for special education teachers. But, states and local government retain control over curricula.

At times, the national government cooperates with or supports programs only if the states meet certain conditions. To receive federal funds for the construction and maintenance of highways, for example, states must follow federal rules about the kinds of roads they build.

To understand the current relationship between the states and the federal government and to better grasp some of the issues that arise from this constantly changing relationship, in this chapter, we'll examine the following topics:

- First, we will look at the *roots of the federal system* created by the Framers, and at their attempt to divide the power and the functions of government between one national and several state governments.

- Second, we will analyze the allocation of *the powers of government* between the national and state governments in the *federal system*.

- Third, we will examine *the evolution and development of federalism*.

- Fourth, we will explore the relationship between *federalism and the Supreme Court*.

- In highlighting *continuity and change* in our political system, we will examine the powers of the states relative to the national government to tax goods and services.

WEB EXPLORATION
For scholarly works on federalism, see
www.ablongman.com/oconnor

THE ROOTS OF THE FEDERAL SYSTEM

The Framers worked to create a particular form of government: one that would be familiar to Americans yet unlike the unitary system found in Great Britain, and one that would remedy many of the problems experienced by the confederated government established by the Articles of Confederation (see chapter 2). (Figure 3.2 illustrates these different forms of government.) The relationship between the national and state governments, and their intertwined powers, are the heart of **federalism** (from the Latin *foedus*, or "covenant"), the philosophy that defines the allocation of power between the national government and the states. Ironically, as discussed in chapter 2, those who supported the government under the Articles of Confederation argued for what they called a federal system. But, the fear of being labeled "nationalists" prompted supporters of the new Constitution to call themselves "Federalists," thus co-opting this popular term of the day. Federalist supporters of the new Constitution articulated three major arguments for federalism: (1) the prevention of tyranny; (2) the provision for increased participation in politics; and, (3) the use of the states as testing grounds or "laboratories" for new policies and programs.

The national government created by the Framers draws its powers directly from the people, so that both national and state governments are ultimately directly accountable to the public. While each government has certain powers in common with the other (such as the ability to tax) and has its own set of public officials, the Framers also envisioned each government to be supreme in some spheres, as depicted in Figure 3.3. In *Federalist No. 51*, James Madison explained what he perceived to be the beauty of this system: The shifting support of the electorate between the two governments would

federalism
The philosophy that describes the governmental system created by the Framers; see also **federal system**.

FIGURE 3.2   The Federal, Confederation, and Unitary Systems of Government
The source of governmental authority and power differs dramatically in various systems of government.

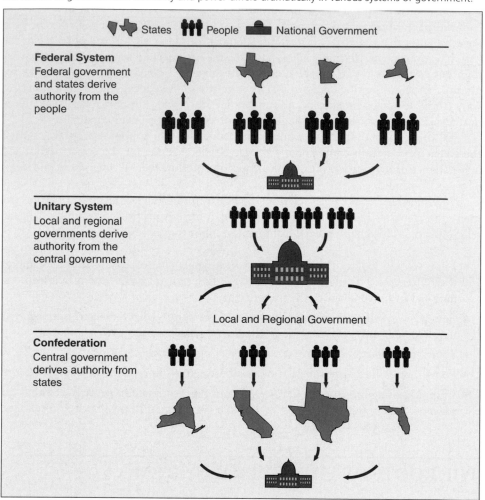

FIGURE 3.3   The Distribution of Governmental Power in the Federal System

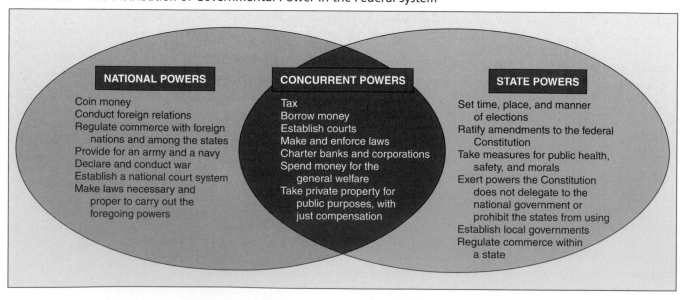

serve to keep each in balance. In fashioning the new federal system of government, the Framers recognized that they could not define precisely how all the relations between the national government and the individual states would work. But, the Constitution makes it clear that separate spheres of government were to be at the very core of the federal system, with some allowances made for concurrent powers. The addition of Article VI to the federal Constitution underscored the notion that the national government always was to be supreme in situations of conflict between state and national law. It declares that the U.S. Constitution, the laws of the United States, and its treaties are to be "the supreme Law of the Land; and the Judges in every State shall be bound thereby."

In spite of this explicit language, the meaning of what is called the **supremacy clause** has been subject to continuous judicial interpretation and reinterpretation. In 1920, for example, Missouri sought to prevent a U.S. game warden from enforcing the Migratory Bird Treaty Act of 1918, which prohibited the killing or capturing of many species of birds as they made their annual migration across the international border from Canada to parts of the United States.[5] Missouri argued that the Tenth Amendment, which reserved a state's powers to legislate for the general welfare of its citizens, allowed Missouri to regulate hunting. But, the Court ruled that since the treaty was legal, it must be considered the supreme law of the land. Thus, when national law and state law come into conflict, national law (including treaties) is supreme. (See also *McCulloch* v. *Maryland* [1819].)

The federal government's right to tax was also clearly set out in the new Constitution. The Framers wanted to avoid the financial problems that the national government had experienced under the Articles of Confederation. If the national government was to be strong, its power to raise revenue had to be unquestionable. Although the new national government lacked the power under the Constitution to levy a national income tax, that was changed by passage of the Sixteenth Amendment in 1913. Eventually, as discussed later in this chapter, this new taxing power was to become a powerful catalyst for the further expansion of the national government.

The new Constitution left the qualifications of suffrage to the individual states. Thus, over time, even the right to vote in national elections has varied.

Here, in an example of concurrent state and national power, birds are protected by both governments.

(Photo courtesy: Judy Gelles/Stock Boston, Inc.)

supremacy clause
Portion of Article VI of the U.S. Constitution that mandates that national law is supreme to (that is, supersedes) all other laws passed by the states or by any other subdivision of government.

THE POWERS OF GOVERNMENT IN THE FEDERAL SYSTEM

The distribution of powers in the federal system often is described as two overlapping systems, as illustrated in Figure 3.3. On the left are powers that were specifically granted to Congress in Article I. Chief among the exclusive powers delegated to the national government are the authorities to coin money, conduct foreign relations, provide for an army and navy, declare war, and establish a national court system. All of these powers set out in Article I, section 8, of the Constitution are called enumerated powers. Article I, section 8, also contains the **necessary and proper clause,** which gives Congress the authority to enact any laws "necessary and proper" for carrying out any of its **enumerated powers.** Thus, for example, Congress's power to charter a national bank was held to be an **implied power** derived from its enumerated power to tax and spend.[6]

The Constitution does not delegate or enumerate many specific powers to the states. Because states had all the power at the time the Constitution was written, the Framers felt no need, as they did for the new national government, to list and restate the powers of the states. Article I, however, allows states to set the "Times, Places and Manner, for holding elections for senators and representatives," and Article II requires that each state appoint electors to vote for president. States also were given the power to ratify amendments to the U.S. Constitution. Nevertheless, the enumeration of so many specific powers to the national government and so few to the states is a clear indication of the

necessary and proper clause
The final paragraph of Article I, section 8, of the U.S. Constitution, which gives Congress the authority to pass all laws "necessary and proper" to carry out the enumerated powers specified in the Constitution; also called the "elastic" clause.

enumerated powers
Seventeen specific powers granted to Congress under Article I, section 8, of the U.S. Constitution; these powers include taxation, coinage of money, regulation of commerce, and the authority to provide for a national defense.

implied power
A power derived from an enumerated power and the necessary and proper clause. These powers are not stated specifically but are considered to be reasonably implied through the exercise of delegated powers.

Tenth Amendment
The final part of the Bill of Rights that defines the basic principle of American federalism in stating "The powers not delegated to the United States by the Constitution, nor prohibited by it to the States, are reserved to the States respectively, or to the people."

reserve (or police) powers
Powers reserved to the states by the Tenth Amendment that lie at the foundation of a state's right to legislate for the public health and welfare of its citizens.

concurrent powers
Authority possessed by both the state and national governments that may be exercised concurrently as long as that power is not exclusively within the scope of national power or in conflict with national law.

bill of attainder
A law declaring an act illegal without a judicial trial.

ex post facto **law**
Law passed after the fact, thereby making previously legal activity illegal and subject to current penalty; prohibited by the U.S. Constitution.

WEB EXPLORATION
For perspectives on the federal system, see
www.ablongman.com/oconnor

Federalist leanings of the Framers. It was not until the addition of the Bill of Rights and the **Tenth Amendment** that the states' powers were better described: "The powers not delegated to the United States by the Constitution, nor prohibited by it to the States, are reserved to the States respectively, or to the people." These powers, often called the states' **reserve** or **police powers,** include the ability to legislate for the public health, safety, and morals of their citizens. Today, the states' rights to legislate under their police powers are used as the rationale for many states' restrictions on abortion, including twenty-four-hour waiting requirements and provisions requiring minors to obtain parental consent. Police powers are also the basis for state criminal laws. That is why some states have the death penalty and others do not. So long as the U.S. Supreme Court continues to find that the death penalty does not violate the U.S. Constitution, the states may impose it, be it by lethal injection, gas chamber, or the electric chair.

As revealed in Figure 3.3, national and state powers also overlap. The area where the systems overlap represents **concurrent powers**—powers shared by the national and state governments. States already had the power to tax; the Constitution extended this power to the national government as well. Other important concurrent powers include the right to borrow money, establish courts, and make and enforce laws necessary to carry out these powers.

Denied Powers

Article I denies certain powers to the national and state governments. In keeping with the Framers' desire to forge a national economy, states are prohibited from entering treaties, coining money, or impairing obligation of contracts. States also are prohibited from entering into "compacts" with other states without express congressional approval. In a similar vein, Congress is barred from favoring one state over another in regulating commerce, and it cannot lay duties on items exported from any state.

Both the national and state governments are denied the authority to take arbitrary actions affecting constitutional rights and liberties. Neither national nor state governments may pass a **bill of attainder,** a law declaring an act illegal without a judicial trial. The Constitution also bars either from passing *ex post facto* **laws,** laws that make an act punishable as a crime even if the action was legal at the time it was committed.

Guarantees to the States

In return for giving up some of their powers, the states received several guarantees in the Constitution. For example, Article I guarantees each state two members in the U.S. Senate and guarantees that Congress would not limit the slave trade before 1808. Article IV guarantees the citizens of each state the privileges and immunities of the citizens of all other states. It also guarantees each state a "Republican Form of Government," meaning one that represents the citizens of the state. It also guarantees that the national government will protect the states against foreign attacks and domestic rebellion.

In 1999, the U.S. Supreme Court dusted off the privileges and immunities clause of the Fourteenth Amendment, which had not been used by the Court to anchor a decision in 126 years. The Court's dramatic 7–2 decision came in a case involving a challenge to a California law that allowed it to pay lower welfare benefits to new state residents.[7] Women who fled from abusive relationships in other states were ineligible for higher California state benefits although they still faced higher California cost of living expenses. Under the challenged provision, California paid new residents only the amounts that they were eligible for in the states that they left. So, if a person traveled from Oklahoma, they would get but $341 their first year in California. Former Alabamans were eligible for only $120, while long-time Californians could receive $631. "The state's legitimate interest in saving money provides no justification for its decision to discriminate among equally eligible citizens," said Justice John Paul Stevens writing for the Court.[8]

The Court said that this two-level benefits system violated citizens' constitutional right to travel and was the justices' first decision dealing with any of the 1996 national welfare reform efforts, which critics charge violate the constitutional rights of many of America's poor. The ruling also was important because of the Court's "revival of a constitutional doctrine making citizens of all states equal."[9] Scores of constitutional scholars immediately weighed in, speculating that the Court's use of the privileges and immunities clause could mean far greater protection for what the Court views as fundamental rights.

Relations Among the States

The Constitution was designed to improve relations among the squabbling states. To that end, to avoid any sense of favoritism it provides that disputes between states be settled directly by the U.S. Supreme Court under its original jurisdiction (see chapter 10). Moreover, Article IV requires that each state give "Full Faith and Credit ... to the public Acts, Records and judicial Proceedings of every other State." This clause ensures that judicial decrees and contracts made in one state will be binding and enforceable in another, thereby facilitating trade and other commercial relationships. In 1997, the Supreme Court ruled that the full faith and credit clause mandates that state courts always must honor the judgments of other state courts, even if to do so is against state public policy or existing state laws. Failure to do so would allow a single state to "rule the world," said Justice Ruth Bader Ginsburg during oral argument.[10] Interestingly, the Violence Against Women Act specifically requires states to give full faith and credit to protective orders issued by other states.[11] (See On Campus: Legislating Against Violence Against Women).

Article IV also requires states to extradite, or return, criminals to states where they have been convicted or are to stand trial. For example, Timothy Reed, an Indian-rights activist, spent five years in New Mexico fighting extradition to Ohio.[12] In 1998, the New Mexico Supreme Court ordered him released from custody in spite of an order from the New Mexico governor ordering his extradition to Ohio. Reed feared that his parole in Ohio would be revoked without due process and that he would be returned to prison and subject to bodily harm. The U.S. Supreme Court found that the Supreme Court of New Mexico went beyond its authority.[13]

The U.S. Constitution gives the Supreme Court the final authority to decide controversies between the states. These kinds of disputes always are decided by the Supreme Court under its original jurisdiction as mandated by Article III of the Constitution. New York and New Jersey, for example, ended up before the Supreme Court arguing over the title to Ellis Island, based on the 1834 compact between the two states that set the boundary lines between them as the middle of the Hudson River. New York got authority over the island, where over 12 million immigrants were processed between 1892 and 1954, but New Jersey retained rights to the submerged lands on its side. Ultimately, the Supreme Court ruled that New Jersey was entitled to all of the new lands that were created when the U.S. government filled in the island's natural shoreline; New York, however, still retained title and thus bragging rights to the museum dedicated to chronicling the history of U.S. immigration.[14]

States are not always in adversarial roles, however. Article 1, section 10, clause 3, of the U.S. Constitution sets the legal foundation for interstate cooperation in the form of **interstate compacts,** contracts between states that carry the force of law. It reads, "No State shall, without the consent of Congress, ... enter into any Agreement or Compact with another state." Before 1920, interstate compacts were largely bistate compacts that addressed boundary disputes such as the 1834 compact between New York and New Jersey or that acted to help two states accomplish some objective. Thus, the New York/New Jersey Port Authority regulates the waters between New York and New Jersey and the port that forms the states' common boundaries.

interstate compacts
Contracts between states that carry the force of law; generally now used as a tool to address multistate policy concerns.

TABLE 3.1 Compacts by the Numbers	
Interstate compacts with 25 or more members	13
Least compact memberships by a state (HI & WI)	14
Most compact memberships by a state (NH & VA)	42
Average compact memberships by a state	27
Compacts developed prior to 1920	36
Compacts developed since 1920	150+
Interstate compacts currently in operation	200+

Source: John Mountjoy, Council of State Governments, "Interstate Cooperation: Interstate Compacts Make a Comeback," (Spring 2001): 6–7.

WEB EXPLORATION
For more information on interstate compacts, see
www.ablongman.com/oconnor

More than 200 interstate compacts exist today; while some deal with rudimentary items such as state boundaries, others help states carry out their policy objectives, and they play an important role in helping states carry out their functions. Although several bistate compacts still exist, other compacts have as many as fifty signatories.[15] The Drivers License Compact was signed by all fifty states to facilitate nationwide recognition of licenses issued in the respective states.

States today find that interstate compacts help them "maintain state control" because compacts with other states allow for sharing resources, expertise, and responses that often are available more quickly than those from the federal government. The Emergency Management Assistance Compact, for example, allows states to cooperate and to share resources in the event of natural and man-made disasters. On September 11, 2001, assistance to New York and Virginia came from a host of states surrounding the areas of terrorist attacks. (For more on compacts, see Table 3.1.)

THE EVOLUTION AND DEVELOPMENT OF FEDERALISM

The victory of the Federalists, those who supported a strong national government, had long-lasting consequences on the future of the nation. Over the course of our nation's history, the nature of federalism and its allocation of power between the national government and the states have changed dramatically. The debate continues today, too, as many Americans, frustrated with the national government's performance on a number of issues, look for a return of more power to the states. Because the distribution of power between the national and state governments is not clearly delineated in the Constitution, over the years the U.S. Supreme Court has played a major role in defining the nature of the federal system.

Interstate speed limits are federalism issues. The National Highway System Designation Act of 1995 allows states to set their own speed limits, reversing an earlier national law that set 55 mph as a national standard. Top state speeds now range from 55 to 75 mph.

(Photo courtesy: Mark Leffingwell/AP/Wide World Photos)

Early Pronouncements on Federalism

The first few years that the Supreme Court sat, it handled few major cases. As described in chapter 9, the Supreme Court was viewed as weak, and many declined the "honor" of serving as a Supreme Court justice. The appointment of John Marshall as chief justice of the United States, however, changed all of this. In a series of decisions, he and his associates carved out an important role for the Court, especially in defining the nature of the federal/state relationship as well as the power of the Court.

McCulloch v. *Maryland* (1819). *McCulloch* v. *Maryland* was the first major decision of the Marshall Court to define the relationship between the national and state governments. In 1816, Congress chartered the Second Bank of the United States. (The charter of the First Bank had been allowed to expire.) In 1818, the Democratic-Republican-controlled Maryland state legislature levied a tax requiring all banks not chartered by Maryland (that is, the Second Bank of the United States) to: (1) buy stamped paper from the state on which the Second Bank's notes were to be issued; (2) pay the state $15,000 a year; or, (3) go out of business. James McCulloch, the head cashier of the Baltimore branch of the Bank of the United States, refused to pay the tax, and Maryland brought suit against him. After losing in a Maryland court, McCulloch appealed his conviction to the U.S. Supreme Court by order of the U.S. secretary of the treasury. In a unanimous opinion, the Court answered the two central questions that had been put to it: First, did Congress have the authority to charter a bank? And, second, if it did, could a state tax it?

Chief Justice John Marshall's answer to the first question—whether Congress had the right to establish a bank or another type of corporation, given that the Constitution does not explicitly mention such a power—continues to stand as the classic exposition of the doctrine of implied powers and as a reaffirmation of the propriety of a strong national government. Although the word "bank" cannot be found in the Constitution, the Constitution enumerates powers that give Congress the authority to levy and collect taxes, issue a currency, and borrow funds. From these enumerated powers, Marshall found, it was reasonable to imply that Congress had the power to charter a bank, which could be considered "necessary and proper" to the exercise of its aforementioned enumerated powers.

Marshall next addressed the question of whether a federal bank could be taxed by any state government. To Marshall, this was not a difficult question. The national government was dependent on the people, not the states, for its powers. In addition, Marshall noted, the Constitution specifically calls for the national law to be supreme. "The power to tax involves the power to destroy," wrote Marshall.[16] Thus, the state tax violated the supremacy clause, because individual states cannot interfere with the operations of the national government, whose laws are supreme.

Gibbons v. *Ogden* (1824). Shortly after *McCulloch*, the Marshall Court had another opportunity to rule in favor of a broad interpretation of the scope of national power. *Gibbons* v. *Ogden* involved a dispute that arose after the New York State legislature granted to Robert Fulton the exclusive right to operate steamboats on the Hudson River. Simultaneously, Congress licensed a ship to sail on the same waters. By the time the case reached the Supreme Court, it was complicated both factually and procedurally. Suffice it to say that both New York and New Jersey wanted to control shipping on the lower Hudson River. But, *Gibbons* actually addressed one simple, very important question: What was the scope of Congress's authority under the commerce clause? The states argued that "commerce," as mentioned in Article I, should be interpreted narrowly to include only direct dealings in products. In *Gibbons*, however, the Supreme Court ruled that Congress's power to regulate interstate commerce included the power to regulate commercial activity as well, and that the commerce power had no limits except those specifically found in the Constitution. Thus, New York had no constitutional authority to grant a monopoly to a single steamboat operator, an act that interfered with interstate commerce.[17]

McCulloch v. *Maryland* (1819)
The Supreme Court upheld the power of the national government and denied the right of a state to tax the bank. The Court's broad interpretation of the necessary and proper clause paved the way for later rulings upholding expansive federal powers.

WEB EXPLORATION
For the full text of *McCulloch* v. *Maryland,* see www.ablongman.com/oconnor

Gibbons v. *Ogden* (1824)
The Court upheld broad congressional power over interstate commerce.

WEB EXPLORATION
For the full text of *Gibbons* v. *Ogden,* see www.ablongman.com/oconnor

The *Gibbons* v. *Ogden* (1824) decision opened the waters to free competition; this is the New York waterfront in 1839.

(Photo courtesy: I. N. Phelps Stokes Collection, Miriam and Ira D. Wallach Division of Art, Prints, and Photographs, The New York Public Library Astor, Lenox, and Tilden Foundations)

dual federalism
The belief that having separate and equally powerful levels of government is the best arrangement.

Dual Federalism

In spite of these nationalist Marshall Court decisions, strong debate continued in the United States over national versus state power. It was under the leadership of Chief Justice Marshall's successor, Roger B. Taney (1835–1863), that the Supreme Court articulated the notions of concurrent power and **dual federalism.** Dual federalism holds that the national government should not exceed its enumerated powers expressly set out in the Constitution.

Federalism and Slavery.   During the Taney era, the comfortable role of the Court as the arbiter of competing national and state interests became troublesome when the Court found itself called upon to deal with the highly political issue of slavery. In cases such as *Dred Scott* v. *Sandford* (1857) and others, the Court tried to manage the slavery issue by resolving questions of ownership, the status of fugitive slaves, and slavery in the new territories. These cases generally were settled in favor of slavery and states' rights within the framework of dual federalism. In its treatment of slavery (see Roots of Government: Dred Scott), the Taney Court erred grievously and thereby contributed to the coming of the Civil War, since its decision seemed to rule out any political (legislative) solution to slavery by the national government.

The Civil War and Beyond

The Civil War (1861–1865) forever changed the nature of federalism, but the Supreme Court continued to adhere to its belief in the concept of dual federalism. The importance and powers of the states were not diminished in spite of the addition of the Thirteenth, Fourteenth, and Fifteenth Amendments to the Constitution.

Between 1865 (the end of the Civil War) and 1933 (when the next major change in the federal system occurred), the Court generally continued to support dual federal-

ism along several lines. State courts, for example, were considered to have the final say on the construction of laws affecting local affairs.[18] Generally, the Court upheld any laws passed under the states' police powers, which allow states to pass laws to protect the general welfare of their citizens. These laws included those affecting commerce, labor relations, and manufacturing. After the Court's decision in *Plessy* v. *Ferguson* (1896), in which the Court ruled that state maintenance of "separate but equal" facilities for blacks and whites was constitutional, most civil rights and voting cases also became state matters, in spite of the Civil War amendments.[19]

The Court also developed legal doctrine in a series of cases that reinforced the national government's ability to regulate commerce. By the 1930s, these two somewhat contradictory approaches led to confusion: States, for example, could not tax gasoline used by federal vehicles,[20] and the national government could not tax the sale of motorcycles to the city police department.[21] In this period, the Court did recognize the need for national control over new technological developments, such as the telegraph.[22] And, beginning in the 1880s, the Court allowed Congress to regulate many aspects of economic relationships such as outlawing monopolies, a type of regulation or power formerly thought to be in the exclusive realm of the states. Passage of laws such as the Interstate Commerce Act in 1887 and the Sherman Anti-Trust Act in 1890 allowed Congress to establish itself as an important player in the growing national economy.

Despite finding that most of these federal laws were constitutional, the Supreme Court did not enlarge the scope of national power consistently. In 1895, for example, the United States filed suit against four sugar refiners, alleging that their sale would give their buyer control of 98 percent of the U.S. sugar-refining business. The Supreme Court ruled that congressional efforts to control monopolies (through passage of the Sherman Anti-Trust Act) did not give Congress the authority to prevent the sale of these sugar-refining businesses, because manufacturing was not commerce. Therefore, the companies and their actions were beyond the scope of Congress's authority to regulate.[23]

DRED SCOTT

(Photo courtesy: Missouri Historical Society)

Dred Scott, born into slavery around 1795, became the named plaintiff in a case that was to have major ramifications on the nature of the federal system. In 1833, Scott was sold by his original owners, the Blow family, to Dr. Emerson in St. Louis, Missouri. The next year he was taken to Illinois and later to the Wisconsin Territory, returning to St. Louis in 1838.[a]

When Emerson died in 1843, Scott tried to buy his freedom. Before he could, however, he was transferred to Emerson's window, who moved to New York leaving Scott in the custody of his first owners, the Blows. Some of the Blows (Henry Blow later founded the antislavery Free Soil Party) and other abolitionists gave money to support a test case seeking Scott's freedom: They believed that his residence in Illinois and later in the Wisconsin Territory, which both prohibited slavery, made him a free man.

After many delays, the U.S. Supreme Court ruled 7–2 that Scott was not a citizen of the United States. "Slaves," said the Court, "were never thought of or spoken of except as property." Chief Justice Roger B. Taney tried to fashion a broad ruling to settle the slavery question. Writing for the majority in *Dred Scott* v. *Sandford* (1857), he concluded that Congress lacked the constitutional authority to bar slavery in the territories. The decision narrowed the scope of national power while it enhanced that of the states. Moreover, for the first time since *Marbury* v. *Madison* (1803), the Court found an act of Congress, the Missouri Compromise, unconstitutional. And, by limiting what the national government could do concerning slavery, it in all likelihood quickened the march toward the Civil War.

[a]Don E. Ferenbacher, "The Dred Scott Case," in John A. Garraty, ed., *Quarrels That Have Shaped the Constitution* (New York: Harper and Row, 1964), ch. 6.

The Sixteenth and Seventeenth Amendments

The Framers purposely omitted a national income tax from the Constitution. But, legislators recognized that the likely entrance of the United States into World War I would be costly, so Congress and the state legislatures were moved to ratify the **Sixteenth Amendment,** although even its chief Republican sponsor supported it only because he believed that the national government must be authorized to raise additional funds during a time of war.[24] The Sixteenth Amendment gave Congress the power to levy and collect taxes on incomes without apportionment among the states. (It was necessary because the Supreme Court earlier had ruled that Congress lacked the authority to levy an income tax.). The revenues taken in by the federal government through taxation of personal income "removed a major constraint on the federal government by giving it access to almost unlimited revenues."[25] If money is power, the income tax and the revenues it generated greatly enhanced the power of the federal government and its ability to enter policy areas where it formerly had few funds to spend.

The **Seventeenth Amendment** similarly enhanced the power of the national government at the expense of the states. This amendment terminated the state legislatures' election of senators and put their election in the hands of the people. With senators no longer directly accountable to the state legislators who elected them, states lost their principal protectors in Congress.

Sixteenth Amendment
Authorized Congress to enact a national income tax.

Seventeenth Amendment
Made senators directly elected by the people; removed their selection from state legislatures.

Cooperative Federalism

The era of dual federalism came to an abrupt end in the 1930s. Its demise began in a series of economic events that ended in the cataclysm of the Great Depression:

- In 1921, the nation experienced a severe slump in agricultural prices.
- In 1926, the construction industry went into decline.
- In the summer of 1929, inventories of consumer goods and automobiles were at an all-time high.
- Throughout the 1920s, bank failures had become common.
- On October 29, 1929, stock prices, which had risen steadily since 1926, crashed, taking with them the entire national economy.

WEB EXPLORATION
For more information
on the Depression, see
www.ablongman.com/oconnor

The New Deal.   Rampant unemployment (historians estimate it was as high as 40 percent to 50 percent) was the hallmark of the Great Depression. In 1933, to combat this unemployment and a host of other problems facing the nation, newly elected President Franklin D. Roosevelt (FDR) proposed a variety of innovative programs under the rubric "the New Deal" and ushered in a new era in American politics. FDR used the full power of the office of the president as well as his highly effective communication skills to sell the American public and Congress on a whole new ideology of government. Not only were the scope and role of national government remarkably altered, but so was the relationship between each state and the national government. It is, in fact, the growth in the federal government that began with the New Deal that many who urge less federal power bemoan today.

The New Deal period (1933–1939) was characterized by intense government activity on the national level. It was clear to most politicians that to find national solutions to the Depression, which was affecting the citizens of every state in the Union, the national government would have to exercise tremendous authority.

In the first few weeks of the legislative session after FDR's inauguration, Congress and the president acted quickly to bolster confidence in the national government. Congress passed a series of acts creating new agencies and programs proposed by the president. These new agencies, often known by their initials, created what many termed an "alphabetocracy." Among the more significant programs were the Federal Housing Administration (FHA), which provided federal financing for new home construction; the Civilian Conservation Corps (CCC), a work relief program for farmers and home-owners; and the Agricultural Adjustment Administration (AAA) and the National Recovery Administration (NRA), both of which imposed restrictions on production in agriculture and many industries.

These programs tremendously enlarged the scope of the national government. Those who feared this unprecedented use of national power quickly challenged the constitutionality of New Deal programs in court. And, at least initially, the Supreme Court often agreed with them.

Through the mid-1930s, the Supreme Court continued to rule that certain aspects of the New Deal went beyond the authority of Congress to regulate commerce.

One of the hallmarks of the New Deal and FDR's presidency was the national government's new involvement of cities in the federal system. Here, New York City Mayor Fiorello La Guardia (for whom one New York airport is named) is commissioned by FDR as the director of civil defense.
(Photo courtesy: AP/Wide World Photos)

Cartoon poking fun at FDR's unpopular plan to expand the size of the Court to allow him to add justices to undo the majority's Anti-New Deal position.

(Photo courtesy: Hulton Archive/Getty Images)

In fact, many believe that the Court considered the Depression to be no more than the sum of the economic woes of the individual states and that it was a problem most appropriately handled by the states. The Court's *laissez-faire*, or "hands-off," attitude toward the economy was reflected in a series of decisions ruling various aspects of New Deal programs unconstitutional.

FDR and the Congress were outraged. FDR's frustration with the *laissez-faire* attitude of the Court prompted him to suggest what ultimately was nicknamed his "Court-packing plan." Knowing that he could do little to change the minds of those already on the Court, FDR suggested enlarging its size from nine to thirteen justices. This would have given him the opportunity to "pack" the Court with a majority of justices predisposed toward the constitutional validity of the New Deal.

Even though Roosevelt was popular, the Court-packing plan was not. Congress and the public were outraged that he even suggested tampering with an institution of government. Nevertheless, the Court appeared to respond to this threat. In 1937, it reversed its series of anti–New Deal decisions, concluding that Congress (and therefore the national government) had the authority to legislate in areas that only affected commerce. Congress then used this newly recognized power to legislate in a wide array of areas, including maximum hour and minimum wage laws, and regulation of child labor. Moreover, the Court also upheld the constitutionality of the bulk of the massive New Deal relief programs, such as the National Labor Relations Act of 1935, which authorized collective bargaining between unions and employees in *NLRB* v. *Jones and Laughlin Steel Co.* (1937);[26] the Fair Labor Standards Act of 1938, which prohibited the interstate shipment of goods made by employees earning less than the federally mandated minimum wage;[27] and the Agricultural Adjustment Act of 1938, which provided crop subsidies to farmers.[28]

The New Deal programs forced all levels of government to work cooperatively with one another. Indeed, local governments—mainly in big cities—became a third partner in the federal system, as FDR relied on big-city Democratic political machines to turn out voters to support his programs. For the first time in U.S. history, in essence, cities were embraced as equal partners in an intergovernmental system and became players in the national political arena because many in the national legislature wanted to bypass state legislatures, where urban interests usually were underrepresented significantly.

The Changing Nature of Federalism: From Layer Cake to Marble Cake.
Before the Depression and the New Deal, most political scientists likened the federal system to a layer cake: Each level or layer of government—national, state, and local—had clearly defined powers and responsibilities. After the New Deal, however, the nature of the federal system changed. Government now looked something like a marble cake:

> Wherever you slice through it you reveal an inseparable mixture of differently colored ingredients.... Vertical and diagonal lines almost obliterate the horizontal ones, and in some places there are unexpected whirls and an imperceptible merging of colors, so that it is difficult to tell where one ends and the other begins.[29]

ANALYZING VISUALS

Federal Grant-in-Aid Outlays, 1940–2005

The table below provides data on grants-in-aid from the national government to state and local governments between 1940 and 2000, with estimates for 2005. Study the data provided in the table and answer the following critical thinking questions: If the amounts were indicated in constant dollars rather than in current dollars, would the figures change significantly? According to the table, which decades experienced a significant increase in federal grants-in-aid in terms of total dollars, percentage of federal outlays, percentage of domestic programs, and percentage of the gross domestic product? How do those increases relate to the various interpretations of federalism (cooperative federalism, creative federalism, and new federalism)? What do you think explains the variations in grants-in-aid over time? See Analyzing Visuals: A Brief Guide for additional guidance in analyzing tables.

Year	Total Grants-in-Aid (billions)	Federal Grants as a Percentage of Federal Outlays[a]			
		Total	Domestic Programs[b]	State and Local Expenditures	Gross Domestic Product
1940	$0.9	9.2	—	—	0.9
1950	2.3	5.3	—	—	0.8
1960	7.0	7.6	18.0	19.0	1.4
1970	24.1	12.3	23.0	24.0	2.4
1980	91.4	15.5	22.0	31.0	3.4
1990	135.3	10.8	17.0	21.0	2.4
1995	225.0	14.8	22.0	25.0	3.1
2000	284.7	15.9	22.7	—[c]	2.9
2005	422.4	18.0	24.6	—[c]	3.5

Note: "—" indicates not available. Amounts are in current dollars. Fiscal years.
[a] Includes off-budget outlays; all grants are on-budget.
[b] Excludes outlays for national defense, international affairs, and net interest.
[c] Data no longer provided by federal government in this form.

Source: Office of Management and Budget, Historical Tables, Budget of the United States Government, Fiscal Year 2003. January 2002. Accessed June 30, 2002, http://www.whitehouse.gov/omb/budget/fy2003/pdf/hi st.pdf.

This kind of "marble cake" federalism is often called **cooperative federalism,** a term that describes the relationship between the national, state, and local governments that began with the New Deal as a stronger, more influential national government was created in response to economic and social crises. States began to take a secondary, albeit important, "cooperative" role in the scheme of governance, as did many cities. Nowhere is this shift in power from the states to the national government more clear than in the growth of federal grant programs that began in earnest during the New Deal. The tremendous growth in these programs and in federal government spending in general, as illustrated in Analyzing Visuals: Federal Grant-in-Aid Outlays, 1940–2005, changed the nature and discussion of federalism from that time to 1995 from "How much power should the national government have?" to "How much say in the policies of the states can the national government buy?" During the 1970s energy crisis, the national government initially imposed a national 55 mph speed limit on the states, for example, and forced states to adopt minimum-age drink restrictions in order to obtain federal transportation funds. (See On Campus: Do You Have ID? Setting a National Alcohol Policy.)

cooperative federalism
The relationship between the national and state governments that began with the New Deal.

Federal Grants.   As early as 1790, Congress appropriated funds for the states to pay debts incurred during the Revolutionary War. But, it wasn't until the Civil War that Congress enacted its first true federal grant program, which allocated federal funds to the states for a specific purpose.

Most view the start of this redistribution of funds with the Morrill Land Grant Act of 1862, which gave each state 30,000 acres of public land for each representative in Congress.

DO YOU HAVE ID? SETTING A NATIONAL ALCOHOL POLICY

The number of fatal crashes involving drivers aged eighteen to twenty-one fell by 14.3 percent from 1983 to 1994. Why? In 1984, after years of often highly emotional lobbying by Mothers Against Drunk Drivers (MADD) and other concerned citizens groups, Congress passed an amendment to the Surface Transportation Act of 1982 designed to withhold 5 percent of federal highway funds from states that did not prohibit people under the age of twenty-one from drinking alcoholic beverages. Prior to that time, MADD had lobbied most state legislators to raise their state drinking ages, with mixed success. Then, its leaders turned their eyes on Congress.[a] In 1984, only sixteen U.S. senators voted against the amendment.

Because the national government did not have the power to regulate the drinking age, it resorted to the carrot-and-stick nature of federalism, whereby the national government dangles money in front of the states but places conditions on its use. To force states to raise their drinking age to twenty-one by 1988, Congress initially decided to withhold 5 percent of all federal highway grants to the recalcitrant states. (This was later raised to 10 percent.) In other words, no raised drinking age, no federal dollars. Even most conservative Republican senators—those most attached to the notion of states' rights—supported the provision, in spite of the fact that it imposed a national ideal on the states. After congressional action, the bill was signed into law by Ronald Reagan, another conservative

long concerned with how the national government had trampled on state power.

States still retain the power to decide who is legally drunk, however. In 1998, Mothers Against Drunk Driving pressured members of Congress to adopt a national blood alcohol level of 0.08 to indicate drunkenness, but that effort failed.[b] Thus, the blood alcohol content required for determining legal intoxication varied dramatically, from a low of 0.05 in Colorado to a high of 0.1 in several states.

In 1999, however, President Bill Clinton signed legislation that contained incentives for states to lower their blood alcohol levels defining drunk driving to 0.08. By late 2000, eighteen states and the District of Columbia adopted that standard. On the twentieth anniversary of its founding, MADD members rallied to convince Congress to set the 0.08 limit as a mandatory national standard, an action supported by a majority of Americans, according to a recent Gallup poll.[c] In October 2000, President Clinton signed the Federal Transportation Appropriations bill, which gave states until October 1, 2003, to enact 0.08 limits or lose 2 percent of their annual federal highway funds per year. By September 2002, 34 states had complied.

[a]Ruth Gastel, "Drunk Driving and Liquor Liability," *Insurance Issues Updates*, (April 1999).
[b]Steve Piacente, "Blood Alcohol Limits Under Fierce Debate," *Post and Courier* (May 27, 1998): B1.
[c]Arthur Santana, "On 20th Anniversary, MADD Urges National 0.08% Standard," *Washington Post* (September 7, 2000): A6.

Income from the sale of these lands was to be earmarked for the establishment and support of agricultural and mechanical arts colleges. Sixty-nine land-grant colleges—including Texas A&M University, the University of Georgia, and Michigan State University—were founded or significantly assisted, making this grant program the single most important piece of education legislation passed in the United States up to that time.

Franklin D. Roosevelt's New Deal program increased the flow of federal dollars to the states with the infusion of massive federal dollars for a variety of public works programs, including building and road construction. These grants made the imposition of national goals on the states easier. No state wanted to decline funds, so states often secured funds for any programs for which money was available—whether they needed it for that specific purpose or not.

In the boom times of World War II, even more new federal programs were introduced; by the 1950s and 1960s, federal grant-in-aid programs were well entrenched. They often defined federal/state relationships and made the national government a major player in domestic policy. Until the 1960s, however, most federal grant programs were constructed in cooperation with the states and were designed to assist the states in the furtherance of their traditional responsibilities to protect the health, welfare, and safety of their citizens. Most of these programs were **categorical grants,** ones for which Congress appropriates funds for specific purposes. Categorical grants allocate federal dollars

categorical grant
Grant for which Congress appropriates funds for a specific purpose.

by a precise formula and are subject to detailed conditions imposed by the national government, often on a matching basis; that is, states must contribute money to match federal funds, although the national government may pay as much as 90 percent of the total.

Creative Federalism

By the early 1960s, as concern about the poor and minorities rose, and as states (especially in the South) were blamed for perpetuating discrimination, those in power in the national government saw grants as a way to force states to behave in ways desired by the national government.[30] If the states would not cooperate with the national government to further its goals, it would withhold funds.

In 1964, the Democratic administration of President Lyndon B. Johnson (LBJ) (1963–1969) launched its "Great Society" program, which included what LBJ called a "War on Poverty." The Great Society program was a broad attempt to combat poverty and discrimination. In a frenzy of activity in Washington not seen since the New Deal, federal funds were channeled to states, to local governments, and even directly to citizen action groups in an effort to alleviate social ills that the states had been unable or unwilling to remedy. There was money for urban renewal, education, and poverty programs, including Head Start and job training. The move to fund local groups directly was made by the most liberal members of Congress to bypass not only conservative state legislatures, but also conservative mayors and councils in cities such as Chicago, who were perceived as disinclined to help their poor, often African American, constituencies. Thus, these programs often pitted governors and mayors against community activists, who became key players in the distribution of federal dollars.

These new grants altered the fragile federal/state balance of power that had been at the core of most older federal grant programs. During the Johnson administration, the national government began to use federal grants as a way to further what federal (and not state) officials perceived to be national needs. Grants based on what states wanted or believed they needed began to decline, while grants based on what the national government wanted states to do to foster national goals increased dramatically. Soon states routinely asked Washington for help: "Pollution, transportation, recreation, economic development, law enforcement and even rat control evoked the same response from politicians: create a federal grant."[31]

Not all federal programs mandating state or local action came with federal money, however. And, while presidents Nixon, Ford, and Carter voiced their opposition to "big government," their efforts to rein it in were largely unsuccessful.

The Reagan Revolution

In 1980, former California Governor Ronald Reagan was elected president pledging to advance what he called a "New Federalism" and a return of power to the states. Reagan's New Federalism had many facets. The Republican "Reagan Revolution" had at its heart strong views about the role of states in the federal system. While many argued that grants-in-aid were an effective way to raise the level of services provided to the poor, others, including Reagan, attacked them as imposing national priorities on the states. Policy decisions were made at the national level. The states, always in search of funds, were forced to follow the priorities of the national government. States found it very hard to resist the lure of grants, even though many were contingent on some sort of state investment of matching or proportional funds.

Shortly after taking office, Reagan proposed massive cuts in federal domestic programs (which had not become federal functions until the New Deal) and drastic income tax cuts. The Reagan administration's budget and its policies dramatically altered the relationships among federal, state, and local governments. For the first time in thirty years, federal aid to state and local governments declined.[32] Reagan persuaded Congress to consolidate many

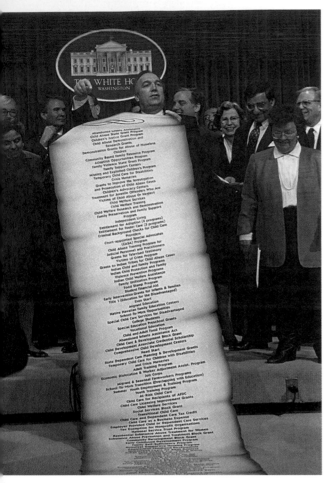

In the mid-1990s, then Michigan Governor John Engler unfurls a scroll of nearly 3,000 federal antipoverty programs that several Republican governors wanted dismantled in favor of lump-sum block grants to allow the states to decide where federal dollars in the states are best spent.

(Photo courtesy: Photo by Jym Wilson. Copyright 2002, Gannett News Service. reprinted with permission.)

block grant
Broad grant with few strings attached; given to states by the federal government for specified activities, such as secondary education or health services.

intergovernmental lobby
The pressure group or groups that are created when state and local governments hire lobbyists to lobby the national government.

WEB EXPLORATION
For more on National Governors Association (NGA) and the Big Seven, see
www.ablongman.com/oconnor

categorical grants (for specific programs that often require matching funds) into far fewer, less restrictive **block grants**—broad grants to states for specific activities such as secondary education or health services, with few strings attached. He also ended general revenue sharing, which had provided significant unrestricted funds to the states.

By the end of the Bush administration in 1992, most block grants fell into one of four categories—health, income security, education, or transportation. Yet, many politicians, including most state governors, urged the consolidation of even more programs into block grants. Calls to reform the welfare system, particularly to allow more latitude to the states in an effort to get back to the Hamiltonian notion of states as laboratories of experiment, seemed popular with citizens and governments alike, as the New Federalism took hold.

Reagan's New "Republican" Federalism initially changed the nature of state politics. Many state governments, as well as cities within a single state, found themselves competing for funds. States were faced with revenue shortfalls caused by the recession of the early 1990s, legal requirements mandating balanced budgets, and growing demands for new social services and the replacement of some formerly provided by the federal government. Many governors around the nation found themselves in political trouble as they had to slash services and ask for tax increases. Legislators in forty-six states narrowly missed deadlines for their new budget authorizations because of rising costs.

In response to budget shortfalls, many states revved up their lobbying activities. What scholars term the "Big Seven," which include the National Governors Association (NGA) and the National League of Cities, among others, are widely recognized as the premier **intergovernmental lobbies** (see Table 3.2).

Several of the Big Seven focus on state issues and on getting more federal dollars. The NGA is composed of incumbent governors from each state. The governors meet twice a year but have a staff and standing committees that meet more regularly. Adoption of policy positions requires a quorum and vote of three-quarters of the governors. Small states tend to be more active within the group than larger states. The Council of State Governments, located in Washington, D.C., is an umbrella organization designed to gather information and provide assistance to the states. The National Conference of State Legislatures, headquartered in Denver, publishes a monthly magazine, *State Legislatures*, and uses its Washington, D.C. office to monitor and publish information about the federal government that is useful to the states. It provides a variety of legislative services to all fifty state legislatures plus Puerto Rico.

Three other groups often are called the "urban lobby." The National League of Cities represents medium and small cities, the U.S. Conference of Mayors represents large cities, and the National Association of Counties represents rural, suburban, and urban counties. The remaining member of the Big Seven is the International City/County Management Association, which represents the country's appointed local chief executives.

The Devolution Revolution

In 1992, Bill Clinton was elected president—the first Democrat in twelve years. Although Clinton was a former governor, he was more predisposed to federal programs than his Republican predecessors.

In 1994, however, Republicans took over both houses of Congress, and every Republican governor who sought reelection was victorious, while some popular Democratic governors, such as Ann Richards of Texas, lost (to George W. Bush). In *Federalist No. 17*, Alexander Hamilton noted that "it will always be far more easy for the State

TABLE 3.2   The "Big Seven" Intergovernmental Associations

Association	Date Founded	Membership
National Governors Association (NGA)	1908	Incumbent governors
Council of State Governments (CSG)	1933	Direct membership by states and territories; serves all branches of government; has dozens of affiliate organizations of specialists
National Conference of State Legislatures (NCSL)	1948	State legislators and staff
National League of Cities (NLC)	1924	Direct, by cities and state leagues of cities
National Association of Counties (NAC)	1935	Direct by counties; loosely linked state associations; affiliate membership for county professional specialists
United States Conference of Mayors (USCM)	1933	Direct membership by cities with population over 30,000
International City/County Management Association (ICMA)	1914	Direct membership by appointed city and county managers, and other professionals

Source: Allan J. Cigler and Burdett A. Loomis, *Interest Group Politics*, 4th ed. (Washington DC: CQ Press, 1995), 135. Reprinted by permission of Congressional Quarterly Inc.

government to encroach upon the national authorities than for the national government to encroach upon the State authorities." He was wrong. By 1994, many state governors and the Republican Party rebelled openly against this growth of national power. (Remember, prior to 9/11, both increases in federal power—FDR's New Deal and LBJ's Great Society program—were launched during Democratic administrations.) They were particularly outraged by the federal government's use of preemption.

Preemption.   **Preemption** allows the national government to override, or preempt, state or local actions in certain areas.[33] The Tenth Amendment expressly reserves to the states and the people all powers not delegated to the national government. The phenomenal growth of preemption statutes, laws that Congress has passed to allow the federal government to assume partial and/or full responsibility for traditional state and local governmental functions, began in 1965 during the Johnson administration. Since then, Congress routinely used its authority under the commerce clause to preempt state laws. New laws not only took authority away from states but also often imposed significant costs on them in the form of unfunded mandates. In fact, the cost to the states—along with the perceived federal interference with local matters—is one reason that the electorate so willingly embraced the campaign message of the Republican Party in 1994.

preemption
A concept derived from the Constitution's supremacy clause that allows the national government to override or preempt state or local actions in certain areas.

Head Start alum and former professional baseball and football player Deion Sanders helps children at a California Head Start center. Sanders was there to launch an educational outreach program designed to provide computers, software, and staff training to selected Head Start centers on the West Coast.

(Photo courtesy: Jill Connelly HO/AP/Wide World Photos)

Join the Debate

SHOULD THE FEDERAL GOVERNMENT PREEMPT STATE LAWS?

Our federal system of government assures a tension among the national government, state governments, and organized interests over which level of government has authority to act and whether policy established at one level can contradict policy established at the other level. At numerous points in our history, the cry of "states' rights" has been heard, while at other times, we hear a demand for the national government to assure uniform (equal) treatment of people across the nation. This tension erupts into political and legal battles over specific policy initiatives. Advocates of a particular policy win at one level of government, then those who lost the battle take the issue to the other level of government in an attempt to block the new policy. The victors then invoke either states' rights or equal protection as justification for their policy.

Sometimes, Congress acts to block state laws. This action is known as "preemption." To preempt a state law is to prevent it from taking effect, to declare that federal policy takes precedence over the state policy. Recent examples of federal preemption include establishing a minimum drinking age for students (see On Campus: Do You Have ID? Setting a National Alcohol Policy) and placement of the nation's high-level nuclear waste dump in Nevada, over that state's objections. Another example is discussed in the following excerpted news article. California voters passed a law (by initiative) requiring food manufacturers to include warnings on food labels if the product contains known cancer-causing ingredients or could be toxic. Consumer advocates argue that the federal government is lax in its food safety regulations, and that requiring such warnings is not only useful information for consumers, but may lead manufacturers to use safer ingredients. The food industry has been trying to get Congress to pass a law preempting such state regulations, arguing that ours is a national market, not a state-by-state market, and that it is too heavy a burden on manufacturers to change ingredients or labels to meet requirements of the various states.

Should the federal government be allowed to preempt state laws in the areas of health and welfare? How far do states' rights go? Alternatively, what should be included in "equal protection" of the laws? In this specific case, should the federal government forbid state food safety regulations that are more stringent than federal requirements? Read and think about the issues raised in the following article. Then, join the debate over whether the federal government should be allowed to preempt state laws in areas of state action protected by the Tenth Amendment by considering the debating points and questions posed at the end of this feature, and sharpen your own arguments for the position you find most viable. While the bill discussed in the article ultimately failed, attempts to pass similar legislation continue today, and Congress frequently considers preemption initiatives in other policy areas, too.

Bills Seek to Preempt State Laws

By Philip Brasher

State laws that require warnings on foods and dietary supplements or regulate the handling of eggs and other products could be nullified under legislation food manufacturers are pushing through Congress.

A top industry priority for years, the legislation was approved on a voice vote by the Senate Agriculture Committee in June—after no hearing and little advance notice. It has at least 35 sponsors, including Senate Democratic leader Tom Daschle of South Dakota....

"If a product needs a warning label, then it shouldn't just be in one state; it should be in all 50 states.... We're one country, we're not 50 countries," said Susan Stout, vice president for public affairs of the Grocery Manufacturers of America.

The food industry has been trying for 12 years to get out from under a California law, known as Proposition 65, that requires a warning label on all products that contain cancer-causing agents or substances that are toxic to the reproductive system.

Manufacturers typically remove or alter products rather than face the negative publicity from a warning label. Because California is such a large market, whatever companies do there they are likely to do nationwide.

After the law was imposed, the state used it to force manufacturers to reduce lead levels in calcium supplements. The law "has been very good at catching loopholes in federal protection, and the feds have often responded by tightening their own standards once California showed the way," said David Roe, a lawyer who helped craft the California law.

The Senate bill, known as the National Uniformity for Food Act of 2000, would bar states from imposing labeling and food safety standards that are tougher than the Food and Drug Administration's. States would have to petition the FDA for exemptions from the law.

Opponents of the legislation say it would block state efforts to act in areas where the FDA has been ineffective or to goad the agency to regulate products it has not. The agency has come under fire recently for not imposing labeling regulations for dietary supplements and "functional foods" containing added nutritional content, such as vitamin-enhanced juices or soups containing St. John's wort.

In a July 11 report, the General Accounting Office said consumers may be buying some potentially unsafe products because the FDA has not set a clear safety standard for new ingredients in dietary supplements or issued regulations for safety information on labels.

A consumer advocacy group, the Center for Science in the Public Interest, has compiled a list of laws and regulations that could be affected by the Senate bill. In addition to Proposition 65, they include:

- Laws in at least 17 states, including California, Florida, Illinois and Texas, that allow them to set tolerances for food additives that are more stringent than the FDA's.
- Michigan and Wisconsin requirements for warning labels on smoked fish. Many states also require warnings on shellfish.
- Illinois and Pennsylvania laws that deem egg products adulterated if they are made in a way that raises the chance of contamination.

Some states also are putting curbs on ephedra, a dietary supplement used to lose weight or boost energy.

The FDA has not taken a position on the Senate bill. The agency is moving forward in regulating and monitoring dietary supplements but is hampered by lack of funding, said Joe Levitt, director of the agency's Center for Food Safety and Applied Nutrition. "The FDA doesn't have the resources at this time to carry out everything that needs to be carried out," he said....

Source: Philip Brasher, *Los Angeles Times* (July 23, 2000): A22. Reprinted with permission of The Associated Press.

JOIN THE DEBATE!

CHECK YOUR UNDERSTANDING: Make sure you understand the following key points from the article; go back and review it if you missed any of them:

- The federal Food and Drug Administration has not set clear safety standards for new ingredients and safety labeling of some food products.
- California citizens enacted a law requiring additional product labeling on food items.
- The intent of the law is to increase safety levels of food products beyond federal requirements.
- The grocery industry has placed a high priority on getting Congress to pass a bill preempting the California and other similar state laws.

ADDITIONAL INFORMATION: News articles don't provide all the information an informed citizen needs to know about an issue under debate. Here are some questions the article does not answer that you may need to consider in order to join the debate:

- Under the California law, how does one determine whether a substance is cancer-causing or toxic?
- Can an industry produce products with differing ingredients for marketing in different states?
- What are the constitutional issues in federal preemption?

What other information might you want to know? Where might you gather this information? How might you evaluate the credibility of the information you gather? Is the information from a reliable source? Can you identify any potential biases?

IDENTIFYING THE ARGUMENTS: Now that you have some information on the issue, and have thought about what else you need to know, see whether you can present the arguments on both sides of the debate. Here are some ideas to get you started. We've provided one example each of "pro" and "con" arguments, but you should be able to offer others:

PRO: Congress should be able to preempt laws such as California's labeling law. Here's why:

- Congress has constitutional authority to regulate interstate commerce; a state law that affects the nationwide marketing of products clearly violates that principle, and Congress must act to protect interstate commerce.

CON: Congress should not be able to preempt laws such as California's labeling law. Here's why:

- People who live in a state where, for instance, food safety is a lower priority than in other states have the right to insist on higher standards, and Congress violates constitutional states' rights if it tries to substitute its judgment for the state's judgment.

TAKING A POSITION AND SUPPORTING IT: After thinking about the information in the article on possible congressional preemption of state food safety labeling laws, placing it in the broader context of federalism, and articulating the arguments in the debate, what position would you take? What information supports your position? What arguments would you use to persuade others to your side of the debate? How would you counter arguments on the other side?

Contract with America
Campaign pledge signed by most
Republican candidates in 1994 to
guide their legislative agenda.

WEB EXPLORATION
For more on the
Devolution Revolution, see
www.ablongman.com/oconnor

mandates
National laws that direct states or
local governments to comply with
federal rules or regulations (such as
clean air or water standards) under
threat of civil or criminal penalties
or as a condition of receipt of any
federal grants.

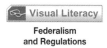

Visual Literacy
**Federalism
and Regulations**

WEB EXPLORATION
To analyze where
your state stands relative
to other states, see
www.ablongman.com/oconnor

The **Contract with America,** proposed by then House Minority Whip Newt Gingrich (R–GA), was a campaign document signed by nearly all Republican candidates (and incumbents) seeking election to the House of Representatives in 1994. In it, Republican candidates pledged themselves to force a national debate on the role of the national government in regard to the states. A top priority was scaling back the federal government, which some called the "devolution revolution." Poll after poll, moreover, revealed that many Americans believed the national government had too much power (48 percent) and that they favored their states assuming many of the powers and functions now exercised by the federal government (59 percent).[34]

Unfunded Mandates.   A key component of the Contract with America was a commitment to end unfunded mandates. From the beginning, most categorical grants were matching grants that came with a variety of strings attached. As categorical grants declined, the national government continued to exercise a significant role in state policy priorities through **mandates**—laws that direct states or local governments to comply with federal rules or regulations (such as clean air or water standards) under threat of civil or criminal penalties or as a condition of receipt of any federal grants (a city might not get federal transportation funds, for example, unless the disabled have access to particular means of transportation).

Prior to 1995, the federal government required the states to shoulder the cost of federal programs it did not fund. Unfunded mandates often made up as much as 30 percent of a local government's annual operating budget. The enactment of federal regulations requiring state and local spending increased tremendously through 1990. During the 1980s, for example, Congress added twenty-seven new programs requiring state spending, and many expensive unfunded provisions were attached to existing grant-in-aid programs. Columbus, Ohio, for example, with 633,000 residents, faced a $1 billion bill to comply with the federal Clean Water Act and the Safe Drinking Water Act at an estimated cost of $685 a year per household.

Unlike the national government, most states are required to have balanced budgets, and these federally mandated outlays were playing havoc with state budgets. In 1993, some state legislatures even passed laws summoning home their senators and representatives to explain why they were imposing costly national regulations on states without providing funds to implement these programs. It is not surprising, then, that the Republican majority was able to secure passage of the Unfunded Mandates Reform Act of 1995, which barred Congress from passing costly programs without debate on how to fund them.

By 1998, the cumulative impact of the federal government's moving some powers back to the states, a tremendously improved economy, and decreasing federal mandates produced record federal and state budget surpluses. States were in the best fiscal shape that they had been in since the 1970s, before federal mandates hurt their ability to prioritize spending. According to the National Conference of State Legislatures, total state budget surpluses in 1998 exceeded $30 billion.

These tax surpluses allowed many states to increase spending, while other states offered their residents steep tax cuts. Mississippi, for example, increased its per capita spending by 42.4 percent, while Alaska opted to reduce taxes by 44.2 percent.[35]

But, by 2000, state revenues were beginning to fall short of projected estimates as costs of health care and education continued to rise and sales tax revenue fell, in part fueled by tax-free Internet commerce. State budget surpluses fell over 4 percent from 1999 to 2000. By 2001, states found themselves in the worst budget shape they had been in since 1992.[36] The stock market crash, lower tax revenues, the increasing cost of Medicaid, Medicare, and prescription drugs, then the tremendous negative economic impact of September 11 all came together to plunge many states into dire economic straits. Figure 3.4 shows the projected shortfalls of the thirty-five states in 2003. By 2005, help from the federal government and tax increases allowed many states to decrease deficits.

FIGURE 3.4   Projected Shortfalls in State Budgets for 2005

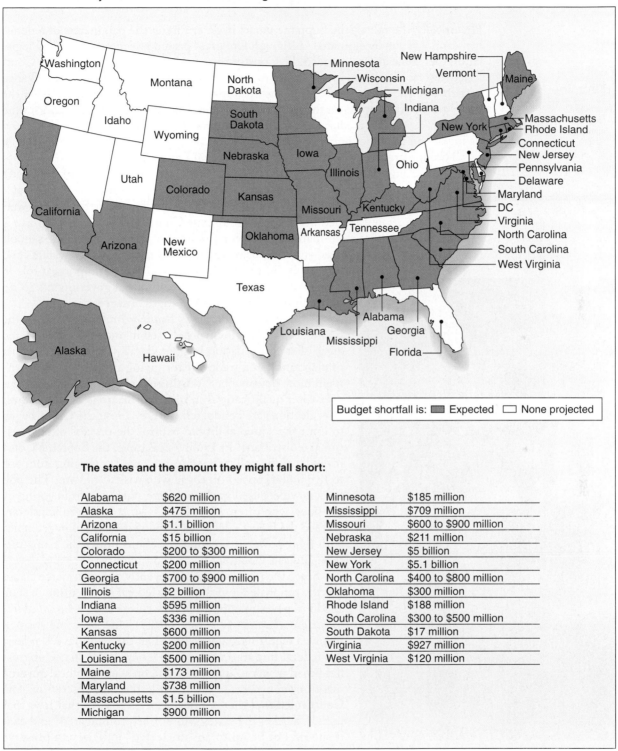

The states and the amount they might fall short:

State	Amount	State	Amount
Alabama	$620 million	Minnesota	$185 million
Alaska	$475 million	Mississippi	$709 million
Arizona	$1.1 billion	Missouri	$600 to $900 million
California	$15 billion	Nebraska	$211 million
Colorado	$200 to $300 million	New Jersey	$5 billion
Connecticut	$200 million	New York	$5.1 billion
Georgia	$700 to $900 million	North Carolina	$400 to $800 million
Illinois	$2 billion	Oklahoma	$300 million
Indiana	$595 million	Rhode Island	$188 million
Iowa	$336 million	South Carolina	$300 to $500 million
Kansas	$600 million	South Dakota	$17 million
Kentucky	$200 million	Virginia	$927 million
Louisiana	$500 million	West Virginia	$120 million
Maine	$173 million		
Maryland	$738 million		
Massachusetts	$1.5 billion		
Michigan	$900 million		

Sources: Nicolas Johnson and Bob Zahradnik, "State Budget Deficits Projected for Fiscal Year 2005," Center on Budget and Policy Priorities (February 2004).

FEDERALISM AND THE SUPREME COURT

Historically, the role of the Supreme Court in determining the parameters of federalism cannot be underestimated. Although Congress passed sweeping New Deal legislation that some argue amended the Constitution, it was not until the Supreme Court finally reversed itself and found those programs to be constitutional that any real change occurred in the federal/state relationship. From the New Deal until the 1980s, the Supreme Court's impact on the nature of the federal system could be found in several areas, but especially in education, the electoral process, and the commerce clause and its impact on the functioning of the states.

Through grant-in-aid programs like the Morrill Land Grant Act of 1862, and into the 1950s, Congress long tried to encourage the states to develop their university and educational systems. Still, education usually was considered a function of the states under their police powers, which allow the states to provide for public health and welfare. That tradition was shattered when the Supreme Court ruled in *Brown* v. *Board of Education* (1954) that state-mandated segregation has no place in the public schools (see chapter 6). *Brown* forced states to dismantle their segregated school systems and ultimately led the federal courts to play an important role in monitoring the efforts of state and local governments to rid their school systems of any vestiges of segregation.

A decade after *Brown* v. *Board of Education* (1954), the Supreme Court again involved itself in one of the most sacred areas of state regulation in the federal system—the conduct of elections. As a trade-off for giving the national government more powers, the Constitution allows the states control over voter qualifications in national elections as well as over how elections are conducted. But, in 1964, the Court began to limit the states' ability to control the process of congressional redistricting. In 1966, for example, the Supreme Court invalidated the poll tax, a state-imposed tax ranging from one to five dollars levied on those who wished to vote. The poll tax was widely used in the southern states to curtail voting by the poor, who often were black.[37] Most southern legislators assailed the Court's decision, viewing it as illegal interference with their powers to regulate elections under the Constitution, and as a violation of state sovereignty.

Since the New Deal, until recently, the commerce clause was the rationale for virtually any federal intervention in state and local governmental affairs. In *Garcia* v. *San Antonio Metropolitan Transit Authority* (1985), for example, which involved requiring states to pay all of their employees at least the federal minimum wage, the Court ruled that Congress has broad power to impose its will on state and local governments, even in areas traditionally left to their discretion. The Court ruled that the "political process ensures that laws that unduly burden the states will not be promulgated" and that it should not be up to an "unelected" judiciary to preserve state powers.[38] Furthermore, the majority of the Court concluded that the Tenth Amendment, which ensures that any powers not given to the national government be reserved for the states or the people, was—at least for the time being— essentially meaningless!

Timeline

Federalism and the Supreme Court

In spite of winning Florida's electoral votes with his brother Jeb's help in 2000 and 2004, George W. Bush rebuffed personal appeals from the Florida governor not to allow drilling for natural gas and oil off the Florida coast.

(Photo courtesy: Reuters/Jeff Mitchell/Hulton Archive)

FEDERALISM IN COMPARATIVE PERSPECTIVE

All governments face the issue of how to divide political authority geographically. Of the variations presented in the table, federal and unitary systems are the most prevalent throughout the world. The Commonwealth of Independent States (made up of most of the former republics of the Soviet Union) is the rare example, a confederation. The countries presented here are split almost evenly between federal and unitary systems, with the latter slightly more common. While these federal systems divide political authority between national and local government, the near balance suggests that there is nothing inherently better, or even more democratic, in a federal system.

Whether a country adopts one or the other tends to be the result of its political history. The United States and Germany were created out of existing confederacies, so the new governments accommodated theoretically strong state governments as the price of union. Canada was formed in 1867 out of three British provinces that voluntarily sought union. In Russia, the current distribution of authority results from the fact that in 1992, the Russian government inherited the geographic divisions of the former Soviet Russian Republic. In France, Italy, and Japan, the creation of modern nation-states was driven by central authorities that imposed geographic political arrangements on their provinces. In all three cases, subnational territories were created by national governments intent on obliterating then-existing regional identities.

The ability of the national government to alter local government at will remains a key feature of unitary systems. No better current example can be found than in the British Parliament's decision in 1998 to provide home parliaments for Scotland, Wales, and Northern Ireland. But, what Parliament created can be abolished by that body at any time: In 2000, dissatisfied with the lack of progress in peace negotiations in Northern Ireland, the Blair government suspended that

Geographic Distribution of Authority		
Country	*System*	*Major Subnational Divisions*
Canada	federal	10 provinces, 3 territories
China	unitary	23 provinces, 9 other units
Egypt	unitary	26 governorates
France	unitary	96 departments
Germany	federal	16 states
India	federal	28 states, 7 union territories
Indonesia	unitary	27 provinces, 3 other units
Italy	unitary	20 regions
Japan	unitary	47 prefectures
Mexico	federal	31 states, 1 federal district
Russia	federal	49 oblasts, 21 republics, 13 other units
United Kingdom	unitary	36 counties, var. others
United States	**federal**	**50 states, 1 federal district**

Source: CIA World Factbook 2000 online. Accessed September 20, 2000, http://www.odci. gov/cia.publications/factbook/geos/.

region's home parliament and reintroduced direct rule by the Parliament in London.

Power is divided differently even among the federal systems. Canada has had a strong federal government with correspondingly weak provinces, although the latter have asserted their power in recent decades. Quebec is the clearest case, with its threat to separate from the rest of the country forcing the federal government to make concessions on issues like the national language and education. German state governments cannot raise their own taxes, but they retain sole control over state police forces, the highest level of regular law enforcement. The Mexican and post-communist Russian federal systems are highly centralized. In the original spirit of the U.S. Constitution, Canadian, German, and Russian regional governments are represented in the upper houses of their respective federal parliaments. This gives state governments a direct say in national law-making.

The Devolution Revolution and the Court

Growth in federal grant-in-aid programs and unfunded mandates to the states, as well as the Court's apparent approval of wide-ranging congressional authority to regulate under the commerce clause, led many states to rethink their position in the federal system. Most were unhappy with it. Some argued that one of the original reasons for federal grants—perceived overrepresentation of rural interests in state legislatures—no longer existed, as the Supreme Court ordered redistricting to ensure better

Comparing
Federal and
Unitary
Systems

TABLE 3.3   Major Cases in the Supreme Court Devolution of Power Back to the States

Case	Year	Issue/Question	Decision	Vote
Webster v. *Reproductive Health Services*	1989	Are several state abortion restrictions constitutional?	Yes. In upholding most of the restrictions, the Court invites the states to begin to enact new state restrictions.	5–4
New York v. *Smith*	1992	Does the Low-Level Waste Act, which requires states to dispose of radioactive waste within their borders, violate the Tenth Amendment?	Yes. The section of the act that requires the states to take legal ownership of waste is unconstitutional because it forces states into the service of the federal government.	6–3
U.S. Term Limits v. *Thornton*	1995	Can the states set qualifications for members of Congress?	No. States do not have the authority to enact term limits for federal elected officials.	5–4
U.S. v. *Lopez*	1995	Does Congress have the authority to regulate guns within 1,000 feet of a public school?	No. Only states have this authority; no connection to commerce found.	5–4
Seminole Tribe v. *Florida*	1996	Can Congress impose a duty on the states to negotiate with Indian tribes?	No. Federal courts have no jurisdiction over an Indian tribe's suit to force state to comply with the Indian Gaming Regulations Act, thus upholding the state's sovereign immunity.	5–4
Boerne v. *Flores*	1997	Constitutionality of the Religious Freedom Restoration Act and its application of local zoning ordinances to a church (see chapter 5)	No. Sections of the act are beyond the power of Congress to force on the states.	5–4
Printz v. *U.S.*	1997	Constitutionality of temporarily requiring local law enforcement officials to conduct background checks on handgun purchasers	No. Congress lacks the authority to compel state officers to execute federal laws.	5–4
Florida Prepaid v. *College Savings Bank*	1999	Can Congress change patent laws to affect state sovereign immunity (immunity from a lawsuit)?	No. Congress lacks authority under the commerce clause and the patent clause to abrogate state sovereign immunity from lawsuits.	5–4
Alden v. *Maine*	1999	Can Congress void state immunity from lawsuit in state courts?	No. Congress lacks the authority to abrogate a state's immunity in its own courts.	5–4
U.S. v. *Morrison*	2000	Does Congress have the authority to provide a federal remedy for victims of gender-motivated violence under the commerce clause of the Fourteenth Amendment?	No. Portions of Violence Against Women Act found unconstitutional.	5–4

representation of urban and suburban interests. Moreover, state legislatures had become more professional, state and local bureaucracies more responsive, and the delivery of services better.

Beginning in the late 1980s, however, as part of the devolution revolution, the Court's willingness to allow Congress to regulate in a variety of areas waned. Once Ronald Reagan was elected president, he attempted to appoint new justices committed to the notion of state rights and to rolling back federal intervention in matters that many Republicans believed properly resided within the province of the states and not Congress or the federal courts.

Mario M. Cuomo, the former liberal Democratic New York governor, has referred to the decisions of what he called the Reagan-Bush Court as creating "a kind of new judicial federalism." According to Cuomo, this new federalism could be characterized by the Court's withdrawal of "rights and emphases previously thought to be national."[39] Illustrative of this trend are the Supreme Court's decisions in *Webster* v. *Reproductive Health Services* (1989)[40] and *Planned Parenthood of Southeastern Pennsylvania* v. *Casey* (1992).[41] In *Webster*, the Court first gave new latitude—and even encouragement—to the states to fashion more restrictive abortion laws, as underscored in Table 3.3. Since *Webster*, most

Simulation

You Are a Federal Judge

ANALYZING VISUALS

State-by-State Report Card on Access to Abortion

According to its concerns, the liberal, pro-choice National Abortion and Reproductive Rights Action League (NARAL) rates each state and the District of Columbia in fourteen categories, including bans on abortion procedures and counseling, clinic violence, the length of waiting periods, access for minors, and public funding, which it then translates into grades. As a pro-choice group, NARAL gives an A only to states it evaluates as pro-choice. After studying the map, answer the following critical thinking questions: What do the states that receive A's have in common? How might factors such as political culture, geography, and social characteristics of the population influence a state's laws concerning abortion? If a group that opposes abortion, such as the National Right to Life Committee, were to grade the states, would their ratings include the same categories or factors? Explain your answer. See Analyzing Visuals: A Brief Guide for additional guidance in analyzing maps.

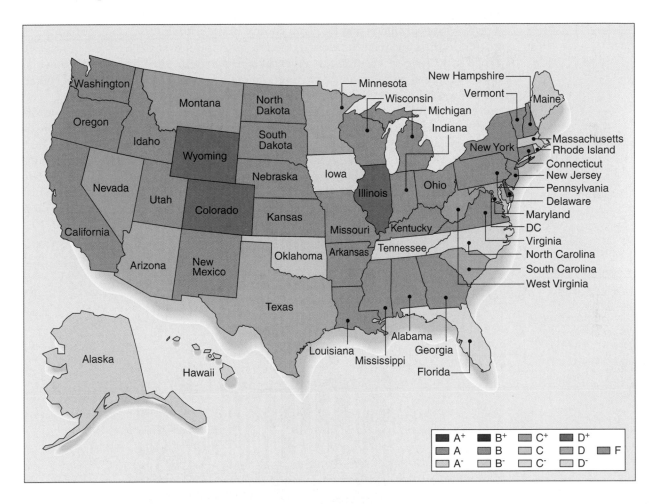

Source: NARAL/NARAL Foundation, "Who Decides? A State-by-State Review of Abortion and Reproductive Rights," 2002. Accessed July 1, 2002, http://www.naral.org/mediaresources/publications/2002/charts_report.pdf. Reprinted by permission.

states have enacted new restrictions on abortion, with spousal or parental consent, informed consent or waiting periods, or bans on late-term abortions being the most common (See Analyzing Visuals: State-by-State Report Card on Access to Abortion.) The Court consistently has upheld the authority of the individual states to limit a minor's access to abortion through imposition of parental consent or notification laws. And, it also consistently has declined to review most other restrictions, including twenty-four-hour

WEB EXPLORATION
For more information on state abortion restrictions, see www.ablongman.com/oconnor

WEB EXPLORATION
For more about local gun control initiatives, see www.ablongman.com/oconnor

sovereign immunity
The right of a state to be free from lawsuit unless it gives permission to the suit. Under the Eleventh Amendment, all states are considered sovereign.

waiting period requirements. In 2000, however, a badly divided 5–4 Court struck down a Nebraska ban on "partial birth" abortions (as discussed in chapter 5).[42]

Personal rights and liberties were not the only issues affected by a Court that became more and more conservative through the Reagan-Bush years. The addition of two justices by President Bill Clinton did little to stem the course of a Court bent on rebalancing the nature of the federal system. Since 1989, the Supreme Court has decided several major cases dealing with the nature of the federal system. Most of these have been 5–4 decisions and most have been decided against increased congressional power or in a manner to provide the states with greater authority over a variety of issues and policies. In *U.S.* v. *Lopez* (1995), for example, which involved the conviction of a student charged with carrying a concealed handgun onto school property, a five-person majority of the Court ruled that Congress lacked constitutional authority under the commerce clause to regulate guns within 1,000 feet of a school.[43] The majority concluded that local gun control in the schools was a state, not a federal, matter. In the same year, the Court reined in state power over the electoral process. In *U.S. Term Limits* v. *Thornton*, however, by a 5–4 margin, the Court struck down as unconstitutional state-imposed term limits on members of Congress.[44] States, of course, are free to set limits on the terms of state lawmakers.

One year later, again a badly divided Court ruled that Congress lacked the authority to require states to negotiate with Indian tribes about gaming.[45] The U.S. Constitution specifically gives Congress the right to deal with Indian tribes, but the Court found that Florida's **sovereign immunity** protected the state from this kind of congressional directive about how to conduct its business. In 1997, the Court decided two more major cases dealing with the scope of Congress's authority to regulate in areas historically left to the province of the states: zoning and local law enforcement. In *Boerne*

Unlike what the majority did in *Bush* v. *Gore* (2000), the conservative Court usually defers to state courts as well as judgments of the state legislatures.

(Photo courtesy: Copyright 2000 by Herblock in The Washington Post)

MARRIAGE IN THE FEDERAL SYSTEM

In 2000, Vermont became the first state to sanction civil unions between same-sex couples. These are not marriages; instead, the Vermont law calls them "civil unions." Couples need pay only $20 to receive a license from a town clerk (there are no residency or blood test requirements) and have a ceremony performed by a judge or clergy member. Once so united, the couple is entitled to all of the benefits, protections, and responsibilities that are granted to married couples under Vermont law.

When the Framers drafted the Constitution, most of them had clear ideas about what marriage was and the authority of the state (as well as the church) to sanction it. Marriage and the laws surrounding it (as well as its dissolution) were solely within the purview of state authority. Under English common law, when a woman married, she ceased to exist in the eyes of the law; in other words, she was civilly dead and could not make contracts or enter into any other kinds of legal arrangements. Beginning in the 1830s, however, most states began to change their laws to give women more rights in marriage. States regularly determine age at marriage (until the 1970s, it was frequently different for males and females), degree of relationship allowed (can cousins marry?), how married individuals dispose of property (inheritance laws) and pay their taxes, and whether they can testify against each other in court. Marriage is not only a legal contract recognized by the state, but it carries certain rights and responsibilities with it. Only when some type of law or practice was viewed as discriminatory under the U.S. Constitution has the force of the federal government come into play. Thus, the Supreme Court has struck down as unconstitutional state laws that prohibit interracial marriages,[a] set differential ages for the age of legal capacity for men and women,[b] or allowed only women to receive alimony upon dissolution of a marriage.[c] As public perceptions of what was appropriate changed, these changes were marked by changes in state law, and when that didn't happen, sometimes by the federal courts.

Until the 1980s, most people in America thought of marriage as a legal relationship between a male and a female. In the 1980s, however, some cities began recognizing what are termed domestic partnerships. Depending on the locale, these domestic partnership ordinances allowed same-sex couples to register with government officials to ensure that their union could be recognized in some way. In some cases, this provided the force of the state in matters of death and inheritance as well as other issues, including a person's ability to make decisions for an incapacitated partner over the wishes of other familial members. Many employers followed suit and began to offer health and insurance benefits to same-sex couples in committed relationships.

In 1993, a decision of the Hawaiian Supreme Court called that state's ban on homosexual marriages into constitutional

Lois Farnham and Holly Puterbaugh challenged Vermont's refusal to allow them to marry, which eventually led to passage of Vermont's civil union law.

(Photo courtesy: Jym Wilson/© USA Today. Reprinted with permission.)

question. While Hawaii was grappling with this issue, several state legislatures and the U.S. Congress were whipped into a frenzy about the specter of gay and lesbian marriages. In 1996 and 1997 alone, half of the states passed provisions to bar legal recognition of same-sex marriages. The U.S. Congress also got into the act and passed the Defense of Marriage Act, which allows states to disregard gay marriages even if they are legal in other states. (The questionable constitutionality of this provision under the full faith and credit clause is discussed on p. 75.)

In 2004, President George W. Bush announced his support of the Federal Marriage Amendment. This proposed amendment to the Constitution states that "marriage in the United States shall consist only of the union of a man and a woman. Neither the Constitution or the constitution of any state, nor state or federal law, shall be construed to require that marital status or the legal incidents thereof be conferred upon unmarried couples or groups." In 2004, lawmakers in eleven states placed various versions of anti-gay marriage and/or civil unions measures on their ballot. Voters in every state approved these measures, some by overwhelming margins.

The idea of gay marriage is still upsetting to some, much as interracial marriage was in many sections of the South. Still, there can be no doubt that our notions of what a family is, as well as what (or who) makes up a married couple, are changing.

[a]*Loving* v. *Virginia*, 388 U.S. 1 (1967).
[b]*Stanton* v. *Stanton*, 421 U.S. 7 (1975).
[c]*Orr* v. *Orr*, 400 U.S. 268 (1979).

LEGISLATING AGAINST VIOLENCE AGAINST WOMEN: A CASUALTY OF THE DEVOLUTION REVOLUTION?

As originally enacted in 1994, the Violence Against Women Act (VAWA) allowed women to file civil lawsuits in federal court if they could prove that they were the victim of rape, domestic violence, or other crimes "motivated by gender." VAWA was widely praised as an effective mechanism to combat domestic violence. In its first five years, $1.6 million was allocated for states and local governments to pay for a variety of programs, including a national toll-free hotline for victims of violence that averages 13,000 calls per month, funding for special police sex crime units, and civil and legal assistance for women in need of restraining orders.[a] It also provided money to promote awareness of campus rape and domestic violence, to enhance reporting of crimes such as what is often termed "date rape."

Most of the early publicity surrounding the act stemmed from a challenge to one of its provisions. In 2000, five justices of the Supreme Court, including Sandra Day O'Connor, ruled that Congress had no authority under the commerce clause to provide a federal remedy to victims of gender-motivated violence, a decision viewed as greatly reining in congressional power.[b]

The suit brought by Christy Brzonkala was the first brought under the act's civil damages provision. While she was a student at Virginia Polytechnic Institute, Brzonkala alleged that two football players there raped her. After the university took no action against the students, she sued the school and the students. No criminal charges were ever filed in her case. The conservative federal appeals court in Richmond, Virginia—in contrast to contrary rulings in seventeen other

Christy Brzonkala, the petitioner in *U.S.* v. *Morrison.*
(Photo courtesy: Cindy Pinkston, January 1996)

courts—ruled that Congress had overstepped its authority because the alleged crimes were "within the exclusive purview of the states."[c] The Clinton administration and the National Organization for Women Legal Defense and Education Fund unsuccessfully appealed this decision to the Supreme Court.

---

[a]Juliet Eilperin, "Reauthorization of Domestic Violence Act Is at Risk," *Washington Post* (September 13, 2000): A6.
[b]*U.S.* v. *Morrison*, 529 U.S. 598 (2000).
[c]Tony Mauro, "Court Will Review Laws of Protection," *USA Today* (September 29, 1999): 4A.

---

v. *Flores* (1997), a majority of the Court ruled that sections of the Religious Freedom Restoration Act were unconstitutional because Congress lacked the authority to meddle in local zoning regulations, even if a church was involved.[46] In *Printz* v. *U.S.* (1997), again a 5–4 majority ruled that Congress lacked the authority to require local law enforcement officials to conduct background checks on handgun purchasers until the federal government was able to implement a national system.[47] In 1999, in another case involving sovereign immunity, a slim majority of the Supreme Court ruled that Congress lacked the authority to change patent laws in a manner that would negatively affect a state's right to assert its immunity from suit.[48]

The combined impact of all of these cases makes it clear that the Court will no longer countenance federal excursions into powers reserved to the states. (See On Campus: Legislating Against Violence Against Women.) As the power of Congress to legislate in a wide array of areas has been limited, the hands of the states have been strengthened.

In 2000, the Supreme Court's decision to stay a ruling of the Florida State Supreme Court ordering a manual recount of ballots surprised many observers, given the majority of the Court's reluctance over the last decade to interfere in areas historically left to the states. The Court's 5–4 decision in *Bush* v. *Gore* (2000),[49] which followed fairly observable liberal/conservative lines, was surprising in that justices normally opposed to federal intervention in state matters found that the Florida Supreme Court, which purportedly based its decisions solely on its interpretation of Florida law, violated federal law and the U.S. Constitution. Thus, the conservative, historically pro–states' rights majority used federal law to justify their decision. Their decision also had the effect of settling the election outcome in favor of George W. Bush, who is expected to appoint more conservative justices to tip the balance of the Court even further toward states' rights at the expense of national power.

Participation

Is Federalism
Dead and
Should It Be?

Continuity & Change

Taxing Sales on the Internet

One of the catalysts for the colonists' revolt against England was the king's imposition of taxes on a variety of goods, including tea. This taxation triggered a colonial boycott and the Boston Tea Party. Although the government under the Articles of Confederation was weak, in part, because of the new government's inability to raise funds, the new Constitution drafted in Philadelphia allowed for no personal income taxes and a limited ability to tax goods and services. While the Sixteenth Amendment eventually gave the national government the ability to tax individuals, the federal government still lacks the constitutional authority to impose a tax on the sale of products. This right, since it was not an enumerated right of the federal government in the new Constitution, was left to the states. Thus, today, the sales of a wide array of goods and services are treated quite differently by 7,500 individual states and taxing jurisdictions around the United States.[50]

Is orange juice a fruit or a beverage, for example? In one state, orange juice is considered a fruit and taxed, but in another, it is a beverage and not taxed. Similarly, in some states, if you board your dog or cat in a kennel, you pay a tax on that service. In most others, you do not. Sales taxes on goods and services provide states with a significant proportion of their revenue. While some states such as Texas and Florida don't have taxes on personal income, all states tax some sales items.

States recently are claiming that they lose billions in revenue from what are termed remote sales. A report by the Institute for State Studies estimates that between 2002 and 2011, states will lose $440 billion in uncollected sales revenues, creating serious shortfalls in budgets for schools, education, and policing, among others.[51]

State governors are banding together to get some assistance from Congress to stop the loss of e-commerce dollars, which has occurred because Congress, in an effort to encourage Internet use, put a moratorium on the states' ability to collect Internet access taxes. In addition, although states can tax sales on all online purchases, the states are prohibited from requiring remote sellers to collect those taxes and forward them to the appropriate state treasuries. Thus, online and catalogue merchants have a significant advantage over stores on Main Street USA. As sales tax revenues plummet, wreaking havoc with their budgets, the governors continue to ask Congress to give them back control of these interstate transactions, to no avail.

CAST YOUR VOTE Should states be allowed to tax items purchased on the Internet? If Congress continues its moratorium, is it a repudiation of the Framers' intentions? To cast your vote, go to
www.ablongman.com/oconnor

SUMMARY

The inadequacies of the confederate form of government created by the Articles of Confederation led the Framers to create an entirely new, federal system of government. From the summer of 1776 until today, the tension between the national and state governments has been at the core of our federal system. In describing the origins of that tension and the renewed debate about the role of the national government in the federal system, we have made the following points:

1. The Roots of the Federal System
The Framers created a federal system to replace the confederate form of government that had existed under the Articles of Confederation.

2. The Powers of Government in the Federal System
The national government has both enumerated and implied powers, and also exercises concurrent powers with the states. Certain powers are denied to both the state and national governments. Certain guarantees concerning representation in Congress and protection

against foreign attacks and domestic rebellion were made to the states in return for giving up some of their powers in the new federal system. Despite limitations, the national government is ultimately supreme.

3. **The Evolution and Development of Federalism**
Over the years, the powers of the national government have increased tremendously at the expense of the states. The Supreme Court, in particular, has played a key role in defining the relationship and powers of the national government through its broad interpretations of the supremacy and commerce clauses. For many years, however, it adhered to the notion of dual federalism, which tended to limit the national government's authority in areas such as slavery and, after the Civil War, civil rights. This notion of a limited role for the national government in some spheres ultimately fell by the wayside after the Great Depression.

The rapid creation of New Deal programs to alleviate many problems caused by the Depression led to a tremendous expansion of the federal government through the growth of federal services and grant-in-aid programs. This growth escalated during the Johnson administration and in the mid to late 1970s. After his election in 1980, Ronald Reagan, upset by the growth of federal services, tried to reverse the tide through what he termed New Federalism. He built on earlier efforts by Richard M. Nixon to consolidate categorical grants into fewer block grant programs, and to give state and local governments greater control over programs. Since 1995, the national government and the states have been in a constant dialogue to reframe the structure of the federal/state relationship.

4. **Federalism and the Supreme Court**
Over the years, the Supreme Court has been a major player in changing trends in the federal/state relationship. Historically, its decisions in the areas of education, the electoral process, and the performance of state functions gave the federal government a wide role in the day-to-day functioning of the states, and limited the scope of the states' police powers. Since the Reagan-Bush era, however, the Supreme Court has been willing to draw the line on congressional power and return important powers to the states while limiting Congress's authority to legislate in areas it believes are the responsibility of the states.

KEY TERMS

SELECTED READINGS

Bowman, Ann O'M., and Richard C. Kearney. *State and Local Government*, 4th ed. Boston: Houghton Mifflin, 1999.

Conlan, Timothy J. *From New Federalism to Devolution: Twenty-Five Years of Intergovernmental Reform*. Washington, DC: Brookings Institution, 1998.

Derthick, Martha. *The Influence of Federal Grants*. Cambridge, MA: Harvard University Press, 1970.

Elazar, Daniel J., and John Kincaid, eds. *The Covenant Connection: From Federal Theology to Modern Federalism*. Lexington, MA: Lexington Books, 2000.

Feingold, Kenneth, and Theda Skocpol. *State and Party in America's New Deal*. Madison: University of Wisconsin Press, 1995.

Gillespie, Ed, and Bob Schellhas, eds. *Contract with America*. New York: Times Books, 1994.

Grodzins, Morton. *The American System*. Chicago: Rand McNally, 1966.

Kenyon, Daphne A., and John Kincaid, eds. *Competition Among States and Local Governments*. Washington, DC: Urban Institute Press, 1991.

McCabe, Neil Colman, ed. *Comparative Federalism in the Devolution Era*. Lanham, MD: Rowman and Littlefield, 2002.

Nagel, Robert F. *The Implosion of American Federalism*. New York: Oxford University Press, 2001.

Ostrom, Vincent. *The Meaning of Federalism*. New York: Institute for Contemporary Studies, 1999.

Riker, William H. *Federalism: Origin, Operation, Significance*. Boston: Little, Brown, 1964.

Rivlin, Alice M. *Reviving the American Dream: The Economy, the States, and the Federal Government*. Washington, DC: Brookings Institution, 1993.

Walker, David B. *The Rebirth of Federalism*. Chatham, NJ: Chatham House, 1994.

Zimmerman, Joseph F. *Interstate Relations: The Neglected Dimension of Federalism*. New York: Praeger, 1996.

NOTES

1. Susan Page, "Suddenly, 'Era of Big Government Is Not Over,'" *USA Today* (October 1, 2001): 4A.
2. Ibid.
3. *Public Opinion Online*, Accession Number 0293831, Question Number 006.
4. In *City of Burbank* v. *Lockheed Air Terminal*, 411 U.S. 624 (1973), the U.S. Supreme Court ruled that the city could not impose curfews on plane takeoff or landing times. The Court said that one uniform national standard was critical for safety and the national interest.
5. *Missouri* v. *Holland*, 252 U.S. 416 (1920).
6. *McCulloch* v. *Maryland*, 17 U.S. 316 (1819).
7. *Saenz* v. *Roe*, 526 U.S. 489 (1999).
8. Ibid.
9. Joan Biskupic, "New-Resident Limits on Welfare Rejected," *Washington Post* (May 18, 1999): A1.
10. Oral argument in *Baker by Thomas* v. *General Motors Corporation*, 522 U.S. 222 (1998), noted in Linda Greenhouse, "Court Weighs Whether One State Must Obey Another's Courts," *New York Times* (October 16, 1997): A25.
11. Catherine F. Klein, "Full Faith and Credit: Interstate Enforcement of Protection Orders Under the Violence Against Women Act of 1994," *Family Law Quarterly* 29 (1995): 253.
12. Nancy Plevin, "Ohio Frees Indian-Rights Activist 'Little Rock' Reed," *Santa Fe New Mexican* (March 12, 1999): B1.
13. *New Mexico* ex rel. *Ortiz* v. *Reed*, 524 U.S. 151 (1998).
14. *New Jersey* v. *New York*, 523 U.S. 767 (1998).
15. John Mountjoy, Council of State Governments, "Interstate Cooperation: Interstate Compacts Make a Comeback" (Spring 2001), 3.
16. *McCulloch* v. *Maryland*, 17 U.S. 316 (1819).
17. *Gibbons* v. *Ogden*, 22 U.S. 1 (1824).
18. *Lane County* v. *Oregon*, 74 U.S. 71 (1869).
19. 163 U.S. 537 (1896).
20. *Panhandle Oil Co.* v. *Knox*, 277 U.S. 218, 223 (1928).
21. *Indian Motorcycle Co.* v. *U.S.*, 238 U.S. 570 (1931).
22. *Pensacola Telegraph* v. *Western Union*, 96 U.S. 1 (1877).
23. *U.S.* v. *E. C. Knight*, 156 U.S. 1 (1895).
24. Christopher Cox, "The 16th Amendment Is the Most Invasive Intrusion by the Government into Citizens' Lives," *Los Angeles Times* (June 20, 1995): B7.
25. John O. McGinnis, "The State of Federalism," Testimony before the Senate Government Affairs Committee, May 5, 1999.
26. 301 U.S. 1 (1937).
27. *U.S.* v. *Darby Lumber Co.*, 312 U.S. 100 (1941).
28. *Wickard* v. *Filburn*, 317 U.S. 111 (1942).
29. Morton Grodzins, "Centralization and Decentralization in the American Federal System," in Robert A. Goldwin, ed., *A Nation of States* (Chicago: Rand McNally, 1963), 3–4.
30. Alice M. Rivlin, *Reviving the American Dream* (Washington, DC: Brookings Institution, 1992), 92.
31. Rivlin, *Reviving the American Dream*, 98.
32. Richard P. Nathan et al., *Reagan and the States* (Princeton, NJ: Princeton University Press, 1987), 4.
33. This discussion of preemption relies heavily on Joseph F. Zimmerman, *Contemporary American Federalism: The Growth of National Power* (New York: Praeger, 1992), 55–81.
34. "Devolutionary Thinking Is Now Part of a Larger Critique of Modern Governmental Experience," *Public Perspective* (April/May 1995): 28.
35. Richard Wolf, "States Bracing for Leaner Times," *USA Today* (July 10, 2000): 1A.
36. Haya El Nasser, "Red Ink Overtakes State Budgets," *USA Today* (December 10, 2001): 3A.
37. *Harper* v. *Virginia Board of Elections*, 383 U.S. 663 (1966).
38. 469 U.S. 528 (1985).
39. Marianne Arneberg, "Cuomo Assails Judicial Hodgepodge," *Newsday* (August 15, 1990): 15.
40. 492 U.S. 490 (1989).
41. 505 U.S. 833 (1992).
42. *Stenberg* v. *Carhart*, 530 U.S. 914 (2000).
43. 514 U.S. 549 (1995).
44. 514 U.S. 779 (1995).
45. *Seminole Tribe* v. *Florida*, 517 U.S. 44 (1996).
46. 521 U.S. 507 (1997).
47. 521 U.S. 898 (1997).
48. *Florida Prepaid* v. *College Savings Bank*, 527 U.S. 627 (1999).
49. 531 U.S. 98 (2000).
50. National Governors Association, "The Streamlined Sales Tax Project Answers the Question," http://www.nga.org/salestax/1,1169.,00.html.
51. National Governors Association, "New Report Shows States to Lose Nearly $440 Billion in Sales Tax Revenue from Remote Sales," http://www.nga.org/newsRoom/1,1169.C_Press_Release^D_2653,00,00.html.

State and Local Government

A fire broke out in a bakery in a neighborhood near downtown Kansas City in 1998. It destroyed or badly damaged nine buildings before firefighters were able to extinguish the flames. Demolition crews moved in quickly to clean up the debris. They had to quit without finishing their work, however. They ran into layers of asbestos and two large underground storage tanks and had to leave for their own safety. For over two years, the area was an abandoned pile of bricks and burnt concrete.

Kansas City was, of course, eager to see this area cleaned and rebuilt. This was a prime location for business. Instead, the eyesore was prompting other businesses to move to the suburbs. The city was losing tax money because the property damaged by the fire was vacant, and it was in jeopardy of losing more if other stores closed. So why was the city not moving to deal with this issue?

The damaged property, with the asbestos and underground storage tanks, is a brownfield—property with environmental contamination. The cleanup itself is hazardous, and anyone who owns a brownfield is liable for any health problems that might occur even after the cleanup is completed. Like other cities, Kansas City can target areas in its jurisdiction for redevelopment by issuing building permits, zoning the land for certain uses, and offering tax breaks. However, the city cannot do anything about liability issues, and it lacks the funds needed for the expense of cleaning up a hazardous site.

Fortunately, Kansas City Mayor Kay Barnes (shown in the photo here) was successful in getting the help she needed from the Missouri State government.[1] Although hazardous cleanups are covered under federal law, the U.S. Environmental Protection Agency has been letting states take responsibility for enforcement. Missouri passed legislation exempting property owners from liability of a former brownfield and, with the federal government, gave Kansas City $5.6 million for cleaning the area. In late 2002, businesses were moving back into the area, revitalizing the community and restoring the city's tax base.

*G*overnance in the United States is by multiple authorities, sometimes in conflict with one another and sometimes in harmony. Some cities in California and Pennsylvania that tried to follow the Kansas City model of dealing with brownfields were not so lucky. Their efforts were complicated because of resistance by other local governments—water and sewerage districts and separate, small towns that have been engulfed in the metropolitan area.

The relationships among the various governments in our country are dynamic. The legal authority, the financial resources, and the political will of the federal government, state and municipal governments, tribal governments, school districts, water districts, and all the other public bodies are constantly changing. On the one hand, this provides groups and individuals with many points of access to government. On the other hand, the multiple, changing jurisdictions that govern our society can be a challenging puzzle, so complex that in effect citizens will have very little access and influence.

This chapter will present the basic patterns and principles of state and local governance so that you might readily understand how public policies in your community are made and applied.

- First, we will review the *evolution of state and local governments.*
- Second, we will identify the nature of *grassroots power and politics.*
- Third, we will describe the *development of state constitutions* and the major institutions of *state governments*, including trends in state elections.
- Fourth, we will examine the different types of *local governments* and explain the bases for their authority as well as the special traits of their institutions.
- Fifth, we will discuss relationships between federal and state governments and the *Indian nations.*
- Sixth, we will explain the budgeting process for state and local *finances.*
- In our exploration of the theme of *continuity and change* in American government, we will review how the importance of state and local governments has been rediscovered and revitalized.

THE EVOLUTION OF STATE AND LOCAL GOVERNMENTS

As pointed out in chapter 3, the basic, original unit of government in this country was the state. The thirteen colonial governments became thirteen state governments and their constitutions preceded the U.S. Constitution. The states initially were loosely tied together in the Articles of Confederation but then formed a closer union and more powerful national government.

State governments, likewise, determined the existence of local governments. As we will later discuss in more detail, in some cases—such as counties and, for most states, school districts—state laws *create* local governments. In others, such as towns and cities, states *recognize* and *authorize* local governments in response to petitions from citizens.

In other words, governance in the United States is not built from the bottom. Local communities do not form states, which then form the United States. Instead, states are the basic units, which on the one hand establish local governments and on the other hand are the building blocks of the federal government.

In the past, state and local governments were primarily part-time governments. This has changed somewhat, but it will never change entirely. Initially, almost all state and local elected officials were part-time. Except for governors and a handful of big-city mayors, people in office were farmers, teachers, lawyers, and shop owners who did public service during their spare time. This was true as well for many judges and local government bureaucrats.

BAKER V. CARR (1962)

State governments have increased with capacity to govern in a dramatic and steady manner since the mid-1960s. A major reason for this is the implementation of the U.S. Supreme Court decision in *Baker* v. *Carr* in 1962. As in most states, Tennessee's legislature had not revised the boundaries of the districts from which lawmakers were elected as urban areas grew. The result was that one legislator from a rural district might represent 700 people while a legislator from an urban area would have 27,000 constituents. The Supreme Court ruled that state legislative boundaries had to be drawn to apply the principle of one-person, one-vote. In other words, the Court realized that rural votes in Tennessee had more impact than urban votes. It mandated that each legislative district within a state have about the same number of people.

The end of rural overrepresentation in state legislatures meant that state governments treated the concerns and issues of everyone throughout the state seriously. States became relevant policy makers. Individuals who seriously wanted to perform public service found state governments attractive. State legislatures and administrative agencies became more professional.

Baker v. *Carr* demonstrated that the democratic principle of one-person, one-vote is important not only for representation, but for professionalism and competence.

As the responsibilities and challenges of government grew, more state and local officials became full-time. Increases in the need for urban services led to more full-time local governments. Likewise, states with high levels of urbanization, industrialization, and economic development needed larger, more professional, and full-time legislatures, courts, and administrative agencies. These states did not, however, always get their needs met. The boundaries of districts from which state legislators got elected did not change in response to population shifts in the post–Civil War period. As a result, state legislatures did not represent the character of their respective states. One legislator from a rural area might represent 50,000 people, whereas a legislator from an urban setting may represent as many as 500,000 constituents. Such a pattern led to low priority for urban needs.

This kind of misrepresentation remained in place until the 1960s. The 1962 ruling by the U.S. Supreme Court in *Baker* v. *Carr* became watershed in the evolution of state and local governments. The Court applied the Fourteenth Amendment to the U.S. Constitution and decreed that equal protection and the **one-person, one-vote** principles required that there be the same number of people in each of the legislative districts within a single state. As a result, state legislatures became more representative, and the agendas of state governments became much more relevant than they had been. This in turn attracted more professional and serious individuals to seek administrative and elective positions in state governments.

The 1960s and 1970s were a period in which the federal government added both to the responsibilities and to the competence of state and local governments. Federal programs to combat poverty, revitalize urban areas, and protect the environment were designed to be administered by state and local officials rather than federal agencies. With this came assistance and sometimes mandates to improve the capacities of subnational governments.

Since the 1980s, some trends in federalism have enhanced the importance of state and local governments. Conscious efforts since the Nixon administration were made to reverse the aggregation of power and authority in Washington, D.C. In part, this was philosophical, but it was also necessary. The federal government found itself unable to expand or even to maintain its presence in domestic policy areas. During the Reagan administration, the debt of the federal government more than tripled, and there was no choice but to cut severely the flow of federal money and mandates that fueled much of the growth of state and local governments.

one-person, one-vote
The principle that each legislative district within a state should have the same number of eligible voters so that representation is equitably based on population.

In 1995, the U.S. Supreme Court placed limitations on the federal government and reasserted the importance of state and local governments. This is best reflected in *U.S. v. Lopez*, where the Court ruled that Congress and the president did not have authority to require the establishment of gun-free zones around local schools and that it was a matter for state and local governments. The Court left open, however, the commonly used option of the federal government attaching conditions states had to meet to receive federal funds. This power had previously been affirmed in *South Dakota* v. *Dole* (1987), in which the Court said it was permissible for the federal government to require states that wanted transportation funds to pass laws setting twenty-one as the legal age for drinking. Congress and the president nonetheless seemed inclined to eliminate strings and to give state and local governments more discretion. For example, they removed the requirement that states have certain speed limits in order to receive federal transportation funds and gave local governments more leeway in determining how they would meet clean water standards.

But, as noted in chapter 3, not all recent developments have enhanced the powers of state and local governments. In 2002, President George W. Bush signed a law that allows the federal government to force state and local authorities to turn over public schools to private businesses to manage if the schools are considered to be failing. In response to the terrorist attacks of September 11, 2001, the federal government expanded its role in domestic security, traditionally the responsibility of state and local police and public health officials.

Despite the conflicting messages, it is still clear that state and local governments have roles and responsibilities of increasing importance. For the most part, these jurisdictions relish these developments. Some states and cities, for example, are taking bold initiatives and even establishing direct ties with other countries in order to spur economic growth.[2] Others, especially in smaller and medium-sized communities, are overwhelmed with all there is to do.

The heroic work of New York City firefighters and rescue workers in response to the terrorist attack on September 11, 2001, was a vivid reminder of the importance of employees of local governments. We depend heavily on state and local agencies for our safety and for services that affect our daily living.

(Photo courtesy: © Gilles Peres)

GRASSROOTS POWER AND POLITICS

The most powerful and influential people in a state or community are not necessarily those who hold offices in government. While there is always a distinction between formal and informal power, the face-to-face character of governance at the grassroots level almost invites informal ties and influence. The part-time officials in particular have a more ambiguous identity than do full-time government officials.

In small to medium-sized communities, it is common for a single family or a traditional elite to be the major decision maker, whether or not one of their members has a formal governmental position.[3] Another frequent pattern is where the owners or managers of the major business in town dominate public decision making. If you want to advocate for some improvements in a local park, a curriculum change in the schools, or a different set of priorities for the police department, it may be more important to get the support of a few key community leaders than the sympathy of the village president or the head of the school board. A newcomer interested in starting a business in a town likewise would be well advised to identify and court the informal elite and not just focus on those who hold a formal office.

Political participation in state and, especially, local politics is both more personal and more issue-oriented than at the national level. Much of what happens is outside the framework of political parties. Elections for some state and local government offices, in fact, are **nonpartisan elections,** which means parties do not nominate candidates and ballots do not include any party identification of those running for office. Access and approaches are usually direct. School board members receive phone calls at their homes. Members of the city council and county board bump into constituents while shopping for groceries or cheering their children in youth sports. The concerns that are communicated tend to be specific and neither partisan nor ideological: A particular grade school teacher is unfair and ineffective; playground equipment is unsafe; it seems to be taking forever for the city to issue a building permit so that you can get started on a remodeling project.

In this setting, local news media invariably play a key role. The major newspaper in the state and what might be the only newspaper in a community can shape the agendas of government bodies and the images of government officials. The mere fact that a problem is covered makes it an issue. If gang or cult activity is just a group of kids acting weird and dressing the same way, public officials might ignore it. News coverage of this or certainly of a violent incident, on the other hand, assures attention. Then the question is how the media define the issue—as an isolated and unusual event or as a signal that certain needs are not being met? Is a brownfield a health hazard or an opportunity for revitalization?

State governments have enhanced the role of reporters by enacting **sunshine laws,** which open meetings and records in government to the public. Perhaps appropriately, Florida—the Sunshine State—passed the first sunshine law in 1967. All fifty states quickly followed suit. The intent of these laws was to ensure access to government to the public, but the major effect has been to make it easier for the news media to cover state and local governments.

Ad hoc, issue-specific organizations are prevalent in state and local governments.[4] Individuals opposed to the plans of a state department of transportation to expand a stretch of highway from two to four lanes will organize, raise funds, and lobby hard to stop the project. Once the project is stopped or completed, that organization will go out of existence. Likewise, neighbors will organize to support or oppose specific development projects or to press for revitalization assistance, and then they will disband once the decision is made. The sporadic but intense activity focused on specific local or regional concerns is an important supplement to the ongoing work of parties and interest groups in state and local governments. A full understanding of what happens at the grass roots requires an appreciation of ad hoc, issue-specific politics as well as the institutions and processes through which state and local governments make and implement public policies.

nonpartisan election
A contest in which candidates run without formal identification or association with a political party.

sunshine law
Legislation that requires government meetings and records to be open to the public.

Specific issues arise from the grass-roots to make their way onto the agendas of state and local governments. Residents in West Virginia are grateful for the jobs provided by mining but object to mining techniques that remove tops from their mountains and fill valleys with waste.

(Photo courtesy: Bob Bird/AP/Wide World Photos)

STATE GOVERNMENTS

State governments have primary responsibility for education, public health, transportation, economic development, and criminal justice. States also are the unit of government that licenses and regulates various professions, such as doctors, lawyers, barbers, and architects. More recently, state governments have been active in welfare and the environment, in part as agents administering federal policies and programs and in part on their own.

State officials, in other words, have been and continue to be in charge of fundamental components of our society. They have also been challenged with problems that seem to defy solutions. Crime, for example, seems to be beyond our ability to do more than try to minimize it. Poverty is another such challenge. Likewise, we have not been fully satisfied with our efforts to provide appropriate high-quality education for every child. Despite these awesome responsibilities, there has been a historic reluctance to make state governments fully capable institutions.

State Constitutions

Whereas a major goal of the writers of the U.S. Constitution in 1787 was to *empower* the national government, the authors of the original **state constitutions** wanted to *limit* government. The Constitutional Convention in Philadelphia was convened, as you recall from chapter 2, because of the perception that the national government under the Articles of Confederation was not strong enough. The debates were primarily over how strong the national, or federal, government should be.

In contrast, the assumption of the authors of the first thirteen state constitutions, based on their backgrounds in the philosophy and experiences of monarchical rule, was that government was all-powerful, and so the question was how to limit it. The state constitutions were written and adopted before the Philadelphia Convention and included provisions that government may not interfere with basic individual liberties.

WEB EXPLORATION
To find statistics on any branch of government in the fifty states, see
www.ablongman.com/oconnor

state constitution
The document that describes the basic policies, procedures, and institutions of the government of a specific state, much as the U.S. Constitution does for the federal government.

These provisions, which were *integral* parts of each of the state constitutions, were *added* to the federal constitution as the first ten amendments, often called the Bill of Rights.

The first state constitutions provided for the major institutions of government, such as governors, legislatures, and courts, with an emphasis on limiting the authority of each institution.[5] These constitutions did not, however, fully embrace the principle of checks and balances that is found in the U.S. Constitution. The office of governor was particularly weak. Not surprisingly, the most powerful institution was the legislature. In fact, initially only South Carolina, New York, and Massachusetts gave their governors the authority to veto legislation.

The first state constitutions set the pattern for what was to come. In one of its last actions, the national Congress under the Articles of Confederation passed the Northwest Ordinance of 1787, which addressed how new states might join the Union. Lawmakers were responding primarily to settlers in what is now Ohio but extended coverage to the territory that includes Wisconsin, Illinois, Michigan, and Indiana—which the people in the original states considered the "northwest." The basic blueprint included in the ordinance was that a territory might successfully petition for statehood if it had at least 60,000 free inhabitants (slaves and American Indians did not count) and a constitution that was both similar to the documents of existing states and compatible with the national constitution. The first white settlers in the territory covered by the Northwest Ordinance were originally from New York and Massachusetts, with some individuals and families direct from Europe. Not surprisingly, the initial constitutions of these states were almost identical to those of New York and Massachusetts.[6]

The traumas of slavery and the Civil War had a profound impact on the constitutions of southern states. Events that led to the secession of southern states included the Missouri Compromise of 1820–1821, which simultaneously admitted Missouri and Maine, the former with a constitution that legalized slavery and the latter as a "free state." The Missouri Compromise also included an agreement that no more states would be admitted that had constitutions allowing slavery. When, in 1854, that provision was violated by the admission of Kansas as a slave state and Nebraska as a free state, the confrontation between the two sides escalated.[7]

Slavery was a unique and very emotional issue. It raised the general question of the extent to which the national Congress could insist on specific clauses in state constitutions. The Civil War, of course, answered that question. That war also precipitated an era in which the states in the Confederacy wrote and discarded constitutions at a rapid pace and ended the process with documents that established state governments that were even weaker than those of the first thirteen states.

Southern states adopted new constitutions when they seceded and formed the Confederacy. After the Civil War, they had to adopt new constitutions acceptable to the Congress in Washington, D.C. These constitutions typically provided former slaves with considerable power and disenfranchised those who had been active in the Confederacy. These were not realistic constitutions. They divorced political power from economic wealth and social status, formal authority from informal influence. White communities simply ignored government and ruled themselves informally as much as possible. After less than ten years of this, whites reasserted political control and rewrote state constitutions.

The new documents reflected white distrust and provided for a narrow scope of authority for state governments and for weak, fragmented institutions. Governors could serve for only two-year terms. Legislatures could only meet for short periods of time and in some cases only once every other year. Law enforcement authority, both police and justices of the peace, rested squarely in local community power structures.

Western states entered the Union with constitutions that also envisioned weak governments. Here the central concerns were not slavery or national government interference, but rather political machines. In large cities in the Northeast and Midwest, machines based on bloc voting by new, non-English-speaking immigrants wrested political control and, sometimes in corrupt ways, began amassing economic wealth.

Progressive movement
Advocated measures to destroy political machines and instead have direct participation by voters in the nomination of candidates and the establishment of public policy.

New states in the West sought to keep machine politics from ever getting started in the first place.

The most effective national anti-machine effort was the **Progressive movement,** led by such figures as Woodrow Wilson, Theodore Roosevelt, Robert M. La Follette, and Hiram Johnson, who advocated changes that involved direct voter participation and bypassed traditional institutions.[8] These reforms included the use of primaries for nominating candidates instead of closed party processes, the initiative for allowing voters to enact laws directly rather than go through legislatures and governors, and the recall for constituents to remove officials from office in the middle of their term. Progressives succeeded in getting their proposals adopted as statutes in existing states and in the constitutions of new states emerging from western territories.

Though weak state government institutions may have been a reasonable response to earlier concerns, they are inappropriate for current issues. The trend since the 1960s, throughout the United States, has been to amend state constitutions in order to enhance the capacity of governors, legislatures, and courts to address problems. In the 1970s alone, over 300 amendments to state constitutions were adopted. Most were to lengthen the terms of governors and provide chief executives with more authority over spending and administration, to streamline courts, and to make legislatures professional and full-time.[9] Constitutional changes have reflected some ambivalence. While there has been recognition that state governments must be more capable, reforms have included severe restrictions on the ability of state and local governments to raise taxes and limits on how long legislators in some states might serve.

States sometimes change their constitutions in response to current policy concerns. In response to a ruling by the Massachusetts Supreme Court, eleven states voted in the November 2004 elections to ban gay marriages. A dozen other states initiated the same change, but the process for amending their constitutions took too long to get on the 2004 ballot.

As compared with the U.S. Constitution, state constitutions are relatively easy to amend. Every state allows for the convening of a constitutional convention, and over 200 have been held. Also, every state has a process whereby the legislature can pass an amendment to the constitution, usually by a two-thirds or three-fourths vote, and then submit the change to the voters for their approval in a referendum. Seventeen states, mostly in the West, allow for amendments simply by getting the proposal on a statewide ballot, without involvement of the legislature or governor.

An implication of the relatively simple amendment processes is frequent changes. All but nineteen states have adopted wholly new constitutions since they were first admitted, and almost 6,000 specific amendments have been adopted. Another effect of the process is that state constitutions include provisions that more appropriately should be statutes or administrative rules. The California constitution, for example, not only establishes state government institutions and protects individual rights, but also defines how long a wrestling match may be. Clearly, these are details that do not belong in a constitution.

Participation

Explore Your State Constitution

Governors

Governors have always been the most visible elected officials in state governments. Initially, that visibility supported the ceremonial role of governors as their primary function. Now that visibility serves governors as they set the agenda and provide leadership for others in state governments. (See Figure 4.1.)

The most important role that current governors play is in identifying the most pressing problems facing their respective states and proposing solutions to those problems. Governors first establish agendas when they campaign for office. After inauguration, the most effective way for the chief executive to initiate policy changes is when submitting the budget for legislative approval.

Budgets are critical to the business of state governments. The ways in which money is raised and spent say a lot about the priorities of decision makers. Until the 1920s, state legislatures commonly compiled and passed budgets and then submitted them for

governor
Chief elected executive in state government.

WEB EXPLORATION
To learn about issues that governors nationwide deem most important, see www.ablongman.com/oconnor

FIGURE 4.1   Party of State Governors, 2002

Democrats made gains in the 2002 elections and there is now an even distribution of governors between the two major parties.

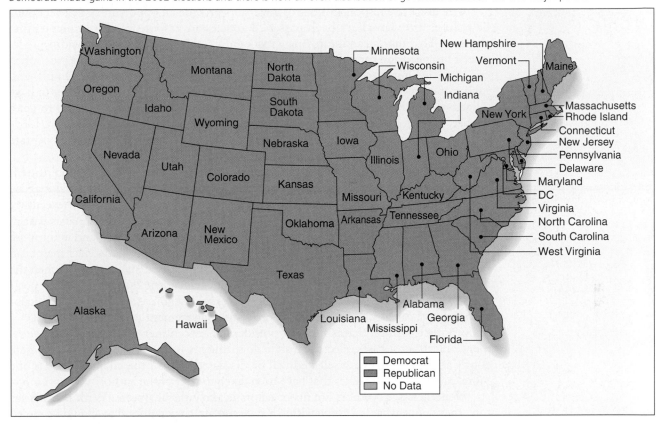

Source: http://www.ncsl.org/statevote2002/govParty_post2002.htm.

gubernatorial approval or veto. As part of the efforts to strengthen the capacities of state governments, governors were, like presidents, given the major responsibility for starting the budget process. Now all but four states have their governors propose budgets.

The role of governor as budget initiator is especially important when coupled with the governor's veto authority and executive responsibilities. Like presidents, governors also have **package** or **general veto** authority, which rejects a bill in its entirety. In addition, governors in all but seven states may exercise a **line-item veto** on bills that involve spending or taxing. A line-item veto strikes only part of a bill that has been passed by the legislature. It allows a chief executive to delete a particular program or expenditure from a budget bill and let the remaining provisions become law. The intent of this authority is to enable governors to revise the work of legislators in order to produce a balanced budget.

When Tommy Thompson was governor of Wisconsin, he was the most extensive and creative user of the line-item veto. He reversed the intent of legislation by vetoing the word "not" in a sentence and created entirely new laws by eliminating specific letters and numerals to make new words and numbers. Voters in Wisconsin were so upset with this free use of the veto pen that in 1993 they passed the "Vanna White amendment" to the state constitution, prohibiting the governor from striking letters within words and numerals within numbers. Not to be outmaneuvered, Governor Thompson then used his veto authority to actually *insert* new words and numbers in bills that had passed the legislature. The Wisconsin state supreme court, in 1995, upheld this interpretation of veto, as long as the net effect of the vetoes was not to increase spending.

While the Wisconsin case is extreme, it illustrates the significant power that veto authority can provide. Legislators can override vetoes, usually with a two-thirds vote in

package or general veto
The authority of a chief executive to void an entire bill that has been passed by the legislature. This veto applies to all bills, whether or not they have taxing or spending components, and the legislature may override this veto, usually with a two-thirds majority of each chamber.

line-item veto
The authority of a chief executive to delete part of a bill passed by the legislature that involves taxing and/or spending. The legislature may override a veto, usually with a two-thirds majority of each chamber.

each of the chambers, but this rarely happens. Only 6 percent of gubernatorial vetoes are overturned.[10]

The executive responsibilities of governors provide an opportunity to affect public policies after laws have been passed. Agencies are responsible for implementing the laws. That may mean improving a road, enforcing a regulation, or providing a service. The speed and care with which implementation occurs are often under the influence of the governor.[11] Likewise, governors can affect the many details and interpretations that must be decided. State statutes require drivers of vehicles to have a license, but they typically let an agency decide exactly what one must do to get a license, where one can take the tests, and what happens if someone fails a test. Governors can influence these decisions primarily through appointing the heads of state administrative agencies.

One of the methods of limiting gubernatorial power is to curtail appointment authority.[12] Unlike the federal government, for example, states have some major agencies headed by individuals who are elected rather than appointed by the chief executive. Forty-three states, for example, elect their attorney general, a position that is part of the president's Cabinet. The positions of secretary of state, treasurer, and auditor are also usually filled by elected rather than appointed officials. Some states elect their head of education, agriculture, or labor. The movement throughout states to strengthen the institutions of their governments has included increasing the number of senior positions that are filled by gubernatorial appointments so that governors, like heads of major corporations, can assemble their own policy and management teams.

Another position that is filled by presidential appointment in the federal government but, in most cases, elected in state governments is judge. The structure of state courts and how judges are selected will be discussed later in the chapter. This is one more example of approaches that have been taken to restrict the authority of governors.

Nonetheless, governors are major actors in the judicial system. With the legislature, they define what is a crime within a state and attach penalties that should be meted out to those convicted of committing crimes. Once someone has been convicted, they will be institutionalized and/or supervised by an agency that is, in every state, headed

As Governor of Minnesota, Tim Pawlenty has set an agenda that emphasizes getting high-quality teachers for public schools and solving fiscal problems without raising taxes.

(Photo courtesy: Marty Lederhandler/AP/Wide World Photos)

by a gubernatorial appointment. Moreover, governors have authority to grant a **pardon** to someone who has been convicted, thereby eliminating all penalties and wiping the court action from an individual's record. Governors may also **commute** all or part of a sentence, which leaves the conviction on record even though the penalty is reduced.

In addition, governors grant **parole** to prisoners who have served part of their terms. Typically, governors are advised by a parole board on whether or not to grant a parole. Paroles usually have conditions that must be met, such as staying in a certain area, avoiding contact with certain people or organizations, and participating in therapy or a work program. Violation of these conditions could mean a return to prison. Beginning in the mid-1990s, a number of states began eliminating parole and requiring convicts to serve their full sentences. This movement was known as "truth in sentencing."

Finally, under the U.S. Constitution, governors have the discretion to **extradite** individuals. This means that a governor may decide to send someone, against his or her will, to another state to face criminal charges. When Mario Cuomo, who opposed the death penalty, was governor of New York, he refused to extradite someone to a state that used capital punishment. That refusal became an issue in Governor Cuomo's unsuccessful bid for reelection in 1994. Shortly after he was inaugurated, the newly elected governor, George Pataki, ordered the extradition. In fact, with the support of Governor Pataki, New York adopted the death penalty.

Gubernatorial participation in the judicial process has led to some of the most colorful controversies in state politics. James E. Ferguson, as governor of Texas, granted 2,253 pardons between 1915 and 1917. His successor, William P. Hobby, granted 1,518 during the next two years, and then Governor Miriam "Ma" Ferguson outdid her husband by issuing almost 3,800 during her term. Texans were used to shady wheeling and dealing in politics, but this volume of pardons seemed a bit excessive. The Texas constitution was amended to remove authority to grant pardons and paroles from the governor; this power was placed in the hands of a board. Governors of the Lone Star State now have the lowest amount of authority among the fifty state chief executives to check actions of the judiciary.[13]

The general trend since the 1960s has been an increase rather than decrease in the power and authority of governors.[14] Given the historic desire to have weak chief executives, some of the enhancement of gubernatorial powers has come at the cost of the prerogatives of other institutions. This is particularly the case with veto authority and the role in the budgetary process. Capacity, however, has both absolute and relative dimensions. Legislatures and courts have also developed into more capable institutions since the 1960s.

State Legislatures

The principles of representative democracy are embodied primarily in the legislature. Legislatures, as mentioned above, were initially established to be the most powerful of the institutions of state government. In over half of the original states, legislatures began without the check of a gubernatorial veto. Until the twentieth century, most state legislatures were responsible for executive chores such as formulating a budget and making administrative appointments.

These tasks were, even more than was envisioned for the U.S. Congress, to be done by "citizen legislators" as a part-time responsibility. The image was that individuals would convene in the state capitol for short periods of time to conduct the state's business. State constitutions and statutes specified the part-time operation of the legislature and provided only limited compensation for those who served.

As mentioned earlier, the one-person, one-vote ruling of the U.S. Supreme Court in *Baker* v. *Carr* (1962) marked a turning point in the history of state legislatures, and state governments generally. Once legislatures more accurately represented their states, agendas became more relevant and policies were more appropriate.[15] State legislatures not only became more representative; they became more professional. Legislators

pardon
The authority of a governor to cancel someone's conviction of a crime by a court and to eliminate all sanctions and punishments resulting from the conviction.

commute
The action of a governor when he or she cancels all or part of the sentence of someone convicted of a crime, while keeping the conviction on the record.

parole
The authority of a governor to release a prisoner before his or her full sentence has been completed and to specify conditions that must be met as part of the release.

extradite
To send someone against his or her will to another state to face criminal charges.

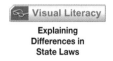

Visual Literacy

Explaining
Differences in
State Laws

worked more days—some of them full-time. In 1960, only eighteen state legislatures met annually. In 2002, forty-three met every year and only seven every other year. Moreover, the floor sessions were longer, and between sessions legislators and their staff increasingly did committee work and conducted special studies.[16]

Ideally, bills are drafted and votes are cast based on informed evaluations. Along with passing laws, legislatures must monitor and assess the activities of administrative agencies. Legislatures consider many initiatives for policy change. Almost 75 percent of the states occasionally force themselves to monitor the implementation of public policy by passing **sunset laws.** These laws state that a particular program or agency will end on a certain date unless the legislature passes a bill to extend it. Typically the legislature mandates that a study be completed before a program or agency is scheduled to end so that lawmakers have an evaluation upon which to base a decision to reauthorize, amend, or terminate.

To develop the capacity to provide oversight, conduct analyses, and serve constituents, state legislatures increased their staff by almost 130 percent between 1968 and 1974.[17] Growth since then has been at a rather steady 4 percent rate. Staff resources have been supplemented by the services of the National Conference of State Legislatures, established in 1973, and increasingly by computer technology and information sharing on the Internet. Like Congress, state legislatures have established library reference services and audit agencies to help serve their needs.

All states except Nebraska have two legislative houses. One, the senate, typically has fewer members than the other, usually called the "house" or the "assembly." The most common ratio between the two chambers is 1:3. In fourteen states the ratio is 1:2, and in New Hampshire it is 1:16. Another difference between the two bodies in thirty-four of the states is that senators serve four-year terms, whereas representatives in the larger house serve two-year terms. In eleven states, everyone in both houses serves two-year terms, and in the remaining, including Nebraska, everyone serves for four years.

Although it has been common to have limits on how many terms someone may serve as governor, **term limits** for legislators is a development of the 1980s and 1990s. By 2002, twenty-one states had passed measures limiting the number of years one might be a state legislator, but the courts in Massachusetts, Oregon, Washington and Wyoming ruled that term limits violated their states' constitutions. In 2002 Idaho's legislature repealed their law and in 2003 Utah followed suit. Depending on the state, limits vary between six and twelve years. (See Table 4.1.)

Proponents of term limits included minority party leaders who calculated—sometimes in error—that they stood a better chance of gaining seats if incumbents had to leave after a certain period of time. Others saw term limits as a way of making the ideal of citizen legislator more probable. They saw intuitive appeal in the concept of having people being a legislator in addition to whatever else they did in life, as opposed to pursuing a career as an elected official.[18]

The movement to limit legislative service is a contrast to the pattern that evolved since the *Baker* v. *Carr* ruling. With an end to rural overrepresentation, state legislatures became relevant and more capable. Urban and economic development issues got serious attention. State budgets included a wider array of programs. The wider scope of state issues, enhanced when the federal government shed some of its responsibilities to the states, attracted individuals seriously interested in public service and required increased staff to help with analysis and evaluation.

State legislatures, although much more capable and serious institutions than they were prior to the early 1960s, are still primarily part-time, citizen bodies.[19] Every election puts new members in about one-fourth of the seats. Only a handful of legislators in each state envision careers as state lawmakers. Those with long-term political aspirations tend to view service in a state chamber as a step on a journey to some other office, in the state capital or in Washington, D.C. For some, their goal is to don a black robe and preside in a courtroom.

sunset law
A law that sets a date for a program or regulation to expire unless reauthorized by the legislature.

WEB EXPLORATION
To learn about the policy issues being addressed in your state legislature, see www.ablongman.com/oconnor

term limits
Restrictions that exist in some states about how long an individual may serve in state and/or local elected offices.

TABLE 4.1   States with Term Limits

	House		Senate	
	Takes Effect	Limit (years)	Takes Effect	Limit (years)
Maine	1996	8	1996	8
California	1996	6	1998	8
Colorado	1998	8	1998	8
Arkansas	1998	6	2000	8
Michigan	1998	6	2002	8
Florida	2000	8	2000	8
Missouri*	2002	8	2002	8
Ohio	2000	8	2000	8
South Dakota	2000	8	2000	8
Montana	2000	8	2000	8
Arizona	2000	8	2000	8
Oklahoma	2004	12	2004	12
Nevada	2008	12	2008	12
Louisiana	2007	12	2007	12
Nebraska	n/a	n/a	2008	8

*Because of special elections, term limits were effective in 1998 for one senator and in 2001 for five House members.

Source: http://www.ncsl.org/programs/legman/about/termlimit.htm

State Courts

Almost everyone is in a courtroom at some point. It may be as a judge, a juror, an attorney, a court officer, or a litigant. It may also be for some administrative function like an adoption, a name change, or the implementation of a will. Few of us will ever be in a federal court; almost all of us will be in a state court.

The primary function of courts is to settle disputes, and most disputes are matters of state, not federal, laws. For the most part, criminal behavior is defined by state legislatures. Family law, dealing with marriage, divorce, adoption, child custody, and the like, is found in state statutes. Contracts, liability, land use, and much that is fundamental to everyday business activity and economic development also are part of state governance.

A common misunderstanding is that the courts in the United States are all part of a single system, with the U.S. Supreme Court at the head. In fact, state and federal courts are separate, with their own rules, procedures, and routes for appeal. The only time state and federal courts converge is when a case involves both federal and state laws or constitutions.

A famous example of overlap between state and federal courts was in 1994, when Los Angeles police officers arrested Rodney King for a traffic violation. An amateur photographer videotaped the arrest and captured shots of the police officers severely beating King. The officers were first tried in California state court for using excessive force. They convinced the jury that King was resisting and thus force was justified. Federal prosecutors nonetheless proceeded to try the officers for violating King's civil rights, a federal crime. In federal court, the jury convicted the officers.

Although the state and federal courts had essentially the same facts, the laws that applied here were somewhat different. The central question posed by state law was whether the police officers used more force than professionally acceptable. The issue focused on professional standards. The federal law centered on racial discrimination and Rodney King's civil rights. Here the racial slurs and jokes made by police officers weighed more heavily and were more relevant than for the state issue of whether excessive force was used.

GRADUATED DRIVER LICENSING

Once upon a time, young adults who were sixteen years old and could pass the required tests could get a driver's license. Now all but thirteen states have Graduated Driver Licensing (GDL) programs that put restrictions on those licenses. Specific provisions vary among the states, but generally new drivers may not drive unsupervised by an older adult for the first thirty to fifty hours after receiving their license, and even after that, they may not drive unsupervised between 10 P.M. and 5 A.M. In ten states, teenagers who drive may not have more than two passengers, and in another eight states, they may not have anyone (other than family members) younger than twenty years old in the car with them.[a]

State legislatures responded to parents, insurance companies, and the federal Department of Transportation's National Highway Traffic Safety Administration in passing GDL programs. Car crashes are the leading killer of teenagers. This age group has the highest accident rate of any cohort, and sixteen-year-olds crash more than twice as often as eighteen- and nineteen-year-olds. After North Carolina adopted GDL, it saw a 26 percent drop in crashes involving sixteen-year-olds. Michigan noted a 31 percent decrease, and in Kentucky it was 32 percent.[b] These are impressive records.

But, placing restrictions on novice drivers has also met opposition. Opponents argue that it is not fair for all sixteen-year-olds to have limits because some are bad drivers. Some families need help from their new drivers, and the GDL rules limit young drivers' abilities to share driving responsibilities without supervision. Those in rural areas, often without access to public transportation, have been particularly unhappy with GDL legislation. In some states, the restrictions are stricter than what many states use as punishments for those convicted of drunk driving.

Despite these arguments, legislators in thirty-seven states were persuaded to place conditions on young drivers. Lawmakers in the remaining states are considering adopting GDL programs. Frequently a legislator proposes GDL in response to a specific tragedy involving a new driver. The tragedy sets the agenda. Then, the pressure of the federal government and local advocates, armed with data about the reduction in accidents where there are GDL laws, generates the support to enact the law.

[a]"U.S. Licensing Systems for Young Drivers. Laws as of June 2002," Insurance Institute for Highway Safety (Arlington, VA).
[b]State Legislative Fact Sheets,
http://www.nhtsa.dot.gov/people/outreach/stateleg/graddriverlic.htm.

---

inclusion
The principle that state courts will apply federal laws when those laws directly conflict with the laws of a state.

Sometimes federal and state laws are directly related. If there is a contradiction between the two, then federal law prevails. A state statute that allowed or encouraged racial hiring, for example, would directly conflict with the 1964 federal Civil Rights Act. Through a rule known as **inclusion,** state courts would be obliged to enforce the federal law.

The issue may be "more or less" rather than "either–or." Since the 1970s, the U.S. Supreme Court has generally taken the position that, especially with regard to individual rights protected in the Constitution, state courts should be encouraged to regard the federal government as setting minimums.[20] If state constitutions and laws provide additional protections or benefits, then state courts should enforce those standards.

common law
Legal traditions of society that are for the most part unwritten but based on the aggregation of rulings and interpretations of judges beginning in thirteenth-century England.

State judges must incorporate **common law** as well as federal law into their analyses. Common law begins with the decisions made by judges in England in the thirteenth century; it has evolved with the interpretation and application of those rulings over the years. While some states and communities have made parts of common law into written laws, most of the rulings and rationale remain unwritten. Courts nonetheless are expected to apply traditional common law as they rule on family disputes, disorderly conduct, charges of indecency, and social conflicts in a community. Louisiana used to follow the Napoleonic Code of French tradition but, like other states, now subscribes to fundamental edicts of Anglo-American common law and culture.

criminal law
Codes of behavior related to the protection of property and individual safety.

Another important distinction is between criminal law and civil law. **Criminal law** consists of incidents in which someone has been killed or injured or has suffered a loss or damage to property. These actions generally involve a victim, but they are considered to be crimes against society. A district attorney or state's attorney, representing society as a whole, prosecutes the alleged criminal. Penalties for those convicted include fines or incarceration or, in some states, death. **Civil law,** on the other hand, involves a dispute between two individuals and/or organizations. At issue may be a verbal or written contract. At stake is usually money. One party typically sues the other for compensation because of damages due to the violation of a contract or agreement. District attorneys or state's attorneys are not involved in civil law cases unless a state agency is suing or being sued.

Like other state government institutions, courts have modernized in the past few decades. Virtually extinct now is the justice of the peace, a judicial position that became part of American lore, humor, and dismay. These were part-time judges. (Some of the ridicule was aimed at justices of the peace who identified their "other" job as the sheriff.) One might count on a justice of the peace for a quick wedding (or divorce), but rarely for consistent, impartial, well-reasoned rulings.

Many states reorganized their court systems in the 1970s to follow a model that relied on full-time, qualified judges and simplified appeal routes, which enabled state supreme courts to have a manageable workload. Figure 4.2 illustrates the court structure that is now common among the states.

Most court cases in urban areas begin in a court that specializes in issues such as family disputes, traffic, small claims (less than $500 or $1,000), or probate (wills) or in a general jurisdiction municipal court. Small towns and rural areas usually do not have specialized courts. If they do, the position of judge is part-time. Cases here start in county-level courts that deal with the full array of disputes.

The specialized courts do not use juries. A single judge hears the case and decides. Other courts at this level do have juries if requested by the litigants. A major responsibility of the judges and juries that deliberate on cases when they are originated is to evaluate the credibility of the witnesses and evidence. Although mistakes can be made, judges and jurors have the opportunity to see and consider the demeanor and apparent confidence of witnesses. When cases are heard on appeal, the only individuals making presentations are attorneys.

Appellate courts have panels of judges. There are no juries in these courtrooms. An important feature of the court reorganizations of the 1970s is that a court of appeals exists between the circuit or county courts and the state supreme court. This court is to cover part of the state and is supposed to accept all appeals. In part, this appellate level is to allow supreme courts to decide whether or not it will hear a case. The basic principle is

civil law
Codes of behavior related to business and contractual relationships between groups and individuals.

FIGURE 4.2   State Court Structure

Most state courts have the basic organization shown in the figure below.

	Jury or Bench Trials	Jurisdiction	Judges
STATE SUPREME COURT	Bench only	Appeal (limited)	Panel of judges, elected/appointed for fixed term
APPEALS COURTS	Bench only	Appeal (readily granted)	Panel of judges, elected/appointed for fixed term
CIRCUIT OR COUNTY COURTS	Jury and Bench	Original and appeal	One judge per court, elected/appointed for fixed term
MUNICIPAL AND SPECIAL COURTS	Bench only	Original	One judge per court, elected/appointed for fixed term

that all litigants should have at least one opportunity to appeal a decision. If the state supreme court is the only place where an appeal can be lodged, that court is almost inevitably going to have too heavy a caseload and unreasonable backlogs will develop.

Most state judges are elected to the bench for a specific term. This differs from the federal government, where the president appoints judges for indefinite terms. Only six states use gubernatorial appointments. The first states had their legislatures elect judges, and that is still the case in Connecticut, Rhode Island, South Carolina, Vermont, and Virginia. As Table 4.2 shows, in sixteen states, voters elect judges and use party identification. In their efforts to limit and even destroy political machines, Progressives at the turn of the twentieth century advocated electing judges without party labels. Today, sixteen states use nonpartisan elections for selecting their judges. The remaining states went a step further and allowed for the election of judges but only after screening for qualifications. The process is referred to as the **Missouri (or Merit) Plan.** The governor selects someone from a list prepared by an independent panel and appoints him or her as a judge for a specific term of years. If a judge wishes to serve for an additional term, he or she must receive approval from the voters, who express themselves on a "yes–no" ballot. If a majority of voters cast a "no" ballot, the process starts all over. Five states (California, Kansas, Missouri, Oklahoma, and Tennessee) use the Missouri Plan for some judicial positions and nonpartisan elections for the others.

Missouri (Merit) Plan
A method of selecting judges in which a governor must appoint someone from a list provided by an independent panel. Judges are then kept in office if they get a majority of "yes" votes in general elections.

Elections

Elections are the vehicle for determining who will fill major state government positions and who will direct the institutions of state government. Almost all contests for state

TABLE 4.2   Judicial Selection Patterns

Partisan Election	Nonpartisan Election	
Alabama	Arizona	
Arkansas	California	
Georgia	Florida	
Indiana	Idaho	
Illinois	Kentucky	
Kansas	Michigan	
Louisiana	Minnesota	
Mississippi	Montana	
Missouri	Nevada	
New Mexico	North Dakota	
New York	Ohio	
North Carolina	Oregon	
Pennsylvania	Oklahoma	
Tennessee	South Dakota	
Texas	Washington	
West Virginia	Wisconsin	

Election by Legislature	Appointment by Governor	
Connecticut	Delaware	
Rhode Island	Hawaii	
South Carolina	Maryland	
Vermont	Massachusetts	
Virginia	New Hampshire	
	New Jersey	

Missouri (Merit) Plan

Alaska	Iowa	Oklahoma
California	Kansas	Tennessee
Colorado	Missouri	Utah
Indiana	Nebraska	Wyoming

Source: The Book of the States, 2003, 247–250. ©2003, Council of State Governments. Reprinted with permission.

government posts are partisan. The major exceptions are judicial elections in many states, as noted above, and the senate in Nebraska's unicameral legislature. Although party labels are not used and political parties are not formally participants in nonpartisan races, the party identity of some candidates may be known and may have some influence.

Political parties have different histories and roles in the various states. The chart in Analyzing Visuals: Patterns of Party Competition in State Legislatures shows the trends in the member of state legislative seats won by Republicans and Democrats. Most states have experienced significant competition between Republicans and Democrats since the Civil War. These states often have party control split between the two houses of the legislature and the governor's office or have frequent changes in party control of state government. This pattern has applied to southern states only once since the 1990s.

The Democratic Party has been dominant in Arkansas, Louisiana, Mississippi, Alabama, and Georgia since 1865—Democrats have elected the governor and majorities in both houses of the legislature over 60 percent of the time. Republicans have occasionally won the governor's race in some of these states, and there have been small blocs of Republicans in state legislatures. No state has experienced long-term dominance by Republicans similar to the Democratic control of these five states.

States are classified as having "majority party rule" if a single party wins the governorship at least 40 percent of the time and both houses of the legislature over 50 percent of the time. There has been Republican majority rule in only two states, New Hampshire and South Dakota. The states of Hawaii, New Mexico, Texas, Oklahoma, Florida, South Carolina, North Carolina, Kentucky, Rhode Island, and Maryland have had Democratic majority rule.

In elections from 1994 through 1997, the Republican Party acquired significant strength that has enhanced party competition generally and might lead to stable Republican dominance in some states. Republicans notched impressive victories throughout the country for federal and state offices. They gained control of the U.S. Senate and House of Representatives, won gubernatorial contests in populous states like New York, Texas, California, Florida, Illinois, and Pennsylvania, and secured the majority of seats in more state legislative chambers than ever before captured by the Republican Party. Democrats made somewhat of a comeback in 1998 and won the governor's race in California, but they lost Florida and generally had to concede that Republican gains in the 1990s were based on long-term changes in the political leanings of the population. After the 2004 elections, Democrats and Republicans were evenly split in their representation in state legislatures and governors' offices.

WEB EXPLORATION
To understand how campaigns are financed in state governments, see www.ablongman.com/oconnor

One of the reasons for Republican success is that voters in the South who had been voting for conservative Democrats began voting for conservative Republicans. Southerners have supported Republican presidential candidates since the Democratic Party began asserting leadership for civil rights following World War II. Alignment with Republicans in contests for state and congressional positions, however, has been much slower and more the exception than the rule. The 1994 elections may represent a threshold. After the votes were counted, six of the eleven southern states had Republican governors. Republicans controlled the Florida state legislature and the house in North Carolina and came close in many chambers throughout the South. This pattern, with slight variations, has continued. In short, Southerners no longer represent a significant minority within the national Democratic Party, but instead are part of the majority within the Republican Party—nationally and regionally.

It is easy to exaggerate the importance of partisanship in state politics. Whether at the state or the national level, the differences between Republicans and Democrats are important but not drastic. While party labels and organizations matter, campaigns are primarily centered on individual candidates. Voters usually have an opportunity to meet face-to-face with those contending for state government offices. A common strategy of candidates is to downplay their party identification, both to emphasize their strengths as individuals and to appeal to independent voters. After the election, party labels are important in determining who is in the majority in the legislature and therefore who will control committees and who will preside. That affects the agenda and the dynamics

ANALYZING VISUALS

Patterns of Party Competition in State Legislatures

This graph presents the trends of the Republican and Democratic Party success in winning seats in state legislatures. Until the 1960s, the Democratic Party dominated the legislatures of southern states and the Republican Party did best outside that region. Based on the information presented in the graph and the chapter discussion on the parties in state legislatures, answer the following critical thinking questions: What trends do you see in the regional patterns of party competition? Do the regional trends allow you to make a summary statement about the national picture of parties in state legislatures? What major movement nationally led to the decline of Democratic dominance in southern states? What major national event contributed to a surge in Democratic strength in the mid-1970s? How would you explain the even competitiveness of the Republicans and Democrats since the mid-1990s?

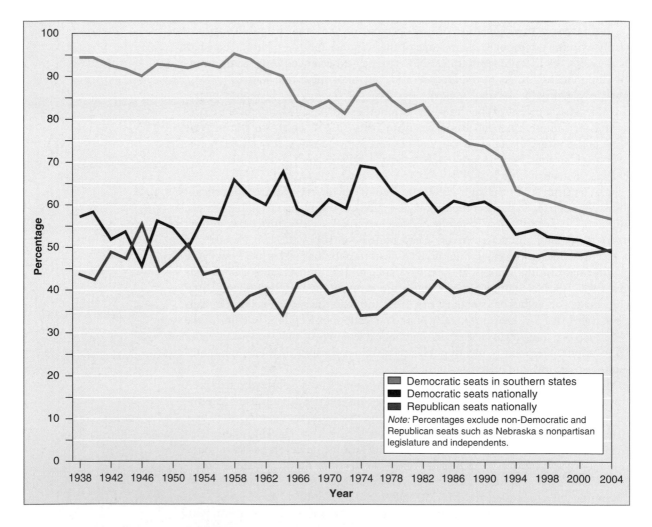

Source: National Conference of State Legislatures, http://www.ncsl.org/programs/legman/elect/demshare2000.htm. Updated by the authors.

of policy making, but even here parties typically lack the homogeneity and the discipline to determine outcomes.

Elections since the 1960s have led increasingly to ethnic and racial diversity among state and local officials. It is now common for African Americans, Latinos, and women to be mayors, including some of the largest cities. In 2002, 22 percent of the 7,424 state legislators were women. This percentage was the lowest in the southern states, and the

TABLE 4.3	Authority for the Initiative and Popular Referendum		
State	Direct Initiative	Indirect Initiative	Popular Referendum
Alaska		X	X
Arizona		X	X
Arkansas	X		X
California	X		X
Colorado	X		
Florida	X		
Idaho	X		X
Illinois	X		
Kentucky			X
Maine		X	X
Maryland			X
Massachusetts		X	X
Michigan	X	X	X
Mississippi		X	
Missouri	X		X
Montana	X		X
Nebraska	X		X
Nevada	X	X	X
New Mexico			X
North Dakota	X		X
Ohio	X	X	X
Oklahoma	X		X
Oregon	X		X
South Dakota	X		X
Utah	X	X	X
Washington	X	X	X
Wyoming		X	X

Source: The Book of the States, 2000–2001, 211. ©2000, Council of State Governments. Reprinted with permission.

range nationally was from 8 percent in Alabama to 39 percent in Washington. Four of the ten women who ran for govenor in 2002 won.

Direct Democracy

Ballots almost always include state and local referenda and initiative questions, as well as the names of candidates. (There is no provision for a national referendum or initiative.) As mentioned earlier, a Progressive reform meant to weaken parties was to provide opportunities for voters to legislate directly and not have to go through state legislatures and governors.[21] That process, known as the **direct initiative,** is available in eighteen states, most of them in the West. (See Table 4.3.) Citizens in these states have been able to enact laws as wide ranging as legalizing physician assisted suicide, limiting property taxes, building mass transit systems, protecting endangered species, and establishing prison terms for certain criminal behaviors.

A disadvantage of the direct initiative is the possibility that a law may be passed solely because of public opinion, which might be shaped largely by thirty-second television commercials and short slogans. There is no opportunity for making amendments as happens frequently when a legislative body debates a measure.

Debate, deliberation, and amendment are included in the **indirect initiative.** In this process, legislatures first consider the issue and then pass a bill that will become law if approved by the voters. The governor plays no role. Of the eleven states that have the indirect initiative, five also have the direct initiative.

Voters in twenty-three states have the opportunity to veto some bills. In these states, voters may circulate a petition objecting to a particular law passed in a recent session of the legislature. If enough signatures are collected, then an item appears on the next statewide ballot, giving the electorate the chance to object and therefore veto the legislation. This is known as a **direct** or **popular referendum.**

direct initiative

A process in which voters can place a proposal on a ballot and enact it into law without involving the legislature or the governor.

indirect initiative

A process in which the legislature places a proposal on a ballot and allows voters to enact it into law, without involving the governor or further action by the legislature.

COLLEGE TOWNS AND BINGE DRINKING

Local governments in communities with a college campus confront the challenge of binge drinking among students. Some may argue that students are just having fun and that bar owners are simply running a business. But, what might be regarded as individual choice and private socializing can have public consequences. City officials face pressure from their constituents to curb disruptive and illegal behavior from college students.

According to a study by the Harvard School of Public Health, 44 percent of U.S. college students engage in binge drinking.[a] Binge drinking is defined for men as having at least five drinks in a row, and for women, at least four drinks—a drink equals a twelve-ounce bottle of beer or wine cooler, a four-ounce glass of wine, or a shot of liquor, either by itself or in a mixed drink. A frequent binge drinker is someone who engages in this behavior at least three times in two weeks.

The Harvard study found that 50 percent of male college students and 39 percent of female students acknowledged that they were binge drinkers. Seventy-three percent of the men and 68 percent of the women said that the reason they drank alcoholic beverages was to get intoxicated.

There are no significant differences in the ages or classes of students and the pattern of binge drinking. Some binge drinkers are not yet twenty-one years old and therefore are breaking the law. Binge drinking, regardless of the legal drinking age, is associated with rowdiness, vandalism, fights, and sexual assault. The Harvard study demonstrated that binge drinkers are more likely than other students to miss class, get behind in school work, have unplanned sexual activity, engage in unprotected sex, damage property, and be hurt or injured.

Local and state governments are responsible for issuing licenses to sell alcoholic beverages. Inevitably, they must balance the pressure from bars and restaurants to do business freely and the need to ensure that alcohol is sold and consumed responsibly. An issue for local governments as well as for universities is that laws are broken when underage students drink and when binge drinking leads to assault and vandalism. Also, neighbors in campus areas want quieter, safer nights on the weekend. More central is the concern for health and safety—of the drinkers as well as of those around them.

An initial and obvious response of local governments has been to enhance policing focused on illegal drinking and unlawful behaviors related to the consumption of alcohol. Cities have revoked liquor licenses from businesses that make little effort to ensure that they are not serving underage drinkers. More innovative and proactive measures have included working with bar owners as well as fraternities and sororities to make sure that alcohol is not served to those who show signs of having had enough, educating students about the effects of binge drinking, eliminating sponsorship of events and programs by the alcohol industry, and sponsoring non-alcoholic alternatives for socializing and having fun. A few universities have sought to keep bars from having special deals during a "happy hour," since offering cheaper drinks in a relatively limited amount of time can encourage binge drinking from patrons trying to "get their money's worth." Some bar owners object strongly that these policing efforts interfere with their businesses.

Universities, health officials, police, and city governments all agree that binge drinking by college students is a serious problem. Attempts to curb the problem, however, have met with only limited success. Local government policies and university programs have not fared well as they confront business and individual choice.

---

[a] Henry Wechsler, George W. Dowdall, Andrea Davenport, and William DeJong, "College Alcohol Study," http://www.hsph.harvard.edu/cas/.

---

direct (popular) referendum
A process in which voters can veto a bill recently passed in the legislature by placing the issue on a ballot and expressing disapproval.

advisory referendum
A process in which voters cast nonbinding ballots on an issue or proposal.

recall
A process in which voters can remove an elected official before his or her term in office has expired.

All state and local legislative bodies may place an **advisory referendum** on a ballot. As the name implies, this is a device to take the pulse of the voters on a particular issue and has no binding effect. In addition, voter approval is required in a referendum to amend constitutions and, in some cases, to allow a governmental unit to borrow money through issuing bonds.

Voters in 17 states can **recall** elected officials from office before their terms have expired. A recall need not be based on criminal charges or malfeasance in office and does not involve the legislative or executive branches of government. In 2003, for example, Wisconsin State Senator Gary George was recalled in part because of charges of corrupt behavior. In contrast, also in 2003, voters in California recalled Governor Gray Davis and replaced him with Arnold Schwarzenegger. Governor Davis was unpopular, not corrupt. As with the initiative process, a recall begins with a petition. If enough valid signatures are submitted on a petition calling for a recall, a special election is scheduled and voters decide whether or not to retain the official that is the subject of the recall.

Arnold Schwarzennegger, campaigning to become California's governor. Utilizing a recall, California voters ousted Governor Gray Davis replaced him with the Republican actor and former Mr. Universe in 2003.

(Photo courtesy: Bob Daemmrich/Stock Boston, Inc.)

LOCAL GOVERNMENTS

The institutions and politics of local governance are even more personalized than state governments. In part this is because officials are friends, neighbors, and acquaintances living in the communities they serve. Except in large cities, most elected officials fulfill their responsibilities on a part-time basis. In part, the personal nature of local governance is due to the immediacy of the issues. The responsibilities of local governments include public health and safety in their communities, education of children in the area, jobs and economic vitality, zoning land for particular uses, and assistance to those in need. Local government policies and activities are the stuff of everyday living.

WEB EXPLORATION
To learn more about the issues currently of concern to local government, see
www.ablongman.com/oconnor

Charters

Romantic notions of democracy in America regard local governments as the building blocks of governance by the people. Alexis de Tocqueville, the critic credited with capturing the essence of early America, described government in the new country as a series of social contracts starting at the grass roots. He said, "the township was organized before the county, the county before the state, the state before the union."[22] It sounds good, but it's wrong.

A more accurate description comes from Judge John F. Dillon. In an 1868 ruling, known as **Dillon's Rule,** Dillon proclaimed:

> The true view is this: Municipal corporations owe their origins to and derive their power and rights wholly from the [state] legislature. It breathes into them the breath without which they cannot exist. As it creates, so it may destroy. If it may destroy, it may abridge and control.[23]

Dillon's Rule applies to all types of local governments.

There are many categories of local governments. Some of these are created in a somewhat arbitrary way by state governments. Counties and school districts are good examples. State statutes establish the authority for these jurisdictions, set the boundaries,

Dillon's Rule
A court ruling that local governments do not have any inherent sovereignty but instead must be authorized by state government.

and determine what these governments may and may not do and how they can generate funds.

Some local governments emerge as people and industries locate together and form a community. These governments must have a **charter** that is acceptable to the state legislature, much as states must have a constitution acceptable to Congress. Charters describe the institutions of government, the processes used to make legally binding decisions, and the scope of issues and services that fall within the jurisdiction of the governmental bodies. There are five basic types of charters:

1. **Special Charters.** Historically, as urban areas emerged, each one developed and sought approval for its own charter. To avoid inconsistencies, most state constitutions now prohibit the granting of special charters.

2. **General Charters.** Some states use a standard charter for all jurisdictions, regardless of size or circumstance.

3. **Classified Charters.** This approach classifies cities according to population and then has a standard charter for each classification.

4. **Optional Charters.** A more recent development is for the state to provide several acceptable charters and then let voters in a community choose from these.

5. **Home Rule Charters.** Increasingly, states are specifying the major requirements that a charter must meet and then allowing communities to draft and amend their own charters. State government must still approve the final product. Every state allows this process except Alabama, Indiana, Illinois, Kentucky, North Carolina, and Virginia.

An important feature of home rule is that the local government is authorized to legislate on any issue that does not conflict with existing state or federal laws. Other approaches list the subjects that a town or city may address.

In the early 1990s, Minnesota, California, and Colorado extended the concept of charters to public schools. They allowed teachers, parents, and/or community leaders to operate a school according to a charter instead of the standard rules and regulations of the state and the school district. To establish a **charter school,** a document would have to be approved that described the administration of the school, its curricula, admission policies, facilities, and general philosophy. States throughout the country have been authorizing charter schools as part of efforts to improve public education. Most states now allow for charter schools. By 2002, there were more than 2,400 of these schools, enrolling over a half-million children.

Types of Local Governments

There are about 87,000 local governments in the United States. The four major categories are as follows.

1. **Counties.** Every state except Connecticut and Rhode Island has **counties,** although in Louisiana they are called parishes, and in Alaska, boroughs. With few exceptions, counties have very broad responsibilities and are used by state governments as basic administrative units for welfare and environmental programs, courts, and the registration of land, births, and deaths. County and city boundaries may and do overlap, although state actions have merged city and county in New York, San Francisco, Denver, St. Louis, Nashville, and Honolulu.

2. **Towns.** In the first states and in the Midwest, "town" refers to a form of government in which everyone in a community is invited to an annual meeting to elect officers, adopt ordinances, and pass a budget. Another use of this term is simply to refer to a medium-sized city.

charter
A document that, like a constitution, specifies the basic policies, procedures, and institutions of a municipality.

charter school
Public school sanctioned by a specific agreement that allows the program to operate outside the usual rules and regulations.

county
A geographic district created within a state with a government that has general responsibilities for land, welfare, environment, and, where appropriate, rural service policies.

3. **Municipalities.** Villages, towns, and cities are established as **municipalities** and authorized by state governments as people congregate and form communities. Some of the most intense struggles among governments within the United States are over the boundaries, scope of authority, and sources of revenue for municipal governments.

4. **Special Districts. Special districts** are the most numerous form of government. A special district is restricted to a particular policy or service area. School districts are the most common form of special district. Others exist for library service, sewerage, water, and parks. Special districts are governed through a variety of structures. Some have elected heads, and others, appointed. Some of these jurisdictions levy a fee to generate their revenues, whereas others depend on appropriations from a state, city, or county. A reason for the recent proliferation of special districts is to avoid restrictions on funds faced by municipalities, schools, or other jurisdictions. The creation of a special park district, for example, may enable the park to have its own budget and sources of funding and relieve a city or county treasury.

municipality
A government with general responsibilities, such as a city, town, or village government, that is created in response to the emergence of relatively densely populated areas.

special district
A local government that is responsible for a particular function, such as K–12 education, water, sewerage, or parks.

The reasons that a particular municipality or special district was established may be sound, but having multiple governments serving the same community and controlling the same area creates incredible complexity and confusion. The challenge is to bridge the separation between cities, school districts, counties, and state agencies to effectively address an issue. A specific response to youth violence, for example, may be to provide a youth center and/or skateboard rink for young people in a community to hang out in a safe and healthy setting. Such a project poses questions about which jurisdictions will provide funding and ensure staffing. Land may have to be rezoned and building permits acquired. Will a park district be involved? Will schools count on this facility for after-school programming? What will be the role and approach of the police department? Who will be in charge?

There are examples of formal and informal arrangements among local governments to cooperate and coordinate their work in a single community. Miami and Dade County in Florida have been an early and visible example. The two jurisdictions have merged their public health services, jointly administer parks, operate a unified mass transit system, and together plan for development and land use. Saint Paul and Minneapolis in Minnesota

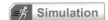
You Are Director of Economic Development for the City of Baltimore, Maryland

You Are a Restaurant Owner

One type of informal local government body is the neighborhood association. Whether or not such associations succeed in communicating clearly and resolving their problems is an open question.

(Photo courtesy: Kevin Jacobus/The Image Works)

*J*oin the Debate

SHOULD PRIVATE ORGANIZATIONS MANAGE PUBLIC SCHOOLS NOT MEETING ACADEMIC GOALS?

States and local governments are responsible for providing every child with an opportunity to get a good quality education. When students in public schools fail to learn effectively, communities expect a response and recommend different strategies for reforming the schools. Some education reform proponents argue that students' academic performance is primarily the responsibility of the teachers and therefore advocate linking pay increases to how well teachers perform and firing those who perform poorly. Another target of reform is the environment in which students learn—namely, the school buildings and equipment. Proposals for change here include renovating old, decrepit buildings and equipping schools with computers and laboratories to assist learning.

A relatively new strategy for making improvements is to remove a school from the control of a local school board and place it under the management of a private for-profit organization. The assumption behind this approach is that private businesses are better than governments at running organizations. With profits to motivate them, the thinking goes, such companies will work harder to provide good education. Opponents of this approach note that many

businesses go bankrupt or have management problems, and so putting schools into private hands means putting schools at risk. Opponents also worry about private firms making decisions about school curricula, discipline policies, and similar issues. Those decisions, they say, should be made by elected officials who represent the public who voted for them. Those in favor of letting private organizations manage schools respond with the argument that local politics is often a major influence on how schools are run. If decisions are made for political reasons rather than out of concern for educational standards, that itself is a problem that hampers sound and efficient management of public schools.

Read and think about the following excerpted news article from 2002 on changes in the Philadelphia public school system. Note the disagreement between the Pennsylvania state government, led by a Republican governor, and the Philadelphia city government, led by a Democratic mayor. Then join the debate over whether private firms should manage public schools by considering the debating points and questions posed at the end of this feature, and sharpen your own arguments for the position you find most viable.

Private Groups Get 42 Schools in Philadelphia

By Jacques Steinberg

In what is believed to be the largest experiment in privatization mounted by an American school district, a state panel charged with improving the Philadelphia public school system voted tonight to transfer control of 42 failing city schools to seven outside managers, including Edison Schools Inc. and two universities.

The three members of the School Reform Commission appointed by Gov. Mark Schweiker voted for the plan, while the two members appointed by Mayor John F. Street voted against it. The vote capped a fiery three-hour meeting in which the two sides had split over whether Edison, the nation's largest for-profit operator of public schools, had the capacity and know-how to improve the 20 schools that it was assigned.

"I want this reform to succeed," Michael Masch, a vice president at the University of Pennsylvania and one of the mayor's two appointees to the panel, said at one point in the debate. "I am gravely concerned that the magnitude of the change being proposed is imprudent."

Moments later, James P. Gallagher, the president of Philadelphia University and one of the governor's three appointees, said, "We should push the envelope and be as aggressive as possible."

The panel's vote today represents a milestone in the decade-long growth of the movement to turn troubled public schools over to private operators. There is no better index of the impact of this effort than Edison's own expansion: over the last six years, it has gone from operating a handful of public schools to more than 130 in 22 states, with a combined student population that is larger than all but a few dozen urban districts.

All told, the Philadelphia panel voted to assign an outside manager to one of every six schools in the city. In addition to Edison, the other organizations involved include two colleges that are in Philadelphia: Temple University, which was assigned five schools, and the University of Pennsylvania, which received three schools.

The panel also tapped four other companies with various degrees of school administrative experience, though each was smaller than Edison....

How much responsibility those managers would be given in the schools that they have been assigned remains to be negotiated with the state panel, as well as with the teachers' union and the parents in those schools. But panel officials said that, in many instances, the outsiders would likely make sweeping changes in school curriculum, as well as seek to replace school administrators and many of the teachers.

After the meeting, Jerry Jordan, a vice president of the Philadelphia Federation of Teachers, said he regretted that the panel had said so little about how the schools would be redesigned by the outsiders....

After the roll was called, several dozen student protesters, who have long argued that it was undemocratic for a for-profit company to operate a public school, chanted, "Shame!" and "I am not for sale!"...

Today's developments were the most significant here since late December, when Mr. Schweiker, a Republican, assumed control of the city school system, which had been operated by a board of education appointed entirely by Mr. Street, a Democrat. At the time, Mr. Schweiker said that only a bold approach could save a system in which more than half of the nearly 200,000 students had failed to achieve minimum proficiency on state reading and math tests.

The governor had also made clear at the time that he wanted Edison, which operates more than 130 public schools in 22 states, to play a major role in Philadelphia. Though the 20 schools that the company was awarded today was more than double the number it manages in any other district, the assignment was far more modest than the 60 Philadelphia schools that it said it was capable of managing.

Indeed, the governor had once argued that Edison should assume control of the system's central administration. Later, he retreated in the face of opposition from many parents and students, as well as the teachers' union and other labor groups representing school employees. They questioned Edison's academic and financial record....

[Still,] a majority of the panel members managed to pass a school reform plan in Philadelphia today that was more ambitious than those mounted in any other district.

The largest such plan previously was believed to have been in Hartford, where all 32 schools in the district were given over to the company Education Alternatives Inc. for less than two years in the mid-1990's. But largely because the Hartford experience failed relatively quickly, other districts have usually embarked on more modest experiments, with Edison now operating nine schools in Chester-Upland, Pa., outside Philadelphia, and seven in Clark County, Nev., the Las Vegas district.

In addition to the 42 schools that the Philadelphia panel assigned to outside managers, it also ordered that 28 other schools undergo substantial reorganization, with some becoming more independent charter schools but most remaining within direct control of the district. In the cases of the schools identified today for private intervention, the panel reserved the right to revoke a contract in instances where the schools fail to improve.

Source: Jacques Steinberg, *New York Times* (April 18, 2002). Copyright ©2002 by the New York Times Co. Reprinted by permission.

JOIN THE DEBATE!

CHECK YOUR UNDERSTANDING: Make sure you understand the following key points from the article; go back and review if you missed any of them:

- The process used to determine that Philadelphia public schools should be placed under private management.
- The number of schools affected and identification of some of the organizations selected to manage the schools.
- Panel officials' assessments of likely changes to the schools under outside management.
- Political dynamics involved in the debate.
- Prior reform plans in other school districts.

ADDITIONAL INFORMATION: News articles do not provide all the information an informed citizen needs to know about an issue under debate. Here are some questions the article does not answer that you may need to consider in order to join the debate:

- Why were the schools judged to be failures?
- What do the private organizations have to offer that would make them successes?
- Why did state and city officials take different positions?
- Why are teachers and students opposed to the change?
- What is Edison's academic and financial record in managing schools in other cities?

What other information might you want to know? Where might you gather this information? How might you evaluate the credibility of the information you gather? Is the information from a reliable source? Can you identify potential biases?

IDENTIFYING THE ARGUMENTS: Now that you have some information on the issue, and have thought about what else you need to know, see whether you can present the arguments on both sides of the debate. Here are some ideas to get you started. We've provided one example each of "pro" and "con" arguments, but you should be able to offer others:

PRO: Private organizations should manage public schools not meeting academic goals. Here's why:

- Private organizations can focus on what is necessary to be effective without having to bend to political pressures from community groups or teachers.

CON: Private organizations should not manage public schools not meeting academic goals. Here's why:

- It is undemocratic for a for-profit company to operate public schools, which should be managed by elected officials.

TAKING A POSITION AND SUPPORTING IT: After thinking about the information in the article, and articulating the arguments in the debate, what position would you take? What information supports your position? What arguments would you use to persuade others to your side of the debate? How would you counter arguments on the other side?

Shirley C. Franklin delivers her inaugural address on January 7, 2002, as mayor of Atlanta. She had been a professional manager in city government and is the first woman to be elected as mayor of Georgia's capital.

(Photo courtesy: Erik S. Lesser/Getty Images)

town meeting
Form of local government in which all eligible voters are invited to attend a meeting at which budgets and ordinances are proposed and voted on.

political machine
An organization designed to solicit votes from certain neighborhoods or communities for a particular political party in return for services and jobs if that party wins.

mayor
Chief elected executive of a city.

city council
The legislature in a city government.

manager
A professional executive hired by a city council or county board to manage daily operations and to recommend policy changes.

district-based election
Election in which candidates run for an office that represents only the voters of a specific district within the jurisdiction.

have also pioneered cooperative arrangements. The establishment of the 911 emergency service can be a catalyst for cooperation by various police, fire, and paramedical agencies in a metropolitan area. The norm, however, continues to be conflict and often a failure to even communicate. Local officials and citizens alike find the legacies of past actions creating local governments a serious challenge.

Executives and Legislatures

Except for the traditional New England **town meeting,** where anyone who attends may vote on policy and management issues, local governments have some or all of the following decision-making offices:

- Elected executive, such as a mayor, village president, or county executive.
- Elected council or commission, such as a city council, school board, or county board.
- Appointed manager, such as a city manager or school superintendent.

Local government institutions are not necessarily bound to the principles of separation of powers or checks and balances that the U.S. Constitution requires of the federal government and most state constitutions require of their governments. School boards, for example, commonly have legislative, executive, and judicial authority. School board members are, with few exceptions, part-time officials, so they hire superintendents and rely heavily on them for day-to-day management and for new policy ideas. It is the school board, however, that makes the policies regarding instruction and facilities. The board also does the hiring and contracting to implement those policies. Similarly, the school board sets student conduct rules, determines if a student should be expelled, and then hears appeals from those who are disciplined.

The patterns of executive and legislative institutions in local government have their roots in some of the most profound events in our history. The influx of non-English-speaking immigrants into urban areas in the North after the Civil War prompted the growth of **political machines.**[24] New immigrants needed help getting settled. They naturally got much of that help from ethnic neighborhoods, where, for example, a family from Poland would find people who spoke Polish, restaurants with Polish food, and stores and churches with links to the old country. Politicians dealt with these ethnic neighborhoods. If the neighborhood voted to help provide victory for particular candidates for **mayor** and **city council,** then city jobs and services would be provided. Political machines were built on these quid pro quo arrangements. The bosses of those machines were either the elected officials or people who controlled the elected officials.

As part of their efforts to destroy the political machines, Progressives sought reforms that minimized the politics in local government institutions.[25] Progressives favored local governments headed by professional **managers** instead of elected executives. Managers would be appointed by councils, the members of which were elected on a nonpartisan ballot, thus removing the role of parties.

As another way of sapping the strength of ethnic bloc voting, Progressive reformers advocated that council members be elected from the city at large rather than from neighborhood districts. The choice between **district-based** and **at-large elections** now, however, raises concerns about discrimination against Latinos and African Americans. At-large elections may keep minority representatives from being elected. On the other hand, a city could be divided into districts that might have an ethnic group constitute a majority within a district. The at-large elections, in short, have the same minimizing effect on these ethnic groups that was intended by Progressives on white ethnic groups.

Progressives argued that the **commission** form of government was an acceptable alternative to mayors and boss politics. The commission evolved as a response to a hurricane in 1900 that killed almost 10,000 people in southern Texas. After the disaster, a

LOCAL AND PROVINCIAL POLITICS IN COMPARATIVE PERSPECTIVE

The United States has a long tradition of political activity at the state and local levels. This is not necessarily the case elsewhere. While the relationship between national and local government in other countries shows a range of variation (in Britain's unitary system, there is no constitutional distinction made between national and local government; in Canada's federal system, local government is directly responsible only to provincial government, not to the federal government in Ottawa), national government and politics often take center stage. Japanese textbooks on politics in that country, for example, include chapters on local autonomy (from national authority) rather than local politics per se. In the centralized political systems of Britain and France, devolution—the decentralization of government authority—has been an important trend in the last two decades, but the national government in each case has retained control over the scope and pace of the changes.

That is not to say that localities play no role in these countries. Local and provincial governments have often been controlled by the parties out of power at the national level, and elections at the lower levels often act as barometers for upcoming national elections. In France, the far right National Front built up political support at the local level, from which it expanded to national significance in the 1990s. Municipal governments controlled by the National Front have introduced anti-immigrant policies (see Global Politics, chapter 6) that are at odds with national policy. In the 1999 elections for the newly created Scottish home parliament, the Scottish Nationalist Party, a minor party in the House of Commons, emerged with the second largest number of seats and denied the local Labour Party a majority. Even China is experimenting with elections at the township and county levels, although few experts see this as necessarily leading to competitive elections at the national level. The government's experiment with local competitive elections has been a top-down process in which the central government has tried to stave off further calls for democracy as provincial and local governments take on more responsibilities for economic development.

The provinces and municipalities have also served as centers of citizen political participation. Public opinion polls taken in postwar Japan suggest that citizens tend to identify with local political symbols more than with national ones, including the Parliament. Environmental movements in Europe began as local organizations, and they remain largely that way in Japan. Those movements have often used the local referendum and recall, borrowed from American practice, to try to remove municipal officials or change their policies.

Vigorous local politics is equated with democracy in the United States. In other countries it is often associated with the loss of central government control. For example, after a prolonged armed conflict, culminating in UN intervention in 1999, East Timor (formerly a Portuguese colony taken over by the Indonesia military in 1976) gained its independence from Indonesia in May 2002. Indonesia also faces insurrections in the provinces of Aceh and Irian Jaya. Canada, Mexico, and Russia also face territorial independence movements, with armed insurgencies (e.g., in Chiapas and Chechnya) in the latter two.

---

group of prominent business leaders in Galveston formed a task force, with each member of the force assuming responsibility for a specific area, such as housing, public safety, and finance. Task force members essentially assumed the roles of both legislators making policy and managers implementing policy. The citizens of Galveston were so impressed with how well this worked that they amended their charter to replace the mayor and city council with a commission, elected at-large and on a nonpartisan basis. The model spread quickly, and by 1917 almost 500 cities had adopted the commission form of government.

As Table 4.4 indicates, half of all U.S. cities have an elected mayor and a council. Mayors differ in how much authority they have. Some are strong and have the power to veto city council action, appoint agency heads, and initiate as well as execute budgets. The charters of other cities do not provide mayors with these formal powers. Except for the largest cities, mayors serve on a part-time basis.

Slightly more than one-third of the municipalities have the Progressive model of government, with an appointed, professional manager and an elected city council. This is the most common pattern among medium-sized cities, whereas the very large and the very small have mayors and councils. Some jurisdictions have both mayors and managers.

Comparing State and Local Governments

at-large election
Election in which candidates for office must compete throughout the jurisdiction as a whole.

commission
Form of local government in which several officials are elected to top positions that have both legislative and executive responsibilities.

TABLE 4.4 Major Forms of Municipal Government

Form of Government	1984	1988	1992	1996	1998	2002
Council–Manager	3,387 (48.5%)	3,232	2,760	2,441	2,356	2,290 (34.7%)
Mayor–Council	3,011 (43.1%)	2,943	3,319	3,635	3,686	3,686 (55.8%)
Commission	143 (2.0%)	146	154	168	173	176 (2.7%)
Town Meeting	337 (4.8%)	333	365	363	369	370 (5.6%)
Representative Town Meeting	63 (.9%)	65	70	79	82	81 (1.2%)
Total	*6,981	*6,719	*6,668	*6,686	*6,666	*6,603 (100%)

*Totals for U.S. local governments represent only those municipalities with populations of 2,500 and greater. There are close to 30,000 local governments with populations under 2,500.

Source: Statistics from "Inside the Year Book: Cumulative Distributions of U.S. Municipalities," *The Municipal Year Books* 1984–2002, International City/County Management Association (ICMA), Washington, DC.

In the aftermath of the devastating 1900 hurricane in Galveston, Texas, the commission form of city government came into being. Although Galveston has abandoned the commission form, the model spread quickly, and by 1917 almost 500 cities had adopted the commission form of government.

(Photo courtesy: © Bettmann/Corbis)

public corporation (authority)
Government organization established to provide a particular service or to run a particular facility that is independent of other city or state agencies and supposed to be operated like a business. Examples include a port authority or a mass transit system.

domestic dependent nation
A type of sovereignty that makes an Indian tribe in the United States outside the authority of state governments but reliant on the federal government for the definition of tribal authority.

Only 2 percent of U.S. cities still use the commission form of government. Tulsa, Oklahoma, and Portland, Oregon, are the largest cities run by commissions. Galveston, however, is one of the cities that has abandoned this structure.

Over 1,800 of the almost 3,000 county governments are run by boards or councils that are elected from geographic districts and without any executive. Committees of the county board manage personnel, finance, roads, parks, social services, and the like. Almost 400 counties elect an executive as well as a board, and thus follow the mayor–council model. Almost 800 hire a professional manager.

School districts, with very few exceptions, follow the council–manager model. Other special districts have boards, sometimes called **public corporations** or **authorities**, that are elected or appointed by elected officials. If the district is responsible for services such as water, sewerage, or mass transit, the board is likely to hire and then supervise a manager.

RELATIONS WITH INDIAN NATIONS

Treaties between the federal government and American Indian nations directly affect thirty-four states. Most of these states are west of the Mississippi River, but New York, Michigan, Florida, Connecticut, and Wisconsin are also included. Although the treaties were between two nations, the United States and an American Indian tribal nation, invariably the tribal leaders signed because of actual or threatened military defeat. The legal status of the various tribes in the United States is that of a **domestic dependent nation,** by which they retain their individual identity and sovereignty but must rely on the U.S. federal government for the interpretation and application of treaty provisions. Under the formal **trust relationship** between the United States and the Indian nations, the federal government is legally and morally obligated to protect Indian interests. State and local governments are clearly affected by federal–tribal relations but have little influence and virtually no legal authority over these relations.

The policy approach of the federal government toward Indians has varied widely (see Table 4.5). From 1830 to 1871, a major goal was to move all Indians to land west of the Mississippi. The policy between 1871 and 1934 was to assimilate Indians into the white culture of the United States. From 1934 until 1953 and then again from 1973 to today, the formal policy was to respect tribal customs, strengthen tribal governments, and promote economic self-determination. Between 1953 and 1973, the federal government terminated the legal status of various tribes, ended services to them, and refused to recognize their treaty rights. This generated protests and led to a resumption of the general policy begun in 1934.[26] While some would argue that the federal government has not been serious or effective enough in supporting treaty rights and

TABLE 4.5	Federal Policies Toward Indian Nations
Up to 1830	Mix conquest and coexistence. Make treaties.
1830–1871	Force all tribes west of Mississippi. Make treaties.
1871–1934	Assimilate Indians into white culture.
1934–1953	Respect tribal customs and government. Encourage economic self-determination.
1953–1973	Terminate legal status of tribes. Ignore treaty provisions.
1973 to present	Recognize tribes and treaty rights. Encourage constitutions and self-determination.

trust relationship
The legal obligation of the United States federal government to protect the interests of Indian tribes.

self-determination, the current policy received new emphasis with the inclusion of tribes in the devolution of responsibilities from Washington to states and local communities.

States are not parties to the treaties between the United States and American Indian nations and have no direct legal authority over tribes. The federal government has in several specific areas granted some powers to states. The Indian Gaming Regulatory Act of 1988, for example, gives state governments limited authority to negotiate agreements, called **compacts,** with tribes who wish to have casino gambling. Also, in 1953, Congress passed Public Law 280, which allows some states to pursue Indians suspected of criminal behavior even if they are on reservation land.

For the most part, however, federal–tribal relations provide given constraints and opportunities as states and communities engage in planning and problem solving. The two most important features of federal–tribal relations for state and local governments are land rights and treaty provisions for hunting, fishing, and gathering. Tribes have **reservation land** and **trust land,** neither of which is subject to taxation or regulation by state or local governments. The former was designated in a treaty. Tribes can acquire trust land by purchasing or otherwise securing ownership of a parcel and then seeking to have it placed in trust status by the secretary of the Department of the Interior. Since a tribe can get trust land at any time and any place, there is the potential for disruption of a community's development plans or tax base and an obvious challenge to cordial, working relationships between tribes, the federal government, and state or local government.

Hunting, fishing, and gathering activities have important cultural and religious significance for many American Indian nations. Treaty provisions giving rights to tribes to hunt, fish, and gather wild rice or berries on their own land and on public lands and waterways in land they once owned are key to tribal identity and dignity. These treaty rights supersede regulations enacted for environmental and recreational purposes. Non-Indian anglers and hunters sometimes protest that Indians have special privileges. Environmental planners worry about the potential implications of unregulated Indian activity. In 1999, for example, the Makah tribe in the Northwest celebrated the successful capture and killing of a whale. While the tribe applauded the preservation of an important cultural tradition, wildlife advocates bemoaned the treaty rights that allowed this destruction of a valued animal. For some, the discord is more racial in nature than based in real environmental or recreational issues. For the states affected, the challenge is to promote harmony between groups and individuals and to deal effectively with any substantive issues that do materialize.

Since Congress passed the Indian Self-Determination and Education Assistance Act in 1975, the federal government has been trying to strengthen tribal governments by encouraging the adoption of constitutions. The Bureau

compact
A formal, legal agreement between a state and a tribe.

reservation land
Land designated in a treaty that is under the authority of an Indian nation and is exempt from most state laws and taxes.

trust land
Land owned by an Indian nation and designated by the federal Bureau of Indian Affairs as exempt from most state laws and taxes.

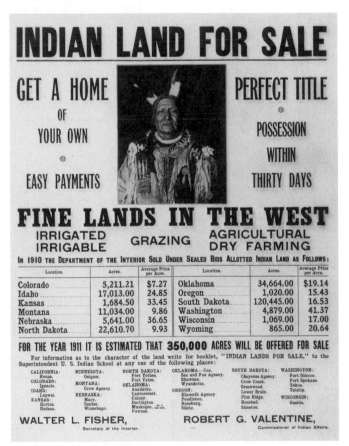

An advertisement from the Department of the Interior (c. 1911) luring individuals to purchase land designated as surplus after tribal allotments were made to Indians.

(Photo courtesy: Library of Congress)

of Indian Affairs offers assistance in writing the constitutions, and other federal agencies, such as the Environmental Protection Agency, are willing to devolve some of their authority for regulating water and air pollution to tribes that have constitutions.

While a tribe may include some traditional patterns of governance in their constitution, the basic concept of a constitution is alien to Indian tribes. The documents read very much like state constitutions, with preambles that espouse principles of democracy and clauses that provide for a familiar separation of powers among executive, legislative, and judicial branches. Not surprisingly, some nations struggle with the mandates of their constitutions and the informal but real power of traditional rule by elders.

WEB EXPLORATION
To learn more about American Indian nations and specific tribes, see www.ablongman.com/oconnor

FINANCES

State, tribal, and local governments must, of course, have money. Getting that money is one of the most challenging and thankless tasks of public officials. Unlike the federal government, state and local governments must balance their budgets. Unlike private businesses, state and local governments may not spend less money than they have. Whereas the goal of a private business is to have significantly more income than expenses, a governor, mayor, or other local public executive would be criticized for taxing too heavily if something akin to profits appeared on the books.

The budgeting process involves making projections of expenses and revenues. State and local officials face some special uncertainties when they make these guesses. One important factor is the health of the economy. If one is taxing sales or income, those will vary with levels of employment and economic growth. Moreover, the public sector faces double jeopardy when the economy declines. Revenues go down as sales and incomes decline, and at the same time expenses go up as more families and individuals qualify for assistance during harsh times.

Another important factor affecting state and local government budgets is the level of funding that governments give to one another. States have been getting about one-fourth of their funds from Washington, D.C. That level has varied over time and, especially with federal deficit spending, is likely to decline. The amount of the decline will depend as much on political dynamics as it will on the health of the national economy. Local governments do not receive as much, but water and sewerage districts have been getting about 15 percent of their funds from the federal government.

Local governments depend heavily on aid from state governments. The pattern varies from one state to another, but on average, school districts get slightly over half of their funds from state governments, counties get almost one-third, and cities about 20 percent.[27]

Not only is federal funding for state and local governments generally declining, but Congress and the president frequently require communities to spend their money for national programs and concerns. The National Governors Association, for example, estimated that states will spend up to $4 billion a year to enhance security at airports, power plants, water sources, and vital infrastructure in the aftermath of the September 11, 2001, terrorist attack.[28] The federal government will reimburse state and local jurisdictions for less than one-third of their costs. Almost 75 percent of the states had to make major adjustments in their budgets in 2002, in part because of unexpected domestic security expenses and in part because of a national economic downturn.

Different governments depend on different types of taxes and fees. Figure 4.3 presents the pattern of funding for state and local governments. Unlike the federal government, which relies primarily on the income tax, state governments rely almost equally on income taxes and sales taxes. States differ among themselves, of course. Alaska, Delaware, Montana, New Hampshire, and Oregon have no sales tax at all, whereas some of the southern states have a double-digit sales tax. Likewise, Alaska, Florida, Nevada, South Dakota, Tennessee, Texas, Washington, and Wyoming do not tax personal incomes. Tax rates differ among those states that do have an income tax, but the levels are generally less than 10 percent.

FIGURE 4.3
State and Local Government Revenues (percentage of total revenues)

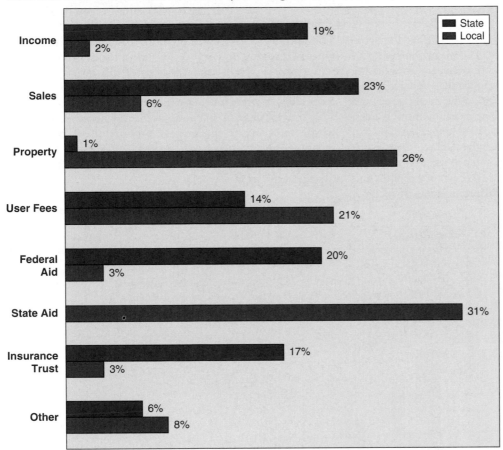

Each of the thirty-nine states with budget deficits in 2002 reduced spending, but only seven balanced their books by raising taxes. Tax increases pose risks for officials seeking reelection. More popular ways of getting needed revenues included using "rainy day funds" established in years when there were surpluses, and selling to investors the rights to funds that states were to receive in a legal settlement with tobacco companies. Investors paid states at the rate of $1 immediately in order to get $5 over 25 years.

Local governments rely primarily on property taxes, have little from levies on sales, and receive virtually nothing from income. Schools, in particular, depend on property taxes for funding. Both local and state governments levy user fees, such as admission to parks, licenses for hunting and fishing, tuition for public universities, and charges based on water use. States, more than local governments, administer retirement systems and insurance programs for public employees. Income from the investment of retirement funds is listed but is not generally available for any use other than paying retirement benefits. Similarly, user fees are typically placed in **segregated funds,** which means they can only be used to provide the service for which the fee was charged. Tuition must, in other words, be used by the university and cannot pay for prison costs or maintaining highways.

Most people accept user fees as the fairest type of taxation. The problem is that the income is both limited and segregated. In general, taxes can be evaluated according to how much money they can raise, whether the revenue is certain, and who bears the burden. See Analyzing Visuals: State and Local Tax Burdens for examples of the impact of different taxes on households with varying levels of income. Income taxes generate large sums of money, although there will be variations with how well the economy is doing, how many people are employed, and the like. Of all the taxes, those

segregated funds
Money that comes in from a certain tax or fee and then is restricted to a specific use, such as a gasoline tax that is used for road maintenance.

ANALYZING VISUALS

State and Local Tax Burdens

In order to pay for the services they provide, state and local governments rely on a variety of taxes. The major source of revenue for cities, towns, villages, school districts, and counties is a tax on the value of property owned by individuals and businesses. Some local governments also use a tax on the sale of goods and services. States get most of their money by taxing income, sales, and cigarettes. Individual states vary widely in what they tax. Some have no income tax and a very high sales tax, whereas others have a relatively high income tax and a low sales tax.

The visual presents a sample breakdown of expenses and taxes for three households with different levels of income.

This allows you to analyze the impact that each of the major types of taxes has on families. Based on the information presented in the graph and the chapter discussion on taxes, answer the following critical thinking questions: Who is most likely to press for lower income taxes? If everyone pays a 5 percent sales tax on food, clothing, and entertainment, whose sales tax is the largest proportion of their total income? If everyone pays $10 in taxes for every $1,000 of value of their property, is the tax progressive or regressive? Is the cigarette tax fair?

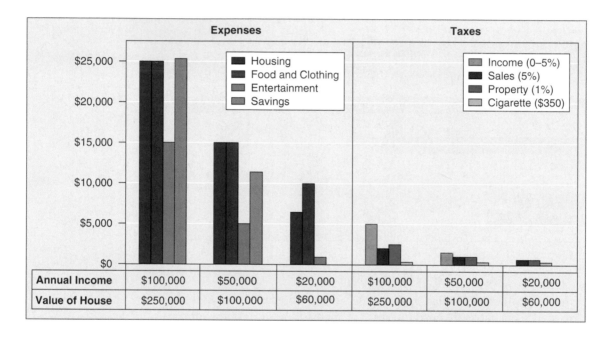

	Expenses			Taxes		
Annual Income	$100,000	$50,000	$20,000	$100,000	$50,000	$20,000
Value of House	$250,000	$100,000	$60,000	$250,000	$100,000	$60,000

Expenses legend: Housing, Food and Clothing, Entertainment, Savings

Taxes legend: Income (0–5%), Sales (5%), Property (1%), Cigarette ($350)

---

progressive tax
The level of tax increases with the wealth or ability of an individual or business to pay.

regressive tax
The level of tax increases as the wealth or ability of an individual or business to pay decreases.

based on income are the most **progressive taxes,** which means that they are based on the ability to pay.

Sales taxes also generate lots of money and they vary with how well the economy is doing. These are not based on earnings, but on purchases. Since those with a low income must spend virtually all that they earn in order to live, sales taxes are **regressive taxes.** To counter the regressive nature of sales taxes, some states exempt food, medicine, and other necessities.

The property tax varies with the value of one's property, not one's current income or spending. Thus, farmers and those with a fixed income, such as retired persons, might bear more of a burden than their current wealth suggests they should carry. The property tax can be a good revenue earner and is stable, since a jurisdiction can set a tax rate that virtually guarantees a certain level of revenue, regardless of economic trends. The local officials who set these rates invariably hear complaints about the regressive nature of property taxes.

Continuity & Change

Rediscovery of Grassroots Governance

Government by the people is the basic principal of politics in the United States. However, by design, state governments initially were weak. In response to the colonial experience, the founders established governments that were very limited in their powers, responsibilities, and abilities. Governors and the executive branch were especially limited. Likewise, governance at the local level was minimal. Officials were part-time, concerns were few, and funds were low. The federal government controlled Indian nations and gave them very little authority to make their own decisions. Tribes found themselves at the receiving end of federal policies that changed drastically, ranging from neglect to assimilation to some forms of self-determination.

The limitations of state, local, and tribal governments became a major problem as technological and economic developments made American society increasingly complex. Crises emerged in the middle of the twentieth century as urban areas emerged and basic government services were lacking. State legislatures commonly had more representatives from rural areas than from urban areas, and city issues got low priority on agendas. Finally, in a 1962 case, the U.S. Supreme Court declared that states had to adhere to the principle of one-person, one-vote and allocate legislative seats according to population. That decision, *Baker* v. *Carr*, marked a threshold. People had a more effective voice and demanded that their state and local governments develop the capacity to address major concerns and issues. On a parallel track, the federal government adopted a policy of promoting more self-governance for the Indian nations.

Subnational units of government today are considerably more competent and more responsive than their predecessors. The governments that provide the services that affect us most directly and regularly have more capable people and more efficient processes than they have ever had before. Although most state, local, and tribal elected officials are still part-time, increasingly professional, full-time staff serves them. Governments run by our neighbors, friends, and co-workers tend to be more accessible and more responsive to our needs.

The challenges of the future rest with reconciling the traditions of desiring a limited government and avoiding high taxes with the demands of a society that is increasingly complex. The federal government has shed much of its responsibilities and many of its programs for local and tribal communities, in part in recognition of the advantages of allowing problem solving by those most directly affected by issues. States, similarly, have delegated considerable authority to their local governments. The health and vitality of local communities will depend greatly on the creativity of their leaders in meeting the challenges of increased responsibilities and limitations on funds.

1. What regulations and services that have affected you during the past week were the responsibilities of state and local government respectively?

2. In what ways can you influence elective and appointed officials in your state and local governments?

CAST YOUR VOTE   What kind of policies, if any, should the federal government impose on state, local, and tribal governments? To cast your vote, go to www.ablongman.com/oconnor

---

SUMMARY

The expectations are that state and local governments are readily accessible to citizens and that they are likely to be responsive to the needs and wishes of a particular community. In this chapter we have examined the changing character of governance at the state and local levels in order to appreciate both the variation and the common patterns in subnational governments. In this chapter, we have made the following points:

1. **Evolution of Sate and Local Governments**
   The initial intent was to limit the capacity and scope of state and local governments. That changed with the increased complexity of our society and economy and with the ruling of the U.S. Supreme Court that legislative districts within a state must each have the same number of people. The trend since the 1960s has been for more representative and more professional state and local governments. These jurisdictions and the federal government are forming partnerships with each other and with the private sector to address issues and provide services.

2. **Grassroots Power and Politics**
   Those who wield the most influence over the making and implementation of public policy in a community are not always the ones elected to formal offices. Sometimes power is in the hands of a family, a small number of individuals, or the local media. Whether or

not those who are most powerful are the ones in government offices, governance at the grass roots is face-to-face, between neighbors, friends, and former high school classmates.

3. State Governments

State governments have traditionally had primary responsibility for criminal justice, education, public health, and economic development. Recently, state officials have assumed a larger role in welfare and environmental policy. State constitutions, which reflect major historical developments in American society, provide the basic framework of institutions and values in which state governments fulfill their roles. Since the 1960s, these governments have dramatically become more competent, professional, and accessible to the general public.

4. Local Governments

Local governance in the United States is conducted by a myriad collection of over 87,000 units, most of which are run by part-time officials. These governments range from general jurisdictions covering densely urbanized areas to special districts functioning for a specific, narrow purpose. The forms of local governments also differ. There are town meetings in which all eligible voters in a community gather to conduct business, elected and appointed boards that have both executive and legislative powers, and governments with distinct legislative councils, elected executives, and professional managers. Local politics is frequently nonpartisan, thanks in part to conscious efforts to prevent control by political party machines.

5. Relations with Indian Nations

American Indian nations obviously affect and are affected by state and local governments. But, due to treaty rights and the domestic dependent sovereignty of the tribes, the Indian nations have a special relationship with the federal government. Tribes have important protections from the potential vagaries of state and local governments. Conversely, the special status of the tribes poses challenges to coherent and consistent policies in a community. Currently, the federal government is encouraging tribal governments to move to self-determination economically and politically and to enter into agreements with state and local governments on financial and policy matters.

6. Finances

Funding government is complex. Revenues are hard to project because governments tax personal and business incomes, sales, and property value—none of which governments can control. State, local, and tribal governments also rely heavily on money given to them by other jurisdictions, including the federal government. The challenge is, given these uncertainties and the general hostility toward taxes, to budget for required services and popular programs.

KEY TERMS

advisory referendum, p. 122
at-large election, p. 128
charter, p. 124
charter school, p. 124
city council, p. 128
civil law, p. 117
commission, p. 128
common law, p. 116
commute, p. 113
compact, p. 131
county, p. 124
criminal law, p. 116
Dillon's Rule, p. 123
direct initiative, p. 121
direct (popular) referendum, p. 122
district-based election, p. 128
domestic dependent nation, p. 130
extradite, p. 113
governor, p. 110
inclusion, p. 116
indirect initiative, p. 121
line-item veto, p. 111
manager, p. 128
mayor, p. 128
Missouri (Merit) Plan, p. 118
municipality, p. 125
nonpartisan election, p. 107
one-person, one-vote, p. 105
package or general veto, p. 111
pardon, p. 113
parole, p. 113
political machine, p. 128
Progressive movement, p. 110
progressive tax, p. 134
public corporation (authority) p. 130
recall, p. 122
regressive tax, p. 134
reservation land, p. 131
segregated funds, p. 133
special district, p. 125
state constitution, p. 108
sunset law, p. 114
sunshine law, p. 114
term limits, p. 107
town meeting p. 128
trust land, p. 131
trust relationship, p. 130

SELECTED READINGS

Banfield, Edward C. *The Unheavenly City.* Boston: Little, Brown, 1970.

Benjamin, Gerald, and Michael J. Malbin, eds. *Limiting Legislative Terms.* Washington, DC: CQ Press, 1992.

Burns, Nancy E. *The Formation of American Local Governments: Private Values in Public Institutions.* New York: Oxford University Press, 1994.

Crenson, Matthew A. *Neighborhood Politics.* Cambridge, MA.: Harvard University Press, 1983.

Dahl, Robert A. *Who Governs? Democracy and Power in an American City.* New Haven, CT.: Yale University Press, 1961.

Erie, Steven P. *Rainbow's End: Irish Americans and the Dilemmas of Urban Machine Politics, 1840–1985.* Berkeley: University of California Press, 1988.

Erikson, Robert S., Gerald C. Wright, and John P. McIver. *Statehouse Democracy: Public Opinion and Policy in the American States.* Cambridge, UK: Cambridge University Press, 1993.

Jewell, Malcolm E., and Marcia Lynn Whicker. *Legislative Leadership in the American States.* Ann Arbor: University of Michigan Press, 1994.

Renzulli, Diane. *Capitol Offenders: How Private Interests Govern Our States.* Washington, DC: Public Integrity Books, 2000.

Stone, Clarence N. *Regime Politics: Governing Atlanta, 1946–1988.* Lawrence: University Press of Kansas, 1989.

Woliver, Laura R. *From Outrage to Action: The Politics of Grass-Roots Dissent.* Urbana: University of Illinois Press, 1993.

NOTES

1. William Fulton and Paul Shigley, "The Greening of the Brown," *Governing* (December 2000): 31–34.
2. Peter K. Eisinger, *The Rise of the Entrepreneurial State* (Madison: University of Wisconsin Press, 1988).
3. Raymond Wolfinger, "Reputation and Reality in the Study of Community Power," *American Sociological Review* 25 (October 1960): 636–44; Nelson Polsby, *Community Power and Political Theory* (New Haven, CT: Yale University Press, 1963); and Robert E. Agger, Daniel Goldrich, and Bert Swanson, *The Rulers and the Ruled: Political Power and Impotence in American Communities* (New York: Wiley, 1964).
4. Laura R. Woliver, *From Outrage to Action: The Politics of Grass-Roots Dissent* (Urbana: University of Illinois Press, 1993); and Matthew A. Crenson, *Neighborhood Politics* (Cambridge, MA: Harvard University Press, 1983).
5. Albert L. Sturm, "The Development of American State Constitutions," *Publius* 12 (Winter 1982): 62–68.
6. Albert L. Kohlmeier, *The Old Northwest as the Keystone of the Arch of the American Federal Union* (Bloomington, IN: Principia Press, 1938); and *Pathways to the Old Northwest* (Indianapolis: Indiana Historical Society, 1988).
7. Theodore Clarke Smith, *Parties and Slavery* (New York: Harper and Brothers, 1906); and Arthur Charles Cole, *The Irrepressible Conflict, 1850–1865* (New York: Macmillan, 1934).
8. George E. Mowry, *The Progressive Era, 1900–1920* (Washington, DC: American Historical Association, 1972).
9. Janice C. May, "Constitutional Amendment and Revision Revisited," *Publius* 12 (Winter 1982): 153–79.
10. Charles Wiggins, "Executive Vetoes and Legislative Overrides in the American States," *Journal of Politics* 54 (November 1980): 42. Also see Glenn Abney and Thomas Lauth, "The Line-Item Veto in the States," *Public Administration Review* 45 (January/February 1985): 66–79.
11. F. Ted Hebert, Jeffrey L. Brudney, and Deil S. Wright, "Gubernatorial Influence and State Bureaucracy," *American Politics Quarterly* 11 (April 1983): 37–52; and Abney and Lauth, "The Governor as Chief Administrator," *Public Administration Quarterly* 3 (January/February 1983): 40–49.
12. Thad L. Beyle and Robert Dalton, "Appointment Power: Does It Belong to the Governor?" *State Government* 54(1) (Winter 1981): 6.
13. Leon W. Blevins, *Texas Government in National Perspective* (Englewood Cliffs, NJ: Prentice-Hall, 1987), 169.
14. James L. Garnett, *Reorganizing State Government: The Executive Branch* (Boulder, CO: Westview, 1980), 8 and 9; and Diane Kincaid Blair, "The Gubernatorial Appointment Power: Too Much of a Good Thing?" *State Government* 55 (Summer 1982): 88–91.
15. Timothy O'Rourke, *The Impact of Reapportionment* (New Brunswick, NJ: Transaction Books, 1980).
16. Council of State Governments, *Book of the States, 2000–01* (Lexington, KY: Council of State Governments, 2000), 49.
17. Gary T. Clarke and Charles R. Grezlak, "Legislative Staffs Show Improvement," *National Civic Review* 65 (June 1976): 292.
18. Gerald Benjamin and Michael J. Malin, eds., *Limiting Legislative Terms* (Washington, DC: CQ Press, 1992).
19. Diana Gordon, "Citizen Legislators—Alive and Well," *State Legislatures* 20 (January 1994): 24–27.
20. Earl M. Maltz, "Federalism and State Court Activism," *Intergovernmental Perspective* (Spring 1987): 23–26.
21. Thomas E. Cronin, *Direct Democracy* (Cambridge, MA: Harvard University Press, 1989); and David B. Magleby, *Direct Legislation* (Baltimore, MD: Johns Hopkins University Press, 1984).
22. Alexis de Tocqueville, *Democracy in America*, Phillips Bradley, ed. (New York: Knopf, 1945), 40.
23. *City of Clinton* v. *Cedar Rapids and Missouri River Railroad Co.* (Iowa, 1868).
24. Steven P. Erie, *Rainbow's End: Irish-Americans and the Dilemmas of Urban Machine Politics, 1840–1985* (Berkeley: University of California Press, 1988); Alfred Steinberg, *The Bosses* (New York: New American Library, 1972); Seymour Mandelbaum, *Boss Tweed's New York* (New York: Wiley, 1955); and Milton Rakove, *Don't Make No Waves—Don't Back No Losers: An Insider's Analysis of the Daley Machine* (Bloomington: Indiana University Press, 1975).
25. Samuel P. Hays, "The Politics of Reform in Municipal Government in the Progressive Era," *Pacific Northwest Quarterly* 55 (October 1964): 157–66.
26. Sharon O'Brien, *American Indian Tribal Governments* (Norman: University of Oklahoma Press, 1989), 261–97.
27. U.S. Census Bureau, *Government Finances in 1993–1994* (Washington, DC: Government Printing Office, 1994), 12–19.
28. http://www.nga.org/center/divisions/1,1188,C_ISSUE_BRIEF^D_2915,00.html.

Civil Liberties

5

In spring 2000, the principal of Highland Springs High School in Virginia entered teacher Liz Armstrong's tenth-grade biology class to announce a "random search."[1] In spite of the cry that went up from the class, the principal and other administrators forced students to empty their pockets, pocketbooks, and backpacks. No weapons or drugs were found.

Armstrong, a nine-year veteran of the classroom, was outraged and promised her students that she would find out more about the public school district's search policy as well as contact the American Civil Liberties Union (ACLU) on her students' behalf. The next day she received a letter from the president of the Virginia ACLU informing her that the search was "clearly illegal" because it violated not only the students' Fourth Amendment right to be free from unlawful and unwarranted searches and seizures, but also the guidelines of the Virginia Board of Education regarding student searches. Upon receipt of the letter, Armstrong sent a letter to her principal informing him of the unlawfulness of the search and suggesting how a legal policy could be implemented.

Armstrong was suspended a few days later. She wasn't charged with speaking up for her students; instead, she was charged with failing to make "effective use of instructional time." How did Armstrong do that? By talking to her students about the search. In May, she was dismissed from her position.

In the wake of the 1999 shootings at Columbine High School in Littleton, Colorado, many school boards and districts instituted zero-tolerance weapons policies for students and teachers. In spite of federal rulings to the contrary, students often fall prey to overzealous administrators as they attempt to keep order in their schools. This balancing of rights—in this case the right of students to be free from unreasonable searches and seizures, as well as to some expectation of privacy for their persons and their belongings, versus a community's and other students' right to be free from violence and harm in the classroom—points out how relevant the writings of John Locke and Thomas Hobbes are today. Although these students were victims of an unlawful search, unless they wish to sue, they have little other recourse.

*W*hen the Bill of Rights, which contains many of the most important protections of individual rights, was written, its drafters were not thinking about issues such as abortion, gay rights, physician assisted suicide, or many of the personal liberties discussed in this chapter. Civil liberties issues often present complex problems. The balancing of civil liberties, especially when competing interests are at stake, is made even more difficult by the non-absolute nature of most civil liberties. Frequently, courts or policy makers are called on to balance competing interests and rights. As a society, for example, how much infringement on our personal liberties do we want to give the police? Do we want to have different rules for our homes, classrooms, lockers, dorm rooms, or cars? Do we want to give the Federal Bureau of Investigation (FBI) the right to tap the phones of suspected terrorists or to hold them in jail without access to a lawyer without probable cause?

In many of the cases discussed in the chapter, there is a conflict between an individual or group of individuals seeking to exercise what they believe to be a right, and the government, be it local, state, or national, seeking to control the exercise of that right in an attempt to keep order and preserve the rights (and safety) of others. In others, two liberties are in conflict, such as a physician's and her patients' rights to easy access to a medical clinic versus a pro-life advocate's liberty to picket that clinic. It generally falls to the judiciary to balance those interests. And, depending on the composition of the Supreme Court and the times, the balance may lean toward civil liberties or toward the power of the government to limit those rights.

Civil liberties are the personal rights and freedoms that the federal government cannot abridge, either by law, or judicial interpretation. Civil liberties guarantees place limitations on the power of the government to restrain or dictate how individuals act. Thus, when we discuss civil liberties such as those found in the Bill of Rights, we are concerned with limits on what governments can and cannot do. Civil rights, in contrast, refer to the positive actions of the government taken to protect individuals against arbitrary or discriminatory treatment. Civil rights are discussed in chapter 6.

In the wake of September 11, 2001, Americans' perceptions about civil liberties and what they are willing to allow the government to do experienced a sea change. As discussed on p. 151 in Politics Now: Civil Liberties and the Bush Administration, with passage of the USA Patriot Act, the federal government was given unprecedented authority to curtail civil liberties on a scope never before seen. When any political commentators or civil libertarians voiced concerns about the act and its consequences—the ability to do so being a hallmark of a free society—their voices were drowned out by many politicians and other pundits and their patriotism attacked. Free speech doesn't seem quite so free anymore.

Moreover, during the 2001–2002 term of the Supreme Court of the United States, the justices were forced from their chambers for the first time since they moved into the Court in 1935. Threats of airborne anthrax closed the Court and several Senate buildings. While the nation was worrying about terrorist attacks from abroad or from within, a quiet revolution in civil liberties continued apace. The five conservative and four moderate Supreme Court justices—who have served together since 1994, longer than any other group of justices since 1820—proceeded to make major changes in long-standing practices in a wide range of civil liberties issues.[2] As the Court continued to veer to the right, the attorney general of the United States, a devout Christian, not only held regular daily prayer meetings for staffers in his office but continued to advocate new restrictions on civil liberties. Many of the Court's recent decisions, as well as actions of the attorney general, are discussed in this chapter as we explore the various dimensions of civil liberties guarantees contained in the U.S. Constitution and the Bill of Rights:

- First, we will discuss *the Bill of Rights*, the reasons for its addition to the Constitution, and its eventual application to the states via the incorporation doctrine.

- Second, we will survey the meaning of *the First Amendment's guarantees of freedom of religion*.

civil liberties
The personal rights and freedoms that the federal government cannot abridge by law, constitution, or judicial interpretation.

Simulation

Balancing Liberty and Security in a Time of War

- Third, we will discuss the meanings of *the free speech and press guarantees found in the First Amendment*.

- Fourth, we will discuss *the right to keep and bear arms found in the Second Amendment*.

- Fifth, we will analyze the reasons for many of *the criminal defendants' rights* found in the Bill of Rights and how those rights have been expanded and contracted by the U.S. Supreme Court.

- Sixth, we will discuss the meaning of *the right to privacy* and how that concept has been interpreted by the Court.

- In our exploration of the theme of *continuity and change* in American politics, we will consider changes in our conceptions of civil liberties over time.

THE FIRST CONSTITUTIONAL AMENDMENTS: THE BILL OF RIGHTS

In 1787, most state constitutions explicitly protected a variety of personal liberties such as speech, religion, freedom from unreasonable searches and seizures, and trial by jury, among others. It was clear that the new Constitution would redistribute power in the new federal system between the national government and the states. Without an explicit guarantee of specific civil liberties, could the national government be trusted to uphold the freedoms already granted to citizens by their states?

Recognition of the increased power that would be held by the new national government led Anti-Federalists to stress the need for a bill of rights. Anti-Federalists and many others were confident that they could control the actions of their own state legislators, but they didn't trust the national government to be so protective of their civil liberties.

The notion of adding a bill of rights to the Constitution was not a popular one at the Constitutional Convention. When George Mason of Virginia proposed that such

WEB EXPLORATION
To view an original copy of the Bill of Rights, see
www.ablongman.com/oconnor

Radio personality Howard Stern was suspended by Clear Channel Communications in February, 2004 for "vulgar, offensive, and insulting" content on his syndicated morning show. Stern and critics of the George W. Bush Administration later speculated that his suspension and subsequent firing were actually the result of his recent, anti-Bush rhetoric.

(Photo courtesy: Patricia Schroeder/ABC Inc.)

a bill be added to the preface of the proposed Constitution, his resolution was defeated unanimously.[3] In the subsequent ratification debates, Federalists argued that a bill of rights was unnecessary. Not only did most state constitutions already contain those protections, but Federalists believed it was foolhardy to list things that the national government had no power to do since the proposed Constitution didn't give the national government the power to regulate speech, religion, and the like.

Some Federalists, however, supported the idea. After the Philadelphia convention, for example, James Madison conducted a lively correspondence about the need for a national bill of rights with Thomas Jefferson. Jefferson was far quicker to support such guarantees than was Madison, who continued to doubt their utility because he believed that a list of "protected" rights might suggest that those not enumerated were not protected. Politics soon intervened, however, when Madison found himself in a close race against James Monroe for a seat in the House of Representatives in the First Congress. The district was largely Anti-Federalist. So in an act of political expediency, Madison issued a new series of public letters similar to *The Federalist Papers* in which he vowed to support a bill of rights.

Once elected to the House, Madison made good on his promise and became the prime mover and author of the Bill of Rights. Still, he considered Congress to have far more important matters to handle and viewed his work on the Bill of Rights "a nauseous project."[4]

The insistence of Anti-Federalists on a bill of rights, the fact that some states conditioned their ratification of the Constitution on the addition of these guarantees, and the disagreement among Federalists about writing specific liberty guarantees into the Constitution, led to prompt congressional action to put an end to further controversy. This was a time when national stability and support for the new government were particularly needed. Thus, in 1789, Congress sent the proposed Bill of Rights to the states for ratification, which occurred in 1791.

The **Bill of Rights,** the first ten amendments to the Constitution, contains numerous specific guarantees, including those of free speech, press, and religion (see Appendix II for the full text). The Ninth and Tenth Amendments in particular highlight Anti-Federalist fears of a too-powerful national government. The **Ninth Amendment,** strongly favored by Madison, makes it clear that this special listing of rights does not mean that others don't exist; and the Tenth Amendment simply reiterates that powers not delegated to the national government are reserved to the states or the people.

The Incorporation Doctrine: The Bill of Rights Made Applicable to the States

The Bill of Rights was intended to limit the powers of the national government to infringe on the rights and liberties of the citizenry. In *Barron* v. *Baltimore* (1833), the Supreme Court ruled that the federal Bill of Rights limited only the U.S. government and not the states.[5] In 1868, however, the Fourteenth Amendment was added to the U.S. Constitution. Its language suggested the possibility that some or even all of the protections guaranteed in the Bill of Rights might be interpreted to prevent state infringement of those rights. Section 1 of the Fourteenth Amendment reads: "No State shall … deprive any person of life, liberty, or property, without due process of law."

Until nearly the turn of the century, the Supreme Court steadfastly rejected numerous arguments urging it to interpret the **due process clause** found in the Fourteenth Amendment as making various provisions contained in the Bill of Rights applicable to the states. In 1897, however, the Court began to increase its jurisdiction over the states.[6] It began to hold states to a **substantive due process** standard whereby state laws had to be shown to be a valid exercise of the state's power to regulate the health, welfare, or public morals of its citizens. Interferences with state power, however, were rare. As a consequence, states continued to pass sedition laws (laws that made it illegal to speak

Bill of Rights
The first ten amendments to the U.S. Constitution, which largely guarantee specific rights and liberties.

Ninth Amendment
Part of the Bill of Rights that reads "The enumeration in the Constitution, of certain rights, shall not be construed to deny or disparage others retained by the people."

due process clause
Clause contained in the Fifth and Fourteenth Amendments. Over the years, it has been construed to guarantee to individuals a variety of rights ranging from economic liberty to criminal procedural rights to protection from arbitrary governmental action.

substantive due process
Judicial interpretation of the Fifth and Fourteenth Amendments' due process clause that protects citizens from arbitrary or unjust laws.

or write any political criticism that threatened to diminish respect for the government, its laws, or public officials), expecting that the Supreme Court would uphold their constitutionality. Then, in 1925, all of this changed dramatically. Benjamin Gitlow, a member of the Socialist Party, was convicted of violating a New York law that, in language very similar to that of the federal Espionage Act, prohibited the advocacy of the violent overthrow of the government. Gitlow had printed 16,000 copies of a manifesto in which he urged workers to rise up to overthrow the U.S. government. Although Gitlow's conviction was upheld, in *Gitlow* v. *New York* (1925) the Supreme Court noted that the states were not completely free to limit forms of political expression:

> For present purposes we may and do assume that freedom of speech and of the press—which are protected by the First Amendment from abridgement by Congress—are among the *fundamental personal rights and "liberties"* protected by the due process clause of the Fourteenth Amendment from impairment by the states [emphasis added].[7]

Until *Gitlow* v. *New York* (1925), involving Benjamin Gitlow, the executive secretary of the Socialist Party, it generally was thought that the Fourteenth Amendment did not apply the protections of the Bill of Rights to the states. Here Gitlow is shown testifying before a congressional committee, which was investigating un-American activities.

(Photo courtesy: AP/Wide World Photos)

Gitlow, with its finding that states could not abridge free speech protections, was the first step in the slow development of the **incorporation doctrine.** After *Gitlow*, it took the Court six more years to "incorporate" another First Amendment freedom—that of the press. *Near* v. *Minnesota* (1931) was the first case in which the Supreme Court found that a state law violated freedom of the press as protected by the First Amendment. Jay Near, the publisher of a weekly Minneapolis newspaper, regularly attacked a variety of groups—African Americans, Catholics, Jews, and labor union leaders. Few escaped his hatred. Near's paper was shut down under the authority of a state criminal libel law banning "malicious, scandalous, or defamatory" publications. Near appealed the closing of his paper, and the Supreme Court ruled that "The fact that the liberty of the press may be abused by miscreant purveyors of scandal does not make any the less necessary the immunity of the press from previous restraint."[8]

As revealed in Table 5.1, not all the specific guarantees in the Bill of Rights have been made applicable to the states through the due process clause of the Fourteenth Amendment. Instead, the Court selectively has chosen to limit the rights of states by protecting the rights it considers most fundamental, and thus subject to the Court's most rigorous strict scrutiny review. This process is referred to as **selective incorporation.**

Selective incorporation requires the states to respect freedoms of press, speech, and assembly among other rights. Other guarantees contained in the Second, Third, and Seventh Amendments, such as the right to bear arms, have not been incorporated because the Court has yet to consider them sufficiently fundamental to national notions of liberty and justice.

incorporation doctrine
An interpretation of the Constitution that holds that the due process clause of the Fourteenth Amendment requires that state and local governments also guarantee those rights.

selective incorporation
A judicial doctrine whereby most but not all of the protections found in the Bill of Rights are made applicable to the states via the Fourteenth Amendment.

Selective Incorporation and Fundamental Freedoms

The rationale for selective incorporation, the judicial application to the states of only some of the rights enumerated by the Bill of Rights, was set out by the Court in *Palko* v. *Connecticut* (1937).[9] Frank Palko was charged with first-degree murder for killing two Connecticut police officers, found guilty of a lesser charge of second-degree murder,

TABLE 5.1   The Selective Incorporation of the Bill of Rights

Date	Amendment	Right	Case
1925	I.	Speech	*Gitlow* v. *New York*
1931		Press	*Near* v. *Minnesota*
1937		Assembly	*DeJonge* v. *Oregon*
1940		Religion	*Cantwell* v. *Connecticut*
	II.	Right to bear arms	*not incorporated* (Generally, the Supreme Court has upheld reasonable regulations of the right of private citizens to bear arms. Should a tough gun-control law be adopted by a state or local government and a challenge to it be made, a test of incorporation might be presented to the Court in the future.)
	III.	No quartering of soldiers	*not incorporated* (The quartering problem has not recurred since colonial times.)
1949	IV.	Unreasonable searches and seizures	*Wolf* v. *Colorado*
1961		Exclusionary rule	*Mapp* v. *Ohio*
1897	V.	Just compensation	*Chicago, B&O R.R. Co.* v. *Chicago*
1964		Self-incrimination	*Malloy* v. *Hogan*
1969		Double jeopardy	*Benton* v. *Maryland* (overruled *Palko* v. *Connecticut*)
		Grand jury indictment	*not incorporated* (The trend in state criminal cases is away from grand juries and toward reliance on the sworn written accusation of the prosecuting attorney.)
1948	VI.	Public trial	*In re Oliver*
1963		Right to counsel	*Gideon* v. *Wainwright*
1965		Confrontation of witnesses	*Pointer* v. *Texas*
1966		Impartial trial	*Parker* v. *Gladden*
1967		Speedy trial	*Klopfer* v. *North Carolina*
1967		Compulsory trial	*Washington* v. *Texas*
1968		Jury trial	*Duncan* v. *Louisiana*
	VII.	Right to jury trial in civil cases	*not incorporated* (While Warren Burger was chief justice, he conducted a campaign to abolish jury trials in civil cases to save time and money.)
1962	VIII.	Freedom from cruel and unusual punishment	*Robinson* v. *California*
		Freedom from excessive fines or bail	*not incorporated*

and sentenced to life imprisonment. Connecticut appealed. Palko was retried, found guilty of first-degree murder, and resentenced to death. Palko then appealed his second conviction on the ground that it violated the Fifth Amendment's prohibition against double jeopardy because the Fifth Amendment had been made applicable to the states by the due process clause of the Fourteenth Amendment.

The Supreme Court upheld Palko's second conviction and the death sentence, thereby choosing not to bind states to the Fifth Amendment's double jeopardy clause. This decision set forth principles that were to guide the Court's interpretation of the incorporation doctrine for the next several decades. Some protections found in the Bill of Rights were absorbed into the concept of due process only because they are so fundamental to our notions of liberty and justice that they cannot be denied by the states unless the state can show what is called a compelling reason for the liberties' curtailment. This is a very high burden of proof for a state. Thus, abridgments of fundamental rights are rarely allowed by the Court. Because the Court concluded that protection from being tried twice (double jeopardy) was not a fundamental right, Palko's appeal was rejected. He died in Connecticut's gas chamber one year later. Fundamental rights include not only less than the whole of the Bill of Rights, but more—that is, other unenumerated rights, such as the right to privacy, while selective incorporation implies that only some enumerated rights enjoy the highest degree of protection.

FIRST AMENDMENT GUARANTEES: FREEDOM OF RELIGION

Today, many lawmakers bemoan the absence of religion in the public schools and voice their concerns that America is becoming a godless nation in spite of the fact that 63 percent of all Americans belong to a church or synagogue. Many of the Framers were religious men, but they knew what evils could arise if the new nation was not founded with religious freedom as one of its core ideals. Despite the fact that many colonists had fled Europe primarily to escape religious persecution, most colonies actively persecuted those who did not belong to their predominant religious groups. Pennsylvania, for example, was a Quaker colony. The Congregationalist Church of Massachusetts, a Puritan colony, taxed and harassed those who held other religious beliefs. Nevertheless, in 1774 the colonists uniformly were outraged when the British Parliament passed a law establishing Anglicanism and Roman Catholicism as official religions in the colonies. The First Continental Congress immediately sent a letter of protest announcing its "astonishment that a British Parliament should ever consent to establish ... a religion [Catholicism] that has deluged [England] in blood and dispersed bigotry, persecution, murder and rebellion through every part of the world."[10]

This distaste for a national church or religion was reflected in the Constitution. Article VI, for example, provides that "no religious Test shall ever be required as a Qualification to any Office or Public Trust under the United States." This simple statement, however, did not reassure those who feared the new Constitution would curtail individual liberty. Thus, the First Amendment to the Constitution soon was ratified to allay those fears.

The **First Amendment** to the Constitution begins, "Congress shall make no law respecting an establishment of religion, or prohibiting the free exercise thereof." This statement sets the boundaries of governmental action. The **establishment clause** ("Congress shall make no law respecting an establishment of religion") directs the national government not to involve itself in religion. It creates, in Thomas Jefferson's words, a "wall of separation" between church and state. The **free exercise clause** ("or prohibiting the free exercise thereof") guarantees citizens that the national government will not interfere with their practice of religion. These guarantees, however, are not absolute. In the mid-1800s, Mormons traditionally practiced and preached polygamy, the taking of multiple wives. In 1879, when the Supreme Court was first called on to interpret the free exercise clause, it upheld the conviction of a Mormon under a federal law barring polygamy. The Court reasoned that to do otherwise would provide constitutional protections to a full range of religious beliefs, including those as extreme as human sacrifice. "Laws are made for the government of actions," noted the Court, "and while they cannot interfere with mere religious belief and opinions, they may with practices."[11] Later, in 1940, the Supreme Court observed that the First Amendment "embraces two concepts—freedom to believe and freedom to act. The first is absolute, but in the nature of things, the second cannot be. Conduct remains subject to regulation of society."[12]

The Establishment Clause

Over the years, the Court has been divided over how to interpret the establishment clause. Does this clause erect a total wall between church and state, or is some governmental

WEB EXPLORATION
For groups with opposing views on how the First Amendment should be interpreted, see www.ablongman.com/oconnor

First Amendment
Part of the Bill of Rights that imposes a number of restrictions on the federal government with respect to the civil liberties of the people, including freedom of religion, speech, press, assembly, and petition.

establishment clause
The first clause in the First Amendment. It prohibits the national government from establishing a national religion.

free exercise clause
The second clause of the First Amendment. It prohibits the U.S. government from interfering with a citizen's right to practice his or her religion.

accommodation of religion allowed? While the Supreme Court has upheld the constitutionality of many kinds of church/state entanglements such as public funding to provide sign language interpreters for deaf students in religious schools,[13] the Court has held fast to the rule of strict separation between church and state when issues of prayer in school are involved. In *Engel* v. *Vitale* (1962), the Court first ruled that the recitation in public school classrooms of a twenty-two-word nondenominational prayer drafted by the New Hyde Park, New York, school board was unconstitutional.[14] In 1992, the Court continued its unwillingness to allow prayer in public schools by finding unconstitutional the saying of prayer at a middle school graduation.[15] In 2000, the Court ruled that student-led, student-initiated prayer at high school football games violated the establishment clause. But, in 2001, it refused to hear a challenge to a Virginia law that requires students to observe a moment of silence at the start of each school day.[16]

The Court has gone back and forth in its effort to come up with a workable way to deal with church/state questions. In 1971, in *Lemon* v. *Kurtzman*, the Court tried to carve out a three-part test for laws dealing with religious establishment issues. According to the *Lemon* test, a practice or policy was constitutional if it: (1) had a secular purpose; (2) neither advanced nor inhibited religion; and, (3) did not foster an excessive government entanglement with religion.[17] But, since the early 1980s, the Supreme Court often has sidestepped the *Lemon* test altogether,[18] and has appeared more willing to lower the wall between church and state so long as school prayer is not involved. In 1981, for example, the Court ruled unconstitutional a Missouri law prohibiting the use of state university buildings and grounds for "purposes of religious worship," which had been used to ban religious groups from using school facilities.[19]

This decision was taken by many members of Congress as a sign that this principle could be extended to secondary and even primary schools. In 1984, Congress passed the Equal Access Act, which bars public schools from discriminating against groups of students on the basis of "religious, political, philosophical or other content of the speech at such meetings." The constitutionality of this law was upheld in 1990 when the Court ruled that a school board's refusal to allow a Christian Bible club to meet in a public high school classroom during a twice-weekly "activity period" violated the act. According to the decision, the primary effect of the act was neither to advance religion nor to excessively entangle government and religion—even though religious meetings would be held on school grounds with a faculty sponsor. The important factor seemed to be that the students had complete choice in their selection of activities with numerous nonreligious options.[20] In 1993, the Court also ruled that religious groups must be allowed to use public schools after hours if that access is also given to other community groups.[21]

Many believed that the 1993 replacement of Justice Byron White by Ruth Bader Ginsburg, a former attorney for the ACLU (see Roots of Government: The American Civil Liberties Union), would halt the trend toward lowering the wall between church and state. But, in 1995, the Court signalled that it was willing to lower the wall even further. Ironically, it did so in a case involving Thomas Jefferson's own University of Virginia. In a 5–4 decision, the majority held that the university violated the First Amendment's

Before members of various faith-based organizations, President George W. Bush signs a presidential executive order creating the controversial Office of Faith-Based and Community Initiatives, which some fear is a lowering of the wall between church and state.

(Photo courtesy: AFB/Corbis)

THE AMERICAN CIVIL LIBERTIES UNION

The American Civil Liberties Union (ACLU) was created in 1920 by a group that had tried to defend the civil liberties of those who were conscientious objectors to World War I. As the nation's oldest, largest, and premier nonpartisan civil liberties organization, the ACLU works in three major areas of the law: freedom of speech and religion, due process, and equality before the law. It lobbies for legislation affecting these areas and litigates to maintain these rights and liberties.

Over time, the national ACLU or one of its state affiliates (as was the case in our opening vignette) has been involved in one way or another in almost every major civil liberties case discussed in this chapter. It was at the fore of the sedition cases brought in the wake of World War I and was involved in the famous *Scopes* case in 1925, which challenged a Tennessee law that made it a crime to teach evolution. It has represented flag burners, Nazis, and skinheads in its zealous and often unpopular defense of the Bill of Rights.

In addition to filing lawsuits challenging governmental actions that it believes do not uphold the many protections contained in the Bill of Rights, the ACLU also lobbies vigorously at the national and state levels against legislation it believes could negatively restrict civil liberties. Thus, for example, in 2002, it opposed a move by the Bush administration to recruit individuals such as telephone or cable service repair persons or mail carriers to report suspicious activity that they see in their daily work. The proposed Terrorism Information and Prevention hotline (TIPS), said the ACLU, would turn the Fourth and Fifth Amendments on their heads.

---

establishment of religion clause by failing to fund a religious student magazine written by a fundamentalist Christian student group even though it funded similar magazines published by 118 other student groups, some of which were religiously based.[22] In dissent, the importance of this decision was highlighted by Justice David Souter, who noted: "The Court today, for the first time, approves direct funding of core religious activities by an arm of the state."[23] And, it continues to do so.

In 1997, in *Agostini* v. *Felton*, the Supreme Court approved of a New York program that sent public school teachers into parochial schools during school hours to provide remedial education to disadvantaged students. The Court concluded that this was not an excessive entanglement of church and state and therefore was not a violation of the establishment clause.[24]

For more than a quarter century, the Supreme Court basically allowed "books only" as an aid to religious schools, noting that the books go to children, not to the schools themselves. In 2000, however, the Court voted 6–3 to uphold the constitutionality of a federal aid provision that allowed the government to lend books and computers to religious schools.[25] And, in 2002, by a bitterly divided 5–4 vote, the Supreme Court in *Zelman* v. *Simmons-Harris* concluded that governments can give money to parents to allow them to send their children to private or religious schools.[26] The majority opinion, written by Chief Justice William H. Rehnquist, concluded that Cleveland's school voucher program gives families freedom of choice to send their children to the school of their choice. He concluded that the voucher system was neutral toward religion and, thus, was not an official sponsorship of religion prohibited by the establishment clause. In dissent, Justice David Souter called the opinion a "potentially tragic" error that "would force citizens to subsidize faiths they do not even share even as it corrupts religion by making it dependent on government."[27] Basically, building on a line of cases that many argue further erode the wall between church and state, the Court now appears willing to support programs so long as they provide aid to religious and nonreligious schools alike, and the money goes to persons who exercise free choice over how it is used.

WEB EXPLORATION
For more information on *Agostini v. Felton*, see www.ablongman.com/oconnor

Snake handling, once more common as part of certain fundamentalist Christian religious services, is banned by law in many parts of the South.

(Photo courtesy: Bettmann/Corbis)

The Free Exercise Clause

The free exercise clause of the First Amendment proclaims that "Congress shall make no law … prohibiting the free exercise [of religion]." Although the free exercise clause of the First Amendment guarantees individuals the right to be free from governmental interference in the exercise of their religion, this guarantee, like other First Amendment freedoms, is not absolute. When secular law comes into conflict with religious law, the right to exercise one's religious beliefs is often denied—especially if the religious beliefs in question are held by a minority or by an unpopular or "suspicious" religious group. State statutes barring the use of certain illegal drugs, snake handling, and polygamy—all practices of particular religious sects—have been upheld as constitutional when states have shown compelling reasons to regulate these practices. Nonetheless, the Court has made it clear that the free exercise clause requires that a state or the national government remain neutral toward religion.

Many critics of rigid enforcement of such neutrality argue that the government should do what it can to accommodate the religious diversity in our nation. Nevertheless, the Court has interpreted the Constitution to mean that governmental interests can outweigh free exercise rights. In 1990, for example, the Supreme Court ruled that the free exercise clause allowed Oregon to ban the use of sacramental peyote (an illegal hallucinogenic drug) in some Native American tribes' traditional religious services. The focus of the case turned on what standard of review the Court should use. Should the Court use the compelling state interest test? In upholding the state's right to deny unemployment compensation to two workers who had been fired by a private drug rehabilitation clinic because they had ingested an illegal substance, a majority of the Court held that the state did not need to show a compelling interest to limit the free exercise of religion.[28] This decision prompted a dramatic outcry. Congressional response was passage of the Religious Freedom Restoration Act, which reinstated strict scrutiny as the required judicial standard of review to make it harder for states to interfere with how citizens practice their religion. In 1997, however, the Supreme Court ruled that the act was unconstitutional.[29]

In contrast, in 1993, the Supreme Court ruled that members of the Santería Church, an Afro-Cuban religion, had the right to sacrifice animals during religious services. In upholding that practice, the Court ruled that a city ordinance banning such practices was unconstitutionally aimed at the group, thereby denying its members the right to free exercise of their religion.[30]

"I'M HOLDING A PRESS CONFERENCE PRAISING THE SUPREME COURT FOR STRIKING DOWN STATE-SPONSORED PRAYER... JUST AS SOON AS THE SENATE CHAPLAIN FINISHES HIS BENEDICTION."

(Photo courtesy: HENRY PAYNE reprinted by permission of United Feature Syndicate, Inc.)

Global Politics

RELIGIOUS FREEDOM

As discussed in earlier chapters, the First Amendment to the U.S. Constitution was based in an understanding of comparative politics. The Framers had seen what religious intolerance meant in Europe, and furthermore understood the establishment of official religions as a basic violation of civil liberties.

In terms of constitutional guarantees of religious freedom, the United States today resembles many countries. As the table to the right shows, most countries have no established state religion. Until recently, however, Britain's Anglicanism guaranteed the right of Anglican bishops to sit in the House of Lords. The Egyptian Constitution establishes Islam as the state religion and stipulates that Islamic law is the principal source of legislation in the country. Atheism is the state religion of the People's Republic of China.

The Canadian, French, Japanese, and German Constitutions all guarantee religious freedom. Reflecting the heavy American involvement in drafting Japan's current Constitution, the guarantee of religious freedom in that document closely paraphrases the First Amendment of the U.S. Bill of Rights. Germany's Basic Law goes further than its U.S. counterpart, guaranteeing the right of conscientious objection as part of religious freedom.

How states interact with religious organizations varies across countries. Many do not share the Jeffersonian insistence on a wall of separation between church and state. Many European countries, including Germany, have religious based parties such as the Christian Democratic Party in their parliaments, most of which emerged out of Catholic parties. The German Basic Law, for example, lacks an establishment clause per se. The government subsidizes both the Catholic Church and the Lutheran Synods within its borders, and citizens designate a portion of their income taxes for that purpose.

Egypt and Indonesia provide an interesting comparison of the separation of church and state in Muslim countries. In both cases, the governments of these Islamic societies have been concerned that religion not become the driving force in national politics. Egypt's Constitution stipulates that Islam is the state religion and Islamic law the basis of the legal system.

The Establishment Clause in Comparative Perspective

Country	State Religion	Main Religion
Canada	None	Christianity
China	Atheism	Confucianism
Egypt	Islam	Islam
France	None	Christianity (Catholicism)
Germany	None	Christianity
India	None	Hinduism
Indonesia	None	Islam
Italy	None	Christianity (Catholicism)
Japan	None	Buddhimsm, Shinto
Mexico	None	Christianity (Catholicism)
Russia	None	Orthodox Christianity
United Kingdom	Christianity (Church of England-Anglicanism)	Christianity (Church of England-Anglicanism)
United States	None	Christianity

Source: *L'Atlas Geopolitique et Cultural du Petit Robert des Noms Propres* (Paris: Dictionnaires les Robert, 1999), 51.

Other countries in which Islam is the state religion include Iran and Malaysia. Acknowledgment of Islam in this manner does not mean that the Egyptian government necessarily views Islamic political organizations with favor. The government has banned the Muslim Brotherhood, a radical Islamic party. Despite its illegal status, however, the Brotherhood's candidates garnered about 3 percent of the vote in the 2000 parliamentary election. In sum, the government has tried to balance constitutional guarantees of Islam's central place in society with the desire to create and maintain a secular state.

Indonesia's population is about 90 percent Muslim (it is the world's most populous Islamic country). Its political elite tends to come from Java, however, where Islam competes with local animistic beliefs. While Indonesia's 1945 Constitution does not acknowledge a state religion, the national ideology of Pancasila identifies monotheism as a component of national identity, and therefore of national policy. In practice, the state has supported Islamic organizations financially. Today, the Indonesian national government faces political and separatist challenges from Muslim groups that threaten the integrity of the state itself.

Although conflicts between religious beliefs and the government are often difficult to settle, the Court has attempted to walk the fine line between the free exercise and establishment clauses. In the area of free exercise, the Court often has had to confront questions of "What is a god?" and "What is a religious faith?"—questions that theologians have grappled with for centuries. In 1965, for example, in a case involving three men who were denied conscientious objector deferments during the Vietnam War because they did not subscribe to "traditional" organized religions, the Court ruled unanimously that belief in a supreme being was not essential for recognition as a conscientious objector.[31] Thus,

Comparative

Comparing
Civil Liberties

149

the men were entitled to the deferments because their views paralleled those who objected to war and who belonged to traditional religions. In contrast, despite the Court's having ruled that Catholic, Protestant, Jewish, and Buddhist prison inmates must be allowed to hold religious services,[32] in 1987, it ruled that Islamic prisoners could be denied the same right for security reasons.[33]

FIRST AMENDMENT GUARANTEES: FREEDOM OF SPEECH AND PRESS

Today some members of Congress criticize the movie industry and television talk shows, including *The Jerry Springer Show,* for pandering to the least common denominator of society. Other groups criticize popular performers such as Eminem for lyrics that promote violence, in general, and against women, in particular. Despite the distastefulness of some talk show topics or musical lyrics, many civil libertarians have resisted even the suggestion that these things be regulated. To learn about recent actions affecting civil liberties, see Politics Now: Civil Liberties and the Bush Administration.

A democracy depends on a free exchange of ideas, and the First Amendment shows that the Framers were well aware of this fact. Historically, one of the most volatile areas of constitutional interpretation has been in the interpretation of the First Amendment's mandate that "Congress shall make no law … abridging the freedom of speech, or of the press." Like the establishment and free exercise clauses of the First Amendment, the speech and press clauses have not been interpreted as absolute bans against government regulation. In fact, over the years the Court has used a hierarchical approach, with some items getting greater protection than others. Generally, thoughts have received the greatest protection, and actions or deeds the least. Words have come somewhere in the middle, depending on their content and purpose.

In the United States, thoughts are considered beyond the scope of governmental regulation, but motives often are considered in assessing the legality of some activities such as hate crimes. Although people may experience a negative reaction for revealing their thoughts, the government has no legal right to punish or sanction Americans for what they think. Words, which stand between thoughts and deeds, are subject to some forms of restraint. Speech that is obscene, libelous (false and causing someone disrepute), or seditious (advocating violent overthrow of the government), or that could incite or cause injury to those to whom it is addressed, has been interpreted as not protected by the First Amendment. Often, however, these exceptions to constitutional protection have troubled the Court. What is considered obscene in rural Mississippi, for example, may not offend someone in another part of the nation.

Actions, or deeds, are given the least constitutional protection. Thus, actions are subject to the greatest governmental restrictions. For example, you may have a right to shoot a pistol in your back yard, but it is illegal to do so on most city streets. Over the years these competing rights have been balanced by the now classic observation that your "right to swing your arm ends at the tip of my nose."[34]

When the First Amendment was ratified in 1791, it was considered to protect only against **prior restraint** of speech or expression, that is, to guard against the prohibition of speech or publication before the fact. As was the case in Great Britain concerning free speech, the First Amendment was not considered to provide absolute immunity from governmental sanction for what speakers or publishers might say or print. Thus, over the years, the meaning of this amendment's mandate has been subject to thousands of cases seeking judicial interpretation of its meaning.

prior restraint
Constitutional doctrine that prevents the government from prohibiting speech or publication before the fact; generally held to be in violation of the First Amendment.

The one-time immense popularity of Jerry Springer's nationally syndicated talk show often was cited by many to underscore declining morals and the need to regulate the airways.

(Photo courtesy: Todd Buchanan/Black Star/Stockphoto)

CIVIL LIBERTIES AND THE BUSH ADMINISTRATION

The Uniting and Strengthening America by Providing Appropriate Tools Required to Enhance Law Enforcement Investigatory Tools legislation—called, for short, the USA Patriot Act—was introduced in the House on October 23, 2001, and the Senate on October 24, and was on President George W. Bush's desk for his signature just two days later. This lengthy act contains many provisions dealing with civil liberties. Key are its amendment of the federal code to allow the interception of wire, oral, and electronic communications for the production of evidence of "(1) specified chemical weapons or terrorism offenses; and (2) computer fraud and abuse." It also provides for "mandatory detention until removal from the United States of an alien certified by the Attorney General as a suspected terrorist or threat to national security." This act gives the attorney general, as chief U.S. law enforcement officer, enormous powers not seen since Attorney General Robert F. Kennedy's campaign against organized crime in the 1960s. Civil libertarians are particularly concerned with how the Department of Justice has implemented all of its newfound powers. Among their key concerns are the following:

- The FBI's ability to spy on domestic groups without having to show any evidence of a crime, including the ability to monitor Internet sites, public meetings, and religious gatherings.
- The Department of Justice's use of "material witness warrants" to hold people secretly and indefinitely without charging them with a crime if the department believes they have critical information about terrorism.
- Immigration hearings that are closed to public scrutiny.
- Attorney General John Ashcroft's authorization of the monitoring of conversations between detainees and their lawyers, ending attorney/client confidentiality.
- Widespread questioning of 5,000 men of Middle Eastern origin.
- Monitoring and tracing of e-mails without probable cause.
- The use of closed circuit cameras to monitor public areas in Washington, D.C.
- Authorizing banks to pool data to monitor and compile data on individual transfers and discern unusual patterns.

Seven in ten Americans report that they are willing to suffer civil liberties restrictions to improve security.[a] Do you agree? Where would you draw the line? What further civil liberties could (or should) be curtailed?

---

[a]Richard Morin, "Poll: Half of All Americans Still Feel Unsafe," *Washington Post* (May 3, 2002): A7.

Attempts to Limit Speech

Although the Supreme Court has allowed few governmental bans on most types of speech, some forms of expression are not protected. In 1942, the Supreme Court set out the rationale by which it would distinguish between protected and unprotected speech. According to the Court, obscenity, lewdness, libel, and fighting words are not protected by the First Amendment because "such expressions are no essential part of any exposition of ideas, and are of such slight social value as a step to truth that any benefit that may be derived from them is clearly outweighed by the social interest in order and morality."[35]

The Alien and Sedition Acts.   In 1798, soon after passage of the Bill of Rights, a constitutional crisis arose when the Federalist Congress enacted the Alien and Sedition Acts. Designed to ban any political criticism by the growing numbers of Jeffersonian Democratic-Republicans, these acts made publication of "any false, scandalous writing against the government of the United States" a criminal offense. Overtly partisan Federalist judges imposed fines and even jail terms on at least ten Democratic-Republican newspaper editors for allegedly violating the acts. The acts became a major issue in the 1800 presidential election campaign, which led to the election of Thomas Jefferson, a vocal opponent of the acts. He quickly pardoned all who had been convicted under their provisions, and the new Democratic-Republican Congress allowed the acts to expire before the Supreme Court had an opportunity to rule on the constitutionality of these serious infringements of the First Amendment.

Timeline

Civil Liberties
and National
Security

Slavery, the Civil War, and Rights Curtailments.　After the public outcry over the Alien and Sedition Acts, the national government largely got out of the business of regulating speech. But, in its place, the states began to prosecute those who published articles critical of governmental policies. In the 1830s, at the urgings of abolitionists, the publication or dissemination of any positive information about slavery became a punishable offense in the North. In the opposite vein, in the South, supporters of the "peculiar institution" of slavery enacted laws to prohibit publication of any antislavery sentiments. Southern postmasters refused to deliver northern abolitionist papers throughout the South, which amounted to censorship of the mails.

During the Civil War, President Abraham Lincoln effectively suspended the free press provision of the First Amendment (as well as many other sections of the Constitution). He even went so far as to order the arrest of the editors of two New York papers who were critical of him. Far from protesting against these blatant violations of the First Amendment, Congress acceded to them. Right after the war, for example, Congress actually prevented the Supreme Court from issuing a judgment because its members feared the Court's decision would be critical of President Lincoln's actions during the war. William McCardle, a Mississippi newspaper editor, had sought to arouse sentiment against Lincoln and the Union occupation. Even though he was a civilian, McCardle was jailed by a military court without having any charges brought against him. He appealed his detainment to the U.S. Supreme Court, arguing that he was being held unlawfully. Congress, fearing that a victory for McCardle would prompt other Confederate newspaper editors to follow his lead, enacted a law barring the Supreme Court from hearing appeals of cases involving convictions for publishing statements critical of the Union. Because Article III of the Constitution gives Congress the power to determine the jurisdiction of the Court, the Court was forced to conclude in *Ex parte McCardle* (1869) that it had no authority to rule in the matter.[36]

After the Civil War, states also began to prosecute individuals for seditious speech if they uttered or printed statements critical of the government. Between 1890 and 1900, for example, there were more than one hundred state prosecutions for sedition in state courts.[37] Moreover, by the dawn of the twentieth century, public opinion in the United States had become exceedingly hostile to the preachings of Socialists and Communists who attempted to appeal to the thousands of new and disheartened immigrants. Groups espousing socialism and communism became the targets of state laws curtailing speech and the written word. By the end of World War I, over thirty states had passed laws to punish seditious speech, and more than 1,900 individuals and over one hundred newspapers were prosecuted for violations.[38]

Anti-Governmental Speech.　The next major national efforts to restrict freedom of speech and the press, however, did not occur until congressional passage of the Espionage Act of 1917. Nearly 2,000 Americans were convicted of violating its various provisions, especially those that made it illegal to urge resistance to the draft or to prohibit the distribution of antiwar leaflets. In *Schenck* v. *U.S.* (1919), the Supreme Court interpreted the First Amendment to allow Congress to restrict speech that was "of such a nature as to create a clear and present danger that will bring about the substantive evils that Congress has a right to prevent."[39] Under the **clear and present danger test,** which allowed Congress to ban speech that could cause a clear and present danger to society, the circumstances surrounding the incident count, according to the Court. Antiwar leaflets, for example, may be permissible in peacetime, but they pose too much of a danger in wartime to be allowed.

For decades, the Supreme Court wrestled with what constituted a "danger." Finally, in *Brandenburg* v. *Ohio* (1969), the Court fashioned a new test for deciding whether certain kinds of speech could be regulated by the government: the **direct incitement test.** Now the government could punish the advocacy of illegal action only if "such advocacy is directed to inciting or producing imminent lawless action and is likely to incite or produce such action."[40] The requirement of "imminent lawless action" makes it more

clear and present danger test
Test articulated by the Supreme Court in *Schenck* v. *U.S.* (1919) to draw the line between protected and unprotected speech; the Court looks to see "whether the words used..." could "create a clear and present danger that they will bring about substantive evils" that Congress seeks "to prevent."

direct incitement test
A test articulated by the Supreme Court in *Brandenburg* v. *Ohio* (1969) that holds that advocacy of illegal action is protected by the First Amendment unless imminent lawless action is intended and likely to occur.

difficult for the government to punish speech and is consistent with the Framers' notion of the special role played by speech in a democratic society.

Libel and Slander.   Today, national tabloid newspapers such as the *National Enquirer* and the *Star* boast headlines that cause many to shake their heads in disbelief. How can they get away with it, some may wonder. The Framers were very concerned that the press not be suppressed. The First Amendment works to allow all forms of speech, no matter how libelous. False or libelous statements are not restrained by the courts, yet the Supreme Court consistently has ruled that individuals or the press can be sued after the fact for untrue or libelous statements. **Libel** is a written statement that defames the character of a person. If the statement is spoken, it is **slander.** In many nations—such as Great Britain, for example—it is relatively easy to sue someone for libel. In the United States, however, the standards of proof are much more difficult. A person who believes that he or she has been a victim of libel, for example, must show that the statements made were untrue. Truth is an absolute defense against the charge of libel, no matter how painful or embarrassing the revelations.

> **libel**
> False written statements or written statements tending to call someone's reputation into disrepute.
>
> **slander**
> Untrue spoken statements that defame the character of a person.

It is often more difficult for individuals the Supreme Court considers to be "public persons or public officials" to sue for libel or slander. *New York Times Co.* v. *Sullivan* **(1964)** was the first major libel case considered by the Supreme Court.[41] An Alabama state court had found the *Times* guilty of libel for printing a full-page advertisement accusing Alabama officials of physically abusing African Americans during various civil rights protests (the ad was paid for by civil rights activists, including former First Lady Eleanor Roosevelt). The Supreme Court overturned the conviction, ruling that a finding of libel against a public official could stand only if there were a showing of "actual malice." Proof that the statements were false or negligent was not sufficient to prove "actual malice." The concept of actual malice (a burden of proof imposed on public officials and public figures suing for defamation and falsity requiring them to prove with clear and convincing evidence that an offending story was published with knowing falsehood or reckless disregard for the truth) can be difficult and confusing. In 1991, the Court directed lower courts to use the phrases "knowledge of falsity" and "reckless disregard of the truth" when giving instructions to juries in libel cases.[42] Given the high degree of proof required, few public officials or public persons have been able to win libel cases. Still, many prominent people file libel suits each year and most are settled out of court. Former Clinton aide Sidney Blumenthal dropped a $30 million suit against cyber columnist Matt Drudge, who apologized for the false charges he reported about Blumenthal,[43] and actor Tom Cruise dropped his $200 million lawsuit against a publisher who claimed he had a videotape of Cruise engaged in a homosexual act when a Los Angeles judge entered a statement that Cruise was not gay into the court records.[44]

> *New York Times Co.* v. *Sullivan* **(1964)**
> The Supreme Court concluded that "actual malice" must be proved to support a finding of libel against a public figure.

Obscenity and Pornography.[45]   Although the Supreme Court has allowed few governmental bans on most types of speech, some forms of expression are not protected. In *Chaplinsky* v. *New Hampshire* (1942), the Supreme Court set out the rationale by which it would distinguish between protected and unprotected speech. According to the Court, obscenity, lewdness, libel, and fighting words are not protected by the First Amendment because "such expressions are no essential part of any exposition of ideas, and are of such slight social value as a step to truth that any benefit that may be derived from them is clearly outweighed by the social interest in order and morality."[46]

What Speech Is Protected by the Constitution?

Through 1957, U.S. courts often based their decisions of what was obscene on an English common-law test that had been set out in 1868: "Whether the tendency of the matter charged as obscenity is to deprive and corrupt those whose minds are open to such immoral influences and into whose hands a publication of this sort might fall."[47]

In *Roth* v. *U.S.* (1957), the Court abandoned that approach and held that to be considered obscene, the material in question must be "utterly without redeeming social importance," and articulated a new test for obscenity: "whether to the average person, applying contemporary community standards, the dominant theme of the material

ANALYZING VISUALS

The Attorney General and the Spirit of Justice

In January 2002, the U.S. Department of Justice spent $8,000 to purchase blue curtains to provide a backdrop for television coverage of then Attorney General John Ashcroft in the Department of Justice's Great Hall. The curtains are strategically placed in front of two aluminum Art Deco statues that have stood in the Great Hall since the 1930s. One of the draped statues, entitled *Spirit of Justice*, depicts a bare-breasted woman half-draped in a toga.

The second statue, entitled *The Majesty of Law*, depicts a man with a cloth covering his midsection. These statues often appeared as the backdrop for public officials' statements to the media, though the *Spirit of Justice* statue, which stands at the left side of the stage, has appeared more frequently in news photographs. Ashcroft was photographed several times in front of the female statue after September 11.

According to a Department of Justice spokesman, the decision to drape the statue was done for "aesthetic" reasons, providing a pleasant background for television cameras. ABC News reported that the decision was made at the request of the conservative attorney general. The photograph shown here was taken in November 2001, at an event in the Great Hall in which the attorney general and deputy attorney general announced plans for restructuring the Department of Justice after September 11. This photograph and others like it accompanied numerous news reports of the event. After examining the photograph, answer the following critical thinking questions about the picture and the decision to drape the statues: What, if anything, do you find objectionable about the statue? Why would ABC News report that Ashcroft ordered the statue draped? Are any civil liberties issues at stake in the decision? For additional guidance in analyzing news photographs, please see Analyzing Visuals: A Brief Guide.

(Photo courtesy: Kamenko PAJIC/AP/Wide World Photos)

taken as a whole appeals to the prurient interests."[48] In many ways the *Roth* test brought with it as many problems as it attempted to solve. Throughout the 1950s and 1960s, "prurient" remained hard to define, as the Court struggled to find a standard by which to judge actions or words. Moreover, it was very difficult to prove that a book or movie was "*utterly* without redeeming social value." In general, even some "hardcore" pornography passed muster under the *Roth* test, prompting some to argue that the Court fostered the increase in the number of sexually oriented publications designed to appeal to those living amidst what many called the "sexual revolution."

Richard M. Nixon made the growth in pornography a major issue when he ran for president in 1968, and he pledged to appoint to federal judgeships only those who would uphold "law and order" and stop coddling criminals and purveyors of porn. Once elected president, Nixon made four appointments to the Court, including Chief Justice Warren Burger, who wrote the opinion in *Miller* v. *California* (1973). There, the Supreme Court set out a test that redefined obscenity. To make it easier for states to regulate obscene materials, the justices concluded that a lower court must ask "whether the work depicts or describes, in a patently offensive way, sexual conduct specifically defined by state law." Moreover, courts were to determine "whether the work, taken as a whole, lacks serious literary, artistic, political or scientific value." And, in place of the contemporary community standards gauge used in earlier cases, the Court defined community standards to mean local, and not national, standards under the rationale that what is acceptable in New York City might not be tolerated in Crawford, Texas.[49]

Time and contexts clearly have altered the Court's and, indeed, much of America's perceptions of what is obscene. But, through the early 1990s, the Court allowed communities greater leeway in drafting statutes to deal with obscenity and, even more important, forms of non-obscene expression. In 1991, for example, the Supreme Court voted 5–4 to allow Indiana to ban totally nude erotic dancing, concluding that its statute did not violate the First Amendment's guarantee of freedom of expression and that it furthered an important or substantial governmental interest (thereby adopting the intermediate standard of review, discussed in detail in chapter 6).[50]

Congress and Obscenity.   While lawmakers have been fairly effective in restricting the sale and distribution of obscene materials, Congress has been particularly concerned with two obscenity and pornography issues: (1) federal funding for the arts; and, (2) the distribution of obscenity and pornography on the Internet.

In 1990, concern over the use of federal dollars by the National Endowment for the Arts (NEA) for works with controversial religious or sexual themes led to passage of legislation requiring the NEA to "[take] into consideration general standards of decency and respect for the diverse beliefs and values of the American public" when it makes its annual awards. Several performance artists believed that congress could not regulate the content of speech solely because it could be offensive; they challenged the statute in federal court.[51] In 1998, the Supreme Court upheld the legislation, ruling that, because decency was only one of the criteria in making funding decisions, the act did not violate the First Amendment.[52]

WEB EXPLORATION
For more information on the NEA, see
www.ablongman.com/oconnor

Monitoring the Internet has proven more difficult for Congress. In 1996, it passed the Communications Decency Act, which prohibited the transmission of obscene materials over the Internet to anyone under age eighteen. In 1997, the Supreme Court ruled in *Reno* v. *American Civil Liberties Union* that the act violated the First Amendment because it was too vague and overbroad.[53] In reaction to the decision, Congress passed the Child Online Protection Act in 1998.[54] The new law broadened the definition of pornography to include any "visual depiction that is, or appears to be, a minor engaging in sexually explicit conduct." The act also redefined "visual depiction" to include computer-generated images, shifting the focus of the law from the children who were involved in pornography to protection of children who see the images via the Internet.[55] The act targeted material "harmful to minors" but applied only to World Wide Web sites, not chat rooms or email. It also targeted only materials used for "commercial purposes."

WEB EXPLORATION
For more information on *Reno v. American Civil Liberties Union*, see
www.ablongman.com/oconnor

The ACLU and online publishers immediately challenged the constitutionality of the act, and a U.S. appeals court in Philadelphia ruled the law was unconstitutional because of its reliance on "community standards," as articulated in *Miller*, which are not enforceable on the Internet. While this case was on appeal to the Supreme Court, Congress enacted the Children's Internet Protection Act, which prohibited public libraries receiving federal funds from allowing minors access to the web without antipornography filters. Meanwhile, in *Ashcroft* v. *Free Speech Coalition* (2002), the Court ruled that Congress had gone too far in a laudable effort to stamp out child pornography.[56] Six justices agreed that the law was too vague because "communities with a narrow view of what words and images are suitable for children might be able to censor Internet content, putting it out of reach of the entire country."[57]

Congressional reaction was immediate. Within two weeks of the Court's decision, lawmakers were drafting more specific legislation to meet the Court's reservations. New regulations were enacted in 2003 as part of an anti-crime bill. In this legislation, Congress further limited the kinds of cyber pornography subject to regulation and allowed those accused to creating and marketing such pornography to "escape conviction if they could show they did not use actual children to produce sexually explicit images.[58] Still, the new law is likely to face immediate legal challenges from the ACLU and other groups.

The act, which made it a crime to sell or own computer-generated photos of children engaged in sex, could not stand, said the Court, because showing sexual images of what only appear to be children would threaten filmmakers who use adult actors to portray underage characters. Makers of films such as *Traffic* or *American Beauty,* or producers of *Romeo and Juliet,* noted Justice Anthony Kennedy writing for the majority, could be prosecuted if the law was applied literally. Justice Sandra Day O'Connor, while agreeing that the law went too far in its coverage of youthful looking actors, noted that she would have upheld the ban on computer-generated pornography, which the majority did not.

What Types of Speech Are Protected?

Not only will the Court not tolerate prior restraint of the press, but certain types of speech also are protected including symbolic speech, and hate speech. (See On Campus: Political Speech and Mandatory Student Fees.)

Prior Restraint.   With only a few exceptions, the Court has made it clear that it will not tolerate prior restraint of speech. In 1971, for example, in *New York Times Co.* v. *U.S.* (also called the "Pentagon Papers" case), the Supreme Court ruled that the U.S. government could not block the publication of secret Department of Defense documents illegally furnished to the *Times* by antiwar activists.[59] In 1976, the Supreme Court went even further, noting that any attempt by the government to prevent expression carried "a 'heavy presumption' against its constitutionality."[60] In this Nebraska case, a trial court issued a "gag order" barring the press from reporting the lurid details of a crime. In balancing the defendant's constitutional right to a fair trial against the press's right to cover a story, the trial judge concluded that the defendant's right carried greater weight. The Supreme Court disagreed, holding the press's right to cover the trial paramount. Still, judges are often allowed to issue gag orders affecting parties to a lawsuit or to limit press coverage of a case.

symbolic speech
Symbols, signs, and other methods of expression generally also considered to be protected by the First Amendment.

Symbolic Speech.   In addition to the general protection accorded to pure speech, the Supreme Court has extended the reach of the First Amendment to other means of expression often called **symbolic speech** such as symbols or signs, as well as to activities like picketing, sit-ins, and demonstrations. In the words of Justice John Marshall Harlan, these kinds of "speech" are part of the "free trade in ideas."[61]

The Supreme Court first acknowledged that symbolic speech was entitled to First Amendment protection in *Stromberg* v. *California* (1931).[62] There the Court overturned the conviction of the director of a communist youth camp under a state statute prohibiting the display of a red flag, a symbol of opposition to the U.S. government. In a similar vein, the right of high school students to wear black armbands to protest the Vietnam War was upheld in *Tinker* v. *Des Moines Independent Community School District* (1969).[63]

Burning the American flag also has been held to be a form of protected symbolic speech. In 1989, a sharply divided Supreme Court (5–4) reversed the conviction of Gregory Johnson, who had been found guilty of setting fire to an American flag during the 1984 Republican national convention in Dallas.[64] As a result, there was a major public outcry against the Court. President George Bush and numerous members of Congress called for a constitutional amendment to ban flag burning to overturn *Texas* v. *Johnson.* Others, including Justice William J. Brennan, noted that if it had not been for acts like that of Johnson, the United States would never have been created nor would a First Amendment guaranteeing a right to political protest exist.

Instead of a constitutional amendment, Congress passed the Federal Flag Protection Act of 1989, which authorized federal prosecution of anyone who intentionally

POLITICAL SPEECH AND MANDATORY STUDENT FEES

In March 2000, the United States Supreme Court ruled unanimously in *Board of Regents* v. *Southworth* that public universities could charge students a mandatory activity fee that could be used to facilitate extracurricular student political speech so long as the programs are neutral in their application.[a]

Scott Southworth, while a law student at the University of Wisconsin, believed that the university's mandatory fee was a violation of his First Amendment right to free speech. He, along with several other law students, objected that their fees went to fund liberal groups. They particularly objected to the support of eighteen of the 125 various groups on campus that benefited from the mandatory activity fee, including the Lesbian, Gay, Bisexual, and Transgender Center, the International Socialist Organization, and the campus women's center.[b]

In ruling against Southworth and for the university, the Court underscored the importance of universities being a forum for the free exchange of political and ideological ideas and perspectives. The *Southworth* case performed that function on the Wisconsin campus even before it was argued before the Supreme Court. A student-led effort called the Southworth Project, for which over a dozen law and journalism students each earned two credits, was begun to make sure that the case was reported on campus in an accurate and sophisticated way. The Southworth Project, said a political science professor, gave "a tremendous boost to the visibility and the thinking process about the case."[c] In essence, the case made the Con-

Colleen Jungbluth, front, and other Wisconsin students as they awaited a ruling on their First Amendment lawsuit.

(Photo courtesy: Tim Dillon/© USA Today. Reprinted with permission)

stitution and what it means come alive on the Wisconsin campus as students pondered the effects of First Amendment protections on their ability to learn in a university atmosphere.

---

[a] 529 U.S. 217 (2000).
[b] "U.S. Court Upholds Student Fees Going to Controversial Groups," *Toronto Star* (March 23, 2000): NEXIS.
[c] Mary Beth Marklein, "Fee Fight Proves a Learning Experience," *USA Today* (November 30, 1999): 8D.

---

desecrated a national flag. Those who originally had been arrested burned another flag and were convicted. Their conviction was again overturned by the Supreme Court. As they had in *Johnson*, the justices divided 5–4 in holding that this federal law "suffered from the same fundamental flaw" as had the earlier state law that was declared in violation of the First Amendment.[65] Since that decision, Congress has tried several times to pass a constitutional amendment to ban flag burning. Those efforts, however, have yet to be successful.

Hate Speech, Unpopular Speech, and Speech Zones.   "As a thumbnail summary of the last two or three decades of speech issues in the Supreme Court," wrote the eminent First Amendment scholar Harry Kalven Jr. in 1966, "we may come to see the Negro as winning back for us the freedoms the Communists seemed to have lost for us."[66] Still, says noted African American scholar Henry Louis Gates Jr., Kalven would be shocked to see the stance that some blacks now take toward the First Amendment, which once protected protests, rallies, and agitation in the 1960s: "The byword among many black activists and black intellectuals is no longer the political imperative to protect free speech; it is the moral imperative to suppress 'hate speech.' "[67]

In the 1990s, a particularly thorny First Amendment area emerged as cities and universities attempted to prohibit what they viewed as offensive hate speech. In *R.A.V.*

(Photo courtesy: ©1999 By Pete Wagner)

v. *City of St. Paul* (1992), a St. Paul, Minnesota, ordinance that made it a crime to engage in speech or action likely to arouse "anger," "alarm," or "resentment" on the basis of race, color, creed, religion, or gender was at issue. The Court ruled 5–4 that a white teenager who burned a cross on a black family's front lawn, thereby committing a hate crime under the ordinance, could not be charged under that law because the First Amendment prevents governments from "silencing speech on the basis of its content" and the ordinance "ruled symbolic speech in or out depending on the groups that the speech targeted."[68] In 2003, the U.S. Supreme Court narrowly ruled that Virginia could ban cross burning so long as it was **intended** to intimidate its targets.[69]

Two-thirds of colleges and universities have banned a variety of forms of speech or conduct that creates or fosters an intimidating, hostile, or offensive environment on campus, such as racial slurs directed at minority groups. Other college codes ban conduct or speech that causes emotional distress.

Speech has been far less protected in the wake of September 11, 2001. Not only have several commentators lost their jobs for criticizing President George W. Bush or U.S. foreign policy, but numerous professors were censored by university administrators for their controversial comments "or visibly symbolic positions" in the aftermath of the 9/11 attacks.[70]

Some universities have created what are called free speech zones, which critics say mean that speech can be limited elsewhere on campus.[71] Often these zones are created by universities to restrict the time, place, or manner of speech or to prevent disruption of university activities. In a way, they are half-full, half-empty policies. On some campuses they actually seem to provide students with more opportunities to speak out; on others, less.

James and Sarah Brady being applauded for their efforts to win congressional approval of the Brady Bill after it was signed into law by President Bill Clinton. Brady, President Reagan's press secretary, was gunned down and permanently injured by Reagan's assailant.

(Photo courtesy: John Ficara/Corbis Sygma)

THE SECOND AMENDMENT: THE RIGHT TO KEEP AND BEAR ARMS

During colonial times, the English tradition of distrust of standing armies was evident: Most colonies required all white men to keep and bear arms, and all white men in whole sections of the colonies were deputized to defend their settlements against Indians and other European powers. These local militias were viewed as the best way to keep order and liberty.

The Second Amendment was added to the Constitution to ensure that Congress could not pass laws to disarm state militias. This amendment appeased Anti-Federalists, who feared that the new Constitution would cause them to lose the right to "keep and bear arms" as well as an unstated right—the right to revolt against governmental tyranny.

Through the early 1920s, few state statutes were passed to regulate firearms (and generally these laws dealt with the possession of

Tens of thousands of mothers, many accompanied by children and husbands, rallied in sight of the Capitol to demand strict control of handguns while memorializing loved ones and strangers killed by bullets during the "Million Mom March," on Mother's Day 2000, in Washington, D.C.

(Photo courtesy: Reuters NewMedia Inc./CORBIS)

firearms by slaves). The Supreme Court's decision in *Barron* v. *Baltimore* (1833), which limited the application of the Bill of Rights to the actions of Congress alone, prevented federal review of those state laws.[72] Moreover, in *Dred Scott* v. *Sandford* (1857) (see chapter 3), Chief Justice Taney listed the right to own and carry arms as a basic right of citizenship.[73]

In 1934, Congress passed the National Firearms Act in response to the increase in organized crime that occurred in the 1920s and 1930s as a result of Prohibition. The act imposed taxes on automatic weapons (such as machine guns) and sawed-off shotguns. In *U.S.* v. *Miller* (1939), a unanimous Court upheld the constitutionality of the act by stating that the Second Amendment was intended to protect a citizen's right to own ordinary militia weapons and not unregistered sawed-off shotguns, which were at issue in the *Miller* case.[74] *Miller* was the last time the Supreme Court directly addressed the Second Amendment. In *Quilici* v. *Village of Morton Grove* (1983), the Supreme Court refused to review a lower court's ruling upholding the constitutionality of a local ordinance banning handguns against a Second Amendment challenge.[75]

In the aftermath of the assassination attempt on President Ronald Reagan in 1981, many lawmakers called for passage of gun control legislation. At the forefront of that effort was Sarah Brady, the wife of James Brady, the presidential press secretary who was badly wounded and left partially disabled by John Hinckley Jr., President Reagan's assailant. In 1993, her efforts helped to win passage of the Brady Bill, which imposed a federal mandatory five-day waiting period on the purchase of handguns.

In 1994, in spite of extensive lobbying by the powerful National Rifle Association (NRA), Congress passed and President Bill Clinton signed, the $30.2 billion Violent

**Gun Rights
and Gun
Control**

Crime Control and Law Enforcement Act. In addition to providing money to states for new prisons and law enforcement officers, the act banned the manufacture, sale, transport, or possession of nineteen different kinds of semi-automatic assault weapons.

In 1997, the U.S. Supreme Court ruled 5–4 that the section of the Brady Bill requiring state officials to conduct background checks of prospective handgun owners violated principles of state sovereignty.[76] The background check provision, while important, is not critical to the overall goals of the Brady Bill because a federal record-checking system went into effect in late 1998. School shootings around the nation heightened interest in gun control legislation.

In 2004, the act banning the sale of assault weapons was allowed to expire by Congress. Many charged that legislators feared a voter backlash in spite of the fact that public opinion polls showed significant support for the measure.

THE RIGHTS OF CRIMINAL DEFENDANTS

due process rights
Procedural guarantees provided by the Fourth, Fifth, Sixth, and Eighth Amendments for those accused of crimes.

The Fourth, Fifth, Sixth, and Eighth Amendments provide a variety of procedural guarantees (often called **due process rights**) for those accused of crimes. Particular amendments, as well as other portions of the Constitution, specifically provide procedural guarantees to protect individuals accused of crimes at all stages of the criminal justice process. As is the case with the First Amendment, many of these rights have been interpreted by the Supreme Court to apply to the states. In interpreting the amendments dealing with what are frequently termed "criminal rights," the courts have to grapple not only with the meaning of the amendments but also with how their protections are to be implemented.

Over the years, many individuals criticized liberal Warren Court decisions, arguing that its rulings gave criminals more "rights" than their victims. The Warren Court made several provisions of the Bill of Rights dealing with the rights of criminal defendants applicable to the states through the Fourteenth Amendment. It is important to remember that most procedural guarantees apply to individuals charged with crimes, that is, before they have been tried. These rights were designed to protect those wrongfully accused, although, of course, they often have helped the guilty. But, as Justice William O. Douglas once noted, "Respecting the dignity even of the least worthy citizen ... raises the stature of all of us."[77]

Many continue to argue, however, that only the guilty are helped by the American system and that criminals should not go unpunished because of simple police error. The dilemma of balancing the rights of the individual against those of society permeates the entire debate, and often even judicial interpretations of the rights of criminal defendants.

The Fourth Amendment and Searches and Seizures

Fourth Amendment
Part of the Bill of Rights that reads: "The right of the people to be secure in their persons, houses, papers, and effects, against unreasonable searches and seizures, shall not be violated, and no Warrants shall issue, but upon probable cause, supported by Oath or affirmation, and particularly describing the place to be searched, and the persons or things to be seized."

The **Fourth Amendment** to the Constitution protects people from unreasonable searches by the federal government. Moreover, in some detail, it sets out what may not be searched unless a warrant is issued, underscoring the Framers' concern with possible government abuses.

> The right of the people to be secure in their persons, houses, papers, and effects, against unreasonable searches and seizures, shall not be violated, and no Warrants shall issue, but upon probable cause, supported by Oath or affirmation, and particularly describing the place to be searched, and the persons or things to be seized.

This amendment's purpose was to deny the national government the authority to make general searches. The English Parliament often had issued general "writs of assistance" that allowed such searches. These general warrants were used against religious and political dissenters, a practice the Framers wanted banned. But, still, the language that they chose left numerous questions to be answered, including, what is an "unreasonable" search?

Over the years, in a number of decisions, the Supreme Court has interpreted the Fourth Amendment to allow the police to search: (1) the person arrested; (2) things in plain view of the accused person; and, (3) places or things that the arrested person could touch or reach or are otherwise in the arrestee's "immediate control." In 1995, the Court also resolved a decades-old constitutional dispute by ruling unanimously that police must knock and announce their presence before entering a house or apartment to execute a search. But, said the Court, there may be "reasonable" exceptions to the rule to account for the likelihood of violence or the imminent destruction of evidence.[78]

Warrantless searches often occur if police suspect that someone is committing or is about to commit a crime. In these situations, police may "stop and frisk" the individual under suspicion. In 1989, the Court ruled that there need be only a "reasonable suspicion" for stopping a suspect—a much lower standard than "probable cause."[79] Thus, a suspected drug courier may be stopped for brief questioning but only a frisk search (for weapons) is permitted. The answers to these questions may shift "reasonable suspicion" to "probable cause," thus permitting the officer to search. But, except at international borders (or international airports), a search requires probable cause.

Simulation

**You Are a
Police Officer**

The Court also ruled in 2001 on a California policy that required individuals, as a condition of their probation, to consent to warrantless searches of their person, property, homes, or vehicles, thus limiting a probationer's Fourth Amendment protections against unreasonable searches and seizures.[80] The Court did not give blanket approval to searches; instead, the unanimous opinion said that a probation officer must have a reasonable suspicion of wrongdoing—a lesser standard than probable cause afforded to most citizens.

Searches can also be made without a warrant if consent is obtained, and the Court has ruled that consent can be given by a variety of persons. It has ruled, for example, that police can search a bedroom occupied by two persons as long as they have the consent of one of them.[81]

In situations where no arrest occurs, police must obtain search warrants from a "neutral and detached magistrate" prior to conducting more extensive searches of houses, cars, offices, or any other place where an individual would reasonably have some expectation of privacy.[82] Police can't get search warrants, for example, to require you to undergo surgery to remove a bullet that might be used to incriminate you, since your expectation of bodily privacy outweighs the need for evidence.[83] But, courts don't require search warrants in possible drunk driving situations. Thus, the police can require you to take a Breathalyzer test to determine whether you have been drinking in excess of legal limits.[84]

Homes, too, are presumed to be private. Firefighters can enter your home to fight a fire without a warrant. But, if they decide to investigate the cause of the fire, they must obtain a warrant before their reentry.[85] In contrast, under the "open fields doctrine" first articulated by the Supreme Court in 1924,[86] if you own a field, and even if you post "No Trespassing" signs, the police can search your field without a warrant to see if you are illegally growing marijuana, because you cannot reasonably expect privacy in an open field.

Participation

**Privacy and Rights
of the Accused**

In 2001, in a decision that surprised many commentators, by a vote of 5–4, the Supreme Court ruled that drug evidence obtained by using a thermal imager (without a warrant) on a public street to locate the defendant's marijuana hothouse was obtained in violation of the Fourth Amendment.[87] In contrast, the use of low-flying aircraft and helicopters to detect marijuana fields or binoculars to look in a yard has been upheld because officers simply were using their eyesight, not a new technological tool like the thermal imager.[88]

Cars have proven problematic for police and the courts because of their mobile nature. As noted by Chief Justice William H. Taft as early as 1925, "the vehicle can quickly be moved out of the locality or jurisdiction in which the warrant must be sought.[89] Over the years, the Court has become increasingly lenient about the scope of automobile searches.

In 2002, an unusually unanimous Court ruled that when evaluating if a border patrol officer acted lawfully in stopping a suspicious minivan, the totality of the circumstances had to be considered. Wrote Chief Justice William H. Rehnquist, the "balance between the public interest and the individual's right to personal security," tilts in favor of a "standard less than probable cause in brief investigatory stops," thus signaling law enforcement officers that there is no neat set of legal rules to determine when officers have "reasonable" suspicion to pull over motorists.[90]

Drug Testing.   Testing for drugs has become an especially thorny search and seizure issue. If the government can require you to take a Breathalyzer test, can it require you to be tested for drugs? In the wake of growing public concern over drug use, in 1986 President Ronald Reagan signed an executive order requiring many federal employees to undergo drug tests. In 1997, Congress passed a similar law authorizing random drug searches of all congressional employees.

While many private employers and professional athletic organizations routinely require drug tests upon application or as a condition of employment, governmental requirements present constitutional questions about the scope of permissible searches and seizures. In 1989, the Supreme Court ruled that mandatory drug and alcohol testing of employees involved in accidents was constitutional.[91] In 1995, the Court upheld the constitutionally of random drug testing of public high school athletes.[92] And, in 2002, the Court upheld the constitutionality of a Tecumseh, Oklahoma, policy that required mandatory drug testing of high school students participating in any extracurricular activities. Thus, prospective band, choir, Technology Student Association (TSA), debate, or drama team members were subject to the same kind of random drug testing undergone by athletes. Two students who wanted to participate on the academic team sued, arguing that the policy violated their Fourth Amendment right to be free from unreasonable searches and seizures. The Supreme Court disagreed, saying that the school policy was "reasonable" in furtherance of the school's interest in the prevention and detection of drug abuse. Relying on its rationale in its earlier opinion allowing for the testing of athletes, the Court went on to say that findings of individual suspicion were not necessary for the search of any one student to be reasonable.[93]

Another question has arisen concerning the constitutionality of compulsory drug testing for pregnant women. In 2001, in a 6–3 decision, the Court ruled that the testing of women for cocaine usage and subsequent reporting of positive tests to law enforcement officials was unconstitutional. When pregnant women in South Carolina sought medical care for their pregnancy, they were not told that their urine tests were also tested for cocaine. Thus, some women were arrested after they unknowingly were screened for illegal drug use and then tested positive. The majority of the Court found that the immediate purpose of the drug test was to generate evidence for law enforcement officials and not medical treatment of the women. Thus, the women's right to privacy was violated unless they specifically consented to the tests.[94]

In *Chandler v. Miller* (1997), the U.S. Supreme Court refused to allow Georgia to require all candidates for state office to pass a urinalysis drug test thirty days before qualifying for nomination or election, concluding that its law violated the search and seizure clause.[95] In general, all employers can require pre-employment drug screening.

WEB EXPLORATION
For more information on
Chandler v. Miller, see
www.ablongman.com/oconnor

Since the Supreme Court has ruled that drug tests are "searches" for the purposes of the Fourth Amendment, public employees enjoy more protections in this area than do employees of private enterprises.[96]

The Fifth Amendment and Self-Incrimination

The **Fifth Amendment** provides that "No person shall be ... compelled in any criminal case to be a witness against himself." "Taking the Fifth" is shorthand for exercising one's constitutional right not to self-incriminate. The Supreme Court has interpreted this guarantee to be "as broad as the mischief against which it seeks to guard,"[97] finding that criminal defendants do not have to take the stand at trial to answer questions, nor can a judge make mention of their failure to do so as evidence of guilt. Moreover, lawyers cannot imply that a defendant who refuses to take the stand must be guilty or have something to hide.

Use of "Voluntary" Confessions. This right not to incriminate oneself also means that prosecutors cannot use as evidence in a trial any of a defendant's statements or confessions that were not voluntary. As is the case in many areas of the law, however, judicial interpretation of the term "voluntary" has changed over time.

In earlier times, it was not unusual for police to beat defendants to obtain their confessions. In 1936, however, the Supreme Court ruled convictions for murder based solely on confessions given after physical beatings unconstitutional.[98] Police then began to resort to other measures to force confessions. Defendants, for example, were "given the third degree"—questioned for hours on end with no sleep or food, or threatened with physical violence until they were mentally "beaten" into a confession. In other situations, family members were threatened. In one case a young mother was told that her welfare benefits would be terminated and her children taken away from her if she failed to talk.[99]

Miranda **v.** *Arizona* (1966) was the Supreme Court's response to these creative efforts to obtain confessions that were not truly voluntary. On March 3, 1963, an eighteen-year-old girl was kidnapped and raped on the outskirts of Phoenix, Arizona. Ten days later police arrested Ernesto Miranda, a poor, mentally disturbed man with a ninth-grade education. In a police-station lineup, the victim identified Miranda as her attacker. Police then took Miranda to a separate room and questioned him for two hours. At first he denied guilt. Eventually, however, he confessed to the crime and wrote and signed a brief statement describing the crime and admitting his guilt. At no time was he told that he did not have to answer any questions or that he could be represented by an attorney.

After Miranda's conviction, his case was appealed on the grounds that his Fifth Amendment right not to incriminate himself had been violated because his confession had been coerced. Writing for the Court, Chief Justice Earl Warren, himself a former district attorney and California state attorney general, noted that because police have a tremendous advantage in any interrogation situation, criminal suspects must be given greater protection. A confession obtained in the manner of Miranda's was not truly voluntary; thus, it was inadmissible at trial.

To provide guidelines for police to implement *Miranda*, the Court mandated that:

> Prior to any questioning, the person must be warned that he has a right to remain silent, that any statements he does make may be used as evidence against him, and that he has a right to the presence of an attorney, either retained or appointed.

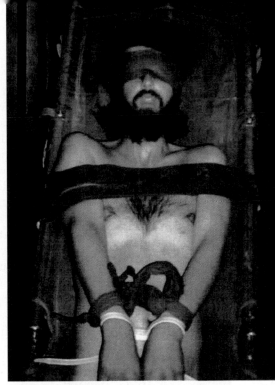

While the FBI insisted that John Walker Lindh signed away his Miranda rights, his lawyers said he repeatedly asked for counsel and was held incommunicado for fifty-four days, while he was mistreated by authorities. Even if he was Mirandized, if the questioning proceeded without breaks or was accompanied by abuse, or if Lindh was shackled, the courts could have found that his confession was involuntary. Public sentiment, however, ran heavily against Lindh and his claims. Thus, he pled guilty in exchange for a twenty-year prison sentence.

(Photo courtesy: AFP/CORBIS)

Fifth Amendment
Part of the Bill of Rights that imposes a number of restrictions on the federal government with respect to the rights of persons suspected of committing a crime. It provides for indictment by a grand jury, protection against self-incrimination, and prevents the national government from denying a person life, liberty, or property without the due process of law. It also prevents the national government from taking property without fair compensation.

Miranda **v.** *Arizona* **(1966)**
A landmark Supreme Court ruling that held the Fifth Amendment requires that individuals arrested for a crime must be advised of their right to remain silent and to have counsel present.

Miranda rights

Statements that must be made by the police informing a suspect of his or her constitutional rights protected by the Fifth Amendment, including the right to an attorney provided by the court if the suspect cannot afford one.

Even though Ernesto Miranda's confession was not admitted as evidence at his retrial, his ex-girlfriend's testimony and that of the victim were enough to convince the jury of his guilt. He served nine years in prison before he was released on parole. After his release, he routinely sold autographed cards inscribed with what are called the Miranda rights now read to all suspects. In 1976, four years after his release, Miranda was stabbed to death in Phoenix in a bar fight during a card game. Two Miranda cards were found on his body, and the person who killed him was read his Miranda rights upon his arrest.

(Photo courtesy: Paul S. Howell/Getty Images)

exclusionary rule

Judicially created rule that prohibits police from using illegally seized evidence at trial.

Sixth Amendment

Part of the Bill of Rights that sets out the basic requirements of procedural due process for federal courts to follow in criminal trials. These include speedy and public trials, impartial juries, trials in the state where crime was committed, notice of the charges, the right to confront and obtain favorable witnesses, and the right to counsel.

In response to this mandate from the Court, police routinely began to read suspects their **Miranda rights,** a practice you undoubtedly have seen repeated over and over in movies and TV police dramas.

Although the Burger Court did not enforce the reading of Miranda rights as vehemently as had the Warren Court, Chief Justice Warren Burger, Warren's successor, acknowledged that they had become an integral part of established police procedures.[100] The Rehnquist Court, however, has been more tolerant of the use of coerced confessions and has employed a much more flexible standard to allow their admissibility. In 1991, for example, it ruled that the use of a coerced confession in a criminal trial does not automatically invalidate a conviction if its admission is deemed a "harmless error," that is, if the other evidence is sufficient to convict.[101]

But, in 2000, in an opinion written by Chief Justice William H. Rehnquist, the Court reaffirmed the central holding of *Miranda*, ruling that defendants must be read Miranda warnings. The Court went on to say that, despite an act of Congress that stipulated that voluntary statements made during custodial interrogations were admissable at trial, without Miranda warnings, no admissions could be trusted to be truly voluntary.[102]

The Fourth and Fifth Amendments and the Exclusionary Rule

In *Weeks* v. *U.S.* (1914), the U.S. Supreme Court adopted the **exclusionary rule,** which bars the use of illegally seized evidence at trial.[103] Thus, although the Fourth and Fifth Amendments do not prohibit the use of evidence obtained in violation of their provisions, the exclusionary rule is a judicially created remedy to deter constitutional violations. In *Weeks*, for example, the Court reasoned that allowing police and prosecutors to use the "fruits of a poisonous tree" (a tainted search) would only encourage that activity.

The Warren Court resolved the dilemma of balancing the goal of deterring police misconduct against the likelihood that a guilty individual would go free in favor of deterrence. In *Mapp* v. *Ohio* (1961), the Warren Court ruled that "all evidence obtained by searches and seizures in violation of the Constitution, is inadmissible in a state court."[104] This historic and controversial case put law enforcement officers on notice that if they "found" evidence in violation of any constitutional rights, those efforts would be for naught because the tainted evidence could not be used in federal or state trials. In contrast, the Burger and Rehnquist Courts and, more recently, Congress gradually have chipped away at the exclusionary rule. Many jurists are uncomfortable with letting the guilty go free. In 1976, the Court noted that the exclusionary rule "deflects the truth-finding process and often frees the guilty."[105] Since then, the Court has carved out a variety of limited "good faith exceptions" to the exclusionary rule, allowing the use of "tainted" evidence in a variety of situations, especially when police have a search warrant, and "in good faith" conduct the search on the assumption that the warrant is valid—though it is subsequently found invalid. Since the purpose of the exclusionary rule is to deter police misconduct, and in this situation there is no police misconduct, the courts have permitted the introduction at trial of the seized evidence. Another exception to the exclusionary rule is "inevitable discovery." Evidence illegally seized may be introduced if it would have been discovered anyway in the course of continuing investigation.

The Sixth Amendment and the Right to Counsel

The **Sixth Amendment** guarantees to an accused person "the Assistance of Counsel in his defense." In the past, this provision meant only that an individual could hire an attorney to represent him or her in court. Since most criminal defendants are impoverished, this provision was of little assistance to many who found themselves on trial. Recognizing this, Congress required federal courts to provide an attorney for defendants too poor to afford one. This was first required in capital cases (where the death penalty is a possibility); eventually, attorneys were provided to the poor in all federal criminal cases.[106] In 1932, the Supreme Court directed states to furnish lawyers to defendants in capital cases.[107] It also began to expand the right to counsel to other state offenses, but did so in a piecemeal fashion that gave the states little direction. Given the high cost of providing legal counsel, this ambiguity often made it cost-effective for the states not to provide counsel at all.

These ambiguities came to an end with the Court's decision in *Gideon* v. *Wainwright* (1963).[108] Clarence Earl Gideon, a fifty-one-year-old drifter, was charged with breaking into a Panama City, Florida, pool hall and stealing beer, wine, and some change from a vending machine. At his trial, he asked the judge to appoint a lawyer for him because he was too poor to hire one himself. The judge refused, and Gideon was convicted and given a five-year prison term for petty larceny. The case against Gideon had not been strong, but as a layperson unfamiliar with the law and with trial practice and procedure, he was unable to point out its weaknesses.

The apparent inequities in the system that had resulted in Gideon's conviction continued to bother him. Eventually, he borrowed some paper from a prison guard, consulted books in the prison library, and then drafted and mailed to the U.S. Supreme Court a petition asking it to overrule his conviction.

In a unanimous decision, the Supreme Court agreed with Gideon and his court-appointed lawyer, Abe Fortas, a future associate justice of the Supreme Court. Writing for the Court, Justice Hugo Black explained that "lawyers in criminal courts are necessities, not luxuries." Therefore, the Court concluded, the state must provide an attorney to poor defendants in felony cases. Underscoring the Court's point, Gideon was acquitted when he was retried with a lawyer to argue his case.

In 1972, the Burger Court expanded the *Gideon* rule, holding that "even in prosecutions for offenses less serious than felonies, a fair trial may require the presence of a lawyer.[109] Seven years later, the Court clarified its decision by holding that defendants charged with offenses where imprisonment is authorized but not actually imposed do not have a Sixth Amendment right to counsel.[110] Thirty years later, the Rehnquist Court expanded *Gideon* even further by revisiting its "actual imprisonment" standard announced in the 1972 and 1979 cases. In 2002, in another 5–4 decision, the majority held that a suspended sentence for a minor crime that may result in imprisonment cannot be imposed unless the defendant was provided with a lawyer at trial even if the sentence never has to be served.[111]

The Sixth Amendment and Jury Trials

The Sixth Amendment (and, to a lesser extent, Article III of the Constitution) provides that a person accused of a crime shall enjoy the right to a speedy and public trial by an impartial jury—that is, a trial in which a group of the accused's peers act as a fact-finding, deliberative body to determine guilt or innocence. It also provides defendants the right to confront witnesses against them. The Supreme Court has held that jury trials must be available if a prison sentence of six or more months is possible.

"Impartiality" is a requirement of jury trials that has undergone significant change, with the method of selecting jurors being the most frequently challenged part of the process. For example, whereas potential individual

When Clarence Earl Gideon wrote out his petition for a writ of *certiorari* to the Supreme Court (asking the Court, in its discretion, to hear his case), he had no way of knowing that his case would lead to the landmark ruling on the right to counsel, *Gideon v. Wainwright* (1963). Nor did he know that Chief Justice Earl Warren actually had instructed his law clerks to be on the lookout for a *habeas corpus* petition (literally, "you have the body," which argues that the person in jail is there in violation of some statutory or constitutional right) that could be used to guarantee the assistance of counsel for defendants in criminal cases.

(Photo courtesy: Supreme Court Historical Society)

jurors who have prejudged a case are not eligible to serve, no groups can be systematically excluded from serving. In 1880, for example, the Supreme Court ruled that African Americans could not be excluded from state jury pools (lists of those eligible to serve).[112] And, in 1975, the Court ruled that to bar women from jury service violated the mandate that juries be a "fair cross section" of the community.[113]

In the 1980s, the Court expanded the requirement that juries reflect the community by invalidating various indirect means of excluding African Americans. While noting that although lawyers historically had used peremptory challenges to select juries they believed most favorable to the outcome they desired, the use of peremptory challenges specifically to exclude African American jurors violated the equal protection clause of the Fourteenth Amendment.[114] In 1994, the Supreme Court answered the major remaining unanswered question about jury selection: Can lawyers exclude women from juries through their use of peremptory challenges? This question came up frequently because in rape trials and sex discrimination cases, one side or another often finds it advantageous to select jurors on the basis of their sex. The Supreme Court ruled that the equal protection clause prohibits discrimination in jury selection on the basis of gender. Thus, lawyers cannot strike all potential male jurors based on the belief that males might be more sympathetic to the arguments of a man charged in a paternity suit, a rape trial, or a domestic violence suit, for example.

The right to confront witnesses at trial also is protected by the Sixth Amendment. In 1990, however, the Supreme Court ruled that this right was not absolute. In *Maryland* v. *Craig* (1990), the Court ruled that the testimony of a six-year-old alleged child abuse victim via one-way closed circuit television was constitutionally permissible. The clause's central purpose, said the Court, was to ensure the reliability of testimony by subjecting it to rigorous examination in an adversary proceeding.[115] In this case, the child was questioned out of the presence of the defendant, who was in communication with this attorney. The defendant, along with the judge and jury, watched the testimony.

The Eighth Amendment and Cruel and Unusual Punishment

The **Eighth Amendment** prohibits "cruel and unusual punishments," a concept rooted in the English common-law tradition. Interestingly, today, the United States is the only Western nation to use executions. Not surprisingly, there are tremendous regional differences in the imposition of the death penalty, with the South leading in the number of men and women executed each year.

In the 1500s, religious heretics and those critical of the Crown were subjected to torture to extract confessions, and then were condemned to an equally hideous death by the rack, disembowelment, or other barbarous means. The English Bill of Rights and its safeguard against "cruel and unusual punishments" was a result of public outrage against those practices. The same language found its way into the U.S. Bill of Rights. Prior to the 1960s, however, little judicial attention was paid to the meaning of that phrase, especially in the context of the death penalty.

The death penalty was in use in all of the colonies at the time the Constitution was adopted, and its constitutionality went unquestioned. In fact, in two separate cases in the late 1800s, the Supreme Court ruled that deaths by public shooting[116] and electrocution were not "cruel and unusual" forms of punishment in the same category as "punishments which inflict torture, such as the rack, the thumbscrew, the iron boot, the stretching of limbs and the like."[117]

In the 1960s, the NAACP Legal Defense Fund, believing that the death penalty was applied more frequently to African Americans than to members of other groups, orchestrated a carefully designed legal attack on its constitutionality.[118] Public opinion polls revealed that in 1971, on the eve of the NAACP's first major death sentence case

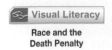

Visual Literacy

Race and the
Death Penalty

to reach the Supreme Court, public support for the death penalty had fallen to below 50 percent. With the timing just right, in *Furman* v. *Georgia* (1972), the Supreme Court effectively put an end to capital punishment, at least in the short run.[119] The Court ruled that because the death penalty often was imposed in an arbitrary manner, it constituted cruel and unusual punishment in violation of the Eighth and Fourteenth Amendments. Following *Furman*, several state legislatures enacted new laws designed to meet the Court's objections to the arbitrary nature of the sentence. In 1976, in *Gregg* v. *Georgia*, Georgia's rewritten death penalty statute was ruled constitutional by the Supreme Court in a 7–2 decision.[120]

Unless the perpetrator of a crime was fifteen years old or younger at the time of the crime or mentally retarded, the Supreme Court currently is unwilling to intervene to overrule state courts' imposition of the death penalty. In *McCleskey* v. *Kemp* (1987), a 5–4 Court ruled that imposition of the death penalty—even when it appeared to discriminate against African Americans—did not violate the equal protection clause.[121] Despite the testimony of social scientists and evidence that Georgia was eleven times more likely to seek the death penalty against a black defendant, the Court upheld Warren McCleskey's death sentence. It noted that even if statistics show clear discrimination, there must be a showing of racial discrimination in the case at hand. Five justices concluded that there was no evidence of specific discrimination proved against McCleskey at his trial. Within hours of that defeat, McCleskey's lawyers filed a new appeal, arguing that the informant who gave the only testimony against McCleskey at trial had been placed in McCleskey's cell illegally.

Four years later, McCleskey's death sentence challenge again produced an equally, if not more important, ruling on the death penalty and criminal procedure from the U.S. Supreme Court. In the second *McCleskey* case, *McCleskey* v. *Zant* (1991), the Court found that the issue of the informant should have been raised during the first appeal, in spite of the fact that McCleskey's lawyers were initially told by the state that the witness was not an informer. *McCleskey* v. *Zant* produced new standards designed to make it much more difficult for death-row inmates to file repeated appeals, a practice frequently decried by many of the justices.[122] Ironically, the informant against McCleskey was freed the night before McCleskey was electrocuted. Justice Powell, one of those in the five-person majority, later said (after his retirement) that he regretted his vote and should have voted the other way. By 2002, executions were commonplace in the United States.

In 2002, the Supreme Court ruled that mentally retarded convicts could not be executed for capital murder because to do so violated the Eighth Amendment's prohibition on cruel and unusual punishments.[123] This 6–3 decision reversed what had been the Court's position on executing the retarded since 1989, a thirteen-year period when several retarded men were executed. It threw the laws of twenty states that permit these executions, including Texas, where the governor recently had vetoed legislation banning execution of the retarded, into chaos because many states have different standards for assessing retardation. And, the opinion represented a rare win in the Supreme Court for death penalty opponents, who have been faring far better in the individual states. In fact, the majority took special note of the fact that eighteen of the thirty-eight states with the death penalty do not allow the execution of the retarded.[124]

At the state level, a move to at least stay executions took on momentum when Governor George Ryan (R–IL) ordered a moratorium on all executions in March 2000. Ryan, a death penalty proponent, became disturbed by new evidence collected as a class project by Northwestern University students. The students unearthed information that led to the release of thirteen men on the state's death row. The specter of allowing death sentences to continue in light of evidence showing so many men were wrongly convicted prompted Ryan's much publicized action. Soon thereafter, the governor of Maryland followed suit after receiving evidence that found that blacks were much more likely

Thousands of demonstrators took to the streets to protest against the death penalty during the 2000 Republican National Convention in Philadelphia. Earlier that year, Governor George Ryan (R–IL) declared a moratorium on executions because of flaws he found in the justice system after several men on death row were proven innocent. Later, he pardoned everyone on death row as he left office.

(Photo courtesy: AFP/Corbis)

Join the Debate

DO "THREE STRIKES" LAWS ABRIDGE CIVIL LIBERTIES?

Public anger and fear over crime has led many states to pass laws requiring life imprisonment for those who commit three serious crimes—so-called "three strikes" laws. The intent of such laws is to get off the streets and into prison forever those violent criminals who have proved that they continue to be a danger to society and cannot be rehabilitated. Yet, such requirements sometimes have led to life prison sentences for petty theft convictions, if the person has two prior convictions.

The U.S. Constitution forbids "cruel and unusual punishment," yet it does not define what it is. In 2003, the U.S. Supreme Court is expected to decide whether three strikes laws constitute cruel and unusual punishment. Meanwhile, the current debate about three-strikes laws raises many related questions: How can public safety be assured in a time of increasing numbers of repeat offenders? Is it right to imprison someone for life for a petty theft? Does commission of a petty theft after commission of two serious crimes constitute a serious danger to society? What is a proper method for dealing with repeat offenders?

Read and think about the following excerpted 2002 news article about three strikes laws in the states. Then, join the debate over three strikes laws and constitutional civil liberties. Should the Supreme Court rule that state and federal three strikes laws unconstitutionally abridge citizens' civil liberties? Consider the debating points and questions posed at the end of this feature, and sharpen your own arguments for the position you find most viable.

Many States Rethinking "Three Strikes" Laws

By V. Dion Haynes

LOS ANGELES-Facing major budgetary strains and concerns that some felons involved in petty crime are being unduly punished, more than a dozen states are rethinking their policies on stiff sentences and so-called "three strikes" laws.

During the 1990s, about 25 states and the federal government passed laws requiring violent offenders convicted of a third felony to be incarcerated 25 years to life without parole. The laws, part of a response to escalating gang and drug activity, followed a move by nearly all states to mandate the number of years felons would serve for specific violent crimes.

The result was a burgeoning prison population and rising costs at a time when state budgets are shrinking. Now several states including California, Texas, Iowa, Connecticut and North Carolina are trying to cut their prison population by loosening

their mandatory minimum laws, shifting more drug users from jail to treatment or by closing facilities.

"The only direction we saw for years and years was for states to increase penalties, increase the number of people going to prison and to abolish early release programs," said Malcolm Young, executive director of The Sentencing Project, a Washington-based non-profit organization that advocates prison alternatives.

"Now politicians are determining that they can take steps to moderate sentences without fear of a public backlash," said Young, whose organization recently released a study on the issue. These developments (by states) are ... driven in part by budget concerns."

Illinois has shuttered the Joliet Correctional Center and has announced several other cuts, in hopes of saving more than $100 million.

In California, a bill seeking to soften the nation's toughest three-strikes law is advancing through the Legislature. The bill would ask voters to decide

whether to restrict the third strike to violent crimes.

The effort is fueled by a recent federal appeals court ruling that overturned the 25 years to life sentences of two felons who had committed petty crimes, such as shoplifting videotapes. The court declared that California's three-strikes law is cruel and unusual punishment and ruled that the sentences should fit the crime....

The movement by the states to toughen penalties for violent criminals has since 1970 contributed to a six-fold increase in the nationwide prison and jail population, which now stands at 1.9 million, according to experts. Since 1980, incarceration costs have jumped to $40 billion, an eight-fold rise. But the recession and the loss of billions in tax revenue have forced many states to make significant cutbacks to prison spending.

For example ... Colorado, Kansas and Arkansas are considering either closing prisons or delaying construction of new ones.

Within the last year, Mississippi has adopted an early release law for non-violent offenders. California, Texas, North Carolina, Connecticut, Idaho and Arkansas passed laws requiring the diversion of non-violent drug users from prison to treatment. And Virginia adopted an early-release program for elderly inmates.

In Louisiana, officials approved a measure last year loosening the state's mandatory minimum sentencing law in the face of a $900 million projected deficit.

In California, a state with a prison population of 160,000, the debate over whether to sentence non-violent criminals to life terms is heating up with the move to soften the 8-year-old three-strikes law. Under the current law, California offenders receive their first and second strikes for a list of serious and violent crimes, including armed robbery, rape, burglary and assault. Judges can double the sentences of second-time offenders. The third offense, which triggers the 25 years to life sentence, can include any felony, such as petty theft. The life sentences in most other three-strikes states result only from violent felonies.

"The benefits of our three-strikes law are evident. Before, 6 percent of criminals were committing 60 percent of the crimes and they were getting out in plea bargains," said California Secretary of State Bill Jones, who authored the three-strikes legislation when he was in the state Assembly.

But in February, the 9th U.S. Circuit Court of Appeals overturned the convictions of two men sentenced under California's three-strikes law to 25 years to life terms for petty theft. The Supreme Court waded into the national debate over sentencing laws this month by agreeing to decide whether California's "three strikes" law violates the Constitution. The court said it would decide whether the long sentences amounted to cruel and unusual punishment. The case could affect laws in up to 40 states and lead to the release of more than 300 other inmates. The court, which will review the issue next fall, has long held that a penalty that is grossly disproportionate to the crime violates the 8th Amendment.

Source: V. Dion Haynes, *Chicago Tribune* (April 30, 2002). Copyrighted 4/30/02 Chicago Tribune Co. All rights reserved. Used with permission.

JOIN THE DEBATE!

CHECK YOUR UNDERSTANDING: Make sure you understand the following key points from the article; go back and review it if you missed any of them:

- Three strikes laws typically provide that violent offenders convicted of a third felony must be imprisoned for twenty-five years to life without parole.
- Three strikes laws added to burgeoning prison populations of the last decade, and current state budget crunches have triggered reconsideration of the laws.
- A federal appeals court declared a three strikes law to be cruel and unusual punishment.

ADDITIONAL INFORMATION: News articles don't provide all the information an informed citizen needs to know about an issue under debate. Here are some questions the article does not answer that you may need to consider in order to join the debate:

- What kinds of punishments have been declared cruel and unusual in the past?
- Is there a common pattern for the repeat criminals convicted under three strikes laws?
- Are there enough "three strikes" prisoners to significantly affect state budgets?

What other information might you want to know? Where might you gather this information? How might you evaluate the credibility of the information you gather? Is the information from a reliable source? Can you identify any potential biases?

IDENTIFYING THE ARGUMENTS: Now that you have some information on the issue, and have thought about what else you need to know, see whether you can present the arguments on both sides of the debate. Here are some ideas to get you started. We've provided one example each of "pro" and "con" arguments, but you should be able to offer others:

PRO: Three strikes laws should be upheld and applied. Here's why:

- For cases where second chances and rehabilitation do not work, society must be able to enforce public safety by locking away incorrigible criminals.

CON: Three strikes laws are unconstitutional. Here's why:

- The constitution restricts government power by forbidding punishments that are cruel and unusual, including onerous punishments for nonviolent crimes.

TAKING A POSITION AND SUPPORTING IT: After thinking about the information in the article on three strikes laws, placing the article in the broader context of the issue of civil liberties, and articulating the arguments in the debate, what position would you take? What information supports your position? What arguments would you use to persuade others to your side of the debate? How would you counter arguments on the other side?

169

ANALYZING VISUALS

Capital Punishment in the United States

Since capital punishment was reinstated in the United States in 1976, more than 780 people have been executed, mostly by lethal injection or electrocution. More than half of the accused (56 percent) were white, over a third (36 percent) were black, and almost a tenth were Hispanic, Native American, or Asian American. Today, more than 3,700 inmates are sitting on death row. Of those inmates, 45 percent are white, 43 percent are black, 9 percent are Hispanic, 1.1 percent are Native American, and 1.1 percent are Asian American. The death row population is overwhelmingly male, with females accounting for only 1.5 percent of inmates awaiting execution. It is also disproportionately African American. Six states (Kansas, South Dakota, New York, New Hampshire, New Jersey, and Connecticut) have the death penalty but have had no executions. After viewing the map, answer the following critical thinking questions: Which states have the largest number of executions? Which states have the fewest executions? What factors—social, economic, and political—might explain the variation among the states in number of executions?

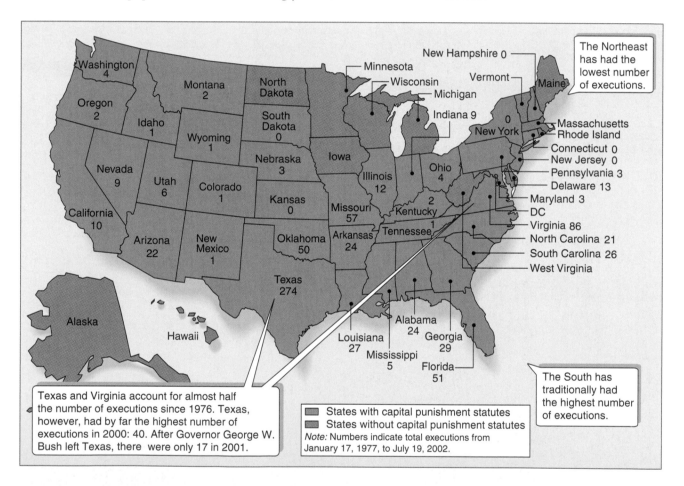

Washington 4
Montana 2
North Dakota
Oregon 2
Idaho 1
Wyoming 1
South Dakota 0
Minnesota
Wisconsin
Michigan
New Hampshire 0
Vermont
Maine

The Northeast has had the lowest number of executions.

Indiana 9
Massachusetts
Rhode Island
Connecticut 0
New Jersey 0
Pennsylvania 3
Delaware 13
Maryland 3
DC
Virginia 86
North Carolina 21
South Carolina 26
West Virginia

New York 0
Nebraska 3
Iowa
Ohio 4
Illinois 12
Nevada 9
Utah 6
Colorado 1
Kansas 0
Missouri 57
Kentucky 2
Tennessee 1
California 10
Arizona 22
New Mexico 1
Oklahoma 50
Arkansas 24
Texas 274

Alaska
Hawaii

Alabama 24
Louisiana 27
Georgia 29
Mississippi 5
Florida 51

The South has traditionally had the highest number of executions.

Texas and Virginia account for almost half the number of executions since 1976. Texas, however, had by far the highest number of executions in 2000: 40. After Governor George W. Bush left Texas, there were only 17 in 2001.

◼ States with capital punishment statutes
◼ States without capital punishment statutes
Note: Numbers indicate total executions from January 17, 1977, to July 19, 2002.

Source: Death Penalty Information Center, http://www.deathpenaltyinfo.org.

to be death sentenced than whites. Other states, such as Ohio, have made offers of free DNA testing to those sitting on death row.

Over the past thirteen years, over a hundred persons have been released from death row after DNA tests proved the did not commit the crimes for which they were convicted.[125] In New York, twenty individuals on death row were later found innocent with evidence derived from evidence other than DNA.[126]

At this writing, proposed legislation called the Innocence Protection Act would provide grants for local prosecutors for DNA testing in death penalty cases. The proposed legislation also makes sure that criminal defendants facing the death penalty would have improved counsel, another chronic problem. In the wake of all of these findings and actions, public support for the death penalty is at its lowest point since 1978, which may be a harbinger of more moves to limit its use, particularly in non-southern states.

THE RIGHT TO PRIVACY

To this point, the rights and freedoms we have discussed have been derived fairly directly from specific guarantees contained in the Bill of Rights. In contrast, the Supreme Court also has given protection to rights not enumerated specifically in the Constitution or Bill of Rights.

Although the Constitution is silent about the **right to privacy,** the Bill of Rights contains many indications that the Framers expected that some areas of life were "off limits" to governmental regulation. The right to freedom of religion guaranteed in the First Amendment implies the right to exercise private, personal beliefs. The guarantee against unreasonable searches and seizures contained in the Fourth Amendment similarly implies that persons are to be secure in their homes and should not fear that police will show up at their doorsteps without cause. As early as 1928, Justice Louis Brandeis hailed privacy as "the right to be left alone—the most comprehensive of rights and the right most valued by civilized men."[127] It was not until 1965, however, that the Court attempted to explain the origins of this right.

right to privacy
The right to be let alone; a judicially created doctrine encompassing an individual's decision to use birth control or secure an abortion.

WEB EXPLORATION
For other privacy issues, see
www.ablongman.com/oconnor

Birth Control

Today, most Americans take access to many forms of birth control as a matter of course. Condoms are sold in the grocery store, and some television stations air ads for them. Easy access to birth control, however, wasn't always the case. Many states often barred the sale of contraceptives to minors, prohibited the display of contraceptives, or even banned their sale altogether. One of the last states to do away with these kinds of laws

In this 1965 photo, Estelle Griswold (left), executive director of the Planned Parenthood League of Connecticut, and Cornelia Jahncke, its president, celebrate the Supreme Court's ruling in *Griswold* v. *Connecticut*.
(Photo courtesy: Bettmann/CORBIS)

was Connecticut. It outlawed the sale of all forms of birth control and even prohibited physicians from discussing it with their married patients until the Supreme Court ruled its restrictive laws unconstitutional.

Griswold v. *Connecticut* (1965) involved a challenge to the constitutionality of an 1879 Connecticut law prohibiting the dissemination of information about and/or the sale of contraceptives.[128] In *Griswold*, seven justices decided that various portions of the Bill of Rights, including the First, Third, Fourth, Ninth, and Fourteenth Amendments, cast what the Court called "penumbras" (unstated liberties on the fringes or in the shadow of more explicitly stated rights), thereby creating zones of privacy, including a married couple's right to plan a family. Thus, the Connecticut statute was ruled unconstitutional because it violated marital privacy, a right the Court concluded could be read into the U.S. Constitution through interpreting several amendments.

Later, the Court expanded the right of privacy to include the right of unmarried individuals to have access to contraceptives. "If the right of privacy means anything," wrote Justice William J. Brennan, "it is the right of the individual, married or single, to be free from unwarranted governmental intrusion into matters so fundamentally affecting a person as the decision to bear or beget a child."[129] Contraceptive rights, however, are often limited for those under age eighteen by state or federal policy.

Abortion

In the early 1960s, two birth-related tragedies occurred: Severely deformed babies were born to women who had been given the drug thalidomide while pregnant, and a nationwide measles epidemic resulted in the birth of more babies with severe problems. The increasing medical safety of abortions and the growing women's rights movement combined with these tragedies to put pressure on the legal and medical establishments to support laws that would guarantee a woman's access to a safe and legal abortion.

By the late 1960s, fourteen states had voted to liberalize their abortion policies, and four states decriminalized abortion in the early stages of pregnancy. But, many women's rights activists wanted more. They argued that the decision to carry a pregnancy to term was a woman's fundamental constitutional right. In 1973, in one of the most controversial decisions ever handed down, seven members of the Court agreed with this position.

The woman whose case became the catalyst for pro-choice and anti-abortion groups was Norma McCorvey, an itinerant circus worker. The mother of one toddler she was unable to care for, McCorvey could not leave another child in her mother's care. So, she decided to terminate her second pregnancy. She was unable to secure a legal abortion and frightened by the conditions she found when she sought an illegal, back-alley abortion. McCorvey turned to two young Texas lawyers who were looking for a plaintiff to bring a lawsuit to challenge Texas's restrictive statute. The Texas law allowed abortions only when they were necessary to save the life of the mother. McCorvey, who was unable to obtain a legal abortion, later gave birth and put the baby up for adoption. Nevertheless, she allowed her lawyers to proceed with the case using her as their plaintiff. They used the pseudonym Jane Roe for McCorvey as they challenged the Texas law as enforced by Henry Wade, the district attorney for Dallas County, Texas.

When the case finally came before the Supreme Court, Justice Harry A. Blackmun, a former lawyer at the Mayo Clinic, relied heavily on medical evidence to rule that the Texas law violated a woman's constitutionally guaranteed right to privacy, which he argued included her decision to terminate a pregnancy. Writing for the majority in *Roe* v. *Wade* (1973), Blackmun divided pregnancy into three stages. In the first trimester, a woman's right to privacy gave her an absolute right (in consultation with her physician), free from state interference, to terminate her pregnancy. In the second trimester, the state's interest in the health of the mother gave it the right to regulate abortions—but only to protect the woman's health. Only in the third trimester—when the fetus becomes potentially viable—did the Court find that the state's interest in potential life

WEB EXPLORATION
To compare the different sides of the abortion debate, see www.ablongman.com/oconnor

Roe v. *Wade* (1973)
The Supreme Court found that a woman's right to an abortion was protected by the right to privacy that could be implied from specific guarantees found in the Bill of Rights applied to the states through the Fourteenth Amendment.

outweighed the woman's privacy interests. Even in the third trimester, however, abortions to save the life or health of the mother were to be legal.[130]

Roe v. *Wade* unleashed a torrent of political controversy. Anti-abortion groups, caught off guard, scrambled to recoup their losses in Congress. Representative Henry Hyde (R–IL) persuaded Congress to ban the use of Medicaid funds for abortions for poor women, and the constitutionality of the Hyde Amendment was upheld by the Supreme Court in 1977 and again in 1980.[131] The issue also polarized both major political parties.

From the 1970s through the present, the right to an abortion and its constitutional underpinnings in the right to privacy have been under attack by well-organized anti-abortion groups. The Reagan and Bush administrations were strong advocates of the anti-abortion position, regularly urging the Court to overrule *Roe*. They came close to victory in *Webster* v. *Reproductive Health Services* (1989).[132] In *Webster*, the Court upheld state-required fetal viability tests in the second trimester, even though these tests would increase the cost of an abortion considerably. The Court also upheld Missouri's refusal to allow abortions to be performed in state-supported hospitals or by state-funded doctors or nurses. Perhaps most noteworthy, however, were the facts that four justices seemed willing to overrule *Roe* v. *Wade* and that Justice Antonin Scalia publicly rebuked his colleague, Justice Sandra Day O'Connor, then the only woman on the Court, for failing to provide the critical fifth vote to overrule *Roe*.

After *Webster*, states began to enact more restrictive legislation. In the most important abortion case since *Roe*, *Planned Parenthood of Southeastern Pennsylvania* v. *Casey* (1992), Justices O'Connor, Anthony Kennedy, and David Souter, in a jointly authored opinion, wrote that Pennsylvania could limit abortions as long as its regulations did not pose "an undue burden" on pregnant women.[133] The narrowly supported decision, which upheld a twenty-four-hour waiting period and parental consent requirements, did not overrule *Roe*, but clearly limited its scope by abolishing its trimester approach and substituting the "undue burden" standard.

In 1993, newly elected pro-choice President Bill Clinton ended bans on fetal tissue research, abortions at military hospitals, and federal financing for overseas population control programs. He also lifted the "gag" rule, a federal regulation enacted in 1987 which barred public health clinics receiving federal dollars from discussing abortion (policies later reversed by George W. Bush).[134] He also lifted the ban on testing of RU-486, the so-called French abortion pill, which ultimately was made available for public consumption late in 2000.

President Clinton used the occasion of his first appointment to the U.S. Supreme Court to select a longtime supporter of abortion rights, Ruth Bader Ginsburg, to replace Justice Byron White, one of the original dissenters in *Roe*. Most commentators believe that this was an important first step in shifting the Court away from any further curtailment of abortion rights, as was the later appointment of Justice Stephen Breyer in 1994.

While President Clinton was attempting to shore up abortion rights through judicial appointments, Congress passed and sent to President Clinton a bill to ban—for the first time—a specific procedure used in late-term abortions.[135] The president vetoed the Partial Birth Abortion Act. Many state legislatures, however, passed their own versions of the act. In 2000, the Supreme Court, however, ruled 5–4 in *Stenberg* v. *Carhart* that a Nebraska "partial birth" abortion statute was unconstitutionally vague and therefore unenforceable, calling into question the laws of twenty-nine other states with their own bans on late-term procedures.[136] At the same time, it ruled that a Colorado law that prohibited protestors from coming within eight feet of women entering clinics was constitutional.[137] This "bubble law" was designed to create an eight-foot buffer zone around women as they walked through protesters into a clinic to receive an abortion. In 2003, the Congress again passed the Partial Birth Abortion Act, which was quickly signed into law by President George W. Bush. At this writing, three federal district court judges have ruled it to be unconstitutional.

A once very popular anti-abortion group, Operation Rescue, staged large-scale protests in front of abortion clinics across the nation gaining a surprising new member—Norma McCorvey, the "Jane Roe" of *Roe* v. *Wade* (1973). In 1995, she announced that she had become pro-life.

(Photo courtesy: Tim Sharp/AP/Wide World Photos)

James Dale, a one-time Boy Scout leader, sued the organization after he was dismissed for being gay. Here he talks to reporters following the Supreme Court's ruling allowing the Boy Scouts of America to refuse to allow gay men to be troop leaders. A closely divided Court ruled that such a private group has the right to set its own moral code, thereby rejecting Dale's claim.

(Photo courtesy: Elizabeth Lippman/Getty Images)

WEB EXPLORATION
For more on gay rights and recent court cases, see
www.ablongman.com/oconnor

Homosexuality

It was not until 2003 that the U.S. Supreme Court ruled that an individual's constitutional right to privacy, which provided the basis for the Griswold (contraceptives) and Roe (abortion) decisions, prevented the state of Texas from criminalizing private sexual behavior. This monumental decision invalidated the laws of thirteen states. In *Lawrence* v. *Texas* (2003), six members of the Court found that the Texas law was unconstitutional; five justices found it to violate fundamental privacy rights. Justice Sandra Day O'Connor agreed that the law was unconstitutional, but concluded that it was an equal protection violation. (See chapter 5 for detailed discussion of the equal protection clause of the Fourteenth Amendment.) Although Justice Antonin Scalia issued a stinging dissent charging that "the Court has largely signed on to the so-called homosexual agenda. . . , " the majority of the Court was unswayed.[138]

Just three years before in *Boy Scouts* v. *Dale* (2000) the Court upheld a challenge to the Boy Scouts' refusal to allow a gay man to become a scoutmaster.[139] There, the majority of the court found that a private club's First Amendment right to freedom of association allowed it to use its own moral code to select troop leaders. While the public largely supported the Boy Scouts' decision, it also approved of the Court's resolution of the challenge to the Texas sodomy law.[140] A poll taken just before the 2003 ruling showed the public against the Court's 1986 decision by a margin of 57 to 38 percent.[141]

Although the Court has refused to expand the right to privacy to invalidate state laws that criminalize some aspects of homosexual behavior, in 1996 it ruled that a state could not deny rights to homosexuals simply because they are homosexuals.[142]

The Right to Die

While the current Supreme Court is unlikely to expand the scope of the privacy doctrine to include greater protections for homosexuals in the near future, it is likely to continue to get more cases involving claims for personal autonomy. More than ten years ago, in 1990, the Supreme Court ruled 5–4 that parents could not withdraw a feeding tube from their comatose daughter after her doctors testified she could live like that for many more years. Writing for the majority, Chief Justice William H. Rehnquist rejected any attempts to expand the right of privacy into this thorny area of social policy. The Court did note, however, that individuals could terminate medical treatment if they were able to express, or had done so in writing via a living will, their desire to have medical treatment terminated in the event they became incompetent.[143]

States, too, have entered into this arena, legislating to prevent what is often called "assisted suicide." Jurors, however, often appear unwilling to find loved ones guilty of helping the terminally ill carry out the decision to take their own lives. In 1999, however, after being acquitted in four other trials, Dr. Jack Kevorkian represented himself and was found guilty of administering a lethal injection of chemicals to a fifty-two-year-old man.

In 1997, the U.S. Supreme Court ruled unanimously that terminally ill persons do not have a constitutional right to physician assisted suicide. The Court's action upheld the laws of New York and Washington state that make it a crime for doctors to give life-ending drugs to mentally competent but terminally ill patients who wish to die.[144] But, Oregon has enacted a "right-to-die" or assisted suicide law approved by Oregon voters that allows physicians to prescribe drugs to terminally ill patients. In November 2001, however, Attorney General John Ashcroft issued a legal opinion determining that assisted suicide is not "a legitimate medical purpose," thereby putting physicians who follow their state law in jeopardy of federal prosecution.[145] His memo also calls for the revocation of physicians' drug prescription licenses, putting the state and the national government in conflict in an area that Republicans historically have argued is the province of state authority. Oregon officials immediately (and successfully) sought a court order blocking Ashcroft's attempt to interfere with implementation of Oregon law.[146] Later, a federal judge ruled that Ashcroft had overstepped his authority on every point.[147]

WEB EXPLORATION
To learn about the right to die movement, see
www.ablongman.com/oconnor

Continuity & Change

Conceptions of Civil Liberties

When the new Constitution was adopted by the citizens in the states, it lacked a bill of rights. This absence was a glaring one in the eyes of many Americans. Their state constitutions often protected their civil liberties, and they feared that they already were giving up too many rights to an untested national government. So, when the first Congress met in 1789, one of the first items on its agenda was the passage of a bill of rights to prevent the national government from infringing the liberties of the citizenry.

In the late 1700s, issues of political speech, freedom of the press, and the right to gather and petition the government were among the rights most cherished. After all, without these rights, the colonists never would have been

(continued)

able to organize and mobilize effectively enough to make the successful break with Great Britain.

Today, our conceptions of civil liberties, as well as their need for protection, are quite different. Poll after poll shows that if Americans were to vote on the Bill of Rights already contained in the Constitution, it would not garner enough votes in the states to be adopted. Over the years the role of the courts—especially the federal courts—in expanding the application of most of the Bill of Rights to the states, as well as in interpreting those provisions, has produced a panoply of rights never envisioned by the Framers. Moreover, the provisions of the Constitution and the Bill of Rights have been interpreted to protect a variety of rights, and liberties that are not explicitly stated, such as protections for criminal defendants, the right to privacy, and reproductive rights.

Today, however, just as was the case in the Civil War and World Wars I and II, many must grapple with how many civil liberties can be curtailed or limited in the name of national security. President George W. Bush, like President Abraham Lincoln before him, believes it is necessary to suspend some civil liberties normally enjoyed by citizens. His TIPS program, noted in Roots of Government: The

American Civil Liberties Union, is just one example of this philosophy. Others believe that in a time of war, the United States should be a model of civil liberties protections for the nations we fight, many of which practice massive civil liberties abuses.

1. Do you believe that war or national emergency justifies curtailments of civil liberties? If so, which ones?
2. Technological advances often are double-edged swords for civil libertarians. DNA testing, for example, can be used to trace parentage or match organ donors. It even can be used to prove the innocence of those already judged guilty. But, the presence of a national DNA data bank, while allowing law enforcement officers the opportunity to apprehend many of the guilty, also is a form of self-incrimination and, some would argue, an unreasonable search and seizure. What are the pros and cons of all Americans having their DNA tested and recorded?

CAST YOUR VOTE   Which civil liberties deserve protection? To cast your vote, go to www.ablongman.com/oconnor

SUMMARY

1. **The First Constitutional Amendments: The Bill of Rights**
   Most of the Framers originally opposed the Bill of Rights. Anti-Federalists, however, continued to stress the need for a bill of rights during the drive for ratification of the Constitution, and some states tried to make their ratification contingent on the addition of a bill of rights. Thus, during its first session, Congress sent the first ten amendments to the Constitution, the Bill of Rights, to the states for their ratification. Later, the addition of the Fourteenth Amendment allowed the Supreme Court to apply some of the amendments to the states through a process called selective incorporation.

2. **First Amendment Guarantees: Freedom of Religion**
   The First Amendment guarantees freedom of religion. The establishment clause, which prohibits the national government from establishing a religion, does not, according to Supreme Court interpretation, create an absolute wall between church and state. While the national and state governments may generally not give direct aid to religious groups, many forms of aid, especially many that benefit children, have been held to be constitutionally permissible. In

contrast, the Court has generally barred prayer in public schools. The Court generally has adopted an accommodationist approach when interpreting the free exercise clause by allowing some governmental regulation of religious practices.

3. **First Amendment Guarantees: Freedom of Speech and Press**
   The First Amendment also guarantees freedom of speech and of the press. The Alien and Sedition Acts in 1798 were the first national efforts to curtail free speech, but they were never reviewed by the U.S. Supreme Court.

   Some forms of speech were punished during the Civil War, and the Supreme Court refused to address their constitutionality directly. By the twentieth century, several states, and later the national government, passed laws restricting freedoms of speech and of the press. These curtailments were upheld by the Court, using the clear and present danger test. Later, the Court used the more liberal direct incitement test, which required a stronger showing of imminent danger before speech could be restricted.

   Symbolic speech has been afforded the same protection as other forms of speech. Historically, the Supreme Court has disfavored any attempts at prior restraint of speech or press; thus, hate speech laws and regulations have come under constitutional challenge.

Libel, slander, and obscenity (as well as some forms of pornography) are not protected by the First Amendment, and the Supreme Court has upheld the authority of Congress to legislate in these areas.

4. **The Second Amendment: The Right to Keep and Bear Arms**
Initially, this right was envisioned as one dealing with state militias. Today, crime in the schools, in particular, has led to a reexamination of this amendment's meaning, with little Supreme Court interpretation as a guide.

5. **The Rights of Criminal Defendants**
The Fourth, Fifth, Sixth, and Eighth Amendments provide a variety of procedural guarantees to individuals accused of crimes. In particular, the Fourth Amendment prohibits unreasonable searches and seizures, and the Court has generally refused to allow evidence seized in violation of this safeguard to be used at trial.

Among other rights, the Fifth Amendment guarantees that "no person shall be compelled to be a witness against himself." The Supreme Court has interpreted this provision to require that the government inform the accused of his or her right to remain silent. This provision has also been interpreted to require that illegally obtained confessions must be excluded at trial.

The Sixth Amendment's guarantee of "assistance of counsel" has been interpreted by the Supreme Court to require that the government provide counsel to defendants unable to pay for it in cases where prison sentences may be imposed. The Sixth Amendment also requires an impartial jury, although the meaning of impartial continues to evolve through judicial interpretation.

The Eighth Amendment's ban against "cruel and unusual punishments" has been held not to bar imposition of the death penalty.

6. **The Right to Privacy**
The right to privacy is a judicially created right carved from the implications of several amendments, including the First, Third, Fourth, Ninth, and Fourteenth Amendments. Statutes limiting access to birth control, abortion rights, the right to physician assisted suicide, and criminalizing homosexual acts have been ruled unconstitutional violations of the right to privacy.

KEY TERMS

SELECTED READINGS

Abernathy, M. Glenn, and Barbara A. Perry, *Civil Liberties Under the Constitution,* 6th ed. Columbia: University of South Carolina Press, 1993.

Dempsey, James X., and David Cole. *Terrorism and the Constitution: Sacrificing Civil Liberties in the Name of National Security,* 2nd ed. Washington, DC: First Amendment Foundation, 2002.

Fiss, Owen M. *The Irony of Free Speech.* Cambridge, MA: Harvard University Press, 1996.

Friendly, Fred W. *Minnesota Rag: The Dramatic Story of the Landmark Case That Gave New Meaning to Freedom of the Press.* New York: Random House, 1981.

Gates, Henry Louis, Jr., ed. *Speaking of Race, Speaking of Sex: Hate Speech, Civil Rights, and Civil Liberties.* New York: New York University Press, 1995.

Greenawalt, Kent. *Fighting Words: Individuals, Communities, and Liberties of Speech.* Princeton, NJ: Princeton University Press, 1995.

Kalven, Harry, Jr. *A Worthy Tradition: Freedom of Speech in America.* New York: Harper and Row, 1988.

Lewis, Anthony. *Gideon's Trumpet* (reissue edition). New York: Vintage Books, 1989.

———. *Make No Law: The Sullivan Case and the First Amendment.* New York: Random House, 1991.

Manwaring, David R. *Render unto Caesar: The Flag Salute Controversy.* Chicago: University of Chicago Press, 1962.

O'Brien, David M. *Constitutional Law and Politics, Vol. 2: Civil Rights and Civil Liberties,* 4th ed. New York: Norton, 1999.

O'Connor, Karen. *No Neutral Ground: Abortion Politics in an Age of Absolutes.* Boulder, CO: Westview Press, 1996.

Regan, Priscilla M. *Legislating Privacy: Technology, Social Values, and Public Policy*. Chapel Hill: University of North Carolina Press, 1995.

Weddington, Sarah. *A Question of Choice*. New York: Grosset/Putnam, 1993.

NOTES

1. This vignette draws heavily from Jamin Raskin, "In Defense of Students' Rights," *Washington Post* (August 27, 2000): B8.
2. Charles Lane, "Court Made Dramatic Shifts in Law," *Washington Post* (June 30, 2002): A6.
3. The absence of a bill of rights led Mason to refuse to sign the proposed Constitution, noting that he "would sooner chop off his right hand than put it to the Constitution as it now stands." (Quoted in Eric Black, *Our Constitution: The Myth That Binds Us* [Boulder, CO: Westview Press, 1988], 75.)
4. Quoted in Jack N. Rakove, "Madison Won Passage of the Bill of Rights but Remained a Skeptic," *Public Affairs Report* (March 1991): 6.
5. 32 U.S. 243 (1833).
6. *Allgeyer* v. *Louisiana*, 165 U.S. 578 (1897).
7. 268 U.S. 652 (1925).
8. 283 U.S. 697 (1931). For more about *Near*, see Fred W. Friendly, *Minnesota Rag: The Dramatic Story of the Landmark Case That Gave New Meaning to Freedom of the Press* (New York: Random House, 1981).
9. 302 U.S. 319 (1937).
10. Continental Congress to the People of Great Britain, October 21, 1774, in Philip Kurland and Ralph Lerner, eds., *The Founders' Constitution*, vol. 5 (Chicago: University of Chicago Press, 1987), 61.
11. *Reynolds* v. *U.S.*, 98 U.S. 145 (1879).
12. *Cantwell* v. *Connecticut*, 310 U.S. 296 (1940).
13. *Zobrest* v. *Catalina Foothills School District*, 506 U.S. 813 (1992).
14. 370 U.S. 421 (1962).
15. *Lee* v. *Weisman*, 505 U.S. 577 (1992).
16. *Santa Fe Independent School District* v. *Doe*, 530 U.S. 290 (2000).
17. 403 U.S. 602 (1971).
18. "An Eternal Debate," *Omaha World-Journal* (November 27, 2002): 6B.
19. *Widmar* v. *Vincent*, 454 U.S. 263 (1981).
20. *Board of Education* v. *Mergens*, 496 U.S. 226 (1990).
21. *Lamb's Chapel* v. *Center Moriches Union Free School District*, 508 U.S. 384 (1993).
22. *Rosenberger* v. *University of Virginia*, 515 U.S. 819 (1995).
23. Ibid.
24. 521 U.S. 203 (1997).
25. *Mitchell* v. *Helms*, 530 U.S. 793 (2000).
26. 2002 U.S. LEXIS 4885 (2002).
27. Charles Lane, "Court Upholds Ohio School Vouchers," *Washington Post* (June 28, 2002): A1, A11.
28. *Employment Division, Dept. of Human Resources of Oregon* v. *Smith*, 494 U.S. 872 (1990).
29. *Boerne* v. *Flores*, 521 U.S. 507 (1997).
30. *Church of the Lukumi Babalu Aye* v. *Hialeah*, 508 U.S. 525 (1993).
31. *U.S.* v. *Seeger*, 380 U.S. 163 (1965).
32. *Cruz* v. *Beto*, 405 U.S. 319 (1972).
33. *O'Lone* v. *Shabazz*, 482 U.S. 342 (1987).
34. See, for example, the opinion in *Boissonneault* v. *Flint City Council*, 392 Mich. 685 (1974).
35. *Chaplinsky* v. *New Hampshire*, 315 U.S. 568 (1942).
36. *Ex parte McCardle*, 74 U.S. 506 (1869).
37. David M. O'Brien, *Constitutional Law and Politics, Vol. 2; Civil Rights and Civil Liberties* (New York: Norton, 1991), 345.
38. See Frederick Siebert, *The Rights and Privileges of the Press* (New York: D. Appleton-Century, 1934), 886, 931–40.
39. 249 U.S. 47 (1919).
40. *Brandenburg* v. *Ohio*, 395 U.S. 444 (1969).
41. 376 U.S. 254 (1964).
42. *Masson* v. *New Yorker Magazine*, 501 U.S. 496 (1991).
43. Howard Kurtz, "Clinton Aide Settles Libel Suit Against Matt Drudge—At a Cost," *Washington Post* (May 2, 2001): C1.
44. Darrell Giles, "Cruise Drops $200m Gay Lawsuit," *Sunday Mail* (December 2, 2001): 1.
45. Technically, obscenity refers to those things considered "disgusting, foul or morally unhealthy." Pornography, in contrast, is often broader in meaning and generally refers to "depictions of sexual lewdness or erotic behavior." While distasteful to many, pornography is not necessarily obscene. While the *Starr Report* contained sexual materials many say were pornographic, no one charged that its contents were obscene. See Donald Downs, "Obscenity and Pornography," in Kermit Hall, ed., *The Oxford Companion to the Supreme Court of the United States* (New York: Oxford University Press, 1992), 602.
46. 315 U.S. 568 (1942).
47. *Regina* v. *Hicklin*, L. R. 2 Q. B. 360 (1868).
48. 354 U.S. 476 (1957).
49. 413 U.S. 15 (1973).
50. *Barnes* v. *Glen Theater*, 501 U.S. 560 (1991).
51. Joan Biskupic, "Decency Can Be Weighed in Arts Funding," *Washington Post* (June 26, 1998): A1, A18.
52. *National Endowment for the Arts* v. *Finley*, 524 U.S. 569 (1998).
53. 521 U.S. 844 (1997).
54. "www.meddling.gov," *Times-Picayune* (October 8, 1998): B6.
55. *Ashcroft* v. *Free Speech Coalition*, 122 S.Ct. 1389 (2002).
56. David G. Savage, "Ban on 'Virtual' Child Porn Is Upset by Court," *Los Angeles Times* (April 17, 2002): A1.
57. Lyle Denniston, "Court Puts 2D Pornography Law on Hold: A Majority Doubt Giving Localities an Internet Veto," *Boston Globe* (May 14, 2002): A2.
58. Nick Anderson and Elizabeth Levin, "Crime Bill Passes Easily in Congress: Measure Includes Expansion of Amber Alert System," *Los Angeles Times* (April 11, 2003): A36.
59. 403 U.S. 713 (1971).
60. *Nebraska Press Association* v. *Stuart*, 427 U.S. 539 (1976).
61. *Abrams* v. *U.S.*, 250 U.S. 616 (1919).
62. 283 U.S. 359 (1931).
63. 393 U.S. 503 (1969).
64. *Texas* v. *Johnson*, 491 U.S. 397 (1989).
65. *U.S.* v. *Eichman*, 496 U.S. 310 (1990).
66. Harry Kalven Jr., *Negro and the First Amendment* (Chicago: University of Chicago Press, 1966).
67. Henry Louis Gates Jr., "Why Civil Liberties Pose No Threat to Civil Rights," *New Republic* (September 20, 1993).
68. Linda Greenhouse, "Supreme Court Roundup: Free Speech or Hate Speech: Court Weighs Cross Burning," *New York Times* (May 28, 2002): A18. *R.A.V.* v. *City of St. Paul*, 505 U.S. 377 (1992).

69. *Virginia* v. *Black,* 538 U.S. 343 (2003).

70. Michael A. Fletcher, "Dissenters Find Colleges Less Tolerant of Discord Following Attacks," *Washington Post* (October 30, 2001): A6.

71. Mary M. Kershaw, "WVU Students Are at Greater Liberty to Protest," *USA Today* (May 13, 2002): D6.

72. 7 Peters 243 (1833).

73. 19 How. 393 (1857).

74. 307 U.S. 174 (1939).

75. 104 U.S. 194 (1983).

76. *Printz* v. *U.S.,* 514 U.S. 898 (1997).

77. *Stein* v. *New York,* 346 U.S. 156 (1953).

78. *Wilson* v. *Arkansas,* 514 U.S. 927 (1995).

79. *U.S.* v. *Sokolov,* 490 U.S. 1 (1989).

80. *U.S.* v. *Knights,* 534 U.S. 112 (2001).

81. *U.S.* v. *Matlock,* 415 U.S. 164 (1974).

82. *Johnson* v. *U.S.,* 333 U.S. 10 (1948).

83. *Winston* v. *Lee,* 470 U.S. 753 (1985).

84. *South Dakota* v. *Neville,* 459 U.S. 553 (1983).

85. *Michigan* v. *Tyler,* 436 U.S. 499 (1978).

86. *Hester* v. *U.S.,* 265 U.S. 57 (1924).

87. *Kyllo* v. *U.S.,* 533 U.S. 27 (2001).

88. David G. Savage, "Court Says No to Home Snooping," *Los Angeles Times* (June 12, 2001): A1.

89. *Carroll* v. *U.S.,* 267 U.S. 132 (1925).

90. *U.S.* v. *Arvizu,* 122 S.Ct. 744 (2002).

91. *Skinner* v. *Railway Labor Executives' Association,* 489 U.S. 602 (1989).

92. *Vernonia School District* v. *Acton,* 515 U.S. 646 (1995).

93. *Board of Education of Independent School District No. 92 of Pottawatomie County* v. *Earls,* 2002 LEXIS 4882 (2002).

94. *Ferguson* v. *City of Charleston,* 532 U.S. 67 (2001).

95. *Chandler* v. *Miller,* 520 U.S. 305 (1997).

96. John Wefing, "Employer Drug Testing: Disparate Judicial and Legislative Responses," *Albany Law Review* 63 (2000): 799–801.

97. *Counselman* v. *Hitchcock,* 142 U.S. 547 (1892).

98. *Brown* v. *Mississippi,* 297 U.S. 278 (1936).

99. *Lynumm* v. *Illinois,* 372 U.S. 528 (1963).

100. *Rhode Island* v. *Innis,* 446 U.S. 291 (1980).

101. *Arizona* v. *Fulminante,* 500 U.S. 938 (1991).

102. *Dickerson* v. *U.S.,* 530 U.S. 428 (2000).

103. 232 U.S. 383 (1914).

104. 367 U.S. 643 (1961).

105. *Stone* v. *Powell,* 428 U.S. 465 (1976).

106. *Johnson* v. *Zerbst,* 304 U.S. 458 (1938).

107. *Powell* v. *Alabama,* 287 U.S. 45 (1932).

108. 372 U.S. 335 (1963).

109. *Argersinger* v. *Hamlin,* 407 U.S. 25 (1972).

110. *Scott* v. *Illinois,* 440 U.S. 367 (1979).

111. *Alabama* v. *LeReed,* 121 S.Ct. 1955 (2002).

112. *Strauder* v. *West Virginia,* 100 U.S. 303 (1880).

113. *Taylor* v. *Louisiana,* 419 U.S. 522 (1975).

114. *Batson* v. *Kentucky,* 476 U.S. 79 (1986).

115. 497 U.S. 836 (1990).

116. *Hallinger* v. *Davis,* 146 U.S. 314 (1892).

117. *O'Neil* v. *Vermont,* 144 U.S. 323 (1892).

118. See Michael Meltsner, *Cruel and Unusual: The Supreme Court and Capital Punishment* (New York: Random House, 1973).

119. 408 U.S. 238 (1972).

120. 428 U.S. 153 (1976).

121. 481 U.S. 279 (1987).

122. 501 U.S. 1224 (1991).

123. *Atkins* v. *Virginia,* 122 S. Ct. 2242 (2002).

124. Joan Biskupic, "Retarded Convicts Can't Be Executed," *USA Today* (June 21, 2002): A1.

125. Henry Weinstein, "Inmate Seeks to Halt Execution for DNA Tests," *Los Angeles Times* (April 28, 2002): A20.

126. Henry Weinstein, "Judge Leans Toward Declaring Death Penalty Unconstitutional," *Los Angeles Times* (April 26, 2002): A22.

127. *Olmstead* v. *U.S.,* 277 U.S. 438 (1928).

128. 381 U.S. 481 (1965).

129. *Eisenstadt* v. *Baird,* 410 U.S. 113 (1972).

130. 410 U.S. 113 (1973).

131. *Beal* v. *Doe,* 432 U.S. 438 (1977), and *Harris* v. *McRae,* 448 U.S. 297 (1980).

132. 492 U.S. 490 (1989).

133. 502 U.S. 1056 (1992).

134. Karen O'Connor, *No Neutral Ground: Abortion Politics in an Age of Absolutes* (Boulder, CO: Westview Press, 1996).

135. "House Sends Partial Birth Abortion Bill to Clinton," *Politics USA* (March 28, 1996): 1.

136. *Stenberg* v. *Carhart,* 530 U.S. 914 (2000).

137. *Hill* v. *Colorado,* 530 U.S. 703 (2000).

138. *Lawrence* v. *Texas,* 539 U.S. 558 (2003).

139. *Boy Scouts* v. *Dale,* 530 U.S. 640 (2000).

140. *Hardwick* v. *Bowers,* 478 U.S. 186 (1986).

141. Charles Lane, "Poll: Americans Say Court Is 'About Right,'" *Washington Post* (July 7, 2002): A15.

142. *Romer* v. *Evans,* 517 U.S. 620 (1996).

143. 530 U.S. 640 (2000).

144. 497 U.S. 261 (1990).

145. *Vacco* v. *Quill,* 521 U.S. 793 (1997).

146. Office of the Attorney General, Memorandum for Asa Hutchinson, Administrator, the Drug Enforcement Administration, November 6, 2001.

147. William McCall, "Oregon Suicide Law Gets Longer Reprieve: Court Allows US Senate 5 Months to Ready Arguments," *Boston Globe* (November 21, 2001): A8.

148. *Oregon* v. *Ashcroft,* 192 F. Supp. 2d 1077 (2002); and Kim Murphy, "U.S. Cannot Block Oregon Suicide Law, Judge Rules," *Los Angeles Times* (April 18, 2002): A1.

Civil Rights

6

On February 4, 1999, Amadou Diallo, a twenty-two-year-old unarmed African immigrant, stood in the vestibule of his apartment building in the Bronx, New York. Four white plainclothed police officers, who were patrolling the neighborhood in an unmarked car, opened fire on him, eventually firing forty-one shots. He died at the scene.[1] There were no witnesses. The four officers, who eventually were charged with second-degree murder, were members of the city's Street Crimes Unit. This unit was created by then-Mayor Rudy Giuliani to help lower New York City's crime rate in the early 1990s. Known to have targeted black citizens, members of the unit admitted to stopping and searching as many as 225,000 citizens since its establishment.[2]

Members of New York City's frightened minority community, African Americans and new immigrants alike, along with liberal activists and everyday citizens, turned their anger on city police and the mayor, who they believed had used overly aggressive, and often racially biased, techniques to reduce crime. In the months after the shooting, citizens from all walks of life, from actress Susan Sarandon to street cleaners, protested at City Hall, and even marched from the federal courthouse over the Brooklyn Bridge and into Manhattan in a procession reminiscent of many 1960s civil rights marches.[3] Over 1,500 protesters were arrested at one demonstration, the largest New York City had seen in twenty-five years.[4] Eventually, all four police officers charged with Diallo's killing were acquitted at trial.

There is no question that in the 1980s, crime in the United States, and in particular New York City, was out of control and Americans demanded that their governments do something about it. Governments at all levels responded with more police and more prisons. But, now that crime is on the wane and no longer even on Americans' list of top ten concerns, ordinary citizens are asking the question that troubled John Locke and Thomas Hobbes over three centuries ago: How much liberty should you give up to the government in return for safety? In the Diallo case, and many others, it is clear that black people in America, whether native- or foreign-born, are being targeted for civil rights deprivations at far higher rates than other identifiable groups. In 1999, for example, it was discovered that 40 percent of those strip-searched at the Chicago O'Hare airport by U.S. Customs officials were African American women.[5] In New Jersey and other states, the use of what is called racial profiling to stop black drivers was challenged in the courts.[6] In 2001, the NAACP announced a boycott of the Adam's Mark hotel chain because employees charged African American college students higher room rates than white students in Daytona Beach during spring break.[7]

Similarly, in the wake of September 11, 2001, men from, or who look as if they may be from, the Middle East are more likely to be stopped by police or taken in for questioning by state or federal law enforcement officials. The ACLU has tried to assist those targeted, but racial profiling continues, especially at airports.

civil rights
Refers to the positive acts governments take to protect individuals against arbitrary or discriminatory treatment by governments or individuals based on categories such as race, sex, national origin, age, or sexual orientation.

WEB EXPLORATION
For more on civil rights generally, see
www.ablongman.com/oconnor

The Declaration of Independence, written in 1776, boldly proclaims: "We hold these truths to be self-evident, that all men are created equal, that they are endowed by their Creator with certain inalienable rights." The Constitution, written eleven years later, is silent on the concept of equality. Only through constitutional amendment and Supreme Court definition and redefinition of the rights contained in that document have Americans come close to attaining equal rights. Even so, as our opening vignette highlights, some citizens have yet to experience full equality and the full enjoyment of **civil rights** many Americans take for granted.

The term civil rights refers to the positive acts governments take to protect individuals against arbitrary or discriminatory treatment by governments or individuals. The Framers considered some civil rights issues. But, as James Madison reflected in *Federalist No. 42*, one entire class of citizens—slaves—were treated in the new Constitution more like property than like people. Without the Three-Fifths Compromise, "No union could possibly have been formed" because the southern states would not have agreed to join the Union if slavery was prohibited by the national government.[8] Under the compromise, slaves were included as three-fifths of a person in counting state population, for representation in the House of Representatives. The Constitution also stipulated that the importation of slaves could not be prohibited for twenty years. Delegates to the Constitutional Convention put political expediency before the immorality of slavery, and basic civil rights. Moreover, the Constitution considered white women full citizens for purposes of determining state population, but voting qualifications were left to the states, and none allowed women to vote at the time the Constitution was ratified.

Since the Constitution was written, concepts of civil rights have changed dramatically. The addition of the Fourteenth Amendment, one of three amendments ratified after the Civil War, introduced the notion of equality into the Constitution by specifying that states could not deny "any person within its jurisdiction equal protection of the laws."

The Fourteenth Amendment has generated more litigation to determine and specify its meaning than any other provision of the Constitution. Within a few years of its ratification, women—and later, African Americans and other minorities and disadvantaged groups—took to the courts to seek expanded civil rights in all walks of life. But, the struggle to augment rights was not limited to the courts. Public protest, civil disobedience, legislative lobbying, and appeals to public opinion have all been part of the arsenal of those seeking equality. The Diallo case incorporates all of those actions. Ordinary citizens and celebrities took to the streets, legislators held hearings, police officers were put on trial, and the media reported it all.

Since passage of the Civil War Amendments (1865–1870), there has been a fairly consistent pattern of the expansion of civil rights to more and more groups. In this chapter, we will explore how notions of equality and civil rights have changed in this country. To do so, we'll discuss slavery, its abolition, and the achievement of voting rights for African Americans and women by examining the evolution of African American rights and women's rights in tandem. To appreciate how each group has drawn ideas, support, and success from the other, throughout this chapter we discuss their parallel developments as well as those of other historically disadvantaged political groups, including Hispanics, now the largest minority group in the United States.

- First, we will discuss *slavery, abolition, and winning the right to vote, 1800–1890*.
- Second, we will examine African Americans' and women's next *push for equality from 1890 to 1954*, using two of the Supreme Court's most famous decisions, *Plessy* v. *Ferguson* and *Brown* v. *Board of Education*, as bookends for our discussion.
- Third, we will analyze the *civil rights movement* and the Civil Rights Act of 1964 and its effects, including its facilitation of the development of a new women's rights movement and its push for an equal rights amendment to the U.S. Constitution.
- Fourth, we will present the efforts of *other groups*, including Hispanic Americans, Native Americans, homosexuals, and Americans with disabilities, to mobilize for rights using methods often modeled after the actions of African Americans and women.
- Using the treatment of African Americans as a lens for examining *continuity and change* in the area of civil rights, we will explore the evolution of affirmative action.

Comparative

Comparing
Civil Rights

SLAVERY, ABOLITION, AND WINNING THE RIGHT TO VOTE, 1800–1890

Today, we take the rights of women and blacks to vote for granted. Since 1980, women have outvoted men at the polls in presidential elections; in the 1990s, in fact, African Americans and women became the core of the Democratic Party. But, it wasn't always this way. The period from 1800 to 1890 was one of tremendous change and upheaval in America. Despite the Civil War and the freeing of the slaves, the promise of equality guaranteed to African Americans by the Civil War Amendments failed to become a reality. Women's rights activists also began to make claims for equality, often using the arguments enunciated for the abolition of slavery, but they too fell far short of their goals.

Slavery and Congress

Congress banned the slave trade in 1808, after the expiration of the twenty-year period specified by the Constitution. In 1820, blacks made up 25 percent of the U.S. population and were in the majority in some southern states. By 1840, that figure had fallen to 20 percent. After the invention of the cotton gin (a machine invented in 1793 that separated seeds from cotton very quickly), the South became even more dependent on agriculture and cheap slave labor as its economic base. At the same time, technological advances were turning the northern states into an increasingly industrialized region, which intensified the cultural and political differences and animosity between the North and the South.

Ever since the first Africans were brought to the American colonies in 1619, slavery had been a divisive issue. But, as the nation grew westward in the early 1800s, conflicts between northern and southern states intensified over the admission of new states to the Union with "free" or "slave" status. The first major crisis occurred in 1820, when Missouri applied for admission to the Union as a "slave state"—that is, one in which slavery would be legal. Missouri's admission would have weighted the Senate in favor of slavery and therefore was opposed by northern senators. The resultant Missouri Compromise of 1820 allowed the admission of Missouri as a slave state, along with the admission of Maine (formed out of a portion of Massachusetts with the permission of Congress and Massachusetts) as a free state. Other compromises concerning slavery eventually were necessitated as the nation continued to grow and new states were added to the Union.

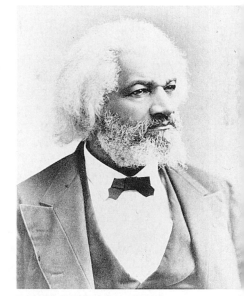

Frederick Douglass (1817–1895) was born into slavery but learned how to read and write. Once he escaped to the North (where 250,000 free blacks lived), he became a well-known orator and journalist. In 1847, he started a newspaper, *The North Star*, in Rochester, New York. The paper quickly became a powerful voice against slavery, and he urged President Lincoln to emancipate the slaves. Douglass was also a firm believer in women's suffrage.

(Photo courtesy: Library of Congress)

The Abolitionist Movement: The First Civil Rights Movement

The Compromise of 1820 solidified the South in its determination to keep slavery legal, but it also fueled the fervor of those who opposed slavery. In the early 1800s, some private charities purchased slaves and transported them to the west coast of Africa, where, in the 1820s, eighty-eight former slaves formed the independent nation of Liberia. But, this solution to the slavery problem was not all that practical. Few owners were willing to free their slaves, and the trip to Africa and conditions there were dangerous. The abolitionist movement might have fizzled had it not been for William Lloyd Garrison, a white New Englander who became active in the movement in the early 1830s. Garrison, a newspaper editor, founded the American Anti-Slavery Society in 1833; by 1838, it had more than 250,000 members—given the U.S. population today, the National Association for the Advancement of Colored People (NAACP) would need 3.8 million members to have the same kind of overall proportional membership. (In 2003, it exceeded 500,000 members.)

WEB EXPLORATION
For more on abolition, the American Anti-Slavery Society, and its leaders, see www.ablongman.com/oconnor

The Women's Rights Tie-in. Slavery was not the only practice that people began to question in the decades following adoption of the Constitution. In 1840, for example, Garrison and even Frederick Douglass, a well-known black abolitionist writer, parted from the Anti-Slavery Society when it refused to accept their demand that women be allowed to participate equally in all its activities. Custom dictated that women not speak out in public, and most laws made women second-class citizens. In most states, for example, women could not divorce their husbands or keep their own wages and inheritances. And, of course, they could not vote.

Elizabeth Cady Stanton and Lucretia Mott, who were to found the women's movement, attended the 1840 meeting of the World's Anti-Slavery Society in London with their husbands. They were not allowed to participate because they were women. As they sat in the balcony apart from the male delegates, they paused to compare their status to that of the slaves they sought to free. They believed that women were not much better off than slaves, and resolved to address these issues. In 1848, they sent out a call for the first women's rights convention. Three hundred women and men, including Frederick Douglass, traveled to the sleepy little town of Seneca Falls, New York, to attend the first meeting for women's rights.

The Seneca Falls Convention (1848). The Seneca Falls Convention attracted people from all over New York State who believed that all men and women should be able to enjoy all rights of citizenship equally. It passed resolutions calling for the abolition of legal, economic, and social discrimination against women. All of the resolutions reflected the attendees' dissatisfaction with contemporary moral codes, divorce and criminal laws, and the limited opportunities for women in education, the church, medicine, law, and politics. Only the call for women's suffrage failed to win unanimous approval. Most who attended the Seneca Falls meeting continued to press for women's rights along with the abolition of slavery.

The 1850s: The Calm Before the Storm. By 1850, much was changing in America—the Gold Rush had spurred westward migration, cities grew as people were lured from

---

THE FIRST CONVENTION

EVER CALLED TO DISCUSS THE

Civil and Political Rights of Women,

SENECA FALLS, N. Y., JULY 19, 20, 1848.

———

WOMAN'S RIGHTS CONVENTION.

———

A Convention to discuss the social, civil, and religious condition and rights of woman will be held in the Wesleyan Chapel, at Seneca Falls, N. Y., on Wednesday and Thursday, the 19th and 20th of July current; commencing at 10 o'clock A. M. During the first day the meeting will be exclusively for women, who are earnestly invited to attend. The public generally are invited to be present on the second day, when Lucretia Mott, of Philadelphia, and other ladies and gentlemen, will address the Convention.*

---

* This call was published in the *Seneca County Courier*, July 14, 1848, without any signatures. The movers of this Convention, who drafted the call, the declaration and resolutions were Elizabeth Cady Stanton, Lucretia Mott, Martha C. Wright, Mary Ann McClintock, and Jane C. Hunt.

This is the announcement that was placed in local newspapers about the upcoming 1848 Seneca Falls Women's Convention.

(Photo courtesy: Library of Congress)

their farms, railroads and the telegraph increased mobility and communication, and immigrants flooded into the United States. Reformers called for change, the women's movement gained momentum, and slavery continued to tear the nation apart. Harriet Beecher Stowe's *Uncle Tom's Cabin*, a novel that showed the evils of slavery by depicting a slave family torn apart, further inflamed the country. *Uncle Tom's Cabin* sold more than 300,000 copies in a single year, 1852.

The tremendous national reaction to Stowe's work, which later prompted Abraham Lincoln to call Stowe "the little woman who started the big war," had not yet faded when a new controversy over the 1820 Missouri Compromise became the lightning rod for the first major civil rights case to be addressed by the U.S. Supreme Court. As discussed in chapter 3, in *Dred Scott* v. *Sandford* (1857), the Court bluntly ruled unconstitutional the 1820 Missouri Compromise, which prohibited slavery north of the geographical boundary at 36 degrees latitude on a map of the United States. Furthermore, the Court found that slaves were not U.S. citizens. Therefore, they could not bring suits in federal court, as the court concluded that "the Negro might justly and lawfully be reduced to slavery for his benefit." Ironically, after the case was decided, Scott's owner freed him.

The Civil War and Its Aftermath: Civil Rights Laws and Constitutional Amendments

The Civil War had many causes, including: (1) the political conflict between the North and the South over nullification, a doctrine allowing states to declare federal laws null and void, and secession, which involved the right of states to leave the Union; (2) the northern states' increasing political strength in Congress, especially in the House of Representatives; (3) southern agriculture versus northern industry; and, (4) the clash of conservative southern culture with more progressive northern ideas. Slavery, though, was clearly the key issue.

During the war (1861–1865), abolitionists continued their antislavery pressure. They were rewarded when President Lincoln issued the Emancipation Proclamation, which provided that all slaves in states still in active rebellion against the United States would be freed automatically on January 1, 1863. Designed as a measure to gain favor for the war in the North, the Emancipation Proclamation did not free all slaves—it freed only those who lived in the Confederacy. Complete abolition of slavery did not occur until congressional passage and ultimate ratification of the Thirteenth Amendment in 1865.

The Civil War Amendments.   The **Thirteenth Amendment** was the first of the three so-called Civil War Amendments. It banned all forms of "slavery [and] involuntary servitude." Although southern states were required to ratify the Thirteenth Amendment as a condition of their readmission to the Union after the war, most of the former Confederate states quickly passed laws that were designed to restrict opportunities for newly freed slaves. These **Black Codes** prohibited African Americans from voting, sitting on juries, or even appearing in public places. Although Black Codes differed from state to state, all empowered local law-enforcement officials to arrest unemployed blacks, fine them for vagrancy, and hire them out to employers to satisfy their fines. Some state codes went so far as to require African Americans to work on plantations or to be domestics. The Black Codes laid the groundwork for Jim Crow laws, which would later institute segregation in all walks of life.

The outraged Reconstructionist Congress enacted the Civil Rights Act of 1866 to invalidate some state Black Codes. President Andrew Johnson vetoed the legislation, but—for the first time in history—Congress overrode a presidential veto. The Civil Rights Act formally made African Americans citizens of the United States and gave the Congress and the federal courts the power to intervene when states attempted to restrict male African American citizenship rights in matters such as voting. Congress reasoned that African Americans were unlikely to fare well if they had to file

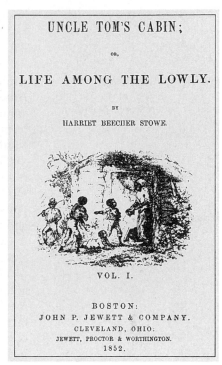

The original title page of *Uncle Tom's Cabin, or Life Among the Lowly,* by Harriet Beecher Stowe.

(Photo courtesy: Library of Congress)

Thirteenth Amendment
One of the three Civil War Amendments; specifically bans slavery in the United States.

Black Codes
Laws denying most legal rights to newly freed slaves; passed by southern states following the Civil War.

Fourteenth Amendment
One of the three Civil War Amendments; guarantees equal protection and due process of the laws to all U.S. citizens.

discrimination complaints in state courts, where judges were elected. Passage of a federal law allowed African Americans to challenge discriminatory state practices in the federal courts, where judges were appointed by the president.

Because controversy remained over the constitutionality of the act (since the Constitution gives states the right to determine qualifications of voters), the **Fourteenth Amendment** was proposed simultaneously with the Civil Rights Act to guarantee, among other things, citizenship to all freed slaves. Other key provisions of the Fourteenth Amendment barred states from abridging "the privileges or immunities of citizenship" or depriving "any person of life, liberty, or property without due process of law."

Unlike the Thirteenth Amendment, which had near-unanimous support in the North, the Fourteenth Amendment was opposed by many women. During the Civil War, women's rights activists, including Elizabeth Cady Stanton and Susan B. Anthony, put aside their claims for expanded rights for women, most notably the right to vote, and threw their energies into the war effort. They were convinced that once slaves were freed and given the right to vote, women similarly would be rewarded with the franchise. They were wrong.

In early 1869, after ratification of the Fourteenth Amendment (which specifically added the word "male" to the Constitution for the first time), women's rights activists met in Washington, D.C., to argue against passage of any new amendment that would extend suffrage to black males and not to women. The convention resolved that "a man's government is worse than a white man's government, because, in proportion as you increase the tyrants, you make the condition of the disenfranchised class more hopeless and degraded."

In spite of these arguments, the **Fifteenth Amendment** was passed by Congress in February 1869. It guaranteed the "right of citizens" to vote regardless of their "race, color or previous condition of servitude." Again, sex was not mentioned.

Fifteenth Amendment
One of the three Civil War Amendments; specifically enfranchised newly freed male slaves.

Women's rights activists were shocked. Abolitionists' continued support of the Fifteenth Amendment, which was ratified by the states in 1870, prompted many women's rights supporters to leave the abolition movement to work solely for the cause of women's rights. Twice burned, Anthony and Stanton decided to form their own National Woman Suffrage Association (NWSA) to achieve that goal. (Another, more conservative group, the American Woman Suffrage Association, also was formed.) In spite of the NWSA's opposition, however, the Fifteenth Amendment was ratified by the states in 1870.

Civil Rights and the Supreme Court

While the Congress was clear in its wishes that the rights of African Americans be expanded and that the Black Codes be rendered illegal, the Supreme Court was not nearly so protective of those rights under the Civil War Amendments. In the first two tests of the scope of the Fourteenth Amendment, the Supreme Court ruled that the citizenship rights guaranteed by the amendment applied only to rights of national citizenship and not to state citizenship. Ironically, neither case involved African Americans. In *The Slaughterhouse Cases* (1873), the Court upheld Louisiana's right to create a monopoly in the operation of slaughterhouses, despite the Butcher's Benevolent Association's claim that this action deprived its members of their livelihood and thus the privileges and immunities of citizenship guaranteed by the amendment.[9]

Similarly, in *Bradwell* v. *Illinois* (1873), when Myra Bradwell asked the U.S. Supreme Court to find that Illinois's refusal to allow her to practice law (although she had passed the bar examination) violated her citizenship rights guaranteed by the privileges and immunities clause of the Fourteenth Amendment, her arguments fell on deaf ears. In *Bradwell*, one justice went so far as to declare that it was reasonable for the state to bar women from the practice of law because "the natural and proper timidity and delicacy which belongs to the female sex evidently unfits it for many of the occupations of civil life."[10]

The combined message of these two cases was that state and national citizenship were separate and distinct. In essence, the Supreme Court ruled that neither African Americans nor any others could be protected from discriminatory state action, because the Fourteenth Amendment did not enlarge the limited rights guaranteed by U.S. citizenship.

Claims for expanded rights and requests for a clear definition of U.S. citizenship rights continued to fall on deaf ears in the halls of the Supreme Court. In 1875, for example, the Court heard *Minor* v. *Happersett*, the culmination of a series of test cases launched by women's rights activists.[11] Virginia Minor, after planning with Anthony and other NWSA members, attempted to register to vote in her hometown of St. Louis, Missouri. When the registrar refused to record her name on the list of eligible voters, Minor sued, arguing that the state's refusal to let her vote violated the privileges and immunities clause of the Fourteenth Amendment. Rejecting her claim, the justices ruled unanimously that voting was not a privilege of citizenship. Until 1999, the Supreme Court never again addressed the possible scope of the privileges and immunities clause.[12]

Southern resistance to African American equality led Congress to pass the Civil Rights Act of 1875, designed to grant equal access to public accommodations such as theaters, restaurants, and transportation. The act also prohibited the exclusion of African Americans from jury service. After 1877, however, as Reconstruction was dismantled, national interest in the legal condition of African Americans waned. Most white Southerners never had believed in equality for "freedmen," as former slaves were called. Any rights freedmen received had been contingent on federal enforcement. Once federal troops were no longer available to guard polls and prevent whites from excluding black voters, southern states moved to limit African Americans' access to the ballot. Other forms of discrimination also were allowed by judicial decisions upholding **Jim Crow laws,** which required segregation in public schools and facilities including railroads, restaurants, and theaters. Many Jim Crow laws also barred interracial marriage. All these laws, at first glance, appeared to conflict with the Civil Rights Act of 1875. In 1883, however, a series of cases decided by the Supreme Court severely damaged the vitality of the 1875 act. The ***Civil Rights Cases*** (1883) were five separate cases involving the convictions of private individuals found to have violated the Civil Rights Act by refusing to extend accommodations to African Americans in theaters, a hotel, and a railroad.[13] In deciding these cases, the Supreme Court ruled that Congress could prohibit only state or governmental action and not private acts of discrimination. The Court thus seriously limited the scope of the Fourteenth Amendment by concluding that Congress had no authority to prohibit private discrimination in public accommodations.

WEB EXPLORATION
For more about the history of Jim Crow in the South, see www.ablongman.com/oconnor

Jim Crow laws
Laws enacted by southern states that discriminated against blacks by creating "whites only" schools, theaters, hotels, and other public accommodations.

Civil Rights Cases (1883)
Name attached to five cases brought under the Civil Rights Act of 1875. In 1883, the Supreme Court decided that discrimination in a variety of public accommodations, including theaters, hotels, and railroads, could not be prohibited by the act because it was private, not state, discrimination.

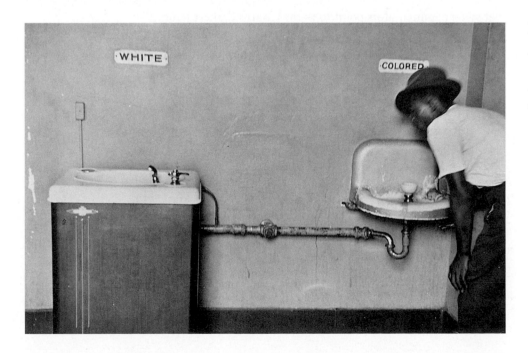

Throughout the South, examples of Jim Crow laws abounded. One such law required separate public drinking fountains, shown here. Notice the obvious difference in quality.
(Photo courtesy: Bettmann/Corbis)

The Court's opinion in the *Civil Rights Cases* provided a moral reinforcement for the Jim Crow system. Southern states viewed the Court's ruling as an invitation to gut the reach and intent of Thirteenth, Fourteenth, and Fifteenth Amendments.

In devising ways to make certain that African Americans did not vote, Southerners had to avoid the intent of the Fifteenth Amendment. This amendment did not guarantee suffrage; it simply said that states could not deny anyone the right to vote on account of race or color. To exclude African Americans in a seemingly racially neutral way, southern states used three devices before the 1890s: (1) poll taxes (small taxes on the right to vote that often came due when poor African American sharecroppers had the least amount of money on hand); (2) some form of property-owning qualifications; and, (3) "literacy" or "understanding" tests, which allowed local registrars to administer difficult reading-comprehension tests to potential voters whom they did not know.

These voting restrictions had an immediate impact. By the late 1890s, black voting fell by 62 percent from the Reconstruction period, while white voting fell by only 26 percent. To make certain that these laws didn't further reduce the numbers of poor or uneducated white voters, many southern states added a **grandfather clause** to their voting qualification provisions, granting voting privileges to those who failed to pass a wealth or literacy test only if their grandfathers had voted before Reconstruction. Grandfather clauses effectively denied the descendants of slaves the right to vote.

While African Americans continued to face wide-ranging racism on all fronts, women also confronted discrimination. During this period, married women, by law, could not be recognized as legal entities. Women often were treated in the same category as juveniles and "imbeciles," and in many states were not entitled to wages, inheritances, or custody of their children.

grandfather clause
Voting qualification provision that allowed only those whose grandfathers had voted before Reconstruction to vote unless they passed a wealth or literacy test.

THE PUSH FOR EQUALITY, 1890–1954

The Progressive era (1890–1920) was characterized by a concerted effort to reform political, economic, and social affairs. Evils such as child labor, the concentration of economic power in the hands of a few industrialists, limited suffrage, political corruption, business monopolies, and prejudice against African Americans all were targets of progressive reform efforts. Distress over the legal inferiority of African Americans was aggravated by the U.S. Supreme Court's decision in ***Plessy v. Ferguson* (1896),**[14] a case that some commentators point to as the Court's darkest hour.

In 1892, a group of African Americans in Louisiana decided to test the constitutionality of a Louisiana law mandating racial segregation on all public trains. They convinced Homer Plessy, a man of seven-eighths Caucasian and one-eighth African descent to board a train in New Orleans and proceed to the "whites only" car.[15] He was arrested when he refused to take a seat in the car reserved for African Americans. Plessy sued the railroad company, arguing that the Fourteenth Amendment prohibited racial segregation.

The Supreme Court disagreed. After analyzing the history of African Americans in the United States, the majority concluded that the Louisiana law was constitutional. The justices based their decision on their belief that separate facilities for blacks and whites provided equal protection of the laws. After all, they reasoned, African Americans were not prevented from riding the train; the Louisiana statute required only that the races travel separately. Justice John Marshall Harlan (1877–1911) was the lone dissenter. He argued that "the Constitution is colorblind" and that it was senseless to hold constitutional a law "which, practically, puts the badge of servitude and degradation upon a large class of our fellow citizens."

Not surprisingly, the separate-but-equal doctrine enunciated in *Plessy* v. *Ferguson* soon came to mean only "separate," as new legal avenues to discriminate against African Americans were enacted into law throughout the South. The Jim Crow sys-

Plessy v. *Ferguson* (1896)
Plessy challenged a Louisiana statute requiring that railroads provide separate accommodations for blacks and whites. The Court found that separate but equal accommodations did not violate the equal protection clause of the Fourteenth Amendment.

Timeline

The Struggle for Equal Protection

tem soon became a way of life in the American South. In 1898, the Supreme Court upheld the constitutionality of literacy tests that were administered to African Americans and indicated its apparent willingness to allow the southern states to define their own suffrage standards, whether or not they disproportionately affected blacks.[16] One year later, the Supreme Court upheld a school district's decision to maintain a whites-only high school but close a blacks-only high school to free up funds for a black elementary school.[17] The Supreme Court unanimously upheld the constitutionality of this disparate treatment.

By 1900, then, equality for African Americans was far from the promise first offered by the Civil War Amendments. Again and again, the Supreme Court nullified the intent of the amendments and sanctioned racial segregation while the states avidly followed its lead. While discrimination was practiced widely in many parts of the North, southern states passed laws legally imposing segregation in education, housing, public accommodations, employment, and most other spheres of life. Miscegenation laws, for example, prohibited blacks and whites from marrying.

Jim Crow laws were not the only practices designed to keep African Americans in a secondary position. Indeed, these laws established a way of life with strong social codes as well. Journalist Juan Williams notes in *Eyes on the Prize:*

> There were Jim Crow schools, Jim Crow restaurants, Jim Crow water fountains, and Jim Crow customs—blacks were expected to tip their hats when they walked past whites, but whites did not have to remove their hats even when they entered a black family's home. Whites were to be called "sir" and "ma'am" by blacks, who in turn were called by their first names by whites. People with white skin were to be given a wide berth on the sidewalk; blacks were expected to step aside meekly.[18]

Notwithstanding these degrading practices, by the early 1900s, a small group of African Americans (largely from the North) had been able to attain some formal education and were ready to push for additional rights. They found some progressive white citizens and politicians amenable to their cause.

The Founding of the National Association for the Advancement of Colored People

In 1909, a handful of individuals active in a variety of progressive causes including women's suffrage and the fight for better working conditions for women and children met to discuss the idea of a group devoted to the problems of "the Negro." Major race riots recently had occurred in several American cities, and progressive reformers who sought change in political, economic, and social relations were concerned about these outbreaks of violence and the possibility of others. Oswald Garrison Villard, the influential publisher of the *New York Evening Post*—and the grandson of William Lloyd Garrison—called a conference to discuss the problem. This group soon evolved into the National Association for the Advancement of Colored People (NAACP). Along with Villard, its first leaders included Jane Addams, a leader of the settlement house and woman suffrage movements; Moorfield Storey, a past president of the American Bar Assoiciation; and W. E. B. DuBois, a founder of the Niagara Movement, a group of educated African Americans who took their name from their first meeting place in Niagara Falls, Ontario, Canada.

W.E.B. DuBois (second from right in the second row, facing left) is pictured with the original leaders of the Niagara Movement. This 1905 photo was taken on the Canadian side of Niagara Falls. The Niagara reformers met in Canada because no hotel on the U.S. side would accommodate them.

(Photo courtesy: Photographs and Prints Division, Schomburg Center for Research in Black Culture, The New York Public Library, Astor, Lenox, and Tilden Foundations)

Key Women's Groups

The struggle for women's rights was revitalized in 1890 when the National and American Woman Suffrage Associations merged. The new organization, the National American Woman Suffrage Association (NAWSA) was headed by Susan B. Anthony. Unlike the National Woman Suffrage Association, which had sought a wide variety of expanded rights for women, this new association was devoted largely to securing women's suffrage. Its task was greatly facilitated by the proliferation of women's groups that emerged during the Progressive era. In addition to the rapidly growing temperance movement—the move to ban the sale of alcohol, which many women blamed for a variety of social ills—women's groups were created to seek protective legislation in the form of maximum hour or minimum wage laws for women and to work for improved sanitation, public morals, education, and the like. Other organizations that were part of what was called the "club movement" were created to provide increased cultural and literary experiences for middle-class women. With increased industrialization, for the first time some women found that they had the opportunity to pursue activities other than those centered on the home.

One of the most active groups lobbying on behalf of women during this period was the National Consumers' League (NCL), which successfully lobbied for Oregon legislation limiting women to ten hours of work a day. Curt Muller was then charged and convicted of employing women more than ten hours a day in his small laundry. When he appealed his conviction to the U.S. Supreme Court, the NCL sought permission from the state to conduct the defense of the statute.

At the urging of NCL attorney and future U.S. Supreme Court Justice Louis Brandeis, NCL members amassed an impressive array of sociological and medical data that were incorporated into what became known as the "Brandeis brief." This contained only three pages of legal argument. More than a hundred pages were devoted to nonlegal, sociological data that were used to convince the Court that Oregon's statute was constitutional. In agreeing with the NCL in *Muller* v. *Oregon* (1908), the Court relied heavily on these data to document women's unique status as mothers to justify their differential legal treatment.[19]

Women seeking the vote used reasoning reflecting the Court's opinion in *Muller.* Discarding earlier notions of full equality, NAWSA based its claim to the right to vote largely on the fact that women, as mothers, should be enfranchised. Furthermore,

In 1908, the U.S. Supreme Court ruled that Oregon's law barring women from working more than ten hours a day in laundries was constitutional. Thus, the conviction of Curt Muller (with arms folded), who owned the laundry where women worked twelve- and fourteen-hour days, was upheld.

(Photo courtesy: Supreme Court Historical Society/Mrs. Neill Whisnant and Portland, Oregon, Chamber of Commerce)

Suffragettes demonstrating for the franchise. Parades like this one took place in cities all over the United States.

(Photo courtesy: Library of Congress)

although many members of the **suffrage movement** were NAACP members, the new women's movement—called the suffrage movement because of its focus on the vote alone and not on broader issues of women's rights—took on racist overtones. Women argued that if undereducated African Americans could vote, why couldn't women? Some NAWSA members even argued that "the enfranchisement of women would ensure immediate and durable white supremacy."

Diverse attitudes clearly were present in the growing suffrage movement, which often tried to be all things to all people. Its roots in the Progressive movement gave it an exceptionally broad base that transformed NAWSA from a small organization of just over 10,000 members in the early 1890s to a true social movement of more than 2 million members in 1917. By 1920, a coalition of women's groups led by NAWSA was able to secure ratification of the **Nineteenth Amendment** to the Constitution. It guaranteed all women the right to vote—fifty years after African American males were enfranchised by the Fifteenth Amendment.

After passage of the suffrage amendment in 1920, the fragile alliance of diverse women's groups that had come together to fight for the vote quickly disintegrated. Women returned to their "home" groups, such as the NCL or the Women's Christian Temperance Union, to pursue their individualized goals. In fact, after the tumult of the suffrage movement, widespread, organized activity on behalf of women's rights did not reemerge until the 1960s. In the meantime, however, the NAACP continued to fight racism and racial segregation. In fact, its activities and those of others in the civil rights movement would later give impetus to a new women's movement.

Litigating for Equality

During the 1930s, leaders of the NAACP began to sense that the time was right to launch a full-scale challenge in the federal courts to the constitutionality of *Plessy's* separate-but-equal doctrine. The NAACP mapped out a long-range strategy that would first target segregation in professional and graduate education. Clearly, the separate-but-equal doctrine and the proliferation of Jim Crow laws were a bar to any hope of full

suffrage movement
The drive for voting rights for women that took place in the United States from 1890 to 1920.

Nineteenth Amendment
Amendment to the Constitution that guaranteed women the right to vote.

equality for African Americans. Traditional legislative channels were unlikely to work, given blacks' limited or nonexistent political power. Thus, the federal courts and a long-range litigation strategy were the NAACP's only hope. The NAACP often relied on Brandeis-type briefs, so-called because they relied heavily on sociological data to support their legal arguments. In fact, the NAACP eventually hired a statistician to help its lawyers amass data to help present evidence of discrimination to the courts.

Test Cases.   The NAACP opted first to challenge the constitutionality of Jim Crow law schools. In 1935, all southern states maintained fully segregated elementary and secondary schools. Colleges and universities also were segregated, but most states did not provide for postgraduate education for African Americans. NAACP lawyers chose to target law schools because they were institutions that judges could well understand, and integration there could prove less threatening to most whites.

Lloyd Gaines, a graduate of Missouri's all-black Lincoln University, sought admission to the all-white University of Missouri Law School in 1936. He was immediately rejected. In the separate-but-equal spirit, the state offered to build a law school at Lincoln (although no funds were allocated for the project) or, if he didn't want to wait, to pay his tuition at an out-of-state law school. Gaines rejected the offer, sued, lost in the lower courts and appealed to the U.S. Supreme Court.

Gaines's case was filed at an auspicious time. As you may recall from chapter 3, a "constitutional revolution" of sorts occurred in Supreme Court decision making in 1937. Before this time, the Court was most receptive to and interested in the protection of economic liberties. In 1937, however, the Court reversed itself in a series of cases and began to place individual freedoms and personal liberties on a more protected footing. Thus, in 1938, Gaines's lawyers pleaded his appeal to a far more sympathetic Supreme Court. NAACP attorneys argued that the creation of a separate law school of any less caliber than that of the University of Missouri would not and could not afford Gaines an equal education. The justices agreed and ruled that Missouri had failed to meet the separate-but-equal requirements of *Plessy*. The Court ordered Missouri either to admit Gaines to the school or to set up a law school for him.[20]

Lloyd Gaines was the subject of the major test case, *Missouri* ex rel. *Gaines* v. *Canada* (1938), which contested the principle of segregated schools. Gaines chose to attend the University of Michigan, from which he strangely disappeared, never to be heard from again.

(Photo courtesy: AP/Wide World Photos)

Recognizing the importance of the Court's ruling, in 1939, the NAACP created a separate, tax-exempt legal defense fund to devise a strategy to build on the Missouri case to bring about equal educational opportunities for all African American children. The first head of the NAACP Legal Defense and Educational Fund (LDF), as it was called, was Thurgood Marshall, who later became the first African American to serve on the Supreme Court (1967–1991). Sensing that the Court would be more amenable to the NAACP's broader goals if it was first forced to address a variety of less threatening claims to educational opportunity, Marshall and the LDF brought a series of carefully crafted test cases to the Court.

The first case involved H. M. Sweatt, a forty-six-year-old African American mail carrier, who applied for admission to the all-white University of Texas Law School in 1946. Rejected on racial grounds, Sweatt sued. The judge gave the state six months to establish a law school or to admit Sweatt to the university. The university then rented a few rooms in downtown Houston and hired two local African American attorneys to be part-time faculty members. (At that time, there was only one full-time African American law school professor in the United States.) The state legislature saw the handwriting on the wall and authorized $3 million for the creation of the Texas State University for Negroes. One hundred thousand dollars of that money was to be for a new law school in Austin across the street from the state capitol building. It consisted of three small basement rooms, a library of more than 10,000 books, access to the state law library, and three part-time first-year instructors as the "faculty." Sweatt declined the opportunity to obtain an education there and instead chose to continue his legal challenge.

While working on the Texas case, the LDF also decided to pursue a case involving George McLaurin, a retired university professor who had been denied admission to the doctoral education program at the University of Oklahoma. Marshall reasoned that McLaurin, at age sixty-eight, would be immune from the charges that African Americans wanted integration in order to intermarry. After a lower court ordered McLaurin's admission, the university reserved a dingy alcove in the cafeteria for him to eat in during off-hours, and he was given his own table in the library behind a shelf of newspapers. In what surely "was Oklahoma's most inventive contribution to legalized bigotry since the adoption of the 'grandfather clause,' "[21] McLaurin was forced to sit outside classrooms while lectures were given and seminars were held inside.

The Supreme Court handled these two cases together.[22] The eleven southern states filed an *amicus curiae* (friend of the court) brief, in which they argued that *Plessy* should govern both cases. The LDF received assistance, however, from an unexpected source— the U.S. government. In a dramatic departure from the past, the administration of Harry S Truman filed a friend of the court brief urging the Court to overrule *Plessy*. Since the late 1870s, the U.S. government never had sided against the southern states in a civil rights matter and never had submitted an *amicus* brief supporting the rights of African American citizens. President Truman believed that because many African Americans had fought and died for their country in World War II, this kind of executive action was proper. The Court traditionally gives great weight to briefs from the U.S. government. The Court, however, again did not overrule *Plessy*, but the justices found that the measures taken by the states in each case failed to live up to the strictures of the separate-but-equal doctrine. The Court unanimously ruled that the "remedies" to each situation were inadequate to afford a sound education. In the *Sweatt* case, for example, the Court declared that the "qualities which are incapable of objective measurement but which make for greatness in a law school ... includ[ing] the reputation of the faculty, experience of the administration, position and influence of the alumni, standing in the community, traditions and prestige" made it impossible for the state to provide an equal education in a segregated setting.

In 1950, after these decisions were handed down, the LDF concluded that the time had come to launch a full-scale attack on the separate-but-equal doctrine. The decisions of the Court were encouraging, and the position of the U.S. government and the population in general appeared to be more receptive to an outright overruling of *Plessy*.

Brown v. *Board of Education* (1954).

Brown v. *Board of Education* actually was four cases brought from different areas of the South and border states involving public elementary or high school systems that mandated separate schools for blacks and whites.[23]

In *Brown*, LDF lawyers, again led by Thurgood Marshall, argued that *Plessy*'s separate-but-equal doctrine was unconstitutional under the **equal protection clause** of the Fourteenth Amendment, and that if the Court was still reluctant to overrule *Plessy*, the only way to equalize the schools was to integrate them. A major component of the LDF's strategy was to prove that the intellectual, psychological, and financial damage that befell African Americans as a result of segregation precluded any court from finding that equality was served by the separate-but-equal policy.

In *Brown*, the LDF presented the Supreme Court with evidence of the harmful consequences of state-imposed racial discrimination. To buttress its claims, the LDF introduced the now-famous "doll study," conducted by Kenneth Clark, a prominent African American sociologist who had long studied the negative effects of segregation on African American children. His research revealed that black children not only preferred white dolls when shown black dolls and white dolls, but that most liked the white

Brown v. Board of Education (1954)
U.S. Supreme Court decision holding that school segregation is inherently unconstitutional because it violates the Fourteenth Amendment's guarantee of equal protection; marked the end of legal segregation in the United States.

equal protection clause
Section of the Fourteenth Amendment that guarantees that all citizens receive "equal protection of the laws"; has been used to bar discrimination against blacks and women.

Seven-year-old Linda Brown lived close to a good public school, but her race precluded her attendance there. When the NAACP LDF sought plaintiffs to challenge this discrimination, her father, a local minister, offered Linda as one of several student plaintiffs named in the LDF's case. Her name came first alphabetically, hence the case name, *Brown* v. *Board of Education* (1954).

(Photo courtesy: Carl Iwasaki/TimePix)

WEB EXPLORATION
To read the full text of *Brown*, see
www.ablongman.com/oconnor

doll better, many adding that the black doll looked "bad." This information was used to illustrate the negative impact of racial segregation and bias on an African American child's self-image.

The LDF's legal briefs were supported by important *amicus curiae* briefs submitted by the U.S. government, major civil rights groups, labor unions, and religious groups decrying racial segregation. On May 17, 1954, Chief Justice Earl Warren delivered the fourth opinion of the day, *Brown* v. *Board of Education*. Writing for the Court, Warren stated:

> To separate [some school children] from others ... solely because of their race generates a feeling of inferiority as to their status in the community that may affect their hearts and minds in a way very unlikely ever to be undone. We conclude, unanimously, that in the field of public education the doctrine of "separate but equal" has no place.

There can be no doubt that *Brown* was the most important civil rights case decided in the twentieth century.[24] It immediately evoked an uproar that shook the nation. Some called the day the decision was handed down "Black Monday." The governor of South Carolina decried the decision, saying, "Ending segregation would mark the beginning of the end of civilization in the South as we know it."[25] The LDF lawyers who had argued these cases and those cases leading to *Brown*, however, were jubilant.

Remarkable changes had occurred in the civil rights of Americans since 1890. Women had won the right to vote, and after a long and arduous trail of litigation in the federal courts, the Supreme Court had finally overturned its most racist decision of the era, *Plessy* v. *Ferguson*. The Court boldly proclaimed that separate but equal (at least in education) would no longer pass constitutional muster. The question then became how *Brown* would be interpreted and implemented. Could it be used to invalidate other Jim Crow laws and practices? Would African Americans be truly equal under the law?

THE CIVIL RIGHTS MOVEMENT

Our notion of civil rights has changed profoundly since 1954. First African Americans and then women built upon existing organizations to forge successful movements for increased rights. *Brown* served as a catalyst for change, sparking the development of the modern civil rights movement. Women's work in that movement and the student protest movement that arose in reaction to the U.S. government's involvement in Vietnam gave women the experience needed to form their own organizations to press for full equality. As African Americans and women became more and more successful, they served as models for others who sought equality—Hispanic Americans, Native Americans, homosexuals, the disabled, and others.

School Desegregation After Brown

One year after *Brown*, in a case referred to as *Brown* v. *Board of Education II*, the Court ruled that racially segregated systems must be dismantled "with all deliberate speed."[26] To facilitate implementation, the Court placed enforcement of *Brown* in the hands of appointed federal district court judges, who were considered more immune to local political pressures than were elected state court judges.

The NAACP and its Legal Defense and Education Fund continued to resort to the courts to see that *Brown* was implemented, while the South entered into a near-conspiracy to avoid the mandates of *Brown II*. In Arkansas, for example, the governor announced that he would not "be a party to any attempt to force acceptance of change to which people are overwhelmingly opposed."[27] The day before school was to begin, he announced that National Guardsmen would surround Little Rock's Central High School to prevent African American students from entering. While the federal courts in Arkansas continued to order the admission of African American children, the governor remained adamant. Finally, President Dwight D. Eisenhower sent federal troops to Little Rock to protect the rights of the nine students who had attempted to attend Central High.

In reaction to the governor's outrageous conduct, the Court broke with tradition and issued a unanimous decision in *Cooper* v. *Aaron* (1958), which was filed by the Little Rock School Board asking the federal district court for a two-and-one-half-year delay in implementation of its desegregation plans. Each justice signed the opinion individually, underscoring his individual support for the notion that "no state legislator or executive or judicial officer can war against the Constitution without violating his undertaking to support it."[28] The state's actions thus were ruled unconstitutional and its "evasive schemes" illegal.

A New Move for African American Rights

In 1955, soon after *Brown II*, the civil rights movement took another step forward—this time in Montgomery, Alabama. Rosa Parks, the local NAACP's Youth Council adviser, decided to challenge the constitutionality of the segregated bus system. First, Parks and other NAACP officials began to raise money for litigation and made speeches around town to garner public support. Then, on December 1, 1955, Rosa Parks made history when she refused to leave her seat on a bus to move to the back to make room for a white male passenger. She was arrested for violating an Alabama law banning integration of public facilities, including buses. After she was freed on bond, Parks and the NAACP decided to enlist city clergy to help her cause. At the same time, they distributed 35,000 handbills calling for African Americans to boycott the Montgomery bus system on the day of Parks's trial. Black ministers used Sunday services to urge their members to support the boycott. On Monday morning, African Americans walked, carpooled, or used black-owned taxicabs. That night, local ministers decided that the boycott should be continued. A twenty-six-year-old minister, Martin Luther King Jr., was selected to lead the newly formed Montgomery Improvement Association. King was new to town, and church leaders had been looking for a way to get him more involved in civil rights work.

As the boycott dragged on, Montgomery officials and local business owners began to harass the city's African American citizens. But, King urged Montgomery's African American citizens to continue their protest. The residents held out, despite suffering personal hardship for their actions, ranging from harassment to bankruptcy to job loss. In 1956, a federal court ruled that the segregated bus system violated the equal protection clause of the Fourteenth Amendment. After a year of walking, African Americans ended their protest as the buses were ordered to integrate. The first effort at nonviolent protest had been successful. Organized boycotts and other forms of nonviolent protest, including sit-ins at segregated restaurants and bus stations, were to follow.

WEB EXPLORATION
For more about the Montgomery bus boycott and Dr. Martin Luther King Jr., see www.ablongman.com/oconnor

Formation of New Groups

The recognition and respect that King earned within the African American community helped him to launch the Southern Christian Leadership Conference (SCLC) in 1957, soon after the end of the Montgomery bus boycott. Unlike the NAACP, which had northern origins and had come to rely largely on litigation as a means of achieving

ANALYZING VISUALS
Police Confront Civil Rights Demonstrators in Birmingham

Civil rights demonstrators in the 1960s sought national attention for their cause, and photos in the print media were a powerful tool in swaying public opinion. In the May 1963 photograph by Charles Moore reprinted below, dogs controlled by police officers in Birmingham, Alabama, attack civil rights demonstrators. This photograph first appeared in the May 17, 1963, issue of the very popular *Life* magazine as part of an eleven-page spread of Moore's photographs of the demonstration in Birmingham. The photo was reprinted often and even frequently mentioned on the floor of Congress during debates on the Civil Rights Act of 1964. After examining the photograph, answer the following critical thinking questions: What do you observe about the scene and the various people shown in the photograph? What do you notice about the man who is being attacked by the dogs? The other demonstrators? The police? What emotions does the picture evoke? Why do you think this image was an effective tool in the struggle for civil rights?

(Photo courtesy: Charles Moore/Black Star)

expanded equality, the SCLC had a southern base and was rooted more closely in black religious culture. The SCLC's philosophy reflected King's growing belief in the importance of nonviolent protest.

On February 1, 1960, students at the all-black North Carolina Agricultural and Technical College participated in the first sit-in. Angered by their inability to be served at local lunch counters and heartened by the success of the Montgomery bus boycott, black students marched to the local Woolworth's store and ordered cups of coffee at the lunch counter there. They were refused service. So, they sat at the counter until police came and carted them off to jail. Soon thereafter, African American college students around the South joined together to challenge Jim Crow laws. These mass actions immediately brought extensive attention from the national news media.

Over spring break 1960, with the assistance of an $800 grant from the SCLC, 200 student delegates—black and white—met at Shaw University in North Carolina to consider recent sit-in actions and to plan for the future. Later that year, two more meetings were held in Atlanta, Georgia, and the Student Nonviolent Coordinating Committee (SNCC) was formed.

Among SNCC's first leaders were Marion Barry, who would later serve as mayor of Washington, D.C. (1978–1990, 1995–1999); John Lewis, a nine-term Democratic member of the House of Representatives; and Marian Wright Edelman, an NAACP lawyer who later became the founder and head of the Children's Defense Fund. While the SCLC generally worked with church leaders in a community, SNCC was much more of a grass-roots organization. Always perceived as more radical than the SCLC, SNCC tended to focus its organizing activities on the young, both black and white.

In addition to joining the sit-in bandwagon, SNCC also came to lead what were called "freedom rides," designed to focus attention on segregated public accommodations. Bands of college students and other civil rights activists traveled by bus throughout the South in an effort to force bus stations to desegregate. Often these protesters were met by angry mobs of segregationists and brutal violence, as local police chose not to defend protesters' basic constitutional rights to free speech and peaceful assembly. African Americans were not the only ones to participate in freedom rides; increasingly, white college students from the North began to play an important role in SNCC.

While SNCC continued to sponsor sit-ins and freedom rides, in 1963, Martin Luther King Jr. launched a series of massive nonviolent demonstrations in Birmingham, Alabama, long considered a major stronghold of segregation. Thousands of blacks and whites marched to Birmingham in a show of solidarity. Peaceful marchers were met there by the Birmingham police commissioner, who ordered his officers to use dogs, clubs, and fire hoses on the marchers. Americans across the nation were horrified as they witnessed the brutality and abuse heaped on the protesters. As the marchers hoped, these shocking scenes helped convince President John F. Kennedy to propose important civil rights legislation.

The Civil Rights Act of 1964

The older faction of the civil rights movement, as represented by the SCLC, and the younger branch, represented by SNCC, both sought a similar goal: full implementation of Supreme Court decisions and an end to racial segregation and discrimination. The cumulative effect of collective actions including sit-ins, boycotts, marches, and freedom rides—as well as the tragic bombings and deaths inflicted in retaliation—led Congress to pass the first major piece of civil rights legislation since the post–Civil War era.

In 1963, President Kennedy requested that Congress pass a law banning discrimination in public accommodations. Seizing the moment and recognizing the potency of a show of massive support, Martin Luther King Jr. called for a monumental march on Washington, D.C., to demonstrate widespread support for legislation to ban discrimination in all aspects of life, not just public accommodations. The March on Washington for Jobs and Freedom was held in August 1963, only a few months after the Birmingham demonstrations. More than 250,000 people heard King deliver his famous "I Have a Dream" speech from the Lincoln Memorial. Before Congress had the opportunity to vote on any legislation, however, John F. Kennedy was assassinated on November 22, 1963, in Dallas, Texas.

It was clear that national laws outlawing discrimination were the only answer: Southern legislators would never vote to repeal Jim Crow laws. It was much more feasible for African Americans to seek national laws and then their implementation from the federal judiciary. But, through the 1960s, African Americans lacked sufficient political power or the force of public opinion to sway enough congressional leaders. Their task was further stymied by loud and strong opposition from southern members of Congress. Many of these legislators, because of the Democratic Party's total control of the South, had been in office far longer than most and therefore held powerful committee chairmanships that were awarded on seniority. The Senate Judiciary Committee was controlled by a coalition of southern Democrats and conservative Republicans. The House Rules Committee was chaired by a Virginian opposed to any civil rights legislation, who by virtue of his position could block such legislation in committee.

Civil rights marchers at the historic gathering on the Mall in Washington, D.C., in August 1963, where Martin Luther King Jr. delivered his famous "I Have a Dream" speech. He was later gunned down at age thirty-nine in Memphis, Tennessee.

(Photo courtesy: DALMAS/SIPA Press)

When Vice President Lyndon B. Johnson, a southern-born, former Senate majority leader, succeeded Kennedy as president, he put civil rights reform at the top of his legislative priority list, and civil rights activists gained a critical ally. Thus, through the 1960s, the movement subtly changed in focus from peaceful protest and litigation to legislative lobbying. Its focus broadened from integration of school and public facilities and voting rights to issues of housing, jobs, and equal opportunity.

The push for civil rights legislation in the halls of Congress was helped by changes in public opinion. Between 1959 and 1965, southern attitudes toward integrated schools changed enormously. The proportion of Southerners who responded that they would not mind their child's attendance at a half-black school doubled.

In spite of strong presidential support and the sway of public opinion, the Civil Rights Act of 1964 did not sail through Congress. Southern senators, led by South Carolina's Strom Thurmond, a Democrat who later switched to the Republican Party, conducted the longest filibuster in the history of the Senate. For eight weeks, they held up voting on the civil rights bill until cloture (see chapter 7) was invoked and the filibuster ended. Once passed, the **Civil Rights Act of 1964:**

Civil Rights Act of 1964
Legislation passed by Congress to outlaw segregation in public facilities and racial discrimination in employment, education, and voting; created the Equal Employment Opportunity Commission.

- Outlawed arbitrary discrimination in voter registration and expedited voting rights lawsuits.
- Barred discrimination in public accommodations engaged in interstate commerce.
- Authorized the Department of Justice to initiate lawsuits to desegregate public facilities and schools.

- Provided for the withholding of federal funds from discriminatory state and local programs.
- Prohibited discrimination in employment on grounds of race, color, religion, national origin, or sex.
- Created the Equal Employment Opportunity Commission (EEOC) to monitor and enforce the bans on employment discrimination.

Other changes were sweeping the United States. Violence rocked the nation as ghetto riots broke out in the Northeast. Although northern African Americans were not subject to Jim Crow laws, many lived in poverty and faced pervasive daily discrimination and its resultant frustration. Some, including Black Muslim leader Malcolm X, even argued that to survive, African Americans must separate themselves from white culture in every way. Given this growing "black power" movement and increased racial tensions, it is not surprising that from 1964 to 1968, many African Americans in the North took to the streets, burning and looting to vent their rage.

Violence also marred the continued activities of civil rights workers in the South. During the summer of 1964, three civil rights workers—one black, two white—were killed in Neshoba County, Mississippi. In 1965, Martin Luther King Jr. again led his supporters on a massive march, this time from Selma, Alabama, to the state capital in Montgomery, in support of a pending voting rights bill. Again, southern officials unleashed a reign of terror in Selma as they used whips, dogs, cattle prods, clubs, and tear gas on the protesters. Again, Americans were horrified as they witnessed this brutality on their television screens. This march and the public's reaction to it led to quick passage of the Voting Rights Act of 1965.

In the late 1960s, court-ordered busing to achieve racial integration frequently required police escorts.
(Photo courtesy: © Bettmann/Corbis)

The Impact of the Civil Rights Act of 1964

Many Southerners were adamant in their belief that the Civil Rights Act of 1964 was unconstitutional because it went beyond the scope of Congress's authority to legislate under the Constitution, and lawsuits were quickly brought to challenge the act. The first challenge to the act was heard by the Supreme Court on an expedited review (which bypasses the intermediate courts). The Court upheld its constitutionality when it found that Congress was within the legitimate scope of its commerce power as outlined in Article I.[29]

Education.   One of the key provisions of the Civil Rights Act of 1964 authorized the Department of Justice to bring actions against school districts that failed to comply with *Brown* v. *Board of Education*. By 1964, a full decade after *Brown*, fewer than 1 percent of African American children in the South attended integrated schools.

After *Brown*, the Charlotte-Mecklenburg School District had assigned students to the school closest to their homes without regard to race, leaving over half of African American students attending schools that were at least 99 percent black. In *Swann* v. *Charlotte-Mecklenburg School District* (1971), the Supreme Court ruled that all vestiges of state-imposed segregation, called ***de jure* discrimination,** or discrimination by law, must be eliminated at once and that lower federal courts had the authority to fashion a wide variety of remedies including busing, racial quotas, and the pairing of schools to end dual, segregated school systems.[30]

de jure discrimination
Racial segregation that is a direct result of law or official policy.

de facto discrimination
Racial discrimination that results from practice (such as housing patterns or other social factors) rather than the law.

You Are the Mayor

In *Swann*, the Court was careful to distinguish *de jure* from **de facto discrimination,** unintentional discrimination often attributable to housing patterns or private acts. The Court noted that its approval of busing was a remedy for intentional, government imposed or sanctioned discrimination only.

Over the years, forced, judicially imposed busing has found less and less favor with the Supreme Court, even in situations where *de jure* discrimination had earlier been proven. In 1992, the Supreme Court even ruled that in a situation where all-black schools still existed despite a 1969 court order to dismantle the *de jure* system, a showing that the persistent segregation was not a result of the school board's actions was sufficient to remove the district from court supervision. In 1995, the Court ruled 5–4 that city school boards can use plans to attract white suburban students to mostly minority urban schools only if both city and suburban schools still show the effects of segregation, thus reversing a lower court desegregation order.[31] Basically, the trend is toward dismantling court-ordered desegregation plans, although school districts still are under orders not to discriminate. Still, especially in the North, school segregation has increased steadily over the past fifteen years.[32] And, in 2002, the Supreme Court declined—without comment—to review efforts in Charlotte-Mecklenburg County, North Carolina, which had been under a desegregation order since 1971.[33]

Employment.   Title VII of the Civil Rights Act of 1964 prohibits employers from discriminating against employees for a variety of reasons, including race, sex, age, and national origin. (In 1978, the act was amended to prohibit discrimination based on pregnancy.)

In 1971, in one of the first major cases decided under the act, the Supreme Court found that employers could be found liable for discrimination if the effect of their employment practices was to exclude African Americans from certain positions.[34] African American employees were allowed to use statistical evidence to show that they had been excluded from all but one department of the Duke Power Company, because it required employees to have a high school education or pass a special test to be eligible for promotion.

The Supreme Court ruled that although the tests did not appear to discriminate against African Americans, their effects—that there were no African American employees in any other departments—were sufficient to shift the burden of proving lack of discrimination on the employer. Thus, the Duke Power Company would have to prove that the tests were "a business necessity" that had a "demonstrable relationship to successful performance" (of a particular job).

The notion of "business necessity," as set out in the Civil Rights Act of 1964 and interpreted by the federal courts, was especially important for women. Women long had been kept out of many occupations on the strength of the belief that customers preferred to deal with male personnel. Conversely, males were barred from flight-attendant positions because the airlines believed that passengers preferred to be served by young, attractive women. Similarly, many large factories, manufacturing establishments, and police and fire departments refused outright to hire women by subjecting them to arbitrary height and weight requirements, which also disproportionately affected Hispanics. Like the tests declared illegal by the Court, these requirements often could not be shown to be related to job performance and were eventually ruled illegal by the federal courts.

The Women's Rights Movement.   Just as in the abolition movement in the 1800s, women from all walks of life also participated in the civil rights movement. Women were important members of SNCC and more traditional groups such as the NAACP and the SCLC, yet they often found themselves treated as second-class citizens. At one point, Stokely Carmichael, chair of SNCC, openly proclaimed: "The only position for women in the SNCC is prone."[35] Statements and attitudes like these led some women to found early women's liberation groups that were generally quite radical, small in membership, and not intended to use more conventional political tactics.

As discussed earlier, initial efforts to convince the Supreme Court to declare women enfranchised under the Fourteenth Amendment were uniformly unsuccessful. The paternalistic attitude of the Supreme Court, and perhaps society as well, continued well into the 1970s. As late as 1961, Florida required women who wished to serve on juries to travel to the county courthouse and register for that duty. In contrast, all men who were registered voters automatically were eligible to serve. When Gwendolyn Hoyt was convicted of bludgeoning her adulterous husband to death with a baseball bat, she appealed her conviction, claiming that the exclusion of women from juries prejudiced her case. She believed that female jurors—her peers—would have been more sympathetic to her and the emotional turmoil that led to her attack on her husband and her claim of "temporary insanity." She therefore argued that her trial by an all-male jury violated her rights as guaranteed by the Fourteenth Amendment. In rejecting her contention, Justice John Harlan (the grandson of the lone dissenting justice in *Plessy*) wrote in *Hoyt* v. *Florida* (1961):

> Despite the enlightened emancipation of women from the restrictions and protections of bygone years, and their entry into many parts of community life formerly considered to be reserved to men, a woman is still regarded as the center of home and family life.[36]

These kinds of attitudes and decisions (*Hoyt* was unanimously reversed in 1975) were not sufficient to forge a new movement for women's rights. Shortly after *Hoyt*, however, three events occurred to move women to action. In 1961, soon after his election, President John F. Kennedy created the President's Commission on the Status of Women. The commission's report, *American Women*, released in 1963, documented pervasive discrimination against women in all walks of life. In addition, the civil rights movement and publication of Betty Friedan's *The Feminine Mystique* (1963), which led some women to question their lives and status in society, added to their dawning recognition that something was wrong.[37] Soon after, the Civil Rights Act of 1964 prohibited discrimination based not only on race but also on sex. Ironically, that provision had been added to Title VII of the Civil Rights Act by southern Democrats. These senators saw a prohibition against sex discrimination in employment as a joke, and viewed its addition as a means to discredit the entire act and ensure its defeat. Thus, it was added at the last minute and female members of Congress seized the opportunity to garner support for the measure.

In 1966, after the **Equal Employment Opportunity Commission** failed to enforce the law as it applied to sex discrimination, women activists formed the National Organization for Women (NOW). From its inception, NOW was modeled closely on the NAACP. Women in NOW were quite similar to the founders of the NAACP; they wanted to work within the system to prevent discrimination. Initially, most of this activity was geared toward two goals: achievement of equality through passage of an equal rights amendment to the Constitution, or by judicial decision. But, because the Supreme Court failed to extend constitutional protections to women, the only recourse that remained was an amendment.

The Equal Rights Amendment (ERA).

Not all women agreed with the notion of full equality for women. Members of the National Consumers' League, for example, feared that an equal rights amendment would invalidate protective legislation of the kind specifically ruled constitutional in *Muller* v. *Oregon* (1908). Nevertheless, from 1923 to 1972, a proposal for an equal rights amendment was made in every session of every Congress. Every president since Harry S Truman backed it, and by 1972, public opinion favored its ratification.

Finally, in 1972, in response to pressure from NOW, the National Women's Political Caucus, and a wide variety of other feminist groups, Congress voted in favor of the

Equal Employment Opportunity Commission
Federal agency created to enforce the Civil Rights Act of 1964, which forbids discrimination on the basis of race, creed, national origin, religion, or sex in hiring, promotion, or firing.

WEB EXPLORATION
To learn more about NOW and the EEOC, see
www.ablongman.com/oconnor

Equal Rights Amendment
Proposed amendment that would bar discrimination against women by federal or state governments.

Equal Rights Amendment (ERA) by overwhelming majorities (84–8 in the Senate; 354–24 in the House). The amendment provided that:

- Equality of rights under the law shall not be denied or abridged by the United States or by any state on account of sex.
- The Congress shall have the power to enforce, by appropriate legislation, the provisions of this article.

Within a year, twenty-two states ratified the amendment, most by overwhelming margins. But, the tide soon turned. In *Roe* v. *Wade* (1973), the Supreme Court decided that women had a constitutionally protected right to privacy that included the right to terminate a pregnancy. Almost overnight, *Roe* gave the ERA's opponents political fuel. Although privacy rights and the ERA have nothing to do with each other, opponents effectively persuaded many people in states that had yet to ratify the amendment that the two were linked. If abortion was legal, why not marriages between and adoptions by homosexuals? They also claimed that the ERA and feminists were anti-family and that the ERA would force women out of their homes and into the workforce because husbands would no longer be responsible for their wives' support.

WEB EXPLORATION
To learn more about the ERA, see
www.ablongman.com/oconnor

These arguments and the amendment's potential to make women eligible for the military draft brought the ratification effort to a near standstill. In 1974 and 1975, the amendment only squeaked through the Montana and North Dakota legislatures, and two states—Nebraska and Tennessee—voted to rescind their earlier ratifications. By 1978, one year before the deadline for ratification was to expire, thirty-five states had voted for the amendment—three short of the three-fourths necessary for ratification. Efforts in key states such as Illinois and Florida failed as opposition to the ERA intensified. Faced with the prospect of defeat, ERA supporters heavily lobbied Congress to extend the deadline for ratification. Congress extended the ratification period by three years, but to no avail. No additional states ratified the amendment and three more rescinded their votes.

What began as a simple correction to the Constitution turned into a highly controversial proposed change. Even though large numbers of the public favored the ERA, opponents needed to stall ratification in only thirteen states while supporters had to convince legislators in thirty-eight. The success that women's rights activists were having in the courts was hurting the effort. When women first sought the ERA in the late 1960s, the Supreme Court had yet to rule that women were protected by the Fourteenth Amendment's equal protection clause from any kind of discrimination, thus clearly showing the need for an amendment. But, as the Court widened its interpretation of the Constitution to protect women from some sorts of discrimination, in the eyes of many, the need for a new amendment became less urgent. The proposed amendment died without being ratified on June 30, 1982. For more on efforts to revive the ERA, see Politics Now: Time for the Equal Rights Amendment?

Litigation for Equal Rights.   While several women's groups worked toward passage of the ERA, NOW and several other groups, including the Women's Rights Project of the American Civil Liberties Union (ACLU), formed litigating arms to pressure the courts. But, women faced an immediate roadblock in the Supreme Court's interpretation of the equal protection clause of the Fourteenth Amendment.

The Equal Protection Clause and Constitutional Standards of Review

The Fourteenth Amendment protects all U.S. citizens from state action that violates equal protection of the laws. Most laws, however, are subject to what is called the rational basis or minimum rationality test. This lowest level of scrutiny means that governments must allege a rational foundation for any distinctions they make. Early on, however, the Supreme Court decided that certain rights were entitled to a heightened standard of review. As early as 1937, the Supreme Court recognized that certain rights were so fundamental that a very heavy burden would be placed on any government that sought to restrict those rights. As discussed in chapter 5, when fundamental rights such as First Amendment freedoms or **suspect classifications** such as race are involved, the Court uses a heightened standard of review called **strict scrutiny** to determine the constitutional validity of the challenged practices, as detailed in Table 6.1. Beginning with *Korematsu* v. *U.S.* (1944), which involved a constitutional challenge to the internment of Japanese Americans, Justice Hugo Black noted that "all legal restrictions which curtail the civic rights of a single racial group are immediately suspect," and should be given "the most rigid scrutiny."[38] In *Brown* v. *Board of Education* (1954), the Supreme Court again used the strict scrutiny standard to evaluate the constitutionality of race-based distinctions. In legal terms, this means that if a statute or governmental practice makes a classification based on race, the statute is presumed to be unconstitutional unless the state can provide "compelling affirmative justifications"; that is, unless the state can prove the law in question is necessary to accomplish a permissible goal and that it is the least restrictive means through which that goal can be accomplished.

During the 1960s and into the 1970s, the Court routinely struck down as unconstitutional practices and statutes that discriminated on the basis of race. "Whites-only" public parks and recreational facilities, tax-exempt status for private schools that discriminated, and statutes prohibiting racial intermarriage were declared unconstitutional. In contrast, the Court refused even to consider the fact that the equal protection clause might apply to discrimination against women. Finally, in a case brought in 1971 by Ruth Bader Ginsburg (now an associate justice of the Supreme Court) as director of the Women's Rights Project of the ACLU, the Supreme Court ruled that an Idaho law granting a male parent automatic preference over a female parent as the administrator of their deceased child's estate violated the equal protection clause of the Fourteenth Amendment.

suspect classification
Category or class, such as race, that triggers the highest standard of scrutiny from the Supreme Court.

strict scrutiny
A heightened standard of review used by the Supreme Court to determine the constitutional validity of a challenged practice.

WEB EXPLORATION
For more about the ACLU Women's Rights Project, see
www.ablongman.com/oconnor

TABLE 6.1 The Equal Protection Clause and Standards of Review Used by the Supreme Court to Determine Whether it Has Been Violated

TYPE OF CLASSIFICATION (What kind of statutory classification is at issue?)	STANDARD OF REVIEW (What standard of review will be used?)	TEST (What does the Court ask?)	EXAMPLE (How does the Court apply the test?)
Fundamental freedoms (including religion, assembly, press, privacy). Suspect classifications (including race, alienage, and national origin)	Strict scrutiny or heightened standard	Is classification necessary to the accomplishment of a permissible state goal? Is it the least restrictive way to reach that goal?	*Brown* v. *Board of Education* (1954): Racial segregation not necessary to accomplish the state goal of educating its students.
Gender	Intermediate standard	Does the classification serve an important governmental objective, and is it substantially related to those ends?	*Craig* v. *Boren* (1976): Keeping drunk drivers off the roads may be an important governmental objective, but allowing eighteen- to twenty-one-year-old women to drink alcoholic beverages while prohibiting men of the same age from drinking is not substantially related to that goal.
Others (including age, wealth, and mental retardation)	Minimum rationality standard	Is there any rational foundation for the discrimination?	*City of Cleburne* v. *Cleburne Living Center* (1985). Zoning restrictions against group homes for the retarded have rational basis.

TIME FOR THE EQUAL RIGHTS AMENDMENT?

In March 2001, Representative Carolyn Maloney (D–NY) reintroduced the Equal Rights Amendment with over 160 co-sponsors on the thirtieth anniversary of its initial approval by both houses of Congress. By mid-2002, that number grew to over 200. Why an Equal Rights Amendment now? According to Maloney, whose action was supported by numerous women's groups, including the National Organization for Women, "There is still discrimination in insurance, in social security, in pensions," with the pension gap being worse than the earnings gap.[a] She specifically mentions the plethora of laws that ban discrimination against women, such as the Civil Rights Act of 1964 and Title IX, but argues that women need to be included in the Constitution, which would afford greater protection to women against discrimination by making sex a suspect classification for judicial review. Even Justice Ruth Bader Ginsburg weighed into the fray, noting that "every constitution that was written after World War II says … men and women are persons of equal stature or words to that effect."[b]

Since the proposed amendment fell short of the three states needed for ratification in 1982, the ERA has been introduced into every session of Congress, but momentum is building. The bill introduced by Maloney places no limit on the time period for ratification. An alternative strategy to win adoption of the ERA uses the Twenty-Seventh or "Madison" Amendment discussed in chapter 2. The acceptance of an amendment 203 years after it was sent to the states for their approval has prompted ERA supporters to "propose that Congress has the power to maintain the legal viability of the ERA's existing thirty-five state ratifications."[c] Proponents of the ERA, backed up by a report for the Congressional Research Service, say that the amendment actually needs only the ratification of three more states to win approval. Ratification bills testing this three-state strategy have been filed in several states that did not ratify the amendment, including Illinois, Missouri, and Virginia, with plans to introduce these bills in all fifteen nonratifying states.

Do you believe that there still is a need for an ERA?

Is this a wise use of resources for the women's movement? Why or why not?

---

[a]Carolyn Maloney press release, "A New E.R.A. for New Era" (March 22, 2001).

[b]"Justice Ginsburg Rueful over ERA," *San Diego Union-Tribune* (May 22, 2002): A14.

[c]Roberta W. Francis, "The History Behind the Equal Rights Amendment," Report of the ERA Task Force, National Council of Women's Organizations, http://www.equalrightsamendment.org/era.htm.

Reed v. *Reed* (1971), the Idaho case, turned the tide in terms of constitutional litigation. While the Court did not rule that sex was a suspect classification, it concluded that the equal protection clause of the Fourteenth Amendment prohibited unreasonable classifications based on sex.[39] In 1976, the Court ruled that sex-discrimination complaints would be judged by a new, judicially created intermediate standard of review a step below strict scrutiny. In *Craig* v. *Boren* (1976), the owner of the Honk 'n' Holler Restaurant in Stillwater, Oklahoma, and Craig, a male under twenty-one, challenged the constitutionality of a state law prohibiting the sale of 3.2 percent beer to males under the age of twenty-one and to females under the age of eighteen.[40] The state introduced a considerable amount of evidence in support of the statute, including:

- Eighteen- to twenty-year-old males were more likely to be arrested for driving under the influence than were females of the same age.
- Youths aged seventeen to twenty-one were the group most likely to be injured or to die in alcohol-related traffic accidents, with males exceeding females.
- Young men were more inclined to drink and drive than females.

The Supreme Court found that this information was "too tenuous" to support the legislation. In coming to this conclusion, the Court carved out a new "test" to be used in examining claims of sex discrimination, "[T]o withstand constitutional challenge, … classifications by gender must serve important governmental objectives and must be substantially related to achievement of those objectives." According to the Court, an intermediate standard of review was created within what previously was a two-tier distinction—strict scrutiny and rational basis.

As *Craig* demonstrates, men, too, can use the Fourteenth Amendment to fight gender-based discrimination. Since 1976, the Court has applied the intermediate standard of constitutional review to most claims that it has heard involving gender. Thus, the following kinds of practices have been found to violate the Fourteenth Amendment:

- Single-sex public nursing schools.[41]
- Laws that consider males adults at twenty-one years but females at eighteen years.[42]
- Laws that allow women but not men to receive alimony.[43]
- State prosecutors' use of peremptory challenges to reject men or women to create more sympathetic juries.[44]
- Virginia's maintenance of an all-male military college, the Virginia Military Institute.[45]

In contrast, the Court has upheld the following governmental practices and laws:

- Draft registration provisions for males only.[46]
- State statutory rape laws that apply only to female victims.[47]

The level of review used by the Court is crucial. Clearly, a statute excluding African Americans from draft registration would be unconstitutional. But, because gender is not subject to the same higher standard of review that is used in racial discrimination cases, the exclusion of women from the requirements of the Military Selective Service Act was ruled permissible because the government policy was considered to serve "important governmental objectives."[48]

This history has perhaps clarified why women's rights activists continue to argue that until the passage of an equal rights amendment, women will never enjoy the same rights as men. An amendment would automatically raise the level of scrutiny that the Court applies to gender-based claims.

U.S. women, many of whom won college athletic scholarships mandated by Title IX, won record numbers of medals at the Summer and Winter Olympics. Vonetta Flowers (left), who won gold in bobsledding along with her teammate Jill Bakken (right), developed her strength and speed as a high school and college track and field star.

(Photo courtesy: Darron Cummings/AP/Wide World Photos)

Statutory Remedies for Sex Discrimination. In part because of the limits of the intermediate standard of review and the fact that the equal protection clause applies only to governmental discrimination, women's rights activists began to bombard the courts with sex-discrimination cases. Many of these cases have been filed under Title VII of the Civil Rights Act, which prohibits discrimination by private (and, after 1972, public) employers, or **Title IX** of the Education Amendments of 1972, which bars educational institutions receiving federal funds from discriminating against female students. Key victories under Title VII include:

- Consideration of sexual harassment as sex discrimination.[49]
- Inclusion of law firms, which many argued were private partnerships, in the coverage of the act.[50]
- A broad definition of what can be considered sexual harassment, which includes same-sex harassment.[51]
- Allowance of voluntary affirmative action programs to redress historical discrimination against women.[52]

Title IX
Provision of the Educational Amendments of 1972 that bars educational institutions receiving federal funds from discriminating against female students.

ANALYZING VISUALS

Sexual Harassment Filings, Fiscal Years 1990–2001

This graph shows the number of sexual harassment charges per fiscal year filed with the Equal Employment Opportunity Commission (EEOC) and state and local Fair Employment Practices Agencies (FEPA) around the country that have a working agreement with the EEOC. The number of these cases filed by males and females are shown as portions of the total for each year. After reviewing the data presented in the graph and reading the related discussion in the chapter, consider the following critical thinking questions: What trends do you see in the overall number of sexual harassment filings from 1990 to 2001? What trends do you see in the percentage of cases filed by males during this period? What might explain these trends?

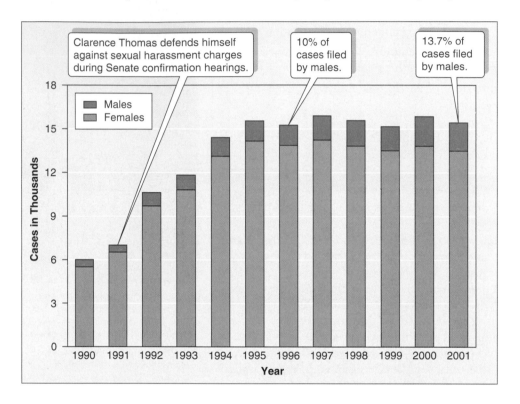

Source: Equal Employment Opportunity Commission, http://www.eeoc.gov/stats/harass.html.

After the hearings concerning whether or not Supreme Court justice nominee Clarence Thomas sexually harassed law professor Anita Hill when she was his employee, sexual harassment claims skyrocketed until 1995 and then leveled off. (See Analyzing Visuals: Sexual Harassment Filings, Fiscal Years 1990–2001.) Claims more than doubled from 1990 to 1998. The Equal Employment Opportunity Commission (EEOC) was able to reach record settlements with employers rising from $7.7 million in 1990 to $53 million in 2001. Complaints have begun to level off as more and more employers have begun education and training programs to avert workplace problems. Women also have won important victories under the Equal Pay Act, but a large wage gap between men and women continues to exist, as underscored in Figure 6.1. In spite of the fact that the Equal Pay Act is forty years old, women in 2000 earned 73 percent of what men earned.

Title IX, which parallels Title VII, also greatly has expanded the opportunities for women in elementary, secondary, and postsecondary institutions. Since women's groups, like the NAACP before them, saw eradication of educational discrimination as key to

FIGURE 6.1   The Wage Gap, 2000

The Equal Pay Act was passed in 1963; still women's wages continue to fall short of men's although the gap is closing among all women with the exception of Hispanic women. What factors might account for these glaring inequities?

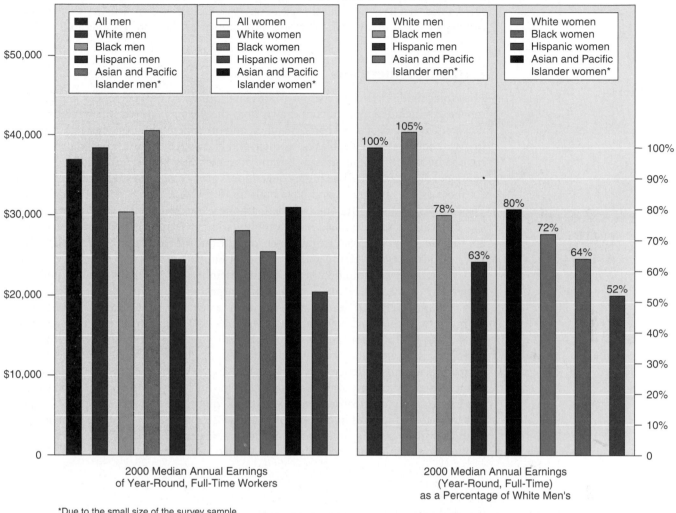

*Due to the small size of the survey sample, these data may not be representative.

Source: National Committee on Pay Equity.

improving other facets of women's lives, they lobbied for it heavily. Most of today's college students did not go through school being excluded from home economics or shop classes because of their sex. Nor, probably, did many attend schools that had no team sports for females. Yet, this was commonly the case in the United States prior to passage of Title IX.[53] The performance of American women athletes in Olympic games shows the impact of the law on women's participation in sports. Record numbers of women compete and win.

OTHER GROUPS MOBILIZE FOR RIGHTS

African Americans and women are not the only groups that suffered unequal treatment under the law. Denial of civil rights led many other disadvantaged groups to mobilize to achieve greater civil rights. Their efforts to achieve those rights have many parallels to the efforts made by African Americans and women. In the wake of the successes of those two groups in achieving enhanced rights, and sometimes even before, other traditionally disenfranchised groups organized to gain fuller equality. Many of them also recognized that litigation and the use of test-case strategies would be key to further civil rights gains, and many of their efforts were funded by the Ford Foundation.

Hispanic Americans

Hispanics made their first real push for equal rights from 1965 to 1975.[54] This new movement included many tactics drawn from the African American civil rights movement, including sit-ins, boycotts, marches, and other activities designed to attract publicity to their cause.[55] Like blacks, women, and Native Americans, Hispanic Americans have some radical militant groups, but the movement has been dominated by more conventional organizations. The more conventional groups have pressed for Chicano/a and Latino/a studies programs and have built up ties with existing, powerful mainstream associations, including unions and the Catholic Church.

Hispanics also have relied heavily on litigation to secure greater rights. Key groups are the Mexican American Legal Defense and Educational Fund (MALDEF) and the Puerto Rican Legal Defense and Educational Fund.

MALDEF was founded in 1968 after members of the League of United Latin American Citizens (LULAC), the nation's largest and oldest Latino/a organization, met with NAACP LDF leaders and, with their assistance, secured a $2.2-million start-up grant from the Ford Foundation. It was created to bring test cases to force school districts to allocate more funds to schools with predominantly low-income minority populations, to implement bilingual education programs, to force employers to hire Hispanics, and to challenge election rules and apportionment plans that undercount or dilute Hispanic voting power. Just as women's rights groups had depended on the legal expertise of their own constituents, MALDEF quickly drew on the talent of Hispanic attorneys to staff offices in San Antonio and Los Angeles. It also started a scholarship fund to train more Hispanic attorneys and established a New Mexico branch office in conjunction with the University of New Mexico Law School.

WEB EXPLORATION
To learn more about MALDEF, see
www.ablongman.com/oconnor

Representatives of the Mexican American Legal Defense and Educational Fund (such as Al Kaufman, pictured second from left), National Council of La Raza, and the League of United Latin American Citizens urge then acting Lt. Gov. Bill Ratliff (R–TX) to retract comments he made that immigrants are "clogging" the state's social services.

(Photo courtesy: Harry Cabluck/AP/Wide World Photos)

IMMIGRATION AND CIVIL RIGHTS

Americans are used to being a nation of immigrants, even as new immigration sparks public debate about how much is enough. Immigration into Western Europe and Japan has been an even more problematic issue. In the last decade or so, right-wing political parties in Western Europe have made immigration a national issue. The divisions it causes in the European political landscape were vividly illustrated in 2002. In the French presidential elections in May, the National Front candidate, Henri Le Pen, edged out the Socialist prime minister on the first ballot, paving the way for a runoff election against conservative President Jacques Chirac. Le Pen ran on an anti-immigrant platform, and his unexpected success in a presidential election stunned the public (he lost in the runoff election). Within days of the French election, Dutch politician Pim Fortuyn, also a nationalist running on an anti-immigration platform, was assassinated. His party had been expected to win up to one-quarter of the seats in the Dutch parliament.

Immigration is a political issue in these countries for three reasons. First, since the nineteenth century European and Japanese nationalism has been based on the notion of the nation as a common ethnic people. Second, most of the postwar immigration into Western Europe and Japan has been from developing countries in Asia, Africa, and the Middle East (many of them former colonies). Third, that immigration, which was assumed after World War II by many governments to be temporary, has been permanent in many cases. Large populations of Turkish "guest workers" and Eastern European refugees in Germany, North Africans in France, and Chinese and Koreans in Japan, present problems of how to assimilate people from different backgrounds without radically altering national identity. In a number of ways, then, immigration issues in Europe and Japan resemble ethnic and racial issues in the United States.

More or less permanent outsider status invites civil rights abuses. Right-wing groups across Western Europe have made rhetorical as well as physical attacks on foreign residents. While the constitutions of these countries typically prohibit discrimination, immigrants who are not citizens often do not enjoy the full protection of the law.

Acquiring citizenship as a way to assimilate is not always easy. Japan and Germany provide a striking contrast to the United States on this point. The United States government subscribes to the doctrine of *jus soli:* People born on American soil automatically acquire citizenship even if their parents are not United States citizens. Moreover, American requirements for citizenship for permanent residents are comparatively lenient. The Japanese and German governments, in contrast, subscribe to the doctrine of *jus sanguinis:* Only the children of citizens (and therefore properly German or Japanese) automatically qualify for citizenship. In 2000, the German government eased this restriction to allow for dual citizenship for second-generation aliens, but preference in immigration and naturalization continues to go to ethnic German immigrants. Naturalization by second- and third-generation immigrants in Germany and Japan remains quite low.

MALDEF lawyers quickly moved to bring major test cases to the U.S. Supreme Court, both to enhance the visibility of their cause and to win cases. MALDEF has been quite successful in its efforts to expand voting rights and opportunities to Hispanic Americans. In 1973, for example, it won a major victory when the Supreme Court ruled that multimember electoral districts (in which more than one person represents a single district) in Texas discriminated against African Americans and Hispanic Americans.[56] In multimember systems, legislatures generally add members to larger districts instead of drawing smaller districts in which a minority candidate could get a majority of the votes necessary to win.

While enjoying greater access to elective office, Hispanics still suffer discrimination. Language barriers and substandard educational opportunities continue to plague their progress. In 1973, the U.S. Supreme Court refused to find that a Texas law under which the state appropriated a set dollar amount to each school district per pupil, while allowing wealthier districts to enrich educational programs from other funds, violated the equal protection clause of the Fourteenth Amendment.[57] The lower courts had found that wealth was a suspect classification entitled to strict scrutiny. Using that test, the lower courts had found the Texas plan discriminatory. In contrast, a divided Supreme Court concluded that education was not a fundamental right (see chapter 5),

Join the Debate

SHOULD WASHINGTON, D.C., RESIDENTS HAVE A VOTE IN CONGRESS?

Voting is considered a fundamental civil right, but, as discussed in this chapter, that right has not always been fully guaranteed for all Americans. Over two centuries, political movements successfully pushed through constitutional amendments to assure voting rights for racial minorities (1870), women (1920), and eighteen-year-olds (1971). But, today, there are still disenfranchised groups—including convicted felons, and residents of the District of Columbia (better known as Washington, D.C.). Since Washington, D.C. is not a state, its residents do not have official representation in the U.S. House and Senate as do Americans who live in the fifty states.

For four decades now, some advocates have pushed for constitutional amendments to assure full voting rights for residents of Washington, D.C. In 1961, the U.S. Constitution was amended (via the Twenty-Third Amendment) to give residents of the District of Columbia the right to vote in presidential elections (with three electoral votes). Residents have long advocated that they also be given the right to vote for full, functioning representation in Congress. The District may send a special delegate to Congress who may vote in committee, but not on any final, official vote on the floor. Congress finally did propose a constitutional amendment extending congressional voting rights to D.C. residents, but the proposal failed ratification among the required three-fourths of the states in 1985. Currently, Washington, D.C. has more people than the state of Wyoming, and nearly as many as Alaska, North Dakota, and Vermont.

Why should more than half a million Americans not be allowed to vote for a full, functioning member of Congress? When Washington, D.C. was originally established as the nation's capital, many people living there were part-time residents, coming to the capital to serve in Congress or in a presidential administration, then returning home. Thus, they retained their right to vote in their home state. While that is still true for some today, most people who now live in Washington are permanent residents. Some vote in home states; others do not.

Read and think about the following news article from 2002. Then, join the debate over whether D.C. residents are unfairly denied a basic civil right—voting. Should the Constitution be amended to extend voting rights to Washington, D.C. residents? Or should this federally owned district remain an area that is distinct from the official states in the union? Consider the debating points and questions posed at the end of this feature, and sharpen your own arguments for the position you find most viable.

Washington Calls for Representation
September 8, 2002

WASHINGTON (Reuters)—Just before he left office in 2001, President Clinton ordered that the presidential limousine bear new Washington license plates emblazoned with the slogan "Taxation Without Representation."

The slogan, born in the American Revolution, replaced the "Celebrate and Discover" license plate motto in a nod to a movement seeking congressional representation for the District of Columbia, which it has lacked for two centuries.

But on the eve of Tuesday's primary election in Washington, right-to-vote campaigners say they are not much closer to securing the same voting rights for America's capital city that residents of the nation's 50 states enjoy.

"It is a shame on our nation," said Kevin Kiger, spokesman for the D.C. Vote group. "We are a disenfranchised people. At the end of the day, nobody in Congress votes for D.C. because we don't vote for them. We are nobody's constituents."

Washingtonians won the right to vote in presidential elections in 1961, but have no senators or members of the House of Representatives despite a legal struggle that reached the Supreme Court in March 2000.

It does have one elected nonvoting representative in Congress, Democrat Eleanor Holmes Norton.

Washington, a city of 572,000 people with landmarks such as the White House and the Washington Monument, has a special status. The land that would become the district was placed under federal control by the framers of the Constitution in 1787. Congress has final authority over each of the city's laws and budgets.

If it were a state, the district would have two senators and, based on population, one member of the House. Democrats, who hold an overwhelming majority in voter registration, would almost certainly win all the seats.

As a result, political observers say, Republicans—who hold a slim majority in the House and are just short of controlling the Senate—tend to oppose district voting rights on political grounds.

Washington Mayor Anthony Williams, seeking the Democratic nomination for re-election in Tuesday's primary, has said the only Americans denied the right to vote are minors, convicted criminals and Washington residents.

All the candidates in Tuesday's Democratic mayoral primary pledged support for congressional representation for the district. Even the district's Republican Party has spoken in favor of the change.

But Republican President Bush opposes voting representation for Washington, and he ordered removed from his presidential limousine the plates that said "Taxation Without Representation."

The full slogan, "Taxation Without Representation Is Tyranny," was a rallying cry against British rule invoked during the Revolutionary War in the 1770s.

Washington residents say they still live in the shadow of a government that ignores them, despite their obligation to pay federal taxes, sit on juries and serve in the armed services. Kevin Moore, 48, a member of the community activist group D.C. Rabble seeking voting rights for the district, said that although lingering racial tensions contributed to foot-dragging on Washington voting rights, the main roadblock lay with partisan politics.

"Part of it does have to do with the fact that D.C. is a majority black city, and most people who live here are Democrats," he said. About 60 percent of Washington residents are black, and 9 percent are Hispanic. "It's a purely political issue, which is very disheartening," Kiger said.

Source: http://www.cnn.com/2002/ ALLPOLITICS/09/08/washington.voting. reut/index.html. Copyright 2002 Reuters. All rights reserved.

JOIN THE DEBATE!

CHECK YOUR UNDERSTANDING: Make sure you understand the following key points from the article; go back and review it if you missed any of them:

- Voting and representation rights in states.
- Voting and representation rights in Washington, D.C., including their special delegate to Congress.
- The campaign to win full voting rights for Washington, D.C. residents.
- The political and racial dynamics involved in the debate.

ADDITIONAL INFORMATION: News articles don't provide all the information an informed citizen needs to know about an issue under debate. Here are some questions the article does not answer that you may need to consider in order to join the debate:

- How many American citizens do not have official representation in Congress?
- How many Washington, D.C., residents vote elsewhere?
- Why may the Washington, D.C delegate vote in committee, but not on the floor?
- Who would benefit if voting rights for Washington, D.C changed?
- Who would be harmed if the voting rules were changed?

What other information might you want to know? Where might you gather this information? How might you evaluate the credibility of the information you gather? Is the information from a reliable source? Can you identify any potential biases?

IDENTIFYING THE ARGUMENTS: Now that you have some information on the issue, and have thought about what else you need to know, see whether you can present the arguments on both sides of the debate. Here are some ideas to get you started. We've provided one example each of "pro" and "con" arguments, but you should be able to offer others:

PRO: Residents of D.C. should have full voting rights. Here's why:

- The original reason for denying them voting rights—most residents of Washington, D.C., had a home state—no longer holds.

CON: Residents of D.C. should not have full voting rights. Here's why:

- Any representatives would almost certainly be Democratic, so this is purely an issue pushed by Democrats for their political advantage.

TAKING A POSITION AND SUPPORTING IT: After thinking about the information in the article on Washington, D.C. congressional voting rights, placing it in the broader context of civil rights, and articulating the arguments in the debate, what position would you take? What information supports your position? What arguments would you use to persuade others to your side of the debate? How would you counter arguments on the other side?

and that a charge of discrimination based on wealth would be examined only under a minimal standard of review (the rational basis test).[58]

Throughout the 1970s and 1980s, inter-school-district inequalities continued, and frequently had their greatest impact on poor Hispanic children, who often had inferior educational opportunities. Recognizing that the increasingly conservative federal courts (see chapter 10) offered no recourse, in 1984, MALDEF filed suit in state court alleging that the Texas school finance policy violated the Texas constitution. In 1989, it won a case in which a state district judge elected by the voters of only a single county declared the state's entire method of financing public schools to be unconstitutional under the state constitution.[59]

MALDEF continues to litigate in a wide range of areas of concern to Hispanics. High on its agenda today are affirmative action, the admission of Hispanic students to state colleges and universities, health care for undocumented immigrants, and challenging unfair redistricting practices that make it more difficult to elect Hispanic legislators. It litigates to replace at-large electoral systems with single district elections to insure the election of more Hispanics, as well as challenging many state redistricting plans to insure that Hispanics are adequately represented. Its highly successful Census 2000 educational outreach campaign, moreover, sought to decrease undercounting of Hispanics.

MALDEF also continues to be at the fore of legal and legislative lobbying for expanded rights. In 2002, it worked to oppose restrictions on proposed California legislation concerning driver's license requirements for undocumented aliens, for the rights of Hispanic workers, and, of course, to monitor the effects of legislative redistricting on the voting strength of Hispanics. In 2002, MALDEF, just as the NAACP LDF before it, was involved in several challenges to the way states drew state legislative and congressional districts arguing against the dilution of Hispanic voters.

Native Americans

Native Americans are the first "true" Americans, and their status under U.S. law is unique. Under the U.S. Constitution, "Indian tribes" are considered distinct governments, a situation that has affected Native Americans' treatment by the Supreme Court in contrast to other groups of ethnic minorities. And, "minority" is a term that accurately describes American Indians. It is estimated that there were as many as 10 million Indians in the New World at the time Europeans arrived in the 1400s, with 3 to 4 million living in what is today the United States. By 1900, the number of Indians in the continental United States had plummeted to less than 2 million. Today, there are 4.1 million.

Many commentators would agree that for years Congress and the courts manipulated Indian law to promote the westward expansion of the United States. The Northwest Ordinance of 1787, passed by the Continental Congress, specified that "the good faith should always be observed toward the Indians; their lands and property shall never be taken from them without their consent, and their property rights, and liberty, they shall never be invaded or disturbed, unless in just and lawful wars authorized by Congress." This is not what happened. Instead, over the years, "American Indian policy has been described as 'genocide-at-law' promoting both land acquisition and cultural extermination."[60] At first, during the eighteenth and nineteenth centuries, the U.S. government isolated Indians on reservations as it confiscated their lands and denied them basic political rights. Indian reservations were administered by the federal government, and Native Americans often lived in squalid conditions.

With passage of the Dawes Act in 1887, however, the government switched policies to promote assimilation over separation. Each Indian family was given land within the reservation; the rest was sold to whites, thus reducing Indian lands from about 140 million acres to about 47 million. Moreover, to encourage Native Americans to assimilate, Indian children were sent to boarding schools off the reservation, and native languages and rituals were banned. In 1924, Native Americans were made U.S. citizens and given the right to vote.

At least in part because tribes were small and scattered (and the number of Indians declining), they formed no protest movement in reaction to these drastic policy changes. It was not until the 1960s, at the same time that women were beginning to mobilize for greater civil rights, that Indians, too, began to mobilize to act. Like the civil rights and women's rights movements, the movement for Native American rights had a radical as well as a more traditional branch. In 1973, for example, national attention was drawn to the plight of Indians when members of the radical American Indian Movement took over Wounded Knee, South Dakota, the site of the massacre of 150 Indians by the U.S. Army in 1890. Just two years before the protest, the treatment of Indians had been highlighted in the best-selling *Bury My Heart at Wounded Knee*, which in many ways served to mobilize public opinion against the oppression of Native Americans in the same way *Uncle Tom's Cabin* had against slavery.[61]

At the same time, just as the growing number of women in the legal profession contributed to the push to secure greater rights for women through litigation, Indians, many trained by the American Indian Law Center at the University of New Mexico, began to file hundreds of test cases in the federal courts involving tribal fishing rights, tribal land claims, and the taxation of tribal profits. The Native American Rights Fund (NARF), founded in 1970, became the NAACP LDF of the Indian rights movement when the "courts became the forum of choice for Indian tribes and their members."[62]

WEB EXPLORATION
For more about the Native American Rights Fund, see
www.ablongman.com/oconnor

Native Americans have won some very important victories concerning hunting, fishing, and land rights. Native American tribes all over America have sued to reclaim lands they say were stolen from them by the United States, often more than 200 years ago. One of the largest Indian land claims was filed in 1972 on behalf of the Passamaquoddie and the Penobscot tribes, that were seeking return of 12.5 million acres in Maine—about two-thirds of the entire state—and $25 billion in damages. The suit was filed by the Native American Rights Fund and the Indian Service Unit of a legal services office that was funded by the U.S. Office of Economic Opportunity. It took intervention from the White House before a settlement was reached in 1980, giving each tribe over $40 million.

Native Americans also are litigating to gain access to their sacred places. All over the nation, they have filed lawsuits to stop the building of roads and new construction on ancient burial grounds or other sacred spots. "We are in a battle for the survival of our very way of life," said one tribal leader. "The land is gone. All we've got left is our religion."[63]

Native Americans have not fared particularly well in areas such as religious freedom, especially where tribal practices come into conflict with state law. As noted in chapter 5, the Supreme Court used the rational basis test to rule that a state could infringe on religious exercise (use of peyote as a sacrament in religious ceremonies) by a neutral law, and limited Indian access to religious sites during timber harvesting.[64] Congress, however, quickly acted to restore some of those rights through passage of the Religious Freedom Restoration Act, although the law later was ruled unconstitutional by the Supreme Court.[65]

Native Americans continue to fight the negative stereotypes that plague their progress. Indians contend that even the popular names of thousands of high school, college, and professional teams are degrading. This has caused some school districts and universities to change the names of their sports teams. Professional teams such as the Atlanta Braves, Cleveland Indians, and Washington Redskins also are under attack. The Washington football team received a request from the Metropolitan Council of Governments to change its name, but to no avail. Even the U.S. Commission on Civil Rights has weighed in on the matter, requesting an end to Indian names, mascots, and logos.

While efforts to pressure teams to change their names wage on, Indian tribes have found themselves locked in a controversy with the Department of the Interior over its handling of Indian trust funds, which are to be paid out to Indians for the use of their lands. In 1996, several Indian tribes filed suit to force the federal government to account for the billions of dollars it has collected over the years for its leasing of Indian land, which it took from the Indians and held in trust since the late-nineteenth century, and to force reform of the system.[66] As the result of years of mismanagement, the trust, administered by the Department of the Interior, has no records of monies taken in or how they were disbursed. The ongoing class action lawsuit includes 500,000 Indians, who claim that they are owed more than $10 billion. The trial judge found massive mismanagement of the funds, which generate up to $500 million a year, and at one time threatened to hold Secretary of the Interior Gail Norton in contempt. In a preliminary resolution of the lawsuit, a total reorganization of the way the federal government treats the trust accounts is now underway. Still, the Indians continue not to hold title to their lands, nor to be compensated adequately for them.

Gays and Lesbians

Gays and lesbians have had an even harder time than other groups in achieving fuller rights.[67] Gays do, however, have on average far higher household incomes and educational levels than do these other groups. They are beginning to convert these advantages into political clout at the ballot box. As discussed in chapter 5, the cause of gay and lesbian rights, like that of African Americans and women early in their quest for greater civil rights, initially did not fare well in the Supreme Court. In the late 1970s, the Lambda Legal Defense and Education Fund, the Lesbian Rights Project, and Gay and Lesbian Advocates and Defenders were founded by gay and lesbian activists dedicated to ending legal restrictions on the civil rights of homosexuals.[68] Although these groups have won important legal victories concerning HIV/AIDS discrimination, insurance policy survivor benefits, and even some employment issues, they generally have not been as successful as other historically legally disadvantaged groups.[69]

WEB EXPLORATION
For more on gay and lesbian rights groups, see
www.ablongman.com/oconnor

In *Bowers* v. *Hardwick* (1986), for example, the Supreme Court ruled constitutional a Georgia law that made private acts of consensual sodomy illegal (whether practiced by homosexuals or by heterosexual married adults). Gay and lesbian rights groups had argued that a constitutional right to privacy included the right to engage in consensual sex within one's home, but the Court disagreed. Although privacy rights may attach to relations of "family, marriage, or procreation," those rights did not extend to homosexuals, wrote Justice Byron White for the Court. In a concurring opinion—his last written on the Court—Chief Justice Warren E. Burger called sodomy "the infamous crime against nature."[70]

The public's and Congress's discomfort with gay and lesbian rights can be seen most clearly in the controversy that occurred after President Bill Clinton attempted to lift the ban on gays in the armed services. Clinton tried to get an absolute ban on discrimination against homosexuals, who were subject to immediate discharge if their sexual orientation was discovered. Military leaders and then-Senator Sam Nunn (D–GA), as chair of the Senate Armed Services Committee, led the effort against Clinton's proposal. Eventually, Clinton and Senate leaders compromised on what was called the "Don't Ask, Don't Tell" policy. It stipulated that gays and lesbians would no longer be asked if they were homosexual, but they were barred from revealing their sexual orientation (under threat of discharge from the service). When the Senate finally voted on the "compromise," however, its version of the new policy labeled homosexuality "an unacceptable risk" to morale. In spite of gay and lesbian groups' labeling the new policy "lie and hide," the Clinton administration chose to back off on the issue, correctly sensing only minimal support in Congress. Over 10,000 men and women have been forced out of the military since this policy was announced.[71]

However, the public's views toward homosexuality were clearly beginning to change, as signaled by the Court's 1996 decision in *Romer* v. *Evans* where the Court ruled that an amendment to the Colorado constitution that denied homosexuals the right to seek protection from discrimination was unconstitutional under the equal protection clause of the Fourteenth Amendment.[72]

Further, in 2000, Vermont became the same state to recognize civil unions, marking another landmark in the struggle for equal rights for homosexuals. However, it was the Court's decision in *Lawrence* v. *Texas* (2003) that really put homosexual rights on the public agenda. In this case, the Court reversed its ruling in *Bowers* v. *Hardwick* by finding a Texas statute that banned sodomy to be unconstitutional. Writing for the majority, Justice Anthony Kennedy stated, "[homosexuals'] right to liberty under the due process clause gives them the full right to engage in their conduct without intervention of the government."[73]

In November 2003, the Massachusetts Supreme court further agreed, ruling that denying homosexuals the right to civil marriage was unconstitutional. Although the U.S. Supreme Court later refused to hear this case, many states rushed to add amendments to their constitutions denying the right to gay marriage, and in some states civil unions. In 2004, all eleven state ballot measures restricting gay marriage were adopted.

Participation

Civil Rights and Gay Adoption

Disabled Americans

Disabled Americans also have lobbied hard for antidiscrimination legislation. In the aftermath of World War II, many veterans returned to a nation unequipped to handle their disabilities. The Korean and Vietnam Wars made the problems of disabled veterans all the more clear. These disabled veterans saw the successes of African Americans, women, and other minorities, and they too began to lobby for greater protection against discrimination.[74] In 1990, in coalition with other disabled people, veterans finally were able to convince Congress to pass the Americans with Disabilities Act (ADA). The statute defines a disabled person as someone with a physical or mental impairment that limits one or more "life activities," or who has a record of such impairment. It thus extends the protections of the Civil Rights Act of 1964 to all of those with physical or mental disabilities. It guarantees access to public facilities, employment, and communication services. It also requires employers to acquire or modify work equipment, adjust work schedules, and make existing facilities accessible. This means, for example, that buildings must be accessible to those in wheelchairs, and telecommunications devices must be provided for deaf employees.

WEB EXPLORATION

For more about disability advocacy groups, see www.ablongman.com/oconnor

In 1999, the U.S. Supreme Court issued a series of four decisions redefining and significantly limiting the scope of the ADA. The cumulative impact of these decisions was to limit dramatically the number of people who can claim coverage under the act. Moreover, these cases "could profoundly affect individuals with a range of impairments—from diabetes and hypertension to severe nearsightedness and hearing loss—who are able to function in society with the help of medicines or aids but whose impairments may still make employers consider them ineligible for certain jobs."[75] Thus, pilots who need glasses to correct their vision cannot claim discrimination when employers fail to hire them because of their correctable vision.[76]

Simply changing the law, while often an important first step in achieving civil rights, is not the end of the process. Attitudes must also change. As history has shown, that can be a very long process and will be longer given the Court's decisions.

Former Senator Max Cleland (D–GA), a Vietnam War veteran, has been a vocal proponent of rights for those with disabilities. He knows first-hand the problems of noncompliance with the American with Disabilities Act. When he was first elected to the U.S. Senate, it took him several months to find housing to accommodate his wheelchair. He lost his 2002 reelection bid.

(Photo courtesy: Mary Ann Chestain/AP/Wide World Photos)

Continuity & Change

Race in America: Affirmative Action

When the Framers met in Philadelphia, they all recognized that the issue of slavery and how it was treated in the new Constitution could make or break their efforts to fashion a new nation and win acceptance in the southern states. In 1861, the Civil War was fought largely over the issue of slavery. And, after slavery was abolished, the southern states did everything in their power to limit opportunities for African Americans. Nearly one hundred years after the Civil War, *Brown* v. *Board of Education* (1954) and passage of the Civil Rights Act of 1964 went a long way toward remedying many onerous forms of discrimination.

Since the mid-1960s, racial tolerance has increased, although discrimination still exists. In 1997, 77 percent of those surveyed by the Gallup organization said they approved of interracial marriage and 93 percent said that they would vote for a black president.[77] Nevertheless, while most Americans agree that discrimination is wrong, most whites—57 percent—believe that **affirmative action** programs, policies designed to give special attention or compensatory treatment to members of a previously disadvantaged group, are no longer needed, although 86 percent thought that those programs were needed thirty years ago.[78]

affirmative action

Policies designed to give special attention or compensatory treatment to members of a previously disadvantaged group.

As early as 1871, Frederick Douglass ridiculed the idea of racial quotas, arguing that they would promote "an image of blacks as privileged wards of the state." They were "absurd as a matter of practice" because some could use them to argue that blacks "should constitute one-eighth of the poets, statesmen, scholars, authors and philosophers."[79]

The debate over affirmative action and equality of opportunity became particularly intense during the Reagan years in the aftermath of two major Supreme Court cases. In 1978, the Supreme Court for the first time addressed the issue of affirmative action in the case of Alan Bakke, a thirty-one-year-old paramedic, who was wait-listed for admission by the University of California at Davis. The Davis Medical School maintained two separate admissions committees—one for white students and another for minority students. Bakke was not admitted, although his grades and standardized test scores were higher than those of all of the African American students admitted to the school. In *Regents of the University of California* v. *Bakke* (1978), a sharply divided Court concluded that Bakke's rejection had been illegal because the use of strict quotas was inappropriate. The medical school, however, was free to "take race into account."[80]

In 1979, the Court ruled that a factory and a union could voluntarily adopt a quota system in selecting black workers over more senior white workers for a training pro-

gram. These kinds of programs outraged blue-collar Americans who had traditionally voted for the Democratic Party. In 1980, they abandoned the party in droves and supported Ronald Reagan, an ardent foe of affirmative action.

For a while, in spite of the addition of Justice Sandra Day O'Connor, the Court continued to uphold affirmative action plans, especially when there was clear-cut evidence of prior discrimination, although it was by 5–4 votes. In 1987, for example, the Court for the first time ruled that a public employer could use a voluntary plan to promote women even if there was no judicial finding of prior discrimination.[81]

In these affirmative action cases, the Reagan administration strongly urged the Court to invalidate the plans in question, but to no avail. With changes on the Court, however, including the 1986 elevation to chief justice of William H. Rehnquist, a strong opponent of affirmative action, the continued efforts of the Reagan administration finally began to pay off as the Court heard a new series of cases signaling an end to the advances in civil rights law. In a three-month period in 1989, the Supreme Court handed down five civil rights decisions limiting affirmative action programs and making it harder to prove employment discrimination.

In February 1990, Congress passed legislation designed to overrule the Court's rulings, but President George Bush vetoed it. In late 1991, however, Congress and the White House reached a compromise on a weaker version of the civil rights bill. The Civil Rights Act of 1991 overruled the Supreme Court rulings noted above but specifically prohibited the use of quotas.

The Supreme Court, however, has not stayed silent on the issue. In 1995, the Court ruled that all federal affirmative action programs based on racial classifications are "inherently suspect," virtually ending affirmative action programs.[82]

The next year, the Court refused to review a challenge to a lower court ruling that upheld the constitutionality of a University of Texas practice that prohibited giving a "plus" to minorities applying to its state law school.[83] Subsequently, the Texas legislature passed a Ten Percent Plan that guarantees all students who graduate in the top ten percent of any public high school are guaranteed college admission.

In 2003, the U.S. Supreme Court heard a pair of affirmative action cases from the University of Michigan and its law school. In deciding these cases, the court ruled that narrowly drawn affirmative action policies, such as those employed by Michigan, promoted an admirable goal of diversity and were therefore constitutional.

1. Is affirmative action now largely a thing of the past? Do you see a need for new civil rights legislation to protect minority populations in the United States?
2. Do you see the Supreme Court as a vehicle to seek expanded rights or one likely to be curtailing civil rights in the future?

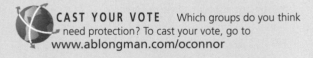

CAST YOUR VOTE   Which groups do you think need protection? To cast your vote, go to www.ablongman.com/oconnor

SUMMARY

While the Framers and other Americans basked in the glory of the newly adopted Constitution and Bill of Rights, their protections did not extend to all Americans. In this chapter, we have shown how rights have been expanded to ever-increasing segments of the population. To that end, we have made the following points:

1. **Slavery, Abolition, and Winning the Right to Vote, 1800–1890**
   When the Framers tried to compromise on the issue of slavery, they only postponed dealing with a volatile question that was later to rip the nation apart. Ultimately, the Civil War was fought to end slavery. Among its results were the triumph of the abolitionist position and adoption of the Thirteenth, Fourteenth, and Fifteenth Amendments. During this period, women also sought expanded rights, especially the right to vote, but to no avail.

2. **The Push for Equality, 1890–1954**
   Although the Civil War Amendments were added to the Constitution, the Supreme Court limited their application. As Jim Crow laws were passed throughout the South, the NAACP was founded in the early 1900s to press for equal rights for African Americans. Women's groups also were active during this period, successfully lobbying for passage of the Nineteenth Amendment, which assured them the right to vote.

   Women's groups such as the National Consumers' League (NCL), and then others, including NOW, began to view litigation as a means to their ends. The NCL was forced to go to court to argue for the constitutionality of legislation protecting women workers; in contrast, NOW and other groups sought the Court's help in securing equality under the Constitution.

3. The Civil Rights Movement

In 1954, the U.S. Supreme Court ruled in *Brown* v. *Board of Education* that state-segregated school systems were unconstitutional. This victory empowered African Americans as they sought an end to other forms of pervasive discrimination. Bus boycotts, sit-ins, freedom rides, pressure for voting rights, and massive nonviolent demonstrations became common tactics. This activity culminated in the passage of the Civil Rights Act of 1964 and the Voting Rights Act of 1965. These acts gave African American and women's rights groups two potential weapons in their legal arsenals: They could attack private discrimination under the Civil Rights Act, or state-sanctioned discrimination under the equal protection clause of the Fourteenth Amendment. Over the years, the Supreme Court developed different tests to determine the constitutionality of various forms of discrimination. In general, strict scrutiny, the most stringent standard, was applied to race-based claims. An intermediate standard of review was developed to assess the constitutionality of sex discrimination claims.

4. Other Groups Mobilize for Rights

Building on the successes of African Americans and women, other groups, including Hispanic Americans, Native Americans, gays and lesbians, and the disabled, organized to litigate for expanded civil rights as well as to lobby for antidiscrimination laws.

KEY TERMS

affirmative action, p. 216
Black Codes, p. 185
Brown v. *Board of Education* (1954), p. 193
civil rights, p. 182
Civil Rights Act of 1964, p. 198
Civil Rights Cases (1883), p. 187
de facto discrimination, p. 200
de jure discrimination, p. 199
Equal Employment Opportunity Commission, p. 201
equal protection clause, p. 193
Equal Rights Amendment, p. 202
Fifteenth Amendment, p. 186
Fourteenth Amendment, p. 186
grandfather clause, p. 188
Jim Crow laws, p. 187
Ninteenth Amendment, p. 191
Plessy v. *Ferguson* (1896), p. 188
strict scrutiny, p. 203
suffrage movement, p. 191
suspect classification, p. 203
Thirteenth Amendment, p. 185
Title IX, p. 205

SELECTED READINGS

Bacchi, Carol Lee. *The Politics of Affirmative Action: 'Women,' Equality and Category Politics*. Thousand Oaks, CA: Sage, 1996.

Bergmann, Barbara R. *In Defense of Affirmative Action*. New York: Basic Books, 1996.

Bullock, Charles, III, and Charles Lamb, eds. *Implementation of Civil Rights Policy*. Pacific Grove, CA: Brooks/Cole, 1984.

Eastland, Terry. *Ending Affirmative Action: The Case for Colorblind Justice*. New York: Basic Books, 1997.

Freeman, Jo. *The Politics of Women's Liberation*. New York: Longman, 1975.

Guinier, Lani. *Who's Qualified?* Boston: Beacon Press, 2001.

Kluger, Richard. *Simple Justice*. New York: Vintage, 1975.

Knobel, Dale T. *'America for the Americans': The Nativist Movement in the United States*. Old Tappan, NJ: Twayne, 1996.

Mansbridge, Jane J. *Why We Lost the ERA*. Chicago: University of Chicago Press, 1986.

McClain, Paula D., and Joseph Stewart Jr. *"Can We All Get Along?" Racial and Ethnic Minorities in American Politics*, 3rd ed. Boulder, CO: Westview Press, 2001.

McGlen, Nancy E., et al. *Women, Politics, and American Society*, 3rd ed. New York: Longman, 2002.

Nobles, Melissa. *Shades of Citizenship: Race and the Census in Modern America*. Palo Alto, CA: Stanford University Press, 2000.

Reed, Adolph, Jr. *Without Justice for All: The New Liberalism and Our Retreat from Racial Equity*. Boulder, CO: Westview Press, 1999.

Rodriguez, Clara E. *Changing Race: Latinos, the Census, and the History of Ethnicity in the United States*. New York: New York University Press, 2000.

Rosales, Francisco A., and Arturo Rosales, eds. *Chicano! The History of the Mexican American Civil Rights Movement*. Houston, TX: Arte Publico Press, 1996.

Verba, Sidney, and Gary R. Orren. *Equality in America: The View from the Top*. Cambridge, MA: Harvard University Press, 1985.

Williams, Juan. *Eyes on the Prize: America's Civil Rights Years, 1954–1965*. New York: Penguin, 1987.

Wilson, William Julius. *The Bridge over the Racial Divide: Rising Inequality and Coalition Politics*. Berkeley: University of California Press, 1999.

NOTES

1. Michael Cooper, "Officers in Bronx Fire 41 Shots, and an Unarmed Man Is Killed," *New York Times* (February 5, 1999): A1.
2. Amy Wilentz, "New York: The Price of Safety in a Police State," *Los Angeles Times* (April 11, 1999): M1.
3. N. R. Kleinfield, "Veterans of 60's Protests Meet the Newly Outraged in a March," *New York Times* (April 16, 1999): B8.
4. Ibid.
5. Jessica Lee, "Women Speak to House About Unwarranted Customs Strip-Searches," *USA Today* (May 21, 1999): 10A.
6. Edward Walsh, "The Racial Issue Looming in the Rear-View Mirror," *Washington Post* (May 19, 1999): A3; and Ralph Siegel, "Turnpike Arrest Cases Explore Use of Racial Profiling Defenses," *Record* (May 12, 1999): A3.
7. Judith Evans, "Suit Claims Race Bias at Fla. Hotel," *Washington Post* (May 21, 1999): A1.

8. Catherine Drinker Bowen, *Miracle at Philadelphia: The Story of the Constitutional Convention May to September 1787* (Boston: Little, Brown, 1986), 201.
9. 83 U.S. 36 (1873).
10. 83 U.S. 130 (1873).
11. 88 U.S. 162 (1875). See also Karen O'Connor, *Women's Organizations' Use of the Courts* (Lexington, MA: Lexington Books, 1980).
12. *Saenz* v. *Roe*, 526 U.S. 471 (1999).
13. 109 U.S. 3 (1883).
14. 163 U.S. 537 (1896).
15. Jack Greenburg, *Judicial Process and Social Change: Constitutional Litigation* (St. Paul, MN: West, 1976), 583–86.
16. *Williams* v. *Mississippi*, 170 U.S. 213 (1898).
17. *Cummins* v. *Richmond County Board of Education*, 175 U.S. 528 (1899).
18. Juan Williams, *Eyes on the Prize: America's Civil Rights Years, 1954–1965* (New York: Penguin, 1987), 10.
19. 208 U.S. 412 (1908).
20. *Missouri* ex rel. *Gaines* v. *Canada*, 305 U.S. 337 (1938).
21. Richard Kluger, *Simple Justice* (New York: Vintage, 1975), 268.
22. *Sweatt* v. *Painter*, 339 U.S. 629 (1950), and *McLaurin* v. *Oklahoma*, 339 U.S. 637 (1950).
23. 347 U.S. 483 (1954).
24. But see Gerald Rosenberg, *Hollow Hope: Can Courts Bring About Social Change* (Chicago: University of Chicago Press, 1991).
25. Quoted in Williams, *Eyes on the Prize*, 10.
26. 349 U.S. 294 (1955).
27. Quoted in Williams, *Eyes on the Prize*, 37.
28. *Cooper* v. *Aaron*, 358 U.S. 1 (1958).
29. *Heart of Atlanta Motel* v. *U.S.*, 379 U.S. 241 (1964).
30. 402 U.S. 1 (1971).
31. *Freeman* v. *Pitts*, 498 U.S. 1081 (1992); *Missouri* v. *Jenkins*, 515 U.S. 70 (1995).
32. Gary Orfield, "Turning Back to Segregation" in Gary Orfield, S. Eaton and the Harvard Project on Desegregation, eds. *Dismantling Desegregation* (New York: The New Press, 1996).
33. *Belk* v. *Charlotte-Mecklenburg Board of Education*, 122 S. Ct. 1538 (2002), 269 F.3d 305 (cert. denied).
34. *Griggs* v. *Duke Power Co.*, 401 U.S. 424 (1971).
35. Jo Freeman, *The Politics of Women's Liberation* (New York: Longman, 1975), 57.
36. 368 U.S. 57 (1961).
37. Betty Friedan, *The Feminine Mystique* (New York: Dell, 1963).
38. 323 U.S. 214 (1944). This is the only case involving race-based distinctions applying the strict scrutiny standard where the Court has upheld the restrictive law.
39. 404 U.S. 71 (1971).
40. 429 U.S. 190 (1976).
41. *Mississippi University for Women* v. *Hogan*, 458 U.S. 718 (1982).
42. *Craig* v. *Boren*, 429 U.S. 190 (1976).
43. *Orr* v. *Orr*, 440 U.S. 268 (1979).
44. *JEB* v. *Alabama* ex rel. *TB*, 440 U.S. 268 (1979).
45. *U.S.* v. *Virginia*, 518 U.S. 515 (1996).
46. *Rostker* v. *Goldberg*, 453 U.S. 57 (1981).
47. *Michael M.* v. *Superior Court of Sonoma County*, 450 U.S. 464 (1981).
48. *Rostker* v. *Goldberg*, 453 U.S. 57 (1981).
49. *Meritor Savings Bank* v. *Vinson*, 477 U.S. 57 (1986).
50. *Oncale* v. *Sundowner Offshore Services, Inc.*, 523 U.S. 75 (1998).
51. *Hishon* v. *King & Spalding*, 467 U.S. 69 (1984).
52. *Johnson* v. *Transportation Agency*, 480 U.S. 616 (1987).
53. Joyce Gelb and Marian Lief Palley, *Women and Public Policies* (Charlottesville: University of Virginia Press, 1996).
54. Ernesto B. Virgil, *The Crusade for Justice* (Madison: University of Wisconsin Press, 1999).
55. F. Chris Garcia, *Latinos and the Political System* (Notre Dame, IN: University of Notre Dame Press, 1988), 1.
56. *White* v. *Register*, 412 U.S. 755 (1973).
57. *San Antonio Independent School District* v. *Rodriguez*, 411 U.S. 1 (1973).
58. *Plyler* v. *Doe*, 457 U.S. 202 (1982).
59. *Edgewood Independent School District* v. *Kirby*, 777 SW.2d 391.
60. Rennard Strickland, "Native Americans," in Kermit Hall, ed., *The Oxford Companion to the Supreme Court of the United States* (New York: Oxford University Press, 1992), 557.
61. Dee Brown, *Bury My Heart at Wounded Knee* (New York: Holt, Rinehart and Winston, 1971).
62. Strickland, "Native Americans," 579.
63. Hugh Dellios, "Rites by Law: Indians Seek Sacred Lands," *Chicago Tribune* (July 4, 1993): C1.
64. *Employment Division of the Oregon Department of Human Resources* v. *Smith*, 494 U.S. 872 (1990).
65. *Boerne* v. *Flores*, 521 U.S. 507 (1997).
66. *Cobell* v. *Norton*, 204 F.3d 1081 (2001). For more on the Indian trust, see http://www.indiantrust.com/overview.cfm.
67. Diane Helene Miller, *Freedom to Differ: The Shaping of the Gay and Lesbian Struggle for Civil Rights* (New York: New York University Press, 1998).
68. Sarah Brewer, David Kaib, and Karen O'Connor, "Sex and the Supreme Court: Gays, Lesbians, and Justice," in Craig A. Rimmerman, Kenneth D. Wald, and Clyde Wilcox, *The Politics of Gay Rights* (Chicago: University of Chicago Press, 2000).
69. Evan Gerstmann, *The Constitutional Underclass: Gays, Lesbians, and the Failure of Class-Based Equal Protection* (Chicago: University of Chicago Press, 1999).
70. 478 U.S. 186 (1986).
71. Deborah Ensor, Gay Veterans Working for Change," *San Diego Union* (April 13, 2002): B1.
72. *Romer* v. *Evans*, 517 U.S. 620 (1996).
73. *Lawrence* v. *Texas*, 539 U.S. 558 (2003).
74. David Pfeiffer, "Overview of the Disability Movement: History, Legislative Record and Political Implications," *Policy Studies Journal* (Winter 1993): 724–42; and "Understanding Disability Policy," *Policy Studies Journal* (Spring 1996): 157–74.
75. Joan Biskupic, "Supreme Court Limits Meaning of Disability," *Washington Post* (June 23, 1999): A1.
76. *Sutton* v. *United Air Lines, Inc.*, 527 U.S. 471 (1999).
77. "Poll: Whites, Blacks Differ on Quality of Race Relations," June 17, 1997. CNN Interactive (http://cnn.com/US/9706/10/gallup.poll/index.html).
78. *United Steelworkers of America* v. *Weber*, 444 U.S. 889 (1979).
79. Frederick Douglass, *Frederick Douglass: Autobiography* (New York: Library of America, 1994), 28.
80. 438 U.S. 186 (1986).
81. *Johnson* v. *Santa Clara County*, 480 U.S. 616 (1987).
82. *Adarand Constructors* v. *Pena*, 515 U.S. 200 (1995).
83. *Texas* v. *Hopwood*, 518 U.S. 1033 (1996) (cert. denied). See also Terrance Stutz, "UT Minority Enrollment Tested by Suit: Fate of Affirmative Action in Education Is at Issue," *Dallas Morning News* (October 14, 1995).
84. *Grutter* v. *Bollinger*, 539 U.S. 306 (2003) and *Gratz* v. *Bollinger*, 539 U.S. 244 (2003).

Congress

On February 6, 2002, Congresswoman Nancy Pelosi (D–CA) broke through a glass ceiling when she was sworn in as the Democratic House whip, becoming the first woman in history to win an elected position in the formal house leadership. It is a position viewed as a stepping stone to becoming the speaker of the House. Both House Speakers Tip O'Neill and Newt Gingrich were former whips. As whip, it became the eight-term Pelosi's responsibility to convince Democratic members of the House to vote together on the full range of bills that came before the 107th Congress.

First elected to Congress from California in 1986, Pelosi quickly made her mark as an advocate for human rights in China and as an effective fund-raiser. Her fund-raising skills and years of experience in the House, in fact, helped her win the hotly contested race for the whip position. As part of the House leadership, she became the first woman to attend critical White House meetings, where, said Pelosi, "Susan B. Anthony and others are with me."

Although the president's party traditionally loses seats in midterm elections, in 2002 House Republicans actually increased their majority. Critics charged that the Democrats lacked a consistent message. Many noted that while House Minority Leader Richard Gephardt (D–MO) voted to support a resolution authorizing the president to use force against Iraq absent approval from the United Nations, Pelosi, as whip, voted in the negative on the highly publicized resolution.

Soon after the election results were in, Gephardt resigned his position, leaving Pelosi in line to succeed him. Representative Harold Ford (D–TN), one of the youngest members of the House, threw his hat into the ring to oppose Pelosi's campaign for the leader's position. Ford, a moderate, charged that Pelosi, who already was being referred to by conservatives as a "San Francisco liberal," was simply too liberal to lead the Democrats back to political viability in the 2004 elections. A majority of the members of the Democratic House Caucus, however, did not appear fazed by these charges. Pelosi was elected the minority leader by an overwhelming majority of the Caucus members. Steny Hoyer (D–MD), who initially had run against Pelosi for the whip position in the 107th Congress, was elected Democratic whip in the 108th Congress.

The election of Pelosi sharply altered the look of power in the House of Representatives. As the leader of all House Democrats, Pelosi automatically is accorded tremendous respect, as well as media attention as the "face" of Democrats in the House. Thus, more than 150 years after woman first sought the right to vote, a woman member of Congress now leads one party in the House of Representatives.

In the Senate, although no women hold top leadership positions, Kay Bailey Hutchison (R–TX) is the Republican Conference Vice-Chair and Susan Collins (R–ME) and Olympia Snowe (R–ME) both chair Senate committees. The representation of women in both Houses of the Congress has come a long way but still has years to go before women and men reach equal proportions in the number of power positions they hold. As more women accrue the seniority that allows them to chair committees, and to join Pelosi as leaders in their respective chambers and parties, more women will be encouraged to consider running for office themselves. Pelosi, in the vanguard, hopes to foster the election of women to more leadership positions, where she, and others, believe women bring a different perspective to the table.

s each congressional representative pursues what appears to be his or her individually rational incentives to act on behalf of their constituents, their actions can create centrifugal pressures that undermine Congress's collective capacity to get things done. Over the past three decades, changes inside and outside Congress have enhanced the ability of congressional representatives to be somewhat more individualistic than in the past; this arguably has weakened the institution's collective capacities even more. Is it any wonder that, before the 1994 midterm elections, public confidence in Congress was at only 8 percent? Although by January 2004, 46 percent of the public voiced approval about the way Congress was doing its job, in general, feelings about Congress as a whole are usually lower than the public's general high support for their individual representatives. Various polls find that as many as 64 percent approve of the way their own representative is handling his or her job (see Analyzing Visuals: Approval Ratings of Congress and District Representatives). Even more significant, the rate at which incumbents are reelected to the House continues to exceed 99 percent, despite the chamber's poor general standing with the public.

Part of the public's strange split on these issues may stem from the dual roles that Congress plays—its members must combine and balance their roles as law and policy makers with their role as representatives, for their district, their state, their party, and sometimes even their race, ethnicity, or gender, as our opening vignette highlights. Not surprisingly, this balancing act often results in role conflict. Moreover, recent studies by political scientists reveal many citizens hold Congress to very high standards, which contributes to negative perceptions of the body as a whole.[4] Increased media negativity, which tends to focus on the foibles of individual members, doesn't help either.[5]

In this chapter, we analyze the powers of Congress and the competing roles members of Congress play as they represent the interests of their constituents, make laws, and oversee the actions of the other two branches of government. We also see that, as these functions have changed throughout U.S. history, so has Congress itself.

WEB EXPLORATION
To find out who your representative is and how he or she votes, see www.ablongman.com/oconnor

- First, we will look at the *roots of the legislative branch* to better understand its place today.

- Second, we will examine what the *Constitution* has to say about Congress—*the legislative branch of government.*

- Third, we will look at the *members of Congress*, including how members get elected, and how they spend their days.

- Fourth, we will describe *how Congress is organized.* We compare the two chambers and how their differences affect the course of legislation.

- Fifth, we will outline the *law-making function of Congress.*

- Sixth, we will examine the various factors that influence *how members of Congress make decisions.*

- Seventh, we will discuss the ever-changing relationship between *Congress and the president.*

- In our examination of the theme of *continuity and change* in American politics, we will explore how members of Congress over time have faced increasing difficulty connecting with their constituents, while many segments of society continue to be underrepresented.

THE ROOTS OF THE LEGISLATIVE BRANCH

As discussed in chapter 2, Congress's powers evolved from Americans' experiences in the colonies and under the Articles of Confederation. When the colonists came to the New World, their general approval of Britain's parliamentary system led them to adopt similar two-house legislative bodies in the individual colonies. One house was directly elected by the people; the other was a Crown-appointed council that worked under the authority of the colonial government.

The colonial assemblies originally were established as advisory bodies to the royal governors appointed by the king. Gradually, however, they assumed more power and authority in each colony, particularly over taxation and spending. The assemblies also legislated on religious issues and established quality standards for such colonial goods as flour, rice, tobacco, and rum. Before the American Revolution, colonists turned to their colonial legislatures (the only bodies elected directly by the "people") to represent and defend their interests against British infringement.

The first truly national legislature in the colonies, the First Continental Congress, met in Philadelphia in 1774 to develop a common colonial response to the Coercive Acts. All of the colonies except Georgia sent a representative. Even though this Congress had no power to force compliance with its actions, it organized an economic boycott of British goods and advised each colony to establish a militia, among other things.

By the time the Second Continental Congress met in Philadelphia in May 1775, fighting had broken out at Lexington and Concord. The Congress quickly helped the now united colonies gear up for war, raise an army, and officially adopt the Declaration of Independence. During the next five years, the Congress directed the war effort and administered a central government. But, it did so with little money or stability; because of the war, it had to move from city to city.

Although the Articles of Confederation were drafted and adopted by the Second Continental Congress in 1777, the states did not ratify them until 1781. Still, throughout the Revolutionary War, the Congress exercised the powers the Articles granted it including the powers to declare war, raise an army, make treaties with foreign nations, and coin money. As described in chapter 2, however, the Congress had no independent sources of income; it had to depend on the states for money and supplies.

After the war, the states began to act once again as if they were separate nations rather than parts of one nation, despite the national government that was created under the Articles of Confederation. Discontent with the Articles and the government they created quickly grew, and ultimately led to the Constitutional Convention in Philadelphia in 1787.

THE CONSTITUTION AND THE LEGISLATIVE BRANCH OF GOVERNMENT

Article I of the Constitution created the legislative branch of government we know today. Any two-house legislature, such as the one created by the Framers, is called a **bicameral legislature.** All states except Nebraska, which has a one-house or *unicameral legislature*, follow this model. As discussed in chapter 2, the Great Compromise at the Constitutional Convention resulted in the creation of an upper house, the Senate, and a lower house, the House of Representatives. Each state is represented in the Senate by two senators,

bicameral legislature
A legislature divided into two houses; the U.S. Congress and the state legislatures are bicameral except Nebraska, which is unicameral.

regardless of the state's population. The number of representatives each state sends to the House of Representatives, in contrast, is determined by that state's population.

The U.S. Constitution sets out the formal, or legal, requirements for membership in the House and Senate. House members must be at least twenty-five years of age; senators, thirty. Members of the House must have resided in the United States for at least seven years; those elected to the Senate, nine. Representatives and senators must be legal residents of the states from which they are elected.

Members of each body were to be elected differently and thus would represent different interests and constituencies. Senators were to be elected to six-year terms by state legislatures. One-third of them would be up for reelection every two years. Senators were to be tied closely to their state legislatures and were expected to represent their states' interests in the Senate. State legislators lost this influence with ratification of the Seventeenth Amendment in 1913, which provides for the direct election of senators by the voters.

In contrast to senators' six-year terms, members of the House of Representatives were to be elected to two-year terms by a vote of the eligible voters in each congressional district. It was expected that the House would be the more "democratic" branch of government because its members would be more responsible to the people (because they were elected directly by them) and more responsive to them (because they were up for reelection every two years).

WEB EXPLORATION
To see more about the legislative branch, see
www.ablongman.com/oconnor

Apportionment and Redistricting

The U.S. Constitution requires that a census, which entails the counting of all Americans, be conducted every ten years. Until the first census could be taken, the Constitution fixed the number of representatives in the House of Representatives at sixty-five. In 1790, then, one member represented 37,000 people. As the population of the new nation grew and states were added to the Union, the House became larger and larger. In 1910, it expanded to 435 members, and in 1929, its size was fixed at that number by statute.

Because the Constitution requires that representation in the House of Representatives be based on state population, congressional districts must be redrawn by state legislatures to reflect population shifts, so that each member in Congress represents approximately the same number of residents. This process of redrawing congressional districts to reflect increases or decreases in seats allotted to the states, as well as population shifts within a state, is called **redistricting**, which every ten years means that some states gain representatives at the expense of others. The effects of redistricting, which played an important role in the 2002 elections and then again in 2004 after Texas re-districted its congressional districts, are discussed in chapter 13.

redistricting
The redrawing of congressional districts to reflect increases or decreases in seats allotted to the states, as well as population shifts within a state.

Constitutional Powers of Congress

The Constitution specifically gives to Congress its most important power—the authority to make laws. (See Table 7.1: The Powers of Congress.) This law-making power is shared by both houses. For example, no **bill** (proposed law) can become law without the consent of both houses. Examples of other constitutionally shared powers include the power to declare war, raise an army and navy, coin money, regulate commerce, establish the federal courts and their jurisdiction, establish rules of immigration and naturalization, and "make all Laws which shall be necessary and proper for carrying into Execution the foregoing Powers." As interpreted by the Supreme Court, the necessary and proper clause, found at the end of Article I, section 8, when coupled with one or more of the specific powers enumerated in Article I, section 8, has allowed Congress to increase the scope of its authority, often at the expense of the states and into areas not necessarily envisioned by the Framers.

bill
A proposed law.

Congress alone is given formal law-making powers in the Constitution, but it is important to remember that presidents issue proclamations and executive orders with the force of law (see chapter 8), bureaucrats issue quasi-legislative rules (see chapter 9), and the Supreme Court and lower federal courts render opinions that generate principles that also have the force of law (see chapter 10).

TABLE 7.1 The Powers of Congress

The powers of Congress, found in Article I, section 8, of the Constitution, include the power to:

- Lay and collect taxes and duties
- Borrow money
- Regulate commerce with foreign nations and among the states
- Establish rules for naturalization (that is, the process of becoming a citizen) and bankruptcy
- Coin money, set its value, and fix the standard of weights and measures
- Punish counterfeiting
- Establish a post office and post roads
- Issue patents and copyrights
- Define and punish piracies, felonies on the high seas, and crimes against the law of nations
- Create courts inferior to (that is, below) the Supreme Court
- Declare war
- Raise and support an army and navy and make rules for their governance
- Provide for a militia (reserving to the states the right to appoint militia officers and to train the militia under congressional rules)
- Exercise legislative powers over the seat of government (the District of Columbia) and over places purchased to be federal facilities (forts, arsenals, dock-yards, and "other needful buildings")
- "Make all Laws which shall be necessary and proper for carrying into Execution the foregoing Powers, and all other Powers vested by this Constitution in the government of the United States" (Note: This "necessary and proper," or "elastic," clause has been interpreted expansively by the Supreme Court, as explained in chapter 2.)

Reflecting the different constituencies and size of each house of Congress (as well as the Framers' intentions), Article I gives special, exclusive powers to each house in addition to their shared role in law-making. For example, as noted in Table 7.2, the Constitution specifies that all revenue bills must originate in the House of Representatives. Over the years, however, this mandate has been blurred, and it is not unusual to see budget bills being considered simultaneously in both houses, especially since each must approve all bills in the end, whether or not they involve revenues. In 1995, for example, when President Clinton submitted his budget deficit reduction plan, both houses deliberated similar proposals simultaneously.

The House also has the power to impeach, the authority to charge the president, vice president, or other "civil officers," including federal judges, with "Treason, Bribery, or other high Crimes and Misdemeanors." Only the Senate is authorized to conduct

Representative Henry Hyde (R–IL) chaired the House Judiciary Committee as it conducted impeachment hearings involving President Bill Clinton. Later, Hyde managed the case against Clinton in the Senate. Because committee chairs no longer can serve more than three terms, Hyde now chairs the House International Relations Committee.

(Photo courtesy: Brad Markel/Getty Source)

TABLE 7.2   Key Differences Between the House and Senate

Constitutional Differences

House	Senate
Initiates all revenue bills	Offers "advice and consent" on many major presidential appointments
Initiates impeachment procedures and passes articles of impeachment	Tries impeached officials
Two-year terms	Six-year terms (one-third up for reelection every two years)
435 members (apportioned by population)	100 members (two from each state)
	Approves treaties

Differences in Operation

House	Senate
More centralized, more formal; stronger leadership	Less centralized, less formal; weaker leadership
Rules Committee fairly powerful in controlling time and rules of debate (in conjunction with the speaker)	No Rules Committee; limits on debate come through unanimous consent or cloture of filibuster
More impersonal	More personal
Power distributed less evenly	Power distributed more evenly
Members are highly specialized	Members are generalists
Emphasizes tax and revenue policy	Emphasizes foreign policy

Changes in the Institution

House	Senate
Power centralized in the speaker's inner circle of advisers	Senate workload increasing and informality breaking down; threat of filibusters more frequent than in the past
House procedures are becoming more efficient	Becoming more difficult to pass legislation
Turnover is relatively high, although those seeking reelection almost always win	Turnover is moderate

impeachment
The power delegated to the House of Representatives in the Constitution to charge the president, vice president, or other "civil officers," including federal judges, with "Treason, Bribery, or other high Crimes and Misdemeanors." This is the first step in the constitutional process of removing such government officials from office.

trials of **impeachment,** with a two-thirds vote being necessary before a federal official can be removed from office. Only two presidents, Andrew Johnson in 1868 and Bill Clinton in 1998, were impeached by the House. Both were acquitted by the full Senate. President Richard M. Nixon resigned from office in 1974 after the House Judiciary Committee voted to impeach him for his role in the Watergate scandal.

The House and Senate share in the impeachment process, but the Senate has the sole authority to approve major presidential appointments, including federal judges, ambassadors, and Cabinet- and sub-Cabinet-level positions. The Senate, too, must approve by a two-thirds vote all treaties entered into by the president. Failure by the president to court the Senate can be costly. At the end of World War I, for example, President Woodrow Wilson worked hard to get other nations to accept the Treaty of Versailles, which contained the charter of the proposed League of Nations. He overestimated his support in the Senate, however. That body refused to ratify the treaty, dealing Wilson and his international stature a severe setback.

THE MEMBERS OF CONGRESS

Today, many members of Congress find the job exciting in spite of public criticism of the institution. But, it wasn't always so. Until Washington, D.C. got air-conditioning and drained its swamps, it was a miserable town. Most representatives spent as little time as possible there, viewing the Congress, especially the House, as a stepping stone to other political positions back home. It was only after World War I that House members became "congressional careerists" who viewed their work in Washington as long term.[6]

Many members of Congress clearly relish their work, although there are indications that the high cost of living in Washington and maintaining two homes, political scandals, intense media scrutiny, the need to tackle hard issues, and a growth of partisan dissension is taking a toll on many members. Those no longer in the majority, in particular, often don't see their service in Congress as satisfying.

Members must attempt to appease two constituencies—party leaders, colleagues, and lobbyists in Washington, D.C., and constituents at home. As revealed in Table 7.3, members spend full days at home as well as in D.C. According to one study of House members in nonelection years, average representatives made thirty-five trips back home to their districts and spent an average 138 days a year there.[7] Hedrick Smith, a Pulitzer Prize–winning reporter for the *New York Times*, has aptly described a member's days as a "kaleidoscopic jumble: breakfast with reporters, morning staff meetings, simultaneous committee hearings to juggle, back-to-back sessions with lobbyists and constituents, phone calls, briefings, constant buzzers interrupting office work to make quorum calls and votes on the run, afternoon speeches, evening meetings, receptions, fund-raisers, all crammed into four days so they can race home for a weekend gauntlet of campaigning. It's a rat race."[8]

TABLE 7.3   A Day in the Life of a Member of Congress

Typical Member's At-Home Schedule[a]			Typical Member's Washington Schedule[b]	
Monday			**Tuesday**	
7:30 A.M.	Business group breakfast, 20 leaders of the business community leaders	(1 hour)	8:30 A.M.	Breakfast with former member
8:45 A.M.	Hoover Elementary School, 6th grade class assembly	(45 min)	9:30 A.M.	Committee on Science, Space, and Technology hearing on research and development in the 1990s
9:45 A.M.	National Agriculture Day speech, Holiday Inn South	(45 min)	10:00 A.M.	Briefing by FAA officials for members of Congress who represent families of victims of Pan Am Flight #103
10:45 A.M.	Supplemental Food Shelf, pass foodstuffs to needy families	(1 hour)	10:00 A.M.	Energy and Commerce Committee mark-up session on Fairness in Broadcasting
12:00 noon	Community College, student/faculty lunch, speech and Q & A	(45 min)	12:00 noon	Reception/photo opportunity with telecommunications officials
1:00 P.M.	Sunset Terrace Elementary School, assembly 4th, 5th, 6th graders, remarks/Q & A	(45 min)	12:00 noon	House convenes
(Travel Time: 1:45 P.M.–2:45 P.M.)			12:00 noon	Lunch with personal friend at Watergate Hotel
2:45 P.M.	Plainview Day Care facility owner wishes to discuss changes in federal law	(1 hour)	1:30 P.M.	Subcommittee on Science Space Applications hearing
4:00 P.M.	Town Hall Meeting, American Legion	(1 hour)	1:30 P.M.	Subcommittee on Health and Environment mark-up session on Trauma Care Systems Planning Act
(Travel Time: 5:00 P.M.–5:45 P.M.)			3:00 P.M.	Meeting with officials of the National Alliance for Animal Legislation
5:45 P.M.	PTA meeting, speech, education issues before Congress (also citizen involvement with national associations)	(45 min)	4:30 P.M.	Meeting with delegates from American Jewish Congress on foreign aid bill
6:30 P.M.	Annual Dinner, St. John's Lutheran Church Developmental Activity Center	(30 min)	5:00 P.M.	New York University reception
7:15 P.M.	Association for Children for Enforcement of Support meeting to discuss problems of enforcing child support payments	(45 min)	5:00 P.M.	Briefing by the commissioner of the Bureau of Labor (statistics on the uninsured)
(Travel Time: 8:00 P.M.–8:30 P.M.)			5:30 P.M.	Reception/fund-raiser for party whip
8:30 P.M.	Students Against Drunk Driving (SADD) meeting, speech, address; drinking age, drunk driving, uniform federal penalties	(45 min)	6:00 P.M.	Reception/fund-raiser for fellow member
			6:00 P.M.	"Cajun" reception/fund-raiser for Louisiana member
9:30 P.M.	State University class, discuss business issues before Congress	(1 hour)	6:00 P.M.	Winetasting reception by New York wine industry

[a]Craig Shultz, ed., *Setting Course: A Congressional Management Guide* (Washington, DC: American University, 1994), 335.
[b]http://congress.indiana.edu/learn_about/schedule.htm.

casework
The process of solving constituents' problems dealing with the bureaucracy.

How do senators and representatives accomplish all that they must and also satisfy their constituents? They send newsletters to stay in touch, hold town meetings throughout their districts, and get important help from their staffs. **Casework,** although rarely indulged in by legislators themselves, is a major responsibility for selected staff members called caseworkers and the many student interns who assist them. Veterans who believe that they are getting the runaround at Veterans Administration hospitals or retirees who experience delays in receiving Social Security checks, for example, often seek help from their representatives.

Increasingly, senators and representatives are placing most of their caseworkers back in their home district offices, where they are more accessible to constituents who can drop by and talk to a friendly face about their problems. In larger districts, caseworkers may "ride the circuit," taking the helping hand of the congressional office to county seats, crossroads, post offices, and mobile offices. The average House member has seventeen full-time staff members; the average size of a senator's office staff is forty-four, although this number varies with state population.[9]

Running for Office and Staying in Office

Visual Literacy

Why Is It So Hard to Defeat an Incumbent?

Despite the long hours, hard work, and sometimes even abuse that senators and representatives experience, thousands aspire to these jobs every year. Yet, only 535 men and women actually serve as voting members of the U.S. Congress. Membership in one of the two major political parties is almost always a prerequisite for election, because election laws in various states often discriminate against independents (those without party affiliation) and minor-party candidates. As discussed in chapter 14, money is the mother's milk of politics—the ability to raise money often is key to any member's victory, and many members spend nearly all of their "free" time on the phone dialing for dollars.

incumbency factor
The fact that being in office helps a person stay in office because of a variety of benefits that go with the position.

The **incumbency factor** helps members to stay in office once they are elected. Simply put, being in office helps you stay in office.[10] It's often very difficult for outsiders to win because they don't have the advantages (enumerated in Table 7.4) enjoyed by incumbents, including name recognition, access to free media, and the inside track on fund-raising. As illustrated in Analyzing Visuals: Approval Ratings of Congress and District Representatives, which compares the way poll respondents feel about their own representatives to how they feel about Congress as an institution, most Americans approve of their own members of Congress.

It is not surprising, then, that from 1980 to 1990, an average of 95 percent of the incumbents who sought reelection won their primary and general election races.[11] More

---

TABLE 7.4   The Advantages of Incumbency

- Name recognition gained through previous campaigns and repeated visits to the district to make appearances at various public events.
- Credit claiming for bringing federal money into the district in the form of grants and contracts.
- Positive evaluations from constituents earned by doing favors (casework) such as helping cut red tape and tracking down federal aid, and tasks handled by publicly supported professional staff members.
- Distribution of newsletters and other noncampaign materials free through the mails by using the "frank" (an envelope that contains the legislator's signature in place of a stamp).
- Access to media—incumbents are news makers who provide reporters with tips and quotes.
- Greater ease in fund-raising—their high reelection rates make them a good bet for people or groups willing to give campaign contributions in hopes of having access to powerful decision makers.
- Experience in running a campaign, putting together a campaign staff, making speeches, understanding constituent concerns, and connecting with people.
- Superior knowledge about a wide range of issues gained through work on committees, review of legislation, and previous campaigns.
- A record for supporting locally popular policy positions.
- Congressional district drawn to maximize their chances of re-election.

ANALYZING VISUALS

Approval Ratings of Congress and District Representatives

For many years, political scientists have noted that approval ratings of Congress as an institution are generally quite low, rarely exceeding 50 percent approval. On the other hand, the public's approval rating of its own member tends to be much higher, usually above 50 percent. The line graph below demonstrates the discrepancy between these ratings since 1990. After studying the graph and the material in this chapter on the incumbency factor, answer the following critical thinking questions: Do the data for approval of Congress and approval of one's own representative follow similar trends over the period covered in the figure? What factors do you think account for the differences in the ratings of Congress and of one's own representative? What are the effects of the differences in these ratings?

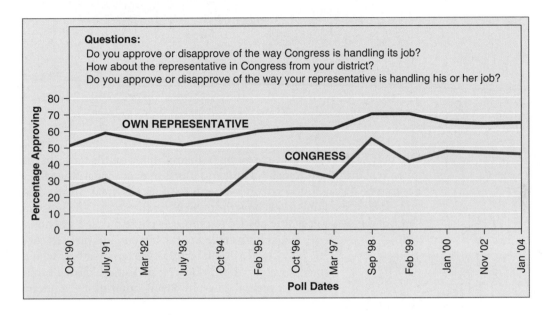

Questions:
Do you approve or disapprove of the way Congress is handling its job?
How about the representative in Congress from your district?
Do you approve or disapprove of the way your representative is handling his or her job?

Source: Data derived from R-Poll, LEXIS/NEXIS.

recent elections saw even higher proportions of incumbents returning to office. One study basically concluded that unless a member of Congress was involved in a serious scandal, his or her chances of defeat were minimal.[12] In 2004, 98 percent of the members seeking re-election won.

Term Limits

A **term-limits** movement began sweeping the nation in the late 1980s because of voter frustration with gridlock and ethics problems in Congress and in state legislatures. Citizens and citizens groups approved referenda limiting the elected terms not only of their state representatives but also of members of Congress. Given the power of incumbency, proponents of term limits argued that election to Congress, in essence, equaled life tenure. The concept of term limits is a simple one that appeals to many who oppose the notion of career politicians.

Term limits aren't a new idea. In 1787, the Framers considered, but rejected, a section of the Virginia Plan that called for members of the House to be restricted to one term. Still, many of the Framers believed in the regular rotation of offices among worthy citizens, and this was generally the practice in the early years of the republic.

In 1994, many Republicans running for Congress signed the Contract with America, which called for congressional passage of federal term limits; in 1995, the U.S.

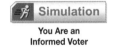

Simulation

You Are an
Informed Voter

term limits

Restrictions that exist in some states about how long an individual may serve in state and/or local elected offices.

WEB EXPLORATION

To evaluate your own representative, see

www.ablongman.com/oconnor

STILL THE BEST CONGRESSIONAL TERM-LIMITING DEVICE.

(Photo courtesy: Oliphant, © Universal Press Syndicate. Reprinted with permission. All rights reserved.)

WEB EXPLORATION
To learn more about the members of the 108th Congress, go to www.ablongman.com/oconnor

Supreme Court ruled that state-imposed limitations on the terms of members of Congress were unconstitutional.[13] Thus, any efforts to enact congressional term limits would necessitate a constitutional amendment—not an easy feat. In the 104th Congress, a term-limits amendment was brought to the floor for a vote. The proposal fell sixty votes short of the two-thirds vote needed to propose a constitutional amendment. In the Senate, Republicans failed to muster enough votes to cut off a Democratic filibuster. In 2000, seven of the ten members who made term limit pledges in 1994 did not seek reelection. Three broke those pledges but were reelected despite strong opposition from term-limits groups.

What Does Congress Look Like?

Congress is better educated, more white, more male, and richer than the rest of the United States. The Senate, in fact, is often called the "Millionaires Club" and its members sport names like Rockefeller and Kennedy. The average age of House members in the 109th Congress is fifty-four; the average age of senators is sixty, and no senator is younger than forty. John Sununu (R–NH) is the youngest senator in the 109th Congress at 41.

As revealed in Figure 7.1, the 1992 elections saw a record number of women, African Americans, and other minorities elected to Congress. In 1992, for the first time ever, both senators elected from a single state—California—were women, Democrats Dianne Feinstein and Barbara Boxer. By the 109th Congress, the total number of women increased to eighty: sixty-six in the House and fourteen in the Senate. In 2005, the number of African Americans serving in the House rose from thirty-nine to forty-two. Barack Obama (D-IL) was elected to the Senate to become the first African American to serve there in several years. In the 109th Congress, only twenty-six Hispanics serve in the House—most of them Democrats. Two Hispanics were elected to the Senate in 2004, Ken Salazar (D-CO), and Mel Martinez (R-FL). Also serving in the 109th Congress were two Asian Pacific Islanders in the Senate and five in the House of Representatives.

Senator Susan Collins (R–ME) meets with U.S. Army soldiers during a visit to the Bagram Air Base, about thirty miles north of Kabul, Afghanistan. A nine-member delegation of U.S. senators arrived at the base for a stopover visit.

(Photo courtesy: Enric Marti/AP/Wide World Photos)

FIGURE 7.1   Numbers of Women and Minorities in Congress

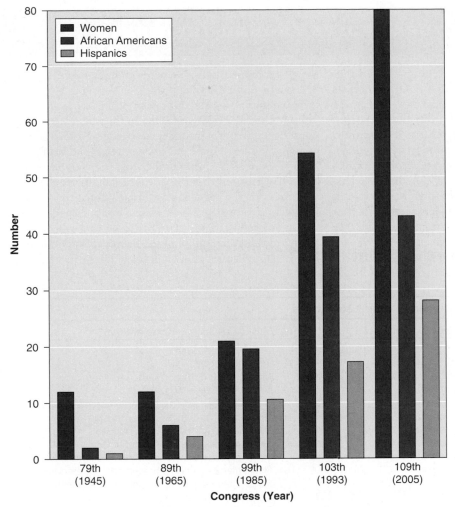

*As of November 4, 2004, two races involving women still undecided.

The Representational Role of Members of Congress

Questions of who should be represented and how that should happen are critical in a republic. Over the years, political theorists have enunciated various ideas about how constituents' interests are best represented in any legislative body. Does it make a difference if the members of Congress come from or are members of a particular group? Are they bound to vote the way their constituents expect them to vote even if they personally favor another policy? Your answer to these questions may depend on your view of the representative function of legislators.

British political philosopher Edmund Burke (1729–1797), who also served in the British Parliament, believed that although he was elected from Bristol, it was his duty to represent the interests of the entire nation. He reasoned that elected officials were obliged to vote as they personally thought best. According to Burke, representatives should be **trustees** who listen to the opinions of their constituents and then can be trusted to use their own best judgment to make final decisions.

A second theory of representation holds that representatives are **delegates.** True delegates are representatives who vote the way their constituents would want them to, whether or not those opinions are the representative's. Delegates, therefore, must be ready and willing to vote against their conscience or policy preferences if they know how their constituents feel about a particular issue. Not surprisingly, members of

Comparing
Legislatures

trustee
Role played by elected representatives who listen to constituents' opinions and then use their best judgment to make final decisions.

delegate
Role played by elected representatives who vote the way their constituents would want them to, regardless of their own opinions.

ELECTORAL RULES AROUND THE WORLD

The representative function of legislatures is critical to a republic. In most of the industrialized democracies, the legislature is the only directly elected part of the national government. In the United States, members of the House of Representatives are first and foremost representatives of electoral districts, which is why district constituents play such a large role in what legislators do. The constitutional requirement that members of the House reside in their districts reinforces that tendency. Other industrialized democracies, such as Japan, Germany, and Italy, mix single-member districts with pro-portional representation, where candidates represent a political party, not a district.

Indonesia and Egypt provide other forms of representation. In the 1999 election for the Indonesian House of Representatives, thirty-eight seats were reserved for the military. Under the New Order government that had been in power from 1966 to 1998, the number had been higher. Reserving seats had ensured that the Suharto dictatorship maintained control over the legislature. Egypt's constitution similarly reserves up to ten legislative seats to be appointed by the president. It also stipulates that "farmers and workers" are to be guaranteed representation in the People's Assembly, reflecting the socialist rhetoric of early postwar Egyptian nationalism.

Electoral Rules and Representation in Selected Legislatures

Country	Lower House of Legislature	Seats	Electoral Rules
Canada	House of Commons	301	Single-member districts
China	National People's Congress	2,979	Indirectly elected
Egypt	People's Assembly	454	Multimember districts, 10 reserved seats
France	National Assembly	577	Single-member districts
Germany	Bundestag	669	Single-member districts, proportional representation
India	People's Assembly	545	Single-member districts, 2 reserved seats
Indonesia	House of Representatives	500	Multimember districts, 38 reserved seats
Italy	Chamber of Deputies	630	Single-member districts, proportional representation
Japan	House of Representatives	480	Single-member districts, proportional representation
Mexico	Chamber of Deputies	500	Single-member districts, proportional representation
Russia	State Duma	500	Single-member districts, proportional representation
United Kingdom	House of Commons	652	Single-member districts
United States	**House of Representatives**	**435**	**Single-member districts**

Source: CIA World Factbook 2000 online, http://www.odci.gov/cia/publications/factbook/geos.

politico

Role played by elected representatives who act as trustees or as delegates, depending on the issue.

Congress and other legislative bodies generally don't fall neatly into either category. It is often unclear how constituents feel about a particular issue, or there may be conflicting opinions within a single constituency. With these difficulties in mind, a third theory of representation holds that **politicos** alternately don the hat of trustee or delegate, depending on the issue. On an issue of great concern to their constituents, representatives most likely will vote as delegates; on other issues, perhaps those that are less visible, representatives will act as trustees and use their own best judgment. Research by political scientists supports this view.[14]

How a representative views his or her role—as a trustee, delegate, or politico—may still not answer the question of whether or not it makes a difference if a representative or senator is male or female, African American or Latino or Caucasian, young or old, gay or straight. Burke's ideas about representation don't even begin to address more practical issues of representation. Can a man, for example, represent the interests of women as well as a woman? Can a rich woman represent the interests of the poor? Are veterans more sensitive to veterans issues? In the 107th Congress, 168 members had some mili-

FIGURE 7.2   Number of Veterans in Congress

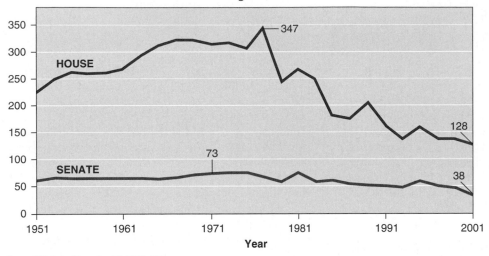

Source: USA Today (November 12, 2001): A12.

tary experience, down considerably from the 1970s, as revealed in Figure 7.2. Only one woman, Representative Heather Wilson (R–NM), had served in the military.

Interestingly, one NBC/*Wall Street Journal* poll conducted in 2000 found that it would be "better for society" if "most of the members of Congress were women."[15] Female representatives historically have played prominent roles in efforts to expand women's rights.[16] One study by the Center for American Women and Politics, for example, found that most women in the 103rd Congress "felt a special responsibility to represent women, particularly to represent their life experiences.... They undertook this additional responsibility while first, and foremost, like all members of Congress, representing their own districts." Said Representative Nancy Johnson (R–CT), "We need to integrate the perspective of women into the policy-making process, just as we have now successfully integrated the perspective of environmental preservation, [and] the perspective of worker safety."[17]

Representative Carolyn Maloney (D–NY) is a regular in the House gym. Women members had to press to get equal access to all the facilities formerly enjoyed by their male colleagues.

(Photo courtesy: ©2001, The Washington Post. Photo by Gerald Martineau. Reprinted with permission.)

A MINORITY BILL OF RIGHTS?

It is customary for the party in control of the House of Representatives to limit the minority's ability to amend bills as well as shape the debate on proposed legislation. But Democrats, as the current minority party are charging that Republicans are wielding their power in unfair ways.

In an effort to allow the minority party more input, Democratic House Leader Nancy Pelosi proposed a "Minority Bill of Rights," which she pledged to follow should the Democrats regain power in 2005. Among its provisions are calls for:

- *Bipartisan Administration of the House.* This would include regular consultation between the leaders of both parties concerning scheduling, administration, and operation of the House. This would include a guarantee that the minority party would get at least one-third of committee budgets and office space.

   In the past, meetings of minority and majority party leaders were routine as were meetings between committee chairs and ranking members. Speaker Dennis Hastert rarely meets with Pelosi, and only a few committee chairs consult with ranking minority members.

- *Regular Order for Legislation.* This would require that bills be developed following full hearings and open committee and subcommittee mark-ups, and that members would have at least twenty-four hours to read any bill before it came to a vote. This would also mandate that all floor votes be completed within fifteen minutes. Republicans have delayed floor votes in order to allow the whips and other leaders to convince members to change their votes. The Republicans held up voting on the Medicare prescription drug bill for nearly three hours to convince Republican dissidents to change their votes after the leadership appeared headed for defeat. Pelosi also called for regular House-Senate conference committee meetings that would allow minority party members some input into final conference committee legislation.

1. Do these suggestions seem just another example of partisanship to you?
2. Given the Pelosi pledged to appy these rules should she become Speaker, would they be a good basis on which to try to end some of the partisanship that affects the kinds of legislation produced in Congress?

Actions of two senators who served as the only Native American and African American senators underscore the representative function that can be played in Congress. Ben Nighthorse Campbell (R–CO), for example, as the only Native American in the Senate, sat on the Committee on Indian Affairs. Earlier, as a member of the House, he led the fight to change the name of Custer Battlefield Monument in Montana to Little Bighorn Battlefield National Monument to honor the Indians who died in battle. He also fought successfully for legislation to establish the National Museum of the American Indian within the Smithsonian Institution.

Before her defeat in 1998, as then the only African American in the Senate, Senator Carol Moseley Braun (D–IL), also tried to sensitize her colleagues about issues of race. In 1993, Senator Jesse Helms (R–NC) sought to amend the national service bill in such a way to preserve the design patent held by the United Daughters of the Confederacy that included the Confederate flag. Most senators had no idea what they were voting on, and the amendment to the bill passed by a vote of 52–48. Then, Senator Moseley Braun took to the floor to express her outrage at Helms's support of a symbol of slavery: "On this issue there can be no consensus. It is an outrage. It is an insult." Although Helms angrily insisted that slavery and race were not the issue, the Senate killed the Helms amendment by a vote of 75–25, as twenty-seven senators changed their votes. Said Senator Barbara Boxer (D–CA), "If there ever was proof of the value of diversity, we have it here today."[18]

President George W. Bush meets with members of the Congressional Black Caucus.

(Photo courtesy: Reuters New Media Inc./CORBIS)

HOW CONGRESS IS ORGANIZED

Every two years, a new Congress is seated. After ascertaining the formal qualifications of new members, the Congress organizes itself as it prepares for the business of the coming session. Among the first items on its agenda are the election of new leaders and the adoption of rules for conducting its business. As illustrated in Figure 7.3, each house has a hierarchical leadership structure.

The House of Representatives

Even in the first Congress in 1789, the House of Representatives was almost three times larger than the Senate. It is not surprising, then, that from the beginning the House has been organized more tightly, structured more elaborately, and governed by stricter rules. Traditionally, loyalty to the party leadership and voting along party lines have been more common in the House than in the Senate. House leaders also play a key role in moving the business of the House along. Historically, the speaker of the House, the majority and minority leaders, and the Republican and Democratic House whips have made up the party leadership that runs Congress. This now has been expanded to include deputy minority whips of both parties.

The Speaker of the House.   The **speaker of the House** is the only officer of the House of Representatives specifically mentioned in the Constitution. The office, the chamber's most powerful position, is modeled after a similar office in the British Parliament—the speaker was the one who spoke to the king and conveyed the wishes of the House of Commons to the monarch.[19]

The speaker is elected formally at the beginning of each new Congress by the entire House of Representatives. Traditionally, the speaker is a member of the **majority party,** the party in each house with the greatest number of members, as are all committee

speaker of the House
The only officer of the House of Representatives specifically mentioned in the Constitution; elected at the beginning of each new Congress by the entire House; traditionally a member of the majority party.

majority party
The political party in each house of Congress with the most members.

FIGURE 7.3   Organizational Structure of the House of Representatives and the Senate Early in the 108th Congress

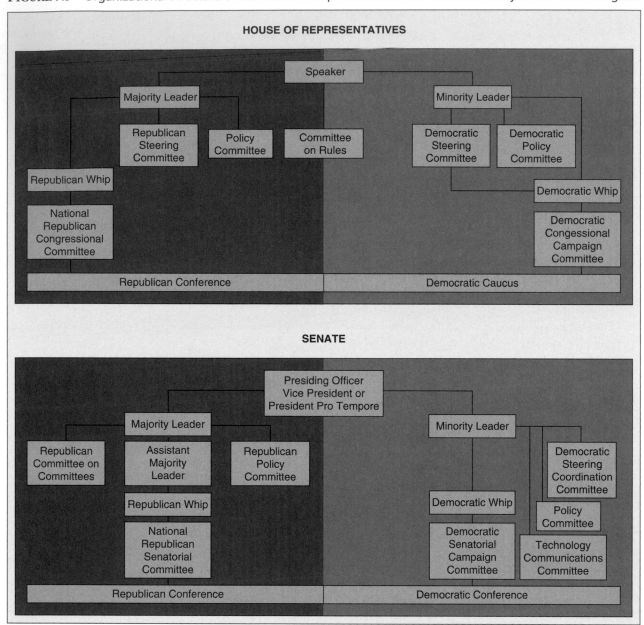

minority party

The political party in each house of Congress with the second most members.

The Power of the Speaker of the House

chairs. (The **minority party** is the party in each house with the second most members.) While typically not the member with the longest service, the speaker generally has served in the House for a long time and in other House leadership positions as an apprenticeship. Dennis Hastert (R–IL) spent twelve years in the House, and his predecessor Newt Gingrich (R–GA) took sixteen years to work his way to the gavel and dais. In the past, a speaker was generally reelected until he chose to retire or his party ceased to be in the majority.

The speaker presides over the House of Representatives, oversees House business, and is the official spokesperson for the House, as well as being second in the line of presidential succession. Moreover, he is the House liaison with the president and generally has great political influence within the chamber. Through his parlia-

WEB EXPLORATION
For more on the offices of the Congress, including the speaker of the House and his activities, see
www.ablongman.com/oconnor

mentary and political skills, he is expected to smooth the passage of party-backed legislation through the House.

The first powerful speaker was Henry Clay. (See Roots of Government: Life on the Floor and in the Halls of Congress.) Serving in Congress at a time when turnover was high, he was elected to the position in 1810, his first term in office. He was the speaker of the House for a total of six terms—longer than anyone else in the nineteenth century.

By the late 1800s, the House ceased to have a revolving door and average stays of members increased. With this professionalization of the House came professionalization in the speakership. Between 1896 and 1910, a series of speakers initiated changes that brought more power to the speaker's office as speakers largely took control of committee assignments and the appointing of committee chairs. Institutional and personal rule reached its height during the tenure of Speaker Joseph Cannon (1903–1910).

Negative reaction to those strong speakers eventually led to a revolt in 1910 and 1911 in the House and to a reduction of the formal powers of the speaker. As a consequence, many speakers between Cannon and Gingrich often relied on more informal powers that came from their personal ability to persuade members of their party.

Newt Gingrich, the first Republican speaker in forty years, convinced fellow Republicans to return important formal powers to the speaker. In return for a rule preventing speakers from serving for more than four consecutive Congresses, the speaker was given unprecedented authority, including the power to refer bills to committee, ending the practice of joint referral of bills to more than one committee, where they might fare better. These formal changes, along with his personal leadership skills, allowed Gingrich to exercise greater control over the House and its agenda than any other speaker since the days of Joe Cannon.

In time, Gingrich's highly visible role as a revolutionary transformed him into a negative symbol outside of the Washington D.C. beltway as his public popularity plunged. Exit polls conducted on Election Day 1996 revealed that 60 percent of the voters had an unfavorable opinion of the speaker, although that dislike did not appear to translate into votes against incumbent House Republicans. But, in 1998, Republicans were stung when they failed to win more seats in the House and Senate. Gingrich's general unpopularity with large segments of the public worked to reinforce Republicans' discontent with Gingrich. The 105th Republican Congress had few legislative successes; members were forced to accept a budget advanced by the White House, and Republicans running for office in 1998 lacked the coherent theme that had been so successful for them in 1994. These were but two of many reasons that prompted several members to announce that they would run against the speaker. Gingrich, who could read the writing on the wall, opted to resign as speaker (later he resigned altogether from the House) rather than face the prospect that he might not be reelected to the position he had coveted for so long.

Representative Bob Livingston (R–LA) quickly emerged as Gingrich's successor. But, amid the Clinton impeachment fervor, news of a longtime Livingston extramarital affair broke and Livingston stunningly announced that he would give up his expected speakership and resign from the House. Scandal-weary Republicans then turned to someone largely unknown to the public: a well-liked and respected one-time high school wrestling coach and social studies teacher, Dennis Hastert.

Representative Barney Frank (D–MA) has been in the rare position of having fun while being in the minority party. Says Frank, "I'm a counterpuncher, happiest fighting on the defensive. Besides, I really dislike what the Republicans are doing. I think they are bad for the country and for vulnerable people. I feel, 'Boy, this is a moral opportunity—you've got to fight this.' Also, I'm used to being in a minority. Hey, I'm a left-handed gay Jew. I've never felt, automatically, a member of any majority. So, I started swinging from the opening bell of this Congress."

(Photo courtesy: Luke Frazza/AFP/Corbis)

WEB EXPLORATION
To get up-to-date data on House leaders, see www.ablongman.com/oconnor

party caucus or conference
A formal gathering of all party members.

majority leader
The elected leader of the party controlling the most seats in the House of Representatives or the Senate; is second in authority to the speaker of the House and in the Senate is regarded as its most powerful member.

minority leader
The elected leader of the party with the second highest number of elected representatives in the House of Representatives or the Senate.

whip
One of several representatives who keep close contact with all members and take "nose counts" on key votes, prepare summaries of bills, and in general act as communications links within the party.

Since coming into his "accidental speakership," Hastert has shown himself to be a "pragmatic and cautious politician" as he tried to deal with his "whisker thin [ten-vote] majority."[20] Through the 106th Congress, Hastert never "lost a vote on the rule to govern floor debate, a feat not seen in at least a decade."[21] His larger majority in the 109th Congress is expected to produce continued unity among House Republicans, a point of concern to House Democratic leader Nancy Pelosi as noted in Politics Now: A Minority Bill of Rights?

Other House Leaders.   After the speaker, the next most powerful people in the House are the majority and minority leaders, who are elected in their individual **party caucuses** or **conferences.** The **majority leader** is the second most important person in the House; his counterpart on the other side of the aisle (the House is organized so that if you are standing on the podium, Democrats sit on the right side and Republicans on the left side of the center aisle) is the **minority leader.** Both work closely with the speaker, and the majority leader helps the speaker schedule proposed legislation for debate on the House floor.

The speaker and majority and minority leaders are assisted in their leadership efforts by the Republican and Democratic **whips,** who are elected by party members in caucuses. The concept of whips originated in the British House of Commons, where they were named after the "whipper in," the rider who keeps the hounds together in a fox hunt. Party whips—who were first designated in the House in 1899 and in the Senate in 1913—do, as their name suggests, try to "whip" fellow Democrats or Republicans into line on partisan issues. They try to maintain close contact with all members on important votes, prepare summaries of content and implications of bills, get "nose counts" during debates and votes, and in general get members to toe the party line. Whips and their deputy whips also serve as communications links, distributing word of the party line from leaders to rank-and-file members and alerting leaders to concerns in the ranks. Whips can be extraordinarily effective. In 1998, for example, when President Bill Clinton returned home from his trip to the Middle East amid calls for his impeachment, he was stunned to learn that moderate Republicans whom he had counted on to vote against his impeachment were "dropping like flies." The reason? Powerful House Republican Whip Tom DeLay (R–TX) threatened Republicans that they would be denied coveted committee assignments and would even face Republican challengers in the next primary season unless they voted the party line. As noted in the opening vignette, Nancy Pelosi became the first female whip in 2002, before becoming minority leader after the 2002 election.

The Senate

The Constitution specifies that the presiding officer of the Senate is the vice president of the United States. Because he is not a member of the Senate, he votes only in the case of a tie. Briefly in 2001, Vice President Dick Cheney became the first vice president since 1881 to preside over an evenly divided Senate.

The official chair of the Senate is the president pro tempore, who is selected by the majority party and presides over the Senate in the absence of the vice president. The position of president pro tempore today is primarily an honorific office that generally goes to the most senior senator of the majority party. Once elected, the pro tem, as he is called, stays in that office until there is a change in the majority party in the Senate. Since presiding

As House speaker, Dennis Hastert has become increasingly powerful as his majority has increased.

(Photo courtesy: Robert Trippett/SIPA Press)

LIFE ON THE FLOOR AND IN THE HALLS OF CONGRESS

Throughout Congress's first several decades, partisan, sectional, and state tensions of the day often found their way onto the floors of the U.S. House and Senate. Many members were armed, and during one House debate thirty members showed their weapons. In 1826, for example, Senator John Randolph of Virginia insulted Henry Clay from the floor of the Senate, referring to Clay as "this being, so brilliant yet so corrupt, which, like a rotten mackerel by moonlight, shined and stunk." Clay immediately challenged Randolph to a duel on the Virginia side of the Potomac River. Both missed, although Randolph's coat fell victim to a bullet hole. Reacting to public opinion, however, in 1839, Congress passed a law prohibiting dueling in the District of Columbia.

Nevertheless, dueling continued. A debate in 1851 between representatives from Alabama and North Carolina ended in a duel, but no one was hurt. In 1856, Representative Preston Brooks of South Carolina, defending the honor of his region and family, assaulted Senator Charles Sumner of Massachusetts on the floor of the Senate. Sumner was dis-

abled and unable to resume his seat in Congress for several years. Guns and knives were abundantly evident on the floor of both House and Senate, along with a wide variety of alcoholic beverages.

over the Senate can be a rather perfunctory duty, neither the vice president nor the president pro tempore performs the task very often. Instead, the duty of actually presiding over the Senate rotates among junior members of the chamber, allowing more senior members to attend more important meetings unless a key vote is being debated.

The true leader of the Senate is the majority leader, elected to the position by the majority party. Because the Senate is a smaller and more collegial body, operating without many of the more formal House rules concerning debate, the majority leader is not nearly as powerful as the speaker of the House, a more overtly partisan body that requires more control by the speaker. The Republican and Democratic whips round out the leadership positions in the Senate and perform functions similar to those of their House counterparts. But, leading and whipping in the Senate can be quite a challenge. Senate rules always have given tremendous power to individual senators; in most cases senators can offer any kind of amendments to legislation on the floor, and an individual senator can bring all work on the floor to a halt indefinitely through a filibuster unless three-fifths of the senators vote to cut him or her off.[22]

Because of the Senate's smaller size, organization and formal rules never have played the same role in the Senate as they do in the House. Through the 1960s, it was a "Gentlemen's Club" whose folkways—unwritten rules of behavior—governed its operation. One such folkway, for example, stipulated that political disagreements not become personal criticisms. A senator who disliked another referred to that senator as "the able, learned, and distinguished senator." A member who really couldn't stand another called that senator "my very able, learned, and distinguished colleague."

In the 1960s and 1970s, senators became more and more active on and off the Senate floor in a variety of issues and extended debates that often occurred on the floor— without the rigid rules of courtesy that had once been the hallmark of the body. These

Senator Hillary Rodham Clinton (D–NY) asks for questions from attendees at a news conference in which she proposed changes to the September 11 Victim Compensation Fund rules as victims' families listen.

(Photo courtesy: Kathy Willens/AP/Wide World Photos)

Representative Bernie Sanders (I–VT), right, shares a toast of milk with Senator Jim Jeffords (I–VT) at a news conference celebrating the Northeast Dairy Compact. This photo was taken shortly before Jeffords disaffiliated himself with Senate Republicans causing Democrats to take control of the Senate in the 107th Congress. Sanders and Jeffords, the only Independents in the 109th Congress, both vote with Democrats.

(Photo courtesy: Tony Talbot/AP/Wide World Photos)

changes weren't accompanied by giving additional powers to the Senate majority leader, who now often has difficulty controlling "the more active, assertive, and consequently less predictable membership" of the Senate.[23] In 2003, Senator Bill Frist (R–TN) became majority leader after Trent Lott (R–MS) resigned after making remarks that were considered racially insensitive.

The Role of Political Parties in Organizing Congress

When the first Congress met in 1789 in the nation's temporary capital in New York City, it consisted of only twenty-two senators and fewer than sixty representatives. Those men faced the enormous task of creating much of the machinery of government as well as that of drafting a bill of rights, for which the Anti-Federalists had argued so vehemently. During their debates, the political differences that divided Americans during the early years of the Union were renewed. For example, when Alexander Hamilton, the first secretary of the treasury and a staunch Federalist, proposed to fund the national debt and create a national bank, he aroused the ire of those who feared vesting the national government with too much power. This conflict led Hamilton's opponents to create the Democratic-Republican Party to counter the Federalists, creating a two-party system in Congress. Control of the political parties quickly gave Congress far more powers. The Democratic-Republican party caucus nominated Thomas Jefferson (1804), James Madison (1808 and 1812), and James Monroe (1816) for president, all of whom were elected.

The organization of both houses of Congress is closely tied to political parties and their strength in each House. For the party breakdowns in the 109th Congress, see Figure 7.4. Parties play a key role in the committee system, an organizational feature of Congress that facilitates its law-making and oversight functions. The committees, controlled by the majority party in each house of Congress, often set the congressional agendas, although under Newt Gingrich's speakership, this power eroded substantially in the House of Representatives as the speaker's power was enhanced.[24]

At the beginning of each new Congress—the 109th Congress, for example, will sit in two sessions, one in 2005 and one in 2006—the members of each party gather in its party caucus or conference. Historically, these caucuses have enjoyed varied powers, but today the party caucuses—now called "caucus" by House Democrats and "conference" by House and Senate Republicans and Senate Democrats—have several roles, including nominating or electing party officers, reviewing committee assignments, discussing party policy, imposing party discipline, setting party themes, and coordinating media, including talk radio. Conference and caucus chairs are recognized party leaders who work with others who are part of the House or Senate leadership.[25]

FIGURE 7.4   The 109th Congress

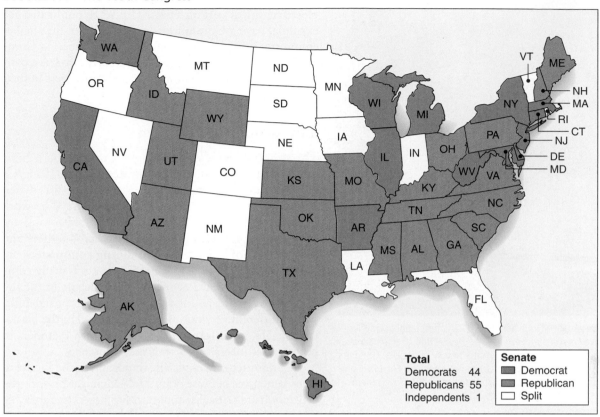

Total
Democrats   44
Republicans 55
Independents 1

Senate
■ Democrat
■ Republican
□ Split

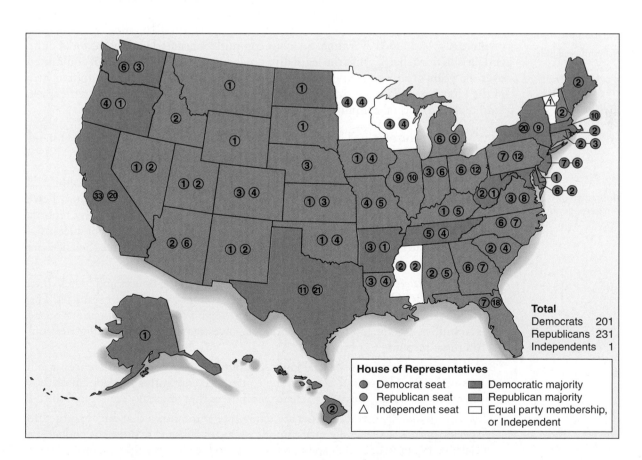

Total
Democrats   201
Republicans 231
Independents   1

House of Representatives
● Democrat seat   ■ Democratic majority
● Republican seat   ■ Republican majority
△ Independent seat   □ Equal party membership,
                             or Independent

Newly elected Representative Linda Sanchez (D–CA), left, laughs with her sister, Representative Loretta Sanchez (D–CA). The election of Linda Sanchez in 2002 makes them the first "sister act" in the history of the U.S. Congress. Loretta Sanchez serves on the Armed Services and Homeland Security Committees in the 109th Congress. Linda Sanchez serves on the Government Reform, Judiciary, and Small Business Committees.

(Photo courtesy: Krista Niles/AP/World Wide Photos)

standing committee
Committee to which proposed bills are referred.

conference committee
Joint committee created to iron out differences between Senate and House versions of a specific piece of legislation.

WEB EXPLORATION
To get information on specific committees, go to
www.ablongman.com/oconnor

Each caucus or conference has specialized committees that fulfill certain tasks. House Republicans, for example, have a Committee on Committees that makes committee assignments. The Democrats' Steering Committee performs this function. Each party also has a congressional campaign committee to assist members in their reelection bids.

The Committee System

The saying "Congress in session is Congress on exhibition, whilst Congress in its committee rooms is Congress at work" may not be as true today as it was when Woodrow Wilson wrote it in 1885.[26] Still, "The work that takes place in the committee and subcommittee rooms of Capitol Hill is critical to the productivity and effectiveness of Congress."[27] **Standing committees** are the first and last places that most bills go. Usually committee members play key roles in floor debate in the full House or Senate about the merits of proposed bills. When different versions of a bill are passed in the House and Senate, a **conference committee** with members of both houses meets to iron out the differences.

Committees are especially important in the House of Representatives because of its size. Organization and specialization are critically important, as noted in Table 7.5. The establishment of subcommittees allows for even greater specialization.

An institutionalized committee system was created in 1816, and more and more committees were added over time. So many committees resulted in duplication of duties and jurisdictional battles that the legislative process suffered. The growth of committees over the years greatly concerned House Republicans. When Republicans took control of the House in 1995, they cut several committees and subcommittees and reorganized (and renamed) several committees to lesson duplication and sharpen focus.[28]

Types of Committees. There are four types of congressional committees: (1) standing; (2) joint; (3) conference; and, (4) ad hoc, special, or select.[29]

1. *Standing committees*, so called because they continue from one Congress to the next, are the committees to which proposed bills are referred for consideration. Fewer than 10 percent of the almost 9,000 measures sent to committees are ever reported out to a vote by the full House or Senate. Standing committees also conduct investigations, such as the Senate Governmental Affairs and Commerce, Science, and Transportation Committees' investigation of Enron.

2. *Joint committees* are set up to expedite business between the houses and to help focus public attention on major matters, such as the economy, taxation, or scandals. They include members from both houses of Congress who conduct investigations or special studies. A joint committee, for example, investigated the U.S. intelligence community's response to terrorism.

3. *Conference committees* are special joint committees that reconcile differences in bills passed by the House and Senate. The conference committee is made up of those members from the House and Senate committees that originally considered the bill.

4. *Ad hoc, special,* or *select committees* are temporary committees that are appointed for specific purposes. Generally such committees are established in order to conduct special investigations or studies and to report back to the chamber that established them.

TABLE 7.5   Committees of the 108th Congress (with a Subcommittee Example)[a]

Standing Committees

House	Senate
Agriculture	Agriculture, Nutrition, and Forestry
Appropriations	Appropriations
Armed Services	Armed Services
Budget	Banking, Housing, and Urban Affairs
Education and the Workforce	Budget
Energy and Commerce	Commerce, Science, and Transportation
Financial Services	Energy and Natural Resources
Government Reform	Environment and Public Works
House Administration	Finance
International Relations	Foreign Relations
Judiciary	Governmental Affairs
Judiciary Subcommittees:	Health, Education, Labor, and Pensions
Courts, the Internet, and Intellectual Property	Judiciary
Immigration, Border Security, and Claims	Judiciary Subcommittees:
Commercial and Administrative Law	Immigration, Border Security, and
Crime, Terrorism, and Homeland Security	Citizenship
Constitution	Antitrust, Competition Policy, and
Resources	Consumer Rights
Rules	Terrorism, Technology, and
Science	Homeland Security
Small Business	Crime, Corrections, and Victims' Rights
Standards of Official Conduct	The Constitution: Civil Rights, and
Transportation and Infrastructure	Property Rights
Veterans Affairs	Terrorism, Technology, and Homeland Security
Ways and Means	Rules and Administration
	Small Business and Entrepreneurship
	Veterans Affairs

Select, Special, and Other Committees

House	Senate	Joint Committees
Select Intelligence	Special Aging	Economics
Select Homeland Security	Select Ethics	Printing
	Select Intelligence	Taxation
	Indian Affairs	Library

The House and Senate standing committees listed in Table 7.5 were created by rule. In the 109th Congress, the House has nineteen standing committees, each with an average of thirty-one members. Together, they have a total of eighty-six subcommittees that collectively act as the eyes, ears, and hands of the House. They consider issues roughly parallel to those of the departments represented in the president's Cabinet. For example, there were committees on agriculture, education, the judiciary, veterans affairs, transportation, and commerce.

Although most committees in one house parallel those in the other, the House Rules Committee, for which there is no counterpart in the Senate, plays a key role in the law-making process. Indicative of the importance of the Rules Committee, majority party members are appointed directly by the speaker. This committee reviews most bills after they come from a committee and before they go to the full chamber for consideration. Performing a "traffic cop" function, the Rules Committee gives each bill what is called a rule, which contains the date the bill will come up for debate and the time that will be allotted for discussion, and often specifies what kinds of amendments can be offered. Bills considered under a closed rule cannot be amended.

Standing committees have considerable power. They can kill bills, amend them radically, or hurry them through the process. In the words of Woodrow Wilson, once a bill is referred to a committee, it "crosses a parliamentary bridge of sighs to dim dungeons of silence from whence it never will return." Committees report out to the full House or Senate only a small fraction of the bills assigned to them. Bills can be "forced" out of a House committee by a **discharge petition** signed by a majority (218) of the House membership, but legislators are reluctant to take this drastic measure.

Until the 103rd Congress, a House rule kept the names of those who signed discharge petitions secret. This prevented members from claiming that they supported legislation when they actually may have tried to keep a bill from coming to the floor for a vote. Discharge petitions are rare, but one was used to force campaign finance reform to a floor vote in 2002. Under a new House rule adopted in 1995, the clerk is required to publish the names of those who sign a discharge petition each week in the *Congressional Record* as well as to make that information available to the public electronically.

In the 109th Congress, the Senate has sixteen standing committees that range in size from fifteen to twenty-nine members. It also has sixty-eight subcommittees, which allow all majority party senators to chair one. For example, the Senate Judiciary Committee has seven subcommittees, as illustrated in Table 7.5.

In contrast to the House, whose members hold few committee assignments (an average of 1.8 standing and three subcommittees), senators are spread more thinly, with each serving on an average of three to four committees and seven subcommittees. Whereas the committee system allows House members to become policy or issue specialists, Senate members often are generalists. In the 109th Congress, Kay Bailey Hutchison (R–TX), for example, serves on several committees including Appropriations, Commerce, Science, and Transportation, Veterans Affairs, and Rules and Administration. She also serves on twelve subcommittees. She also chairs two of those subcommittees and is the vice chair of the Republican Conference.

Senate committees enjoy the same power over framing legislation as do House committees, but the Senate, being an institution more open to individual input than the House, gives less deference to the work done in committees. In the Senate, legislation is more likely to be rewritten on the floor, where all senators can participate and add amendments at any time.

Committee Membership.   Many newly elected members of Congress come into the body with their sights set on certain committee assignments. Others are more flexible. Many legislators seeking committee assignments inform their party's selection committee of their preferences. They often request assignments based on their own interests or expertise or on a particular committee's ability to help their prospects for reelection. Political scientist Kenneth Shepsle has noted that committee assignments are to members what stocks are to investors—they seek to acquire those that will add to the value of their portfolios.[30]

Representatives often seek committee assignments that have access to what is known as the **pork barrel.** Historically, pork barrel legislation has allowed representatives to "bring home the bacon" to their districts in the form of public works programs, military bases, or other programs designed to benefit districts directly. In the past, a seat on the Armed Services Committee, for example, would allow a member to bring lucrative defense contracts back to his or her district, or to discourage base closings within his or her district or state. The 1999 "emergency relief" bill for Kosovo well illustrates the pervasiveness of pork. The Senate version of that bill had something for everyone: In it was a $1 billion request for aid for ailing steel companies in Senator Robert Byrd's West Virginia (Byrd is known as the "Prince of Pork"), $500 million in loans for faltering oil and gas interests, and a provision to prevent the Mississippi sturgeon in the Senate majority leader's home state, from being listed as an endangered species.[31]

discharge petition
Petition that gives a majority of the House of Representatives the authority to bring an issue to the floor in the face of committee inaction.

pork barrel
Legislation that allows representatives to "bring home the bacon" to their districts in the form of public works programs, military bases, or other programs designed to benefit their districts directly.

Legislators who bring jobs and new public works programs back to their districts are hard to beat. But, ironically, these programs are the ones that attract much of the public criticism directed at the federal government in general and Congress in particular. Thus, it is somewhat paradoxical that pork barrel improves a member's chances for reelection or for election to higher office. In 1984, Jesse Helms (R–NC), for example, turned down the chairmanship of the Senate Committee on Foreign Relations to stay on the less prestigious Committee on Agriculture, Nutrition, and Forestry, where he could better ensure continued support for the tobacco industry so vital to his home state's economy.

Pork isn't the only motivator for those seeking strategic committee assignments.[32] Some committees, such as Energy and Commerce, facilitate reelection by giving House members influence over decisions that affect large campaign contributors. Other committees, such as Education and the Workforce or Judiciary, attract members eager to work on the policy responsibilities assigned to the committee even if the appointment does them little good at the ballot box. Another motivator for certain committee assignments is the desire to have power and influence within the chamber. The Appropriations and Budget Committees provide that kind of reward for some members.

Depending on whether or not his party controls the Senate, Robert Byrd (D–VA) has served as president pro tem of the Senate as well as the chair of the powerful Appropriations Committee. Senator Byrd is known as the "Prince of Pork" for his ability to "bring home the bacon" in the form of public works projects to West Virginia.

(Photo courtesy: Hillery Smith Garrison/AP/Wide World Photos)

In both the House and the Senate, committee membership generally reflects the party distribution within that chamber. For example, at the outset of the 109th Congress, Republicans held a majority of House seats and thus claimed about a 55 percent share of the seats on several committees, including International Relations, Energy and Commerce, and Education and the Workforce. On committees more critical to the operation of the House or to setting national policy, the majority often takes a disproportionate share of the slots. Since the Rules Committee regulates access to the floor for legislation approved by other standing committees, control by the majority party is essential for it to manage the flow of legislation. For this reason, no matter how narrow the majority party's margin in the chamber, it makes up at least two-thirds of Rules's membership. In the Senate, during its brief 50–50 split in 2001, the leaders agreed to equal representation on committees, along with equal staffing, office space, and budget.

Committee Chairs.   Before recent changes giving the House speaker more power, committee chairs long enjoyed tremendous power and prestige. Even today's House and Senate chairs may choose not to schedule hearings on a bill to kill it. Chairs also carry with them the power to draft legislation, manage a million-plus dollar staff budget, and "hear pleas from lobbyists, Cabinet secretaries and even presidents who need something only a committee can provide."[33] Chairs also may convene meetings when opponents are absent, or they may adjourn meetings when things are going badly. Personal skill, influence, and expertise are a chair's best allies.

Historically, committee chairs generally have been the majority party member with the longest continuous service on the committee. Reforms made by Republicans in 1995 dramatically limited the long-term power of committee chairs. House rules prevent chairs from serving more than six years—three consecutive Congresses—or heading their own subcommittees. Committee chairs, however, still have some important powers. They are authorized to select all subcommittee chairs, call meetings, strategize, and recommend majority members to sit on conference committees. Committee chairs in the House no longer are selected by seniority, as is the case in the Senate. Thus, in the 107th Congress, the first Congress after the new rules took effect, thirteen House committee chairs were new.[34]

THE LAW-MAKING FUNCTION OF CONGRESS

The organization of Congress allows it to fulfill its constitutional responsibilities, chief among which is its law-making function. It is through this power that Congress affects the day-to-day lives of all Americans as well as sets policy for the future. Proposals for legislation—be they about education, violence against women, trade with China, gun control or foreign aid—can come from the president, executive agencies, committee staffs, interest groups, or even private individuals. Only members of the House or Senate, however, formally can submit a bill for congressional consideration. Once a bill is proposed, it usually reaches a dead end. Of the approximately 9,000 or so bills introduced during any session of Congress, fewer than 10 percent are made into law.

It is probably useful to think of Congress as a system of multiple vetoes, which was what the Framers desired. They wanted to disperse power, and as Congress has evolved, it has come closer and closer to the Framers' intentions. As a bill goes through Congress, a dispersion of power occurs as roadblocks to passage must be surmounted at numerous steps in the process. In addition to realistic roadblocks, caution signs and other opportunities for delay abound. A member who sponsors a bill must get through every obstacle. In contrast, successful opposition means "winning" at only one of many stages, including: (1) the subcommittee; (2) the House full committee; (3) the House Rules Committee; (4) the House; (5) the Senate subcommittee; (6) the full Senate committee; (7) the Senate; (8) floor leaders in both Houses; (9) the House-Senate conference committee; and, (10) the president.

The story of how a bill becomes a law in the United States can be told in two different ways. The first is the "textbook" method, which provides a greatly simplified road map of the process to make it easier to understand. We'll review this method first. But real life, of course, rarely goes according to plan, as underscored in Analyzing Visuals: Gun Control Legislation Following Publicized Shootings Since 1968.

How a Bill Becomes a Law: The Textbook Version

Simulation

You Are a Member of Congress

A bill must survive three stages before it becomes a law. It must be approved by one or more standing committees and both chambers, and, if House and Senate versions differ, a conference report resolving those differences must be accepted by each house. A bill may be killed during any of these stages, so it is much easier to defeat a bill than it is to get one passed. The House and Senate have parallel processes, and often the same bill is introduced in each chamber at the same time.

A bill must be introduced by a member of Congress, but it is often sponsored by a whole list of other members in an early effort to show support for it.[35] Once introduced, the bill is sent to the clerk of the chamber, who gives it a number (for example, HR 1 or S 1—indicating House or Senate bill number one for the Congress). The bill is then printed, distributed, and sent to the appropriate committee or committees for consideration.

The first action takes place within the committee, after it is referred there by the speaker. The committee usually refers the bill to one of its subcommittees, which researches the bill and decides whether to hold hearings on it. The subcommittee hearings provide the opportunity for those on both sides of the issue to voice their opinions. Most of these hearings are now open to the public because of 1970s sunshine laws, which require open sessions. After the hearings, the bill is revised, and the subcommittee votes to approve or defeat the bill. If the subcommittee votes in favor of the bill, it is returned to the full committee, which then either rejects the bill or sends it to the House or Senate floor with a favorable recommendation (see Figure 7.5).

The second stage of action takes place on the House or Senate floor. In the House, before a bill may be debated on the floor, it must be approved by the Rules Committee and given a rule and a place on the calendar, or schedule. (House budget bills don't go

ANALYZING VISUALS

Gun Control Legislation Following Publicized Shootings Since 1968

Machine gun violence during Prohibition and the attempted assassination of President Franklin D. Roosevelt in 1933 were followed by the National Firearms Act of 1934, which required registration of automatic weapons. Other gun control legislation has followed highly publicized shootings. The path of a particular piece of legislation is often as varied as the content of the legislation itself. In the wake of so many workplace and school shooting tragedies in the 1990s, many Americans began to regard some form of gun control legislation as a must. Congress frequently reacts to external stimuli that produce citizen demands for action. Still, gun control legislation was defeated in spite of public opinion favoring

its passage, perhaps underscoring the potency of the powerful gun lobby. Since 2000, little headway has been made by gun control advocates who seek additional federal laws, in spite of efforts by some members to link stricter background checks, for example, with measures to fight terrorism. After studying the timeline below, answer the following critical thinking questions about the information presented: What generalization about incidents and government action follows from the timeline? Is gun control legislation more likely when Congress is controlled by Democrats rather than by Republicans? Why do you think gun control legislation did not follow some gun violence incidents?

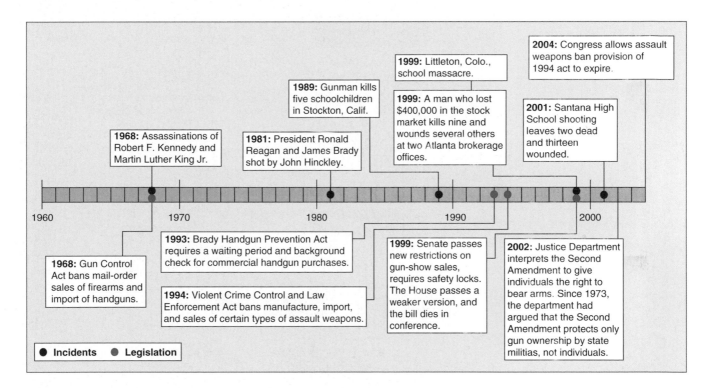

2004: Congress allows assault weapons ban provision of 1994 act to expire.

1999: Littleton, Colo., school massacre.

1989: Gunman kills five schoolchildren in Stockton, Calif.

1999: A man who lost $400,000 in the stock market kills nine and wounds several others at two Atlanta brokerage offices.

2001: Santana High School shooting leaves two dead and thirteen wounded.

1968: Assassinations of Robert F. Kennedy and Martin Luther King Jr.

1981: President Ronald Reagan and James Brady shot by John Hinckley.

1993: Brady Handgun Prevention Act requires a waiting period and background check for commercial handgun purchases.

1968: Gun Control Act bans mail-order sales of firearms and import of handguns.

1994: Violent Crime Control and Law Enforcement Act bans manufacture, import, and sales of certain types of assault weapons.

1999: Senate passes new restrictions on gun-show sales, requires safety locks. The House passes a weaker version, and the bill dies in conference.

2002: Justice Department interprets the Second Amendment to give individuals the right to bear arms. Since 1973, the department had argued that the Second Amendment protects only gun ownership by state militias, not individuals.

● Incidents   ● Legislation

Source: USA Today (May 26, 1999): A2. Reprinted with permission. Revised and updated by the authors.

to the Rules Committee.) In the House, the rule given to a bill determines the limits on the floor debate and specifies what types of amendments, if any, may be attached to the bill. Once the Rules Committee considers the bill, it is put on the calendar.

When the day arrives for floor debate, the House may choose to form a Committee of the Whole. This allows the House to deliberate with only one hundred members present to expedite consideration of the bill. On the House floor, the bill is debated, amendments are offered, and a vote ultimately is taken by the full House. If the bill survives, it is sent to the Senate for consideration if it was not considered there simultaneously.

FIGURE 7.5   How a Bill Becomes a Law

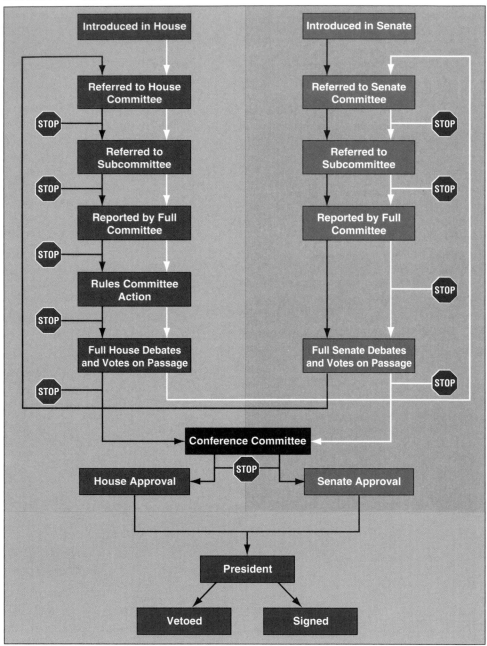

Unlike the House, where debate is necessarily limited given the size of the body, bills may be held up by a hold or a filibuster in the Senate. A **hold** is a tactic by which a senator asks to be informed before a particular bill is brought to the floor. This request signals the Senate leadership and the sponsors of the bill that a colleague may have objections to the bill and should be consulted before further action is taken. Because any single member can filibuster a bill or other action to death, the Senate leadership is very reluctant to bring actions with a hold on them to the floor. Explained one Senate staffer, "Four or five years ago it started to mean that if you put a hold on something, it would never come up. It became, in fact, a veto."[36]

In the first sessions of the 103rd and 104th Congresses, for example, holds were placed on more than two-thirds of the 250 bills reported out of committee in the Senate. In the 105th Congress, holds also were used to prevent votes on many judicial nominees, prompting criticism from Chief Justice William H. Rehnquist. Since holds were not made public, it was difficult to know how many actually were placed and who exercised the privilege. The secrecy attached to holds made them particularly powerful as a personal means to stall action. In March 1999, however, the Senate changed its rules. Senators who want to place a hold on legislation now must send written notification to the bill or nomination's sponsor and to the committee with jurisdiction over the issue. "What this means," said Senator Ron Wyden (D–OR), long a critic of holds, "is that the fog is starting to lift over the Senate."[37] Still, holds are powerful tools. In 2002, for example, Senator Joe Biden (D–DE) became so upset with congressional failure to fund Amtrak security (Biden takes Amtrak back and forth to his home in Delaware when the Senate is in session) that he put holds on two Department of Transportation nominees, whom he called "fine, decent, and competent people."[38] In return, the administration retaliated by withholding a third of the funding for a University of Delaware research project on high-speed trains. As the *Washington Post* noted in reporting this story, "Welcome to the wild wacky world of Washington politics, where people sometimes destroy a village to save it."[39]

Filibusters, which allow for unlimited debate on a bill, grew out of the absence of rules to limit speech in the Senate and often are used to "talk a bill to death." In contrast to a hold, a filibuster is a more formal and public way of halting action on a bill by means of long speeches or unlimited debate in the Senate. Senate Rule 22 allows for unlimited debate on a motion before it is brought to a vote.[40] There are no rules on the content of a filibuster as long as a senator keeps on talking. A senator may read from a phone book, recite poetry, or read cookbooks in order to delay a vote. Often, a team of senators will take turns speaking to keep the filibuster going in the hope that a bill will be tabled or killed. In 1964, for example, a group of northern liberal senators continued a filibuster for eighty-two days in an effort to prevent amendments that would weaken a civil rights bill. Still, filibusters often are more of a threat than an actual event on the Senate floor.

To end a filibuster, **cloture** must be invoked. To cut off debate, sixteen senators must first sign a motion for cloture, then sixty senators must vote to end debate. If cloture is invoked, no more than thirty additional hours can be devoted to debate before the legislation at issue is brought to a vote.

The third stage of action takes place when the two chambers of Congress approve different versions of the same bill. When this happens, a conference committee is established to iron out the differences between the two versions. The conference committee, whose members are from the original House and Senate committees, hammers out a compromise, which is returned to each chamber for a final vote. Sometimes the conference committee fails to agree and the bill dies there. No changes or amendments to the compromise version are allowed. If the bill is passed, it is sent to the president, who either signs it or vetoes it. If the bill is not passed in both houses, it dies.

The president has ten days to consider a bill. He has four options: (1) he can sign the bill, at which point it becomes law; (2) he can veto the bill, which is more likely to occur when the president is of a different party from the majority in Congress (In the 103rd Congress, when Democrats controlled both houses of Congress, President Bill Clinton became the first president in 140 years not to veto a single bill during a two-year Congress. Congress may override the president's veto with a two-thirds vote in each chamber, a very difficult task); (3) he can wait the full ten days, at the end of which time the bill becomes law without his signature if Congress is still in session; and, (4) if the Congress adjourns before the ten days are up, the president can choose not to sign the bill, and it is considered "pocket vetoed." A **pocket veto** figuratively allows bills stashed in the president's pocket to die. The only way for a bill then to become law is for it to be reintroduced in the next session and go through the process all over again. Because Congress sets its own date of adjournment, technically the session could be continued the few extra days necessary to prevent a pocket veto. Extensions are unlikely,

filibuster
A formal way of halting action on a bill by means of long speeches or unlimited debate in the Senate.

cloture
Motion requiring sixty senators to cut off debate.

pocket veto
If Congress adjourns during the ten days the president has to consider a bill passed by both houses of Congress, without the president's signature, the bill is considered vetoed.

line-item veto
The authority of a chief executive to delete part of a bill passed by the legislature that involves taxing and/or spending. The legislature may override a veto, usually with a two-thirds majority of each chamber.

however, as sessions are scheduled to adjourn close to the November elections or the December holidays. For a short while, the last action that the president could take was to exercise a **line-item veto.**

Presidents since Ulysses S. Grant urged Congress to give them a line-item veto as a way to curb wasteful spending, particularly in pork barrel projects added to bills to assure member support. As adopted by Congress, the line-item veto allowed the president to strike or reduce any discretionary budget authority or eliminate any targeted tax provision (the line item) in any bill sent to him by the Congress. The president was then required to prepare a separate recisions package for each piece of legislation he wished to veto and then submit his proposal to Congress within twenty working days. The president's proposed recisions were to take effect unless both houses of Congress passed a disapproval bill by a two-thirds vote within twenty days of receiving the proposed deletions from the budget.[41]

President Bill Clinton used the line-item veto eighty-two times to reject a range of pork barrel provisions in legislation that was sent to him for his approval. In 1998, however, the U.S. Supreme Court struck down the line-item veto as unconstitutional. In a 6–3 decision, a majority of the Court concluded that the veto violates a constitutional provision mandating that legislation be passed by both houses of Congress and then be sent to the president—in its entirety—for his signature or veto.[42] Allowing the president to pick and choose among budget authorizations submitted to him by Congress gives the president the power "to enact, to amend or to repeal statutes," said the Court, a constitutional power the Framers never intended the president to have.

How a Bill Really Becomes a Law: The China Trade Act of 2000

For each bill introduced in Congress, enactment is a long shot. A bill's supporters struggle to get from filing in both houses of Congress to the president's signature, and each bill follows a unique course. The progress of the trade legislation described below is probably even quirkier than most bills that actually become law.

Under the Trade Act of 1974, part of a two-decades-old American Cold War policy, the president of the United States was empowered to grant any nation most favored trade status, a designation that brings favorable U.S. tariff treatment. By law, however, the president was limited to extending that status to communist countries on a year by year (instead of permanent) basis subject to congressional review. Thus, since passage of that act, China, as a communist nation, could receive this status only a year at a time although it provided a huge potential market for U.S. goods. President Bill Clinton and many members of the business community wanted this year by year reauthorization dropped once China was scheduled to join the World Trade Organization. To do that required a new act of Congress. Ironically, the Clinton administration's push for this bill also allied President Clinton with many Republicans who favored opening trade to a nation with billions of new consumers. Many of the Republicans' biggest financial and political supporters would benefit from opening Chinese markets and removing barriers to service providers such as banks and telecommunications companies. In contrast, unions, a traditionally Democratic constituency, feared further loss of jobs to foreign shores.

Legislation to extend what is called permanent normal trade relations (PNTR) was viewed by Clinton as a means of putting "his imprint on foreign policy [as] the president who cemented in place the post-Cold-War experiment of using economic engagement to foster political change among America's neighbors and its potential adversaries."[43] He had begun this effort in 1993 after he pushed through Congress passage of the North American Free Trade Agreement (NAFTA) with Mexico and Canada. Now, as his time in office was coming to an end, he wanted Congress to act to allow him to cement PNTR with China.

As soon as the United States completed a bilateral agreement to make China a member of the World Trade Organization in November 1999 and early 2000, Clinton met with more than one hundred lawmakers individually or in groups, called scores more on the phone, and traveled to the Midwest and California to build support for the proposed legislation, which was necessary to implement this agreement. While Clinton was setting the stage for congressional action, the U.S. Chamber of Commerce and the Business Roundtable launched a $10 million ad campaign—the largest ever for a single legislative issue.[44]

WEB EXPLORATION
To learn about the details of Clinton's transmittal letter to Congress on permanent normal trade relations with China, go to www.ablongman.com/oconnor

On March 8, 2000, Clinton transmitted the text of legislation he was requesting to Congress. This proposed legislation, called S 2277, formally introduced in the Senate on March 23 by Senator William Roth Jr. (R–DE). It was then read twice and referred to the Finance Committee. In the House, hearings on the China trade policy were held throughout the spring, even before the Clinton legislation formally was introduced. Anticipating concern from colleagues about China's human rights abuses, labor market issues, and the rule of law, some members proposed that Congress create (under separate legislation) a U.S. Congressional-Executive Commission on China to monitor those issues. HR 4444, the bill that Clinton sought, was introduced formally in Congress on May 15, 2000, by Representative Bill Archer (R–TX). It was referred to the House Ways and Means Committee shortly thereafter and a mark-up session was held on May 17. It was reported out of committee on the same day by a vote of 34–4. On May 23, 2000, HR 4444 received a rule from the Rules Committee allowing for three hours of debate. The bill was closed to amendments except motions to recommit, and the House Republican leadership "closed ranks behind the bill," claiming that economic change would foster political change.[45] But, they still had to sell this idea to their colleagues, many of whom balked at extending trade advantages to a communist government with a history of rights violations including religious persecution and the denial of political rights to many. The rights legislation was designed to assuage those fears.

While the House Committee on International Relations was holding hearings (and even before), the Clinton administration sprang into action. Secretary of Commerce William Daley and several other Cabinet members were sent out to say the same thing over and over again: The bill will mean jobs for Americans and stability in Asia. Republican leaders got Chinese dissidents to say that the bill would improve human rights in China, and televangelist Billy Graham was recruited by the leadership to endorse the measure. At the same time, interest groups on both sides of the debate rushed to convince legislators to support their respective positions. Organized labor, still stinging from its NAFTA loss, was the biggest opponent of the bill. Teamsters and members of the United Auto Workers roamed the halls of Congress, trying to lobby members of the House.[46] Vice President Al Gore, knowing that he would need union support in the upcoming presidential election, broke ranks with the president and said that the bill would only serve to move American jobs to China.

On the other side, lobbyists from large corporations, including Procter & Gamble, and interest groups such as the Business Roundtable, used their cell phones and personal contacts to cajole legislators. "It's like a big wave hitting the shore," said one uncommitted Republican legislator from Staten Island, New York.[47] For the first time, he was lobbied by rank-and-file office workers at the request of their corporate offices, as well as union members. Another member of Congress was contacted by former President George Bush and Secretary of Defense William Cohen, and he received a special defense briefing from the Central Intelligence Agency. The president of the AFL-CIO also personally visited him. All stops were out, and this was the kind of treatment most undecided members received.

House debate on the bill began on May 24, 2000. That morning, House Republican Whip Tom DeLay (R–TX) didn't know if he had enough votes to support the measure to ensure its passage. The bare minimum he needed was 150 Republicans if he was to push the bill over the top.[48] DeLay lined up lots of assistance. Somewhat ironically, Texas Governor George W. Bush and retired General Colin Powell were enlisted to help convince wavering Republicans to support the Democratic president's goals. Powell, in particular, was called on to assuage national security concerns of several conservative representatives. Scores of pro-trade lobbyists spread out over Capitol Hill like locusts looking to light on any wavering legislators. A last-minute amendment to create a twenty-three-member commission to monitor human rights and a second to monitor surges in Chinese imports helped garner the votes of at least twenty more legislators.

Debate then came on a motion from House Democratic Whip David Bonior (D–MI) to recommit the bill to the Ways and Means and International Relations Committees to give them the opportunity to add an amendment to the bill to provide conditions under which withdrawals of normal trade relations with China could occur should China attack or invade Taiwan. This motion failed on a vote of 176–258. As lobbyists stepped up their efforts, their actions and those of the Republican leadership and the Clinton administration bore fruit. Every single uncommitted Republican voted for the bill, joining seventy-three Democrats to grant China permanent normal trade status as the bill passed by a surprisingly large margin of 237–197. "Frankly, they surprised me a bit. Members in the last few hours really turned around and understood how important this was," said DeLay, who earned the nickname "The Hammer" for his efforts to have members vote his way. Stunned labor leaders admitted that they were outgunned. "The business community unleashed an unprecedented campaign that was hard for anyone to match," said the president of the United Auto Workers.[49]

As the bill was transmitted to the Senate, critics sprang into action. Senator Jesse Helms (R–NC), chair of the Foreign Relations Committee and a major critic of the Beijing government, immediately put fellow Republicans on notice that he would not rubber stamp the actions of the House. Although amendments were not allowed in the House, Senate rules that permit amendment were seen as a way of changing the nature of the bill and causing the amended version to go back to the House for a vote. Secretary Daley immediately went to see the Senate majority leader and members of the Senate Finance Committee, which had jurisdiction over the bill, to ask their assistance in fending off amendments.

While hearings on China were being held in the House, the Senate Finance Committee had been considering the bill. Once it passed the House, however, it was reported out of the Senate Finance Committee immediately on May 25. On that day, Senators Fred Thompson (R–TN) and Robert Torricelli (D–NJ) held a press conference to announce that they would offer parallel legislation based on their concerns about Chinese proliferation of weapons of mass destruction to continue a yearly review of China as a condition of open trade with that nation. They viewed the opening of PNTR to China as a national security as well as a trade issue.

The Senate began debating S 2277 on July 26, 2000. The next day, after a filibuster was begun by several opponents of the bill including Senators Robert Byrd (D–WV), Jesse Helms (R–NC), Barbara Mikulski (D–MD), and Ben Nighthorse Campbell (R–CO), a move to invoke cloture was brought by the majority leader and several others. Cloture then was invoked by a vote of 86–12, well over the sixty votes required. The Senate recessed shortly thereafter. Debate on S 2277 began anew on September 5, after the Labor Day recess. At that time, until the final vote on September 19, 2000, scores of amendments were offered by senators; all failed by various margins. On September 19, 2000, the bill passed without amendment on a 83–15 vote with most senators voting as they had done on the cloture motion. Throughout that period, however, lobbyists kept up their pressure on the committed to make sure that no amendments were added to the bill that would require House reconsideration.

The bill was signed by President Clinton on October 10, 2000, amid considerable fanfare. Throughout the course of this bill becoming law, Clinton used his office in a way reminiscent of Lyndon B. Johnson's cajoling of recalcitrant legislators. One member got a new zip code for a small town and another got a natural gas pipeline for his district.[50] In the end, these kinds of efforts were crucial to House passage of the bill.

China became a member of the World Trade Organization on December 11, 2001. On December 28, 2001, President George W. Bush signed a formal proclamation granting normal trading status to China, ending annual reviews.

HOW MEMBERS MAKE DECISIONS

As a bill makes its way through the labyrinth of the law-making process described above, members are confronted with the question: How should I vote? Members often listen to their own personal beliefs on many matters, but those views can often be moderated by other considerations. To avoid making any voting mistakes, members look to a variety of sources for cues.

Constituents

Constituents—the people who live and vote in the home district or state—are always in the member's mind when casting a vote.[51] It is rare for a legislator to vote against the wishes of his or her constituency regularly, particularly on issues of welfare rights, domestic policy, or other highly salient issues such as civil rights, abortion, or war. Most constituents often have strong convictions on one or more of these issues. For example, during the 1960s, representatives from southern states could not hope to keep their seats for long if they voted in favor of proposed civil rights legislation. But, gauging how voters feel about any particular issue often is not easy. Because it is virtually impossible to know how the folks back home feel on all issues, a representative's perception of their preferences is important. Even when voters have opinions, legislators may get little guidance if their district is narrowly divided. Abortion is an issue about which many voters feel passionately, but a legislator whose district has roughly equal numbers of pro-choice and pro-life advocates can satisfy only a portion of his or her constituents.

If an issue affects their constituents, a representative often will try to determine how the people back home feel about it. Staff members often keep running tallies of the letters and phone calls for and against a policy that will be voted on soon. Only if a legislator has strong personal preferences will he or she vote against a clearly expressed desire of their constituents. Studies by political scientists show that members vote in conformity with prevailing opinion in their districts about two-thirds of the time.[52] On average, Congress passes laws that reflect national public opinion at about the same rate.[53] Legislators tend to act on their own preferences as trustees when dealing with topics that have come through the committees on which they serve or issues that they know about as a result of experience in other contexts, such as their vocation. On items of little concern to people back in the district or for which the legislator has little firsthand knowledge, the tendency is to turn to other sources for voting cues. The opinions of one's colleagues, especially those who belong to one's party, often weigh heavily when casting a roll-call vote.

Senator Mitch McConnell (R–KY) meets with constituents at a naval gun plant in Louisville. McConnell toured the plant and touted the more than $30 million in pork barrel spending he helped to secure from the Department of Defense budget.

(Photo courtesy: Brian Bohannon/AP/Wide World Photos)

Colleagues

The range and complexity of issues confronting Congress means that no one can be up to speed on more than a few topics. When members must vote on bills about which they know very little, they often turn for advice to colleagues who have served on the committee that handled the legislation. On issues that are of little interest to a legislator, logrolling, or vote trading, often occurs. Logrolling often takes place on specialized bills targeting money or projects to selected congressional districts. A yea vote by an unaffected member often is given to a member in exchange for the promise of a future yea vote on a similar piece of specialized legislation.

Other appeals are of a more personal nature. During the China trade bill effort, for example, representatives often lobbied each other.

Party

Political parties are another important source of influence. Members often look to party leaders for indicators of how to vote. Indeed, it is the whips' job in each chamber to reinforce the need for party cohesion, particularly on issues of concern to the party. From 1970 to the mid-1990s, the incidence of party votes in which majorities of the two parties took opposing sides roughly doubled to more than 60 percent of all roll-call votes. When the Republicans took control of Congress in 1995, the parties divided over three-quarters of the time in both the House and the Senate, making 1995 the most partisan year in generations. Partisan voting decreased in 1999 to 47.1 percent,[54] its lowest in a decade. These numbers surprised many, given media attention to political acrimony on the Hill. Still, party makes a big difference, especially in times of **divided government,** the term used to describe the political condition in which different political parties control the White House and Congress (see Figure 7.6). Although public opinion polls have found that Americans tend to like divided government, it does make it harder for either party to govern and often results in congressional leaders pulling out all the stops to keep their partisans together.[55]

Today, many members of Congress elected on a partisan ticket feel a degree of obligation to their party and to the president if he is of the same party. The national political parties have little say in who gets a party's nomination for the U.S. Senate or the House. But, once a candidate has emerged successfully from a primary contest (see chapter 13), both houses have committees that provide campaign assistance. It is to each party's advantage to win as many seats as possible in each house. If a member is elected with the financial support or campaign visits from popular members and party leaders, he or she is much more inclined to toe the party line.

divided government
The political condition in which different political parties control the White House and Congress.

FIGURE 7.6   Divided Government

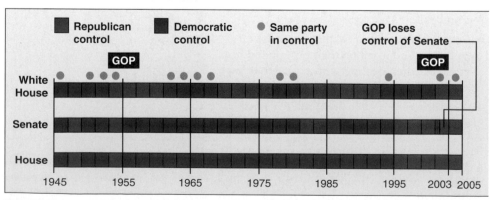

Source: "Total Control," Washington Post (January 20, 2001). © 2001, The Washington Post, reprinted with permission. Updated by authors.

Caucuses

Special-interest caucuses were created to facilitate member communication—often across party lines—over issues of common concern. Caucuses also complement and counterbalance the informational roles played by the committee system.[56] By 1994, there were at least 140 special-interest caucuses, including many formed to promote certain industries, such as textile, tourism, wine, coal, steel, mushrooms, and cranberries, or to advance particular views or interests.

Before 1995, twenty-seven caucuses enjoyed special status as legislative service organizations (LSOs), and Congress provided staff, office space, and budgets for them. Included among these were the liberal Congressional Black Caucus, the Congressional Caucus for Women's Issues, and the Democratic Study Group. In 1995, the Republican majority voted to abolish LSOs.[57] Without institutional support, most of the caucuses have died while others have lost influence and members. Said Representative Charles Rangel (D–NY) of the bipartisan Narcotics Abuse and Control Caucus, "We just couldn't keep it together."[58] The Congressional Caucus for Women's Issues reorganized to form an informal caucus with the same name but without a paid staff or budget. Its Republican and Democratic co-chairs and co-vice chairs use their own staff to conduct caucus business.

State and regional caucuses are another important source of information exchange among members and across party lines. Large state delegations, such as those of California, New York, and Texas, often work together, regardless of party lines, to bring the bacon home to their states. Some state caucuses hold weekly meetings to assure that their interests are adequately represented on important committees and to keep abreast of pending legislation that might affect their states.

Interest Groups and Lobbyists

A primary function of most lobbyists, whether they work for interest groups or large corporations, is to provide information to supportive or potentially supportive legislators, committees, and their staffs.[59] It's likely, for example, that a representative knows the National Rifle Association (NRA) position on gun control legislation. What the legislator needs to get from the NRA is information and substantial research on the feasibility and impact of such legislation. How could the states implement such legislation? Is it constitutional? Will it really have an impact on violent crime or crime in schools? Organized interests can win over undecided legislators or confirm the support of their friends by providing information that legislators use to justify the position they have embraced. They also can supply direct campaign contributions, volunteers, and publicity to members seeking reelection.

Pressure groups also use grassroots appeals to pressure legislators by urging their members in a particular state or district to call, write, fax, or e-mail their senators or representatives. Lobbyists can't vote, but voters back home can and do. Lobbyists and the corporate or other interests they represent, however, can contribute to political campaigns and are an important source of campaign contributions. Many have political action committees to help support members seeking reelection.

Political Action Committees

While a link to a legislator's constituency may be the most effective way to influence behavior, that is not the only path of interest group influence on member decision making.[60] The high cost of campaigning has made members of Congress, especially those without huge personal fortunes, attentive to those who help pay the tab for the high cost of many campaigns. The almost 5,000 political action committees (PACs) organized by interest groups are a major source of most members' campaign funding. When

Otilie English, left, a lobbyist for the Afghani Northern Alliance, stands with photos of Afghanistan refugee children in need, during a Congressional Caucus for Women's Issues briefing co-chaired by Representative Judy Biggert (R–IL) in the 107th Congress. Committee staffers are instrumental in setting up briefings for members.

(Photo courtesy: Kenneth Lambert/AP/Wide World Photos)

an issue comes up that is of little consequence to his or her constituents, which the legislator has no strong opinion there is, not surprisingly, a tendency to support the positions of those interests who helped pay for the last campaign. After all, who wants to bite the hand that feeds him or her? (Interest groups and PACs are discussed in detail in chapter 16. PACs are also discussed in chapter 14.)

Staff and Support Agencies

Members of Congress rely heavily on members of their staffs for information on pending legislation.[61] Staff members prepare summaries of bills and brief the representative or senator based on their research. If the bill is nonideological or one on which the member has no real position, staff members can be very influential. Staff members also do research on and even draft bills that a member wishes to introduce.

Staff aides are especially crucial in the Senate. Because senators have so many committee assignments and often are spread so thin, they frequently rely heavily on aides. Every legislator has personal staff and other staff who work for each committee and subcommittee.

The support personnel at the Congressional Budget Office and the Congressional Research Service at the Library of Congress also are considered to be staff working for Congress (see Table 7.6). Even with the reduction in House committee staffers enacted by Republicans in 1995, the ranks of congressional staff total almost 14,000, albeit a number down from the 1980s.

The next time you see a televised Senate hearing, notice how each senator has at least one aide sitting behind him or her, ready with information and often even with questions for the senator to ask. Members also rely on the support agencies described in Table 7.6.

CONGRESS AND THE PRESIDENT

The Constitution envisioned that the Congress and the president would have discrete powers and that one branch would be able to hold the other in check. Over the years, and especially since the 1930s, the president often has held the upper hand. In times

TABLE 7.6 Congressional Support Agencies

Congressional Research Service (CRS)	General Accountability Office (GAO)	Congressional Budget Office (CBO)
Created in 1914 as the Legislative Research Service (LRS), the CRS is administered by the Library of Congress and responds to more than a quarter of a million congressional requests for information each year. The service provides nonpartisan studies of public issues, compiling facts on both sides of issues, and it conducts major research projects for committees at the request of members. The CRS also prepares summaries of all bills introduced and tracks the progress of major bills.	The GAO was established in 1921 as an independent regulatory agency for the purpose of auditing the financial expenditures of the executive branch and federal agencies. Today, the GAO performs four additional functions: It sets government standards for accounting, it provides a variety of legal opinions, it settles claims against the government, and it conducts studies upon congressional request.	The CBO was created in 1974 to evaluate the economic effect of different spending programs and to provide information on the cost of proposed policies. It is responsible for analyzing the president's budget and economic projections. The CBO provides Congress and individual members with a valuable second opinion to use in budget debates.

of crisis or simply when it was unable to meet public demands for solutions, Congress willingly has handed over its authority to the chief executive. Even though the chief executive has been granted greater latitude, legislators do, of course, retain ultimate legislative authority to question executive actions and to halt administration activities by cutting off funds. Congress also wields the ultimate oversight power—the power to impeach and even remove the president from office.

The Shifting Balance of Power

The balance of power between Congress and the executive branch has seesawed over time. The post–Civil War Congress attempted to regain control of the vast executive powers that President Abraham Lincoln, recently slain, had assumed. Angered at the refusal of Lincoln's successor, Andrew Johnson, to go along with its radical "reforms" of the South, Congress passed the Tenure of Office Act, which prevented the president, under the threat of civil penalty, from removing any Cabinet-level appointees of the previous administration. Johnson accepted the challenge and fired Lincoln's secretary of war, who many believed was guilty of heinous war crimes. The House voted to impeach Johnson, but the desertion of a handful of Republican senators prevented him from being removed from office. (The effort fell short by one vote.) Nonetheless, the president's power had been greatly weakened, and the Congress again became the center of power and authority in the federal government.

Beginning in the early 1900s, however, a series of strong presidents acted at the expense of congressional power. Theodore Roosevelt, Franklin D. Roosevelt, and Lyndon B. Johnson, especially, viewed the presidency as carrying with it enormous powers.

Over the years, especially since the presidency of Franklin D. Roosevelt, Congress has ceded to the president a major role in the legislative process. Today, for example, Congress often finds itself responding to executive branch proposals, as illustrated by the law-making process surrounding trade relations with China. Critics of Congress point to its slow and unwieldy nature as well as the complexity of national problems as reasons that Congress often doesn't seem to act on its own.

Congressional Oversight of the Executive Branch

Since the 1960s, there has been a substantial increase in the **oversight** of the executive branch by Congress.[62] Oversight subcommittees became particularly prominent in the 1970s and 1980s as a means of promoting investigation and program review, to determine if an agency, department, or office is carrying out its responsibilities as intended by Congress.[63] It also includes checking on possible abuses of power by governmental officials, including the president.

oversight
Congressional review of the activities of an agency, department, or office.

Join the Debate

From the 1970s to the mid-1990s, Congress granted the president "fast track" negotiating authority over trade agreements with some countries. Fast track means that Congress agrees to vote on the president's negotiated agreement, up or down, with no amendments. Such authority had to be renewed every few years. However, Congress refused to extend the authority to President Bill Clinton, despite his aggressive push for its renewal.

Fast track authority is controversial for two reasons. First, it features battles between business lobbyists, who prefer trade policies with few restrictions, and labor union and environmental lobbyists, who fear that business and presidential trade agreements will hurt workers and environmental protection. Second, such an arrangement is an explicit grant of power from Congress to the president and, thus, shifts the balance of power away from Congress.

In 2001 and 2002, President George W. Bush pressed aggressively for, and finally received (in a series of very close votes), fast track authority under the name Trade Promotion Authority. Yet, electoral politics and interest group battles are likely to assure that this battle repeats itself in each presidential administration. Read and think about the following excerpted news article from 2002, when Congress and President Bush were very much in the heat of the battle on his effort and Congress's response. Then, join the debate. Should Congress authorize fast track authority? Who gains and who loses from such a decision? Consider the debating points and questions posed at the end of this feature, and sharpen your own arguments for the position you find most viable.

House Backs Trade Power for President

Narrow Vote Ends 8 Years of Battle over Authority

By Mike Allen and Juliet Eilperin

The House ended an eight-year battle with two White Houses yesterday by voting 215 to 212 to restore presidential power to negotiate iron-clad trade deals, which the Bush administration plans to use to open markets around the world for U.S. crops, machinery and other products. President Bush argued for trade promotion authority, formerly known as "fast track," in every economic speech since taking office, and it is one of the plans he cites in contending that he has a blueprint to put the juice back in economic recovery.

The Republican-controlled House had refused similar entreaties from former president Bill Clinton. The power, which was held by Bush's five predecessors and

had expired in 1994, prevents Congress from amending trade deals and instead restricts lawmakers to voting them up or down....

Trade bills have traditionally been more problematic in the House than in the Senate, where lawmakers have to worry less about a particular factory or industry because they represent an entire state instead of a district.

Commerce Secretary Donald L. Evans said the vote "sends a powerful signal to the markets in America."

Hailing the agreement, U.S. Trade Representative Robert B. Zoellick said that in the past eight years, "we have paid a price. America fell behind other nations."

Another trade official said the measure will allow the administration to begin work immediately on agreements with Chile and Singapore to allow tariff-free trading with those nations. Several American fast-food chains in Chile now use Canadian potatoes in their french fries, because that nation has a free-trade agreement and the products are

cheaper. "Now, those will be our potatoes," the official said.

The administration also hopes to secure a free-trade accord with countries in Central America and with Morocco, the official said. U.S. wheat, vegetable oil and other farm products will have many new markets, as will road graders and other heavy machinery by manufacturers such as Caterpillar, the official said....

Bush, celebrating a major victory after several weeks on the defensive about economic issues, praised the House for what he called landmark legislation that "will open markets, expand opportunity and create jobs for American workers and farmers."

Bush golfed at Andrews Air Force Base yesterday with three senior House Republicans. "We're celebrating a victory in the House, playing golf with House members who helped convince their fellow members that trade is good for the economy and trade is good for the working people," he said before teeing off with Reps. Dan Burton (Ind.), Tom DeLay (Tex.) and Michael G. Oxley (Ohio).

House Ways and Means Committee Chairman Bill Thomas (R-Calif.) joked about the narrow margin as he triumphantly left the Capitol after a battle that forced the White House and GOP leadership to threaten, beg and sweat. "I wasted two votes," he said. "I don't want to be profligate with these votes."

Republicans voted for the bill 190 to 27, with five not voting. Democrats opposed the bill, 183 to 25, with two not voting. Both independents—Reps. Virgil H. Goode Jr. (Va.) and Bernard Sanders (Vt.)—voted against the bill.

The key to passage was the defection of several New Democrats, who generally favor free trade and try to work with business. The bill was a top priority of business interests, which have spent weeks in the legislative cross hairs because of mushrooming corporate accounting scandals. Labor unions fought the change, but sponsors were able to pick up some Democratic votes by including health and training benefits for some laid-off workers....

House Democrats hope to use the trade issue to unseat several vulnerable Republicans, although the defections yesterday of a handful of centrist Democrats allowed some vulnerable GOP lawmakers to switch and vote against the bill. Among them was Rep. Robin Hayes (R-N.C.), who, in December, provided the one-vote margin for a previous version of the bill but voted against it this time.

Trade could still emerge as a contentious issue in several House races where two incumbents face each other because of redistricting, since in each case the Republican backed the bill while the Democrat opposed it. AFL-CIO President John J. Sweeney vowed that GOP lawmakers would pay a price for their votes.

For some centrist Democrats, supporting presidential trade authority gave them an opportunity to make amends with the business community after voting against the bill the first time....

Source: Mike Allen and Juliet Eilperin, *Washington Post* (July 28, 2002): A1. ©2001, The Washington Post, reprinted with permission.

JOIN THE DEBATE!

CHECK YOUR UNDERSTANDING: Make sure you understand the following key points from the article; go back and review it if you missed any of them:

- All recent presidents except Clinton have had fast track authority.
- Business groups support fast track authority, while labor unions oppose it.
- Most House Republicans traditionally support fast track authority, while most House Democrats oppose it.
- President George W. Bush won fast track negotiating authority, though in very close votes in the House.

ADDITIONAL INFORMATION: News articles don't provide all the information an informed citizen needs to know about an issue under debate. Here are some questions the article does not answer that you may need to consider in order to join the debate:

- Why were side deals necessary for President George W. Bush to win House Republican votes?
- Why do labor unions oppose fast track authority?
- What might congressional oversight over the trade negotiating process entail?
- How effective is use of the fast track issue in congressional elections?

What other information might you want to know? Where might you gather this information? How might you evaluate the credibility of the information you gather? Is the information from a reliable source? Can you identify any potential biases?

IDENTIFYING THE ARGUMENTS: Now that you have some information on the issue, and have thought about what else you need to know, see whether you can present the arguments on both sides of the debate. Here are some ideas to get you started. We've provided one example each of "pro" and "con" arguments, but you should be able to offer others:

PRO: Congress should grant presidents fast track trade promotion authority. Here's why:

- Members of Congress face too much pressure from district-centered forces to make trade decisions that have national implications. Only the president can truly represent the interests of the entire nation, so such a grant of authority serves the national interest.

CON: Congress should NOT grant presidents fast track trade promotion authority. Here's why:

- In our current era of presidential government, further concessions of power from Congress only weakens the balance of power built into our political system, creating a too-powerful presidency, and empowering those interests (such as economic powers) that have a greater ability to influence big decisions over those interests (such as labor and environmental protection) that have power in other centers of the political system.

TAKING A POSITION AND SUPPORTING IT: After thinking about the information in the article on fast track trade authority and articulating the arguments in the debate, what position would you take? What information supports your position? What arguments would you use to persuade others to your side of the debate? How would you counter arguments on the other side?

Former Homeland Security Secretary Tom Ridge, center, is greeted by Representatives John Peterson (R–PA), left, and Don Sherwood (R–PA) at an informal hearing of a House Appropriations Committee subcommittee on Capitol Hill in April 2002.
(Photo courtesy: Tim Sloan/AFP Photo)

Key to Congress's performance of its oversight function is its ability to question members of the administration and the bureaucracy to see if they are enforcing and interpreting the laws passed by Congress as the members intended. These committee hearings, now routinely televised, are among Congress's most visible and dramatic actions. Millions, for example, tuned in to watch the House's investigations of Presidents Richard M. Nixon and Bill Clinton, the Senate's investigation of the Iran-Contra affair, and the Senate's trial of President Clinton.

By the late 1990s, a series of costly congressional investigations led some to question the high cost of Senate oversight. Executive branch investigations by the Republican Congress cost over $200 million through 2000. In contrast, Congress allotted far less for the arts and job training programs.[64]

Hearings are not used simply to gather information. Hearings that focus on particular executive branch actions often signal that Congress believes changes in policy need to be made before an agency next comes before the committee to justify its budget. Recent research reveals that the more the legislative body sees the oversight committee as not representative of the House or Senate as a whole, the more likely it will allow the executive branch leeway in adopting regulations to implement congressional policy.[65]

Hearings also are used to improve the administration of programs. Since most members of House and Senate committees and subcommittees are interested in the issues under their jurisdiction, they often want to help bureaucrats and not hinder them.

Although most top government officials appear before various House and Senate committees regularly to update them on their activities, this is not necessarily the case for those who do not require Senate confirmation, such as Tom Ridge when he became the Office of Homeland Security Director (before becoming the secretary of the department) or former National Security Advisor Condoleezza Rice. Sometimes members of the administration are reluctant to appear before Congress. Tom Ridge, for example, repeatedly refused requests to testify before Congress from a variety of committees looking into important homeland security issues, including the creation of a shadow government. Members believe that they are being left in the dark while asked to allocate money for a wide array of new programs.

In refusing to allow Ridge to testify, the Bush administration cited what it called "executive prerogative," a term that also was used to justify Vice President Dick Cheney's refusal to turn over information to lawmakers concerning private conversations he had with top Enron and other energy company officials when he was formulating administration energy policies. That standoff prompted Congress's investigative office to file suit to get the information it wanted from Cheney.[66] In response to Ridge's refusal, angry members of the then Democratic-controlled Senate approved legislation requiring Ridge to testify. Both situations represent the constant tension between the two branches of government as well as between a Democratic Senate and a Republican executive branch. When Democrats controlled the Senate, President Bush sought "to set limits on congressional oversight of his administration," while Congress tried to reassert its role in the governing process.[67]

Legislators augment their formal oversight of the executive branch by allowing citizens to appeal adverse bureaucratic decisions to agencies, Congress, and even the courts. The Congressional Review Act of 1996 allows Congress to nullify agency regulations by joint resolutions of legislative disapproval. This process, called **congressional review,** is another method of exercising congressional oversight.[68] The act provides Congress with sixty days to disapprove newly announced agency regulations, often passed to implement some congressional action. A regulation is disapproved if the res-

congressional review
The process by which Congress can nullify an executive branch regulation by a resolution jointly passed in both houses within sixty days of announcement of the regulation and accepted by the president.

olution is passed by both chambers and signed by the president, or when Congress overrides a presidential veto of a disapproving resolution. This act was not used until 2001 when Congress reversed Clinton administration ergonomics regulations.

Congressional review differs only marginally from another form of legislative oversight called the legislative veto. The **legislative veto,** a procedure by which one or both houses of Congress can disallow an act of an executive agency by a simple majority vote, was first added to statutes in 1932, but the vetoes were not used frequently until the 1970s. They usually were included in laws that delegated congressional powers to the executive branch while retaining the power of Congress to restrict their use. By 1981, more than 200 statutes contained legislative veto provisions. In *Immigration and Naturalization Service* v. *Chadha* (1983), however, the U.S. Supreme Court ruled that the legislative veto as it was used in many circumstances was unconstitutional because it violated separation of powers principles.[69] The Court concluded that although the Constitution gave Congress the power to make laws, the Framers were clear in their intent that Congress should separate itself from executing or enforcing the laws. It is the president's responsibility to sign or veto legislation, not the Congress's.[70] In spite of *Chadha,* however, the legislative veto continues to play an important role in executive-legislative relations. In signing the Omnibus Consolidation Recision and Appropriation Act in April 1996, for example, President Clinton noted that Congress had included a legislative veto that the Supreme Court in all likelihood would find unconstitutional under *Chadha.* Nevertheless, he signed the bill. Some scholars believe that congressional review, the constitutionality of which has yet to be reviewed, may emerge as an alternative to the legislative veto.[71]

legislative veto
A procedure by which one or both houses of Congress can disallow an act of the president or executive agency by a simple majority vote; ruled unconstitutional by the Supreme Court.

Foreign Affairs Oversight.

The Constitution divides foreign policy powers between the executive and the legislative branches. The president has the power to wage war and negotiate treaties, whereas the Congress has the power to declare war and the Senate has the power to ratify treaties. The executive branch, however, has become preeminent in foreign affairs despite the constitutional division of powers. This is partly due to a series of crises and the development of nuclear weapons in the twentieth century; both have necessitated quick decision making and secrecy, which are much easier to manage in the executive branch. Congress, with its 535 members, has a more difficult time reaching a consensus and keeping secrets.

After years of playing second fiddle to a series of presidents from Theodore Roosevelt to Richard M. Nixon, a "snoozing Congress" was "aroused"[72] and seized for itself

The War Powers Act, passed during the height of the Vietnam War, requires a president to obtain congressional approval before committing troops to a combat zone.

(Photo courtesy: J.P. Fizet/Corbis Sygma)

War Powers Act
Passed by Congress in 1973; the president is limited in the deployment of troops overseas to a sixty-day period in peacetime (which can be extended for an extra thirty days to permit withdrawal) unless Congress explicitly gives its approval for a longer period.

the authority and expertise necessary to go head-to-head with the chief executive. In a delayed response to Lyndon B. Johnson's 1964–1969 conduct of the Vietnam War, Congress passed in 1973 the **War Powers Act** over President Nixon's veto. This act requires any president to obtain congressional approval before committing U.S. forces to a combat zone and to notify Congress within forty-eight hours of committing troops to foreign soil. In addition, the president must withdraw troops within sixty days unless Congress votes to declare war. The president also is required to consult with Congress, if at all possible, prior to committing troops.

The War Powers Act has been of limited effectiveness in claiming a larger congressional role in international crisis situations. Presidents Gerald Ford, Jimmy Carter, and Ronald Reagan never consulted Congress in advance of committing troops, citing the need for secrecy and swift movement, although each president did notify Congress shortly after the incidents. They contended that the War Powers Act was probably unconstitutional because it limits presidential prerogatives as commander in chief. When Congress does try to get into the foreign affairs area, it often seems to botch it. In 1999, for example, the House voted to bar President Bill Clinton from deploying ground troops to Kosovo without its approval. But, ultimately, it took six often contradictory votes on intervention in Kosovo to formulate policy. With these kinds of confusing signals, it is not surprising that many presidents have insisted on quite a bit of autonomy in conducting foreign affairs.

In 2001, when Congress passed a joint resolution authorizing the president to use force against terrorists, the resolution included language that met War Powers Act requirements and waived the sixty-day limit on the president's authority to involve U.S. troops abroad. This action prompted two senators who served in Vietnam, John McCain (R–AZ) and John Kerry (D–MA), to express concern over handing over to the president such open-ended use of military force. President George W. Bush largely has taken the congressional resolution as a blank check to conduct the war in Iraq. Said one high-ranking Department of Justice official, "the president enjoys broad unilateral authority to use force in the war on terrorism—with or without specific congressional authorization."[73]

Confirmation of Presidential Appointments.   The Senate plays a special oversight function through its ability to confirm key members of the executive branch, as well as presidential appointments to the federal courts. As discussed in chapters 9 and 10, although the Senate generally confirms most presidential nominees, it does not always do so. A wise president considers senatorial reaction before nominating potentially controversial individuals to his administration or to the federal courts. In the case of federal district court appointments, senators often have a considerable say in the nomination of judges from their states through what is called **senatorial courtesy,** a process by which presidents generally defer selection of district court judges to the choice of senators of their own party who represent the state in which a vacancy occurs.

senatorial courtesy
A process by which presidents, when selecting district court judges, defer to the senator in whose state the vacancy occurs.

Clinton administration nominees faced a particularly hostile Congress. "Appointments have always been the battleground for policy disputes," says political scientist Calvin MacKenzie. But now, "what's new is the rawness of it—all of the veneer is off."[74] Thus, while Congress's power seems to have waned over the years, its oversight function gives it a potent weapon to thwart presidential abuses of power. Most of George W. Bush's executive appointments went fairly smoothly in spite of the 50–50 party division in the Senate that existed early in his administration. His most controversial appointee, John Ashcroft, the former Republican senator from Missouri, withstood one of the closest votes in history—58–42 to be confirmed as attorney general. Still, Democrats in the Senate sent a clear message to the Bush administration. Although they were willing to allow the new president to fill his administration with like-minded conservatives, they would not allow him to appoint the same kind of partisans to the federal courts, which has been underscored by the Senate Judiciary Committee's refusal to send some of Bush's nominees to the courts of appeals to the floor for a vote. The larger majority enjoyed by Republicans in the Senate is expected to make confirmation of President Bush's appointments in his second term fare better.

The Impeachment Process. The impeachment process is Congress's ultimate oversight of the U.S. president (as well as federal court judges). The U.S. Constitution is quite vague about the impeachment process, and much of the debate about it concerns what is an impeachable offense. The Constitution specifies that a president can be impeached for treason, bribery, or other "high crimes and misdemeanors." Most commentators agree that this phrase was meant to mean significant abuses of power. The question for the U.S. House, then, in considering whether President Bill Clinton should be removed from office was, were President Clinton's statements to the grand jury lies, and if so, did lying to a grand jury constitute a "high crime and misdemeanor" deserving of possible removal from office? In *The Federalist Papers*, Alexander Hamilton noted his belief that impeachable offenses "are of a nature which may with peculiar propriety be denominated political, as they relate chiefly to injuries done immediately to society itself."

House and Senate rules control how the impeachment process operates. (See Table 7.7.) Yet, because the process is used so rarely, and under such disparate circumstances, there are few hard and fast rules. Until 1998, the U.S. House of Representatives had voted to impeach only sixteen federal officials—and only one of those was a president, Andrew Johnson. (Of those, seven were convicted and removed from office and three resigned before the process described below was completed.)

Until late 1998, only three resolutions against presidents had resulted in further action: (1) John Tyler, charged with corruption and misconduct in 1843; (2) Andrew Johnson, charged with serious misconduct in 1868; and, (3) Richard M. Nixon, charged with obstruction and the abuse of power in 1974. The House rejected the charges against Tyler; Johnson was acquitted by the Senate by a one-vote margin; and Nixon resigned before the full House voted on the articles of impeachment. Four articles of impeachment against President Clinton were considered in the House; two of these were sent to the Senate, where the president was found not guilty of the charges contained in both articles.

TABLE 7.7 The Eight Stages of the Impeachment Process

1. **The Resolution.** A resolution, called an inquiry of impeachment, is sent to the House Judiciary Committee. Members also may introduce bills of impeachment, which are referred to the Judiciary Committee.

2. **The Committee Vote.** After the consideration of voluminous evidence, the Judiciary Committee votes on the resolution or bill of impeachment. A positive vote from the committee indicates its belief that there is sufficiently strong evidence for impeachment in the House.

3. **The House Vote.** If the articles of impeachment are recommended by the House Judiciary Committee, the full House votes to approve (or disapprove) a Judiciary Committee decision to conduct full-blown impeachment hearings.

4. **The Hearings.** Extensive evidentiary hearings are held by the House Judiciary Committee concerning the allegations of wrongdoing. Witnesses may be called and the scope of the inquiry may be widened at this time. The committee heard only from the independent counsel in the Clinton case.

5. **The Report.** The committee votes on one or more articles of impeachment. Reports supporting this finding (as well as dissenting views) are forwarded to the House and become the basis for its consideration of specific articles of impeachment.

6. **The House Vote.** The full House votes on each article of impeachment. A simple majority vote on any article is sufficient to send that article to the Senate for its consideration.

7. **The Trial in the Senate.** A trial is conducted on the floor of the Senate with the House Judiciary Committee bringing the case against the president, who is represented by his own private attorneys. The Senate, in essence, acts as the jury, with the chief justice of the United States presiding over the trial.

8. **The Senate Vote.** The full Senate votes on each article of impeachment. If there is a two-thirds vote on any article, the president automatically is removed from office and the vice president assumes the duty of the president. Both articles issued against President Clinton, charging him with lying to a grand jury and encouraging a grand jury witness to lie or mislead, were defeated in the Senate.

Continuity & Change

Representatives—In or Out of Touch?

When the Framers met in Philadelphia, they were concerned that their representatives not get too far away from the American people. Thus, the House of Representatives was created with members to stand for election every two years. The House was truly to be "the people's house." The Framers envisioned those elected to this body would well represent the interests of their constituents, go back home frequently, and not view the House as their ultimate career.

Over time, not only did members come to represent more people, making it nearly impossible for members to stay in touch with their constituents, but the kinds of people who could vote for members changed. Thus, as those who didn't own property, blacks, and women were added to the rolls of voters, the kinds of interests that members were expected to represent should have changed, but did not necessarily.

Today, although women make up more than half of the population, they make up only about 15 percent of our national lawmakers. African Americans constitute more than 12 percent of the population, but only one African American, Barack Obama (D-IL), elected in 2004, is a member of the United States Senate. When members of the Congressional Black Caucus wanted to challenge the joint session's counting of Electoral College votes in the 2000 election, they could not do so when they failed to get the signature of a single senator.

Hispanics, now the largest minority in the United States, suffer even poorer representation. Although they make up more than 13 percent of the population, they hold a small share of the seats in Congress and two seats in the Senate.

As the nation becomes more diverse ethnically and racially, and minorities as well as women hold so few seats in Congress, can that body still be seen as a representative body? Representative of whom, some might ask. Particularly when one sees the power of corporate interests, as evident in the section How a Bill Really Becomes a Law, one begins to wonder how much drastic change might take place before the interests of the citizens, as the citizenry has developed in this new century, are truly being represented.

1. Do you see the present racial, economic, and male/female composition of the Congress as a problem in truly representing the interests of "the people"?
2. Does former Senate Majority Leader Trent Lott's (R–MS) forced resignation, made after a furor about his racially insensitive remarks, signal a change in making representatives more careful to represent all of "the people"?

CAST YOUR VOTE   Is Congress representative of the American people? To cast your vote, go to **www.ablongman.com/oconnor**

SUMMARY

The size and scope of Congress, and demands put on it, have increased tremendously over the years. In presenting the important role that Congress plays in American politics, we have made the following points:

1. **The Roots of the Legislative Branch**
   Congress was molded after the bicameral British Parliament, but with an important difference. The U.S. Senate is probably the most powerful upper house in any national legislature. The Senate has unique powers to ratify treaties and to approve presidential nominees.

2. **The Constitution and the Legislative Branch of Government**
   The Constitution created a bicameral legislature with members of each body to be elected differently, and thus to represent different constituencies. Article I of the Constitution sets forth qualifications for office, states age minimums, and specifies how legislators are to be distributed among the states. The Constitution also requires seats in the House of Representatives to be apportioned by population. Thus, after every census, district lines must be redrawn to reflect population shifts. The Constitution also provides a vast array of enumerated and implied powers to Congress. Some, such as law-making and oversight, are shared by each house of Congress; others are not.

3. **The Members of Congress**
   Members of Congress live in two worlds—in their home districts and in the District of Columbia. Casework is one way to keep in touch with the district, since members, especially those in the House, never stop running for office. Incumbency is an important factor in winning reelection. Thus, many have called for limits on congressional terms of office.

4. How Congress Is Organized

Political parties play a major role in the way Congress is organized. The speaker of the House is traditionally a member of the majority party, and members of the majority party chair all committees. In 1995, Speaker Newt Gingrich became the most powerful speaker since the first decade of this century. Because the House of Representatives is large, the speaker enforces more rigid rules on the House than exist in the Senate.

In addition to the party leaders, Congress has a labyrinth of committees and subcommittees that cover the entire range of government policies, often with a confusing tangle of shared responsibilities. Each legislator serves on one or more committees and multiple subcommittees. It is in these environments that many policies are shaped and that members make their primary contributions to solving public problems.

5. The Law-making Function of Congress

The road to enacting a bill into law is long and strewn with obstacles, and only a small share of the proposals introduced become law. Legislation must be approved by committees in each house and on the floor of each chamber. In addition, most House legislation initially is considered by a subcommittee and must be approved by the Rules Committee before getting to the floor. Legislation that is passed in different forms by the two chambers must be resolved in a conference before going back to each chamber for a vote and then to the president, who can sign the proposal into law, veto it, or allow it to become law without his signature. If Congress adjourns within ten days of passing legislation, that bill will die if the president does not sign it.

6. How Members Make Decisions

A multitude of factors impinge on legislators as they decide policy issues. The most important of the many considerations are constituents' preferred options and the advice given by better informed colleagues. When clear and consistent cues are given by voters back home, legislators usually heed their demands. In the absence of strong constituency preferences, legislators may turn for advice to colleagues who are experts on the topic or to interest-group lobbyists, especially those who have donated to their campaigns.

7. Congress and the President

Although the Framers intended for Congress and the president to have discrete spheres of authority, over time, power shifted between the two branches, with Congress often appearing to lose power to the benefit of the president. Still, Congress has attempted to oversee the actions of the president and the executive branch through committee hearings where members of the administration testify. Congress also has used the legislative veto and, more recently, congressional review to take back power from the president. Congress also has attempted to rein in presidential power through passage of the War Powers Act, to little practical effect. Congress, through the Senate, also possesses the power to confirm or reject presidential appointments. Its ultimate weapon is the power of impeachment and conviction.

KEY TERMS

bicameral legislature, p. 223
bill, p. 224
casework, p. 228
cloture, p. 249
conference committee, p. 242
congressional review, p. 260
delegate, p. 231
discharge petition, p. 244
divided government, p. 254
filibuster, p. 249
hold, p. 248
impeachment, p. 226
incumbency factor, p. 228
legislative veto, p. 261
line-item veto, p. 250
majority leader, p. 238
majority party, p. 235
minority leader, p. 238
minority party, p. 236
oversight, p. 257
party caucus or conference, p. 238
pocket veto, p. 249
politico, p. 232
pork barrel, p. 244
redistricting, p. 224
senatorial courtesy, p. 262
speaker of the House, p. 235
standing committee, p. 242
term limits, p. 229
trustee, p. 231
War Powers Act, p. 262
whip, p. 238

SELECTED READINGS

Aberbach, Joel D. *Keeping a Watchful Eye*. Washington, DC: Brookings Institution, 1990.

Bianco, William T., ed. *Congress on Display, Congress at Work*. Ann Arbor: University of Michigan Press, 2000.

Deering, Christopher J., and Steven S. Smith, *Committees in Congress*, 3rd ed. Washington, DC: CQ Press, 1997.

Dodd, Lawrence C., and Bruce I. Oppenheimer, eds. *Congress Reconsidered*, 7th ed. Washington, DC: CQ Press, 2000.

Fenno, Richard F., Jr. *Home Style: House Members in Their Districts*. Boston: Little, Brown, 1978.

Fox, Richard Logan. *Gender Dynamics in Congressional Elections*. Beverly Hills, CA: Sage, 1996.

Gill, Laverne McCain. *African American Women in Congress: Forming and Transforming History*. New Brunswick, NJ: Rutgers University Press, 1997.

Hibbing, John R., and Elizabeth Theiss-Morse. *Congress as Public Enemy: Public Attitudes Toward American Political Institutions*. New York: Cambridge University Press, 1996.

Kaptur, Marcy. *Women of Congress*. Washington, DC: CQ Press, 1996.

Loomis, Burdett A., ed. *Esteemed Colleagues: Civility and Deliberation in the U.S. Senate*. Washington, DC: Brookings Institution, 2000.

Mayhew, David R. *Congress: The Electoral Connection*. New Haven, CT: Yale University Press, 1986.

Oleszek, Walter J. *Congressional Procedures and the Policy Process*, 5th ed. Washington, DC: CQ Press, 2000.

Price, David E. *The Congressional Experience: A View from the Hill*, 2nd ed. Boulder, CO: Westview Press, 2000.

Schickler, Eric. *Disjointed Pluralism: Institutional Innovation and the Development of the U.S. Congress*. Princeton, NJ: Princeton University Press, 2001.

Swers, Michele. *The Difference Women Make: The Policy Impact of Women in Congress*. Chicago: University of Chicago Press, 2002.

Thurber, James A., and Roger H. Davidson, eds. *Remaking Congress: Change and Stability in the 1990s*. Washington, DC: CQ Press, 1995.

Wawro, Gregory. *Legislative Entrepreneurship in the U.S. House of Representatives*. Ann Arbor: University of Michigan Press, 2001.

Wolfensberger, Donald R. *Congress and the People: Deliberative Democracy on Trial*. Washington, DC: Woodrow Wilson Center, 2001.

NOTES

1. For an outstanding account of Pelosi's campaign for the whip post, see Juliet Eilperin, "The Making of Madam Whip: Fear and Loathing—and Horse Trading—The Race for the House's No. 2 Democrat," *Washington Post* (January 6, 2002): W27.

2. "Mother of All Whips," *Pittsburgh Post-Gazette* (February 9, 2002): A11.

3. Sue Thomas, *How Women Legislate* (New York: Oxford University Press, 1994); and Karen O'Connor, ed., *Women and Congress: Running, Winning and Ruling* (New York: Haworth Press, 2001).

4. David C. Kimball and Samuel C. Patterson, "Living Up to Expectations: Public Attitudes Toward Congress," *Journal of Politics* 59 (August 1997): 701–28.

5. John R. Hibbing and Elizabeth Theiss-Morse, "The Media's Role in Fomenting Public Disgust with Congress," *Extensions* (Fall 1996): 15–18.

6. Charles S. Bullock III, "House Careerists: Changing Patterns of Longevity and Attrition," *American Political Science Review* 66 (December 1972): 1295–1300.

7. Richard F. Fenno Jr., *Home Style: House Members in Their Districts* (Boston: Little, Brown, 1978), 32.

8. Hedrick Smith, *The Power Game* (New York: Ballantine Books, 1989), 108.

9. Norman Ornstein, ed., *Vital Statistics on Congress* (Washington, DC: CQ Press, 1998), 135.

10. Gary W. Cox and Jonathan N. Katz, "Why Did the Incumbency Advantage in U.S. House Elections Grow?" *American Journal of Political Science* 40 (May 1996): 478–97; and Kenneth N. Bickers and Robert M. Stein, "The Electoral Dynamics of the Federal Pork Barrel," *American Journal of Political Science* 40 (November 1996): 1300–26.

11. Marjorie Randon Hershey, "Congressional Elections," in Gerald M. Pomper et al., *The Election of 1992: Reports and Interpretations* (Chatham, NJ: Chatham House, 1993), 159.

12. Alan I. Abramowitz, "Incumbency, Congressional Spending, and the Decline of Competition in House Elections," *Journal of Politics* 53 (February 1991): 34–56.

13. *U.S. Term Limits* v. *Thornton*, 115 U.S. 1842 (1995).

14. Warren E. Miller and Donald Stokes, "Constituency Influence in Congress," *American Political Science Review* 57 (March 1963): 45–57.

15. Public Opinion Online, Accession Number 0363310, Question Number 054, June 14–18, 2000, R-Poll (NEXIS).

16. See also Cindy Simon Rosenthal, *Women Transforming Congress* (Norman: University of Oklahoma Press, 2002); O'Connor, *Women and Congress*; and Susan J. Carroll, ed., *The Impact of Women in Public Office* (Bloomington: Indiana University Press, 2002).

17. Center for American Women and Politics, *Voices, Views, Votes: The Impact of Women in the 103rd Congress* (New Brunswick, NJ: Eagleton Institute of Politics, Rutgers, 1995), 15.

18. Adam Clymer, "Daughter of Slavery Hushes Senate," *New York Times* (July 23, 1993): B6.

19. Barbara Hinckley, *Stability and Change in Congress*, 3rd ed. (New York: Harper & Row, 1983), 166.

20. Katharine Seelye, "Congressional Memo: New Speaker, New Style, Old Problem," *New York Times* (March 12, 1999): A18.

21. Karen Foerstel, "Hastert and the Limits of Persuasion," *CQ Weekly* (September 30, 2000): 2252.

22. Barbara Sinclair, "The Struggle over Representation and Lawmaking in Congress: Leadership Reforms in the 1990s," in James A. Thurber and Roger H. Davidson, eds., *Remaking Congress: Change and Stability in the 1990s* (Washington, DC: CQ Press, 1995), 105.

23. Quoted in Donald R. Matthews, *U.S. Senators and Their World* (Chapel Hill: University of North Carolina Press, 1960), 97–8.

24. Steven S. Smith and Eric D. Lawrence, "Party Control of Congress in the Republican Congress," in Lawrence C. Dodd and Bruce I. Oppenheimer, eds. *Congress Reconsidered*, 6th ed. (Washington, DC: CQ Press, 1997), 163–4. For more on the role of parties in the organization of Congress, see Forrest Maltzman, *Competing Principals: Committees, Parties, and the Organization of Congress* (Ann Arbor: University of Michigan Press, 1997).

25. "What Is the Democratic Caucus?" http://dcaucusweb.house.gov/about/what_is.asp.

26. Woodrow Wilson, *Congressional Government: A Study in American Government* (New York: Meridian Books, 1956, originally published in 1885), 79.

27. Roger H. Davidson, "Congressional Committees in the New Reform Era: From Combat to the Contract," in Thurber and Davidson, *Remaking Congress*, 28.

28. See E. Scott Adler, *Why Congressional Reforms Fail: Reelection and the House Committee System* (Chicago: University of Chicago Press, 2002).

29. For more about committees, see Christopher Deering and Steven S. Smith, *Committees in Congress*, 3rd ed. (Washington, DC: CQ Press, 1997).

30. Kenneth A. Shepsle, *The Giant Jigsaw Puzzle: Democratic Committee Assignments in the Modern House* (Chicago: University of Chicago Press, 1978).

31. Jack Anderson, "Subcontractor Oversight Absent," *Press Journal* (May 17, 1999): A8.

32. Tim Groseclose and Charles Stewart III, "The Value of Committee Seats in the House, 1947–91," *American Journal of Political Science* 42 (April 1998): 453–74.

33. Guy Gugliotta, "Term Limits on Chairman Shake Up House," *Washington Post* (March 22, 1999): A4.

34. Miles Benson, "New Faces Inevitable Among House Leadership," *Times-Picayune* (June 15, 2000): A7.

35. Keith Krehbiel, "Cosponsors and Wafflers from A to Z." *American Journal of Political Science* 39 (November 1995): 906–23.

36. Barbara Sinclair, *The Transformation of the U.S. Senate* (Baltimore, MD: Johns Hopkins University Press, 1989).

37. Helen Dewar, "Senate Lifts Veil on Bill 'Holds': Leaders Remove Anonymity from Long-Used Delay Tactic," *Washington Post* (March 4, 1999): A8.

38. Don Phillips, "Biden Stalls Transportation Picks," *Washington Post* (March 28, 2002): A4.

39. Ibid.

40. Sarah A. Binder and Steven S. Smith, *Politics or Principle: Filibustering in the United States* (Washington, DC: Brookings Institution, 1997).

41. James A. Thurber, "If the Game Is Too Hard, Change the Rules: Congressional Budget Reform in the 1990s," in Thurber and Davidson, *Remaking Congress*, 140.

42. *Clinton v. City of New York*, 524 U.S. 417 (1998).

43. David E. Sanger, "Rounding Out a Clear Clinton Legacy," *New York Times* (May 25, 2000): A1.

44. Sanger, "Rounding Out," A1, A10.

45. Eric Schmitt, "How a Hard-Driving G.O.P. Gave Clinton a Trade Victory," *New York Times* (May 26, 2000): A1.

46. John Burgess, "A Winning Combination: Money, Message, and Clout," *Washington Post* (May 25, 2000): A4.

47. David E. Rosenbaum, "With Smiles and Cell Phones, a Last-Minute Assault on the Undecided," *New York Times* (May 25, 2000): A11.

48. Schmitt, "How a Hard-Driving."

49. Ibid.

50. Sanger, "Rounding Out," A1, A10.

51. See L. Martin Overby, "The Senate and Justice Thomas: A Note on Ideology, Race, and Constituent Pressures," *Congress & the Presidency* 21 (Autumn 1994): 131–6.

52. John W. Kingdon, *Congressmen's Voting Decisions*, 3rd ed. (Ann Arbor: University of Michigan Press, 1989).

53. Ibid. See also Lee Sigelman, Paul J. Wahlbeck, and Emmett H. Buell Jr., "Vote Choice and the Preference for Divided Government: Lessons of 1992," *American Journal of Political Science* 41 (July 1997): 879–94.

54. Daniel Jo Parks, "Partisan Voting Holds Steady," *CQ Weekly*, (December 11, 1999): 2975–7.

55. *National Journal* 26 (December 17, 1994): 2996.

56. Scott H. Ainsworth and Francis Akins, "The Informational Role of Caucuses in the U.S. Congress," *American Politics Quarterly* 25 (October 1997): 407–30.

57. Jonathan D. Salant, "LSOs Are No Longer Separate, the Work's Almost Equal," *Congressional Quarterly* 53 (May 27, 1995): 1483.

58. A. B. Stoddard, "Caucuses Lose Influence After LSOs Abolished," *The Hill* (February 14, 1996): 2.

59. Ken Kollman, "Inviting Friends to Lobby: Interest Groups, Ideological Bias, and Congressional Committees," *American Journal of Political Science* 41 (April 1997): 519–44. See also Marie Hojnacki and David C. Kimball, "Organized Interests and the Decision of Whom to Lobby in Congress," *American Political Science Review* 92 (December 1998): 775–90.

60. Robert Beirsack, Paul Herrnson, and Clyde Wilcox, *After the Revolution: PACs, Lobbies and the Republican Congress* (Boston: Allyn and Bacon, 1999).

61. Barbara S. Romzek and Jennifer A. Utter, "Congressional Legislative Staff: Political Professionals or Clerks?" *American Journal of Political Science* 41 (October 1997): 1251–79; and Susan Webb Hammond, "Recent Research on Legislative Staffs," *Legislative Studies Quarterly* (November 1996): 543–76.

62. Joel D. Aberbach, *Keeping a Watchful Eye: The Politics of Congressional Oversight* (Washington, DC: Brookings Institution, 1990).

63. William F. West, "Oversight Subcommittees in the House of Representatives, *Congress & the Presidency* 25 (Autumn 1998): 147–60.

64. Jonathan D. Salant, "GOP Reveals the Cost of Senate Oversight," *Washington Post* (January 9, 1998): A19.

65. Steven J. Balla, "Legislative Organization and Congressional Review of Agency Regulations," paper delivered at the 1999 annual meeting of the Midwest Political Science Association.

66. Nick Anderson, "Ridge's Refusal to Testify Irks Lawmakers," *Los Angeles Times* (March 16, 2002): A14.

67. Ibid.

68. This discussion draws heavily on Balla, "Legislative Organization and Congressional Review."

69. 462 U.S. 919 (1983).

70. Daniel Baracskay, Review of *The Power of Separation: American Constitutionalism and the Myth of the Legislative Veto*, in *Journal of Politics* 61 (May 1999): 555–7.

71. Wayne Washington, "Wrangling Intensifies on US Rules: Little-Known Law Becomes Weapon in Partisan Fights," *Boston Globe* (March 26, 2001): A1.

72. *Wall Street Journal* (April 13, 1973): 10.

73. Craig Gilbert, "Use of Force Is President's Call," *Milwaukee Journal Sentinel* (April 18, 2002): A8.

74. Quoted in Stewart M. Powell, "Lee Fight Signals Tougher Battles Ahead on Nomination," *Commercial Appeal* (December 21, 1997): A15.

The Presidency

When Ronald Reagan died on June 5, 2004, many Americans were able to see, for the first time in recent memory, the grandeur of a presidential state funeral. As Americans first in California, and then in Washington, D.C., lined up for hours to pay their respects to the fortieth president of the United States. Reagan was the first president to lie in state in the Rotunda of the Capitol since Lyndon B. Johnson did in January 1973, and one of only nine American presidents to do so.

The 200 plus years of presidential funerals underscore the esteem with which most Americans accord the office of the president, regardless of its occupant. Just before the first president, George Washington, died, he made it known that he wanted his burial to be a quiet one, "without parade of funeral oration."[1a] He also asked that he not be buried for three days; at that time, it was not without precedent to make this kind of request out of fear of being buried alive.[1b] Despite these requests, Washington's funeral was a state occasion as hundreds of soldiers with their rifles held backward, marched to Mount Vernon, Virginia, where he was interred. Across the nation, imitation funerals were held, and the military wore black arm bands for six months.[1c] It was during his memorial service that Henry Lee declared that Washington was "first in war, first in peace, and first in the hearts of his countrymen."[1d]

When Abraham Lincoln died in 1865 after being wounded by an assassin's bullet, more than a dozen funerals were held for him as hundreds of thousands of mourners lined the way as the train carrying his open casket traveled the 1,700 miles to Illinois, where he was buried, along with the body of his young son, who had died three years earlier.

One of the first things that a president is asked to do upon taking office is to consider his funeral plans. The military alone has a book 138 pages long devoted to the kind of ceremony and traditions that were so evident in the Reagan funeral, from the horse-drawn caisson to the riderless horse with boots hung backward in the stirrups to indicate that the deceased will ride no more, to the twenty-one gun salute to the flyover by military aircraft. Each president's family, however, has personalized their private, yet also public opportunity to mourn. The Reagan family, for example, filed a 300 page plan for his funeral in 1989 and updated it regularly. Former Presidents Ford, Carter, and Bush all have filed formal plans; Bill Clinton has yet to do so.

The Reagan funeral also created a national timeout from the news of war, and even presidential campaigns were halted in respect to the deceased president. Said one historian, the event gave Americans the opportunity to "rediscover . . . what holds us together instead of what pulls out apart."[1e] This is often the role of presidents . . . in life or in death.

*T*he constitutional authority, statutory powers, and burdens of the presidency make it a powerful position and an awesome responsibility. Most of the men who have been president in the past two decades have done their best, yet many have come up short. Not only did the Framers not envision such a powerful role for the president, but they could not have foreseen the skepticism with which many presidential actions are now greeted in the press, on talk radio, and on the Internet. Presidents have gone into policy arenas never dreamed of by the Framers. Imagine, for example, what the Framers might have thought about President Clinton's 1998 State of the Union message, which advocated eighteen as a national norm for class size in the lower grades. But, by the 2000 presidential campaign, both major party candidates embraced education and smaller class sizes as national priority, further underscoring the key role presidents can play in setting national policy agendas.

The modern media, used by successful presidents to help advance their agendas, have brought us "closer" to our presidents, making them seem more human, a mixed blessing for those trying to lead. Only two photographs exist of Franklin D. Roosevelt in a wheelchair—his paralysis was a closely guarded secret. Five decades later, Bill Clinton was asked on national TV what kind of underwear he preferred (briefs). Later, revelations about his conduct with Monica Lewinsky made this exchange seem tame. This demystifying of the president and increased mistrust of government make governing a difficult job. A president relies on more than the formal powers of office to lead the nation: Public opinion and public confidence are key components of his ability to get his programs adopted and his vision of the nation implemented. As political scientist Richard E. Neustadt has noted, the president's power often rests on his power to persuade.[1f] To persuade, he not only must be able to forge links with members of Congress; he also must have the support of the American people and the respect of foreign leaders.

The ability to persuade and to marshal the informal powers of the presidency have become more important over time. In fact, the presidency of George W. Bush and the circumstances that surround it are dramatically different from the presidency of his father (1989–1993). America is changing dramatically and so are the responsibilities of the president and people's expectations of the person who holds that office. Presidents in the last century battled the Great Depression, fascism, communism, and several wars involving American soldiers. With the Cold War over, until the war in Afghanistan, there were few chances for recent presidents to demonstrate their leadership in the face of adversity. Moreover, it is hard to lead on the domestic front when divided government or gridlock has become the norm.

The tension between public expectations about the presidency and the formal powers of the president permeate our discussion of how the office has evolved from its humble origins in Article II of the Constitution to its current stature. In this chapter,

- First, we will examine the *roots of the office of president of the United States* and discuss how the Framers created a chief executive officer for the new nation.
- Second, we will discuss Article II and the *constitutional powers of the president*.
- Third, we will examine the *development of presidential power* and a more personalized presidency: How well a president is able to execute the laws often depends strongly on his personality, popularity, and leadership style.

- Fourth, to help you understand more fully the development of the office of the president as a central focus of power and action in the American political system, we will also discuss the development of what is called the *presidential establishment*. Myriad departments, special assistants, and a staff of advisers help the president but also make it easier for a president to lose touch with the common citizen.

- Fifth, we will focus on the *role of the president in the legislative process*. Since the days of Franklin D. Roosevelt, most presidents have played major roles in setting the national policy agenda—a power that Congress is now trying to reclaim.

- Sixth, we will examine the *president and public opinion*, including the effect that public opinion has on the American presidency as well as the role the president plays in molding public opinion.

- In our exploration of the theme of *continuity and change*, we will examine the case for a woman president in the context of the historical efforts to elect a woman to that office.

THE ROOTS OF THE OFFICE OF PRESIDENT OF THE UNITED STATES

The earliest example of executive power in the colonies was the position of royal governor. The king of England appointed a royal governor to govern a colony. He normally was entrusted with the "powers of appointment, military command, expenditure, and—within limitations—pardon, as well as with large powers in connection with the powers of law making."[2] Royal governors often found themselves at odds with the colonists and especially with the elected colonial legislatures. As representatives of the Crown, the governors were distrusted and disdained by the people, many of whom had fled from Great Britain to escape royal domination. Others, generations removed from England, no longer felt strong ties to the king.

When the colonists declared their independence from England in 1776, their distrust of a strong chief executive remained. Most state constitutions reduced the office of governor to a symbolic post elected annually by the legislature. Governors were stripped of most rights we assume an executive must have today, including the right to call the legislature into session or to veto its acts. The constitution adopted by Virginia in 1776 illustrates prevailing colonial sentiment. It cautioned that "the executive powers of government" were to be exercised "according to the laws" of the state, and that no powers could be claimed by the governor on the basis of "any law, statute, or custom of England."[3]

Although most of the states opted for a more "symbolic" governor, some states did entrust wider powers to their chief executives. The governor of New York, for example, was elected directly by the people. Perhaps because he was directly accountable to the people, he was given the power to pardon, the duty to execute the law faithfully to the best of his ability, and the power to act as commander in chief of the state militia.

The Constitutional Convention

As we saw in chapter 2, the delegates to the Philadelphia Convention quickly decided to dispense with the Articles of Confederation and fashion a new government composed of three branches—the legislative (to make the laws), the executive (to execute, or implement, the laws), and the judicial (to interpret the laws). The Framers had little difficulty in agreeing that executive authority should be vested in one person, although some delegates suggested multiple executives to diffuse the power of the executive branch. Under the Articles of Confederation, there had been no executive branch

John Hanson was the first president of the United States. Hanson, a representative from Maryland, became president of the Continental Congress of America on November 5, 1781. The position of president under the Articles of Confederation, however, was largely ceremonial.

(Photo courtesy: Maryland Historical Society, Baltimore, Maryland)

WEB EXPLORATION
To learn more about specific presidents, see www.ablongman.com/oconnor

Twenty-Second Amendment
Adopted in 1951, prevents a president from serving more than two terms or more than ten years in office.

impeachment
The power delegated to the House of Representatives in the Constitution to charge the president, vice president, or other "civil officers," including federal judges, with "Treason, Bribery, or other high Crimes and Misdemeanors." This is the first step in the constitutional process of removing such government officials from office.

of government; the eighteen different men who served as the president of the Continental Congress of the United States of America were president in name only—they had no actual authority or power in the new nation. Yet, because the Framers were so sure that George Washington—whom they had trusted with their lives during the Revolutionary War—would become the first president of the new nation, many of their deepest fears were calmed. They agreed on the necessity of having one individual speak on behalf of the new nation, and they all agreed that one individual should be George Washington.

The Framers also had no problem in agreeing on a title for the new office. Borrowing from the constitutions of Pennsylvania, Delaware, New Jersey, and New Hampshire, the Framers called the new chief executive the president. How the president was to be chosen and by whom was a major stumbling block. James Wilson of Philadelphia suggested a single, more powerful president, who would be elected by the people and "independent of the legislature." Wilson also suggested giving the executive an absolute veto over the acts of Congress. "Without such a defense," he wrote, "the legislature can at any moment sink it [the executive] into non-existence."[4]

The manner of the president's election haunted the Framers for a while, and their solution to the dilemma is described in detail in chapter 13. We leave the resolution of that issue—the creation of the electoral college—aside for now and turn instead to details of the issues the Framers resolved quickly.

Qualifications for Office.   The Constitution requires that the president (and the vice president, whose major function is to succeed the president in the event of his death or disability) be a natural-born citizen of the United States, at least thirty-five years old, and a resident of the United States for at least fourteen years. In the 1700s, it was not uncommon for those engaged in international diplomacy to be out of the country for substantial periods of time, and the Framers wanted to make sure that prospective presidents spent some time on this country's shores before running for its highest elective office. Most presidents have prior elective experience, too, as revealed in Table 8.1.

Terms of Office.   Although three of the five last presidents were not reelected to a second term, at one time, the length of a president's term was controversial. Four-, seven-, and eleven-year terms with no eligibility for reelection were suggested by various delegates to the Constitutional Convention. Alexander Hamilton suggested that a president serve during "good behavior." The Framers ultimately reached agreement on a four-year term with eligibility for reelection.

The first president, George Washington (1789–1797), sought reelection only once, and a two-term limit for presidents became traditional. Although Ulysses S. Grant unsuccessfully sought a third term, the two terms established by Washington remained the standard for 150 years, avoiding the Framers' much-feared "constitutional monarch," a perpetually reelected tyrant. In the 1930s and 1940s, however, Franklin D. Roosevelt ran successfully in four elections as Americans fought first the Great Depression and then World War II. Despite Roosevelt's popularity, negative reaction to his long tenure in office ultimately led to passage (and ratification in 1951) of the **Twenty-Second Amendment.** It limits presidents to two four-year terms, or a total of ten years in office, should a vice president assume a portion of a president's remaining term.

Removal.   During the Constitutional Convention, Benjamin Franklin was a staunch supporter of **impeachment,** a process by which to begin to remove an official from office. He noted that "historically, the lack of power to impeach had necessitated recourse to assassination."[5] Not surprisingly, then, he urged the rest of the delegates to formulate a legal mechanism to remove the president and vice president.

Just as the veto power was a check on the power of Congress, the impeachment provision ultimately included in Article II was adopted as a check on the power of the president. Each house of Congress was given a role to play in the impeachment process

TABLE 8.1   Personal Characteristics of the Men Who Became President

President	Place of Birth	Higher Education	Occupation	First Political Office/ Last Political Office Before Presidency	Years in Congress	Years as Governor	Years as Vice President	Age at Becoming President
George Washington	VA	William & Mary	Farmer/ surveyor	County surveyor/ military general	2	0	0	57
John Adams	MA	Harvard	Farmer/ lawyer	Highway surveyor/ vice president	5	0	4	61
Thomas Jefferson	VA	William & Mary	Farmer/ lawyer	State legislator/ vice president	5	3	4	58
James Madison	VA	Princeton	Farmer	State legislator/ secretary of state	15	0	0	58
James Monroe	VA	William & Mary	Farmer/ lawyer	State legislator/ secretary of state	7	4	0	59
John Quincy Adams	MA	Harvard	Lawyer	Minister to Netherlands/ secretary of state	0[a]	0	0	58
Andrew Jackson	SC	None	Lawyer	Prosecuting attorney/ U.S. senator	4	0	0	62
Martin Van Buren	NY	None	Lawyer	County surrogate/ vice president	8	0	4	55
William H. Harrison	VA	Hampden	Military	Territorial delegate/ minister to Colombia	0	0	0	68
John Tyler	VA	William & Mary	Lawyer	State legislator/ vice president	12	2	0	51
James K. Polk	NC	North Carolina	Lawyer	State legislator/ governor	14	3	0	50
Zachary Taylor	VA	None	Military	None/military general	0	0	0	65
Millard Fillmore	NY	None	Lawyer	State legislator/ vice president	8	0	1	50
Franklin Pierce	NH	Bowdoin	Lawyer	State legislator/ district attorney	9	0	0	48
James Buchanan	PA	Dickinson	Lawyer	County prosecutor/ minister to Great Britain	20	0	0	65
Abraham Lincoln	KY	None	Lawyer	State legislator/ U.S. representative	2	0	0	52
Andrew Johnson	NC	None	Tailor	City alderman/ vice president	14	4	0	57
Ulysses S. Grant	OH	West Point	Military	None/military general	0	0	0	47
Rutherford B. Hayes	OH	Kenyon	Lawyer	City solicitor/governor	3	6	0	55
James A. Garfield	OH	Williams	Educator/ lawyer	State legislator/ U.S. senator	18	0	0	50
Chester A. Arthur	VT	Union	Lawyer	State engineer/ vice president	0	0	1	51
Grover Cleveland	NJ	None	Lawyer	District attorney/ governor	0	2	0	48
Benjamin Harrison	OH	Miami (Ohio)	Lawyer	City attorney/ U.S. senator	6	0	0	56
Grover Cleveland	NJ	None	Lawyer	District attorney/ governor	0	2	0	53
William McKinley	OH	Allegheny	Lawyer	Prosecuting attorney/ governor	14	4	0	54
Theodore Roosevelt	NY	Harvard	Lawyer/ author	State legislator/ vice president	0	2	1	43
William H. Taft	OH	Yale	Lawyer	Prosecuting attorney/ secretary of war	0	0	0	52
Woodrow Wilson	VA	Princeton	Educator	Governor/governor	0	2	0	56
Warren G. Harding	OH	Ohio Central	Newspaper editor	State legislator/ U.S. senator	6	0	0	56

(continued)

TABLE 8.1   (continued)

President	Place of Birth	Higher Education	Occupation	First Political Office/ Last Political Office Before Presidency	Years in Congress	Years as Governor	Years as Vice President	Age at Becoming President
Calvin Coolidge	VT	Amherst	Lawyer	City council/ vice president	0	2	3	51
Herbert Hoover	IA	Stanford	Engineer	Relief administrator/ secretary of commerce	0	0	0	55
Franklin D. Roosevelt	NY	Harvard	Lawyer	State legislator/ governor	0	4	0	49
Harry S Truman	MO	None	Clerk/store owner	County judge/ vice president	10	0	0	61
Dwight D. Eisenhower	TX	West Point	Military	None/military general	0	0	0	63
John F. Kennedy	MA	Harvard	Lawyer	U.S. representative/ U.S. senator	14	0	0	43
Lyndon B. Johnson	TX	Southwest Texas State Teachers' College	Educator	U.S. representative/ vice president	24	0	3	55
Richard M. Nixon	CA	Whittier/Duke	Lawyer	U.S. representative/ vice president	6	0	8	56
Gerald R. Ford	NE	Michigan/Yale	Lawyer	U.S. representative/ vice president	25	0	2	61
Jimmy Carter	GA	Naval Academy	Farmer/ business owner	County board of education/governor	0	4	0	52
Ronald Reagan	IL	Eureka	Actor	Governor/governor	0	8	0	69
George Bush	MA	Yale	Business owner	U.S. representative/ vice president	4	0	8	64
Bill Clinton	AR	Georgetown/ Yale	Lawyer	State attorney general/governor	0	12	0	46
George W. Bush	CT	Yale/Harvard	Business owner	Governor/governor	0	6	0	54

[a] Adams served in the U.S. House for six years after leaving the presidency.

Sources: Adapted from *Presidential Elections Since 1789*, 4th ed. (Washington, DC: CQ Press, 1987), 4; Norman Thomas, Joseph Pika, and Richard Watson, *The Politics of the Presidency*, 3rd ed. (Washington, DC: CQ Press, 1993), 490; Harold W. Stanley and Richard G. Niemi, eds., *Vital Statistics on American Politics 2001–2002* (Washington, DC: CQ Press, 2001).

WEB EXPLORATION
For a chronology of the Clinton impeachment hearings, see www.ablongman.com/oconnor

articles of impeachment
The specific charges brought against a president or a federal judge by the House of Representatives.

to assure that the chief executive could be removed only for "Treason, Bribery, or other high Crimes and Misdemeanors."

The Constitution gives the House of Representatives the power to conduct a thorough investigation in a manner similar to a grand jury proceeding to determine whether or not the president has engaged in any of those offenses (see chapter 7). If the finding is positive, the House is empowered to vote to impeach the president by a simple majority vote. The Senate then acts as a court of law and tries the president for the charged offenses, which are called **articles of impeachment**. (The chief justice of the United States presides over the Senate hearing and the vote on the articles.) A two-thirds majority vote in the Senate on any count contained in the articles of impeachment is necessary to remove the president from office. Only two presidents, Andrew Johnson and Bill Clinton, were impeached by the House of Representatives. Neither man, however, was removed from office by the Senate. (For more on how the impeachment process works, see The Eight Stages of the Impeachment Process, Table 7.7, p. 263.)

Succession.   Through 2005, eight presidents died in office from illness or assassination. William H. Harrison was the first president to die in office—he caught a cold at his inauguration in 1841 and died one month later. (John Tyler thus became the first vice president to succeed to the presidency.) In 1865, Abraham Lincoln became the first president to be assassinated. In 1974, Richard M. Nixon, facing impeachment and likely conviction, became the first president to resign from office. The Framers were aware that a system of orderly transfer of power was necessary, so they created the office of the vice president. Moreover, the Constitution directs Congress to select a successor if the office of vice president is vacant. To clarify this provision, Congress passed the Presidential Succession Act of 1947, which lists—in order—those in line (after the vice president) to succeed the president:

1. Speaker of the House of Representatives
2. President pro tempore of the Senate
3. Secretaries of state, treasury, and defense, and other Cabinet heads in order of the creation of their department

The Succession Act has never been used because there has always been a vice president to take over when a president died in office. The **Twenty-Fifth Amendment,** in fact, was added to the Constitution in 1967 to assure that this will continue to be the case. Should a vacancy occur in the office of the vice president, the Twenty-Fifth Amendment directs the president to appoint a new vice president, subject to the approval (by a simple majority) of both houses of Congress.

The Twenty-Fifth Amendment has been used twice in its relatively short history. In 1973, President Richard M. Nixon selected House Minority Leader Gerald R. Ford (R–MI) to replace Vice President Spiro Agnew after Agnew resigned in the wake of charges of bribe taking, corruption, and income tax evasion. Less than a year later, when Vice President Ford became the thirty-eighth president after Nixon's resignation, he nominated, and the House and Senate approved, former New York Governor Nelson A. Rockefeller to be his vice president. This chain of events set up for the first time in U.S. history a situation in which neither the president nor the vice president had been elected to those positions.

The Twenty-Fifth Amendment also contains a section that allows the vice president and a majority of the Cabinet (or some other body determined by Congress) to deem a president unable to fulfill his duties. It sets up a procedure to allow the vice

Twenty-Fifth Amendment
Adopted in 1967 to establish procedures for filling vacancies in the office of president and vice president as well as providing for procedures to deal with the disability of a president.

When President Abraham Lincoln was shot by John Wilkes Booth in Ford's Theater, he became the first of four presidents assassinated in office.

(Photo courtesy: Museum of the City of New York)

Immediately after September 11, 2001, Vice President Dick Cheney was moved to an "undisclosed location." The formerly very visible vice president was no longer around, and in the wake of a Government Accountability Office request for documents about his and the administration's connections to the oil industry, political cartoonists used his being unavailable at an undisclosed location for continued security reasons as an opportunity to poke fun at him.

(Photo courtesy: Danziger/©Tribune Media Services, Inc. All Rights Reserved. Reprinted with permission.)

Questions Arise About Mr. Cheney's Connection to ENRON

president to become "acting president" if the president is incapacitated. The president also voluntarily can relinquish his power. In 1985, following the spirit of the amendment, President Ronald Reagan sent Vice President George Bush a letter that made Bush the acting president during Reagan's eight-hour surgery for colon cancer.

The Vice President

The Framers paid little attention to the office of vice president beyond the need to have an immediate official "stand-in" for the president. Initially, for example, the vice president's one and only function was to assume the office of president in the case of the death of the president or some other emergency. After further debate, the delegates made the vice president the presiding officer of the Senate (except in cases of presidential impeachment). They feared that if the Senate's presiding officer was chosen from the Senate itself, one state would be short a representative. However, the vice president was given the authority to vote in the event of a tie.

With so little authority, for many years the vice presidency was considered a sure place for a public official to disappear into obscurity. When John Adams wrote to his wife, Abigail, about his position as America's first vice president, he said it was "the most insignificant office that was the invention of man … or his imagination conceived."[6]

Power and fame generally come only to those vice presidents who become president. Just "one heartbeat away" from the presidency, the vice president serves as a constant reminder of the president's mortality. In part, this situation quickly gave rise to a series of uneasy relationships between presidents and vice presidents that began as early as Adams and Thomas Jefferson. As historian Arthur M. Schlesinger Jr. once noted, "The Vice President has only one serious thing to do: that is, to wait around for the President to die. This is hardly the basis for a cordial and enduring friendship."[7]

In the past, presidents chose their vice presidents largely to "balance," politically, geographically, or otherwise, the presidential ticket, with little thought given to the possibility of the vice president becoming president. Franklin D. Roosevelt, for example, a liberal New Yorker, selected John Nance Garner, a conservative Texan, to be his running mate in 1932. After serving two terms, Garner—who openly disagreed with Roosevelt over many policies, including Roosevelt's decision to seek a third term—unsuccessfully sought the 1940 presidential nomination himself.

The Bush/Cheney and Gore/Lieberman tickets in 2000 also showed an effort to balance the ticket, but in ways different from the past. Many speculated that Gore selected Senator Joe Lieberman (D–CT), one of the first Democrats to speak out against President Clinton's moral lapses, to counter attacks on his own character and early support of Clinton. In contrast, most commentators agreed that Dick Cheney was chosen to provide "gravitas"—i.e., a sense of national governmental experience, especially in foreign affairs, that Governor Bush neither had nor claimed.

How much power a vice president has depends on how much the president is willing to give him. Although Jimmy Carter, a Southerner, chose Walter Mondale, a Northerner, as his running mate in 1976 to balance the ticket, he was also the first president to give his vice president more than ceremonial duties. In fact, Mondale was the first vice president to have an office in the White House. (It wasn't until 1961 that a vice president even had an office in the Executive Office Building next door to the White House!) Mondale, a former senator from Minnesota with Washington connections, became an important adviser to President Carter, a former governor who had run for office as a Washington "outsider."

The "Mondale model" of an active vice president has become the norm. In fact, both Presidents Bill Clinton and George W. Bush expanded tremendously on the Mondale model. Al Gore and Clinton forged a close working (and apparently personal) relationship when they traveled the country campaigning by bus in 1992. President George W. Bush's sharing of power with his vice president, Dick Cheney, a former secretary of defense in his father's administration, has been unprecedented. Cheney was at Bush's side when every major appointment to his new administration was announced. His greater interest and experience in foreign affairs were showcased on September 11, 2001, when he, and not the president, was at the White House. No matter how much authority President Bush has opted to share with Vice President Cheney, it is clear that the days of inactive, out-of-the-loop vice presidents in America are over.

The question still exists, however, as to whether or not the vice presidency is a stepping stone to the presidency. As the 2000 campaign underscores, the vice president of a very popular president at a time of unprecedented economic prosperity was unable to translate that good will into election for himself. Since the presidency of Franklin D. Roosevelt, several vice presidents have become president. In fact, as revealed in Table 8.2, five of the twelve men who served as vice president from 1945 until 2001 became president. Three of those five, however—Presidents Truman, Johnson, and Ford—came to the office through the death or resignation of the president. (Truman and Johnson were then later elected in their own right.) Only two, Republican presidents, Nixon and Bush, were elected after serving as vice president. Richard M. Nixon actually was defeated by John F. Kennedy when he ran for president in 1960 while vice president; it wasn't until 1968, when he ran as a private citizen, that he was elected president. Two vice presidents, Democrats Hubert H. Humphrey and Al Gore, ran for president and lost. Vice President Dan Quayle unsuccessfully sought the Republican Party nomination for the presidency. Thus, since 1945, the vice presidency no longer can be viewed as an especially advantageous place from which to make a run for the presidency.

In 1919, President Woodrow Wilson had what many believed to be a nervous collapse in the summer and a debilitating stroke in the fall that incapacitated him for several months. His wife, Edith Bolling Galt Wilson, refused to admit his advisers to his sickroom, and rumors flew about the "First Lady President," as many suspected it was his wife and not Wilson who was issuing the orders.

(Photo courtesy: Stock Montage, Inc.)

WEB EXPLORATION
For more on the vice president, see
www.ablongman.com/oconnor

TABLE 8.2 The Vice Presidency: A Modern Stepping Stone to the Presidency?

President	Vice President	President Through Death or Resignation	Ran for Office	Won
Franklin D. Roosevelt	Harry S Truman	Death	1948	Won
Harry S Truman	(vacant 1945–1949)			
	Alben Barkley			
Dwight D. Eisenhower	Richard M. Nixon		1960	Lost
			1968	Won
John F. Kennedy	Lyndon B. Johnson	Death	1964	Won
Lyndon B. Johnson	Hubert H. Humphrey		1968	Lost
Richard M. Nixon	Spiro T. Agnew (resigned 1973)			
	Gerald R. Ford	Resignation	1976	Lost
Gerald R. Ford	Nelson A. Rockefeller			
	Ford ran as president			
Jimmy Carter	Walter Mondale		1984	Lost
Ronald Reagan	George Bush		1988	Won
George Bush	Dan Quayle		Sought party nomination	Lost
Bill Clinton	Al Gore		2000	Lost

THE CONSTITUTIONAL POWERS OF THE PRESIDENT

Though the Framers nearly unanimously agreed about the need for a strong central government and a greatly empowered Congress, they did not agree about the proper role of the president or the sweep of his authority. In contrast to Article I's laundry list of enumerated powers for the Congress, Article II details few presidential powers. Distrust of a powerful chief executive led to the intentionally vague prescriptions for the presidency in Article II. Nevertheless, it is these constitutional powers, when coupled with a president's own personal style and abilities, that allow him to lead the nation.

Despite the Framers' faith in George Washington as their intended first president, it took considerable compromise to overcome their continued fear of a too-powerful president. The specific powers of the executive branch that the Framers agreed on are enumerated in Article II of the Constitution. Perhaps the most important section of Article II is its first sentence: "The executive Power shall be vested in a President of the United States of America."

Over the years, the expected limits of these specific constitutional powers have changed as individual presidents asserted themselves in the political process. Some presidents are powerful and effective; others just limp along in office. Much of the president's authority stems from his position as the symbolic leader of the nation and his ability to wield power, whether those powers are enumerated specifically in the Constitution or not. When the president speaks, especially in the area of foreign affairs, he speaks for the whole nation. But, the base of all presidential authority is Article II, which outlines only a limited policy-making role for the president. Thus, as administrative head of the executive branch, the president is charged with taking "Care that the Laws be faithfully executed," but he has no actual power to make Congress enact legislation he supports. Nonetheless, the sum total of his powers, enumerated below, allows him to become a major player in the policy process.

Simulation

Presidential Leadership: Which Hat Do You Wear?

The Appointment Power

To help the president enforce laws passed by Congress, the Constitution authorizes him to appoint, with the advice and consent of the Senate, "Ambassadors, other public Ministers and Consuls, judges of the supreme Court, and all other Officers of the United States, whose Appointments are not herein otherwise provided for, and which shall be established by Law." Although this section of the Constitution deals only with appointments, behind that language is a powerful policy-making tool. The president has the authority to make more than 6,000 appointments to his administration (of which 1,125 require Senate confirmation),[8] and more than 75,000 military personnel also technically are appointed by the president. Many of these appointees are in positions to wield substantial authority over the course and direction of public policy. Although Congress has the authority "to make all laws" through the president's enforcement power—and his chosen assistants—he often can set the policy agenda for the nation. And, especially in the context of his ability to make appointments to the federal courts, his influence can be felt far past his term of office.

It is not surprising, then, that selecting the "right" people is often one of a president's most important tasks. Presidents look for a blend of loyalty, competence, and integrity. Identifying these qualities in people is a major challenge that every new president faces. Recent presidents, especially Bill Clinton and George W. Bush, have made an effort to make their Cabinets and staffs look, in President Clinton's terms, "more like America," as is underscored in Table 8.3. In fact, of the first five major appointments announced by then President-elect Bush in 2000, all but one were women and/or minorities: retired General Colin Powell (secretary of state), Condoleezza Rice (national security advisor), Texas Supreme Court Justice Alberto Gonzales (White House counsel), and long-time Bush adviser Karen Hughes (counselor to the president)*—two blacks, two women, and a Hispanic. By June 2002, when 75 percent of all appointments had been made, 21 percent of his top appointments were women and 20 to 25 percent were minorities.

In the past, when a president forwarded a nomination to the Senate for its approval, his selections traditionally were given great respect—especially those for the **Cabinet,** an advisory group selected by the president to help him make decisions and execute the laws. In fact, until the Clinton administration, the vast majority (97 percent) of all presidential nominations were confirmed.[9]

Rejections of as well as onerous delays in approving presidential nominees can have a major impact on the course of an administration. Rejections leave a president without first choices, and rejections and delays have a chilling effect on other potential nominees, affect a president's relationship with the Senate, and affect how the president is perceived by the public. George W. Bush's nomination of conservative John Ashcroft as attorney general unleashed a torrent of liberal criticism and protracted hearings. But, in the end, Ashcroft was confirmed on a 58–42 vote. It wasn't until fourteen months into his presidency that president Bush saw the defeat of one of his nominees, Charles Pickering to the U.S. Court of Appeals. Other judicial nominees faced the same kind of delays in the Democratic Senate that Clinton appointees faced in the Republican Senate.

You Are Appointing a Supreme Court Justice

Cabinet
The formal body of presidential advisers who head the fourteen executive departments. Presidents often add others to this body of formal advisers.

WEB EXPLORATION
For more on President George W. Bush's appointments, see
www.ablongman.com/oconnor

---

*Hughes later resigned to spend more time with her family, but continued to work closely with the president.

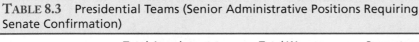

TABLE 8.3 Presidential Teams (Senior Administrative Positions Requiring Senate Confirmation)

	Total Appointments	Total Women	Percentage Women
Jimmy Carter	1,087	191	17.6%
Ronald Reagan	2,349	277	11.8%
George Bush	1,079	215	19.9%
Bill Clinton	1,257	528	42%
George W. Bush	862[a]	182	21%

[a] As of June 2002.

Sources: "Insiders Say White House Has Its Own Glass Ceiling," *Atlanta Journal and Constitution* (April 10, 1995): A4; and Judi Hasson, "Senate GOP Leader Lott Says He'll Work With Clinton," *USA Today* (December 4, 1996): 8A. Updated by the authors from data available at http://www.appointee.org.

The Power to Convene Congress

The Constitution requires the president to inform the Congress periodically of "the State of the Union," and authorizes the president to convene either or both houses of Congress on "extraordinary Occasions." In *Federalist No. 77*, Hamilton justified the latter by noting that because the Senate and the chief executive enjoy concurrent powers to make treaties, "It might often be necessary to call it together with a view to this object, when it would be unnecessary and improper to convene the House of Representatives." The power to convene Congress was important when Congress did not sit in nearly year-round sessions. Today this power has little more than symbolic significance.

The Power to Make Treaties

The president's power to make treaties with foreign nations is checked by the Constitution's stipulation that all treaties must be approved by at least two-thirds of the members of the Senate. The chief executive can also "receive ambassadors," wording that has been interpreted to allow the president to recognize the very existence of other nations.

Historically, the Senate ratifies about 70 percent of the treaties submitted to it by the president.[10] Only sixteen treaties that have been put to a vote have been rejected, often under highly partisan circumstances. Perhaps the most notable example of the Senate's refusal to ratify a treaty was its defeat of the Treaty of Versailles submitted by President Woodrow Wilson. The treaty was an agreement among the major nations to end World War I. At Wilson's insistence, it also called for the creation of the League of Nations—a precursor of the United Nations—to foster continued peace and international disarmament. In struggling to gain international acceptance for the League, Wilson had taken American support for granted. This was a dramatic miscalculation. Isolationists, led by Senator Henry Cabot Lodge (R–MA), opposed U.S. participation in the League on the grounds that the League would place the United States in the center of every major international conflict. Proponents countered that, League or no League, the United States had emerged from World War I as a world power and that membership in the League of Nations would enhance its new role. The vote in the Senate for ratification was very close, but the isolationists prevailed—the United States stayed out of the League, and Wilson was devastated.

The Senate also may require substantial amendment of a treaty prior to its consent. When President Carter proposed the controversial Panama Canal Treaty in 1977, for example, the Senate required several conditions to be ironed out between the Carter and Torrijos administrations before its approval was forthcoming.

When trade agreements are at issue, presidents often also are forced to be mindful of the wishes of Congress. The North American Free Trade Agreement (NAFTA) and the General Agreement on Tariffs and Trade (GATT) came to Congress after President Clinton and his aides had negotiated these trade agreements under special rules referred to as "fast track" procedures. These special rules are designed to protect a president's ability to negotiate with confidence that the accords will not be altered by Congress. The rules bar amendment and require an up or down vote in Congress within ninety days of introduction.

executive agreement
Formal government agreement entered into by the executive branch that does not require the advice and consent of the U.S. Senate.

Presidents often try to get around the "advice and consent" requirement for ratification of treaties and the congressional approval required for trade agreements by entering into an **executive agreement,** which allows the president to enter into secret and highly sensitive arrangements with foreign nations without Senate approval. Presidents have used these agreements since the days of George Washington, and their use has been upheld by the courts. Although executive agreements are not binding on subsequent administrations, since 1900 they have been used far more frequently than treaties, further cementing the role of the president in foreign affairs as revealed in Table 8.4.

Years	Number of Treaties	Number of Executive Agreements
1789–1839	60	27
1839–1889	215	238
1889–1929	382	763
1930–1932	49	41
1933–1944 (F. Roosevelt)	131	369
1945–1952 (Truman)	132	1,324
1953–1960 (Eisenhower)	89	1,834
1961–1963 (Kennedy)	36	813
1964–1968 (L. Johnson)	67	1,083
1969–1974 (Nixon)	93	1,317
1975–1976 (Ford)	26	666
1977–1980 (Carter)	79	1,476
1981–1988 (Reagan)	125	2,840
1989–1992 (Bush)	67	1,350
1993–2000 (Clinton)	209	2,047
2001–2002 (Bush)	21	262

TABLE 8.4 Treaties and Executive Agreements Concluded by the U.S., 1789–2002

Note: Number of treaties includes those concluded during the indicated span of years. Some of these treaties did not receive the consent of the U.S. Senate. Varying definitions of what an executive agreement comprises and their entry-into-force date make the above numbers approximate.

Source: Harold W. Stanley and Richard E. Niemi, eds., *Vital Statistics on American Politics,* 2003–2004 (Washington, DC: CQ Press, 2003): 337.

Veto Power

Presidents can affect the policy process through the **veto power,** the authority to reject any congressional legislation. "Presidential vetoes have been vital to the development of the twentieth-century presidency."[11] The threat of a presidential veto often prompts members of Congress to fashion legislation that they know will receive presidential acquiescence, if not support. Thus, simply threatening to veto legislation often gives a president another way to influence law-making.

During the Constitutional Convention, proponents of a strong executive argued that the president should have an absolute and final veto over acts of Congress. Opponents of this idea, including Benjamin Franklin, countered that in their home states the executive veto "was constantly made use of to extort money" from legislators. James Madison made the most compelling argument for a compromise on the issue:

> Experience has proven a tendency in our governments to throw all power into the legislative vortex. The Executives of the States are in general little more than Ciphers, the legislatures omnipotent. If no effectual check be devised for restraining the instability and encroachments of the latter, a revolution of some kind or other would be inevitable.[12]

In keeping with the system of checks and balances, then, the president was given the veto power, but only as a "qualified negative." Although the president was given the authority to veto any act of Congress (with the exception of joint resolutions that propose constitutional amendments), Congress was given the authority to override an executive veto by a two-thirds vote in each house. The veto is a powerful policy tool because Congress cannot usually muster enough votes to override a veto. Thus, in over 200 years, there have been approximately 2,500 presidential vetoes and only about a hundred have been overridden, as revealed in Table 8.5.

During Bill Clinton's first two years in office, he became the first president since James A. Garfield (1881) not to veto any act of Congress. But, beginning in August 1995, when he exercised his first veto involving Congress's passage of legislation to require the United States to lift its embargo of arms sales to Bosnian Muslims, Clinton found himself

veto power
The formal, constitutional authority of the president to reject bills passed by both houses of Congress, thus preventing their becoming law without further congressional action.

THE PRESIDENT'S MANY HATS

Chief law enforcer: National Guard troops sent by President Dwight D. Eisenhower enforce federal court decisions ordering the integration of public schools in Little Rock, Arkansas.

(Photo courtesy: John Bryson/Time Pix)

Leader of the party: George W. Bush accepts his party's nomination for president at the 2000 Republican National Convention.

(Photo courtesy: Mark Wilson/Newsmakers/Getty Images)

Commander in chief: President George Bush and his wife, Barbara, with troops in the Persian Gulf.

(Photo courtesy: Wally McNamee/Folio, Inc.)

Shaper of domestic policy: President Jimmy Carter announces new energy policies. Here, he wears a sweater to underscore that thermostats in the White House were turned down to save energy.

(Photo courtesy: Bettmann/CORBIS)

Key player in the legislative process: President Bill Clinton proposes legislation to Congress and the nation.

(Photo courtesy: Dirck Halstead/Getty Images)

Chief of state: President John F. Kennedy and his wife, Jacqueline, with the president of France and his wife during the Kennedys' widely publicized 1961 trip to that nation.

(Photo courtesy: Bettmann/CORBIS)

at odds with the Republican-controlled Congress and was forced to veto thirty-seven pieces of legislation through the end of his term. Only two were overridden.

The Line-Item Veto. As early as 1873, in his State of the Union message, President Ulysses S. Grant proposed a constitutional amendment to give to presidents a **line-item veto,** a power enjoyed by many governors to disapprove of individual items within a spending bill and not just the bill in its entirety. Over the years, 150 resolutions calling for a line-item veto were introduced in Congress. Presidents from Gerald R. Ford to Bill Clinton supported the concept. Finally, in 1996, Congress enacted legislation that gave the president the authority to veto specific spending provisions within a bill without vetoing the bill in its entirety. This move allowed the president to project his policy priorities into the budget by vetoing any programs inconsistent with his policy goals. It also allowed President Clinton to do away with more outrageous examples of "pork" (legislators' pet projects which often find their way into a budget). The city of New York soon challenged the line-item veto law when the president used it to stop payment of some congressionally authorized funds to the city. In *Clinton* v. *City of New York* (1998), the U.S. Supreme Court ruled that the line-item veto was unconstitutional because it gave powers to the president denied him by the U.S. Constitution. Significant alterations of executive/congressional powers, said the Court, require constitutional amendment.[13]

The Power to Preside over the Military as Commander in Chief

One of the most important constitutional executive powers is the president's authority over the military. Article II states that the president is "Commander in Chief of the Army and Navy of the United States." While the Constitution specifically grants Congress the authority to declare war, presidents since Abraham Lincoln have used the commander-in-chief clause in conjunction with the chief executive's duty to "take Care that the Laws be faithfully executed" to wage war (and to broaden various powers).

Modern presidents continually clash with Congress over the ability to commence hostilities. The Vietnam War, in which 58,000 American soldiers were killed and 300,000 were wounded, was conducted (at a cost of $150 billion) without a congressional declaration of war. In fact, acknowledging President Lyndon B. Johnson's claim to war-making authority, in 1964 Congress passed—with only two dissenting votes—the Gulf of Tonkin Resolution, which authorized a massive commitment of U.S. forces in South Vietnam.

During that highly controversial war, Presidents Johnson and then Nixon routinely assured members of Congress that victory was near. In 1971, however, publication of what were called *The Pentagon Papers* revealed what many had suspected all along—Lyndon B. Johnson systematically had altered casualty figures and distorted key facts to place

President	Regular Vetoes	Vetoes Overridden	Pocket Vetoes	Total Vetoes
Washington	2	0	0	2
J. Adams	0	0	0	0
Jefferson	0	0	0	0
Madison	5	0	2	7
Monroe	1	0	0	1
J. Q. Adams	0	0	0	0
Jackson	5	0	7	12
Van Buren	0	0	1	1
W. H. Harrison	0	0	0	0
Tyler	6	1	4	10
Polk	2	0	1	3
Taylor	0	0	0	0
Fillmore	0	0	0	0
Pierce	9	5	0	9
Buchanan	4	0	3	7
Lincoln	2	0	5	7
A. Johnson	21	15	8	29
Grant	45	4	48	93
Hayes	12	1	1	13
Garfield	0	0	0	0
Arthur	4	1	8	12
Cleveland	304	2	110	414
B. Harrison	19	1	25	44
Cleveland	42	5	128	170
McKinley	6	0	36	42
T. Roosevelt	42	1	40	82
Taft	30	1	9	39
Wilson	33	6	11	44
Harding	5	0	1	6
Coolidge	20	4	30	50
Hoover	21	3	16	37
F. Roosevelt	372	9	263	635
Truman	180	12	70	250
Eisenhower	73	2	108	181
Kennedy	12	0	9	21
L. Johnson	16	0	14	30
Nixon	26	7	17	432
Ford	48	12	18	66
Carter	13	2	18	31
Reagan	39	9	39	78
Bush	29	1	17	46
Clinton	37	2	1	38
G. W. Bush[a]	0	0	0	0
Total	1,485	107	1,068	2,553

[a]As of March 2005.

Sources: Harold W. Stanley and Richard G. Niemi, eds., *Vital Statistics on American Politics,* 2001–2002 (Washington, DC: CQ Press, 2001): 256. Data for Clinton and G. W. Bush from Office of the Clerk, U.S. House of Representatives, http://clerk.house.gov/histHigh/Congressional_History/vetoes.php.

line-item veto
The authority of a chief executive to delete part of a bill passed by the legislature that involves taxing and/or spending. The legislature may override a veto, usually with a two-thirds majority of each chamber.

In 2002, Jimmy Carter became the first U.S. president to visit Cuba since its 1959 revolution, prompting President George W. Bush to reiterate his belief that Castro is a dictator.

(Photo courtesy: Jose Goita/AP/Worldwide Photos)

War Powers Act

Passed by Congress in 1973; the president is limited in the deployment of troops overseas to a sixty-day period in peacetime (which can be extended for an extra thirty days to permit withdrawal) unless Congress explicitly gives its approval for a longer period.

pardon

An executive grant providing restoration of all rights and privileges of citizenship to a specific individual charged or convicted of a crime.

WEB EXPLORATION
To learn more about presidential pardons, go to
www.ablongman.com/oconnor

the progress of the war in a more positive light. In 1973, Congress passed the **War Powers Act** to limit the president's authority to introduce American troops into hostile foreign lands without congressional approval. President Nixon vetoed the act, but it was overridden by a two-thirds majority in both houses of Congress.

Presidents since Nixon have continued to insist that the War Powers Act is an unconstitutional infringement of their executive power. Over and over again, presidents, both Democratic and Republican, have ignored one or more provisions of the act. In 1980, Jimmy Carter failed to inform members of Congress before he initiated an unsuccessful effort to rescue American hostages at the U.S. Embassy in Iran. In 1983, President Reagan ordered the invasion of Grenada. In 1990, President Bush ordered 13,000 troops to invade Panama. And, in 1993, President Clinton sent U.S. troops to Haiti to restore its president to power. On each of these occasions, members of Congress criticized the president. Yet the president's actions in each case were judged in terms of his success and not on his possible abuse of power.

In 2001, President George W. Bush sought, and both houses of Congress approved, a joint resolution authorizing the use of force against "those responsible for the recent [September 11] attacks launched against the United States." This resolution actually gave the president more open-ended authority to wage war than his father received in 1991 to conduct the Gulf War or President Johnson received after the Gulf of Tonkin Resolution in 1964.[14] Later, in October 2002, the House (296–133) and Senate (77–23) voted overwhelmingly to allow the president to use force in Iraq "as he determines to be necessary and appropriate," thereby conferring tremendous authority on the president to wage war.

The Pardoning Power

Presidents can exercise a check on judicial power through their constitutional authority to grant reprieves or pardons. A **pardon** is an executive grant releasing an individual from the punishment or legal consequences of a crime before or after conviction, and restores all rights and privileges of citizenship. Presidents exercise complete pardoning power for federal offenses except in cases of impeachment, which cannot be pardoned. President Gerald R. Ford granted the most famous presidential pardon when he pardoned former President Nixon—who had not been formally charged with any crime—"for any offenses against the United States, which he, Richard Nixon, has committed or may have committed while in office." This unilateral, absolute pardon, prevented the former president from ever being tried for any crimes he may have committed. It also unleashed a torrent of public criticism against Ford and questions about whether or not Nixon had discussed the pardon with Ford before Nixon's resignation. Many attribute Ford's defeat in his 1976 bid for the presidency to that pardon.

In the waning days of his term, George Bush was showered with a torrent of criticism when he pardoned former Secretary of Defense Caspar Weinberger and five other administration officials on Christmas Eve 1992 for their conduct related to the Iran-Contra affair. Bush tried to place his pardons in the context of the historic use of the pardoning power to "put bitterness behind us and to look to the future."

Even though pardons are generally directed toward a specific individual, presidents have also used them to offer general amnesties. Presidents Washington, John Adams,

Madison, Lincoln, Andrew Johnson, Theodore Roosevelt, Truman, and Carter used general pardons to grant amnesty to large classes of individuals for illegal acts. Carter, for example, incurred the wrath of many veterans' groups when he made an offer of unconditional amnesty to approximately 10,000 men who had fled the United States or gone into hiding to avoid being drafted to serve in the Vietnam War.

While the pardoning power normally is not considered a key presidential power, its use by a president can get him in severe trouble with the electorate. Three presidents defeated in their reelection bids—Ford, Carter, and Bush—all incurred the wrath of the voters for unpopular pardons.

It is much less risky politically for two-term presidents to use their pardoning power. Still, President Bill Clinton found himself in hot water over the number and kinds of pardons he issued on his last day in office: 140. Just as controversial were who got them. Critics were especially concerned with his pardon of financier Marc Rich, whose ex-wife was a major Clinton contributor. In reaction to this controversy, Senators Arlen Specter (R–PA), Hillary Rodham Clinton (D–NY), and others co-sponsored legislation to require anyone lobbying for a pardon for themselves or a client to register as a lobbyist. See Figure 8.1 for a graphic illustration of presidential pardons.

THE DEVELOPMENT OF PRESIDENTIAL POWER

Each president brings to the position not only a vision of America, but also expectations about how to use presidential authority. Through 2005, the forty-two men who have held the nation's highest office have been a diverse lot. (While there have been forty three presidents, only forty-two men have held the office—Grover Cleveland served as the twenty-second and twenty-fourth president because he was elected to nonconsecutive terms in 1884 and 1892.) Most presidents find accomplishing their goals much more difficult than they envisioned. After President John F. Kennedy was in office two years, for example, he noted publicly that there were "greater limitations upon our ability to bring about a favorable result than I had imagined."[15] Similarly, as he was leaving office, President Harry S Truman mused about what surprises awaited his successor, Dwight D. Eisenhower, a former general: "He'll sit here and he'll say, 'Do this! Do that!' *And nothing will happen.* Poor Ike—it won't be a bit like the army. He'll find it very frustrating."[16]

A president's authority is limited by the formal powers enumerated in Article I of the Constitution and by the Supreme Court's interpretation of those constitutional provisions. How a president wields these powers is affected by the times in which the president serves, his confidantes and advisers, and the president's personality and leadership abilities. The 1950s postwar era of good feelings and economic prosperity presided over by the grandfatherly former war hero Dwight D. Eisenhower, for instance, called for a very different leader than that needed by the Civil War–torn nation governed by Abraham Lincoln. Furthermore, not only do different times call for different kinds of leaders; they also often provide limits, or conversely, wide opportunities, for whoever serves as president at the time. Crises, in particular, trigger expansions of presidential power. The danger to the Union posed by the Civil War in the 1860s required a strong leader to take up the reins of government. Because of his leadership during this crisis, Lincoln is generally ranked by historians as the best president (see Table 8.6).

FIGURE 8.1   Presidential Pardons
Although President Bill Clinton's pardons were more controversial than those of preceding presidents, he didn't issue significantly more. His last-minute burst of pardons, however, did produce more pardons in one year than at any time since Richard M. Nixon was president. In 2002, President George W. Bush actually appointed Elliot Abrams, who his father pardoned after he was found guilty of withholding information from Congress, as Director of the National Security Council's Office of Democracy, Human Rights and International Operations.

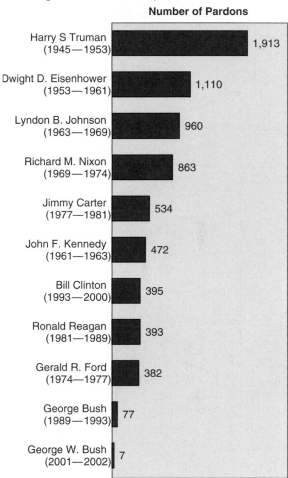

Number of Pardons

President	Number of Pardons
Harry S Truman (1945—1953)	1,913
Dwight D. Eisenhower (1953—1961)	1,110
Lyndon B. Johnson (1963—1969)	960
Richard M. Nixon (1969—1974)	863
Jimmy Carter (1977—1981)	534
John F. Kennedy (1961—1963)	472
Bill Clinton (1993—2000)	395
Ronald Reagan (1981—1989)	393
Gerald R. Ford (1974—1977)	382
George Bush (1989—1993)	77
George W. Bush (2001—2002)	7

Source: Elizabeth Wing, *USA Today* (February 2, 2001): 11A. Updated by authors.

| TABLE 8.6   The Best and the Worst Presidents |

Who was the best president and who was the worst? Many surveys of scholars have been taken over the years to answer this question, and virtually all have ranked Abraham Lincoln the best. A 2000 C-SPAN survey of fifty-eight historians, for example, came up with these results:

Ten Best Presidents	Ten Worst Presidents
1. Lincoln (best)	1. Buchanan (worst)
2. F. Roosevelt	2. A. Johnson
3. Washington	3. Pierce
4. T. Roosevelt	4. Harding
5. Truman	5. W. Harrison
6. Wilson	6. Tyler
7. Jefferson	7. Fillmore
8. Kennedy	8. Hoover
9. Eisenhower	9. Grant
10. L. Johnson (10th best)	10. Arthur (10th worst)

Source: Susan Page, "Putting Presidents in Their Place," *USA Today* (February 21, 2000): 8A.

The First Three Presidents

The first three presidents, and their conceptions of the presidency, continue to have a profound impact. When President Washington was sworn in on a cold, blustery day in New York City on April 30, 1789, he took over an office and a government that really yet were to be created. Eventually, a few hundred postal workers were hired and Washington appointed a small group of Cabinet advisers and clerks. During Washington's two terms, the entire federal budget was only about $40 million, or approximately $10 for every citizen in America. In contrast, in 2002, the federal budget was $1.96 trillion, or $6,829 for every man, woman, and child.

In furtherance of his belief in the importance of the executive office to the development of the new nation, George Washington set several important precedents for future presidents:

- He took every opportunity to establish the primacy of the national government. In 1794, for example, Washington used the militia of four states to put down the Whiskey Rebellion, an uprising of 3,000 western Pennsylvania farmers opposed to the payment of a federal excise tax on liquor. Leading those 1,500 troops was Secretary of the Treasury Alexander Hamilton, whose duty it was to collect federal taxes. Washington's action helped establish the idea of federal supremacy and the authority of the executive branch to collect the taxes levied by Congress.

- Washington began the practice of regular meetings with his advisers (called the Cabinet), thus establishing the Cabinet system.

- He asserted the prominence of the role of the chief executive in the conduct of foreign affairs. He sent envoys to negotiate the Jay Treaty with Great Britain. Then, over senatorial objection, he continued to assert his authority to negotiate treaties first and then simply submit them to the Senate for its approval. Washington made it clear that the Senate's function was limited to approval of treaties and did not include negotiation with foreign powers.

- He claimed the inherent power of the presidency as the basis for proclaiming a policy of strict neutrality when the British and French were at war. Although the Constitution is silent about a president's authority to declare neutrality, Washington's supporters argued that the Constitution granted the president **inherent powers**, that is, powers that can be derived or inferred from what is formally described in the Constitution. Thus, they argued, the president's power to conduct diplomatic relations could be inferred from the Constitution. Since neither Congress nor the

inherent powers
Powers of the president that can be derived or inferred from specific powers in the Constitution.

Supreme Court later disagreed, this power was presumed added to the list of specific, enumerated presidential powers found in Article II.

Like Washington, the next two presidents, John Adams and Thomas Jefferson, acted in ways that were critical to the development of the presidency as well as to the president's role in the political system. Adams's poor leadership skills, for example, heightened the divisions between Federalists and Anti-Federalists and probably quickened the development of political parties (see chapter 12). Soon thereafter, Jefferson used the party system to cement strong ties with the Congress and expanded the role of the president in the legislative process. He claimed that certain presidential powers were inherent and used those inherent powers to justify his expansion of the size of the nation through the **Louisiana Purchase** in 1803.

Louisiana Purchase
The 1803 land purchase authorized by President Thomas Jefferson, which expanded the size of the United States dramatically.

Congressional Triumph: 1804–1933

Although the first three presidents made enormous contributions to the office of the chief executive, the very nature of the way government had to function in its formative years caused the balance of power to be heavily weighted in favor of a strong Congress. Americans routinely had close contacts with their representatives in Congress, while to most, the president seemed a remote figure. Members of Congress frequently were at home where they were seen by voters; few citizens ever even gazed on a president.

By the end of Jefferson's first term, it was clear that the Framers' initial fear of an all-powerful, monarchical president was unfounded. The strength of Congress and the relatively weak presidents who came after Jefferson allowed Congress quickly to assert itself as the most powerful branch of government. In fact, with but few exceptions, most presidents from Jefferson to Franklin D. Roosevelt failed to exercise the powers of the presidency in any significant manner.

Andrew Jackson was the first president to act as a strong national leader, representing more than just a landed, propertied elite. By the time Jackson ran for president in 1828, eleven new states had been added to the Union, and the number of white males eligible to vote had increased dramatically as property requirements for voting were removed by nearly all states. When Jackson, a Tennessean, was elected the seventh president, it signaled the end of an era: He was the first president not to be either a Virginian or an Adams. His election launched the beginning of "Jacksonian democracy," a concept that embodied the western, frontier, egalitarian spirit personified by Jackson, the first "common man" elected president. The masses loved him, and legends were built around his down-to-earth image. Jackson, for example, once was asked to give a postmastership to a soldier who had lost his leg on the battlefield and needed the job to support his family. When told that the man hadn't voted for him, Jackson responded: "If he lost his leg fighting for his country, that is vote enough for me."[17]

Jackson used his image and personal power to buttress the developing party system by rewarding loyal followers of his Democratic Party with presidential appointments. He frequently found himself at odds with Congress and made extensive use of the veto power. His veto of twelve bills surpassed the combined total of nine vetoes used by his six predecessors. Jackson also reasserted the supremacy of the national government (and the presidency) by facing down South Carolina's nullification of a federal tariff law.

Abraham Lincoln's approach to the presidency was similar to Jackson's. Moreover, the unprecedented emergency of the Civil War allowed Lincoln to assume powers that no president before him had claimed. Because Lincoln believed he needed to act quickly for the very survival of the Union, he frequently took action without first obtaining the approval of Congress. Among many of Lincoln's "questionable" acts:

- He suspended the writ of *habeas corpus*, which allows those in prison to petition to be released, citing the need to jail persons even suspected of disloyal practices.

- He expanded the size of the U.S. army above congressionally mandated ceilings.
- He ordered a blockade of southern ports, in effect initiating a war without the approval of Congress.
- He closed the U.S. mails to treasonable correspondence.

Lincoln argued that the inherent powers of his office allowed him to circumvent the Constitution in a time of war or national crisis. Since the Constitution conferred on the president the duty to make sure that the laws of the United States are faithfully executed, reasoned Lincoln, the acts enumerated above were constitutional. He simply refused to allow the nation to crumble because of what he viewed as technical requirements of the Constitution. Noting the secession of the southern states and their threat to the sanctity of the Union, Lincoln queried, "Are all of the laws *but one* to go unexecuted, and the Government itself go to pieces lest that one be violated?"[18]

Later, both Theodore Roosevelt (1901–1909) and Woodrow Wilson (1913–1921) expanded the powers of the presidency. Roosevelt worked closely with Congress, sending it several messages defining his legislative program. Roosevelt also followed the **stewardship theory** of executive power, believing that Article II conferred on the president not only the power, but the duty to take whatever actions are deemed necessary in the national interest, unless prohibited by the Constitution or by law.[19] Wilson helped formulate bills and reinstated the practice of personally delivering the State of the Union message to Congress. World War I also forced him to take a pivotal role in international affairs.

Few presidents other than Jackson, Lincoln, Theodore Roosevelt, and Wilson subscribed to a broad and expansive interpretation of executive power prior to the administration of Franklin D. Roosevelt (1933–1945), possibly because the nation was not ready to submit to a series of strong presidents and because the times and national events did not seem to call for strong, charismatic leaders. Instead, most other presidents adopted what is known as the **Taftian theory** of presidential power, which holds that the president is limited by the specific grants of executive power found in the Constitution.[20] President William Howard Taft argued explicitly for this literalist view of presidential power, a view shared by Presidents Warren G. Harding and Calvin Coolidge, among others.

stewardship theory
The theory that holds that Article II confers on the president the power and the duty to take whatever actions are deemed necessary in the national interest, unless prohibited by the Constitution or by law.

Taftian theory
The theory that holds that the president is limited by the specific grants of executive power found in the Constitution.

The Growth of the Modern Presidency

Before the days of instantaneous communication, the nation could afford to allow Congress, with its relatively slow deliberative processes, to make most decisions. Furthermore, decision making might have been left to Congress because its members, and not the president, were closest to the people. As times and technology have changed, however, so have the public's expectations of anyone who becomes president. For example, the breakneck speed with which the electronic media such as the Cable News Network (CNN) report national and international events has intensified the public's expectation that in a crisis the president will be the individual to act quickly and decisively on behalf of the entire nation. Congress often is just too slow to respond to fast-changing events—especially in foreign affairs.

In the twentieth and twenty-first centuries, the general trend has been for presidential—as opposed to congressional—decision making to be more and more important. The start of this trend can be traced to the four-term presidency of Franklin D. Roosevelt (FDR), who led the nation through several crises. This growth of presidential power and the growth of the federal government and its programs in general are now criticized by many. To understand the basis for many of the calls for reform of the political system being made today, it is critical to understand how the growth of government and the role of the president occurred.[21]

FDR took office in 1933 in the midst of a major crisis—the Great Depression—during which a substantial portion of the U.S. workforce was unemployed. Noting the sorry state of the national economy in his inaugural address, FDR concluded, "This nation asks for action and action now." To jump-start the American economy, FDR asked Congress for and was given "broad executive powers to wage a war against the emergency, as great as the power that would be given to me if we were in fact invaded by a foreign foe."[22]

Just as Lincoln had taken bold steps on his inauguration, Roosevelt also acted quickly. He immediately fashioned a plan for national recovery called the **New Deal,** a package of bold and controversial programs designed to invigorate the failing American economy. As part of that plan, Roosevelt:

- Declared a bank holiday to end public runs on the depleted resources of many banks.
- Persuaded Congress to pass legislation to provide for emergency relief, public works jobs, regulation of farm production, and improved terms and conditions of work for thousands of workers in a variety of industries.
- Made standard the executive branch practice of sending legislative programs to Congress for its approval; before, the executive branch had generally just reacted to congressional proposals.
- Increased the size of the federal bureaucracy from fewer than 600,000 to more than 1 million workers.

New Deal
The name given to the program of "Relief, Recovery, Reform" begun by President Franklin D. Roosevelt in 1933 designed to bring the United States out of the Great Depression.

Roosevelt served an unprecedented twelve years in office (he was elected to four terms but died shortly after beginning the last one). The nation went from the economic "war" of the Great Depression to the real international conflict of World War II. The institution of the presidency changed profoundly and permanently and new federal agencies were created to implement New Deal programs as the executive branch became responsible for implementing a wide variety of new programs.

Not only did FDR create a new bureaucracy to implement his pet programs, but he also personalized the presidency by establishing a new relationship between the presidency and the people. In his radio addresses, or "fireside chats," as he liked to call them, he spoke directly to the public in a relaxed and informal manner about serious issues. He opened his radio addresses with the words, "My friends …," which made it seem as though he were speaking directly to each listener. In response to these chats, Roosevelt began to receive about 4,000 letters per day, in contrast to the forty letters per day received by his predecessor, Herbert Hoover. The head of the White House correspondence section remembered that "the mail started coming in by the truckload. They couldn't even get the envelopes open."[23] One letter that found its way to the White House was simply addressed "My Friend, Washington, D.C."

To his successors, FDR left the "modern presidency," including a burgeoning federal bureaucracy (see chapter 9), an active and usually leading role in both domestic and foreign policy and legislation, and a nationalized executive office that used technology—first radio and then television—to bring the president closer to the public than ever before.

The communication and leadership styles of post-FDR presidents are very different from those of eighteenth- and nineteenth-century presidents. George Washington believed that the purpose of public appearances was to "see

President Franklin D. Roosevelt delivering one of his famous "fireside chats" to the American people. Roosevelt projected the voice and image of such a vigorous and active president that no one listening to him or seeing him in the newsreels would have guessed that he was confined to a wheelchair as a result of polio.
(Photo courtesy: AP/Wide World Photos)

and be seen," and not to discuss policy issues. Abraham Lincoln was applauded for refusing to speak about the impending Civil War. Today, presidents use every opportunity to sell their economic, domestic, and foreign programs, as well as to support their favorite candidates. In addition, the modes of communication have changed greatly. The rhetoric of early presidents was written, formal, and addressed principally to Congress. Today press conferences and speeches addressed directly to the public are the norm.

THE PRESIDENTIAL ESTABLISHMENT

As the responsibilities and scope of presidential authority grew over the years, especially since FDR's time, so did the executive branch, including the number of people working directly for the president in the White House, itself. While the U.S. Constitution makes no special mention of a Cabinet, it does imply that a president will be assisted by advisers. Just think of the differences in governance faced by two Georges—Washington and George W. Bush. George Washington supervised the nation from a temporary headquarters with a staff of but one aide—his nephew, paid out of Washington's own funds—and only four Cabinet members. In contrast, in 2005, George W. Bush presides over a White House staff of nearly 400, a Cabinet of fifteen members, and an executive branch of government that employs more than 1.7 million people. Today, the president is surrounded by policy advisers of all types—from the attorney general, who advises him on legal issues, to the surgeon general, who advises him on health matters. The vice president and his staff, the Cabinet, the first lady and her staff, the Executive Office of the President, and the White House staff all help the president fulfill his duties as chief executive.

WEB EXPLORATION
For more on the modern White House, see
www.ablongman.com/oconnor

The Cabinet

The Cabinet, which has no basis in the Constitution, is an informal institution based on practice and precedent whose membership is determined by tradition and presidential discretion. By custom, this advisory group selected by the president includes the heads of major executive departments. Presidents today also include their vice presidents in Cabinet meetings, as well as any other agency heads or officials to whom they would like to accord Cabinet-level status.

As a body, the Cabinet's major function is to help the president execute the laws and assist him in making decisions. Although the Framers had discussed the idea of

In the Oval Office of the White House, President George W. Bush meets with some of his closest advisers: Vice President Dick Cheney, then Secretary of State Colin Powell, and then National Security Advisor Condoleezza Rice.

(Photo courtesy: Mark Wilson/Getty Images)

some form of national executive council, they did not include a provision for one in the Constitution. They did recognize, however, the need for departments of government and departmental heads.

As revealed in Table 8.7, over the years the Cabinet has grown as departments have been added to accommodate new pressures on the president to act in areas that initially were not considered within the scope of concern of the national government. As interest groups, in particular, pressured Congress and the president to recognize their demands for services and governmental action, they often were rewarded by the creation of an executive department. Since each was headed by a secretary who automatically became a member of the president's Cabinet, powerful groups including farmers (Agriculture), business people (Commerce), workers (Labor), and teachers (Education) saw the creation of a department as increasing their access to the president.

The size of the president's Cabinet has increased over the years at the same time that most presidents' reliance on their Cabinet secretaries has decreased, although some individual members of a president's Cabinet may be very influential. Because the Cabinet secretaries and high-ranking members of their departments routinely are subjected to congressional oversight and interest group pressures, they often have divided loyalties. In fact, Congress, through the necessary and proper clause, has the authority to reorganize executive departments, create new ones, or abolish existing ones altogether. For this reason, most presidents now rely most heavily on members of their inner circle of advisers for advice and information. (Chapter 9 provides a more detailed discussion of the Cabinet's role in executing U.S. policy.)

The First Lady

From Martha Washington to Laura Bush, first ladies (a term coined during the Civil War) have assisted presidents as informal advisers while making other, more public, significant contributions to American society. Until recently, the only formal national recognition given to first ladies was an exhibit of inaugural ball gowns at the Smithsonian

TABLE 8.7 The U.S. Cabinet

Department	Date of Creation	Responsibilities
Department of State	1789	Responsible for the making of foreign policy, including treaty negotiation
Department of the Treasury	1789	Responsible for government funds and regulation of alcohol, firearms, and tobacco
Department of Defense	1789, 1947	Created by consolidating the former Departments of War, the Army, the Navy, and the Air Force; responsible for national defense
Department of Justice	1870	Represents U.S. government in all federal courts, investigates and prosecutes violations of federal law
Department of the Interior	1849	Manages the nation's natural resources, including wildlife and public lands
Department of Agriculture	Created 1862; elevated to Cabinet status 1889	Assists the nation's farmers, oversees food-quality programs, administers food stamp and school lunch programs
Department of Commerce	1903	Aids businesses and conducts the U.S. Census (originally the Department of Commerce and Labor)
Department of Labor	1913	Runs labor programs, keeps labor statistics, aids labor through enforcement of laws
Department of Health and Human Services	1953	Runs health, welfare, and Social Security programs; created as the Department of Health, Education, and Welfare (lost its education function in 1979)
Department of Housing and Urban Development	1965	Responsible for urban and housing programs
Department of Transportation	1966	Responsible for mass transportation and highway programs
Department of Energy	1977	Responsible for energy policy and research, including atomic energy
Department of Education	1979	Responsible for the federal government's education programs
Department of Veterans Affairs	1989	Responsible for programs aiding veterans
Department of Homeland Security	2003	Responsible for all issues pertaining to homeland security.

WEB EXPLORATION
For more on
first ladies, see
www.ablongman.com/oconnor

Institution. Not any more. Heightened interest—undoubtedly at least partially attributable to the highly visible role Hillary Rodham Clinton played in the Clinton administration—led the Smithsonian to launch an exhibit that highlights the personal accomplishments of first ladies since Martha Washington. The new exhibit is built around three themes: (1) the political role of the first ladies, including how they were portrayed in the media and perceived by the public; (2) their contributions to society, especially their personal causes; and, (3) still, of course, their inaugural gowns.

Hillary Rodham Clinton was not the first instance of a first lady working for or with her husband. Martha Washington followed George to all the winter camps. At Valley Forge, she helped feed the troops and nurse the wounded. Abigail Adams was a constant sounding board for her husband. An early feminist, as early as 1776 she cautioned him "to Remember the Ladies" in any new code of laws. Edith Bolling Galt Wilson was probably the most powerful first lady. When Woodrow Wilson collapsed and was left partly paralyzed in 1919, she became his surrogate and decided whom and what the stricken president saw. Her detractors dubbed her "Acting First Man."

First Lady Laura Bush addresses the International Women's Day Conference on Afghani Women at the United Nations headquarters on March 8, 2002. The first lady callled for international support for women who suffered under the oppresive Taliban regime.

(Photo courtesy: Osamu Honda/AP/Wide World Photos)

Eleanor Roosevelt also played a powerful and much criticized role in national affairs. Not only did she write a nationally syndicated daily newspaper column, but she traveled and lectured widely, worked tirelessly on thankless Democratic Party matters, and raised six children. After FDR's death, she shone in her own right as U.S. delegate to the United Nations, where she headed the commission that drafted the covenant on human rights. Later, she headed John F. Kennedy's Commission on the Status of Women. Rosalyn Carter also took an activist role by attending Cabinet meetings and traveling to Latin America as her husband's policy representative.

Initially, Laura Bush, a former librarian, seemed to be following the path of her mother-in-law, former First Lady Barbara Bush. She adopted a behind-the-scenes role and made literacy the focus of her activities. In the aftermath of the tragedy of September 11, 2001, the first lady immediately took on a more public role. She gave the president's weekly radio address, highlighting the status of women in Afghanistan under the oppressive Taliban regime, and then continued to speak out, calling for improvements in the legal status of women. She even went to the United Nations to call for international support for women under the Taliban. She also took to the campaign trail in 2002 on behalf of Republican candidates. In 2004, she was an effective campaigner raising millions of dollars for the presidential campaign as well as other Republican candidates.

The Executive Office of the President (EOP)

Executive Office of the President (EOP)
Establishment created in 1939 to help the president oversee the bureaucracy.

The **Executive Office of the President (EOP)** was established by FDR in 1939 to oversee his New Deal programs. It was created to provide the president with a "general staff" to help him direct the diverse activities of the executive branch. In fact, it is a minibureaucracy of several advisers and offices located in the ornate Executive Office Building next to the White House on Pennsylvania Avenue, as well as in the White House itself, where his closest advisers often are located.

The EOP has expanded over time to include several advisory and policy-making agencies and task forces, each of which is responsible to the executive branch. Over time, the units of the EOP have become more responsive to individual presidents rather than to the executive branch as an institution. They are often now the prime policy makers in their fields of expertise as they play key roles in advancing the president's policy preferences. Among the EOP's most important members are the National Security

Council, the Council of Economic Advisers, the Office of Management and Budget, the Office of the Vice President, and the U.S. Trade Representative.

The National Security Council (NSC) was established in 1947 to advise the president on American military affairs and foreign policy. The NSC is composed of the president, the vice president, and the secretaries of state and defense. The chairman of the Joint Chiefs of Staff and the Director of the Central Intelligence Agency also participate. Others such as the chief of staff and White House counsel may attend. The assistant to the president for national security affairs runs the staff of the NSC, coordinates information and options, and advises the president.

Although the president appoints the members of each of these bodies, they must perform their tasks in accordance with congressional legislation. Thus, like the Cabinet, depending on who serves in key positions, these mini-agencies may not be truly responsible to the president.

Presidents can give clear indications of their policy preferences by the kinds of offices they include in the EOP. President George W. Bush, for example, not only moved or consolidated several offices when he became president in 2001, but he quickly sought to create a new Office of Faith Based and Community Initiatives, which critics immediately attacked as an unconstitutional mingling of the church and state.

The White House Staff

Often more directly responsible to the president are the members of the White House staff: the personal assistants to the president, including senior aides, their deputies, assistants with professional duties, and clerical and administrative aides. As personal assistants, these advisers are not subject to Senate confirmation, nor do they have divided loyalties. Their power is derived from their personal relationship to the president, and they have no independent legal authority.

George Washington's closest confidantes were Alexander Hamilton and Thomas Jefferson—both Cabinet secretaries—but that has often not been the case with modern presidents. As the size and complexity of the government grew, Cabinet secretaries had to preside over their own ever-burgeoning staffs, and presidents increasingly looked to a different inner circle of loyal informal advisers. By the 1830s, Andrew

NBC's highly rated *The West Wing* has given the American public a greater appreciation of the inner workings of the White House.

(Photo courtesy: James Sorensen/NBC/Zuma Press)

Jackson had chosen to rely on his own inner circle, nicknamed his "Kitchen Cabinet," instead of his department heads to advise him. FDR surrounded himself with New York political operatives and an intellectual "brain trust"; Jimmy Carter brought several Georgians to the White House with him; Ronald Reagan initially surrounded himself with fellow Californians.

Although presidents organize the White House staff in different ways, they typically have a chief of staff whose job is to facilitate the smooth running of the staff and the executive branch of government. Successful chiefs of staff also have protected the president from mistakes and helped implement policies to obtain the maximum political advantage for the president. Other key White House aides include those who help plan domestic policy, maintain relations with Congress and interest groups, deal with the media, provide economic expertise, and execute political strategies.

As presidents have tried to consolidate power in the White House, and as public demands on the president have grown, the size of the White House staff has increased—from fifty-one in 1943, to 247 in 1953, to a high of 583 in 1972. Since that time, staffs have been trimmed, generally running around 500. During his 1992 presidential campaign, Bill Clinton promised to cut the size of the White House staff and that of the Executive Office of the President, and eventually he reduced the size of his staff by approximately 15 percent. President George W. Bush's White House has fewer than 400 staffers.

While White House staffers prefer to be located in the White House in spite of its small offices, many staffers are relegated to the old Executive Office Building next door because White House office space is limited. In Washington, the size of the office is not the measure of power that it often is in corporations. Instead, power in the White House goes to those who have the president's ear and the offices closest to the Oval Office.

THE ROLE OF THE PRESIDENT IN THE LEGISLATIVE PROCESS: THE PRESIDENT AS POLICY MAKER

When FDR sent his first legislative package to Congress, he broke the traditional model of law-making.[24] As envisioned by the Framers, it was to be Congress that made the laws. Now FDR was claiming a leadership role for the president in the legislative process. Said the president of this new relationship, "It is the duty of the President to propose and it is the privilege of the Congress to dispose."[25] With those words and the actions that followed, FDR shifted the presidency into a law- and policy-maker role. Now not only did the president and the executive branch execute the laws, he and his aides generally suggested them, too.

presidentialist
One who believes that Article II's grant of executive power is a broad grant of authority allowing a president wide discretionary powers.

FDR's view of the role of the president in the law-making process of government is often called a **presidentialist** view. Thus, a president such as FDR could claim that his power to oversee and direct the vast and various executive departments and their policies is based on the simple grant of executive power found in Article II that includes the duty to take care that the laws be faithfully executed. Presidentialists take an expansive view of their powers and believe that presidents should take a key role in policy making. For various reasons, Democratic presidents since FDR have tended to embrace this view of the president's role in law and policy making. In contrast, Republicans in the White House and in Congress generally have subscribed to what is called the **congressionalist** view, which holds that Article II's provision that the president should ensure "faithful execution of the laws" should be read as an injunction against substituting presidential authority for legislative intent.[26] These conflicting views of the proper role of the president in the law-making process should help you understand why presidents, especially Democratic presidents who have faced Republican majorities in the Congress or Republican presidents who have faced Democratic majorities, have experienced difficulties in governing in spite of public expectations.

congressionalist
One who believes that Article II's provision that the president should ensure "faithful execution of the laws" should be read as an injunction against substituting presidential authority for legislative intent.

President Lyndon B. Johnson signs the long awaited Civil Rights Act of 1964. Immediately to his right is Senator Edward Brooke (R–MA), the first African American to be popularly elected as a U.S. senator. On his left is Senator Walter Mondale (D–MN), who later served as vice president. In 2002, Mondale lost his Senate race to succeed Paul Wellstone (D–MN), who was killed in a plane crash only a few days before the election.

(Photo courtesy: Bettmann/Corbis)

Visual Literacy

Presidential Success in Polls and Congress

From FDR's presidency to the Republican-controlled 104th Congress, the public routinely looked to the president to formulate concrete legislative plans to propose to Congress, which then adopted, modified, or rejected his plans for the nation. Then, in 1994, it appeared for a while that the electorate wanted Congress to reassert itself in the legislative process. In fact, the Contract with America was a Republican call for Congress to take the reins of the law-making process. But several Republican Congresses failed to pass many of the items of the Contract, and President Clinton's continued forceful presence in the budgetary process made a resurgent role for Congress largely illusory. The same holds true for George W. Bush.

Modern presidents thus continue to play a major role in setting the legislative agenda, especially in an era when the House and Senate are so narrowly divided along partisan lines. Without working majorities, "merely placing a program before Congress is not enough," as President Lyndon B. Johnson (LBJ) once explained. "Without constant attention from the administration, most legislation moves through the congressional process at the speed of a glacier."[27] The president's most important power (and often the source of his greatest frustration), then, in addition to support of the public, is his ability to construct coalitions within Congress that will work for passage of his legislation. FDR and LBJ were among the best presidents at "working" Congress, but they were helped by Democratic majorities in both houses of Congress.[28]

On the whole, presidents have a hard time getting Congress to pass their programs.[29] Passage is especially difficult if the president presides over a divided government, which occurs when the presidency and Congress are controlled by different political parties (see chapter 7). Recent research by political scientists, however, shows that presidents are much more likely to "win" on bills central to their announced agendas, such as President George W. Bush's victory on the Iraq war resolution, than to secure passage of legislation proposed by others.[30]

Presidents generally experience declining support for policies they advocate throughout their terms. That's why it is so important for a president to propose key plans early in his administration during the honeymoon period, a time when the good-will toward the president often allows a president to secure passage of legislation that he would not be able to gain at a later period. Even LBJ, who was able to get about 57 percent of his programs through Congress, noted: "You've got to give it all you can, that first year … before they start worrying about themselves…. You can't put anything through when half the Congress is thinking how to beat you."[31]

George W. Bush moved quickly to take advantage of his honeymoon period, which was marred by a precipitous decline in the stock market. Still, he was able to sell his tax cut plan to the House and took several decisive actions to reverse liberal Clinton era policies, as discussed in Politics Now: What a Difference a President Makes. Said former House Majority Leader Dick Armey (R–TX), "Our new president says he wants to take us in a new direction, and we should say, 'we're with you, Mr. President.'" While not a sentiment shared by all, many would agree that a new president deserves some time to act without rancorous partisan division.[32]

Presidential Involvement in the Budgetary Process

WEB EXPLORATION
To try your hand at balancing the budget, see
www.ablongman.com/oconnor

Since the 1970s, Congress has spent more time debating the budget than it has legislating.[33] The annual high-stakes showdowns that occur nearly every November are a way for presidents to exert their authority over Congress and to demonstrate leadership at the same time they drive home to the public and the Congress their policy priorities.

In addition to proposing new legislation or new programs, a president can also set national policy and priorities through his budget proposals and his continued insistence on their congressional passage. The budget proposal not only outlines the programs he wants, but indicates the importance of each program by the amount of funding requested for each program and its associated agency or department.

Because the Framers gave Congress the power of the purse, Congress had primary responsibility for the budget process until 1930. The economic disaster set off by the stock market crash of 1929, however, gave FDR, once elected in 1932, the opportunity to assert himself in the congressional budgetary process, just as he inserted himself into the legislative process. In 1939, the Bureau of the Budget, which had been created in 1921 to help the president tell Congress how much money it would take to run the executive branch of government, was made part of the newly created Executive Office of the President. In 1970, President Nixon changed its name to the Office of Management and Budget (OMB) to clarify its function in the executive branch.

The OMB works exclusively for the president and employs hundreds of budget and policy experts. Key OMB responsibilities include preparing the president's annual budget proposal, designing the president's program, and reviewing the progress, budget, and program proposals of the executive department agencies. It also supplies economic forecasts to the president and conducts detailed analyses of proposed bills and agency rules. OMB reports allow the president to attach price tags to his legislative proposals and defend the presidential budget. The OMB budget is a huge document, and even those who prepare it have a hard time deciphering all of its provisions. Even so, the expertise of the OMB directors often gives them an advantage over members of Congress.

The importance of the executive branch in the budget process has increased in the wake of the Balanced Budget and Emergency Deficit Reduction Act of 1985 (often called Gramm-Rudman, for two of the three senators who sponsored it). This act outlined debt ceilings and targeted a balanced budget for 1993. To meet that goal, the act required that the president bring the budget in line by reducing or even eliminating cost-of-living and similar automatic spending increases found in programs such as Social Security. It also gave tremendous power to the president's director of the Office of Management and Budget, who was made responsible for keeping all appropriations in line with congressional understanding and presidential goals.

WHAT A DIFFERENCE A PRESIDENT MAKES

Although George W. Bush came into office without any kind of clear mandate, down nearly a half million popular votes from his opponent, Al Gore, he did not let that stop him from setting to work immediately to put his stamp on a wide array of bold public policies. One of his first actions found tremendous approval from the conservative wing of his party. On his third day in office he reimposed what is called the "Mexico City Policy" of the previous Reagan and Bush administrations, which bans federal aid to organizations that use their own money to perform or promote abortions, whether through counseling, public information campaigns, or lobbying to legalize abortions.

This change in policy was predicted by pro-choice activists during the campaign. Other quick steps by the new Bush administration, however, appeared to catch some—even members of his Cabinet—by surprise. During the 2000 presidential campaign, for example, Bush pledged to seek reductions in carbon dioxide emissions from the nation's power plants. Christine Todd Whitman, head of the Environmental Protection Agency, in fact, told her staff to come up with a plan to brand carbon dioxides as a pollutant, but her actions were suspended when the president announced that he had changed his mind because limits on carbon dioxide would cause energy costs to escalate further. His actions were hailed by industry lobbyists but triggered widespread condemnation from environmentalists.

President Bush's affinity with big business showed through loud and clear again with his support of bankruptcy reform legislation, which the Clinton administration opposed. Over the strong objections of consumer groups, the Bush administration urged Congress to pass legislation to make it harder for individuals to go bankrupt and to make it easier for banks to collect consumer loans.

President Bush also quickly moved to create an Office of Faith Based and Community Initiatives to allow for an increased participation in the nation's churches in implementing executive policies, a move that never would have happened during the Clinton administration. He also acted forcefully to support congressional efforts to overrule Clinton era ergonomics regulations hotly contested by big business, showing organized labor that they no longer had a friend in the White House.

President Bush also made it quickly evident that the United States no longer was to be a peace negotiator around the world. In meetings with Britain's Tony Blair, he made it clear that he would not take the kind of role that his predecessor did in the Northern Ireland peace process. Ditto to the previous administration's resolve to intervene in the Middle East peace process, a position Bush had to abandon as violence in the Middle East escalated in 2002.

President Bush also ended the American Bar Association's fifty-year role in evaluating nominees to the federal bench, finding that the liberal ABA is often too critical in its evaluation of conservative judges of the kind that Bush seeks to nominate to the federal courts.

Quick out of the starting gate in spite of a protracted election that shortened the time to put his administration in place, President Bush, the first president with an advanced degree in business administration, has shown himself to be an effective manager able to get policies he wants in place quickly.

In 1990, Congress, recognizing that its goal of a balanced budget would not be met, gave the OMB the authority to access each appropriations bill. Although this action gutted the Gramm-Rudman Balanced Budget Act, it "had the effect of involving [the OMB] even more directly than it already is in congressional law-making."[34] Growing public (and even congressional) concern over the deficit contributed to the president's and executive branch's increasing role in the budget process. As a single actor, the president may be able to do more to harness the deficit and impose order on the federal budget and its myriad programs than the 535 members of Congress who are torn by several different loyalties.

Interestingly, many critics hailed the joint efforts of the president and Congress in coming up with a balanced budget in 1998—a goal that long eluded Bill Clinton's predecessors and earlier Congresses. The feat of avoiding a deficit budget was achieved without benefit of a balanced budget amendment. Although both parties to the budget dance sought to take credit for their thriftiness, much of the surplus that occurred was a result of savings brought about by the end of the Cold War, which led to much lower military spending, and a strong economy. Still, the president was happy to take credit for the balanced budget when he became the first president since Richard M. Nixon to sign a budget that had no red ink.

President Bill Clinton and Vice President Al Gore celebrate the first balanced budget in years, a feat not likely to be repeated soon in light of federal tax cuts and huge spending increases.

(Photo courtesy: J. Scott Applewhite/AP/Wide World Photos)

During the 2000 presidential campaign, the budget surplus was cited by then Governor George W. Bush as a reason to give more money back to the taxpayers, which became the basis of massive tax cuts in 2001. Checks ranging from $300 to $600, depending on whether the taxpayer was single, married, or the head of a household, were sent to many federal taxpayers. But, the failing economy and the massive spending on defense and homeland security brought about by the September 11 attacks quickly put the federal budget back into red ink. The war in Iraq, tax cuts and continued unemployment led to increasing budget deficits, which did not defer voters from re-electing President Bush.[35]

Ruling Through Regulation

Proposing legislation and using the budget to advance policy priorities are not the only ways that presidents can affect the policy process, especially in times of highly divided government. Executive orders (further discussed in chapter 9) offer the president an opportunity to make policy without legislative approval. Major policy changes have been made when a president has issued an **executive order,** a rule or regulation issued by the president that has the effect of law. While many executive orders are issued to help clarify or implement legislation enacted by Congress, other executive orders have the effect of making new policy. President Harry S Truman ordered an end to segregation in the military through an executive order, and affirmative action was institutionalized as national policy through Executive Order 11246, issued by Lyndon B. Johnson in 1966.

Executive orders have been used since the 1980s to set national policies toward abortion. Ronald Reagan, for example, used an executive order to stop federal funding of fetal tissue research and to end federal funding of any groups providing abortion counseling. Bill Clinton immediately rescinded those orders when he became president. One of George W. Bush's first acts upon taking office was to reverse those Clinton orders.

executive order

A rule or regulation issued by the president that has the effect of law. All executive orders must be published in the *Federal Register*.

With the
Stroke of a
Pen:
The Executive
Order

Like presidents before him, George W. Bush has used executive orders to put his policy stamp on a wide array of important issues. After much soul searching, for example, he signed an executive order limiting federal funding of stem cell research to the sixty or so cell lines currently in the possession of scientific researchers.[36] He also established several boards and agencies in the wake of September 11, 2001, including the Office of Homeland Security and the Critical Infrastructure Protection Board to create a national plan to secure cyberspace from terrorist attack. An executive order also was used to allow military tribunals to try any foreigners captured by U.S. forces in Afghanistan or linked to the terrorist acts of September 11.

One of George W. Bush's more controversial executive orders eviscerated the 1978 Presidential Records Act. This act was written after the Watergate scandal and "established that the records of presidents belong to the American people."[37] It allowed former presidents to block the release of some documents from their presidency for up to twelve years. But, in general, it allowed the national archivist to make as many records public as quickly as possible. Bush's executive order "incorporates a much more expansive view of executive privilege than the law supposes,"[38] and requires the permission of former and incumbent presidents while extending the privilege to family members. (See Join the Debate: Should Presidents Have the Power to Restrict Access to Official Papers of Previous Administrations?) Former vice presidents also now have veto power under the new order. The order allows access for scholars or journalists or other interested persons who demonstrate a specific "need to know" when requesting documents.[39] Critics of the act believe that it was written to "hide the actions of the president's father, George H.W. Bush,"[40] during the Reagan administration's conduct of the Iran-Contra affair. For whatever reason the order was issued, it demonstrates how easily presidents may thwart the wishes of Congress and substitute their own policy preferences through executive orders, which require congressional action to make them unenforceable.

Winning Support for Programs

The ability to govern often comes down to a president's ability to get his programs through Congress. He may want those programs for policy or political reasons. According to political scientist Thomas Cronin, a president has three ways to improve his role as a legislative lobbyist to get his favored programs passed.[41] The first two involve what you may think of as traditional political avenues.

President George W. Bush signs a controversial farm subsidy bill that raised spending on existing programs by 80 percent. Critics charged that Bush signed the bill to curry favor of voters in farm belt states whose votes were needed to elect more Republicans to the Senate in 2002.

(Photo courtesy: Paul J. Richards/AFP Photo)

Join the Debate

SHOULD PRESIDENTS HAVE THE POWER TO RESTRICT ACCESS TO OFFICIAL PAPERS OF PREVIOUS ADMINISTRATIONS?

The president of the United States, as its chief executive, has the power to issue orders to federal agencies—called executive orders. Upon entering office in 2001, President George W. Bush issued many executive orders, just as his predecessors had done. In the modern era of divided government, presidents have sometimes issued executive orders putting into effect significant public policy changes (for instance, the chapter discussion notes Presidents Reagan, Bush, and Clinton's orders on abortion counseling). Sometimes Congress had considered those policy changes but not enacted them. Other times, Congress has reacted to an executive order by passing a law countering or restricting it. Clearly, with executive orders, presidents can be policy initiators.

Under the 1978 Presidential Records Act, some presidential and vice presidential papers become public twelve years after the end of a president's term. The Reagan/Bush administration ended in January 1989, and thus their papers were scheduled to be released in January 2001. However, as noted in the chapter discussion, President George W. Bush issued an executive order forbidding the release of those records. His decision triggered a storm of criticism from historians and members of Congress arguing that freedom of information was more important than protecting the reputation of former officials.

Read and think about the following transcript of a public radio news commentary on the presidential papers secrecy order. Then, join the debate over whether presidents should have the power to restrict access to official papers. Should a president be able to unilaterally change major public policies, despite congressional action to the contrary? Should presidents and their successors be allowed to decide the issue of access to their papers? Does the desire for freedom of information contravene the desire of former officials to protect their reputations? Consider the debating points and questions posed at the end of this feature, and sharpen your own arguments for the position you find most viable.

Analysis: New Executive Order Restricting Access to Papers of Past Presidents

Noah Adams and Daniel Schorr

8:00-9:00 PM, Both Republican and Democratic lawmakers are unhappy with an executive order that President Bush issued last week. At stake, presidential papers and whether, in some cases, they should be kept secret forever. News analyst Daniel Schorr says that would be a chilling development.

DANIEL SCHORR: Michael Beschloss's new book, *Reaching for Glory*, based on White House tapes and records, reveals the depths of depression into which President Johnson sank as he privately concluded that the Vietnam War was unwinnable. Richard Reeves's new book, *President Nixon*, drawing on documents and diaries from the Nixon White House, fills out the picture of this tormented, paranoid man who was driven from office.

How much we will learn about the inner workings of more recent presidencies has been thrown into doubt by an executive order signed by President Bush. In 1978 after a court fight over the Nixon records, Congress passed a law permitting the release of presidential records 12 years after the end of the term. The first to become eligible for release last January were some 68,000 pages of Reagan records. But the current White House three times postponed their release, saying that further review was needed. Finally, last Friday, the president signed the order permitting an incumbent, or former president, in some cases even the family of a dead president, to veto the release of his papers.

The whole idea of the Presidential Records Act was to avoid another Nixon tapes battle by taking the decision out of the hands of the one most concerned and putting it in the hands of the National Archives and historians. President Bush has put himself in the odd position of asserting the right to rule on papers of a period when his father was vice president and claiming to be out of the loop in the Iran Contra scandal. There may also be in the Reagan papers references to officials now serving under the incumbent, like Secretary of State Colin Powell and budget director Mitch Daniels.

Republican Representative Doug Ose, member of a House subcommittee with jurisdiction over presidential records, says the Bush order undercuts the public's right to be fully informed about how the government operated in the past. Inevitably the question arises: What is it about old Reagan documents that has this president so concerned? This is Daniel Schorr.

JOIN THE DEBATE

CHECK YOUR UNDERSTANDING: Make sure you understand the following key points from the news commentary; go back and review it if you missed any of them:

- The 1978 Presidential Records Act permits the National Archives to release some presidential papers twelve years after the end of an administration.
- The act was passed as a response to clashes between former President Nixon and the government over control of his administration's papers.
- President George W. Bush's executive order allows former presidents to veto release of records from their administration.

ADDITIONAL INFORMATION: News commentaries don't provide all the information an informed citizen needs to know about an issue under debate. Here are some questions the commentary does not answer that you may need to consider in order to join the debate:

- What legal authority does a president have to issue executive orders?
- What happens if Congress or others believe that an executive order violates a federal law?
- What papers are not covered by the 1978 Presidential Records Act?
- Did the act contemplate the possibility of policy makers still being in decision-making positions when their records are released twelve years later?
- How are national security concerns addressed by releasing or withholding records?

What other information might you want to know? Where might you gather this information? How might you evaluate the credibility of the information you gather? Is the information from a reliable source? Can you identify any potential biases?

IDENTIFYING THE ARGUMENTS: Now that you have some information on the issue, and have thought about what else you need to know, see whether you can present the arguments on both sides of the debate. Here are some ideas to get you started. We've provided one example each of "pro" and "con" arguments, but you should be able to offer others:

PRO: Presidents should have the right to issue executive orders protecting presidential papers. Here's why:

- A president must govern within the constraints of earlier governmental decisions, and release of relatively recent documents could harm his or her ability to administer the laws.

CON: Presidents should not be allowed to make earlier presidential records secret. Here's why:

- Congress has the constitutional authority and responsibility for initiating policy, and a presidential decision to block the 1978 Presidential Records Act violates the constitutional principle of separation of powers.

TAKING A POSITION AND SUPPORTING IT: After thinking about the information in the news commentary on President George W. Bush's executive order, placing the information in the broader context of the issue of policy making and freedom of information, and articulating the arguments in the debate, what position would you take? What information supports your position? What arguments would you use to persuade others to your side of the debate? How would you counter arguments on the other side?

patronage
Jobs, grants, or other special favors that are given as rewards to friends and political allies for their support.

Patronage and Party Ties.   Presidents can use **patronage** (jobs, grants, or other special favors that are given as rewards to friends and political allies for their support) and personal rewards to win support. Invitations to the White House and campaign visits to the home districts of members of Congress running for office are two ways to curry favor with legislators, and inattention to key members can prove deadly to a president's legislative program. Then Speaker of the House Tip O'Neill (D–MA) reportedly was quite irritated when the Carter team refused O'Neill's request for extra tickets to Carter's inaugural. This did not exactly get the president off to a good start with the powerful speaker.

A second way a president can bolster support for his legislative package is to call on his political party. As the informal leader of his party, he should be able to use that position to his advantage in Congress, where party loyalty is very important. This strategy works best when the president has carried members of his party into office on his coattails, as was the case in the Johnson and Reagan landslides of 1964 and 1984, respectively. In fact, many scholars regard LBJ as the most effective legislative leader.[42] Not only had he served in the House and as Senate majority leader, but he also enjoyed a comfortable Democratic Party majority in Congress.[43] As governor of Texas, President George W. Bush was able to work well with members of his own party as well as Democrats. This kind of across the aisle cooperation, however, is for more difficult to achieve in a Congress where many of the leading Republicans are quite conservative and possibly less inclined to compromise with Democrats than is the president.

Presidential Style.   The third way a president can influence Congress is a less "political" and far more personalized strategy. A president's ability to lead and to get his programs adopted or implemented depends on many factors, including his personality, his approach to the office, others' perceptions of his ability to lead, and his ability to mobilize public opinion to support his actions.

Some presidents have been modest in their approach to the office. Jimmy Carter, for example, adopted an unassuming approach to the presidency. During the energy crunch of the 1970s, he ordered White House thermostats set to a chilly 65 degrees and suggested that his advisers wear sweaters to work. Carter often appeared before the nation in cardigan sweaters instead of suits. He tried to build his "common man" image by carrying his own luggage and prohibiting the Marine band from playing the traditional fanfare, "Hail to the Chief," to signal his arrival on official occasions. In contrast, other presidents have been much more attuned to the trappings of office. Many believe that Kennedy did it best.

Frequently, the difference between great and mediocre presidents centers on their ability to grasp the importance of leadership style. Truly great presidents, such as Abraham Lincoln and Franklin D. Roosevelt, understood that the White House was a seat of power from which decisions could flow to shape the national destiny. They recognized that their day-to-day activities and how they went about them should be designed to bolster support for their policies and to secure congressional and popular backing that could translate their intuitive judgment into meaningful action. Mediocre presidents, on the other hand, have tended to regard the White House as "a stage for the presentation of performances to the public" or a fitting honor to cap a career.[44] Many agree that George W. Bush has proven to be a much more effective leader than his detractors had hoped.

Presidential Leadership.   Leadership is not an easy thing to exercise, and it remains an elusive concept for scholars to identify and measure, but it is important to all presidents seeking support for their programs and policies. Moreover, ideas about the importance of effective leaders have deep roots in our political culture. The leadership abilities of the "great presidents"—Washington, Jefferson, Lincoln, and FDR—have been

extolled over and over again, leading us to fault modern presidents who fail to cloak themselves in the armor of leadership. Americans thus have come to believe that "If presidential leadership works some of the time, why not all of the time?"[45] This attitude, in turn, directly influences what we expect presidents to do and how we evaluate them (see Analyzing Visuals: Barber's Presidential Personalities). Research by political scientists shows that presidents can exercise leadership by increasing public attention to particular issues. Analyses of presidential State of the Union Addresses, for example, reveal that mentions of particular policies translate into more Americans mentioning those policies as the most important problems facing the nation.[46]

The presidency often transforms its occupants. There is an old adage that great crises make great presidents. President Franklin D. Roosevelt's handling of the Great Depression solidified his place in American history, as did Abraham Lincoln's handling of the Civil War. Many critics argue that September 11 transformed George W. Bush's presidency to the degree that commentators now refer to the pre- and post-9/11 president.[47] President Bush not only cast himself as the strong leader of the United States but has portrayed himself as the worldwide leader in the war against terrorism, transforming himself from the candidate who disavowed interest in or much knowledge of international affairs. His newfound self-confidence is what Americans look for in a time of crisis.

The Power to Persuade.   In trying to lead against long odds, a president must not only exercise the constitutional powers of the chief executive but also persuade enough of the country that his actions are the right ones so that he can carry them out without national strife.[48] A president's personality and ability to persuade others are key to amassing greater power and authority.

Presidential personality and political skills often determine how effectively a president can exercise the broad powers of the modern presidency. To be successful, says political scientist Richard E. Neustadt, a president not only must have a will for power but must use that will to set the agenda for the nation. In setting that agenda, in effect, he can become a true leader. According to Neustadt, "Presidential power is the *power to persuade*," which comes largely from an individual's ability to bargain. Persuasion is key, Neustadt says, because constitutional powers alone don't provide modern presidents with the authority to meet rising public expectations.[49]

ANALYZING VISUALS

Barber's Presidential Personalities

Does presidential character, which James David Barber defines as the "way the president orients himself toward life," seriously affect how a president handles his job? Many of the presidents ranked highest by historians had major character flaws. Not all discussions of presidential character center on lying, as was the case with Richard M. Nixon, or womanizing and possible lying about his draft status, as was the case with Bill Clinton. In an approach to analyzing and predicting presidential behavior criticized and rejected by many political scientists, political scientist James David Barber has suggested that patterns of behavior, many that may be ingrained during childhood, exist and can help explain presidential behavior.

Barber believes that there are four presidential character types, based on energy level (whether the president is active or passive) and the degree of enjoyment a president finds in the job (whether the president has a positive or negative attitude). Barber believes that active and positive presidents are more successful than passive and negative presidents. Active-positive presidents, he argues, generally enjoyed warm and supportive childhood environments and are basically happy individuals open to new life experiences. They approach the presidency with a characteristic zest for life and have a drive to lead and succeed. In contrast, passive-negative presidents find themselves reacting to circumstances, are likely to take directions from others, and fail to make full use of the enormous resources of the executive office.

	Active	Passive
Positive	F. Roosevelt Truman Kennedy Ford Carter[a] Bush	Taft Harding Reagan
Negative	Wilson Hoover L. Johnson Nixon	Coolidge Eisenhower

[a]Some scholars think that Carter better fits the active-negative typology.

The table classifies presidents from Taft through George Bush according to Barber's categories. After reviewing the table, answer the following critical thinking questions based on your understanding of the president's performance in office: Would you consider Jimmy Carter, whom Barber considers an active-positive character type, a successful president? Why might some of the highest-rated presidents have character flaws? What actions or policy failures are associated with the four active-negative presidents? What factors in addition to personality could influence presidential behavior? How would you classify President Bill Clinton? President George W. Bush?

Source: James David Barber, *The Presidential Character: Predicting Performance in the White House*, 4th ed. (Englewood Cliffs, NJ: Prentice Hall, 1992).

THE PRESIDENT AND PUBLIC OPINION

executive privilege
An assertion of presidential power that reasons that the president can withhold information requested by the courts in matters relating to his office.

U.S. v. Nixon (1974)
The Supreme Court ruled that there is no constitutional absolute executive privilege that would allow a president to refuse to comply with a court order to produce information needed in a criminal trial.

Presidents have long recognized the power of the "bully pulpit" and the importance of going public. Since the 1970s, however, the American public has been increasingly skeptical of presidential actions, and few presidents have enjoyed extended periods of the kind of popularity needed to help win support for programmatic change.

In 1974, President Richard M. Nixon resigned from office rather than face the certainty of impeachment, trial, and removal from office for his role in covering up details about a break-in at Democratic Party national headquarters in the Watergate office complex. What came to be known simply as Watergate also produced a major decision from the Supreme Court on the scope of what is termed **executive privilege,** which later became an issue for Bill Clinton. In *U.S. v. Nixon* (1974), the Supreme Court ruled unanimously that there was no overriding executive privilege that sanctioned the president's refusal to comply with a court order to produce information to be used in the trial of the Watergate defendants.

Watergate forever changed the nature of the presidency. Because the president long had been held up as a symbol of the nation, the knowledge that corruption could exist at the highest levels of government changed how Americans viewed all institutions of government, and mistrust of government ran rampant. Watergate demystified the office and its occupant. As Richard M. Nixon toppled from office so did the prestige of the office itself. After Watergate, no longer was the president to be considered above the law or the scrutiny of the public or of the press.

Watergate not only forever changed the public's relationship to the president but also spurred many reforms in how government and politics were run. Ethics and campaign finance laws were tightened up, and an independent counsel law, which allowed for independent investigation of the executive branch, was enacted. Perhaps even more than these changes, Watergate bruised Americans' optimism about what was good about America. Furthermore, intensive media attention to the president and the presidency brought him closer to the people (and to their intense public criticism) at the same time that the public expectations about the presidency itself increased. People began to look to the president rather than Congress to solve pressing and increasingly complex national problems even as their respect for the office—and often even its occupant—declined.

Writing in the 1940s, decades before Watergate, the great author John Steinbeck said, "We give the president more work than a man can do, more responsibility than a man should take, more pressure than a man can bear. We abuse him often, and rarely praise him. We wear him out, use him up, eat him up. And with all this, Americans have a love for the president that goes beyond party loyalty or nationality; he is ours, and we exercise the right to destroy him."[50]

The complex interaction of public opinion and the president are of considerable interest to scholars as well as members of the media and politicians. The president can mold public opinion and use public opinion to garner support for his favored programs. While all presidents try to manipulate public opinion to win support of their programs, they also are very mindful of their own standing in the polls.

Paula Jones charged President Bill Clinton with sexual harassment for actions that she alleged took place while she worked for the Arkansas state government and Clinton was governor. While her charges became just one of many allegations of sexual misconduct by the president, they resulted in an important decision from the U.S. Supreme Court about the scope of executive privilege also addressed by the Court in *U.S* v. *Nixon* (1972). In *Clinton* v. *Jones* (1997), the Supreme Court ruled that a sitting president was not immune from civil litigation during the course of his presidency for conduct before he took office. Thus, no president has unqualified immunity from the judicial process.

(Photo courtesy: Linda Spillers/AP/Wide World Photos)

Going Public

On average, President Bill Clinton spoke to the public in a variety of venues about 550 times a year. President Reagan, often remembered as a master of public relations and the media, averaged 320 appearances a year; the folksy President Truman, only 88 times a year.[51] What's the difference? The postmodern president has to try to govern amidst the din of several competing twenty-four-hour news channels, the Internet, and a news cycle that makes events of an hour ago old news. This rapid change provides presidents with rare opportunities while at the same time representing daunting challenges.

Historically, even before the days of radio and television, presidents tried to reach out to the public to gain support for their programs through what President Theodore Roosevelt (1901–1909) called "the bully pulpit." In this century, the development of commercial air travel and radio, newsreels, television, and communication satellites have made direct communication to larger numbers of voters easier. Presidents, first ladies, and other presidential advisers no longer stay at home but instead travel all over the world to expand their views and to build personal support as well as support for administration programs.

Direct, presidential appeals to the electorate like those often made by Bill Clinton are referred to as "going public."[52] Going public means that a president goes over the heads of members of Congress to gain support from the people, who can then place pressure on their elected officials in Washington.

WEB EXPLORATION
For more details on Watergate, see
www.ablongman.com/oconnor

Russian President Vladimir Putin speaks with President George W. Bush. Both are wearing traditional Chinese silk coats as they walk to a family photo session of the 2001 Asia Pacific Economic Cooperation (APEC) summit in Shanghai. The two-day summit focused on measures to counter terrorism and on ways to boost trade to support the slumping global economy. Interactions such as these solidified the personal relationships between the two leaders.

(Photo courtesy: AFP/CORBIS)

Like most presidents, Clinton was keenly aware of the importance of maintaining his connection with the public. Beginning with his 1992 campaign, Clinton often appeared on Larry King's TV talk show on CNN. Even after becoming president, Clinton continued to take his case directly to the people. He launched his healthcare reform proposals, for example, on a prime-time edition of *Nightline* hosted by Ted Koppel. For an hour and a half, the president took audience questions about his health plan, impressing even those who doubted the plan with his impressive grasp of details. Moreover, at a black-tie dinner honoring radio and television correspondents, Clinton responded to criticisms leveled against him for not holding traditional press conferences by pointing out how clever he was to ignore the traditional press. "You know why I can stiff you on the press conferences? Because Larry King liberated me from you by giving me to the American people directly," quipped Clinton.[53]

Throughout his first term, President George W. Bush believed he was far better to go directly to the people than to hold regular press conferences. Like President Clinton before him, he gave very few solo press conferences. Interestingly, 82 percent of President Bush's press conferences were joint conferences, most with foreign leaders such as Tony Blair, the British prime minister. These joint occassions allow a president to reinforce his image as a world leader to the American electorate.

Presidential Approval Ratings

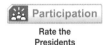

Participation

Rate the Presidents

Historically, a president has the best chances of convincing Congress to follow his policy lead when his public opinion ratings are high. Presidential popularity, however, generally follows a cyclical pattern. These cycles have occurred since 1938, when pollsters first began to track presidential popularity.

Typically, presidents enjoy their highest level of popularity at the beginning of their terms and try to take advantage of this honeymoon period to get their programs passed by Congress as soon as possible. Each action a president takes, however, is divisive—some people will approve, and others will disapprove. Disapproval tends to have a cumulative effect. Inevitably, as a general rule, a president's popularity wanes, although Bill Clinton, who ended with a higher approval rating than any president in recent history, was a notable exception.

As revealed in Analyzing Visuals: Presidential Approval Ratings Since 1938, since Lyndon B. Johnson's presidency, only four presidents finished their term with approval rating of more than 50 percent. Many credit this trend to events such as Vietnam, Watergate, the Iran hostage crisis, and the Iran-Contra scandal, which have made the public increasingly skeptical of presidential performance. Presidents George Bush, Bill Clinton, and George W. Bush, however, experienced increases in their presidential performance scores during the course of their presidencies. Bush's rapid rise in popularity occurred after the major and, perhaps more important, quick victory in the 1991 Persian Gulf War. His popularity, however, plummeted as the good feelings faded and Americans began to feel

ANALYZING VISUALS

Presidential Approval Ratings Since 1938

Presidential approval ratings traditionally have followed a cyclical pattern. Presidents generally have enjoyed their highest ratings at the beginning of their terms and experienced lower ratings toward the end. Presidents George Bush and Bill Clinton, however, enjoyed popularity surges during the course of their terms. Despite the Monica Lewinsky crisis and the threat of impeachment, Clinton's approval ratings continued to rise in 1998 and 1999. They peaked at 73 percent at the end of 1998—the highest rating of his administration. Clinton left office with a 66 percent approval rating. Similarly, President George W. Bush got a spectacular and sustained boost after September 11, 2001. After viewing the line graph of presidential approval scores and reading the related chapter material, answer the following critical thinking questions about presidential approval: What types of events (domestic or international) tend to boost presidential approval? Why do you think that the cyclical pattern of presidential approval exists? What do you think enabled George W. Bush to sustain his high approval rating for a relatively long period after the terrorist attacks of September 11?

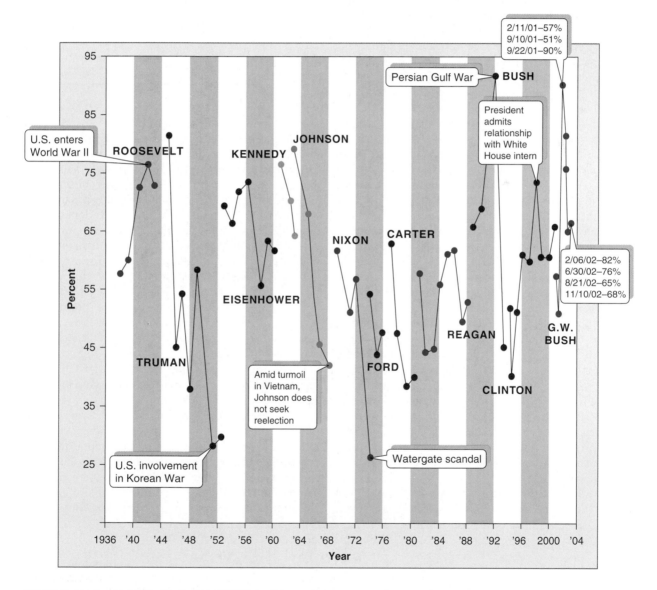

Sources: USA Today (August 14, 2000): 6A. © 2000, USA Today. Reprinted by permission. "President Bush: Job Ratings," Gallup Poll and CNN/USA Today/Gallup Poll. PollingReport.com. 2002. Accessed November 10, 2002, http://www.pollingreport.com/BushJob.htm

THE PRESIDENCY IN COMPARATIVE PERSPECTIVE

Presidents in the industrial democracies, faced with the difficulties of leading governments, often wish they had those powers exercised by the other kind of executive, the prime minister. Is the president of the United States more powerful than the prime ministers of the parliaments of Europe, Canada, and Japan?

In some ways, the president has significant powers that prime ministers do not. First, presidents typically appoint 3,000 positions in the executive branch and judiciary, two to three times the number prime ministers appoint. Second, presidents have larger staffs than prime ministers, a significant information-gathering resource. Third, the separation of powers places presidents at the center of the political system, which gives them the ability to focus popular attention on key issues and to appeal to the public.

Presidents are harder to remove from office than are prime ministers. Impeachment proceedings in the United States, for example, require that the president have committed "high crimes or misdemeanors." Prime ministers can be removed by a vote of no confidence, which requires only that a simple majority of the legislature's lower house agrees that it does not support the prime minister's leadership.

Prime ministers, on the other hand, have powers American presidents often wish they had. Prime ministers do not face formal term limits and, with the exception of Germany's chancellor, can call for elections whenever they choose (within limits). Unlike recent American presidents, prime ministers have long prior experience in the legislature (an informal requirement for the position) and Cabinet: "Outsiders" do not take over the reins of government. Finally, because the majority party or coalition in the lower house of parliament elects the prime minister, the latter is virtually assured of support from the legislature. Unlike both the American and French presidents in 1999, for example, no prime minister in the G-8 faced a hostile majority in the legislature. As a result, prime ministers have a much easier time getting their legislative agendas passed into law; the success rate for Cabinet-sponsored bills in the parliamentary systems is 80–90 percent, which no American president can match.

When we look farther afield, we run into a problem of comparison. "President" in countries such as Mexico, Egypt,

Chief Executives, 2005		
Country	Chief Executive	Office
Canada	Paul Martin	Prime minister
China	Jiang Zemin	President
Egypt	Hosni Mubarak	President
France	Jacques Chirac	President
Germany	Gerhard Schröder	Chancellor
India	Manmohan Singh	Prime minister
Indonesia	Susilo Bambang Yudhoyono	President
Italy	Silvio Berlusconi	Prime minister
Japan	Junichiro Koizumi	Prime minister
Mexico	Vicente Fox	President
Russia	Vladimir Putin	President
United Kingdom	Tony Blair	Prime minister
United States	George W. Bush	President

China, and Indonesia means something different from what it means in the United States. In many developing countries, for different reasons, presidents typically have powers no American president enjoys. Among many of these presidencies, the chief executives are not faced with courts that can overturn their decisions. In China and Indonesia, the president is elected by the legislature, a device intended (until recently in Indonesia's case) to ensure that the incumbent remained in office. The domination of Mexican national politics by the Institutional Revolutionary Party until the 1990s had similar consequences; President Vicente Fox represents a break from the domination. Egypt's president, Hosni Mubarak, has been chief executive since 1981. He has been reelected in four successive referenda, and the vote in each case was largely mobilized.

The existence of a president doesn't guarantee a government based on meaningful checks and balances. China represents an extreme in this regard. Jiang Zemin is not chief executive because he is president so much as because he occupies a number of positions in the government and the Communist Party that enable him and his supporters to control government. Jiang's predecessor, Deng Xiao-Ping, was commonly referred to as "paramount leader," a term that fully conveys the idea that the executive power in China lies outside the constitutional provisions of any particular office.

Comparing Chief Executives

the pinch of recession. In contrast, Bill Clinton's approval scores skyrocketed after the 1996 Democratic National Convention. More interestingly, Clinton's high approval ratings continued in the wake of allegations of wrongdoing in the Oval Office, his eventual admission of inappropriate conduct, and through his impeachment proceedings. In fact, when Clinton went to the American public and admitted that he misled them about his rela-

TABLE 8.8   Temporary Rises in Presidential Popularity

Gallup poll measurements of the size and duration of the largest increase in each president's approval rating before and after dramatic international events.

President	Event	Percentage Point Increase in Public Approval	Duration of the Increase in Weeks
Franklin D. Roosevelt	Pearl Harbor	12	30
Harry S Truman	Truman Doctrine;	12	n/a[a]
	Korea invaded	9	10
Dwight D. Eisenhower	Bermuda Conference/Atoms for Peace speech	10	20
John F. Kennedy	Cuban Missile Crisis	13	31
Lyndon B. Johnson	Speech halting bombing of North Vietnam	14	19
Richard M. Nixon	Vietnam peace agreement	16	15
Gerald R. Ford	Mayaguez incident	11	25
Jimmy Carter	Hostages seized in Iran	19	30
Ronald Reagan	Beirut bombing/Grenada invasion;	8	n/a[b]
	First summit with Gorbachev	7	4
George Bush	War with Iraq	18	30
George W. Bush	September 11, 2001, terrorist attacks	31	58[c]

[a]No polls conducted.

[b]Overlapping events.

[c]As of November, 2002.

Source: *New York Times* (May 22, 1991): A10. Information from the Gallup Organization. Reprinted by permission of NYT Graphics. Updated by the authors. Copyright ©1991 by the New York Times Co. Reprinted by permission.

tionship with Monica Lewinsky, an ABC poll conducted immediately after his speech showed a 10-point jump in his job approval rating.[54]

Most presidents experience surges in popularity after major international events, but they generally don't last long. As revealed in Table 8.8, each of the last ten presidents before Bill Clinton experienced at least one "rallying" point based on a foreign event. Before George W. Bush, rallies lasted an average of ten weeks, with the longest being seven months.[55] These popularity surges allow presidents to make some policy decisions that they believe are for the good of the nation, even though the policies are unpopular with the public. This phenomenon has led some to ask if presidents launch bold international initiatives to distract critics of their personal or domestic policy problems and to enhance their popularity with the public. Of course, this was not the case with President George W. Bush's actions against terrorists in Afghanistan.

Presidential popularity in domestic or foreign affairs is likely to have some effect on the president's ability to build support for programs, although some political scientists question direct linkages between presidential support and policy influence.[56] Still, it is critical to remember that the president—whether you voted for him, like him, or agree with him on any particular issue or philosophical debate—is the elected leader of the nation and a key player in the policy process. A president is many things to many people: a symbol of the nation, a political organizer, a moral teacher. As we discussed in chapter 1, until the 1960s, most Americans looked up to their president. Watergate heightened cynicism about the president and government in general. Nevertheless, until the 1990s, it was highly unusual for a sitting president to be vilified on radio or television talk shows. Never before have Americans known so much about the activities of their presidents, their background, whom they dated in high school and college, what affairs they've had, and what they eat. Bill Clinton's legs, his running shorts, and even his undershorts were objects of public attention and comment. The Monica Lewinsky affair opened a whole new line of what is considered fair game. In fact, in 2000, one of the strength's of George W. Bush's candidacy was the absence of a recent scandal in his personal life; in 2004, when morals again were of concern to the public, George W. Bush was even more successful.

Continuity & Change

A Woman President?

When the Constitution was first adopted, women could not vote, let alone dream of being president. By the mid-1800s, however, some women had begun to mobilize for expanded rights and opportunities, and the right to vote in particular. As early as 1871, Victoria Woodhull, an outspoken proponent of "free love" and editor of a weekly newspaper, tried to convince women suffrage leaders to form their own political party, the Cosmo-Political Party.[57] Woodhull would then run for president in the 1872 elections. Susan B. Anthony soon vetoed the idea because she was distrustful of Woodhull and her motives.[58]

Campaigning for Woodhull in 1872, was Belva Lockwood, who founded the first D.C. franchise group, the Universal Suffrage Association, in 1867. Lockwood was a strong believer in using publicity to serve the cause of women's rights. In 1884, Lockwood, along with a handful of other women, met in California and founded the National Equal Rights Party, which nominated Lockwood for president.[59] Her platform included equal rights for all, liquor restrictions, uniform marriage and divorce laws, and universal peace. Her run for the presidency was opposed by most women suffrage leaders; still, she received 4,149 votes in the six states where she was on the ballot. She ran again in 1888, but received even fewer votes.

In 1964, Senator Margaret Chase Smith (R–ME), the only woman in the U.S. Senate, announced her candidacy for her party's nomination; her name was placed in nomination at the convention, but she garnered few votes. In 1984, the Democratic Party and its presidential candidate, former Vice President Walter Mondale, thought it could capitalize on its growing support from women voters and reenergize the party by nominating Representative Geraldine Ferraro (D–NY) as his vice-presidential running mate.[60] Several women's groups, including the Women's Presidential Project, openly advocated that the Democrats add a woman to their party's ticket. The Mondale/Ferraro ticket was trounced by the popular incumbent Ronald Reagan. Still, women's hopes to have a woman president did not die. In fact, in 1998, a nonpartisan group called the White House Project was founded to change the political climate so that the public would be more receptive to the idea of a woman president. In 2000, it cooperated with Mattel to produce "Madame President Barbie" to help socialize young girls to think about being president. In 2001, the Girl Scouts added a Ms. President badge.

Today, the idea of a woman president is becoming more and more accepted. In 1937, only 33 percent of those polled said they would vote for a woman for president.[61] By 1999, when Elizabeth Dole announced her exploratory committee for president, 92 percent of those polled said that they could vote for a woman, up 10 percentage points since 1987.[62] To facilitate the election of a woman to the White House by the year 2004, the White House Project launched a campaign in 1998 with a straw ballot in women's magazines offering twenty women as potential nominees. Over 100,000 people responded; the top five winners were then First Lady Hillary Rodham Clinton, Elizabeth Dole, Senator Dianne Feinstein, then New Jersey Governor Christine Todd Whitman, and Lt. General Claudia Kennedy, then the highest-ranking woman in the U.S. military.[63] The election of Representative Nancy Pelosi (D–CA) to the House leadership, first as Democratic whip and then as minority leader, brings a woman's face to power for the first time in U.S. history. And, in 2002, a push was made by several women's groups to elect more women governors—an office that has produced most of our recent presidents.

1. What kind of barriers face women seeking the presidency?
2. Why have so many other nations elected women presidents? Senator Hillary Clinton (D–NY) is already considered to be a front runner for the 2008 Democratic nomination for president.

CAST YOUR VOTE   What female candidate would you elect as President of the United States? To cast your vote, go to www.ablongman.com/oconnor

---

SUMMARY

Because the Framers feared a tyrannical monarch, they gave considerable thought to the office of the chief executive. Since ratification of the Constitution, the office has changed considerably—more through practice and need than from changes in the Constitution. In chronicling these changes, we have made the following points:

1. **The Roots of the Office of President of the United States**

   Distrust of a too-powerful leader led the Framers to create an executive office with limited powers. They mandated that a president be at least thirty-five years old and opted not to limit the president's term of office. To further guard against tyranny, they also made provisions for the removal of the president and created an office of vice president to provide for an orderly transfer of power.

2. **The Constitutional Powers of the President**
   The Framers gave the president a variety of specific constitutional powers in Article II, including the appointment power, the power to convene Congress, the power to make treaties, and the power to veto. The president also derives considerable power from being commander in chief of the military. The Constitution also gives the president the power to grant pardons.

3. **The Development of Presidential Power**
   The development of presidential power has depended on the personal force of those who have held the office. George Washington, in particular, took several actions to establish the primacy of the president in national affairs and as true chief executive of a strong national government. But, with only a few exceptions, subsequent presidents often let Congress dominate in national affairs. The election of FDR, however, forever changed all that, as a new era of the modern presidency began. A hallmark of the modern presidency is the close relationship between the American people and their chief executive.

4. **The Presidential Establishment**
   As the responsibilities of the president have grown, so has the executive branch of government. FDR established the Executive Office of the President to help him govern. Perhaps the most key policy advisers are those closest to the president—the White House staff, some members of the Executive Office of the President, and sometimes, the first lady.

5. **The Role of the President in the Legislative Process: The President as Policy Maker**
   Since FDR, the public has looked to the president to propose legislation to Congress. The modern president also plays a major role in the budgetary process. To gain support for his programs or proposed budget, the president can use patronage, personal rewards, party connections, and direct appeals to the public. How the president goes about winning support is determined by his leadership and personal style, affected by his character and his ability to persuade.

6. **The President and Public Opinion**
   Presidents have long recognized the power of the "bully pulpit" and the importance of going public. Since the 1970s, however, the American public has been increasingly skeptical of presidential actions, and few presidents have enjoyed extended periods of the kind of popularity needed to help win support for programmatic change.

KEY TERMS

articles of impeachment, p. 274
Cabinet, p. 279
congressionalist, p. 294
executive agreement, p. 280
Executive Office of the President (EOP), p. 292
executive order, p. 298
executive privilege, p. 304
impeachment, p. 272
inherent powers, p. 286
line-item veto, p. 283
Louisiana Purchase, p. 287
New Deal, p. 289
pardon, p. 284
patronage, p. 302
presidentialist, p. 294
stewardship theory, p. 288
Taftian theory, p. 288
Twenty-Fifth Amendment, p. 275
Twenty-Second Amendment, p. 272
U.S. v. Nixon (1974), p. 304
veto power, p. 281
War Powers Act, p. 284

SELECTED READINGS

Barber, James David. *The Presidential Character: Predicting Presidential Performance in the White House*, 4th ed. Englewood Cliffs, NJ: Prentice Hall, 1992.

Campbell, Karlyn Kohr, and Kathleen Hall Jamieson. *Deeds Done in Words: Presidential Rhetoric and the Genres of Governance*. Chicago: University of Chicago Press, 1990.

Cooper, Philip J. *By Order of the President: The Use and Abuse of Executive Direct Action*. Lawrence: University Press of Kansas, 2002.

Corwin, Edwin S. *The Presidential Office and Powers*, 4th ed. New York: New York University Press, 1957.

Dallek, Robert. *Hail to the Chief: The Making and Unmaking of American Presidents*. New York: Oxford University Press, 2001.

Daynes, Byron W., and Glen Sussman. *The American Presidency and the Social Agenda*. Upper Saddle River, NJ: Prentice Hall, 2001.

Edwards, George C., III. *Presidential Leadership: Politics and Policy Making*, 5th ed. New York: Bedford Books, 2000.

Greenstein, Fred I. *The Presidential Difference: Leadership Style from Roosevelt to Clinton*. New York: Free Press, 2000.

Kellerman, Barbara. *The Political Presidency*. New York: Oxford University Press, 1986.

Kernell, Samuel. *Going Public: New Strategies for Presidential Leadership*, 3rd ed. Washington, DC: CQ Press, 1997.

Levy, Leonard W., and Louis Fisher, eds. *Encyclopedia of the American Presidency*. Englewood Cliffs, NJ: Prentice Hall, 1994.

Nelson, Michael, ed. *The Presidency and the Political System*, 6th ed. Washington, DC: CQ Press, 2000.

Neustadt, Richard E. *Presidential Power and the Modern Presidency.*, New York: Free Press, 1991.

Pfiffner, James P. *Modern Presidency*. New York: Bedford Press, 2000.

Pious, Richard M. *The Presidency*. Boston: Allyn and Bacon, 1996.

Ragsdale, Lyn. *Vital Statistics on the Presidency: Washington to Clinton*. Washington, DC: CQ Press, 1998.

Rossiter, Clinton. *The American Presidency*. Baltimore, MD: Johns Hopkins University Press, 1987.

Skowronek, Stephen. *The Politics Presidents Make: Leadership from John Adams to Bill Clinton*. Cambridge, MA: Harvard University Press, 1997.

Walcott, Charles E., and Karen Hult. *Governing the White House*. Lawrence: University Press of Kansas, 1995.

Warshaw, Shirley Anne. *The Domestic Presidency: Policy Making in the White House*. Boston: Allyn and Bacon, 1996.

———. *The Keys to Power: Managing the Presidency*. New York: Addison-Wesley, 1999.

NOTES

1a. "Two Hundred Years of Presidential Funerals," *Washington Post*, June 10, 2004, C14.

1b. "Two Hundred Years."

1c. "Two Hundred Years."

1d. "The Fold: Presidential Funerals; Farewell to the Chiefs," *Newsday*, June 9, 2004, A38.

1e. Gail Russell Chaddock, "The Rise of Mourning in America," *Christian Science Monitor*, June 11, 2004, 1.

1f. Richard E. Neustadt, *Presidential Power and the Modern Presidency* (New York: Free Press, 1991).

2. Edward S. Corwin, *The President: Office and Powers, 1787–1957*, 4th ed. (New York: New York University Press, 1957), 5.

3. F. N. Thorpe, ed., *American Charters, Constitutions, Etc.* (Washington, DC, 1909), VIII, 3816–17.

4. Quoted in Corwin, *The President*, 11.

5. Winston Solberg, *The Federal Convention and the Formation of the Union of the American States* (Indianapolis, IN: Bobbs-Merrill, 1958), 235.

6. Alfred Steinberg, *The First Ten: The Founding Presidents and Their Administrations* (New York: Doubleday, 1967), 59.

7. "Is the Vice Presidency Necessary?" *Atlantic* 233 (May 1974): 37.

8. James P. Pfiffner, "Recruiting Executive Branch Leaders," *Brookings Review* 19 (Spring 2001): 41–3.

9. Benjamin I. Page and Mark P. Petracca, *The American Presidency* (New York: McGraw-Hill, 1983), 262.

10. Ibid., 268.

11. Todd Shields and Chi Huang, "Executive Vetoes: Testing Presidency Versus President Centered Perspectives of Presidential Behavior," *American Politics Quarterly* (October 1997): 431–2.

12. Quoted in Solberg, *The Federal Convention*, 91.

13. 524 U.S. 417 (1998).

14. "War Powers: Resolution Grants Bush Power He Needs," *Rocky Mountain News* (September 15, 2001): 6B.

15. *Public Papers of the Presidents* (1963), 889.

16. Quoted in Richard E. Neustadt, *Presidential Power*, 9.

17. Quoted in Paul F. Boller Jr., *Presidential Anecdotes* (New York: Penguin Books, 1981), 78.

18. Abraham Lincoln, "Special Session Message," July 4, 1861, in Edward Keynes and David Adamany, eds., *Borzoi Reader in American Politics* (New York: Knopf, 1973), 539.

19. "The Stewardship Presidency," in James Pfiffner and Roger H. Davidson, *Understanding the Presidency* (Boston: Allyn and Bacon, 1995), 29–30.

20. "The Strict Constructionist Presidency," in Pfiffner and Davidson, *Understanding the Presidency*, 27–8.

21. Lyn Ragsdale and John Theis III, "The Institutionalization of the American Presidency, 1924–1992," *American Journal of Political Science* 41 (October 1997): 1280–1318.

22. Quoted in Page and Petracca, *The American Presidency*, 57.

23. Merlin Gustafson, "The President's Mail," *Presidential Studies Quarterly* 8 (1978): 36.

24. See Louis Fisher, *Constitutional Conflicts Between Congress and the President*, 4th ed. (Lawrence: University Press of Kansas, 1997).

25. Franklin D. Roosevelt, Press Conference, July 23, 1937.

26. See, generally, Richard Pious, *The American Presidency* (Boston: Allyn and Bacon, 1996), 213, 254, 255.

27. Lyndon B. Johnson, *The Vantage Point* (New York: Holt, Rinehart and Winston, 1971), 448.

28. Morris Fiorina, *Divided Government*, 2nd ed. (New York: Macmillan, 1995).

29. See Lance LeLoup and Steven Shull, *The President and Congress: Collaboration and Conflict in National Policymaking* (Boston: Allyn and Bacon, 1999).

30. See Cary Covington, J. Mark Wrighton, and Rhonda Kinney, "A 'Presidency-Augmented' Model of Presidential Success on House Roll Call Votes," *American Journal of Political Science* 39 (November 1995): 1001–24; and Wayne P. Steger, "Presidential Policy Initiation and the Politics of Agenda Control," *Congress & the Presidency* 24 (Spring 1997): 102–14.

31. Quoted in Thomas E. Cronin, *The State of the Presidency*, 2nd ed. (Boston: Little, Brown, 1980), 169.

32. "House Passes Bush's Budget and Tax Plan," *St. Louis Post-Dispatch* (March 29, 2001): A1.

33. Michael Waldman, "Bush's Presidential Power."

34. *Congressional Quarterly Weekly Report* (December 1, 1990): 4034.

35. For more on sources of budget deficits, see George Krause, "Partisan and Ideological Sources of Fiscal Deficits in the United States," *American Journal of Political Science* 44 (July 2000): 541–59.

36. Mary Leonard, "Bush Begins Talks on Human Cloning," *Boston Globe* (January 17, 2002): A6.

37. "Resisting Secrecy," *Plain Dealer* (April 30, 2002): B8.

38. "Resisting Secrecy."

39. Richard Reeves, "Writing History to Executive Order," *New York Times* (November 16, 2001): A25.

40. "Resisting Secrecy."

41. Thomas Cronin, *The State of the Presidency* (Boston: Little, Brown, 1975).

42. Robert A. Caro, *Master of the Senate: The Years of Lyndon Johnson* (New York: Knopf, 2002).

43. Paul C. Light, *The President's Agenda: Domestic Policy Choice from Kennedy to Carter* (Baltimore, MD: Johns Hopkins University Press, 1983).

44. George Reedy, *The Twilight of the Presidency* (New York: New American Library), 38–9.

45. Samuel Kernell, *New Strategies of Presidential Leadership*, 2nd ed. (Washington, DC: CQ Press, 1993), 3.

46. Jeffrey Cohen, "Presidential Rhetoric and the Public Agenda," *American Journal of Political Science* 39 (February 1995): 87–107.

47. Brian Kates and Kenneth R. Bazinet, "Crisis Forges a New Bush First-Year," *Daily News* (January 20, 2002): 9.

48. Reedy, *Twilight of the Presidency*, 33.

49. Neustadt, *Presidential Power*, 1–10.

50. Quoted in "Dear Abby," *Atlanta Journal and Constitution* (March 13, 1996): D11.

51. Michael Waldman, "Bush's Presidential Power."

52. Samuel Kernell, *Going Public: New Strategies of Presidential Leadership*, 3rd ed. (Washington, DC: CQ Press, 1996).

53. Dan Balz, "Strange Bedfellows: How Television and Presidential Candidates Changed American Politics," *Washington Monthly* (July 1993).

54. William E. Gibson, "Job Approval Ratings Steady: Personal Credibility Takes a Hit," *News and Observer* (August 19, 1998): A16.

55. Michael R. Kagay, "History Suggests Bush's Popularity Will Ebb," *New York Times* (May 22, 1991): A10.

56. See Kenneth Collier and Terry Sullivan, "New Evidence Undercutting the Linkage of Approval with Presidential Support and Influence," *Journal of Politics* 57 (February 1995): 197–209; and George C. Edwards III, "Aligning Tests with Theory: Presidential Approval as a Source of Influence in Congress," *Congress & the Presidency* 24 (Autumn 1997): 113–30.

57. *Woodhull and Clafin's Weekly* (April 22, 1871).

58. Carol Hymowitz and Michaele Weissman, *A History of Women in America* (New York: Bantam Books, 1978), 172.

59. Louis Filler, "Belva Lockwood," in Edward T. James, ed., *Notable American Women*, vol. 2 (Cambridge, MA: Harvard University Press, 1971), 413–6.

60. Nancy E. McGlen et. al. *Women, Politics, and American Society*, 3rd ed. (New York: Longman, 2002), 53–4.

61. Frank Newport, "Americans Today Much More Accepting of a Woman, Black, Catholic, or Jew as President," *Poll Releases*, Gallup Organization, March 29, 1999.

62. Ibid.

63. Gloria Negri, "Liswood's Goal: A Woman in the White House," *Boston Globe City Weekly,* (May 2, 1999): 1.

The Executive Branch and the Federal Bureaucracy

9

Sometimes, as you are trying to obtain some sort of a government service—be it a student loan or a driver's license—it may seem as though the right hand doesn't know what the left hand is doing. Frequently, critics of the bureaucracy argue, the maze of administrative regulations, rules, and procedures makes it difficult for individual citizens to find their way through Internal Revenue Service or Immigration and Naturalization Service requirements. One bureaucrat might tell you to do X; another one will tell you to do Y—after you have stood in the wrong line for an hour or two.

But it is unusual for major actors in the bureaucracy not to know what each other is doing. And, when it comes to issues of national security, public acknowledgement of these information vacuums can be particularly troubling.

In the wake of the terrorist attacks of 9/11, Congress eventually authorized the creation of a new Department of Homeland Security. Its first director was Tom Ridge, who had chaired the Office of Homeland Security that was created in the White House immediately after the September tragedy. Under the Homeland Security Act of 2002, the Department of Homeland Security alone can issue threat warnings, and the process is a very complicated one involving several agencies and the White House.

On May 27, 2004, then Attorney General John Ashcroft and FBI Director Robert Mueller called a major news press conference to ask the public's help in capturing seven suspected terrorists within the United States. In the same press conference they talked about an imminent terrorism threat to the United States. Both men concluded that a terrorist attack on the United States was likely in the next few months—just as the nation was gearing up for the opening of the World War II Veteran's Memorial, Memorial Day celebrations around America, and the presidential conventions of the two national parties. News accounts quickly revealed that the Secretary of Homeland Security had heard about Ashcroft's and Mueller's concerns as he watched the television report along with

Chapter Outline

- **The Roots and Development of the Executive Branch and the Federal Bureaucracy**
- **The Modern Bureaucracy**
- **Policy Making**
- **Making Agencies Accountable**

315

millions of other Americans. In fact, earlier that morning Ridge had appeared on several morning news shows downplaying any increased risks.

Lawmakers, whose job it is to oversee the Department of Homeland Security, were irate and said that the efforts of Ashcroft and Mueller undermined efforts of the national government to assure the safety of its citizens. "The reason that Congress created the Department of Homeland Security is that we need to merge the various parts of government responsible for pieces of the war on terrorism into one coordinated effort," said Representative Christopher Cox (R-CA), who chairs the House committee overseeing the Department.[1]

bureaucracy
A set of complex hierarchical departments, agencies, commissions, and their staffs that exist to help a chief executive officer carry out his or her duty to enforce the law.

The bureaucracy often is called the "fourth branch of government" because of the tremendous power that agencies and bureaus can exercise. Politicians often charge that the **bureaucracy,** the thousands of federal government agencies and institutions that implement and administer federal law and federal programs, is too large, too powerful, and too unaccountable to the people or even to elected officials. Many politicians, elected officials, and voters complain that the bureaucracy is too wasteful. Interestingly, few critics discuss the fact that laws and policies also are implemented by state and local bureaucracies and bureaucrats whose numbers are far larger, and often far less efficient, than those working for the federal government.

While many Americans are uncomfortable with the large role of the federal government in policy making, current studies show that most users of federal agencies rate the agencies and the services received quite favorably. Many of those polled by the Pew Research Center as part of its efforts to assess America's often seemingly conflicting views about the federal government and its services were frustrated by complicated rules and the slowness of a particular agency. Still, a majority gave most agencies overall high marks. Most of those polled drew sharp distinctions between particular agencies and the government as a whole, although the federal government, especially the executive branch, is largely composed of agencies, as we will discuss later in this chapter. For example, 84 percent of physicians and pharmacists rated the Food and Drug Administration favorably, while only one half were positive about the government in general.[2] The survey also found that attitudes toward particular agencies were related to public support for their function. Thus, the public, which views clean air and water as a national priority, was much more likely to rate the Environmental Protection Agency highly. Since missions of most agencies aren't likely to change, most agencies are trying to improve their service to the public, and the public appears to be responding.

Harold D. Lasswell once defined political science as the "study of who gets what, when, and how."[3] It is by studying the bureaucracy that those questions can perhaps best be answered. To allow you to understand the role of the bureaucracy in the policy and governmental processes, this chapter explores the following issues:

- First, we will trace *the roots and development of the executive branch and the federal bureaucracy.*
- Second, we will examine *the modern bureaucracy* by discussing bureaucrats and the formal organization of the bureaucracy.
- Third, we will discuss *policy making,* including the role of rule making and adjudication.
- Fourth, we will analyze *how agencies are held accountable.*
- We will illustrate our theme of *continuity and change* by examining the executive branch's use of technology over time.

THE ROOTS AND DEVELOPMENT OF THE EXECUTIVE BRANCH AND THE FEDERAL BUREAUCRACY

In the American system, the bureaucracy can be thought of as the part of the government that makes policy as it links together the three branches of the national government in the federal system. Although Congress makes the laws, it must rely on the executive branch and the bureaucracy to enforce and implement them. Commissions such as the Equal Employment Opportunity Commission (EEOC) have the power not only to make rules, but also to settle disputes between parties concerning the enforcement and implementation of those rules. Often, agency determinations are challenged in the courts. Because most administrative agencies that make up part of the bureaucracy enjoy reputations for special expertise in clearly defined policy areas, the federal judiciary routinely defers to bureaucratic administrative decision makers.

German sociologist Max Weber believed bureaucracies were a rational way for complex societies to organize themselves. Model bureaucracies, said Weber, are characterized by certain features, including:

1. A chain of command in which authority flows from top to bottom.
2. A division of labor whereby work is apportioned among specialized workers to increase productivity.
3. A specification of authority where there are clear lines of authority among workers and their superiors.
4. A goal orientation that determines structure, authority, and rules.
5. Impersonality, whereby all employees are treated fairly based on merit and all clients are served equally, without discrimination, according to established rules.
6. Productivity, whereby all work and actions are evaluated according to established rules.[4]

Clearly, this Weberian idea is somewhat idealistic, and even the best-run agencies don't always work this way, but most are trying.

It is quite unusual for agencies or bureaus to switch their priorities, even minimally. But, after it became clear that the FBI failed to recognize or act on tips about potential terrorists before September 11, 2001, then FBI Director Robert Mueller unveiled plans to transform the agency then with a new set of priorities.

(Photo courtesy: Mike Theiler/AFP Photo)

In 2003, the executive branch had approximately 1.8 million civilian employees employed directly by the president or his advisers or in independent agencies or commissions. The Department of Defense had an additional 667,750 civilian employees, with an additional 2.3 million in the military. The Postal Service, which is a quasi-governmental corporation not part of the executive branch, has nearly 860,000 employees (and is second only to Wal-Mart in employees).[5]

In 1789, conditions were quite different. Only three departments existed under the Articles of Confederation: Foreign Affairs, War, and Treasury. George Washington inherited those departments, and soon, the head of each department was called its secretary and Foreign Affairs was renamed the Department of State.

To provide the president with legal advice, Congress created the office of attorney general. The original status of the attorney general, however, was unclear—was he a member of the judicial or executive branch? That confusion was remedied in 1870 with the creation of the Department of Justice as part of the executive branch, with the attorney general as its head. From the beginning, individuals appointed as Cabinet secretaries (as well as the attorney general) were subject to approval by the U.S. Senate but were removable by the president alone. Even the First Congress realized how important it was for a president to be surrounded by those in whom he had complete confidence and trust.

From 1816 to 1861, the size of the federal executive branch and the bureaucracy grew as increased demands were made on existing departments and new departments were created. The Postal Service, for example, which Article I constitutionally authorized the Congress to create, was forced to expand to meet the needs of a growing and westward-expanding population. Andrew Jackson removed the Post Office from the jurisdiction of the Department of the Treasury in 1829 and promoted the postmaster general to Cabinet rank.

The Civil War and Its Aftermath

Timeline

Evolution of the Federal Bureaucracy

The Civil War (1861–1865) permanently changed the nature of the federal bureaucracy. As the nation geared up for war, thousands of additional employees were added to existing departments. The Civil War also spawned the need for new government agencies. A series of poor harvests and marketing problems led President Abraham Lincoln (who understood that you need well-fed troops to conduct a war) to create the Department of Agriculture in 1862, although it was not given full Cabinet-level status until 1889.

After the Civil War, the need for big government continued unabated. The Pension Office was established in 1866 to pay benefits to the thousands of Union veterans who had fought in the war (more than 127,000 veterans initially were eligible for benefits). Justice was made a department in 1870, and other departments were added through 1900. Agriculture became a full-fledged department and began to play an important role in informing farmers about the latest developments in soil conservation, livestock breeding, and planting techniques. The increase in the types and nature of government services resulted in a parallel rise in the number of federal jobs, as illustrated in Analyzing Visuals: Number of Federal Employees in the Executive Branch, 1789–2001. Many of the new jobs were used by the president or leaders of the president's political party for **patronage,** that is, jobs, grants, or other special favors given as rewards to friends and political allies for their support. Political patronage often is defended as an essential element of the party system because it provides rewards and inducements for party workers.

patronage
Jobs, grants, or other special favors that are given as rewards to friends and political allies for their support.

From Spoils to Merit

spoils system
The firing of public-office holders of a defeated political party and their replacement with loyalists of the newly elected party.

In 1831, describing a "rotation in office" policy for bureaucrats supported by President Andrew Jackson, Senator William Learned Marcy of New York commented, "To the victors belong the spoils." From his statement derives the term **spoils system** to describe the firing of public-office holders of the defeated political party and their replacement

ANALYZING VISUALS

Number of Federal Employees in the Executive Branch, 1789–2004

The federal government grew slowly until the 1930s, when Franklin D. Roosevelt's New Deal programs were created in response to the high unemployment and weak financial markets of the Great Depression. A more modest spike in the federal workforce occurred in the mid-1960s during Lyndon B. Johnson's Great Society program. Through 2005, seven new executive departments were created: the Department of Housing and Urban Development (1965), the Department of Transportation (1966), the Department of Energy (1977), the Department of Education and the Department of Health and Human Services (1979—created out of the old Department of Health, Education, and Welfare), the Department of Veterans Affairs (1989), and the Department of Homeland Security. It is important to note that while the number of federal employ-

ees has gone down, agencies increasingly make use of outside contractors to do their work.

After reviewing the data and balloons in the line graph and reading the material in this chapter on the roots and development of the executive branch and federal bureaucracy, answer the following critical thinking questions: Before the United States' involvement in World War II, what was the principal reason for the growth in the number of federal employees? The rapid decline in federal employees between 1945 and 1950 resulted from the end of World War II, but why do you think the number of federal employees declined after 1970? What do you think caused the increase in federal employees between 1975 and 1990?

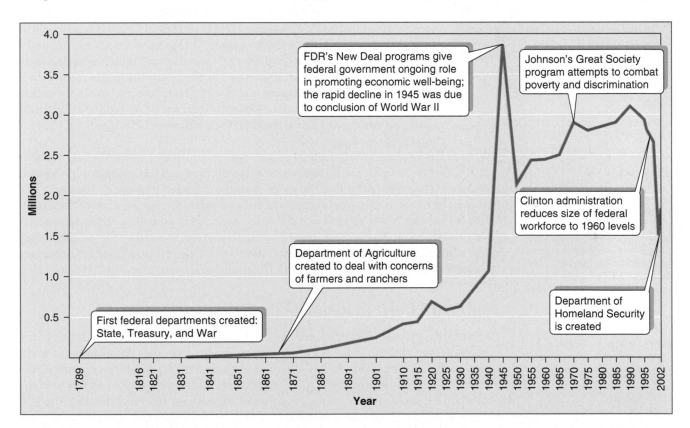

Sources: Office of Personnel Management, *The Fact Book,* http://www.opm.gov/feddata/032factbk.pdf.

with loyalists of a new administration. Jackson, in particular, faced severe criticism for populating the federal government with his political cronies. But, many presidents, including Jackson, argued that to implement their policies, they had to be able to appoint those who subscribed to their political views.

A political cartoonist's view of how President Andrew Jackson would be immortalized for his use of the spoils system.

(Photo courtesy: Bettmann/CORBIS)

Pendleton Act

Reform measure that created the Civil Service Commission to administer a partial merit system. The act classified the federal service by grades, to which appointments were made based on the results of a competitive examination. It made it illegal for federal political appointees to be required to contribute to a particular political party.

civil service system

The system created by civil service laws by which many appointments to the federal bureaucracy are made.

merit system

The system by which federal civil service jobs are classified into grades or levels, to which appointments are made on the basis of performance on competitive examinations.

independent regulatory commission

An agency created by Congress that is generally concerned with a specific aspect of the economy.

The spoils system reached a high-water mark during Abraham Lincoln's presidency. By the time James A. Garfield, a former distinguished Civil War officer, was elected president in 1880, many reformers were calling for changes in the patronage system. On his election to office, Garfield, like many presidents before him, was besieged by office seekers. Washington, D.C., had not seen such a demand for political jobs since Abraham Lincoln became the first president elected as a Republican. Garfield's immediate predecessor, Rutherford B. Hayes, had favored the idea of the replacement of the spoils system with a merit system based on test scores and ability. Congress, however, failed to pass the legislation he proposed. Possibly because potential job seekers wanted to secure positions before Congress had the opportunity to act on an overhauled civil service system, thousands pressed Garfield for positions. This siege prompted Garfield to record in his diary: "My day is frittered away with the personal seeking of people when it ought to be given to the great problems which concern the whole country."[6] Garfield resolved to reform the civil service, but his life was cut short by the bullets of an assassin who, ironically, was a frustrated job seeker.

Public reaction to Garfield's death and increasing criticism of the spoils system prompted Congress to pass the Civil Service Reform Act in 1883, more commonly known as the **Pendleton Act,** named in honor of its sponsor, Senator George H. Pendleton (D–OH). It established the principle of federal employment on the basis of open, competitive exams and created a bipartisan three-member Civil Service Commission, which operated until 1978. Initially, only about 10 percent of the positions in the federal **civil service system** were covered by the law, but later laws and executive orders extended coverage of the act to over 90 percent of all federal employees. This new system was called the **merit system,** one characteristic of Weber's model bureaucracy.

As it has evolved today, the civil service system provides a powerful base for federal agencies and employees. Federal workers have tenure and the leverage of politicians is reduced. The good part is that the spoils system was gutted (but not eliminated). The bad part, however, is that federal agencies can and often do take on a life of their own. With 90 percent of the federal workforce secure in their positions, some bureaucrats have been able to thwart reforms passed by legislators and wanted by the people as they make administrative law, pass judgments, and so on. This often makes the bureaucracy the target of public criticism and citizen frustration.

National Efforts to Regulate the Economy

As the nation grew, so did the bureaucracy. In the wake of the tremendous growth of big business (especially railroads), widespread price fixing, and other unfair business practices that occurred after the Civil War, Congress created the Interstate Commerce Commission (ICC). In creating the ICC, Congress was reacting to public outcries over the exorbitant rates charged by railroad companies for hauling freight. It became the first **independent regulatory commission,** an agency outside of a major executive department. Independent regulatory commissions such as the ICC, generally concerned with particular aspects of the economy, are created by Congress to be independent of direct presidential authority. Commission members are appointed by the president and hold their jobs for fixed terms, but they are not removable by the president unless they fail to uphold their oaths of office. In 1887, the creation of the ICC also marked a shift in the focus of the bureaucracy from service to regulation. Its creation gave the government—in the shape of the bureaucracy—vast powers over individual and property rights.

The 1900 election of Theodore Roosevelt, a progressive Republican, strengthened the movement toward governmental regulation of the economic sphere; the size of the bureaucracy was further increased when, in 1903, Roosevelt asked Congress to estab-

An artist's interpretation of President James A. Garfield's assassination at the hands of an unhappy office seeker.

(Photo courtesy: Bettmann/CORBIS)

lish a Department of Commerce and Labor to oversee employer-employee relations. At the turn of the twentieth century, many workers toiled long hours for low wages in substandard conditions. Many employers refused to recognize the rights of workers to join unions, and many businesses had grown so large and powerful that they could force workers to accept substandard conditions.

In 1913, President Woodrow Wilson divided the Department of Commerce and Labor when it became clear that one agency could not well represent the interests of both employers and employees, creating two separate departments: Commerce and Labor. One year later, in 1914, Congress created the Federal Trade Commission (FTC). Its function was to protect small businesses and the public from unfair competition, especially from big business. Bureaus within departments also were created to concentrate on a variety of issues. The Women's Bureau, for example, was created in 1920 in the Department of Labor to represent working women's interests.

The ratification of the Sixteenth Amendment to the Constitution in 1913 also affected the size of government and the possibilities for growth. It gave Congress the authority to implement a federal income tax to supplement the national treasury and provided an infusion of funds to support new federal agencies, services, and governmental programs, as discussed in chapter 3.

WEB EXPLORATION
For more about the Women's Bureau in the Department of Labor, see www.ablongman.com/oconnor

What Should Government Do?

During the early 1900s, while Progressives raised the public cry for governmental regulation of business, many Americans, especially members of the business community, continued to resist such moves. They believed that any federal government regulation was wrong. Instead they favored governmental facilitation of the national economy through a commitment to *laissez-faire*, a French term that means to leave alone. In America, the term was used to describe a governmental hands-off policy concerning the economy, as discussed in chapter 1. This philosophical debate about the role of government in regulating the economy had major ramifications on the size of government and the bureaucracy. A *laissez-faire* attitude, for example, implied little need for the creation of new independent regulatory commissions or executive departments, a view held by many, especially Republicans, in Congress.

A political cartoonist satirizes President Franklin D. Roosevelt's criticisms of the Supreme Court's repeated rulings against the constitutionality of New Deal programs.

(Photo courtesy: Richmont Times Dispatch)

The New Deal and Bigger Government.

In the wake of the high unemployment and weak financial markets of the Great Depression, Franklin D. Roosevelt planned to revitalize the economy by creating hundreds of new government agencies to regulate business practices and various aspects of the economy. Roosevelt proposed, and the Congress enacted, far-ranging economic legislation. The desperate mood of the nation supported these moves, as most Americans began to change their ideas about the proper role of government and the provision of governmental services. Formerly, most Americans had believed in a hands-off approach; now they considered it the government's job to get the economy going and get Americans back to work.

Congress approved every new regulatory measure proposed by Roosevelt during his first hundred days in office. Also passed were the National Industrial Recovery Act (NIRA), an unprecedented attempt to regulate industry, and the Agricultural Adjustment Act (AAA), to provide government support for farm prices and to regulate farm production to ensure market-competitive prices. Congress also created the Federal Deposit Insurance Corporation (FDIC) to insure bank deposits, and it passed the Federal Securities Act, giving the Federal Trade Commission the authority to supervise and regulate the issuance, buying, and selling of stocks and bonds.

Until 1937, the Supreme Court refused to allow Congress or the president to delegate to the executive branch or the bureaucracy such far-ranging authority to regulate the economy. *Laissez-faire* was alive and well at the Court, and attempts to end the economic slump through greater governmental involvement repeatedly were stymied by the justices. In a series of decisions made through 1937, the Supreme Court invalidated key provisions in congressional legislation designed to regulate various aspects of the economy. The Court and others who subscribed to the *laissez-faire* principles of a free enterprise system argued that natural economic laws at work in the marketplace control the buying and selling of goods. Advocates of *laissez-faire* believed that the government simply had no right to regulate business.

In response, frustrated by the decisions of the Court, FDR proposed to increase the size of the Court to dilute the majority. This famous Court-packing plan (see chapter 10), outraged the public, yet the Court quickly reversed a number of its earlier decisions and upheld what some have termed the "alphabetocracy." For example, the Court upheld the constitutionality of the National Labor Relations Act (NLRA) of 1935, which allowed recognition of unions and established formal arbitration procedures for employers and employees.[7] Subsequent decisions upheld the validity of the Fair Labor Standards Act (FLSA) and the Agricultural Adjustment Act (AAA).[8]

Once these new programs were declared constitutional, the proverbial floodgates were open to the creation of more governmental agencies. With the growth in the bureaucracy came more calls for reform of the system.

World War II and Its Aftermath.

During World War II, the federal government grew tremendously to meet the needs of a nation at war. Tax rates were increased to support the war, and they never again fell to prewar levels. After the war, this infusion of new monies and veterans' demands for services led to a variety of new programs and a much bigger government. The G.I. (Government Issue) Bill, for example, provided college loans for returning veterans and reduced mortgage rates to allow them to buy homes. The national government's involvement in these programs not only affected more people but also led to its greater involvement in more regulation. Homes bought with Veterans Housing Authority loans, for example, had to meet certain specifications. With these programs, Americans became increasingly accustomed to the national government's role in entirely new areas such as affordable middle-class housing, which never would have existed without government assistance.

Within two decades after World War II, the civil rights movement and President Lyndon B. Johnson's War on Poverty produced additional growth in the bureaucracy. The Equal Employment Opportunity Commission (EEOC) was created in 1964 (by the Civil Rights Act of 1964), and the Departments of Housing and Urban Development (HUD) and Transportation were created in 1966. These expansions of the bureaucracy corresponded to increases in the president's power and his ability to persuade Congress that new agencies would be an effective way to solve pressing social problems. Remember from chapter 8 that most major expansions of presidential power occurred during times of war, social crisis, or economic emergency, as is underscored by the recent creation of the new, huge Department of Homeland Security.

THE MODERN BUREAUCRACY

Critics continually lament that the national government is not run like a business. Private businesses as well as all levels of government have their own bureaucratic structures. But, the national government differs from private business in numerous ways. Governments exist for the public good, not to make money. Businesses are driven by a profit motive; government leaders, but not bureaucrats, are driven by reelection. Businesses get their money from customers; the national government gets its money from taxpayers. Another difference between a bureaucracy and a business is that it is difficult to determine to whom bureaucracies are responsible. Is it the president? Congress? The citizenry? Still, governments can learn much from business, and recent reform efforts have tried to apply business solutions to create a government that works better and costs less.

The different natures of government and business have tremendous consequences on the way the bureaucracy operates. Because all of the incentive in government "is in the direction of not making mistakes," public employees view risks and rewards very differently than their private-sector counterparts.[9] The key to the modern bureaucracy is to understand how the bureaucracy is organized, who bureaucrats are, and how organization and personnel affect each other. It also is key to understand that government cannot be run like a business. An understanding of these facts and factors can help in the search for ways to motivate positive change in the bureaucracy.

Bureaucrats perform all kinds of jobs. The cast of CBS's *The Agency,* a series about the people who work in the Central Intelligence Agency (CIA), actually can be considered bureaucrats.

(Photo courtesy: Everett Collection)

Who Are Bureaucrats?

Federal bureaucrats are career government employees who work in the executive branch in the Cabinet-level departments and independent agencies that comprise more than 2,000 bureaus, divisions, branches, offices, services, and other subunits of the federal government. There are approximately 1.8 million federal workers in the executive branch, a figure that does not include postal workers and uniformed military personnel. Nearly one-third of all civilian employees work in the Postal Service, as illustrated in Figure 9.1. The remaining federal civilian workers are spread out among the various executive departments and agencies throughout the United States. Most of these federal employees are paid according to what is called the "General Schedule" (GS). They advance within GS grades and into higher GS levels and salaries as their careers progress.

FIGURE 9.1   Distribution of Federal Civilian Employment by Branch, 2002

Non–U.S. Postal
Service
1,838,300
(67.7%)

Legislative 30,900 (1.1%)
Judicial 34,700 (1.2%)

Executive
2,649,900
(97.6%)

U.S. Postal
Service
811,600
(29.9%)

Total Employment: 2,704,015

Source: Office of Personnel Management, The Fact Book.

As a result of reforms during the Truman administration that built on the Pendleton Act, most civilian federal governmental employees today are selected by merit standards, which include tests (such as civil service or foreign service exams) and educational criteria. Merit systems protect federal employees from being fired for political reasons. (For a description of how a federal employee can be fired, see Table 9.1.)

At the lower levels of the U.S. Civil Service, most positions are filled by competitive examinations. These usually involve a written test, although the same position in the private sector would not. Mid-level to upper ranges of federal positions don't normally require tests; instead, applicants simply submit a resume, or even apply by phone. Personnel departments then evaluate potential candidates and rank candidates according to how well they fit a particular job opening. Only the names of those deemed "qualified" are then forwarded to the official filling the vacancy. This can be a time-consuming process; it is not unusual for it to take six to nine months before a position can be filled in this manner.

The remaining 10 percent of the federal workforce is made up of persons not covered by the civil service system. These positions generally fall into three categories:

WEB EXPLORATION
To examine the federal workforce by gender, race, and ethnicity, see
www.ablongman.com/oconnor

1. Appointive policy-making positions. About 600 persons are appointed directly by the president. Some of these, including Cabinet secretaries, are subject to Senate confirmation. These appointees, in turn, are responsible for appointing the high-level policy-making assistants who form the top of the bureaucratic hierarchy.

2. Independent regulatory commissioners. Although each president gets to appoint as many as one hundred commissioners, they become independent of his direct political influence once they take office.

3. Low-level, nonpolicy patronage positions. At one time, the U.S. Postal Service was the largest source of these government jobs. In 1971, Congress reorganized the Postal Service and removed positions such as local postmaster from the political patronage/rewards pool. Since then, these types of positions generally refer to secretarial assistants to policy makers.

TABLE 9.1   How to Fire a Federal Bureaucrat

Removing federal employees for poor performance is very difficult and rare. In 1997, for example, of the federal government's 2.7 million employees, 3,550 were terminated for poor performance. Only 100 were demoted and only 1,257 failed to get a pay raise based on their poor performance.[a] Civil service rules make it easier to fire someone for misconduct than poor performance. Incompetent employees must be given notice by their supervisors and given an opportunity for remedial training.

To fire a member of the competitive civil service, explicit procedures must be followed:

1. At least thirty days' written notice must be given to an employee in advance of firing or demotion for incompetence or misconduct.
2. The written notification must contain a statement of reasons for the action and specific examples of unacceptable performance.
3. The employee has the right to reply both orally and in written form to the charges, and has the right to an attorney.
4. Appeals from any adverse action against the employee can be made to the three-person Merit Systems Protection Board (MSPB), a bipartisan body appointed by the president and confirmed by the Senate.
5. All employees have the right to a hearing and to an attorney in front of the MSPB.
6. All decisions of the MSPB may be appealed by the employee to the U.S. Court of Appeals.

[a]D. Mark Wilson, "Inadequate Remedies for Poorly Performing Federal Workers Would Undermine Airport Security," Heritage Foundation WebMemo 54 (November 8, 2001).

Federal employees are stereotyped as "paper pushers," but more than 15,000 job skills are represented in the federal government, and its workers are perhaps the best trained and most skilled and efficient in the world. Government employees, whose average age is 46.3 years, with an average length of service at 17.1 years, include forest rangers, FBI agents, foreign service officers, computer programmers, security guards, librarians, administrators, engineers, plumbers, lawyers, doctors, postal carriers, and zoologists, among others.

The graying of the federal workforce is of concern to many. By 2005, "more than two-thirds of those in the Senior Executive Service and large numbers of mid-level managers will be eligible to retire,"[10] taking with them "a wealth of institutional knowledge."[11] Many in government hope that the Presidential Management Fellows Program, which was begun twenty years ago to hire and train future managers and executives, will be enhanced to make up for the shortfall in experienced managers that the federal government is expected to face soon. Moreover, the proposed "Good People, Good Government Act" is designed to improve recruiting and training of federal employees, recognizing the critical shortages that are expected soon in the civil service workforce.[12] Agencies even are contemplating ways to pay the college loans of prospective recruits.[13] Lacking sufficient skilled employees to carry out critical functions, the government often uses outside contractors.

The diversity of government jobs mirrors the diversity of jobs in the private sector. The federal workforce, itself, is also diverse. As revealed in Analyzing Visuals: Characteristics and Rank Distribution of Federal Civilian Employees, the federal workforce largely reflects the racial and ethnic composition of the United States as a whole, although the employment of women lags behind that of men. Women still make up nearly 70 percent of the lowest GS level, but have raised their proportion of positions in the GS 13–15 ranks from 18 percent in 1990 to nearly 30 percent in 2000.[14]

Only about 325,000 federal bureaucrats work in the nation's capital; the rest are located in regional, state, and local offices scattered throughout the country. To enhance efficiency, the United States is broken up into several regions, with most agencies having regional offices in one city in that region. (See Figure 9.2.) The decentralization of the bureaucracy facilitates accessibility to the public. The Social Security Administration, for example, has numerous offices so that its clients may have a place nearby to take their paperwork, questions, and problems. Decentralization also helps distribute jobs and incomes across the country.

Participation

Who Wants to
Be a
Bureaucrat?

FIGURE 9.2   Federal Agency Regions and City Headquarters

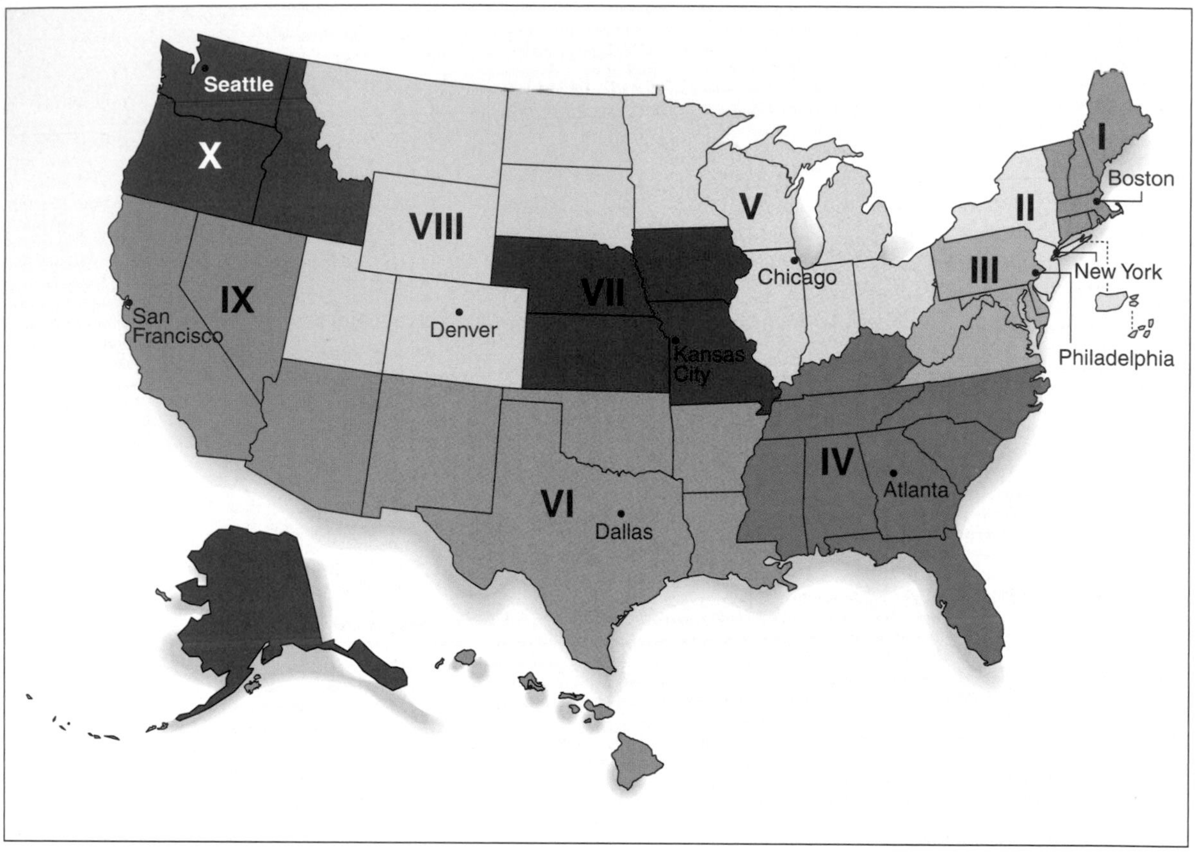

Source: Department of Health and Human Services, http://www.hhs.gov/images/regions.gif.

Many Americans believe that the federal bureaucracy is growing bigger each year, but they are wrong. Efforts to reduce the federal workforce have had an effect. Although it is true that the number of total government employees has increased over time, most growth has taken place at the state and local levels. And, as more federal programs are shifted back to the states, the size of state payrolls and state bureaucracies is likely to rise to reflect these new responsibilities.

Formal Organization

While even experts can't agree on the exact number of separate governmental agencies, commissions, and departments that make up the federal bureaucracy, there are at least 1,149 civilian agencies.[15] A distinctive feature of the executive bureaucracy is its traditional division into areas of specialization. For example, one agency, the Occupational Safety and Health Administration, handles occupational safety, the Department of State specializes in foreign affairs, the Environmental Protection Agency in the environment, and so on. It is not unusual, however, for more than one agency to be involved in a particular issue or for one agency to be involved in myriad issues. In fact, numerous agencies often have authority in the same issue areas, making administration even more difficult. Agencies fall into four general types; (1) Cabinet departments; (2) government corporations; (3) independent agencies; and, (4) regulatory commissions.

ANALYZING VISUALS

Characteristics and Rank Distribution of Federal Civilian Employees

The bar graph depicts the percentage of the federal civilian workforce in several categories: gender, gender and rank, race or ethnicity, disability, age, length of service, and union representation. After reviewing the data displayed in the graph, answer the following critical thinking questions: What do you notice about the percentages of males and females in the lowest (GS-01-04) and the highest (GS-13) grades? How would you explain the differences in percentages of males and females in those grades? Which racial/ethnic groups are represented in percentages that are greater than their percentages in the population (see the population statistics in the Changes in Racial and Ethnic Distributions section in chapter 1)? What do you think would explain the high percentage of federal civilian workforce represented by a union?

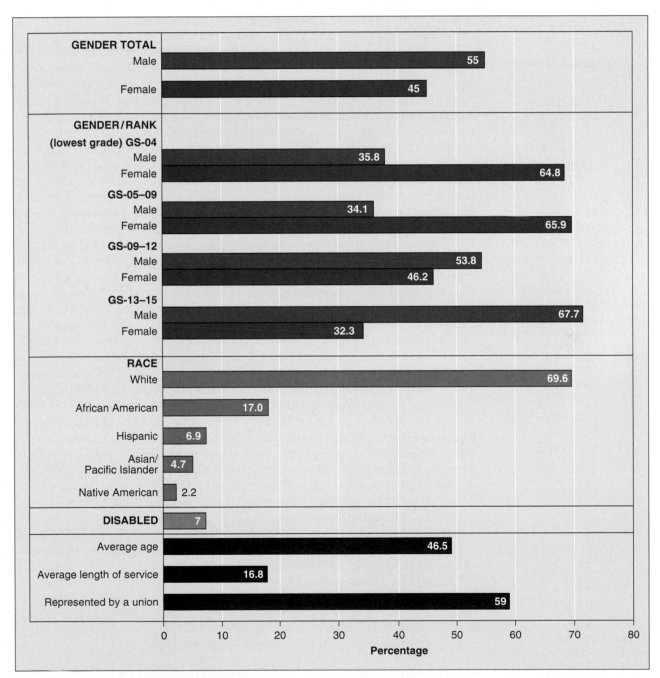

Source: Office of Personnel Management, *2003 Fact Book.*

departments
Major administrative units with responsibility for a broad area of government operations. Departmental status usually indicates a permanent national interest in that particular governmental function, such as defense, commerce, or agriculture.

The Cabinet Departments.   The fifteen Cabinet **departments** are major administrative units that have responsibility for conducting a broad area of government operations. Cabinet departments account for about 60 percent of the federal workforce. The vice president, the heads of all of the departments, as well as the heads of the EPA, OMB, Office of National Drug Control Policy, the U.S. Trade Representative, and the President's chief of staff make up his formal Cabinet.

The executive branch departments depicted in Figure 9.3 are headed by Cabinet members called secretaries (except the Department of Justice, which is headed by the attorney general). The secretaries are responsible for establishing their department's general policy and overseeing its operations. As discussed in chapter 8, Cabinet secretaries are responsible directly to the president but are often viewed as having two masters—the president and those affected by their department. Cabinet secretaries also are tied to Congress, from which they get their appropriations and the discretion to implement legislation and make rules and policy.

Although departments vary considerably in size, prestige, and power, they share certain features. Each department covers a broad area of responsibility generally reflected by its name. Each secretary is assisted by one or more deputies or undersecretaries who take part of the administrative burden off the secretary's shoulders, as well as by several assistant secretaries who direct major programs within the department. In addition, each secretary, like the president, has numerous assistants who help with planning, budgeting, personnel, legal services, public relations, and other key staff functions. Most departments are subdivided into bureaus, divisions, sections, or other smaller units, and it is at this level that the real work of each agency is done. Most departments are subdivided along functional lines, but the basis for division may be geography, work processes (for example, the new Transportation Security Agency, which initially was housed in the Department of Transportation, until its relocation to the new Department of Homeland Security), or clientele (such as the Bureau of Indian Affairs in the Department of the Interior).

Departmental status generally signifies a strong permanent national interest to promote a particular function. Moreover, some departments are organized to foster and promote the interests of a given clientele—that is, a specific social or economic group. Such departments are called **clientele agencies.** The Departments of Agriculture, Education, Energy, Labor, Veterans Affairs, and the Bureau of Indian Affairs in the Department of the Interior are examples of clientele agencies or bureaus. The Department of Labor's Women's Bureau is a good example of a clientele agency. "Created by Congress in 1920, the Women's Bureau has played a central role in representing and protecting the needs of wage-earning women."[16] Over time, it helped ease women into the war industry in World War II, played an important role in establishing President Kennedy's Commission on the Status of Women, and worked to get the Equal Pay Act passed in 1963 and the Family and Medical Leave Act in 1993. In early 2002, the Bush administration announced that it planned to eliminate all of the regional offices of the bureau. This action was met with an outcry from women's rights groups and labor unions. When even Secretary of Labor Elaine Chao protested, these plans were dropped for the time being.

clientele agencies
Executive departments directed by law to foster and promote the interests of a specific segment or group in the U.S. population (such as the Department of Education).

Because many of these agencies were created at the urging of well-organized interests to advance their particular objectives, it is not surprising that clientele groups are powerful lobbies with their respective agencies in Washington. The clientele agencies and groups also are active at the regional level, where the agencies devote a substantial part of their resources to program implementation. One of the most obvious examples of regional outreach is the Extension Service of the Department of Agriculture. Agricultural extension agents are scattered throughout the farm belt and routinely work with farmers on farm productivity and other problems. Career bureaucrats in the Department of Agriculture know that farm interests will be dependable allies year in and year out. Congress and the president are not nearly so reliable, because they must balance the interests of farmers with those of other segments of society.

government corporations
Businesses established by Congress that perform functions that could be provided by private businesses (such as the U.S. Postal Service).

Government Corporations.   **Government corporations** are the most recent addition to the bureaucratic maze. Dating from the early 1930s, they are businesses

FIGURE 9.3   The Executive Branch

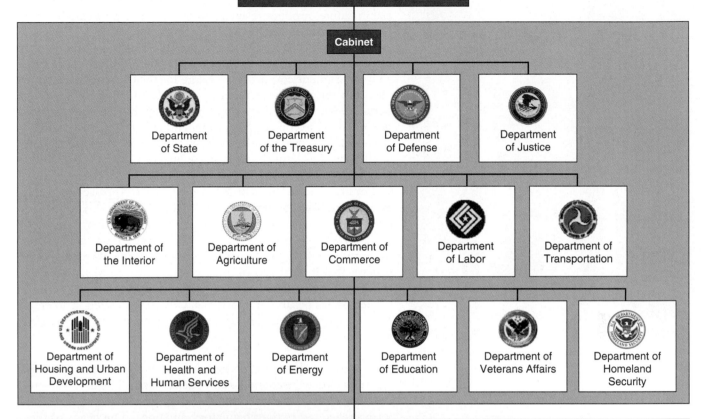

THE PRESIDENT OF THE UNITED STATES

Cabinet

Department of State | Department of the Treasury | Department of Defense | Department of Justice

Department of the Interior | Department of Agriculture | Department of Commerce | Department of Labor | Department of Transportation

Department of Housing and Urban Development | Department of Health and Human Services | Department of Energy | Department of Education | Department of Veterans Affairs | Department of Homeland Security

Independent Agencies and Government Corporations

Advisory Council on Historic Preservation
African Development Foundation
American Battle Monuments Commission
Appalachian Regional Commission
Architectural and Transportation
    Barriers Compliance Board
Arctic Research Commission
Armed Forces Retirement Home
Barry M. Goldwater Scholarship and
    Excellence in Education Foundation
Broadcasting Board of Governors
Central Intelligence Agency
Civil Air Patrol Great Lakes Region
Commission on Civil Rights
Commission of Fine Arts
Committee for Purchase from People
    Who Are Blind or Severely Disabled
Commodity Futures Trading Commission
Consumer Product Safety Commission
Corporation for National Service
Defense Nuclear Facilities Safety Board
Delaware River Basin Commission
Environmental Protection Agency
Equal Employment Opportunity Commission
Export-Import Bank of the U.S.
Farm Credit Administration
Federal Communications Commission
Federal Deposit Insurance Corporation
Federal Election Commission
Federal Emergency Management Agency
Federal Energy Regulatory Commission
Federal Housing Finance Board
Federal Labor Relations Authority
Federal Maritime Commission

Federal Mediation and Conciliation Service
Federal Mine Safety and Health Review Commission
Federal Reserve System
Federal Retirement Thrift Investment Board
Federal Trade Commission
General Services Administration
Harry S Truman Scholarship Foundation
Inter-American Foundation
International Boundary and Water Commission,
    United States and Mexico
International Broadcasting Bureau
Interstate Commission on the Potomac River Basin
James Madison Memorial Fellowship Foundation
Japan–United States Friendship Commission
Marine Mammal Commission
Merit Systems Protection Board
National Aeronautics and Space Administration
National Archives and Records Administration
National Capital Planning Commission
National Commission on Libraries and
    Information Science
National Council on Disability
National Credit Union Administration
National Foundation on the Arts
    and the Humanities
National Labor Relations Board
National Mediation Board
National Performance Review
National Railroad Passenger Corporation (Amtrak)
National Science Foundation
National Transportation Safety Board
Nuclear Regulatory Commission
Occupational Safety and Health Review Commission
Office of Government Ethics

Office of Navajo and Hopi Indian Relocation
Office of Personnel Management
Office of Special Counsel
Overseas Private Investment Corporation
Peace Corps
Pension Benefit Guaranty Corporation
Physician Payment Review Commission
Postal Rate Commission
President's Commission on White House
    Fellowships
President's Committee on Employment
    of People with Disabilities
Railroad Retirement Board
Securities and Exchange Commission
Selective Service System
Small Business Administration
Smithsonian Institution
Social Security Administration
Surface Transportation Board
Susquehanna River Basin Commission
Tennesse Valley Authority
Trade Development Agency
U.S. Arms Control and Disarmament Agency
U.S. Chemical Safety and Hazard
    Investigation Board
U.S. Holocaust Memorial Council
U.S. Information Agency
U.S. Institute of Peace
U.S. International Development
    Corporation Agency
U.S. International Trade Commission
U.S. Postal Service
Woodrow Wilson International Center
    for Scholars

Source: Library of Congress, http://www.loc.gov/global/executive/fed.html.

A U.S. Postal Service employee delivers mail while wearing a mask and rubber gloves along his route as a precaution against contracting anthrax, which paralyzed the Washington, D.C. mail system post 9/11.

(Photo courtesy: C. Todd Sherman/The Vicksburg Post/AP/World Wide Photos)

independent executive agencies
Governmental units that closely resemble a Cabinet department but have a narrower area of responsibility (such as the Central Intelligence Agency) and are not part of any Cabinet department.

You Are the President of Medicorp

established by Congress to perform functions that could be provided by private businesses. The corporations are formed when the government chooses to engage in activities that primarily are commercial in nature, produce revenue, and require greater flexibility than Congress generally allows regular departments. Some of the better-known government corporations include Amtrak and the Federal Deposit Insurance Corporation. Unlike other governmental agencies, government corporations charge for their services. For example, the largest government corporation, the U.S. Postal Service—whose functions could be handled by a private corporation, such as Federal Express or the United Parcel Service (UPS)—exists today to ensure delivery of mail throughout the United States at cheaper rates than those a private business might charge. Similarly, the Tennessee Valley Authority (TVA) provides electricity at reduced rates to millions of Americans in the Appalachian region of the Southeast, generally a low-income area that had failed to attract private utility companies to provide service there.

In cases such as that of the TVA, where the financial incentives for private industry to provide services are minimal, Congress often believes that it must act. In other cases, it steps in to salvage valuable public assets. For example, when passenger rail service in the United States became unprofitable, Congress stepped in to create Amtrak, nationalizing the passenger-train industry to keep passenger trains running.

Independent Executive Agencies. **Independent executive agencies** closely resemble Cabinet departments but have narrower areas of responsibility. Generally speaking, independent agencies perform service rather than regulatory functions. The heads of these agencies are appointed by the president and serve, like Cabinet secretaries, at his pleasure.

Independent agencies exist apart from executive departments for practical or symbolic reasons. The National Aeronautics and Space Administration (NASA), for example, could have been placed within the Department of Defense. That, however, could have conjured up thoughts of a space program dedicated solely to military purposes, rather than to civilian satellite communication or scientific exploration. Similarly, the Environmental Protection Agency (EPA) was created in 1970 to administer federal programs aimed at controlling pollution and protecting the nation's environment. It administers all congressional laws concerning the environment and pollution. Along with the Council on Environmental Quality, a staff agency in the Executive Office of the President, the EPA advises the president on environmental concerns, and its head, Mike Leavitt, is considered a member of the president's Cabinet.[17] It also administers programs transferred to it with personnel detailed from the Departments of Agriculture, Energy, Interior, and Health and Human Services, as well as the Nuclear Regulatory Commission, among others. The expanding national focus on the environment, in fact, has brought about numerous calls to elevate the EPA to Cabinet-level status to reinforce a long-term national commitment to improved air and water and other environmental issues.

Independent Regulatory Commissions. Independent regulatory commissions are agencies that were created by Congress to exist outside of the major departments to regulate a specific economic activity or interest. Because of the complexity of modern economic issues, Congress sought to create agencies that could develop expertise and provide continuity of policy with respect to economic issues because neither Congress nor the courts have the time or talent to do so. Examples include the National Labor Relations Board, the Federal Reserve Board, the Federal Communications Commission, and the Securities and Exchange Commission (SEC).[18] Congress started setting up regulatory commissions as early as 1887, recognizing the need for close and continuous guardianship of particular economic activities. Older boards and commissions, such as the SEC and the Federal Reserve Board, generally are charged with overseeing a certain industry. Regulatory agencies created since the 1960s are more concerned with how the business sector relates to public health and safety. The Occupational Safety and Health Administration, for example, promotes job safety.

Most of the older independent agencies were created specifically to be free (relatively) from immediate (partisan) political pressure. Each is headed by a board composed of five to seven members (always an odd number, to avoid tie votes) who are selected by the president and confirmed by the Senate for fixed, staggered terms to increase the chances of a bipartisan board. Unlike executive department heads, they cannot easily be removed by the president. In 1935, the U.S. Supreme Court ruled that in creating independent commissions, the Congress had intended that they be independent panels of experts as far removed as possible from immediate political pressures.[19]

Newer regulatory boards lack this kind of autonomy and freedom from political pressures; they are generally headed by a single administrator who can be removed by the president. These boards and commissions, such as the Equal Employment Opportunity Commission, therefore, are far more susceptible to political pressure and to the political wishes of the president who appoints them.

Politics and Government Workers

As an increasing proportion of the American workforce came to work for the U.S. government as a result of the New Deal recovery programs, many began to fear that the members of the civil service would play major roles not only in implementing public policy but also in electing members of Congress and even the president. Consequently, Congress enacted the Political Activities Act of 1939, commonly known as the **Hatch Act.** It was designed to prohibit federal employees from becoming directly involved in working for political candidates.

Hatch Act
Law enacted in 1939 to prohibit civil servants from taking activist roles in partisan campaigns. This act prohibited federal employees from making political contributions, working for a particular party, or campaigning for a particular candidate.

Although presidents as far back as Thomas Jefferson had advocated efforts to limit the opportunities for federal civil servants to influence the votes of others, over the years many criticized the Hatch Act as too extreme. Critics argued that it denied millions of federal employees First Amendment guarantees of freedom of speech and association and discouraged political participation among a group of people who might otherwise be strong political activists. Critics also argued that civil servants should become more involved in campaigns, particularly at the state and local level, to understand better the needs of the citizens they serve.

In 1993, in response to criticisms of the Hatch Act and at the urgings of President Bill Clinton, Congress enacted the **Federal Employees Political Activities Act.** This liberalization of the Hatch Act allows employees to run for public office in nonpartisan elections, contribute money to political organizations, and campaign for or against candidates in partisan elections. They still, however, are prohibited from engaging in political activity while on duty, soliciting contributions from the general public, or running for office in partisan elections. During the signing ceremony, Clinton said the law will "mean more responsive, more satisfied, happier, and more productive federal employees."[20] Some, however, didn't even realize that they were federal employees. Recently, the Hatch Act had a surprising effect when a teacher in the D.C. public schools was fired for running for the D.C. city council, a race he lost in a landslide. Prior to the 1993 amendments, D.C. employees were exempted from the Hatch Act's reach. But, political wrangling led to their being covered in the 1993 amendments. Thus, because D.C. employees are treated as federal workers, they are not exempt from Hatch Act provisions that bar federal workers from running for public office in partisan elections. Initially, the teacher wasn't aware of the prohibition, but he refused to terminate his candidacy even after being notified that it could cost him his job.[21] See Table 9.2 for more specifics about this law.

Federal Employees Political Activities Act
1993 liberalization of the Hatch Act. Federal employees are now allowed to run for office in nonpartisan elections and to contribute money to campaigns in partisan elections.

TABLE 9.2   The Liberalized Hatch Act

Here are some examples of permissible and prohibited activities for federal employees under the Hatch Act, as modified by the Federal Employees Political Activities Act of 1993.

Federal employees

- **May** be candidates for public office in nonpartisan elections
- **May** assist in voter registration drives
- **May** express opinions about candidates and issues
- **May** contribute money to political organizations
- **May** attend political fund-raising functions
- **May** attend and be active at political rallies and meetings
- **May** join and be active members of a political party or club
- **May** sign nominating petitions
- **May** campaign for or against referendum questions, constitutional amendments, and municipal ordinances
- **May** campaign for or against candidates in partisan elections
- **May** make campaign speeches for candidates in partisan elections
- **May** distribute campaign literature in partisan elections
- **May** hold office in political clubs or parties

- **May not** use their official authority or influence to interfere with an election
- **May not** collect political contributions unless both individuals are members of the same federal labor organization or employee organization and the one solicited is not a subordinate employee
- **May not** knowingly solicit or discourage the political activity of any person who has business before the agency
- **May not** engage in political activity while on duty
- **May not** engage in political activity in any government office
- **May not** engage in political activity while wearing an official uniform
- **May not** engage in political activity while using a government vehicle
- **May not** solicit political contributions from the general public
- **May not** be candidates for public office in partisan elections

Source: U.S. Special Counsel's Office.

POLICY MAKING

One of the major functions of the bureaucracy is policy making—and bureaucrats can be, and often are, major policy makers.[22] When Congress creates any kind of department, agency, or commission, it is actually delegating some of its powers listed in Article I, section 8, of the U.S. Constitution. Therefore, the laws creating departments, agencies, corporations, or commissions carefully describe their purpose and give them the authority to make numerous policy decisions, which have the effect of law. Congress recognizes that it does not have the time, expertise, or ability to involve itself in every detail of every program; therefore, it sets general guidelines for agency action and leaves it to the agency to work out the details. How agencies execute congressional wishes is called **implementation,** the process by which a law or policy is put into operation. Much of the policy-making process occurs in the form of what some call iron triangles or issue networks.

Senator John McCain (R–AZ) addresses a veterans' group. The son and grandson of Navy admirals, McCain was shot down over Vietnam and held as a prisoner of war for five years.

(Photo courtesy: M. Spencer Green/AP/Wide World Photos)

Iron Triangles and Issue Networks

The relatively stable relationships and patterns of interaction that occur among an agency, interest groups, and congressional committees or subcommittees as policy is made are often referred to as **iron triangles,** or subgovernments (see Figure 9.4).

Policy-making subgovernments are "iron" because they virtually are impenetrable to outsiders and largely are autonomous. Even presidents have difficulty piercing the workings of these subgovernments, which have endured over time. Examples of iron triangles abound. Senior citizens' groups (especially the American Association of Retired Persons), the Social Security Administration, and the House Subcommittee on Aging all are likely to agree on the need for increased Social Security benefits. Similarly, the Department of Veterans Affairs, the House Committee on Veterans Affairs, and the American Legion and Veterans of Foreign Wars—the two largest organizations representing veterans—usually agree on the need for expanded programs for veterans.

The policy decisions made within these iron triangles often foster the interests of a clientele group and have little to do with the advancement of national policy goals. In part, subgovernmental decisions often conflict with other governmental policies and tend to tie the hands of larger institutions such as Congress and the president. The White House often is too busy dealing with international affairs or crises to deal with smaller issues such as the scope of benefits for veterans. Likewise, Congress defers to its committees and subcommittees. Thus, these subgovernments decentralize policy making and make policy making difficult to control.[23]

Today, iron triangles no longer dominate most policy processes for three main reasons: (1) problems are increasingly complex; (2) issues cut across several policy areas; and, (3) there has been a phenomenal increase in the number of Washington, D.C.–based interest groups. As these three changes have occurred, many iron triangles have become rusty. New terms have been coined to

FIGURE 9.4   An Iron Triangle

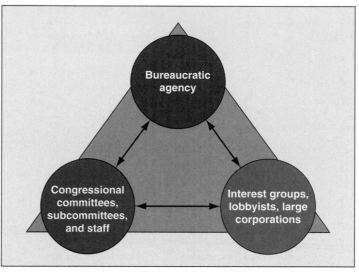

describe the policy-making process and the bureaucracy's role in it. Hugh Heclo argues that this system of separate subgovernments is overlaid with an amorphous system of **issue networks,** that is, the fuzzy set of relationships among a large number of actors in broad policy areas.[24] In general, like iron triangles, issue networks are made up of agency officials, members of Congress (and committee staffers), and interest group lobbyists. But, they also often include lawyers, consultants, academics, public relations specialists, and sometimes even the courts.[25] Unlike iron triangles, issue networks constantly are changing as members with technical expertise become involved in various issues.

Issue networks reflect the complexity of the problems and issues that lawmakers and policy makers try to solve. As an example, let's look at the plight of many American children. All kinds of complex and interrelated issues are involved. Improving their lives is, for example, a health issue because many children don't have access to medical care; an education issue because many can't read, go to poor schools, or are dropouts; a labor issue because many have no job skills; and a drug and crime issue because many of these children live in drug-infested neighborhoods and often ultimately turn to crime, ending up in jail as a result. But, given the segmented nature of policy making, relevant and related policies are made and implemented by myriad agencies, including the Departments of Health and Human Services, Education, Labor, and Justice—plus all their associated House and Senate subcommittees, interest groups, and experts, as well as state and local governmental agencies.

As policy issues become more and more complex, they often need cooperation across agencies to get the job done. To that end, all kinds of **interagency councils,** or working groups, have been created to facilitate the coordination of policy making and implementation. Depending on how well these councils are funded, they can be the prime movers of administration policy in any area where an interagency council exists. The U.S. Interagency Council on the Homeless, for example, was created in 1987 to coordinate the activities of the more than fifty governmental agencies and programs that work to alleviate homelessness. Lack of funding during the 1990s, however, caused it to lie dormant, until it got a $500,000 budget authorization in 2001.[26] Better funded is the Interagency Council on Community Living, which was created to implement a presidential executive order to expand community-based services for people with disabilities. Representatives from the Departments of Health and Human Services, Education, and Labor form this interagency council that has over $9 million in grants to dispense to the states.[27] The initial Office of Homeland Security, which involved far more agencies, bureaus, departments, and people (see Figure 9.5), provides an interesting perspective on potential problems faced when agencies try to cooperate, as illustrated in Politics Now: Homeland Security.

implementation
The process by which a law or policy is put into operation by the bureaucracy.

iron triangles
The relatively stable relationships and patterns of interaction that occur among an agency, interest groups, and congressional committees or subcommittees.

issue networks
The loose and informal relationships that exist among a large number of actors who work in broad policy areas.

interagency councils
Working groups created to facilitate coordination of policy making and implementation across a host of governmental agencies.

E-GOVERNMENT

In 1992, the White House first went up on the World Wide Web. Now all government agencies and bureaus have web sites and provide a plethora of information to the American public that formerly would have taken numerous trips to the library and even Washington, D.C., to obtain.[a]

By 1998, the Government Paperwork Elimination Act required that federal agencies allow persons transacting business with the government to have the option of submitting information or transacting business with them electronically. It is from this act that you or members of your family now have the option of submitting your tax returns electronically.

In 2002, the Bush administration took additional steps to take advantage of changing technologies and an increasing number of American's access to it whether in their homes or at local public libraries (as well as Internet cafes). The E-Government Act of 2002 was an effort to mandate that all government agencies used "Internet-based information technologies to enhance citizen's access to government information and services."

According to the E-Gov web site, E-Gov is not simply about putting forms on line; its major purpose is to harness technology to make it easier for citizens to learn more about government services. GovBenefits.gov, for example, has been created so that citizens can answer a range of questions dealing with their individual circumstances and will immediately be given a list of government programs that they may be eligible for. Recreation.gov allows individuals to find out about national parks and recreation sites and to make on-line reservations at those facilities.

The newest addition to the E-Government effort under the Bush administration is its eRulemaking Initiative. Managed by the Environmental Protection Agency, this new use of technology is designed to transform "the federal rule making process by enhancing the public's ability to participate in their government's regulatory decision making." Regulations.gov was launched in 2002 to allow the public to "search, view, and comment on proposed federal regulations open for comment."

While the regulatory process was one formerly almost exclusively a process that saw the near exclusive involvement of interest groups and affected industries, this new initiative allows the public to search proposed regulations easily. Agencies are in the process of posting their proposed regulations on this central site, although some agencies still have their own sites. One 2004 study revealed that some agencies had failed to post proposed regulations on the central site, but efforts are being made to remedy these lapses.

By 2006, individuals should be able to track and comment on regulations from the 173 rule-making entities of the federal government as each of these units adapts to this new technology.

OMB Watch, a nonprofit group that monitors government actions as they affect citizen participation, has applauded the notion of a centralized, one-stop methods to allow concerned citizens great input into the policy process.

1. Will the bureaucracy become more responsive to citizens and less captured by special interests as E-Government increases?
2. Are there any downside to E-Regulations?

---

[a]About E-Gov, www.whitehouse.gov/omb/egov/about_leg.htm.
[b]www.regulations.gov.
[c]Ibid.

Policy making and implementation often take place on informal and formal levels. Practically, many decisions are left to individual government employees on a day-to-day basis. Department of Justice lawyers, for example, make daily decisions about whether or not to prosecute someone. Similarly, street-level Internal Revenue Service agents make many decisions during personal audits. These street-level bureaucrats make policy on two levels. First, they exercise wide discretion in decisions concerning citizens with whom they interact. Second, taken together, their individual actions add up to agency behavior.[28] Thus, how bureaucrats interpret and apply (or choose not to apply) various policies are equally important parts of the policy-making process. Administrative discretion allows decision makers (whether they are in a Cabinet-level position or at the lowest GS levels) a tremendous amount of leeway.

FIGURE 9.5 Department of Homeland Security

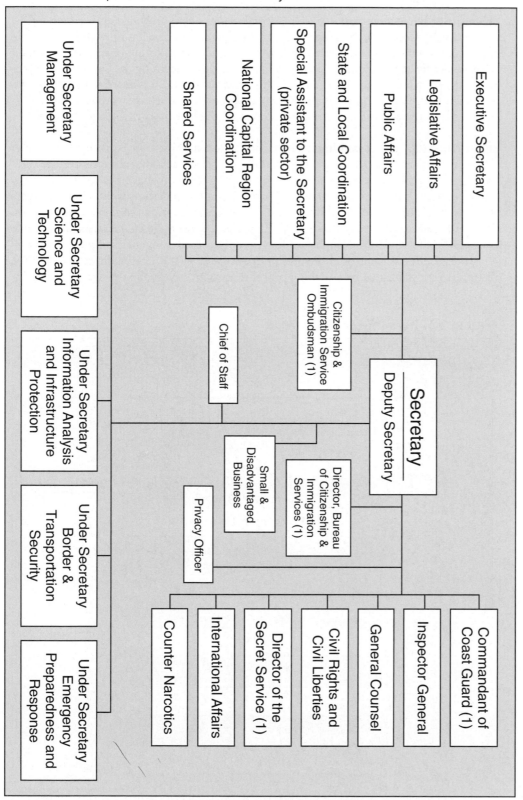

Although very complex, the Department of Homeland Security was created to make America safer.
Note (1): Effective March 1st, 2003.

Administrative Discretion

Essentially, bureaucrats make as well as implement policy. They take the laws and policies made by Congress, the president, and the courts, and develop rules and procedures for making sure they are carried out. Most implementation involves what is called **administrative discretion,** the ability to make choices concerning the best way to implement congressional intentions. Administrative discretion also is exercised through two formal administrative procedures: rule making and administrative adjudication. This process is illustrated in On Campus: Enforcing Gender Equity in College Athletics.

administrative discretion
The ability of bureaucrats to make choices concerning the best way to implement congressional intentions.

Rule Making.   **Rule making** is a quasi-legislative administrative process that results in regulations and has the characteristics of a legislative act. **Regulations** are the rules that govern the operation of all government programs and have the force of law. In essence, then, bureaucratic rule makers often act as lawmakers as well as law enforcers when they make rules or draft regulations to implement various congressional statutes. The rule-making process is illustrated in Figure 9.6. Some political scientists say that rule making "is the single most important function performed by agencies of government."[29]

rule making
A quasi-legislative administrative process that has the characteristics of a legislative act.

regulations
Rules that govern the operation of a particular government program that have the force of law.

Because regulations often involve political conflict, the 1946 Administrative Procedures Act established rule-making procedures to give everyone the chance to partic-

FIGURE 9.6   How a Regulation Is Made

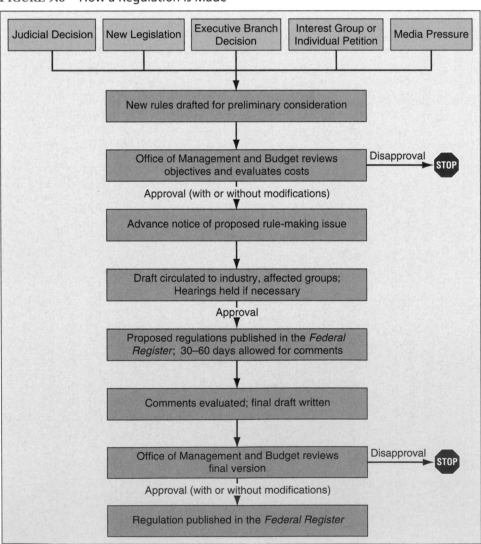

ipate in the process. The act requires that: (1) public notice of the time, place, and nature of the rule-making proceedings be provided in the *Federal Register*; (2) interested parties be given the opportunity to submit written arguments and facts relevant to the rule; and, (3) the statutory purpose and basis of the rule be stated. Once rules are written, generally, thirty days must elapse before they take effect.

Sometimes an agency is required by law to conduct a formal hearing before issuing rules. Evidence is gathered, and witnesses testify and are cross-examined by opposing interests. The process can take weeks, months, or even years, at the end of which agency administrators must review the entire record and then justify the new rules. Although cumbersome, the process has reduced criticism of some rules and bolstered the deference given by the courts to agency decisions.

Administrative Adjudication. **Administrative adjudication** is a quasi-judicial process in which a bureaucratic agency settles disputes between two parties in a manner similar to the way courts resolve disputes. Administrative adjudication, like rule making, is referred to as "quasi" (Latin for "seemingly") judicial, because law-making by any body other than Congress or adjudication by any body other than the judiciary would be a violation of the constitutional principle of separation of powers.

Agencies regularly find that persons or businesses are not in compliance with the federal laws the agencies are charged with enforcing, or that they are in violation of an agency rule or regulation. To force compliance, some agencies resort to administrative adjudication, which generally is less formal than a trial. Several agencies and boards employ administrative law judges to conduct the hearings. Although these judges are employed by the agencies, they are strictly independent and cannot be removed except for gross misconduct. Congress, for example, empowers the Federal Trade Commission (FTC) to determine what constitutes an unfair trade practice.[30] Its actions, however, are reviewable in the federal courts. So are the findings of EEOC judges.

administrative adjudication
A quasi-judicial process in which a bureaucratic agency settles disputes between two parties in a manner similar to the way courts resolve disputes.

WEB EXPLORATION
To see federal agency rules and regulations contained in the *Federal Register*, see
www.ablongman.com/oconnor

MAKING AGENCIES ACCOUNTABLE

The question of to whom bureaucrats should be responsible is one that continually comes up in any debate about governmental accountability. Should the bureaucracy be answerable to itself? To organized interest groups? To its clientele? To the president? To Congress? Or to some combination of all of these? At times an agency becomes so removed from the public it serves that Congress must step in. This is what happened with the Internal Revenue Service (IRS). Throughout 1997 and 1998, Congress held extensive hearings about abuses at the IRS, one of the most hated and feared federal agencies in America. Senate hearings in particular exposed abuses of ordinary citizens who found themselves in a nightmare of bureaucratic red tape and agency employee abuse of power. As a result of these hearings, Congress ordered the new IRS commissioner to overhaul the way the IRS deals with the public.[31]

While many would argue that federal employees should be responsive to the public interest, the public interest is difficult to define. As it turns out, several factors work to control the power of the bureaucracy, and to some degree, the same kinds of checks and balances that operate among the three branches of government serve to check the bureaucracy (see Table 9.3).

Many argue that the president should be in charge of the bureaucracy because it is up to him to see that popular ideas and expectations are translated into administrative action. But, under our constitutional system, the president is not the only actor in the policy process. Congress creates the agencies, funds them, and establishes the broad rules of their operation. Moreover, Congress continually reviews the various agencies through oversight committee investigations, hearings, and its power of the purse. And, the federal judiciary, as in most other matters, has the ultimate authority to review administrative actions.

TABLE 9.3	Making Agencies Accountable

The president has the authority to:

- Appoint and remove agency heads and a few additional top bureaucrats.
- Reorganize the bureaucracy (with congressional approval).
- Make changes in an agency's annual budget proposals.
- Ignore legislative initiatives originating within the bureaucracy.
- Initiate or adjust policies that would, if enacted by Congress, alter the bureaucracy's activities.
- Issue executive orders.
- Reduce an agency's annual budget.

Congress has the authority to:

- Pass legislation that alters the bureaucracy's activities.
- Abolish existing programs.
- Investigate bureaucratic activities and compel bureaucrats to testify about them.
- Influence presidential appointments of agency heads and other top bureaucratic officials.
- Write legislation to limit the bureaucracy's discretion.

The judiciary has the authority to:

- Rule on whether bureaucrats have acted within the law and require policy changes to comply with the law.
- Force the bureaucracy to respect the rights of individuals through hearings and other proceedings.
- Rule on the constitutionality of all rules and regulations.

Executive Control

As the size and scope of the American national government, in general, and of the executive branch and the bureaucracy, in particular, have grown, presidents have delegated more and more power to bureaucrats. But, most presidents have continued to try to exercise some control over the bureaucracy, although they have often found that task more difficult than they first envisioned. As president, John F. Kennedy, for example, once lamented that to give anyone at the Department of State an instruction was comparable to putting your request in a dead-letter box.[32] No response would ever be forthcoming.

The Environmental Protection Agency (EPA) is charged with administering most of the federal government's environmental legislation. Here, EPA inspectors oversee the handling and storing of hazardous waste.

(Photo courtesy: A. Ramey/Woodfin Camp and Associates)

Recognizing these potential problems, presidents try to appoint the best possible persons to carry out their wishes and policy preferences. Presidents make hundreds of appointments to the executive branch; in doing so, they have the opportunity to appoint individuals who share their views on a range of policies. Although presidential appointments make up a very small proportion of all federal jobs, presidents usually fill most top policy-making positions.

Presidents, with the approval of Congress, can reorganize the bureaucracy. They also can make changes in an agency's annual budget requests and ignore legislative initiatives originating within the bureaucracy. Several presidents have made it a priority to try to tame the bureaucracy to make it more accountable. Thomas Jefferson was the first president to address the issue of accountability. He attempted to cut waste and bring about a "wise and frugal government." But, it wasn't until the Progressive era (1890–1920) that calls for reform began to be taken seriously. Later, President Calvin Coolidge urged spending cuts and other reforms. His Two Percent Club was created to cut staff, as its name implies, by

ENFORCING GENDER EQUITY IN COLLEGE ATHLETICS

In 2002, there were approximately 157,000 female student-athletes,[a] a number up dramatically from 1971 when there were only about 30,000 women participating in collegiate athletics.[b] Male participation has grown much more slowly while the number of women's teams in the NCAA nearly doubled, from 4,776 to 8,414.[c] A major source of that difference? The passage in 1972 of legislation popularly known as Title IX, which prohibits discrimination against girls and women in federally funded education, including athletics programs. This legislation mandates that "No person in the United States shall, on the basis of sex, be excluded from participation in, be denied the benefits of, or be subjected to discrimination under any education program or activity receiving federal financial assistance." It wasn't until December 1978—six years after passage of the Education Amendments—that the Office for Civil Rights in the Department of Health, Education, and Welfare released a "policy interpretation" of the law, dealing largely with the section that concerned intercollegiate athletics.[d] More than thirty pages of text were devoted to dealing with a hundred or so words from the statute. Football was recognized as unique, because of the huge revenues it produces, so it could be inferred that male-dominated football programs could continue to outspend women's athletic programs. The more than sixty women's groups that had lobbied for equality of spending were outraged and turned their efforts toward seeking more favorable rulings on the construction of the statute from the courts.

Increased emphasis on Title IX enforcement has led many women to file lawsuits to force compliance. In 1991, in an effort to trim expenses, Brown University cut two men's and two women's teams from its varsity rosters. Several women on the downgraded gymnastics team filed a Title IX complaint against the school, arguing that it violated the act by not providing women varsity sport opportunities in relation to their population in the university. The women also argued that cutting the two women's program saved $62,000, whereas the men's cuts saved only $16,000. Thus, the women's varsity programs took a bigger hit, in violation of federal law.

A U.S. district court refused to allow Brown to cut the women's programs. A U.S. court of appeals upheld that action, concluding that Brown had failed to provide adequate opportunities for its female students to participate in athletics.[e] In 1997, in *Brown University* v. *Cohen*, the U.S. Supreme Court declined to review the appeals court's decision.[f] This put all colleges and universities on notice that discrimination against women would not be tolerated, even when, as in the case of Brown University, the university had expanded sports opportunities for women tremendously since the passage of Title IX.

Women have made significant strides on all college campuses, but true equity in athletics is still a long way away at many colleges and universities. While the number of women partici-

Title IX of the Education Amendments of 1972 mandated nondiscrimination in sports. Since its passage, there has been a dramatic increase in the number of high school and college women competing in school sports. Soccer was added as a team sport for women in 846 colleges.
(Photo courtesy: Karen O'Connor)

pating in college level sports is increasing, the proportion of women coaches is decreasing (at the same time the pool of women who could be coaches is increasing). Most colleges still provide far fewer opportunities to women given their numbers in most universities, and enforcement still lags. This has required groups including the National Women's Law Center to take the lead in the *Brown* case and to spend millions of dollars in legal fees to press for fuller enforcement, because Title IX is not self-enforcing.[g] Individual colleges and universities must comply with the law, aggrieved students must complain of inequities, and the Department of Education's Office of Civil Rights must enforce the law. This may become more difficult given the mixed messages being put out by the Bush administration. In 2002, for example, the National Wrestling Coaches Association filed suit against the Department of Education, arguing that Title IX guidelines force universities to discriminate against low-profile men's sports such as wrestling. To the surprise of many women's rights organizations, the Bush administration asked the court to dismiss the wrestling challenge. The government brief, however, offered no praise or support for Title IX, leaving its supporters wary of future administration actions.

[a]Bill Pennington, "Colleges: More Men's Teams Benched as Colleges Level the Playing Field," *New York Times* (May 9, 2002): A1.
[b]*Intercollegiate Athletics: Status of Efforts to Promote Gender Equity*, General Accounting Office, October 25, 1996.
[c]Pennington, "Colleges."
[d]See Joyce Gelb and Marian Lief Palley, *Women and Public Policies* (Charlottesville: University of Virginia Press, 1996), ch. 5.
[e]*Cohen* v. *Brown University*, 101 F.3d 155 (1996).
[f]520 U.S. 1186 (1997).
[g]http://www.edc.org/WomensEquity/resource/title9/report/athletic.html.

2 percent each year; his Correspondence Club was designed to reduce bureaucratic letter writing by 30 percent.[33]

All recent presidents since John F. Kennedy have tried to streamline the bureaucracy to make it smaller and thus more accountable. President Richard M. Nixon, for example, proposed a plan to combine fifty domestic agencies and seven different departments into four large "super departments." But, according to his former aide John Erlichman, this plan to "disrupt iron triangles" was dead on arrival. "Why? Because such a reorganization would have broken up the hoary congressional committee organization that corresponded to the existing departments and agencies." Said Erlichman, "A subcommittee chairman with oversight of the Agriculture Department would lose power, perks and status if we were authorized to fold Agriculture into a new Department of Natural Resources. The powerful farm lobbies were equally hostile to the idea."[34]

The Clinton administration was especially bullish on reform. The President's Task Force on Reinventing Government cut the size of the federal workforce, halved the growing number of federal regulations, and set customer service standards to direct agencies to put the people they serve first. President George W. Bush also put bureaucratic reform as a priority, but that effort lost momentum in the aftermath of September 11, 2001, which necessitated the creation of additional federal programs and offices and even a new Department of Homeland Security.

Presidents also can shape policy and provide direction to bureaucrats by issuing **executive orders,**[35] presidential directives to an agency that provide the basis for carrying out laws or for establishing new policies. Even before Congress acted to protect women from discrimination by the federal government, for example, the National Organization for Women convinced President Lyndon B. Johnson to sign Executive Order 11375 in 1967. This amended an earlier order prohibiting the federal government from discriminating on the basis of race, color, religion, or national origin in the awarding of federal contracts, by adding to it the category of "gender." Nevertheless, although the president signed the order, the Office of Federal Contract Compliance, part of the Department of Labor's Employment Standards Administration, failed to draft appropriate guidelines for implementation of the order until several years later.[36] A president can direct an agency to act, but it may take some time for the order to be carried out. Given the many jobs of any president, few can ensure that all their orders will be carried out or that they will like all the rules that are made.

Congressional Control

Congress, too, plays an important role in checking the power of the bureaucracy. Constitutionally, it possesses the authority to create or abolish departments and agencies as well as to transfer agency functions, as was recently seen in the protracted debate over the creation of the Department of Homeland Security. It can also expand or contract bureaucratic discretion. The Senate's authority to confirm (or reject) presidential appointments also gives Congress a check on the bureaucracy. Congress exercises considerable oversight over the bureaucracy in several ways. Table 9.4 contains data from a study conducted by the Brookings Institution detailing this authority.

Political scientists distinguish between two different forms of oversight: police patrol and fire alarm oversight.[37] As the names imply, police patrol oversight is proactive and allows Congress to set its own agenda for programs or agencies to review. In contrast, fire alarm oversight is reactive and generally involves a congressional response to a complaint filed by a constituent or politically significant actor. The range of congressional responses can vary from simple inquiries about an issue to full-blown hearings. Congress, at times, even responds to constituent complaints about the bureaucracy, as was the case when its intense and often hostile hearings resulted in total reorganization of the IRS.

Given the prevalence of iron triangles and issue networks, it is not surprising that the most frequently used form of oversight and the most effective is communication between house staffers and agency personnel. Various forms of program evaluations

Visual Literacy

The Changing Face of the Federal Bureaucracy

executive orders
Rules or regulations issued by the president that have the effect of law. All executive orders must be published in the *Federal Register*.

WEB EXPLORATION
For more about the IRS and its modernization efforts, see
www.ablongman.com/oconnor

TABLE 9.4	**Frequency and Effectiveness of Oversight Techniques in a Single Congress**	

Oversight technique	Number of Cases in Which Technique Was Used	Effectiveness Ranking
Staff communication with agency personnel	91	1
Member communication with agency personnel	86	2
Program reauthorization hearings	73	3
Oversight hearings	89	4
Hearings on bills to amend ongoing programs	70	5
Staff investigations	90	6
Program evaluations done by committee staff	89	7
Program evaluations done by congressional support agencies	89	8
Legislative veto	82	9
Analysis of proposed agency rules and regulations	90	10
Program evaluations done by outsiders	88	11
Agency reports required by Congress	91	12
Program evaluations done by the agencies	87	13
Review of casework	87	14

Source: Joel Aberbach, *Keeping a Watchful Eye* (Washington, DC: Brookings Institution, 1990), 132, 135.

make up the next most commonly used forms of congressional control. Congress and its staff routinely conduct evaluations of programs and conduct oversight hearings.

Congress also uses many of its constitutional powers to exercise control over the bureaucracy. These include its investigatory powers. It is not at all unusual for a congressional committee or subcommittee to hold hearings on a particular problem and then direct the relevant agency to study the problem or find ways to remedy it. Representatives of the agencies also appear before these committees on a regular basis to inform members about agency activities, ongoing investigations, and so on.

Congress also has its power of the purse. To control the bureaucracy, Congress uses its ability to fund or not fund an agency's activities like the proverbial carrot and stick. The House Appropriations Committee routinely holds hearings to allow agency heads to justify their budget requests. Authorization legislation originates in the various legislative committees that oversee particular agencies (such as Agriculture, Veterans Affairs, Education, and Labor) and sets the maximum amounts that agencies can spend on particular programs. While some authorizations, such as those for Social Security, are permanent, others, including the Departments of State and Defense procurements, are watched closely and are subject to annual authorizations.

Once funds are authorized, they must be appropriated before they can be spent. Appropriations originate with the House Appropriations Committee, not the specialized legislative committees. Often the Appropriations Committee allocates sums smaller than those authorized by legislative committees. Thus, the Appropriations Committee, a budget cutter, has an additional oversight function.

To help Congress's oversight of the bureaucracy's financial affairs, in 1921 Congress created the General Accountability Office (GAO) at the same time that the Office of the Budget (now the Office of Management and Budget) was created in the executive branch. With the establishment of the GAO, the Congressional Research Service, and later, the Congressional Budget Office (CBO), Congress essentially created its own bureaucracy to keep an eye on what the executive branch and its bureaucracy were doing. Today, the GAO not only tracks how money is spent in the bureaucracy, but it also monitors how policies are implemented. The CBO also conducts oversight studies. If it or the GAO uncovers problems with an agency's work, Congress is notified immediately.

Legislators also augment their formal oversight of the executive branch by allowing citizens to appeal adverse bureaucratic decisions to agencies, Congress, and even

Global Politics

BUREAUCRATS IN OTHER COUNTRIES

The bureaucracy plays a significant role in several European and Japanese governments. Unlike in the United States, in a number of other countries, employment in the national bureaucracy is considered an elite career that competes for prestige with the best private sector positions. In Britain, France, and Japan, top civil servants are recruited from elite institutions of higher education and are recognized as having professional qualifications specifically to manage government and the economy.

The higher levels of the civil service in these parliamentary systems are intimately involved in all aspects of policy making. Cabinet ministers drawn from the ranks of the legislature typically do not have expertise in the specific policy areas that their ministries oversee, so they rely on high-level civil service bureaucrats to draft the bills that will be introduced in their names. Top bureaucrats, of course, oversee the implementation of that legislation. In Germany and France, bureaucrats frequently run for election in the parliament without giving up their civil service status; retired Japanese bureaucrats have often done the same. In these countries, the elite civil service therefore is represented not only in the bureaucracy but in the legislature and executive as well.

The table above shows the proportion of women in cabinet-level positions. We should be careful interpreting the numbers because they reflect government situations at a particular time. In Japan, for example, no women held a cabinet position at the time of the United Nations survey from which the data are drawn on, but women have held such portfolios before and since. They have

Women in Cabinet-Level Positions, 1998	
Country	Percentage
Canada	14[a]
China	6[a]
Egypt	6
France	12
Germany	8
India	3[a]
Indonesia	3
Italy	13
Japan	0
Mexico	5
Russia	8
United Kingdom	24
United States	**26**

[a]1994 figure. Not all countries provided data for the 1998 survey.

Source: World Development Indicators, 1998 (Washington, DC: World Bank).

never numbered more than three in any cabinet, however. It is fairly clear that women do not hold high office proportionate to their numbers in the total population, the workforce (see Global Politics table, chapter 1), or the national legislature. As the World Bank points out, it is difficult for women to influence public policy without representation in the executive parts of government. Of countries for which there was 1998 data available, twenty-seven had no women in such positions. The highest concentration of such countries was in Southwest Asia, but African, Asian, and East European countries also were represented.

Comparing Bureaucracies

the courts. Congressional review, a procedure adopted by the 104th Congress, by which agency regulations can be nullified by joint resolutions of legislative disapproval, is another method of exercising congressional oversight. This form of oversight is discussed in greater detail in chapter 7.

Judicial Control

While the president's and Congress's control over the actions of the bureaucracy is very direct, the judiciary's oversight function is less so. The federal judiciary, for example, can directly issue injunctions or orders to an executive agency even before a rule is promulgated formally. The courts also have ruled that agencies must give all affected individuals their due process rights guaranteed by the U.S. Constitution. A Social Security recipient's checks cannot be stopped, for example, unless that individual is provided with reasonable notice and an opportunity for a hearing. On a more informal, indirect level, litigation, or even the threat of litigation, often exerts a strong influence on bureaucrats. Injured parties can bring suit against agencies for their failure to enforce the law, and can challenge agency interpretations of the law. In general, however, the courts give great weight to the opinions of bureaucrats and usually defer to their expertise.[38]

Research by political scientists also shows that government agencies are strategic. They often implement Supreme Court decisions "based on the costs and benefits of alternative policy choices." Specifically, the degree to which agencies appear to respond to Supreme Court decisions is based on the "specificity of Supreme Court opinions, agency policy preferences, agency age, and *amicus curiae* support."[39]

The development of specialized courts has altered the relationship of some agencies with the federal courts, apparently resulting in less judicial deference to agency rulings. Research by political scientists reveals that specialized courts such as the Court of International Trade, because of its expertise, defers less to agency decisions than do more generalized federal courts. Conversely, decisions from executive agencies are more likely to be reversed than those from more specialized independent regulatory commissions.[40]

Continuity & Change

Technology and the Bureaucracy

We rely on government bureaucrats to make sure that our cars are registered, to get our drivers' licenses, voter registration, and passports, and even to keep track of our contributions to the Social Security system. That is a far cry from what government did in the late 1700s or what citizens expected of it. When the United States first was founded, there were but three departments in the executive branch, and an attorney general who provided the president with legal advice. The Department of State, headed by Democrat-Republican Thomas Jefferson, a consistent opponent of big government, had but nine employees. The Department of the Treasury, headed by Federalist Alexander Hamilton, had a much larger staff.

The bureaucracy continued to increase in size, albeit slowly. From 1816 to 1861, the size of the bureaucracy grew as demands on the national government increased. The Civil War and its aftermath greatly accelerated the growth of government.

Technology was barely existent. Ledgers and federal records were compiled and maintained with pen and ink. The development of the typewriter, carbon paper, and copying machines while making the maintenance of records easier, contributed tremendously to the red tape and paper woes of the bureaucracy. Computers totally revolutionized the way the federal government did business. Detailed records now are maintained about individuals by several different agencies, and some fear that the government knows way too much about them. But, even computers become obsolete.

Today, the local, state, and national governments are adopting and embracing technology at breathtaking speed. States, in particular, are using the Internet to provide information and services to their citizens, cutting costs, increasing efficiency, and making government more responsive to the people, just as the Framers intended. "Well-run, efficiently organized Web sites [improve] the attitude of citizens toward government," concluded one major study of federal and state Web sites that ranked them according to twenty-seven factors, including the ability to register a vehicle online and access searchable records. In September 2000, the federal government went online with a new home page to allow Americans to access all of its services from a single location. Firstgov.gov provides connections to over 27 million federal agency Web pages on 20,000 sites.[41] Unlike the federal government, this site is accessible twenty-four hours a day. Better yet, for those who aren't familiar with federal bureaucratic structures, the site contains a search engine to allow the public to connect with the correct agency. This site contains connections to all branches of government and federal agencies, as well as to state and local governments.

The IRS's effort to ease online tax filing in 2002 is another example of the use of technology. The IRS also redesigned its Web site, www.irs.gov, and President Bush's budget calls for making online filings free. The public is responding positively to these changes. In 2002, 67 percent of the American public reported that they had confidence in the IRS.[42]

How technology can be used to make government more efficient and effective—especially as the number of federal employees decreases—may have important implications for how the federal government of the future operates.

1. What uses do you see for technology?
2. How could governmental services and accountability be improved through the use of new technologies?

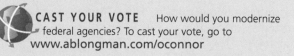

CAST YOUR VOTE   How would you modernize federal agencies? To cast your vote, go to www.ablongman.com/oconnor

SUMMARY

The bureaucracy plays a major role in America as a shaper of public policy, earning it the nickname the "fourth branch" of government. To explain the evolution and scope of bureaucratic power, in this chapter we have made the following points:

1. **The Roots and Development of the Executive Branch and the Federal Bureaucracy**
   According to Max Weber, all bureaucracies have similar characteristics. These characteristics can be seen in the federal bureaucracy as it developed from George Washington's time, when the executive branch had only three departments—State, War, and Treasury—through the Civil War. Significant gains occurred in the size of the federal bureaucracy as the government geared up to conduct a war. As employment opportunities within the federal government increased, concurrent reforms in the civil service system assured that more and more jobs were filled according to merit and not by patronage. By the late 1800s, reform efforts led to further increases in the size of the bureaucracy, as independent regulatory commissions were created. In the wake of the Depression, many new agencies were created to get the national economy back on course as part of President Franklin D. Roosevelt's New Deal.

2. **The Modern Bureaucracy**
   The modern bureaucracy is composed of nearly two million civilian workers from all walks of life. In general, bureaucratic agencies fall into four general types: departments, government corporations, independent agencies, and independent regulatory commissions.

3. **Policy Making**
   Bureaucrats not only make but implement public policy. Iron triangles or issue networks often can be used to describe how this policy making occurs. Much policy making occurs at the lowest levels of the bureaucracy, where administrative discretion can be exercised on an informal basis. More formal policy is often made through rule making and administrative adjudication.

4. **Making Agencies Accountable**
   Agencies enjoy considerable discretion, but they are also subjected to many formal controls. The president, Congress, and the judiciary all exercise various degrees of control over the bureaucracy.

KEY TERMS

administrative adjudication, p. 337
administrative discretion, p. 336
bureaucracy, p. 316
civil service system, p. 320
clientele agencies, p. 328
departments, p. 328
executive orders, p. 340
Federal Employees Political Activities Act, p. 331
government corporation, p. 328
Hatch Act, p. 331
implementation, p. 333
independent executive agency, p. 330
independent regulatory commission, p. 320
interagency councils, p. 333
iron triangles, p. 333
issue networks, p. 333
merit system, p. 320
patronage, p. 318
Pendleton Act, p. 320
regulations, p. 336
rule making, p. 336
spoils system, p. 318

SELECTED READINGS

Aberbach, Joel D., and Bert A. Rockman. *In the Web of Politics: Three Decades of the U.S. Federal Executive.* Washington, DC: Brookings Institution, 2000.

Bennett, Linda L. M., and Stephen E. Bennett. *Living with Leviathan: Americans Coming to Terms with Big Government.* Lawrence: University Press of Kansas, 1990.

Borrelli, Mary Anne. *The President's Cabinet: Gender, Power, and Representation.* New York: Lynn Reiner Publishers, 2002.

Brehm, John, and Scott Gates. *Working, Shirking, and Sabotage: Bureaucratic Response to a Democratic Public.* Ann Arbor: University of Michigan Press, 1997.

Derthick, Martha, and Paul J. Quirk. *The Politics of Deregulation.* Washington, DC: Brookings Institution, 1985.

Goodsell, Charles T. *The Case for Bureaucracy: A Public Administration Polemic.* Chatham, NJ: Chatham House, 1994.

Gormley, William T., Jr. *Taming the Bureaucracy: Muscles, Prayers and Other Strategies.* Princeton, NJ: Princeton University Press, 1989.

Handler, Joel F. *Down the Bureaucracy: The Ambiguity of Privatization and Empowerment.* Princeton, NJ: Princeton University Press, 1996.

Ingraham, Patricia Wallace. *The Foundation of Merit: Public Service in American Democracy.* Baltimore, MD: Johns Hopkins University Press, 1995.

Kerwin, Cornelius M. *Rulemaking: How Government Agencies Write Law and Make Policy,* 2nd ed. Washington, DC: CQ Press, 1999.

Mackenzie, G. Calvin. *The Irony of Reform: Roots of Political Disenchantment.* Boulder, CO: Westview Press, 1996.

Osborne, David, and Peter Plastrik. *Banishing Bureaucracy: The Five Strategies for Reinventing Government.* Boston: Addison-Wesley, 1997.

Peters, B. Guy. *The Politics of Bureaucracy,* 4th ed. New York: Longman, 1995.

Richardson, William D. *Democracy, Bureaucracy and Character.* Lawrence: University Press of Kansas, 1997.

Rourke, Francis E. *Bureaucracy, Politics and Public Policy.* Boston: Little, Brown, 1988.

Stivers, Camilla. *Gender Images in Public Administration: Legitimacy and the Administrative State*. Thousand Oaks, CA: Sage, 2002.

Twight, Charlotte. *Dependent on DC: The Rise of Federal Control over the Lives of Ordinary Americans*. New York: Palgrave Macmillan, 2002.

Wilson, James Q. *Bureaucracy: What Government Agencies Do and Why They Do It*. (reprint ed.) New York: Basic Books, 2000.

NOTES

1. Jack Kelly, "Poll: Most Support Elian Raid," *USA Today* (April 25, 2000): A1.
2. Stephen Barr, "Users Mostly Rate Agencies Favorably," *Washington Post* (April 13, 2000): A29.
3. Harold D. Lasswell, *Politics: Who Gets What, When and How* (New York: McGraw-Hill, 1938).
4. H. H. Gerth and C. Wright Mills, *From Max Weber* (New York: Oxford University Press, 1958).
5. The Postal Service, like the rest of the federal government, continues to downsize. "20,000 Job Cuts at Postal Service," *Newsday* (January 9, 2002): A38.
6. Quoted in Robert C. Caldwell, *James A. Garfield* (Hamden, CT: Archon Books, 1965).
7. *NLRB v. Jones & Laughlin Steel Corp.*, 301 U.S. 1 (1937).
8. *U.S. v. Darby Lumber Co.* 312 U.S. 100 (1941); and *Wickward v. Filburn*, 317 U.S. 111 (1942).
9. David Osborne and Ted Gaebler, *Reinventing Government* (Reading, MA: Addison-Wesley, 1992), 20–21.
10. Stephen Barr, "Some Trainees Voice Frustration with Presidential Management Intern Program," *Washington Post* (November 26, 2001): B2.
11. A Report of the U.S. Merit Systems Protection Board, Executive Summary. http://www.mspb.gov/studies/rpt%2008-01%20pmi-program/pmi_program.pd8.
12. Stephen Barr, "Morella Civil Service Bill Would Boost Government's Share of Health Costs," *Washington Post* (April 23, 2002): B21.
13. Kenneth J. Cooper, "U.S. May Repay Loans for College," *Washington Post* (December 13, 2001): A45.
14. Office of Personnel Management, *2001 Fact Book*. See also Julie Dolan, "The Senior Executive Service: Gender, Attitudes and Representative Bureaucracy," *Journal of Public Administration Research and Theory* 10(3): 513–29.
15. "A Century of Government Growth," *Washington Post* (January 3, 2000): A17. On the difficulty of counting the exact number of government agencies, see David Nachmias and David H. Rosenbloom, *Bureaucratic Government: U.S.A.* (New York: St. Martin's Press, 1980).
16. Ruth Rosen, "Bush's Political Payoff," *San Francisco Chronicle* (January 14, 2002): B7.
17. For the EPA to become a department and its head a formal member of the president's Cabinet, Congress would have to act.
18. The classic work on regulatory commissions is Marver Bernstein, *Regulating Business by Independent Commission* (Princeton, NJ: Princeton University Press, 1955).
19. *Humphrey's Executor v. U.S.*, 295 U.S. 602 (1935).
20. "Federal News: Hatch Act," *Inc.: Government Employee Relations Report* (October 11, 1993): 1317.
21. Avram Goldstein, "Teacher to Lose Job Under Hatch Act," *Washington Post* (April 15, 2002): A8.
22. Deborah A. Stone, *Policy Paradox: The Art of Political Decision Making* (New York: Norton, 1997).
23. For more on iron triangles, see Randall Ripley and Grace Franklin, *Congress, Bureaucracy and Public Policy*, 4th ed. (Homewood, IL: Dorsey Press, 1984). See also George A. Krause, "The Institutional Dynamics of Policy Administration: Bureaucratic Influence over Securities Regulation," *American Journal of Political Science* 40 (November 1996): 1083–1121.
24. "Issue Networks and the Executive Establishment," in Anthony King, ed., *The New American Political System* (Washington, DC: American Enterprise Institute, 1978), 87–124.
25. Martin Shapiro, "The Presidency and the Federal Courts," in Arnold Meltsner, ed., *Politics and the Oval Office* (San Francisco: Institute for Contemporary Studies, 1981), ch. 8.
26. Ellen Nakashima, "HUD Secretary Focuses on Chronic Homelessness," *Washington Post* (July 21, 2001): A15.
27. Health and Human Services, Office for Civil Rights, "Bush Cabinet to Review Barriers to Disabled," http://www.hhs.gov/ocr/bushada.html.
28. Michael Lipsky, *Street-Level Bureaucracy: Dilemmas of the Individual in Public Services* (New York: Russell Sage Foundation, 1980).
29. Cornelius M. Kerwin, *Rulemaking: How Government Agencies Write Law and Make Policy*, 2nd ed. (Washington, DC: CQ Press, 1999), xv.
30. Jack C. Plano and Milton Greenberg, *The American Political Dictionary*, 6th ed. (New York: Holt, Rinehart and Winston, 1982), 236.
31. Stephen Barr, "For IRS, a Deadline to Draft a Smile," *Washington Post* (January 31, 1999): H1.
32. Quoted in Arthur Schlesinger Jr., *A Thousand Days* (Greenwich, CT: Fawcett Books, 1967), 377.
33. Thomas V. DiBacco, "Veep Gore Reinventing Government—Again!" *USA Today* (September 9, 1993): 13A.
34. John Erlichman, "Government Reform: Will Al Gore's Package of Changes Succeed Where Others Failed? Washington's 'Iron Triangles,'" *Atlanta Journal and Constitution* (September 16, 1993): A15.
35. George A. Krause, "Presidential Use of Executive Orders, 1953–1994," *American Politics Quarterly* 25 (October 1997): 458–81.
36. Irene Murphy, *Public Policy on the Status of Women* (Lexington, MA: Lexington Books, 1974).
37. Matthew McCubbins and Thomas Schwartz, "Congressional Oversight Overlooked: Police Patrols Versus Fire Alarms," *American Journal of Political Science* 28 (1987): 165–79.
38. Rosemary O'Leary, *Environmental Change: Federal Courts and the EPA* (Philadelphia: Temple University Press, 1993).
39. James F. Spriggs III, "The Supreme Court and Federal Administrative Agencies: A Resource-Based Theory and Analysis of Judicial Impact," *American Journal of Political Science* 40 (November 1996): 1122.
40. Wendy Hansen, Renee Johnson, and Isaac Unah, "Specialized Courts, Bureaucratic Agencies, and the Politics of U.S. Trade Policy," *American Journal of Political Science* 39 (August 1995): 529–57.
41. Bob Dart, "Feds Open 'All-in-One' Web Site for Public," *Atlanta Journal and Constitution* (September 23, 2000): A1.
42. *Public Opinion Online*, FOX News, Opinion Dynamics Poll, April 4, 2002.

The Judiciary

On December 1, 2000, hundreds of protesters gathered outside the U.S. Supreme Court in spite of the bone-chilling temperatures. People had started lining up two days before to be one of the 250 lucky individuals who would be given tickets to hear the first of the two cases that ultimately would decide the outcome of the 2000 presidential election.[1] All of the surrounding roads were closed by Court police to ensure public safety. Hundreds of media crews staked out positions outside the building.

As the new century dawned, Americans were accustomed to seeing Congress deliberate a full range of issues from the most mundane to presidential impeachment on C-SPAN or one or more of the other networks. Political junkies could get their fill of the 2000 presidential election contest as the trial, circuit, and Florida Supreme Court proceedings were televised in their entirety. But, the U.S. Supreme Court hearings were not televised. In the first challenge, after Bush campaign lawyer Theodore Olson (now George W. Bush's solicitor general) finished his presentation, Roger Cossack of CNN rushed out of the Court to report breathlessly on what had happened. Greta Van Susteren remained in the courtroom to cover the opposing arguments offered by Harvard University law professor Laurence Tribe on behalf of the Gore campaign.

Olson's arguments were dramatic as he attempted to fend off attacks from various justices who questioned whether Governor Bush even had a federal case. The mood and nature of the questioning then shifted during Tribe's turn at the lectern. But, very few people in America were able to see either presentation, even though the gallery looked like a who's who in American politics. Among the onlookers were retired Justice Byron White, several senators, and even Caroline Kennedy Schlossberg. The drama was similarly high when the second case involving the presidential contest was argued less than two weeks later.

Members of the news media, as well as the American Political Science Association, have urged the U.S. Supreme Court to open its arguments to the public for years, to no avail. With the outcome of the presidential contest at stake, the call was raised anew, with C-SPAN and CNN leading the charge for a one-time deal. Still, it was a no go at the Court, where many of the justices have taken an "over my dead body" stand on the issue of cameras in the Court while condoning their use in other courts. The Court's lone concession to the magnitude of the cases before it? Recordings of both sets of oral arguments were released in their entirety one hour after conclusion of the attorneys' presentations, instead of being made available two weeks later on the Court's Web site.

Even before the high-stakes presidential case was accepted by the Court, several members of the Senate were upset with the Court's refusal to make its "public" appearances more public. In fact, Senators Arlen Specter (R–PA) and Joe Biden (D–DE) of the Judiciary Committee sponsored a bill to require television cameras in the Supreme Court, which went nowhere. Although many commentators argued that the legitimacy of the Court was on the line because of the high stakes in *Bush* v. *Gore* (2000),[2] the justices remained undeterred in their commitment to keep their proceedings as private as possible.

*I*n 1787, when Alexander Hamilton wrote to urge support of the U.S. Constitution, he firmly believed that the judiciary was the weakest of the three departments of government. In its formative years, the judiciary was, in Hamilton's words, "the least dangerous" branch. The judicial branch seemed so inconsequential that when the young national government made its move to the District of Columbia in 1800, Congress actually forgot to include any space to house the justices of the Supreme Court! Last-minute conferences with the Capitol architects led to the allocation of a small area in the basement of the Senate wing of the Capitol Building for a courtroom. No other space was allowed for the justices, however. Noted one commentator, "A stranger might traverse the dark avenues of the Capitol for a week, without finding the remote corner in which Justice is administered to the American Republic..."[3]

Today, the role of the courts, particularly the U.S. Supreme Court, is significantly different from that envisioned in 1788, the year the national government came into being. The "least dangerous branch" is now perceived by many as having too much power, and critics charge that the Framers would not recognize the current federal government, especially the judiciary.

During different periods of the judiciary's history, the role and power of the federal courts have varied tremendously. They have often played a key role in creating a strong national government and boldly have led the nation in social reform. Yet, at other times, the federal courts, especially the U.S. Supreme Court, stubbornly have stood as major obstacles to social and economic change.

In addition to being unaware of the expanded role of the federal judiciary, only recently have many Americans become aware of the political nature of the courts. They were raised to think of the federal courts, especially the Supreme Court, as above the fray of politics. That, however, is simply not the case. Elected presidents nominate judges to the federal courts and justices to the Supreme Court, often to advance their personal politics, and elected senators ultimately confirm (or decline to confirm) presidential nominees to the federal bench. Not only is the selection process political, but the process by which cases ultimately get heard—if they are heard at all—by the Supreme Court often is political as well. Interest groups routinely seek out good test cases to advance their policy positions. Even the U.S. government, generally through the Department of Justice and the U.S. solicitor general (another political

Protesters gathered outside the U.S. Supreme Court during arguments in *Bush* v. *Gore* (2000).

(Photo courtesy: Sylvia Johnson/Woodfin Camp & Associates)

appointee), seeks to advance its version of the public interest in court. Interest groups then often line up on opposing sides to advance their positions, much in the same way lobbyists do in Congress.

In this chapter, we explore these issues and the scope and development of judicial power:

- First, we will look at *the Constitution and the creation of the national judiciary*. Article III of the Constitution created a Supreme Court but left it to Congress to create any other federal courts, a task it took up quickly.

- Second, we will examine *the Judiciary Act of 1789* and explore the structure and the *creation of the federal judicial system*. The American legal system contains parallel court systems for the fifty states and the national government. Each court system has courts of original and appellate jurisdiction.

- Third, we will discuss *the American legal system* and the concepts of civil and criminal law.

- Fourth, we will discuss *the federal court system*. The federal court system is composed of specialized courts, district courts, courts of appeals, and the Supreme Court, which is the ultimate authority on all federal law.

- Fifth, we will see *how federal court judges are selected*. All appointments to the federal district courts, courts of appeals, and the Supreme Court are made by the president and are subject to Senate confirmation.

- Sixth, we will take a look at *the Supreme Court today*. Only a few of the millions of cases filed in courts around the United States every year eventually make their way to the Supreme Court through the lengthy appellate process, as cases are filtered out at a variety of stages.

- Seventh, we will learn *how justices vote and make decisions* and discuss how judicial decision making is based on a variety of legal and extra-legal factors.

- Eighth, we will discuss *judicial policy making and implementation*.

- In our examination of the *continuity and change* theme in American politics, we will explore how the granting of suffrage to black men and then women has had consequences in the judicial system far greater than simply voting rights.

A note on terminology: When we refer to the "Supreme Court," the "Court," or the "high Court" here, we always mean the U.S. Supreme Court, which sits at the pinnacle of the federal and state court systems. The Supreme Court is referred to by the name of the chief justice who presided over it during a particular period (for example, the Marshall Court is the Court presided over by John Marshall from 1801 to 1835). When we use the term "courts," we refer to all federal or state courts unless otherwise noted.

THE CONSTITUTION AND THE CREATION OF THE NATIONAL JUDICIARY

The detailed notes James Madison took at the Philadelphia Convention make it clear that the Framers devoted little time to the writing of, or the content, of Article III, which created the judicial branch of government. The Framers believed that a federal judiciary posed little of the threat of tyranny that they feared from the other two branches. One scholar has even suggested that, for at least some delegates to the Constitutional Convention,

> provision for a national judiciary was a matter of theoretical necessity…more in deference to the maxim of separation [of powers] than in response to clearly formulated ideas about the role of a national judicial system and its indispensability.[4]

Alexander Hamilton argued in *Federalist No. 78* that the judiciary would be the "least dangerous branch of government." Anti-Federalists, however, did not agree with Hamilton. They particularly objected to a judiciary whose members had life tenure and the ability to interpret what was to be "the supreme law of the land," a phrase that Anti-Federalists feared would give the Supreme Court too much power.

The Framers also debated the need for any federal courts below the level of the Supreme Court. Some argued in favor of deciding all cases in state courts, with only appeals going before the Supreme Court. Others argued for a system of federal courts. A compromise left the final choice to Congress, and Article III, section 1, begins simply by vesting "The judicial Power of the United States...in one supreme Court, and in such inferior Courts as the Congress may from time to time ordain and establish." Although there is some debate over whether the Court should have the power of **judicial review,** which allows the judiciary to review acts of the other branches of government and the states, the question was left unsettled in Article III—and not finally resolved until *Marbury* v. *Madison* (1803), regarding acts of the national government, and *Martin* v. *Hunter's Lessee* (1816), regarding state law.[5] This vagueness was not all that unusual, given the numerous compromises that took place in Philadelphia.

Article III, section 1, also gave Congress the authority to establish other courts as it saw fit. Section 2 specifies the "judicial power" of the Supreme Court (see Table 10.1) and discusses the Court's original and appellate jurisdiction. This section also specifies that all federal crimes, except those involving impeachment, shall be tried by jury in the state in which the crime was committed. The third section of the article defines treason, and mandates that at least two witnesses appear in such cases.

Although it is the duty of the chief justice of the United States to preside over presidential impeachments, this is not mentioned in Article III. Instead, Article I, section 3, notes in discussing impeachment, "When the President of the United States is tried, the Chief Justice shall preside."

Had the Supreme Court been viewed as the potential policy maker it is today, it is highly unlikely that the Framers would have provided for life tenure with "good behavior" for federal judges in Article III. This feature was agreed on because the Framers did not want the justices (or any federal judges) subject to the whims of politics, the public, or politicians. Moreover, Alexander Hamilton argued in *Federalist No. 78* that the "independence of judges" was needed "to guard the Constitution and the rights of individuals." Because the Framers viewed the Court as quite powerless, Hamilton stressed the need to place federal judges above the fray of politics. Yet, although there is no denying that judges are political animals and carry the same prejudices and preferences to the bench that others do to the statehouse, Congress, or the White House, the provision of life tenure for "good behavior" generally has functioned well.

Some checks on the power of the judiciary were nonetheless included in the Constitution. The Constitution gives Congress the authority to alter the Court's jurisdiction (its ability to hear certain kinds of cases). Congress can also propose constitutional

judicial review
Power of the courts to review acts of other branches of government and the states.

TABLE 10.1   The Judicial Power of the United States Supreme Court

The following are the types of cases the Supreme Court was given the jurisdiction to hear as initially specified in the Constitution:

- All cases arising under the Constitution and laws or treaties of the United States
- All cases of admiralty or maritime jurisdiction
- Cases in which the United States is a party
- Controversies between a state and citizens of another state
- Controversies between two or more states
- Controversies between citizens of different states
- Controversies between citizens of the same states claiming lands under grants in different states
- Controversies between a state, or the citizens thereof, and foreign states or citizens thereof
- All cases affecting ambassadors or other public ministers

KAL
THE ECONOMIST
London
ENGLAND

In this cartoon, the Chief Justice of the United States, William H. Rehnquist, is shown presiding over the impeachment of President Bill Clinton, which the cartoonist depicts as "grillling."

(Photo courtesy: KAL/Cartoonists & Writers Syndicate)

amendments that, if ratified, can effectively reverse judicial decisions, and it can impeach and remove federal judges. In one further check, it is the president who (with the "advice and consent" of the Senate) appoints all federal judges.

THE JUDICIARY ACT OF 1789 AND THE CREATION OF THE FEDERAL JUDICIAL SYSTEM

In spite of the Framers' intentions, the pervasive role of politics in the judicial branch quickly became evident with the passage of the Judiciary Act of 1789. Congress spent nearly the entire second half of its first session deliberating the various provisions of the act to give form and substance to the federal judiciary. As one early observer noted, "The convention has only crayoned in the outlines. It left it to Congress to fill up and colour the canvas."[6]

The **Judiciary Act of 1789** established the basic three-tiered structure of the federal court system. At the bottom are the federal district courts—at least one in each state— each staffed by a federal judge. If the people participating in a lawsuit (called litigants) were unhappy with the district court's verdict, they could appeal their case to one of three circuit courts. Each circuit court, initially created to function as a trial court for important cases, was composed of one district court judge and two itinerant Supreme Court justices who met as a circuit court twice a year. Thus, Supreme Court Justice Samuel Chase, in his capacity as a circuit court judge, presided over a Sedition Act trial resulting in the conviction of a Jeffersonian newspaper editor who was critical of the Federalist-led government. It wasn't until 1891 that circuit courts (also often called courts of appeals, as we know them today) took on their exclusively appellate function.

The third tier of the federal judicial system fleshed out by the Judiciary Act of 1789 was the Supreme Court of the United States. Although the Constitution mentions "the supreme Court," it was silent on its size. In the Judiciary Act, Congress set the size of the Supreme Court at six—the chief justice plus five associate justices.

When the justices met in their first public session in New York City in 1790, they were garbed magnificently in black and scarlet robes in the English fashion, but they had discarded what Thomas Jefferson termed "the monstrous wig which makes English judges look like rats peeping through bunches of oakum!"[7] The elegance of their attire,

Judiciary Act of 1789
Established the basic three-tiered structure of the federal court system.

The Supreme Court held its first two sessions in this building, called the Exchange, located in New York City.

(Photo courtesy: Bettmann/Corbis)

however, could not make up for the relative ineffectiveness of the Court. Its first session presided over by John Jay, who was appointed chief justice of the United States by George Washington, initially had to be adjourned when a quorum of the justices failed to show up. Later, once a quorum assembled, the justices decided only one major case—*Chisholm* v. *Georgia* (1793) (discussed below). Moreover, as an indication of its lowly status, one associate justice left the Court to become chief justice of the South Carolina Supreme Court. (Although such a move would be considered a step down today, keep in mind that in the early years of the United States, many viewed the states as more important than the new national government.)

Hampered by frequent changes in personnel, limited space for its operations, no clerical support, and no system of reporting its decisions, the Court and its meager activities did not impress many people. From the beginning, the circuit court duties of the Supreme Court justices presented problems for the prestige of the Court. Few good lawyers were willing to accept nominations to the high Court because its circuit court duties entailed a substantial amount of travel—most of it on horseback over poorly maintained roads in frequently inclement weather. Southern justices often rode as many as 10,000 miles a year on horseback. George Washington tried to prevail on several friends and supporters to fill vacancies on the Court as they appeared, but most refused the "honor." John Adams, the second president of the United States, ran into similar problems. When he asked John Jay to resume the position of chief justice after he resigned to become governor of New York, Jay declined the offer. Jay once had remarked of the Court that it lacked "energy, weight, and dignity" as well as "public confidence and respect." Given Jay's view of the Court and its performance statistics, his refusal to serve was not surprising.

In spite of all its problems, in its first decade, the Court took several actions to help mold the new nation. First, by declining to give George Washington advice on the legality of some of his actions, the justices attempted to establish the Supreme Court as an independent, nonpolitical branch of government. Although John Jay, as an individual, frequently gave the president advice in private, the Court refused to answer questions Washington posed to it concerning the construction of international laws and treaties. The justices wanted to avoid the appearance of prejudging an issue that could arise later before them.

The early Court also tried to advance principles of nationalism and to maintain the national government's supremacy over the states. As circuit court jurists, the justices rendered numerous decisions on such matters as national suppression of the Whiskey Rebellion and the constitutionality of the Alien and Sedition Acts, which made it a crime to criticize national governmental officials or their actions (see chapter 5).

During the ratification debates, Anti-Federalists had warned that Article III extended federal judicial power to controversies "between a State and Citizens of another State"—meaning that a citizen of one state could sue any other state in federal court, a prospect unthinkable to defenders of state sovereignty. Although Federalists, including Hamilton and Madison, had scoffed at the idea, the nationalist Supreme Court quickly proved them wrong in *Chisholm* v. *Georgia* (1793).[8] In *Chisholm* the justices interpreted the Court's jurisdiction under Article III, section 2, to include the right to hear suits brought by a citizen of one state against another state. For example, writing in *Chisholm*, Justice James Wilson denounced the "haughty notions of state independence, state sovereignty, and state supremacy." The states' reaction to this perceived attack on their authority led to passage and ratification (in 1798) of the Eleventh Amendment to the Constitution, which specifically limited judicial power by stipulating that the authority of the federal courts could not "extend to any suit ... commenced or prosecuted against one of the United States by citizens of another State."

Finally, in a series of circuit and Supreme Court decisions, the justices paved the way for announcement of the doctrine of judicial review by the third chief justice, John Marshall. (Oliver Ellsworth served from 1796 to 1800.) Justices "riding circuit" occasionally held state laws unconstitutional because they violated the U.S. Constitution. In 1796, the Court for the first time evaluated the constitutionality of an act of Congress, finding the law, however, to be constitutional.[9]

The Marshall Court (1801–1835)

John Marshall brought much-needed respect and prestige to the Court through his leadership in a progression of cases and a series of innovations. Marshall was appointed chief justice by President John Adams in 1801, three years after he declined to accept a nomination as associate justice (see Roots of Government: John Marshall). An ardent Federalist who also earlier had declined Washington's offer to become attorney general, Marshall later came to be considered the most important justice ever to serve on the high Court. Part of his reputation is the result of the duration of his service and the historical significance of this period in our nation's history.

As chief justice, Marshall instituted several innovations and led the Court to issue several important rulings to establish the Court as a co-equal branch of government:

- Discontinued the practice of *seriatim* (Latin for "in a series") opinions, which was the custom of the King's Bench in Great Britain. Prior to the Marshall Court, the justices delivered their individual opinions in order. There was no single "opinion of the Court," as we are accustomed to today. For the Court to take its place as an equal branch of government, Marshall strongly believed, the justices needed to speak as a Court and not as six individuals. In fact, during Marshall's first four years in office, the Court routinely spoke as one, and the chief justice wrote twenty-four of its twenty-six opinions.

- Claimed for the Court the right of judicial review, from which the Supreme Court derives much of its day-to-day power and impact on the policy process. This established the Court as the final arbiter of constitutional questions, with the right to declare congressional acts void (*Marbury* v. *Madison* [1803]).[10]

- Established the authority of the Supreme Court over the judiciaries of the various states, including the Court's power to declare state laws invalid (*Fletcher* v. *Peck* [1810];[11] *Martin* v. *Hunter's Lessee* [1816];[12] and, *Cohens* v. *Virginia* [1821]).[13]

- Established the supremacy of the federal government and Congress over state governments through a broad interpretation of the "necessary and proper" clause (*McCulloch* v. *Maryland* [1819]).[14]

Asserting Judicial Review: *Marbury* v. *Madison*

During the Philadelphia Convention, the Framers debated and rejected the idea of judicial veto of legislation or executive acts, and they rejected the Virginia Plan's proposal to give the judiciary explicit authority over Congress. They did, however, approve Article VI, which contains the supremacy clause (see chapter 3).

In *Federalist No. 78*, Alexander Hamilton first publicly endorsed the idea of judicial review, noting, "Whenever a particular statute contravenes the Constitution, it will be the duty of the judicial tribunals to adhere to the latter and disregard the former." Nonetheless, because the power of judicial review is not mentioned in the U.S. Constitution, the

JOHN MARSHALL

A single person can make a major difference in the development of an institution. Such was the case with John Marshall, who dominated the Supreme Court during his thirty-four years as chief justice. As one commentator noted, "Marshall found the Constitution paper, and he made it power. He found a skeleton, and he clothed it with flesh and blood."

Who was this man still so revered today? John Marshall (1755–1835) was born in a log cabin in Virginia, the first of fifteen children of Welsh immigrants. Although tutored at home by two clergymen, Marshall's inspiration was his father, who introduced him to English literature and Sir William Blackstone's influential work, *Commentaries on the Laws of England*. After serving in the Continental Army and acquiring the rank of captain, Marshall taught himself the law. He attended only one formal course at the College of William & Mary before being admitted to the bar. Marshall practiced law in Virginia, where he and his wife lived and raised a family. Of their ten children, only six survived childhood.

More of a politician than a lawyer, Marshall served as a delegate to the Virginia legislature from 1782 to 1785, 1787 to 1790, and 1795 to 1796, and played an instrumental role in Virginia's ratification of the U.S. Constitution in 1787. As the leading Federalist in Virginia, Marshall was offered several positions in the Federalist administrations of George Washington and John Adams—including attorney general and associate justice of the Supreme Court—but he refused them all. Finally, in 1799, Washington persuaded him to run for the House of Representatives. Marshall was elected, but his career in the House was brief, for he became secretary of state in 1800

(Photo courtesy: Boston Athenaeum)

under John Adams. When Oliver Ellsworth resigned as chief justice of the United States in 1800, Adams nominated Marshall. Marshall was an ardent Federalist and a third cousin of Democratic-Republican President Thomas Jefferson, whose administration he faced head-on in *Marbury v. Madison*.

Marshall came to head the Court with little legal experience and no judicial experience, unlike the situation on the current Supreme Court, where all of the justices except Chief Justice William H. Rehnquist had prior judicial experience. Still, it is unlikely that any contemporary justice will have anywhere near the impact that Marshall had on the Court and the course of U.S. politics.

Marbury v. Madison (1803)
Supreme Court first asserted the power of judicial review in finding that the congressional statute extending the Court's original jurisdiction was unconstitutional.

actual authority of the Supreme Court to review the constitutionality of acts of Congress was an unsettled question. But, in **Marbury v. Madison (1803)**, Chief Justice John Marshall claimed this sweeping authority for the Court by asserting that the right of judicial review was a power that could be implied from the Constitution's supremacy clause.[15]

Marbury v. Madison arose amidst a sea of political controversy. In the final hours of the Adams administration, William Marbury was appointed a justice of the peace for the District of Columbia. But, in the confusion of winding up matters, Adams's secretary of state failed to deliver Marbury's commission. Marbury then asked James Madison, Thomas Jefferson's secretary of state, for the commission. Under direct orders from Jefferson, who was irate over the Adams administration's last-minute appointment of several federal judges (quickly confirmed by the Federalist Senate), Madison refused to turn over the commission. Marbury and three other Adams appointees who were in the same situation then filed a writ of *mandamus* (a legal motion) asking the Supreme Court to order Madison to deliver their commissions.

Political tensions ran high as the Court met to hear the case. Jefferson threatened to ignore any order of the Court. Marshall realized that he and the prestige of the Court could be devastated by any refusal of the executive branch to comply with the decision.

Responding to this challenge, in a brilliant opinion that in many sections reads more like a lecture to Jefferson than a discussion of the merits of Marbury's claim, Marshall concluded that although Marbury and the others were entitled to their commissions, the Court lacked the power to issue the writ sought by Marbury. In *Marbury* v. *Madison*, Marshall further ruled that the parts of the Judiciary Act of 1789 that extended the jurisdiction of the Court to allow it to issue writs were inconsistent with the Constitution and therefore unconstitutional.

Although the immediate effect of the decision was to deny power to the Court, its long-term effect was to establish the principle of judicial review, a power that Marshall concluded could be implied from the Constitution. Said Marshall, writing for the Court, "[I]t is emphatically the province and duty of the judicial department to say what the law is."

Through judicial review, an implied power, the Supreme Court most dramatically exerts its authority to determine what the Constitution means. Since *Marbury*, the Court has routinely exercised the power of judicial review to determine the constitutionality of acts of Congress, the executive branch, and the states.

WEB EXPLORATION
To learn more about the workings of the U.S. justice system, go to
www.ablongman.com/oconnor

THE AMERICAN LEGAL SYSTEM

The judicial system in the United States can best be described as a dual system consisting of the federal court system and the judicial systems of the fifty states. Cases may arise in either system. Both systems are basically three tiered. At the bottom of the system are **trial courts,** where litigation begins. In the middle are appellate courts in the state systems and the courts of appeals in the federal system. At the top of each pyramid sits a high court. (Some states call these supreme courts; New York calls it the Court of Appeals; Oklahoma and Texas call the highest state court for criminal cases the Court of Criminal Appeals.) The federal courts of appeals and Supreme Court as well as state courts of appeals and supreme courts are **appellate courts** that, with few exceptions, review on appeal only cases that already have been decided in lower courts. These courts generally hear matters of both civil and criminal law.

trial court
Court of original jurisdiction where a case begins.

appellate court
Court that generally reviews only findings of law made by lower courts.

Jurisdiction

Before a state or federal court can hear a case, it must have **jurisdiction,** which means the authority to hear and decide the issues in that case. The jurisdiction of the federal courts is controlled by the U.S. Constitution and by statute. Jurisdiction is conferred based on issues, money involved in a dispute, or the type of offense. Procedurally, we speak of two types of jurisdiction: original and appellate. **Original jurisdiction** refers to a court's authority to hear disputes as a trial court. O.J. Simpson's criminal and civil trials, for example, were heard in state trial courts of original jurisdiction. The case against "Unabomber" Theodore Kaczynski was begun in federal district court. More than 90 percent of all cases, whether state or federal, end at this stage. **Appellate jurisdiction** refers to a court's ability to review cases already decided by a trial court. Appellate courts ordinarily do not review the factual record; instead, they review legal procedures to make certain that the law was applied properly to the issues presented in the case. Table 10.2 shows the jurisdiction of the three major federal courts.

jurisdiction
Authority vested in a particular court to hear and decide the issues in any particular case.

original jurisdiction
The jurisdiction of courts that hear a case first, usually in a trial. Courts determine the facts of a case under their original jurisdiction.

appellate jurisdiction
The power vested in an appellate court to review and/or revise the decision of a lower court.

Criminal and Civil Law

Criminal law is the body of law that regulates individual conduct and is enforced by the government.[16] Crimes are graded as felonies, misdemeanors, or offenses, according to their severity. Some acts—for example, murder, rape, and robbery—are considered crimes in all states. Although all states outlaw murder, their penal, or criminal, codes treat the crime quite differently; the penalty for murder differs considerably from state

criminal law
Codes of behavior related to the protection of property and individual safety.

TABLE 10.2   Federal Court Jurisdiction

The Supreme Court rarely exercises its original jurisdiction. Instead, most cases are heard by the Court under its appellate jurisdiction.

	Original Jurisdiction (Usually 1–3% of Cases Heard)	Appellate Jurisdiction (Approximately 97–99% of Cases Heard)
The Supreme Court	Cases are heard by the Supreme Court first when they involve: • Two or more states • The United States and a state • Foreign ambassadors and other diplomats • A state and a citizen of another state (if the action is begun by the state)	The Supreme Court can agree to hear cases first heard or decided on in lower courts or the state courts (generally the highest state court) involving appeals from: • U.S. courts of appeals • State highest courts (only in cases involving federal questions) • Court of Military Appeals
U.S. Courts of Appeals	None	Hears appeals of cases from: • Lower federal courts • U.S. regulatory commissions • Legislative courts, including the U.S. Court of Federal Claims and the U.S. Court of Veterans Appeals
U.S. District Courts	Cases are heard in U.S. district courts when they involve: • The federal government • Civil suits under federal law • Civil suits between citizens of different states if the amount in issue is more than $75,000 • Admiralty or maritime disputes • Bankruptcy • Other matters assigned to them by Congress	None

---

WEB EXPLORATION

To view the trial progressions of criminal and civil actions, go to www.ablongman.com/oconnor

civil law
Codes of behavior related to business and contractual relationships between groups and individuals.

to state. Other crimes—such as sodomy and some forms of gambling, such as lotteries or bingo—are illegal only in some states.

Criminal law assumes that society itself is the victim of the illegal act; therefore, the government prosecutes, or brings an action, on behalf of an injured party (acting as a plaintiff) in criminal but not civil cases. The murder charges against O.J. Simpson were styled as *The State of California* v. *Orenthal James Simpson*.

Criminal cases are traditionally in the purview of the states. But, a burgeoning set of federal criminal laws is contributing significantly to delays in the federal courts.

Civil law is the body of law that regulates the conduct and relationships between private individuals or companies. Because the actions at issue in civil law do not constitute a threat to society at large, people who believe they have been injured by another party must take action on their own to seek judicial relief. Civil cases, then, involve lawsuits filed to recover something of value, whether it is the right to vote, fair treatment, or monetary compensation for an item, or service that cannot be recovered. Most cases seen on *The People's Court* or *Judge Judy* are civil cases, as was *Bush* v. *Gore*, discussed in our opening vignette.

Before a criminal or civil case gets to court, much has to happen. In fact, most legal disputes that arise in the United States never get to court. Individuals and companies involved in civil disputes routinely settle their disagreements out of court. Often these settlements are not reached until minutes before the case is to be tried. Many civil cases that go to trial are settled during the course of the trial—before the case can be handed over to the jury or submitted to a judge for a decision or determination of guilt.

Each civil or criminal case has a plaintiff, or petitioner, who brings charges against a defendant, or respondent. Sometimes the government is the plaintiff. The government may bring civil charges on behalf of the citizens of the state or the national government against a person or corporation for violating the law, but it is always the government that brings a criminal case. When cases are initiated, they are known first by the name of the petitioner. In *Marbury* v. *Madison*, William Marbury was the plaintiff, suing the defendants, the U.S. government and James Madison as its secretary of state, for not delivering his judicial commission.

During trials, judges must often interpret the intent of laws enacted by Congress and state legislatures as they bear on the issues at hand. To do so, they read reports, testimony, and debates on the relevant legislation and study the results of other similar legal cases. They also rely on the presentations made by lawyers in their briefs and at trial. If it is a jury trial, the jury ultimately is the finder of fact, while the judge is the interpreter of the law.

WEB EXPLORATION

To view the hierarchy of the U.S. court system, go to www.ablongman.com/oconnor

THE FEDERAL COURT SYSTEM

The federal district courts, circuit courts of appeals, and the Supreme Court are called **constitutional** (or Article III) **courts** because Article III of the Constitution either established them (as is the case with the Supreme Court) or authorizes Congress to establish them. Judges who preside over these courts are nominated by the president (with the advice and consent of the Senate), and they serve lifetime terms, as long as they engage in "good behavior."

In addition to constitutional courts, **legislative courts** are set up by Congress, under its implied powers, generally for special purposes. The U.S. Territorial Courts (which hear federal cases in the territories) and the U.S. Court of Veterans Appeals are examples of legislative courts, or what some call Article I courts. The judges who preside over these federal courts are appointed by the president (subject to Senate confirmation) and serve fixed, limited terms.

constitutional courts
Federal courts specifically created by the U.S. Constitution or by Congress pursuant to its authority in Article III.

legislative courts
Courts established by Congress for specialized purposes, such as the Court of Military Appeals.

District Courts

Congress recognized the need for federal trial courts of original jurisdiction soon after ratification of the Constitution. The district courts were created by the Judiciary Act of 1789. By 2005, there were ninety-four federal district courts staffed by a total of 655 active judges, assisted by more than 300 retired judges who still hear cases on a limited basis. No district court cuts across state lines. Every state has at least one federal

FIGURE 10.1   The Dual Structure of the American Court System

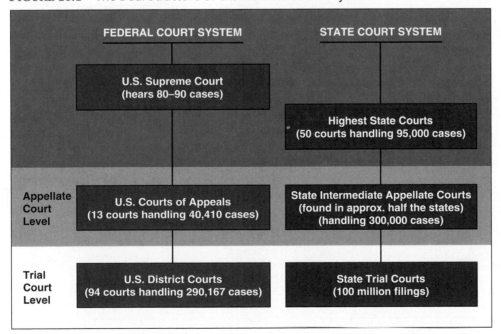

WEB EXPLORATION

To learn more about U.S. district courts, go to www.ablongman.com/oconnor

district court, and the most populous states—California, Texas, and New York—each have four (see Figure 10.2).[17]

Federal district courts, where the bulk of the judicial work takes place in the federal system, have original jurisdiction over only specific types of cases, as indicated in Table 10.2. (Cases involving other kinds of issues generally must be heard in state courts.) Although the rules governing district court jurisdiction can be complex, cases heard in federal district courts by a single judge (with or without a jury) generally fall into one of three categories:

1. They involve the federal government as a party.

2. They present a federal question based on a claim under the U.S. Constitution, a treaty with another nation, or a federal statute. This is called federal question jurisdiction and it can involve criminal or civil law.

3. They involve civil suits in which citizens are from different states, and the amount of money at issue is more than $75,000.[18]

Since 1789, the federal court system and the number of federal court judges who preside within it have grown tremendously. As illustrated in Figure 10.3, there were only thirteen federal judges and six Supreme Court justices nominated and confirmed in 1789. By 2003, that number had grown to 812. Although John Adams and the lame-duck Federalist Congress created eighteen courts of appeals judgeships in 1801, those positions were quickly abolished by the Democratic-Republican Congress. It wasn't until 1869 that judges were selected specifically for the courts of appeals. By 2005, there

FIGURE 10.2   The Federal Court System

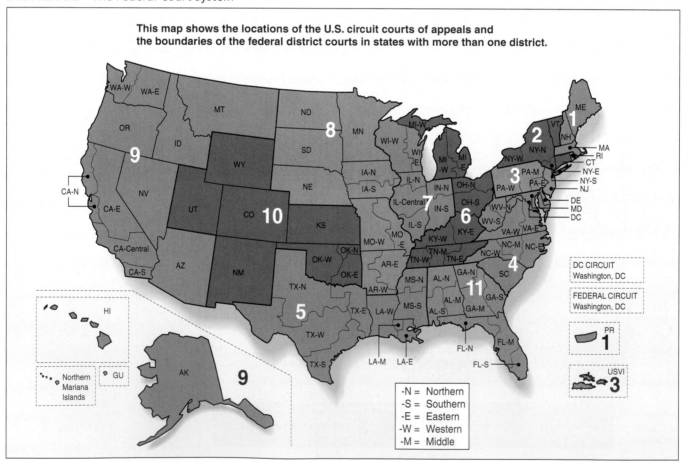

FIGURE 10.3   A Growing Federal Judiciary

Since the 1950s, the number of federal judges has been increased dramatically by Congress to help meet demands by litigants. Still, most judges argue that their case loads are too heavy.

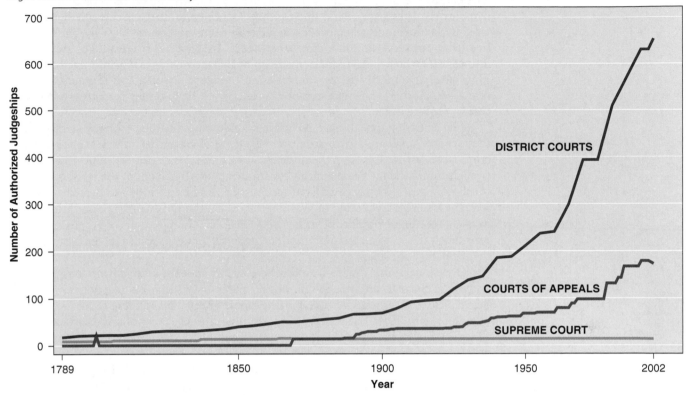

were 167 court of appeals judges and 655 district court judges, although many of those seats remained unfilled, as discussed later in this chapter.

Each federal judicial district has a U.S. attorney, who is nominated by the president and confirmed by the Senate. The U.S. attorney in each district is that district's chief law enforcement officer. The size of the staff and the number of assistant U.S. attorneys who work in each district depend on the amount of litigation in each district. U.S. attorneys, like district attorneys within the states, have a considerable amount of discretion as to whether they pursue criminal or civil investigations or file charges against individuals or corporations. These highly visible positions often serve as spring boards for elective office. Former New York City Mayor Rudy Giuliani earlier was the U.S. attorney for the Southern District of New York.

The Courts of Appeals

The losing party in a case heard and decided in a federal district court can appeal the decision to the appropriate court of appeals. The United States courts of appeals (known as the circuit courts of appeals prior to 1948) are the intermediate appellate courts in the federal system and were established in 1789 to hear appeals from federal district courts. The present structure of the appeals courts, however, dates from the Judiciary Act of 1891. There are eleven numbered circuit courts (see Figure 10.2). A twelfth, the D.C. Court of Appeals, handles most appeals involving federal regulatory commissions and agencies, including, for example, the National Labor Relations Board and the Securities and Exchange Commission. The thirteenth federal appeals court is the U.S. Court of Appeals for the Federal Circuit, which deals with patents and contract and financial claims against the federal government.

WEB EXPLORATION

To learn more about the courts of appeals, go to www.ablongman.com/oconnor

In 2005, the courts of appeals were staffed by 167 active and more than eighty senior judges, who were appointed by the president, subject to Senate confirmation. The number of judges within each circuit varies—depending on the workload and the complexity of the cases—and ranges from six to nearly thirty. Each circuit is supervised by a chief judge, the most senior judge in terms of service below the age of sixty-five, who can serve no more than seven years. In deciding cases, judges are divided into rotating three-judge panels, made up of the active judges within the circuit, visiting judges (primarily district judges from the same circuit), and retired judges. In rare cases, all the judges in a circuit may choose to sit together (*en banc*) to decide a case by majority vote.

The courts of appeals have no original jurisdiction. Rather, Congress has granted these courts appellate jurisdiction over two general categories of cases: appeals from criminal and civil cases from the district courts, and appeals from administrative agencies. Criminal and civil case appeals constitute about 90 percent of the workload of the courts of appeals, with appeals from administrative agencies about 10 percent. Because so many agencies are located in Washington, D.C., the D.C. Circuit Court of Appeals hears an inordinate number of such cases. The D.C. Circuit Court of Appeals, then, is considered the second most important court in the nation because its decisions govern the regulatory agencies.

Once a decision is made by a federal court of appeals, a litigant no longer has an automatic right to an appeal. The losing party may submit a petition to the U.S. Supreme Court to hear the case, but the Court grants few of these requests, as illustrated in Figure 10.4. The courts of appeals, then, are the courts of last resort for almost all federal litigation. Keep in mind, however, that most cases, if they actually go to trial, go no further than the district court level.

In general, courts of appeals try to correct errors of law and procedure that have occurred in lower courts or administrative agencies. Courts of appeals hear no new tes-

Visual Literacy

Case Overload

FIGURE 10.4 Supreme Court Caseload, 1950–2003 Terms

The caseload of the Supreme Court has remained fairly consistent from its 1992 through 2003–2004 terms, although the Court accepted far fewer cases for its review than it did in earlier decades. Still, the Court decides only a small percentage of the cases filed.

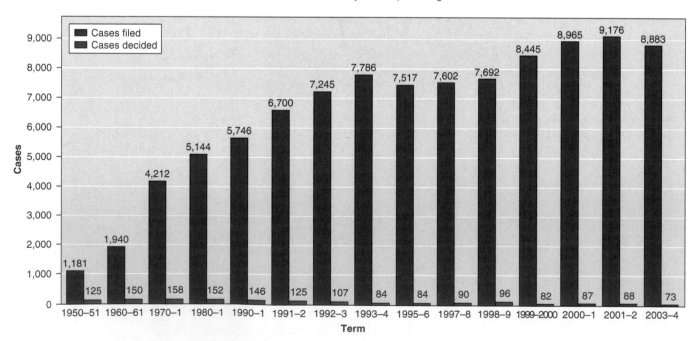

Source: Administrative Office of the Courts; Supreme Court Public Information Office.

timony; instead, lawyers submit written arguments, in what is called a **brief** (also submitted in trial courts), and then appear to present and argue the case orally to the court.

Decisions of any court of appeals are binding on only the district courts within the geographic confines of the circuit, but decisions of the U.S. Supreme Court are binding throughout the nation and establish national **precedents.** This reliance on past decisions or precedents to formulate decisions in new cases is called *stare decisis* (a Latin phrase meaning "let the decision stand"). The principle of *stare decisis* allows for continuity and predictability in our judicial system. Although *stare decisis* can be helpful in predicting decisions, at times judges carve out new ground and ignore, decline to follow, or even overrule precedents in order to reach a different conclusion in a case involving similar circumstances. In one sense, that is why there is so much litigation in America today. Parties know that one cannot always predict the outcome of a case; if such prediction were possible, there would be little reason to go to court.

The Supreme Court

The U.S. Supreme Court is often at the center of the storm of highly controversial issues that have yet to be resolved successfully in the political process. As the court of last resort at the top of the judicial pyramid, it reviews cases from the U.S. courts of appeals and state supreme courts and acts as the final interpreter of the U.S. Constitution. It not only decides many major cases with tremendous policy significance each year, but it also ensures uniformity in the interpretation of national laws and the Constitution, resolves conflicts among the states, and maintains the supremacy of national law in the federal system.

Since 1869, the U.S. Supreme Court has consisted of eight associate justices and one chief justice, who is nominated by the president specifically for that position. There is no special significance about the number nine, and the Constitution is silent about the size of the Court. Between 1789 and 1869, Congress periodically altered the size of the Court. The lowest number of justices on the Court was six; the most, ten. Through 2004, only 108 justices had served on the Court, and there had been fifteen chief justices (see Appendix V).

The chief justice presides over public sessions of the Court, conducts the Court's conferences, and assigns the writing of opinions (if he is in the majority; otherwise, the most senior justice in the majority makes the assignment). By custom, he administers the oath of office to the president and the vice president on Inauguration Day (any federal judge can administer the oath, as has happened when presidents have died in office).

Compared with the president or Congress, the Supreme Court operates with few support staff. Along with the three or four clerks each justice employs, there are about 400 staff members at the Supreme Court.

HOW FEDERAL COURT JUDGES ARE SELECTED

Although specific, detailed provisions in Articles I and II specify the qualifications for president, senator, and member of the House of Representatives, the Constitution is curiously silent on the qualifications for federal judges. This may have been because of an assumption that all federal judges would be lawyers, but to make such a requirement explicit might have marked the judicial branch as too elitist for the tastes of common men and women. Also, it would have been impractical to require formal legal training, given that there were so few law schools in the nation, and that most lawyers became licensed after clerking or apprenticing with other attorneys.[19]

The selection of federal judges is often a very political process with important political ramifications because judges are nominated by the president and must be confirmed

brief
A document containing the legal written arguments in a case filed with a court by a party prior to a hearing or trial.

precedent
Prior judicial decision that serves as a rule for settling subsequent cases of a similar nature.

stare decisis
In court rulings, a reliance on past decisions or precedents to formulate decisions in new cases.

WEB EXPLORATION
To take a virtual tour of the Court and examine current cases on its docket, go to
www.ablongman.com/oconnor

Timeline
The Chief Justice of the United States

by the U.S. Senate. During the administrations of Ronald Reagan and George Bush, for example, 553 basically conservative Republican judges were appointed to the lower federal bench, remolding it in a conservative image (see Figure 10.5). The cumulative impact of this conservative block of judges led many liberal groups to abandon their efforts to expand rights through the federal courts.

Presidents, in general, try to select well-qualified men and women for the bench. But, these appointments also provide a president with the opportunity to put his philo-

FIGURE 10.5   How a President Affects the Federal Judiciary

This figure depicts the number of judges appointed by each president and how quickly a president can make an impact on the make-up of the Court.

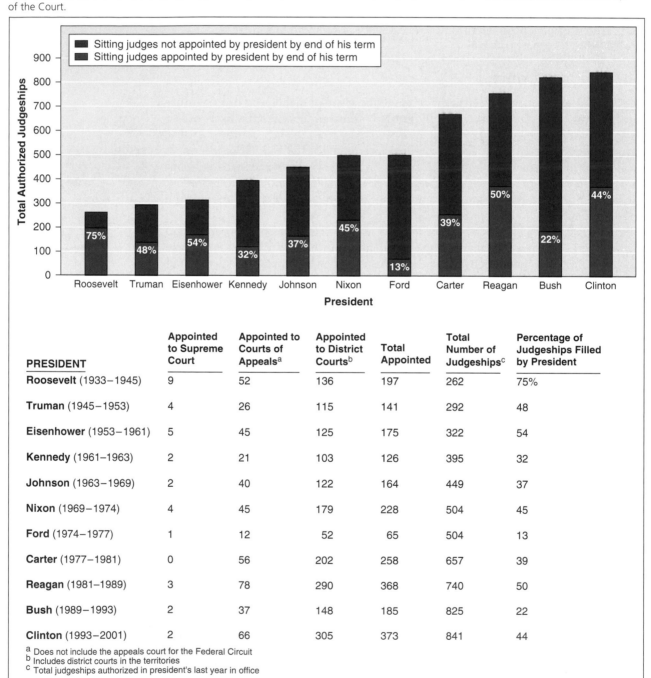

PRESIDENT	Appointed to Supreme Court	Appointed to Courts of Appeals[a]	Appointed to District Courts[b]	Total Appointed	Total Number of Judgeships[c]	Percentage of Judgeships Filled by President
Roosevelt (1933–1945)	9	52	136	197	262	75%
Truman (1945–1953)	4	26	115	141	292	48
Eisenhower (1953–1961)	5	45	125	175	322	54
Kennedy (1961–1963)	2	21	103	126	395	32
Johnson (1963–1969)	2	40	122	164	449	37
Nixon (1969–1974)	4	45	179	228	504	45
Ford (1974–1977)	1	12	52	65	504	13
Carter (1977–1981)	0	56	202	258	657	39
Reagan (1981–1989)	3	78	290	368	740	50
Bush (1989–1993)	2	37	148	185	825	22
Clinton (1993–2001)	2	66	305	373	841	44

[a] Does not include the appeals court for the Federal Circuit
[b] Includes district courts in the territories
[c] Total judgeships authorized in president's last year in office

Source: "Imprints on the Bench," *CQ Weekly Report* (January 19, 2001): 173. Reprinted by permission of Copyright Clearance Center on behalf of Congressional Quarterly, Inc.

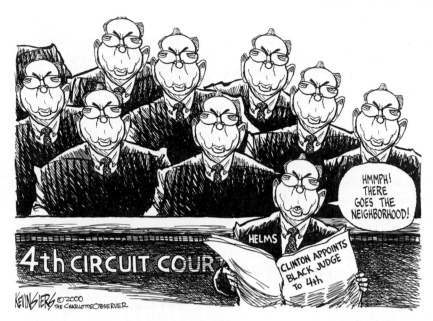

Jesse Helms (R–NC), originally blocked the nomination of Roger Gregory to the fourth Circuit Court of Appeals, headquartered in North Carolina. President Bill Clinton responded with a recess appointment of Gregory to be the first African American to sit on that court. Later, President George W. Bush surprised many when he formallly nominated Gregory, a Democrat, for the seat.

(Photo courtesy: Kevin Siers/Reprinted with special permission of North America Syndicate)

sophical stamp on the federal courts. Nominees, however, while generally members of the nominating president's party, usually are vetted through the senator's offices of the states where the district court or court of appeals vacancy occurs. In the Clinton White House, candidates for district court generally came from recommendations by Democratic senators, "or in the absence of a Democratic senator, from the Democratic members of the House of Representatives or other high ranking Democratic Party politicians."[20] At least in part because of the conservative make-up of the Republican-controlled Senate Judiciary Committee, President Clinton attempted to appoint moderates to the federal courts. But, many of his nominations were met with unprecedented delay even though studies by political scientists found that his appointees were more moderate than earlier Republican or Democratic appointees.[21] In early 1998, Chief Justice William H. Rehnquist spoke out, uncharacteristically criticizing the Senate for its failure to approve presidential nominees for the bench in a timely manner. These delays, charged Rehnquist, were contributing to lengthy delays in the federal courts, already overburdened by an "upward spiral" in case filings brought about, at least in part, by Congress's expanding federal jurisdiction over crimes involving drugs and firearms.

According to Rehnquist, in the 1990s the number of cases filed in courts of appeals rose 21 percent; district court filings increased by 24 percent. At the same time, not only did Congress refuse to expand the number of federal judges,[22] but the Senate refused to confirm many appointees to the federal courts. In 1998, the Court of Appeals for the Ninth Circuit, for example, had vacancies in nearly one-quarter of its seats, and five had been vacant for over eighteen months. The Senate, said Clinton White House Communications Director Ann Lewis, "has the right to advice and consent, but not to duck and delay, and what they have effectively done by a delaying process is causing some courts to almost grind to a halt."[23]

There is a saying that what goes around comes around, and that is what first happened to many of George W. Bush's nominations to the federal bench. Through Election Day, 2002, only eighty of Bush's 130 nominees were confirmed by the Democratic-controlled Senate. One appeals court nominee, District Court Judge Charles W. Pickering, was voted down by the Senate Judiciary Committee on a 10–9 vote along straight party lines. Liberal groups charged that Pickering was racist and against reproductive rights.[24]

WEB EXPLORATION

To learn about the U.S. Senate's Judiciary Committee and judicial nominations currently under review, go to www.ablongman.com/oconnor

The White House tried to make the Democrats' failure to act an issue in the 2002 congressional elections. President Bush even announced a plan to speed up action on his judicial nominees, a move that many saw as an effort to energize conservative Republican voters to go to the polls. Democratic Senators responded by filibustering several Judicial nominations.

In later 2003, the Republican leadership attempted to counter these filibusters by holding a forty-hour talkathon to bring attention to the Senate's failure to confirm these nominees. Although this event received a good deal of press, it achieved little success. President George W. Bush further irritated Senate Democrats when he made several recess appointments of contested appointees including Charles W. Pickering, which allowed them to serve for the remainder of the 108th Congress. Finally, in 2004, President Bush and Senate Democrats reached an agreement that no further recess appointments would occur if the Senate confirmed twenty-five of the president's nominees.[25]

Who Are Federal Judges?

Typically, federal district court judges have held other political offices, such as those of state court judge or prosecutor, as illustrated in Table 10.3. Most have been involved in politics, which is what usually brings them into consideration for a position on the federal bench. Griffin Bell, a former federal court of appeals judge, once remarked, "For me, becoming a federal judge wasn't very difficult. I managed John F. Kennedy's presidential campaign in Georgia."[26]

TABLE 10.3   Characteristics of District Court Appointees from Carter to Bush

	Carter Appointees	Reagan Appointees	Bush Appointees	Clinton Appointees	Bush Appointees[a]
Occupation					
Politics/gov't	5.0%	13.4%	10.8%	11.5%	12.5%
Judiciary	44.6	36.9	41.9	48.2	46.9
Lawyer	49.9	49.0	45.9	38.7	37.4
Other	0.5	0.7	1.4	2.6	3.1
Experience					
Judicial	54.0%	46.2%	46.6%	52.1%	53.1%
Prosecutorial	38.1	44.1	39.2	41.3	40.6
Neither	30.7	28.6	31.8	28.9	18.8
Political Affiliation					
Democrat	90.6%	4.8%	5.4%	87.5%	3.1%
Republican	4.5	91.7	88.5	6.2	84.3
Independent	5.0	3.4	6.1	5.9	12.5
ABA Rating					
Extremely/Well Qualified	51.0%	53.5%	57.4%	59.0%	65.6%
Qualified	47.5	46.6	42.6	40.0	31.2
Not Qualified	1.5	—	—	1.0	3.1
Net Worth					
Under $200,000	35.8%	17.6%	10.1%	13.4%	6.2%
200,000–499,999	41.2	37.6	31.1	21.6	28.1
500,000–999,999	18.9	21.7	26.4	26.9	15.6
1,000,000+	4.0	23.1	32.4	32.4	50.0
Average age at nomination (years)	49.6	48.7	48.1	49.5	49.4
Total number of appointees	202	290	148	305	32

[a]George W. Bush appointee data is through February 19, 2002.

Source: Sheldon Goldman and Elliot E. Slotnick, "Clinton's First Term Judiciary: Many Bridges to Cross," *Judicature* (May–June 1997): 261. Reprinted by permission. Updated data from Sheldon Goldman, University of Massachusetts, Amherst.

Increasingly, most judicial nominees have had prior judicial experience. White males continue to dominate the federal courts, but the Clinton administration sought to appoint nontraditional judges, as is revealed in Analyzing Visuals: Race/Ethnicity and Gender of District Court Appointees. His female appointees, however, experienced far greater problems in their confirmation hearings than did white males. Since the 1970s, in fact, most presidents have pledged (with varying degrees of success) to do their best to appoint more African Americans, women, and others traditionally under-represented on the federal bench.

Appointments to the U.S. Supreme Court

The Supreme Court is not now, nor has it ever been, above politics, as its foray into settling the 2000 national election underscores. Further, during the 2004 presidential campaign, Chief Justice William H. Rehnquist's diagnosis of thyroid cancer as well as the ages of several other justices refocused attention on the president's ability to appoint justices to the Court. Much of that speculation was based on the ages of the justices. Politics permeates the selection process of federal court judges, including those on the Supreme Court. On occasion, some individuals or their friends have actively lobbied for a spot on the bench. In their classic insiders' view of the Supreme Court, *The Brethren*, Bob Woodward and Scott Armstrong wrote critically of then Court of Appeals Judge Warren E. Burger's somewhat clumsy efforts to lobby Richard M. Nixon for the position of chief justice of the Supreme Court.[27] Burger's lobbying for the position was portrayed as unseemly (but ultimately effective).

The Constitution is silent on the qualifications for appointment to the Supreme Court (as well as to other constitutional courts), although Justice Oliver Wendell Holmes once remarked that a justice should be a "combination of Justinian, Jesus Christ and John Marshall."[28]

Like other federal court judges, the justices of the Supreme Court are nominated by the president and must be confirmed by the Senate. Few appointments, however, have been subject to the kind of lobbying that occurred when Court of Appeals Judge Ruth Bader Ginsburg was nominated to the U.S. Supreme Court in 1993. Ginsburg's husband, a prominent tax attorney and Georgetown University law professor, unabashedly orchestrated a letter-writing campaign on behalf of his wife's nomination. He contacted his wife's former students, the presidents of Stanford and Columbia Universities, academics, legal scholars, and even then Texas Governor Ann Richards, urging them to call or write the White House to support his wife's nomination to the Court.

Presidents always have realized how important their judicial appointments, especially their Supreme Court appointments, were to their ability to achieve all or many of their policy objectives. After all, Franklin D. Roosevelt proposed his infamous Court-packing plan because he wanted to add like-minded jurists to the Court to outweigh the votes of those opposed to federal governmental expansion and intervention into the economy. But, even though most presidents have tried to appoint jurists with particular political or ideological philosophies, they have often been wrong in their assumptions about their appointees. President Dwight D. Eisenhower, a moderate/conservative, was appalled by the liberal opinions written by his appointee, Earl Warren, concerning criminal defendants' rights. Similarly, Justices Sandra Day O'Connor, Anthony Kennedy, and David Souter, appointed by Presidents Ronald Reagan and George Bush, are not as conservative as some predicted. Souter, in particular, has surprised many commentators with his moderate to liberal decisions in a variety of areas, including free speech, criminal rights, race and gender discrimination, and abortion.

Historically, because of the special place the Supreme Court enjoys in our constitutional system, its nominees have encountered more opposition than district court or court of appeals nominees. As the role of the Court has increased over time, so too has the amount of attention given to nominees. With this increased attention has come greater opposition, especially to nominees with controversial views.

ANALYZING VISUALS

Race/Ethnicity and Gender of District Court Appointees

Traditionally, white males have dominated federal court appointments. Of President Ronald Reagan's 290 appointees to federal district courts, for example, 92.4 percent were white males. By the end of the Clinton administration, however, the percentage of white males had decreased significantly, to only 52.1 percent of Clinton's 305 appointments. George W. Bush reversed the trend during the first eighteen months of his term, by appointing a large proportion of white males. While most presidents in recent years have pledged to appoint more African Americans, women, and Hispanics to the federal bench, Clinton was the most successful. After reviewing the bar graph below, answer the following critical thinking questions: Is there a difference between appointments made by Democratic presidents (Carter and Clinton) and Republican presidents? Which group is most underrepresented in appointments? What factors do presidents consider, in addition to the nominee's gender and race/ethnicity, in making appointments to the federal bench? Should gender and race/ethnicity be considered by a president? Explain your answers.

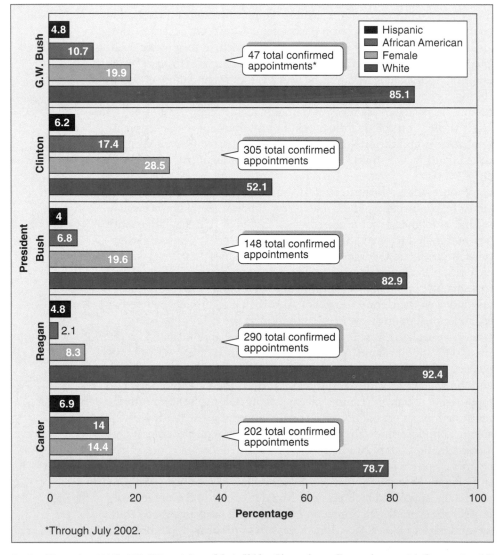

*Through July 2002.

Sources: *Fordham Law Review* (December 1992): 497–539; and Anne Marie Kilday, "Amendment Expert Agrees with Congressional Pay Ruling," *Dallas Morning News* (February 14, 1993): 13A. Clinton data from Sheldon Goldman, University of Massachusetts, Amherst. George W. Bush data from Federal Judicial Center, "Judges of the United States." The Federal Judges Biographical Database. July 16, 2002. Accessed July 16, 2002, http://air.fjc.gov/history/judges_frm.html.

Nomination Criteria

Justice Sandra Day O'Connor once remarked that "You have to be lucky" to be appointed to the Court.[29] Although luck is certainly important, over the years nominations to the bench have been made for a variety of reasons. Depending on the timing of a vacancy, a president may or may not have a list of possible candidates or even a specific individual in mind. Until recently, presidents often have looked within their circle of friends or their administration to fill a vacancy. Nevertheless, whether the nominee is a friend or someone known to the president only by reputation, at least six criteria are especially important: competence, ideology or policy preferences, rewards, pursuit of political support, religion, and race and gender.

Competence. Most prospective nominees are expected to have had at least some judicial or governmental experience. John Jay, the first chief justice, was one of the authors of *The Federalist Papers* and was active in New York politics. Most have had some prior judicial experience. In 2004, eight sitting Supreme Court justices had prior judicial experience (see Table 10.4). If Chief Justice Rehnquist's service as associate justice is included, all nine justices have prior judicial experience.

Ideology or Policy Preferences. Most presidents seek to appoint to the Court individuals who share their policy preferences, and almost all have political goals in mind when they appoint a justice. Presidents Franklin D. Roosevelt, Richard M. Nixon, and Ronald Reagan were very successful in molding the Court to their own political beliefs. Roosevelt was able to appoint eight justices from 1937 to his death in 1945, solidifying

TABLE 10.4 The Supreme Court, 2004

Name	Year of Birth	Year of Appointment	Political Party	Law School	Appointing President	Religion	Prior Judicial Experience	Prior Government Experience
William H. Rehnquist	1924	1971/1986[a]	R	Stanford	Nixon	Lutheran	Associate Justice U.S. Supreme Court	Assistant U.S. Attorney General
John Paul Stevens	1920	1975	R	Chicago	Ford	Nondenominational Protestant	U.S. Court of Appeals	
Sandra Day O'Connor	1930	1981	R	Stanford	Reagan	Episcopalian	Arizona Court of Appeals	State Legislator
Antonin Scalia	1936	1986	R	Harvard	Reagan	Catholic	U.S. Court of Appeals	
Anthony Kennedy	1936	1988	R	Harvard	Reagan	Catholic	U.S. Court of Appeals	
David Souter	1939	1990	R	Harvard	Bush	Episcopalian	U.S. Court of Appeals	New Hampshire Assistant Attorney General
Clarence Thomas	1948	1991	R	Yale	Bush	Catholic	U.S. Court of Appeals	Chair, Equal Employment Opportunity Commission
Ruth Bader Ginsburg	1933	1993	D	Columbia	Clinton	Jewish	U.S. Court of Appeals	
Stephen Breyer	1938	1994	D	Harvard	Clinton	Jewish	U.S. Court of Appeals	Chief Counsel, Senate Judiciary Committee

[a]Promoted to chief justice by President Reagan in 1986.

strict constructionist
An approach to constitutional inter-
pretation that emphasizes the
Framers' original intentions.

support for his liberal New Deal programs. In contrast, Presidents Nixon and Reagan publicly proclaimed that they would nominate only conservatives who favored a **strict constructionist** approach to constitutional decision making—that is, an approach emphasizing the original intentions of the Framers.

Rewards.   Historically, many of those appointed to the Supreme Court have been personal friends of presidents. Abraham Lincoln, for example, appointed one of his key political advisers to the Court. Lyndon B. Johnson appointed his longtime friend Abe Fortas to the bench. Most presidents select justices of their own party affiliation. Chief Justice Rehnquist was long active in Arizona Republican Party politics, as was Justice O'Connor before her appointment to the bench; both were appointed by Republican presidents. Party activism also can be used by presidents as an indication of a nominee's commitment to certain ideological principles.

Pursuit of Political Support.   During Ronald Reagan's successful campaign for the presidency in 1980, some of his advisers feared that the "gender gap" would hurt him. Polls repeatedly showed that he was far less popular with female voters than with men. To gain support from women, Reagan announced during his campaign that should he win, he would appoint a woman to fill the first vacancy on the Court. When Justice Potter Stewart, a moderate, announced his early retirement from the bench, President Reagan nominated Sandra Day O'Connor of the Arizona Court of Appeals to fill the vacancy. It probably did not hurt President Bill Clinton that his first appointment (Ruth Bader Ginsburg) was a woman and Jewish (at a time when no Jews served on the Court).

Religion.   Ironically, religion, which historically has been an important issue, was hardly mentioned during the most recent Supreme Court vacancies. Some, however, hailed Clinton's appointment of Ginsburg, noting that the traditionally "Jewish" seat on the Court had been vacant for over two decades.

Through 2004, of the 108 justices who have served on the Court, almost all have been members of traditional Protestant faiths.[30] Only nine have been Catholic and only seven have been Jewish.[31] Twice during the Rehnquist Court, more Catholics—William Brennan, Antonin Scalia, and Anthony Kennedy, and then Scalia, Kennedy, and Clarence Thomas—served on the Court at one time than at any other period in history. Today, however, it is clear that religion cannot be taken as a sign of a justice's conservative or liberal ideology. When William Brennan was on the Court, he and fellow Catholic Antonin Scalia were at ideological polar extremes.

Race and Gender.   Only two African Americans and two women have served on the Court. Race was undoubtedly a critical issue in the appointment of Clarence Thomas to replace Thurgood Marshall, the first African American justice. But, President George Bush refused to acknowledge his wish to retain a "black seat" on the Court. Instead, he announced that he was "picking the best man for the job on the merits," a claim that was met with considerable skepticism by many observers.

In contrast, Sandra Day O'Connor pointedly was picked because of her gender. Ruth Bader Ginsburg's appointment, in contrast, surprised many because the Clinton administration initially appeared to be considering several men for the appointment.

The Supreme Court Confirmation Process

The Constitution gives the Senate the authority to approve all nominees to the federal bench. Before 1900, about one-fourth of all presidential nominees to the Supreme Court were rejected by the Senate. In 1844, for example, President John Tyler sent six nominations to the Senate, and all but one were defeated. In 1866, Andrew Johnson nominated his brilliant attorney general, Henry Stanberry, but the Senate's hostility to Johnson led it to abolish the seat to prevent Johnson's filling it. Ordinarily, nominations are referred to the Senate Judiciary Committee. As detailed later, this committee investigates the nominees, holds hearings, and votes on its recommendation for Senate action. At this stage, the Committee may reject a nominee or send the nomination to the full Senate for a vote. The full Senate then deliberates on the nominee before voting. A simple majority vote is required for confirmation.

Investigation.   As a president begins to narrow the list of possible nominees to the Supreme Court, those names are sent to the Federal Bureau of Investigation before a nomination formally is made. At the same time, until the current president, the president forwarded names of prospective nominees to the American Bar Association (ABA), the politically powerful organization that represents the interests of the legal profession. Republican President Dwight D. Eisenhower started this practice, believing it helped "insulate the process from political pressure."[32] After its own investigation, the ABA rated each nominee, based on his or her qualifications, as Well Qualified (previously "Highly Qualified"), Qualified, or Not Qualified. (The same system was used for lower federal court nominees; over the years, however, the exact labels have varied.)

WEB EXPLORATION
To learn the extent of the ABA's legislative and government advocacy, go to
www.ablongman.com/oconnor

David Souter, George Bush's first nominee to the Court, received a unanimous rating of Highly Qualified from the ABA, as did both of Clinton's nominees, Ruth Bader Ginsburg and Stephen Breyer. In contrast, another Bush nominee, Clarence Thomas, was given only a Qualified rating (well before sexual harassment charges against him became public), with two members voting Not Qualified. Unlike the twenty-two previous successful nominees rated by the ABA, he was the first to receive less than a unanimous Qualified rating.

Early in his administration, President George W. Bush announced that the ABA would no longer play this key role. Earlier, the 1996 Republican presidential candidate, Bob Dole, went so far as to pledge, if elected, he would remove the ABA from the selection process, viewing it as "another blatantly partisan liberal advocacy group."[33] Bush agrees with this view and instead has looked to the more conservative Federalist Society to vet his nominees.

After a formal nomination is made and sent to the Senate, the Senate Judiciary Committee begins its own investigation. (The same process is used for nominees to the lower federal courts, although such investigations generally are not nearly as extensive as for Supreme Court nominees.) To begin its task, the Senate Judiciary Committee asks each nominee to complete a lengthy questionnaire detailing previous work (dating as far back as high school summer jobs), judicial opinions written, judicial philosophy, speeches, and even all interviews ever given to members of the press. Committee staffers also contact potential witnesses who might offer testimony concerning the nominee's fitness for office.

Lobbying by Interest Groups.   While historically the ABA was the only organization that was asked formally to rate nominees, other groups also are keenly interested in the nomination process. Until recently, interest groups played a minor and backstage role in most appointments to the Supreme Court. Although interest groups generally have not lobbied on behalf of any one individual, in 1981

The scrutiny by the public and press of President Ronald Reagan's Supreme Court nominee Robert H. Bork set a new standard of inquiry into the values—political and personal—of future nominees. Bork's nomination was rejected by the Senate in 1987. Here, Kate Michelman, president of the National Abortion and Reproductive Rights Action League, speaks at an anti-Bork rally.

(Photo courtesy: Frank Fournier/Contact Press Images)

The Senate Judiciary Committee, with the blessings of liberal interest groups, delayed hearings on the nomination of Miguel Estrada to the U.S. Court of Appeals for the District of Columbia. After Democratic senators exercised a modified filibuster to delay further a vote on Estrada, he eventually withdrew his name from consideration.

(Photo courtesy: Terry Ashe/AP/Wide World Photos)

women's rights groups successfully urged President Ronald Reagan to honor his campaign commitment to appoint a woman to the high Court.

It is more common for interest groups to lobby against a prospective nominee, as revealed in Table 10.5. Even this, however, is a relatively recent phenomenon. In 1987, the nomination of Robert H. Bork to the Supreme Court produced an unprecedented amount of interest group lobbying on both sides of the nomination. The Democratic-controlled Senate Judiciary Committee delayed the hearings, thus allowing liberal interest groups time to mobilize the most extensive radio, television, and print media campaign ever launched against a nominee to the U.S. Supreme Court. This opposition was in spite of the fact that Bork sat with distinction on the D.C. Court of Appeals and was a former U.S. solicitor general, a top-ranked law school graduate, and a Yale Law School professor. His actions as solicitor general, especially his firing of the Watergate special prosecutor at the request of President Richard M. Nixon, made him a special target for traditional liberals.

More and more, interest groups are getting involved in district court and court of appeals nominations. They recognize that these appointments often pave the way for future nominees to the Supreme Court, as was the case with most of the members of the current Court. (See Table 10.4.) The Senate Judiciary Committee, in fact, with the blessings of liberal groups including the Alliance for Justice and the Mexican American Legal Defense and Education Fund, delayed hearings on the nomination of Miguel Estrada to the U.S. Court of Appeals for the District of Columbia. Senator Orrin Hatch (R–UT), then the ranking member on the Senate Judiciary Committee, noted that "Estrada is likely to be the first Hispanic American to sit on the Supreme Court," a notion that struck fear in the hearts of many Democrats, who viewed Estrada as a "Latino Clarence Thomas and the darling of the right wing."[34] Estrada was a member of George W. Bush's legal team in Florida during the wrangling over the 2000 election, and he was opposed to the Supreme Court's rulings on abortion, criminal defendants' rights, and affirmative action.

The Senate Committee Hearings and Senate Vote.   As the relatively uneventful 1994 hearings of Stephen Breyer attest, not all nominees inspire the kind of intense reaction that kept Bork from the Court and almost blocked the confirmation of

TABLE 10.5   Interest Groups Appearing in Selected Senate Judiciary Committee Hearings

Nominee	Year	Liberal	Conservative	ABA Rating	Senate Vote
Stevens	1976	2	3	Well-Q	98–0
O'Connor	1981	8	7	Well-Q	99–0
Scalia	1986	5	7	Well-Q	98–0
Rehnquist	1986	6	13	Well-Q	68–36
Bork	1987	18	68	Well-Q[a]	42–58
Kennedy	1987	12	14	Well-Q	97–0
Souter	1990	13	18	Well-Q	90–9
Thomas	1991	30	46	Q[b]	52–48
Ginsburg	1993	6	5	Well-Q	96–3
Breyer	1994	8	3	Well-Q	87–9

[a]Four ABA committee members evaluated him as Not Qualified.

[b]Two ABA committee members evaluated him as Not Qualified.

Source: Karen O'Connor, "Lobbying the Justices or Lobbying for Justice," in Paul S. Herrnson, Ronald G. Shaiko, and Clyde Wilcox, eds., *The Interest Group Connection* (Chatham, NJ: Chatham House, 1998), 273. Reprinted by permission of Chatham House Publishers, Inc.

Clarence Thomas. Until 1929, all but one Senate Judiciary Committee hearing on a Supreme Court nominee was conducted in executive session—that is, closed to the public. The 1916 hearings on Louis Brandeis, the first Jewish justice, were conducted in public and lasted nineteen days, although Brandeis himself never was called to testify. In 1939, Felix Frankfurter became the first nominee to testify in any detail before the committee. Subsequent revelations about Brandeis's secret financial payments to Frankfurter to allow him to handle cases of social interest to Brandeis (while Brandeis was on the Court and couldn't handle them himself) raise questions about the fitness of both Frankfurter and Brandeis for the bench. Still, no information about Frankfurter's legal arrangements with Brandeis was unearthed during the committee's investigations or Frankfurter's testimony.[35]

Until recently, modern nomination hearings were no more thorough in terms of the attention given to nominees' backgrounds. In 1969, for example, Chief Justice Warren E. Burger was confirmed by the Senate on a vote of 94–3, just nineteen days after he was nominated. Since the 1980s, it has become standard for senators to ask the nominees probing questions. Most nominees (with the notable exception of Robert H. Bork) have declined to answer most of them on the grounds that these issues raised ultimately might come before the Court.

After hearings are concluded, the Senate Judiciary Committee usually makes a recommendation to the full Senate. Any rejections of presidential nominees to the Supreme Court generally occur only after the Senate Judiciary Committee has recommended against a nominee's appointment. Few recent confirmations have been close; prior to Clarence Thomas's 52–48 vote in 1991, William H. Rehnquist's nomination in 1971 as associate justice (68–26) and in 1986 as chief justice (65–33) were the closest in recent history. (See Table 10.5.)

THE SUPREME COURT TODAY

Given the judicial system's vast size and substantial, although often indirect, power over so many aspects of our lives, it is surprising that so many Americans know next to nothing about the judicial system, in general, and the Supreme Court, in particular.

Even today, after the unprecedented attention the Supreme Court received when the fate of the 2000 presidential election was in its hands, nearly two-thirds of those sampled in 2002 could not name one member of the Court; only 32 percent knew that the Court had nine members. In sharp contrast, 75 percent knew that there are three Rice Krispies characters. As revealed in Table 10.6, Sandra Day O'Connor, the first woman appointed to the Court, is the most well-known justice. Still, less than a quarter of those polled could name her. To fill in any gaps in your knowledge of the current Supreme Court, see Table 10.4.

Much of this ignorance can be blamed on the American public's lack of interest. But, the Court has taken great pains to ensure its privacy and sense of decorum. Its rites and rituals contribute to the Court's mystique and encourage a "cult of the robe."[36] Consider, for example, the way Supreme Court proceedings are conducted. Oral arguments are not televised, and deliberations concerning the outcome of cases are conducted in utmost secrecy. In contrast, C-SPAN brings us daily coverage of various congressional hearings and floor debate on bills and important

TABLE 10.6 Don't Know Much About ... the Supreme Court

	% Responding Correctly
Rice Krispies Characters:	
Crackle	67
Snap	66
Pop	66
Supreme Court Justices:	
Sandra Day O'Connor	24
Clarence Thomas	19
William H. Rehnquist	11
Antonin Scalia	8
Ruth Bader Ginsburg	7
Anthony Kennedy	5
David Souter	5
Stephen Breyer	3
John Paul Stevens	2

Source: The Polling Company. Accessed May 30, 2002, http://www.pollingcompany.com/News.asp?FormMode=ViewReleases&ID=50. Reprinted by permission of The Polling Company.

WEB EXPLORATION

To examine the major Supreme Court decisions from the past to the present, go to www.ablongman.com/oconnor

national issues, and Court TV (and sometimes other networks) provides gavel-to-gavel coverage of many important state court trials. The Supreme Court, however, remains adamant in its refusal to televise its proceedings—including public oral arguments, as discussed in the opening vignette.

Deciding to Hear a Case

Although nearly 9,000 cases were filed at the Supreme Court in its 2003–2004 term, this was not always the case. From 1790 to 1801, the Court heard only eighty-seven cases under its appellate jurisdiction.[37] In the Court's early years, the bulk of the justices' workload involved their circuit-riding duties. From 1862 to 1866, only 240 cases were decided. Creation of the courts of appeals in 1891 resulted in an immediate reduction in Supreme Court filings—from 600 in 1890 to 275 in 1892.[38] As recently as the 1940s, fewer than 1,000 cases were filed annually. Since that time, filings increased at a dramatic rate until the mid 1990s and then shot up again in the late 1990s, as revealed earlier in Figure 10.4. The increased number of filings does not mean the Court is deciding more cases. In fact, of the 8,883 petitions it received during the 2003–2004 term, ninety cases were argued and seventy-three signed opinions were issued. The process by which cases get to the Supreme Court is outlined in Figure 10.6.

SKAKEL GETS 20 TO LIFE
▶ DORTHY MOXLEY: DAUGHTER'S KILLER SENTENCED TODAY

Nancy Grace, a former Fulton County, Georgia prosecutor, anchors Court TV's daily trial coverage on *Trial Heat*. She also serves as a legal commentator on several national news shows, including CNN's *Larry King Live* and *Crossfire*.

(Photo courtesy: CNN/Getty Images)

The Supreme Court today. From left to right: Clarence Thomas, Antonin Scalia, Sandra Day O'Connor, Anthony Kennedy, David Souter, Stephen Breyer, John Paul Stevens, William H. Rehnquist, and Ruth Bader Ginsburg.

(Photo courtesy: Ken Heinen/Pool/AP/Wide World Photos)

Just as it is up to the justices to "say what the law is," they can also exercise a significant role in policy making and politics by opting not to hear a case. The content of the Court's docket is, of course, every bit as significant as its size. Prior to the 1930s, the Court generally heard cases of interest only to the immediate parties. During the 1930s, however, cases requiring the interpretation of constitutional law began to take a growing portion of its workload, leading the Court to take a more important role in the policy-making process. At that time, only 5 percent of the Court's cases involved questions concerning the Bill of Rights. By the late 1950s, one-third of filed cases involved such questions; by the 1960s, half did.[39] More recently, 42 percent of the cases decided by the Court dealt with issues raised in the Bill or Rights.[40]

The Supreme Court's Jurisdiction

The Court has two types of jurisdiction, as indicated in Table 10.2. Its original jurisdiction is specifically set out in the Constitution. The Court has original jurisdiction in "all Cases affecting Ambassadors, other public Ministers and Consuls, and those in which a State shall be a party." Most cases arising under the Court's original jurisdiction involve disputes between two states, usually over issues such as ownership of off-shore oil deposits, territorial disputes caused by shifting river boundaries, or controversies caused by conflicting claims over water rights, such as when a river flows through two or more states.[41] In earlier days, the Court would actually sit as a trial court and hear evidence and argument. Today, the Court usually appoints a Special Master—often a retired judge or an expert on the matter at hand—to hear the case in a district court on behalf of the Supreme Court and then report his or her findings and recommendations to the Court. It is rare for more than two or three of these cases to come to the Court in a year.

FIGURE 10.6 How a Case Goes to the Supreme Court
This figure illustrates how cases get on the Court's docket; what happens after a case is accepted for review is detailed in Figure 10.7.

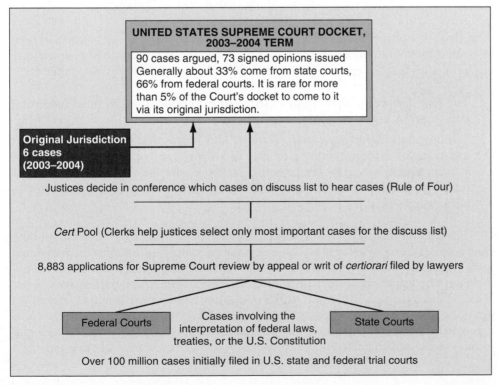

A second kind of jurisdiction enjoyed by the Court is its appellate jurisdiction (see Table 10.2). The appellate jurisdiction of the Court can be changed by the Congress at any time, a power that has been a potent threat to the authority of the Court. The Judiciary Act of 1925 gave the Court discretion over its own case load, meaning that it does not have to accept all appeals that come to it. The idea behind the act was that the intermediate courts of appeals should be the final word for almost all federal litigants, thus freeing the Supreme Court to concentrate on constitutional issues, unless the Court decided that it wanted to address other matters. The Court, then, is not expected to exercise its appellate jurisdiction simply to correct errors of other courts. Instead, appeal to the Supreme Court should be taken only if the case presents important issues of law, or what is termed "a substantial federal question." Since 1988, nearly all appellate cases that had gone to the Supreme Court arrived there on a petition for a **writ of** *certiorari* (from the Latin "to be informed"), which is a request for the Supreme Court—at its discretion—to order up the records of the lower courts for purposes of review.

About one-third of all Supreme Court filings involve criminal law issues.[42] Many of these, in fact more than half of all petitions to the Court, are filed as *in forma pauperis* (IFP) motions (literally from the Latin, "as a pauper"), which is a way for an indigent or poor person to appeal a case to the Supreme Court. About 80 percent of these petitions are filed by indigent prison inmates seeking review of their sentences. Permission to proceed *in forma pauperis* allows the petitioner to avoid expensive filing and printing costs. Any criminal defendant who has had a court-appointed lawyer in a lower court proceeding automatically is entitled to proceed in this fashion.

In recent years, the Court has tended more and more to deny requests to file *in forma pauperis*. In *In re Sindram* (1991), for example, the Rehnquist Court chastised Michael Sindram for filing his petition *in forma pauperis* to require the Maryland courts to expedite his request to expunge a $35 speeding ticket from his record. Sindram was no stranger to the Supreme Court. During the previous three years, he had filed forty-two separate motions on various legal matters, twenty-four of them in the 1990 term. In denying Sindram's request to file as an indigent, the majority noted that "[t]he goal of fairly dispensing justice ... is compromised when the Court is forced to devote its limited resources to the processing of repetitious and frivolous requests." Along with the order denying the petition, the Court issued new rules to provide for denial of "frivolous" or "malicious" *in forma pauperis* motions.[43]

The Rule of Four.   Unlike other federal courts, the Supreme Court controls its own caseload through the *certiorari* process, deciding which cases it wants to hear, and rejecting most cases that come to it. All petitions for *certiorari* must meet two criteria:

1. The case must come either from a U.S. court of appeals, a special three-judge district court, or a state court of last resort.

2. The case must involve a federal question. This means that the case must present questions of interpretation of federal constitutional law or involve a federal statute, action, or treaty. The reasons that the Court should accept the case for review and legal argument supporting that position are set out in the petition (also called a brief).

The clerk of the Court's office transmits petitions for writs of *certiorari* first to the chief justice's office, where his clerks review the petitions, and then to the individual justices' offices. All the justices on the Rehnquist Court except Justice John Paul Stevens (who lets his clerks dispose of most cases without memos) participate in what is called the "*cert* pool."[44] As part of the pool, they review their assigned fraction of petitions and share their notes with each other. Those cases that the justices deem noteworthy are then placed on what is called the "discuss list" prepared by the chief justice's clerks and circulated to the chambers of the other justices. All others are dead

writ of *certiorari*
A request for the Court to order up the records from a lower court to review the case.

in forma pauperis
Literally, "as a pauper"; a way for an indigent or poor person to appeal a case to the Supreme Court.

listed and go no further unless a justice asks that a case be removed from the dead list and discussed at conference. Only about 30 percent of submitted petitions make it to the discuss list. During one of the justices' weekly conference meetings, the cases on the discuss list are reviewed. The chief justice speaks first, then the rest of the justices, according to seniority. The decision process ends when the justices vote, and by custom, *certiorari* is granted according to the **Rule of Four**—when at least four justices vote to hear a case.

Rule of Four
At least four justices of the Supreme Court must vote to consider a case before it can be heard.

The Role of Clerks.   As early as 1850, the justices of the Supreme Court beseeched Congress to approve the hiring of a clerk to assist each justice. Congress denied the request, so when Justice Horace Gray hired the first law clerk in 1882, he paid the clerk himself. Justice Gray's clerk was a top graduate of Harvard Law School whose duties included cutting Justice Gray's hair and running personal errands. Finally, in 1886, Congress authorized each justice to hire a "stenographer clerk" for $1,600 a year.

Simulation
You Are a Clerk to Supreme Court Justice Judith Gray

Clerks typically are selected from candidates at the top of the graduating classes of prestigious law schools. They perform a variety of tasks, ranging from searching for arcane facts to playing tennis or taking walks with the justices. Clerks spend most of their time researching material relevant to particular cases, reading and summarizing cases, and helping justices write opinions. The clerks also make the first pass through the petitions that come to the Court, undoubtedly influencing which cases get a second look. Just how much help they provide in the writing of opinions is unknown.[45] (See Table 10.7 for more on what clerks do.)

Over time, the number of clerks employed by the justices has increased. Through the 1946 to 1969 terms, most justices employed two clerks. By 1970, most had three, and by 1980 all but three had four. In 2004, there were thirty-four clerks. This growth in clerks has had many interesting ramifications for the Court. "Between 1969 and 1972—the period during which the justices each became entitled to a third law clerk— … the number of opinions increased by about 50 percent and the number of words tripled."[46] And, until recently, the number of cases decided annually increased as more help was available to the justices.

The relationship between clerks and the justices for whom they work is close and confidential, and many aspects of the relationship are kept secret. Clerks may sometimes talk among themselves about the views and personalities of their justices, but rarely has a clerk leaked such information to the press. In 1998, a former clerk to Justice Harry A. Blackmun broke the silence. Edward Lazarus published a book that shocked many Court watchers by penning an insider's account of how the Court really works.[47] He also charged that the justices give their young, often ideological, clerks far too much power.

How Does a Case Survive the Process?

It can be difficult to determine why the Court decides to hear a particular case. Sometimes it involves a perceived national emergency, as was the case with appeals concerning the outcome of the 2000 presidential election. The Court does not offer reasons, and "the standards by which the justices decide to grant or deny review are highly personalized and necessarily discretionary," noted former Chief Justice Earl Warren, although sometimes individual justices publicly dissent from the Court's denial of *certiorari*. Moreover, he continued, "those standards cannot be captured in rules or guidelines that would be meaningful."[48] Political scientists nonetheless have attempted to

TABLE 10.7   What Do Supreme Court Clerks Do?

Supreme Court clerks are among the best and brightest recent law school graduates. Almost all first clerk for a judge on one of the courts of appeals. After their Supreme Court clerkship, former clerks are in high demand. Firms often pay signing bonuses of up to $80,000 to attract clerks to their firms, where salaries start at over $130,000 a year.

Tasks of a Supreme Court clerk include the following:

- Perform initial screening of the 9,000 or so petitions that come to the Court each term
- Draft memos to summarize the facts and issues in each case, recommending whether the case should be accepted by the Court for full review
- Write a "bench memo" summarizing an accepted case and suggesting questions for oral argument
- Write the first draft of an opinion
- Be an informal conduit for communicating and negotiating between other justices chambers as to the final wording of an opinion

Theodore Olson was appointed by President George W. Bush as solicitor general. As a private lawyer, Olson represented Bush before the Supreme Court throughout the 2000 presidential election recount dispute. He narrowly won confirmation on a 51–47 vote in the Senate. His wife, conservative political commentator Barbara Olson, was killed when an American Airlines flight crashed into the Pentagon on September 11. Olson resigned his post in 2004.

(Photo courtesy: Reuters NewMedia Inc./Corbis)

amicus curiae
"Friend of the court"; a third party to a lawsuit who files a legal brief for the purpose of raising additional points of view in an attempt to influence a court's decision.

solicitor general
The fourth-ranking member of the Department of Justice; responsible for handling all appeals on behalf of the U.S. government to the Supreme Court.

WEB EXPLORATION
To examine the recent filings of the office of solicitor general, go to www.ablongman.com/oconnor

determine the characteristics of the cases the Court accepts; not surprisingly, they are similar to those that help a case get on the discuss list. Among the cues are the following:

- The federal government is the party asking for review.
- The case involves conflict among the circuit courts.
- The case presents a civil rights or civil liberties question.
- The case involves ideological and/or policy preferences of the justices.
- The case has significant social or political interest, as evidenced by the presence of interest group *amicus curiae* briefs.

The Federal Government. One of the most important cues for predicting whether the Court will hear a case is the position the solicitor general takes on it. The **solicitor general,** appointed by the president, is the fourth-ranking member of the Department of Justice and is responsible for handling most appeals on behalf of the U.S. government to the Supreme Court. The solicitor's staff is like a small, specialized law firm within the Department of Justice. But, because this office has such a special relationship with the Supreme Court, even having a suite of offices within the Supreme Court building, the solicitor general often is referred to as the Court's "ninth and a half member."[49] Moreover, the solicitor general, on behalf of the U.S. government, appears as a party or as an *amicus curiae* in more than 50 percent of the cases heard by the Court each term.

This special relationship with the Court helps explain the overwhelming success the solicitor general's office enjoys before the Supreme Court. The Court generally accepts 70 to 80 percent of the cases where the U.S. government is the petitioning party, compared with about 5 percent of all others.[50] But, because of this special relationship, the solicitor general often ends up playing two conflicting roles: representing in Court both the president's policy interests and the broader interests of the United States. At times, solicitors find these two roles difficult to reconcile. Former Solicitor General Rex E. Lee (1981–1985), for example, noted that on more than one occasion he refused to make arguments in Court that had been advanced by the Reagan administration (a stand that ultimately forced him to resign his position). Said Lee, "I'm not the pamphleteer general; I'm the solicitor general. My audience is not 100 million people; my audience is nine people.... Credibility is the most important asset that any solicitor general has."[51]

Conflict Among the Circuits. Conflict among the lower courts is apparently another reason that the justices take cases. When interpretations of constitutional or federal law are involved, the justices seem to want consistency throughout the federal court system.

Often these conflicts occur when important civil rights or civil liberties questions arise. Political scientist Lawrence Baum has commented, "Justices' evaluations of lower court decisions are based largely on their ideological position."[52] Thus, it is not uncommon to see conservative justices voting to hear cases to overrule liberal lower court decisions, or vice versa.

Interest Group Participation.   A quick way for the justices to gauge the ideological ramifications of a particular case is by the amount of interest group participation. Richard C. Cortner has noted that "Cases do not arrive on the doorstep of the Supreme Court like orphans in the night."[53] Instead, most cases heard by the Supreme Court involve either the government or an interest group—either as the sponsoring party or as an *amicus curiae*. Liberal groups such as the ACLU, People for the American Way, the NAACP Legal Defense Fund, and conservative groups including the Washington Legal Foundation, Concerned Women for America, or Americans United for Life Legal Defense Fund, routinely sponsor cases or file *amicus* briefs either urging the Court to hear a case or asking it to deny *certiorari*. Research by political scientists has found that "not only does [an *amicus*] brief in favor of *certiorari* significantly improve the chances of a case being accepted, but two, three and four briefs improve the chances even more."[54]

Clearly, it's the more the merrier, whether or not the briefs are filed for or against granting review.[55] Interest group participation may highlight lower court and ideological conflicts for the justices by alerting them to the amount of public interest in the issues presented in any particular case.

Starting the Case

Once a case is accepted for review, a flurry of activity begins (see Figure 10.7). If a criminal defendant is proceeding *in forma pauperis*, the Court appoints an expert lawyer to prepare and argue the case. Unlike the situation in many state courts, where appointed lawyers are often novices, it is considered an honor to be asked to represent an indigent before the Supreme Court even though such representation is on a *pro bono*, or no fee, basis.

Whether they are being paid or not, lawyers on both sides of the case begin to prepare their written arguments for submission to the Court. In these briefs, lawyers cite prior case law and make arguments as to why the Court should find in favor of their client.

More often than not, these arguments are echoed or expanded in *amicus curiae* briefs filed by interested parties, especially interest groups. (The vast majority of the cases decided by the Court in the 1990s had at least one *amicus* brief.)

Since the 1970s, interest groups have increasingly used the *amicus* brief as a way to lobby the Court. Because litigation is so expensive, few individuals have the money (or time or interest) to pursue a perceived wrong all the way to the U.S. Supreme Court. All sorts of interest groups, then, find that joining ongoing cases through *amicus* briefs is a useful way of advancing their policy preferences. Major cases such as *Brown v. Board of Education* (1954), *Planned Parenthood of Southeastern Pennsylvania v. Casey* (1992),

Simulation
You Are a
Young Lawyer

FIGURE 10.7   How Supreme Court Decisions Get Made

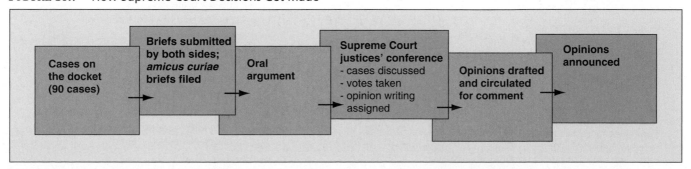

and *Harris* v. *Forklift Systems* (1993),[56] which involved the degree of psychological damage a victim of sexual harassment must show, all attracted large numbers of *amicus* briefs as part of interest groups' efforts to lobby the judiciary and bring about desired political objectives (see Table 10.8).

TABLE 10.8   *Amicus Curiae* Briefs in a Sexual Harassment Case

Teresa Harris celebrates her victory after the Supreme Court ruled that her employer's conduct was illegal sexual harassment.

(Photo courtesy: Fritz Hofmann/The Image Works)

In *Harris* v. *Forklift Systems* (1993), the U.S. Supreme Court unanimously ruled that federal civil rights law created a "broad rule of work-place equality." In *Harris*, the Court found that Title VII of the Civil Rights Act was violated when Teresa Harris was subjected to "intimidation, ridicule, and insults" of a sexually harassing nature by her supervisor. The following groups or governments filed *amicus* briefs:

In support of Teresa Harris
1. U.S. Equal Employment Opportunity Commission
2. National Conference of Women's Bar Associations
3. National Organization for Women Legal Defense and Education Fund
    American Jewish Committee
    American Medical Women Association
    Asian American Legal Defense and Education Fund
    Association for Union Democracy
    Center for Women's Policy Studies
    Chicago Women in Trades
    Illinois Coalition Against Sexual Harassment
    National Organization for Women
    Northern Tradeswomen's Network
    Northern New England Tradeswomen Institute
    Puerto Rican Legal Defense and Education Fund
    Women's Law Project
4. NAACP Legal Defense and Education Fund
    National Conference of Jewish Women
5. Women's Legal Defense Fund
    National Women's Law Center
    AFL-CIO
    Ayuda, Inc.
    Bar Association of San Francisco
    California Women Lawyers
    Center for Women Policy Studies
    Coalition of Labor Union Women
    Committee for Justice for Women of North Carolina
    Federally Employed Women, Inc.
    Federation of Organizations for Professional Women
    Institute for Women's Policy Research

    Mexican American Women's National Association
    National Association of Female Executives
    National Association of Social Workers, Inc.
    National Center for Lesbian Rights
    National Council of Negro Women, Inc.
    National Association of Working Women
    9 to 5
    Older Women's League
    Trial Lawyers for Public Justice
    Wider Opportunities for Women
    Women Employed
    Women's Action Alliance
    Women's Bar Association of the District of Columbia
    Women's Law Center of Maryland
    YWCA of the U.S.A.
6. Employment Law Center
    California Women Lawyer's Committee
    Equal Rights Advocates
7. National Employment Lawyers Association
8. American Civil Liberties Union
    American Jewish Congress
9. Feminists for Free Expression
10. Southern States Police Benevolent Association
    North Carolina Police Benevolent Association
11. National Conference of Women's Bar Associations

In Support of Forklift Systems
1. Equal Employment Advisory Council

For Neither Party
1. American Psychological Association

Interest groups also provide the Court with information not necessarily contained in the major-party briefs, help write briefs, and assist in practice moot-court sessions. In these sessions, the lawyer who will argue the case before the nine justices goes through a complete rehearsal, with prominent lawyers and law professors role playing the various justices.

Oral Arguments.   Once a case is accepted by the Court for full review, and after briefs and *amicus* briefs are submitted on each side, oral argument takes place. The Supreme Court's annual term begins the first Monday in October, as it has since the late 1800s, and runs through late June or early July. In the early 1800s, sessions of the Court lasted only a few weeks twice a year. Today, justices hear oral arguments from the beginning of the term until early April. Special cases, such as *U.S. v. Nixon* (1974), have been heard even later in the year.[57] During the term, "sittings," periods of about two weeks in which cases are heard, alternate with "recesses," also about two weeks long. Oral arguments are usually heard Monday through Wednesday during two-week sitting sessions.

Oral argument generally is limited to the immediate parties in the case, although it is not uncommon for the U.S. solicitor general to appear to argue orally as an *amicus curiae*. Oral argument at the Court is fraught with time-honored tradition and ceremony. At precisely ten o'clock every morning when the Court is in session, the Court Marshal (dressed in a cutaway—a formal morning coat) emerges to intone "Oyez! Oyez! Oyez!" as the nine justices emerge from behind a reddish-purple velvet curtain to take their places on the raised and slightly angled bench. (From 1790 to 1972, the justices sat on a straight bench. Chief Justice Warren E. Burger modified it so that justices at either end could see and hear better.) The chief justice sits in the middle with the justices to his right and left, alternating in seniority.

Almost all attorneys are allotted one half hour to present their cases, and this allotment includes the time taken by questions from the bench. Justice John Marshall Harlan once noted that there was "no substitute for this method in getting at the heart of an issue and in finding out where the truth lies."[58] As the lawyer for the appellee approaches the mahogany lectern, a green light goes on, indicating that the attorney's time has begun. A white light flashes when five minutes remain. When a red light goes on, Court practice mandates that counsel stop immediately. One famous piece of Court lore told to all attorneys concerns a counsel who continued talking and reading from his prepared argument after the red light went on. When he looked up, he found an empty bench—the justices had quietly risen and departed while he continued to talk. On another occasion, Chief Justice Charles Evans Hughes stopped a leader of the New York bar in the middle of the word "if."

Although many Court watchers have tried to figure out how a particular justice will vote based on the questioning at oral argument, most find that the nature and number of questions asked does not help much in predicting the outcome of a case. Nevertheless, many believe that oral argument has several important functions. First, it is the only opportunity for even a small portion of the public (who may attend the hearings) and the press to observe the workings of the Court. Second, it assures lawyers that the justices have heard their case, and it forces lawyers to focus on arguments believed important by the justices. Last, it provides the Court with additional information, especially concerning the Court's broader political role, an issue not usually addressed in written briefs. For example, the justices can ask how many people might be affected by its decision or where the Court (and country) would be heading if a case were decided in a particular way. Justice Stephen Breyer also notes that oral arguments are a good way for the justices to try to highlight certain issues for other justices.

The Conference and the Vote.   The justices meet in closed conference once a week when the Court is hearing oral argument. Since the ascendancy of Chief Justice Roger B. Taney to the Court in 1836, the justices have begun each conference session with a round of handshaking. Once the door to the conference room closes, no others are allowed to enter. The justice with the least seniority acts as the doorkeeper for the other eight, communicating with those waiting outside to fill requests for documents, water, and any other necessities.

Conferences highlight the importance and power of the chief justice, who presides over them and makes the initial presentation of each case. Each individual justice then discusses the case in order of his or her seniority on the Court, with the most senior justice speaking next. Most accounts of the decision-making process reveal that at this point some justices try to change the minds of others, but that most enter the conference room with a clear idea of how they feel. Although other Courts have followed different procedures, on the Rehnquist Court the justices generally vote at the same time they discuss the case, with each justice speaking only once. Initial conference votes are not final, allowing justices to change their minds before final votes are taken later.

Writing Opinions.   There are basically five kinds of opinions that can be written:

1. A *majority opinion* is written by one member of the Court and reflects the views of at least a majority of the justices. This opinion usually sets out the legal reasoning justifying the decision, and this legal reasoning becomes a precedent for deciding future cases.

2. A *concurring opinion* is one written by a justice who agrees with the outcome of the case but not with the legal rationale for the decision.

3. A *plurality opinion* is one that attracts the support of three or four justices. Generally, this opinion becomes the controlling opinion of the Court. Usually one or more justices agree with the outcome of the decision in a concurring opinion, but there is no solid majority for the legal reasoning behind the outcome. Plurality opinions do not have the precedential value of majority opinions.

4. A *dissenting opinion* is one that is written by one or more justices who disagree with the opinion of a majority or plurality of the Court.

5. A *per curiam opinion* is an unsigned opinion issued by the Court. Justices may dissent from *per curiam* opinions but do so fairly rarely. The seventy-page *Bush* v. *Gore* (2000) was an unsigned, *per curiam* opinion.

WEB EXPLORATION

For an analysis of the Court's 2000 election decision by constitutional scholars, go to www.ablongman.com/oconnor

The chief justice, if he is in the majority, has the job of assigning the writing of the opinion. This privilege enables him to wield tremendous power. (If he is in the minority, the assignment falls to the most senior justice in the majority.)

The justice assigned to write the majority opinion circulates drafts of the opinion to all members of the Court. The Court must provide legal reasons for its positions. The reasoning behind any decision is often as important as the outcome. Under our system of *stare decisis*, both are likely to be relied on as precedent later by lower courts confronted with cases involving similar issues. The justice who drafts the opinion can have an important impact on how any legal issues are framed. Informal caucusing and negotiation then often take place, as justices may "hold out" for word changes or other modifications as a condition of their continued support of the majority opinion. At the same time, dissenting opinions and/or concurring opinions also circulate through the various chambers. The justices often are assisted in their writing of opinions by their clerks, who also can serve as intermediaries between the justices as they talk among themselves.

A good example of how politics can be involved at the opinion-writing stage is evident in *Bowers* v. *Hardwick* (1986), the Georgia consensual sodomy case discussed in chapters 5 and 6.[59] Chief Justice Warren E. Burger and Justice Byron White voted for *certiorari*, believing that the Constitution doesn't protect homosexual acts. Liberal Justices Thurgood Marshall and William Brennan thought they had enough votes to overturn the law, but when Brennan perceived he would lose, he withdrew his vote for *certiorari*, albeit too late. Once the case was argued, coalitions quickly shifted. According to papers kept by Justice Marshall, Justice Lewis Powell originally indicated at conference that he would vote with the majority to find the law unconstitutional. After drafts of the majority and minority opinions were circulated, however, he changed his mind, thus changing a 5–4 majority to strike down the law into a 5–4 majority to uphold it.[60]

This kind of communal work can result in poorly written opinions, as was the case with *U.S.* v. *Nixon* (1974).[61] Although the opinion involving President Richard M. Nixon's refusal to turn over tape recordings of his conversations was issued under Chief Justice Warren E. Burger's name, many believe that it was a combination of several justices' contributions and additions. Sensing the need for the Court to speak unanimously in such an important opinion—one that pitted two branches of government against each other—Chief Justice Burger apparently made concessions to get support.[62] This process led to some very confused prose in some sections of the opinion.

Recently, tensions have grown on the Court concerning some issues, and dissents or concurring opinions have become quite pointed. The protocol of the Court has always been characterized by politeness, but this has not stopped some justices from openly ridiculing their colleagues from the bench. Justice Antonin Scalia, for example, publicly criticized Justice Sandra Day O'Connor's opinion in *Webster* v. *Reproductive Health Services* (1989), saying that her "assertion that a fundamental rule of judicial restraint requires [the Court] to avoid reconsidering *Roe* [v. *Wade*] cannot be taken seriously."[63] This kind of ridicule was unprecedented and perhaps simply reflects how manners in politics are on the decline.

Not all cases result in split decisions from the justices. In *Clinton* v. *Jones* (1997), which involved President Bill Clinton's attempt to defer Paula Jones's action for civil damages against him, a unanimous Court affirmed the lower court ruling allowing the case to go forward. Justice Stephen Breyer, who was appointed by Clinton, concurred with the opinion of the other eight justices, but did so only to underscore his belief that a federal judge could not schedule judicial proceedings that could interfere with the president's discharge of his public duties.[64] So here, in a decision that was to set the stage for debating articles of impeachment against the president, all nine justices—including two justices appointed by Clinton—were in agreement.

HOW THE JUSTICES VOTE

Justices are human beings, and they do not make decisions in a vacuum. Principles of *stare decisis* dictate that the justices follow the law of previous cases in deciding cases at hand. But, more factors are usually operating. A variety of legal and extra-legal factors have been found to affect Supreme Court decision making. As Politics Now: Educating or Lobbying? indicates, there may be other ways too.

Legal Factors

Legal scholars long have argued that judges decide cases based on the Constitution and their reading of various statutes. Determining what the Framers meant—if that is even important today—often appears to be based on an individual jurist's philosophy.

Judicial Philosophy and Original Intent.   One of the primary issues concerning judicial decision making focuses on what is called the activism/restraint debate. Advocates of **judicial restraint** argue that courts should allow the decisions of other branches to stand, even when they offend a judge's own sense of principles.[65] Restraintists defend their position by asserting that the federal courts are composed of unelected judges, which makes the judicial branch the least democratic branch of

judicial restraint
A philosophy of judicial decision making that argues courts should allow the decisions of other branches of government to stand, even when they offend a judge's own sense of principles.

EDUCATING OR LOBBYING?

By now you should realize that judges, appointed and confirmed through an often highly political process, may reflect political or ideological biases. How else might we explain the growing number of 5–4 decisions, including *Bush* v. *Gore* (2000), from the U.S. Supreme Court? Today, some judges and justices lobby for spots on the federal bench, and interest groups bring cases to courts they believe are amenable to their causes. Interest groups are also involved in another form of perhaps more insidious lobbying that has received very little attention.

From 1992 to 1998, more than 230 federal judges took all-expenses-paid trips to resort locations (some might call these vacations) to attend legal seminars paid for by corporations and foundations that have interests in cases already in or likely to be soon in federal court. These seminars are always held in warm places and have been occurring since the early 1980s. The most recent seminars have been devoted to issues of environmental litigation, where the message from the seminar sponsors was that regulation should be limited

and that "the free market should be relied upon to protect the environment."[a]

In fact, judges who attended those seminars wrote ten of the most crucial rulings handed down during the 1990s dealing with curbing environmental protection, including decisions invalidating a provision of the Endangered Species Protection Act and another regulation that attempted to abate soot and smog. Although judges are asked each year to report outside sources of income, which itself is also controversial, many judges do not note these seminars on their financial disclosure forms. Whether undue influence is felt at these seminars, there is at least the appearance of a conflict of interest. Chief Justice William H. Rehnquist, however, has defended these trips, saying that judges "are getting valuable education unavailable elsewhere."[b] Do you think that judges who go on these trips should rule on cases involving the parties hosting these events?

[a]Abner Mikva, "The Wooing of Our Judges," *New York Times* (August 28, 2000): A17.
[b]"Rehnquist Defends Groups' Trips for Judges," *Milwaukee Journal Sentinel* (May 15, 2001): 4A.

---

judicial activism
A philosophy of judicial decision making that argues judges should use their power broadly to further justice, especially in the areas of equality and personal liberty.

government. Consequently, the courts should defer policy making to other branches of government as much as possible.

Restraintists refer to *Roe* v. *Wade* (1973), the case that liberalized abortion laws, as a classic example of **judicial activism** run amok. They maintain that the Court should have deferred policy making on this sensitive issue to the states or to the other branches of the federal government—the legislative and executive—because their officials are elected and therefore are more receptive to the majority's will.

Advocates of judicial activism contend that judges should use their power broadly to further justice, especially in the areas of equality and personal liberty. Activists argue that it is the courts' appropriate role to correct injustices committed by the other branches of government. Explicit in this argument is the notion that courts need to protect oppressed minorities.[66]

Activists point to *Brown* v. *Board of Education* (1954) as an excellent example of the importance of judicial activism.[67] In *Brown*, the Supreme Court ruled that racial segregation in public schools violated the equal protection clause of the Fourteenth Amendment. Segregation was nonetheless practiced after passage of the Fourteenth Amendment. An activist would point out that if the Court had not reinterpreted provisions of the amendment, many states probably would still have laws or policies mandating segregation in public schools.

The debate over judicial activism versus judicial restraint often focuses on how the Court should interpret the meaning of the Constitution. See Join the Debate: Should the Senate Rein in Judicial Activism? Advocates of judicial restraint generally agree that judges should be strict constructionists; that is, they should interpret the Constitution as it was written and intended by the Framers. They argue that in determining the constitutionality of a statute or policy, the Court should rely on the explicit meanings of the clauses in the document, which can be clarified by looking at the intent of the Framers.

Precedent.   Most Supreme Court decisions are laced with numerous references to previous Court decisions. Some justices, however, believe that *stare decisis* and adherence to precedent is no longer as critical as it once was. Chief Justice William H. Rehnquist, for example, has noted that while "*stare decisis* is a cornerstone of our legal system … it has less power in constitutional cases."[68] In contrast, Justices Sandra Day O'Connor, Anthony Kennedy, and David Souter explained their reluctance to overrule *Roe* v. *Wade* (1973) in *Planned Parenthood of Southeastern Pennsylvania* v. *Casey* (1992): "to overrule under fire in the absence of the most compelling reason to reexamine a watershed decision would subject this Court's legitimacy beyond any serious question."[69]

Interestingly, a 2001 study of the American public's knowledge and perceptions of the Court indicated that 52 percent believed that judges were controlled by special interests.[70] Seventy-six percent reported that they believed judges were political,[71] and 36 percent of those polled believed that judges make decisions based more on politics and pressure from special interests than from a strict reading of the law.[72]

The "zipper" in New York's Times Square announces the Supreme Court's decision in *Bush* v. *Gore* regarding the recounting of Florida's votes after the 2000 presidential election. Some saw political reasons as motivating the Court's decision.

(Photo courtesy: Robert Mecea/AP/Wide World Photos)

Extra-Legal Factors

Most political scientists who study what is called judicial behavior conclude that a variety of forces shape judicial decision making. Of late, many have attempted to explain how judges vote by integrating a variety of models to offer a more complete picture of how judges make decisions.[73] Many of those models attempt to take into account justices' behavioral characteristics and attitudes as well as the fact patterns of the case.

Behavioral Characteristics.   Originally, some political scientists argued that social background differences, including childhood experiences, religious values, education, earlier political and legal careers, and political party loyalties, are likely to influence how a judge evaluates the facts and legal issues presented in any given case. Justice Harry A. Blackmun's service at the Mayo Clinic often is pointed to as a reason that his opinion for the Court in *Roe* v. *Wade* (1973) was grounded so soundly in medical evidence. Similarly, Justice Potter Stewart, who was generally considered a moderate on most civil liberties issues, usually took a more liberal position on cases dealing with freedom of the press. Why? It may be that Stewart's early job as a newspaper reporter made him more sensitive to these claims.

Ideology.   Critics of the social background approach argued that attitudes or ideologies can better explain the justices' voting patterns. Since the 1940s, the two most prevailing ideologies in the United States have been conservative and liberal. On the Supreme Court, justices with "conservative" views generally vote against affirmative action, abortion rights, expanded rights for criminal defendants, and increased power for the national government. In contrast, "liberals" tend to support the parties advancing these positions.

Over time, scholars have generally agreed that identifiable ideological voting blocs have occurred on the Court. During Franklin D. Roosevelt's first term, for example,

Join the Debate

Americans long have disagreed about the proper role for federal judges to play in enforcing the U.S. Constitution. From the time of the Constitutional Convention, and especially since the Supreme Court asserted the right of judicial review in *Marbury* v. *Madison* (1803), judicial authority to invalidate state and federal laws has been controversial. Some argue that the only way that the Constitution can truly be supreme is if judges protect individual rights when legislative bodies or majorities do not. Otherwise, governmental bodies can ignore the Constitution, and it becomes irrelevant. Others argue that democracy requires that decisions by the elected representatives of the people be respected, and that an elite group of appointed judges does not and should not have the power to block the will of the majority as expressed through the electoral or legislative process.

Those holding the latter view describe judges who often rule to invalidate state or congressional laws as "judicial activists." They argue that judges should defer to legislative decisions, and that presidents and the Senate should appoint and confirm as judges those who support such legislative supremacy. Yet, others claim that judicial activism is in the eye of the beholder. These arguments often occur over policy and ideological differences. For instance, conservatives often have decried judges who invalidate laws on the grounds of violation of constitutional standards of civil rights as judicial activists; however, liberals argue that conservatives do not label judges who invalidate laws that regulate economic activities as judicial activists, and that they desire judicial imposition of a conservative ideology, rather than pure judicial nonintervention.

Attorney General John Ashcroft, as a U.S. senator from Missouri, suggested that judges who impose policy decisions on government bodies and individuals are judicial activists, and that the Senate should stop confirming nominees who would be judicial activists. His views were at the center of debates in 2001 over whether the Senate should confirm him as attorney general (and the Senate did so in a divided vote). Read and think about the following excerpted news article written during the Ashcroft attorney general confirmation hearings. Then, join the debate over whether the Senate should reject nominees whom it considers to be judicial activists. Consider the debating points and questions posed at the end of this feature, and sharpen your own arguments for the position you find most viable.

Ashcroft Complained of Judges

By Larry Margasak

WASHINGTON (AP)—Attorney General–designate John Ashcroft, who would likely help make judicial selections if confirmed, complained in a 1997 lecture that there were too many "renegade judges" who imposed their personal will on the people.

In the remarks, ... then-Sen. Ashcroft said it was time to stop "judicial tyranny" on issues including school desegregation, abortion and affirmative action in education.

"Consider how far the federal judiciary has strayed," Ashcroft said in a lecture at the conservative Heritage Foundation think tank. He offered these examples:

- In 1987, U.S. District Judge Russell Clark ordered a tax increase to "remedy vestiges of segregation" in the Kansas City, Mo., school system. Ashcroft called the ruling "an appalling judicial activism" and said it imposed on taxpayers a $2 billion cost that "turned the city's school district into a gold-plated Taj Mahal…."

- The Supreme Court in 1992 reaffirmed a woman's right to an abortion, with three judges appointed by President Reagan joining the majority. "So much for recapturing the court," Ashcroft complained. "Together, Roe, Casey (abortion rulings) and their illegitimate progeny have occasioned the slaughter of 35 million children—35 million innocents denied standing before the law."

- A ruling by U.S. District Judge Thelton Henderson in 1996 that prohibited the state of California from implementing Proposition 209, a voter-approved initiative that prohibited preferences for women and minorities in state and local contracting, employment and education. Henderson ruled that minorities would face "irreparable harm" from the initiative. Ashcroft denounced the decision, saying: "What of the irreparable harm racial preference programs are inflicting right now?"

The initiative went into effect after Henderson's ruling was overturned by a federal appellate court and the U.S. Supreme Court let the appeals decision stand.

Ashcroft asked whether "people's lives and fortunes [have] been relinquished to renegade judges—a robed, contemptuous, intellectual elite…."

During his confirmation hearings last week, Ashcroft pulled back on some of the views he expressed as a Republican senator from Missouri—saying his role as attorney general would be different than that of a senator....

But in the 1997 lecture, Ashcroft called rulings on such issues "a page of snapshots in an album of liberties lost." He argued, "Over the past half-century, the federal courts have usurped from school boards the power to determine what a child can learn, removed from the people the ability to establish equality under the law, and challenged God's ability to mark when life begins and ends."

He said Americans can end "judicial tyranny" by "asking ourselves why modern judicial activism exists in the first place. Could it be that we have been lax in demanding that judges place our constitutional rights before their policy objectives? Could it be we have failed to reject judges who are willing to place their private preferences above the people's will?"

In the speech, given while Bill Clinton was in the White House, Ashcroft insisted, "There must be a dialogue between the president and the Senate regarding judicial nominees. And if the White House fails to solicit our advice, perhaps we should withhold our consent." ...

Source: Larry Margasak, Associated Press Online, January 22, 2001. Reprinted with permission of The Associated Press.

JOIN THE DEBATE!

CHECK YOUR UNDERSTANDING: Make sure you understand the following key points from the article; go back and review it if you missed any of them:

- Attorney General John Ashcroft previously served as U.S. Senator from Missouri.
- Senate hearings on Ashcroft's nomination for attorney general explored his views on controversial issues and how he would enforce laws and implement policy concerning those issues.
- While serving as a senator, Ashcroft strongly opposed what he called "judicial tyranny," federal judges' decisions that restricted freedom of action by governmental units, in areas such as school desegregation, abortion, and affirmative action in education.
- While serving as a senator, Ashcroft suggested a closer dialogue between the Senate and president over judicial selection.

ADDITIONAL INFORMATION: News articles don't provide all the information an informed citizen needs to know about an issue under debate. Here are some questions the article does not answer that you may need to consider in order to join the debate:

- What actions by judges would constitute judicial activism, and what actions would not?
- What is the Heritage Foundation to which Ashcroft addressed his remarks?
- What actions could an attorney general take in the judicial selection process?
- What would constitute a dialogue between the president and senators over judicial selection and judicial activism?

What other information might you want to know? Where might you gather this information? How might you evaluate the credibility of the information you gather? Is the information from a reliable source? Can you identify any potential biases?

IDENTIFYING THE ARGUMENTS: Now that you have some information on the issue, and have thought about what else you need to know, see whether you can present the arguments on both sides of the debate. Here are some ideas to get you started. We've provided one example each of "pro" and "con" arguments, but you should be able to offer others:

PRO: The Senate should refuse to confirm judicial activists. Here's why:

- The Senate has a constitutional obligation to give its advice and consent on judicial appointments and should use that role to advance democratic control of public policy by helping create a judiciary that is responsive to decisions of representative democracy.

CON: The Senate should not base its confirmation decisions on supposed predictions of judicial activism. Here's why:

- The phrase "judicial activism" has become code words for ideological liberalism, and confirmation decisions made on predictions of judicial activism simply become battles between liberal and conservative policy postures.

TAKING A POSITION AND SUPPORTING IT: After thinking about the information in the article on Attorney General Ashcroft's views on judicial activism, placing it in the broader context of democracy and ideology, and articulating the arguments in the debate, what position would you take? What information supports your position? What arguments would you use to persuade others to your side of the debate? How would you counter arguments on the other side?

five justices, a critical conservative bloc, routinely voted to strike down the constitutionality of New Deal legislation. Traditionally, such voting blocs or coalitions have centered on liberal/conservative splits on issues such as states' rights (conservatives supporting and liberals opposing), economic issues (conservatives being pro-business; liberals, pro labor), and civil liberties and civil rights (conservatives being less supportive than liberals). In death penalty cases, for example, Justices William Brennan and Thurgood Marshall (sometimes joined by John Paul Stevens) consistently voted against the imposition of capital punishment.

The Attitudinal and Strategic Models.   The attitudinal approach hypothesizes that there is a substantial link between judicial attitudes and decision making.[74] Simply stated, the attitudinal model holds that Supreme Court justices decide cases in light of the facts of the cases according to their personal preferences toward issues of public policy. Among some of the factors used to derive attitudes are a justice's party identification,[75] the party of the appointing president,[76] and the liberal/conservative leanings of a justice. Although by 1995, many judicial scholars were claiming that the attitudinal model could be used to explain all judicial decision making, by 2000 that was no longer the case. Now, several scholars who study the courts are advocating their belief that judges act strategically, meaning that they weigh and assess their actions against those of other justices to optimize the chances that their preferences will be adopted by the whole Court.[77] Moreover, this approach seeks to explain not only a justice's vote but also the range of forces such as congressional/judicial relations and judicial/executive relations that also affect the outcome of legal disputes.

Public Opinion.   Many political scientists also have examined the role of public opinion in Supreme Court decision making.[78] Not only do the justices read legal briefs and hear oral arguments, but they also read newspapers, watch television, and have some knowledge of public opinion—especially on controversial issues. According to Chief Justice William H. Rehnquist,

> Judges, so long as they are relatively normal human beings, can no more escape being influenced by public opinion in the long run than can people working at other jobs. And if a judge on coming to the bench were to decide to hermetically seal himself off from all manifestations of public opinion, he would accomplish very little; he would not be influenced by current public opinion, but instead would be influenced by the state of public opinion at the time he came to the bench.[79]

Political scientist Thomas R. Marshall has discovered substantial variation in the degree to which particular justices' decisions were congruent with public opinion.[80] Whether or not public opinion actually influences some justices, public opinion can act as a check on the power of the courts as well as an energizing factor. Activist periods on the Supreme Court have generally corresponded to periods of social or economic crisis. For example, the Marshall Court supported a strong national government, much to the chagrin of a series of pro–states' rights Democratic-Republican presidents in the early crisis-ridden years of the republic. Similarly, the Court capitulated to political pressures and public opinion when, after 1936, it reversed many of its earlier decisions that had blocked President Roosevelt's New Deal legislation.

The courts, especially the Supreme Court, also can be the direct target of public opinion. When *Webster* v. *Reproductive Health Services* (1989) was about to come before the Supreme Court, the Court was subjected to unprecedented lobbying as groups and individuals on both sides of the abortion issue marched and sent appeals to the Court. Earlier, in the fall of 1988, Justice Harry A. Blackmun, author of *Roe* v. *Wade* (1973), had warned a law school audience in a public address that he feared that the decision was in jeopardy.[81] This in itself was a highly unusual move; until recently, it was the practice of the justices never to comment on cases or the Court.

Speeches such as Blackmun's put pro-choice advocates on guard, and many took advantage of the momentum that had built around their successful campaign against the nomination of Robert H. Bork. In 1989, their forces mounted one of the largest demonstrations in the history of the United States—more than 300,000 people marched from the Mall to the Capitol, just across the street from the Supreme Court. In addition, full-page advertisements appeared in prominent newspapers, and supporters of *Roe* v. *Wade* were urged to contact members of the Court to voice their support. Justice Sandra Day O'Connor, at the time the Court's lone woman, was targeted by many who viewed her as the crucial swing justice in the case. Mail at the Court, which usually averages about 1,000 pieces a day, rose to an astronomical 46,000 pieces when *Webster* reached the Court, virtually paralyzing normal lines of communication. Several justices spoke out against this kind of "extra-judicial" communication and voiced their belief in its ineffectiveness. In *Webster* v. *Reproductive Health Services* (1989), Justice Scalia lamented in a concurrence:

> We can now look forward to at least another term with carts full of mail from the public, and streets full of demonstrators, urging us—their unelected and life tenured judges who have been awarded those extraordinary, undemocratic characteristics precisely in order that we might follow the law despite the popular will—to follow the popular will.[82]

But, the fact remains that the Court is very dependent on the public for its prestige as well as for compliance with its decisions. In times of war and other emergencies, for example, the Court frequently has decided cases in ways that commentators have attributed to the sway of public opinion and political exigencies. In *Korematsu* v. *U.S.* (1944), for example, the high Court upheld the obviously unconstitutional internment of Japanese American citizens during World War II.[83] Moreover, Chief Justice William H. Rehnquist himself has suggested that the Court's restriction on presidential authority in *Youngstown Sheet & Tube Co.* v. *Sawyer* (1952), which invalidated President Harry S Truman's seizure of the nation's steel mills,[84] was largely attributable to Truman's unpopularity and that of the Korean War.[85] As Table 10.9 reveals, the public and the Court often are in agreement on many controversial issues.

Public confidence in the Court, like other institutions of government, has ebbed and flowed. Public support for the Court was highest after the Court issued *U.S.* v. *Nixon*

TABLE 10.9 The Supreme Court and the American Public

In recent years, the Court's rulings have agreed with or diverged from public opinion on various questions, such as:

Issue	Court Decision	Public Opinion
Should TV and other recording devices be permitted in the Supreme Court?	No	Yes (59%)
Should a parent be forced to reveal the whereabouts of a child even though it could violate Fifth Amendment rights?	Yes	Maybe (50%)
Should homosexual relations between consenting adults be legal?	Yes	Maybe (50%)
Before getting an abortion, whose consent should a teenager be required to gain?	One parent	Both parents (38%) One parent (37%) Neither parent (22%)
Is the death penalty constitutional?	Yes	Yes (72% favor)
Should members of Congress be subject to term limits?	No	Yes (77% favor)

Source: Table compiled from General Social Surveys, Gallup Poll data, and a Tarrance Group Poll.

(1974).[86] At a time when Americans lost faith in the presidency, they could at least look to the Supreme Court to do the right thing. Of late, however, the Court and the judicial system as a whole have taken a beating in public confidence. In the aftermath of the O. J. Simpson trial, many white Americans faulted the judicial system. This dissatisfaction was reflected in low levels of confidence in the judicial system, although the Supreme Court enjoys greater popular support than the other two branches of government. In 2001, 66 percent of those sampled by Zogby International had a favorable opinion of the Supreme Court.[87] Still, race seems to color individuals' perceptions of the Court. Nearly 90 percent of blacks polled thought that the Court ruled politically in *Bush* v. *Gore* (2000) instead of the good of the country. Only 43 percent of the whites polled agreed with this assessment.[88]

The Supreme Court also appears to affect public opinion. Political scientists have found that the court affects public opinion when it first rules in controversial cases such as those involving abortion or capital punishment but that subsequent decisions have little effect.[89]

JUDICIAL POLICY MAKING AND IMPLEMENTATION

Clearly, the American public regards the Supreme Court as a powerful policy maker. In a 1990 poll, most respondents said they believed that the Court was more powerful than the president (31 percent versus 21 percent), and that the Court was close to being as powerful as Congress (38 percent).

All judges, whether they like it or not, make policy. In 1996, when the U.S. Supreme Court ruled that Colorado could not prevent states and local governments from extending any constitutional protections to gay, lesbian, and bisexual citizens, the justices were making policy.[90] When the Court ruled that prayer at public school ceremonies was a violation of separation of church and state, the Court made policy.[91] It is through interpreting statutes or the Constitution that federal courts, and the Supreme Court, in particular, make policy in several ways. Judges can interpret a provision of a law to cover matters not previously understood to be covered by the law, or they can "discover" new rights, such as that of privacy, from their reading of the Constitution. They also can affect lives, with the extreme being death penalty cases.

This power of the courts to make policy presents difficult questions for democratic theory, as noted by Justice Antonin Scalia in *Webster*, because democratic theorists believe that the power to make law resides only in the people or their elected representatives. Yet, court rulings, especially Supreme Court decisions, routinely affect policy far beyond the interests of the immediate parties.

Policy Making

One measure of the power of the courts and their ability to make policy is that more than one hundred federal laws have been declared unconstitutional. Although many of these laws have not been particularly significant, others have. For example, in *Immigration and Naturalization Service* v. *Chadha* (1983) (discussed in chapter 7), the Court found that legislative vetoes were unconstitutional.[92]

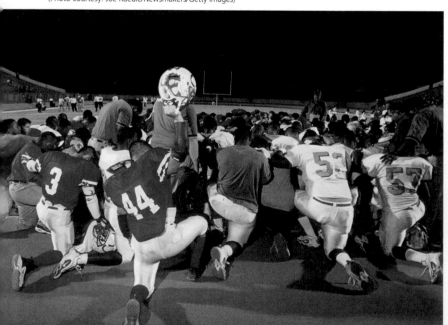

Football players at Odessa High School in Texas pray after their season opening game in September 2000. The players joined together for an unsanctioned prayer session as the Supreme Court's June ruling banning school-sanctioned pre-game prayer came into effect.

(Photo courtesy: Joe Raedle/Newsmakers/Getty Images)

Another measure of the policy-making power of the Supreme Court is its ability to overrule itself. Although the Court generally abides by the informal rule of *stare decisis*, by one count, it has overruled itself in more than 140 cases since 1810. *Brown* v. *Board of Education* (1954), for example, overruled *Plessy* v. *Ferguson* (1896), thereby reversing years of constitutional interpretation concluding that racial segregation was not a violation of the Constitution. Moreover, in the past few years, the Court has repeatedly reversed earlier decisions in the areas of criminal defendants' rights, affirmative action, and the establishment of religion, thus revealing its powerful role in determining national policy.

A measure of the growing power of the federal courts is the degree to which they now handle issues that, after *Marbury* v. *Madison* (1803), had been considered political questions more appropriately left to the other branches of government to decide. Prior to 1962, for example, the Court refused to hear cases questioning the size (and population) of congressional districts, no matter how unequal they were.[93] The boundary of a legislative district was considered a political question. Then, in 1962, writing for the Court, Justice William Brennan concluded that simply because a case involved a political issue, it did not necessarily involve a political question. This opened up the floodgates to cases involving a variety of issues that the Court formerly had declined to address.[94]

Implementing Court Decisions

President Andrew Jackson, annoyed about a particular decision handed down by the Marshall Court, is alleged to have said, "John Marshall has made his decision; now let him enforce it." Jackson's statement raises a question: How do Supreme Court rulings translate into public policy? In fact, although judicial decisions carry legal and even moral authority, all courts must rely on other units of government to carry out their directives. If the president or Congress, for example, doesn't like a particular Supreme Court ruling, they can underfund programs needed to implement a decision or seek only lax enforcement. **Judicial implementation** refers to how and whether judicial decisions are translated into actual public policies affecting more than the immediate parties to the lawsuit.

judicial implementation
Refers to how and whether judicial decisions are translated into actual public policies affecting more than the immediate parties to a lawsuit.

How well a decision is implemented often depends on how well crafted or popular it is. Hostile reaction in the South to *Brown* v. *Board of Education* (1954) and the absence of precise guidelines to implement the decision meant that the ruling went largely unenforced for years. The *Brown* experience also highlights how much the Supreme Court needs the support of both federal and state courts as well as other governmental agencies to carry out its judgments. For example, you probably graduated from high school after 1992, when the Supreme Court ruled that public middle school and high school graduations could not include a prayer, yet your own commencement ceremony may have included one.

The implementation of judicial decisions involves what political scientists call an implementing population and a consumer population.[95] The implementing population consists of those people responsible for carrying out a decision. It varies, depending on the policy and issues in question, but can include lawyers, judges, public officials, police officers and police departments, hospital administrators, government agencies, and corporations. In the case of school prayer, the implementing population could include teachers, school administrators, or the school board. The consumer population consists of those people who might be directly affected by a decision, that is, students and parents.

For effective implementation of a judicial decision, the first requirement is that the members of the implementing population must act to show that they understand the original decision. For example, the Supreme Court ruled in *Reynolds* v. *Sims* (1964) that every person should have an equally weighted vote in electing governmental representatives.[96] This "one person, one vote" decision might seem simple enough at first glance, but in practice it can be very difficult to understand. The implementing population in this case consists chiefly of state legislatures and local governments, which determine voting districts for federal, state, and local offices (see chapter 7). If a state legislature

ANALYZING VISUALS

The Supreme Court and the 2000 Presidential Election

Following the 2000 election, the Supreme Court's decision in *Bush* v. *Gore* ended the possibility of recounts in Florida and thus secured the state and its electoral votes for George W. Bush. Despite the fact that Al Gore received more than one-half million more popular votes than Bush nationwide, the Supreme Court's decision and Florida's electoral votes effectively decided the election. The bizarre 2000 presidential election was the subject of countless political cartoons. Here, Mike Luckovich offers one view. Analyze the cartoon by answering the following questions: How is George W. Bush portrayed in the two panels of the cartoon? What message is conveyed by the words in the speech bubbles in the panel? Which effect do you think the cartoonist is attempting to achieve: exaggeration, irony, or juxtaposition? How does the cartoon achieve the desired effect?

(Photo courtesy: By permission of Mike Luckovich and Creators Syndicate, Inc.)

Comparing Judiciaries

draws districts in such a way that African American voters are spread thinly across a number of separate constituencies, the chances are slim that any particular district will elect a representative who is especially sensitive to blacks' concerns. Does that violate "equal representation"? (In practice, through the early 1990s, courts and the Department of Justice intervened in many cases to ensure that elected officials would include minority representation, only ultimately to be overruled by the Supreme Court.)

The second requirement is that the implementing population must actually follow Court policy. Thus, when the Court ruled that men could not be denied admission to a state-sponsored nursing school, the implementing population—in this case, university administrators and the board of regents of the nursing school—had to enroll qualified male students.[97]

Judicial decisions are most likely to be implemented smoothly if responsibility for implementation is concentrated in the hands of a few highly visible public officials, such

THE POWERS OF THE COURTS

Judicial review is an American innovation that reflects the concern with balancing the branches of government under a system of separation of powers. It does not exist in all political systems, and how it is used varies. The United Kingdom and China occupy one extreme; these two countries do not afford the courts judicial review. In the British case, judicial review is seen as a violation of the principle of parliamentary sovereignty, that Parliament is the supreme organ of government. Consistent with this principle, the House of Lords, which combines a history of legislative and judicial functions, acts as the highest court. Judicial review is also inconsistent with socialist legality, which places the Communist Party above the law, so Chinese courts do not exercise judicial review.

A number of constitutions afford their courts limited powers of judicial review. In Russia and Mexico, the courts can overturn legislative acts but not executive actions. Even more striking in the Mexican case, the president appoints the justices on the Supreme Court of Justice. It has become accepted practice for the members of that court to resign after each presidential election to make room for the new president's appointees.

France stands out in this group because the Constitutional Council is not a court. It is a body of eminent persons appointed respectively by the president and the two houses of the legislature, and it rules only on the constitutionality of legislation currently under debate. The deliberations of the council can be seen as part of the legislative process.

Japan's experience illustrates another aspect of judicial review. Japan's 1947 constitution was written during the American occupation at the end of World War II (as was West Germany's), and judicial review was accordingly given to the courts. Yet, Japan's Supreme Court has been reluctant to use that power. In the 1950s, the court made a series of declarations stating that issues involving national defense, operations of the parliament, and the imperial household were the responsibility of the parliament and were therefore not proper concerns of the judiciary. In so doing, the Supreme Court removed itself from the most controversial issues of the time, issues that had engendered numerous lawsuits by citizens.

Malapportionment of electoral seats in the Japanese parliament illustrates the high court's reluctance to intervene in parliamentary operations. As the Japanese population shifted from the countryside to the cities in the postwar era, rural electoral districts became overrepresented at the expense of their urban counterparts. In extreme cases, voters in some districts had the equivalent of nearly five times as many votes as did citizens in certain other districts, a violation of the constitutional principle of one person, one vote. Japan's supreme court first weighed in on a suit brought after elections in 1976, ruling that although overrepresented rural districts violated the constitution, it was up to the parliament to provide a remedy. Using similar arguments, the courts have continued to issue rulings that refuse to overturn the results of parliamentary elections. In the most recent case, involving the 1998 elections to the lower house, plaintiffs sued the government, alleging that malapportionment continues despite electoral reforms enacted in the mid-1990s (which had had the support of the judiciary). Japan's supreme court again refused to nullify the election results.

Japan's case suggests that judicial activism is not necessarily part and parcel of judicial review. Whether the courts are active in shaping politics has to do with how the courts perceive their role in relation to other parts of government.

Judicial Review in Selected Countries

Country	Highest Court	Power of the Court
Canada	Supreme Court	judicial review
China	Supreme People's Court	no judicial review
Egypt	Supreme Constitutional Court	judicial review
France	Constitutional Council	limited judicial review
Germany	Federal Constitutional Court	judicial review
India	Supreme Court	no judicial review
Indonesia	Supreme Court	judicial review
Italy	Constitutional Court	judicial review
Japan	Supreme Court	judicial review
Mexico	Supreme Court of Justice	limited judicial review
Russia	Constitutional Court	limited judicial review
United Kingdom	House of Lords	no judicial review
United States	Supreme Court	judicial review

as the president or a governor. By the same token, these officials also can thwart or impede judicial intentions. Recall from chapter 6, for example, the effect of Governor Orval Faubus's initial refusal to allow black children to attend all-white public schools in Little Rock, Arkansas.

The third requirement for implementation is that the consumer population must be aware of the rights that a decision grants or denies them. Teenagers seeking an abortion, for example, are consumers of the Supreme Court's decisions on abortion. They need to know that most states require them to inform their parents of their intention to have an abortion or to get parental permission to do so. Similarly, criminal defendants and their lawyers are consumers of Court decisions and need to know, for example, the implications of recent Court decisions for evidence presented at trial.

Continuity & Change

Participation in the Judicial Process

At the time the Constitution was adopted, women and African Americans were largely excluded from the judicial process. Neither could vote, and largely on that basis, both groups were excluded from jury service. Similarly, no women or African Americans were lawyers or judges. A handful of black lawyers practiced in the North in the mid-1880s, and John Swett Rock was admitted to practice before the Supreme Court in 1861. The first women lawyers were admitted to practice in the late 1860s. When Belva Lockwood's petition to be admitted to the Supreme Court bar was denied in 1876, she energetically lobbied Congress, which passed a law requiring the Court to admit qualified women to practice. In 1879, she became the first woman admitted to practice before the Supreme Court.

Women and blacks often were excluded from jury service because many states selected jurors from those registered to vote. African Americans systematically were excluded from the voter rolls throughout the South until after passage of the Voting Rights Act of 1965. They have only recently begun to be part of the judicial system as the Voting Rights Act has been implemented. As early as 1888, however, the Supreme Court ruled that Negro citizens could not be barred from serving as jurors.[98] It was not until 1975 that the Supreme Court was to rule that states could not exclude women from jury service.[99]

As a result of the civil rights and women's rights movements detailed in chapter 6, the number as well as percentage of women and minority lawyers and judges has grown tremendously. Today, 29 percent of all lawyers are women, and 7 percent are African American, Hispanic, or Native American. Similarly, beginning with President Jimmy Carter's efforts to appoint more women and minorities to the federal courts, they have become a rising proportion of the federal judiciary. In 1993, when President Bill Clinton took office, just 10 percent of the federal bench were minori-

ties; 11 percent were women. He appointed more African Americans to judgeships than presidents serving in the last sixteen years combined. Similarly, he appointed three times as many female judges as Presidents Ronald Reagan and George Bush before him. While no state can bar African Americans or women from serving on a jury, it was not all that unusual, until recently, for lawyers to use their peremptory challenges (those made without a reason) systematically to dismiss women or African Americans if they believed that they would be more hostile jurors to their side. In two cases, however, the Supreme Court ruled that race or gender could not be used as reasons to exclude potential jurors.[100] Thus, today, juries are much more likely to be truly representative of the community and capable of offering litigants in a civil or criminal matter a jury of their peers.

Many studies of the judicial process have concluded that male and female justices decide cases differently. Women and African American judges tend to be more liberal than their white male counterparts. Thus, the presence of more women and more minority judges could lead to enhanced public support for the judiciary. The O. J. Simpson case brought home to most Americans quite vividly that whites and blacks view the judicial process quite differently, often based on group treatment within that process.

1. Will greater participation by women and minority judges affect how cases are decided and the ways that laws are interpreted?
2. As we move into a society with more minority and female jurists, lawyers, and jurors, what consequences will this have on public perceptions of the American legal system?

CAST YOUR VOTE   What changes, if any, do you foresee in the judicial process? To cast your vote, go to www.ablongman.com/oconnor

SUMMARY

The judiciary and the legal process—on both the national and state levels—are complex and play a far more important role in the setting of policy than the Framers ever envisioned. To explain the judicial process and its evolution, we have made the following points:

1. **The Constitution and the Creation of the National Judiciary**
Many of the Framers viewed the judicial branch of government as little more than a minor check on the other two branches, ignoring Anti-Federalist concerns about an unelected judiciary and its potential for tyranny.

2. **The Judiciary Act of 1789 and the Creation of the Federal Judicial System**
The Judiciary Act of 1789 established the basic federal court system we have today. It was the Marshall Court (1801–1835), however, that interpreted the Constitution to include the Court's major power, that of judicial review.

3. **The American Legal System**
Ours is a dual judicial system consisting of the federal court system and the separate judicial systems of the fifty states. In each system there are two basic types of courts: trial courts and appellate courts. Each type deals with cases involving criminal and civil law. Original jurisdiction refers to a court's ability to hear a case as a trial court; appellate jurisdiction refers to a court's ability to review cases already decided by a trial court.

4. **The Federal Court System**
The federal court system is made up of constitutional and legislative courts. Federal district courts, courts of appeals, and the Supreme Court are constitutional courts.

5. **How Federal Court Judges Are Selected**
District court and court of appeals judges are nominated by the president and subject to Senate confirmation. Senators often play a key role in recommending district court appointees from their home state. Supreme Court justices are nominated by the president and must also win Senate confirmation. Presidents use different criteria for selection, but important factors include competence, standards, ideology, rewards, pursuit of political support, religion, race, and gender.

6. **The Supreme Court Today**
Several factors go into the Court's decision to hear a case. Not only must the Court have jurisdiction, but at least four justices must vote to hear the case, and cases with certain characteristics are most likely to be heard. Once a case is set for review, briefs and *amicus curiae* briefs are filed and oral argument scheduled. The jus-

tices meet after oral argument to discuss the case, votes are taken, and opinions are written and circulated.

7. **How the Justices Vote**
Several legal and extra-legal factors affect how the Court arrives at its decision. Legal factors include judicial philosophy, the original intent of the Framers, and precedent. Extra-legal factors include public opinion and the behavioral characteristics, ideology, and strategic preferences of the justices.

8. **Judicial Policy Making and Implementation**
The Supreme Court is an important participant in the policy-making process. The process of judicial interpretation gives the Court powers never envisioned by the Framers.

KEY TERMS

amicus curiae, p. 376
appellate court, p. 355
appellate jurisdiction, p. 355
brief, p. 361
constitutional courts, p. 357
criminal law, p. 355
civil law, p. 356
in forma pauperis, p. 374
judicial activism, p. 382
judicial implementation, p. 389
judicial restraint, p. 381
judicial review, p. 350
Judiciary Act of 1789, p. 351
jurisdiction, p. 355
legislative courts, p. 357
Marbury v. *Madison* (1803), p. 354
original jurisdiction, p. 355
precedent, p. 361
Rule of Four, p. 375
solicitor general, p. 376
stare decisis, p. 361
strict constructionist, p. 368
trial court, p. 355
writ of *certiorari*, p. 374

SELECTED READINGS

Abraham, Henry J. *The Judicial Process*, 7th ed. New York: Oxford University Press, 1997.

Barrow, Deborah J., Gary Zuk, and Gerard S. Gryski, *The Federal Judiciary and Institutional Change*. Ann Arbor: University of Michigan Press, 1996.

Baum, Lawrence. *The Supreme Court*, 7th ed. Washington, DC: CQ Press, 2000.

———. *The Puzzle of Judicial Behavior*. Ann Arbor: University of Michigan Press, 1997.

Clayton, Cornell, and Howard Gillman, eds. *Supreme Court Decision-Making: New Institutionalist Approaches*. Chicago: University of Chicago Press, 1999.

Epstein, Lee, et al. *The Supreme Court Compendium:* 3rd ed. Washington, DC: Congressional Quarterly Inc., 2002.

Goldman, Sheldon. *Picking Federal Judges: Lower Court Selection from Roosevelt Through Reagan*. New Haven, CT: Yale University Press, 1997.

Hall, Kermitt L., ed. *The Oxford Companion to the Supreme Court of the United States*. New York: Oxford University Press, 1992.

Lazarus, Edward. *Closed Chambers: The First Eyewitness Account of the Epic Struggles Inside the Supreme Court*. New York: Times Books, 1998.

Maveety, Nancy. *Justice Sandra Day O'Connor: Strategist on the Supreme Court*. Lanham, MD: Rowman & Littlefield, 1996.

O'Brien, David M. *Storm Center: The Supreme Court in American Politics*, 6th ed. New York: Norton, 2002.

Perry, H. W. *Deciding to Decide: Agenda Setting in the United States Supreme Court*. Cambridge, MA: Harvard University Press, 1994.

Provine, Doris Marie. *Case Selection in the United States Supreme Court*. Chicago: University of Chicago Press, 1980.

Salokar, Rebecca Mae. *The Solicitor General: The Politics of Law*. Philadelphia: Temple University Press, 1992.

Slotnick, Elliot E., and Jennifer A. Segal. *Television News and the Supreme Court: All the News That's Fit to Air*. Boston: Cambridge University Press. 1998.

Spaeth, Howard, and Jeffrey A. Segal. *Majority Rule or Minority Will: Adherence to Precedent on the U.S. Supreme Court*. New York: Cambridge University Press, 2001.

Sunstein, Cass R. *One Case at a Time: Judicial Minimalism on the Supreme Court*, 2nd ed. Cambridge, MA: Harvard University Press, 2001.

Woodward, Bob, and Scott Armstrong. *The Brethren: Inside the Supreme Court*. New York: Avon, 1996.

NOTES

1. *Bush* v. *Palm Beach County Canvassing Board*, 531 U.S. 70 (2000).
2. 531 U.S. 98 (2000).
3. Bernard Schwartz, *The Law in America* (New York: American Heritage, 1974), 48.
4. Julius Goebel Jr., *History of the Supreme Court of the United States*, vol. 1: *Antecedents and Beginnings to 1801* (New York: Macmillan, 1971), 206.
5. 14 U.S. 304 (1816).
6. Quoted in Goebel, *History of the Supreme Court*, 280.
7. Schwartz, *The Law in America*, 11.
8. 2 Dall. 419 (1793).
9. 3 Dall. 171 (1796). In *Hylton* v. *U.S.*, the Court ruled that a congressional tax on horse-drawn carriages was an excise tax and not a direct tax and therefore it need not be apportioned evenly among the states (as direct taxes must be, according to the Constitution).
10. 5 U.S. 137 (1803).
11. 10 U.S. 87 (1810).
12. 14 U.S. 304 (1816).
13. 19 U.S. 264 (1821).
14. 17 U.S. 316 (1819).
15. 5 U.S. 137 (1803).
16. This discussion draws heavily on Jack C. Plano and Milton Greenberg, *The American Political Dictionary*, 10th ed. (Fort Worth TX: Harcourt Brace, 1996), 247.
17. David W. Neubauer, *Judicial Process: Law, Courts, and Politics* (Pacific Grove, CA: Brooks/Cole, 1991), 57.
18. Cases involving citizens from different states can be filed in state or federal court.
19. John R. Vile and Mario Perez-Reilly, "The U.S. Constitution and Judicial Qualifications: A Curious Omission," *Judicature* (December/January 1991): 198–202.
20. Sheldon Goldman and Elliot E. Slotnick, "Clinton's First Term Judiciary: Many Bridges to Cross," *Judicature* (May/June 1997): 254–55.
21. William H. Rehnquist, "The 1997 Year-End Report on the Federal Judiciary," http://www.uscourts.gov/cj97.html.
22. "Rehnquist Sees Threat to Judicial System," *Washington Post* (January 2, 1998): A21.
23. Quoted in Thomas B. Edsall, "Clinton Plans Judicial Offensive," *Washington Post* (January 16, 1998): A1.
24. Joan Biskupic, "Partisanship Delays Action on Judicial Nominees," *USA Today* (May 9, 2002): 4A.
25. Neil Lewis, "Deal Ends Impasse Over Judicial Nominees," *New York Times* (May 19, 2004): A19.
26. Quoted in Nina Totenberg, "Will Judges Be Chosen Rationally?" *Judicature* (August/September 1976): 93.
27. Bob Woodward and Scott Armstrong, *The Brethren* (New York: Simon and Schuster, 1979).
28. Quoted in Judge Irving R. Kaufman, "Charting a Judicial Pedigree," *New York Times* (January 24, 1981): A23.
29. Quoted in Lawrence Baum, *The Supreme Court*, 3rd ed. (Washington, DC: CQ Press, 1989), 108.
30. See Barbara A. Perry, *A Representative Supreme Court? The Impact of Race, Religion, and Gender on Appointments* (New York: Greenwood Press, 1991).
31. Clarence Thomas was raised a Catholic but attended an Episcopalian church at the time of his appointment, having been barred from Catholic sacraments because of his remarriage. He again, however, is attending Roman Catholic services.
32. Amy Goldstein, "Bush Set to Curb ABA's Role in Court Appointments," *Washington Post* (March 18, 2001): A2.
33. Saundra Torry, "ABA's Judicial Panel Is a Favorite Bipartisan Target," *Washington Post* (April 29, 1996): F7.
34. Lawrence M. O'Rourke, "Judicial Nomination Sparks Partisan Fight," *Sacramento Bee* (April 22, 2002): A1.
35. See Bruce Allen Murphy, *The Brandeis/Frankfurter Connection* (New York: Oxford University Press, 1982).
36. John Brigham, *The Cult of the Court* (Philadelphia: Temple University Press, 1987).
37. Stephen L. Wasby, *The Supreme Court in the Federal Judicial System*, 4th ed. (Chicago: Nelson-Hall, 1988), 194.
38. Ibid., 194.
39. Ibid., 199. Much of this change occurred as the result of an increase in state criminal cases, of which nearly 100 percent concerned constitutional questions.
40. Data compiled by authors for 2001–2002 term of the Court.
41. Neubauer, *Judicial Process*, 370.
42. William P. McLauchan "The Business of the United States Supreme Court, 1971–1983: An Analysis of Supply and Demand," paper presented at the 1986 annual meeting of the Midwest Political Science Association.
43. 498 U.S. 177 (1991).

44. Justice Stevens chooses not to join this pool. According to one former clerk, "He wanted an independent review," but Stevens examines only about 20 percent of the petitions, leaving the rest to his clerks. Tony Mauro, "Ginsburg Plunges into the Cert Pool," *Legal Times* (September 6, 1993): 8.

45. Paul Wahlbeck, James F. Spriggs II, and Lee Sigelman, "The Influence of Law Clerks on Supreme Court Opinions," paper delivered at the 1999 annual meeting of the Midwest Political Science Association.

46. Richard A. Posner, *The Federal Courts: Crisis and Reform* (Cambridge, MA: Harvard University Press, 1985), 114.

47. Edward Lazarus, *Closed Chambers: The First Eyewitness Account of the Epic Struggles Inside the Supreme Court* (New York: Random House, 1998).

48. "Retired Chief Justice Warren Attacks … Freund Study Group's Composition and Proposal," *American Bar Association Journal* 59 (July 1973): 728.

49. Kathleen Werdegar, "The Solicitor General and Administrative Due Process," *George Washington Law Review* (1967–1968): 482.

50. Rebecca Mae Salokar, *The Solicitor General: The Politics of Law* (Philadelphia: Temple University Press, 1992), 3.

51. Quoted in Elder Witt, *A Different Justice: Reagan and the Supreme Court* (Washington, DC: CQ Press, 1986), 133.

52. Lawrence Baum, *The Supreme Court*, 4th ed. (Washington, DC: CQ Press, 1992), 106.

53. Richard C. Cortner, *The Supreme Court and Civil Liberties* (Palo Alto, CA: Mayfield, 1975), vi.

54. Gregory A. Caldeira and John R. Wright, "*Amicus Curiae* Before the Supreme Court: Who Participates, When and How Much?" *Journal of Politics* 52 (August 1990): 803.

55. See also John R. Hermann, "American Indians in Court: The Burger and Rehnquist Years," Ph.D. dissertation, Emory University, 1996.

56. 347 U.S. 483 (1954); 585 U.S. 833 (1992); 510 U.S. 17 (1993).

57. 418 U.S. 683 (1974).

58. Quoted in Wasby, *The Supreme Court*, 229.

59. 478 U.S. 186 (1986).

60. "Justices' Files Show Struggle over Georgia Sodomy Case," *Atlanta Journal and Constitution* (May 25, 1993): A9. The Marshall papers also reveal politics at the *certiorari* stage.

61. 418 U.S. 683 (1974).

62. Woodward and Armstrong, *The Brethren*, 65, 288–347.

63. 492 U.S. 490 (1989).

64. *Clinton* v. *Jones*, 520 U.S. 681 (1997).

65. Stanley C. Brubaker, "Reconsidering Dworkin's Case for Judicial Activism," *Journal of Politics* 46 (1984): 504.

66. Donald L. Horowitz, *The Courts and Social Policy* (Washington, DC: Brookings Institution, 1977), 538.

67. 347 U.S. 483 (1954).

68. *Webster* v. *Reproductive Health Services*, 492 U.S. 518 (1989).

69. 505 U.S. 833 (1992).

70. Justice at Stake Survey, *Public Opinion Online*, Accession Number 0404703, Question Number 029 (October 30–November 7, 2001).

71. Ibid., Question Number 030.

72. Ibid., Question Number 043.

73. See, for example, Tracy E. George and Lee Epstein, "On the Nature of Supreme Court Decision Making," *American Political Science Review* 86 (1992): 323–37; Melinda Gann Hall and Paul Brace, "Justices' Responses to Case Facts: An Interactive Model," *American Politics Quarterly* (April 1996): 237–61; Lawrence Baum, *The Puzzle of Judicial Behavior* (Ann Arbor: University of Michigan Press, 1997); and Gregory N. Flemming, David B. Holmes, and Susan Gluck Mezey, "An Integrated Model of Privacy Decision Making in State Supreme Courts," *American Politics Quarterly* 26 (January 1998): 35–58.

74. Jeffrey A. Segal and Harold Spaeth, *The Supreme Court and the Attitudinal Model* (New York: Cambridge University Press, 1993).

75. Gerard Gryski, Eleanor C. Main, and William Dixon, "Models of State High Court Decision Making in Sex Discrimination Cases," *Journal of Politics* 48 (1986): 143–55; and C. Neal Tate and Roger Handberg, "Time Binding and Theory Building in Personal Attribute Models of Supreme Court Voting Behavior, 1916–1988," *American Political Science Review* 35 (1991): 460–80.

76. Donald R. Songer and Sue Davis, "The Impact of Party and Region on Voting Decisions in the U.S. Courts of Appeals, 1955–86," *Western Political Quarterly* 43 (1990): 830–44.

77. See, generally, Lee Epstein and Jack Knight, "Field Essay: Toward a Strategic Revolution in Judicial Politics: A Look Back, A Look Ahead," *Political Research Quarterly* 53 (September 2000): 663–76.

78. Thomas R. Marshall, "Public Opinion, Representation and the Modern Supreme Court," *American Politics Quarterly* 16 (1988): 296–316.

79. William H. Rehnquist, "Constitutional Law and Public Opinion," paper presented at Suffolk University School of Law, Boston, April 10, 1986, 40–41.

80. Thomas R. Marshall, *Public Opinion and the Supreme Court* (Boston: Unwin and Hyman, 1989).

81. Curtis J. Sitomer, "High Court to Rethink Abortion?" *Christian Science Monitor* (September 16, 1988): 3.

82. 492 U.S. 490 (1989).

83. 323 U.S. 214 (1944).

84. 343 U.S. 579 (1952).

85. The Supreme Court ruled that President Truman's seizure and operation of U.S. steel mills in the face of a strike threat were unconstitutional, because the Constitution implied no such broad executive power. See Alan Westin, *Anatomy of a Constitutional Law Case* (New York: Macmillan, 1958); and Maeva Marcus, *Truman and the Steel Seizure Case* (New York: Columbia University Press, 1977).

86. 418 U.S. 683 (1984).

87. Zogby Poll, *Public Opinion Online*, Accession Number 0388197, Question Number 001 (July 16–19, 2001).

88. Jim Cullen, "Corporations Beat Voters Again," *Progressive Populist* (February 1, 2001): 1.

89. Timothy R. Johnson and Andrew D. Martin, "The Public's Conditional Response to Supreme Court Decisions," *American Political Science Review* 92 (June 1998): 299–309.

90. *Romer* v. *Evans*, 517 U.S. 620 (1996).

91. *Lee* v. *Weisman*, 505 U.S. 577 (1992).

92. 462 U.S. 919 (1983).

93. See *Colegrove* v. *Green*, 328 U.S. 549 (1946), for example.

94. *Baker* v. *Carr*, 369 U.S. 186 (1962).

95. Charles Johnson and Bradley C. Canon, *Judicial Policies: Implementation and Impact*, 2nd ed. (Washington, DC: CQ Press, 1998), ch. 1.

96. 377 U.S. 533 (1964).

97. *Mississippi University for Women* v. *Hogan*, 458 U.S. 718 (1982).

98. *Strauder* v. *West Virginia*, 100 U.S. 303 (1888).

99. *Duren* v. *Missouri*, 439 U.S. 357 (1979).

100. *Batson* v. *Kentucky*, 476 U.S. 79 (1986) (African Americans), and *JEB* v. *Alabama*, 511 U.S. 127 (1994) (women).

Public Opinion and Political Socialization

At 2:18 A.M. on November 9, 2000, one of the major television networks made the call that George W. Bush would become the forty-third president of the United States. All the major networks quickly followed suit. But, as we all know now, that was not the end of it. As calls for recounts and litigation went on, one of the longest presidential elections in the nation's history became a field day for pollsters and their critics. Interestingly, the original call awarding Florida to Al Gore came early in the evening and was based not on actual vote totals, but on projections from the Voter News Service, an exit poll service used by a consortium of news organizations to hold down costs.

Pollsters sprang into action after Gore decided to retract his concession call he had made to Governor Bush. The Gallup Organization polled Americans to determine if they favored or opposed hand recounts in Florida. Nationwide, on November 11–12, 2000, 55 percent favored a recount, 85 percent of the Gore voters but only 20 percent of those who voted for Bush. Sixty percent believed that those votes should be included in the final totals.[1] On November 26, 2000, when asked whom they considered the real winner in Florida to be, 51 percent said Bush, but 32 percent were unsure. By then, only 15 percent thought Gore was the "real" winner. But, after the U.S. Supreme Court's decision that stopped all further vote counting, and, in essence, declared George W. Bush the winner, voters were asked on December 15–17, "Just your best guess, if the Supreme Court had allowed the vote recount to continue in Florida, who do you think would have ended up with the most votes in Florida?" Of the national sample, 46 percent said Gore; 45 percent said Bush. As in the November 11–12 poll, there was a huge chasm between Bush and Gore voters. Nearly three-quarters (74 percent) of the Gore voters continued to believe that he was the rightful winner; 77 percent of the Bush voters believed that their man would have ended up the winner. The same poll found that only 51 percent of those sampled believed that the Electoral College outcome was "fair." Again, huge gaps were evident in Bush and Gore voters. Eighty-five percent of the Bush voters thought the election outcome was fair; only 23 percent of the Gore voters did. Nationally, 68 percent of black voters believed that their votes were less likely to have been counted fairly in Florida than the votes of whites. Still, 61 percent of the public reported their belief that George W. Bush would work hard to "represent the interests of all Americans," but only 22 percent of blacks polled agreed with this statement.

Polling gives us a unique view into the psyche of Americans. Politicians read the polls, as do their advisers. George W. Bush, who prided himself on his good relations with Hispanic and African American communities in Texas, undoubtedly was shocked and troubled by the feelings of Gore supporters and African Americans. Some might even argue that the diversity of his first Cabinet appointments reflected his concern with American sentiment as he sought to lead the nation and establish the legitimacy of his victory.

Candidates, news services, and elected officials, including presidents, are not the only ones who look at poll data. Professional pollsters routinely question Americans from all walks of life about their beliefs and opinions on a variety of things from washing detergent, to favorite television and radio programs, to their attitudes about government and democracy. Americans hold myriad views on most issues, and on many political issues they often are divided nearly evenly.

In 1787, John Jay wrote glowingly of the sameness of the American people. He and the other authors of *The Federalist Papers* believed that Americans had more in common than not. Wrote Jay in *Federalist No. 2*, we are "one united people—a people descended from the same ancestors, speaking the same language, professing the same religion, attached to the same principles of government, very similar in manners and customs." Many of those who could vote were of English heritage; almost all were Christian. Moreover, most believed that certain rights—such as freedom of speech, association, and religion—were unalienable rights. Jay also spoke of shared public opinion and of the need for a national government that reflected American ideals.

(Photo courtesy: Rick McKee/The Augusta Chronicle)

Today, however, Americans are a far more heterogeneous lot. Election after election and poll after poll reveal this diversity, but nonetheless, Americans appear to agree on many things. Most want less government, particularly at the national level. So did many citizens in 1787. Most want a better nation for their children. So did the Framers. But, the Framers did not have sophisticated public opinion polls to tell them this, nor did they have national news media to tell them the results of those polls. Today, many people wonder what shapes public opinion: poll results or people's opinions? Do the polls drive public opinion, or does public opinion drive the polls?

The role of public opinion in elections as well as the making of policy are just two issues we explore in this chapter. In analyzing the role of public opinion in a democracy, the development of polling, and how politicians respond to public opinion, in this chapter we look at the following issues:

- First, we will examine the question, *what is public opinion?* We offer a simple definition and then note the role of public opinion polls in determining public perception of political issues.

- Second, we will describe *early efforts to influence and measure public opinion.* From the writing of *The Federalist Papers* to now, parties and public officials have tried to sway as well as gauge public opinion for political purposes.

- Third, we will discuss *political socialization and other factors that influence opinion* formation about political matters. We also examine the role of political ideology in public opinion formation.

- Fourth, we will examine *how Americans form political opinions.*

- Fifth, we will analyze *how we measure public opinion* and note problems with various kinds of polling techniques.

- Sixth, we will look at *how polling and public opinion affect politicians* as well as how politicians affect public opinion.

- In exploring our theme of *continuity and change,* we will look at how election forecasting has changed over time.

WHAT IS PUBLIC OPINION?

At first blush, **public opinion** seems to be a very straightforward term: It is what the public thinks about a particular issue or set of issues at a particular time. Since the 1930s, governmental decision makers have relied heavily on **public opinion polls**—interviews with samples of citizens that are used to estimate what the public is thinking. According to George Gallup, the founder of modern-day polling, polls have played a key role in defining issues of concern to the public, shaping administrative decisions, and helping "speed up the process of democracy" in the United States.[2]

According to Gallup, leaders must constantly take public opinion—no matter how short-lived—into account. Like the Jacksonians of a much earlier era, Gallup was distrustful of leaders who were not in tune with the "common man." According to Gallup:

> In a democracy we demand the views of the people be taken into account. This does not mean that leaders must follow the public's view slavishly; it does mean that they should have an available appraisal of public opinion and take some account of it in reaching their decision.[3]

Even though Gallup undoubtedly had a vested interest in fostering reliance on public opinion polls, his sentiments accurately reflect the feelings of many political thinkers concerning the role of public opinion and governance. Some, like Gallup, believe that

public opinion
What the public thinks about a particular issue or set of issues at any point in time.

public opinion polls
Interviews or surveys with samples of citizens that are used to estimate the feelings and beliefs of the entire population.

the government should do what a majority of the public wants done. Others argue that the public as a whole doesn't have consistent opinions on day-to-day issues but that subgroups within the public often hold strong views on some issues. These pluralists believe that the government must allow for the expression of these minority opinions and that democracy works best when these different voices are allowed to fight it out in the public arena.

But, as we will see later in this chapter, what the public or even subgroups think about various issues is difficult to know with certainty, simply because public opinion can change so quickly. For example, two weeks before the United States bombed Iraq in January 1991, public opinion polls revealed that only 61 percent of the American public believed that the United States should engage in combat in Iraq. One week after the invasion, however, 86 percent reported that they approved of the bombings.

EARLY EFFORTS TO INFLUENCE AND MEASURE PUBLIC OPINION

You can hardly read a newspaper or news magazine or watch television without hearing the results of the latest public opinion poll on confidence in government, the war on terrorism, the economy, or the president's performance. But, long before modern polling, politicians tried to mold and win public opinion. *The Federalist Papers* were one of the first major attempts to change public opinion—in this case, to gain public support for the newly drafted U.S. Constitution. Even prior to publication of *The Federalist Papers*, Thomas Paine's *Common Sense* and later his *Crisis* papers were distributed widely throughout the colonies to stimulate patriotic feelings and to increase public support for the Revolutionary War.

From the very early days of the republic, political leaders recognized the importance of public opinion and used all of the means at their disposal to manipulate it for political purposes. By the early 1800s, the term "public opinion" frequently was being used by the educated middle class. As more Americans became educated, they became more vocal about their opinions and were more likely to vote. A more educated, reading public led to increased demand for newspapers, which in turn provided more information about the process of government. As the United States grew, there were more elections and more opportunities for citizens to express their political opinions through the ballot box. As a result of these trends, political leaders were forced more frequently to try to gauge public opinion to remain responsive to the wishes and desires of their constituents.

An example of the power of public opinion is the public's response to the 1851–1852 serialization of Harriet Beecher Stowe's *Uncle Tom's Cabin*. This novel was one of the most powerful propaganda statements ever issued about slavery. By the time the first shots of the Civil War were fired at Fort Sumter in 1861, more than 1 million copies of the book were in print. Even though Stowe's words alone could not have caused the public outrage over slavery that contributed to northern support for the war, her book convinced the majority of the American people of the justness of the abolitionist cause and solidified public opinion in the North against slavery.

During World War I, some people argued that public opinion didn't matter at all. But, President Woodrow Wilson argued that public opinion would temper the actions of international leaders. Therefore, only eight days after the start of the war, Wilson created a Committee on Public Information. Run by a prominent journalist, the committee immediately undertook to unite U.S. public opinion behind the war effort. It used all of the tools available—pamphlets, posters, and speakers who exhorted the patrons of local movie houses during every intermission—in an effort to garner support

Timeline

War, Peace, and Public Opinion

and favorable opinion for the war. In the words of the committee's head, it was "the world's greatest adventure in advertising."[4]

After World War I, Walter Lippmann, a well-known journalist and author who was involved extensively in propaganda activities during the war, openly voiced his concerns about how easily governments could manipulate public opinion and voiced his reservations about the weight it should be given.

Governments continually try to manipulate public opinion internally and abroad. In November 2001, for example, an Office of Strategic Influence was created within the Pentagon "to oversee military propaganda and other information-related operations, which could have blurred the lines between public relations and covert actions."[5] The *New York Times* then reported that the office was planning a "disinformation campaign" to "provide news items, possibly even false ones, to foreign media organizations as part of a new effort to influence public sentiment and policy makers in both friendly and unfriendly countries."[6] Bush administration officials then announced that this action would not occur, and Secretary of Defense Donald Rumsfeld announced that the office would be closed. Still, the flap over this effort highlights how governments continue to try to manipulate information and public opinion.

Early Efforts to Measure Public Opinion

Public opinion polling as we know it today did not begin to develop until the 1930s. Earlier, in his seminal work, *Public Opinion* (1922), Lippmann wrote, "Since Public Opinion is supposed to be the prime mover in democracies, one might reasonably expect to find a vast literature [examining it]. One does not find it."[7] Researchers in a variety of disciplines, including political science, heeded Lippmann's call to learn more about public opinion. Some tried to use scientific methods to measure political thought through the use of surveys or polls. As methods for gathering and interpreting data improved, survey data began to play an increasingly important role in all walks of life, from politics to retailing.

As part of "the world's greatest adventure in advertising," the Committee on Public Information created a vast gallery of posters designed to shore up public support for World War I.
(Photo courtesy: Bettmann/Corbis)

Early Election Forecasting.   As early as 1824, one Pennsylvania newspaper tried to predict the winner of that year's presidential contest. Later, in 1883, the *Boston Globe* sent reporters to selected election precincts to poll voters as they exited voting booths, in an effort to predict the results of key contests. In 1916, *Literary Digest*, a popular magazine, began mailing survey postcards to potential voters in an effort to predict election outcomes. *Literary Digest* drew its survey sample from "every telephone book in the United States, from the rosters of clubs and associations, from city directories, lists of registered voters [and] classified mail order and occupational data."[8] Using the data it received from the millions of postcard ballots it received from all over the United States, *Literary Digest* correctly predicted every presidential election from 1920 to 1932.

Literary Digest used what were called **straw polls** to predict the popular vote in those four presidential elections. Its polling methods were hailed widely as "amazingly right" and "uncannily accurate."[9] In 1936, however, its luck ran out. *Literary Digest* predicted that Republican Alfred M. Landon would beat incumbent President Franklin D. Roosevelt by a margin of 57 percent to 43 percent of the popular vote. Roosevelt, however, won in a landslide election, receiving 62.5 percent of the popular vote and carrying all but two states.

straw polls
Unscientific surveys used to gauge public opinion on a variety of issues and policies.

Not only did advance polls in 1948 predict that Republican nominee Thomas E. Dewey would defeat Democratic incumbent Harry S Truman, but based on early and incomplete vote tallies, some newspapers' early editions published the day after the election declared Dewey the winner. Here a triumphant Truman holds aloft the *Chicago Daily Tribune*.

(Photo courtesy: Bettmann/Corbis)

What Went Wrong?   *Literary Digest* reached out to as many potential respondents as possible, with no regard for modern sampling techniques that require that respondents be selected or sampled according to strict rules of cross-sectional representation. Respondents, in essence, were like "straws in the wind," hence the term "straw polls."

Literary Digest's sample had three fatal errors. First, its sample was drawn from telephone directories and lists of automobile owners. This technique oversampled the upper middle class and the wealthy, groups heavily Republican in political orientation. Moreover, in 1936, voting polarized along class lines. Thus, the oversampling of wealthy Republicans was particularly problematic because it severely underestimated the Democratic vote.

Literary Digest's second problem was timing. Questionnaires were mailed in early September. The changes in public sentiment that occurred as the election drew closer were not measured.

Its third error occurred because of a problem we now call self-selection. Only highly motivated individuals sent back the cards—a mere 22 percent of those surveyed responded. Those who respond to mail surveys (or today, online surveys) are quite different from the general electorate; they often are wealthier and better educated and care more fervently about issues. *Literary Digest*, then, failed to observe one of the now well-known cardinal rules of survey sampling: "One cannot allow the respondents to select themselves into the sample."[10]

At least one pollster, however, correctly predicted the results of the 1936 election: George Gallup. Gallup had written his dissertation on how to measure the readership of newspapers and then expanded his methods to study public opinion about politics. He was so confident about his methods that he gave all of his newspaper clients a money-back guarantee: If his poll predictions weren't closer to the actual election out-come than those of the highly acclaimed *Literary Digest*, he would refund their money to them. The *Digest* predicted Alfred M. Landon to win; Gallup predicted Roosevelt. Although he underpredicted Roosevelt's victory by nearly 7 percent, the fact that he got the winner right was what everyone remembered, especially given *Literary Digest*'s dramatic miscalculation.

Polling Matures.   Through the late 1940s, the number of polling groups and increas-ingly sophisticated polling techniques grew by leaps and bounds as new businesses and politicians relied on the information they provide to market products and candidates. But, in 1948, the polling industry suffered a severe, although fleeting, setback when Gallup and many other pollsters incorrectly predicted that Thomas E. Dewey would defeat President Harry S Truman.

Nevertheless, as revealed in Figure 11.1, the Gallup Organization, now co-chaired by George Gallup Jr., continues to predict the winners of the presidential popular vote successfully. But, as the 2000 presidential election reminded most Americans, it is the vote in the Electoral College—not the popular vote—that ultimately counts. Thus, while George W. Bush's lead in the polls continued to shrink in the final days of 2000 polling, he won a 271–266 vote in the Electoral College. On November 7, 2000, the Gallup Organization announced what turned out to be a major understatement: The election was too close to call. Ultimately, Bush got 48 percent of the popular vote; Gore 49 percent. In 2004, although many polls were all over the place, Gallup predicted the winner while underpredicting George W. Bush's popular vote. Still, in spite of its rep-utation for accuracy, even the Gallup Organization is not immune from error, as is illustrated in Politics Now: Polling: When the Numbers Don't Add Up.

WEB EXPLORATION
To learn more about the Gallup Organization and poll trends, see
www.ablongman.com/oconnor

FIGURE 11.1   The Success of the Gallup Poll in Presidential Elections, 1936–2004

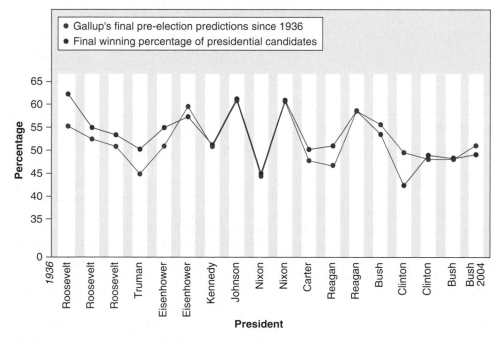

Sources: USA Today & CNN/Gallup Tracking Poll, USAtoday.com

POLLING: WHEN THE NUMBERS DON'T ADD UP

In the wake of the September 11, 2001, attacks on the World Trade Center and the Pentagon, many Americans were surprised by the reactions of numerous people in the Middle East. All of the major news networks showed images of Muslim men, women, and children in the Middle East celebrating in the streets. To many Americans and commentators, the question soon became: Do Muslims in other parts of the world really view Americans so unfavorably?

To answer that question, the Gallup Organization surveyed citizens in nine predominantly Muslim nations, asking them if they disliked Americans. The answer to the question was, "Yes, quite a bit." Relying on Gallup's findings, *USA Today* proclaimed in a page one headline, "In poll, Islamic world says Arabs not involved in 9/11."[a] The newspaper article and CNN's coverage of it were picked up by other news outlets around the United States and, indeed, the world, as it was reported that 53 percent of those polled had unfavorable views of the United States and that only 18 percent believed that Arabs carried out the September 11 attacks on the United States.

However, there were several significant problems with this poll. Three of the nine nations polled wouldn't let Gallup poll takers ask the question concerning who carried out the attacks, less than half of the world's Muslims lived in the nine nations surveyed, and Gallup didn't require respondents to be citizens of a particular nation or even Muslims to be included in its poll. In addition, too few countries were sampled and two nations were oversampled.

In response to these shoddy polling methods and the hype the poll initially got, the National Council on Public Polls (NCPP) publicly chastised *USA Today* and CNN for "the way they reported the results of the project."[b] The results reported "actually were the average for the countries surveyed regardless of the size of their populations," NCPP noted. Thus, "Kuwait, with fewer than 2 million Muslims, was treated the same as Indonesia, which has more than 200 million Muslims."[c] Reporters were sent the aggregate numbers but failed to "do the arithmetic," said one of the reporters who ran with the initial data provided by Gallup that misinterpreted the numbers.[d] Thus, not only was the poll itself flawed, but so was the way it was reported, which was partly due to the incomplete way in which Gallup released it.

The Gallup Organization is one of the most respected polling companies. Still, it made major, obvious errors in taking its poll, as well as in disseminating the results to news organizations. Not only did the poll present an inaccurate picture of public opinion, but it probably fueled anti-Muslim sentiments within the United States.

Do you recall hearing about the results of this poll? If you do, did you ever hear subsequent criticisms of it?

What lessons can be learned from this poll as well as how it was reported?

---

[a]Richard Morin and Claudia Deane, "The Poll That Didn't Add Up: Spin on Data Blurs Findings from Gallup's Muslim Survey," *Washington Post* (March 23, 2002): C1.
[b]Ibid.
[c]NCPP Report quoted in Morin and Deane, "The Poll That Didn't Add Up."
[d]Morin and Deane, "The Poll That Didn't Add Up."

POLITICAL SOCIALIZATION AND OTHER FACTORS THAT INFLUENCE OPINION FORMATION

political socialization
The process through which an individual acquires particular political orientations; the learning process by which people acquire their political beliefs and values.

Political scientists believe that many of our attitudes about issues are grounded in our political values. We learn these values through a process called **political socialization,** "the process through which an individual acquires his particular political orientations—his knowledge, feeling and evaluations regarding his political world."[14]

The American Voter was published in 1960.[11] This book "intellectually contributed the dominant model for thinking about mass attitudes and mass behavior in the social science research that followed."[12] Drawing on data from the 1952 and 1956 presidential elections, *The American Voter* showed how class coalitions, which were originally formed around social-welfare issues, led to party affiliations—the dominant force in presidential elections. This book also led directly to the "institutionalization of regular surveys of the American electorate, through a biennial series now recognized as the National Election Study (NES)."[13]

The NES surveys are conducted by social scientists at the Center for Political Studies of the Institute for Social Research at the University of Michigan. NES surveys focus only on the political attitudes and behavior of the electorate. They include questions about how respondents voted, their party affiliation, and their opinions of major political parties and candidates. NES surveys also include questions about interest in political matters and political participation, including participation in non-election-related activities, such as church attendance.

WEB EXPLORATION

To use NES data sets, go to www.ablongman.com/oconnor

NES surveys are conducted before and after midterm and presidential elections. A random sample of those eligible to vote on Election Day and living in the continental United States is used. Some of the same questions are used in each survey to compile long-term studies of the electorate to facilitate political scientists' understanding of how and why people vote and participate in politics. These studies help us understand how political values and political socialization occur.

Family, the mass media, school, and peers are often important influences or agents of political socialization. For example, try to remember your earliest memory of the president of the United States. It may have been George Bush or Bill Clinton (older students probably remember earlier presidents). What did you think of him? Of the Republican or Democratic Party? It's likely that your earliest feelings or attitudes were shaped by what your parents thought about that particular president and his party. Your experiences at school and your friends also probably influenced your political beliefs today. Similar processes also apply to your early attitudes about the flag of the United States, or the police. Other factors, too, often influence how political opinions are formed or reinforced. These include political events; the social groups you belong to, including your church; your demographic group, including race, gender, and age; and even the region of the country in which you live, all items surveyed in the NES surveys.

The Family

The influence of the family can be traced to two factors: communication and receptivity. Children, especially during their preschool years, spend tremendous amounts of time with their parents; early on they learn their parents' political values, even though these concepts may be vague. One study, for example, found that the most important visible public figures for children under the age of ten were police officers and, to a much lesser extent, the president.[15] Young children almost uniformly view both as "helpful." But, by the age of ten or eleven, children become more selective in their perceptions of the president. By this age, children raised in Democratic households are much more likely to be critical of a Republican president than are those raised in Republican households. In 1988, for example, 58 percent of children in Republican households identified themselves as Republicans, and many had developed strong positive feelings toward Ronald Reagan, the Republican president. Support for and the popularity of Ronald Reagan translated into support for the Republican Party through the 1988 presidential election and also contributed to the decline of liberal ideological self-identification of first-year college students. (See Figure 11.2.)

Political values are shaped in childhood.
(Photo courtesy: Nancy O'Connor Zeigler)

School and Peers

Researchers report mixed findings concerning the role of schools in the political socialization process, which affects how individuals perceive events. There is no question that, in elementary school, children are taught respect for their nation and its symbols. Most school days begin with the Pledge of Allegiance, and patriotism and respect for country are important, although subtle,

FIGURE 11.2   The Ideological Self-Identification of First-Year College Students

Like the general population, many students who call themselves liberals or conservatives accept only part of the liberal or conservative ideology. During the Ronald Reagan era of the 1980s, the number of people who considered themselves conservative increased. But, by far, most students continue to identify their ideology as middle of the road.

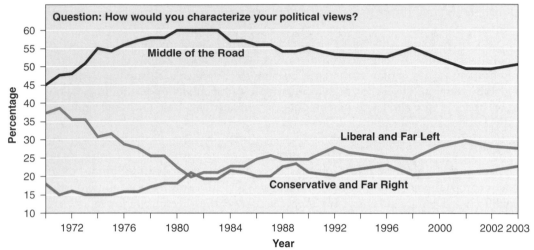

Sources: Reprinted from Howard W. Stanley and Richard G. Niemi, *Vital Statistics on American Politics, 2001–2002* (Washington, DC: CQ Press, 2001), 119. 2003 data from Cooperative Institutional Research Program (CIRP), The American Freshman: National Norms for Fall 2003 (December 2003).

components of most school curricula. The terms "flag" and the "United States" evoke very positive feelings from a majority of Americans. Support for these two icons serves the purpose of maintaining national allegiance and underlies the success of the U.S. political system in spite of frequently held negative views about Congress, or the courts, for example. In 1991, for instance, few schoolchildren were taught to question U.S. involvement in the Persian Gulf. Instead, at almost every school in the nation, children were encouraged or even required to write to service men and women stationed in the Gulf. These activities involved children in the war effort and underscored public support for the war.

In 1994, Kids Voting USA was launched nationwide. This civic education project was designed to have a short-term impact on student political awareness and lead to a higher voter turnout among parents. In 2002, Congress appropriated nearly $400,000 to Kids Voting USA to further teach "young people about the value of voting and democratic participation."[16] Over 2 million students participate annually, and adult turnout frequently goes up 3 to 5 percent in communities where the program operates.[17] Thus, a school-based program actually uses children to affect their parents.

The *Weekly Reader*, read by elementary students nationwide, not only attempts to present young students with newsworthy stories, but also tries to foster political awareness and a sense of civic duty. Each presidential election, moreover, the *Weekly Reader* conducts a nationwide student election, which except for 1992, has been surprisingly accurate. The 1992 results were thrown off because students liked the alligator pointer that Ross Perot used to point to key ideas on charts!

A child's peers—that is, children about the same age as a young person—also seem to have an important effect on the socialization process. Whereas parental influences are greatest from birth to age five, a child's peer group becomes increasingly important as the child gets older, especially as he or she gets into middle school or high school.[18] Groups such as the Girl Scouts of the USA recognize this and are trying to influence more young women to participate in, and have a positive view of, politics. The Girl Scouts' new Ms. President merit badge engages girls as young as five to learn "herstory" and to emulate women leaders.

High schools also can be important agents of political socialization. They continue the elementary school tradition of building good citizens and often reinforce textbook learning with trips to the state or national capital. They also offer courses on current

To heighten young girls' interest in politics, the Girl Scouts of the USA, in conjunction with The White House Project, has created a Ms. President merit badge.

(Photo courtesy: Girl Scouts of the USA and The White House Project)

U.S. affairs. Many high schools impose a compulsory community service requirement, which some studies report positively affects later political participation.[19] Although the formal education of many people in the United States ends with high school, research shows that better-informed citizens vote more often as adults. Therefore, presentation of civic information is especially critical at the high school level.

At the college level, teaching style often changes. Many college courses and texts like this one are designed in part to provide you with the information necessary to think critically about issues of major political consequence. It is common in college for students to be called on to question the appropriateness of certain political actions or to discuss underlying reasons for certain political or policy decisions. Therefore, most researchers believe that college has a liberalizing effect on students. Since the 1920s, studies have shown, students become more liberal each year they are in college. As we show in Figure 11.2, however, students entering college in the 1980s were more conservative than in past years. The 1992 and 1996 victories of Bill Clinton and his equally youthful running mate Al Gore, who went out of their way to woo the youth vote, probably contributed to the small bump in the liberal ideological identification of first-year college students.

The Mass Media

The media today are taking on a growing role as a socialization agent. Adult Americans spend nearly thirty hours a week in front of their television sets; children spend even more.[20] Television has a tremendous impact on how people view politics, government, and politicians. TV talk shows, talk radio, and now even online newsletters and magazines are important sources of information about politics for many, yet the information that people get from these sources often is skewed. In 2000, one study estimated that 51 percent of all adults regularly got information about the election or candidates from alternative sources such as *Saturday Night Live*, MTV, or Comedy Central. For those younger than thirty, that figure soared to 79 percent.[21]

Visual Literacy

The Media and the American Public

Television can serve to enlighten voters and encourage voter turnout. For example, MTV began coverage of presidential campaigns in 1992 and had reporters traveling with both major candidates to heighten young people's awareness of the stakes in the campaign. Its "Choose or Lose" campaign conducted during recent presidential elections was designed to change the abysmal turnout rates of young voters. When an MTV poll found only 33 percent of those aged eighteen to twenty-four planned to vote, it stepped up its efforts.[22]

Over the years, more and more Americans have turned away from traditional sources of news to different outlets. As one analyst put it, "Letterman, Jay Leno, Oprah Winfrey, *Saturday Night Live*, and MTV became the deliverers of the news mainstream Americans want."[23] Several studies have found that the average media sound bite in the 2000 election was just seven seconds, three less than in 1998, which gives the electorate little opportunity to evaluate a candidate. In sharp contrast, George W. Bush got thirteen minutes of airtime on Letterman, and the public saw him unfiltered by packaging. When he went on popular programs hosted by Oprah Winfrey and Regis Philbin, he got to discuss his political and personal views, and his poll ratings went up.[24]

Colin Powell's ninety-minute appearance before a live audience on MTV is another example of how an administration can get its message out and sway public opinion. Powell's views on the conflict in Afghanistan were broadcast to over 370 million viewers worldwide.[25]

All of the major candidates in the 2000 and 2004 presidential elections also attempted to use another form of media to sway and inform voters: the Internet, a form of campaigning that was considered new in 1996. Each presidential and most other major and minor campaigns launched their own Internet sites, and all of the major networks and newspapers had their own Internet sites reporting on the election. There was even an Internet Alley at the Republican and Democratic National Conventions. On Election Night, millions of hits were counted on election-related news sites as voters logged on to get the most up-to-date coverage. In fact, in 2000, the outcome of the

The Amish are a religious group who eschew involvement in national politics.
(Photo courtesy: Dan Loh/AP/Wide World Photos)

presidential election was first called online, prompting other forms of media to follow quickly. One poll conducted after the 2000 election found that one in three voters followed the campaign online—three times the number who did in 1996. Nationwide, 11 percent of voters listed the Internet as their major source of information about campaign news; an additional 19 percent reported that they got some of their information about the election online.[26] Forty-two percent of voters under age thirty reported that the Internet was their major source of information about the campaign.

Social Groups

Group effects, that is, certain characteristics that allow persons to be lumped into categories, also affect the development and continuity of political beliefs and opinions. Among the most important of these are religion, education level, income, and race. More recently, researchers have learned that gender and age are becoming increasingly important determinants of public opinion, especially on certain issues. Region, too, while not a social group, per se, appears to influence political beliefs and political socialization.

Religion.   Today, religion plays a very important role in the life of Americans and is credited by many as a source of political mobilization.[27] Numerous scholars have found that organized religion provides both organizational and psychological resources to adherents whose effects differ on black and white Americans.[28] Although only one in five citizens in 1776 belonged to a church or synagogue, today 67 percent of all Americans report such membership. Moreover, almost all Americans (94 percent) believe in God and 86 percent report that religion is "very" (64 percent) or "fairly" important in their own lives.[29] Nearly half of all Americans attend church regularly, and 61 percent believe that religion "can answer all or most of today's problems."[30]

More specifically, in 2000, 56 percent of Americans identified themselves as Protestant, 27 percent as Catholic, 2 percent as Jewish, and 7 percent as other. Only 8 percent claimed to have no religious affiliation. Over the years, analysts have found continuing ideological differences among these groups, with Protestants being the most conservative and Jews the most liberal, as shown in Figure 11.3. Still, a rising number

FIGURE 11.3   The Ideological Self-Identification of Protestants, Catholics, and Jews

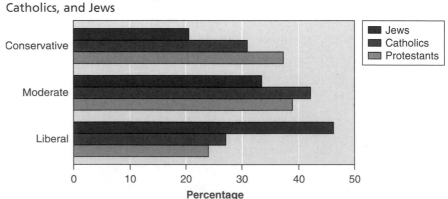

Source: Data compiled by Sarah Brewer from the General Social Survey Cumulative File, 1999.

408

of people report that they don't attend any religious services—14 percent of the population. Thus, it is important to remember that although religious preferences and participation affect personal political views and participation, a growing segment of the population is not swayed by a religious affiliation.[31]

Shared religious attitudes tend to affect voting and stances on particular issues. Catholics tend to vote Democratic more than do Protestants, and they tend to vote for other Catholics. For example, in 1960, Catholics overwhelmingly cast their ballots for John F. Kennedy, who became the first Catholic president. Catholics as a group also favor aid to parochial schools, and many fundamentalist Protestants support organized prayer in public schools. Seventy-eight percent of white evangelical protestants voted Republican in the 2004 elections, contributing substantially to George W. Bush's re-election.[32] Jews, in contrast, tend to be more liberal and to vote more Democratic.[33] In 2004, for example, Senator John Kerry and his running mate Senator John Edwards captured 74 percent of the Jewish vote. That proportion of the Jewish vote, however, was down slightly from the vote captured by Al Gore in 2000. Figure 11.4 reveals other voting differences based on the factors discussed in this chapter.

Recent research by political scientists reveals that a new religious cleavage is emerging, as defined by the "orthodoxy of religious beliefs, affiliations, and practices on religious behavior." Thus, conservative evangelical Christians are becoming increasingly Republican and more likely than less religious Protestants to vote for Republican candidates.[34]

Vice presidential candidate Joe Lieberman (D–CT) became the first Jewish candidate to run for national office. Al Gore and Lieberman were defeated by George W. Bush and Dick Cheney in one of the closest presidential elections in American history. In 2004, Lieberman made a short, unsuccessful bid to be the Democratic Party nominee.

(Photo courtesy: Arnold Gold/New Haven Register/The Image Works)

Race and Ethnicity. Differences in political socialization of African Americans and whites appear at a very early age. Young black children, for example, generally show very positive feelings about the national political community, but this attachment lessens considerably over time. Black children fail to hold the president in the esteem accorded him by white children; indeed, older African American children in the 1960s viewed the government primarily in terms of the U.S. Supreme Court.[35] These differences continue through adulthood.

During the O.J. Simpson trial, public opinion poll after public opinion poll revealed in stark numbers the immense racial divide that continues to exist in the nation. Blacks distrust governmental institutions far more than do whites, and are much more likely to question police actions. Not surprisingly, then, while a majority of whites believed that Simpson was guilty, a majority of blacks believed that he was innocent.

Race and ethnicity are exceptionally important factors in elections and in the study of public opinion. The direction and intensity of African American opinion on a variety of hot-button issues often are quite different from those of whites. As revealed in Analyzing Visuals: Racial and Ethnic Attitudes on Selected Issues, whites are much more likely to believe that police treat all races fairly than are blacks or Hispanics. Likewise, differences can be seen in other issue areas, including abortion.[36] Other issues, however, such as school vouchers, show much smaller racial dimensions.

Hispanics, Asians/Pacific Islanders, and Native Americans are other identifiable ethnic minorities in the United States who often respond differently to issues than do whites. Generally, Hispanics and Native Americans hold similar opinions on many issues, largely because so many of them have low incomes and find themselves targets of discrimination. Government sponsored health insurance for the working poor is a hot-button issue

FIGURE 11.4   Group-Identified Voting Differences in the 2004 Presidential Election

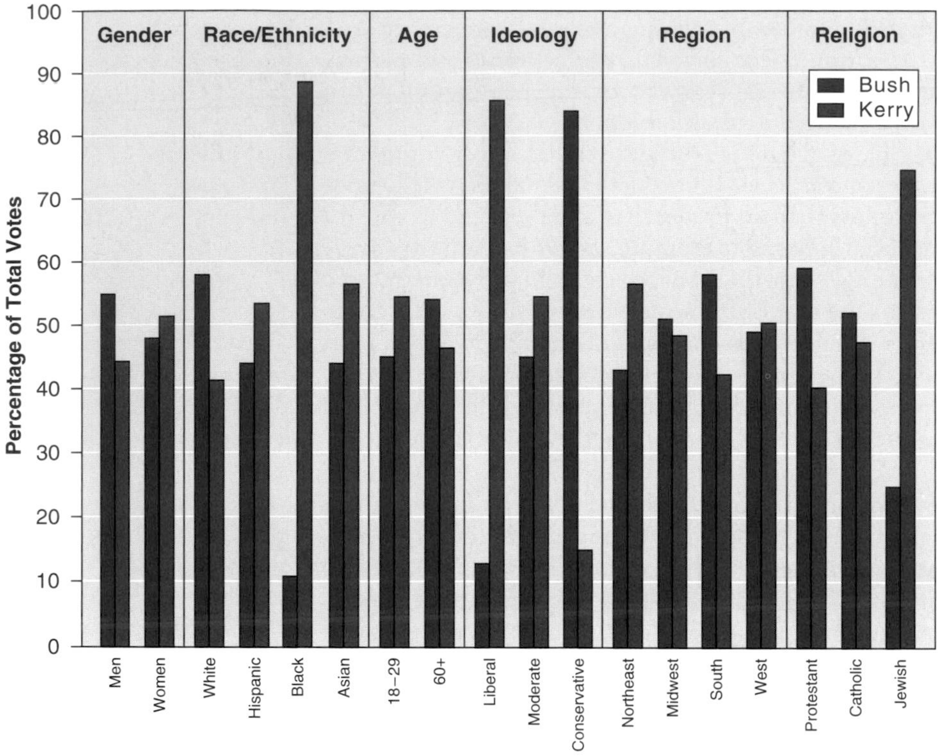

Source: CNN Exit Polls, www.cnn.com/election/2004/pages/results/states/us/p/00/epolls.0/html

with Hispanic voters, with 94 percent favoring it.[37] Unlike many other Americans, they also favor bilingual education and liberalized immigration policies.[38]

Within the Hispanic community, however, existing divisions often depend on national origin. Generally, Cuban Americans who cluster in Florida and in the Miami–Dade County area, in particular, are more likely to be conservative. They fled from communism and Fidel Castro in Cuba, and they generally vote Republican. In contrast, Hispanics of Mexican origin who vote in California, New Mexico, Arizona, Texas, or Colorado, are more likely to vote Democratic.[39]

On issues directly affecting a particular group, sentiments often are markedly different. As our opening vignette illustrated, black voters perceived the fairness of Florida vote counting procedures very differently from whites. Similarly, public sentiment in the Cuban community about the proper fate of Elian Gonzalez was quite different from that in the rest of the nation. Although 56 percent of the American public believed that Elian should be returned to his father in Cuba,[40] nearly 90 percent of the Cuban community in Miami believed that he should be allowed to stay in the United States.[41]

Gender.   Poll after poll reveals that women hold very different opinions from men on a variety of issues, as shown in Analyzing Visuals: Gender Differences on Political Issues. From the time that the earliest public opinion polls were taken, women have been found to hold more negative views about war and military intervention than do men, and more strongly positive attitudes about issues touching on social-welfare concerns, such as education, juvenile justice, capital punishment, and the environment. Some suggest that women's more "nurturing" nature and their prominent role as moth-

ANALYZING VISUALS

Racial and Ethnic Attitudes on Selected Issues

Political opinions held by racial and ethnic groups in the United States differ on many issues. In the figure below, the opinions of whites, blacks, and Hispanics are compared on a number of political issues. After studying the bar graph and the material in this chapter on race, ethnicity, and public opinion, answer the following critical thinking questions: What do you observe about the differences and similarities in opinions among the different groups? On which issues do blacks and whites, Hispanics and blacks, and Hispanics and whites have similar or diverging opinions? What factors might explain these similarities and differences?

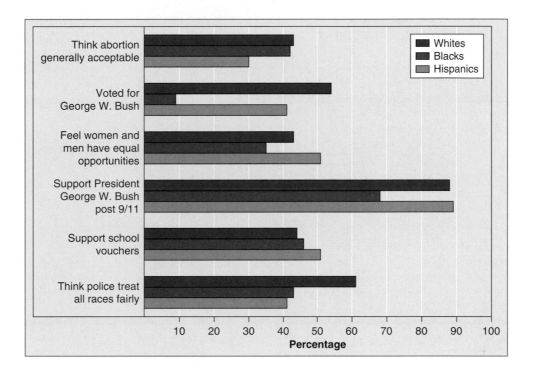

Source: http://nationaljournal.qpass.com/members/polltrack/2001/issues/01education.htm

ers lead women to have more liberal attitudes on issues affecting the family or the safety of their children. Research by political scientists, however, finds no support for a maternal explanation.[42]

These differences on political issues have often translated into substantial gaps in the way women and men vote. Women, for example, are more likely to be Democrats, and they often provide Democratic candidates with their margin of victory.[43]

The historic gender gap in views on military issues began to disappear in the late 1990s. In 1999, public opinion polls on Kosovo showed no more than a ten-point gap. One NBC News/*Wall Street Journal* poll showed only a four-point difference. Experts offer several reasons for this shrinking gap, including the increased participation of women in the workforce and in the military, the "sanitized nature of much of the war footage" shown on TV, and the humanitarian reasons offered for NATO involvement in Yugoslavia.[44]

The terrorist attacks of September 11, 2001, appear to have erased the gender gap concerning military affairs, at least in the short run. Although only 24 percent of the women polled (versus 41 percent of the men) favored an increase in defense

ANALYZING VISUALS

Gender Differences on Political Issues

Public opinion polls reveal that men and women hold different views on a number of political issues. Yet, on some political issues, little difference is evident. In the table below, the opinions of men and women on several political issues are compared. After studying the table and reading the material in this chapter on the impact of gender on public opinion, answer the following critical thinking questions: On which issues are the opinions of men and women the least different? What, if anything, do these issues have in common? On which issues are the opinions of men and women most different? What, if anything, do these issues have in common? How would you explain the results?

	Males (%)	Females (%)
Support initial sending of troops to Gulf (1991)	62	41
Support return of Elian Gonzalez to his father (2000)	63	32
Believe crime influences the way they live (2000)	47	66
Favor the death penalty (2000)	72	60
Favor gun control legislation (2000)	55	77
Believe health care important in presidential vote (2000)	76	89
Approve George W. Bush's handling of the presidency (2001)	54	44
Approve of George W. Bush's handling of the presidency (2002)	85	83
Believe war on terrorism will spread (2002)	24	74
Have a favorable view of Saudi Arabia (2002)	42	23

Sources: Data from CNN/*USA Today* (December 28–30, 1994); Roper Center *Public Opinion Online,* 1998; Gallup Organization, *WashingtonPost*/ABC Poll (May 7–10, 2000): Harris Poll February 22–March 3, 2001); Harris Interactive 2001, 2002, CBS News; and http://national journal.qpass.com/members/polltrack/2001/issues.htm.

spending before the attacks, 47 percent voiced their support post-9/11 (versus 53 percent of the men).[45] Still, far more women than men fear the effects of terrorism—41 versus 17 percent—a difference that undoubtedly colors their perceptions of many political phenomena. Interestingly, young women (aged eighteen to twenty-five), while following the news about terrorism more than do young men (73 percent versus 51 percent), don't follow news about the war in Afghanistan as closely (27 versus 39 percent).[46]

Age. As Americans live longer, senior citizens are becoming a potent political force. In states such as Florida, to which many northern retirees have flocked seeking relief from cold winters and high taxes, the elderly have voted as a bloc to defeat school tax increases and to pass tax breaks for themselves. As a group, senior citizens are much more likely to favor an increased governmental role in the area of medical insurance and to oppose any cuts in Social Security benefits.

In the future, the "graying of America" will have major social and political consequences. As we discuss in chapter 13, the elderly under age seventy vote in much larger numbers than do their younger counterparts. Moreover, the fastest-growing age group in the United States is that of citizens over the age of sixty-five. Thus, not only are there more people in this category, but they are more likely to be registered to vote, and often vote conservatively.

The elderly continue to be a potent voting bloc with high concern about particular issues, but the youth vote that was mobilized in 1992 appears to have burned itself out by 1996. Turnout among those eighteen to twenty-one dropped from 38 to 31 percent; for those twenty-one to twenty-four, the drop was from 45 to 33 percent.[47] Young voters are least likely to follow campaigns; only 15 percent of those under thirty years of age report that they followed campaigns "very closely." For those over sixty years of age, the figure was 43 percent.[48] One 1996 poll found that only 28 percent of young people thought that "keeping up with politics" was "important"; in 1966, 57 percent believed it was important.[49]

Age seems to have a decided effect on one's view of the proper role of government, with older people continuing to be affected by having lived through the Depression and World War II. One political scientist predicts that as Baby Boomers age, the age gap in political beliefs about political issues, especially governmental programs, will increase.[50] Young people, for example, resist higher taxes to fund Medicare, while the elderly resist all efforts to limit it or Social Security.

As highlighted in Figure 11.5, young people are far more likely to see government as too controlling, and they follow local politics much less than do their older counterparts.

Region.   Regional and sectional differences have been important factors in the development and maintenance of public opinion and political beliefs since colonial times. As the United States developed into a major industrial nation, waves of immigrants with different religious traditions and customs entered the United States and often settled in areas they viewed as hospitable to their way of life. For example, thousands of Scandinavians settled in cold, snowy, rural Minnesota, and many Irish settled in the urban centers of the Northeast, as did many Italians and Jews. All brought with them unique views about many issues, as well as about the role of government. Many of these regional differences continue to affect public opinion today and sometimes result in conflict at the national level.

Recall, for example, that during the Constitutional Convention most Southerners staunchly advocated a weak national government. Nearly a hundred years later, the Civil War was fought in part because of basic differences in philosophy toward government (states' rights in the South versus national rights in the North). As we know from the results of modern political polling, the South has continued to lag behind the rest of

FIGURE 11.5   Comparing Three Age Cohorts on Political Issues, 2002

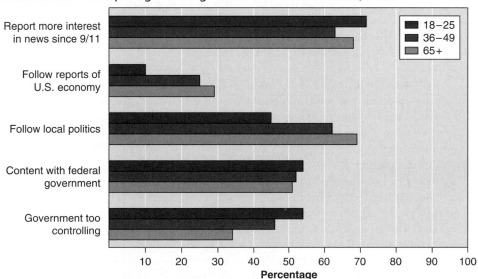

Source: Center for Information and Research on Civil Learning and Engagement.

the nation on support for civil rights, while continuing to favor return of power to the states at the expense of the national government.

The South also is much more religious than the rest of the nation, as well as more Protestant. Sixty-four percent of the South is Protestant (versus 39 percent for the rest of the nation), and 45 percent identify themselves as born-again Christians. Nearly half of all Southerners believe that "the United States is a Christian country, and the government should make laws to keep it that way."[51] Church attendance is highest in the South, where 38 percent report weekly visits. In contrast, only 26 percent of those living in the Midwest and 19 percent of those residing in the West go to church or synagogue on a weekly basis.[52] Given the South's higher churchgoing rates, it is not surprising that the Christian Coalition has been very successful at mobilizing voters in that region.

Southerners also are much more supportive of a strong national defense. They accounted for 41 percent of the troops in the Persian Gulf in the early days of that war, even though they made up only 28 percent of the general population.

The West, too, now appears different from other sections of the nation. Some people have moved there to avoid city life; other residents have an anti-government bias. Many who have sought refuge there are staunchly against any governmental action, especially on the national level. One need only look at a map of the vote distribution in the 2004 presidential election to see stark differences in candidate appeal. John Kerry carried 60 percent of big city voters. In contrast, George W. Bush carried 59 percent of the rural voters.[53] Republicans won the South and the West; Democrats carried the Northeast and West Coast.

The Impact of Events

Key political events play a very important role in a person's political socialization. You probably have some professors who remember what they were doing on the day that President John F. Kennedy was killed—November 22, 1963. This dramatic event is indelibly etched in the minds of virtually all people who were old enough to be aware of it. Similarly, most college students today remember where they were when they heard of Princess Diana's death, or when they learned about the Oklahoma City bombing. Americans' collective memory of many events is fading, as is revealed in Table 11.1, but prior to September 11, 2001, John F. Kennedy's assassination was the most compelling. No one old enough to have been aware of the events will ever forget where they were when they first heard about or saw the attacks on the World Trade Center and the Pentagon. These attacks on American shores brought out a profound sense of patriotism. American flags were displayed from windows, doors, balconies, and cars. For many Americans, the attacks were life-changing political events.

One has to go back to 1974 to find a political event that similarly affected what people thought about the political process. President Richard M. Nixon's resignation in 1974 made a particular impression on young people, who were forced to realize that their government was not always right or honest. This general distrust of politicians was reignited during Kenneth Starr's investigation of President Bill Clinton and his subsequent impeachment.

One problem in discussing political socialization is that many of the major studies on this topic were conducted in the aftermath of Watergate and other crucial events, including the civil rights movement and the Vietnam War, all of which produced a marked increase in Americans' distrust of government. The findings reported in Table 1.3, in chapter 1, reveal the dramatic drop-off of trust in government that began in the mid-1960s and continued through the election of Ronald Reagan in 1980. In a study of Boston children conducted in the aftermath of the Watergate scandal, for

TABLE 11.1	America's Collective Memory			

Memories often define generations, and the memories (and experiencing) of key events often affect how individuals perceive other political events. Today, nearly all Americans know what they were doing when they first heard of the 9/11 attacks.

Early Events Fading		Events Most Compelling	
Percentage of public who remember hearing the news of:		Percentage who remember what they were doing when they heard the news of:[a]	
Princess Diana's death	87	John F. Kennedy's assassination	90
Oklahoma City bombing	86	Princess Diana's death	87
Challenger explosion	78	Oklahoma City bombing	86
Beginning of Gulf War	75	Attack on Pearl Harbor	85
Reagan shot by Hinckley	67	Challenger explosion	82
Fall of Berlin Wall	59	Armstrong walking on moon	80
Armstrong walking on moon	54	End of World War II	79
John F. Kennedy's assassination	53	Beginning of Gulf War	76
Nixon's resignation	53	Reagan shot by Hinckley	72
Martin Luther King assassination	43	Franklin Roosevelt's death	71
Tiananmen Square massacre	41	Nixon's resignation	67
End of World War II	21	Martin Luther King assassination	67
Attack on Pearl Harbor	18	Fall of Berlin Wall	60
Franklin Roosevelt's death	17	N. Korea invading S. Korea	43
N. Korea invading S. Korea	15	Tiananmen Square massacre	42
Paris falling to the Nazis	7	Paris falling to the Nazis	38
1929 stock market crash	4	1929 stock market crash	38

[a]Based on those who are old enough to remember.

Source: "Public Perspectives on the American Century," 1999 Millennium Survey 1: Section 4, http://people-press.org/reports/display.ph3?PageID=283

example, one political scientist found that children's perception of the president went from that of a benevolent to a "malevolent" leader.[54] These findings are indicative of the low confidence most Americans had in government in the aftermath of Watergate and President Richard M. Nixon's ultimate resignation from office to avoid impeachment. Interestingly, confidence in government remained high during the Clinton scandal, although still down from the Watergate years. But, the issues surrounding the Clinton impeachment raised concerns about their impact on young people, especially Generation Y. Some studies show that their views toward the president and political affairs are significantly more negative than ever seen before—including during and immediately after Watergate.[55]

The tragedy of September 11, 2001, at least in the short term, had the opposite effect of the Watergate and Clinton scandals. They were scandals, and the public reacted negatively toward those in power. In contrast, in times of war, the public generally rallies round the flag, which happened after the 1991 invasion of Iraq as well as during the effort to remove the Taliban from Afghanistan in 2001. Children nationwide collected pennies as part of the Pennies for Patriots program announced by President George W. Bush, raised funds for the Red Cross, made flags, and expressed their patriotism in numerous ways, as did their parents and the rest of the nation.

Political Ideology and Public Opinion About Government

As discussed in chapter 1, an individual's coherent set of values and beliefs about the purpose and scope of government is called his or her **political ideology**. Americans' attachment to strong ideological positions has varied over time. In sharp contrast to spur-of-the-moment responses, these sets of values, which are often greatly affected by political socialization, can prompt citizens to favor a certain set of policy programs and adopt views about the proper role of government in the policy process.

political ideology
An individual's coherent set of values and beliefs about the purpose and scope of government.

WEB EXPLORATION
For the most recent
Roper Center polls, see
www.ablongman.com/oconnor

Visual Literacy

**Who Are
Liberals and
Conservatives?
What's the
Difference?**

Conservatives generally are likely to support smaller, less activist governments, limited social welfare programs, and reduced government regulation of business. In contrast, liberals generally believe that the national government has an important role to play in a wide array of areas, including helping the poor and the disadvantaged. Unlike most conservatives, they generally favor activist governments. Most Americans today, however, identify themselves as moderates.

Political scientists and politicians often talk in terms of conservative and liberal ideologies, and most Americans believe that they hold a political ideology. When asked by the Roper Center, most Americans (37 percent) responded that their political beliefs were moderate, although a substantial number called themselves conservatives (34 percent), with only 20 percent describing themselves as liberal. Nine percent of those polled "didn't know" or refused to label themselves.

HOW WE FORM POLITICAL OPINIONS

Many of us hold opinions on a wide range of political issues, and our ideas can be traced to our social group and the different experiences each of us has had. Some individuals (called ideologues) think about politics and vote strictly on the basis of liberal or conservative ideology. Others use the party label. Most people, however, do neither. Most people filter their ideas about politics through the factors discussed above, but they are also influenced by: (1) personal benefits; (2) political knowledge; and, (3) cues from various leaders or opinion makers.

Personal Benefits

Participation

**Are You
a Liberal or a
Conservative?**

Most polls reveal that Americans are growing more and more "I" centered. This perspective often leads people to choose policies that best benefit them personally. You've probably heard the adage, "People vote with their pocketbooks." Taxpayers generally favor lower taxes, hence the popularity of candidates pledging "No new taxes." Similarly, an elderly person is likely to support Social Security increases, while a member of Generation X, worried about the continued stability of the Social Security program, is not likely to be very supportive of federal retirement programs. Those born in Generation Y appear even less willing to support retirement programs. Similarly, an African American is likely to support strong civil rights laws and affirmative action programs, while a majority of nonminorities will not.

Some government policies, however, don't really affect us individually. Legalized prostitution and the death penalty, for example, are often perceived as moral issues that directly affect few citizens. Individuals' attitudes on these issues often are based on underlying values they have acquired through the years.

When we are faced with policies that don't affect us personally and don't involve moral issues, we often have difficulty forming an opinion. Foreign policy is an area in which this phenomenon is especially true. Most Americans often know little of the world around them. Unless moral issues such as ethnic cleansing in Kosovo are involved, American public opinion is likely to be volatile in the wake of any new information.

Political Knowledge

Political participation and political knowledge "affect each other reciprocally"—an increase in one will increase the other.[56] Knowledge about the political system is essential to "successful political engagement," which, in turn, teaches citizens about politics and "increases attentiveness to public affairs."[57]

Americans enjoy a relatively high literacy rate, and most Americans (82 percent) graduate from high school. Most Americans, moreover, have access to a range of higher education opportunities. In spite of that access to education, however, Americans' level of knowledge about history and politics is quite low. A 2002 Department of Education report found that most high school seniors had a poor grasp of history and that levels of knowledge haven't changed in nearly a decade.[58] Fifty-two percent didn't know that Russia was an ally of the U.S. in World War II, and 63 percent didn't know that Richard M. Nixon opened diplomatic relations with China. According to the Department of Education, today's college graduates have less civic knowledge than high school graduates did fifty years ago.[59]

The lack of historical perspective hurts many Americans' understanding of current political events. Moreover, knowledge about current leaders or routine facts that everyone should know often is as abysmal as the answers given in Jay Leno's "Jaywalking" segments on the *Tonight Show*. As revealed in Table 11.2, in 1996, the vast majority of Americans could not identify the chief justice of the United States. Less than half could name both senators from their state or the party with the most members in the Senate. In 2002, only 51 percent of people aged eighteen to twenty-five could correctly identify Dick Cheney as the vice president.[60]

Americans also don't appear to know much about foreign policy, and some would argue that many Americans are geographically illiterate. One Gallup study done in 1988, for example, found that 75 percent of all Americans were unable to locate the Persian Gulf on a map. Two-thirds couldn't find Vietnam. Americans aged eighteen to twenty-four scored the lowest, with two-thirds not being able to point to France on an outline map.[61]

There are also significant gender differences in political knowledge. One 2000 survey found that only 27 percent of the women polled knew that Republicans controlled the House and the Senate; 46 percent of the men did. Another 1996 study found that 75 percent of the women scored well below men on political information questions.[62] Moreover, in a survey one month before the 2000 presidential election, MTV found that one quarter of those aged eighteen to twenty-four could not name both presidential candidates; 70 percent couldn't name the running mates.[63] Knowledge, however, is often related to interest. Given both major candidates' emphasis on issues of concern to the elderly, such as Social Security, Medicare, and prescription drugs, it may be that young people, turned off, tuned out in 2000.

In 1925, Walter Lippmann critiqued the American democratic experience and highlighted the large but limited role the population plays. Citizens, said Lippmann, cannot know everything about candidates and issues but they can, and often do, know enough to impose their views and values as to the general direction the nation should take.[64] This generalized information often stands in contrast and counterbalance to the views held by more knowledgeable political elites "inside the Beltway."

As early as 1966, V. O. Key Jr. argued in his book *The Responsible Electorate* that voters "are not fools."[65] Since then, many political scientists have argued that generalizable knowledge is enough to make democracy work. Research, for example, shows citizens' perception "of the policy stands of parties and candidates were considerably more clear and accurate when the stands themselves were more distinct: in the highly ideological election of 1964, for example, as opposed to that of 1956, or in the primaries rather than the general election of 1968."[66] In elections with sharper contrasts between candidates, voters also seem to pay more attention to issues and to have more highly structured liberal–conservative belief systems.[67] In addition, the use of more sophisticated analytical methods involving perceived issue distances between candidates and voters reveals more issue voting, in general, than previously had been discovered.[68]

WEB EXPLORATION

To test your own political knowledge, go to www.ablongman.com/oconnor

TABLE 11.2   Americans' Political Knowledge

Percentage	unable to identify
Number of Senators	52
Representative in the House	53
Who has the power to declare war	60
Chief Justice of the United States	69
Source of the phrase "government of the people, by the people, for the people"	78

Sources: "A Nation that is in the Dark," *San Diego Union-Tribune* (November 3, 2002): E3; John Wilkens, "America Faces a Crisis of Apathy," *San Diego Union-Tribune* (November 3, 2002); E3.

Cues from Leaders

Low levels of knowledge can lead to rapid opinion shifts on issues. The ebb and flow of popular opinion can be affected dramatically (some might say "manipulated") by political leaders. Given the visibility of political leaders and their access to the media, it is easy to see the important role they play in influencing public opinion. Political leaders, members of the news media, and a host of other experts have regular opportunities to influence public opinion because of the lack of deep conviction with which most Americans hold many of their political beliefs.[69]

The president, especially, is often in a position to mold public opinion through effective use of the "bully pulpit," as discussed in chapter 8.[70] Political scientist John E. Mueller concludes, in fact, that there is a group of citizens—called followers—who are inclined to rally to the support of the president no matter what he does.[71]

According to Mueller, the president's strength, especially in the area of foreign affairs (where public information is lowest), derives from the "majesty" of his office and his singular position as head of state. Recognizing this phenomenon, presidents often take to television in an effort to drum up support for their programs.[72] President George W. Bush, borrowing a page from Presidents Ronald Reagan and Bill Clinton, clearly realizes the importance of mobilizing public opinion. He took his case for his tax cut, as well as his plans for the war in Afganistan, directly to the public, urging citizens to support his efforts.

There is always a question, however, of who is leading, the president or the people? Bill Clinton, for example, often was criticized for appearing to govern by public opinion poll. Still, according to one report, the Republican National Committee was on track to pay President George W. Bush's pollsters more than 1 million dollars in 2002 to let him know the pulse of the people.[73]

Peter Steiner

HOW WE MEASURE PUBLIC OPINION

Public officials at all levels use a variety of measures as indicators of public opinion to guide their policy decisions. These measures include election results; the number of telephone calls, faxes, or e-mail messages received pro and con on any particular issue; letters to the editor in hometown newspapers; and the size of demonstrations or marches. But, the most commonly relied-on measure of public sentiment continues to be the public opinion survey, more popularly called a public opinion poll. Opinion polls are big news—especially during an election year. However, even the most accurate polls can be very deceiving. In the past sixty years, polls have improved so much that we may be dazzled—and fooled— by their apparent statistical precision.

Polls often can mislead. "Slight differences in question wording or in the placement of the questions in the interview can have profound consequences," says David Moore, vice president of the Gallup Organization. He points out that poll findings "are very much influenced by the polling process itself."[74] Consider, for instance, what researchers discovered in a 1985 national poll: Only 19 percent of the public agreed that the country wasn't spending enough money on "welfare." When the question contained the phrase "assistance to the poor" instead of "welfare," affirmative responses jumped to 63 percent. That 44 percent shift explains how people can make opposite—and equally vehement— claims about what "polls show." The truth is that, at best, polls offer us flat snapshots of a three-dimensional world.

Traditional Public Opinion Polls

The polling process most often begins when someone says, "Let's find out about X and Y." Potential candidates for local office may want to know how many people have heard of them (the device used to find out is called a name recognition survey). Better-known candidates contemplating running for higher office might want to know how they might fare against an incumbent. Polls also can be used to gauge how effective particular ads are or if a candidate is being well (or negatively) perceived by the public. Political scientists have found that public opinion polls are critical to successful presidents and their staffs, who use polls to "create favorable legislative environment(s) to pass the presidential agenda, to win reelection, and to be judged favorably by history."[75] These polls and others have several key phases, including: (1) determining the content and phrasing the questions; (2) selecting the sample; and, (3) contacting respondents.

Determining the Content and Phrasing the Questions. Once a candidate, politician, or news organization decides to use a poll to measure the public's attitudes, special care has to be taken in constructing the questions to be asked. For example, if your professor asked you, "Do you think my grading procedures are fair?" rather than asking, "In general, how fair do you think the grading is in your American Politics course?" you might give a slightly different answer. The wording of the first question tends to put you on the spot and personalize the grading style; the second question is more neutral. Even more obvious differences appear in the real world of polling, especially when interested groups want a poll to yield particular results. Responses to highly emotional issues such as abortion, busing, and affirmative action often are skewed depending on the wording of a particular question.

Selecting the Sample. Once the decision is made to take a poll, pollsters must determine the universe, or the entire group whose attitudes they wish to measure. This universe could be all Americans, all voters, all city residents, all women, or all Republicans. In a perfect world, each individual would be asked to give an opinion, but such comprehensive polling is not practical. Consequently, pollsters take a sample of the universe in which they are interested. One way to obtain this sample is by **random sampling.** This method of selection gives each potential voter or adult the same chance of being selected. In theory, this sounds good, but it is actually impossible to achieve because no one has lists of every person in any group. This is why the method of poll taking is extremely important in determining the validity and reliability of the results.

Nonstratified Sampling. *Literary Digest* polls suffered from an oversampling of voters whose names were drawn from telephone directories and car registrations; this group was hardly representative of the general electorate in the midst of the Depression. Thus, the use of a nonstratified or nonrepresentative sample led to results that could not be used to predict accurately how the electorate would vote.

Perhaps the most common form of unrepresentative sampling is the kind of straw poll used today by local television news programs or online services. Many have regular features asking viewers to call in their sentiments (with one phone number for pro and another for con) or asking those logged on to indicate their preferences. The results of these unscientific polls are not very accurate because those who feel very strongly about the issue often repeatedly call in to vote more than once. One American Online straw poll from late September 2004, for example, recorded a slightly different outcome from the general presidential election. George W. Bush led the field with 65 percent of the vote, followed by Democratic Party candidate John Kerry at 35 percent. Green Party candidate Ralph Nader drew only one percent of the vote. At the same time, a Zogby online poll showed 46 percent for Bush, 43 percent for Kerry and Nader with one percent of the vote.

Simulation
You Are a
Polling
Consultant

random sampling
A method of poll selection that gives each person in a group the same chance of being selected.

WEB EXPLORATION
To see an example of a nonstratified poll, go to www.ablongman.com/oconnor

A typical polling instrument.

(Photo courtesy: Council for Marketing and Opinion Research)

Model Introduction

Hello, my name is _____ and I'm calling from (company). Today/Tonight we are calling to gather opinions regarding (general subject), and are not selling anything. This study will take approximately (length) and may be monitored (and recorded) for quality purposes. We would appreciate your time. May I include your opinions?

Closing

- At the conclusion of the survey, thank the respondent for his/her time.

- Express the desired intention that the respondent had a positive survey experience and will be willing to participate in future market research projects.

- Remind the respondent that his/her opinions do count.

MODEL CLOSING

Thank you for your time and cooperation. I hope this experience was a pleasant one and you will participate in other market research projects in the future. Please remember that your opinion counts! Have a good day/evening.

Alternative: Participate in collecting respondent satisfaction data to improve survey quality.

Thank you very much for taking part in this survey. Because consumers like you are such a valued part of what we do, I'd like you to think about the survey you just participated in. On a scale from 1 to 10 where ten means "it was a good use of my time", and one means "it was not a good use of my time", which number between 1 and 10 best describes how you feel about your experience today? That's all the questions I have. Please remember that your opinion counts! Have a good day/evening.

A more reliable method is a quota sample, in which pollsters draw their sample based on known statistics. Assume that a citywide survey has been commissioned. If the city is 30 percent African American, 15 percent Hispanic, and 55 percent white, interviewers will use those statistics to determine the proportion of particular groups to be questioned. These kinds of surveys often are conducted in local shopping malls. Perhaps you've wondered why the man or woman with the clipboard has let you pass by but has stopped the next shopper. Now you know it is likely that you did not match the subject profile that the interviewer was instructed to locate. Although this kind of sampling technique can produce relatively accurate results, the degree of accuracy falls short of those surveys based on probability samples. Moreover, these surveys generally oversample the visible population, such as shoppers, while neglecting the stay-at-homes who may be glued to the Home Shopping Network or prefer to buy online.

stratified sampling

A variation of random sampling; census data are used to divide a country into four sampling regions. Sets of counties and standard metropolitan statistical areas are then randomly selected in proportion to the total national population.

Stratified Sampling.   Most national surveys and commercial polls use samples of 1,000 to 1,500 individuals and use a variation of the random sampling method called **stratified sampling.** Simple random, nonstratified samples aren't very useful at predicting voting because they may undersample (or oversample) key populations that are not likely or particularly likely to vote. To avoid these problems, reputable polling organizations use stratified sampling based on census data that provide the number of residences in an area and their location. Researchers divide the country into four sampling regions. They then randomly select a set of counties and standard metropolitan statistical areas in proportion to the total national population. Once certain primary sampling units are selected, they are often used for many years, because it is cheaper for polling companies to train interviewers to work in fixed areas.

About twenty respondents from each primary sampling unit are selected to be interviewed. Generally four or five city blocks or areas are selected, and then four or five target families from each district are used. Large, sophisticated surveys like the National Election Study and General Social Survey, which produce the data commonly used by political scientists, attempt to sample from lists of persons living in each household.

Doonesbury

BY GARRY TRUDEAU

The key to the success of the stratified sampling method is not to let people volunteer to be interviewed—volunteers as a group often have different opinions from those who don't volunteer.

Stratified sampling (the most rigorous sampling technique) generally is not used by those who do surveys reported in the *New York Times* and *USA Today* or on network news programs. Instead, those organizations or pollsters working for them randomly survey every tenth, hundredth, or thousandth person or household. If those individuals are not at home, they go to the home or apartment next door.

Contacting Respondents.   After selecting the methodology to conduct the poll, the next question is how to contact those to be surveyed. Television stations often ask people to call in, and some surveyors hit the streets. Telephone polls, however, are becoming the most frequently used mechanism by which to gauge the temper of the electorate.

Telephone Polls.   The most common form of telephone polls are random-digit dialing surveys, in which a computer randomly selects telephone numbers to be dialed. Because it is estimated that as many as 95 percent of the American public have telephones in their homes, samples selected in this manner are likely to be fairly representative.

In spite of some problems (such as the fact that many people don't want to be bothered, especially at dinner time), most polls done for newspapers and news magazines are conducted this way. Most polls, in fact, contain language similar to that used by the Gallup Organization in reporting its survey results:

SPEED BUMP   **Dave Coverly**

> The current results are based on telephone interviews with a randomly selected national sample of 1,008 adults, conducted ____ to ____. For results based on a sample of this size, one can say with 95 percent confidence that the error attributable to sampling and other random effects could be plus or minus 3 percentage points. In addition to sampling error, question wording and practical difficulties in conducting surveys can introduce error or bias into the findings of public opinion polls.[76]

In-Person Polls.   Individual, in-person interviews are conducted by some groups, such as the University of Michigan for the National Election Study. Some analysts favor such in-person surveys, but others argue that the unintended influence of the questioner or pollster is an important source of errors. How the pollster dresses, relates to the person being interviewed, and even asks the questions can affect responses. (Some of these factors, such as tone of voice, can also affect the results of telephone surveys.)

Political Polls

As polling has become increasingly sophisticated and networks, newspapers, and magazines compete with each other to report the most up-to-the-minute changes in public opinion on issues or politicians, new types of polls have been suggested and put into use. Each type of poll has contributed much to our knowledge of public opinion and its role in the political process.

Push Polls.   All good polls for political candidates contain push questions. These questions produce information that helps campaigns judge their own strengths and weaknesses as well as those of their opponents.[77] They might, for example, ask if you would be more likely to vote for candidate X if you knew that candidate was a strong environmentalist. These kinds of questions are accepted as an essential part of any poll, but there are concerns as to where to draw the line. Questions that go over the line result in **push polls,** which are telephone polls with an ulterior motive. Push polls are designed to give respondents some negative or even untruthful information about a candidate's opponent in order to "push" them away from that candidate toward the one paying for the poll. Reputable polling firms eschew these tactics. A typical push poll might ask a question such as "If you knew Candidate X beat his wife, would you vote for him?" Push poll takers don't even bother to record the responses because they are irrelevant. The questions are designed simply to push as many voters away from a candidate as possible. Push poll calls are made to thousands; legitimate polls survey much smaller samples.

Tracking Polls.   During the 1992 presidential elections, **tracking polls,** which were taken on a daily basis by some news organizations, were first introduced to allow presidential candidates to monitor short-term campaign developments and the effects of their campaign strategies. Tracking polls involve small samples (usually of registered voters contacted at certain times of day) and are conducted every twenty-four hours. They usually are combined with some kind of a moving statistical average to boost the sample size and therefore the statistical reliability.[78] As revealed in Figure 11.6, the 2004 tracking polls, in spite of receiving significant criticism for their performance in 2000, performed quite well and predicted a Bush victory.

push polls
"Polls" taken for the purpose of providing information on an opponent that would lead respondents to vote against that candidate.

tracking polls
Continuous surveys that enable a campaign to chart its daily rise or fall in support.

FIGURE 11.6   A Daily Tracking Poll for the 2004 Presidential Election

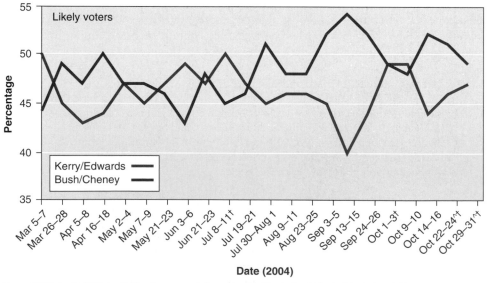

Source: USA Today & CNN/Gallop Poll Results, www.usatoday.com/news/politicselections/nation/polls/usatodaypolls.htm.

Exit Polls.   **Exit polls** are polls conducted at selected polling places on Election Day. Generally, large news organizations send pollsters to selected precincts to sample every tenth voter as he or she emerges from the polling place. The results of these polls are used to help the television networks predict the outcome of key races, often just a few minutes after the polls close in a particular state and generally before voters in other areas—sometimes in a later time zone—have cast their ballots. They also provide an independent assessment of why voters supported particular candidates "free from the spin that managers and candidates alike place on the 'meaning of an election.' "[79]

In 1980, President Jimmy Carter's own polling and the results of network exit polls led him to concede defeat three hours before the polls closed on the West Coast. Many Democratic Party officials and candidates criticized Carter and network predictions for harming their chances at victories, arguing that with the presidential election already "called," voters were unlikely to go to the polls. In the aftermath of that controversy, all networks agreed not to predict the results of presidential contests until all polling places were closed. Exit polls continue to be problematic. In 2000, they led newscasters to inaccurately call Florida in the Gore column as discussed below. In 2004, midafternoon exit poll results were leaked on the Internet making many believe a Kerry victory was at hand. Whether Republicans voted later, Democrats were more willing to be polled, or for other reasons, the exit polls were wrong.[80]

exit polls
Polls conducted at selected polling places on Election Day.

Shortcomings of Polling

In 1990, the networks consolidated their polling operations under the umbrella of Voter News Service (VNS), which was a major cost-saving measure for all involved. But, the construction of a single questionnaire and one data set meant that problems could arise, as was evident in the 2000 Election Night projections. In 1992, the VNS data significantly overpredicted the support for Republican candidate Patrick Buchanan in the New Hampshire primary, and showed President George Bush to be in much more trouble than he was. Armed with these erroneous survey results, commentator after commentator (all relying on the same data) predicted a narrow victory for Bush—who actually went on to win by a healthy sixteen-point margin. Nevertheless, "[M]any Americans went to bed believing that the president had been badly damaged.[81] This kind of reporting based on inaccurate polls can skew the rest of a campaign, particularly in an era when campaigns are viewed as horse races and everyone wants to know who's winning and by how much. VNS also provided all of the major networks with exit poll data in 2000 that prompted them to call Florida, and then the entire presidential contest, too early.

According to a confidential report of VNS, its polling was plagued with errors all night long in Florida. The polling firm had no reliable way of estimating the number of Florida's absentee ballots, which were nearly double the expected number. It estimated that the absentee ballots would make up 7.2 percent of all of the ballots cast; instead, they were 12 percent. VNS also misprojected how many of those absentee votes would go to Governor Bush, estimating 22.4 percent when it actually was 23.7. "That mistake alone accounted for 1.3 percentage points of the 7.3 percent lead that Gore was projected to hold at 7:50 that night."[82]

Prior to the election, VNS failed to conduct any telephone polling in Florida as it had done in traditionally absentee-heavy states such as California, Oregon, and Washington, in an effort to estimate the magnitude or direction of absentee voting. Essentially, it overlooked the politics of the state where the Republican Party was headed by the brother of one of the candidates. Phone polling is labor intensive and expensive, and according to VNS, its budget simply didn't allow it to sample every state.

An additional part of Gore's projected lead—2.8 percent—was inflated because of results from forty-five sample polls. This error, while in the range of acceptable error for exit polls, added to the inaccuracy of VNS's actions on Election Night. The rest of its error—3.2 percent—came from the exit poll model that it used. Instead of relying on the vote model of 1996 Republican presidential candidate Bob Dole, VNS used the 1998 Florida gubernatorial vote for Jeb Bush as an indicator of how his older brother would fare in 2000. Critics charge that since more voters turn out in presidential elections, 1996 should have been used as a baseline instead of 1998 when comparisons were being made to project the winner in 2000. Finally, to correct exit poll errors, VNS turned to actual vote data. At 7:50 P.M., the Tampa exit poll was off by 16 percentage points, but no actual votes were yet reported there or in Miami. Thus, VNS was unable to modify any of its exit poll errors in Tampa and Miami, where its polls were the most inaccurate.

It got worse in 2002. VNS, in spite of pledges to improve its act, announced midday that there would be no exit poll data revealed, leaving the networks with no data to project winners or discuss turnout or issues. Finally, in January 2003, VNS was disbanded. In November 2004, the major networks and the Associated Press again joined in a new polling consortium, National Election Pool. Its data, like that of VNS, also was riddled with errors. Its subscribers were quite unhappy, and on Election Day remained in doubt given their poor track record in predicting winners in the last three national elections.

Sampling Error.   The accuracy of any poll depends on the quality of the sample that was drawn. Small samples, if properly drawn, can be very accurate if each unit in the universe has an equal opportunity to be sampled. If a pollster, for example, fails to sample certain populations, his or her results may reflect that shortcoming. Often the opinions of the poor and homeless are underrepresented because insufficient attention is given to making certain that these groups are representatively sampled. In the case of tracking polls, if you choose to sample only on weekends or from 5 P.M. to 9 P.M., you may get more Republicans, who are less likely to have jobs that require them to work in the evening or on weekends. There comes a point in sampling, however, where increases in the size of the sample have little effect on a reduction of the **sampling error** (also called **margin of error**), the difference between the actual universe and the sample.

All polls contain errors. Standard samples of approximately 1,000 to 1,500 individuals provide fairly good estimates of actual behavior (in the case of voting, for example). Typically, the margin of error in a sample of 1,500 will be about 3 percent. If you ask 1,500 people "Do you like ice cream?" and 52 percent say "yes" and 48 percent say "no," the results are too close to tell whether more people like ice cream than not. Why? Because the margin of error implies that somewhere between 55 percent (52 + 3) and 49 percent (52 − 3) of the people like ice cream, while between 51 percent (48 + 3) and 45 percent (48 − 3) do not. The margin of error in a close election makes predictions very difficult.

The introduction of tracking polls into the 1992 election scenario brought more criticism of political polling. According to one political scientist, their advent "played upon the worst tendencies of journalists to focus almost entirely upon who is ahead and by how much."[83] Moreover, the one-day polls were fraught with other problems. Sampling is conducted with limited or no callbacks and may be skewed because certain groups may not be at home at certain times. The 1992 CNN/Gallup poll, for example, used two different time periods—weekdays 5 P.M. to 9 P.M. and all day on the weekends. Midweek surveys produced candidate distributions that disproportionately favored George Bush over Bill Clinton, while weekend surveys showed the reverse.

This problem was exacerbated by two shifts in the way data were collected. First, pollsters moved from surveying "registered" voters to surveying "likely" voters[84]; second, Gallup changed the way it allocated "undecided" voters. All of these methodologies created the impression that the race was closer than it was and gave a boost to Bush. Thus, some argue that the danger of tracking polls needs to be highlighted and discussed before more emphasis is placed on them.

sampling error or margin of error
A measure of the accuracy of a public opinion poll.

PUBLIC OPINION ON THREATS TO PERSONAL SAFETY

The American media have repeated frequently the comment that the United States and the world have changed since the September 11, 2001, terrorist attacks on the World Trade Center and the Pentagon. That changes have occurred is undoubtedly true, but the extent to which people perceive such events as affecting their lives differs greatly from country to country.

In early 2002, the University of British Columbia and the *Asahi Shimbun* (one of Japan's largest daily newspapers) conducted a public opinion survey in the eleven countries listed in the table below. Respondents were asked a series of questions about their perceptions of world safety, including what they considered the one threat or danger that was of most concern to them at the time of the survey. While at least two-thirds of respondents in every country thought the world had gotten more dangerous in the previous twelve months (which included the 9/11 attacks), they ranged widely on the threats

they thought likeliest to occur. Criminal violence was by far the most serious perceived threat in every country but Japan and South Korea, both of which are relatively crime-free societies.

Although citizens in the developed countries allied with the United States tended to be more concerned about the threat of terrorism than citizens in other parts of the world, they did not perceive it as an overwhelming priority. Almost twice as many Japanese respondents thought natural disaster was more likely than a terrorist attack. Japanese, Russians, Germans, and Britons were also more worried about the possibility of nuclear war than they were about terrorism. India's high response rate for terrorism—highest of the eleven countries surveyed, including the United States—can be attributed to ongoing communal violence between the Hindu majority and Muslim minority, in which, incidentally, Muslims have largely been the victims of violence by Hindus. Based on these poll results, it seems clear that, given a range of possible threats to life and limb, most people see terrorism as one of a variety threats, but not the most immediate concern.

Citizen Attitudes About Likely Threats and Dangers (percentage mentioning a specific danger)

Country	Nuclear War	Terrorism	Natural Disaster	Criminal Violence	Health Threats	Economic Threats
Brazil	1	1	3	84	4	3
Canada	4	8	17	24	14	9
France	4	10	14	46	8	2
Germany	10	9	8	14	3	13
India	5	19	13	24	5	21
Japan	19	12	24	6	12	20
Russia	15	13	10	22	9	7
South Africa	2	4	7	47	22	6
South Korea	6	3	21	6	14	14
United Kingdom	10	6	13	26	6	2
United States	5	15	13	22	9	7
Average	9	11	14	23	9	7

Source: *Asahi Shimbun* (May 17, 2002): 15. Reprinted by permission of The Asahi Shimbun Company.

Limited Respondent Options. Polls can be inaccurate when they limit responses. If you are asked, "How do you like this class?" and are given only like or dislike options, your full sentiments may not be tapped if you like the class very much or feel only so-so about it.

Lack of Information. Public opinion polls may also be off when they attempt to gauge attitudes about issues that some or even many individuals don't care about or about which the public has little information. For example, until the 2000 election, few Americans cared about the elimination of the Electoral College. If a representative sample were polled prior to 2000, many would answer pro or con without having given

Comparing
Public
Opinion

Join the Debate

SHOULD POLITICAL AND LEGISLATIVE STRATEGIES BE DRIVEN BY PUBLIC OPINION?

Democratic theory holds that governments should be responsive to the popular will. We want our public policy to reflect the opinions of the public, rather than just the values of the elite. Yet, one of the criticisms we often have of our political leaders is that they make up their policy positions depending on what public opinion surveys show is popular, with little regard for whether the idea in question is sound public policy. What is the proper balance between a government that is responsive to public opinion and government leaders who pursue policies that may not be popular at the time but may prove beneficial in the long run?

In the context of elections, campaign advisers often advise candidates to take positions that "poll well"—i.e., that the majority agree with in public opinion surveys. In the modern era, of course, many candidates are incumbent officeholders, and campaign advice becomes not only

advice about what position to state on an issue, but also what policy decisions to make as officeholders.

In the 2002 election cycle, in the wake of the Enron and WorldCom–MCI bankruptcies, indictments of some of their officials, and accounting industry scandals, public opinion surveys showed the public to be very concerned about corporate fraud issues and the close relationship between political leaders and corporations. Read and think about the following excerpted 2002 news article on guidance that public opinion analysts provided to Republican politicians concerning their policy stance on corporate fraud issues. Then, join the debate. Should political and legislative strategies be driven by public opinion? Consider the debating points and questions posed at the end of this feature, and sharpen your own arguments for the position you find most viable.

GOP Pollsters Warn of Economic News

By David Espo

WASHINGTON (AP)—Corporate wrongdoing and economic jitters have soured the national mood noticeably in recent weeks, according to prominent Republican pollsters who warn of "GOP turnout problems" in midterm elections if the trend persists.

"The bottom has fallen out on the mood of the country," Public Opinion Strategies cautioned party strategists in and out of Congress in recent days. Based on soundings taken recently in Georgia, the pollsters concluded that "WorldCom's announcement may have been the straw

that broke the camel's back," a reference to the major telecommunications company's disclosure last month that it had erroneously accounted for nearly $4 billion in expenses. WorldCom late Sunday filed for protection under federal bankruptcy statutes....

Republicans and Democrats alike have scrambled for political gain in the wake of WorldCom's announcement, and the polling report urged the GOP to be aggressive in doing so.

"The issue agenda seems tilted slightly toward the Democrats as our party struggles to right the economy and get a handle on the corporate corruption issue. Voters attitudes toward corporate offenders are hostile. Legislation punishing wrongdoers can't be too tough," Public Opinion Strategies

said in a report obtained by The Associated Press. It advised Republicans: "Get out in front of this issue now. Don't wait for the Democrats to tee off on you." ...

At the same time, polling shows that the percentage of Americans who believe the country has moved off in the wrong direction is at 52 percent, up from 39 percent as recently as May. The percentage of people who said the country is moving in the right direction was pegged at 37 percent, down from 50 percent in May. At the same time, President Bush's approval ratings have slipped.

"If the negative mood of the country is sustained over the next few months, look for GOP turnout problems," the pollsters cautioned. "'Wrong track' voters always turn out at higher rates than those believing the country is headed in the right direction."

Republicans were cautioned that senior citizens, who often vote in disproportionately large numbers in midterm elections, also show increasing concern about the direction of the country. And among female voters who swing between the parties, the economy was not the only issue, the report said. "Of the dozens of issues we tested among swing women voters, getting tough on HMOs and prescription drugs for vulnerable seniors top the list."

Democrats have attacked Republicans vigorously in recent weeks on the issue of corporate scandals, attempting to depict the GOP as captive to special interests. For their part, Senate Republicans responded by swinging behind a series of tough new penalties for corporate wrong-doers, and helping pass legislation 97–0. In the House, GOP leaders moved swiftly to bring their own bill to the floor for a vote to toughen some penalties even further....

Source: David Espo, Associated Press Online, July 23, 2002. Reprinted with permission of The Associated Press.

JOIN THE DEBATE!

CHECK YOUR UNDERSTANDING: Make sure you understand the following key points from the article; go back and review it if you missed any of them:

- Public Opinion Strategies is a polling firm that advises Republicans.
- In 2002, WorldCom disclosed that it had used improper accounting in reporting $4 billion worth of activity, and filed for bankruptcy protection.
- Public Opinion Strategies reported that potential voters were leaning Democratic for the 2002 elections as a response to the corporate corruption scandals.
- Public Opinion Strategies advised its Republican clients that the negative mood of voters could dampen Republican turnout.
- Public Opinion Strategies reported voters' views that possible legislation punishing corporate wrongdoers "can't be too tough," and that Republicans should embrace that philosophy.

ADDITIONAL INFORMATION: News articles don't provide all the information an informed citizen needs to know about an issue under debate. Here are some questions the article does not answer that you may need to consider in order to join the debate:

- How influential are partisan public opinion analysts with officeholders?
- How does advice from public opinion analysts compare with promises made in party platforms?
- Did these scandals adversely affect the GOP in the 2002 races?

What other information might you want to know? Where might you gather this information? How might you evaluate the credibility of the information you gather? Is the information from a reliable source? Can you identify any potential biases?

IDENTIFYING THE ARGUMENTS: Now that you have some information on the issue, and have thought about what else you need to know, see whether you can present the arguments on both sides of the debate. Here are some ideas to get you started. We've provided one example each of "pro" and "con" arguments, but you should be able to offer others:

PRO: Policymakers should be responsive to public opinion as expressed in polls. Here's why:

- Modern public opinion survey methodology is sophisticated and accurate, and using such information is a good way for an elected representative to serve as a delegate of the voters' wishes.

CON: Political and legislative strategies should not be driven tightly by public opinion. Here's why:

- Public opinion is measured in such a way that it discourages deliberation; policy that is driven by snap judgment answers to difficult questions is not likely to be as good as policy that considers public opinion, but places greater emphasis on deliberation over the issues.

TAKING A POSITION AND SUPPORTING IT: After thinking about the information in the article on pollsters' advice to Republican clients, placing it in the broader context of public opinion in a democracy, and articulating the arguments in the debate, what position would you take? What information supports your position? What arguments would you use to persuade others to your side of the debate? How would you counter arguments on the other side?

much consideration to the question. Of course, all of this changed in the wake of public attention to the Electoral College after the 2000 presidential election.

Most academic public opinion research organizations, such as the National Election Study, use some kind of filter question that first asks respondents whether or not they have thought about the question. These screening procedures generally allow surveyors to exclude as many as 20 percent of their respondents, especially on complex issues like the federal budget. Questions on more personal issues such as moral values, drugs, crime, race, and women's role in society get far fewer "no opinion" or "don't know" responses.

Intensity.   Another shortcoming of polls concerns their inability to measure intensity of feeling about particular issues. Whereas a respondent might answer affirmatively to any question, it is likely that his or her feelings about issues such as abortion, the death penalty, or support for U.S. troops in Afghanistan or Iraq are much more intense than are his or her feelings about the electoral college or even types of voting machines.

HOW POLLING AND PUBLIC OPINION AFFECT POLITICIANS, POLITICS, AND POLICY

As early as the founding period, the authors of *The Federalist Papers* noted that "all government rests on public opinion," and as a result, public opinion inevitably influences the actions of politicians and public officials. (For a broader perspective, see Global Politics: Public Opinion on Threats to Personal Safety.) The public's perception of crime as a problem, for example, was the driving force behind the comprehensive crime bill President Bill Clinton submitted to Congress in 1994 and congressional passage of the Brady gun control bill in 1993. The public's concern with crime skyrocketed to an all-time high in 1994, when 37 percent of the public rated crime as the nation's most important problem, and politicians at all levels were quick to convert that concern into a campaign issue.

Politicians and government officials spend millions of dollars each year taking the pulse of the public. Even the federal government spends millions annually on polls and surveys designed to evaluate programs and to provide information for shaping policies. But, as political scientist Benjamin Ginsberg noted, "the data reported by opinion polls are actually the product of an interplay between opinion and the survey instrument." They interact with each other and, in essence, often change the "character of the views receiving public expression."[85] Polls thus can help transform public opinion.

We know that politicians rely on polls, but it's difficult to say to what degree. Several political scientists have attempted to study whether public policy is responsive to public opinion, with mixed results.[86] As we have seen, public opinion can fluctuate, making it difficult for a politician or policy maker to assess. Some critics of polls and of their use by politicians argue that polls hurt democracy and make leaders weaker. Ginsberg, one of these critics, argues that these polls weaken democracy.[87] He claims that these polls allow governments and politicians to say they have considered public opinion even though polls don't always measure the intensity of feeling on an issue or might overreflect the views of the responders who lack sufficient information to make educated choices. Ginsberg further argues that democracy is better served by politicians' reliance on telephone calls and letters—active signs of interest—than on the passive voice of public opinion. Some say that politicians are simply driven by the results of polls that do not reflect a serious debate of issues. In response to this argument, George Gallup retorted, "One might as well insist that a thermometer makes the weather."[88]

Polls can clearly distort the election process by creating what are called "bandwagon" and "underdog" effects. In a presidential campaign, an early victory in the Iowa caucuses or the New Hampshire primary, for example, can boost a candidate's standings in the polls as the rest of the nation begins to think of him or her in a more positive light. New supporters jump on the bandwagon. A strong showing in the polls, in turn, can generate more and larger donations, the lifeblood of any campaign. One political scientist has noted that "bad poll results, as well as poor primary and caucus standings, may deter potential donors from supporting a failing campaign."[89]

Continuity & Change

Election Forecasting

The first attempts to measure public opinion were quite crude.[90] While politicians attempted to influence how Americans would vote, as well illustrated by the Federalist/Anti-Federalist debates in local newspapers and in political tracts circulated among the thirteen states, the true test of public opinion was the election results. It wasn't until the development of more sophisticated methods of communication such as mass-circulation magazines and a reliable mail service that organizations such as *Literary Digest* even attempted to tap the pulse of American voters in any systematic fashion.

The development of the telephone truly revolutionized the polling industry. As more and more households got telephone service, the ability to use sampling techniques to draw representative samples, and quickly administer surveys and polls, proved a real boon to the political polling industry. Since their widespread use in the 1970s, "telephone polls, on the whole, have proved to be remarkably accurate predictors of voter behavior—the gold standard of all polling research." Problems with telephone polls are rapidly increasing, however. Over 40 percent of those contacted now refuse to participate, and such polls get more and more costly each year.[91]

In the 1990s, American pollsters and social scientists began to experiment with a variety of other kinds of polls, often spurred on by news agencies' desire to be the "first" with the "news." Sophisticated exit polls, often conducted to allow a network to be the first on the air with a prediction, and tracking polls, often conducted to make political races seem closer than they are, thereby enhancing their "newsworthiness," are particularly popular today. A changing American electorate has made it more difficult for pollsters to conduct accurate political polls, particularly exit polls. In 2002, when the Voters News Service announced that its polls were too flawed to be released, the networks and political analysts were left with little to report about other than totals. How did women, African Americans, or white men vote in 2002? In most cases, we just don't know. Problems like these may result in major changes. New forms of measuring public sentiment are being devised using the Internet as a new medium. One company, DiscoveryWhy.com, used Internet polling to measure the instantaneous responses of potential voters to the 2000 Democratic presidential nomination acceptance speech of Al Gore.[92] Participants rated his performance with mouse clicks as they watched the address on television, and the results could be known almost instantaneously. The 300 watchers—a smaller sample than used for phone polls—were drawn from lists created by the company and were by invitation only. DiscoveryWhy.com, however, went out of business in the dot-com bust.

Harris Interactive, an Internet-based marketing firm, used the Internet to achieve a 99 percent accuracy rate in seventy-three political contests in November 2000.[93] Harris's margin of error was 1.9 percent; conventional polling was off by 3.9 percent. Harris even predicted that Gore would win the popular vote but lose the electoral college vote. How did they do it? Over 300,000 members of the voting-age public participated in the poll online from October 30 through November 6, 2000. The company processed over 40,000 online interviews per hour, including 7,800 simultaneous interviews. The final data were then weighted and tabulated. The results were remarkable and could change the face of polling as we know it, especially in light of the errors in traditional methods that occurred in 2000, and with Voters News Service in 2002.

1. What potential problems do you see with Internet polling?
2. Can huge sample sizes reduce polling problems regardless of the way the sample was drawn?

CAST YOUR VOTE   Will the Internet serve as an effective and accurate tool for political polling? To cast your vote, go to www.ablongman.com/oconnor

SUMMARY

Public opinion is a subject constantly mentioned in the media, especially in presidential election years or when important policies (such as health care, balancing the budget, race, or crime) are under consideration. What public opinion is, where it comes from, how it's measured, and how it's used are aspects of a complex subject. To that end, this chapter has made the following points:

1. **What Is Public Opinion?**
   Public opinion is what the public thinks about an issue or a particular set of issues. Public opinion polls are used to estimate public opinion.

2. **Early Efforts to Influence and Measure Public Opinion**
   Almost since the beginning of the United States, various attempts have been made to influence public opinion about particular issues or to sway elections. Modern-day polling did not begin until the 1930s, however. Over the years, polling to measure public opinion has become increasingly sophisticated and more accurate because pollsters are better able to sample the public in their effort to determine their attitudes and positions on issues. Pollsters recognize that their sample must reflect the population whose ideas and beliefs they wish to measure.

3. **Political Socialization and Other Factors That Influence Opinion Formation**
   The first step in forming opinions occurs through a process called political socialization. Our family, school, peers, social groups—including religion, race, gender, and age—as well as where we live and the impact of events all affect how we view political events and issues. Our political ideology—whether we are conservative, liberal, or moderate—also provides a lens through which we filter our political views. Even the views of other people affect our ultimate opinions on a variety of issues, including race relations, the death penalty, abortion, and federal taxes.

4. **How We Form Political Opinions**
   Myriad factors enter our minds as we form opinions about political matters. These include a calculation about the personal benefits involved, degree of personal political knowledge, and cues from leaders.

5. **How We Measure Public Opinion**
   Measuring public opinion can be difficult. The most frequently used measure is the public opinion poll. Determining the content, phrasing the questions, selecting the sample, and choosing the right kind of poll are critical to obtaining accurate and useful data.

6. **How Polling and Public Opinion Affect Politicians, Politics, and Policy**
   Knowledge of the public's views on issues is often used by politicians to tailor campaigns or to drive policy decisions. Polls, however, have several shortcomings, including sampling error and inadequate respondent information.

KEY TERMS

exit polls, p. 423
margin of error, p. 424
political ideology, p. 415
political socialization, p. 404
public opinion, p. 399
public opinion polls, p. 399
push polls, p. 422
random sampling, p. 419
sampling error, p. 424
stratified sampling, p. 420
straw polls, p. 401
tracking polls, p. 422

SELECTED READINGS

Alvarez, R. Michael, and John Brehm. *Easy Answers, Hard Choices: Values, Information, and American Public Opinion.* Princeton, NJ: Princeton University Press, 2002.

Asher, Herbert. *Polling and the Public: What Every Citizen Should Know,* 5th ed. Washington, DC: CQ Press, 2001.

Erikson, Robert S., and Kent L. Tedin. *American Public Opinion: Its Origins, Contents, and Impact,* 6th ed. New York: Longman, 2001.

Fishkin, James S. *The Voice of the People: Public Opinion and Democracy.* New Haven, CT: Yale University Press, 1996.

Ginsberg, Benjamin. *The Captive Public.* New York: Basic Books, 1986.

Herbst, Susan. *Numbered Voices: How Opinion Polling Has Shaped American Politics.* Chicago: University of Chicago Press, 1993.

Jamieson, Kathleen Hall. *Everything You Think You Know About Politics … And Why You Were Wrong.* New York: Basic Books, 2000.

Jennings, M. Kent, and Richard G. Niemi. *Generations and Politics: A Panel Study of Young Adults and Their Parents.* Princeton, NJ: Princeton University Press, 1981.

Key, V. O., Jr. *Public Opinion and American Democracy.* New York: Alfred E. Knopf, 1961.

Manza, Jeff, ed. *Navigating Public Opinion: Polls, Policy, and the Future of American Democracy.* New York: Oxford University Press, 2002.

Mutz, Diana Carole. *Impersonal Influence: How Perceptions of Mass Collectives Affect Political Attitudes.* New York: Cambridge University Press, 1998.

Norrander, Barbara, and Clyde Wilcox, eds. *Understanding Public Opinion*, 2nd ed. Washington, DC: CQ Press, 2001.

Rubenstein, Sondra Miller. *Surveying Public Opinion*. Belmont, CA: Wadsworth Publishing, 1994.

Shafer, Byron E., and William J. M. Claggett. *The Two Majorities: The Issue Context of Modern American Politics*. Baltimore, MD: Johns Hopkins University Press, 1995.

Stimson, James A. *Public Opinion in America: Moods, Cycles, and Swings*, 2nd ed. Boulder, CO: Westview Press, 1998.

Warren, Kenneth F. *In Defense of Public Opinion Polling*. Boulder, CO: Westview Press, 2001.

Zaller, John. *The Nature and Origins of Mass Opinions*. New York: Cambridge University Press, 1992.

NOTES

1. The Gallup Organization, "Poll Releases: The Florida Recount Controversy from the Public's Perspective: 25 Insights," http://www.gallup.com/poll/releases. All data discussed here are drawn from this compendium of polls concerning the Florida recount.
2. Allan M. Winkler, "Public Opinion," in Jack Greene, ed., *The Encyclopedia of American Political History* (New York: Charles Scribner's Sons, 1988), 1038.
3. Quoted in *Public Opinion Quarterly* 29 (Winter 1965–1966): 547.
4. Winkler, "Public Opinion," 1035.
5. Mike Allen, "White House Angered at Plan for Pentagon Disinformation," *Washington Post* (February 25, 2002): A17.
6. Stephanie Salter, "War of the Words," *San Francisco Chronicle* (February 10, 2002): A21.
7. Quoted in Winkler, "Public Opinion," 1035.
8. *Literary Digest* 122 (August 22, 1936): 3.
9. *Literary Digest* 125 (November 14, 1936): 1.
10. Robert S. Erikson, Norman Luttbeg, and Kent Tedin, *American Public Opinion: Its Origin, Contents, and Impact* (New York: Wiley, 1980), 28.
11. Angus Campbell, et al. *American Voter* (New York: Wiley, 1960).
12. Byron E. Shafer and William J. M. Claggett, *The Two Majorities: The Issue Context of Modern American Politics* (Baltimore, MD: Johns Hopkins University Press, 1995), 12.
13. Ibid., 13.
14. Richard Dawson et al. *Political Socialization*, 2nd ed. (Boston: Little, Brown, 1977), 33.
15. Robert D. Hess and David Easton, "The Child's Changing Image of the President," *Public Opinion Quarterly* 14 (Winter 1960): 632–42; and Fred I. Greenstein, *Children and Politics* (New Haven, CT: Yale University Press, 1965).
16. "Kids Voting USA Gains Support in Two Congressional Actions: Rep. Pastor Praised for His Continued Efforts," http://www.kidsvoteusa.org/march1502.htm.
17. "Kids Voting USA."
18. James Simon and Bruce D. Merrill, "Political Socialization in the Classroom Revisited: The Kids Voting Program," *Social Science Journal* 35 (1998): 29–42.
19. Ibid.
20. *Statistical Abstract of the United States, 1997* (Washington, DC: Government Printing Office, 1997), 1011.
21. Peggy Fikas, "A Funny Thing Happened on the Way to the White House," *San Antonio Express* (October 31, 2000): 1F.
22. Anne Miller, "Students Fighting National Apathy Trend," *San Antonio Express* (November 1, 2000): 3H.
23. Sean H. Smith, "Breaking News: ABC Had It Right," *Washington Post* (March 29, 2002): A23.
24. Julie Mason, "Avalanche of Politico-tainment Seems to Benefit Presidential Candidates," *Houston Chronicle* (October 1, 2000): A38; and Lois Romano, "For the Candidates, It's Showtime," *Washington Post* (October 20, 2000): A11.
25. Smith, "Breaking News."
26. Andrew Glass, "News About the Net," *Atlanta Journal and Constitution* (November 17, 2000): 2D.
27. Frederick C. Harris, "Something Within: Religion as a Mobilizer of African-American Political Activism," *Journal of Politics* 56 (February 1994): 42–68. See also Rory McVeigh, "God, Politics, and Protest: Religious Beliefs and the Legitimation of Contentious Tactics," *Social Forces* 79 (2001).
28. Harris, "Something Within."
29. "Church Membership Trend," http://www.gallup.com/POLL_ARCHIVES/970329.html.
30. "Basic Religious Beliefs," *Public Perspective* (October/November 1995): 4–5; and "America's Religious Makeup," http://www.gallup.com/POLL_ARCHIVES/970329.html.
31. Alfred Lubrano, "America's Religious Ties Are Loosening," *Houston Chronicle* (April 13, 2002): R1.
32. CNN Exit Polls. www.cnn.com/election/2004/pages/results/states/us/p/00/epolls.0.html.
33. Steven M. Cohen and Charles S. Liebman, "American Jewish Liberalism," *Public Opinion Quarterly* 61 (1997): 405–30.
34. Geoffrey C. Layman, "Religion and Political Behavior in the United States: The Impact of Beliefs, Affiliations, and Commitment from 1980 to 1994," *Public Opinion Quarterly* 61 (1997): 288.
35. Edward S. Greenberg, "The Political Socialization of Black Children," in Edward S. Greenberg, ed., *Political Socialization* (New York: Atherton Press, 1970), 181.
36. Elaine J. Hall and Myra Marx Ferree, "Race Differences in Abortion Attitudes," *Public Opinion Quarterly* 50 (Summer 1986): 193–207; and Jon Hurwitz and Mark Peffley, "Public Perceptions of Race and Crime: The Role of Racial Stereotypes," *American Journal of Political Science* 41 (April 1997): 375–401.
37. Elaine S. Povich, "Courting Hispanics: Group's Votes Could Shift House Control," *Newsday* (April 21, 2002): A4.
38. Ibid.
39. Alejandro Portest and Rafael Mozo, "The Political Adaptation Process of Cubans and Other Ethnic Minorities in the United States: A Preliminary Analysis," in F. Chris Garcia, ed., *Latinos and the Political System* (Notre Dame, IN: University of Notre Dame Press, 1988), 161.
40. The Gallup Organization, "Poll Releases: Americans Approve of U.S. Government Decision to Return Boy to Cuba," http://www.gallup.com/poll/releases/pr000112.asp.
41. Wes Allison and David Adams, "Family to Dad: Elian Stays with Us," *St. Petersburg Times* (April 1, 2000): 1A.

42. Pamela Johnson Conover and Virginia Sapiro, "Gender, Feminist Consciousness and War," *American Journal of Political Science* 37 (November 1993): 1079–99.

43. Margaret Trevor, "Political Socialization, Party Identification, and the Gender Gap," *Public Opinion Quarterly* 63 (Spring 1999): 62–89.

44. Alexandra Marks, "Gender Gap Narrows over Kosovo," *Christian Science Monitor* (April 30, 1999): 1.

45. Pew Research Center for People and the American Press (2002).

46. Center for Information and Research on Civil Learning and Engagement (2002).

47. Danny Goldberg, "As Politicians Demonize Pop Culture, Young Voters Tune Out," *Los Angeles Times* (September 3, 2000): M3.

48. William Booth, "Younger Voters Reflect Rise in Apathy, Discontent with Politics," *Washington Post* (November 5, 1996): A10.

49. Tanya Bricking, "Young Voters May Not," *Cincinnati Enquirer* (October 19, 1996): A1.

50. Susan A. MacManus, *Young v. Old: Generational Combat in the 21st Century* (Boulder, CO: Westview Press, 1995).

51. Richard Morin, "Southern Exposure," *Washington Post* (July 14, 1996): A18.

52. "Church Pews Seat More Blacks, Seniors, and Republicans," http://www.gallup.com/POLL_ARCHIVES/970329.html.

53. CNN Exit Polls. www.cnn.com/election/2004/pages/results/states/us/p/00/epolls.0.html.

54. F. Christopher Arterton, "The Impact of Watergate on Children's Attitudes Toward Political Authority," *Political Science Quarterly* 89 (June 1974): 273.

55. Diana Owen and Jack Dennis, "Kids and the Presidency: Assessing Clinton's Legacy," *Public Perspective* (April 1999): NEXIS.

56. Suzanne Soule, "Will They Engage? Political Knowledge, Participation and Attitudes of Generations X and Y," paper prepared for the 2001 German and American Conference, 6.

57. Soule, "Will They Engage?" quoting Richard G. Niemi and Jane Junn, *Civic Education* (New Haven, CT: Yale University Press, 1998).

58. Tamara Henry, "Kids Get 'Abysmal' Grade in History," *USA Today* (May 10, 2002): 1A.

59. "Don't Know Much About ..." *Christian Science Monitor* (May 16, 2002): 8.

60. Center for Information and Research on Civil Learning and Engagement (2002).

61. "Geography: A Lost Generation," *The Nation* (August 8, 1988): 19.

62. Kate O'Bierne, "Clueless: What Women Don't Know About Politics," *National Review* (October 9, 2000): NEXIS.

63. David Bauder, "Young Voters Turning Out in Droves, MTV Says," *Dayton Daily News* (October 20, 2000): 6A.

64. Quoted in Everett Carl Ladd, "Fiskin's 'Deliberative Poll' Is Flawed Science and Dubious Democracy," *Public Perspective* (December/January 1996): 41.

65. V. O. Key Jr., *The Responsible Electorate: Rationality in Presidential Voting, 1936–1960* (Cambridge, MA: Belknap Press of Harvard University, 1966).

66. Gerald M. Pomper, *The Performance of American Government* (New York: Free Press, 1972); and Benjamin I. Page, *Choices and Echoes in Presidential Elections* (Chicago: University of Chicago Press, 1978).

67. Norman H. Nie, Sidney Verba, and John R. Petrocik, *The Changing American Voter* (Cambridge, MA: Harvard University Press, 1976).

68. Ladd, "Fiskin's 'Deliberative Poll,'" 42.

69. Richard Nodeau et al., "Elite Economic Forecasts, Economic News, Mass Economic Judgments and Presidential Approval," *Journal of Politics* 61 (February 1999): 109–35.

70. Michael Towle, Review of *Presidential Responsiveness and Public Policy-making: The Public and the Policies* by Jeffrey E. Cohen, *Journal of Politics* 61 (February 1999): 230–32.

71. John E. Mueller, *War, Presidents, and Public Opinion* (New York: Wiley, 1973), 69.

72. Roderick P. Hart, *The Sound of Leadership: Presidential Communication in the Modern Age* (Chicago: University of Chicago Press, 1987).

73. Dana Milbank, "At the White House, 'The People' Have Spoken—Endlessly," *Washington Post* (June 4, 2002): A15.

74. David W. Moore, *The Superpollsters: How They Measure and Manipulate Public Opinion in America*, 2nd ed. (New York: Four Walls Eight Windows, 1995).

75. Diane J. Heith, "Staffing the White House Public Opinion Apparatus 1969–1988," *Public Opinion Quarterly* 62 (Summer 1998): 165.

76. David W. Moore, "Public Opposes Gay Marriages," Gallup Organization, April 4, 1996.

77. Francis J. Connolly and Charley Manning, "What 'Push Polling' Is and What It Isn't," *Boston Globe* (August 16, 2001): A21.

78. Michael W. Traugott, "The Polls in 1992: Views of Two Critics: A Good General Showing, but Much Work Needs to Be Done," *Public Perspective* 4 (November/December 1992): 14–16.

79. Michael W. Traugott, "The Polls in 1992: It Was the Best of Times, It Was the Worst of Times," *Public Perspective* (December/January 1992): 14.

80. Adam Berinsky, "A Tale of Two Elections: An Investigation of Pre-election Polling in Biracial Contests," paper presented at the 1999 annual meeting of the Midwest Political Science Association.

81. Traugott, "The Polls in 1992."

82. This account of errors in the VNS poll draws heavily on "News Group Admits Poll Errors: Probe Also Reveals Use of Risky Techniques," *Washington Post* (December 24, 2000): A7.

83. Traugott, "The Polls in 1992."

84. Michael W. Traugott and Clyde Tucker, "Strategies for Predicting Whether a Citizen Will Vote and Estimation of Electoral Outcomes," *Public Opinion Quarterly* (Spring 1984): 330–43.

85. Benjamin Ginsberg, "How Polls Transform Public Opinion," in Michael Margolis and Gary A. Mauser, eds., *Manipulating Public Opinion* (Pacific Grove, CA: Brooks/Cole, 1989), 273.

86. See, for example, Benjamin Page and Robert Shapiro, "Effects of Public Opinion on Policy," *American Political Science Review* 57 (March 1983): 175–90; Alan D. Monroe, "Public Opinion and Public Policy, 1980–1993," *Public Opinion Quarterly* 62

(Spring 1998): 6–28; and Kathleen M. McGraw, Samuel Best, and Richard Timpone, "'What They Say or What They Do?' The Impact of Elite Explanation and Policy Outcomes on Public Opinion," *American Journal of Political Science* 39 (February 1995): 53–74.

87. Benjamin Ginsberg, *The Captive Public* (New York: Basic Books, 1986), ch. 4.

88. Quoted in Pace, "George Gallup Is Dead at 82," *New York Times* (July 28, 1984): A1.

89. Herbert Asher, *Polling and the Public: What Every Citizen Should Know* (Washington, DC: CQ Press, 1988), 109.

90. For an interesting discussion of measuring public opinion before surveys, see Karen Hoffman, "Going Public in the Eighteenth and Nineteenth Centuries: Measuring the Influence of Public Opinion Before Surveys," paper prepared for delivery at the 1999 annual meeting of the Midwest Political Science Association.

91. Gordon S. Black and George Terhanian, "Using the Internet for Election Forecasting," http://www.pollingreport.com/internet.html.

92. Steve Marantz, "Dotcom Finds a Future Cyber Polling," *Boston Herald* (September 25, 2000): 21.

93. "2000 Election Winners: George W. Bush and Online Polling," *Business Wire* (December 14, 2000).

Political Parties

In the summer of 2004, the two major political parties met and held their national conventions. The primary focus of these conventions was the nomination of their presidential candidates. In July, the Democrats used the city of Boston to formally launch John Kerry's campaign for the presidency. A few weeks later in New York City, the Republicans followed suit and renamed President George W. Bush their candidate for President of the United States. The televised convention proceedings and morning papers focused on the nominations of these two men and their personal attributes. Relatively little attention, however, was paid to something of similar importance: the passage at both party conventions of the party platforms, which are official statements that detail the party's beliefs, as well as its positions on various policy issues. The platforms are often taken for granted, certainly by the news media, and even by many political activists.

How wrong the cynics are. The Democrats outlined very substantial programmatic differences from those that had been supported by the Bush administration on a wide range of foreign policy, domestic, and social issues. The Republicans strongly defended the policies of the previous four years including the invasion of Iraq as a "great and gathering" danger to American interests at home and abroad; the Democrats, on the other hand, offered intense criticism by referring to the utter lack of weapons of mass destruction constituting such a threat and to the failure for the administration to bring peace to the region. The Republicans insisted that President Bush's 2001 and 2003 tax cut bills were essential to rebuilding a weakened American economy; the Democrats argued that the tax cuts had created enormous national deficits to be paid off by future generations. In particular, Democrats deemed tax cuts as fiscally irresponsible in light of rising defense costs while Republicans defended tax cuts by pointing to the reinvigorated stock market and the increase in jobs. The Republicans continued their strong pro-life stance on the issue of abortion, their most recent success being a federal partial birth abortion ban. Trying to stay committed to their pro-choice stance, Democrats remained split over whether to oppose the ban, thus supporting the most extreme form of abortion, or to support the ban, in order to satisfy politically moderate constituents. Finally, Republicans opposed extending marriage rights to homosexuals, while not eliminating the option of civil unions as the legal equivalent, forcing Democrats either to hold the unpopular and most radical position, the legalization of gay marriage, or support the Republicans.

As this chapter will discuss, these party positions really do matter, since they affect who will hold hundreds of elective offices across the nation. The winning party attempts to act on the positions laid out in its platform, and these positions are used as guidelines for the major legislative initiatives that will be pursued during the president's term. Given the results of the 2004 election, we can expect an aggressive foreign policy that will continue to assert American and international security abroad and pursue terrorists into other countries during President Bush's second term, with an equally aggressive domestic security policy geared toward preventing terrorism, as outlined in the Patriot Act. We can expect a preservation of the current tax cuts and perhaps even an expansion in their provisions. Conservative positions will continue to be advanced on a wide range of social issues including abortion, the definition of marriage, and faith-based initiatives.

These policies affect millions of people. They are as important, if not more important, than the personal aspects of politics, which tend to dominate media coverage.

*I*t is difficult to reject the assertion that we are now entering a new, more fluid era of party politics. But, while some maintain that our two-party system is likely to be replaced by a chaotic multiparty system, or that a system in which presidential hopefuls bypass party nominations altogether and compete on their own is on the horizon, it is important to remember that political parties have been staples of American life since the late 1700s and, in one form or another, most likely will continue to be. As this chapter explains, political scientist E. E. Schattschneider was not exaggerating when he wrote, "Modern democracy is unthinkable save in terms of the parties."[1]

The chapter addresses contemporary party politics and attempts to help you understand political parties by examining them from many vantage points. Our examination of political parties traces their development from their infancy in the late 1700s to today.

- First, we will discuss *what a political party is.*
- Second, we will look at the *parties' evolution* through U.S. history.
- Third, we will examine the *roles of the American parties* in our political system.
- Fourth, we will present the *basic structure of American political parties.*
- Fifth, we will explore the *party in government*, the office holders and candidates who run under the party's banner.
- Sixth, we will examine the *modern transformation of the parties*, paying special attention to how political parties have moved from the labor-intensive, person-to-person operations of the first half of the century toward the use of technology and communication strategies.
- Seventh, we will look at the *party in the electorate*, showing that a political party's reach extends well beyond the relative handful of men and women who are the party in government.
- Eighth, we will discuss *one-partyism and third-partyism*, as well as independent and third-party candidates and the history of party alignment.
- In continuing our investigation of *continuity and change* in American politics, we will consider the fate of third parties from the 1990s and into the new millennium.

WHAT IS A POLITICAL PARTY?

Any definition of "political party" must be kept general because there are so many kinds of parties in the United States. In some states and localities, party organizations are strong and well entrenched, whereas in other places the parties exist more on paper than in reality. A definition of "party" might also be shaped by what people expect of parties. Some people expect parties to seek policy changes, while others expect them to win elections. This distinction flavors some of the debate over the effectiveness of political parties. If you expect parties to help candidates win office, then you might conclude that they are healthy. But, if you believe that the main goal of political parties should be to promote and accomplish policy changes, then you might believe they frequently fail. We will be concerned here primarily with the electoral functions served by political parties, but it is important to remember these distinctions.[2]

At the most basic level, a **political party** is a group of office holders, candidates, activists, and voters who identify with a group label and seek to elect to public office individuals who run under that label. Notice how pragmatic this concept of party is. The goal is to win office, not just compete for it. This objective is in keeping with the practical nature of Americans and the country's historical aversion to most ideologically driven, "purist" politics (as we discuss later in this chapter). Nevertheless, the group label, also called party identification for the voters who embrace the party as their own, can carry with it clear messages about ideology and issue positions. Although this is especially true of minor, less broad-based parties that have little chance of electoral success, it also applies to the national, dominant political parties in the United States, the Democrats and the Republicans.

When it comes to providing a formal definition of political parties, political scientists have often disagreed.[3] Some political scientists, for example, conceive of political parties as being made up of three separate but related entities: (1) the office holders and candidates who run under the party's banner (the **governmental party**); (2) the workers and activists who staff the party's formal organization (the **organizational party**); and, (3) the voters who consider themselves to be allied or associated with the party (the **party in the electorate**).[4] Other political scientists take issue with this definition, arguing that, especially in the American political system, voters should not be included in the definition of political parties. Voters, they note, are not part of the parties but choosers among them, in much the same way that fans of a sports team are not actually part of the team.[5] In this chapter, we examine all three components of political parties—the governmental party, the organizational party, and the party in the electorate—including voters if only because they are so important in driving the actions of the other two components. First, however, we turn to the history and development of political parties in the United States.

political party
A group of office holders, candidates, activists, and voters who identify with a group label and seek to elect to public office individuals who run under that label.

governmental party
The office holders and candidates who run under a political party's banner.

organizational party
The workers and activists who staff the party's formal organization.

party in the electorate
The voters who consider themselves allied or associated with the party.

National security was a prominent theme at both parties' conventions in 2004. Here, delegates hold signs in support of President Bush at the Republican National Convention in New York City.

(Photo courtesy: AP/World Wide Photos)

THE EVOLUTION OF AMERICAN PARTY DEMOCRACY

It is one of the great ironies of the early republic that George Washington's public farewell, which warned the nation against parties, marked the effective end of the brief era of partyless politics in the United States (see Figure 12.1). Washington's unifying influence ebbed as he stepped off the national stage, and his vice president and successor, John Adams, occupied a much less exalted position. Adams was allied with Alexander Hamilton. To win the presidency in 1796, Adams narrowly defeated Thomas Jefferson, Hamilton's former rival in Washington's Cabinet. Before ratification of the Constitution, Hamilton and Jefferson had been leaders of the Federalists and Anti-Federalists, respectively (see chapter 2). Over the course of Adams's single term, two competing congressional party groupings (or caucuses) gradually organized around these clashing men and their principles: Hamilton's Federalists supported a strong central government; the Democratic-Republicans of Thomas Jefferson and his ally James Madison inherited the mantle of the Anti-Federalists and preferred a federal system in which the states were relatively more powerful. (Jefferson actually preferred the simpler name "Republicans," a very different group from today's party of the same name, but Hamilton insisted on calling them "Democratic-Republicans" to link them to the radical democrats of the French Revolution.) In the presidential election of 1800, the Federalists supported Adams's bid for a second term, but this time the Democratic-Republicans prevailed with their nominee, Jefferson, who became the first U.S. president elected as the nominee of a political party.

Jefferson was deeply committed to the ideas of his party, but not nearly as devoted to the idea of a party system. He regarded his party as a temporary measure necessary to defeat Adams and Hamilton. Neither Jefferson's party nor Hamilton's enjoyed widespread "party identification" among the citizenry akin to that of today's Democrats and Republicans. Although Southerners were overwhelmingly partial to the Democratic-Republicans and New Englanders to the Federalists, no broad-based party organizations existed on either side to mobilize popular support. Rather, as political scientist John H. Aldrich observes, the congressional factions organized around Hamilton and Jefferson were primarily governmental parties designed to settle the dispute over how strong the new federal government would be.[6] Just as the nation was in its infancy, so, too, was the party system, and attachments to both parties were weak at first.

The Early Parties Fade

After the spirited confrontations of the republic's early years, political parties faded somewhat in importance for a quarter of a century. The Federalists ceased nominating presidential candidates by 1816, having failed to elect one of their own since Adams's victory in 1796, and by 1820 the party had dissolved. James Monroe's presidency from 1817 to 1825 produced the so-called Era of Good Feelings, when party politics was nearly suspended at the national level. Even during Monroe's tenure, though, party organizations continued to develop at the state level. Party growth was fueled in part by the enormous increase in the electorate that took place between 1820 and 1840, as the United States expanded westward and most states abolished property requirements as a condition of white male suffrage. During this twenty-year period, the number of votes cast in presidential contests rose from 300,000 to more than 2 million.

At the same time, U.S. politics was being democratized in other ways. By the 1820s, all the states except South Carolina had switched from state legislative selection of presidential electors to popular election of electoral college members. This change helped transform presidential politics. No longer just the concern of society's upper crust, the election of the president became a matter for all qualified voters to decide.

FIGURE 12.1   American Party History at a Glance

This table shows the transformations and evolution of the various parties that have always made up the basic two-party structure of the American political system.

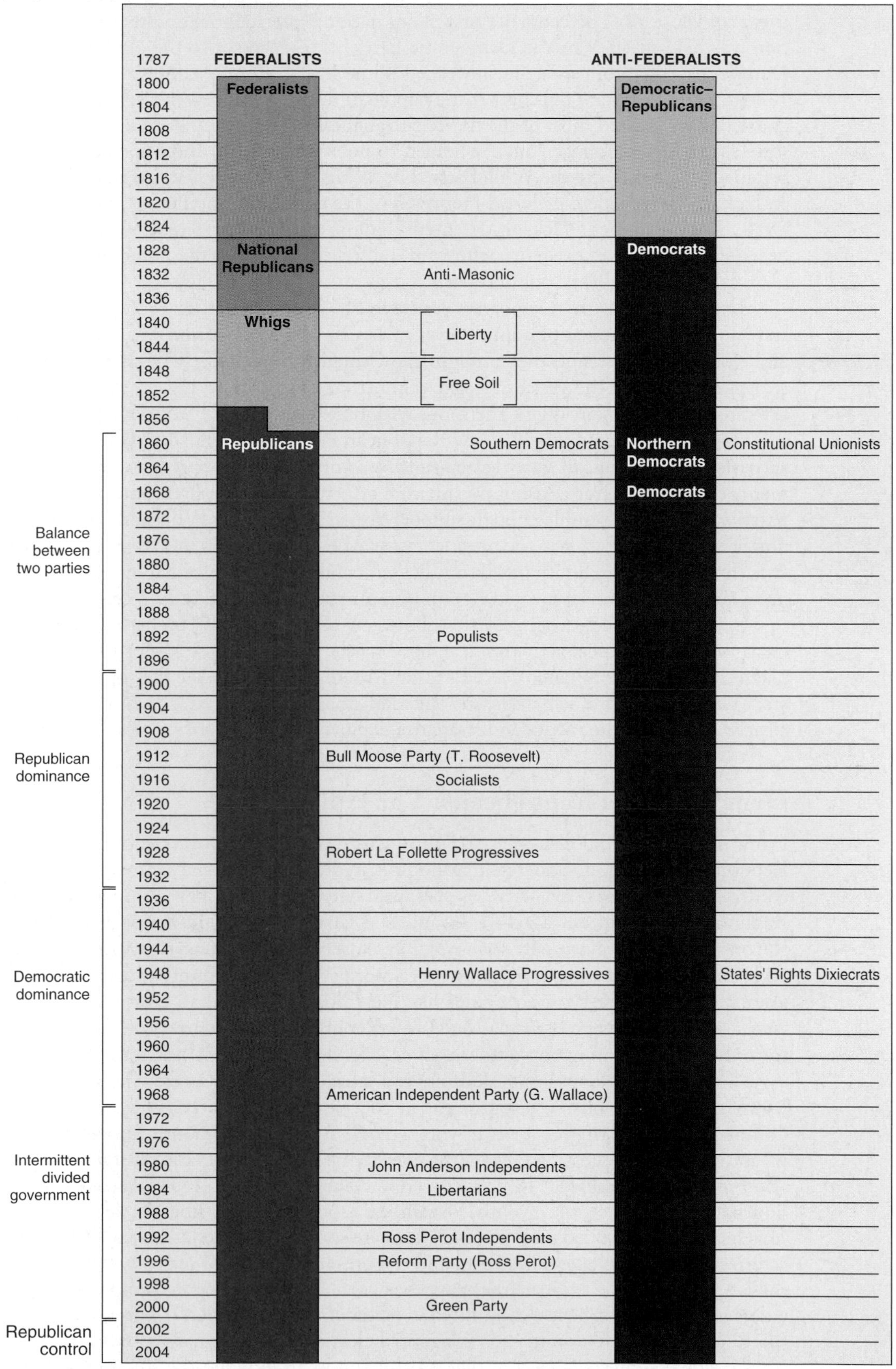

		FEDERALISTS			ANTI-FEDERALISTS	
	1787	FEDERALISTS			ANTI-FEDERALISTS	
	1800	Federalists			Democratic–Republicans	
	1804					
	1808					
	1812					
	1816					
	1820					
	1824					
	1828	National Republicans			Democrats	
	1832		Anti-Masonic			
	1836					
	1840	Whigs	Liberty			
	1844					
	1848		Free Soil			
	1852					
	1856					
Balance between two parties	1860	Republicans	Southern Democrats	Northern Democrats	Constitutional Unionists	
	1864					
	1868			Democrats		
	1872					
	1876					
	1880					
	1884					
	1888					
	1892		Populists			
	1896					
Republican dominance	1900					
	1904					
	1908					
	1912		Bull Moose Party (T. Roosevelt)			
	1916		Socialists			
	1920					
	1924					
	1928		Robert La Follette Progressives			
	1932					
Democratic dominance	1936					
	1940					
	1944					
	1948		Henry Wallace Progressives		States' Rights Dixiecrats	
	1952					
	1956					
	1960					
	1964					
	1968		American Independent Party (G. Wallace)			
Intermittent divided government	1972					
	1976					
	1980		John Anderson Independents			
	1984		Libertarians			
	1988					
	1992		Ross Perot Independents			
	1996		Reform Party (Ross Perot)			
	1998					
	2000		Green Party			
Republican control	2002					
	2004					

The party base broadened along with the electorate. Small caucuses of congressional party leaders had previously nominated candidates, but after much criticism of the process as elitist and undemocratic, this system gave way to nominations at large party conventions. The country's first major national presidential nominating convention was held in 1832 by the Democratic Party,[7] the successor to the old Jeffersonian Democratic–Republicans (the shortened name had gradually come into use in the 1820s). Formed around the charismatic populist President Andrew Jackson, the Democratic Party attracted most of the newly enfranchised voters, who were drawn to Jackson's style. His strong personality helped to polarize politics, and opposition to the president coalesced into the Whig Party. The Whig Party was descended from the Federalists; its early leaders included Henry Clay, the speaker of the House from 1811 to 1820. The incumbent Jackson defeated Clay in the 1832 presidential contest. He became the first chief executive who won the White House as the nominee of a truly national, popularly based political party.

The Whigs and the Democrats continued to strengthen after 1832, establishing state and local organizations almost everywhere. Their competition was usually fierce and closely matched, and they brought the United States the first broadly supported two-party system in the Western world.[8] Unfortunately for the Whigs, the issue of slavery sharpened the many divisive tensions within the party, which led to its gradual dissolution and replacement by the new Republican Party. Formed in 1854 by antislavery activists, the Republican Party set its sights on the abolition (or at least the containment) of slavery. After a losing presidential effort for John C. Fremont in 1856, the party was able to assemble enough support primarily from the Whigs and antislavery northern Democrats to win the presidency for Abraham Lincoln in a fragmented 1860 vote. In that year, the South voted solidly Democratic, beginning a habit so strong that not a single southern state voted Republican for president again until 1920.

It should also be recognized that, between 1838 and 1890, many minor parties engaged in the political activities developed by the major parties. Minor parties organized themselves, nominated candidates, and attempted to mobilize the support of voters.[9] Thus, despite the self-imposed "outsider" image of minor parties in this era, they clearly adhered to the tactics and strategies deployed by the major parties.

Democrats and Republicans: The Golden Age

From the presidential election of 1860 to this day, the same two major parties, the Republicans and the Democrats, have dominated elections in the United States, and control of an electoral majority has seesawed between them. The dominance of the Republicans (now often called the Grand Old Party, or GOP) in the post–Civil War Reconstruction era eventually gave way to a closely competitive system from 1876 to 1896 in part because the Democrats were more successful at integrating new immigrants into U.S. society in port cities like New York, Boston, and Chicago. Another factor was the exclusion of virtually all black Republicans and many pro-Union whites from the electorate in many southern states.[10] In the later years of the nineteenth century, however, the Republicans skillfully capitalized on fears of a growing anti-establishment, anti–big business sentiment in the Democratic Party. They fashioned a dominant and enduring majority of voters that essentially lasted until the early 1930s, when the Great Depression created the conditions for a Democratic resurgence.

President Franklin D. Roosevelt's New Deal coalition of 1932 consisted of the South, racial and ethnic groups, organized labor, farmers, liberals, and big-city "machines," as well-oiled party organizations are sometimes called. This coalition characterized both the Democratic Party and the prevailing national majority until at least the late 1960s. Since 1970, neither party has been clearly dominant, as more and more voters have seemed to be less committed to either of the two parties. In this same period, the Republicans have dominated presidential elections and Democrats have won most congressional contests, a pattern that was broken in 1994 when the Republicans, two years after the Democrats regained the White House, won control of both congressional houses. (The development of "divided government" is discussed later in this chapter.)

The Modern Era Versus the Golden Age

The modern era seems very distant from the "golden age" of parties that existed from the 1870s to the 1920s. Emigration from Europe (particularly from Ireland, Italy, and Germany) fueled the development of big-city party organizations that ruled their domains with an iron hand. Party and government were virtually interchangeable, and the parties were the providers of much-needed services, entertainment, and employment. These big-city party organizations were called **machines.** A political machine is a party organization that recruits its members with tangible incentives—money, political jobs, an opportunity to get favors from government—and that is characterized by a high degree of leadership control over member activity. Machines were a central element of life for millions of people: They sponsored community events, such as parades and picnics, and provided social services, such as helping new immigrants settle in and giving food and temporary housing to those in immediate need, all in exchange for votes.

The parties offered immigrants not just services but also the opportunity for upward social mobility as they rose in the organization. Because they held the possibility of social advancement, the parties engendered among their supporters and office holders intense devotion that helped to produce startlingly high voter turnouts—75 percent or better in all presidential elections from 1876 to 1900, compared with only about 50 percent to 55 percent today.[11] They also fostered the greatest party-line voting ever achieved in Congress and many state legislatures.[12] (See Roots of Government: Plunkitt of Tammany Hall.)

Recent scholarship, however, shows that the effect of political machines on immigrant communities was not all positive. In his book *Rainbow's End*, Steven P. Erie concludes that machines retarded the social mobility of the Irish. The exclusion of other groups from the machine-controlled jobs forced them to get more education and work their way up the social ladder, while the Irish as part of the machine tended to get stuck in these relatively low-wage, low-advancement jobs.[13]

As several political scientists have observed, political machines have not been exclusive to urban areas.[14] Although the most prominent and colorful political machines existed in cities, political machines could be found in some rural and suburban areas as well. Even today, for example, a traditional, machine-style Republican Party organization continues to exist in Nassau County, New York—a wealthy suburb of New York City situated on Long Island.[15]

Is the Party Over?

In the twenty-first century, many social, political, technological, and governmental changes have contributed to party decline. Historically, the government's gradual assumption of important functions previously performed by the parties, such as printing ballots, conducting elections, and providing social welfare services, had a major impact. Social services began to be seen as a right of citizenship rather than as a privilege extended in exchange for a person's support of a party. Also, as the flow of immigrants slowed dramatically in the 1920s, party organizations gradually withered in most places.

The **direct primary,** whereby party nominees were determined by the ballots of qualified voters rather than at party conventions, was widely adopted by the states in the first two decades of the twentieth century. The primary removed the power of nomination from party leaders and workers and gave it instead to a much broader and more independent electorate, thus loosening the tie between the party nominee and the party organization. **Civil service laws** also removed much of the patronage used by the parties to reward their followers. Civil service laws require appointment on the basis of merit and competitive examinations, whereas **patronage** and the **spoils system** award

machine
A party organization that recruits its members with tangible incentives and is characterized by a high degree of control over member activity.

direct primary
The selection of party candidates through the ballots of qualified voters rather than at party nomination conventions.

civil service laws
These acts removed the staffing of the bureaucracy from political parties and created a professional bureaucracy filled through competition.

patronage
Jobs, grants, or other special favors that are given as rewards to friends and political allies for their support.

spoils system
The firing of public-office holders of a defeated political party and their replacement with loyalists of the newly elected party.

PLUNKITT OF TAMMANY HALL

Tammany Hall was a powerful New York City political organization during the mid-nineteenth and early twentieth centuries. Originally formed as a social club in 1797, it had been transformed into an influential political machine by 1850, with membership including most of the city's prominent Democrats.

Of all the organization's politicians, one of the most renowned at the turn of the twentieth century was ward boss George Washington Plunkitt. Starting as a teenager, this son of Irish immigrants worked his way up through the ranks of the organization to become the leader of the city's Fifteenth Assembly District. (An assembly district is made up of many smaller units, called election districts.) He is remembered as one of the shrewdest politicians of his time. Plunkitt was born poor but died a millionaire, acquiring most of his wealth through what he called "honest graft," a term best described in his own candid words:

> My party's in power in the city, and its goin' to make a lot of public improvements. Well, I'm tipped off, say, that they're going to lay out a new park at a certain place.
>
> I see my opportunity and I take it. I go to that place and I buy up all the land I can in the neighborhood. Then the board of this or that makes it public, and there is a rush to get my land, which nobody cared particular for before.
>
> Ain't it perfectly honest to charge a good price and make a profit on my investment and foresight? Of course, it is. Well, that's honest graft.

For Plunkitt, there was a difference between dishonest and honest graft, "between [dishonest] political looters and [honest] politicians who make a fortune out of politics by keepin' their eyes wide open":

> The looter goes in for himself alone without considerin' his organization or his city. The politician looks after his own interests, the organization's interests, and the city's interests all at the same time.

Plunkitt certainly looked after his constituents' interests. During Tammany's reign, the population of New York City was made up predominantly of poor immigrants, mostly Irish, for whom Plunkitt and his fellow district leaders served as a bridge between the Old and New Worlds and also as a way out of the slums. Besides assimilating these newcomers into life in the United States and acquainting them with the processes of self-government, the ward bosses used the patronage at their disposal to provide tangible benefits. Be it a job, liquor, a push-cart license, or even cash, the ward boss was always happy to help out a needy constituent—in exchange, of course, for loyalty at the ballot box during election time.

In contrast to the issue-oriented or image-appeal politics we know today, Plunkitt's politics were *personal*. As Plunkitt put it, "[I] learned how to reach the hearts of the great mass of voters. I don't bother about reaching their heads." Plunkitt understood the value of this personalized, community-oriented politics to both voters and leaders. His advice to aspiring politicians was simply to know and study the members of their communities and to "study human nature and act accordin'."

Plunkitt's brand of politics had all but disappeared by the mid-twentieth century. First, a drastic decline of immigration during the 1920s strangled the fuel line that fed the fires of city machines. Second, many of the services the parties provided gradually came to be viewed as rights of citizenship rather than as rewards for supporting a particular party; therefore, government replaced party organizations as the dispenser of benefits. Most important, however, and much to the chagrin of Plunkitt himself, were the new civil service laws passed by reformers in the 1920s to combat the alleged corruption of machine politics. These laws, which struck at the heart and soul of machine politics—patronage and the spoils system—induced Plunkitt to deem the civil service laws "the biggest fraud of the age" and the ruin of the nation:

> There can't be no real patriotism while it lasts. How are you goin' to interest our young men in their country if you have no offices to give them when they work for their party?...I know more than one man in the past years who worked for the ticket and was just overflowin' with patriotism, but when he was knocked out by the civil service humbug he got to hate his country and became an anarchist.

For better or worse, however, the reformers prevailed, and by the mid-twentieth century, civil service had come to dominate government at every level, consigning Plunkitt's brand of politics to America's past.

Source: William L. Riordon, ed., *Plunkitt of Tammany Hall* (New York: Dutton, 1963), 11, 89.

jobs on the basis of party loyalty. These changes were encouraged by the Progressive movement (consisting of politically liberal reformers), which flourished in the first two decades of the twentieth century.

In the post–World War II era, extensive social changes contributed to the move away from strong parties. Broad-based education gave rise to **issue-oriented politics,** politics that focuses on specific issues, such as civil rights, tax cutting, environmental-

issue-oriented politics
Politics that focuses on specific issues rather than on party, candidate, or other loyalties.

ism, or abortion, rather than on party labels. Issue politics tends to cut across party lines and encourages voters to **ticket-split,** that is, to vote for candidates of different parties for various offices in the same election. Recent studies by political scientists indicate that split-ticket voting is not the result of a conscious effort on behalf of voters to moderate the government by pitting the parties against each other. It is rather a result of decisions made by individual voters about individual candidates' positions on specific issues important to them. This issue-based vote, combined with often lopsided congressional campaigns favoring well-funded and well-known candidates over little-known upstarts, contributes greatly to split-ticket voting.[16]

Another post–World War II social change that has affected the parties is the growth in population and the shift from urban to suburban locales. Millions of people have moved out of the cities, which are easily organizable because of population density, and into the sprawling suburbs, where a sense of privacy and detachment can deter the most energetic organizers. In addition, the population boom in the last half-century has created districts with far more people, making it unfeasible to knock on every door or shake every hand. Such changes have required new methods for reaching voters. One example of this is the voter mobilization activities of the Christian Coalition in the 1990s. When first organized, Pat Robertson's conservative evangelical Christian organization relied on the traditional political precinct-level method of organizing communities to turn out and vote. By the middle of the 1990s, however, Robertson retired this method in favor of a church-based model of literature distribution and voter activation. In modern suburbs, the Christian Coalition found it easier to reach their target audience in church on Sunday rather than in sprawling neighborhoods on other days of the week.[17]

Politically, many other trends have contributed to the parties' decline. Television, which has come to dominate U.S. politics, naturally emphasizes personalities rather than abstract concepts such as party labels. Other technological advances such as the autodialer, a computer that leaves pre-recorded messages on voters' answering machines, have often alienated voters and further eroded precinct organization. In addition, the modern parties have many rivals for the affections of their candidates, including **political consultants,** the hired guns who manage campaigns and design television

ticket-split
To vote for candidates of different parties for various offices in the same election.

political consultant
Professional who manages campaigns and political advertisements for political candidates.

Senior members of Republican presidential candidate George W. Bush's campaign staff watch the televised Florida Supreme Court hearing on the vote recounts at the Bush 2000 Campaign headquarters in Austin, Texas. From left are Chief Strategist Karl Rove, Campaign Chairman Don Evans, and Communications Director Karen Hughes. All three took positions in the Bush administration. Hughes later resigned in April 2002 to spend more time with her family in Texas, but continues to work closely with the president.

(Photo courtesy: Harry Cabluck/AP/Wide World Photos)

advertisements. Both technology and consultants have replaced the party as the intermediary between candidate and voter. It is little wonder that many candidates and office holders who have reached their posts without much help from their parties remain as free as possible of party ties.

The Parties Endure

Despite the challenges described in the preceding section, the parties' decline can easily be exaggerated. Viewing parties in the broad sweep of U.S. history, it becomes clear that, first, although political parties have evolved considerably and changed form from time to time, they usually have been reliable vehicles for mass participation in a representative democracy. In fact, the gradual but steady expansion of suffrage was orchestrated by the parties. As political scientist E. E. Schattschneider concluded, "In the search for new segments of the populace that might be exploited profitably, the parties have kept the movement to liberalize the franchise well ahead of the demand.... The enlargement of the practicing electorate has been one of the principal labors of the parties, a truly notable achievement for which the parties have never been properly credited."[18] It is important to mention, however, that there are notable exceptions in which parties have worked to contract the electorate. Southern Democrats, for example, worked to exclude blacks from the end of Reconstruction through the civil rights movement.

Second, the parties' journey through U.S. history has been characterized by the same ability to adapt to prevailing conditions that is often cited as the genius of the Constitution. Flexibility and pragmatism are characteristics of both and help ensure their survival and the success of the society they serve.

Third, despite massive changes in political conditions and frequent dramatic shifts in the electorate's mood, the two major parties not only have achieved remarkable longevity, but they also have almost always provided strong competition for each other and the voters at the national level. Of the thirty-one presidential elections from 1884 to 2004, for instance, the Republicans won seventeen and the Democrats fourteen. Even when calamities have beset the parties—the Great Depression in the 1930s or the Watergate scandal of 1973–1974 for the Republicans (see chapter 8), and the Civil War or left-wing McGovernism in 1972 for the Democrats—the two parties have proved tremendously resilient, sometimes bouncing back from landslide defeats to win the next election. Indeed, political scientist Philip A. Klinkner argues that the national committees have been at their most innovative in adapting to changing political conditions precisely when they are responding to electoral defeat.[19]

Fourth, although much research indicated that parties were declining for much of the twentieth century, new research suggests that parties have begun to rebound from this period of decline. Marc J. Hetherington points out that "Americans in the 1990s [were] more likely to think about one party positively and one negatively, less likely to feel neutral toward either party, and better able to list why they like and dislike the parties than they were ten to thirty years ago."[20] Hetherington asserts that this increase in partisanship is a function of the polarization so much decried among political elites. As he puts it, "Greater ideological polarization in Congress has clarified public perceptions of party ideology, which has produced a more partisan electorate."[21] In other words, there are fewer liberal Republicans and conservative Democrats, making it easier for voters to identify with the party that best represents their personal ideology.

Perhaps most of all, history teaches us that the development of parties in the United States (outlined in Figure 12.1) has been inevitable, as James Madison feared. Human nature alone guarantees conflict in any society; in a free state, the question is simply how to contain and channel conflict productively without infringing on individual liberties. The Founders' utopian hopes for the avoidance of partisan faction, Madison's chief concern, have given way to an appreciation of the parties' constructive contributions to conflict definition and resolution during the years of the American republic.

THE ROLES OF THE AMERICAN PARTIES

For 150 years, the two-party system has served as the mechanism American society uses to organize and resolve social and political conflict. (Of course, third parties have periodically made important contributions to American politics, and they will be discussed later in the chapter.) Although political parties are arguably less popular today than in previous times, it is important both to remember that political parties often are the chief agents of change in our political system and to discuss the vital services to society the parties provide and how difficult political life would be without them.

Mobilizing Support and Gathering Power

Party affiliation is enormously helpful to elected leaders. They can count on disproportionate support among their fellow partisans not just in times of trouble and in close judgment calls, but also on general political and legislative matters. Therefore the parties aid office holders by giving them room to develop their policies and by mobilizing support for them. When the president addresses the nation and requests support for his policies, for example, his party's activists are usually the first to respond to the call, perhaps by flooding Congress with telegrams urging action on the president's agenda. Additionally, a recent study found that the more liberal and competitive the Democratic Party is in a state, the greater the level of mobilization and voter turnout among the lower classes. The lower classes, after activation by the Democrats, presumably then vote and participate in ways favorable to the Democratic Party or their position on issues.[22]

Because there are only two major parties, pragmatic citizens who are interested in politics or public policy are mainly attracted to one or the other standard, creating natural majorities or near-majorities for party office holders to command. The party creates a community of interest that bonds disparate groups over time into a **coalition.** This continuing mutual interest eliminates the necessity of creating a new coalition for every campaign or every issue. Imagine the constant chaos and mad scrambles for public support that would ensue without the continuity provided by the parties.

coalition
A group of interests or organizations that join forces for the purpose of electing public officials.

A Force for Stability and Moderation

As mechanisms for organizing and containing political change, the parties are a potent force for stability. They represent continuity in the wake of changing issues and personalities, anchoring the electorate in the midst of the storm of new political policies and people. Because of its unyielding, practical desire to win elections (not just to contest them), each party in a sense acts to moderate public opinion. The party tames its own extreme elements by pulling them toward an ideological center in order to attract a majority of votes on Election Day.

Another aspect of the stability the parties provide is found in the nature of the coalitions they forge. There are inherent contradictions in these coalitions that, oddly enough, strengthen the nation even as they strain party unity. Franklin D. Roosevelt's Democratic New Deal coalition, for example, included many African Americans and most southern whites, opposing elements nonetheless joined in common political purpose. This party union of the two groups, as limited a context as it may have been, provided a framework for acceptance of change and contributed to reconciliation of the races in the civil rights era. Nowhere can this reconciliation be more clearly seen than in the South, where most state Democratic parties remained predominant after the mid-1960s by building on the ingrained Democratic voting habits of both whites and blacks to create new, moderate, generally integrated societies.

In fact, a recent study of the voting patterns of southern Democratic senators from 1960 to 1995 found that, as the years progressed, the senators became more and more liberal in their policy positions compared to their predecessors. The study determined that the liberalization of the formerly conservative southern Democratic Party was a direct result of the growth of the viable and conservative southern Republican Party, and the extension of greater voting rights to African Americans.[23] It should also be noted that the development of liberalism among southern Democrats is at least partly a story of segregation; as whites abandoned the Democratic Party for the GOP, the Democrats became even more dependent on black votes.[24]

Unity, Linkage, and Accountability

Parties provide the glue that holds together the disparate elements of the fragmented U.S. governmental and political apparatus. The Framers designed a system that divides and subdivides power, making it possible to preserve individual liberty but difficult to coordinate and produce action in a timely fashion. Parties help compensate for this drawback by linking all the institutions of power one to another. Although rivalry between the executive and legislative branches of U.S. government is inevitable, the partisan affiliations of the leaders of each branch constitute a common basis for cooperation, as any president and his fellow party members in Congress usually have demonstrated daily. Often when President Bill Clinton proposed a major new program (such as health care or crime control), Democratic members of the Congress usually were the first to speak up in favor of the program and to orchestrate efforts for its passage. Political scientist Kelly D. Patterson shows that presidential candidates tend to advocate policies similar to those advocated by their party's congressional leaders, suggesting that the diminished power of party elites in the presidential nomination process has not weakened parties' linkage function.[25]

Even within each branch, there is intended fragmentation, and the party once again helps narrow the differences between the House of Representatives and the Senate, or between the president and the chiefs in the executive bureaucracy. Similarly, the division of national, state, and local governments, while always an invitation to conflict, is made more workable and easily coordinated by the intersecting party relationships that exist among office holders at all levels. Party affiliation, in other words, is a basis for mediation and negotiation laterally among the branches and vertically among the layers.

The party's linkage function does not end there. Party identification and organization are natural connectors and vehicles for communication between the voter and the candidate, as well as between the voter and the office holder. The party connection is one means of increasing accountability in election campaigns and in government. Candidates on the campaign trail and elected party leaders in office are required from time to time to account for their performance at party-sponsored forums, nominating primaries, and conventions.

Political parties, too, can take some credit for unifying the nation by dampening sectionalism. Because parties must form national majorities in order to win the presidency, any single, isolated region is guaranteed minority status unless it establishes ties with other areas. The party label and philosophy build the bridge that enables regions to join forces; in the process, a national interest, rather than a merely sectional one, is created and served.

One of the last of the big-city party bosses, Chicago Mayor Richard J. Daley controlled a powerful political machine for more than twenty-five years.

(Photo courtesy: Bettmann/Corbis)

The Electioneering Function

The election, proclaimed author H. G. Wells, is "democracy's ceremonial, its feast, its great function," and the political parties assist this ceremony in essential ways. First, the parties funnel eager, interested individuals into politics and government. Thousands of candidates are recruited each year by the two parties, as are many of the candidates' staff members—the people who manage the campaigns and go on to serve in key governmental positions once the election has been won.

Elections can have meaning in a democracy only if they are competitive, and in the United States, they probably could not be competitive without the parties. Even in the South, traditionally the least politically competitive U.S. region, the parties today regularly produce reasonably vigorous contests at the state (and increasingly the local) level.

Party as a Voting and Issue Cue

A voter's party identification acts as an invaluable filter for information, a perceptual screen that affects how he or she digests political news. Therefore, party affiliation provides a useful cue for voters, particularly for the least informed and least interested, who can use the party as a shortcut or substitute for interpreting issues and events they may not fully comprehend. Better-educated and more involved voters also find party identification helpful. After all, no one has the time to study every issue carefully or to become fully knowledgeable about every candidate seeking public office.

Policy Formulation and Promotion

U.S. Senator Huey Long (D–LA), one of the premier spokesmen for "the people," was usually able to capture the flavor of the average person's views about politics. Considering an independent bid for president before his assassination in 1935, Long liked to compare the Republican and Democratic parties to the two patent medicines offered by a traveling salesman. Asked the difference between them, the salesman explained that the "High Populorum" tonic was made from the bark of the tree taken from the top down, while "Low Populorum" tonic was made from bark stripped from the root up. The analogous moral, according to Long, was this: "The only difference I've found in Congress between the Republican and Democratic leadership is that one of 'em is skinning us from the ankle up and the other from the ear down!"[26]

Long would certainly have insisted that his fable applied to the **national party platform,** the most visible instrument by which parties formulate, convey, and promote public policy. Every four years, each party writes for the presidential nominating conventions a lengthy platform explaining its positions on key issues. Many citizens in our own era undoubtedly believe that party platforms are relatively undifferentiated, a mixture of pabulum and pussyfooting. Yet, political scientist Gerald M. Pomper's study of party platforms from 1944 through 1976 has demonstrated that each party's pledges were consistently and significantly different, a function in part of the varied groups in their coalitions.[27] Interestingly, about 69 percent of the specific platform positions were taken by one party but not the other. The trend observed by Pomper continues. On abortion, for example, the Democrats are strongly for abortion rights while the Republicans are firmly against them in their most recent platforms.

Granted, then, party platforms are quite distinctive. Does this elaborate party exercise in policy formulation mean anything? One could argue that the platform is valuable, if only as a clear presentation of a party's basic philosophy and as a forum for activist opinion and public education. But, platforms have much more impact than that. About two-thirds of the promises in the victorious party's presidential platform have been completely or mostly implemented; even more astounding, one-half or more of the pledges of the losing party find their way into public policy (with the success rate

national party platform
A statement of the general and specific philosophy and policy goals of a political party, usually promulgated at the national convention.

State Control
and National
Platforms

Senator Huey Long (D–LA) campaigned for the presidency in 1935 on a populist platform, arguing in fiery speeches that neither of the major parties' policies had the people's best interests at heart.
(Photo courtesy: Bettmann/Corbis)

depending on whether the party controls one, both, or neither house of Congress).[28] The party platform also has great influence on a new presidential administration's legislative program and on the president's State of the Union Address. While party affiliation is normally the single most important determinant of voting in Congress and in state legislatures,[29] the party–vote relationship is even stronger when party platform issues come up on the floor of Congress. Pomper concludes: "We should therefore take platforms seriously, because politicians appear to take them seriously."[30] More recent analyses of the role of party platforms, however, tend to discount their electoral significance in the 1990s. L. Sandy Maisel, for instance, states that in the 1990s and beyond, party platforms "really are not party platforms" anymore. They are instead "presidential candidate-centered platforms." They are documents written to be generally noncontroversial and acceptable to broad coalitions of voters, not to set the national policy agenda nor spur debate on the direction of government. They are written by and for the candidate seeking office, not as representations of the party positions on current and philosophical issues.[31]

Besides mobilizing Americans on a permanent basis, then, the parties convert the cacophony of hundreds of identifiable social and economic groups into a two-part semi-harmony that is much more comprehensible, if not always on key and pleasing to the ears. The simplicity of two-party politics may be deceptive, given the enormous variety in public policy choices, but a sensible system of representation in the American context might be impossible without it. The people who would suffer most from its absence would not be the few who are individually or organizationally powerful; their voices would be heard under almost any system. As political scientist Walter Dean Burnham has pointed out, the losers would be the many individually powerless for whom the parties are the only effective devices yet created that can generate collective power on their behalf.[32]

THE BASIC STRUCTURE OF AMERICAN POLITICAL PARTIES

While the distinctions might not be as clear today as they were two or three decades ago, the two major parties remain fairly simply organized, with national, state, and local branches (see Figure 12.2). The different levels of each party represent diverse interests in Washington, D.C., state capitals, and local governments throughout the nation.

The pyramid shown in Figure 12.2 illustrates the hierarchy of party organization in the United States, and it will help you to see how parties operate in a general sense. This very simple diagram, however, is deceptive in one important way: Not shown is that the national, state, and local parties overlap. Frequently, state and local parties have more influence than the national party in their region, and their decisions can override the national party. This is especially true in the Republican Party. A diagram this simple cannot fully represent the dynamic and complex interrelationships of national, state, and local parties.

National Committees

The first national party committees were skeletal and formed some years after the creation of the presidential nominating conventions in the 1830s. First the Democrats in 1848 and then the Republicans in 1856 established national governing bodies—the Democratic National Committee, or DNC, and the Republican National Committee, or RNC—to make arrangements for the conventions and to coordinate the subsequent presidential campaigns. The DNC and RNC were each composed of one representative

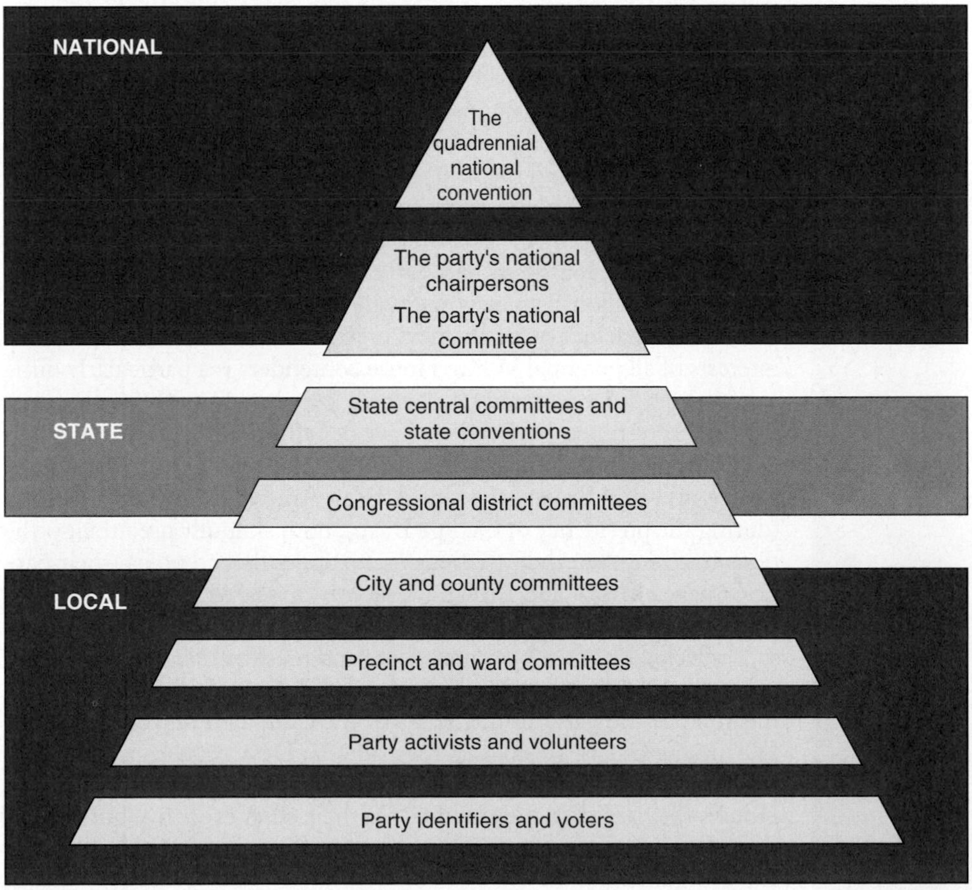

FIGURE 12.2   Political Party Organization in America: From Base to Pinnacle

from each state; this was expanded to two in the 1920s after the post of state committeewoman was established. The states had complete control over the selection of their representatives to the national committees. In addition, to serve their interests, the congressional party caucuses in both houses organized their own national committees, loosely allied with the DNC and RNC. The National Republican Congressional Committee (NRCC) was started in 1866 when the Radical Republican congressional delegation was feuding with Abraham Lincoln's moderate successor, President Andrew Johnson, and wanted a counterweight to his control of the RNC. At the same time, House and Senate Democrats set up a similar committee.

After the popular election of U.S. senators was initiated in 1913 with the ratification of the Seventeenth Amendment to the Constitution, both parties organized separate Senate campaign committees. This three-part arrangement of national party committee, House party committee, and Senate party committee has persisted in both parties to the present day, and each party's three committees are located together in Washington, D.C. There is, however, an informal division of labor among the national committees. Whereas the DNC and RNC focus primarily on aiding presidential campaigns and conducting general party-building activities, the congressional campaign committees work primarily to maximize the number of seats held by their respective parties in Congress. In the past two decades, all six national committees have become major, service-oriented organizations in American politics.[33]

Leadership

The key national party official is the chairperson of the national committee. Although the chair is formally elected by the national committee, he or she is usually selected by the sitting president or newly nominated presidential candidate, who is accorded the right to name the individual for at least the duration of his or her campaign. Only the post-campaign, out-of-power party committee actually has the authority to appoint a chairperson independently. The committee-crowned chairpersons generally have the greatest impact on the party, because they come to their posts at times of crisis when a leadership vacuum exists. (A defeated presidential candidate is technically the head of the national party until the next nominating convention, but the reality is naturally otherwise as a party attempts to shake off a losing image.) The chair often becomes the prime spokesperson and arbitrator for the party during the four years between elections. He or she is called on to damp down factionalism, negotiate candidate disputes, raise money, and prepare the machinery for the next presidential election. Balancing the interests of all potential White House contenders is a particularly difficult job, and strict neutrality is normally expected from the chair.

In recent times, both parties have benefited from adept leadership while out of power. William Brock, RNC chair during the Carter presidency, and Ron Brown, the first African American to chair the DNC (during the presidency of George Bush), both skillfully used their positions to strengthen their parties organizationally and polish their parties' images. Brock and Brown frequently appeared on news shows to give the out-of-power party's viewpoint. By contrast, party chairpersons selected by incumbent presidents and presidential candidates tend to be close allies of the presidents or candidates and often subordinate the good of the party to the needs of the campaign or White House. During the Carter presidency, for example, DNC Chairman Kenneth Curtis and his successor John White were creatures of the White House; they acted as cheerleaders for their chief executive but did little to keep the Democratic Party competitive with the strengthening GOP organization.

Chrissy Gephardt appears with her father, Representative Richard Gephardt (D-MO), during the 2004 primary season. Richard Gephardt, who abandoned his bid for the presidency after a disappointing showing in the Iowa Caucus, served as the Democratic Leader of the House of Representatives from 1989 to 2003.

(Photo courtesy: Sal DiMarco/Black Star)

Because of their command of presidential patronage and influence, a few national party chairpersons selected by presidents have become powerful and well known, such as Republican Mark Hanna during the McKinley presidency (1897–1901) and Democrat James Farley under President Franklin D. Roosevelt. Most presidentially appointed chairs, however, have been relatively obscure; the chance for a chairperson to make a difference and cut a memorable figure generally comes when there is no competition from a White House nominee or occupant.

National Conventions

Every four years, each party holds a **national convention** to nominate its presidential and vice presidential candidates. Much of any party chairperson's work involves planning the presidential nominating convention, the most publicized and vital event on the party's calendar. Until 1984, gavel-to-gavel coverage was standard practice on all national television networks. Even after the recent cutbacks by some news organizations, a substantial block of time is still devoted to the conventions. (In 2004, for example, networks devoted up to three hours of nightly prime-time convention coverage.) Although the nomination of the presidential ticket naturally receives the lion's share of attention, the convention also fulfills its role as the ultimate governing body for the party. The rules adopted and the platform passed at the quadrennial conclave are durable guidelines that steer the party for years after the final gavel has been brought down.

Most of the recent party chairpersons, in cooperation with the incumbent president or likely nominee, have tried to orchestrate every minute of the conventions in order to project just the right image to voters. By and large, they have succeeded, though at the price of draining some spontaneity and excitement from the convention process.

national convention
A party conclave (meeting) held in the presidential election year for the purposes of nominating a presidential and vice presidential ticket and adopting a platform.

States and Localities

Although national committee activities of all kinds attract most of the media attention, the party is structurally based not in Washington, D.C., but in the states and localities. Except for the campaign finance arena, virtually all governmental regulation of political parties is left to the states, for example, and most elected officials give their allegiance to the local party divisions they know best. Most important, the vast majority of party leadership positions are filled at subnational levels.

The pyramid arrangement of party committees provides for a broad base of support. The smallest voting unit, the precinct, usually takes in a few adjacent neighborhoods and is the fundamental building block of the party. Each of the more than 100,000 precincts in the United States potentially has a committee member to represent it in each party's councils. The precinct committee members are the key foot soldiers of any party, and their efforts are supplemented by party committees above them in the wards, cities, counties, towns, villages, and congressional districts.

The state governing body supervising this collection of local party organizations is usually called the state central (or executive) committee. It comprises representatives from all major geographic units, as determined by and selected under state law. Generally, state parties are free to act within the limits set by their state legislatures without interference from the national party, except in the selection and seating of presidential convention delegates. National Democrats have been particularly inclined to regulate this aspect of party life. With the decline of big-city political machines, few local parties have the clout to object to the national party's dictates.

Research conducted by political scientists shows that state and local parties have become significantly stronger over the past three decades. Comparing the same county parties in 1964 and 1980, for example, a team of political scientists found considerable increases in several important campaign activities: fund-raising, campaign events, registration drives, publicity of party and candidate activity, and the distribution of campaign literature.[34] A subsequent study indicates that local parties have continued to increase their levels of activity in these areas.[35] While all this renewed party activity surely helps the parties' candidates, recent research indicates that higher levels of party organizational strength also lead to greater public support for political parties as institutions.[36]

Many states have also seen the emergence of state legislative campaign committees.[37] These party committees resemble the congressional campaign committees at the national level in that they are run by a party's legislative incumbents and exist primarily to help maximize the number of legislative seats held by the party of which they are part. (For example, the Democratic Assembly Campaign Committee in the New York State assembly seeks primarily to maximize the number of Democrats elected to the assembly.) Importantly, legislative campaign committees are playing an increasingly vital role in the financing of state legislative elections.[38] One scholar, however, points out that these committees care little about the overall party ticket and thus resemble big political consulting firms more than they do traditional political parties.[39]

Examining separately the national, state, and local parties should not lead us to overlook the increasing integration of these committees. The national parties have become fund-raising powerhouses during the last two decades, and they now channel significant financial support—much of it in soft money—to state parties. This financial support has given the national parties considerable leverage over the state committees—many of which have become dependent on the funding—and the national parties have increasingly used the state committees to help execute national campaigns.

The growing reliance of state parties on national party funding has changed fundamentally the balance of power in the American party system. Whereas power previously flowed up from the state and local parties to the national committees, the national committees now enjoy considerable leverage over state and local parties.[40] That said, the relationships among the national, state, and local party committees were altered once again with the implementation of the Bipartisan Campaign Reform Act for the 2004 elections (see chapter 14 for details of the Bipartisan Campaign Reform Act).

Informal Groups

The formal structure of party organization is supplemented by numerous official, semi-official, and unaffiliated groups that combine and clash with the parties in countless ways. Both the DNC and RNC have affiliated organizations of state and local party women (the National Federation of Democratic Women and the National Federation of Republican Women). The youth divisions (the Young Democrats of America and the Young Republicans' National Federation) have a generous definition of "young," up to and including age thirty-five. The state governors in each party have their own party associations, too.

Just outside the party orbit are the supportive interest groups and associations that often provide money, labor, or other forms of assistance to the parties. Labor unions, progressive political action committees (PACs), teachers, African American and liberal women's groups, and the Americans for Democratic Action are some of the Democratic Party's organizational groups. Business PACs, the U.S. Chamber of Commerce, fundamentalist Christian organizations, and some anti-abortion groups work closely with the Republicans. Similar party–interest group pairings occur in Britain, where trade unions have aligned themselves with the Labour Party, providing the bulk of the party's contributions, and business has been closely allied with the Conservatives.

Each U.S. party has several institutionalized sources of policy ideas. Though unconnected to the parties in any official sense, these so-called *think tanks* (institutional collections of policy-oriented researchers and academics) are quite influential. During the Reagan administration, for instance, the right-wing Heritage Foundation placed many dozens of its conservatives in important governmental positions, and its issue studies on subjects ranging from tax reform to South Africa carried considerable weight with policy makers. The more moderate and bipartisan American Enterprise Institute also supplied the Reagan team with people and ideas. On the Democratic side, liberal think tanks

WEB EXPLORATION
To explore the ideological agendas of unaffiliated think tanks and search for connections to specific parties or politicians, go to www.ablongman.com/oconnor

proliferated during the party's Reagan- and Bush-induced exile from 1981 to 1993. More than a half-dozen policy institutes formed in an attempt to nurse the Democrats back to political health. The Center for National Policy and the Progressive Policy Institute, to cite two, sponsored conferences and published papers on Democratic policy alternatives.

Finally, there are extra-party organizations that form for a wide variety of purposes, including "reforming" a party or moving it ideologically to the right or left. In New York City, for example, Democratic reform clubs were established in the late 1800s to fight the Tammany Hall machine, the city's dominant Democratic organization at the time. About seventy clubs still prosper by attracting well-educated activists committed to various liberal causes. More recently, both national parties have been favored (or bedeviled) by the formation of new extra-party outfits. The Democrats have been pushed by both halves of the ideological continuum. The Democratic Leadership Council (DLC) was launched in 1985 by moderate and conservative Democrats concerned about what they perceived as the leftward drift of their party and its image as the captive of liberal special interest groups. It is composed of more than one hundred current and former Democratic office holders (such as Congressman Harold Ford of Tennessee and Senator John Edwards of North Carolina). The DLC has not always been popular with the national party leadership, which has sometimes viewed it as a potential rival, but it nurtured and strongly backed Bill Clinton's candidacy in 1992 and 1996. Several DLC leaders were appointed to positions in the Clinton administration.

The DLC formed in part to counter a left-leaning force organizing from within the partisan ranks, Jesse Jackson's National Rainbow Coalition. The coalition is partly a vehicle for Jackson's ambitions. Beyond that, its goals of mass membership, hundreds of state and local charter affiliates, and endorsements of independent candidates when Democratic nominees are found to be "unacceptable" present a challenge to the Democratic Party in the eyes of at least some party officials.

On the Republican side, GOPAC was prominent throughout the 1990s but lost influence after the resignation of its leader, Newt Gingrich. The void in the Republican organization is now being filled less formally by leading conservative representatives such as House Majority Leader Tom DeLay (R–TX) and Chair of the House Republican Caucus Deborah Pryce (R–OH), and the Head of the House Republican Campaign Committee, Tom Reynolds of New York.

Over the past decade, informal groups allied with the two parties have become more fully (if informally) integrated into the increasingly complex party network, often working closely with the national and state parties in conducting campaigns. Indeed, as political scientist John F. Bibby observes, parties and interest group allies now work together so closely that "the traditional lines of demarcation between parties and interest groups are no longer clear."[41]

WEB EXPLORATION

To learn about the informal factions and interest groups that strive for influence with the major parties, go to www.ablongman.com/oconnor

THE PARTY IN GOVERNMENT

Political parties are not restricted to their role as grassroots organizations of voters; they also have another major role inside government institutions. Parties are the organizing mechanisms for the branches and layers of American government.

The Congressional Party

In no segment of U.S. government is the party more visible or vital than in the Congress. In this century, the political parties have dramatically increased the sophistication and impact of their internal congressional organizations. Prior to the beginning of every session, the parties in both houses of Congress gather (or "caucus") separately to select party leaders (House speaker and minority leader, Senate majority and minority leaders, party whips, and so on) and to arrange for the appointment of members of each chamber's committees. In effect, then, the parties organize and operate the Congress. Their management

Senate Majority Leader Bill Frist (R-TN) witnessed his party's margin of control increase by four seats in the 2004 elections. Frist has been mentioned frequently as a possible Republcian presidential candidate in 2008.

(Photo courtesy: AP/World Wide Photos)

systems have grown quite elaborate; the web of deputy and assistant whips for House Democrats now extends to about one-fourth of the party's entire membership. Although not invulnerable to pressure from the minority, the majority party in each house generally holds sway, even fixing the size of its majority on all committees—a proportion frequently in excess of the percentage of seats it holds in the house as a whole.

Discipline.   Congressional party leaders have some substantial tools at their disposal to enforce a degree of discipline in their troops. Even though seniority usually determines most committee assignments, an occasional choice plum may be given to the loyal or withheld from the rebellious. For example, Newt Gingrich, speaker of the House for the 104th and 105th Congresses, rewarded his most loyal freshmen representatives with plum slots on major committees, such as Ways and Means, when he took the reins in January 1995. Gingrich also took the unprecedented step of appointing committee chairs, and on several committees he disregarded seniority altogether and awarded chairmanships to members he believed would fight most aggressively for the GOP's program.[42] A member's bill can be lovingly caressed through the legislative process, or it can be summarily dismissed without so much as a hearing. Pork barrel projects—government projects yielding rich patronage benefits that sustain many a legislator's electoral survival—may be included or deleted during the appropriations process. Small favors and perquisites (such as the allocation of desirable office space or the scheduling of floor votes for the convenience of a member) can also be useful levers. Then, too, there are the campaign aids at the command of the leadership: money from party sources, endorsements, appearances in the district or at fund-raising events, and so on. On rare occasions the leaders and their allies in the party caucus may even impose sanctions of various sorts (such as stripping away seniority rights or prized committee berths) in order to punish recalcitrant lawmakers.[43]

There are, however, limits to coordinated, cohesive party action. For example, the separate executive branch, the bicameral power-sharing, and the extraordinary decentralization of Congress's work all constitute institutional obstacles to effective party action. Moreover, party discipline is hurt by the individualistic nature of U.S. politics: campaigns that are candidate-centered rather than party-oriented; diverse electoral constituencies to which members of Congress must understandably be responsive; the largely private system of election financing that indebts legislators to wealthy individuals and nonparty interest groups more than to their parties; and the importance to lawmakers of attracting the news media's attention—often more easily done by showmanship than by quiet, effective labor within the party system.

Despite all of the barriers to cohesive party action, events occasionally move a party in that direction. One such example occurred in 1994, when most Republican U.S. House candidates signed onto the "Contract with America," a party platform for Congressional campaigns similar in some respects to a formal presidential platform. The Contract included such popular items as tax relief, term limits for members of Congress, and welfare reform, and it became the basis for the House of Representatives' legislative activity in early 1995. While not all of these items were passed by the legislature or signed into law by the president, in debating and voting on the Contract, both the Republicans and Democrats showed that cohesive party action can still be achieved.

Indeed, given the previously discussed barriers to coordinated party activity, it is impressive to discover that party labels have consistently been the most powerful predictor of congressional roll-call voting, and in the last few years even more votes have closely followed the partisan divide. While not invariably predictive, as in strong parliamentary systems, a member's party affiliation has proven to be the indicator of his or her votes more than 70 percent of the time in recent years; that is, the average representative or senator sides with his or her party on about 70 percent of the votes that divide a majority of Democrats from a majority of Republicans. In most recent years, more than half of the roll-call votes in the House and Senate also found majorities of Democrats and Republicans on opposite sides.

In the past several years, party voting has increased noticeably, as reflected in the upward trend demonstrated in Figure 12.3. While in 1992 Democrats and Republicans already voted with their party 79 percent of the time, the number sky-rocketed to 88 percent of the time for the first year of President Bill Clinton's first term in 1993. The number started to reduce until after the 1994 midterm elections that saw "Republican Revolution" during which the Republicans reclaimed majorities of both Houses of Congress. When the Republicans arrived in Washington, D.C., in 1995, they voted together an astounding 91 percent of the time while Democrats remained high at 80 percent. Ordinarily, party unity decreases when the party controlling Congress is different from the one controlling the Presidency; however, the Republican Party voted with high party unity during Clinton's very popular second term, the percentage of party unity only slightly increasing during George W. Bush's first term. In 2005, the wider margins for Republicans in Congress and the re-election of Bush will likely lead to a continuation of high party unity, a problem particularly for the Senate, since Republicans there lack the 60 Senator majority (having only 53 Republican Senators) necessary to break a filibuster.[44]

There are many reasons for the recent growth of congressional party unity and cohesion. Some are the result of long-term political factors. Both congressional parties, for instance, have gradually become more ideologically homogeneous and internally consistent. Southern Democrats today are more moderate and much closer philosophically to their northern counterparts than the South's legislative barons of old ever were. Similarly, there are few liberal Republicans left in either chamber of Congress, and GOP House members from all regions of the country are—with a few exceptions—moderately to solidly conservative. As each party became more ideologically homogeneous, rank-and-file members of Congress (especially in the House) delegated to party leaders enhanced powers with which to push through the party's agenda.[45] At the same time, strong two-party competition has come to almost all areas of the nation. The electoral insecurity produced by vigorous competition seems to encourage party unity and cooperation in a legislature (perhaps as a kind of "circling the wagons" effect).[46]

FIGURE 12.3 Congressional Party Unity Scores, 1959–2003

Note how party-based voting has increased conspicuously since the 1970s.

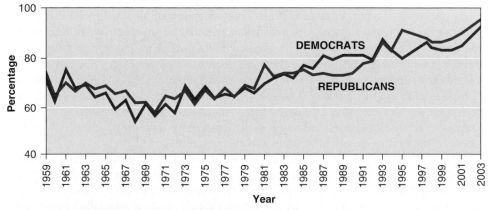

Source: Congressional Quarterly Almanacs (Washington, DC: CQ Press).

The circumstances of contemporary politics are also producing greater party cohesion. The militancy of Speaker of the House Newt Gingrich (R–GA) raised the partisan hackles of many Democrats, polarizing the House a bit more along party lines. In fact, Gingrich's Contract with America generated very strong party voting in the House in early 1995; most floor votes found virtually all Republicans supporting the provisions of the Contract, with most Democrats voting in opposition. On the other side of the Capitol, the continuing, close partisan struggle since 1980 over control of the Senate has appeared to increase the party consciousness of both groups of senators.

The recent defections of legislators from both parties ironically support the strengthening of party cohesion. Conservative Democratic Representative Virgil Goode of Virginia left the Democratic Party in January 2000 and is now a Republican. Similarly, liberal Republican Senator Jim Jeffords bolted the GOP and became an independent in spring 2001, shifting control of the Senate to the Democrats. These and other defections underscore that the polarization of the electorate is continuing. Liberals are moving more firmly into the Democratic camp, and conservatives are aligning strongly with the Republican party. Rather than consistently vote against the party with which they were identified on Election Day, legislators are crossing over to the party that more accurately reflects their own ideology and, in most cases, the ideology of their constituents.

The political party campaign committees have also played a role in the renewed cohesiveness observed within Congress. Each national party committee has been recruiting and training House and Senate candidates as never before, and devising common themes for all nominees in election seasons—work that may help to produce a consensual legislative agenda for each party. Party money and campaign services, such as media advertisements and polling, may also help convert candidates into team players. The evidence for this, however, is mixed, with some research showing that party money increases party loyalty among House members[47] while other research reveals no such effect.[48]

The Presidential Party

Political parties may be more central to the operation of the legislative branch than the executive branch, but it is the presidential party that captures the public imagination and shapes the electorate's opinion of the two parties. In our very personalized politics, voters' perceptions of the incumbent president and the presidential candidates determine to a large extent how citizens perceive the parties.

The chief executive's successes are his party's successes; his failures are borne by the party as much as by the individual. The image projected by a losing presidential candidate is incorporated into the party's contemporary portrait, whether wanted or not. As the highest elected candidate of the national party, the president naturally assumes the role of party leader, as does the nominee of the other party (at least during the campaign).

The juggling of contradictory roles is not always easy for a president. Expected to bring the country together as ceremonial chief of state and also to forge a ruling consensus as head of government, the president must also be an effective commander of a sometimes divided party. Along with the inevitable headaches party leadership brings, though, are clear and compelling advantages. Foremost among them is a party's ability to mobilize support among voters for a president's program. Also, the executive's legislative agenda might be derailed more quickly without the common tie of party label between the chief executive and many members of Congress; all presidents appeal for some congressional support on the basis of shared party affiliation, and they generally receive it depending on circumstances and their executive skill.

These party gifts to the president are reciprocated in many ways. In addition to compiling a record for the party and giving substance to its image, presidents appoint many activists to office, recruit candidates, raise money for the party treasury, campaign extensively for party nominees during election seasons, and occasionally provide some "coattail" help to fellow office seekers who are on the ballot in presidential election years.

ANALYZING VISUALS

Parties and the Presidency

As you know, political cartoons express commentary about current events and leaders in a sharp and often entertaining way. The cartoon below by Mike Luckovich was published in the *Atlanta Journal and Constitution* in March 2002. Study the cartoon for a few moments, and then answer the following critical thinking questions: What can you infer about the pres-ident's popularity at the time the cartoon was published? What, specifically, may have been the reason for the president's popularity at that time? Why, more generally, do the public and even politicians from the opposing party sometimes unite behind the president? Would the cartoon make much sense if it were published today? Why or why not?

(Photo courtesy: By permission of Mike Luckovich and Creators Syndicate, Inc.)

Pro-Party Presidents.   Some presidents take their party responsibilities more seriously than others. Democrats Woodrow Wilson and Franklin D. Roosevelt were exceptionally party oriented and dedicated to building their party electorally and governmentally. Republican Gerald R. Ford, during his brief tenure from 1974 to 1977, also achieved a reputation as a party builder. He was willing to undertake campaign and organizational chores for the GOP (especially in fund-raising and in barnstorming for nominees) that most other presidents minimized or shunned. Perhaps Ford's previous role as House minority leader made him more sensitive to the needs of his fellow party office holders.

Ronald Reagan and George Bush exemplified the "pro-party" presidency. Reagan was one of the most party-oriented presidents of recent times.[49] In 1983 and 1984, during his own reelection effort, Reagan made more than two dozen campaign and fund-raising appearances for all branches of the party organization and candidates at every level. He taped more than 300 television endorsements as well, including one for an obscure Honolulu city council contest. Reagan also showed a willingness to get involved in the nitty-gritty of candidate recruitment, frequently calling strong potential candidates to urge them to run. Unlike Dwight D. Eisenhower, Reagan was willing to attempt a popularity transfer to his party and to campaign for Republicans whether or not they were strongly loyal to him personally. Unlike Lyndon B. Johnson, Reagan was willing to put his prestige and policies to the test on the campaign trail. Unlike Richard M. Nixon, Reagan spent time and effort helping underdogs and long-shot candidates,

Join the Debate

For four brief months in 2001, the presidency, the U.S. Senate, and the U.S. House were all controlled by Republicans. Then, in May 2001, Vermont's U.S. Senator Jim Jeffords shocked the political world by renouncing his lifelong affiliation with the Republican Party and declaring that he was independent and that he would vote with Democrats to organize the Senate. Occasionally, members of Congress have switched party affiliation in the middle of their term of office (for instance, in the 1990s, eight House members and three senators switched parties). But this time, since the Senate was tied 50–50 Democratic-Republican (with Republican Vice President Cheney breaking the tie), Jeffords's decision turned control of the Senate over to the Democrats.

Ultimately, the Senate returned to Republican control following the 2002 midterm elections, but the Jeffords party switch (and the possibility of other legislators switching parties) raises an important issue. As noted in the text, party control is critical in Congress. Senator Jeffords's decision stoked the fires of a debate over whether an official elected in a partisan election should be allowed to renounce that party affiliation in the middle of a term and serve out the term aligned with the opposing party. Or should he or she resign his seat and run again as an independent or with another party's nomination, as then-Representative Phil Gramm of Texas did in 1983? Does a party switch violate the trust of the voters? Does it undo the results of the election? In a democracy, should one person have the power to unilaterally decide who controls a governmental body? Or are policy convictions good grounds for making such a switch? Obviously in the Jeffords case, Republicans and Democrats differed in their assessment of the issue. Read and think about the issues the following 2002 news article raises. Then, join the debate over congressional party switchers by considering the debating points and questions posed at the end of this feature, and sharpen your own arguments for the position you find most viable.

GOP, Dems Squabble over Senate Control with November Elections Looming

By Jill Zuckman

WASHINGTON—One year after a lone Republican senator dramatically altered the balance of power in Washington, Democrats and Republicans are engaged in an intense public relations battle to convince voters that the move was either a godsend or a disaster.

In the wake of the May 24, 2001, decision by Sen. James Jeffords of Vermont to leave the Republican Party and become an independent, President Bush's domestic agenda has faltered in Congress, with the Senate now serving as a graveyard for Republican priorities.

Whether that has helped or hurt the country is an open question, and the parties are urgently making their case in hopes of influencing the midterm elections in November [2002]. The elections could either solidify the Democrats' hold on the Senate, which they control 51–49 with Jeffords' vote, or tilt power back to the Republicans.

The campaign to influence voters' view of the Democrats' unprecedented assumption of power in a non-election year includes: television ads vilifying Senate leaders; verbal accusations of abuse of power; frequent appearances by Jeffords, a lifelong Republican, on behalf of Democrats.

Jeffords said he has no regrets about his decision, though he worries about what would happen if Republicans were to prevail in November. "I'm campaigning for Democrats to make sure that (the Republicans) don't take it back," Jeffords said. "I'm worried for the country."

Jeffords said he left the GOP because Republicans had too much power when they controlled the House, the Senate and the White House. He wanted more money spent on education, he said, but Republican leaders refused, and he fears that would happen again. "I'm worried they'll gobble up all the money," he said. "They have this war. They talk about the war, the war, the war. They do that to build up more money for defense."

Democrats … brag that their ascent has been invaluable in countering what they portray as a group of extreme House Republicans and a president who is more conservative than most voters anticipated.

They plan to highlight such issues as education, the environment and Social Security, and they are importing Michele Forman, the 2001 teacher of the year, who is from Vermont. When Jeffords was still a Republican, Bush excluded him from the Rose Garden ceremony recognizing Forman—a snub that some say was among the incidents that prompted Jeffords' defection. Senate Majority Leader Tom Daschle, D–SD, said in an interview that with control of the Senate, Democrats have been able to prevent drilling in the Arctic

National Wildlife Refuge, stop Bush nominee Charles Pickering of Mississippi from becoming a federal appeals judge, halt additional tax cuts and keep the administration from increasing the cost of student loans.

"What Jim Jeffords did was to create brakes in the governmental car here," Daschle said. "Before this, there was nothing to check the administration and check the Republicans. We were able to do that in a very profound way." Sen. Harry Reid, D–Nev., the assistant majority leader, agreed: "We've been able to stop a lot of things from happening."

… [T]he significance of the Democrats' seizure of power a year ago can hardly be overestimated. Republicans controlled the Senate after the 2000 elections, despite a 50–50 split, because Vice President Dick Cheney cast the tie-breaking vote under the Constitution.

Jeffords' switch to independent gave Democrats all committee chairmanships and the ability to schedule—or not schedule—legislation for consideration by the full Senate.

On the flip side, Republicans are pointing to all that has gone wrong from their perspective since Jeffords switched—and their list of failures does not sound that different from the Democrats' list of victories. Republicans cite stalled and stymied judicial nominations, a big-spending farm bill, the Senate's refusal to allow drilling in the arctic refuge and a bogged-down trade measure sought by the president.

Republicans complain that Daschle has used his power unfairly. Sen. Rick Santorum of Pennsylvania, a member of the Republican leadership team, said that since May 2001, the Senate has become more polarized and partisan. "It put the Democrats in control and in position to attempt to thwart Bush's agenda and increase the size and scope of government," Santorum said….

Source: Jill Zuckman, *Chicago Tribune* (May 21, 2002): 8. Copyright 5/21/02 Chicago Tribune Co. All rights reserved. Used with permission.

JOIN THE DEBATE!

CHECK YOUR UNDERSTANDING: Make sure you understand the following key points from the article; go back and review it if you missed any of them:

- Senator Jeffords's switch to independent status gave Democrats all the committee chairmanships in the Senate.
- Senator Jeffords's reason for switching parties was that the Republican Party was too conservative and too powerful in holding both chambers of Congress and the presidency.
- By reinstating divided government, Senator Jeffords's party switch hurt President Bush's success rate for his domestic agenda.

ADDITIONAL INFORMATION: News articles don't provide all the information an informed citizen needs to know about an issue under debate. Here are some questions the article does not answer that you may need to consider in order to join the debate:

- How often does party switching actually affect political and policy outcomes?
- How many party switchers are there currently in Congress, and which parties do they represent?
- Could a member of Congress be forced to resign and, if so, how?

What other information might you want to know? Where might you gather this information? How might you evaluate the credibility of the information you gather? Is the information from a reliable source? Can you identify any potential biases?

IDENTIFYING THE ARGUMENTS: Now that you have some information on the issue, and have thought about what else you need to know, see whether you can present the arguments on both sides of the debate. Here are some ideas to get you started. We've provided one example each of "pro" and "con" arguments, but you should be able to offer others:

PRO: Members of Congress should be required to resign if they switch parties. Here's why:

- Party affiliation is a fundamental part of the "contract" between a candidate and voters, and party-switching after an election violates an essential element of democracy—voter approval.

CON: Members of Congress must be allowed to reconsider their partisan affiliation. Here's why:

- Voters elect an individual to Congress, not a party, and if party philosophy changes, the elected member must be free to act according to his or her conscience.

TAKING A POSITION AND SUPPORTING IT: After thinking about the information in the article on Senator Jeffords's switch of party affiliation, placing it in the broader context of popular control of elected officials, and articulating the arguments in the debate, what position would you take? What information supports your position? What arguments would you use to persuade others to your side of the debate? How would you counter arguments on the other side?

not just likely winners. Unlike Jimmy Carter, Reagan signed more than seventy fund-raising appeals for party committees and took a personal interest in the further strengthening of his party's organizational capacity. George Bush, a former RNC chairman, emulated the Reagan model during his own presidency.

coattail effect
The tendency of lesser-known or weaker candidates lower on the ballot to profit in an election by the presence on the party's ticket of a more popular candidate.

However, neither Reagan nor Bush had long enough coattails to help elect their party's nominees lower down on the ballot. Reagan's initial victory in 1980 was one factor in the election of a Republican Senate, but his landslide reelection in 1984, like Nixon's in 1972, had almost no impact on his party's congressional representation. Bush provided no coattails at all to the GOP in 1988. There is little question that the **coattail effect,** the tendency of lesser-known or weaker candidates lower on the ballot to profit in an election by the presence on the party's ticket of a more popular candidate, has diminished sharply compared with a generation ago.[50] Partly, the decreased competitiveness of congressional elections has been produced by artful redistricting and the growing value of incumbency.[51] However, voters are also less willing to think and cast ballots in purely partisan terms, a development that limits presidential leadership and hurts party development. (We return to this subject in the next chapter.) One study concluded that the coattails of Ross Perot in 1992 benefited challengers to House incumbents, regardless of party. In this case, Perot's coattails went toward a general feeling of anti-incumbency, not toward (or against) any one party.[52]

George W. Bush, like his father, is also considered a "pro-party" president, but in the aftermath of September 11, Bush suspended campaigning for Republican gubernatorial candidates Mark Earley in Virginia and Bret Schundler in New Jersey, although it is unlikely that his strong support could have salvaged either campaign. Bush's focus on governing rather than politics in that crucial time garnered him even higher approval ratings among the public. In 2002, however, Bush transferred his strong approval into political capital, as he and Vice President Cheney campaigned and raised a record sum of money for their party, and secured a legislative majority for the second half of his term. These efforts reemerged in 2004 and while campaigning strongly for reelection, The Bush-Cheney campaign also made efforts to secure or increase the Republican margin in Congress.

Nonpartisan Presidents.   Most modern American chief executives have been cast in an entirely different mold from the pro-party presidents of more recent times. Dwight D. Eisenhower elevated "nonpartisanship" to a virtual art form; while this may

Democratic presidential candidate John Kerry addresses the International Association of Fire Fighters, who endorsed his campaign for president. The IAFF was one of dozens of labor unions to endorse Kerry in 2004.

(Photo courtesy: Susan Walsh/AP/World Wide Photos)

have preserved his personal popularity, it proved a disaster for his party. Despite a full two-term occupancy of the White House, the Republican Party remained mired in minority status among the electorate, and Eisenhower never really attempted to transfer his high ratings to the party. Lyndon B. Johnson kept the DNC busy with such trivial tasks as answering wedding invitations sent to the first family. When many of the Democratic senators and representatives elected on his presidential coattails were endangered in the 1966 midterm election, LBJ canceled a major campaign trip on their behalf lest his policies get tied too closely to their possible defeats. Democrats lost forty-seven House seats, three Senate seats, and eight governorships in the 1966 debacle.

In 1972, Richard M. Nixon discouraged the GOP from nominating candidates against conservative southern Democrats in order to improve his own electoral and congressional position, since the grateful unopposed legislators would presumably be less likely to cause Nixon trouble on the campaign trail or in Congress. Nixon also subordinated the party's agenda almost wholly to his own reelection. Shunting aside the Republican National Committee, Nixon formed the Committee to Re-Elect the President, which became known by the acronym CREEP. So removed were party leaders from CREEP's abuses that the Republican Party organization escaped blame during the Watergate investigations.

Jimmy Carter also showed little interest in his national party. Elected as an outsider in 1976, Carter and his top aides at first viewed the party as another extension of the Washington establishment they had pledged to ignore. Carter and his DNC chairmen failed to develop the Democratic Party organizationally and financially in order to keep it competitive during a critical period, while the Republicans were undergoing a dramatic revitalization stimulated by their desire to recover from the Watergate scandal. Later, during his unsuccessful 1980 reelection campaign, Carter was properly criticized for diverting DNC personnel and resources to his presidential needs, such as travel and Christmas cards, rather than permitting them to pursue essential partywide electoral tasks.

Clearly, then, some presidents have taken their party responsibilities more seriously than have others. In general, argues political scientist Sidney Milkis, most presidents since Franklin D. Roosevelt have been less supportive of their respective political parties than have been earlier presidents.[53]

Recent Presidents.   Because Bill Clinton won with such a small plurality (43 percent) in 1992, he produced little coattail for his party's candidates. Like Reagan and Bush before him, though, he campaigned vigorously for many of his party's candidates across the country. Unlike his predecessors, however, Clinton enjoyed little success in transferring popularity. Democrats lost both governor's races in 1993 and a special Senate election in Texas after Clinton won the presidency. Then came the Republican deluge in 1994, when the GOP won fifty-two House seats and nine Senate seats in an election widely regarded as a repudiation of Clinton's presidency.

Before the ink was dry on the obituaries penned by journalists and political pundits, however, Clinton and his party rose from the ashes of the 1994 elections. After outmaneuvering congressional Republicans during the costly government shutdowns of late 1995 and early 1996, Clinton and congressional Democrats saw their popularity ratings climb. Meanwhile, the Republicans tried to regroup, a task made difficult by an acrimonious presidential primary season. Two months later, Clinton was returned to the White House and Democrats significantly cut into the Republican Party's hold on the U.S. House of Representatives, proving again that we should not be too quick to write off any politician, let alone an entire political party. Underlining this conclusion is the remarkable survival of Bill Clinton during 1998, when scandals of various sorts sprouted like daisies in spring. The final proof came in the November pudding, when Clinton's party defied all the rules and predictions. Profiting from the unpopular partisan antagonism between the Republican Congress and Democratic White House, Clinton's party did not lose, but actually won, five seats in the House of Representatives! Through it all, Clinton's high popularity was hardly dented.

Having lost the popular vote and only narrowly capturing a majority in the electoral college, George W. Bush came into the White House with arguably one of the weakest and most bitterly contested mandates in recent history. When Bush took office in January 2001, the Republicans held a six-seat majority in the House and tie-breaking control of a Senate tied 50–50. For the first time in forty-six years, Republicans controlled (however slightly) both branches of the legislature and the White House. Bush was very aware that he would need strong bipartisan support to push through his legislative priorities in the opening months of his term. Most observers were struck, however, by Bush's strong partisanship despite the closeness of the 2000 election and the slim majority in Congress. Difficult odds were made even more perilous by the defection of moderate three-term Senator Jim Jeffords of Vermont from the Republican Party on May 24, 2001. By becoming an independent but caucusing with the Democrats, Jeffords tipped control of the Senate to the Democrats, making Tom Daschle of South Dakota the new majority leader.

Despite the embarrassment and political expense of the Jeffords defection, Bush successfully lobbied for a $1.35 trillion federal income tax cut in June, a signature piece of Bush's presidential campaign. He was also able to move his education plan into the forefront of the legislative agenda before the devastation of the terrorist attacks of September 11, 2001. In the aftermath of September 11, a new political landscape emerged. All of Bush's energy went into helping the country recover from the attacks and preparing the nation for the pursuit of terrorists in Afghanistan and beyond, and he did so with near universal bipartisan support. Both houses overwhelmingly passed an anti-terrorism bill (dubbed the Patriot Act) and legislation improving airline security, providing economic aid to New York City, and bailing out the struggling airline industry.

In 2002, George W. Bush effectively used his still high approval ratings from handling the War on Terror and the aftermath of the September 11 attacks to campaign for Republican Congressional candidates, winning a few more seats in Congress and retaining his Republican majority there. Bush's victory was significant both because it made it easier for him to pass major legislation like programs giving American seniors prescription drug benefits but also because, historically, the president's party loses seats in Congress during midterm elections. The setting for Congressional elections in 2004 was very different, with Bush under heavy criticism for the lack of an apparent exit strategy in Iraq, slower than expected job recovery, and no immediate plan to reduce deficit spending. However, Bush won even more seats for Congress largely because redistricting in strongly Republicans states gave Republicans electoral advantages, especially in Texas. Texas state lawmakers redistricted Democratic incumbents into new largely Republican districts controlled by strong Republican incumbents, resulting in a six seat loss for Congressional Democrats alone.

The Parties and the Judiciary

Many Americans view the judiciary as "above politics" and certainly as nonpartisan, and many judges are quick to agree. Yet, not only do members of the judiciary sometimes follow the election returns and allow themselves to be influenced by popular opinion, but they are also products of their party identification and possess the same partisan perceptual screens as all other politically aware citizens.

Legislators are much more partisan than judges, but it is wrong to assume that judges reach decisions wholly independent of partisan values. First, judges are creatures of the political process, and their posts are considered patronage plums. Judges who are not elected are appointed by presidents or governors for their abilities but also as members of the executive's party and increasingly as representatives of a certain philosophy of or approach to government. Most recent presidents have appointed judges overwhelmingly from their own party; Jimmy Carter and Ronald Reagan, for instance, drew 95 percent or more of their judicial choices from their respective parties. Furthermore, Democratic executives are naturally inclined to select for the bench liberal individuals who may be friendly to the welfare state or critical of some business practices. Republican executives generally lean toward conservatives for judicial posts, hoping they will be tough on criminal defendants, opposed to abortion, and restrained in the use of court power. During the Clinton administration, when Republicans were in charge of both Houses of Congress, the GOP not only refused to confirm many of President Clinton's judicial nominations but also failed to bring many of the nominations to a vote. The result was numerous judicial vacancies across the country and a backlog of cases. Unfortunately, this was an inevitable effect of divided government in a very partisan and ideologically polarized era marked by a mutual lack of trust. Even the strongly Republican chief justice of the Supreme Court, William H. Rehnquist, was moved to criticize the Republican Senate's failure to confirm Clinton nominees. After reclaiming control of the Senate in 2001, Democrats extracted a measure of revenge by refusing to confirm many of George W. Bush's judicial nominees, further compounding the problem of judicial vacancies.

Research has long indicated that party affiliation is a moderately good predictor of judicial decisions in some areas.[54] One specific example involves judicial approval of new congressional districts created by state legislatures every ten years based on the U.S. Census. Randall D. Lloyd found that judges "vote against [redistricting] plans presented from legislatures of their own party at a much lower rate than in cases where the party opposite their own controls the district drawing process.[55] In other words, party matters in the judiciary just as it does in the other two branches of government, although it certainly matters less on the bench than in the legislature and in the executive.

Many judges appointed to office have had long careers in politics as loyal party workers or legislators. Supreme Court Justice Sandra Day O'Connor, for example, was an active member of the National Republican Women's Club and is a former Republican state legislator. Jurists who are elected to office are even more overtly political. In a majority of states, at least some judicial positions are filled by election, and seventeen states hold outright partisan elections, with both parties nominating opposing candidates and running hard-hitting campaigns. In some rural counties across the United States, local judges are not merely partisanly elected figures; they are the key public officials, controlling many patronage jobs and the party machinery.

Clearly, in many places in the United States, judges by necessity and by tradition are not above politics but are in the thick of it. Although election of the judiciary is a questionable practice in light of its specially sanctioned role as impartial arbiter, partisan influence exerted both by jurists' party loyalties and by the appointment (or election) process is useful in retaining some degree of accountability in a branch often accused of being arrogant and aloof.

The Parties and State Governments

Most of the conclusions just discussed about the party's relationship to the legislature, the executive, and the judiciary apply to those branches on the state level as well. The national parties, after all, are organized around state units, and the basic structural arrangement of party and government is much the same in Washington and the state capitals. Remarkably, too, the major national parties are the dominant political forces in all fifty states. This has been true consistently; unlike Great Britain or Canada, the United States has no regional or state parties that displace one or both of the national parties in local contests. Occasionally in U.S. history, a third party has proven locally potent, as did Minnesota's Farmer-Labor Party and Wisconsin's Progressives, both of which elected governors and state legislative majorities in the twentieth century. But, over time, no such party has survived,[56] and every state's two-party system mirrors national party dualism, at least as far as labels are concerned.

Parties and Governors.   Following the 2004 elections, Republicans hold twenty-eight and Democrats hold twenty-one governorships (with Washington State still too close to call at the time of printing). The powerful position of governor is a natural launching pad for a presidential candidacy. Just since 1900, Woodrow Wilson, Franklin D. Roosevelt, Jimmy Carter, Ronald Reagan, Bill Clinton, and most recently, George W. Bush have all gone from statehouses to the White House. In 2000, governors played a very prominent auxiliary role in George W. Bush's victory. During his bid for office, Bush relied heavily on fellow GOP governors, such as former Montana governor Mark Racicot, now chairman of the Republican Party. Of course, Bush received great help during his 2004 reelection campaign from his brother Jeb, who used his position as Florida governor to campaign all throughout the battle-ground state to assure Bush would keep the state in his column on November 2. Bush won Florida in 2004 by a tight margin but one wider than the 537 votes in 2000, and, in part, he has his brother to thank.

Governors in many states tend to possess greater influence over their parties' organizations and legislators than do presidents. Many governors have more patronage positions at their command than does a president, and these material rewards and incentives give governors added clout with activists and office holders. In addition, tradition in some states permits the governor to play a role in selecting the legislature's committee chairs and party floor leaders, and some state executives even attend and help direct the party legislative caucuses, activities no president would ever undertake. Moreover, forty- one governors possess the power of the line-item veto, which permits the governor to veto single items (such as pork barrel projects) in appropriations bills. Many governors have gained enormous leverage with legislators by means of the line-item veto. A Republican-sponsored measure in 1996 gave President Clinton this potent tool, but the presidential line-item veto was ruled unconstitutional in 1998 by the U.S. Supreme Court.

Parties and State Legislatures.   Unlike the partisan make-up of state executives, state legislatures are nearly evenly split, with neither party having a significant advantage. However, the party role in the legislature tends to be more high-profile and effective at the state level than at the national level. Most state legislatures surpass the U.S. Congress in partisan unity and cohesion. Even though fewer than half of congressional roll calls in the post–World War II era have produced majorities of the two parties on opposite sides, a number of state legislatures (including Massachusetts, New York, Ohio, and Pennsylvania) have achieved party voting levels of 70 percent or better in some years. Not all states display party cohesion of this magnitude, of course. Nebraska has a nonpartisan legislature, elected without party labels on the ballot.

One other party distinction is notable in many state legislatures. Compared with the Congress, state legislative leaders have much more authority and power; this is one reason party unity is usually higher in the state capitols.[57] The strict seniority system that usually controls committee assignments in Congress is less absolute in most states, and legislative leaders often have considerable discretion in appointing the committee chairs and members. The party caucuses, too, are usually more active and influential in state legislatures than in their Washington counterparts. In some legislatures, the caucuses meet weekly or even daily to work out strategy and count votes, and nearly one-fourth of the caucuses bind all the party members to support the group's decisions on key issues (such as appropriations measures, tax issues, and procedural questions).

In 2004, female candidates across the country were victorious in races at the local, state, and federal level. In South Dakota, where President Bush won by 21 percent, Stephanie Herseth (D) won the state's only U.S. House seat.   Below, Herseth addresses supporters at the Democratic campaign headquarters in Sioux Falls, shortly after being declared the winner on November 3.

(Photo courtesy: Roy Dabner/AP/Wide World Photos)

Not just the leaders and caucuses but the party organizations as well have more influence over legislators at the state level. State legislators are much more dependent than their congressional counterparts on their state and local parties for election assistance. Whereas members of Congress have large government-provided staffs and lavish perquisites to assist (directly or indirectly) their reelection efforts, state legislative candidates need party workers and, increasingly, the party's financial support and technological resources at election time.

THE MODERN TRANSFORMATION OF PARTY ORGANIZATION

Political parties have moved from the labor-intensive, person-to-person operations of the first half of the century toward the use of modern high technologies and communication strategies. Nevertheless, the capabilities of each party's organization vary widely.

Republican Party Strengths

Until 1992, the modern Republican Party thoroughly outclassed its Democratic rival in almost every category of campaign service and fund-raising. There are a number of explanations for the disparity between the two major parties: From 1932 until 1980, the Republicans were almost perennially disappointed underdogs, especially in congressional contests; they therefore felt the need to give extra effort. The GOP had the willingness, and enough electoral frustrations, to experiment with new campaign technologies that might hold the key to elusive victories. Also, since Democrats held most of the congressional offices and thus had most of the benefits of incumbency and staff, Republican nominees were forced to rely more on their party to offset built-in Democratic advantages. The party staff, in other words, compensated for the Democratic congressional staff, and perhaps also for organized labor's divisions of election troops, which were usually at the beck and call of Democratic candidates. Then, too, one can argue that the business and middle-class base of the modern GOP has a natural managerial and entrepreneurial flair, demonstrated by the party officers drawn from that talented pool.

Whatever the causes, the contemporary national Republican Party has organizational prowess unparalleled in American history. The Republicans have surpassed the Democrats in fund-raising by large margins in recent election cycles—never by less than two to one and usually by a considerably higher ratio (see Figure 12.4). Democrats must struggle to raise enough money to meet the basic needs of most of their candidates, while, in the words of a past chairman of the Democratic Senatorial Campaign Committee, "The single biggest problem the Republicans have is how to legally spend the money they have."[58] In 2004, Republicans still outspent the Democrats in Senate and House races, but the Democrats came closer to matching the Republicans than they have historically. Money played a particularly interesting role in the Democratic primaries. Former Vermont governor Howard Dean, because of outspoken criticism of President Bush's war in Iraq, took a significant lead in early fundraising, but his stuffed war chest was still insufficient to battle early losses against Massachusetts Senator John Kerry in the Iowa caucus and New Hampshire primary. Eventually, Kerry took away Dean's momentum and eventually surpassed him in fundraising.

Most of the Republican money is raised through highly successful mail solicitation. This procedure started in the early 1960s and accelerated in the mid-1970s, when postage and production costs were relatively low. From a base of just 24,000 names in 1975, for example, the national Republican Party has expanded its mailing list of proven donors to several million in the 1990s. Mailings produce about three-fourths of total revenue, and they do so with an average contribution of less than $35. In this fashion, the GOP may have broadened its committed base, because contributing money usually strengthens the tie between a voter and any organization. Most of the rest of the GOP's funds come from donors of larger amounts who secure membership

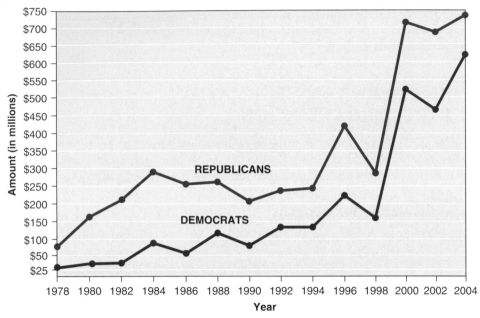

FIGURE 12.4   Political Party Finances, 1978–2004: Total Receipts
Note how the Republican Party has consistently taken in substantially higher receipts than their Democratic competitors—especially in the 1980s, when the Republican Party consolidated and prospered during Ronald Reagan's administration.

Source: Federal Election Commission (http://www.fec.gov/press/press2004/20041025party/20041025party.htm).

in various Republican contributor groups. For instance, the Republican National Committee designates any $15,000 annual giver an "Eagle."

A party or candidate with a considerable financial advantage can daunt opponents. Recent empirical evidence shows that large campaign war chests of incumbents act to deter high-quality challengers from entering political races. Faced with the prospect of raising huge sums of money to match incumbents, many potentially competitive opposition candidates simply decide to sit races out.[59]

The Republican cash is used to support a dazzling variety of party activities and campaign services. These include party staff, voter contact, polling, media advertising, and campaign staff training and research.

Party Staff.   Several hundred operatives are employed by the national GOP in election years. Even in the off years, more than one hundred people hold full-time party positions. There is great emphasis on field staff, that is, on staff members stationed in key districts and states who maintain close communication between local and national party offices.

Voter Contact.   The Republicans frequently conduct massive telephone canvassing operations to identify likely Republican voters and to get them to the polls on Election Day. In 1986, for instance, the GOP used paid callers in seventeen phone centers across the country to reach 10.5 million prospective voters in twenty-five states during the general election campaign. Nearly 5.5 million previously identified Republicans were called again just before Election Day. Many of them heard an automated message from the president that began: "This is Ronald Reagan and I want to remind you to go out and vote on Tuesday." In addition, 12 million pieces of "persuasive" (non-fund-raising) mail were sent to households in the last two weeks of the campaign.

The Republican National Committee also pioneered the use of interactive technologies to attract voters. The RNC's award-winning "Main Street" Internet site has offered "chats" with the RNC chair and links to a variety of sites of interest to voters.

Polling.   The national Republican committees have spent millions of dollars for national, state, and local public opinion surveys, and they have accumulated an enormous storehouse of data on American attitudes in general and on marginal districts in particular. Many of the surveys are provided to GOP nominees at a cut-rate cost. In important contests, the party will frequently commission tracking polls to chart its daily rise or fall. The information provided in such polls is invaluable in the tense concluding days of an election.

Media Advertising.   The national Republican Party operates a sophisticated in-house media division that specializes in the design and production of television advertisements for party nominees at all levels. About seventy to one hundred candidates are helped in an election cycle. They obtain expert and technically superior media commercials, and the party offers its wares for a minimal fee, often including the purchase of specific time slots on television shows for broadcasting the advertising spots. The candidates thus save the substantial commissions and fees usually charged by independent political consultants for the same services.

The Republican Party pioneered the use of "morphing" in television advertising. This negative campaigning technique was first used in 1994 congressional election ads that transformed the faces of Democratic candidates for Congress into the face of Bill Clinton. A 1996 Republican spot revived the issue of Clinton's alleged draft-dodging and attacked his Achilles' heel by asking if he could be trusted to tell the truth.

The Republicans' use of party advertising is even more significant. Since 1978, the Republicans have aired spots designed to support not specific candidates, but the generic party label. Beginning with the 1980 election, the GOP has used institutional advertising to establish basic election themes. "Vote Republican, for a Change" spots attacked the Democratic Congress in 1980. In another spot, House Speaker Thomas P. O'Neill was lampooned by an actor lookalike who ignored all warning signs and drove a car until it ran out of fuel. ("The Democrats are out of gas," announced the narrator as the actor futilely kicked the automobile's tire.)

Campaign Staff Training and Research.   The party trains many of the political volunteers and paid operatives who manage the candidates' campaigns. Since 1976, the Republicans have held annually about a half-dozen week-long "Campaign Management Colleges" for staffers. In 1986, the party launched an ambitious million-dollar "Congressional Campaign Academy" that offers two-week, all-expenses-paid training courses for prospective campaign managers, finance directors, and press relations staff. Early in each election cycle, the national party staff also prepares voluminous research reports on Democratic opponents, analyzing their public statements, votes, and attendance records. The reports are made available to GOP candidates and their aides.

Democratic campaign staffers and volunteers call on the party faithful to vote on Election Day. Phone banks are a significant part of party-related activity around election time.

(Photo courtesy: Bob Daemmrich/The Image Works)

Party Reliance on Money and Technology

Despite its noted financial edge and service sophistication, all is not well in the Republican organization. Success has bred self-satisfaction and complacency, encouraged waste, and led the party to place too much reliance on money and technology and not enough on the foundation of any party movement—people. As former Senator Paul Laxalt (R–NV), outgoing general chair of the national Republican Party, was forced to admit in 1987: "We've got way too much money, we've got way too many political operatives, we've got far too few volunteers.... We are substituting contributions and high technology for volunteers in the field. I've gone the sophisticate route, I've gone the television route, and there is no substitute for the volunteer route."[60] Because of the very narrow margin of victory Bush won in 2000, both political parties placed a great deal of focus on grassroots organizations and get-out-the-votes efforts. At least one report claims that Republicans won the "ground game" in battle-ground states like Florida.[60a]

As Laxalt's comments imply, technology and money can probably add only two or three percentage points to a candidate's margin, and one recent study even put the advantage of higher spending for Senate incumbents at about six percentage points.[61] The rest is determined by the nominee's quality and positions, the general electoral tide prevailing in any given year, and the energy of party troops in the field. Republicans were to learn this anew in 1992, when George Bush's large war chest could not stave off defeat. Similarly, many Democratic senators and representatives outspent their opponents by a wide margin in the 1994 elections, but they tasted defeat nonetheless. In 2004, Senate candidates in Oklahoma and South Dakota outspent their Republican opponents and yet failed to win. Have the two major parties learned that while money helps, having more than your opponent by no means guarantees electoral success, especially when running against incumbents? Only time and future elections will tell.

Democratic Party Gains

Parties, like people, change their habits slowly. The Democrats were reluctant to alter a formula that had been a winning combination for decades of New Deal dominance. The prevailing philosophy was, "Let a thousand flowers bloom"; candidates were encouraged to go their own way, to rely on organized labor and other interest groups allied with the Democrats, and to raise their own money, while the national party was kept subservient and weak. The massive Democratic defeats suffered in 1980 forced a fundamental reevaluation of the party's structure and activities. Democrats, diverse by nature, came to an unaccustomed consensus that the party must change to survive, that it must dampen internal ideological disputes and begin to revitalize its organization. Thus was born the commitment to technological and fund-raising modernization, using the Republican Party's accomplishments as a model, that drives the Democratic Party today.

Comprehension of the task is the first step to realization of the goal, so even after more than a decade, Democrats still trail their competitors by virtually every significant measure of party activity. Yet, the party finances (receipts) graphed in Figure 12.4 can be read a different way. While the GOP has consistently maintained an enormous edge, the Democrats have considerably increased their total receipts, now raising many times more than just a few years ago. More importantly, Democrats are contributing much more to their candidates and have actually come close to the GOP's larger total recently (see Analyzing Visuals: Political Party Finances, 1978–2002). Several national party chairs (Paul Kirk, Ron Brown, David Wilhelm, and Roy Romer) aggressively sought more funds from party supporters and friendly interest groups.

With the 1992 elections, the Democrats reaped the benefits of their substantially increased receipts, winning the presidency for the first time in sixteen years. The Clinton administration also redoubled Democratic Party efforts as the midterm elections of 1994 approached, and their exertions again made the Democrats more competitive with the Republicans. In the 2004, George W. Bush outspent John Kerry, but significantly, independent liberal groups, such as MoveOn.org and Media Fund, and labor unions spent more to support Kerry than partisan conservative organizations spent in support of Bush.

The Bush-Cheney campaign received nearly $300 million in donations from individuals, PACs, and parties in 2004. Here President Bush speaks to a group of senior citizens at a campaign fund raiser.

(Photo courtesy: AP/World Wide Photos)

ANALYZING VISUALS

Political Party Finances, 1978–2004

Both major parties give money—a small portion of what they actually raise—directly to specific candidates, and they also provide millions of dollars in coordinated expenditures (which are federally limited) on behalf of the candidates. The Republican Party historically has raised and spent far more campaign money than the Democratic Party (notice the especially large difference in the 1980s). But, since the 1990s, the Democrats have made tremendous strides in fund-raising and contributions to candidates and are now much more competitive with their opponents. Democrats also receive an invisible boost from labor unions, which are not required to report politically oriented expenditures. After studying the graph, answer the following critical thinking questions: What general trend do you notice about fund-raising and spending by both parties over time? What appears to be significant about 1998 and 2004? Drawing on what you know about recent election results, does there seem to be a strong correlation between which party spends the most money and which party wins on Election Night?

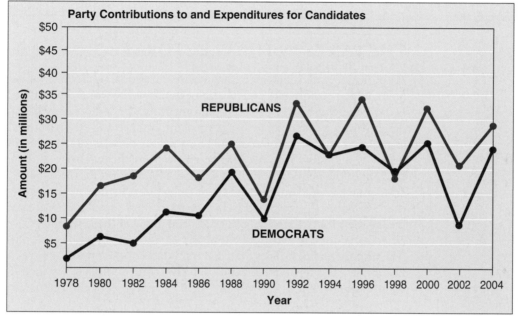

Includes totals for national, senatorial, and congressional committees as well as all other reported national, state, and local spending; all presidential, Senate, and House candidates are included. Not included are "soft money" expenditures. 2004 amounts include monies spent between January 1, 2003 and October 13, 2004.

Source: Federal Election Commission release, October 25, 2004. (http://www.fec.gov/press/press2004/20041025party/20041025party.htm)

The decision in 1981 to begin a direct-mail program for the national party was a turning point for Democrats. From a list of only 25,000 donors before the program began, the DNC's support base has grown to 500,000. The Democrats have imitated the Republicans not just in fund-raising but also in the uses to which the money is put. For instance, in 1986, the party opened a $3 million media center that produces television and radio spots at rates much lower than those charged by independent political consultants. The Democratic Party is attempting to do more for its candidates and their campaign staffs, too, creating the Democratic National Training Institute in 1985. The institute coordinates campaign schools for party workers from around the country.

"Smart money" is a term used to describe campaign contributions that flow to the candidates and political party expected to win in an election year. With Bill Clinton leading every public opinion poll taken after mid-July during the 1992 campaign and almost every public opinion poll taken during the 1996 campaign, Democrats were flooded with smart money. The Democratic Party dramatically increased both its receipts and expenditures in 1996 and then again in 2004. The Republicans did equally well, but the GOP's well-oiled fund-raising machinery has regularly produced massive war chests. For the Democrats, being financially well off was a new and delightful experience.

Interestingly, the party campaign committees in Congress have also begun to raise significant sums of money from their own congressional incumbents. For example, under former campaign committee chair Vic Fazio (D–CA), the DCCC began in 1991 requesting a $5,000 contribution from all House Democratic incumbents.[62] During the 1993–1994 election cycle, the NRCC instituted a similar program to encourage financial support from incumbents.[63] Both parties' efforts to raise funds from incumbents have been remarkably successful. Indeed, during the 2001-2002 cycle, Republican candidates contributed $17.4 million to their party committees, while Democratic candidates contributed $18.0 million to theirs.[64]

Thus, both party organizations have grown mightier in recent years, even though political parties have seemed to be in decline in other ways. Most important, many voters appear to have less partisan identification and loyalty today than in generations past. Why is this so?

THE PARTY IN THE ELECTORATE

A political party is much more than its organizational shell, however dazzling the technologies at its command, and its reach extends well beyond the relative handful of men and women who are the party in government. In any democracy, where power is derived directly from the people, the party's real importance and strength must come from the citizenry it attempts to mobilize. The party in the electorate—the mass of potential voters who identify with the Democratic or Republican labels—is the most significant element of the political party, providing the foundation for the organizational and governmental parties. But, in some crucial respects, it is the weakest of the components of the U.S. political party system. In recent decades, fewer citizens have been willing to pledge their fealty to the major parties, and many of those who have declared their loyalties have done so with less intensity. Moreover, voters of each partisan stripe are increasingly casting ballots for some candidates of the opposing party. Partisan identification is a less reliable indicator of likely voting choices today than it once was. (For a more detailed discussion of patterns in American vote choice, see chapter 13.)

Party Identification

Most American voters identify with a party but do not belong to it. There is no universal enrolled party membership; there are no prescribed dues, no formal rules concerning an individual's activities, and no enforceable obligations to the party assumed by the voter. A party has no real control over or even an accurate accounting of its adherents, and the party's voters subscribe to few or none of the commonly accepted tenets of organizational membership, such as regular participation and some measure of responsibility for the group's welfare. Rather, **party identification** or affiliation is an informal and impressionistic exercise whereby a citizen acquires a party label and accepts its standard as a summary of his or her political views and preferences. (See Figure 12.5 for trends in party identification.)

However, just because the acquisition is informal does not mean that it is unimportant. The party label becomes a voter's central political reference symbol and perceptual screen, a prism or filter through which the world of politics and government flows and is interpreted. For many Americans, party identification is a significant aspect of their political personality and a way of defining and explaining themselves to others. The loyalty generated by the label can be as intense as any enjoyed by sports teams and alma maters; in a few areas of the country, "Democrat" and "Republican" are still fighting words. Some studies of aggregate personal party identification in the electorate, such as one conducted by Michael MacKuen, Robert S. Erikson, and James A. Stimson, argue that a great variability of individual partisan leanings exists, stemming from

party identification
A citizen's personal affinity for a political party, usually expressed by his or her tendency to vote for the candidates of that party.

Participation
Deciding on a Political Party

FIGURE 12.5   Party Identification, 1952–2004

Simply defined, party identification is the response a voter gives to the poll question, "With what political party do you identify?" Notice how, despite the varying party of the president over time, party identification has remained fairly stable from the 1950s to the early 1990s. Not until an era of acute partisan strife in the mid-1990s have the independents made significant gains in party identification.

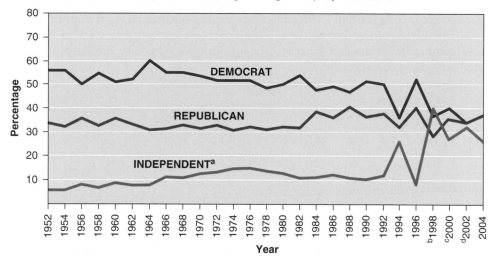

Note: Partisan totals do not add up to 100 percent because "apolitical" and "other" responses were deleted. Sample size varied from poll to poll, from a low of 1,130 to a high of 2,850.
a Pure Independents only. Independent "leaners" have been added to Democratic and Republican totals.
b 1998 figures were provided from a Gallup poll. Due to differences in wording from the Center for Political Studies Poll, the Gallup Poll may overstate the number of Independents.
c 2000 figures based on Voter News Service exit poll.
d 2002 figures were provided from a November 4, 2002, Gallup Poll survey.

Sources: Center for Political Studies/Survey Research Center of the University of Michigan, made available through the Inter-University Consortium for Political and Social Research. Also, Leon D. Epstein, *Political Parties in the American Mold* (Madison: University of Wisconsin Press, 1986), table 8.1, 257. Data for 1996 provided by exit poll conducted by Voter Research and Surveys. Data for 2004 from http://www.cnn.com/ELECTION/2004/pages/results/states/US/P/00/epolls.0.html.

short-term evaluations of the state of the economy, approval of the incumbent president, and other factors.[65] Other, more recent studies of a greater amount of polling data, however, support the traditional view of partisanship, finding much smaller permanent variability in party identification. Donald Green, Bradley Palmquist, and Eric Schickler, for example, claim that the partisanship of the electorate changes in response to temporal features only in the short term. Long-term partisanship remains stable after the condition causing the shock subsides.[66]

On the whole, Americans regard their partisan affiliation as a convenience rather than a necessity. The individual identifications are reinforced by the legal institutionalization of the major parties. Because of restrictive ballot laws, campaign finance rules, the powerful inertia of political tradition, and many other factors, voters for all practical purposes are limited to a choice between a Democrat and a Republican in almost all elections—a situation that naturally encourages the pragmatic choosing up of sides. About half of the states require a voter to state a party preference (or independent status) when registering to vote, and they restrict voter participation in primaries to party registrants, which is an incentive for voters to affiliate themselves with a party.[67]

Sources of Party Identification.   Whatever the societal and governmental forces undergirding party identification, the explanations of partisan loyalty at the individual's level are understandably more personal. Not surprisingly, parents are the single greatest influence in establishing a person's first party identification. Politically active parents with the same party loyalty raise children who will be strong party identifiers, whereas parents without party affiliations or with mixed affiliations produce offspring more likely to be independents (see chapter 11).

Early socialization is hardly the last step in the acquisition and maintenance of a party identity; marriage and other aspects of adult life can change one's loyalty. So can charismatic political personalities, particularly at the national level (such as Franklin D. Roosevelt and Ronald Reagan), cataclysmic events (the Civil War and the Great Depression are the best examples), and maybe intense social issues (for instance, abortion). Interestingly, social class is not an especially strong indicator of likely partisan choice in the United States, at least in comparison with Western European democracies. Not only are Americans less inclined than Europeans to perceive class distinctions, preferring instead to see themselves and most other people as members of an exceedingly broad middle class, but other factors, including sectionalism and candidate-oriented politics, tend to blur class lines in voting.

Declining Loyalty?

Over the past two decades, many political scientists as well as other observers, journalists, and party activists have become increasingly anxious about a perceived decline in partisan identification and loyalty. Many public opinion surveys have shown a significant growth in independents at the expense of the two major parties. The Center for Political Studies/Survey Research Center (CPS/SRC) of the University of Michigan, for instance, has charted the rise of self-described independents from a low of 19 percent in 1958 to a peak of 38 percent twenty years later. Before the 1950s (although the evidence for this research is more circumstantial because of the scarcity of reliable survey research data), there are indications that independents were fewer in number, and party loyalties considerably firmer.

Yet, the recent decline of party identification can be exaggerated, and in some ways there has been remarkable stability in the voters' party choices. Over more than thirty years, during vast political, economic, and social upheavals that have changed the face of the nation, the Democratic Party has nearly consistently drawn the support of a small majority and the Republican Party has attracted a share of the electorate in the low-to-mid-30-percent range. Granted, there have been peaks and valleys for both parties. The Lyndon B. Johnson landslide of 1964 helped Democrats top the 60 percent mark, and the Reagan landslide of 1984 and the post–Persian Gulf War glow of 1991 sent Democratic stock below the majority midpoint. However, these sorts of gradations are more akin to rolling foothills than towering mountain ranges. The steady nature of modern partisanship goes beyond the fortunes of each party. Identification with the two parties in modern times has never dipped below 83 percent of the U.S. electorate (recorded during the disillusionment spawned by Watergate in 1974) and can usually be found in the mid-to-upper-80-percent range. Finally, political scientist Martin Wattenberg suggests that Americans' attitudes about political parties are not so much negative as they are neutral—leaving the door open for strengthened party attachments in the American electorate.[68]

When pollsters ask for party identification information, they generally proceed in two stages. First, they inquire whether a respondent considers himself or herself a Democrat, Republican, or independent. Then the party identifiers are asked to categorize themselves as "strong" or "not very strong" supporters, while the independents are pushed to reveal their leanings with a question such as, "Which party do you normally support in elections, the Democrats or the Republicans?" (See Figure 12.5.) It may be true that some independent respondents are thereby prodded to pick a party under the pressure of the interview situation, regardless

Simple messages and catchy phrases have earned campaign buttons a permanent place in American Politics. These popular campaign novelties serve to increase candidate name recognition in the general public and to reinforce the support of the button wearer. These are a few examples from the Republican National Convention in 2004.

(Photo courtesy: Corbis)

THE LIMITS OF RED AND BLUE

Journalists, analysts, and academics have generally described the growing political division in the United States as being between the so-called "blue" and "red" states. Blue states are largely composed of New England, the Pacific Coast, and some Rust Belt states. Red States make up the South, the Midwest, Southwest, the Rockies, and Alaska. The origins of the colors come from the electoral map of the 2000 presidential election, which showed a striking geographical continuity (with the exception of a blue New Mexico and a red New Hampshire). Many supposed that the stark contrast on the political map indicates a growing division among the American people.

Of course, the belief that the American people are divided into two camps is not new. Conservative and liberal ideologues constantly refer to a cultural war perpetrated by the other side trying to subvert the appropriate path for America.

Recently, however, scholars[a] have taken issue with associating political divisions with cultural ones, claiming that there is a big difference between the greater political organization one sees in the growing divisions between red and blue states and the existing moral consensus shared among all of them. They posit that the culture war is largely a consequence of the "mis-

interpretation of election returns, lack of hard examination of polling data, systematic and self-serving misrepresentation by issue activists, and selective coverage by an uncritical media more concerned with news value than with getting the story right."[b] The image of a culture war is actually more a function of how right-leaning communities vote in hard right candidates far right of the community's values, just as left-leaning communities vote in candidate on their ideological extreme. The extreme positions of successful candidates hide rather than reveal the general moral consensus among Americans.

Activists and extremists often receive more attention, giving us the impression that everyone is an activist or an extremist. Nevertheless, according to exit polls, 22 percent of 2004 voters cited "moral values" as their primary issue while voting, and these voters voted 80 percent in favor of Bush. With datum like this, it is hard to discount entirely the belief in a cultural division among Americans; however, the relative calm after the 2004 election demonstrates that Americans at least share the principles of peace and democracy in spite of their different interpretations.

---

[a] Morris P. Fiorina, et al. *Culture War? The Myth of a Polarized America.* Longman: New York, 2005.
[b] Ibid 5.

of their true feelings. But, research has demonstrated that independent "leaners" in fact vote very much like real partisans, in some elections more so than the "not very strong" party identifiers. There is reason to count the independent leaners as closet partisans, though voting behavior is not the equivalent of real partisan identification.

In fact, the reluctance of leaners to admit their real party identities is in itself worrisome, because it reveals a change in attitudes about political parties and their role in our society. Being a socially acceptable, integrated, and contributing member of one's community once almost demanded partisan affiliation; it was a badge of good citizenship, signifying that one was a patriot. Today, the labels are avoided as an offense to a thinking person's individualism, and a vast majority of Americans insist that they vote for "the person, not the party."

The reasons for these anti-party attitudes are not hard to find. The growth of issue-oriented politics that cuts across party lines for voters who feel intensely about certain policy matters is partly the cause. So, too, is the emphasis on personality politics by the mass media (especially television) and political consultants. Party splits have also played a role. Fiscal conservatives in the GOP often have little in common with social conservatives who care most about the abortion issue, for example. Underlying these causes, though, are two much more disturbing and destructive long-term phenomena: the perceived loss of party credibility, and the decline of the party's tangible connections to the lives of everyday citizens. Although the underlying partisanship of the American people has not declined significantly since 1952, voter-admitted partisanship has dropped considerably. About three-fourths or more of the electorate volunteered a party choice without prodding from 1952 to 1964, but since 1970, an average of less than two-thirds has been willing to do so. Professed independents (including leaners) have increased from around one-fifth of the electorate in the 1950s to one-third or more during the last three decades. Also cause for concern is the marginal decline in strong Democrats and strong Republicans. Strong partisans are a party's backbone, the source of its volunteer force, candidates, and dependable voters. Even a slight shrinkage in these ranks can be troublesome.

Group Affiliations

Just as individuals vary in the strength of their partisan choice, so, too, do groups vary in the degree to which they identify with the Democratic Party or the Republican Party. There are enormous variations in party identification from one region or demographic group to another, particularly in geographic region, gender, race and ethnicity, age, social and economic status, religion, marital status, and ideology.

Geographic Region.   While all other geographic regions in the United States are relatively closely contested between the parties, the South still exhibits some of the Democratic Party affinity cultivated in the nineteenth century and hardened in the fires of the Civil War. This is only still true in local elections, however, and even there, it is changing rapidly. In the 1994 election, for instance, Southerners elected Republicans to a majority of the U.S. House seats in the states of the old Confederacy, and dozens of sheriffs won under the GOP banner, too. This increase in the number of southern elected officials matches changes in party identification in the South as calculated by Alan I. Abramowitz and Kyle L. Saunders. Abramowitz and Saunders found that Democratic Party identification among white Southerners fell by 16 percentage points between 1987 and 1994, from 64 percent to 48 percent. For the first time since the Civil War, a majority of southern whites no longer identify with the Democratic Party, either nationally or within their own state.[69] In all regions, party strengths vary by locality, with central cities almost everywhere heavily Democratic, the swelling suburbs serving as the main source of GOP partisans, and the small-town and rural areas split evenly between the two major parties.

Gender.   Some political scientists argue that the difference in the way men and women vote first emerged in 1920, when newly enfranchised women registered overwhelmingly as Republicans. It was not until the 1980 presidential election, however, that a noticeable and possibly significant *gender gap* emerged. This time, the Democratic Party was the apparent beneficiary. While Ronald Reagan trounced incumbent Democratic President Jimmy Carter, he did so with the votes of only 46 percent of the women, compared with 54 percent of the men.

This gender gap continues to persist at all levels of elections. In 1990, exit polls conducted after seventy races revealed a gender gap in 61 percent of the races analyzed. In 1992, as in previous elections, more voters were women (54 percent) than men (46 percent). Again, more women—47 percent—voted for the Democrat (Clinton) than men—41 percent. Among working women, the gap was even more pronounced—51 percent voted for Clinton, only 31 percent for Bush.

In 1996, the gender gap persisted. Women favored Clinton by 7- to 12-point margins in polls taken during the summer leading up to the Democratic and Republican conventions, while men favored Dole by margins ranging from 8 to 16 points. Two months later, the largest gender gap in the nation's history was recorded. While men split their vote evenly between the two candidates (Dole received 45 percent of the male vote and Clinton 44 percent), according to exit polls, women supported Clinton by a 54–37 margin.

The 2004 exit polls showed that the gender gap was smaller but still with us. Women still favored Democrats, and men still favored Republicans. George W. Bush received 55 percent of the men's vote to 44 percent for Kerry, while Bush received only 48 percent to Kerry's 51 percent of women's vote.

One of the biggest challenges facing Republicans is how to gain the support of women without alienating their male base. Besides abortion and women's rights issues, women's concerns for peace and social compassion may provide much of the gap's distance. For instance, women are usually much less likely than men to favor American military action. As noted in chapter 11, however, there is some evidence that the terrorist attacks of September 11, 2001, may have erased much of the gender gap concerning military affairs, at least in the short run. Women are also less inclined to support cuts in government funding of social welfare programs. This is not, however, the only explanation for the gender gap. One recent study has pointed the finger not at Republican Party difficulties in attracting female voters, but rather at the Democratic Party's inability to attract the votes of males. In other words, the gender gap exists because of the lack of support for the Democratic Party among men, and the corresponding male preference for the Republican Party, stemming from the same differences in opinions about social welfare and military issues identified above.[70]

Race and Ethnicity.   African Americans are the most dramatically different population subgroup in party terms. The 80-percent-plus advantage they offer the Democrats dwarfs the edge given to either party by any other segment of the electorate, and their proportion of strong Democrats (about 40 percent) is three times that of whites. African Americans account almost entirely for the slight lead in party affiliation that Democrats normally enjoy over Republicans, since the GOP has recently been able to attract a narrow plurality of whites to its standard. Perhaps as a reflection of the massive party chasm separating blacks and whites, the two races differ greatly on many policy issues, with blacks overwhelmingly on the liberal side and whites closer to the conservative pole. Two recent studies of African American voting behavior show this, contending that whites of middle to upper income are most concerned with issues of the economy and defense, while blacks of all income levels nearly uniformly identify health care and problems of the poor as their key voting issues. Both Michael Dawson and Louis Bolce therefore conclude that while whites tend to vote differently depending on their socio-economic class interest, African Americans' policy concerns are the same regardless of their socio-economic class. The belief of most blacks that their fate is linked causes upper-income blacks to vote the same as lower-income blacks. Whites see no such class-based obligation.[71] An exception, incidentally, is abortion, where religious beliefs may lead African Americans to the more conservative stance. Hispanics supplement this group as a Democratic stalwart; by more than three to one, Hispanics prefer the Democratic label. Voting patterns of Puerto Ricans are very similar to African Americans, while Mexican Americans favor the Democrats by smaller margins. An exception is the Cuban American population, whose anti–Fidel Castro tilt leads to Republicanism.

Age.   Young people are once again becoming more Democratic. Polls in 1972 indicated that the group of eighteen- to twenty-four-year-olds, and particularly students, was the only age group to support Democratic presidential nominee George McGovern. But, by the 1990s, the eighteen-to-twenty-four-year-old age group was the most Republican of all. Much of this margin was derived from strong student affiliation with the Republicans. Perhaps because of the bad economy from 1990 to 1992, which limited job availability for college graduates, young people swung back to the Democrats in 1992. Bill Clinton ran strongly among eighteen- to twenty-four-year-olds, and they were among his best groups in the electorate. In 2004, Kerry won the young vote (18–29 year olds) by a 9 percent margin, receiving 54 percent to Bush's 45 percent. Nader received nearly none of the youth vote, which in 2000 reached 8 percent.

Social and Economic Factors.   Some traditional strengths and weaknesses persist for each party by occupation, income, and education. The GOP remains predominant among executives, professionals, and white-collar workers, whereas the Democrats lead substantially among blue-collar workers and the unemployed. Labor union members are also Democratic by two-and-a-half to one. The more conservative, retired population leans Republican. Women who do not work outside the home are less liberal and Democratic than those who do. Occupation, income, and education are closely related, of course, so many of the same partisan patterns can be detected in all three classifications. Democratic support usually drops steadily as one climbs the income scale. Similarly, as years of education increase, identification with the Republican Party climbs; in graduate school, however, the Democrats rally a bit and only narrowly trail GOP partisans.

Religion.   The party preferences by religion are also traditional, but with modern twists. Protestants—especially Methodists, Presbyterians, and Episcopalians—favor the Republicans, whereas Catholics and, even more so, Jews are predominantly Democratic in affiliation. Decreased polarization is apparent all around, though.[72] Democrats have made inroads among many Protestant denominations over the past three decades, and Republicans can now sometimes claim up to 25 percent of the Jewish population and nearly 40 percent of the Catholics. Recent studies have confirmed this, finding empirical evidence of liberal Protestants leaving their traditional home in the Republican Party, and conservative Catholics and conservative Protestants remaining relatively stable, if not voting more for the Republicans, between 1960 and 1992.[73] The "born again" Christians, who have received much attention in recent years, are somewhat less Republican than commonly believed. The GOP usually has just about a 10 percent edge among them, primarily because so many blacks classify themselves as members of this group.

Marital Status.   Even marital status reveals something about partisan affiliation. People who are married, a traditionally more conservative group, and people who have never married, a segment weighted toward the premarriage young who currently lean toward the Republicans, are closely divided in party loyalty. But, the widowed are Democratic in nature, probably because there are many more widows than widowers; in this, the gender gap is again expressing itself. Proof of the "marriage gap" is found in a study that determined married people vote 10–15 percent more for Republicans than their unmarried counterparts. This difference, the study says, is key, for the proportion of unmarried people, including divorcees, has doubled since 1964.[74] The divorced and the separated, who may be experiencing economic hardship and appear to be more liberal than the married population, are a substantially Democratic group.

Ideology.   Ideologically, there are few surprises. Lending credence to the belief that both parties are now relatively distinct philosophically, liberals are overwhelmingly Democratic and conservatives are staunchly Republican in most surveys and opinion studies.

However, as party identification has weakened, so, too, has the likelihood that voters will cast ballots predictably and regularly for their party's nominees. (Chapter 13 discusses this in some detail.) In the present day, as at the founding of the republic, Americans are simply not wedded to the idea or the reality of political parties. Said one Democratic pollster: "It took a lot of years for the trust and loyalty to dissipate, and it will take a lot of years to bring it back."[75] If this is true, then the dealigning patterns we have witnessed in recent times are likely to remain the norm in the foreseeable future.

ONE-PARTYISM AND THIRD-PARTYISM

The two-party system has not gone unchallenged. At the state level, two-party competition was severely limited or nonexistent in much of the country for most of the twentieth century.[76] Formerly in the one-party Democratic states of the Deep South and the rock-ribbed Republican states of Maine, New Hampshire, and Vermont, the dominant party's primary nomination was often equivalent to election, and the only real contest was an unsatisfying intraparty one in which colorful personalities often dominated and a half-dozen major candidacies in each primary proved confusing to voters.[77] Even in most two-party states, many cities and counties had a massive majority of voters aligned with one or the other party and thus were effectively one-party in local elections.

Historical, cultural, and sectional forces primarily accounted for the concentration of one party's supporters in certain areas. The Civil War's divisions, for instance, were mirrored for the better part of a century in the Democratic predisposition of the South and the Republican proclivities of the Yankee northern states. Whatever the combination of factors producing **one-partyism**—a political system in which one party dominates and wins virtually all contests—the condition has certainly declined precipitously in the last quarter century.[78]

The spread of two-party competition, especially in the South, is one of the most significant political trends of recent times, and virtually no one-party states are left. The once solidly Democratic South has been reduced to, at most, Louisiana and Arkansas. (Note, though, that even in each of these two states, one or more Republicans have been elected to the governorship or U.S. Senate since 1970, and the Deep South states usually vote Republican in presidential contests as well, unless a Southerner heads the Democratic ticket.) At the same time, there are no longer any purely Republican states.

Ironically, the growth of two-party competition has been spurred less by the developing strength of the main parties than by party weakness, as illustrated by the decline in partisan loyalty among the voters. In other words, citizens now are somewhat more inclined to cross party lines in order to support an appealing candidate regardless of party affiliation, thus making a victory for the minority party possible whether or not it has earned the victory through the party's own organizational hard work. It should also be noted that the elimination of pockets of one-party strength adds an element of instability to the system, since at one point, even in lean times of national electoral disaster, each party was assured of a regional base from which a comeback could be staged. Nonetheless, the increase in party competitiveness can be viewed positively, since it eliminates the effects of one-partyism and guarantees a comprehensible and credible partisan choice to a larger segment of the electorate than ever before.

Minor Parties: Third-Partyism

Third-partyism has proved more durable than one-partyism, though its nature is sporadic and intermittent, and its effects on the political system are on the whole less weighty. Given all the controversy third parties generate, one could be excused for thinking that they were extraordinarily important on the American scene. But, as Frank J. Sorauf has concluded, third parties in fact "have not assumed the importance that all the [academic] attention lavished on them suggests."[79] No minor party has ever come close to winning the presidency, and only eight minor parties have won so much as a single state's electoral college votes (see Table 12.1). Eight third parties (including the farmer-backed Populists in 1892, Theodore Roosevelt's Bull Moose Party in 1912, the reform-minded Progressives in 1924, former Alabama Governor George Wallace's racially based American Independent Party in 1968, and Ross Perot's independents in 1992) have garnered more than 10 percent of the popular vote for president. Theodore Roosevelt's 1912 effort was the most successful; the Bull Moose Party won 27 percent of the popular vote for president (although only 17 percent of the electoral college votes). Roosevelt's is also the only third party to run ahead of one of the two major parties (the Republicans). Roosevelt, incidentally, abandoned the Republican Party, under whose banner he had won the presidency in 1904, in order to form the Bull Moose Party, composed mainly of reformist Republicans.

Third parties find their roots in sectionalism (as did the South's states' rights Dixiecrats, who broke away from the Democrats in 1948); in economic protest (such as the agrarian revolt that fueled the Populists, an 1892 prairie-states party); in specific issues (such as the Green Party's support of the environment); in ideology (the Socialist, Communist, and Libertarian Parties are examples); and in appealing, charismatic personalities (Theodore Roosevelt is perhaps the best case). Many of the minor parties have

one-partyism
A political system in which one party dominates and wins virtually all contests.

WEB EXPLORATION
Independents proliferate, but finding one that represents your views on several issues is difficult. To compare the planks of several different independent parties, go to
www.ablongman.com/oconnor

third-partyism
The tendency of third parties to arise with some regularity in a nominally two-party system.

Timeline

Third Parties in American History

TABLE 12.1   Third-Party and Independent Presidential Candidates
Receiving 5 Percent or More of Popular Vote

Candidate (Party)	Year	Percentage of Popular Vote	Electoral Votes
Ross Perot (Reform Party)	1996	8.5	0
Ross Perot (Independent)	1992	18.9	0
John B. Anderson (Independent)	1980	6.6	0
George C. Wallace (American Independent)	1968	13.5	46
Robert M. La Follette (Progressive)	1924	16.6	13
Theodore Roosevelt (Bull Moose)	1912	27.4	88
Eugene V. Debs (Socialist)	1912	6.0	0
James B. Weaver (Populist)	1892	8.5	22
John C. Breckinridge (Southern Democrat)	1860	18.1	72
John Bell (Constitutional Union)	1860	12.6	39
Millard Fillmore (Whig-American)	1856	21.5	8
Martin Van Buren (Free Soil)	1848	10.1	0
William Wirt (Anti-Masonic)	1832	7.8	7

Source: Congressional Quarterly Weekly Report (October 18, 1980): 3147 (as adapted), and official election returns for 1992, 1996.

drawn strength from a combination of these sources. The American Independent Party enjoyed a measure of success because of a dynamic leader (George Wallace), a firm geographic base (the South), and an emotional issue (civil rights). In 1992, Ross Perot, the billionaire with a folksy Texas manner, was a charismatic leader whose campaign was fueled by the deficit issue (as well as by his personal fortune).

The 2000 election saw Green Party nominee Ralph Nader, the environmentalist and consumer advocate who ran for president in 1996, lead a nationwide grassroots, anti-establishment campaign to oppose the corporate-backed main party candidates, Vice President Al Gore and Texas Governor George W. Bush. Although Nader collected just 2.86 million votes (or 2.72 percent nationwide, well below the 5 percent required for the Green Party to receive matching federal funding in 2004), there is little question that Nader cost Democrat Al Gore the presidency in 2000. In the critical state of Florida—the state that effectively decided the presidential election—Nader received 97,488 votes, while the official margin between Al Gore and George W. Bush in that state was 537 votes out of 5,963,070 votes cast. At least half of all Nader voters indicated in exit polls that they would have voted for Gore in a two-way race, while

Ralph Nader has run for president in the last three election cycles in an effort to draw attention to issues he believes have been ignored by Republicans and Democrats.

(Photo courtesy: AFP/Corbis)

most of the rest said they would not have voted at all, and only a small percentage of Nader voters said that they would have voted for Bush over Gore. Nader's 22,188 votes in New Hampshire also cost Gore that state, which Bush won by a mere 7,211 votes out of 567,795 cast.

Gore came to the brink of winning the presidential election and carried, albeit closely, some states where Nader did well: Wisconsin, Oregon, New Mexico, California, and Washington. However, because of narrow losses in states like Florida and New Hampshire, Democratic Party anger at Ralph Nader was intense, since many Nader voters would have likely voted for Gore had Nader not run. In 2004, Nader had no measurable impact on the election, although many states still had very narrow margins. For instance, Bush defeated Kerry in Iowa, which Gore carried in 2000, by a slim 14,000 votes, but Nader only received a total of 6,000 votes, meaning Kerry would still have lost had Nader not run (and assuming Nader voters would all vote for Kerry). While recent research in political science raises the chicken-or-egg question of which comes first, political dissatisfaction leading to third parties[80] or third-party movements leading to political dissatisfaction,[81] the conclusion that third parties are at some point linked to discontent with government and party leaders is widely accepted.

Importantly, minor-party and independent candidates are not limited to presidential elections; many also run in congressional elections, and the numbers appear to be growing. In the 2000 congressional elections, for example, more than 850 minor-party and independent candidates ran for seats in the House and Senate—almost eight times as many as in 1968 and nearly three times the number that ran in 1980. A recent study shows that minor-party candidates for the House are most likely to emerge under three conditions: (1) when a House seat becomes open; (2) when a minor party candidate has

Minnesota Governor Jesse Ventura, who did not seek reelection in 2002, supported Independence Party candidate Tim Penny (left) in his unsuccessful bid for the Minnesota governorship. Despite leading his two opponents in early polls, Penny secured only 16 percent of the vote on Election Day.

(Photo courtesy: Tom Olmscheid/AP/Wide World Photos)

previously competed in the district; and, (3) when partisan competition between the two major parties in the district is close.[82]

Above all, third parties make electoral progress in direct proportion to the failure of the two major parties to incorporate new ideas or alienated groups or to nominate attractive candidates as their standard-bearers. One study, for instance, found that in 1992, the independent candidacy of Ross Perot increased voter turnout by 3 percentage points. Perot presumably activated previous nonvoters who were ignored, disenchanted, or frustrated with the current two-party system.[83] Other recent studies have found that third parties do best when declining trust in the two major political parties plagues the electorate.[84] Usually, though, third parties are eventually co-opted by one of the two major parties, each of them eager to take the politically popular issue that gave rise to the third party and make it theirs in order to secure the allegiance of the third party's supporters. For example, the Republicans of the 1970s absorbed many of the "states' rights" planks of George Wallace's 1968 presidential bid. Both parties have also more recently attempted to attract independent voters by sponsoring reforms of the governmental process, such as limitations on the activities of Washington lobbyists.

Why Third Parties Tend to Remain Minor

proportional representation
A voting system that apportions legislative seats according to the percentage of the vote won by a particular political party.

Third parties in the United States are akin to shooting stars that appear briefly and brilliantly but do not long remain visible in the political constellation. In fact, the United States is the only major Western nation that does not have at least one significant, enduring national third party. There are a number of explanations for this. Unlike many European countries that use **proportional representation** (awarding legislative seats according to the percentage of votes a political party receives), the United States has a "single-member, plurality" electoral system. The U.S. system requires a party to get one more vote than any other party in a legislative district or in a state's presidential election in order to win. In contrast, countries that use proportional representation often guarantee parliamentary seats to any faction securing as little as 5 percent of the vote. To paraphrase the legendary football coach Vince Lombardi, finishing first is not everything, it is the *only* thing in U.S. politics; placing second, even by a smidgen, doesn't count. This condition encourages the grouping of interests into as few parties as possible (the democratic minimum being two). Moreover, the two parties will often move to the left or right on issues in order to gain popular support. Some observers go so far as to say that parties in the United States have no permanent positions at all, only permanent interests—winning elections. Regardless of one's position on this issue, it is clear that the adaptive nature of the two parties further forestalls the growth of third parties in the United States. Nonetheless, we should not write off the possibility that an enduring third party will emerge.

Other institutional and historical factors also undergird the two-party system:

- Most states have laws that require third parties to secure a place on the ballot by gathering large numbers of signatures, whereas the Democratic and Republican Parties are often granted automatic access.

- Democrats and Republicans in the state legislatures may have little in common, but both want to make sure that the political pie is cut into only two sizable pieces, not three or more smaller slices.

- The public funding of campaigns (financing from taxpayer dollars), where it exists, is much more generous for the two major parties. At the national level, for instance, third-party presidential candidates receive money only after the general election, if they have garnered more than 5 percent of the vote, and only in proportion to their total vote; the major-party candidates, by contrast, get large, full general-election grants immediately upon their summer nominations. (This funding difference does not affect wealthy politicians like Perot.)

■ The news media give relatively little coverage to minor parties compared with that given to major-party nominees. The media's bias is legitimate—it only reflects political reality, and it would be absurd to expect them to offer equal time to all comers. Still, this is a vicious cycle for minor-party candidates: A lack of broad-based support produces slight coverage, which minimizes their chances of attracting more adherents. Of course, once a third-party candidate such as Ross Perot becomes prominent, the media flock to his appearances and clamor to schedule him on their news shows.

■ Voters tend to flirt with independent candidates early in the election process, but they routinely return to the two-party fold by late fall.

■ Independents and third-party candidates suffer from a "can't win" syndrome. Voters tell pollsters that they like the non-major-party candidate but ultimately decide not to cast their vote for him or her if they suspect the candidate cannot win. In other words, many voters are hesitant to "waste" their vote on a third-party candidate.

Beyond the institutional explanations are historical, cultural, and social theories of two-partyism in the United States. The **dualist theory,** frequently criticized as overly simplistic, suggests that there has always been an underlying binary nature to U.S. politics. Whether it was the early conflict between eastern financial interests and western frontiersmen, the sectional division of North and South, the more current urban-versus-rural or urban-versus-suburban clashes, or even the natural tensions of democratic institutions (the government against the opposition, for instance), dualists believe that the processes and interests of politics inevitably push the players into two great camps.

dualist theory
The theory that there has always been an underlying binary party nature to U.S. politics.

Other political scientists emphasize the basic social consensus existing in American life. Despite great diversity in our heritage, the vast majority of Americans accept without serious question the fundamental structures of our system: the Constitution, the governmental setup, a lightly controlled free enterprise economy, for example. This consensus, when allied with certain American cultural characteristics developed over time (pragmatism, acceptance of the need for compromise, a lack of extreme and divisive social-class consciousness), produces the conditions necessary for relatively non-ideological, centrist politics that can naturally support two moderate alternative parties but has little need for more.

The passion for power and victory that drives both Democrats and Republicans overrides ideology and prevents rigidity. Unless a kind of rigor mortis takes hold in the future in one or both major parties—with, say, the capture of the party organization by unyielding extremists of right or left—it is difficult to imagine any third party becoming a major, permanent force in U.S. politics. The corollary of this axiom, though, is that the major parties must be eternally vigilant if they are to avoid ideologically inspired takeovers.

For the foreseeable future, however, third parties likely will continue to play useful supporting roles similar to their historically sanctioned ones: They can popularize ideas that might not receive a hearing otherwise. They can serve as vehicles of popular discontent with the major parties and thereby induce change in major-party behavior and platforms, such as in 1992 when Ross Perot forced the two major parties to acknowledge and address the deficit issue. They may presage and assist party realignments in

POLITICAL PARTIES IN COMPARATIVE PERSPECTIVE

The United States has a number of minor political parties, but since the Civil War, the Republican and Democratic Parties have always controlled the federal government. Very few members of Congress do not belong to either of the two major parties.

Election rules offer a partial explanation for this. The "winner-take-all" single-member district system found here tends to produce a two-party system. Yet, Canada and the United Kingdom also use the winner-take-all election rule, with two parties dominating their parliaments, but other parties also have at least a few members representing them in the legislature. In Britain's House of Commons, for example, Sinn Fein, the political arm of the Irish Republican Army, now has four seats (currently vacant because the party opposes British government policy in Northern Ireland). Canada and the United Kingdom are thus better described as two-plus party systems. India is off the charts, with national political parties representing the entire political spectrum. There are many regional parties as well.

The European countries and Japan have multiparty systems. Typically, several parties are competitive in campaigns to control the executive branch, and a coalition of parties in the Cabinet is a frequent feature of these systems. Again, election rules tend to produce such a party configuration. Germany, Italy, and Japan have two-ballot elections in which voters elect part of the legislature from single-member districts and part by proportional representation based on party lists. Proportional representation tends to benefit smaller parties, because their electoral bases are not confined to districts. Not only do these countries' parliaments have several medium-sized parties (Japan is a bit different because the conservative party is far larger than any of its rivals), but they have parties that span the political spectrum. On the left, social democratic parties are represented in every legislature. France, Germany, and Japan have communist parties (a reformed one in Germany's case). In France, the reactionary National Front has emerged in the last decade as a powerful alternative to the mainstream conservative Union for French Democracy and the Rally for the Republic.

Number of Political Parties in the Lower House of National Legislatures, 2002	
Country	*Number of Parties*
Canada	5
China	9
Egypt	6
France	6
Germany	6
India	38
Indonesia	20
Italy	8
Japan	8
Mexico	5
Russia	11
United Kingdom	9
United States	2

China, Egypt, Mexico, and Indonesia challenge American assumptions about what the term "political party" means. China is a one-party state in which the Communist Party is guaranteed the leading role in politics by the constitution. The eight other parties represented in the National People's Congress form a token opposition that publicly acknowledges the Communist Party's preeminent position as the price for being allowed to exist. Egyptian law requires political parties be approved by the government before they can legally enter politics. Not surprisingly, the president's party, the National Democratic Party, now holds nearly 90 percent of the seats in the People's Assembly. Until the 1999 elections, Indonesian legislative politics was dominated by GOLKAR, an official party created and supported by the military and the civil service. Since 1999, the once dominant GOLKAR finds itself in the uncomfortable position of being the second largest of twenty parties, but it still dwarfs the smaller parties in the legislature. The Institutional Revolutionary Party (PRI) in Mexico dominated politics there until recently, although less by statutory provision than by skillful manipulation of patronage.

Comparing Political Parties

the future as they have sometimes done in the past. In a few states, third parties will also continue to take a unique part in political life, as the Conservative and Liberal Parties of New York State do. But, in a two-party system that is supplemented by generous means of expressing dissent and registering political opposition in other ways (court challenges and interest group organizing, for example), third parties will probably continue to have a limited future in the United States.

Continuity & Change

The Decline of the Reform Party and the Rise of the Greens

In 1992, the economy was in a slump and voters were angry. Their discontent coalesced behind Ross Perot's presidential candidacy. Perot announced that he would run for president if citizens would get the required number of signatures on petitions to put him on the ballot in every state, and from this populist beginning, his clever and idiosyncratic campaign was as unconventional as any of the twentieth century. Perot, running as an independent, gained an astonishing 19 percent of the popular vote. Building on this success, Perot founded the Reform Party and was their presidential candidate in 1996. Unfortunately for Perot, the economy had improved, and his message, falling on prosperous ears, earned him only 8 percent of the vote. Jesse Ventura's successful Reform Party bid for the Minnesota governorship gave the party a boost in 1998, but his departure from the party a few years later clearly stole back that energy. Internecine struggles among various contenders to be the party's 2000 presidential nominee—ultimately and preposterously won by Pat Buchanan—unmistakably signaled the end of the Reform Party, which was promptly confirmed at the polls.

In 2000, however, the dramatic change in the fortunes of the Reform Party was matched by a very significant sign of continuity in the role of a third party in American politics. Just as Perot's 19 percent of the popular vote may have deprived George Bush of some crucial votes against newcomer Bill Clinton in 1992, so did Green Party candidate Ralph Nader's share of the vote likely play a role in taking the 2000 election from Clinton's vice president, Al Gore, and giving it to George W. Bush. Nader's less than 3 percent of the popular vote was only a fraction of Perot's record, but the unprecedented closeness of the election meant that every vote had exceptional importance in key states such as Florida. Had Nader's third-party appeal cost Gore only a few hundred votes less in Florida, the 2000 election might have told a very different story.

Despite the decline and fall of the Reform Party, the rise of the Green Party offers hope to those who believe the American system needs a strong third party. The Green Party may fare better than previous third parties because it seems to recognize that the only way to build a party is from the ground up. In the near future, Green Party leaders are likely to focus not so much on the presidential races as on local races, for city councils and resources management officials, in more liberal areas across the country, including New Mexico, California, Oregon, Washington, Wisconsin, Vermont, and Minnesota. Indeed, in 2002, twenty-two Green Party candidates were elected to local offices across the United States. So, while a minor-party candidate has yet to attain the nation's highest office, third parties continue to play an erratic and unpredictable, but very important, role in American politics.

1. Many people would argue that America currently suffers from a political disease in which there is a real or perceived gap between our political leaders and the electorate. What connection, if any, do you find between our traditional binary (two-party) political system and the current political malaise?

2. Despite their best efforts, third-party candidates have failed to win election to the White House. Would you ever consider voting for a third-party candidate, even if you didn't think he or she had a good chance to win? Why, and what is the significance of such a vote?

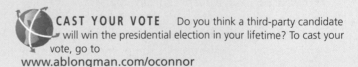

CAST YOUR VOTE   Do you think a third-party candidate will win the presidential election in your lifetime? To cast your vote, go to
www.ablongman.com/oconnor

SUMMARY

A political party is a group of office holders, candidates, activists, and voters who identify with a group label and seek to elect to public office individuals who run under that label. Parties encompass three separate components: (1) the governmental party comprises office holders and candidates who run under the party's banner; (2) the electoral party comprises the workers and activists who staff the party's formal organization; and, (3) the party in the electorate refers to the voters who consider themselves allied or associated with the party. In this chapter, we have made the following points:

1. What Is a Political Party?

The goal of American political parties is to win office. This objective is in keeping with the practical nature of Americans and the country's long-standing aversion to most ideologically driven, "purist" politics.

2. **The Evolution of American Party Democracy**
The evolution of U.S. political parties has been remarkably smooth, and the stability of the Democratic and Republican groupings, despite name changes, is a wonder, considering all the social and political tumult in U.S. history.

3. **The Roles of the American Parties**
For 150 years, the two-party system has served as the mechanism American society uses to organize and resolve social and political conflict. The Democratic and Republican Parties, through lengthy nominating processes, provide a sort of screening mechanism for those who aspire to the presidency, helping to weed out unqualified individuals, expose and test candidates' ideas on important policy questions, and ensure a measure of long-term continuity and accountability.

4. **The Basic Structure of American Political Parties**
While the distinctions might not be as clear today as they were two or three decades ago, the basic structure of the major parties remains simple and pyramidal. The state and local parties are more important than the national ones, though campaign technologies and fund-raising concentrated in Washington are invigorating the national party committees.

5. **The Party in Government**
Political parties are not restricted to their role as grass-roots organizations of voters; they also have another major role *inside* government institutions. The party in government comprises the office holders and candidates who run under the party's banner.

6. **The Modern Transformation of Party Organization**
Political parties have moved from labor-intensive, person-to-person operations toward the use of modern high technologies and communication strategies. Nevertheless, the capabilities of the party organizations vary widely from place to place.

7. **The Party in the Electorate**
The party in the electorate refers to the voters who consider themselves allied or associated with the party. This is the most significant element of the political party, providing the foundation for the organizational and governmental parties.

8. **One-Partyism and Third-Partyism**
The U.S. party system is uniquely a two-party system. While periods of one-partyism, third-partyism, or independent activism (such as the 1992 Perot phenomenon) can arise, the greatest proportion of all federal, state, and local elections are contests between the Republican and Democratic Parties only.

KEY TERMS

civil service laws, p. 441
coalition, p. 445
coattail effect, p. 460
direct primary, p. 441
dualist theory, p. 481
governmental party, p. 437
issue-oriented politics, p. 442
machine, p. 441
national convention, p. 451
national party platform, p. 447
one-partyism, p. 477
organizational party, p. 437
party identification, p. 470
party in the electorate, p. 437
patronage, p. 441
political consultant, p. 443
political party, p. 437
proportional representation, p. 480
spoils system, p. 441
third-partyism, p. 477
ticket-split, p. 443

SELECTED READINGS

Abramowitz, Alan I., and Jeffrey A. Segal. *Senate Elections*. Ann Arbor: University of Michigan Press, 1993.

Aldrich, John Herbert. *Why Parties? The Origin and Transformation of Political Parties in America*. Chicago: University of Chicago Press, 1995.

Beck, Paul Allen, and Majorie Randon Hershey. *Party Politics in America*, 10th ed. New York: Pearson Longman, 2002.

Cox, Gary W., and Mathew D. McCubbins. *Legislative Leviathan: Party Government in the House*. Berkeley: University of California Press, 1993.

Epstein, Leon. *Political Parties in the American Mold*, reprint ed. Madison: University of Wisconsin Press, 1989.

Fiorina, Morris P. *Divided Government*, 2nd ed. New York: Longman, 2002.

Gierzynski, Anthony. *Legislative Party Campaign Committees in the American States*. Lexington: University Press of Kentucky, 1992.

Klinkner, Philip A. *The Losing Parties: Out-Party National Committees, 1956–1993*. New Haven, CT: Yale University Press, 1995.

Maisel, L. Sandy, ed. *The Parties Respond: Changes in American Parties and Campaigns*, 4th ed. Boulder, CO: Westview Press, 2002.

Milkis, Sidney M. *The President and the Parties: The Transformation of the American Party System Since the New Deal*, New ed. New York: Oxford University Press, 1993.

Patterson, Kelly D. *Political Parties and the Maintenance of Liberal Democracy*. New York: Columbia University Press, 1996.

Polsby, Nelson W. *Consequences of Party Reform*, 2nd ed. Berkeley, CA: Institute of Governmental Studies Press, 1983.

Pomper, Gerald M. *Passions and Interests: Political Party Concepts of American Democracy*. Lawrence: University Press of Kansas, 1992.

Reichley, James. *The Life of the Parties: A History of American Political Parties*. Lanham, MD: Rowman and Littlefield, 2000.

Riordan, William L., ed. *Plunkitt of Tammany Hall: A Series of Very Plain Talks on Very Practical Politics*, reprint ed. New York: Signet, 1995.

Rohde, David W. *Parties and Leaders in the Postreform House*. Chicago: University of Chicago Press, 1991.

Sabato, Larry J. and Bruce A. Larson. *The Party's Just Begun: Shaping Political Parties for America's Future*, 2nd ed. New York: Longman, 2002.

Schattschneider, E. E. *Party Government*, Reprint ed. Westport, CT: Greenwood Press, 1977.

Shea, Daniel M. *Transforming Democracy: Legislative Campaign Committees and Political Parties*. Albany: SUNY Press, 1995.

Sifry, Micah L. *Spoiling for a Fight: Third-Party Politics in America*. New York: Routledge, 2002.

Sundquist, James L. *Dynamics of the Party System: Alignment and Realignment of Political Parties in the United States*, rev. ed. Washington, DC: Brookings Institution, 1983.

Wattenberg, Martin P. *The Decline of American Political Parties, 1952–1996*. Cambridge, MA: Harvard University Press, 1998.

NOTES

1. E. E. Schattschneider, *Party Government* (New York: Holt, Rinehart and Winston, 1942), 1. Schattschneider's book stands as one of the most eloquent arguments for a strong political party system ever penned.

2. For more information on this topic, see Larry J. Sabato and Bruce A. Larson, *The Party's Just Begun: Shaping Political Parties for America's Future*, 2nd ed. (New York: Longman, 2002).

3. For a sampling of some alternative definitions of political parties put forth by political scientists, see Paul Allen Beck, *Party Politics in America*, 8th ed. (New York: Longman, 1998), 8–9.

4. This conception of a political party was originally put forth by V. O. Key in *Politics, Parties, and Pressure Groups* (New York, Crowell, 1958).

5. Joseph Schlesinger, *Political Parties and the Winning of Office* (Ann Arbor: University of Michigan, 1991); and Mildred A. Schwartz, *The Party Network: The Robust Organization of Illinois Republicans* (Madison: University of Wisconsin, 1990).

6. John H. Aldrich, *Why Parties? The Origin and Transformation of Party Politics in America* (Chicago: University of Chicago Press, 1995).

7. The National Republican (one forerunner of the Whig Party) and the Anti-Masonic parties each had held more limited conventions in 1831.

8. By contrast, Great Britain did not develop truly national, broad-based parties until the 1870s.

9. Joel H. Silbey, "The Rise and Fall of American Parties, 1790–2000," in L. Sandy Maisel, ed., *The Parties Respond: Changes in American Parties and Campaigns*, 3rd ed. (Boulder, CO: Westview Press, 1998), 11.

10. J. Morgan Kousser, *The Shaping of Southern Politics* (New Haven, CT: Yale University Press, 1974).

11. See *Historical Statistics of the United States: Colonial Times to 1970*, part 2, series Y-27-28 (Washington, DC: Government Printing Office, 1975), based on unpublished data prepared by Walter Dean Burnham.

12. Frank J. Sorauf, *Party Politics in America*, 5th ed. (Boston: Little, Brown, 1984), 22.

13. Steven P. Erie, *Rainbow's End: Irish-Americans and the Dilemmas of Urban Machine Politics, 1840–1985* (Berkeley: University of California Press, 1990).

14. Leon Esptein, *Political Parties in the American Mold* (Madison: University of Wisconsin, 1986), 135. Paul Allen Beck, *Party Politics in America*, 8th ed. (New York: Longman, 1998), 75.

15. Tom Watson, "All Powerful Machine of Yore Endures in New York's Nassau," *Congressional Quarterly Weekly Report* 43 (August 17, 1985): 1623–5.

16. Lee Sigelman, Paul J. Wahlbeck, and Emmett H. J. Buell Jr., "Vote Choice and the Preference for Divided Government: Lessons of 1992," *American Journal of Political Science* 41 (July 1997): 879–94; Barry C. Burden and David C. Kimball, "A New Approach to the Study of Ticket-Splitting," *American Political Science Review* 92 (September 1998): 533–44; and Paul Frymer, Terri Bimes, and Thomas Kim, "Party Elites, Ideological Voters, and Divided Party Government," *Legislative Studies Quarterly* 22 (May 1997): 195–216.

17. Robert Boston, "How to Eat an Elephant: The Christian Coalition's Precinct-Based Political Strategy," *Church and State* 52 (November 1999): 9.

18. Schattschneider, *Party Government*, 48.

19. Philip A. Klinkner, *The Losing Parties: Out-Party National Committees, 1956–1993* (New Haven, CT: Yale University Press, 1994).

20. Marc J. Hetherington, "Resurgent Mass Partisanship: The Role of Elite Polarization," *American Political Science Review* 95 (September 2001): 628.

21. Ibid., 629.

22. Kim Hill and Jan Leighley, "Political Parties and Class Mobilization in Contemporary United States Elections," *American Journal of Political Science* 40 (August 1996): 787–804.

23. M. V. Hood, Quentin Kidd, and Irwin L. Morris, "Of Byrds and Bumpers: Using Democratic Senators to Analyze Political Change in the South, 1960–1995," *American Journal of Political Science* 43 (April 1999): 465–87.

24. Earl Black and Merle Black, *The Rise of Southern Republicans* (Cambridge, MA: Harvard University Press, 2002).

25. Kelly D. Patterson, *Political Parties and the Maintenance of Liberal Democracy* (New York: Columbia University Press, 1996).

26. Quoted in Ken Bode, "Hero or Demagogue?" *New Republic* 195 (March 3, 1986): 28.

27. Gerald M. Pomper with Susan Lederman, *Elections in America*, 2nd ed. (New York: Longman, 1980), 145–50, 167–73.

28. See David E. Price, *Bringing Back the Parties* (Washington, DC: CQ Press, 1984), 284–8.

29. See, for example, Sarah McCally Morehouse, "Legislatures and Political Parties," *State Government* 59 (1976): 23.

30. Pomper with Lederman, *Elections in America*, 150.

31. L. Sandy Maisel, "The Platform-Writing Process: Candidate-Centered Platforms in 1992," *Political Science Quarterly* 108 (Winter 1993–1994): 671–98.

32. Walter Dean Burnham, *Critical Elections and the Mainsprings of American Politics* (New York: Norton, 1970), 132–3.

33. Paul S. Herrnson, "National Party Organizations at Century's End," in L. Sandy Maisel, ed., *The Parties Respond: Changes in American Parties and Campaigns*, 3rd ed. (Boulder, CO: Westview Press, 1998).

34. Cornelius P. Cotter, James L. Gibson, John F. Bibby, and Robert J. Huckshorn, *Party Organizations in American Politics* (Pittsburgh: University of Pittsburgh Press, 1989).

35. Paul Allen Beck, et al., "Local Party Organizations in the 1992 Presidential Elections," paper presented at the 1993 annual meeting of the Southern Political Science Association. See also Paul Allen Beck, et al., "Party Efforts at the Grass Roots: Local Presidential Campaigning in 1992," paper presented at the 1994 annual meeting of the Midwest Political Science Association.

36. John J. Coleman, "Party Organization Strength and Public Support for Parties," *American Journal of Political Science* 40 (August 1996): 805–24.

37. Anthony Gierzynski, *Legislative Party Campaign Committees in the American States* (Lexington: University Press of Kentucky, 1992).

38. Anthony Gierzynski and David A. Breaux, "The Financing Role of Parties," in Joel A. Thompson and Gary Moncrief, eds., *Campaign Finance in State Legislative Elections* (Washington, DC: CQ Press, 1998).

39. Daniel M. Shea, *Transforming Democracy: Legislative Campaign Committees and Political Parties* (Albany: SUNY Press, 1995).

40. John F. Bibby, "Party Networks: National-State Integration, Allied Groups, and Issue Activists," in John C. Green and Daniel M. Shea, eds., *The State of the Parties: The Changing Role of Contemporary American Parties*, 3rd ed. (Lanham, MD: Rowman and Littlefield, 1999).

41. Ibid.

42. Steven S. Smith and Eric D. Lawrence, "Party Control of Committees in the Republican Congress," in Lawrence C. Dodd and Bruce I. Oppenheimer, eds., *Congress Reconsidered*, 6th ed. (Washington, DC: CQ Press, 1997).

43. Such cases are few, but a deterrent nonetheless. Several U.S. senators were expelled from the Republican Caucus in 1925 for having supported the Progressive candidate for president the previous year. In 1965, two southern House Democrats lost all their committee seniority because of their 1964 endorsement of GOP presidential nominee Barry Goldwater, as did another southerner in 1968 for backing George Wallace's third-party candidacy. In early 1983, the House Democratic Caucus removed Texas Representative Phil Gramm from his Budget Committee seat because of his "disloyalty" in working more closely with Republican committee members than with his own party leaders. (Gramm resigned his seat in Congress, changed parties, and was reelected as a Republican. He then used the controversy to propel himself into the U.S. Senate in 1984.)

44. Gregory R. Thorson, "Divided Government and the Passage of Partisan Legislation, 1947–1990," *Political Research Quarterly* 51 (September 1998): 751–65.

45. David W. Rohde, *Parties and Leaders in the Postreform House* (Chicago: University of Chicago Press, 1991); and John A. Aldrich and David W. Rohde, "The Transition to Republican Rule in the House: Implications for Theories of Congressional Politics," *Political Science Quarterly* 112 (1997–1998): 541–67.

46. Joseph A. Schlesinger, "The New American Political Party," *American Political Science Review* 79 (1985): 1168.

47. Kevin M. Leyden and Stephen A. Borrelli, "An Investment in Goodwill: Party Contributions and Party Unity Among U.S. House Members in the 1980s," *American Politics Quarterly* 22 (1994): 421–52.

48. Richard A. Clucas, "Party Contributions and the Influence of Campaign Committee Chairs on Roll-Call Voting," *Legislative Studies Quarterly* 22 (1997): 179–94; and David M. Cantor and Paul S. Herrnson, "Party Campaign Activity and Party Unity in the U.S. House of Representatives," *Legislative Studies Quarterly* 22 (1997): 393–415.

49. Rhodes Cook, "Reagan Nurtures His Adopted Party to Strength," *Congressional Quarterly Weekly Report* 43 (September 28, 1985): 1927–30.

50. George C. Edwards III, *Presidential Influence in Congress* (New York: Freeman, 1980); and Herbert M. Kritzer and Robert B. Eubank, "Presidential Coattails Revisited: Partisanship and Incumbency Effects," *American Journal of Political Science* 23 (1979): 615–26.

51. Lyn Ragsdale, "The Fiction of Congressional Elections as Presidential Events," *American Politics Quarterly* 8 (1980): 375–98; and Thomas E. Mann and Raymond E. Wolfinger, "Candidates and Parties in Congressional Elections," *American Political Science Review* 74 (1980): 617–32.

52. Gregory R. Thorson and Stephen J. Stambough, "Anti-Incumbency and the 1992 Elections: The Changing Face of Presidential Coattails," *Journal of Politics* 57 (February 1995): 210–20.

53. Sidney M. Milkis, *The President and the Parties: The Transformation of the American Party System Since the New Deal* (New York: Oxford University Press, 1993).

54. See S. Sidney Ulmer, "The Political Party Variable on the Michigan Supreme Court," *Journal of Public Law* 11 (1962): 352–62; Stuart Nagel, "Political Party Affiliation and Judges' Decisions," *American Political Science Review* 55 (1961): 843–50; David W. Adamany, "The Party Variable in Judges' Voting: Conceptual Notes and a Case Study," *American Political Science Review* 63 (1969): 57–73; Sheldon Goldman, "Voting Behavior on the United States Courts of Appeals, 1961–1964," *American Political Science Review* 60 (1966): 374–83; and Robert A. Carp and C. K. Rowland, *Policymaking and Politics in the Federal District Courts* (Knoxville: University of Tennessee Press, 1983).

55. Randall D. Lloyd, "Separating Partisanship from Party in Judicial Research: Reapportionment in the U.S. District Courts," *American Political Science Review* 89 (June 1995): 413–20.

56. The Farmer-Labor Party did survive in a sense; having endured a series of defeats, it merged in 1944 with the Democrats, and Minnesota's Democratic candidates still officially bear the standard of the Democratic-Farmer-Labor (DFL) Party. At about the same time, also having suffered severe electoral reversals, the Progressives stopped nominating candidates in Wisconsin. The party's members either returned to the Republican Party, from which the Progressives had split early in the century, or became Democrats.

57. Morehouse, "Legislatures and Political Parties," 19–24.

58. Senator George J. Mitchell (D–ME), as quoted in the *Washington Post* (February 9, 1986): A14.

59. Janet M. Box-Steffensmeier, "A Dynamic Analysis of the Role of War Chests in Campaign Strategy," *American Journal of Political Science* 40 (May 1996): 352–71.

60. In a speech to the RNC as quoted by the Associated Press, January 24, 1987, and in the *Washington Post* (January 24, 1987): A3.

60a. S. V. Date "President won Florida with better ground game," Palm Beach Post, November 4, 2004: http://www.palmbeachpost.com/politics/content/news/epaper/2004/11/04/a1aa_FLA PRES1104.html

61. Alan Gerber, "Estimating the Effect of Campaign Spending on Senate Election Outcomes Using Instrumental Variables," *American Political Science Review* 92 (June 1998): 401–12.

62. Tim Kenworthy, "Collaring Colleagues for Cash," *Washington Post* (14 May 1991): A17.

63. Jennifer Babson and Beth Donovan, "GOP Fundraiser Raises Sights and Tightens Belt," *Congressional Quarterly Weekly Report* (April 2, 1994): 809–11.

64. Bruce A. Larson, "Ambition and Money in the U.S. House of Representatives: Analyzing Campaign Contributions from Incumbents' Leadership PACs and Reelection Committees" (Ph.D. dissertation, University of Virginia, 1998); Paul S. Herrnson, "Money and Motives: Spending in House Elections," in Lawrence C. Dodd and Bruce I. Oppenheimer, eds., *Congress Reconsidered*, 6th ed. (Washington, DC: CQ Press, 1997); and Bibby, "Party Networks."

65. Michael B. McKuen, Robert S. Erikson, and James A. Stimson, "Macropartisanship," *American Political Science Review*, 83 (December 1989): 1125–42.

66. Donald Green, Bradley Palmquist, and Eric Schickler, "Macropartisanship: A Replication and Critique," *American Political Science Review* 92 (December 1998): 883–900.

67. See Steven E. Finkel and Howard A. Scarrow, "Party Identification and Party Enrollment: The Difference and the Consequence," *Journal of Politics* 47 (May 1985): 620–42.

68. Martin P. Wattenberg, *The Decline of American Political Parties, 1952–1994* (Cambridge, MA: Harvard University Press, 1996).

69. Alan I. Abramowitz and Kyle L. Saunders, "Ideological Realignment in the U.S. Electorate," *Journal of Politics* 60 (August 1998): 634–52.

70. Karen M. Kaufmann and John R. Petrocik, "The Changing Politics of American Men: Understanding the Sources of the Gender Gap," *American Journal of Political Science* 43 (July 1999): 864–87.

71. Michael Dawson, *Behind the Mule: Race and Class in African-American Politics* (Princeton, NJ: Princeton University Press, 1994); and Louis Bolce, Gerald DeMaio, and Douglas Muzzio, "Blacks and the Republican Party: The 20 Percent Solution," *Political Science Quarterly* 107 (Spring 1992): 63–79.

72. The presidential election of 1960 may be an extreme case, but John F. Kennedy's massive support among Catholics and Nixon's less substantial but still impressive backing by Protestants demonstrates the polarization that religion could once produce. See Philip E. Converse, "Religion and Politics: The 1960 Election," in Angus Campbell et al., *Elections and the Political Order* (New York: Wiley, 1966), 96–124.

73. Jeff Manza and Clem Brooks, "The Religious Factor in U.S. Presidential Elections, 1960–1992," *American Journal of Sociology* 103 (July 1997): 38–81.

74. Herbert F. Weisberg, "The Demographics of a New Voting Gap: Marital Differences in American Voting," *Public Opinion Quarterly* 51 (Autumn 1987): 335–43.

75. Richard Benedetto, "Fed-Up Voters in Search of a Better Candidate," *USA Today* (August 11, 1995): A4.

76. See V. O. Key Jr., *American State Politics: An Introduction* (New York: Knopf, 1956).

77. See V. O. Key Jr., *Southern Politics in State and Nation* (New York: Knopf, 1949).

78. See John F. Bibby et al., "Parties in State Politics," in Virginia Gray, Herbert Jacob, and Kenneth Vines, eds., *Politics in the American States*, 4th ed. (Boston: Little, Brown, 1983), table 3.3, 66; also see Larry J. Sabato, *Goodbye to Good-Time Charlie: The American Governorship Transformed*, 2nd ed. (Washington, DC: CQ Press, 1983), 116–38.

79. Sorauf, *Party Politics in America*, 51.

80. Todd Donovan, Shaun Bowler, and Tammy Terrio, "Support for Third Parties in California," *American Politics Quarterly* 28 (January 2000): 50–71.

81. Jeffrey Koch, "The Perot Candidacy and Attitudes Toward Government and Politics," *Political Research Quarterly* 51 (March 1998): 141–54.

82. Christian Collet and Martin P. Wattenberg, "Strategically Unambitious: Minor Party and Independent Candidates in the 1996 Congressional Elections," in John C. Green and Daniel M. Shea, eds., *The State of the Parties: The Changing Role of Contemporary American Parties*, 3rd ed. (Lanham, MD: Rowman and Littlefield, 1999).

83. Dean Lacy and Barry C. Burden, "The Vote-Stealing and Turnover Effects of Ross Perot in the 1992 U.S. Presidential Election," *American Journal of Political Science* 43 (January 1999): 233–55.

84. Mark J. Hetherington, "The Effect of Political Trust on the Presidential Vote, 1968–1996," *American Political Science Review* 93 (June 1999): 311–26.

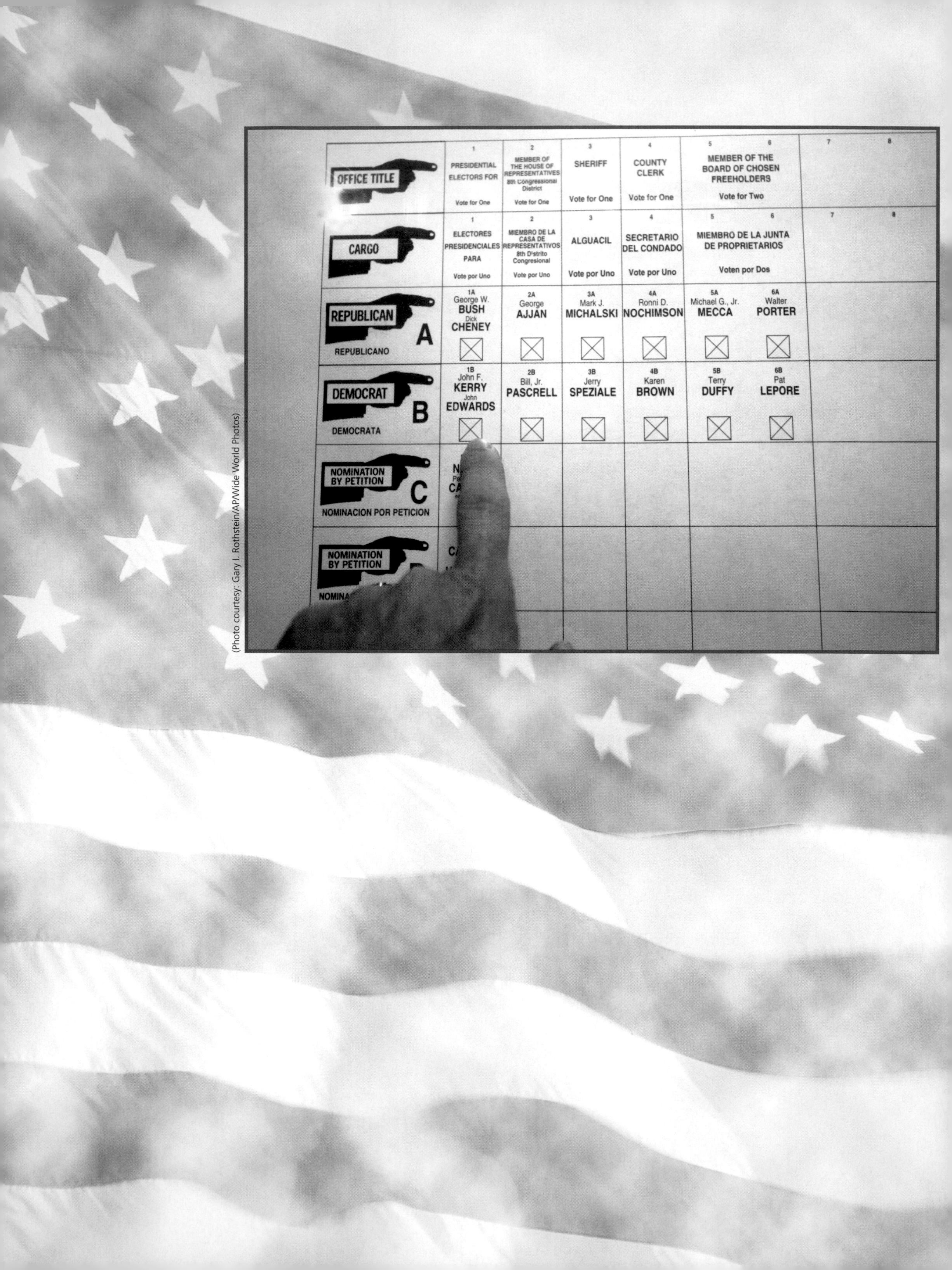

(Photo courtesy: Gary I. Rothstein/AP/Wide World Photos)

Voting and Elections

During the months leading up to the 2004 presidential election, no one doubted that the election between Republican President George W. Bush and the Democratic challenger, Massachusetts Senator John Kerry, would be close. The question everyone wanted answered was exactly how close it would be. Although the presidential election is national, both candidates focused on specific states that showed either narrow margins or even ties. Many of these so-called "battle-ground states" were located in the Rust Belt—Minnesota, Iowa, Wisconsin, Michigan, Ohio, and Pennsylvania; however, others were spread across the country, such as Florida, New Hampshire, New Mexico, and even Hawaii.

Of these several battle-ground states, three stood out as the most valuable because of their razor-thin margins of victory in 2000 and their large number of electoral votes. The first was Pennsylvania, a state the 2000 Democratic candidate Al Gore had won narrowly with 220,000 votes, had 21 electoral votes. Second, Florida, with the miniscule and heavily contested 537 vote margin for Bush in 2000, had 27 electoral votes up for grabs. Finally, there was Ohio with 20 electoral votes, a state no Republican candidate has been able to lose and still go on to win the presidency. By Election Day, it was conventional wisdom that either candidate had to win at least two of these two states if they were going to win an election. By early evening, it was clear that Bush would take Florida by a much wider margin than 2000, and Kerry would narrowly win Pennsylvania. This left the election down to Ohio, which both candidates had visited more than twenty-five times in 2004. Throughout the night, Bush appeared to hold a 2 percent voter margin over Kerry, leading some television stations—Fox News and NBC—to call the state for Bush, while others like ABC, CBS, and CNN left it too close to call. However, fears that Ohio might become the 2004 version of Florida quickly abated when it became clear that Kerry could not rely on the provisional and absentee ballots to overtake Bush's voter lead. By the morning after Election Day, Bush took Ohio.

Ohio alone would not have been enough for Bush to win the election. To push his vote count over the 270 needed for victory, Bush also won New Mexico and Iowa states that Gore carried in 2000, but he lost New Hampshire to Kerry. The remaining battle-ground states also went to Kerry, but they did not collectively have enough electoral votes for him to win. When looking at how the 2004 map changed from the 2000 map, one can see that the division of coastal "blue" (Democratic) states and the "red" (Republican) states became even more contiguous. New England is now completely Democratic like the Pacific states (except Alaska), while the South from Florida to Arizona is solidly Republican. Because of these geographical differences, many students of politics raise questions about whether blue and red Americans see America the same way and respond differently or if America is actually two nations fighting a cultural war in the Mid-western battlegrounds, a question the 2008 presidential elections may help to answer.

*E*very four years, on the first Tuesday following a Monday in November, a plurality of the voting electorate, simply by casting ballots peacefully across a continent-sized nation, reelects or replaces politicians at all levels of government—from the president of the United States, to members of the U.S. Congress, to state legislators. A number of other countries do not have the luxury of a peaceful transition of political power. We tend to take this process for granted, but in truth it is a marvel. The relatively uneventful conclusion of a second very close presidential race in 2004 demonstrates that Americans, in spite of their political differences, have a common commitment to peaceful politics. Fortunately, most Americans, though not enough, understand why and how elections serve their interests. Elections take the pulse of average people and gauge their hopes and fears; the study of elections permits us to trace the course of the American revolution over 200 years of voting.

Today, the United States of America is a democrat's paradise in many respects, because it probably conducts more elections for more offices more frequently than any nation on earth. Moreover, in recent times, the U.S. electorate (those citizens eligible to vote) has been the most inclusive in the country's history; no longer can one's race or sex or creed prevent participation at the ballot box. But, challenges still remain. After all the blood spilled and energy expended to expand the suffrage (as the right to vote is called), little more than half the potentially eligible voters bother to go to the polls!

(Photo courtesy: Mike Luckovich and Creators Syndicate, Inc., by permission)

This chapter focuses on the purposes served by elections, the various kinds of elections held in the United States, and patterns of voting over time. We concentrate in particular on presidential and congressional contests, both of which have rich histories that tell us a great deal about the American people and their changing hopes and needs. We conclude by returning to contemporary presidential elections and addressing some topics of electoral reform.

- First, we will examine the *purposes served by elections*, pointing out that they confer a legitimacy on regimes better than any other method of change.
- Second, we will analyze *different kinds of elections*, including the many different types of elections held at the presidential and congressional levels.
- Third, we will take a closer look at the elements of *presidential elections*, including primaries, conventions, and delegates.
- Fourth, we will explore how *congressional elections*, although they share similarities with presidential elections, are really quite different.
- Fifth, we will discuss *how voters behave* in certain distinct ways and exhibit unmistakable patterns each election cycle.
- Sixth, we will present arguments for *reforming the electoral process* for the most powerful official in the world, the president of the United States.
- In exploring our theme of *continuity and change*, we will conclude the chapter with a discussion of the ongoing revolution in voting technology.

THE PURPOSES SERVED BY ELECTIONS

Both the ballot and the bullet are methods of governmental change around the world, and surely the former is preferable to the latter. Although the United States has not escaped the bullet's awful effects, most leadership change has come to this country through the election process. Regular free elections guarantee mass political action and enable citizens to influence the actions of their government. Election campaigns may often seem unruly, unending, harsh, and even vicious, but imagine the stark alternatives: violence and social disruption. Societies that cannot vote their leaders out of office are left with little choice other than to force them out by means of strikes, riots, or coups d'état.

Popular election confers on a government the legitimacy that it can achieve no other way. Even many authoritarian systems around the globe, including Singapore, Syria, and Iraq, recognize this. From time to time, they hold "referenda" to endorse their regimes or one-party elections, even though these so-called elections offer no real choice that would ratify their rule. The symbolism of elections as mechanisms to legitimize change, then, is important, but so is their practical value. After all, elections are the means to fill public offices and staff the government. The voters' choice of candidates and parties helps to organize government as well. Because candidates advocate certain policies, elections also involve a choice of platforms and point the society in certain directions on a wide range of issues, from abortion to civil rights to national defense to the environment.

Regular elections also ensure that government is accountable to the people it serves. At fixed intervals the **electorate,** citizens eligible to vote, is called on to judge those in power. If the judgment is favorable, and the incumbents are reelected, the office holders may continue their policies with renewed resolve. Should the incumbents be defeated and their challengers elected, however, a change in policies will likely result. Either way, the winners will claim a **mandate** (literally, a command) from the people to carry out their platform.

electorate
Citizens eligible to vote.

mandate
A command, indicated by an electorate's votes, for the elected officials to carry out their platforms.

retrospective judgment
A voter's evaluation of the performance of the party in power.

prospective judgment
A voter's evaluation of a candidate based on what he or she pledges to do about an issue if elected.

Sometimes the claim of a mandate is suspect because voters are not so much endorsing one candidate and his or her beliefs as rejecting his or her opponent. Frequently, this occurs because the electorate is exercising **retrospective judgment;** that is, voters are rendering judgment on the performance of the party in power. This judgment makes sense because voters can evaluate the record of office holders much better than they can predict the future actions of the out-of-power challengers.

At other times, voters might vote using **prospective judgment,** that is, they vote based on what a candidate pledges to do about an issue if elected. This forward-looking approach to choosing candidates voters believe will best serve their interests requires that the electorate examine the views that the rival candidates have on the issues of the day and then cast a ballot for the person they believe will best handle these matters. Unfortunately, prospective voting requires lots of information about issues and candidates. Voters who cast a vote prospectively must be willing to spend a great deal of time seeking out information and learning about issues and how each candidate stands on them. As the authors of a classic study on the American electorate note, three requirements exist in order for voters to engage in prospective voting: (1) Voters must have an opinion on an issue; (2) voters must have an idea of what action, if any, the government is taking on the issue; and, (3) voters must see a difference between the two parties on the issue.[1] Only a small minority of voters, the authors concluded, could meet these requirements, although scholars studying more recent elections have found voters better equipped to engage in prospective voting.[2] Consider for a moment how voters retrospectively and prospectively judged recent presidential administrations in reaching their ballot decisions:

- *1972:* The American people were satisfied with Richard M. Nixon's stewardship of foreign affairs, especially his good relationship with the Soviet Union, the diplomatic opening of China, and the "Vietnamization" of the war. Thus, they retrospectively judged his administration to have been a success and looked to the future, believing that he, rather than Democrat George McGovern, could best lead the country. The Watergate scandal (involving Nixon's cover-up of his campaign committee's bugging of the Democrats' national headquarters) was only in its infancy, and the president was rewarded with a forty-nine-state sweep.

- *1976:* Retrospective judgments clearly prevailed over prospective considerations. Despite confusion about Jimmy Carter's real philosophy and intentions, the relatively unknown Georgia Democrat was elected president as voters held President Gerald R. Ford responsible for an economic recession and deplored his pardon of Richard M. Nixon for Watergate crimes.

- *1980:* Burdened by difficult economic times and the Iranian hostage crisis (one year before Election Day, Iranian militants had seized fifty-three Americans, whom they held until January 20, 1981, Inauguration Day), Carter became a one-term president as the electorate rejected the Democrat's perceived weak leadership. At age sixty-nine, Ronald Reagan was not viewed as the ideal replacement by many voters, nor did a majority agree with some of his conservative principles. But, the retrospective judgment on Carter was so harsh, and the prospective outlook of four more years under his stewardship so glum, that an imperfect alternative was considered preferable to another term of the Democrat.

- *1984:* A strong economic recovery from a midterm recession and an image of strength derived from a defense buildup and a successful military venture in Grenada combined to produce a satisfied electorate whose retrospective judgment granted Ronald Reagan four more years. A forty-nine-state landslide reelected Reagan over Jimmy Carter's vice president, Walter Mondale.

- *1988:* Continued satisfaction with Reagan, a product of strong economic expansion and superpower summitry, produced an electoral endorsement of Reagan's vice president, George Bush. Bush was seen as Reagan's understudy and natural successor; the Democratic nominee, Michael Dukakis, offered too few convincing reasons to alter the voters' retrospective judgment.

- *1992:* A prolonged recession, weak job growth, and Ross Perot's candidacy—which split the Republican base—denied a second term to George Bush, despite many significant foreign policy triumphs. In the end, voters decided to vote retrospectively and gamble on little-known Arkansas Governor Bill Clinton.

- *1996:* Similar to 1984, only with the party labels reversed, a healthy economy prompted Americans to retrospectively support President Bill Clinton in his quest for reelection over Bob Dole. Voters also looked prospectively at the two candidates and again registered their support for President Clinton and his vision for the country's future.

- *2000:* Eight years of peace and record economic prosperity should have worked in favor of Vice President Al Gore. While he received more votes than any Democratic candidate in U.S. history, Gore's Clinton-era baggage and credibility questions helped to nullify any advantage over Texas Governor George W. Bush, an opponent with an undistinguished record but no significant liabilities. Given the unusual circumstances of the actual election, it is difficult to say more precisely to what extent the outcome represents a retrospective or prospective political opinion.

- *2004:* Ordinarily, incumbent reelections become a referendum on the incumbent's performance, making Americans likely to think retrospectively. However, President George W. Bush, the incumbent, managed to make the election not merely about his own economic performance but also former President Clinton's, whose last year in office Bush credits as the beginning of a recession, and on the September 11 attacks, which shook consumer confidence. Finally, Bush used retrospective opinion on his opponent, Senator John Kerry, claiming his Senate voting record actually shows tax increases that hindered economic progress.

Whether one agrees or disagrees with these election results, there is a rough justice at work here. When parties and presidents please the electorate, they are rewarded; when they preside over hard times, they are punished. Presidents usually are not responsible for all the good or bad developments that occur on their watch, but the voters nonetheless hold them accountable, not an unreasonable way for citizens to behave in a democracy.

On rare occasions, off-year congressional elections can produce mandates. In 1974, a tidal wave for Democrats produced a mandate to clean up politics after Watergate. In

Controversy over vote counting in the 2000 presidential election brought people to West Palm Beach, Florida, to protest on behalf of Al Gore and George W. Bush.

(Photo courtesy: Kirk Condyles)

1994, backlash against Clinton's decision to push liberal policies like national health-care and a large government stimulus package helped Representative Newt Gingrich (R–GA) to lead Republicans to a similar wave, claiming the House of Representatives and a mandate for limiting government.

DIFFERENT KINDS OF ELECTIONS

So far, we have referred mainly to presidential elections, but in the U.S. system, elections come in many varieties: primary elections, general elections, initiatives, referenda, and recalls.

Primary Elections

primary election
Election in which voters decide which of the candidates within a party will represent the party in the general election.

closed primary
A primary election in which only a party's registered voters are eligible to vote.

open primary
A primary in which party members, independents, and sometimes members of the other party are allowed to vote.

crossover voting
Participation in the primary of a party with which the voter is not affiliated.

raiding
An organized attempt by voters of one party to influence the primary results of the other party.

blanket primary
A primary in which voters may cast ballots in either party's primary (but not both) on an office-by-office basis.

runoff primary
A second primary election between the two candidates receiving the greatest number of votes in the first primary.

nonpartisan primary
A primary used to select candidates regardless of party affiliation.

general election
Election in which voters decide which candidates will actually fill elective public offices.

In **primary elections,** voters decide which of the candidates within a party will represent the party's ticket in the general elections. The primaries themselves vary in kind. For example, **closed primaries** allow only a party's registered voters to cast a ballot, and **open primaries** allow independents and sometimes members of the other party to participate. (Figure 13.1 shows the states with open and closed primaries for presidential delegate selection.) Closed primaries are considered healthier for the party system because they prevent members of one party from influencing the primaries of the opposition party. Studies of open primaries indicate that **crossover voting**—participation in the primary of a party with which the voter is not affiliated—occurs frequently.[3] On the other hand, the research shows little evidence of much **raiding**—an *organized* attempt by voters of one party to influence the primary results of the other party.[4] In a **blanket primary,** voters are permitted to vote in either party's primary (but not both) on an office-by-office basis. When none of the candidates in the initial primary secures a majority of the votes, most states have a **runoff primary,** a contest between the two candidates with the greatest number of votes. One final type of primary, used in Nebraska and Louisiana (in state wide, non-presidential primaries), and in hundreds of cities large and small across America, is the **nonpartisan primary,** which is used to select candidates without regard to party affiliation. A nonpartisan primary could produce two final candidates of the same party from a slate of several candidates from many parties.

General Elections

Once the party candidates for various offices are chosen, general elections are held. In the **general election,** voters decide which candidates will actually fill the nation's elective public offices. These elections are held at many levels, including municipal, county, state, and national. While primaries are contests between the candidates within each party, general elections are contests between the candidates of opposing parties.

General elections come in many varieties, because Americans perceive the various offices as substantially different from one another. In sizing up presidential candidates, voters look for leadership and character, and they base their judgments partly on foreign policy and defense issues that do not arise in state and local elections. Leadership qualities are vital for gubernatorial and mayoral candidates, as are the nuts-and-bolts issues (such as taxes, schools, and roads) that dominate the concerns of state and local governments. Citizens often choose their congressional representatives very differently than they select presidents. Knowing much less about the candidates, people will sometimes base a vote on simple name identification, visibility, or party identification. This way of deciding one's vote obviously helps incumbents and therefore to some degree explains the high reelection rates of incumbent U.S. representatives. Since World War

II, 92 percent of all U.S. House members seeking another term have won; in several recent election years, the proportion has been above 95 percent. In 2004, fully 97 percent of the lawmakers who sought reelection won. Still, as political scientist Gary Jacobson observes, greater name recognition is probably not the most important factor driving the incumbency advantage. More important is that incumbents are typically able to cultivate more favorable public images than are challengers.[5]

Initiative, Referendum, and Recall

Three other types of elections are the initiative, the referendum, and the recall. Used in twenty-four states and the District of Columbia, initiatives involve voting on issues (as opposed to voting for candidates). An **initiative** is a process that allows citizens to propose legislation and submit it to the state electorate for popular vote, as long as they get a certain number of signatures on petitions supporting the proposal. Ballot initiatives have been the subject of growing controversy in the past decades. Critics charge that the process—which was intended to give citizens more direct control over policy making—is now unduly influenced by interest groups and "the initiative industry"— "law firms that draft legislation, petition management firms that guarantee ballot access, direct-mail firms, and campaign consultants who specialize in initiative contests."[6]

Colorado's Amendment 36, one of the more publicized and controversial initiatives, failed to receive a majority of votes in 2004. This proposed amendment to the state constitution would have changed Colorado's election law so that the state's nine electoral votes would be awarded proportionally, according to the popular vote.

Timeline

The Initiative and the Referendum

initiative
A process that allows citizens to propose legislation and submit it to the state electorate for popular vote.

WEB EXPLORATION

To select, evaluate, and debate upcoming referenda or initiatives currently under consideration in California, the "Referendum State," go to
www.ablongman.com/oconnor

FIGURE 13.1 Methods of Selecting Presidential Delegates

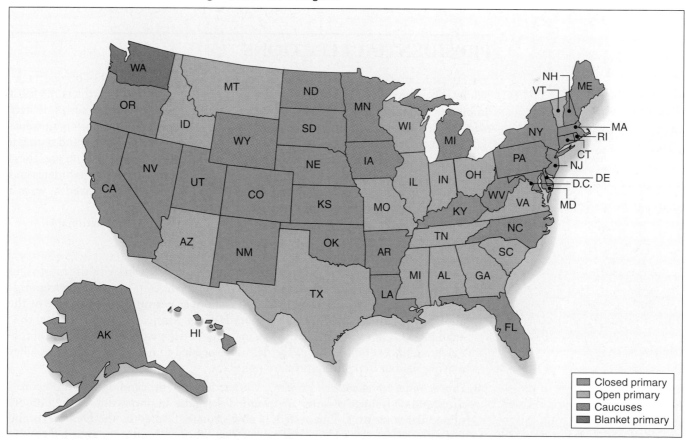

Closed primary
Open primary
Caucuses
Blanket primary

Note: Methods of selection current as of December 2002.

referendum
A procedure whereby the state legislature submits proposed legislation to the state's voters for approval.

A **referendum** is a procedure whereby the state legislature submits proposed legislation to the state's voters for approval. Although both the referendum and the initiative provide for more direct democracy, they are not problem free. In the 1990 elections, for instance, California had so many referenda and initiatives on its ballot that the state printed a lengthy two-volume guide in an attempt to explain them all to voters. In addition, the wording of the question can have an enormous impact on the outcome. In some cases, a "yes" vote will bring about a policy change, in other cases, a "no" vote will cause a change, depending on how the question is presented.[7]

Other problems with initiatives and referenda are identified in a recent study by Edward L. Lascher. Lascher and his co-researchers found, among other things, that referenda are imperfect representations of the public will because only a small, self-selected portion of the voting public choose to participate in the referenda voting process. Those who decide to study and form an opinion on the numerous questions are generally of higher socio-economic class, and therefore the votes of the lower classes are underrepresented. Additionally, Lascher found that the expense of first getting thousands of signatures to place a question on the ballot, and then waging a political campaign for it, dissuades private citizens from taking part in the process. He therefore concludes referenda are not the voice of the people, but rather the voice of well-funded special interest groups who can afford the cost and time commitment of a major campaign.[8]

recall
Removal of an incumbent from office by popular vote.

The third type of election (or "deelection") found in many states is the **recall,** whereby an incumbent can be removed from office by popular vote. Recall elections are very rare, and sometimes they are thwarted by the official's resignation or impeachment prior to the vote. For example, Arizona Governor Evan Mecham was impeached and ousted in 1988 by the state legislature for mishandling campaign finances (among other offenses) just a few weeks before a recall election had been scheduled.

PRESIDENTIAL ELECTIONS

Variety aside, no U.S. election can compare to the presidential contest. This spectacle, held every four years, brings together all the elements of politics and attracts the most ambitious and energetic politicians to the national stage. Through the series of state primary elections and caucuses, delegates to each party's national convention are allotted. The election of delegates is followed in midsummer by the parties' grand national conventions and then by a final set of fifty separate state elections all held on the Tuesday after the first Monday in November. This lengthy process exhausts candidates and voters alike, but it allows the diversity of the United States to be displayed in ways a shorter, more homogeneous presidential election process could not.

The state party organizations use a number of methods to elect national convention delegates:

WEB EXPLORATION
To see how presidential candidates presented themselves in the technology age of the 2000 race, go to
www.ablongman.com/oconnor

1. *Winner-take-all primary:* Under this system the candidate who wins the most votes in a state secures all of that state's delegates. The Democrats moved away from this mode of delegate selection in 1976 and no longer permit its use because of the arguable unfairness. Republicans generally favor winner-take-all contests, thus enabling a GOP candidate to amass a majority of delegates more quickly. California alone has over one-fifth of the delegates needed to nominate, making it a key playing field in Republican primary politics.

2. *Proportional representation primary:* Under this system, candidates who secure a threshold percentage of votes are awarded delegates in proportion to the number of popular votes won. This system is now strongly favored by the Democrats and is used in many states' Democratic primaries, where delegates are awarded to anyone who wins more than 15 percent in any congressional district. Although proportional representation is probably the fairest way of allocating delegates to

candidates, its downfall is that it renders majorities of delegates more difficult to accumulate and thus can lengthen the contest for the nomination.

3. *Proportional representation with bonus delegates primary; beauty contest with separate delegate selection; delegate selection with no beauty contest:* Used rarely, the first of these awards delegates to candidates in proportion to the popular vote won and then gives one bonus delegate to the winner of each district. The second serves as an indication of popular sentiment for the conventions to consider as they choose the actual delegates. Under the third system, the primary election chooses delegates to the national conventions who are not linked on the ballot to specific presidential contenders.

4. *The caucus:* Under this system, party members meet in small groups throughout a state to select the party's delegates to the national convention.

Primaries Versus Caucuses

The mix of preconvention contests has changed over the years, with the most pronounced trend being the shift from caucuses to primaries: Only seventeen states held presidential primaries in 1968, compared with thirty-eight in 1992, forty-two in 1996, forty-three in 2000, and thirty-six in 2004. Figure 13.1 shows which states use primaries (open and closed) and which use caucuses to select presidential delegates.

WEB EXPLORATION

To learn about the functions of the Federal Election Commission, the government agency that monitors and enforces campaign finance and election laws, go to www.ablongman.com/oconnor

The caucus is the oldest, most party-oriented method of choosing delegates to the national conventions. Traditionally, the caucus was a closed meeting of party activists in each state who selected the party's choice for presidential candidate. In the late-nineteenth and early twentieth centuries, however, these caucuses came to be viewed by many people as elitist and anti-democratic, and reformers succeeded in replacing them with direct primaries in most states. While there are still presidential nominating caucuses today (in Iowa, for example), they are now more open and attract a wider range of the party's membership. Indeed, political scientists Elaine Ciulla Kamarck and Kenneth M. Goldstein note that the new participatory caucuses more closely resemble primary elections than they do the old, exclusive party caucuses.[9]

The increase in the number of primaries is supported by some people who claim that this type of election is more democratic. The primaries are open not only to party activists, but also to anyone, wealthy or poor, urban or rural, northern or southern, who wants to vote. Theoretically, then, representatives of all these groups have a chance of winning the presidency. Related to this idea, advocates argue that presidential primaries are the most representative means by which to nominate presidential candidates. They are a barometer of a candidate's popularity with the party rank and file. While conventional wisdom holds that both primaries and caucuses attract more extreme voters in each party, recent research posits that primaries help nominate more moderate and appealing candidates—those that primary voters believe can win in the general election. Paul Abramson, for instance, describes "sophisticated voting," where primary voters vote for their second or third choice because they believe he or she will more easily win in November than will their first choice, perhaps because of less extreme policy positions.[10] Finally, the proponents of presidential primaries claim that they constitute a rigorous test for the candidates, a chance to display under pressure some of the skills needed to be a successful president.

Critics of presidential primaries, however, see the situation somewhat differently. First, they argue that although it may be true that primaries attract more participants than do caucuses, this quantity is more than matched by the quality of caucus participation. Compared with the unenlightening minutes spent at the primary polls, caucus attendees spend several hours learning about politics and the party, listening to speeches by candidates or their representatives, and taking cues from party leaders and elected officials, culminating often in a public vote (which is somewhat at odds with our conception of voting being a private act). Moreover, voters may not know very much about any of the field of candidates in a primary, or they may be excessively swayed by popularity polls, television ads, and other media presentations, such as newspaper and magazine coverage.

Critics also argue that the scheduling of primaries unfairly affects their outcomes. For example, the earliest primary is in the small, atypical state of New Hampshire, which is heavily white and conservative, and it receives much more media coverage than it warrants simply because it is first. Such excessive coverage undoubtedly skews the picture for more populous states that hold their primaries later. The critics also argue that the qualities tested by the primary system are by no means a complete list of those a president needs to be successful. For instance, skill at playing the media game is by itself no guarantee of an effective presidency. Similarly, the exhausting schedule of the primaries may be a better test of a candidate's stamina than of his or her brain power.

The primary proponents have obviously had the better of the arguments so far, though the debate continues, as do efforts to experiment with the schedule of primaries. From time to time, proposals are made for **regional primaries.** Under this system, the nation would be divided into five or six geographic regions (such as the South or the Midwest). All the states in each region would hold their primary elections on the same day, with perhaps one regional election day per month from February through June of presidential election years. This change would certainly cut down on candidate wear and tear. Moreover, candidates would be inspired to focus more on regional issues. On the other hand, regional primaries would continue to favor wealthy candidates who can afford to advertise on television throughout the large regions, and the system might needlessly amplify the differences and create divisive rifts among the nation's regions.

Occasionally, a regional plan is adopted. In 1988, for instance, fourteen southern and border South states joined together to hold simultaneous primaries on "Super Tuesday" (March 8) in order to maximize the South's impact on presidential politics. This was an attempt by conservative Democrats to influence the choice of the party nominee. Their effort failed, however, since the two biggest winners of Super Tuesday were liberals Jesse Jackson (who won six southern states) and Michael Dukakis, who carried the megastates of Texas and Florida. This outcome occurred because, in general, the kinds of citizens who vote in Democratic primaries in the South are not greatly different from those who cast ballots in northern Democratic primaries—most tend toward the liberal side of the ideological spectrum. This trend was repeated in the 1996 "Yankee Primary," when five of the six New England states held their contests on March 5 (Massachusetts, Connecticut, Rhode Island, Vermont, and Maine), followed by New York on March 7, and a scaled-down Super Tuesday on March 12.

The primary schedule has also been altered by a process called **front-loading,** the tendency of states to choose an early date on the primary calendar. Seventy percent of all the delegates to both party conventions are now chosen before the end of March. This trend is hardly surprising, given the added press emphasis on the first contests and the voters' desire to cast their ballots before the competition is decided. The focus on early contests (such as the Iowa caucus and the New Hampshire primary), coupled with front-loading, can result in a party's being saddled with a nominee too quickly, before press scrutiny and voter reflection are given enough time to separate the wheat from the chaff. Front-loading has also had other important effects on the nomination process. First, a front-loaded primary schedule generally benefits the

regional primary
A proposed system in which the country would be divided into five or six geographic areas and all states in each region would hold their presidential primary elections on the same day.

front-loading
The tendency of states to choose an early date on the primary calendar.

Former Vermont governor Howard Dean (right) challenged Senator John Kerry for the 2004 Democratic presidential nomination. Dean was the early frontrunner, thanks in part to his tremendously successful on-line fundraising strategy, and his grassroots campaign served to energized party activists.

(Photo courtesy: Jack Kurtz/The Image Works)

front-runner, since opponents have little time to turn the contest around once they fall behind. Second, front-loading advantages the candidate who can raise the bulk of the money *before* the nomination season begins, since there will be little opportunity to raise money once the process begins and since candidates will need to finance campaign efforts simultaneously in many states. Finally, front-loading has amplified the importance of the "invisible primary"—the year or so prior to the start of the official nomination season when candidates begin raising money and unofficially campaigning.[11]

The Party Conventions

The seemingly endless nomination battle does have a conclusion: the national party convention held in the summer of presidential election years. The out-of-power party traditionally holds its convention first, in late July, followed in mid-August by the party holding the White House. Preempting some of prime-time television for four nights, these remarkable conclaves are difficult for the public to ignore; indeed, they are pivotal events in shaping the voters' perceptions of the candidates.

Yet, the conventions once were much more: They were deliberative bodies that made actual decisions, where party leaders held sway and deals were sometimes cut in "smoke-filled rooms" to deliver nominations to little-known contenders called "dark horses." This era predated the modern emphasis on reform, primaries, and proportional representation, all of which have combined to make conventions the ratifying agencies for nominees preselected through the various primaries and caucuses.[12]

The first national convention was held in 1831 by the Anti-Masonic Party. In 1832, Andrew Jackson's nomination for reelection was ratified by the first Democratic National Convention. Just four years later, in 1836, Martin Van Buren became the first nonincumbent candidate nominated by a major party convention (the Democrats) to win the presidency.

From the 1830s to the mid-twentieth century, the national conventions remained primarily under the control of the important state and local party leaders, the so-called bosses or kingmakers, who would bargain within a splintered, decentralized party. During these years, state delegations to the convention consisted mostly of *uncommitted delegates* (that is, delegates who had not pledged to support any particular candidate). These delegates were selected by party leaders, a process that enabled the leaders to broker agreements with prominent national candidates. Under this system, a state party leader could exchange delegation support for valuable political plums—for instance, a Cabinet position or even the vice presidency—for an important state political figure.

Today, the convention is fundamentally different. First, its importance as a party conclave, at which compromises on party leadership and policies can be worked out, has diminished. Second, although the convention still formally selects the presidential ticket, most nominations are settled well in advance. Three preconvention factors have lessened the role of the current parties and conventions: delegate selection, national candidates and issues, and the news media.

Delegate Selection. The selection of delegates to the conventions is no longer the function of party leaders but of primary elections and grassroots caucuses. Moreover, recent reforms, especially by the Democratic Party, have generally weakened any remaining control by local party leaders over delegates. A prime example of such reform is the Democrats' abolition of the **unit rule,** a traditional party practice under which the majority of a state delegation (say, twenty-six of fifty delegates) could force the minority to vote for its candidate. Another new Democratic Party rule decrees that a state's delegates be chosen in proportion to the votes cast in its primary or caucus (so that, for example, a candidate who receives 30 percent of the vote gains about 30 percent of the convention delegates). This change has had the effect of requiring delegates to indicate their presidential preference at each stage of the selection process.

unit rule
A traditional party practice under which the majority of a state delegation can force the minority to vote for its candidate.

Consequently, the majority of state delegates now come to the convention already committed to a candidate. Again, this diminishes the discretionary role of the convention and the party leaders' capacity to bargain.

In sum, the many complex changes in the rules of delegate selection have contributed to the loss of decision-making powers by the convention. Even though many of these changes were initiated by the Democratic Party, the Republicans were carried along as many Democratic-controlled state legislatures enacted the reforms as state laws. There have been new rules to counteract some of these changes, however. For instance, since 1984, the number of delegate slots reserved for elected Democratic Party officials—called **superdelegates**—has been increased in the hope of adding stability to the Democratic convention. Before 1972, most delegates to a Democratic National Convention were not bound by primary results to support a particular candidate for president. This freedom to maneuver meant that conventions could be exciting and somewhat unpredictable gatherings, where last-minute events and deals could sway wavering delegates. Superdelegates are supposed to be party professionals concerned with winning the general election contest, not simply amateur ideologues concerned mainly with satisfying their policy appetites. All Democratic governors and 80 percent of the congressional Democrats, among others, are now included as voting delegates at the convention.

superdelegate
Delegate slot to the Democratic Party's national convention that is reserved for an elected party official.

The 2004 fields of presidential candidates. On top, the Democratic field, including presidental nominee John Kerry and vice-presidential nominee John Edwards. On bottom, President George Bush and Vice President Dick Cheney.

(Photos courtesy: AP/World Wide Photos)

Two recent studies of the role of superdelegates in the Democratic Party offer differing conclusions about the usefulness of those party insiders in the nomination process. Priscilla Southwell posits that if the superdelegate rule were relaxed in 1984, as it was in 1992, "the 1984 [Democratic primary] race could have changed the outcome of the Democratic nomination," as the eventual nominee, Walter Mondale, was the overwhelming choice of the party insiders who were unpledged superdelegates. Without support among this numerous group for Mondale, the nomination fight would have been much tighter.[13] In contrast, Richard Herrera, using data on the views of both regular and superdelegates to the 1988 Democratic convention, concludes that the common belief (and fear) that the regularly chosen delegates are amateurs who do not understand the true interests of the party is overstated. Regular delegates and superdelegates are more similar to each other than previously believed, according to Herrera.[14]

National Candidates and Issues.   The political perceptions and loyalties of voters are now influenced largely by national candidates and issues, a factor that has undoubtedly served to diminish the power of state and local party leaders at the convention. The national candidates have usurped the autonomy of state party leaders with their preconvention ability to garner delegate support. Issues, increasingly national in scope, are significantly more important to the new, issue-oriented party activists than to the party professionals, who, prior to the late 1960s, had a monopoly on the management of party affairs.

The News Media.   The mass media have helped to transform the national conventions into political extravaganzas for the television audience's consumption. They have also helped to preempt the convention, by keeping count of the delegates committed to the candidates; as a result, the delegates and even the candidates now have much more information about nomination politics well before the convention. From the strategies of candidates to the commitments of individual delegates, the media cover it all. Even the bargaining within key party committees, formerly done in secret, is now subject to some public scrutiny, thanks to open meetings.

The business of the convention has been irrevocably shaped to accommodate television. Desirous of presenting a unified image to kick off a strong general election campaign, the parties assign important roles to attractive speakers, and most crucial party affairs are saved for prime-time viewing hours. During the 1990s, the networks gradually began to reduce their convention coverage, citing low viewer ratings. In 2004, the major networks changed their coverage slightly, providing no prime-time coverage on some days, and extending coverage to as much as three hours on the final day of each convention. While this likely reflects a change in the political culture away from meaningful convention activity overall, the increased final-night coverage indicates a greater interest in the candidates themselves. Fortunately, C-SPAN still gives gavel-to-gavel coverage.

Extensive media coverage of the convention has its pros and cons. On the one hand, such exposure helps the party launch its presidential campaign with fanfare, usually providing a boost to the party's candidate. President George Bush went from a seventeen-point deficit to a slim lead following the 1988 Republican convention. On the other hand, it can expose rifts within a party, as happened in 1968 at the Democratic convention in Chicago. Dissension was obvious when "hawks," supporting the Vietnam War and President Lyndon B. Johnson, clashed with the antiwar "doves" both on the convention floor and in street demonstrations outside the convention hall. Whatever the case, it is obvious that saturation media coverage of preelection events has led to the public's loss of anticipation and exhilaration about convention events.

Some reformers have spoken of replacing the conventions with national direct primaries, but it is unlikely that the parties would agree to this. Although its role in nominating the presidential ticket has often been reduced to formality, the convention is still a valuable political institution. After all, it is the only real arena where the national political parties can command a nearly universal audience while they celebrate past achievements and project their hopes for the future.

Who Are the Delegates?   In one sense, party conventions are microcosms of the United States: Every state, most localities, and all races and creeds find some representation there. (For some historic "firsts" for women at the conventions, see Table 13.1.) Yet, delegates are an unusual and unrepresentative collection of people in many ways. It is not just their exceptionally keen interest in politics that distinguishes delegates. These activists also are ideologically more pure and financially better off than most Americans.

TABLE 13.1   Historic Moments for Women at the Conventions

Since 1980, Democratic Party rules have required that women constitute 50 percent of the delegates to its national convention. The Republican Party has no similar quotas. Nevertheless, both parties have tried to increase the role of women at the convention. Some "firsts" and other historic moments for women at the national conventions include:

1876	First woman to address a national convention
1890	First women delegates to conventions of both parties
1940	First woman to nominate a presidential candidate
1951	First woman asked to chair a national party
1972	First woman keynote speaker
1984	First major-party woman nominated for vice president (Democrat Geraldine Ferraro)
1996	Wives of both nominees make major addresses
2000	Daughter of a presidential candidate nominates her father
2004	Both candidates introduced by their daughters

Source: Center for American Women in Politics.

Kwesi Mfume, president of the National Association for the Advancement of Colored People, addresses the 2004 Democratic National Convention in Boston. Mfume is also a former U.S. Congressman from the state of Maryland.

(Photo courtesy: AP/World Wide Photos)

In 2004, for example, both parties drew their delegates from an elite group that had income and education levels far above the average American's; however the parties also showed their differences. Nearly 40 percent of delegates at the Democratic convention were minorities, and half of those were also women.[14a] This percentage exceeds Republican diversity, whose delegates are 17 percent minorities; however, this actually marks how the GOP has made a concerted effort to increase minority representation at its Convention, since the 2000 delegates were only 9 percent minorities.[14b]

The contrast in the two parties' delegations is no accident; it reflects not only the differences in the party constituencies, but also conscious decisions made by party leaders. After the tumultuous 1968 Democratic National Convention (which, as noted, was torn by dissent over the Vietnam War), Democrats formed a commission to examine the condition of the party and to propose changes in its structure. As a direct consequence of the commission's work, the 1972 Democratic convention was the most broadly representative ever of women, African Americans, and young people, because the party required these groups to be included in state delegations in rough proportion to their numbers in the population of each state. (State delegations failing this test were not seated.) This new mandate was very controversial, and it has since been watered down considerably. Nonetheless, women and blacks are still more fully represented at Democratic conventions than at Republican conventions. GOP leaders have placed much less emphasis on proportional representation, and instead of procedural reforms, Republicans have concentrated on strengthening their state organizations and fundraising efforts, a strategy that has clearly paid off at the polls in the elections of 1980, 1984, and 1988, which saw Republicans elected as president. Yet, overall, the representation of women and minorities at the convention is largely symbolic, as delegates no longer have a great deal of power in determining the nominee.

The delegates in each party also exemplify the philosophical gulf separating the two parties. Democratic delegates are well to the left of their own party's voters on most issues, and even farther away from the opinions held by the nation's electorate as a whole. Republican delegates are a mirror image of their opponents—considerably to the right of GOP voters and even more so of the entire electorate. Although it is sometimes said that the two major parties do not present U.S. citizens with a "clear choice" of candidates, it is possible to argue the contrary. Our politics are perhaps too polarized, with the great majority of Americans, moderates and pragmatists overwhelmingly, left underrepresented by parties too fond of ideological purity. Political scientists James L. Hutter and Steven E. Schier conducted a study of 1980 Iowa caucus and convention delegates for both the Republican and Democratic parties that confirms the above conclusion. Hutter and Schier found that, among the Democrats, the delegates to the state convention were the most liberal of the group of voters studied, followed closely by Democratic caucus attenders. Republican delegates, similarly, were the most conservative members of the group studied, followed closely by Republican caucus attenders. Hutter and Schier also found that while both groups of party decision makers were more ideological than other party members, Republican Party leaders were "closer to their followers in representativeness of opinions than were Democratic leaders and followers,"[15] although the difference was small. The philosophical divergence is usually reflected in the party platforms, even in years such as 1996, when both parties attempted to water down their rhetoric and smooth over ideological differences.

The Electoral College: How Presidents Are Elected

Given the enormous amount of energy, money, and time expended to nominate two major-party presidential contenders, it is difficult to believe that the general election could be more arduous than the nominating contests, but it usually is. The actual campaign for the presidency (and other offices) is described in chapter 14, but the object of the exercise is clear: winning a majority of the **electoral college.** The total number of electors for each state is equivalent to the number of senators and representatives that state has in the U.S. Congress. This uniquely American institution consists of representatives of each state who cast the final ballots that actually elect a president.

The electoral college was the result of a compromise between Framers like Roger Sherman and Elbridge Gerry, who argued for selection of the president by the Congress, and those such as James Madison, James Wilson, and Gouverneur Morris, who favored selection by direct popular election. The electoral college compromise, while not a perfect solution, had practical benefits. Since there were no mass media in those days, it is unlikely that common citizens, even reasonably informed ones, would know much about a candidate from another state. This situation could have left voters with no choice but to vote for someone from their own state, thus making it improbable that any candidate would secure a national majority. On the other hand, the **electors** (members of the electoral college) would be men of character with a solid knowledge of national politics who were able to identify, agree on, and select prominent national statesmen. There are three essentials to understanding the Framers' design of the electoral college. The system was constructed (1) to work without political parties; (2) to cover both the nominating and electing phases of presidential selection; and, (3) to produce a nonpartisan president.

The machinery of the electoral college was somewhat complex. Each state designated electors (through appointment or popular vote) equal in number to the sum of its representation in the House and Senate. (Figure 13.2 shows a map of the United States drawn in proportion to each state's 2004 Electoral College votes.) The electors met in their respective states. Each elector had two votes to cast in the electoral college's selection for the president and vice president, although electors could not vote for more than one candidate from their state. The rules of the college stipulated that each elector was allowed to cast only one vote for any single candidate, and by extension obliged each elector to use his second vote for another candidate. There was no way to designate votes for president or vice president; instead, the candidate with the most votes (provided he also received votes from a majority of the electors) won the presidency and the runner-up won the vice presidency. If two candidates received the same number of votes and both had a majority of electors, the election was decided in the House of Representatives, with each state delegation acting as a unit and casting one vote. In the event that no candidate secured a majority, the election would also be decided in the House, with each state delegation casting one vote for any of the top five electoral vote-getters. In both these scenarios, a majority of the total number of states was necessary for victory.

This system seems almost insanely unpredictable, complex, and unwieldy until one remembers that the Framers devised it specifically for the type of political system that existed when they framed the Constitution and which they (erroneously) foresaw for America in perpetuity: a nonpartisan (one-party), consensus-based, indirectly representative, multi-candidate system. In such a system, the electoral college would function admirably. In practice, it was hoped that electors with a common basic political understanding would arrive at a consensus preference for president, and most, if not all, would plan to cast one of their votes for that candidate, thereby virtually guaranteeing one clear winner, who would then become president; a tie was an unlikely and unhappy outcome. Each would then plan to cast his remaining vote for another candidate, the one whom the elector implicitly preferred for vice president. Consensus on the vice

electoral college
Representatives of each state who cast the final ballots that actually elect a president.

elector
Member of the electoral college chosen by methods determined in each state.

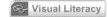

American Electoral Rules: How Do They Influence Campaigns?

FIGURE 13.2   The States Drawn in Proportion to their Electoral College Votes

This map visually represents the respective electoral weights of the fifty states in the 2004 presidential election. For each state, the gain or loss of electoral college votes based on the 2000 Census is indicated in parentheses.

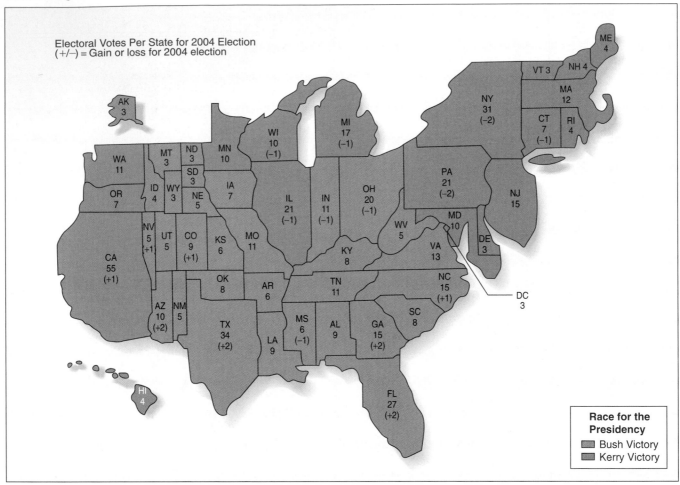

Electoral Votes Per State for 2004 Election
(+/−) = Gain or loss for 2004 election

Race for the Presidency
Bush Victory
Kerry Victory

Note: States drawn in proportion to number of electoral votes. Total electoral votes: 538.
Source: *New York Times* 2004 Election Guide, http://www.nytimes.com/packages/html/politics/2004_ELECTIONGUIDE_GRAPHIC/.

presidency would presumably be less clear than for the more important position of president, so there might be a closer spread among the runners-up, but in any case, the eventual president and vice president—indeed, all the candidates—would still have been members of the same one party.

The Framers' idea of nonpartisan presidential elections, however, lasted barely a decade, ending for the most part after George Washington's two terms. In 1796, their arrangement for presidential selection produced a president and vice president with markedly different political philosophies, a circumstance much less likely in modern times.

The Electoral College in the Nineteenth Century

The republic's fourth presidential election revealed a flaw in the Framers' electoral college plan. In 1800, Thomas Jefferson and Aaron Burr were, respectively, the presidential and vice presidential candidates advanced by the Democratic-Republican Party, and supporters of the Democratic-Republican Party controlled a majority of the electoral college. Accordingly, each Democratic-Republican elector in the states cast one of his two votes for Jefferson and the other one for Burr, a situation that resulted in a tie for the presidency between Jefferson and Burr, since there was no way under the constitutional arrangements for electors to earmark their votes separately for president and vice president. Even though most understood Jefferson to be the actual choice for president, the Constitution mandated that a tie be decided by the House of Representatives. It was, of course, and in Jefferson's favor, but only after much energy was expended to persuade lame-duck Federalists not to give Burr the presidency.

The Twelfth Amendment, ratified in 1804 and still the constitutional foundation for presidential elections, was an attempt to remedy the confusion between the selection of vice presidents and presidents that beset the election of 1800. The amendment provided for separate elections for each office, with each elector having only one vote to cast for each. In the event of a tie or when no candidate received a majority of the total number of electors, the election still went to the House of Representatives; now, however, each state delegation would have one vote to cast for one of the three candidates who had received the greatest number of electoral votes.

The electoral college modified by the Twelfth Amendment has fared better than the college as originally designed, but it has not been problem free. For example, in the 1824 election between John Quincy Adams and Andrew Jackson, neither presidential candidate secured a majority of electoral votes, once again throwing the election into the House. Despite the fact that Jackson had more electoral and popular votes than Adams, the House voted for the latter as president. On two other occasions in the nineteenth century, the presidential candidate with fewer popular votes than his opponent won the presidency. In the 1876 contest between Republican Rutherford B. Hayes and Democrat Samuel J. Tilden, no candidate received a majority of electoral votes; the House decided in Hayes's favor even though he had only one more (disputed) electoral vote and 250,000 fewer popular votes than Tilden. In the election of 1888, President Grover Cleveland secured about 100,000 more popular votes than did Benjamin Harrison, yet Harrison won a majority of the electoral college vote, and with it the presidency.

Timeline

And the
Winner Is . . .
Close Calls in
Presidential
Elections

The Electoral College in the Twentieth and Twenty-First Centuries

A number of near crises pertaining to the electoral college occurred in the twentieth century. The election of 1976 was almost a repeat of those nineteenth-century contests in which the candidate with fewer popular votes won the presidency: Even though Democrat Jimmy Carter received about 1.7 million more popular votes than Republican Gerald Ford, a switch of some 8,000 popular votes in Ohio and Hawaii would have secured for Ford enough votes to win the electoral college, and hence the presidency. Had Ross Perot stayed in the 1992 presidential contest without a hiatus, it is possible that he could have thrown the election into the House of Representatives. His support had registered from 30 percent to 36 percent in the polls in early 1992. When he reentered the race, some of that backing had evaporated, and he finished with 19 percent of the vote and carried no states. However, Perot drained a substantial number of Republican votes from George Bush, thus splitting the GOP base and enabling Clinton to win many normally GOP-leaning states.

During the 2004 presidential campaign, many foresaw that the election would be as close as the 2000 election. Although President George W. Bush defeated challenger Senator John Kerry (MA), both candidates won states by very small margins, with many in the news media being unable to project winners in Iowa and New Mexico for several days. Bush beat Kerry in 2004 by a larger margin than he did Gore in 2000, but the fact remains that electoral college votes could have been much closer with only a few thousand votes difference.

WEB EXPLORATION

To access the most up-to-date, high-quality data on voting, public opinion, and political participation, go to www.ablongman.com/oconnor

It is important to note that the representation of states in the electoral college is altered every ten years to reflect population shifts. The number of congressional seats has been fixed at 435 since 1910 (with a temporary increase to 437 in 1959 to accommodate the entrance of Hawaii and Alaska to the Union). Since that time, the average size of congressional districts has tripled in population, from 211,000 following the 1910 Census to 647,000 in the 2000 Census. Following the 2000 Census, Arizona, Florida, Georgia, and Texas gained two congressional districts (and therefore two additional seats in the electoral college), while California, Colorado, Nevada, and North Carolina picked up one seat. Two states, New York and Pennsylvania, lost two seats, while eight states lost a single electoral vote: Connecticut, Illinois, Indiana, Michigan, Mississippi, Ohio, Oklahoma, and Wisconsin. The Census figures show a sizable population shift from the Northeast to the South and West. (Figure 13.2 shows the gains and losses in electoral college votes per state.)

The political implications of the decennial reapportionment of the congressional seats and the electoral college are likely to favor Republican presidential candidates in the near future; with the exception of California, George W. Bush carried all of the states that gained seats in 2000. Had the current congressional apportionment been in effect for the November 2000 elections, Bush would have had 278 electoral votes (compared to the 271 he officially received), and Gore would have gone from 267 to 260 electoral votes.

It is worth remarking that the existing winner-take-all system mandated by the Constitution is a major obstacle to the creation, success, and endurance of third parties, which have a uniquely high hurdle to clear in securing a plurality of votes in a state in order to secure any electoral votes.

Given the periodically recurring dissatisfaction expressed by the public, especially in the wake of the 2000 election, reformers have seized the opportunity to bring forward several proposals for improving the American electoral college system. Three major reform ideas have developed; each is described below.

Abolition. This reform proposes to abolish the electoral college entirely and have the president selected by popular vote. George W. Bush's election in 2000 marked the fourth time in U.S. history that a president was elected without the majority of the popular vote. Many believe that the electoral college is archaic and that the only way to have a true democracy in the United States is to have the president elected directly by a popular vote. This reform is by far the most unlikely to succeed, given that the Constitution of the United States would have to be amended to change the electoral college. Even assuming that the House of Representatives could muster the two-third majority necessary to pass an amendment, the proposal would almost certainly never pass the Senate. This is because small states have the same representation in the Senate as populous ones, and the Senate thus serves as a bastion of equal representation for all states, regardless of population—a principle generally reinforced by the existing configuration of the electoral college, which ensures a minimum of electoral influence for even the smallest states. In addition, the likelihood of engaging a national recount in the event of a close election would wreak havoc on our electoral system.

Congressional District Plan. Under this plan, each candidate would receive one electoral vote for each congressional district that he or she wins in a state, and the winner of the overall popular vote in each state would receive two bonus votes (one for each senator) for that state. Take for example Virginia, which has eleven representatives and two senators for a total of thirteen electoral votes. If the Democratic candidate wins five congressional districts, and the Republican candidate wins the other six districts and also the statewide majority, the Democrat wins five electoral votes and the Republican wins a total of eight. The interesting fact about this reform is that it can be adopted without a constitutional amendment. This electoral system currently exists only in Maine and Nebraska; neither state has had to split its votes. Any state can adopt this system on its own because the Constitution gives states the right to determine the place and manner by which electors are selected.

There are, however, some unintended consequences to this reform. First, the winner of the overall election might change in some circumstances. Richard M. Nixon would have won the 1960 election instead of John F. Kennedy under a congressional district plan. George W. Bush would have likely won by a wider margin if the entire nation used this system in 2000. Second, this reform would further politicize the redistricting process that takes place every ten years according to U.S. Census results. Fair and objective redistricting already suffers at the hands of many political interests, and if electoral votes were at stake, it would suffer further as the parties made nationwide efforts to maximize the number of safe electoral districts for their presidential nominee while minimizing the number of competitive districts.

The third consequence of state-by-state adoption is that the nation would quickly come to resemble a patchwork of different electoral methods, with some states being awarded by congressional districts and some states awarded solely by popular vote. California, for example, would be unlikely to adopt this system because it would tremendously reduce the power of the state that comes with having fifty-four electoral votes in one package and induces California legislators to keep their electoral votes together.

In the end, the United States and its democracy might be better served by preserving the more uniform system that currently prevails, despite its other shortcomings. Finally, candidates would quickly learn to focus their campaigning on competitive districts while ignoring secure districts, since secure districts would contribute electoral votes only through the senatorial/statewide-majority component.

Keep the College, Abolish the Electors. This proposal calls for the preservation of the college as a statistical electoral device but would remove all voting power from actual human electors and their legislative appointers. This would eliminate the threat of so-called faithless electors—that is, electors who are appointed by state legislators to vote for the candidate who won that state's vote, but who then choose, for whatever reason, to vote for the other candidate. This reform is widely accepted, although—perhaps even because—the problem of faithless electors is only a secondary and little-realized liability of the electoral college.

While the fate of these three reform proposals has yet to be determined, any change in the existing system would inevitably have a profound impact on the way that candidates go about the business of seeking votes for the U.S. presidency.

Patterns of Presidential Elections

The electoral college results reveal more over time than simply who won the presidency. They show which party and which regions are coming to dominance and how voters may be changing party allegiances in response to new issues and generational changes.

Party Realignments. Usually such movements are gradual, but occasionally the political equivalent of a major earthquake swiftly and dramatically alters the landscape. During these rare events, called **party realignments,**[16] existing party affiliations are subject to upheaval: Many voters may change parties, and the youngest age group of voters may permanently adopt the label of the newly dominant party. The existing party cleavage fades over time, allowing new issues to emerge. Until recent times, at least, party realignments have been spaced about thirty-six years apart in the U.S. experience.

A major realignment is often precipitated by one or more **critical elections,** which may polarize voters around new issues and personalities in reaction to crucial developments, such as a war or an economic depression. In Britain, for example, the first postwar election held in 1945 was critical, since it ushered the Labour Party into power for the first time and introduced to Britain a new interventionist agenda in the fields of economic and social welfare policies.

In the entire history of the United States, there have been six party realignments. Three tumultuous eras in particular have produced significant elections (see Figure 13.3).

Participation

The Electoral College

WEB EXPLORATION

To learn more about the electoral college, go to www.ablongman.com/oconnor

party realignment
A shifting of party coalition groupings in the electorate that remains in place for several elections.

critical election
An election that signals a party realignment through voter polarization around new issues.

FIGURE 13.3   Electoral College Results for Three Realigning Presidential Contests
This figure shows the electoral votes in three crucial U.S. elections.

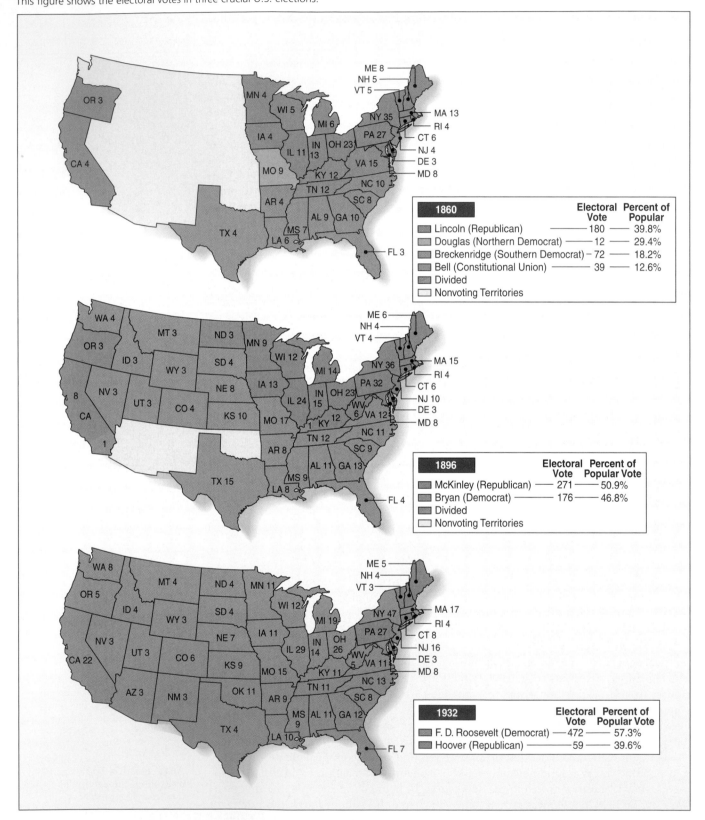

First, during the period leading up to the Civil War, the Whig Party gradually dissolved and the Republican Party developed and won the presidency in 1860. Second, the populist radicalization of the Democratic Party in the 1890s enabled the Republicans to greatly strengthen their majority status and make lasting gains in voter attachments. Third, the Great Depression of the 1930s propelled the Democrats to power, causing large numbers of voters to repudiate the GOP and embrace the Democratic Party. In each of these cases, fundamental and enduring alterations in the party equation resulted.

The last confirmed major realignment, then, happened in the 1928–1936 period, as Republican Herbert Hoover's presidency was held to one term because of voter anger about the Depression. In 1932, Democrat Franklin D. Roosevelt swept to power as the electorate decisively rejected Hoover and the Republicans. This dramatic vote of "no confidence" was followed by substantial changes in policy by the new president, who demonstrated in fact or at least in appearance that his policies were effective. The people responded to his success, accepted his vision of society, and ratified their choice of the new president's party in subsequent presidential and congressional elections.

With the aid of timely circumstances, realignments are accomplished in two main ways.[17] Some voters are converted from one party to the other by the issues and candidates of the time. New voters may also be mobilized into action: Immigrants, young voters, and previous nonvoters may become motivated and then absorbed into a new governing majority, especially if they have been excluded previously. However vibrant and potent party coalitions may be at first, as they age, tensions increase and grievances accumulate. The majority's original reason for existing fades, and new generations neither remember the traumatic events that originally brought about the realignment nor possess the stalwart party identifications of their ancestors. New issues arise, producing conflicts that can be resolved only by a breakup of old alignments and a reshuffling of individual and group party loyalties. Viewed in historical perspective, party realignment has been a mechanism that ensures stability by controlling unavoidable change.

A critical realigning era is by no means the only occasion when changes in partisan affiliation are accommodated. In truth, every election produces realignment to some degree, since some individuals are undoubtedly pushed to change parties by events and by their reactions to the candidates. Recent research suggests that partisanship is much more responsive to current issues and personalities than had been believed earlier, and that major realignments are just extreme cases of the kind of changes in party loyalty registered every year.[18]

Secular Realignment.   Although the term *realignment* is usually applied only if momentous events such as war or depression produce enduring and substantial alterations in the party coalitions, political scientists have long recognized that a more gradual rearrangement of party coalitions could occur.[19] Called **secular realignment,** this piecemeal process depends not on convulsive shocks to the political system, but on slow, almost barely discernible demographic shifts—the shrinking of one party's base of support and the enlargement of the other's, for example—or simple generational replacement (that is, the dying off of the older generation and the maturing of the younger generation). A recent version of this theory, termed "rolling realignment,"[20] argues that in an era of weaker party attachments (such as we currently are experiencing), a dramatic, full-scale realignment may not be possible. Still, a critical mass of voters may be attracted for years to one party's banner in waves or streams, if that party's leadership and performance are consistently exemplary.

Some scholars and political observers also contend that the decline of party affiliation has in essence left the electorate dealigned and incapable of being realigned as long as party ties remain tenuous for so many voters.[21] Voters shift with greater ease between the parties during dealignment, but little permanence or intensity exists in identifications made and held so lightly. If nothing else, the obsolescence of realignment theory may be indicated by the calendar; if major realignments occur roughly every thirty-six years, then we are long overdue. The last major realignment took place

secular realignment
The gradual rearrangement of party coalitions, based more on demographic shifts than on shocks to the political system.

between 1928 and 1936, and so the next one might have been expected in the late 1960s and early 1970s.

As the trends toward ticket-splitting, partisan independence, and voter volatility suggest, there is little question that we have been moving through an unstable and somewhat "dealigned" period at least since the 1970s. The foremost political question today is whether dealignment will continue (and in what form) or whether a major realignment is in the offing. Each previous dealignment has been a precursor of realignment,[22] but realignment need not succeed dealignment, especially under modern conditions.

WEB EXPLORATION

To learn more about candidates you have supported in the past or to familiarize yourself with other political candidates so you can make informed choices, go to www.ablongman.com/oconnor

incumbency
The condition of already holding elected office.

U.S. Senator Edward Kennedy (D–MA) knows full well the advantages of incumbency. Elected to the Senate in 1962 to complete the term of his brother, President John F. Kennedy, Edward Kennedy has been reelected every term since. His name recognition and campaign war chest enabled him to handily defeat Republican challenger Jack Robinson 73 percent to 13 percent in the 2000 election.

(Photo courtesy: David McNew/Newsmakers/Getty Source)

CONGRESSIONAL ELECTIONS

Many similar elements are present in different kinds of elections. Candidates, voters, issues, and television advertisements are constants. But, there are distinctive aspects of each kind of election as well. Compared with presidential elections, congressional elections are a different animal. Unlike major-party presidential contenders, most candidates for Congress labor in relative obscurity. There are some celebrity nominees for Congress—television stars, sports heroes, even local TV news anchors. In 2004, Coors Brewing Company CEO Pete Coors' U.S. Senate campaign in Colorado gained national attention. (See Politics Now: Senate Race Steals Spotlight.) The vast majority of party nominees, however, are little-known state legislators and local office holders who receive remarkably little coverage in many states and communities. For them, just getting known, establishing name identification, is the biggest battle.

The Incumbency Advantage

Under current circumstances, the advantages of **incumbency** (that is, already being in office) are enhanced, and a kind of electoral inertia takes hold: Those people in office tend to remain in office. Every year, the average member of the U.S. House of Representatives expends about $750,000 in taxpayer funds to run the office. Much of this money directly or indirectly promotes the legislator by means of mass mailings and *constituency services*, the term used to describe a wide array of assistance provided by a member of Congress to voters in need (for example, tracking a lost Social Security check, helping a veteran receive disputed benefits, or finding a summer internship for a college student). Indeed, one political scientist found that constituents for whom a House incumbent did casework gave the incumbent considerably higher evaluations than constituents who did not benefit from such casework.[23]

In addition to these institutional means of self-promotion, most incumbents are highly visible in their districts. They have easy access to local media, cut ribbons galore, attend important local funerals, and speak frequently at meetings and community events. Nearly a fourth of the people in an average congressional district claim to have met their representative, and about half recognize their legislator's name without prompting. This spending and visibility pay off. Reelection rates for sitting House members range well above 90 percent in most election years, and research shows district attentiveness is at least partly responsible for incumbents' electoral safety.[24]

Recent research also identifies an indirect advantage of incumbency: the ability of the office holder to fend off challenges from strong opposition candidates. Gary Cox and Jonathan Katz's research calls it a "scare-off" effect. Incumbents have the ability to scare off high-quality challengers because of the institutional advantages of office, such as high name recognition, large war chests, staffs attached to legislative offices, and overall experience in running a successful campaign. Potential strong challengers facing this initial uphill battle will, according to Cox and Katz, wait until the incumbent retires rather than challenge him. This only strengthens the arguments for advantages to reelection related to incumbency.[25]

SENATE RACE STEALS SPOTLIGHT

You may recognize the name Pete Coors. He is the great-grandson of Adolph Coors, who started the Golden brewery in 1873. Needless to say, Mr. Coors has no problem with name recognition in Colorado. The Coors name appears on everything from beer cans in the local grocery store to the Colorado Rockies' baseball stadium, Coors Field. Coors ran on a platform of traditional family values, tax reform, and a strong hand in the war on terror. While he believed we should not second-guess the President now that we know about the unlikelihood of weapons of mass destruction existing, he did believe the outcome of the vote that gave President Bush the authority to go to war would have been different. Coors was also vehemently opposed to gay marriage; however, some conservatives criticized him because Coors beer sponsored events like the Black & Blue 2004 Festival in Montreal, a weekend long gay-benefit. The Coors tax plan was what one would expect from a businessman. He believed less taxes and regulation on small and large businesses will stimulate the economy and offset the jobs Colorado has lost in the past few years.

Ken Salazar, the current Attorney General, grew up as a farmer and ran for Senate along side his brother, John, who ran for Colorado's 3rd Congressional District. He criticized his opponent for being a rubber-stamp for the Bush administration.

Salazar cited his humble roots and his experience in dealing with security issues through meetings with President Bush and Homeland Security Director Tom Ridge as the reason he is best qualified to serve as Colorado's next Senator. His opponent, he argues, had zero experience. Furthermore, Salazar said that Coors' plan for tax reform would drive the nation farther into debt. On the issue of homosexuality, Salazar believed marriage should be between a man and a woman, but that a constitutional amendment was not necessary. Also, he favored the right of gay couples to adopt a child, something that Coors' opposed.

Taxes and jobs, experience with security issues, and traditional family values seem to be the main issues in Colorado. Coors portrays himself as a traditional conservative, while Salazar distanced himself from Kerry and paints himself as a conservative Democrat. Salazar's tactic worked. Running both on his political experience and his more moderate position, Salazar managed to draw moderate Republicans to split their ticket. Even though Bush won Colorado, Coors was not able to rely on the President's coattails to carry him into the Senate. John Salazar won his race as well, leading one journalist to refer to the brothers as the new "Colorado Kennedys."*

*Eddie Pells, "Colorado Kennedys' head to Washington", *Cortez Journal*, November 4, 2004: http://www.cortezjournal.com/asp-bin/article_generation.asp?article_type=news&article_path=/news/news041104_3.htm

---

The 1994 congressional elections, regarded as a year of massive change in the make-up of electoral politics, provide yet another example of the power of incumbency. The press focused on the Republican takeover of both houses of Congress, naturally enough, but another perspective is provided by the reelection rates for incumbents. More than 90 percent of the sitting representatives and senators who sought reelection won another term, despite electoral conditions that were termed a tidal wave.

Frequently, the reelection rate for senators is as high, but not always. In a "bad" year for House incumbents, "only" 88 percent will win (as in the Watergate year of 1974), but the senatorial reelection rate can drop much lower on occasion (to 60 percent in the 1980 Reagan landslide, for example). There is a good reason for this lower senatorial reelection rate. A Senate election is often a high-visibility contest; it receives much more publicity than a House race. So, while House incumbents remain protected and insulated in part because few voters pay attention to their little-known challengers, a Senate-seat challenger can become well known more easily and thus be in a better position to defeat an incumbent. In addition, studies by Jonathan Krasno show that the quality of the challengers in Senate races is higher than in House races, making it more likely that an incumbent could be upset.[26]

Redistricting, Scandals, and Coattails

For the relatively few incumbent members of Congress who lose their reelection bids, three explanations are paramount: redistricting, scandals, and coattails.

511

redistricting
The redrawing of congressional districts to reflect increases or decreases in seats allotted to the states, as well as population shifts within a state.

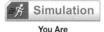
Simulation

You Are Redrawing the Districts in Your State

gerrymandering
The legislative process through which the majority party in each statehouse tries to assure that the maximum number of representatives from its political party can be elected to Congress through the redrawing of legislative districts.

Redistricting.   Every ten years, after the U.S. Census, all congressional district lines are redrawn (in states with more than one congressperson) so that every legislator represents about the same number of citizens. The U.S. Constitution requires that a Census, which entails the counting of all Americans, be conducted every ten years. Until the first U.S. Census could be taken, the Constitution fixed the number of representatives in the House at sixty-five. In 1790, then, one member represented 37,000 people. As the population of the new nation grew and states were added to the Union, the House became larger and larger. In 1910, it expanded to 435 members, and in 1929, its size was fixed at that number by statute.

Because the Constitution requires that representation in the House be based on state population, and that each state have at least one representative, congressional districts must be redrawn by state legislatures to reflect population shifts, so that each member in Congress will represent approximately the same number of residents. Exceptions to this rule are states like Wyoming and Vermont, whose statewide populations are less than average congressional districts. This process of redrawing congressional districts to reflect increases or decreases in seats allotted to the states, as well as population shifts within a state, is called **redistricting.** When shifts occur in the national population, states gain or lose congressional seats through a process called reapportionment. In the spring of 2000, the U.S. Census Bureau announced its results from the 2000 Census, which showed the largest population growth in American history. Since the 1990 Census, the U.S. population had increased 13.2 percent, from 248.7 million people to an estimated 281.4 million people, with western and southern states (the sunbelt) gaining residents at the expense of the Northeast. This has been a trend since the 1960 Census, causing the Northeast to lose congressional seats in every recent decade. It is also important to consider that the substantial increase in the Hispanic population (from 9 percent in 1990 to 14 percent in 2004) has magnified its collective political clout and will play an important role in redistricting and politics in general in the twenty-first century.

Redistricting is a largely political process that is used in many cases by the majority party to insure formation of voting districts conducive to retaining or expanding their majority. In Michigan, for example, the Republican legislature redrew the congressional districts in such a way as to place the dean of the House of Representatives, John Dingell, in a single district with fellow Democratic Representative Lynn Rivers. Dingell and Rivers were forced to square off against each other in a hard-fought Democratic primary which Dingell won, leaving incumbent Rivers without a seat in the Congress. Some states, however, including Iowa and Arizona, appoint nonpartisan commissions or use some independent means of drawing district lines. Although the processes vary in detail, most states require legislative approval of the plans.

This redistricting process, which has gone on since the first U.S. Census in 1790, often involves what is called **gerrymandering** (see Figure 13.4). Because of the enormous population growth, the partisan implications of redistricting, and the requirement under the Voting Rights Act for minorities to have special "majority-minority districts" in order to get an equal chance to elect candidates of their choice, legislators end up drawing oddly shaped districts to achieve their goals.[27] Redistricting plans routinely meet with court challenges across the country. Following the 2000 Census and the subsequent redistricting in 2002, courts have thrown out legislative maps in a half-dozen states, primarily because of state constitutional concerns about compactness. The circuitous boundaries of improper districts often cut across county lines or leap over natural barriers and split counties and long-standing communities.[28] Despite the obviously abnormal shape of many districts (including Texas' 6th district, Illinois 17th district, and North Carolina's 12th district), gerrymandering is very difficult to prove and its interpretation often depends on partisan factors.

Over the years, the Supreme Court has ruled that:

- Congressional as well as state legislative districts must be apportioned on the basis of population.[29]

FIGURE 13.4   Gerrymandering

Two drawings—one a mocking cartoon, the other all too real—show the bizarre geographical contortions involved in gerrymandering.

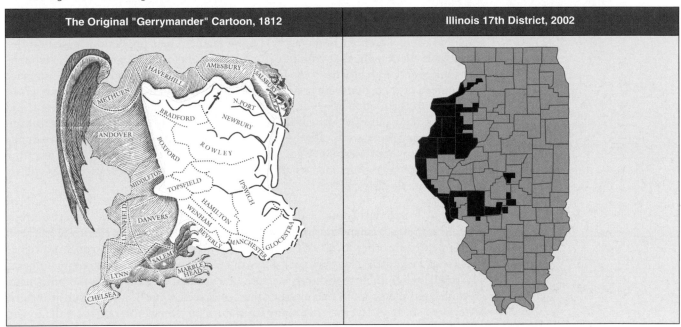

| The Original "Gerrymander" Cartoon, 1812 | Illinois 17th District, 2002 |

Sources: David Van Biema, "Snakes or Ladders?" *Time* (July 12, 1993). © 1993, Time Inc. Reprinted by permission. Illinois General Assembly.

- Purposeful gerrymandering of a congressional district to dilute minority strength is illegal under the Voting Rights Act of 1965.[30]
- Redrawing of districts for obvious racial purposes to enhance minority representation is constitutional if race is not the "predominate" factor over all other factors that are part of traditional redistricting, including compactness.[31]

New software has made it easier to draw more politically reliable electoral maps, which have an adverse impact on competitiveness. Until the 1990s, legislators had to draw districts using colored pens on acetate sheets spread out on large maps. Computers appeared in the 1990s, but only big, sophisticated ones could handle the demographic data, putting the cost beyond all but a few states. Now the U.S. Census Bureau makes available digitized maps, and new geographic information systems for mapping and analyzing demographic data can draw up partisan maps automatically. These developments have turned redistricting (and gerrymandering) from an art into a science.[32] Yet the process is probably more resource intensive and time consuming than ever.

Recent research has added yet another actor into the redistricting process: the individual member. In an analysis of 1992 redistricting in North Carolina, Paul Gronke maintains that members' partisanship is balanced with their own ambition. He finds that "individual ambition generally outweighs partisan loyalty." If, in other words, voting for the other party's district lines will help individual members obtain higher office, they will vote in their own self-interest over the better interests of their party.[33]

For the dominant party, redistricting is often used to make their incumbents safer. But redistricting can also be used to punish the out-of-power party. Some incumbents can be put in the same districts as other incumbents, or the base of other congresspersons can be weakened by adding territory favorable to the opposition party. In 1992, ten incumbents were paired together—five therefore lost—and about a dozen more incumbents were defeated in part because of unfavorable redistricting. The number of incumbents who actually lose their reelections because of redistricting is lessened by the strategic behavior of redistricted members—who often choose to retire rather than wage an expensive (and likely unsuccessful) reelection battle.[34]

One innovative analysis of the post-1990 redistricting conducted by political scientists John Swain, Stephen Borrelli, and Brian Reed finds that the redistricting of 1990 increased the number of Republican seats overall. The researchers created a model of partisan support in each congressional district and assumed that all seats were open seats—in other words, incumbency was not a factor. Their projections based on this model gave the Republicans twenty more seats than before the redistricting. Republicans took over dominance from the Democrats in three districts and gained dominance in seventeen districts that were previously evenly divided. When incumbency was added as a factor to the model, however, the Republican projected gain was eliminated, and the parties came out even. Swain therefore concludes that Republican strength from the redistricting process was effectively masked by the power of incumbency. The implication of this partially explains the Republican rise in congressional power after the 1990 redistricting. As incumbents retired, Republicans picked up seats in these newly created favorable districts.[35]

Scandals.   Scandals come in many varieties in this age of the investigative press. The old standby of financial impropriety (bribery and payoffs, for example) has been supplemented by other forms of career-ending incidents, such as personal improprieties (sexual escapades, for instance). As with redistricting, the number of incumbents who actually lose their reelections because of a scandal is reduced by the propensity of implicated members to retire rather than seek reelection.[36] The power of incumbency is so strong, however, that many legislators survive even serious scandal to win reelection.

On the first day of the 2004 Republican National Convention in New York City, the party's attention was briefly turned to the second congressional district in the state of Virginia, where two-term Congressman Ed Schrock surprised the political world by announcing that he would not run for a third term. Having been unopposed in the party primary and faced with meager Democratic opposition in a heavily Republican district, this came as a surprise to many observers. In his withdrawal announcement, Schrock cited unspecific allegations that would prevent him from representing his constituents to the fullest. Party members rallied around the congressman, but conceded that the controversy surrounding an internet announcement by a gay activist had prompted the move.

The most famous recent political scandal is that of New Jersey Governor Jim McGreevey. In August 2004, the Garden State's first-term Democratic governor announced that he would be resigning from office effective November 15, in response to a sexual harassment lawsuit being prepared by a former security aide. While the suit was never filed, it alleged that while working as the governor's lead homeland security adviser, Golan Cipel was the subject of improper sexual conduct and intimidating behavior at the hands of McGreevey. Cipel, an Israeli citizen, initially resigned in 2002, but was kept on the state payroll for several months afterward.

Coattails.   The defeat of a congressional incumbent can also occur as a result of the presidential coattail effect. As shown in Analyzing Visuals: Congressional Election Results, 1948–2002, successful presidential candidates usually carry into office congressional candidates of the same party in the year of their election. Notice the overall decline in the strength of the coattail effect in modern times, however, as party identification has weakened and the powers and perks of incumbency have grown. Whereas Harry S Truman's party gained seventy-six House seats and nine additional Senate seats in 1948, George Bush's party actually lost three House seats and one Senate berth in 1988, despite Bush's handsome 54 percent majority. The gains can be minimal even in presidential landslide reelection years, such as 1972 (Nixon) and 1984 (Reagan). Occasionally, though, when the issues are emotional and the voters' desire for change is strong enough, as in Reagan's original 1980 victory, the coattail effect can still be substantial.

Midterm Congressional Elections

Elections in the middle of presidential terms, **midterm elections,** present a threat to incumbents. This time it is the incumbents of the president's party who are most in jeopardy. Just as the presidential party usually gains seats in presidential election years, it usually loses seats in off years. The problems and tribulations of governing normally cost a president some popularity, alienate key groups, or cause the public to want to send the president a message of one sort or another. An economic downturn or a scandal can underline and expand this circumstance, as the Watergate scandal of 1974 and the recession of 1982 demonstrated. The 2002 midterm elections, however, bucked that trend, marking the first time since Franklin D. Roosevelt in 1934 that a first-term president gained seats for his party in a midterm election.

What is most apparent from the midterm statistics presented in Analyzing Visuals: Congressional Elections Results, 1948–2004, is the tendency of voters to punish the president's party much more severely in the sixth year of an eight-year presidency, a phenomenon associated with retrospective voting. After only two years, voters are still willing to "give the guy a chance," but after six years, voters are often restless for change.

In 1994, the United States seemed to experience a sixth-year itch in the second year of a presidency, such was the dissatisfaction with the Clinton administration. To their credit, Democrats, despite the scandals that plagued Clinton's presidency, avoided a true sixth-year itch in 1998. During this midterm election, Democrats actually gained five seats in the U.S. House of Representatives.

Senate elections are less inclined to follow these off-year patterns than are House elections. The idiosyncratic nature of Senate contests is due to their intermittent scheduling (only one-third of the seats come up for election every two years) and the existence of well-funded, well-known candidates who can sometimes swim against whatever political tide is rising. Also worth remembering is that midterm elections in recent history have a much lower voter turnout than presidential elections. A midterm election may draw only 35 percent to 40 percent of adult Americans to the polls, whereas a presidential contest usually attracts between 50 percent and 55 percent. (See Analyzing Visuals: Voter Turnout in American Presidential and Midterm Congressional Elections.)

As noted, the 1994 midterm elections were extraordinary, a massacre for the Democrats and a dream come true for the Republicans. Not since Harry S Truman's loss in 1946 had a Democratic president lost both houses of Congress in a midterm election, but such was President Clinton's fate. For the first time since popular elections for the U.S. Senate began in the early 1900s, the entire freshman Senate class (that is, all newly elected senators) was Republican. Moreover, every incumbent House member, senator, and governor who was defeated for reelection was a Democrat. Even the speaker of the House, Thomas Foley (D–WA), fell in the onslaught. Republican George Nethercutt became the first person to unseat a House speaker since 1862. Looking specifically at the House, political scientist Gary C. Jacobson concludes that Republicans scored their impressive victory in 1994 "by fielding (modestly) superior candidates who were on the right side of the issues that were important to voters in House elections and by persuading voters to blame a unified Democratic government for government's failures."[37]

Republicans had just as much success at the state level. The GOP took control of nineteen houses in state legislatures, securing a majority of the legislative bodies. From just nineteen governors before the election, Republicans wound up with thirty governorships, including eight of the nine largest. (Only Florida, which reelected Democratic Governor Lawton Chiles, resisted the trend.)

Cynics frequently say that elections do not matter, but the 1998 midterm elections effectively and dramatically refuted the cynics. A loss of just five seats for the Republicans in the U.S. House of Representatives toppled a speaker, and not just any speaker of the House, but one of the most powerful speakers of the twentieth century— Newt Gingrich of Georgia. The Republicans were expected to gain seats in both the House

midterm election
Election that takes place in the middle of a presidential term.

ANALYZING VISUALS

Congressional Election Results, 1948–2004

Take a few moments to study the table, which indicates whether or not the president's party gained or lost seats in each election since 1948, and then answer the following critical thinking questions: Are there any striking patterns in the outcomes of congressional elections that occur in presidential election years? Are there any striking patterns in the outcomes of congressional elections that occur in nonpresidential (midterm) election years? Drawing on what you've learned from this chapter, how might you explain the patterns in midterm elections?

GAIN (+) OR LOSS (–) FOR PRESIDENT'S PARTY					
PRESIDENTIAL ELECTION YEARS			NONPRESIDENTIAL ELECTION YEARS		
President/Year	House	Senate	Year	House	Senate
Truman (D): 1948	+76	+9	1950	–29	–6
Eisenhower (R): 1952	+24	+2	1954	–18	–1
Eisenhower (R): 1956	–2	0	1958	–48	–13
Kennedy (D): 1960	–20	–2	1962	–4	+3
Johnson (D): 1964	+38	+2	1966	–47	–4
Nixon (R): 1968	+7	+5	1970	–12	+2
Nixon (R): 1972	+13	–2	Ford: 1974	–48	–5
Carter (D): 1976	+2	0	1978	–15	–3
Reagan (R): 1980	+33	+12	1982	–26	+1
Reagan (R): 1984	+15	–2	1986	–5	–8
G. Bush (R): 1988	–3	–1	1990	–9	–1
Clinton (D): 1992	–10	0	1994	–52	–9[a]
Clinton (D): 1996	+10	–2	1998	+5	0
G. W. Bush (R): 2000	–2	–4	2002	+6	+2
G. W. Bush (R): 2004	+4	+4 (House results pending two Dec. run-offs in LA)			

[a]Includes the switch from Democrat to Republican of Alabama U.S. Senator Richard Shelby.

of Representatives and, especially, in the Senate, as well as a few governorships. They, however, did not do so, for several reasons. First, Republicans had pushed hard for severe punishment against President Clinton because of the Monica Lewinsky scandal. While the public disapproved of President Clinton's embarrassing and demeaning behavior in that scandal, most Americans believed that impeachment was simply too severe a penalty. Second, the Republicans had made a strategic miscalculation by shifting into neutral governmentally; that is, Republicans accomplished virtually nothing in the second session of the 105th Congress. Their assumption was that the Clinton scandal would be enough to deliver substantial gains for the GOP, and they bet wrong. President Clinton's Democratic Party scored a moral victory by actually gaining five seats in the U.S. House of Representatives and maintaining their share of seats in the Senate. The most surprising election result of all, however, occurred on the Friday after the November 3 election, when Gingrich shocked the nation by announcing his resignation from the speakership and from Congress itself.

The 2002 Midterm Elections

As discussed earlier, the president's party historically loses congressional seats in midterm elections. George. W. Bush's first midterm election, however, was a remarkable exception. In the previous fourteen midterms, the opposing party has lost an average of twenty-six seats in the House and four in the Senate. It was more than a statistical anomaly, however, when the Republicans gained a handful of seats in House and Senate races. This year marks the first time since 1934 that a first-term president picked

TABLE 13.2   Results of Selected Elections, 2004

State	Contest	Winner	Loser	Significance
Alaska	Senate	Lisa Murkowski (R)	Tony Knowles (D)	Murkowski, son of the current Alaska governor who appointed her to replace him, suffered from claims of nepotism but eked out a victory against strong challenger Knowles. Both candidates set the record for the most expensive race in Alaskan history.
Florida	Senate	Mel Martinez (R)	Betty Castor (D)	Former housing secretary Martinez won by the smallest of margins against the former state education commissioner, after the two spent $40 million in television ads. Martinez joins Salazar in a growing Hispanic presence in the U.S. Senate.
Georgia	House	John Barrow (D)	Max Burns (R)	Freshman Representative Burns loses to Barrow in close election, giving the Republicans in the Georgia House delegation a very slight 7-6 advantage, in spite of Georgia's increasing Republican leanings.
Kentucky	House	Geoff Davis (R)	Nick Clooney (D)	Davis, a military veteran who lost a House election only two years before, defeated Clooney, whose political credentials include being the father of actor George Clooney.
Louisiana	Senate	David Vitter (R)	several candidates	In the Bayou State's open primary system, a candidate must garner over 50 percent of the vote in order to avoid a run-off in December. Vitter—the only Republican in the race—did just that in defeating four Democratic opponents.
Montana	Governor	Brian Schweitzer (D)	Bob Brown (R)	Schweitzer, a rancher, beat a more experienced Secretary of State Brown in the heavily Republican state of Montana by effectively campaigning to independent voters as a political outsider.
New Hampshire	Governor	John Lynch (D)	Craig Benson (R)	For the second time in 78 years, New Hampshire voters ousted a freshman governor. Lynch won among college graduates and women, who turned out in large numbers to defeat the incumbent.
Oklahoma	Senate	Tom Coburn (R)	Brad Carson (D)	In what was expected to be a close race between a current and a former Congressman, Coburn won by 12 percentage points in a state that voted heavily for Bush.
South Carolina	Senate	Jim DeMint (R)	Inez Tenenbaum (D)	Former U.S. Congressman Jim DeMint, from the 4th Congressional District of the Palmetto State, benefited from Bush's strong showing to defeat the former state superintendent of education.
South Dakota	Senate	John Thune (R)	Tom Daschle (D)	Representative Thune unseats Senate Minority Leader Daschle in a bitter and expensive upset. Thune nearly defeated Senator Tim Johnson (D) in 2000.
Texas	House	Peter Sessions (R)	Martin Frost (D)	After redistricting in Texas, Frost's original district no longer existed, forcing the leader of the Texan House delegation to run in Sessions' district. Both were incumbents, but district lines obviously favored the Republican candidate, who won easily.

up seats in both houses of Congress. How did this occur? While there is no definitive answer, the remarkable time and energy President George W. Bush devoted to stumping for Republican candidates in key battleground states (under White House strategist Karl Rove's watchful direction) cannot be overlooked. Between April and November, Bush and Vice President Dick Cheney raised more than $141 million campaigning for Republican candidates, capitalizing on Bush's approval ratings, which remained high more than a year after the September 11 terrorists attacks. Some Democrats felt that the war on terrorism and the administration's focus on impending hostility with Iraq constrained the voice of opposition by monopolizing the political agenda, preventing Democratic candidates from gaining ground on a weak economy, corporate scandals, and traditionally Democratic domestic issues. In addition, the D.C.-area snipers dominated media coverage, quite justifiably becoming a fixture of public consciousness that eclipsed virtually all political discourse until the final twelve days before the election.

Following the 2000 election, the Senate was tied at 50–50 with Republicans holding leadership capacity because of Vice President Dick Cheney's tie-breaking vote. In May of 2001, the defection of Senator Jim Jeffords of Vermont allowed Democrats to take a control of the Senate by the smallest of margins, while Republicans narrowly held a six-vote majority in the House. The near parity of the balance of power in the Senate and House produced an election where even marginal gains for either side made a crucial

ANALYZING VISUALS
Voter Turnout in Presidential and Midterm Elections

Various factors influence voter turnout in the United States. The high percentages of 1876 and 1960 both occurred in open races (that is, when no incumbent was running). In the latter, the new TV debates energized and engaged the electorate. Following the historic 2000 presidential election, many correctly anticipated high voter turnout in 2004. Take a few moments to study the graph below, and then answer the following critical thinking questions: What general trend do you notice about voter turnout during the twentieth century? What is generally true about turnout in midterm elections as opposed to turnout in presidential elections? Drawing on what you've learned from this and other chapters, why do you think voter turnout, generally speaking, increased over the course of the nineteenth century? Why do you think voter turnout declined during the twentieth century?

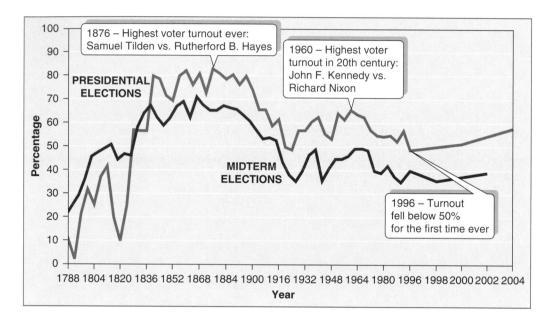

Source: Adapted from Harold W. Stanley and Richard G. Niemi, *Vital Statistics on American Politics, 2001–2002* (Washington, DC: CQ Press, 2001), figure 1-1, 12. Updated by the authors.

difference. In 2002, thirty-four Senate seats, thirty-six governorships, and the entire House were up for grabs. Republicans capitalized on a late wave that expanded their House majority by six seats and regained control of the Senate, 51–49, possibly giving Bush the mandate that eluded him in the 2000 election. The Louisiana Senate election was decided in a December 7 runoff in which Democratic incumbent Mary Landrieu defeated Republican Suzanne Haik Terrell. The runoff was a result of Louisiana election law that requires winners to post fifty percent or more of the vote; Landrieu only secured 46 percent of the vote in an election that featured nine candidates.

Consistent with historical norm, most contests tended to favor incumbents regardless of party. Only four incumbent governors lost, and only three incumbent senators who were on the Election Day ballot lost: Democrats Jean Carnahan of Missouri and Max Cleland of Georgia, and Republican Tim Hutchinson of Arkansas. (In addition, Republican Senator Bob Smith of New Hampshire was defeated in the primary.) Because many of the Republican governors elected in the 1994 GOP landslide and reelected in 1998 were term-limited, Democrats were expected to make big gains in several open gubernatorial races. Wins by Republicans in heavily Democratic states Massachusetts and Maryland, as well as the surprise victory of Republican Sonny Perdue over the Georgia governor helped mute the number of Democratic pick-ups, leaving the Republicans with twenty-six governorships and the Democrats twenty-four when the dust settled.

The 2002 elections were unique not only for delivering big wins for the incumbent president, but also for the unusual and unexpected conditions that preceded a number of contests. In Minnesota, Senator Paul Wellstone, along with his family and several staff members, died tragically in a plane crash while campaigning on October 25, only days before the November elections. Amid the disbelief, Minnesotans desperately scanned the political landscape for a qualified replacement. Former Vice President Walter Mondale accepted the Democratic Party's appointment, but lost the race to Republican Norm Coleman, who capitalized on a remarkable backlash to Senator Wellstone's memorial service, which was seen by some as a Democratic pep rally. In New Jersey, former Senator Frank Lautenberg became the Democrats' late nominee when Senator Robert Torricelli abruptly withdrew his candidacy after a wave of criticism over professional ethics made it clear that he was not likely to win the election. Following the decisive ruling by the New Jersey Supreme Court, Lautenberg was permitted to replace Torricelli on the ballot, ultimately defeating his Republican opponent Douglas Forrester.

By and large, control by the Republicans over the two branches of elected government should hasten the flow of legislative business and improve the ability of the White House to promote and control the agenda. Representative Tom Delay (R–TX), newly elected as majority leader in the House, will be able to help President Bush promote legislation for the remainder of his term. They must not forget, however, the lessons learned from 1994—the last time the GOP held both houses of Congress—when Newt Gingrich's overconfidence hurt Republicans in 1996. Under the leadership of new House Minority Leader Nancy Pelosi, a liberal Democrat from San Francisco, Democrats tried to oppose Republican economic policies; however, House Republicans held to the party line, giving Bush the ability to move his tax cuts through the House with little difficulty. Pelosi has an even more difficult job ahead of her now that the Republicans have expanded their majority in the House. It would not be fair to blame the Democratic losses entirely on Pelosi, however, since many of the Republican gains in the House came from favorable redistricting plans, especially in Texas.

VOTING BEHAVIOR

Research on voting behavior seeks primarily to explain two phenomena: voter turnout (that is, what factors contribute to an individual's decision to vote or not to vote) and vote choice (once the decision to vote has been made, what leads voters to choose one candidate over another). Accordingly, in this section, we will discuss salient patterns in voter turnout and analyze the possible causes of the recent decline in voter turnout, and then turn our attention to similar patterns in vote choice. Finally, we will discuss ticket-splitting, an important contemporary development in American politics.

turnout
The proportion of the voting-age public that votes.

Patterns in Voter Turnout

Turnout is the proportion of the voting-age public that votes. About 40 percent of the eligible adult population in the United States votes regularly, whereas 25 percent are occasional voters. Thirty-five percent rarely or never vote. Turnout is important because voters have the ability to influence election outcomes. The presidential election of 2000 will forever be the classic example of the power of an individual's single vote. As recount succeeded recount in several states, and the fate of the presidency rested on razor-thin margins representing perhaps a handful of ballots, many

ALL THOSE APATHETIC AMERICANS WHO DID NOT VOTE IN THE LAST ELECTION TODAY SPENT FIFTY CENTS APIECE TO DIAL IN THEIR OPINIONS TO "ENTERTAINMENT TONIGHT" ON THE QUESTION OF WHETHER JOHN TRAVOLTA SHOULD HAVE A CHIN TUCK.

WEB EXPLORATION

To look at what voters said before going to the polls and whom they actually voted for, go to www.ablongman.com/oconnor

Visual Literacy

Voting Turnout:
Who Votes?

nonvoters in Florida, New Mexico, and Oregon must have wished they had taken the trouble to exercise their right to choose their leader. (For the various methods citizens use once they turn out to vote, see Table 13.3.) Some of the factors known to influence voter turnout include education, income, age, race and ethnicity, and interest in politics.

Education.   People who vote are usually more highly educated than nonvoters. Other things being equal, college graduates are much more likely to vote than those with less education. People with more education tend to learn more about politics, are less hindered by registration requirements, and are more self-confident about their ability to affect public life. Therefore, one might argue that institutions of higher education provide citizens with opportunities to learn about and become interested in politics.

Income.   There is also a relationship between income and voting. A considerably higher percentage of citizens with annual incomes over $40,000 vote than do citizens with incomes under $10,000. Income level, to some degree, is connected to education level, as wealthier people tend to have more opportunities for higher education, and more education also may lead to higher income. Wealthy citizens are more likely than poor ones to think that the "system" works for them and that their votes make a difference. People with higher income also find the opportunity cost of participation cheaper than do the poor and are more likely to have a direct financial stake in the decisions of the government, thus spurring them into action.[38]

By contrast, lower-income citizens often feel alienated from politics, possibly believing that conditions will remain the same no matter for whom they vote. A factor that contributes to this feeling of alienation is that American political parties, unlike parties in many other countries that tend to associate themselves with specific social classes, do not attempt to link themselves intimately to one major class (such as the "working class"). Therefore, the feelings of alienation and apathy about politics prevalent among many lower-income Americans should not be unexpected. For another view that stresses that education level supercedes income as a primary factor in voter participation, see Raymond Wolfinger and Steven Rosenstone's *Who Votes?*[39]

Age.   A strong correlation exists between age and voter participation rates. The Twenty-Sixth Amendment, ratified in 1971, lowered the voting age to eighteen. While this amendment obviously increased the number of *eligible* voters, it did so by enfranchising the group that is least likely to vote. A much higher percentage of citizens age thirty and older vote than do citizens younger than thirty, although voter turnout decreases over the age of seventy, primarily because of physical infirmity, which makes it difficult to get to the polling location. Regrettably, less than half of eligible eighteen- to twenty-four-year-olds are even registered to vote. The most plausible reason for this is that younger people are more mobile; they have not put down roots in a community.

TABLE 13.3   Voting Equipment for the 2004 Elections

Type of Voting Equipment	Counties		Registered Voters*	
	Number	Percentage	Number	Percentage
Punch card	307	9.86	32,224,103	18.64
Lever	270	8.67	22,165,917	12.82
Paper Ballots	299	9.60	1,038,800	0.60
Optical Scan	1,418	45.54	55,668,695	32.20
Electronic	669	21.48	50,035,070	28.94
Mixed	151	4.85	11,742,150	6.79
Total	3,114	100.00	172,874,735	100.00

*Registered voter counts are from the November 2002 general elections

Because voter registration is not automatic, people who relocate have to make an effort to register. Therefore, the effect of adding this low-turnout group to the electorate has been to lower the overall turnout rate. As young people marry, have children, and settle down in a community, their likelihood of voting increases.[40]

Race and Ethnicity.   Another pattern in voter turnout is related to race: Whites tend to vote more regularly than do African Americans. This appears to be holding true for 2004. Examining exit polls from both years reveals that African Americans increased as a proportion of the total turnout by one point, from 10 to 11 percent. Whites, who made up 81 percent of the voting population in 2000, only comprised 77 percent in 2004.[40a] In 2000, white turnout was just over 50 percent, while African Americans hovered in the mid-40s.

This difference is due primarily to the relative income and educational levels of the two racial groups. African Americans tend to be poorer and have less formal education than whites; as mentioned earlier, both of these factors affect voter turnout. Significantly, though, highly educated and wealthier African Americans are as likely to vote as whites of similar background, and sometimes more likely.

Race also helps explain why the South has long had a lower turnout than the rest of the country (see Figure 13.5). In the wake of Reconstruction, the southern states made it extremely difficult for African Americans to register to vote, and only a small percentage of the eligible African American population was registered throughout the South. The Voting Rights Act (VRA) of 1965 helped to change this situation. The VRA was intended to guarantee voting rights to African Americans nearly a century after passage of the Fifteenth Amendment. Often now heralded as the most successful piece of civil rights legislation ever passed, the VRA targeted states that had used literacy or morality tests or poll taxes to exclude blacks from the polls. The act bans any voting device or procedure that interferes with a minority citizen's right to vote and requires approval for any changes in voting qualifications or procedures in certain areas where minority registration was not in proportion to the racial composition of the district. It also authorized the federal government to monitor all elections in areas where discrimination was found to be practiced or where less than

FIGURE 13.5   The South Versus the Non-South for Presidential Voter Turnout
After a century-long discrepancy caused by discrimination against African American voters in the South, regional voting turnouts have grown much closer together with the increasing enfranchisement of these voters.

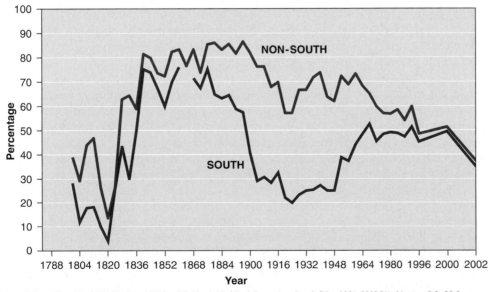

Source: Adopted from Harold W. Stanley and Richard G. Niemi, *Vital Statistics on American Politics, 2001–2002* (Washington, DC: CQ Press, 2001), 14.

Maria Gonzalez Mabbutt, Director of Idaho Latino Vote, holds a sample ballot flyer from Nampa, Idaho. The project "Get the Vote Out" was created to inform the Hispanic Community where and when to vote, as well as who the candidates are.

(Photo courtesy: Greg Wahl-Stephens/AP/Wide World Photos)

50 percent of the voting-age public was registered to vote in the 1964 election.

The impact of the act was immediate. African American voter registration skyrocketed, as did the number of African Americans elected to office. For example, in 1965 there were 280 black elected officials at any level in the United States. Since 1965, African American voters have used their strength at the ballot box to elect more black officials at all levels of government. But, while the results have been encouraging, the percentage of elected offices held by African Americans in the eleven southern states covered by the VRA remains relatively small.

The 2000 Census revealed that the Hispanic community in the United States is now about equal in size to the African American community, which means that Hispanics have the potential to wield enormous political power. In California, Texas, Florida, Illinois, and New York, five key electoral states, Hispanic voters have emerged as powerful allies for candidates seeking office. However, just as voter turnout among African Americans is historically much lower than whites, the turnout among Hispanics is much lower than that among African Americans. In 1996, 50.6 percent of African Americans voted in the presidential election; only 27.6 percent of Hispanics turned out to vote.[41]

Like any voting group, Hispanics and Latinos are not easily categorized and voting patterns cannot be neatly generalized. However, several major factors play out as key decision-making variables: one's point of origin, length of time in United States, and income levels. Despite having citizenship, Puerto Ricans can vote in a presidential election only if they live on the mainland and establish residency. Cuban Americans are concentrated in South Florida and tend to be conservative and vote for GOP candidates because of their historically anti-communist position. Mexican American voting patterns are very issue-oriented, divided according to income levels and generation.[42]

As more Hispanic candidates run for office, the excitement level and participation of Hispanic voters is likely to increase. The 2004 elections featured several high profile Hispanic candidates, including Colorado's Salazar brothers, Ken, who won a Senate seat, and John, who won a seat in the House. Mel Martinez ran for a Senate seat in Florida and won as well.

Interest in Politics.   Although socio-economic factors undoubtedly weigh heavily in voter participation rates, an interest in politics must also be included as an important factor. Many citizens who vote have grown up in families interested and active in politics, and they in turn stimulate their children to take an interest. Additionally, recent research has determined that interest in politics is not dependent on any one especially mobilizing candidate. Those citizens involved in the process remain so even if their favored candidate loses. Political scientist James McCann, for instance, found that "preconvention mobilization into presidential politics tends to increase participation on behalf of House candidates," even if the candidate for which the individual was mobilized lost the party's presidential nomination.[43] Likewise, based on data from 1984 presidential nomination caucus attenders political scientists Walter Stone and colleagues say that voters become mobilized for later party work and support after participating in presidential nominating campaigns, whether their favored candidate won or lost. Such workers, Stone maintains, care more about the outcome of elections and the political process than they do about individual candidates.[44] Conversely, many nonvoters simply do not care about politics or the outcome of elections, never having been taught their importance at a younger age.

People who are highly interested in politics constitute only a small minority of the U.S. populace. For example, the most politically active Americans—party and issue-group activists—make up less than 5 percent of the country's more than 285 million people. Those who contribute time or money to a party or a candidate during a campaign make up only about 10 percent of the total population. On the other hand, although these percentages appear low, they translate into millions of Americans who contribute more than just votes to the system.

Why Is Voter Turnout So Low?

There is no getting around the fact that the United States has one of the lowest voter participation rates of any nation in the industrialized world. In 1960, 62 percent of the eligible electorate voted in the presidential election, but by 1996, American voter participation had fallen to a record low of 48.8 percent—the lowest general presidential election turnout since 1824. Because of massive voter registration drives and the closeness of the election, the 2004 elections saw the largest voter turnout since 1968 at just under 60 percent. In contrast, turnout for postwar British elections has fluctuated between 72 percent and 84 percent. Figure 13.6 shows several reasons U.S. nonvoters give for not voting. A number of contributing factors are discussed below.

Too Busy.   Over 39 million voters did not cast a ballot in the 2002 midterm elections. According to the U.S. Census Bureau, 27 percent of registered non-voters surveyed said that they did not vote because they were too busy or had conflicting work or school schedules. Another 13 percent said that they did not vote because they were ill, disabled, or had a family emergency. While these reasons seem to account for a large portion of the people surveyed, the results may likely also reflect the respondents' desire not to seem uneducated about the candidates and issues or apathetic about the political process. While some would-be voters are undoubtedly busy, infirm, or otherwise unable to make it to the polls, it is likely that many of these nonvoters are offering an easy excuse, and may be in fact more directly affected by another reason.

Difficulty of Registration.   Of those citizens who are registered, the overwhelming majority vote. The real source of the participation problem in the United States seems to be that a relatively low percentage of the adult population is registered to vote. There are a number of reasons for the low U.S. registration rates. First, while nearly every other democratic country places the burden of registration on the government rather than on the individual, in the United States the registration process requires individual initiative—a daunting impediment in this age of political apathy. Thus, the cost (in terms of time and effort) of registering to vote is higher in the United States than it is in other industrialized democracies. Second, many nations automatically register all of their citizens to vote. In the United States, however, citizens must jump the extra hurdle of remembering on their own to register. Indeed, it is no coincidence that voter

Citizen Change was one of many organizations in 2004 that endeavored to educate, register, and turn out young voters. Here, Sean "P. Diddy" Combs is seen wearing a shirt featuring the group's much-publicized slogan.

(Photo courtesy: AP/World Wide Photos)

FIGURE 13.6   Why People Don't Vote

According to the U.S. Census Bureau's Current Population Survey taken after the 2004 elections, "too busy" was the single biggest reason Americans gave for not voting on Election Day. Anger toward politicians and disenchantment with the current political system also drove Americans away from the polls.

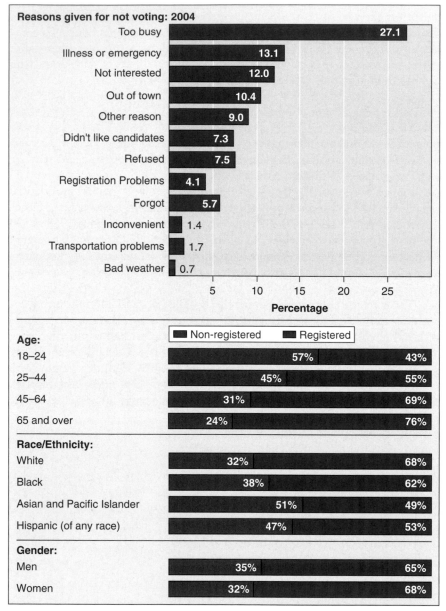

Source: U.S. Census Bureau, Current Population Survey, July 2004.

participation rates dropped markedly after reformers pushed through strict voter registration laws in the early part of the twentieth century. Correspondingly, several recent studies of the effects of relaxed state voter registration laws show that easier registration leads to higher levels of turnout. Stephen Knack and J. White, for instance, found that when states adopted Election Day registration of new voters, large and significant improvements in turnout occurred among younger voters and the poor.[45] Similarly, Daniel Franklin, in a 1992 study of states with a "motor voter" law (allowing citizens to register to vote at the Department of Motor Vehicles), found that those states had levels of registration and turnout that were significantly higher than in states lacking such a law.[46]

Difficulty of Absentee Voting.   Stringent absentee ballot laws are another factor in the United States' low voter turnout. Many states, for instance, require citizens to apply in person for absentee ballots, a burdensome requirement given that one's inability to be present in his or her home state is often the reason for absentee balloting in the first place. Recent literature in political science links liberalized absentee voting rules and higher turnout. One study, for instance, concluded that lax absentee voting restrictions reduced the "costs of voting" and increased turnout when the parties mobilized their followers to take advantage of new lenient absentee voting laws.[47]

Number of Elections.   Another explanation for low voter turnout in this country is the sheer number and frequency of elections, which few if any other democracies can match. Yet, an election cornucopia is the inevitable result of federalism and the separation of powers, which result in layers of often separate elections on the local, state, and national levels.

Voter Attitudes.   Although some of the reasons for low voter participation are due to the institutional factors we have just reviewed, voter attitudes play an equally important part. Some nations, such as Australia and Belgium, try to get around the effects of voter attitudes with compulsory voting laws. Not surprisingly, voter turnout rates in Australia and Belgium are often greater than 95 percent. Other nations fine citizens who do not vote. (See Global Politics: Voter Turnout Around the World.)

As noted previously, alienation afflicts some voters, and others are just plain apathetic, possibly because of a lack of pressing issues in a particular year, satisfaction with the status quo, or uncompetitive (even uncontested) elections. Furthermore, many citizens may be turned off by the quality of campaigns in a time when petty issues and personal mudslinging are more prevalent than ever. Additionally, one recent study finds that divided government affects voter turnout, with turnout declining by 2 percent in each consecutive election conducted when the presidency and Congress are controlled by different parties.[48] Finally, perhaps turnout has declined due to rising levels of distrust of government. More and more people are telling pollsters that they lack confidence in political leaders. In the past, some scholars argued that there is no correlation between distrust of political leaders and nonvoting. But, as the levels of distrust rise, these preliminary conclusions might need to be revisited.

Weak Political Parties.   Political parties today are no longer as effective as they once were in mobilizing voters, ensuring that they are registered, and getting them to the polls. As we discussed in chapter 12, the parties once were grassroots organizations which forged strong party-group links with their supporters. Today, these bonds have been stretched to the breaking point for many. Candidate-centered campaigns and the growth of expansive party bureaucracies have resulted in a somewhat more distant party with which most people do not identify very strongly.

How Can the United States Improve Voter Turnout?

Reformers have suggested many ideas to increase voter turnout in the United States. Always on the list is raising the political awareness of young citizens, a reform that inevitably must involve our nation's schools. Political scientists Steven J. Rosenstone and John Marc Hansen's research shows that the rise in formal education levels among Americans played a significant role in preventing an even greater decline in voter turnout.[49] No less important, and perhaps simpler to achieve, are institutional reforms, though many of the reforms discussed below, if enacted, may result in only a marginal increase in turnout.

Comparative

Comparing Voting and Elections

Easier Registration and Absentee Voting.   Registration laws vary by state, but in every state except North Dakota, registration is required in order to vote. Many observers believe that voter turnout could be increased if registering to vote were made

VOTER TURNOUT AROUND THE WORLD

The problem of declining voter turnout over the last two decades has been a cause of concern across the industrial democracies. Nowhere is the issue seen as more acute than in the United States, which has the lowest voter turnout of any country surveyed here. Why do other countries have higher voter turnouts?

One explanation has to do with when elections are held. Every other government listed in the table holds elections on weekends, usually on Sunday, when voters are not at work. Another explanation is that parliamentary systems require their voters to vote less often. Elections for the parliament typically happen every three to four years. Prime ministers are elected by the lower house of Parliament, so a vote for a legislative candidate is also an indirect vote for a chief executive. Thus, in a parliamentary system, there are no midterm legislative elections, which is when turnout in the United States drops from presidential election levels.

Most important, voter registration is automatic, or nearly so, in the other countries. Voters are placed on the election rolls when they register their residence at the local government office. The Canadian government actively canvasses citizens of voting age to ensure their inclusion on the rolls. This is significant because the percentage recorded for the United States in the table shows voter turnout as a proportion of the voting-age population (including people ineligible to vote); the proportion of actual voters to registered voters is nearly two-thirds, close to the other industrial democracies' levels. Automatic registration would undoubtedly increase the number of registered voters, and therefore turnout, as it does in Europe, Canada, and Japan.

The high voter turnout in the 1999 election for the Indonesian House of Representatives highlights another issue. That election, and the presidential election that took place the same year, was the first democratic election since the 1950s. The number of new political parties that competed in the election suggests a broad public enthusiasm for the turn to democracy. We may see the 1999 election as a repudiation of the previous dictatorship as well as support for a new political system. Given the magnitude of the shift in government, we may also conclude that the stakes were much higher in that election

Voter Turnout in Selected National Elections		
Country	*Year, Election*	*Turnout (%)*
Canada	1997, parliamentary	69.6
Egypt	1999, presidential	79.7
France	2002, presidential	80
Germany	2002, parliamentary	71.9
India	1999, parliamentary	59.7
Indonesia	1999, parliamentary	93.3
Italy	1996, parliamentary	82.9
Japan	2000, parliamentary	62.4
Mexico	2000, presidential	64.0
Russia	2000, presidential	68.6
United Kingdom	2000, parliamentary	54.9
United States	**2000, presidential**	**50.7**

Sources: Parliaments Around the World, http://www.electionworld.org.parliaments.htm, and selected national government sites.

than in any American election in recent history, with a correspondingly high voter participation.

Compulsory voting is one way to avoid low turnout. Albania, Australia, Belgium, Egypt, and Mexico are among the countries that use this device. Voting in presidential elections is compulsory in Austria (the Austrian president acts as the ceremonial executive). Typically, a voter is fined if she or he does not vote, a fact that can be ascertained by checking voting rolls. Countries in which voting is compulsory have higher turnouts than the United States: 90.6 percent of Belgian voters participated in the 1999 elections, and 64 percent of Mexican voters went to the polls in the 2000 presidential election. Yet, that still means a significant number of voters stay away from the polls despite threat of sanction. Nearly 80 percent of Egyptian voters turned out for the 1999 presidential referendum in which President Mubarak was handily reelected to a fourth term. Turnout was very low, however, for the parliamentary elections held the following year (see www.electionworld.org).

Austria presents an interesting anomaly. Just over 80 percent of Austrian voters participated in the October 1999 parliamentary election (which is not compulsory), while just over 74 percent voted in the presidential election the previous year (which is compulsory).

The Prepared Voter Kit

simpler for citizens. The typical thirty-days-before-an-election registration deadline could be shortened to a week or ten days. After all, most people become more interested in voting as Election Day nears. Indeed, one political scientist calculated that allowing citizens to register on the same day as they vote would boost national turnout by five percentage points.[50] Better yet, all U.S. citizens could be registered automatically at the age of eighteen. Absentee ballots could also be made easier to obtain by eliminating the in-person requirement.

In 1993, a major advance toward easier registration was achieved with the passage by Congress of the so-called motor-voter bill, which required states to permit individuals to register by mail, not just in person. The law, strongly backed by President Clinton, also allows citizens to register to vote when they visit any motor vehicles office, public assistance agency, or military recruitment division. Proponents of the law say it will result in the registration of roughly 49 million Americans of voting age with driver's licenses or identification cards. Opponents claim the new law is yet another in a long line of intrusive and costly federal mandates that do not appropriate money to pay for the costs involved in implementing the programs. However, research on motor-voter laws passed by states prior to the passage of federal legislation indicates that such laws indeed have a positive impact on voter registration levels.[51] Indeed, the Federal Election Commission reports that while there was a slight increase in voter registration in those states covered by the motor-voter law, there was actually a slight decrease in voter registration in those states not covered by the legislation.[52]

Make Election Day a Holiday.   Besides removing an obstacle to voting (the busy workday), making Election Day a national holiday might focus more voter attention on the contests in the critical final hours.

Strengthen Parties.   Reformers have long argued that strengthening the political parties would increase voter turnout, because parties have historically been the organizations in the United States best suited for and most successful at mobilizing citizens to vote. During the late 1800s and early 1900s, the country's "Golden Age" of powerful political parties, one of their primary activities was getting out the vote on Election Day. Even today, the parties' Election Day get-out-the-vote drives increase voter turnout by as many as several million in national contests.

Other Suggestions.   Other ideas to increase voter turnout are less practical or feasible. For example, holding fewer elections might sound appealing, but it is difficult to see how this could be accomplished without diluting many of the central tenets of federalism and separation of powers that the Founders believed essential to the protection of liberty. Political scientist Arend Lijphart suggests other changes that he believes could increase voter turnout, including proportional representation of the congressional vote to encourage third parties and combat voter apathy toward the two major parties, changing Election Day to Saturday or Sunday, and making voting mandatory, which he contends has benefits that far outweigh most Americans' aversion to the idea.[53]

Does Low Voter Turnout Matter?

Some political observers have argued that nonvoting is not a critical problem. For example, some believe that the preferences of nonvoters are not much different from those who do vote. If this is true, the results would be about the same if everyone voted. Others contend that since legal and extralegal denials of the vote to previously disfranchised groups—African Americans, women, Hispanics—have now been outlawed, nonvoting is voluntary. Some say that nonvoters are indicating their acceptance of things as they are, or that we should not attempt to make it easier for people characterized as apathetic and lazy to vote. Finally, some claim that low voter turnout is a positive benefit, based on the dubious supposition that less-educated people are more easily swayed. Thus, low turnout supposedly increases the stability of the system and discourages demagogic, populist appeals.

We should not be too quick to accept these arguments, which have much in common with the early nineteenth-century view that the Nineteenth Amendment to the Constitution (which enfranchised women) need not be passed because husbands could protect the interests of their wives. First, the social make-up and attitudes of present-day nonvoters are significantly different from those of voters. Nonvoters tend to be low income, younger, blue collar, less educated, and more heavily minority. Even if their

A worker at a state motor vehicles office displays the form that makes it easy to register to vote.

(Photo courtesy: Dennis Brack/Black Star)

expressed preferences about politics do not look very distinctive, their objective circumstances as well as their need for government services differ from the majority of those who do vote. These people—who require the most help from government—currently lack a fair share of electoral power. A political system that actively seeks to include and mobilize these people might well produce broader-based policies that differ from those we have today.

In 2004, nationwide voter turnout was just under 60 percent of the voting age population, nearly 9 percentage points up from 51 percent in 2000. The sudden surge in voter turnout surprised no one. Both political parties and non-partisan groups had been registering voters throughout the year and in unprecedented numbers. Voters also had much to motivate them with the election predicted to be as close as in 2000, putting critical issues such as the war in Iraq, the fate of Social Security, and the possible appointments to the Supreme Court (an issue which came up after Supreme Court Justice William Rehnquist underwent thyroid cancer surgery a week before the election). With nearly 60 million viewers watching the first debate, voters also acquainted themselves with the candidates and their stances on the issues. For the first time in decades, the American people seemed political engaged, and the stakes could not be any higher.

This significant improvement from the 2000 election is encouraging, and hopefully is the beginning of a trend toward an increased level of participation. The 2000 outcome had offered a mixed message of idealism and cynicism, and we learned anew how one vote really can make a difference. An older generation of Americans learned this in 1960 in the extremely close election where one vote per precinct in the United States made John F. Kennedy the president of the United States. This was so few votes in a handful of states that clearly the power of the individual vote became clear, and perhaps this is a lesson that Americans need to learn and relearn.

On the other hand, the carelessness with which the media handled the election in its early stages, especially in Florida, did nothing to dispel the doubly false belief of many Americans that their votes would be no more important than usual. Of course, there is bitterness from the realization that for many Americans who did trouble to vote, their vote went uncounted. Thousands of ballots were discarded due to machine or human error; several thousand ballots from Americans living overseas or serving in the military were not counted in the initial tabulation; some polling stations may have unfairly turned away rightful voters.

Turnout in some states exceeded even the national average. South Dakota experienced a 78 percent turnout of registered voters during their elections, very likely because of the high stakes race between the then Senate Minority Leader and a popular challenger. Even in states with fewer high profile races saw a huge increase in voter turnout. Early reports show that Maine reached 73 percent voter turnout, only the third time the state has passed the 70 percent mark in its history. Such a sharp increase in voter participation is exciting and undoubtedly good for democracy, but it is uncertain whether such gains are permanent or simply unique to this highly contested presidential race. The best test will be the level of turnout in the 2006 midterm elections.

Patterns in Vote Choice

Just as there are certain predictable patterns when it comes to American voter turnout (discussed above), so, too, are there predictable features of vote choice. One of the most prominent and consistent correlates of vote choice is partisan identification, which is discussed in the previous chapter. Some other consistent and notable correlates of vote choice include race and ethnicity, gender, income, ideology, and issues and campaign-specific developments.

Race and Ethnicity.   One of the most striking and enduring patterns in American vote choice concerns the voting patterns of different racial groups. While whites have shown an increasing tendency to vote Republican in recent elections, African American voters remain overwhelmingly Democratic in both their partisan identification and in their voting decisions. In their book *The New American Voter*, Warren E. Miller and J. Merrill Shanks point out that "since ... the civil rights voting legislation of 1964 and 1965, the Black vote has been monolithically Democratic."[54] Miller and Shanks report that in presidential elections from 1980–1992, "Blacks cast approximately 90 percent of their two-party ballots for the Democratic candidates."[55] Despite the best efforts of the Republican Party to garner African American support, this pattern shows no signs of waning. In 2004, for example, 88 percent of the votes cast by African Americans were cast for Kerry, while Bush received a mere 11 percent of the African American vote.[56]

Hispanics also tend to identify with and vote for Democrats, although not as monolithically as do African Americans.[57] In 2004, for example, Kerry received 53 percent of the votes cast by Latinos; Bush received only 44 percent. These exit poll data indicate that, in fact, Bush is closing the Democratic lead among Latinos; however, more research must be done to verify whether the exit poll data were skewed.

The Asian American segment of the electorate is less monolithic and more variable in its voting than either the Hispanic or the African American communities. It is worth noting the considerable political diversity within this group: Chinese Americans tend to prefer Democratic candidates, but Vietnamese Americans, with a strong anticommunist leaning, tend to support Republicans. A typical voting split for the Asian American community in general, though, might run about 60 percent Democratic and 40 percent Republican, though it can reach the extreme of a 50–50 split, depending on the election.

Gender.   There have been elections throughout the twentieth century in which gender was a factor, although precise data are not always available to prove the conventional wisdom. For example, journalists in 1920 claimed that women—in their first presidential election after the passage of the Nineteenth Amendment granted women suffrage—were especially likely to vote for Republican presidential candidate Warren G. Harding. In the sexist view of the day, women were supposedly taken in by the handsome Harding's charm. Recent evidence is more clear that women act and react differently than men to some candidacies, including those of other women. For instance, Democratic women were more likely than Democratic men to support Walter Mondale's presidential ticket in 1984 because of former Vice President Mondale's selection of Representative Geraldine Ferraro (D–NY) for the second slot on his presidential ticket. However, Republican women at the time were more likely than GOP men to support Ronald Reagan's candidacy because of Ferraro's presence on the Democratic ticket; Republican women were opposed to Ferraro's liberal voting record and views. Since 1980, the so-called "gender gap" (the difference between the voting choices of men and women) has become a staple of American politics.

Simply put, in most elections today, women are more likely to support the Democratic candidate and men are more likely to support the Republican candidate. The size of the gender gap varies considerably from election to election, though normally the gender gap is between 5 and 7 percentage points. That is, women support the average Democrat 5 to 7 percent more than men support the average Republican candidate. Some elections result in an expanded gender gap though, such as the presidential election of 1996, where the gender gap was an enormous 17 percentage points, about 10 points larger than in 1992. Bob Dole narrowly won among men in 1996, while Bill Clinton scored a landslide among women. Of importance here is the fact that women now constitute a majority of the adult population in all the American states, and they are a majority of the registered electorate in virtually all of those states. This means it has become increasingly important for both Democrats and Republicans to seek the votes and support of women.

Income.   Over the years, income has been a remarkably stable correlate of vote choice. As Miller and Shanks put it, "Both vote turnout and vote divisions consistently conform to well-established stereotypes; the poor vote less often and more Democratic, the well-to-do vote more often and heavily Republican."[59] Indeed in the 2004 presidential election, those voters who earned less than $15,000 yearly voted for Kerry over Bush by 63 to 36 percent, whereas those voters who earned more $100,000 yearly supported Bush over Kerry by 59 to 41 percent.[60]

Ideology.   Ideology represents one of the most significant cleavages in contemporary American politics. Liberals, generally speaking, favor government involvement in society to try to solve problems, and they are committed to the ideals of tolerance and diversity. Conservatives, on the other hand, think individuals and private organizations, *not* government, should be responsible for solving most problems, and they are dedicated to the promotion of traditional and family values. Moderates, as the name implies, lie somewhere between liberals and conservatives on the ideological spectrum.

Not surprisingly, ideology is very closely related to vote choice. Liberals tend to vote for Democrats, and conservatives tend to vote for Republicans. In 2004, 85 percent of self-described liberals voted for Kerry, whereas only 13 percent voted for Bush. Conservatives, on the other hand, voted for Bush over Kerry at a rate of 84 to 15 percent.[61]

Issues and Campaign-Specific Developments.   In addition to the underlying influences on vote choice discussed above, issues and campaign-specific developments can have important effects on vote choice in any given election year. Miller and Shanks, for example, found that in the 1992 presidential election, one's positions on whether or not government should do more to aid the disadvantaged and on whether or not homosexuals should be permitted to serve in the military were related to the eventual choice between voting for Bill Clinton or George Bush.[62]

The 2004 had two major campaign-specific issues, Iraq and the War on Terror. Early in the campaign, Bush attempted to link the two issues together with the hope that the general support he received in his handling the War on Terror could help boost flagging ratings on how Bush was handling the war in Iraq. The Kerry efforts to keep the two issues separate, however, succeeded. Exit polls showed that voters who considered terrorism the most important issue voted 86 to 14 percent for Bush, while those who considered Iraq the most important issue voted 73 to 26 for Kerry. Amazingly, while terrorism and Iraq dominated the 2004 election, and even the 2004 Democratic primaries, voters actually cited the economy (20 percent of respondents) and moral values (22 percent) as the most important issues. Terrorism and Iraq only received 19 and 15 percent, respectively. Those voters citing the economy as most important voted 82 to 18 percent in favor of Kerry, and those stating moral values as most important voted 80 to 20 percent in favor of Bush. In the end, the campaign-specific issues ran side by side with the perennial problems Americans and their representatives face every day.

Ticket-Splitting

Citizens have been increasingly deserting their party affiliations in the polling booths. The practice of **ticket-splitting,** voting for candidates of different parties for various offices in an election, rose dramatically since the 1950s, but has levelled off and started to decline since the early 1990s.[64] The evidence of this development abounds. As already reviewed in this chapter, Republican presidential landslides in 1956, 1972, 1980, and 1984 were accompanied by the election of substantial Democratic majorities in the House of Representatives. Divided government, with the presidency held by one party and one or both houses of Congress held by the other party, has never been as frequent in U.S. history as it has been recently. From 1920 to 1944, about 15 percent of the congressional districts voted for presidential and House candidates of different parties. But, from 1960 to 1996, at least 25 percent of the districts cast split tickets in any presidential year; and in 1984 nearly 50 percent of the districts did so.

Similarly, at the statewide level, only 17 percent of the states electing governors in presidential years between 1880 and 1956 elected state and national executives from different parties. Yet, from 1960 to 1992, almost 40 percent of states holding simultaneous presidential and gubernatorial elections recorded split results. (In 1992 and 1996, this proportion was somewhat lower, just 25 percent and 27 percent, respectively.) Whereas the proportion of states voting for a governor of a different party than the president stayed even in 2004 at 44 percent (45 percent in 2000), the proportion of states splitting their ticket between a presidential candidate of one party and a senatorial candidate of the other remained low at 18 percent. Perhaps the disparity between state level and federal level ticket splitting indicates that voters set different agendas for their state than for whole nation or that the closer proximity state voters have to their governors makes them more likely to make decisions based on personal experience of the candidates rather than because of partisanship.

These percentages actually understate the degree of ticket-splitting by individual voters. The Gallup poll has regularly asked its respondents, "For the various political offices, did you vote for all the candidates of one party, that is, a straight ticket, or did you vote for the candidates of different parties [ticket-splitting]?" Since 1968, the proportion of voters who have ticket-split in presidential years has consistently been around 60 percent of the total.[66] Other polls and researchers have found reduced straight-ticket balloting and significant ticket-splitting at all levels of elections, especially since 1952.

Not surprisingly, the intensity of party affiliation is a major determinant of a voter's propensity to split the ticket. Strong party identifiers are the most likely to cast a straight-party ballot; pure independents are the least likely. Somewhat greater proportions of ticket-splitters are found among high-income and better-educated citizens, but there is little difference in the distribution by gender or age. African Americans exhibit the highest straight-party rate of any population subgroup; about three-quarters of all black voters stay in the Democratic Party column from the top to the bottom of the ballot.

ticket-splitting
Voting for candidates of different parties for various offices in the same election.

Scholars have posited several potential explanations for ticket-splitting. For example, political scientist Morris P. Fiorina argues that voters split their tickets, consciously or not, because they trust neither party to govern.[67] Under this interpretation, ticket-splitters are aware of the differences between the two parties and split their tickets to augment the checks and balances already present in the Constitution. Alternatively—and in contrast to Fiorina—political scientist Martin P. Wattenberg argues that voters split their tickets because party has become less relevant as a voting cue.[68] Other explanations for ticket-splitting abound. The growth of issue-oriented politics, the mushrooming of single-interest groups, the greater emphasis on candidate-centered personality politics, and broader-based education are all often cited. A strong independent presidential candidacy also helps to loosen party ties among many voters. So, too, does the marked gain in the value of incumbency. Thanks in part to the enormous fattening of congressional constituency services, incumbent U.S. representatives and senators have been able to attract a steadily increasing share of the other party's identifiers.[69]

REFORMING THE ELECTORAL PROCESS

Most proposals for electoral reform in America center on the electoral college, as discussed earlier. Abolition of the electoral college, the establishment of a congressional district plan, and the elimination of electors are at once the most dramatic and apparently urgent reforms, especially in light of the events of the 2000 election, and the least likely to succeed, given the many entrenched interests they serve and the difficulty of amending the Constitution. Changes to the electoral college, however, are not the only ways in which the election of public officials in America might be improved.

Another possible electoral reform, one which focuses on the nomination rather than the general election stage of presidential elections, is the idea of holding a series of regional primaries throughout the United States during the first week of each month, beginning in February of a presidential election year. Under this system, the country would be divided into five regions: the Southeast, Southwest, Far West, Midwest, and Northeast. In December of the year prior to the presidential election, a lottery would be held to determine the order in which the regions would hold their nomination races, with all regional contests held on the first of every month from Feb-

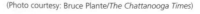
(Photo courtesy: Bruce Plante/*The Chattanooga Times*)

ruary through June. The goals of this reform would be twofold: First, it would end the current "permanent campaign" by preventing candidates from "camping out" in Iowa and New Hampshire for one to two years in the hopes of winning or doing better than expected in these small, unrepresentative states. Second, some rational order would be imposed on the electoral process, allowing candidates to focus on each region's concerns and people in turn.

Another area of electoral reform that has gained attention in recent years involves campaign finance. The Bipartisan Campaign Reform Act, sponsored by Senators John McCain (R–AZ) and Russ Feingold (D–WI), was signed into law in March 2002. This legislation bans unregulated "soft-money" donations to political parties, restricts the use of political ads, and increases political contribution limits for private individuals. Supporters heralded its passage as a major victory in lessening the influence of big money on politics. Unfortunately, political consultants have already found ways around the new legislation, leaving many voters to wonder what change the legislation will effect, if any. Campaign finance will be discussed more thoroughly in chapter 14.

These possible reform ideas should convince you that although individual elections may sometimes be predictable, the electoral system in the United States is anything but static. New generations, and party changers in older generations, constantly remake the political landscape. At least every other presidential election brings a change of administration and a focus on new issues. Every other year, at least a few fresh personalities and perspectives infuse the Congress, as newly elected U.S. senators and representatives claim mandates and seek to shake up the established order. Each election year, the same tumult and transformation can be observed in the fifty states and in thousands of localities.

The welter of elections may seem like chaos, but from this chaos comes the order and often explosive productivity of a democratic society. For, the source of all change in the United States, just as Hamilton and Madison predicted, is the individual citizen who goes to the polls and casts a ballot.

Continuity & Change

Election Technology—Past, Present, Future

In the nineteenth century, political parties ran the elections, supplying not only paper ballots but also many of the poll watchers and election judges. This was a formula for fraud, of course—there was not even a truly secret ballot, as people voted on ballots of different colors, depending on their choice of party. The twentieth century saw widespread improvements in election practices and technology. The states now oversee the election process through official state boards of election, and the use of voting machines, nearly universal in America by the 1970s, permits truly secret mechanical voting. These measures helped effect enormous reductions in fraud and electoral ambiguity—though as the irregularities of the election of 2000 proved, there is still a long way to go.

As more and more Americans become computer savvy, and as computer technology continues to evolve, Internet voting has become a likely way to cast votes in the coming years. Rightly or wrongly, Internet voting equates in the minds of many Americans with the ideals of instant democracy and greater citizen input in major decisions. Many states are formally studying the feasibility and impact of Internet voting. In 2000, Arizona pioneered online balloting by allowing citizens to vote via the Internet in the state's Democratic presidential primary. Opponents and proponents alike recognize potential problems, but technical solutions draw ever nearer.

The use of mail-in ballots, whereby registered voters are mailed ballots and given several weeks to mail them back with their votes, increases participation but delays final tabulation of the ballots for several weeks. Oregon, the only state that votes entirely by mail-in ballots, did not have its 2000 presidential results finalized until several weeks

(continued)

after Election Day. The state of Washington, which has extremely liberal laws regarding mail-in votes, was also much later than the rest of the country in announcing its presidential and congressional winners.

The nation also lacks a standardized method by which votes should be recounted in close elections. Many reformers favor a national uniform ballot system for the entire country—every voting locale would use the same kind of ballot. A national ballot is highly unlikely, however. If the federal government mandates a ballot form, it would almost certainly have to pay for it, at a price tag of up to several billion dollars. In addition, there are over 41,000 voting localities in states and jurisdictions across the United States, electing hundreds of thousands of officials, making it extremely difficult to create a uniform type of ballot.

Another change likely to result from the chaos of the 2000 election addresses the technology of the ballot itself. America can look forward to the elimination of the "butterfly ballot," which featured prominently in the heavily contested county of Palm Beach, Florida. Although the ballot was approved for use, it gained national attention because of its confusing layout. After the debacle of ambiguously punched ballots, Americans can also expect to see fewer stylus punch-card ballots, a technologically obsolete method of voting whereby voters use increasingly antiquated and faulty voting machines to stamp out a small bit of paper, or chad, to indicate their vote.

Many Americans believe that the federal government should assist states in updating outdated and faulty voting equipment. Some localities across the country use computerized touch-screen machines, which are expensive but much more secure and accurate than the older mechanical devices still in widespread use. An analysis of Florida's voting machines found that older, punch-card machines failed to indicate a vote for president on 1.5 percent of the ballots, while newer, optical-scanning machines failed on only 0.3 percent of the ballots. Additionally, older, error-ridden machines are commonly assigned to low-income and African American precincts, which reintroduces a troublesome discriminatory dimension into the voting process. Indeed, prior to the 2002 midterm elections the Florida

legislature undertook massive voting reforms, including banning punch-card ballots and investing $30 million in new touch-screen voting systems, with the individual counties spending tens of millions more. Unfortunately, the tragic scene of election 2000 was replayed in south Florida on September 12, 2002, as problems plagued the Democratic gubernatorial primary. Confusion abounded as voters and poll workers misused the expensive new machines. Election administrators had difficulty tabulating the electronic votes, leading to a week-long delay in naming an official winner. Florida was once again the electoral laughingstock of the nation, and everyone learned an important lesson: technology is not a panacea that will cure all election problems.

Updating election equipment and ensuring fair elections across the country should be a legislative priority, but emphasis must be placed on training poll workers, administrators, and voters how to effectively use the new equipment. As Charles M. Vest, the president of the Massachusetts Institute of Technology, said, "A nation that can send a man to the moon, that can put a reliable ATM machine on every corner, has no excuse not to deploy a reliable, affordable, easy-to-use voting system."

1. What kind of voting machine does your precinct use? What about the precincts of your friends and family? Did you or someone you know vote by mail? Ask around, and then determine how the perceived experience of voting, especially after the year 2000, differs depending on the technology one uses.

2. We tend to take fair elections and private voting for granted in the United States, but in many countries such conditions are still not widespread. What do the lessons of election reform in America teach us about ways of improving the integrity of elections in other nations? What can a country without a long stable democratic tradition do to ensure fraud-free elections and private voting?

CAST YOUR VOTE How can America improve voter turnout? To cast your vote, go to
www.ablongman.com/oconnor

SUMMARY

The explosion of elections we have experienced in over 200 years of voting has generated much good and some harm. But, all of it has been done, as Hamilton insisted, "on the solid basis of the consent of the people." In our efforts to explain the complex and multilayered U.S. electoral system, we covered these points in this chapter:

1. **The Purposes Served by Elections**
   Regular elections guarantee mass political action and governmental accountability. They also confer

legitimacy on regimes better than any other method of change.

2. **Different Kinds of Elections**
   When it comes to elections, the United States has an embarrassment of riches. There are various types of primary elections in the country, as well as general elections, initiatives, referenda, and recall elections. In presidential elections, primaries are sometimes replaced by caucuses, in which party members choose a candidate in a closed meeting, but recent years have seen fewer caucuses and more primaries.

3. **Presidential Elections**

Variety aside, no U.S. election can compare to the presidential contest. This spectacle, held every four years, brings together all the elements of politics and attracts the most ambitious and energetic politicians to the national stage.

4. **Congressional Elections**

Many similar elements are present in different kinds of elections. Candidates, voters, issues, and television advertisements are constants. But, there are distinctive aspects of each kind of election as well. Compared with presidential elections, congressional elections are a different animal.

5. **Voting Behavior**

Whether they are casting ballots in congressional or presidential elections, voters behave in certain distinct ways and exhibit unmistakable patterns to political scientists who study them.

6. **Reforming the Electoral Process**

The American political system uses indirect electoral representation in the form of the electoral college. Events of the 2000 election have renewed a longstanding debate over the legitimacy and efficacy of this institution and sparked controversial calls for change. Other suggested reforms are regional primaries and campaign finance limits.

KEY TERMS

SELECTED READINGS

Bartels, Larry M. *Presidential Primaries and the Dynamics of Public Choice.* Princeton, NJ: Princeton University Press, 1988.

Campbell, Angus, Philip E. Converse, Warren E. Miller, and Donald E. Stokes. *The American Voter.* Chicago: University of Chicago, Reprint ed. 1980.

Carroll, Susan J. *Women as Candidates in American Politics.* Bloomington: Indiana University Press, 2nd ed., 1994.

Conway, M. Margaret. *Political Participation in the United States,* 3rd ed. Washington, DC: CQ Press, 2000.

Darcy, Robert, Susan Welch, and Janet Clark. *Women, Elections, and Representation,* 2nd ed. Lincoln: University of Nebraska Press, 1994.

Herrnson, Paul S. *Congressional Elections: Campaigning at Home and in Washington,* 4th ed. Washington, DC: CQ Press, 2003.

Jacobson, Gary C. *The Politics of Congressional Elections,* 6th ed. New York: Longman, 2003.

Nie, Norman H. *The Changing American Voter,* Reprint ed. Lincoln, NE: iUniverse, 1999.

Patterson, Thomas E. *The Vanishing Voter: Public Involvement in an Age of Uncertainty.* New York: Vintage, 2003.

Sabato, Larry J., Howard R. Ernst, and Bruce A. Larson. *Dangerous Democracy?: The Battle Over Ballot Initiatives in America.* Lanham, MD: Rowman and Littlefield, 2001.

Sabato, Larry J. *Midterm Madness: The Elections of 2002.* Lanham, MD: Rowman and Littlefield, 2003.

Sundquist, James L. *Dynamics of the Party System: Alignment and Realignment of Political Parties in the United States.* Washington, DC: Brookings Institution, 1983.

Teixeira, Ruy A. *The Disappearing American Voter.* Washington, DC: Brookings Institution, 1992.

Verba, Sidney, Norman H. Nie, and Jae-On Kim. *Participation and Political Equality,* Reissue ed. Chicago: University of Chicago Press, 1987.

Verba, Sidney, Kay Lehman Schlozman, and Henry E. Brady. *Voice and Equality: Civic Voluntarism in American Politics.* Cambridge, MA: Harvard University Press, 1996.

Wayne, Stephen J. *The Road to the White House 2004: The Politics of Presidential Elections,* 7th ed. New York: Wadsworth, 2003.

Weisberg, Herbert F., ed. *Democracy's Feast: Elections in America.* Chatham, NJ: Chatham House, 1995.

NOTES

1. Angus Cambell, Philip E. Converse, Warren E. Miller, and Donald E. Stokes, *The American Voter* (New York: Wiley, 1960).

2. Paul Abramson, John H. Aldrich, and David W. Rohde, *Change and Continuity in the 1996 Elections* (Washington, DC: CQ Press, 1998).

3. Paul Allen Beck, *Party Politics in America*, 8th ed. (New York: Longman, 1998); David Adamany, "Cross-over Voting and the Democratic Party's Reform Rules," *American Political Science Review* 70 (1976): 536–41; Ronald Hedlund and Meredith W. Watts, "The Wisconsin Open Primary: 1968 to 1984," *American Politics Quarterly* 14 (1986): 55–74; and Gary D. Wekkin, "The Conceptualization and Measurement of Crossover Voting," *Western Political Quarterly* 41 (1988) 105–14.

4. Beck, *Party Politics in America*; Alan Abromowitz, John McGlennon, and Ronald Rapoport, "A Note on Strategic Voting in a Primary Election," *Journal of Politics* 43 (1981): 899–904; and Gary D. Wekken, "Why Crossover Voters Are Not 'Mischievous' Voters," *American Politics Quarterly* 19 (1991): 229–47.

5. Gary C. Jacobson, *The Politics of Congressional Elections*, 5th ed. (New York: Addison Wesley, 2000), 107–8.

6. Shaun Bowler, Todd Donovan, and Caroline Tolbert, eds., *Citizens as Legislators: Direct Democracy in the United States* (Columbus: Ohio State University Press, 1998).

7. For a more in-depth discussion of initiative, referendum, and recall voting please see Larry J. Sabato, Howard R. Ernst, and Bruce Larson, *Dangerous Democracy: The Battle over Ballot Initiatives in America* (Lanham, MD: Rowman and Littlefield, 2001) and David S. Broder *Democracy Derailed: Initiative Campaigns and the Power of Money* (New York: Harcourt, 2000).

8. Edward L. Lascher Jr., Michael G. Hagen, and Steven A. Rochlin, "Gun Behind the Door?" *Journal of Politics* 58 (August 1996): 766–75.

9. Elaine Ciulla Kamarck and Kenneth M. Goldstein, "The Rules Matter: Post-Reform Presidential Nominating Politics," in L. Sandy Maisel, *The Parties Respond: Changes in American Parties and Campaigns* (Boulder, CO: Westview Press, 1994), 174.

10. Paul R. Abramson, John H. Aldrich, Phil Paolino, and David W. Rohde, "'Sophisticated' Voting in the 1998 Presidential Primaries," *American Political Science Review* 86 (March 1992): 55–69.

11. Larry J. Sabato, "Presidential Nominations: The Front-loaded Frenzy of 1996," in Larry J. Sabato, ed., *Toward the Millennium: The Elections of 1996* (New York: Allyn and Bacon, 1997).

12. Byron Shafer, *Bifurcated Politics: Evolution and Reform in the National Party Convention* (Cambridge, MA: Harvard University Press, 1988).

13. Priscilla Southwell, "Rules as 'Unseen Participants' " *American Politics Quarterly* 20 (January 1992): 54–68.

14. Richard Herrera, "Are 'Superdelegates' Super?" *Political Behavior* 16 (March 1994): 79–92.

14a. Mary Lynn F. Jones, "Diverse delegates", *The Hill*. July 15, 2004 Thursday, 9.

14b. Ken Herman, Jim Tharpe, "GOP convention to showcase diversity", *The Atlanta Journal-Constitution*. August 6, 2004 Friday, 1A

15. James L. Hutter and Steven E. Schier, "Representativeness: From Caucus to Convention in Iowa," *American Politics Quarterly* 12 (October 1984): 431–48.

16. On the subject of party realignment, see Walter Dean Burnham, *Critical Elections and the Mainsprings of American Politics* (New York: Norton, 1970); Kristi Andersen, *The Creation of a Democratic Majority* (Chicago: University of Chicago Press, 1979); and John R. Petrocik, "Realignment: New Party Coalitions and the Nationalization of the South," *Journal of Politics* 49 (May 1987): 347–75.

17. Barbara Farah and Helmut Norpoth, "Trends in Partisan Realignment, 1976–1986: A Decade of Waiting," paper prepared for the annual meeting of the American Political Science Association, Washington, DC, August 27–31, 1986.

18. Morris P. Fiorina, *Retrospective Voting in American National Elections* (New Haven, CT: Yale University Press, 1981); and Charles H. Franklin and John E. Jackson, "The Dynamics of Party Identification," *American Political Science Review* 77 (1983): 957–73.

19. See, for example, V. O. Key Jr., "A Theory of Critical Elections," *Journal of Politics* 17 (February 1955): 3–18.

20. The less dynamic term "creeping realignment" is also sometimes used by scholars and journalists.

21. Everett Carl Ladd, "Like Waiting for Godot: The Uselessness of 'Realignment' for Understanding Change in Contemporary American Politics," in Byron Shafer, ed., *The End of Realignment? Interpreting American Electoral Eras* (Madison: Wisconsin, 1991).

22. See Paul Allen Beck, "The Dealignment Era in America," in Russell J. Dalton et al., *Electoral Change in Advanced Industrial Democracies: Realignment or Dealignment?* (Princeton, NJ: Princeton University Press, 1984), 264. See also Philip M. Williams, "Party Realignment in the United States and Britain," *British Journal of Political Science* 15 (January 1985): 97–115.

23. George Serra, "What's in It for Me? The Impact of Congressional Casework on Incumbent Evaluation," *American Politics Quarterly* 22 (1994): 403–20.

24. Glenn R. Parker and Suzanne L. Parker, "Correlates and Effects of Attention to District by U.S. House Members," *Legislative Studies Quarterly* 10 (May 1985): 223–42.

25. Gary W. Cox and Jonathan N. Katz, "Why Did the Incumbency Advantage in U.S. House Elections Grow?" *American Journal of Political Science* 40 (May 1996): 478–97.

26. Jonathan Krasno, *Challengers, Competition and Reelection: Comparing Senate and House Elections* (New Haven, CT: Yale University Press, 1994).

27. "How to Rig an Election," *The Economist* (April 25, 2002).

28. Matthew Mosk and Lori Montgomery, "Md. Court Spurns Assembly Map: Glendening Plan Ruled Unconstitutional; Judges to Redraw Lines," *Washington Post* (June 12, 2002).

29. *Wesberry* v. *Sanders*, 376 U.S. 1 (1964).

30. *Thornburg* v. *Gingles*, 478 U.S. 30 (1986).

31. *Shaw* v. *Reno*, 113 S.Ct. 2816 (1993).

32. "How to Rig an Election," *The Economist* (April 25, 2002).

33. Paul Gronke and J. Wilson, "Competing Plans as Evidence of Political Motives: The North Carolina Case," *American Politics Quarterly* 27 (April 1999): 147–76.

34. Sunhil Ahuja et al., "Modern Congressional Election Theory Meets the 1992 House Elections," *Political Research Quarterly* 47 (1994): 909–21; and Paul S. Herrnson, *Congressional Elections: Campaigning at Home and in Washington*, 2nd ed. (Washington, DC: CQ Press, 1998).

35. John W. Swain, Stephen A. Borrelli, and Brian C. Reed, "Partisan Consequences of the Post-1990 Redistricting for the U.S. House of Representatives," *Political Research Quarterly* 51 (December 1998): 945–67.

36. Gary C. Jacobson and Michael A. Dimock, "Checking Out: The Effects of Bank Overdrafts on the 1992 House Elections," *American Journal of Political Science* 38 (1994): 601–24; and Herrnson, *Congressional Elections*.

37. Gary C. Jacobson, "The 1994 House Elections in Perspective," *Political Science Quarterly* 111 (1996): 203–23.

38. Steven J. Rosenstone and John Mark Hanson, *Mobilization, Participation, and Democracy in America* (New York: Macmillan, 1993).

39. Raymond E. Wolfinger and Steven J. Rosenstone, *Who Votes?* (New Haven, CT: Yale University Press, 1980).

40. See, for example, Laura Stoker and M. Kent Jennings, "Life-Cycle Transitions and Political Participation: The Case of Marriage," *American Political Science Review* 89 (1995): 421–36; and Abramson et al., *Change and Continuity in the 1996 Elections*.

40a. National Election Pool Exit Poll, http://www.CNN.com.

41. Federal Election Commission, http://www.fec.gov/pages/Raceto.htm.

42. League of United Latin American Citizens, http://www.lulac.org.

43. James A. McCann, Randall W. Partin, Ronald B. Rapoport, and Walter J. Stone, "Presidential Nomination Campaigns and Party Mobilization: An Assessment of Spillover Effects," *American Journal of Political Science* 40 (August 1996): 756–67.

44. Walter Stone, Lonna Rae Atkeson, and Ronald B. Rapoport, "Turning On or Turning Off? Mobilization and Demobilization Effects of Participation in Presidential Nomination Campaigns," *American Journal of Political Science* 36 (August 1992): 665–91.

45. Stephen Knack and J. White, "Election-Day Registration and Turnout Inequality," *Political Behavior* 22 (March 2000): 29–44.

46. Daniel Franklin and Eric Grier, "Effects of Motor Voter Legislation: Voter Turnout, Registration, and Partisan Advantage in the 1992 Presidential Election," *American Politics Quarterly* 25 (January 1997): 104–17.

47. J. Eric Oliver, "The Effects of Eligibility Restrictions and Party Activity on Absentee Voting and Overall Turnout," *American Journal of Political Science* 40 (May 1996): 498–513.

48. Marg N. Franklin and Wolfgang P. Hirczy, "Separated Powers, Divided Government, and Turnout in U.S. Presidential Elections," *American Journal of Political Science* 42 (January 1998): 316–26.

49. Steven J. Rosenstone and John Marc Hansen, *Mobilization, Participation, and Democracy in America* (New York: Macmillan, 1993).

50. Mark J. Fenster, "The Impact of Allowing Day of Registration Voting on Turnout in U.S. Elections from 1960 to 1992: A Research Note," *American Politics Quarterly* 22 (January 1994), 74–87.

51. Stephen Knack, "Does 'Motor Voter' Work? Evidence from State-Level Data," *Journal of Politics* 57 (1995): 796–811.

52. "The Impact of the National Voter Registration Act on Federal Elections, 1999–2000," http://www.fec.gov/pages/nvrareport2000/nvrareport2000.htm.

53. Arend Lijphart, "Unequal Participation: Democracy's Unsolved Dilemma," *American Political Science Review* 91 (March 1997): 1–14.

54. Warren E. Miller and J. Merrill Shanks, *The New American Voter* (Cambridge, MA: Harvard University Press, 1996), 254–5.

55. Ibid., 255.

56. Voter News Service Exit Poll, http://www.CNN.com.

56.a http://www.cnn.com/ELECTION/2004/pages/results/states/US/P/00/epolls.0.html

57. Miller and Shanks, *The New American Voter*, 256.

58. Voter News Service Exit Poll, http://www.CNN.com.

59. Miller and Shanks, *The New American Voter*, 270.

60. Voter News Service Exit Poll, http://www.CNN.com.

61. Ibid.

62. Warren E. Miller and J. Merrill Shanks, "Multiple-Stage Explanation of Political Preferences," in Richard G. Niemi and Herbert F. Weisberg, eds., *Controversies in Voting Behavior* (Washington, DC: CQ Press, 2001), 227–32.

63. Charles Babington, "Campaigns Matter: The Proof of 2000," in Larry J. Sabato, ed., *Overtime! The Election 2000 Thriller* (New York: Longman, 2002), 65.

64. Gary C. Jacobson, *The Politics of Congressional Elections*, 5th ed. (New York: Addison Wesley, 2000.)

65. Barry C. Burden and David C. Kimball, *Why Americans Split Their Tickets: Campaigns, Competition, and Divided Government* (Ann Arbor, MI: University of Michigan Press, 2002).

66. Cited in Everett Carl Ladd Jr., "On Mandates, Realignments, and the 1984 Presidential Election," *Political Science Quarterly* 100 (Spring 1985): 23.

67. Morris P. Fiorina, *Divided Government* (Boston: Allyn and Bacon, 1996).

68. Martin P. Wattenberg, *The Decline of American Political Parties, 1952–1994* (Cambridge, MA: Harvard University Press, 1996).

69. Thomas E. Mann and Raymond E. Wolfinger, "Candidates and Parties in Congressional Elections," *American Political Science Review* 74 (September 1980): 617–32; Albert D. Cover, "One Good Term Deserves Another: The Advantage of Incumbency in Congressional Elections," *American Journal of Political Science* 21 (August 1977): 535; and Gary C. Jacobson, *The Politics of Congressional Elections*, 2nd ed. (Boston: Little, Brown, 1987), 86.

The Campaign Process

In early 2003, the field for the Democratic nomination for President was crowded and seemingly wide open. But many Democratic insiders, when pushed to name the "real" frontrunner, picked John Kerry. The Senator's life story seemed to lend itself to this path. As he was about to graduate from Yale University, he volunteered to go to Vietnam, came home a decorated veteran, and gained national fame as spokesman of the Vietnam Veterans Against the War. After attending law school at Boston College, he began his career as a prosecutor in his home state of Massachusetts. In 1982 he won his first political office, Lieutenant Governor, and two years later began the first of his four consecutive terms as a U.S. Senator.

But this life story was no guarantee that John Kerry would win his party's nomination or the presidency. He was easily targeted from the right as a "patrician Massachusetts liberal," and was assailed from the left wing of his party for his votes supporting the Iraq War and the Patriot Act. The nomination process began with nine candidates, including the fiery doctor-turned-Governor Howard Dean of Vermont. In the fall of 2003 Howard Dean was the frontrunner in most polls, and his anti-war stance seemed to energize the grassroots of his party. However, in the end John Kerry wrapped up the nomination remarkably quickly after gaining strong momentum following his surprise victory in the Iowa caucus.

In the general election John Kerry would face incumbent President George W. Bush, a Texas Republican and wartime president with a loyal base and impressive fundraising capabilities. At one point he held the highest approval ratings of any sitting president, a result of the outpouring of unity after the terrorist attacks of September 11, 2001. The nation's increased concern with Homeland Security as a result of these attacks also seemed to give the President an advantage, as polls have classically shown the GOP to be preferable to the Democrats on military issues. Even history also seemed to be Bush's side. No wartime president seeking re-election—not James Madison, not Abraham Lincoln, not FDR, and not Richard Nixon had lost. Still, his re-election was by no means secure. The success of the Iraqi occupation was hotly debated, and the economy showed many signs of distress that the President's tax cuts—the centerpiece of his economic program—had not remedied. As is usually the case with an incumbent, Bush would spend the election season ardently defending his presidency. Kerry's task, typical of a challenger, would be to discredit the President's administration and convince voters to accept him as the alternative to their current Commander-in-Chief.

"Next time, why don't you run? You're a well-known figure, people seem to like you, and you haven't had an original idea in years."

(Photo courtesy: *Playboy* magazine, reproduced by special permission. Copyright 1992 by Playboy)

WEB EXPLORATION

To compare the development of presidential candidates, go to www.ablongman.com/oconnor

nomination campaign
That part of a political campaign aimed at winning a primary election.

Up to this point in the book, we have focused on the election decision and have said little about the campaign conducted prior to the balloting. Many today denounce electioneering and politicians for their negative use of the airwaves and the perceived disproportionate influence of a few wealthy donors and a handful of well-endowed and well-organized political action committees and interest groups. Nonetheless, the basic purpose of modern electioneering remains intact: one person asking another for support, an approach unchanged since the dawn of democracy.

The art of campaigning involves the science of polls, the planning of sophisticated mass mailings, and the coordination of electronic telephone banks to reach voters. More importantly, it also involves the diplomatic skill of unifying disparate individuals and groups to achieve a fragile but election-winning majority. How candidates perform this exquisitely difficult task is the subject of this chapter, in which we discuss the following topics:

- First, we will explore the *structure of a campaign*, the process of seeking and winning votes in the run-up to an election, which consists of five separate components: the nomination campaign, the general election campaign, the personal campaign, the organizational campaign, and the media campaign.

- Second, we will look at the question of *which we vote for: the candidate or the campaign*. Although campaign methods have clearly become very sophisticated, in most cases the candidate wins or loses the race according to his or her abilities, qualifications, communication skills, issues, and weaknesses.

- Third, we will see the opportunities and challenges presented to the campaign by *the modern media*.

- Fourth, we will analyze the *campaign finance system* as it has evolved since the Federal Election Campaign Act (FECA) of 1971, and will pay special attention to the features and potential implications of the Bipartisan Campaign Reform Act of 2002.

- Fifth, we will discuss the 2004 presidential campaign and election, one of the most contentious elections in United State history.

- In keeping with our theme of *continuity and change,* we will examine the evolution of campaign ethics.

THE STRUCTURE OF A CAMPAIGN

A campaign for high office (such as the presidency, a governorship, or a U.S. Senate seat) is a highly complex effort akin to running a multimillion-dollar business. Campaigns for local offices are usually less complicated, but all campaigns, no matter what their size, have certain aspects in common. Indeed, each campaign really consists of several campaigns run simultaneously:

- The **nomination campaign.** The target is the party elite, the leaders and activists who choose nominees in primaries or conventions. Party leaders are concerned with electability, while party activists are often ideologically and issue oriented, so a candidate must appeal to both bases.

- The **general election campaign.** A farsighted candidate never forgets the ultimate goal: winning the general election. Therefore the candidate tries to avoid taking stands that, however pleasing to party activists in the primary, will alienate a majority of the larger general election constituency.

- The **personal campaign.** This is the public part of the campaign. The candidate and his or her family and supporters make appearances, meet voters, hold press conferences, and give speeches.

- The **organizational campaign.** Behind the scenes, another campaign is humming. Volunteers telephone voters and distribute literature, staffers organize events, and everyone raises money to support the operation.

- The **media campaign.** On television and radio, the candidate's advertisements (*paid media*) air frequently in an effort to convince the public that the candidate is the best person for the job. Meanwhile, campaigners attempt to influence the press coverage of the campaign by the print and electronic news reporters—the *free media*.

general election campaign
That part of a political campaign aimed at winning a general election.

personal campaign
That part of a political campaign concerned with presenting the candidate's public image.

organizational campaign
That part of a political campaign involved in fund-raising, literature distribution, and all other activities not directly involving the candidate.

media campaign
That part of a political campaign waged in the broadcast and print media.

Election campaigns in the United States are very different from those in parliamentary democracies. In British elections, for example, candidate selection is controlled by local party organizations, not by any sort of primary system. The national parties control key facets of the campaign. For example, they provide all the financing, which is regulated by national statute, and execute the campaign strategy. As a result, national party platforms—not candidate personalities—play a dominant role in British campaigns. The power of the prime minister to call elections at his or her discretion—literally at a moment's notice—produces campaigns of a mere four to five weeks in duration, instead of the two-year (for a Senate seat) to four-year (for president) campaigns we endure in the United States.

To better comprehend the various campaigns that make up U.S. elections, let's examine a few aspects of each, remembering that they must all mesh successfully for the candidate to win.

The Nomination Campaign

New candidates get their sea legs early on, as they adjust to the pressures of being in the spotlight day in and day out. This is the time for the candidates to learn that a single careless phrase could end the campaign or guarantee a defeat. This is also the time to seek the support of party leaders and interest groups and to test out themes, slogans, and strategies. The press and public take much less notice of shifts in strategy at this time than they will later in the general election campaign.

This is a critical time for gaining and maintaining the aura of support both within the party and with the larger electorate. Patrick Kenney and Tom Rice explain this in a study of momentum and the "bandwagon effect" in the 1988 Republican presidential primary. They found that Vice President George Bush, the eventual nominee, converted support from other Republican candidates through a variety of means. Some party members switched their allegiance from their favored candidate to Bush because they became caught up in his media-driven sense of upward momentum. Others switched to him simply because they perceived him to be the eventual nominee and liked the feeling of supporting a winner. Still others voted for Bush in the later primaries because they perceived him as the strongest Republican candidate heading into the November general election. Much of Bush's eventual support, therefore, grew out of his previous success and a sense of inevitability, not necessarily out of support for his issue positions or campaign themes or slogans.[1]

At this point in the nomination campaign, there is a danger not widely recognized by candidates: Surrounded by friendly activists and ideological soulmates in the quest to win the party's nomination, a candidate can move too far to the right or the left and become too extreme for the November electorate. Diehard activists, who are often more extreme than other members of their own party, tend to participate in primaries and caucuses, and candidates are forced to try to appeal to their interests. Conservative Barry Goldwater, the 1964 Republican nominee for president, and liberal George McGovern, the 1972 Democratic nominee for president, both fell victim to this phenomenon in seeking their party's nomination, and they were handily defeated in the general elections by Presidents Lyndon B. Johnson and Richard M. Nixon, respectively.

The General Election Campaign

Once the choice between the two major-party nominees is clear, both candidates can get to work. Most significant interest groups are courted for money and endorsements, although the results are mainly predictable: Liberal, labor, and minority groups usually back Democrats, while conservative and business organizations support Republicans. The most active and intense groups are often coalesced around emotional issues such as abortion and gun control, and these organizations can produce a bumper crop of money and activists for favored candidates. Race and class divisions can often play an important role in general elections, although this tends not to be true in the United States.

Virtually all candidates adopt a brief theme, or slogan, to serve as a rallying cry in their quest for office. The first to do so was William H. Harrison in 1840, with the slogan "Tippecanoe and Tyler, too." Tippecanoe was a nickname given to Harrison, a reference to his participation in the battle of Tippecanoe, and Tyler was Harrison's vice presidential candidate, John Tyler of Virginia. Some presidential campaign slogans have entered national lore, like Herbert Hoover's 1928 slogan "A chicken in every pot, a car in every garage." Bill Clinton used two memorable slogans: "Time for a change" and "Building a bridge to the twenty-first century." Most slogans can fit many candidates ("She thinks like us," "He's on our side," "She hears you," "You know where he stands"). Candidates try to avoid controversy in their selection of slogans, and some openly eschew ideology. (An ever-popular one of this genre is "Not left, not right—forward!") The clever candidate also attempts to find a slogan that cannot be lampooned easily. In 1964, Barry Goldwater's handlers may have regretted their choice of "In your heart, you know he's right" when Lyndon B. Johnson's supporters quickly converted it into "In your guts, you know he's nuts." (Democrats were trying to portray Goldwater as a warmonger after the Republican indicated a willingness to use nuclear weapons in Vietnam and elsewhere under some conditions.)

Right-wing 1964 Republican candidate Barry Goldwater's famous slogan, "In your heart, you know he's right," was quickly lampooned by incumbent Democratic opponent President Lyndon B. Johnson's campaign as "In your guts, you know he's nuts."

(Photo courtesy: Bettmann/Corbis)

Candidates must also decide which issues they want to focus on during the campaign, and they must also define their stances on other topics that may be of interest to voters. A variety of factors influence candidates' positions and core issues, including personal conviction, party platform, and experience in a certain area. Candidates also utilize public opinion polling to gauge whether or not the issues that they care about are issues that the voters care about.

The Personal Campaign

In the effort to show voters that they are hardworking, thoughtful, and worthy of the office they seek, candidates try to meet personally as many citizens as possible in the course of a campaign. Often, these opportunities are carefully staged and timed to ensure maximum media coverage. To some degree, these events are symbolic, especially for presidential candidates, since it is only possible to have direct contact with a limited number of people. But, one cannot underestimate the value of visiting numerous localities (or states for presidential candidates) to increase media coverage and motivate local activists who are working for the campaigns.

In a typical campaign, a candidate for high office may deliver up to a dozen speeches a day, and that is only part of the exhausting schedule most contenders maintain. The day may begin at 5 A.M. at the entrance gate to an auto plant with an hour or two of handshaking, followed by similar gladhanding at subway stops until 9 A.M. Strategy sessions with key advisers and preparation for upcoming presentations and forums may fill the rest of the morning. A luncheon talk, afternoon fund-raisers, and a series of television and print interviews crowd the afternoon agenda. The light fare of cocktail parties is followed by a dinner speech, perhaps telephone or neighborhood canvassing of voters, and a civic-forum talk or two. More meetings with advisers and planning for the next day's events can easily take a candidate past midnight. Following only a few hours of sleep, the candidate starts all over again. After months of this grueling pace, the candidate may be functioning on automatic pilot and unable to think clearly.

Beyond the strains this fast-lane existence adds to a candidate's family life, the hectic schedule leaves little time for reflection and long-range planning. Is it any wonder that under these conditions many candidates commit gaffes and appear to have foot-in-mouth disease?

It's not all drudgery, however. The considerable rewards to be had on the campaign trail can balance the personal disadvantages. A candidate can affect the course of the government and community, and in so doing become admired and respected by peers. Meeting all kinds of people, solving problems, gaining exposure to every facet of life in one's constituency—these experiences help a public person live life fully and compensate for the hardships of campaigning.

The Organizational Campaign

If the candidate is the public face of the campaign, the organization behind the candidate is the private face. Depending on the level of the office sought, the organizational staff can consist of a handful of volunteers or hundreds of paid specialists supplementing and directing the work of thousands of volunteers. The most elaborate structure is found in presidential campaigns. Tens of thousands of volunteers distribute literature and visit neighborhoods. They are directed by paid staff that may number 300 or more, including a couple of dozen lawyers and accountants.

Senator John Kerry (D-MA) announces his choice for a running mate, John Edwards (D-NC), at a rally in Pittsburgh, Pennsylvania. Both John Kerry and George W. Bush made numerous personal stops in this pivotal state throughout the 2004 campaign for the presidency.

(Photo courtesy: Corbis.com)

campaign manager
The individual who travels with the candidate and coordinates the many different aspects of the campaign.

political consultant
Professional who manages campaigns and political advertisements for political candidates.

WEB EXPLORATION
To find out what Americans have to say on a range of political issues and to experience poll taking firsthand, go to www.ablongman.com/oconnor

media consultant
A professional who produces political candidates' television, radio, and print advertisements.

pollster
A professional who takes public opinion surveys that guide political campaigns.

direct mailer
A professional who supervises a political campaign's direct-mail fund-raising strategies.

finance chair
A professional who coordinates the fund-raising efforts for the campaign.

Simulation
You are a Professional Campaign Manager

voter canvass
The process by which a campaign gets in touch with individual voters, either by door-to-door solicitation or by telephone.

get-out-the-vote (GOTV)
A push at the end of a political campaign to encourage supporters to go to the polls.

At the top of the organizational chart is the **campaign manager,** who coordinates and directs the various aspects of the campaign. Beside the manager is the **political consultant,** whose position is one of the most important developments in campaigning for office in this century. The political consultant is a private-sector individual (or, more often now, a team of individuals or a firm) who sells to a candidate the technologies, services, and strategies required to get that candidate elected to his or her office of choice. The number of consultants has grown exponentially since they first appeared in the 1930s, and their specialties and responsibilities have increased accordingly, to the point that they are now an obligatory part of campaigns at almost any level of government. Candidates hire generalist consultants to oversee their entire campaign from beginning to end, which often includes responsibilities ranging from defining campaign objectives to formulating strategy, developing tactics, and fighting individual battles alongside the candidate. Alongside the generalist consultant, or perhaps hired by the generalist, are more specialized consultants who focus on the new and complex technologies for only one or two specialties, such as fund-raising, polling, mass mailings, media relations, advertising, and speech writing.

The best-known consultants for any campaign are usually the **media consultant,** who produces the candidate's television and radio advertisements; the **pollster,** who takes the public opinion surveys that guide the campaign; and the **direct mailer,** who supervises direct-mail fund-raising. After the candidate, however, the most important person in the campaign is probably the **finance chair,** who is responsible for bringing in the large contributions that pay most of the salaries of the consultants and staff.

Many critics claim that consultants strip campaigns of substance and reduce them to a clever bag of tricks for sale. Many see a degeneration of American politics in the rise of the political consultant. Disappointed office seekers sometimes blame their loss entirely on their consultants, while successful candidates often retain their consultants after the election as political advisers, thereby lending even more credibility to the claim that politics now is all about appearance and not about issues. Candidates, always busy with making public appearances and canvassing, often entrust the entire management of campaigns to their consultants without understanding entirely what those consultants do. Sometimes, as in the notable case of Mary Matalin and James Carville in the 1992 presidential campaign, the consultants become media stars in their own right.

Others insist that despite the consultants, running for office is still about the bread and butter of campaigns: shaking hands, speaking persuasively, and listening to the voters. Voters, they say, are smart enough to tell the difference between a good candidate and a bad one, regardless of the smoke and mirrors erected by their consultants. Nevertheless, consultants do make a difference. Recent research on political consultants conducted by political scientists indicates that consultants have a significant impact in elections. In campaigns for the U.S. House of Representatives, for example, the use of professional campaign consultants has been shown to have a positive impact on candidates' fund-raising ability[2] and on candidates' final vote shares.[3]

In addition to raising money, the most vital work of the candidate's organization is to get in touch with voters. Some of this is done in person by volunteers who walk the neighborhoods, going door to door to solicit votes. Some is accomplished by volunteers who use computerized telephone banks to call targeted voters with scripted messages. (See Politics Now: High-Tech Campaigning for a discussion of the types of technologies contemporary campaigns rely on.) Both contact methods are termed **voter canvass.** Most canvassing, or direct solicitation of support, takes place in the month before the election, when voters are paying attention. Close to Election Day, the telephone banks begin the vital **get-out-the-vote (GOTV)** effort, reminding supporters to vote and arranging for their transportation to the polls if necessary. As the media becomes less effective in encouraging political education and participation, candidates increasingly realize the value of identifying base voters and getting them to the polls.

The Media Campaign

What voters actually see and hear of the candidate is primarily determined by the **paid media** (such as television advertising) accompanying the campaign and the **free media** (newspaper and television coverage). The two kinds of media are fundamentally different: Paid advertising is completely under the control of the campaign, whereas the press is independent. Great care is taken in the design of the television advertising, which takes many approaches. (For information on the first national political ad campaign, see Roots of Government: The Television Advertising Campaign of 1952.) **Positive ads** stress the candidate's qualifications, family, and issue positions with no direct reference to the opponent. These are usually favored by the incumbent candidate. **Negative ads** attack the opponent's character and platform. The campaign finance reforms of 2002 stipulate that candidates must now appear in their ads and deliver a disclaimer that they approved the ads; previously, negative ads may not have even mentioned the candidate who is paying for the airing (except for a brief identification at the ad's conclusion). In 2004, most of the negative advertising was not carried out directly by the campaigns. Instead, independent organizations did most of the dirty work. Bush supporters from a group called "Swift Boat Veterans for Truth" sought to discredit Kerry's military record by running ads that called into question the validity of the medals he had won in Vietnam. Kerry supporters, through MoveOn PAC, ran ads criticizing the Bush presidency, most notably one which showed children performing various tasks—working in factories, hauling trash—with the message that America's children would be paying off the president's enormous deficit. **Contrast ads** compare the records and proposals of the candidates, with a bias toward the sponsor.

Whether the public likes them or not, all three kinds of ads can inject important (as well as trivial) issues into a campaign. Incidentally, some of the negative ads aired in modern campaigns are sponsored *not* by candidates but by interest groups. These ads usually focus on issues and are independent of the actual campaigns, though it may be easy to tell which candidate the interest group favors.

Occasionally, advertisements are relatively long (ranging from four-and-one-half-minute ads up to thirty-minute documentaries). Ross Perot, for example, bought half-hour blocks repeatedly during the 1992 and 1996 presidential elections. Usually, however, the messages are short **spot ads,** sixty, thirty, or even ten seconds long.

While there is little question that negative advertisements have shown the greatest growth in the past two decades, they have been a part of American campaigns for some time. In 1796, Federalists portrayed Thomas Jefferson, a Founder of the nation and the chief author of the Declaration of Independence, as an atheist and a coward. In 1800, Federalists again attacked Jefferson, spreading a rumor that Jefferson was dead! Clearly, although negative advertisements are more prevalent today, they are not solely the function of the modern media. Furthermore, their effects are well documented. While voters normally need a reason to vote for a candidate, they also frequently vote *against* the other candidate—and negative ads can provide the critical justification for such a vote.

After some well-publicized defeats of incumbents in the early 1980s in which negative television advertising played a prominent role,[4] incumbents began attacking their challengers in earnest. The new rule of politics became "An attack unanswered is an attack agreed to." In a further attempt to stave off brickbats from challengers, incumbents began anticipating the substance of their opponents' attacks and airing **inoculation ads** early in the campaign to protect themselves in advance of the other side's spots. (Inoculation advertising attempts to counteract an anticipated attack from the opposition before the attack is launched.) For example, a senator who fears a

paid media
Political advertisements purchased for a candidate's campaign.

free media
Coverage of a candidate's campaign by the news media.

positive ad
Advertising on behalf of a candidate that stresses the candidate's qualifications, family, and issue positions, without reference to the opponent.

negative ad
Advertising on behalf of a candidate that attacks the opponent's platform or character.

contrast ad
Ad that compares the records and proposals of the candidates, with a bias toward the sponsor.

spot ad
Television advertising on behalf of a candidate that is broadcast in sixty-, thirty-, or ten-second duration.

inoculation ad
Advertising that attempts to counteract an anticipated attack from the opposition before the attack is launched.

Rear Admiral Roy Hoffman, who commanded a Swift boat during the Vietnam War, appears in an ad by Swift Boat Veterans for Truth. These ads, which attacked John Kerry's character and service in Vietnam and called into question his honor and truthfulness, had a major impact in the 2004 election.
(Photo courtesy: AFP Photo/HO)

THE TELEVISION ADVERTISING CAMPAIGN OF 1952

The initial, landmark year for political television was 1952. Television had become truly national, not just regional, and portions of the political parties' national conventions were telecast for the first time. With 45 percent of the nation's households owning television sets, the presidential campaign was forced to take notice. Republican presidential nominee Dwight D. Eisenhower's advisers were particularly intrigued with the device, seeing it as a way to counter Eisenhower's stumbling press conference performances and to make him appear more knowledgeable.

Eisenhower's advertising campaign was a glimpse of the future. The three primary themes of the commercials (corruption, high prices, and the Korean War) were chosen after consultation with pollster George Gallup. There was an extraordinarily large number of spots (forty-nine produced for television, twenty-nine for radio). Most spots were twenty seconds in length; the rest, sixty seconds. They played repeatedly in forty-nine selected counties in twelve non-southern states as well as in a few targeted southern states. The GOP's media strategy appeared to have been successful, and the Nielsen ratings showed that Eisenhower's telecasts consistently drew higher ratings than those of his Democratic opponent, Adlai Stevenson.

The commercials were simplistic and technically very primitive in comparison with modern fare. Eisenhower had a peculiarly stilted way of speaking while reading cue cards, and his delivery was amateurish, albeit sincere and appealing. If nothing else, the GOP commercials from 1952 reveal that the issues in U.S. politics never seem to change. Eisenhower's slogan, "It's Time for a Change," for example, is a perennial production.

By the best estimates, this first media blitz cost the Republicans close to $1.5 million. During that campaign, the Democrats spent only about $77,000 on television, and the new spots they produced played on New Deal themes and Republican responsibility for the Great Depression: "Sh-h-h-h. Don't mention it to a soul, don't spread it around…but the Republican party was in power back in 1932…13 million people were unemployed…bank doors shut in your face." The Democrats, who had wanted to run an ad blitz but could not raise the money to pay for it, turned instead to broadsides about the GOP's "soap campaign." Stevenson's supporters charged that the Republican ad managers conceived a multimillion-dollar production designed to sell a political party ticket to the American people in precisely the way they sell soap.

The poet Marya Mannes was moved to write "Sales Campaign" in reaction to the Eisenhower advertising effort. Her poem read, in part: "Philip Morris, Lucky Strike, Alka Seltzer, I Like Ike." For better or worse, the pattern was set for future campaigns.

broadside about her voting record on Social Security issues might air advertisements featuring senior citizens praising her support of Social Security.

There has been significant debate among political scientists about the impact of negative advertising on American electoral politics. Particularly prominent have been studies investigating the influence of negative advertising on voter turnout. In an important study, political scientists Stephen Ansolabehere and Shanto Iyengar concluded that negative advertising decreases voter turnout (especially among political independents), and worse yet, that political consultants use negative advertising precisely for such purposes.[5] However, this study by no means constitutes the last word on the subject. Indeed, several studies have cast doubt on the demobilizing effect of negative advertising. Steven Finkel and John Geer, for instance, find no demobilizing effects of negative ads, even among independent voters, and suggest that negative advertising might actually increase turnout by increasing knowledge and a sense of urgency about the campaign.[6] Similarly, Paul Freedman and Ken Goldstein also suggest a mobilizing effect of negative ads when they took into account viewing behavior and the total mix of positive, negative, and contrast ads actually broadcast, something that previous studies had omitted.[7] At this time, the weight of the evidence in the scholarly literature appears to be with those who, like Freedman and Goldstein, assert that negative political advertisements do not have a pronounced demobilizing effect on the electorate. Nevertheless, the question as to whether or not widespread negative advertisements are inherently harmful to democracy remains open to debate.

Politics Now

HIGH-TECH CAMPAIGNING: THE CHANGING NATURE OF RUNNING FOR OFFICE

The age of modern technology has brought many changes to the traditional campaign. Labor-intensive community activities have been replaced by carefully targeted messages disseminated through the mass media, and candidates today are able to reach voters more quickly than at any time in our nation's history. Consequently, the well-organized party machine is no longer essential to winning an election. The results of this technological transformation are candidate-centered campaigns in which candidates build well-financed, finely tuned organizations centered around their personal aspirations.

At the heart of the move toward today's candidate-centered campaigns is an entire generation of technological improvements. Contemporary campaigns have an impressive new array of weapons at their disposal: faster paper printing technologies, instantaneous Internet publishing and mass e-mail, fax machines and video technology, and enhanced telecommunications and teleconferencing. As a result, candidates can gather and disseminate information better than ever.

One outcome of these changes is the ability of candidates to employ "rapid-response" techniques: the formulation of prompt and informed responses to changing events on the campaign battlefield. In response to breaking news of a scandal or issue, for example, candidates (as well as journalists) can conduct background research, implement an opinion poll and tabulate the results, devise a containment strategy and appropriate "spin," and deliver a reply. This makes a strong contrast with the campaigns of the 1970s and early 1980s, which were dominated primarily by radio and TV advertisements, which took much longer to prepare and had little of the flexibility enjoyed by contemporary campaigners.

The first widespread use of the Internet in national campaigning came in 1996. Republican presidential candidate Bob Dole urged voters to log onto his Web site, and many did. According to one source, 26 percent of the public regularly logged onto the Internet to get campaign and election information.[a] In 1996, CNN's AllPolitics site reported an estimated 50 million hits on Election Night—a number that paled in comparison with the 2000 results when they were released. All the candidates for the 2000 presidential campaign maintained a Web site—and did so even when their candidacies were only in the exploratory stage, before their formal declarations. These sites have always presented platforms, offered easily accessible information on how to get involved in the campaign, and for the very enthusiastic Web-surfer, information on how to contribute money.

As bandwidth on the Internet continues to improve, real-time video clips enable Web users to view speeches, press conferences, state-of-the-nation addresses, and other typically "live" events at their own convenience, independent of the schedule of the original television coverage or rebroadcast. Campaign sites often offer the text of the speech as well as multiple video and audio versions of the real public event.

In the campaign of 2004, the Internet's prominence in campaign organizing and fundraising exceeded its use even just four years earlier. At MeetUp.com each presidential candidate's supporters were put in contact with other local activists. These groups—formed entirely through the Internet—"met up" in local restaurants and coffee shops throughout the country to engage in grassroots organizing. Candidate web sites provided supporters with materials to throw "House Parties" with their friends (and strangers finding the party posted on the campaign website) at which all guests would make a campaign contribution. Incentives to attend sometimes included a nationwide conference call from the candidate.

Whatever the real benefit of such an embarrassment of riches, the goal is to suggest a candidate's technological mastery, sophistication, and depth of resources. The new media appear to be serving the current paradigm of mass-media, candidate-centered campaigns, but it is possible that with time, they may reshape the campaign landscape. One possibility is that political parties might use new technologies to organize and manage massive voter bases, in an effort to return to an older mode of campaign that supports the party, rather than just one individual candidate. Another possible outcome is that with increasing ease of public access and the tendency of "underdog" messages to resonate on the Web, the number of candidates or parties might increase, while elections and voting become increasingly private, solitary events.

---

[a]*Public Perspective* (December/January 1997): 42.

THE CANDIDATE OR THE CAMPAIGN: WHICH DO WE VOTE FOR?

Much is said and written about media and organizational techniques during the campaign, and they are often presented as political magic. Despite their sophistication, however, the technologies often fail the candidates and their campaigns. The political consultants who develop and master the technologies of polling, media, and other

Vice Presidential candidate and former Senator John Edwards (D-NC) had appeared regularly on a number of national news shows before the 2004 election, which helped him raise his profile as a contender for the Democratic presidential nomination.

(Photo courtesy: Alex Wong/Getty Images)

techniques frequently make serious mistakes in judgment. Despite popular lore and journalistic legend, few candidates are the creations of their clever consultants and dazzling campaign techniques. Partly, this is because politics always has been (and always will be) much more art than science, not subject to precise manipulation or formulaic computation. Of course, campaign techniques can enhance the candidate's strengths and downplay his or her weaknesses, and in that respect, technique certainly matters. In the end—in most cases—the candidate wins or loses the race according to his or her abilities, qualifications, communication skills, issues, and weaknesses. Although this simple truth is warmly reassuring, it has been remarkably overlooked by election analysts and reporters seemingly mesmerized by the exorbitant claims of consultants and the flashy computer lights of their technologies.[8]

The voter deserves much of the credit for whatever encouragement we can draw from this candidate-centered view of politics. Granted, citizens are often inattentive to politics, almost forcing candidates to use empty slogans and glitz to attract their attention. But, it is also true that most voters want to take the real measure of candidates, and they retain a healthy skepticism about the techniques of running for office. Political cartoonist Tom Toles suggested as much when he depicted the seven preparatory steps the modern candidate takes: (1) Set out to discover what voters want; (2) conduct extensive polling; (3) study demographic trends; (4) engage in sophisticated interpretation of in-depth voter interviews; (5) analyze results; (6) discover that what the voters want is a candidate who doesn't need to do steps one through five; and, (7) pretend you didn't. The chastened politician then tells his assembled throng, "I follow my conscience."[9]

Not all political scientists believe that the campaign or even the candidate matters to a great degree, however. A strain of thought in political science contends that citizens vote for the president based on their evaluations of past, current, or prospective states of the economy. This is based on the early work of political scien-

"And, if elected, I will take the money out of politics and put it into a portfolio of high-yielding instruments."

(Photo courtesy: ©The New Yorker Collection 2000 Bernard Schoenbaum from Cartoonbank.com. All Rights Reserved.)

tist V. O. Key Jr., who posited, "voters are not fools"—they may not understand the details of economic policy, but they know its effects on them and vote accordingly.[10] Later, Morris Fiorina analyzed election results from 1964 to 1972 and found that voters chose candidates based on retrospective evaluations of changes in their economic welfare under the incumbent party. If it went up, they voted for the status quo. If it went down, they voted for a change in government.[11] To this end, much of the recent literature in political science proposes to be able to predict election outcomes based on measures of economic growth and incumbent popularity measured prior to the start of the campaign. Robert S. Erikson, for instance, asserts from his analysis of post–World War II election outcomes that the change in per capita income measured prior to the election is a better predictor of presidential election outcomes than the affect in the electorate for the Democratic or Republican Parties or their candidates.[12] Likewise, Steven Finkel finds that the overwhelming majority of individual vote decisions are accounted for by party identification and presidential approval measured before the start of the fall campaign. He argues that the campaigns do not make a difference in most individuals' vote choice or the outcome of most elections, except to remind people of their preexisting preferences and activate them to vote on those preconceived notions.[13]

During the election of 2004, many political scientists and journalists avoided making predictions based on theoretical or statistical modeling because of the uncertainty of the 2000 election. Despite strong indications, based on economic data and past experience, of a substantial Gore victory in 2000, the election proved to be extremely close. The uncertainty caused by the ongoing Iraq war and threat of international terrorism made the 2004 election very difficult to predict. For example, Bush won a close election despite the fact that no incumbent president had ever succeeded when he was tied with his electoral challenger on election eve. Campaigns do matter, often making predictive modeling or prior experience uncertain guides to electoral outcomes.

THE CAMPAIGN AND THE NEWS MEDIA

The news media present quite a challenge to candidates. Although politicians and their staffs cannot control the press, they nonetheless try to manipulate press coverage. They use three techniques to accomplish this aim. First, the staff often seeks to isolate the candidate from the press, thus reducing the chances that reporters will bait a candidate into saying something that might damage the candidate's cause. Naturally, the media are frustrated by such a tactic and insist on as many open press conferences as possible.

Second, the campaign stages media events—activities designed to include brief, clever quotes called *sound bytes* and staged with appealing backdrops so that they are all but irresistible, especially to television news. In this fashion, the candidate's staff can successfully fill the news hole reserved for campaign coverage on the evening news programs and in the morning papers, often by pounding in the same message over and over throughout the day.

Third, the handlers and consultants have cultivated the technique termed *spin*— that is, they put the most favorable possible interpretation for their candidate on any circumstance occurring in the campaign, and they work the press to sell their point of view or at least to ensure that it is included in the reporters' stories. The two 2004 presidential contenders offered a classic example of spin before and after their first debate. In 2000, George W. Bush was widely believed to have benefited from low expectations. Al Gore was expected to perform better in the debate, so Bush's exceeding the low expectations set for him added to the generally positive evaluation of his performance. The Bush and Kerry campaigns remembered this phenomenon, and attempted to paint their opponents as superior debaters going into the debate. Bush strategist Matthew Dowd called Kerry "the best debater since Cicero." The Kerry campaign countered that "Bush had never lost a debate." Each campaign tried to spin the press to call its opponent the superior debater, hoping that its candidate would come out as "exceeding expectations."

Simulation

You Are a Media
Consultant to
a Political Candidate

candidate debate
Forum in which political candidates face each other to discuss their platforms, records, and character.

Timeline

**Television
and
Presidential
Campaigns**

Candidate debates, especially the televised presidential variety, are also showcases for the consultants' spin patrol, and teams of staffers from each side swarm the press rooms to declare victory even before the candidates finish their closing statements.

Televised Debates.   Candidate debates are media extravaganzas that are a hybrid of free and paid media. As with ads, much of the candidate dialogue (jokes included) is canned and prepackaged. Spontaneity, however, cannot be completely eliminated, and gaffes, quips, and slips of the tongue can sometimes be revealing. President Gerald R. Ford's insistence during an October 1976 debate with Jimmy Carter that Poland was not under Soviet domination may have cost him a close election. Ronald Reagan's refrain, "Are you better off today than you were four years ago?" neatly summed up his case against Carter in 1980. Moreover, Reagan's easygoing performance reassured a skeptical public that wanted Carter out of the White House but was not certain it wanted Reagan in.

Senator John F. Kennedy's visually impressive showing in the first 1960 presidential debate dramatically reduced the edge that experience gave two-term Vice President Richard M. Nixon. Not only was Nixon ill at the time, but he also was poorly dressed and poorly made up for television. Interestingly, most of those who heard the debate on radio—and therefore could not see the contrast between the pale, anxious, sweating Nixon and the relaxed, tanned Kennedy—thought that Nixon had won.

The importance of debates can easily be overrated, however. A weak performance by Reagan in his first debate with Walter Mondale in 1984 had little lasting effect, in part because Reagan did better in the second debate. Most of the debates in 1960, 1976, 1980, and 1988 were unmemorable and electorally inconsequential. Debates usually just firm up voters' predispositions and cannot change the fundamentals of an election (the state of the economy, scandal, and presidential popularity, for example). This is what appeared to happen in 1992 and 1996, when none of the three presidential debates and one vice presidential debate changed the underlying pro-Clinton trends in the election. In 2000, Al Gore was universally expected to best George W. Bush, on the basis of his greater experience in both foreign and domestic policy. However, while in command of his facts, Gore was generally thought to have been aggressive and peevish, often sighing at Bush's responses. Bush, with a calm and earnest demeanor, managed to hold his own with Gore in all three debates. Polls afterward showed the public found Bush's more easygoing style preferable, but only narrowly. Bush benefited chiefly from his ability to exceed very low expectations, and proved he was not unqualified. Both campaigns took the debates extremely seriously in 2004. Television ratings were exceptionally high, with the

Presidential debates have come a long way—at least in terms of studio trappings—since the ill-at-ease Richard M. Nixon was visually bested by John F. Kennedy in the first televised debate. John Kerry's strong performance in the three presidential debates of 2004 helped him stay within striking distance of President Bush's lead going into the final weeks of the campaign.

(Photos courtesy: left, Bettmann/Corbis; right, Al Behrman/AP/Wide World Photos)

ANALYZING VISUALS

Playing for All the Marbles

Candidates for public office, whether for president of the United States or a local office, create photo opportunities, hoping that the press coverage of a staged event will promote their candidacy. In the Associated Press photograph below, George W. Bush is depicted shooting marbles with children during a visit to a Washington school as he campaigned for the presidency in 2000. What does the picture imply about George W. Bush and the policies that he would promote as president? What do you notice about the children shooting marbles with Bush? What caption would you write for the picture?

(Photo courtesy: Jackie Johnson/AP/Wide World Photos)

first debate being watched by 62.5 million viewers, the most since 1992. Senator Kerry, long considered a strong debater, was favored to win the debates. Bush was again subject to low expectations, and was thought to appear tired and unenthusiastic during the first debate. Kerry was generally considered by opinion polls to have an edge on Bush in each debate, and helped even public opinion in the final days of the campaign. However, despite Kerry's strong performance, none of the three debates proved to be decisive in helping Kerry win. Thus, while debates do not usually remake an election, they are potentially educational and focus the public's mind on the upcoming election.

Political scientists have recently found some effects resultant from presidential debates. John Geer, for instance, using panel-study poll data, finds that "a sizable minority of the public altered their preferences for president" after watching debates. In 1976, he found that 16 percent of viewers altered the intensity of their choice for president, and 10 percent switched candidate allegiance altogether, with the largest changes occurring among undecided voters and those weakly allied to a candidate.[14] Similarly, David Lanoue, in a study of the 1980 debates, finds significant shifts occurred in candidate preference among viewers with low levels of political knowledge.[15] The debates of 2004 reinforced and added to these studies, as polling during the three presidential debates showed Kerry's strong performance helped to lower Bush's favorability rating significantly, and placed the race on a very even footing all the way to election day. So, while debates do not appear to alter the results of elections, they do tend to increase knowledge about the candidates and their respective personalities and issue positions, especially among voters who have not previously paid attention to the campaign. Since they have been held in every presidential campaign since 1976, debates are now likely to be an expected and standard part of the presidential election process. They are also an established feature of campaigns for governor, U.S. senator, and many other offices.

Can the Press Be Handled?   Candidates and their consultants constantly try to spin (or influence) the thinking of the press. For example, campaigns today will often fax a dozen or more statements or releases a day to key journalists. Efforts by candidates to manipulate the news media often fail because the press is wise to their tactics and determined to thwart them. Not even the candidates' paid media are sacrosanct anymore. Major newspapers throughout the country have taken to analyzing the accuracy of the television advertisements aired during the campaign—a welcome and useful addition to journalists' scrutiny of politicians.

Less welcome are some other news media practices in campaigns. For example, the news media often regard political candidates with suspicion—looking for possible deception even when a candidate is simply trying to share his or her message with the public. This attitude makes it difficult for candidates to appear in a positive light or to have a genuine opportunity to explain their basic ideas via the news media without being on the defensive. Candidates have found ways to circumvent the news media by appearing on talk shows such as *The Oprah Winfrey Show* and *Larry King Live,* where they have an opportunity to present their views and answer questions in a less critical forum.

In addition, many studies have shown that the media are obsessed with the horse-race aspect of politics—who's ahead, who's behind, who's gaining—to the detriment of the substance of the candidates' issues and ideas. Public opinion polls, especially tracking polls, many of them taken by the news outlets themselves, dominate coverage, especially on network television, where only a few minutes a night are devoted to politics. (Tracking polls were discussed in chapter 11.)

Related to the proliferation of polls is the media's expectations game in presidential primary contests. With polls as the objective backdrop, journalists set the margins by which contenders are expected to win or lose—so much so that even a clear victory of 5 percentage points can be judged a setback if the candidate had been projected to win by 12 or 15 points. Additionally, research in political science shows that media coverage of the horse race in presidential primaries affects campaign contributions to candidates at this critical time. The tone of the media coverage—that a candidate is either gaining or losing support in polls—can affect, positively or negatively, the frequency with which citizens decide to give money and other types of support to a candidate.[16] Finally, the news media often overemphasize trivial parts of the campaign, such as a politician's minor gaffe, and give too much attention to the private lives of candidates. This superficial coverage and the resources needed to generate it are displacing serious journalism on the issues. These subjects are taken up again in the next chapter, which deals with the news media.

WEB EXPLORATION

To get an insider's look at the detail and urgency with which campaigns are now covered, go to www.ablongman.com/oconnor

CAMPAIGN FINANCE

Campaign finance reform has been a major source of discussion among politicians and pundits in recent years. For the past thirty years, campaign finance has been governed by the provisions of the Federal Election Campaign Act (FECA). The most recent bout of reforms were set in motion by the Senator John McCain, who ran for the 2000 Republican presidential nomination on a platform to take elections out of the hands of the wealthy. McCain lost to Bush, who ironically used soft money in the primaries to defeat McCain; however, McCain's credibility on the issue skyrocketed. Once corporate soft money donors at Enron, WorldCom, and Global Crossing (to name a few) became embroiled in accounting scandals and alleged criminal behavior, the possibility of corruption became too strong for Congress to ignore. Senators John McCain (R-AZ) and Russ Feingold (D-WI) co-sponsored the Bipartisan Campaign Reform Act of 2002 (BCRA) in the Senate, while Representatives Chris Shays (R-CT) and Martin Meehan (D-MA) sponsored the House version. On Valentine's Day, the bills passed, and, in March of 2002, President George W. Bush signed BCRA into law, which has altered the campaign finance landscape in ways we perhaps have yet to discover.

Included within BCRA was a "fast track" provision that any suits challenging the constitutionality of the reforms would be immediately placed before a U. S. District Court and giving appellate powers to the U.S. Supreme Court. The reason for this provision was simple, to thwart the numerous lobbying groups and several high profile elected officials who threatened to tie up BCRA in the courts for as long as they could until they could find a judge who could kill it. No sooner did Bush sign BCRA than U.S. Senator Mitch McConnell (R-KY) and the National Rifle Association separately filed lawsuits claiming that BCRA violated free speech rights, specifically by equated financial contributions with symbolic political speech.

In May 2003, a three-judge panel of the U.S. District Court in the District of Columbia found that the BCRA restrictions on soft money donations violated free speech rights, although the BCRA restrictions on political advertising did not. The decision was immediately appealed to the Supreme Court, which stayed the district court's decision. After oral arguments in September, the Court handed down its 5-4 decision, *McConnell* v. *FEC*, in December, concluding that the government's interest in preventing political party corruption overrides the free speech rights to which the parties would otherwise be entitled. In other words, the Supreme Court very narrowly upheld the BCRA measures restricting speech both in the form of political contributions and in political advertising. There are some serious questions about whether the Court has really solved the problem of campaign finance reform, since the attempt to avoid the corruption that so often plagues a democracy necessarily means limiting the political speech necessary to sustain democracy. For now, we will investigate the compromise over campaign finance laws that the federal government has most recently struck.

Sources of Political Contributions

To run all aspects of a campaign successfully requires a great deal of money. In 2004 alone, the Center for Responsive Politics estimates that more than $3.9 billion dollars was spent on the Presidential and congressional elections, a 30 percent increase on the $3 billion spent in 2000. The congressional elections account for $2.7 billion, with the majority going to incumbents. As of the last filing before the election, Democrat incumbents in the House spent an average of nearly $918,879. Republican incumbents in the House spent an average of $1,086,616. Their challengers, in contrast, spent an average of $299,328. As humorist Will Rogers once remarked, "Politics has got so expensive that it takes lots of money even to get beat with."

Political money is regulated by the federal government under the terms of the Federal Election Campaign Act (FECA) of 1971, first passed in 1971 and substantially strengthened by amendments several times during the 1970s. Table 14.1 summarizes some of the important provisions of this law, which limits the amounts that individuals, interest groups, and political parties can give to candidates for president, U.S. senator, and U.S. representative. The goal of all limits is the same: to prevent any single group or individual from gaining too much influence over elected officials, who naturally feel indebted to campaign contributors (see Figure 14.4).

Given the cash flow required by a campaign and the legal restrictions on political money, raising the funds necessary to run a modern campaign is a monumental task. Consequently, presidential and congressional campaigns have squads of fund-raisers on staff. These professionals rely on several standard sources of campaign money.

Individual Contributions.   Individual contributions are donations from individual citizens. Citizens typically donate because they like the candidate or party or a particular stand on issues they care about, or to feel involved in the political process, or

TABLE 14.1   Contribution Limits for Congressional Candidates Before and After Bipartisan Campaign Reform Act, 2002

Contributions from	Given to Candidate (per election)[a]	Given to National Party (per calendar year)	Total Allowable Contributions (per calendar year)
	Before/After	Before/After	Before/After
Individual	$1,000/$2,000	$20,000/$25,000	$25,000/$95,000 per two-year cycle
Political action committee[b]	$5,000/$5,000	$15,000/$15,000	No limit/No Limit
Any political party committee[c]	$5,000/$10,000	No limit/No limit	No limit/No limit
All national and state party committees taken together	To House candidates: $30,000 plus "coordinated expenditures"[d] To Senate candidates: $27,500 plus "coordinated expenditures"[d]		

Note: The regulations under the Bipartisan Campaign Reform Act did not take effect until *after* the 2002 election.

[a]Each of the following is considered a separate election: primary (or convention), runoff, general election.

[b]Multi-candidate PACs only. Multi-candidate committees have received contributions from at least fifty persons and have given to at least five federal candidates.

[c]Multi-candidate party committees only. Multi-candidate committees have received contributions from at least fifty persons and have given to at least five federal candidates.

[d]Coordinated expenditures are party-paid general election campaign expenditures made in consultation and coordination with the candidate under the provisions of section 441(a)(d) of the Federal Code.

political action committee (PAC)
Federally mandated, officially registered fund-raising committee that represents interest groups in the political process.

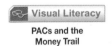

Visual Literacy

PACs and the
Money Trail

because they want access to the candidate. The maximum allowable contribution under federal law for congressional and presidential elections is $2,000 per election to each candidate, with primary and general elections considered separately. Individuals are also limited to a total of $47,500 in gifts to all candidates combined in each calendar year. Most candidates receive a majority of all funds directly from individuals, and most individual gifts are well below the maximum level. Finally, individuals who spend over $10,000 to air "electioneering communication", that is, "any broadcast, cable, or satellite communication which refers to a clearly identified candidate for Federal office" that airs within sixty days of a general election or thirty days of a primary election, is now subject to a strict disclosure laws. The rationale behind the last regulation is that spending any more on an ad favoring a candidate is effectively the same as a contribution to the candidate's campaign and requires the same scrutiny as other large donations do.

Political Action Committee (PAC) Contributions.   When interest groups such as labor unions, corporations, trade unions, and ideological issue groups seek to make donations to campaigns, they must do so by establishing **political action committees (PACs)**. PACs are officially recognized fundraising organizations that are allowed by federal law to participate in federal elections (Some states have similar requirements for state elections). Approximately 4,000 PACs are registered with the Federal Election Commission—the governmental agency charged with administering the election laws. In 2004, PACs contributed $266 million to Senate and House candidates, while individuals donated $657 million. On average, PAC contributions account for 36 percent of the war chests (campaign funds) of House candidates and 18 percent of the treasuries of Senate candidates. Incumbents benefit the most from PAC money; incumbents received $233 million, much more than the $33 million given to challengers and open-seat candidates in the 2004 election cycle. By making these contributions, PACs hope to secure entree to the candidate after he or she has been elected in order to influence them on issues important to the PAC, since a candidate might reciprocate campaign donations with loyalty to the cause. Therefore, PACs give primarily to incumbents because incumbents tend to win.

Because donations from a small number of PACs make up such a large proportion of campaign war chests, PACs have influence disproportionate to that of individuals. Studies, in fact, have shown that PACs effectively use contributions to punish legislators and affect policy, at least in the short run.[18] Legislators who vote contrary to the wishes of a PAC see their donations withheld, but those who are successful in legislating in the PAC's wishes are rewarded with even greater donations.[19] (Interest groups are treated in more detail in chapter 16.)

In an attempt to control PACs, BCRA has a limit on the way PACs attempt to influence campaigns. The law strictly forbids PACs from using corporate or union funds for the electioneering communications discussed earlier. PACs can only use corporate or labor contributions for administrative costs. The purpose of the limit is to prevent corporations or unions from having an undue influence on the outcome of elections, as they have in the past, by heavily advertising towards specific audiences the weeks leading up to elections.

Political Party Contributions.   Candidates also receive donations from the national and state committees of the Democratic and Republican Parties. As mentioned in chapter 12, political parties can give substantial contributions to their congressional nominees. In 2004, the national committees of the two major parties spent over $875 million dollars to support their candidates. In competitive races, the parties may provide 15 percent to 17 percent of their candidates' total war chests. In addition to helping elect party members, campaign contributions from political parties have another, less obvious benefit: helping to ensure party discipline in voting. One study of congressional voting behavior in the 1980s, for instance, found that those members who received a large percentage of their total campaign funds from their party voted with their party more often than they were expected to.[20]

Some nations favor contributions to the party over contributions to individual campaigns. Parliamentary forms of government are much less candidate oriented and much more party oriented; therefore, the political monies raised flow to the *party coffers*. For example, in Great Britain, rather than receiving direct contributions, candidates for prime minister obtain campaign funds through party donations.

Member-to-Candidate Contributions.   In Congress and in state legislatures, well-funded, electorally secure incumbents now often contribute campaign money to their party's needy incumbent and nonincumbent legislative candidates.[21] This activity began in some state legislatures (notably California), but it is now well-established at the congressional level.[22] Generally, members contribute to other candidates in one of two ways. First, some members have established their own PACs-informally dubbed "leadership" PACs—through which they distribute campaign support to candidates. For example, as of the last reporting before the 2004 election, a PAC established by House Majority Leader Tom DeLay (R-TX), allowed him to contribute to 221 House and 19 Senate incumbents. In total, his PAC spent over $3 million dollars to help retain the House and Senate. Second, individual members can give up to $2,000 per candidate per election and $10,000 per candidate for each cycle: $5,000 for the primary election and $5,000 for the general election from a leadership PAC.

These contributions from members, whether individually or via a PAC, can add up. Republican Larry Diedrich, who was challenging newly-elected Democrat

TABLE 14.2   Amount Spent on Presidential Elections (in Millions), 1980–2004

Year	Primary Receipts	General Election Public Funding	Convention Public Funding	Total
2004	$701.5	$149.2	$29.8	$880.5
2000	$351.7	$147.7	$29.5	$528.9
1996	$248.3	$152.7	$24.7	$425.7
1992	$198.5	$110.5	$22.1	$331.1
1988	$213.8	$92.2	$18.4	$324.4
1984	$105.0	$80.8	$16.2	$202.0
1980	$94.2	$58.9	$8.8	$161.9

Source: The Center for Responsive Politics, www.opensecrets.org. The data for 2004 is through August 20, 2004.

Stephanie Herseth for South Dakota's sole seat in the House of Representatives, received large donations from numerous leadership PACs, including the PACs of Ralph Regula (R-OH), Rob Portman (R-OH), Tom DeLay (R-TX), Jim McCrery (R-LA), Jerry Lewis (R-CA), and Speaker Dennis Hastert (R-IL). In fact, 17 of Diedrich's 27 top contributors in 2004 were leadership PACs. In general, members give their contributions to the same candidates who receive the bulk of congressional campaign committee resources. Thus, member contributions at the congressional level have emerged as a major supplement to the campaign resources contributed by the party campaign committees.[23]

Candidates' Personal Contributions.

Candidates and their families may donate to the campaign. The Supreme Court ruled in 1976 in *Buckley* v. *Valeo* that no limit could be placed on the amount of money candidates can spend from their own families' resources, since such spending is considered a First Amendment right of free speech.[24] For wealthy politicians, this allowance may mean personal spending in the millions. John Corzine (D-NJ) spent over $60 million of his vast personal fortune in 2000 to capture a U.S. Senate seat. In 2004, twenty-one candidates for House or Senate seats spent over $1 million of their own money to finance their campaigns; only one of the candidates, Michael McCaul (R-TX), was victorious. The biggest spender by far was Blair Hull (D-IL), who invested $28.7 million into his losing efforts in the primary against Barrack Obama. While self-financed candidates often garner a great deal of attention, most candidates commit much less than $100,000 in family resources to their election bids.

public funds
Donations from the general tax revenues to the campaigns of qualifying presidential candidates.

matching funds
Donations to presidential campaigns from the federal government that are determined by the amount of private funds a qualifying candidate raises.

Public Funds.

Public funds are donations from general tax revenues. Only presidential candidates (and a handful of state and local contenders) receive public funds. Under the terms of the FECA (which first established public funding of presidential campaigns), a candidate for president can become eligible to receive public funds during the nominating contest by raising at least $5,000 in individual contributions of $250 or less in each of twenty states. The candidate can apply for federal **matching funds**, whereby every dollar raised from individuals in amounts less than $251 is matched by the federal treasury on a dollar-for-dollar basis. Of course, this assumes there is enough money in the Presidential Election Campaign Fund to do so. The fund is accumulated by taxpayers who designate $3 of their taxes for this purpose each year when they send in their federal tax returns. (Only about 20 percent of taxpayers check off the appropriate box, even though participation does not increase their tax burden.) During the 2004 Democratic primaries, John Kerry and Howard Dean, like George W. Bush in 2000, opted out of the federal matching funds, allowing them to raise considerably more money than the government would have provided.

For the general election, the two major-party presidential nominees can accept a $75 million lump-sum payment from the federal government after the candidate accepts his or her nomination. If the candidate accepts the money, it becomes the sole source for financing the campaign. A candidate could refuse the money and be free from the spending cap the government attaches to it. John Kerry considered doing just that in order to help finance general election campaign operations. Because the Democratic convention, during which Kerry accepted his nomination, occurred five weeks before the Republican convention, Kerry actually had five weeks more than Bush during which he had to stretch out the $75 million the government provided. Kerry first considered not accepting his party's nomination until after the Republican convention, a possibility that proved unpopular.[25] A third-party candidate receives a smaller amount proportionate to his or her November vote total if that candidate gains a minimum of 5 percent of the vote. Note that in such a case, the money goes to third-party campaigns only *after* the election is over; no money is given in advance of the general election. Only two third party candidates have qualified for public campaign funding, John B. Anderson in 1980, gaining 7 percent of the of the vote, and colorful Texan billionaire Ross Perot in 1992, gaining 19 percent of the vote.

FIGURE 14.1   Expenditures by PACs in 2004 Election Cycle
Notice how PACs use a majority of their expenditures to support congressional candidates. Of independent expenditures by PACs, a majority of the money is spent positively to support candidates and only a small fraction to attack opponents in presidential campaigns. Notice how PAC spending has a slight bias toward Republican candidates and a strong bias toward incumbents.

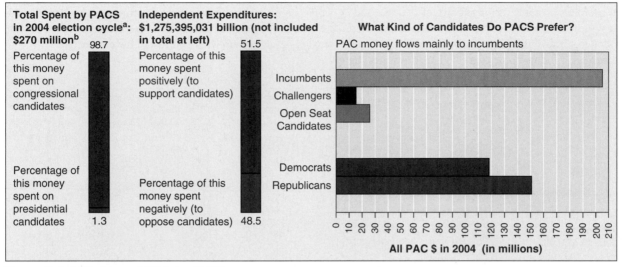

[a]The amount is the total from January 1, 2003 to June 30, 2004.
[b]Total amount spent by PACs does not include $21 million in independent expenditures.
Source: Federal Election Commission.

Independent Expenditures.

Because of two Supreme Court decisions,[26] individuals, PACs, and now political parties may spend unlimited amounts of money directly advocating the election or defeat of a candidate as long as these expenditures are not made in coordination with the candidate's campaign. For example, in the summer of 2004, the Swift Boat Veterans for Truth, a 527 supporting Bush, created television advertisements questioning Kerry's Vietnam service. However, because independent expenditure advertisements expressly advocate the election or defeat of a specific federal candidate, they must be paid for with **hard money**—that is, with money raised under the FECA guidelines.).

hard money
Legally specified and limited contributions that are clearly regulated by the Federal Election Campaign Act and by the Federal Election Commission.

The Internet

The Internet, like campaign finance reform, has the potential to alter radically the way candidates raise funds for their campaigns. After all, making an online appeal for campaign contributions costs significantly less than raising funds through expensive direct-mail campaigns or pricey fund-raising events—the standard means of attaining campaign resources. Nevertheless, the potential weaknesses of Internet fund-raising are unlikely to stop candidates from experimenting with it. Former Republican presidential candidate John McCain became the first political candidate to raise over $1 million online in forty-eight hours after his victory in the New Hampshire primary in 2000. The Internet converted McCain's momentum into money and volunteers virtually overnight. McCain eventually took in over $5 million online—nearly 25 percent of his total contributions.

The Internet also promises to create headaches for the Federal Election Commission. The FEC had to rule on issues such as whether a business site link to a campaign site constitutes in-kind contribution from the business to the campaign, and whether funds raised online by presidential candidates are eligible to be matched with public funds from the Presidential Election Campaign Fund. (In the first case, the FEC ruled yes; in the second case, it ruled no.) Clearly, these issues are only the beginning of a seemingly limitless plethora of concerns regarding the Internet and campaign finance which the FEC will be asked to address. Campaign finance experts question whether

ANALYZING VISUALS

Campaign for the Senate, 2004

Take a few moments to study the breakdown of a sample budget for a typical senate campaign, shown below, and then answer the following critical thinking questions: Where does the majority of campaign funding come from? What constitutes the single largest expense for the typical campaign? About what proportion of campaign funds come from PACs? Is this proportion smaller or larger than what you would have expected?

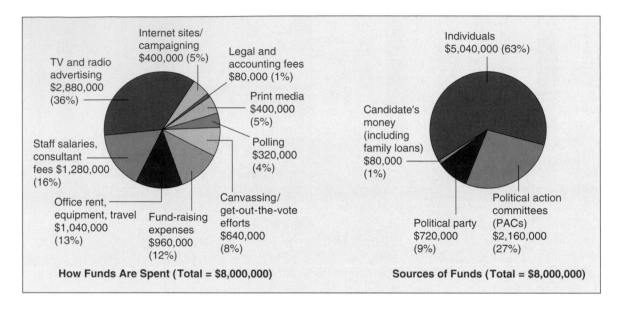

How Funds Are Spent (Total = $8,000,000)

- Internet sites/campaigning $400,000 (5%)
- Legal and accounting fees $80,000 (1%)
- TV and radio advertising $2,880,000 (36%)
- Print media $400,000 (5%)
- Polling $320,000 (4%)
- Staff salaries, consultant fees $1,280,000 (16%)
- Canvassing/get-out-the-vote efforts $640,000 (8%)
- Office rent, equipment, travel $1,040,000 (13%)
- Fund-raising expenses $960,000 (12%)

Sources of Funds (Total = $8,000,000)

- Individuals $5,040,000 (63%)
- Candidate's money (including family loans) $80,000 (1%)
- Political action committees (PACs) $2,160,000 (27%)
- Political party $720,000 (9%)

the agency has the resources to regulate and monitor the newly unfolding campaign activity on the Internet.[27]

Soft Money and Issue Advocacy Advertisements.

soft money
The virtually unregulated money funneled by individuals and political committees through state and local parties.

Soft money is campaign money raised and spent by political parties for expenses—such as overhead and administrative costs—and for grassroots activities such as political education and GOTV efforts. In a 1978 advisory opinion, the Federal Election Commission ruled that political parties could raise these funds without regulation. Then, in 1979, Congress passed an amendment allowing parties to *spend* unlimited sums on these same activities.[28] In the years immediately following the rule changes, the national parties began raising five- and six-figure sums from individuals and interest groups to pay for expenses such as rent, employee salaries, and building maintenance. The national parties also began transferring large sums of soft money to state parties in order to help pay for grassroots activities (such as get-out-the-vote drives) and campaign paraphernalia (such as yard signs and bumper stickers).

However, the line separating expenditures that influence federal elections from those that do not proved to be quite blurry, and this blurriness resulted in a significant campaign finance loophole. The largest controversy came in the area of campaign advertisements. The federal courts have ruled that only campaign advertisements that use explicit words—for example, "vote for," "vote against," "elect," or "support"—qualify as *express advocacy* advertisements. Political advertisements that do not use these words were considered *issue advocacy* advertisements.[29] The distinction here is crucial. Because express advocacy advertisements were openly intended to influence federal elections, they could only be paid for with strictly regulated hard money. Issue advocacy advertisements, on the other hand, were paid for with unregulated soft money. The parties' response to these rules was to create issue advocacy advertisements that very much resemble express advocacy ads, for such advertisements call attention to the voting record of the candidate supported or opposed and are replete with images of the candidate. However, the parties ensured that the magic words "vote for" or "vote against" were never uttered in the advertisements, allowing them to be paid for with soft rather than hard money.

Soft money donations are now prohibited under BCRA, and third-party issue ads, if coordinated with a federal candidate's campaign, can now be considered campaign contributions, thus regulated by the FEC. The last election cycle for the parties to use soft money was 2001-2002, and the amount raised, nearly $430 million for Republican and Democrats combined,[30] highlights why the reform seemed necessary. Republicans raised $219 million in soft money from pharmaceutical, insurance, and energy companies. Democrats came in just under $211 million in soft money from unions and law firms. With soft money banned, wealthy donors and interest groups now lack the privileged and potentially corrupting influence on parties and candidates. Like every other citizen, they must donate within the hard money limits placed on individuals and PACs. With BCRA in place and supported by the courts in *McConnell* v. *FEC*, the reforms appear to be working. A preliminary study of the effects of BCRA on the 2004 Democratic primaries revealed that hard money donations have increased and are increasingly used for grassroots efforts.[31] However, reforms usually necessitate more reform, since the correction of one problem usually creates a new one.

Are PACs Good or Bad for the Process?

Of all the forms of campaign spending, probably the most controversial is that involving PAC money. Some observers claim that PACs are the embodiment of corrupt special interests that use campaign donations to buy the votes of legislators. Furthermore, they argue that the less affluent and minority members of our society do not enjoy equal access to these political organizations.

These charges are serious and deserve consideration. Although the media relentlessly stress the role of money in determining policy outcomes, the evidence that PACs buy votes is less than overwhelming.[32] Political scientists have conducted many studies to determine the impact of interest group PAC contributions on legislative voting, and the conclusions reached by these studies have varied widely.[33] Whereas some studies have found that PAC money affects legislators' voting behavior, other studies have uncovered no such correlation. It may be, of course, that interest group PAC money has an impact at earlier stages of the legislative process. One innovative study found that PAC money had a significant effect on legislators' participation in congressional committees on legislation important to the contributing group.[34] Thus, interest group PAC money may mobilize something more important than votes—the valuable time and energy of members.

Also serious is the charge that some interests are significantly better represented by the PAC system than are others. This view was put forth by a political scientist, who argues that laws regulating PAC activity inherently favor PACs with parent organizations—corporate, labor, and trade PACs—over citizen-based PACs without parent organizations.[35] Thus, he argues that any campaign finance reform should raise substantially the limits on the amount of money an individual may contribute to a PAC— to the point where a single person could underwrite a citizen group's formation and maintenance costs.

Although a good number of PACs of all persuasions existed prior to the 1970s, it was during the 1970's—the decade of campaign reform—that the modern PAC era began. Spawned by the Watergate-inspired revisions of the campaign finance laws, PACs grew in number from 113 in 1972 to 4,268 by the late 1980s (see Figure 14.2), and their contributions to congressional candidates multiplied almost thirty-fold, from $8.5 million in 1971 and 1972 to $258 million in 2002 (see Figure 14.3). But, these

FIGURE 14.2   PACS

Created in the early 1970s, PACs allowed individuals to collect money and contribute to political campaigns. PACs saw explosive growth in the 1980s, but their numbers have declined in recent years, although their ability to raise money has increased.

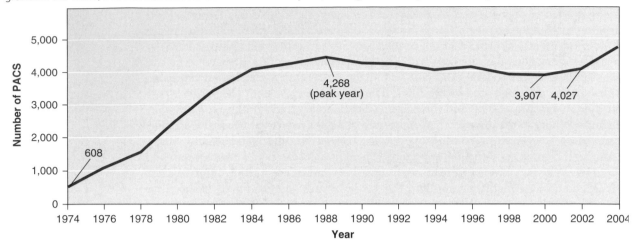

Note: Numbers are as of December 31 of every other year, starting in 1972. 2004 numbers through July 1, 2002.
Source: Federal Election Commission.

numbers should not obscure a basic truth about the PAC system: that a very small group of PACs conducts the bulk of total PAC activity. Indeed, as political scientist Paul Herrnson observes, a mere 6 percent of all PACs contributed a full 62 percent of the total dollars given to congressional candidates by PACs during the 2001-2002 election cycle.

Some people argue that PACs are newfangled inventions that have flooded the political system with money. Although the widespread use of the PAC structure is new, special-interest money of all types has always found its way into politics. Before the 1970s, it did so in less traceable and much more disturbing and unsavory ways, because little of the money given to candidates was regularly disclosed to public inspection. Although it is true that PACs contribute a massive sum to candidates in absolute terms, it is not clear that there is proportionately more interest group money in the system than earlier. The proportion of House and Senate campaign funds provided by PACs has certainly increased since the early 1970s, but individuals, most of whom are unaffiliated with PACs, together with the political parties still supply more than 60 percent of all the money spent by or on behalf of House candidates, 75 percent of the campaign expenditures for Senate contenders, and 85 percent of the campaign expenditures for presidential candidates. So, while the importance of PAC spending has grown, PACs clearly remain secondary as a source of election funding and therefore pose no overwhelming threat to the system's legitimacy.

The election outlays of PACs, like the total amount expended in a single election season, seem huge. However, the cost of elections in the United States is less than or approximately the same as elections in some other nations, measured on a per-voter basis.[36] Moreover, the cost of all elections in the United States taken together is less than the amount many individual private corporations spend on advertising their cereals, dog food, cars, and toothpaste. These days, it is expensive to communicate, whether the message is political or commercial. The costs of television time, polling, consultants, and other items have soared over and above the inflation rate.

Future Campaign Finance Reform

Despite the overblown promises of campaign finance nirvana by some of those pushing the McCain-Feingold Bipartisan Campaign Reform Act, many problems remain in this complicated area of politics and constitutional law. For example, the McCain-Feingold law banned donations of "soft money" to the political parties (as explained

FIGURE 14.3 Growth in Total Contributions by PACs to House and Senate Candidates

The growth of campaign spending by PACs has roughly paralleled the increasing number of PACs over their thirty-year history.

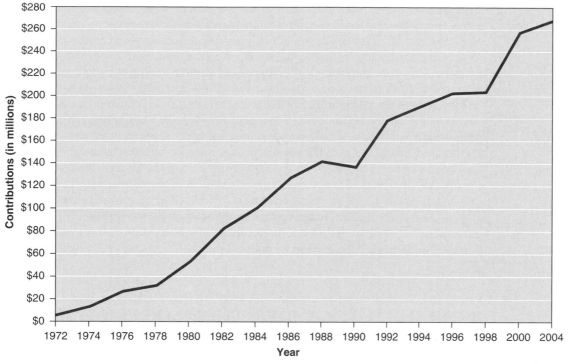

Note: Contributions are for two-year election cycles ending in years shown. The 2004 numbers are only through November 2, 2004.
Source: http://www.opensecrets.org/overview/stats.asp?Cycle=2004

earlier). Did that money disappear? Of course not! Much of it has shown up in new "527 political committees"—the number 527 coming from the provision of the Internal Revenue tax code that gives life to these committees.

The 527s exist on all sides of the political fence, though the Democrats were the first to aggressively pursue them in 2004. Two of the largest Democratic committees are the Media Fund and Americans Coming Together (ACT), both run by allies of presidential nominee John Kerry and raising millions of dollars from people who desired to see President Bush defeated, such as billionaire George Soros. These committees bought TV, radio, and print advertising to sell their message, focusing on the battleground or

Participation

The Debate over
Campaign
Finance Reform

Senators John McCain (R–AZ) and Russ Feingold (D–WI) co-authored the Bipartisan Campaign Reform Act of 2002, legislation which bans unregulated soft money contributions. The crusade to reform the campaign finance system was aided significantly by McCain's 2000 presidential candidacy.

(Photo courtesy: AP/World Wide Photos)

"swing" states that were not firmly in the Bush or Kerry camps. Ohio is an excellent example, and in that state, not only did the groups air thousands of media ads, but they also helped organize many thousands of volunteers who went door-to-door, recruiting voters and volunteers for Democratic campaigns. Even though most political observers predicted that President Bush would easily outspend Senator Kerry in the presidential contest, the Democratic 527s helped Senator Kerry catch up and level the playing field against Bush's campaign war chest. Fundraising records in almost every category were shattered in 2004, so the campaign reform law clearly had no effect on overall spending.

It is easy to see that reformers will once again attempt to reform their reforms. The next target may well be the 527s. Their abolition is highly unlikely—and the money supporting them would simply reappear in some other form—but there is a need for greater transparency. The 527s have far less required disclosure than other forms of finance committees, and that does cry out for a legislative fix. Overall, however, the lesson of McCain-Feingold is obvious. No amount of clever legislating will rid the American system of campaign money. Interested individuals and groups will always give lots of cash. The challenge is to find a way to get that cash disclosed in a timely fashion for the press and the public. As always, disclosure and its sunshine is the ultimate check on potential misbehavior in the realm of political money.

BRINGING IT TOGETHER: THE 2004 PRESIDENTIAL CAMPAIGN AND ELECTIONS

The 2004 election for president may go down in history for how extremely it divided the nation. An entire month before the election, polls showed that only 3 percent of Americans remained undecided on a candidate. Despite his status as an incumbent,

FIGURE 14.4   How the Campaign Finance Bill Alters Money Flow

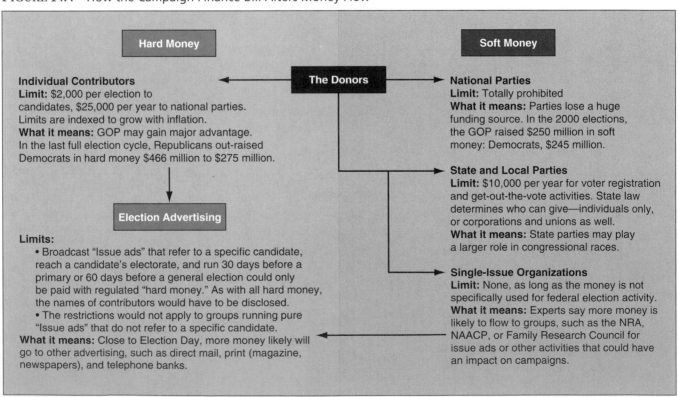

Source: Adapted from *CQ Weekly* (March 23, 2002): 800.

implementation of tax cuts, and reputation for decisiveness, President George W. Bush faced an incredibly heated race again Massachusetts Senator John Kerry. At the most basic level Americans knew that John Kerry had the knowledge and experience to serve in the highest office in the nation. Many were also unhappy with the situation in Iraq, job losses, and healthcare costs. However, Americans were casting their first presidential vote in the post–9-11 world, and had reservations about electing a president whose leadership during a national security crisis had not yet been proven.

The Party Nomination Battle

Although few remember, the Republican Party *did* hold presidential primaries in 2004. Few noticed, as is usually the case when there is an incumbent candidate, because there was no significant opposition within the party to George W. Bush's reelection. Any speculation that Senator John McCain, Bush's 2004 primary rival, might challenge the President again in 2004 was silenced by a Bush campaign ad released in May featuring the Arizona Senator praising the President's leadership. Without any significant Republican activity, the Democrats were the focus of media attention for the entire primary season.

The Democrats, meanwhile, would have ten candidates competing for their party's nomination. Although some assumed that Al Gore would make a second attempt at winning the White House, the former Vice President announced in December 2002 that he had no intentions to do so. The media were also fixated on the prospect of a run by Senator Hillary Rodham-Clinton (NY), but her insistence to the contrary left the field wide open for four Democratic Party veterans: Representative Dick Gephardt (MO), Senator and 2000 vice presidential nominee Joseph Lieberman (CT), Senator Bob Graham (FL), and Senator John Kerry (MA).

The five other "original" candidates *appeared* marginal. Senator John Edwards (NC) threw his hat into the ring before even completing his first term in the Senate. Former Illinois Senator Carol Moseley-Braun, the first African American woman in the Senate, had been absent from the national political stage for several years. Former Governor Howard Dean came from the small state of Vermont and had done little during his term as governor to attract national attention. Representative Dennis Kucinich (OH) was also rather obscure, held extreme political beliefs, and appeared to be running more to get across an ideological message than in hopes of winning in November 2004. Similarly, the Reverend Al Sharpton, an African American activist from New York, appeared primarily interested in gaining national fame rather than winning over primary voters. Retired General Wesley Clark entered late in the race after some Democrats ran a "Draft Clark" effort. Despite an inconsistent partisan past (Clark voted for Nixon, Reagan, and George H.W. Bush, and spoke at a Republican Committee dinner in 2001), supporters believed his military credentials would render him the best candidate to compete in the fall of 2004.

The Democratic candidates spent the spring and summer of 2003 in the typical primary season fashion: fund-raising, debating, giving speeches, and concentrating on the key states of Iowa and New Hampshire. By the fall, Senator Graham had dropped out of the race, citing fund-raising problems. The fall also brought the rise of the once "fringe" candidate Howard Dean. His solid stance against the Iraq War and harsh criticism of President Bush appealed to Democratic partisans, providing him with impressive grassroots support and a large war chest. Although in the spring of 2003 Democratic insiders were predicting John Kerry would emerge as the front-runner, the fall brought Howard Dean the endorsements of party leaders such as Iowa Senator Tom Harkin and former Vice President Al Gore.

Initially the Democrats' campaigns were focused on contrasting themselves with President Bush. However, as Dean emerged as the apparent front-runner, his rivals began aiming many of their attacks in his direction rather than at the President. The former Governor's third place finish in the Iowa caucuses, behind both John Kerry and John Edwards, may be partially attributed to these attacks. Others blame the campaign's mismanagement of Dean's resources—not spending enough on ads and appearances and overspending on other items, for the Iowa upset. Perhaps most fatal to Dean's translating partisan excitement into caucus and primary victories was his reputation as having a short temper. During a rally after his Iowa defeat, Dean tried to encourage his campaign staff by giving a bombastic speech giving a litany of states he would win. This speech ended with a notorious yelp known by some as "the scream heard round the world." For the many already concerned that Dean's temper could be a liability in the general election season, this yelp confirmed their fears and symbolized the downfall of the Dean candidacy. He would win only one primary, in Vermont, and dropped out of the race by February.

After Iowa, the race centered on Kerry and Edwards. Gephardt and Lieberman's appeal proved narrow, the former dropping out after Iowa and the latter after losing in Arizona. Moseley-Braun, Sharpton, and Kucinich's poll numbers never reached double digits. Even John Edwards never seemed to have had much of a chance. His strategy had been to dominate southern primaries, demonstrating to the Party that he could be a national candidate because his appeal extended into the GOP's regional stronghold. However, with the exception of a victory in his home state of South Carolina, Kerry defeated Edwards handily in other southern states. Edwards dropped out of the race in March, leaving Senator John Kerry of Massachusetts as the "presumptive" Democratic candidate. Democrats appeared united, at least in their determination to defeat George Bush in the general election. For this reason, many suggest, they chose a candidate quickly and channeled their energies towards winning in the fall.

WEB EXPLORATION

To get involved and find out what you can do about campaign reform, go to www.ablongman.com/oconnor

The Third Force

The impact of third parties on the 2004 presidential election was insignificant as compared to 2000. In 2000 Green Party candidate Ralph Nader gathered 3 percent of the national vote, which was 2 percent short of the vote needed to receive federal funding for the next election season. Still, he played the spoiler in key states, including Florida and New Hampshire. Nader received over 97,000 votes in Florida in 2000, far more than the 537 Gore needed to carry the state and the election.

Consumer activist Ralph Nader sought the presidency again in 2004, although this time he was not the Green Party nominee. The Green Party would not decide whether or under which conditions they would run a presidential candidate until June, and Nader felt that he could not wait that long to begin the process of getting on each state's ballot. The Green Party nominated its own General Counsel, David Cobb, for president, while Nader ran as an Independent and received the endorsement of the Reform Party (made famous in 1992 by the presidential candidacy of Ross Perot). Despite his efforts, by October Nader was only officially on the ballot in 34 states and the District of Columbia, 9 fewer than he was on in 2000.

Members of the two major parties were not quick to forget Nader's impact on the 2000 presidential election, resulting in highly controversial campaign tactics. There were reported instances of Republicans donating to his campaign and assisting in his efforts to get on ballot, with the goal of reducing the vote count for John Kerry. Similarly, there were accusations of obstruction on the part of Democrats, who would most likely benefit from Nader's absence from the ballot.

The 2004 election indicated that left-leaning voters had become risk-averse after their experience in 2000. The "Nader effect" was a mere 1 percent nationally, not enough to swing any states. Whereas in 2000 some left-leaning voters complained that there was not much of a difference between Bush and Gore and voted for Nader, four years of a Bush presidency contributed to a mentality that came to be known as "anything but Bush." "Anything but Bush" adherents were not necessarily enthusiastic about

AMERICAN AND PARLIAMENTARY CAMPAIGNS IN COMPARISON

Election campaigns in the United States have the distinction of being the longest and most expensive of any in the industrial democracies. Institutions like Political Action committees (PACs), the horse-race media coverage of presidential campaigns, and the concentration on momentum in presidential primaries are unknown in other democracies.

Observers in the European countries have worried in recent years about the "Americanization" of parliamentary campaigns, by which they mean in particular the growing use of television as a campaign tool. In recent rounds of parliamentary elections in Great Britain and Germany, the winning parties' campaign teams closely studied how the Clinton campaign had used media techniques to deliver effective messages. In 1998, Gerhard Schröder's winning team used focus groups and speeches deliberately geared to television during the campaign for the German Bundestag. It is not clear, however, how far American-style campaigning can go; in France and Japan, the government carefully regulates media coverage of campaigns, and candidates are prohibited from buying television and radio time. Polling, a key tool in any national campaign in the United States, is less widely used in other democracies. In France, Italy, and Canada, the government prohibits public dissemination of poll results in the days prior to an election.

In most parliamentary systems (Japan until recently was an exception) the parties are the candidates' major source of funding. Sympathetic interest groups channel their campaign contributions through the parties. Not only do PACs not exist,

but pronouncements such as U.S. Senator Russ Feingold's that one way to lessen the expense of campaigns is to refuse "soft money" from the national parties and their committees[a] would baffle a candidate in other democracies.

In addition, no other major democratic political system has primaries (Mexico's PRI experimented with presidential primaries in the mid-1990s). Candidates are selected by the political party organizations, not the rank-and-file voters. Except in France and Egypt, where elections are carried out over two or more weekends, the public in most countries does not have to go to the polls twice in a year to elect a government.

Parliamentary general election campaigns in other countries are short. The campaign season typically lasts less than a month. Japan's 2000 parliamentary election campaign lasted less than two weeks, and prompted some observers to ask whether the campaigns were too short to allow the public to make informed candidate choices. The two top candidates in France's 2002 presidential election did not even announce their candidacies officially until two months before the election (everyone knew they would run well before that, of course). Election dates are not fixed in the parliamentary systems. Except for Germany and France, elections occur whenever the prime minister calls for them (the French president has that power). Moreover, the Parliament elects the prime minister, so direct election of the executive (except for the presidents of France and Russia) is not possible.

---

[a]Russ Feingold, "Running and Winning a 'Restrained' Campaign," *Extensions* (Spring 1999): 4.

John Kerry, but were so determined to get the President out of office that they gave Kerry their votes. Low levels of third party voting therefore did not necessarily indicate increased popularity of the major parties; rather, they demonstrated that Florida had made liberal voters unwilling to take the risk of voting for a third party.

Comparative

Comparing Political Campaigns

Democratic Convention

Twenty days before the start of the Democratic National Convention, Senator John Kerry made public his selection for vice presidential running mate: North Carolina Senator John Edwards, Kerry's most persistent rival in the Democratic primaries. Not since Ronald Reagan in 1980 had a nominee picked a primary rival as a running mate. This choice was also notable as the earliest vice presidential selection in a modern presidential campaign, which may have been a strategic move by the Kerry campaign to demonstrate party unity and to get the charismatic Edwards on the campaign trail as much as possible. Whereas other vice presidential hopefuls might have carried a particular state for the Democrats, the choice of John Edwards was viewed as a classic attempt to balance the ticket. When detractors characterized Kerry as a blue blooded, Northeastern liberal, Edwards, a more moderate Southern Democrat of humble beginnings, would stand by his side. Edwards was only serving his first term in the U.S. Senate (prior to his presidential bid he had gained prominence as a highly successful trial lawyer) and, in light of Kerry's long tenure of public service, was not viewed as bringing particular experience or expertise to the ticket. However, his energy and skill at connecting with voters were thought to be significant assets in the campaign.

With Kerry entering the national convention in a virtual tie with George W. Bush, he and Edwards would take this opportunity to define their candidacy, woo new voters, and rally their party faithful at the July 26-29 Democratic National Convention. The convention was held in Boston, Massachusetts, Kerry's home state and solid Democratic territory.

The first night started with a flourish, with former Presidents Bill Clinton and Jimmy Carter taking center stage, joined by former Vice President Al Gore. Bill Clinton was introduced by his wife, Senator Hillary Rodham-Clinton. Bill Clinton contrasted the peace and prosperity of his presidency with the international turmoil and job losses of the Bush presidency. With polls showing Americans giving Bush higher marks than Kerry on national security issues, Clinton sought to highlight the Democratic nominee's credentials in this area. "Their opponents will tell you we should be afraid of John Kerry and John Edwards because they won't stand up to terrorists. Don't you believe it," he said. *"Strength and wisdom . . . are not opposing values."* While defending Kerry's national security credentials, this statement simultaneously played on the perception held by some that Bush lacked "wisdom." Harsher criticism of the sitting President came from Jimmy Carter, the Democrats' elder statesmen, who took aim at Bush's foreign policy: "The United States has alienated its allies, dismayed its friends and inadvertently gratified its enemies by proclaiming a confused and disturbing strategy of pre-emptive war. In the world at large, *we cannot lead if our leaders mislead."* Some Democratic strategists worried that Al Gore, who in recent months had been giving forceful speeches critical of president Bush, would be overly negative at the convention. His speech was not of this character, however, and attempted to reach across party lines on behalf of the Kerry-Edwards ticket. "Did you really get what you expected from the candidate [Bush] you voted for?" he asked. "Do you still believe there was no difference between the candidates?"

The second night of the convention featured a diverse series of speakers. The most surprising speaker was Ron Reagan, son of the late Republican President Ronald Reagan. His speech focused on the controversial topic of embryonic stem cell research. In

FIGURE 14.5   Landmarks in the 2004 Campaign

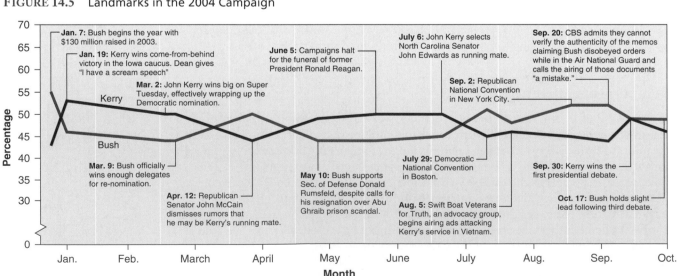

Source: Polling data based on polls by CNN-Gallup-USA Today, or Gallup when combined poll unavailable.

2001 President Bush limited the use of federal funds for this practice, which was opposed by some conservatives who linked it to abortion. Reagan's speech detailed stem cell research's potential to cure disease, labeling it the "future of medicine," and implored voters to vote for Kerry, who supports this type of research. Democrats also featured Massachusetts Senator Ted Kennedy, another Party elder statesman, on the second night. His speech was filled with images of patriotism and history, in which he called on Americans to return to a nobler, stronger leadership by electing John Kerry.

If Ron Reagan was the most unlikely speaker of the second night, it was Barack Obama, a Democratic Senate candidate from Illinois, who really stole the spotlight. The multi-racial son of a Kenyan immigrant father and poor, Kansas-born mother, Obama used his own story, of "a skinny kid with a funny name who believes that America has a place for him, too," to illustrate his party's hope for creating opportunity and unity in America. "There are those who are preparing to divide us, the spin masters and negative ad peddlers who embrace the politics of anything goes," he said. "Well, I say to them tonight, there is not a liberal America and a conservative America—there is the United States of America." This appearance launched Obama into fame on the national political scene.

The final speaker of the night was the John Kerry's wife, Teresa Heinz Kerry. No one was sure what to expect from Heinz Kerry, the unconventional, outspoken, wealthy benefactress from Mozambique. Her speech focused, as one would expect, on "humanizing" her sometimes aloof husband. In addition, however, she reached out to women, stressed environmental issues, and demonstrated her worldliness by peppering her speech with words from each of the five languages she speaks.

The next night, Senator John Edwards addressed the delegates. True to form, Edwards delivered a populist pitch for his and John Kerry's candidacy. He returned to his primary race theme of "two different Americas." "John Kerry and I believe that we shouldn't have two different economies in America: one for people who are set for life . . . and then one for most Americans, people who live paycheck to paycheck." Edwards used one of his signature phrases, "it's wrong," to describe moral problems he sees with our current system. "We have millions of Americans who work full-time every day to support their families, working for minimum wage, and still live in poverty. It's wrong." His speech's refrain, "Hope is on the way," summarized his pledge to the nation to improve their everyday lives.

The overarching theme of the Democrats' convention was, "Respected abroad, stronger at home." This emphasis of national security was most prominent on the final night of the convention, which featured testimonials from former Senator Max Cleland and Kerry's Vietnam swiftboat crewmates. Kerry opened his speech in military style with a literal salute, "I am John Kerry, and I am reporting for duty." In Kerry's speech, foreign affairs and his personal biography vastly overshadowed other topics. The biographical portion was most likely in response to polls that showed Kerry as not yet having established a personal connection with Americans. Strategists hoped that his other focus, national security, would convince Americans that he would handle threats of terrorism and the wars in Iraq and Afghanistan better than President Bush had been. "In these dangerous days, there is a right way and a wrong way to be strong," he said. "Strength is more than tough words." Kerry also took his speech as an opportunity to defend against GOP accusations that he "flip flops." "Now I know that there are those who criticize me for seeing complexities," he said. "And I do, because some issues just aren't all that simple. Saying there are weapons of mass destruction doesn't make it so. Saying we can fight a war on the cheap doesn't make it so. And proclaiming 'mission accomplished' certainly doesn't make it so." In one of his most direct attacks on the integrity of President Bush, Kerry pledged that his leadership would "start by telling the truth to the American people."

Despite what most pundits considered a solid performance, Kerry-Edwards did not receive any significant post-convention "bounce." This was unusual in that there had not been another candidate since George McGovern in 1972 whose convention had not yielded at least a small bounce. In their candidate's defense, the Kerry cam-

Democratic presidential candidates Rev. Al Sharpton, Sen. John Edwards, Sen. John Kerry, Vermont Gov. Howard Dean listen as Dick Gephardt, center, addresses the audience during their debate on October 9, 2003 in Phoenix.

(Photo courtesy: AP/World Wide Photos)

paign argued that challengers historically run behind incumbents by about 15 points heading into a convention, whereas Kerry entered the convention already polling neck and neck with Bush. Regardless whether one is interested in spin of the issue, John Kerry and John Edwards left Boston with an energized (and financially generous) base, increased familiarity to the electorate, and a *very* close race.

Republican Convention

It may come as a surprise that even though George W. Bush was an incumbent, there was still pre-convention debate regarding who would run as his Vice President. Cheney had significantly lower approval ratings with voters than did the President, and some doubted Cheney's objectivity in the Iraqi rebuilding efforts because of his connections to oil company Halliburton. Rumors flew that Secretary of State Colin Powell or Arizona Senator John McCain might be asked to take over Cheney's job. The Bush campaign, however, continuously affirmed that Cheney would remain on the ticket and was viewed as an asset to the campaign and administration. Cheney, a conservative from Wyoming who had served in the U.S. House of Representatives, was thought to bring vast foreign and domestic policy experience and a certain *gravitas* to the administration. Although perhaps McCain, Powell, or Director or Secretary of Homeland Security Tom Ridge (PA) would have won the GOP some moderates' votes (or even a key state), to change Vice Presidents between terms would have been shocking and politically risky. The possibility of this happening was most likely pure rumor.

The Republican National Convention was held from August 30 to September 2, beginning a full month after the Democratic National Convention ended. It was held in Madison Square Garden in New York City, considered to be among the most heavily liberal, Democratic locales in the nation and most certainly Kerry territory. It was clear that the GOP picked New York City not to win over its residents, but rather in an effort to use the symbolism of the September 11, 2001, terrorist attacks to their advantage. By bringing voters back to a time when they gave Bush had enormously high approval ratings, and reminding them of the "post–9-11" era of heightened homeland security, the Republican Party hoped to build on its perceived strength in issues relating to national defense.

Under the theme "A Nation of Courage," the 2004 Republican National Convention had an unmistakable focus on showcasing moderate Republicans. The right-wing branch of the Republican Party that had captured the stage at past conventions—Pat Buchanan, Jerry Falwell, Pat Robertson, and Ralph Reed—would stand aside as the more moderate Arnold Schwarzenegger, Rudy Giuliani, and John McCain spoke on behalf of their party and President Bush. The convention would be a delicate balancing act between reaching out to the swing voters (who were charmed in 2000 by Bush's "compassionate conservative" agenda) without alienating the socially conservative Republican base.

On the first night of the convention, both Arizona Senator John McCain and former New York City Mayor Rudolph Giuliani sought to make terrorism, and what they viewed as Bush's strong, decisive, management of the issue, the dominant issue of the campaign. McCain, who is known to have butted heads with the President on many occasions, made it clear that he supported his re-election and his handling of the Iraq War unwaveringly: "This president will not rest until America is stronger and safer still and this hateful iniquity is vanquished," he said. "He has been tested and has risen to the most important challenge of our time, and I salute him." McCain's speech also seemed to adopt the moral, religious tone for which Bush is famous. "[The war on terror] is a fight between a just regard for human dignity and a malevolent force that defiles an honorable religion by disputing God's love for every soul on earth," he declared. "It's a fight between right and wrong, good and evil." The GOP hoped that these words from Senator McCain, well known for reaching across party lines, would appeal to moderate and independent voters.

Rudy Giuliani speech's was more unabashedly pro-Bush than was John McCain's. Whereas McCain made overtures of unity and bipartisan cooperation, Giuliani spent seven minutes directly attacking the Democratic nominee's position on the Iraq War. Overall, however, the former mayor's speech shied away from defending the war in Iraq in favor of personal remembrances of the tragedies of September 11, 2001. He spoke of the time Bush spent at Ground Zero, despite the Secret Service's wishes to keep him away from the area, talking with construction workers, firefighters, and police officers. He described his own arrival at the north tower as "seeing the flames of hell emanating from those buildings, and realizing that what [he] was actually seeing was a human being on the 101st, 102nd floor, that was jumping out of the building." In keeping with his party's attempts to woo Jewish voters in the 2004 election, Giuliani referred to events following the attack on the Israeli team at the 1972 Olympics, the Holocaust, and Palestinian leader Yasser Arafat's winning a Nobel Peace Prize as examples of inadequate responses to terrorism.

Republicans spent the second night of the convention less on national security than on domestic issues, such as education and health care, under the banner "People with Compassion." Former movie actor and bodybuilder Arnold Schwarzenegger, who had become governor of California less than a year earlier after the state recalled Democratic Governor Gray Davis, used his star power and reputation as a moderate to bring support to President Bush. Schwarzenegger peppered his speech with references to his films, asserting that Bush would "terminate" terrorism and referring to the Democratic Convention as "True Lies." He also used his own experience as an immigrant to the United States from Austria to reach out to immigrants, who have been traditionally attracted to the Democratic Party. "To my fellow immigrants listening tonight," he said. "I want you to know how welcome you are in this party. We Republicans admire your ambition. We encourage your dreams. We believe in your future." Schwarzenegger continued, "And one thing I've learned about America is that if you work hard and if you play by the rules, this country is truly open to you. You can achieve anything." The GOP hoped that this appeal to immigrants would win the Party support from the growing and increasingly important Latino population, whose population in key states such as New Mexico, Florida, and even Colorado could swing the election.

If Ron Reagan was most surprising speaker at the Democratic National Convention, his equivalent at the Republican National Convention was undoubtedly Georgia Democratic Senator Zell Miller. Miller, who was by then thought of as a Democrat in name only, sharply attacked John Kerry and his party's positions on national defense. "Motivated more by partisan politics than by national security, today's Democratic leaders see America as an occupier [in Iraq] rather than liberators," he said. "Listing all the weapon systems that Senator Kerry tried his best to shut down sounds like an auctioneer selling off our national security." He also criticized Kerry's beliefs in diplomacy and multilateralism. "Senator Kerry has made it clear that he would use military force only if approved by the United Nations," he said. "Kerry would let Paris decide when America need defending. I want Bush to decide."

Vice President Dick Cheney also took the stage on the third night of the Republican National Convention, accepting his party's nomination for a second term. In harmony with the Bush campaign strategy, he sought to portray Kerry as a "flip-flopper." "On Iraq, Senator Kerry has disagreed with many of his fellow Democrats. But Senator Kerry's liveliest disagreement is with himself," he said. "His back-and-forth reflects a habit of indecision and sends a message of confusion. And it's all part of a pattern. He has, in the last several years, been for the No Child left Behind Act and against it. He has spoken in favor of the North American Free Trade Agreement and against it. He is for the Patriot Act and against it." In defense of Bush's foreign policy decisions and willingness to act without approval from the United Nations or many of our NATO allies, Cheney repeated a famously successful line from the President's State of the Union speech. "George W. Bush," he said, "will never seek a permission slip to defend the American people." Although the vice president made mention of domestic issues such as reforming medical liability laws, job creation and health care, his speech had the same general focuses as did the entire convention: the War on Terror, Iraq, and Homeland Security.

The final night was reserved for the Republican Party's official nomination of George W. Bush for a second term as President. In addition to his vows to stay the course on terrorism, he discussed education, health care, jobs and taxes. More specifically, Bush said that his second term would prioritize simplifying the federal tax code, reducing federal regulations, revamping labor laws, providing incentives for small businesses to provide health care, increasing funding for job training, revamping social security, and placing limits on lawsuits. Although he highlighted these types of issues—those which would be most salient with moderate and independent voters—he was careful to assure his conservative base that he would be uncompromising on social issues such as abortion and gay marriage. Bush also took advantage of his location— New York City—to remind voters of his handling of the crisis and reawaken the emotion, unity and fear surrounding September 11 attacks. "My fellow Americans, for as long as our country stands, people will look to the resurrection of New York City and they will say: Here buildings fell, and here a nation rose," he said. "Having come this far, our tested and confident nation can achieve anything." Despite the emotional strength of this imagery, perhaps the most effective aspect of the President's speech was its simple patriotic appeal. "I will never relent in defending America," he said. "Whatever it takes."

The 2004 Republican National Convention was not only a depiction of the Party's agenda and campaign strategy, but also a vivid demonstration of how polarized the nation had become this election season. Bush's speech was interrupted twice by hecklers, who were removed by security guards. Thousands of New Yorkers and protesters from other states took to the streets during the convention for primarily peaceful protests against Bush, the Iraq War, and the Republican Party. One such protest included a three-mile long symbolic unemployment line, in which each individual held a pink slip, as an expression of anger over the job losses during Bush's presidency. Over 1,700 individuals were arrested for reasons related to their protesting the convention, and accusations of police misconduct abounded.

Still, the GOP had reason to be pleased with its convention performance. Whereas the Democratic National Convention did not give Kerry a "bounce" in public opinion polls, Bush left New York with the prize of a modest 2 percent post-convention bounce, giving him the support of 52 percent of likely voters. With only two months left before Election Day, a gain of any size would be welcomed.

The Presidential Debates

In an up-and-down campaign season, the candidate debates promised a rare decisive moment. Conventional wisdom suggests that debates rarely alter the complexion of a contest, but with such a tight election, the three meetings between President George W. Bush and Senator John Kerry proved an exception to the rule.

The weeks and months preceding these face-offs were filled with traditional jockeying and posturing by the Democrats and Republicans with much of the back-and-forth reported by the media. With suggestions from the nonpartisan Commission on Presidential Debates, the candidates agreed to three presidential debates as well as one

Vice Presidential debate between vice president Dick Cheney and Senator John Edwards. Each debate lasted ninety minutes and presented a different format.

With both campaigns having agreed to the Commission's recommendations, Republican and Democratic representatives worked out over thirty pages of rules for the television networks, moderators, and candidates. Though the dozens of regulations were agreed upon by the campaigns, Democrats and Republicans even suggested that the media not show traditional reaction shots of the candidates in addition to various other rules. The media, not part of the negotiating team, did not follow all suggestions and instead showed split screens and reaction shots.

With such a tight election, both campaigns downplayed their candidate's debating abilities through the media prior to the first debate hoping to lower the American public's expectations. Kerry, a champion debater at Yale and throughout his Senate career, trailed in most polls prior to the first meeting of the candidates. With a successful track record of debating, his campaign quietly asserted the match ups between Kerry and Bush would offer the Democrat a chance to make his comeback in the polls after trailing the president for most of September. While Kerry was known to excel in formal settings, it was well known that Bush disliked prescribed speaking engagements. In 2000, Bush managed to connect with American voters through his plain spoken demeanor and his team hoped to capitalize on the same success against Kerry.

The first debate took place on September 30 in Coral Gables, Florida. The candidates format for this event featured questions posed by the moderator, PBS host Jim Lehrer, with responses and rebuttals by the candidates. During the discussion on foreign policy, Bush and Kerry clashed sharply on the war in Iraq and on fighting terrorism. Bush hammered at Kerry's inconsistent statements and policies throughout the ninety minutes while Kerry stressed the failure of the Bush Administration to prove that Iraq posed a large enough threat to the United States to have warranted invasion. Television ratings were exceptionally high, with the first debate being watched by 62.5 million viewers, the most since 1992. Viewer, generally found Kerry to have won the debate, and many pundits commented on Bush's lack of energy and focus.

Senator John Edwards and Vice President Dick Cheney faced off in a heated debate on October 5, managing very high television ratings despite airing alongside Major League baseball playoffs. The vice presidential debates almost managed slightly higher ratings than the first presidential debate of 2000. Edwards created some controversy by highlighting the fact that Cheney's daughter Mary was a lesbian when talking about his stance on gay marriage. Some commentators took this as a covert signal by the Kerry campaign to religious conservative voters in hopes of diminishing support for Bush. Kerry himself brought up this fact during the final debate. Lynne Cheney angrily responded that Kerry and Edwards' maneuver was "a cheap and tawdry political trick." Opinion polls showed that almost two-thirds of the public agreed Kerry and Edwards' comments were "inappropriate," but the incident did not prove to be an enduring problem for their campaign going into the final stages of the election.

A town hall format was used for the second presidential debate, wherein voters found to be undecided by the Gallop polling organization were allowed to ask questions of each candidate in turn. Reacting against the criticism that he seemed tired and unfocused, Bush was extremely forthright and energetic throughout the night. For example, Bush was so adamant in responding fully to a response by Kerry that he talked over Charlie Gibson of ABC News who was attempting to ask a follow up question. Debate questions were selected to give more weight to the Iraq war, but little new emerged about either candidate's positions.

On the campaign trail, candidates frequently rely on sound bytes and media devices to convey their messages. Here, George W. Bush uses dollar bills to illustrate how the budget surplus could be used to finance an across-the-board tax cut and save Social Security.

(Photo courtesy: Iikka Uimonen/Corbis Sygma)

The candidates met for the last time in Tempe, Arizona, on October 13. This debate followed a similar structure to the first debate with the candidates standing behind podiums, and answering questions in turn from CBS News anchor Bob Schieffer. For the first time during the debates, the questions were geared toward domestic issues. Bush worked hard to portray Kerry as a liberal, pointing to his voting record on taxes and defense. Kerry battled back, attacking the president's record on health care, education, and tax policy. The last debate was generally considered to have been won by Kerry by the public and media commentators. Ultimately, Kerry managed to even the playing field going in to the final days of the campaign with his debate performances.

The 2004 presidential debates managed to change public opinion in an already highly publicized campaign. Kerry entered the debate season down in the polls, and he finished virtually tied with Bush in the polls. Having met expectations, the candidates moved forward with their messages into the final weeks of the campaign season.

The Fall Campaign and General Election

In the final weeks of the campaign public opinion was deadlocked, and many began to fear the closeness and uncertainty of 2000 was again possible in 2004. There was even the real possibility of a tie in the Electoral College, which would throw the election into the House of Representatives. The election was especially close in the key battleground states of Ohio, Florida, Pennsylvania, New Mexico, Iowa, and Wisconsin. Bush had won Florida, but only narrowly and controversially, in 2000, and very narrowly lost New Mexico, Wisconsin, and Iowa. Bush had won Ohio by four points in 2000, but his support was waning, and Ohio was very much in play until the last hours of the campaign. Both candidates spent considerable amounts of time in all of these states, crisscrossing the nation in an attempt to carve out a slight victory on election day.

Bush stayed on message during the last days of the campaign, emphasizing the need to continue the effort in Iraq and strongly prosecute the war on terrorism. Kerry continued to hack away at the president's choice to invade Iraq as misguided and without a plan for victory. Kerry especially criticized Bush's handling of foreign relations, and the bad blood in Europe and around the world created out of his Iraq policy. Kerry promised a change in international relations in which the United States would be more attuned to the concerns of allies, and spend more effort building alliances to fight the global war on terrorism. In a number of television commercials, and in public appearances, Bush fought back, attempting to paint Kerry as a "flip-flopper" who constantly switched his positions to better fit public opinion. Bush also used a *New York Times* interview where Kerry likened terrorism before September 11 to a "nuisance" like illegal gambling or prostitution to attack Kerry's credibility on defense.

Three weeks before the election, a few polls in Hawaii found the presidential race to be too close to call. In a surprising move, Vice President Cheney flew out to Hawaii as part of a last swing through the western states, making the first campaign visit by a member of a presidential ticket since Richard Nixon in 1960. The Democrats sent Al Gore in response to try and even the score. Hawaii had elected its first Republican governor in forty years two years before, and some considered the Aloha State a possible Bush win. Despite this, Hawaii was still considered a long shot for Bush, as it had not voted for a Republican presidential candidate since 1984.

Hollywood made an appearance in the waning days of the campaign for both candidates to help swing key states. Arnold Schwarzenegger, the Republican governor of California, made an appearance with President Bush in Ohio, promising to "pump" the crowd to re-elect the president. Overshadowing even Schwarzenegger's fame, the Kerry campaign brought out significantly more star power in the last month of the campaign. Kerry appeared with Bruce Springsteen in Cleveland, Stevie Wonder in Detroit, and Bette Midler in Miami, all during the month of October. John Edwards also appeared with Jimmy Buffet in Pompano Beach, Florida. While celebrity endorsements did not

PRESIDENTIAL DEBATES: COMING TO A CAMPUS NEAR YOU?

Televised presidential debates offer the American electorate a unique opportunity to see and hear the candidates for the presidency. It is a means by which millions of Americans gather information regarding each candidate's personality and platform. Recognizing the profound educational value of these debates to the voting public, two bipartisan national study groups recommended that steps be taken to establish an organization whose main function was the sponsorship of presidential and vice presidential debates during the general election period. In response to the recommendations put forward by the two study groups, the Commission on Presidential Debates (CPD) was established in 1987.

The CPD's formal charge is to ensure that debates are a permanent part of every general election and that they provide the best possible information to viewers and listeners. The organization sponsored all the presidential debates since 1988, heavily favoring institutions of higher learning as the host sites. The last four presidential elections have included fourteen debates sponsored by the CPD, eleven of which have been held on college campuses. Both Wake Forest University and Washington University in St. Louis were chosen on two separate occasions to serve as the debate sites. Although Washington

University was selected twice, it ultimately hosted only one debate in 2000. In 1996, the Clinton and Dole camps restructured the commission's debate proposal, eliminating Washington University as a host site. Other sites have included the University of California at Los Angeles, the University of Richmond in Virginia, Michigan State University, and the University of San Diego.

Prospective debate hosts must conform to a rigorous set of criteria as dictated by the CPD. The selection criteria encompass a broad range of categories, including the physical structure of the debate hall (over 17,000 square feet with a 35 foot ceiling and 65-foot stage); the transportation and lodging networks available; and the ability to raise $550,000 to cover production costs.

Why would a college or university go through so much trouble to host a presidential debate? The answer is that the benefits are plentiful and diverse. The host sites inevitably bring in revenue with masses of people migrating into town, purchasing community services and products. The colleges gain immediate international exposure, perhaps becoming a more attractive option to prospective students. Students and professors benefit from first hand exposure to a very important aspect of the American political process.

---

[a]Commission on Presidential Debates, http://www.debates.org.

---

bring victory, they helped draw crowds and attention to the Kerry campaign in several key battleground states.

Despite the efforts of each campaign, public opinion remained very divided in key states like Ohio and Florida up until the election. Realizing this, both candidates made a marathon sprint through battleground states the last few days before the election. Bush covered several states in the final week, but spent seven consecutive days traveling through Ohio, including Election Day. Kerry visited Michigan, Wisconsin, Florida, and Ohio in the final days of the campaign. After voting in his home state of Texas, Bush flew back to Washington to await the election results. Kerry returned to Massachusetts to cast his vote and follow an Election Day tradition of lunch at a Boston oyster bar. With the election close, and both candidates confident of their chances, the afternoon wore on in anticipation of the first exit polls.

Election Results

Network and cable news bureaus were extremely cautious about election night, with the painful memories of 2000 still fresh in their minds. Exit polling had proved unreliable, leading many networks to have incorrectly called an early victory for Al Gore in Florida. Because Florida is in two time zones, the polls had not yet closed in the panhandle when the news that Gore had won Florida began to come in. This early call helped to depress turnout in the predominantly Republican panhandle and contributed to the overall closeness of the election. Wary of causing another election debacle, the networks used extreme caution in declaring winners in 2004. As CNN vice president

David Bohrman said of the media the day of the election, "I think we're all pretty much in a race not to be first."

Exit polling for the major broadcast and cable networks was performed by the Voter News Service (VNS) during the 2000 and 2002 elections. Because of the flawed data VNS provided in both elections, the networks retooled their exit polling system and created a new service for 2004 called the National Election Pool (NEP). The polling information gathered by the NEP was available only to subscribers, and the general public was not privy to its first early results the afternoon of Election Day. However, despite the vows of the media to keep a lid on early exit polling, rumors began leaking out on the Internet, primarily on weblogs and political sites, of a Kerry lead across the country. By the time polls had first closed at 7:00 p.m. on the east coast, many felt a Kerry victory to be the result. As the first precincts began reporting, some anxiety spread through the Bush campaign, as states like Virginia seemed to be too close to call initially. Bush had won Virginia by eight points in 2000, so this seemed to confirm the strong Kerry numbers in the exit polling.

FIGURE 14.6   Exit Poll Results for 2004 Elections

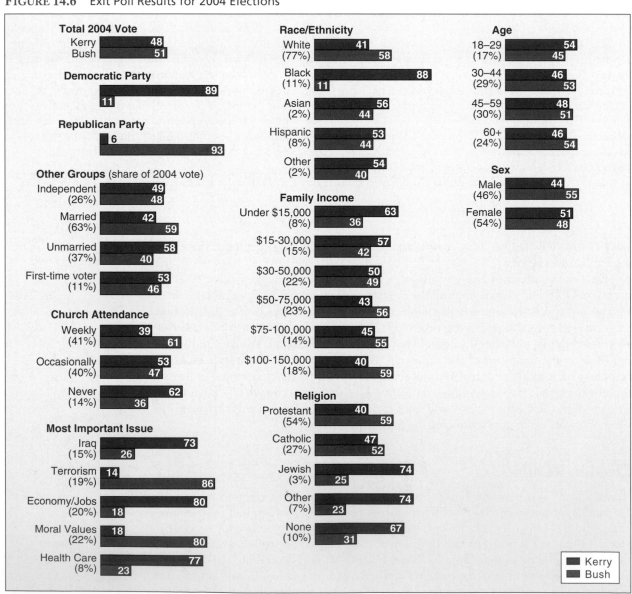

Source: Exit Poll conducted by Edison Media Research and Mitofsky International. For more information and further results, see http://www.cnn.com/ELECTION/2004/.

As the night wore on and more states began to close their polls, Bush began to show a convincing lead in the key battleground state of Florida. However, the networks remained extremely cautious, only calling the states that had given a clear and commanding victory to either candidate. As Election Day approached midnight, Florida had been called for Bush, but Ohio still remained too close to call for some networks, despite a significant lead by the president. By early the next morning, neither candidate had yet to capture the necessary 270 electoral votes. Around 2:00 a.m., Edwards addressed the expectant crowd at the Kerry victory celebration in Boston to say they were not conceding the election. Appearing confident and energetic, Edwards said, "It's been a long night but we've waited four years for this victory, and we can wait one more night." Despite a lead of over a hundred thousand votes for Bush in Ohio, the Kerry campaign believed there might be enough late votes to turn the tide. In Ohio, when a person is not listed on the voting roles, or is otherwise deemed ineligible, they are allowed to vote a provisional ballot to be validated later. Nearly two hundred thousand provisional ballots had been cast, and the Kerry campaign held on through the night convinced these might push them over the top to victory.

By later that morning, the Bush campaign was confident that they had carried the election, and had informed the Kerry campaign that they would be declaring victory. Giving Kerry the courtesy of giving his concession speech first, the Bush campaign waited until the early afternoon for Kerry to speak. Kerry spoke at the historic Faneuil Hall in Boston to concede, speaking of the need for unity after such a divisive campaign. About an hour later, Bush gave his victory speech at the Ronald Reagan building in Washington, D.C., also speaking of the need for unity, but also emphasizing his victory as ratification by the people of his policies.

Turnout in the 2004 Election

The 2004 election had the highest voter turnout rate since 1968, with 59.6% of eligible citizens participating, or an estimated 120,200,000 votes. An additional 15 million

TABLE 14.3   2004 Election Results (Popular Vote Percentage)

State	Bush (%)	Kerry (%)	State	Bush (%)	Kerry (%)
Alabama	62	35	Montana	59	39
Alaska	63	37	Nebraska	67	32
Arizona	55	44	Nevada	51	48
Arkansas	54	45	New Hampshire	49	50
California	44	55	New Jersey	46	53
Colorado	53	46	New Mexico	50	49
Connecticut	44	54	New York	40	58
Delaware	46	53	North Carolina	56	44
District of Columbia	9	90	North Dakota	63	36
Florida	52	47	Ohio	51	49
Georgia	58	41	Oklahoma	66	34
Hawaii	45	54	Oregon	48	52
Idaho	68	30	Pennsylvania	49	51
Illinois	45	55	Rhode Island	39	60
Indiana	60	39	South Carolina	58	41
Iowa	50	49	South Dakota	60	39
Kansas	62	37	Tennessee	57	43
Kentucky	60	40	Texas	61	38
Louisiana	57	42	Utah	71	27
Maine	45	53	Vermont	39	59
Maryland	43	56	Virginia	54	45
Massachusetts	37	62	Washington	46	53
Michigan	48	51	West Virginia	56	43
Minnesota	48	51	Wisconsin	49	50
Mississippi	60	40	Wyoming	69	29
Missouri	54	46			

Source: Unofficial election results as from CNN, as of November 4, 2004. http://www.cnn.com/ELECTION/2004/.

President Bush and First Lady Laura Bush are joined on-stage by Vice President Dick Cheney and his wife, Lynne Cheney, during a victory rally Wednesday, November 3, 2004, at the Ronald Reagan Building and International Trade Center in Washington, D.C.

(Photo courtesy: AP/World Wide Photos)

Americans voted in 2004 than in 2000, despite long lines that kept some voters waiting for over 7 hours. Not surprisingly, the largest turnouts occurred in "swing states," where a majority of campaign time and resources were spent. Six states and the District of Columbia had record turnout: Alabama, Georgia, Florida, South Carolina, Tennessee, and Virginia. According to the Committee for the Study of the American Electorate (CSAE), the highest turnout overall presidential vote was seen in Minnesota, where 76.2 percent of eligible voters cast ballots; Wisconsin, New Hampshire, and South Dakota followed closely. As of the time of publication, only one state, Arizona, appeared to have a lower turnout in 2004 than in 2000.

The major partisan divide is seen as a primary cause for such high numbers. Emotions about the presidency of Bush, both good and bad, made the campaign more bitter and vicious than any election in recent memory. Yet Bush still received more than 30 percent of the eligible vote, which no candidate has done since Bush Sr. won in 1988. Scholars cite many reasons for Kerry's defeat. According to Curtis Gans, director of CSAE, Kerry was never seen as a strong candidate, but rather undistinguished and distant. Gans also cites poor decisions on the part of DNC chairman Terry McAuliffe to truncate the nomination process and hold the Democratic convention in Boston, as well as the inability of the Democratic Party to clearly define a Democratic vision that resonates with voters, as key contributing factors to Kerry's loss. In addition, the Republicans' centralized voter drive bested the Democrats decentralized get-out-the-vote mobilization, which had been farmed out to other mobilizing groups.

Despite the highly publicized youth vote campaign on both sides, increases among college-attending youth were seen in the battleground states, and there only slightly. Across the board, young people accounted for 17 percent of the overall turnout, exactly the same percentage as 2000.

Because of such a polarized campaign and election, the third party factor was almost completely nonexistent in 2004. A little over 1 million votes went to the four different third-party candidates. If this political division between Republican and Democrats continues, the role of the third party will decline. However, this same divide that brought about such large turnouts may prove to be temporary if such polarization does not exist in the future.

Bush's Second Term

Now that the votes have been counted, George W. Bush has been granted four more years as the President of the United States. This overwhelming 3.5 million vote victory, complete with increased Republican majorities in the House of Representatives and the Senate, presents the question "What next?" for several players in American politics. The first is President Bush himself. Although he is the first president to win a majority of the popular vote since his father in 1988, the president has inherited an electorate deeply divided by a contentious and emotional political campaign. Bush finds himself at a crossroads. He could be a "uniter," moderating his positions to bring in

President George W. Bush greets supporters at a campaign rally. The 2004 election marks the first time since 1988 that the winner received more than 50 percent of the popular vote.

(Photo courtesy: Tannen Maurey/The Image Works)

lawmakers from the Democratic Party and build a consensus. Or he can spend the political capital that he has earned to assert conservative policy initiatives that he has kept on the backburner during the first term. These initiatives are likely to find a way onto the president's agenda: Social Security reform, medical liability and health care reform, and making his tax cuts permanent. At the time of this writing, it appears very likely that one of Bush's first efforts will be to make an appointment to the Supreme Court, which will undoubtedly generate intense discussion of divisive social issues such as abortion and gay marriage. After an ugly election season, Bush has several reasons to reach out to moderates and liberals, but he also feels buoyed by the GOP's gains in the White House and Congress and will like take advantage of that mandate and momentum.

One could also argue that the Republican Party also finds itself at a crossroads. Now that the election is over, several moderates within the party may look to assert themselves at the beginning of the legislative session. Pennsylvania Senator Arlen Specter, the chairman of the Senate Judiciary Committee, has cautioned President Bush not to nominate overly conservative judges for judicial positions. Senator Charles Lugar and outgoing Senator Charles Hagel have been critical of the president's handling of the war in Iraq and may place more pressure on President Bush to reform how the situation is being handled. The Republicans are cognizant of the polarization of the country and are fearfully aware of the "6 year itch" that may scratch out congressional majorities for the president's party. With all of this tension, the battle lines are also being drawn for 2008, in which moderates such as Arizona Senator John McCain, New York Governor George Pataki, and former New York Mayor Rudolph Giuliani are likely compete for the Republican presidential nomination against traditional conservatives such as Senate Majority Leader Bill Frist of Tennessee and Virginia Senator George Allen, chairman of the National Republican Senatorial Committee. This contest will be shaped in the next four years by the level of success President Bush has in pushing his agenda, as well as how the Republicans manage the midterm Congressional elections.

Overall, the next four years is an eternity in politics. President Bush and the Republican majorities in Congress will have to decide how much they want to push through their agenda and make a legacy for themselves, versus how much they want to reach out to lawmakers across the aisle. This balancing act will not only be based on principle—whether it is better to reconcile the country or pass policies that conservatives

Continuity & Change

Campaign Ethics in American Politics

American politics has never been particularly clean or ethical, and even the Founders were much maligned in their campaigns. The rumors about Jefferson's black mistress, Sally Hemmings, first came to prominence during his presidential campaign in 1800, and Jefferson's campaigns were the subject of much acrimonious and partisan strife in newly emerging American newspapers.

When Andrew Jackson campaigned for president in 1828, his opponents widely published the fact that the divorce of his wife's first marriage had not been finalized by the time of their marriage, though this was unbeknownst to her or Jackson at the time. Rachel Jackson was completely humiliated by the ensuing public scandal, and historians have read this as a major contribution to the physical and emotional breakdown that took her life between the time of Jackson's election and his swearing-in as president.

America did not leave campaign corruption behind in the nineteenth century. The country's greatest political scandal, Watergate, is still well within the nation's living memory. The Watergate scandal developed from Richard Nixon's flagrantly illegal measures to investigate anti-Vietnam activists and to ensure his reelection in 1972—including misusing the CIA, FBI, and IRS and accepting huge concealed campaign contributions. What brought the scandal into the open was the Nixon Campaign Committee's bugging and breaking into the Democratic National Committee, headquartered in the Watergate Building, which gave the scandal its name. Laws passed after Watergate to compel campaign finance reform have had some limited success in cleaning up the campaign process in America, although the disguising and misreporting of fund-raising inevitably continues in new forms.

Personal political attacks, especially in TV advertising, are still par for the course today. The most egregious example of negative campaigning at the presidential level occurred in 1988, when George Bush ran the infamous "Willie Horton ad." This ad featured the face of Willie Horton—a convicted African American criminal who had committed a rape while on a weekend furlough program advocated by Bush's Democratic presidential opponent, Massachusetts Governor Michael Dukakis. The advertisement was extremely effective in casting doubt on some of Dukakis's policies, though many criticized it for brazenly exploiting racial and cultural prejudices to asperse Dukakis.

Push-polling, the dissemination of negative and often inaccurate information about a candidate under the guise of asking opinion-poll questions, is a dirty but increasingly popular campaign tactic that remains unregulated and can only worsen in upcoming campaigns. In push-polling, a pollster for Candidate Y might make a phone call and ask the respondent, "Would you be less likely to vote for Candidate X if you found out that she had voted for six consecutive tax increases?" (Notice how the question implies that Candidate X actually has voted for six increases, whether or not she really has.) As Americans become increasingly immersed in the Internet, it is not hard to imagine how push-polling might rear its ugly head in the form of e-mail messages.

In the 2004 election the Kerry campaign was accused of questionable ethics during the debates. Both John Edwards and John Kerry mentioned the fact that Vice President Dick Cheney's daughter Mary was a lesbian when referring to his stance on gay marriage. While Cheney was cordial about the comment during his debate, even thanking Edwards for his kind words about his daughter, some suspected foul play. Later, Kerry, during the last presidential debate, mentioned Cheney's daughter in relation to gay marriage. Lynne Cheney, Mary's mother, responded angrily to what she construed as "a cheap and tawdry political trick" by the Kerry campaign to use her daughter to scare away religious conservative voters. The public reaction was very negative, with almost two-thirds of voters finding the comments by Kerry and Edwards inappropriate. Some candidates will always push the envelope on ethics, sometimes even crossing the line to win elected office—it will always be true that campaign ethics is an oxymoron for many. The public can only keep a close eye on campaign antics and do its best to judge the conduct of the campaigns and hold them accountable.

1. Do you remember ever viewing a negative political advertisement, or an attack ad? In your opinion, are such advertisements a useful tactic in political campaigning, or might they do more harm than good for the political system? Should government take steps to limit negative advertising, or would this constitute a violation of the First Amendment?

2. Debate the specific merit of the "no-limits, full-disclosure" system of campaign finance, in which unlimited campaign contributions are allowed if they are fully declared in a publicly accessible manner. Will it ever be possible to close all the loopholes in laws governing campaign ethics? What would be the particular advantages and disadvantages of such an open system—not only to politicians, but to PACs and other lobbyists, and to the interest of the general public? Do you believe that the general public is smart enough to track political contributions and take them into account when voting for a candidate?

CAST YOUR VOTE   Should there be a limit on campaign contributions, or should there be no limits, but full disclosure on the contributors? To cast your vote, go to
www.ablongman.com/oconnor

believe in—but also on electoral self-interest: a desire to expand the GOP's appeal and the need to keep together the conservative base that pushed the President to victory in 2004.

Which Way the Democratic Party?

As the Democrats emerge from the 2004 defeat, the party finds itself grappling with disappointment and self-doubt, as well as needing to reevaluate its fundamental message and overhaul its leadership. The party itself is divided over whether to move further left, in the spirit of Howard Dean and Hillary Clinton, or move closer to the middle of the political spectrum in a country that has proven to be more center-right than the Democrats had anticipated. There is further debate over whether the basic political philosophy of the Democrats is out of touch with mainstream America, or if this cycle's leadership failed to articulate a potentially successful ideology. Either way, the Republicans won this battle of the culture war, and the Democrats must hone a message that resonates with the masses of Southern and Midwestern Americans who decided to keep the President and GOP in power. In order to win nationally, the Democrats will need to show the American people that liberal values are not antithetical to traditional Christian values.

To be successful in the 2006 midterm elections and ultimately in 2008, the Democrats must focus their message and find a strong voice (or voices) to deliver it. With Tom Daschle out of the Senate Minority Leader's seat, and Terry McAuliffe likely to resign his chairmanship of the DNC, the Democrats have a much-needed opportunity to revamp the party leadership. Now out that he is out of the Senate, John Edwards will have the next four years to build support among the party faithful for his 2008 nomination. For Edwards and the Democrats, his best shot may be to may revisit his 2004 campaign theme of "two Americas" divided by wealth, as opposed to the two Americas divided by morality that the Republicans so deftly used to their advantage.

At the time of printing, it appears that Minority Whip Harry Reid of Nevada will likely take over Daschle's seat as Senate Minority Leader, and McAuliffe's successor has yet to be determined. It may behoove the Democrats to consider selecting a woman to chair the DNC, given the apparent shift in the women's vote to the Republicans. John Kerry will return to the Senate, where he is likely to be an even more outspoken and effective legislator than he was in his first twenty years. While the Northeast and the West Coast have become solidly Democratic, the next generation of Democratic leadership will probably come from the heartland of America. Plausible options for reviving the Democratic Party include Senator Blanche Lincoln of Arkansas, Iowa Governor Tom Vilsack, Michigan Governor Jennifer Granholm, Indiana Senator Evan Bayh, and newly-elected Senator Barack Obama of Illinois. Senator Hillary Clinton is a passionate spokeswoman for her party, but she is also a polarizing figure who may be too risky for the Democrats to elevate to leadership at this sensitive period. However, Clinton will certainly join the pool of rumored 2008 presidential candidates, which already includes Edwards, Bayh, New Mexico Governor Bill Richardson, and possibly former Vice President Al Gore. Future success for the Democrats will be determined by their willingness to learn from this election's mistakes, return to its populist roots, and find a voice that speaks to all Americans.

SUMMARY

With this chapter, we switched our focus from the election decision and turned our attention to the actual campaign process. What we have seen is that while modern campaigning makes use of dazzling new technologies and a variety of strategies to attract voters, campaigns still tend to rise and fall on the strength of the individual candidate. In this chapter we have stressed the following observations:

1. **The Structure of a Campaign**
   A campaign, the process of seeking and winning votes in the run-up to an election, consists of five separate components: the nomination campaign, in which party leaders and activists are courted to ensure that the candidate is nominated in primaries or conventions; the general election campaign, in which the goal is to appeal to the nation as a whole; the personal campaign, in which the candidate and his or her family make appearances, meet voters, hold press conferences, and give speeches; the organizational campaign, in which volunteers telephone voters, distribute literature, organize events, and raise money; and the media campaign waged on television and radio and in newspapers.

   Campaign staffs combine volunteers, a manager to oversee them, and key political consultants including media consultants, a pollster, and a direct mailer. In recent years media consultants have assumed greater and greater importance, partly because the cost of advertising has skyrocketed, so that campaign media budgets consume the lion's share of available resources.

2. **The Candidate or the Campaign: Which Do We Vote For?**
   Despite the dazzle of technology and the celebrity of well-known consultants, the candidate remains the most important component of any campaign. The candidate's strengths, weaknesses, and talents are central to the success or failure of the campaign.

3. **The Campaign and the News Media**
   Candidates tell their story directly in paid broadcast media advertising. They are much less successful in managing and directing their press coverage.

4. Campaign Finance

Since the 1970s, campaign financing has been governed by the terms of the Federal Election Campaign Act (FECA). Due to the rise of soft money, the FECA was amended in 2002 by the Bipartisan Campaign Finance Reform Act, which was promptly challenged by opponents in the Courts.

5. Bringing It Together: The 2004 Presidential Campaign and Election

A very competitive Democratic primary season, that had Howard Dean leading for much of the winter, ended in victory for John Kerry in Iowa. Kerry's momentum carried him on to a quick primary victory, and began the unofficial general campaign far in advance of the summer. Public opinion remained extremely close until the conventions, where President Bush benefited from a well orchestrated effort by the Republicans. Bush's slight lead over Kerry was diminished by a lackluster performance during three televised debates, and the end of the race was a photo finish. Turnout was very brisk, and President Bush managed a close but convincing win in both the Electoral College and the popular vote.

KEY TERMS

campaign manager, p. 544
candidate debate, p. 550
contrast ad, p. 545
direct mailer, p. 544
finance chair, p. 544
free media, p. 545
general election campaign, p. 541
get-out-the-vote (GOTV), p. 544
hard money, p. 556
inoculation ad, p. 545
matching funds, p. 555
media campaign, p. 541
media consultant, p. 544
negative ad, p. 545
nomination campaign, p. 540
organizational campaign, p. 541
paid media, p. 545
personal campaign, p. 541
political action committee (PAC), p. 554
political consultant, p. 544
pollster, p. 544
positive ad, p. 545
public funds, p. 555
soft money, p. 556
spot ad, p. 545
voter canvass, p. 544

SELECTED READINGS

Abramson, Paul R., John H. Aldrich, and David W. Rohde. *Change and Continuity in the 2000 and 2002 Elections.* Washington, DC: CQ Press, 2003.

Ansolabehere, Stephen, and Shanto Iyengar. *Going Negative: How Attack Ads Shrink and Polarize the Electorate.* New York: Free Press, 1995.

Ceaser, James W., and Andrew E. Busch. *Losing to Win: The 1996 Elections and American Politics.* Lanham, MD: Rowman and Littlefield, 1997.

———. *The Perfect Tie: The True Story of the 2000 Presidential Election.* Lanham, MD: Rowman and Littlefield, 2001.

Fenno, Richard F. *Senators on the Campaign Trail: The Politics of Representation.* Norman: University of Oklahoma Press, 1996.

Goldenberg, Edie, and Michael W. Traugott. *Campaigning for Congress.* Washington, DC: CQ Press, 1984.

Greive, R. R. Bob. *The Blood, Sweat, and Tears of Political Victory—And Defeat.* Lanham, MD: University Press of America, 1996.

Herrnson, Paul S. *Congressional Elections: Campaigning at Home and in Washington,* 3rd ed. Washington, DC: CQ Press, 2000.

Hertzke, Allen D. *Echoes of Discontent: Jesse Jackson, Pat Robertson, and the Resurgence of Populism.* Washington, DC: CQ Press, 1993.

Holbrook, Thomas M. *Do Campaigns Matter?* Thousand Oaks, CA: Sage Publications, 1996.

Jackson, Brooks. *Honest Graft: Big Money and the American Political Process.* Washington, DC: Farragut, 1990.

Kern, Montague. *30-Second Politics: Political Advertising in the Eighties.* New York: Praeger, 1989.

Mayer, William G., ed. *In Pursuit of the White House: How We Choose Our Presidential Nominees.* Chatham, NJ: Chatham House Publishers, 2000.

Nelson, Michael, ed. *The Elections of 1996.* Washington, DC: CQ Press, 1997.

Orren, Gary R., and Nelson W. Polsby, eds. *Media and Momentum: The New Hampshire Primary and Nomination Politics.* Chatham, NJ: Chatham House, 1987.

Patterson, Thomas E. *The Mass Media Election.* New York: Praeger, 1980.

Pika, Josepha A., and Richard A. Watson. *The Presidential Contest,* 5th ed. Washington, DC: CQ Press, 1995.

Pomper, Gerald M., ed. *The Election of 1992: Reports and Interpretations.* Chatham, NJ: Chatham House, 1993.

———. *The Election of 2000.* Chatham, NY: Chatham House, 2001.

Sabato, Larry J., ed. *Campaigns and Elections: A Reader in Modern American Politics.* Glenview, IL: Scott, Foresman, 1989.

———. *PAC Power: Inside the World of Political Action Committees.* New York: Norton, 1985.

———. *Paying for Elections: The Campaign Finance Thicket.* New York: Priority Press for the Twentieth Century Fund, 1989.

———. *The Rise of Political Consultants: New Ways of Winning Elections.* New York: Basic Books, 1981.

———. *Toward the Millennium: The Elections of 1996.* Boston: Allyn and Bacon, 1997.

———. *Overtime! The Election 2000 Thriller.* New York: Longman, 2002.

Sabato, Larry J., and Glenn R. Simpson. *Dirty Little Secrets: The Persistence of Corruption in American Politics.* New York: Times Books, 1996.

Sorauf, Frank J. *Inside Campaign Finance.* New Haven, CT: Yale University Press, 1992.

Thurber, James A. and Candice J. Nelson. *Campaign Warriors: Political Consultants in Elections.* Washington, D.C.: The Brookings Institution, 2000.

Troy, Gil. *See How They Ran: The Changing Role of the Presidential Candidate.* Cambridge, MA: Harvard University Press, 1996.

NOTES

1. Patrick J. Kenney and Tom W. Rice, "The Psychology of Political Momentum," *Political Research Quarterly* 47 (December 1994): 923–38.

2. Paul S. Herrnson, "Campaign Professionalism and Fundraising in Congressional Elections," *Journal of Politics* 54 (1992): 859–70.

3. Stephen K. Medvic and Silvo Lenart, "The Influence of Political Consultants in the 1992 Congressional Elections," *Legislative Studies Quarterly* 22 (February 1997): 61–77.

4. Five liberal Democratic U.S. senators, including George McGovern of South Dakota, were defeated in this way in 1980, for example.

5. Stephen Ansolabehere and Shanto Iyengar, *Going Negative: How Political Advertisements Shrink and Polarize the Electorate* (New York: Free Press, 1995).

6. Steven E. Finkel and John G. Geer, "A Spot Check: Casting Doubt on the Demobilizing Effect of Attack Advertising," *American Journal of Political Science* 42 (April 1998): 573–95.

7. Paul Freedman and Ken Goldstein, "Measuring Media Exposure and the Effects of Negative Campaign Ads," *American Journal of Political Science* 43 (October 1999): 1189–1208.

8. See Larry J. Sabato, ed., *Campaigns and Elections: A Reader in Modern American Politics* (Glenview, IL: Scott, Foresman, 1989), 3–4.

9. From a 1987 cartoon by Tom Toles, copyrighted by the *Buffalo News.*

10. V. O. Key Jr., with Milton C. Cummings Jr., *The Responsible Electorate: Rationality in Presidential Voting, 1936–1960* (Cambridge, MA: Harvard University Press, 1966).

11. Morris Fiorina, *Retrospective Voting in American National Elections* (New Haven, CT: Yale University Press, 1981).

12. Robert S. Erikson, "Economic Conditions and the Presidential Vote," *American Political Science Review* 82 (June 1989): 567–73.

13. Steven E. Finkel, "Reexamining the 'Minimal Effects' Model in Recent Presidential Campaigns," *Journal of Politics* 55 (February 1993): 1–21.

14. John G. Geer, "The Effects of Presidential Debates on the Electorate's Preferences for Candidates," *American Politics Quarterly* 16 (October 1988): 486–501.

15. David J. Lanoue, "One That Made a Difference: Cognitive Consistency, Political Knowledge, and the 1980 Presidential Debate," *Public Opinion Quarterly* 56 (Summer 1992): 168–84.

16. Diana C. Mutz, "Effects of Horse-Race Coverage on Campaign Coffers: Strategic Contributing in Presidential Primaries," *Journal of Politics* 57 (November 1995): 1015–42.

17. Data provided by the Federal Election Commission.

18. Steven T. Engel and David J. Jackson, "Wielding the Stick Instead of Its Carrot: Labor PAC Punishment of Pro-NAFTA Democrats," *Political Research Quarterly* 51 (September 1998): 813-28.

19. Janet M. Box-Steffensmeier and J. Tobin Grant, "All in a Day's Work: The Financial Rewards of Legislative Effectiveness," *Legislative Studies Quarterly* 24 (November 1999): 511-23.

20. Kevin M. Leyden and Stephen A. Borrelli, "An Investment in Goodwill: Party Contributions and Party Unity Among U.S. House Members in the 1980s," *American Politics Quarterly* 22 (October 1994): 421-52.

21. Amy Keller, "Helping Each Other Out: Members Dip into Campaign Funds for Fellow Candidates," *Roll Call* (June 15, 1998): 1.

22. For member contribution activity at the state level, see Jay K. Dow, "Campaign Contributions and Intercandidate Transfers in the California Assembly," *Social Science Quarterly* 75 (1994): 867-80. For member contribution activity at the congressional level, see Bruce A. Larson, "Ambition and Money in the U.S. House of Representatives: Analyzing Campaign Contributions from Incumbents' Leadership PACs and Reelection Committees" (Ph.D. dissertation, University of Virginia, 1998). For a briefer account, see Paul S. Herrnson, "Money and Motives: Spending in House Elections," in Lawrence C. Dodd and Bruce I. Oppenheimer, eds., *Congress Reconsidered*, 6th ed. (Washington, DC: CQ Press, 1997).

23. Larson, "Ambition and Money in the U.S. House of Representatives."

24. 424 U.S. 1 (1976).

25. Marisa Katz. "Matching Funds" *The New Republic Online.* (July 13, 2004) http://www.tnr.com/doc.mhtml?i=express&s=katz071304

26. 424 U.S. 1 (1976), 116 S.Ct. 2309 (1996).

27. Amy Keller, "Experts Wonder About FEC's Internet Savvy: Regulating Web Is a Challenge for Watchdog Agency," *Roll Call* (May 6, 1999): 1, 21.

28. Anthony Corrado, "Party Soft Money," in Anthony Corrado et al., eds., *Campaign Finance Reform: A Sourcebook* (Washington, DC: Brookings Institution, 1997).

29. Trevor Potter, "Issue Advocacy and Express Advocacy," in Anthony Corrado et al., eds., *Campaign Finance Reform: A Sourcebook* (Washington, DC: Brookings Institution, 1997).

30. http://www.commoncause.org/laundromat/stat/topdonors01.htm

31. Mann, Thomas E. and Norman J. Ornstein. "Separating Myth From Reality in *McConnell v. FEC*". *Election Law Journal.* March 2004, pg. 14. Taken from the Brookings Institute website: http://www.brook.edu/views/articles/mann/20040204.pdf

32. Frank Sorauf, *Inside Campaign Finance: Myths and Realities* (New Haven, CT: Yale University Press, 1992), ch. 6.

33. Richard A. Smith, "Interest Group Influence in the U.S. Congress," *Legislative Studies Quarterly* 20 (1995): 89-139. See also Janet Grenzke, "PACs and the Congressional Supermarket: The Currency Is Complex," *American Journal of Political Science* 33 (1989): 1-24.

34. Richard L. Hall and Frank W. Wayman, "Buying Time: Moneyed Interests and the Mobilization of Bias in Congressional Committees," *American Political Science Review* 84 (1990): 797-820.

35. Thomas Gais, *Improper Influence: Campaign Finance Law, Political Interest Groups, and the Problem of Equality* (Ann Arbor: University of Michigan Press, 1996).

36. See Howard Penniman, "U.S. Elections: Really a Bargain?" *Public Opinion* (June/July 1984): 51.

The News Media

In the four years following the 2000 presidential election, Americans faced challenges at home and abroad including September 11 and the war in Iraq. The media served as an outlet for information and patriotism during the times of crises with more Americans relying on them in the face of terrorism than previous years. By the spring of 2002, however, as the presidential primary and general election took off, the around-the-clock news services returned to their previous stories centered on scandals and character issues surrounding candidates.

In the fall of 2003, Howard Dean, the former governor of Vermont, quickly turned into the frontrunner among the Democratic presidential candidates after proving himself to be the media darling, much like Senator John McCain did in 2000. Though Dean had little name recognition before his run for the White House, the media's constant coverage helped propel him to America's consciousness within a few short months. With a stronghold of young, Internet-driven supporters backing his run for president, the media quickly formed stories about his campaign, personal background and rise to the top. Yet, Dean's popularity with the media was not to last through the general election. Instead, the media began questioning Dean's electability in a match-up election against President George W. Bush beginning in December, 2003.

The media found the answer to their electability question on the eve of the Iowa caucus, after Dean's infamous scream speech following a dismal third-place finish. They recounted the scream in the days and weeks ahead on television, radio and the Internet during the most crucial primaries, ultimately lending support to the downfall of Dean's bid for the presidency.

While Senator John Kerry benefited from the foibles of Howard Dean, the media turned to character issues surrounding Kerry and Bush during the general election. With heavy emphasis on Senator Kerry's record in Vietnam and President Bush's service in the National Guard, major networks and newspapers saturated the American public in covering a war fought over 30 years before. In what proved to be faulty information, CBS anchorman Dan Rather, relied heavily on information from a source who later turned out to have forged the documents that formed the basis of Rather's interview which suggested Bush did not report for mandatory duty in the National Guard in the 1970s.

Perhaps "Rathergate" will be most remembered for the role that the internet, particularly the loose collection of political weblogs known as the "blogosphere," played in breaking the story.

*T*he media have the potential to exert enormous influence over Americans. Not only do they tell us what is important by setting the agenda for what we will watch and read, but they can also influence what we think about issues through the content of their news stories. The simple words of the First Amendment, "Congress shall make no law … abridging the freedom of speech, or of the press," have shaped the American republic as much as or more than any others in the Constitution. With the Constitution's sanction, as interpreted by the Supreme Court over two centuries, a vigorous and highly competitive press has emerged. This freedom has been crucial in facilitating the political discourse and education necessary for the maintenance of democracy. But, does this freedom also entail responsibility on the part of the press and other media? Have the media, over the years, met their obligation to provide objective, issue-based coverage of our politicians and political events, or do they tend to focus on the trivial and sensational, ignoring the important issues and contributing to voter frustration with government and politicians? How this freedom evolved, the ways in which it is manifested, and whether it is used responsibly are subjects we examine further in this chapter.

The chapter reviews the historical development of the press in the United States and then explores the contemporary media scene. Do the media go too far in their coverage of public figures and issues, and are they biased in their reporting? Do the media influence public opinion, and are they manipulated by skilled politicians? We also explore the ways in which government controls the organization and operation of the media, attempting to promote a balance between freedom and responsibility on the one hand, and competitiveness and consumer choice on the other. In discussing the changing role and impact of the media, we will address the following:

- First, we will discuss the *evolution of the press*, from the founding of the country up to modern times.
- Second, we will examine the *current structure and role of the media*.
- Third, we will discuss *how the media cover politicians and government*, and the trend away from the attention given to investigative journalism during the Watergate era and, more recently, toward character issues and intrusive examination of the private lives of public figures.
- Fourth, we will investigate the *media's influence on the public*, and whether public opinion is significantly swayed by media coverage.
- Fifth, we will examine the *public's perception of the media*.
- Sixth, we will observe *how politicians use the media* and attempt to influence coverage for their own ends.
- Seventh, we will explain how *government regulates the electronic media* and identify the motivations for and evolution of such control.
- In exploring our theme of *continuity and change*, we will examine how television has transformed American politics.

THE AMERICAN PRESS OF YESTERYEAR

Journalism—the process and profession of collecting and disseminating the news (that is, new information about subjects of public interest)—has been with us in some form since the dawn of civilization.[1] (See Table 15.1 for a history of the media in the United States.) Yet, its practice has often been remarkably uncivilized, and it was much more so at the beginning of the American republic than it is today.

The first newspapers were published in the American colonies in 1690. The number of newspapers grew throughout the 1700s, as colonists began to realize the value of a press free from government oversight and censorship. Thus, it was not surprising that

TABLE 15.1	Landmarks of the American Media
1760	First newspaper published
1789	First party newspapers circulated
1833	First penny press
1890	Yellow journalism spreads
1900	Muckraking in fashion
1928	First radio broadcast of an election
1948	First election results to be covered by television
1952	First presidential campaign advertisements aired on television
1960	Televised presidential campaign debates
1979	The Cable Satellite Public Affairs Network (C-SPAN) is founded, providing live, round-the-clock coverage of politics and government.
1980	Cable News Network (CNN) is founded by media mogul Ted Turner, making national and international events available instantaneously around the globe.
1992	Talk-show television circumvents the news, allowing candidates to go around journalists to reach the voting public directly.
1996	Official candidate home pages addresses appear on the World Wide Web.
2000	Explosion of World Wide Web as a primary campaign tool for candidates, and a continuous twenty-four-hour news cycle.
2004	Web logs, or blogs, create a popular forum for the disbursement of political news and commentary.

one of the most important demands made by Anti-Federalists (see chapter 2) during our country's constitutional debate was that an amendment guaranteeing the freedom of the press be included in the final version of the Constitution. When beginning a discussion of the media in American history, it is important to remember that, by and large, that history is one of private enterprise, and that the reference to the media as "the fourth branch of government," while a provocative notion, is a complete fiction. In other words, an American media outlet might choose, or have chosen, stridently to support a particular political party, platform, issue, or official, but it would do so as an independent voice of private citizens or a private organization, not as the concealed organ of the government in power (contrast this system with those of totalitarian regimes, in which a state news agency is often the only, and inevitably a highly biased, source of information). This distinction can be difficult to maintain under some circumstances, as this chapter will discuss, but its basic reliability continues to provide the basis for journalistic integrity in America.

During his presidency, George Washington escaped most press scrutiny but detested journalists nonetheless; his battle tactics in the Revolutionary War had been much criticized in print, and an early draft of his "Farewell Address to the Nation" at the end of his presidency (1796) contained a condemnation of the press that has often been described as savage.[2] Thomas Jefferson was treated especially harshly by elements of the early U.S. press. For example, one Richmond newspaper editor, angered by Jefferson's refusal to appoint him as postmaster, printed a rumor sparked an enduring debate: that Jefferson kept a slave Sally Hemmings as his concubine and had several children by her.[3] One can understand why Jefferson, normally a defender of a free press, commented that "even the least informed of the people have learned that nothing in a newspaper is to be believed." Jefferson, of course, probably did not intend that statement literally, since he was instrumental in establishing the *National Gazette*, the newspaper of his political faction and viewpoint. Recent DNA testing has verified that Jefferson most likely fathered Hemmings's children, but the saga to this day is still being carried out in the media.

The partisan press eventually gave way to the penny press. In 1833, Benjamin Day founded the *New York Sun*, which cost a penny at the newsstand. Because it was not tied to one party, it was politically more independent than the party papers. The *Sun* was the forerunner of the modern press built on mass circulation and commercial

Timeline

Three Centuries
of American
Mass Media

advertising to produce profit. By 1861, the penny press had so supplanted partisan papers that President Abraham Lincoln announced that his administration would have no favored or sponsored newspaper.

The press thus became markedly less partisan but not necessarily more respectable. Mass-circulation dailies sought wide readership, and readers were clearly attracted by the sensational and the scandalous. The sordid side of politics became the entertainment of the times. One of the best-known examples occurred in the presidential campaign of 1884, when the *Buffalo Evening Telegraph* headlined "A Terrible Tale" about Grover Cleveland, the Democratic nominee.[4] In 1871, while sheriff of Buffalo, the bachelor Cleveland had allegedly fathered a child. Even though paternity was indeterminate because the child's mother had been seeing other men, Cleveland willingly accepted responsibility since all the other men were married, and he had dutifully paid child support for years. Fortunately for Cleveland, another newspaper, the *Democratic Sentinel*, broke a story that helped to offset this scandal: Republican presidential nominee James G. Blaine and his wife had had their first child just three months after their wedding.

In the late 1800s and early 1900s, the era of the intrusive press was in full flower. First yellow journalism and then muckraking were in fashion. Pioneered by prominent publishers such as William Randolph Hearst and Joseph Pulitzer, **yellow journalism**—the name strictly derived from printing the comic strip "Yellow Kid" in color—featured pictures, comics, and color designed to capture a share of the burgeoning immigrant population market. These newspapers also oversimplified and sensationalized many news developments. The front-page editorial crusade became common, the motto for which frequently seemed to be, "Damn the truth, full speed ahead."

After the turn of the century, the muckrakers—so named by President Theodore Roosevelt after a special rake designed to collect manure[5]—took charge of a number of newspapers and nationally circulated magazines. **Muckraking** journalists such as Upton Sinclair and David Graham Phillips searched out and exposed real and apparent misconduct by government, business, and politicians in order to stimulate reform.[6] There was no shortage of corruption to reveal, of course, and much good came from these efforts. In particular, muckrakers stimulated demands for the increased regulation of

yellow journalism
A form of newspaper publishing in vogue in the late-nineteenth century that featured pictures, comics, color, and sensationalized, oversimplified news coverage.

muckraking
A form of newspaper publishing, in vogue in the early twentieth century, concerned with reforming government and business conduct.

"Uncle Sam's Next Campaign—the War Against the Yellow Press." In this 1898 cartoon in the wake of the Spanish-American War, yellow journalism is attacked for its threats, insults, filth, grime, blood, death, slander, gore, and blackmail, all of which are "lies." The cartoonist suggests that, after winning the foreign war, the government ought to attack its own yellow journalists at home.

(Photo courtesy: Stock Montage, Inc.)

public trusts. But, an unfortunate side effect of the emphasis on crusades and investigations was the frequent publication of gossip and rumor without sufficient proof.

The modern press corps may also be guilty of this offense, but it has achieved great progress on another front. Throughout the nineteenth century, payoffs to the press were not uncommon. Andrew Jackson, for instance, gave one in ten of his early appointments to loyal reporters.[7] During the 1872 presidential campaign, the Republicans slipped cash to about 300 newsmen.[8] Wealthy industrialists also sometimes purchased editorial peace or investigative cease-fire for tens of thousands of dollars. Examples of such press corruption are exceedingly rare today, and not even the most extreme of the modern media's critics believe otherwise.

As the news business grew, its focus gradually shifted from passionate opinion to corporate profit. Newspapers, hoping to maximize profit, were more careful to avoid alienating the advertisers and readers who produced their revenues, and the result was less harsh, more objective reporting. Meanwhile, media barons such as Joseph Pulitzer and William Randolph Hearst became pillars of the establishment; for the most part, they were no longer the anti-establishment insurgents of yore.

Technological advances had a major impact on this transformation in journalism. High-speed presses and more cheaply produced paper made mass-circulation dailies possible. The telegraph and then the telephone made news gathering easier and much faster, and nothing could compare to the invention of radio and television. When radio became widely available in the 1920s, millions of Americans could hear national politicians instead of merely reading about them. With television—first introduced in the late 1940s, and nearly a universal fixture in U.S. homes by the mid-1950s—citizens could see and hear candidates and presidents. The removal of newspapers and magazines as the foremost conduits between politicians and voters had profound effects on the electoral process, as we discuss shortly.

WEB EXPLORATION
For examples of nineteenth-century yellow journalism, go to www.ablongman.com/oconnor

Timeline

Major Technological Innovations That Have Changed the Political Landscape

THE CONTEMPORARY MEDIA SCENE

The editors of the first partisan newspapers could scarcely have imagined what their profession would become more than two centuries later. The number and diversity of media outlets existing today are stunning. The **print press** consists of many thousands of daily and weekly newspapers, periodicals, magazines, newsletters, and journals. The **electronic media** are radio and television stations and networks, computerized information services, and the Internet. In some ways, the news business is more competitive now than at any time in history. Paradoxically, the news media have expanded in some ways and contracted in others, dramatically changing the ways in which they cover politics.

The growth of the political press corps is obvious to anyone familiar with government or campaigns. Since 1983, for example, the number of print (newspaper and magazine) reporters accredited at the U.S. Capitol has jumped from 2,300 to more than 4,100; the gain for broadcast (television and radio) journalists was equally impressive and proportionately larger, from about 1,000 in 1983 to an average of 3,000 by 1999.[9] On the campaign trail, a similar phenomenon has occurred. In the 1960s, a presidential candidate in the primaries would attract a press entourage of at most a couple of dozen reporters, but in the 1990s, a hundred or more print and broadcast journalists can be seen tagging along with a front-runner. Consequently, a politician's every public utterance is reported and intensively scrutinized and interpreted in the media.

Although there are more journalists, they are not necessarily attracting a larger audience, at least on the print side. Daily newspaper circulation has been declining for more than twenty years (see Analyzing Visuals: Circulation of Daily Newspapers, 1850–2003). On a per-household basis, circulation fell 47 percent from 1976 to 1998.[10] Barely half of the adult population reads a newspaper every day. Among people age eighteen to twenty-nine, fewer than one-third are daily readers—a decline of 50 percent in two decades.

print press
The traditional form of mass media, comprising newspapers, magazines, and journals.

electronic media
The broadcast media, including television, radio, computerized information services, and the Internet.

Along with the relative decline of readership has come a drop in the overall level of competition. In 1880, 61 percent of U.S. cities had at least two competing dailies, but by 1990, a mere 2 percent of cities did so. Not surprisingly, the number of dailies has declined significantly, from a peak of 2,600 in 1909 to around 1,500 today (Sunday papers are an exception to the trend).[11] Most of the remaining dailies are owned by large media conglomerates called chains, such as Gannett, Hearst, Knight-Ridder, and Newhouse. In 1940, 83 percent of all daily newspapers were independently owned, but by 1990, just 24 percent remained independent of a chain. Chain ownership usually reduces the diversity of editorial opinions and can result in the homogenization of the news.

Part of the cause of the newspapers' declining audience has been the increased numbers of television sets and cable and satellite television subscribers (see Figure 15.1) and the increased popularity of television as a news source. At the dawn of the 1960s, a substantial majority of Americans reported that they got most of their news from newspapers; by the latter half of the 1980s, television was the people's choice by an almost two-to-one margin.[12] Moreover, by a margin of 55 percent to 21 percent, Americans now say that they are inclined to believe television over newspapers when conflicting reports about the same story arise. Of course, most individuals still rely on both print *and* broadcast sources,[13] but there can be little question that television news is increasingly important. Despite its many drawbacks (such as simplicity, brevity, and entertainment orientation), television news is "news that matters." It has the power to greatly affect which issues viewers say are important.[14]

Although not totally eclipsing newspapers, television frequently overshadows them, even though it often takes its agenda and lead stories from the headlines produced by print reporters (especially those working for the print elite—papers such as the *New York Times, Washington Post,* and *Wall Street Journal*; wire services such as the Associated Press and United Press International; and journals such as *Time, Newsweek,* and *U.S. News & World Report*). Regrettably, busy people today appear to have less time to review the printed word, and consequently they rely more on television's brief headline summaries. Additionally, at least one study of television and print news finds differences in the level of independence each shows in their reporting. Television news was less questioning of the "government line" during the 1991 Persian Gulf War, while newspapers exhibited greater journalistic autonomy and diversity of opinion about the conduct of the war in their coverage.[15] Perhaps over time the Internet will nudge Americans back to the printed word—not in newspapers but on Web sites sponsored by the major news organizations.

The television news industry differs from its print counterpart in a variety of ways. The number of outlets has been increasing, not declining, as with newspapers. The three

FIGURE 15.1   Television in the American Home
The growth of cable television has been tremendous over the last thirty years. Today, the majority of American households possess access to cable television. Satellite television, bringing hundreds of channels to viewers, is also on the rise. Smaller satellite dishes and lower prices are sure to make satellite television a more attractive media source in the future.

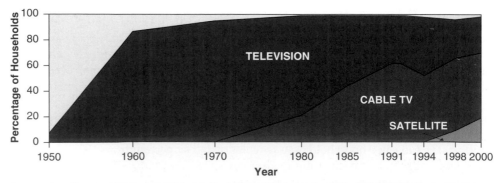

Sources: Adapted from Harold W. Stanley and Richard G. Niemi, *Vital Statistics on American Politics, 2001–2002* (Washington, DC: CQ Press, 2001), 170; 1 Television Bureau of Advertising.

ANALYZING VISUALS

Circulation of Daily Newspapers, 1850–2003

Take a few moments to study these figures and accompanying graph, and then answer the following critical thinking questions: What do you notice about newspaper circulation from 1850 to 1970? What do you notice about newspaper circulation after 1970? Drawing on what you have learned from the chapter, what might be the underlying reasons behind these patterns in newspaper circulation?

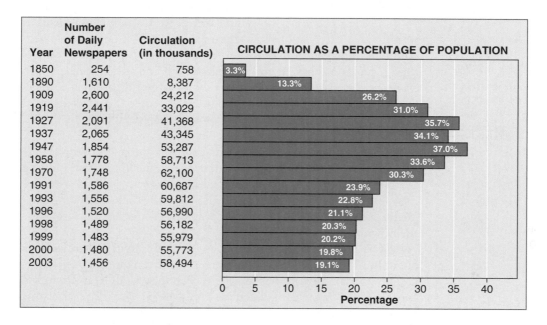

Year	Number of Daily Newspapers	Circulation (in thousands)
1850	254	758
1890	1,610	8,387
1909	2,600	24,212
1919	2,441	33,029
1927	2,091	41,368
1937	2,065	43,345
1947	1,854	53,287
1958	1,778	58,713
1970	1,748	62,100
1991	1,586	60,687
1993	1,556	59,812
1996	1,520	56,990
1998	1,489	56,182
1999	1,483	55,979
2000	1,480	55,773
2003	1,456	58,494

Sources: Adapted from Harold W. Stanley and Richard G. Niemi, *Vital Statistics on American Politics, 2001–2002* (Washington, DC: CQ Press, 2001), 171–172; *Editor & Publisher Yearbook 1999*; Newspaper Association of America, http://www.nad.org.

major networks now receive broadcast competition from Cable News Network (CNN), Fox News Channel, MSNBC, Headline News, Cable Satellite Public Affairs Network (C-SPAN), and the PBS *News Hour with Jim Lehrer.* Although the audiences of all the alternative shows are relatively small compared with those of the network news shows, they are growing while the networks' audience shares contract. The potential for cable expansion is large: Nearly half of all U.S. households are currently wired for cable. In addition, the rise of cable has had important implications for the political system. For instance, political scientists Matthew Baum and Samuel Kernell suggest that the splintering of television audiences caused by cable makes it much more difficult for the president to drum up support for his favored policies. Whereas the president could at one time command the attention of all television consumers by appearing on network television, this is no longer possible.[16] The increasing satellite television access, with its expanded choices of channels, further splinters the core audience for network television.

Adding to television's diversity, the national television news corps is often outnumbered on the campaign trail by local television reporters. Satellite technology has provided any of the 1,300 local stations willing to invest in the hardware an opportunity to beam back reports from the field. On a daily basis, local news is watched by more people (67 percent of adults) than is network news (49 percent), so increased local attention to politics has some real significance. Unfortunately, however, studies also show that local news, compared to newspapers and network reports, contains the least substantive coverage. Criticism and analysis of policy positions and candidates are much more likely to be found in national news reports than local broadcasts.[17]

The decline of the major networks' audience shares and the local stations' decreasing reliance on the major networks for news—coupled with stringent belt tightening ordered by the networks' corporate managers—resulted in severe news staff cutbacks at NBC, CBS, and ABC during the 1980s and 1990s. These economy measures have affected the quality of broadcast journalism. Many senior correspondents bemoan the loss of desk assistants and junior reporters, who did much of the legwork necessary to get less superficial, more in-depth pieces on the air. As a consequence, stories requiring extensive research are often discarded in favor of simplistic, eye-catching, "sexy" items that increasingly seem to dominate campaign and government coverage.

There has also been a substantial increase in the number of media mergers in recent years, so that each national television network now is only a piece of a massive corporation. These mergers have had at least two important effects. One effect is that the large corporations have their financial bottom line as the alpha and the omega of their existence. As a consequence, if news shows cannot be profitable, the corporate executives will either cut the news divisions back or force the news divisions to do virtually anything to expand the audience. Unfortunately, what expands the audience is sleazy, tabloid coverage of gossip, innuendo, and sex.

Another suspected effect is that the media megacorporations are censoring news that reflects badly on products created by the nonnews divisions of those corporations.[18] While conservative critics say that media bias is mainly liberal—and in coverage of politics this criticism may well be valid—it is also true that another form of bias in the news media is conservative, since these corporations are making sure that the coverage of their own products stays positive.

Every newspaper, radio station, and television station is influential in its own area, but only a handful of media outlets are influential nationally. The United States has no nationwide daily newspapers to match the influence of Great Britain's *Times, Guardian*, and *Daily Telegraph*, all of which are avidly read in virtually every corner of the United Kingdom. The national orientation of the British print media can be traced to the smaller size of the country and also to London's role as both the national capital and the largest cultural metropolis. The vastness of the United States and the existence of many large cities, such as New York, Los Angeles, and Chicago, effectively preclude a nationally united print medium in this country.

However, national distribution of the *New York Times, Wall Street Journal, USA Today*, and *Christian Science Monitor* does exist, and other newspapers, such as the *Washington Post* and *Los Angeles Times*, have substantial influence from coast to coast. These six newspapers also have a pronounced effect on what the five major national **networks** (ABC, CBS, NBC, CNN, and Fox) broadcast on their evening news programs—or, in the case of CNN and Fox, air on cable around the clock. A major story that breaks in one of these papers is nearly guaranteed to be featured on one or more of the network news shows. These news shows are carried by hundreds of local stations—called **affiliates**—that are associated with the national networks and may choose to carry their programming. A **wire service,** such as the Associated Press (AP) (established in 1848), also nationalizes the news. Most newspapers subscribe to the service, which not only produces its own news stories but also puts on the wire major stories produced by other media outlets.

The national newspapers, wire services, and broadcast networks are supplemented by a number of national news magazines, whose subscribers number in the millions. *Time, Newsweek*, and *U.S. News & World Report* bring the week's news into focus and headline one event or trend for special treatment. Other news magazines stress commentary from an ideological viewpoint, including the *Nation* (left-wing), *New Republic* (moderate-liberal), and the *Weekly Standard* (conservative). These last three publications have much smaller circulations, but because their readerships are composed of activists and opinion leaders, they have disproportionate influence.

In politics, as in every other field, the World Wide Web is truly the wave of the future. Already, Web-based information has become standard fare for anyone interested in politics. Three Web sites among the dozens now available are those of the

WEB EXPLORATION

To see how the media are diversifying and repackaging themselves through the use of pundits, go to www.ablongman.com/oconnor

network
An association of broadcast stations (radio or television) that share programming through a financial arrangement.

affiliates
Local television stations that carry the programming of a national network.

wire service
An electronic delivery of news gathered by the news service's correspondents and sent to all member news media organizations.

Simulation
You Are a News Editor

Congressional Quarterly (www.cq.com); the *Washington Post*, whose site is widely considered the best political site on the Web (www.washingtonpost.com); and an all-politics collaboration between CNN, *Time* magazine, and other media sources (www.cnn.com/ALLPOLITICS). Virtually every major newspaper, opinion magazine, and news magazine maintains a site, as do the television networks, which endlessly offer not only the pieces that appear on the evening news, but also additional commentary and information too lengthy to include on the original thirty-minute broadcast. Furthermore, those Americans not satisfied with the news coverage provided by traditional media can find additional information at alternative news sites. Sites such as freerepublic.com provide news and commentary for those with a conservative perspective, while those with a more liberal bent may prefer to get their news from sites such as salon.com.

Many people wonder if the media are cutting into their own subscription revenues, since it is not feasible to charge for the use of a public site associated with a newspaper or TV network. However, there is very little evidence that this is happening. By and large, the people who use media Web sites are highly informed voters who devour additional information about politics and government and use the Web for updates and supplements to their traditional media services. Indeed, a recent study by Scott L. Althaus and David Tewksbury concluded that "using the Web as a source of news may be positively related to reading printed newspapers."[19] Web sites thus appear to be building interest in traditional media rather than detracting from them.

The future relationship between the Internet and politics remains hard to predict. Some believe that as the current generation of computer-literate children and young people become adult voters, the Web is likely to become the primary means by which America informs itself about politics and government on a regular and current basis. (Table 15.2 shows the public's media choices by age group.) Others, such as Althaus and Tewksbury, assert that "it appears unlikely that more than a small portion of the existing audience for traditional news media will abandon those media for Internet news sources."[20] More generally, some scholars in political science and psychology have expressed concern that extensive use of the Internet may actually harm the polity because it "weakens real-world ties, and reduces community involvement."[21] Communications scholars Dhavan Shah, Nojin Kwak, and R. Lance Holbert, however, find

WEB EXPLORATION

To see which newspapers, magazines, and networks have a Web presence, and how that coverage differs from or complements their standard coverage, go to www.ablongman.com/oconnor

TABLE 15.2 The News Generation Gap				
	18–29 %	*30–49* %	*50–64* %	*65+* %
Did yesterday				
Watched TV news	40	52	62	73
Local TV news	28	41	49	52
Network evening	17	25	38	46
Cable TV news	16	23	30	35
Morning news	11	16	21	27
Read a newspaper	26	37	52	59
Listened to radio news	34	49	42	29
No news yesterday	33	19	15	12
Watch/listen/read regularly				
Local TV news	46	54	64	69
Cable TV news	23	31	42	38
Nightly network news	19	23	45	53
Network TV magazines	15	22	30	33
Network morning news	16	22	23	31
Call-in radio shows	16	19	20	10
National Public Radio	14	18	15	11
Time/Newsweek/US News	12	13	15	13
Online news 3+ times/week	31	30	24	7

Source: "Public's Habits Little Changed by September 11," June 9, 2002. Pew Research Center for the People and the Press, http://people-press.org.

that those who "use the Internet for information exchange (i.e., searching for information and exchanging email)... may be able to exert greater control over their environments, encouraging participation and enhancing trust and contentment."[22] Only continued observation and research will reveal all of the influences of the information age on American politics.

HOW THE MEDIA COVER POLITICIANS AND GOVERNMENT

Much of the news media's attention is focused on our politicians and the day-to-day operations of our government. In this section, we will discuss coverage of the three constitutionally created branches of government (Congress, the president, and the courts), and show how the tenor of this coverage has changed since the Watergate scandal of the early 1970s.

Covering the Presidency

The three branches of the U.S. government—the executive, the legislative, and the judicial—are roughly equal in power and authority, but in the world of media coverage, the president is first among equals. All television cables lead to the White House, and a president can address the nation on all networks almost at will. On television, Congress and the courts appear to be divided and confused institutions—different segments contradicting others—whereas the commander in chief is in clear focus as chief of state and head of government. The situation is scarcely different in other democracies. In Great Britain, for example, all media eyes are on No. 10 Downing Street, the office and residence of the prime minister.

Since Franklin D. Roosevelt's time, chief executives have used the office and presidential press conference as a bully pulpit to shape public opinion and explain their actions (see Figure 15.2). The presence of the press in the White House enables a president to appear even on very short notice and to televise live, interrupting regular programming. The White House's press briefing room is a familiar sight on the evening news, not just because presidents use it so often, but also because the presidential press secretary has almost daily question-and-answer sessions there.

press release
A document offering an official comment or position.

press briefing
A relatively restricted session between a press secretary or aide and the press.

press conference
An unrestricted session between an elected official and the press.

It is useful to distinguish between several terms associated with the release and discussion of information by elected officials, public figures, and their staff. A **press release** is a written document offering an official comment or position on an issue or news event; it is usually printed on paper and handed directly to reporters, or increasingly, released by e-mail or fax. A **press briefing** is a relatively restricted live engagement with the press, in which the range of questions accepted is limited to one or two specific topics and a public figure or elected official is usually represented by his or her press secretary or other aides but does not appear in person. In a full-blown **press conference,** an elected official appears in person to talk with the press at greater length about an unrestricted range of topics. Press conferences are still significant media events, providing a field on which reporters struggle to get the answers they need and public figures attempt to retain control of their message and spin the news and issues in ways favorable to them.

The press secretary's post has existed only since Herbert Hoover's administration (1929–1933), and the individual holding it is the president's main disseminator of information to the press. For this vital position, a number of presidents have chosen close aides who were very familiar with their thinking. For example, John F. Kennedy had Pierre Salinger (an ABC News foreign correspondent), Lyndon B. Johnson had Bill Moyers (who now hosts many PBS documentaries), and Jimmy Carter had longtime Georgia associate Jody Powell. Probably the most famous recent presidential press secretary is James Brady, who was wounded and disabled in the March 1981 assassination attempt on President

FIGURE 15.2 Presidential News Conferences, 1929–2004

U.S. presidents give fewer news conferences than in the past. Today, presidents prefer to give a limited number of well-planned news conferences rather than make more regular appearances. However, presidential advisers and a press team provide the media with daily briefings.

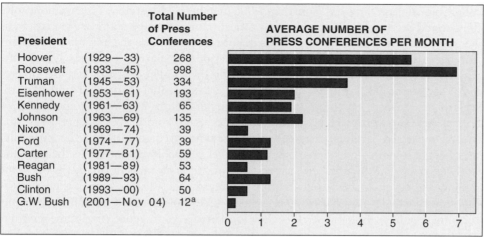

President		Total Number of Press Conferences	AVERAGE NUMBER OF PRESS CONFERENCES PER MONTH
Hoover	(1929—33)	268	
Roosevelt	(1933—45)	998	
Truman	(1945—53)	334	
Eisenhower	(1953—61)	193	
Kennedy	(1961—63)	65	
Johnson	(1963—69)	135	
Nixon	(1969—74)	39	
Ford	(1974—77)	39	
Carter	(1977—81)	59	
Reagan	(1981—89)	53	
Bush	(1989—93)	64	
Clinton	(1993—00)	50	
G.W. Bush	(2001—Nov 04)	12[a]	

Note: Any count of news conferences is only an approximation given the variety of contacts presidents have with the press.

[a]On March 28, 2001, White House spokesman Ari Fleischer said President George W. Bush planned to conduct no formal news conferences but intended to be accessible to reporters during public appearances. The total number shown is for solo press conferences through November 8, 2004.

Sources: Adapted from Harold W. Stanley and Richard G. Niemi, *Vital Statistics on American Politics, 2003–2004* (Washington, DC: CQ Press 2001), table 4.3, 174..

Ronald Reagan. Texas native Scott McClellan, the current White House press secretary, began working for Governor Bush in early 1999 as deputy communications director and then traveling press secretary for the Bush-Cheney 2000 presidential campaign. McClellan took over the job on July 15, 2003 from Ari Fleischer, who was highly regarded for his strong communication skills during the tumultuous first years of the Bush presidency. The White House press secretary job is one of the most contentious in politics. Considering the Bush administration's obsession with staying "on message" and frequently cold relationship with the media, McClellan's job is perhaps even tougher than past press secretaries.

On any given day, presidents, their advisers, and their families do any number of things that might become news. In deciding what *does* become news, presidents and the press engage in a continuous "debate about newsworthiness." This debate occurs not only between the White House and the news media but within the two entities as well, and it involves "what gets covered, who gets asked about a story, and how and for how long the story is covered."[23]

Although the president receives the vast majority of the press's attention, political scientist Thomas Patterson suggests that much of this focus is unfavorable. Since the 1960s, press coverage of the president has become dramatically more negative. In fact, all three major presidential contenders in 1992 and 1996 received more negative than positive coverage. Patterson also finds that coverage of President George Bush's handling of important national problems was almost solely negative.[24]

The media have faced a more difficult challenge in covering the administration of George W. Bush, a president who prides himself on the tight-lipped, no leaks nature of his White House. The staff does not speak to the media without permission, and reporters have a more difficult time penetrating the inner circle. This arrangement works well for Bush, but is not good for reporters, or perhaps, the public.

White House Press Secretary Scott McClellan gestures as he briefs reporters about al-Qaeda in March 2004.

(Photo Courtesy: AP/World Wide Photos)

Covering Congress

The size of Congress (535 members) and its decentralized nature (bicameralism, the committee system, and so on) make it difficult for the media to survey. Nevertheless, the congressional press corps has more than 3,000 members.[25] Most news organizations solve the size and decentralization problems by concentrating coverage on three groups of individuals. First, the leaders of both parties in both houses receive the lion's share of attention because only they can speak for a majority of their party's members. Usually the majority and minority leaders in each house and the speaker of the House are the preferred spokespersons, but the whips also receive a substantial share of air time and column inches. Second, key committee chairs command center stage when subjects in their domain are newsworthy. Heads of the most prominent committees (such as Ways and Means or Armed Services) are guaranteed frequent coverage, but even the chairs and members of minor committees or subcommittees can achieve fame when the time and issue are right. Third, local newspapers and broadcast stations normally devote some resources to covering their local senators and representatives, even when these legislators are junior and relatively lacking in influence. Most office holders, in turn, are mainly concerned with meeting the needs of their local media contingents, since these reporters are the ones who directly and regularly reach the voters in their home constituencies. Political scientist Timothy Cook showed this in his 1984 survey of congressional press secretaries. Local print and television news, if applicable, occupied much of the House members' time when dealing with the press. Members only contacted the national news media when they sought to become a national spokesperson on some issue.[26]

One other kind of congressional news coverage is worth noting: investigative committee hearings. Occasionally, a sensational scandal leads to televised congressional committee hearings that transfix and electrify the nation. In the early 1950s, Senator Joseph R. McCarthy (R–WI) held a series of hearings to root out what he claimed were Communists in the Department of State and other U.S. government agencies, as well as in Hollywood's film industry. The senator's style of investigation, which involved many wild charges made without proof and the smearing and labeling of some innocent opponents as Communists, gave rise to the term *McCarthyism*.

The Watergate hearings of 1973 and 1974—which stemmed from White House efforts to eavesdrop on officials of the Democratic National Committee and then to cover up presidential involvement in the scheme—made heroes out of two committee chairs, Senator Sam Ervin (D–NC) and Representative Peter Rodino (D–NJ). They uncovered many facts behind the Watergate scandal and then pursued the impeachment of President Richard M. Nixon. (Nixon resigned in August 1974, before the full House could vote on his impeachment.)

In 1987, the Iran-Contra hearings—set up to investigate a complicated Reagan administration scheme in which arms were sold to Iran and the profits were then diverted to the anti-Communist Nicaraguan Contras—also created a popular, if controversial, hero. This time, however, the most memorable impressions were cast by a witness, Lieutenant Colonel Oliver North, a White House aide deeply involved in the plot. North's boyish appeal and patriotic demeanor projected well on television, on which all the hearings were carried live (as were the McCarthy and Watergate hearings). North capitalized on his notoriety and in 1994 launched an unsuccessful campaign for a U.S. Senate seat from Virginia. In October 1991, the nation viewed another televised committee spectacle when Supreme Court nominee Clarence Thomas was accused of sexual harassment.

In 1995 and 1996, Whitewater hearings led by Senator Alfonse D'Amato (R–NY) questioned the actions of President Clinton and Hillary Rodham Clinton in a failed investment venture while Clinton was governor of Arkansas. On much the same subject, even more sensational hearings were convened under Senator Fred Thompson (R–TN) in 1997 concerning the financing of President Clinton's 1996 reelection campaign. Though containing much sound and fury and a number of very serious charges, the hearings seemed to fizzle as the year wore on, since hard evidence was difficult to come by. Similar hearings were held on the House side, headed by Representative Dan Burton (R–IN) in 1998. Burton was a highly controversial choice as chairman because of his staunchly anti-Clinton perspective and was not viewed as credibly as the moderate Thompson. Nonetheless, far more information was revealed, not only by his hearings but by newspaper and television coverage surrounding his hearings.

In July 2004, the bipartisan, independent 9/11 Commission, issued their final report. The panel had heard highly charged and closely watched testimony from members of the Clinton and Bush administrations, New York City emergency personnel, and the families of 9/11 victims. Though the media did not escape censure in the final report, which charged that "between May 2001 and September 11, there was very little in newspapers or on television to heighten anyone's concern about terrorism," the commission's final report and recommendations were extensively covered and often hotly debated.

Coverage of Congress has been greatly expanded through cable channels C-SPAN and C-SPAN2, which provide gavel-to-gavel coverage of House and Senate sessions as well as many committee hearings. For the first time, Americans can watch their representatives in action (or inaction, as the case may be), and do so twenty-four hours a day.

During the Clinton impeachment hearings C-SPAN provided extensive live congressional coverage for cable viewers across the United States.
(Photo courtesy: C-SPAN Archive)

As with coverage of the president, media coverage of Congress is disproportionately negative. Much media attention given to the House and Senate focuses on conflict between members. Political scientists John Hibbing and Elizabeth Theiss-Morse believe that such reporting is at least partially responsible for the public's negative perceptions of Congress.[27]

Covering the Courts

Media coverage of the judiciary differs from coverage of the other two branches of government. Cloaked in secrecy—because judicial deliberations and decision making are conducted in private—the courts receive scant coverage under most circumstances. However, a volatile or controversial issue, such as abortion, can change the usual type of coverage, especially when the Supreme Court is rendering the decision. Each network and major newspaper has one or more Supreme Court reporters, people who are usually well schooled in the law and whose instant analysis of court opinions interprets the decisions for the millions of people without legal training. Gradually, the admission of cameras into state and local courtrooms across the United States is offering people a more in-depth look at the operation of the judicial system. As yet, though, the Supreme Court does not permit televised proceedings. Interestingly, during the case of *Bush* v. *Gore* (2000), the Supreme Court did release tapes of oral argument an hour after the case was heard. Although the proceedings of the U.S. Supreme Court are conducted in public, the justices continue to resist attempts to have oral arguments televised. State courts, however, often allow television cameras in the courtroom. First the Palm Beach rape trial of William Kennedy Smith and then the O. J. Simpson trial attracted millions of viewers. The Simpson trial even spawned two legal-oriented television programs: *Burden of Proof*, a CNN program originally hosted by Greta Van Susteren and Roger Cossack (who had served as commentators during the Simpson trial), and *Geraldo Live*, on CNBC. Court TV, which provides full televised coverage of many highly publicized trials, such as those of Scott Peterson and Martha Stewart, also draws significant viewership.

The work of Independent Counsel Ken Starr and the grand juries investigating Whitewater and President Bill Clinton's relationship with Monica Lewinsky also

WEB EXPLORATION

To learn more about the debate on cameras in the courtroom, particularly the Supreme Court, go to www.ablongman.com/oconnor

attracted the attention of the mass media, overshadowing the pope's historic visit to Cuba in almost all media outlets. In addition, the aftermath of the election 2000 debacle generated intense media coverage of the various courts in Florida, as well as the Supreme Court in Washington, D.C. The operations of the federal and state courts, as well as the judges and attorneys who appear in them, are now regular fodder for media pundits and legal experts.

Watergate and the Era of Investigative Journalism

The Watergate scandal of the Nixon administration had the most profound impact of any modern event on the manner and substance of press conduct. In many respects, Watergate began a chain reaction that today allows for intense media scrutiny of public officials' private lives. Moreover, coupled with the Civil Rights movement and Vietnam War, Watergate shifted the orientation of journalism away from mere description (providing an account of happenings) and toward prescription—helping to set the campaign's (and society's) agenda by focusing attention on the candidates' shortcomings as well as on certain social problems.

A new breed and a new generation of reporters were attracted to journalism, particularly to its investigative role. As a group, they were idealistic, although aggressively mistrustful of authority, and they shared a contempt for "politics as usual." The Vietnam and Watergate generation dominates journalism today. They and their younger colleagues hold sway over most newsrooms, with two-thirds of all reporters now under the age of thirty-six, and an ever-increasing number of editors and executives who had their start in journalism in the Watergate era.[28]

The Post-Watergate Era

A volatile mix of guilt and fear is at work in the post-Watergate press. The guilt stems from regret that experienced Washington reporters failed to detect the telltale signs of the Watergate scandal early on; that even after the story broke, most journalists underplayed the unfolding disaster until forced to take it more seriously by two young *Washington Post* reporters; that over the years journalism's leading lights had become too close to the politicians they were supposed to check and therefore for too long failed to tell the public about dangerous excesses in the government. The press's ongoing fear is deep-seated and complements the guilt. Every political journalist is apprehensive about missing the next big story, of being left on the platform when the next scandal train leaves Union Station.

Washington Post reporters Bob Woodward, right, and Carl Bernstein won a Pulitzer Prize for their reporting of the Watergate case.

(Photo courtesy: AP/Wide World Photos)

In the post-Watergate era, the sizable financial and personnel investments many major news organizations have made in investigative units almost guarantee that greater attention will be given to scandals, and that probably more of them—some real and some manufactured—will be uncovered.

The Character Issue in Media Coverage of Politicians. Another clear consequence of Watergate has been the increasing emphasis by the press on the character of candidates. The issue of character has always been present in U.S. politics—George Washington was not made the nation's first president for his policy positions— but rarely if ever has character been such an issue as it has in elections from 1976 onward. (See

Roots of Government: The Presidency in the Television Age.) Jimmy Carter's 1976 presidential campaign was characterized by moral posturing in the wake of Watergate. Edward M. Kennedy's 1980 presidential candidacy was destroyed in part by lingering character questions. The 1988 race witnessed an explosion of character concerns so forceful that several candidates (including Gary Hart) were badly scarred by it, and the 1992 contest for the White House included probing about the alleged mistresses of Bill Clinton. While Clinton did not suffer irreversible damage in the election, interest in his tawdry affairs set the stage for more serious public revelations. Character was also a major issue in the 2004 presidential election. George W. Bush tried to portray himself as more steadfast in his beliefs than Kerry, and campaigned on the notion that Kerry flip-flopped on major issues including the war in Iraq. Kerry, on the other hand, attempted to show Bush as uncompromising in the face of international opposition to the war. Each charge brought increased media attention to the candidates' character with respect to broad political topics.

The character issue may in part have been an outgrowth of the "new journalism" popularized by author Tom Wolfe in the 1970s.[29] Contending that conventional journalism was sterile and stripped of color, Wolfe and others argued for a reporting style that expanded the definition of news and, novel-like, highlighted all the personal details of the newsmaker. Then, too, reporters had witnessed the success of such books as Theodore H. White's *The Making of the President* series and Joe McGinniss's *The Selling of the President 1968*, which offered revealing, behind-the-scenes vignettes of the previous election's candidates.[30] Why not give readers and viewers this information before the election, the press reasoned. There was encouragement from academic quarters as well. "Look to character first" when evaluating and choosing among presidential candidates, wrote Duke University political science professor James David Barber in a widely circulated 1972 volume, *The Presidential Character* (see chapter 8).[31]

Communications scholar Roderick Hart believes that this shift in focus from issues to character is the result of the shift from newspaper to television news. Unlike print, television is a visual medium, which best portrays faces and images. As a result, voters who receive their political information from television are significantly more likely to rely on candidate traits (rather than issue positions) in casting their ballots than are voters who receive their political information primarily from newspapers.[32]

Whatever the precise historical origins of the character trend in reporting, it is undergirded by certain assumptions. First, the press sees that it has mainly replaced the political parties as the screening committee that winnows the field of candidates and filters out the weaker or more unlucky contenders. (This fact may be another reason to

Representative Gary Condit (D–CA) is surrounded by the media after voting in the March 2002 Democratic primary. Condit was defeated in the primary, due largely to allegations that he was romantically involved with Chandra Levy, an intern who was found murdered in Washington, D.C. after a national search into her disappearance.

(Photo courtesy: Paul Sakuma/AP/Wide World Photos)

We have come to expect most of our presidential candidates to be media-genic—that is, able to look good on television and use their media appearance to achieve their political ends. From their hairstyles and suits to their televised personas, candidates aim to please the unblinking eye of the camera. But, what of the period when television was first emerging as a mass medium? How did the presidency adapt to this strange new cultural force?

Television first became a phenomenon for the mass public at the end of Harry S Truman's presidency in the early 1950s. While historians now rate Truman as a near-great president—that is, among our top fifteen presidents—he was clearly not cut out for the cathode ray tube. He was not a gifted public speaker, and his looks were pedestrian. Had television been universal in those days, it is doubtful that Truman could have been elected without great difficulty. Democrat Truman was followed by Republican Eisenhower, but while their policies and outlooks were very different, they shared the same aversion to television. Eisenhower was, if anything, an even worse public speaker than Truman. While the former World War II general had a dazzling smile that inspired Americans to like and trust him (thus the famous slogan, "I like Ike"), he was particularly inarticulate when delivering official speeches. Eisenhower's inadequacy in communicating with the American people may have been one reason that, despite his enormous personal popularity, he was unable to pass the presidency along to his chosen successor, Richard M. Nixon, in 1960.

Television had its inevitable effect on politics in 1960. In that presidential campaign, John F. Kennedy clearly loved the television camera, and it loved him. His vigor (he pronounced it "vigah," with a Massachusetts accent), the Kennedy family touch football games, his beautiful wife, and his handsome young family all combined to give Kennedy an intangible but powerful media edge against the jowly Nixon. In the famous televised Nixon-Kennedy debate, which probably tipped an extremely close election in JFK's favor, Kennedy's tanned and handsome visage was as much a part of his victory as any argument he employed. In contrast to television viewers, many radio listeners, judging the performance without visual aid, thought that Nixon had won the debate.

Kennedy's time in office was brief, but he set the style that has dominated the presidency in the media ever since. All presidents have tried to live up to the Kennedy standard, some with more success than others, but it is difficult to imagine a talented but TV-phobic president like Truman or Eisenhower coming to the fore of the American political system again.

support the strengthening of the political parties. Politicians are in a much better position than the press to provide professional peer review of colleagues who are seeking the presidency.) Second, many journalists believe it necessary to tell people about any of a candidate's foibles that might affect his or her public performance. The press's third supposition is that it is giving the public what it wants and expects, more or less. Perhaps television has conditioned voters to think about the private lives of the rich and famous. The rules of television prominence now seem to apply to all celebrities equally, whether they reside in Hollywood or Washington. Perhaps more important, scandal sells papers and attracts television viewers.

Loosening of the Libel Law. Another factor permits the modern press to undertake character investigations. In the old days, a reporter would think twice about filing a story critical of a politician's character, and the editors probably would have killed the story had the reporter been foolish enough to do so. The reason? Fear of a libel suit. (Recall from chapter 5 that libel is written defamation of character that unjustly injures a person's reputation.) The first question editors would ask about even an ambiguous or suggestive phrase about a public official was, "If we're sued, can you prove beyond a doubt what you've written?"

Such inhibitions were ostensibly lifted in 1964, when the Supreme Court ruled in **New York Times Co. v. Sullivan** that simply publishing a defamatory falsehood is not enough to justify a libel judgment.[33] Henceforth, a public official would have to prove "actual malice," a requirement extended three years later to all public figures, such as Hollywood stars and prominent athletes.[34] The Supreme Court declared that the First Amendment requires elected officials and candidates to prove that the publisher either

New York Times Co. v. Sullivan (1964)
The Supreme Court concluded that "actual malice" must be proved to support a finding of libel against a public figure.

believed the challenged statement was false or at least entertained serious doubts about its truth and acted recklessly in publishing it in the face of those doubts. The actual malice rule has made it very difficult for public figures to win libel cases.

Despite *Sullivan*, the threat of libel litigation (and its deterrent effect on the press) persists for at least two reasons. First, the *Sullivan* protections do little to reduce the expense of defending defamation claims. The monetary costs have increased enormously, as have the required commitments of reporters' and editors' time and energy. Small news organizations without the financial resources of a national network or the *New York Times* are sometimes reluctant to publish material that might invite a lawsuit, because the litigation costs could threaten their existence. The second reason for the continuing libel threat is a cultural phenomenon of heightened sensitivity to the harm that words can do to an individual's emotional tranquility. As a result, politicians are often more inclined to sue their press adversaries, even when success is unlikely.

But, high costs and the politicians' propensity to sue cut both ways. The overall number of libel suits filed in recent years had dropped because plaintiffs also incur hefty legal expenses, and—perhaps more important—they have despaired of winning. Some news outlets have added another disincentive by filing countersuits charging their antagonists with bringing frivolous or nuisance actions against them.

In practice, then, the loosening of libel law has provided journalists with a safer harbor from liability in their reporting on elected officials and candidates. Whether it has truly diminished press self-censorship, especially for financially less well-endowed media outlets, is a more difficult question to answer. However, at least for the wealthy newspapers and networks, the libel laws are no longer as severe a restraint on the press as they once were.

The Question of Ideological Bias. Whenever the media break an unfavorable story about a politician, the politician usually counters with a cry of "biased reporting"—a claim that the press has told an untruth, has told only part of the truth, or has reported facts out of the complete context of the event. Who is right? Are the news media biased? The answer is simple and unavoidable: Of course they are. Journalists are fallible human beings who inevitably have values, preferences, and attitudes galore—some conscious, others subconscious, but all reflected at one time or another in the subjects selected for coverage or the slant of that coverage. Given that the press is biased, it is important to know in what ways it is biased and when and how the biases are shown.

Truth be told, most journalists lean to the left. First of all, those in the relatively small group of professional journalists (not many more than 100,000, while there are more than 4 million teachers in the United States) are drawn heavily from the ranks of highly educated social and political liberals, as a number of studies, some conducted by the media themselves, have shown.[35] Journalists are substantially Democratic in party affiliation and voting habits, progressive and anti-establishment in political orientation, and well to the left of the general public on most economic, foreign policy, and social issues (such as abortion, affirmative action, gay rights, and gun control). Indeed, a recent survey revealed that, whereas 35 percent of the general public describes themselves as being ideologically conservative, only 6 percent of those in the media would do the same.[36] Second, dozens of the most influential reporters and executives entered (or reentered) journalism after stints of partisan involvement in campaigns or government, and a substantial majority worked for Democrats.[37]

Third, this liberal bias does indeed show up frequently on screen and in print. A study of reporting on the abortion issue, for example, revealed a clear slant to the pro-choice side on network television news, matching in many ways the reporters' own abortion-rights views.[38]

Conservative bias exists in the media as well. Fox News Channel, which has overtaken many CNN shows in cable ratings, features several conservative hosts, including Sean Hannity, Bill O'Reilly, and Brit Hume. Most observers agree that Fox is generally further to the right of most other mainstream media conglomerates. Another more

WEB EXPLORATION

To compare news coverage on a particular news story for evidence of political bias, go to www.ablongman.com/oconnor

Bill O'Reilly, host of the Fox News Channel's television show *The O'Reilly Factor* is one of the country's most visible conservative commentators.

(Photo courtesy: Marc Asnin/Corbis Saba)

extreme example is the world of AM radio talk shows. Some studies have indicated that liberal programs actually enjoy more airtime than conservative ones, but there is no question that conservatives have hosted by far the most popular shows, as exemplified by Rush Limbaugh, G. Gordon Liddy (of Watergate infamy), and Sean Hannity. These radio hosts are the political equivalent of "shock jocks." They strive for controversy and attack liberals (they especially targeted Sen. John Kerry and liberal filmmaker Michael Moore) with ferocious and inflammatory rhetoric.

Of course, these conservative hosts are within their First Amendment rights, and their programs only exist because an audience exists to support them. The Limbaugh show, for example, which attracts millions of listeners every day, is tremendously profitable and successful in increasing voter preferences for Republican candidates, according to one analysis of panel-study data.[39] At the same time, others worry that these programs have a corrosive effect on political discourse and are unfair to their appointed targets. However, it must be said that these conservative organs provide some balance to the liberal orientation of much of the other media, especially in the evening news programs televised on the major networks and cable channels.

Other Sources of Bias.   From left to right on the political spectrum, the charge of ideological bias has some validity in different times and circumstances, in one media forum or another. But, these critiques ignore some nonideological factors probably more essential to an understanding of media bias. Owing to competition and the reward structure of journalism, the deepest bias most political journalists have is the desire to get to the bottom of a good campaign story—which is usually negative news about a candidate. The fear of missing a good story, more than bias, leads all media outlets to develop the same headlines and to adopt the same slant.

A related nonideological bias is the effort to create a horse race where none exists. Newspeople, whose lives revolve around the current political scene, naturally want to add spice and drama, minimize their boredom, and increase their audience. Other human, not just partisan, biases are also at work. Whether the press likes or dislikes a candidate personally is often vital. Former Governor Bruce Babbitt and U.S. Representative Morris K. Udall, both wisecracking, straight-talking Arizona Democrats, were press favorites in their presidential bids (in 1988 and 1976, respectively), and both enjoyed favorable coverage. Richard M. Nixon, Jimmy Carter, and Gary Hart—all aloof politicians—were disliked by many reporters who covered them, and they suffered from a harsh and critical press. More recently, as House speaker, Newt Gingrich was a favorite target of the press. Repeatedly, the stories newspaper editors decided to print about Gingrich when he was speaker of the House cast him in a negative light. This treatment contributed to his negative popularity ratings. But, like any other institution, the press develops a relationship with political figures, who assume some responsibility for the images and impressions they transmit. One possible explanation for Gingrich's poor relationship with the media is that he mismanaged, or simply overexposed himself. The higher a politician's profile, the more open they are to scrutiny, and must take great care in their handling of the press.

Some research even suggests that candidates may charge the media with bias as a strategy for dealing with the press, and that bias claims are part of the dynamic between elected officials and reporters. If a candidate can plausibly and loudly decry bias in the media as the source of his negative coverage, for example, reporters might temper future negative stories or give the candidate favorable coverage to mitigate the calls of bias.[40]

One other source of bias, or at least of non-objectivity, in the press is the increasing celebrity status of many people involved in reporting the news. In an age of media stardom and blurring boundaries between forms of entertainment, journalists in prominent media positions have unprecedented opportunities to attain fame and fortune, of which they often take full advantage. Already commanding multimillion-dollar salaries, jour-

Are the Media Biased?

nalists can often secure lucrative speaker's fees by addressing corporations, trade societies, private political organizations, universities, and media gatherings. Especially in the case of journalists with highly ideological perspectives, close involvement with wealthy or powerful special-interest groups can blur the line between reporting on policy issues and influencing them. Some journalists even find work as political consultants or members of government—which seems reasonable, given their prominence, abilities, and expertise, but which can become problematic when they move between spheres not once, but repeatedly. A good example of this troublesome revolving-door phenomenon is the case of Pat Buchanan, who has repeatedly and alternately enjoyed prominent positions in media (as a host of CNN's *Crossfire* and later on MSNBC) and politics (as a perennial presidential candidate). If American journalism is to retain the watertight integrity for which it is justly renowned, it is essential that key distinctions between private and media enterprise and conscientious public service continue to command our respect.

But, does media bias affect election outcomes? Perhaps. In the 1970s, political scientist Eric Veblen showed that the net advantage that the *Manchester Union-Leader*, New Hampshire's most influential newspaper, provided its favored candidate could increase that candidate's vote share significantly.[41] On the other hand, media darlings such as Howard Dean (former Vermont governor) and Senator John McCain (R–AZ) failed in their quest to become president, while those less popular with the media, such as Jimmy Carter and Richard M. Nixon, succeeded. Clearly, bias is not the be-all and end-all that critics on both the right and left often insist that it is. Press tilt has a marginal to moderate effect, and is merely one piece in the media's mosaic.

THE MEDIA'S INFLUENCE ON THE PUBLIC

How much influence do the media have on the public? In most cases the press has surprisingly little effect. To put it bluntly, people tend to see what they want to see; that is, human beings will focus on parts of a report that reinforce their own attitudes and ignore parts that challenge their core beliefs. Most of us also selectively tune out or ignore reports that contradict our preferences in politics and other fields. Therefore, a committed Democrat will remember certain portions of a televised news program about a current campaign—primarily the parts that reinforce his or her own choice—and an equally committed Republican will recall very different sections of the report or remember the material in a way that supports the GOP position. In other words, most voters are not empty vessels into which the media can pour their own beliefs. This fact dramatically limits the ability of news organizations to sway public opinion.

However, this is not the only view. Some political scientists argue that the content of network television news accounts for a large portion of the volatility and change in policy preferences of Americans, when measured over relatively short periods of time.[42] These changes are called **media effects.** Let's examine how these media-influenced changes might occur.

First, reporting can sway people who are uncommitted and have no strong opinion in the first place. So, for example, the media have a greater influence on political independents than on strong partisans.[43] Indeed, many studies from the 1940s and 1950s, an era when partisanship was very strong, suggested that the media had no influence at all on public opinion. The last forty years, however, have seen the rapid decline in political partisanship,[44] thereby opening the door to greater media influence. On the other hand, the sort of politically unmotivated individual who is open to media effects is probably unlikely to vote in a given election, and therefore the media influence is of no particular consequence.

Second, the media have a much greater impact on topics far removed from the lives and experiences of its readers and viewers. News reports can probably shape public opinion about events in foreign countries fairly easily. Yet, what the media say about domestic issues such as rising prices, neighborhood crime, or child rearing may have relatively

Visual Literacy

The Media and the
American Public

media effects
The influence of news sources on public opinion.

little effect, because most citizens have personal experience of and well-formed ideas about these subjects.

Third, news organizations can help tell us what to think about, even if they cannot determine what we think. As mentioned earlier, the press often sets the agenda for government or a campaign by focusing on certain issues or concerns. For example, in the weeks following the Littleton, Colorado, school massacre in 1999, every national network devoted extensive coverage to the incident. Sure enough, concern about gun control, school safety, and cultural violence began to top the list of national problems considered most pressing by the public, as measured in opinion polls. Without the dramatic pictures and lavish attention that accompanied the shooting, it is doubtful that these issues would have risen so quickly to the forefront of the national agenda.

Thus, perhaps not so much in *how* they cover an event, but in *what* they choose to cover, the media make their effect felt. By deciding to focus on one event while ignoring another, the media can determine to a large extent the country's agenda, an awe-inspiring power. Unfortunately, the media has increasingly focused on the horse-race aspects of a campaign, rather than giving candidates a chance to address issues in more than a six-second soundbyte.

The media's power to shape citizens' perceptions—though limited—can have important implications for the success of politicians. For example, voters' choice in presidential elections is often related to their assessments of the economy. In general, a healthy economy motivates voters to reelect the incumbent president, whereas a weak economy motivates voters to choose the challenger. Hence, if the media paint a consistently dismal picture of the economy, that picture may well hurt the incumbent president seeking reelection. In fact, political scientist Marc Hetherington convincingly shows that the media's relentlessly negative coverage of the economy in 1992 shaped voters' retrospective assessments of the economy, which in turn helped lead to George Bush's defeat in the 1992 presidential election.[45]

Another primary determinant of election outcomes relates to matters of war and peace. In times of relative peace, or in times of popular and successful war, incumbent presidents have a pronounced advantage. Alternatively, if the country is engaged in an unpopular and unsuccessful war, incumbent presidents can pay the price on Election Day. The 2004 election featured copious coverage and debate on the war in Iraq. Despite a high number of casualties and a large percentage of Americans against the war, President Bush did not suffer in the polls. One primary explanation is that he was able to successfully link the war in Iraq to the on-going war against terror, which was one of his strongest positions.

On Election Night 2000, all the networks assigned Florida to Al Gore's list of wins fairly early in the evening. In fact, their call was extremely premature, and their actions had disastrous consequences for the dignity and credibility of both the networks and the election. Most viewers did not catch the nuance that the networks had given Florida to Gore based purely on exit-poll predictions, before any Florida precincts had reported a single actual return, and the ensuing reversal, counter-reversal, and confusion—reminiscent of the famous *Chicago Daily Tribune's* "Dewey Defeats Truman"—have become legendary. Although the media did a much better job on Election Night 2004 than they did four years ago, it is worth remembering the debacle of the 2000 election and discussing an important way in which the media can influence public behavior. It was later discovered that a series of errors had contributed to the debacle, including: network over-eagerness to break the news; underestimating the number of absentee ballots in Florida; network projections based on inadequate poll data in key Florida cities; and flaws in the sampling techniques of exit-pollers in Florida. Many of these errors can be laid at the feet of Voter News Service, a company created and owned by the major networks and the Associated Press for the specific purpose of reporting uniform and reliable election results. For their part, VNS blames budget limitations for their inability to do their job accurately.[46]

Due to VNS's poor performance in both 2000 and 2002, the media consortium funding it decided to pull the plug on it in early 2003, preferring to make other

arrangements with pollsters and analysts for the 2004 elections. The exit poll results in 2004 were not much better, with the pre-results being widely criticized for showing Senator John Kerry with a commanding lead throughout the day.

THE PUBLIC'S PERCEPTION OF THE MEDIA

The news media has long felt the brunt of public discontent and criticism, more so than other institutions essential to the operation of the American government. When asked in the summer of 2002 how much confidence they had in various institutions, only 11 percent of the public said they had a great deal of confidence in the media, ranking them just behind the Internal Revenue Service. By comparison, 50 percent had a great deal of confidence in the president, and 71 percent felt the same way about the military.[47] The Pew Research Center for the People and the Press, which has been studying public opinion of the media since 1985, found that survey participants when asked to describe the national news media use the words "biased" and "sensational" nearly as often as "good" and "informative."[48] A majority of Americans perceive the media to be politically biased (generally in favor of the Democrats, with the exception of Fox News favoring Republicans); believe they stand in the way of solving society's problems; and think that they usually report inaccurately and are unwilling to admit mistakes. Most pejoratively, over two-thirds of the people interviewed in 1999 believed that the news media did not care about the people they report on.[49]

One of the most common perceptions of the media is that it has a liberal political bias that influences how journalists and news organizations cover stories. Over the past decade, there has been an increase in the number of voters who believe that reporters allow their political preferences to shape news coverage. Just prior to the 2000 presidential election, 57 percent of voters held that view, compared to 49 percent in 1992. Twice as many voters (47 percent) believed that the media were pulling for a Gore victory compared to those who thought the media was hoping for a Bush victory (23 percent). The gap shrank considerably from the 1996 election, where 59 percent of voters said that most members of the media wanted Bill Clinton to win, while just 17 percent believed that reporters wanted a Bob Dole victory.[50]

Despite obvious displeasure expressed by the majority of Americans about political bias and sensationalism, credibility ratings for the national news media have remained relatively high. Broadcast news outlets tend to get higher believability ratings than print, with CNN, C-SPAN, and the major networks leading the way. Anchormen Tom Brokaw, Dan Rather, and Peter Jennings rate as the most trusted journalists (around 80 percent positive ratings), while cable journalists Geraldo Rivera ranks at the bottom (less than 9 percent believe all or most of what he says).[51] The main exception to the domination of broadcast outlets is the *Wall Street Journal*, which consistently ranks with CNN at the top of credibility polls. In addition, more people tend to trust their local news organizations more than national news networks.

The terrorist attacks of September 11, 2001, caused a temporary shift in the public's attitude toward the media. In addition to Americans following the news more closely and relying more heavily on cable network coverage of the attacks and the war on terrorism, 69 percent of those polled believed that the news media stands up for America, and the professionalism rating of the news media soared to 73 percent (See Table 15.3). Improvements cut across demographic and political lines, and criticism abated as a confidence in the media rose. This bounce in popularity, however, was to be short-lived. By July of 2002, less than a year after the attacks, the public's perception and support of the media was essentially the same as pre-September 11 levels. The percentage of Americans who believed that the news media stands up for America plummeted twenty points to 49 percent, and the percent of people who believed the news organizations were highly professional dropped to below half, down from 73 percent in November 2001. Despite the less favorable view of the press, Americans continue to value the watchdog role that the media serves, with 59 percent believing that press scrutiny keeps political leaders from doing things they should not do. In addition, a substantial majority thinks that the media's influence is increasing, rather than decreasing. Whether that is a positive or negative assessment remains to be seen.[52]

With the expansion of Internet news sources and around the clock cable news networks, citizens have come to rely on more than their own judgment to discern whether or not the media is performing their duties sufficiently. In addition to the Pew Research Center for the People and the Press, numerous polling organizations survey voters to gather and analyze public opinion regarding the news media. Several major newspapers and magazines, including the *Washington Post* and the *Boston Globe*, have media critics, who write about how well the media is performing their duties. Some non-profits, such as the Center for Media and Public Affairs in Washington, D.C., conduct scientific studies of the news and entertainment media. Other groups, including Accuracy In Media, are self-proclaimed conservative watchdogs. They critique news stories and attempt to set the record straight on important issues that they believe have received biased coverage. All of these organizations have a role in ensuring that the media provides fair and balanced coverage of topics that are of importance to citizens.

TABLE 15.3   News Media Ratings Backslide

	Feb 1999 %	Early Sept 2001 %	Nov 2001 %	July 2002 %
Percentage polled responding that news organizations …				
Usually get facts straight	37	35	**46**	35
Usually report inaccurately	58	57	45	56
Don't know	5	8	9	9
Are highly professional	52	54	**73**	49
Are not professional	32	27	12	31
Neither/Don't know	16	19	15	20
Stand up for America	41	43	**69**	49
Too critical of America	42	36	17	35
Neither/Don't know	17	21	14	16
Are moral	40	40	**53**	39
Are immoral	38	34	23	36
Neither/Don't know	22	26	24	25
Care about the people they report on	21	23	**47**	30
Don't care	67	64	38	55
Neither/Don't know	12	13	15	15

Source: "News Media's Improved Image Proves Short-Lived," August 4, 2002. Pew Research Center for the Public and the Press, http://people-press.org. Reprinted by permission of Pew Research Center.

HOW POLITICIANS USE THE MEDIA

Although the media are powerful actors in any election campaign, they can also be used and manipulated by politicians in a variety of ways. The use of focus groups, in which campaign consultants attempt to gauge the strengths and weaknesses of presenting candidates or policy positions in particular ways, is a powerful tool in a politician's pocket when attempting to discern how best to tailor a media campaign. Additionally, politicians can attempt to bypass the national news media through paid advertising and by appearing on talk shows and local news programs (see Table 15.4). Some of these and other techniques for dealing with the media during a campaign are discussed in greater detail in chapter 14. Politicians also use the media to attempt to retain a high level of name recognition and to build support for their ideological and policy ideas.

As president, Bill Clinton was an acknowledged master of media manipulation. Despite all of the negative coverage he endured over his long political career, or perhaps because of it, Clinton knew how to push the right media buttons. For example, in his initiative to encourage better race relations, which he labeled a prime goal of his second term, President Clinton staged a series of town meetings and televised encounters among people of all colors. Most of these events were carefully orchestrated and resulted in little frank talk, something experts in the field of race relations believe is a necessity if real progress is to be made. Yet, reams of positive publicity resulted, so at least from a public relations perspective, the race initiative could be termed a success. Presidents are often pulled in many directions by interest groups, constituencies, and even their own bureaucracy. Whether any substantive progress came out of the town meetings may have been, to the administration, less important than the gesture of drawing national attention to an issue and using the press to create a favorable public discourse. President Clinton was not always the leader in getting the media to focus attention on a particular issue, however. Indeed, often the relationship was exactly the opposite—the president *reacted* to attention given to an issue by the news media. This seemed to be especially true in foreign policy.[53]

Politics once again met policy on the day before President Clinton was scheduled to be impeached by the House of Representatives, when the president decided to launch the largest attack on Iraq since the Persian Gulf War. Clinton's military advisers urged this action, but the timing was naturally highly suspicious to many on the Republican side of the aisle as well as in the news media. Some went so far as to suggest

TABLE 15.4	Senators Most Often on Sunday News Shows, 2002					
	Total	*Face the Nation*	*Meet the Press*	*This Week*	*Late Edition*	*Fox News Sunday*
Joe Lieberman (D–CT)	7	2	1	0	2	2
John McCain (R–AZ)	7	2	2	1	1	1
Tom Daschle (D–SD)	6	2	1	1	1	1
Mitch McConnell (R–KY)	5	1	0	0	3	1
Richard Shelby (R–AL)	5	0	1	1	3	0
Joe Biden (D–DE)	4	1	1	0	1	1
John Edwards (D–NC)	4	0	0	0	2	2
Bob Graham (D–FL)	4	0	1	1	1	1
Trent Lott (R–MS)	4	1	1	0	0	2
Chuck Hagel (R–NE)	3	0	0	1	1	1
Chris Dodd (D–CT)	2	0	0	0	2	0
Byron Dorgan (D–ND)	2	0	1	0	1	0
Dianne Feinstein (D–CA)	2	0	1	0	1	0
Carl Levin (D–MI)	2	1	0	1	0	0
Don Nickles (R–OK)	2	0	0	0	1	1
Arlen Specter (R–PA)	2	1	0	0	1	0

Note: Table shows number of 2002 appearances through April.

Source: Roll Call (April 11, 2002): 4. ©Copyright 2002, Roll Call.

During the 2000 presidential campaign, George W. Bush appeared on talk shows such as the *Oprah Winfrey Show*.

(Photo courtesy: Wilfredo Lee/AP/Wide World Photos)

on background
A term for when sources are not specifically named in a news story.

deep background
Information gathered for news stories that must be completely unsourced.

off the record
Term applied to information gathered for a news story that cannot be used at all.

on the record
Term applied to information gathered for a news story that can be used and cited.

that the president was following the script of a recent movie, *Wag the Dog*, in which a president attempts to divert attention from his sex scandal by starting a war. This was but the latest example of real-life politics seeming to imitate the art and entertainment of our time.

In October 2004, Jon Stewart, host of Comedy Central's popular faux-news program "The Daily Show," appeared on CNN's "Crossfire" debate show with hosts Paul Begala and Tucker Carlson. In a very testy and personal discussion, Stewart criticized "Crossfire" and other debate shows as being political theater, much like professional wrestling. He said that they were "hurting America" and that instead of being real journalists asking tough question, "Crossfire" and other shows like it were part of the strategy of the campaigns—they help get the partisan message out to a wider (and unexpecting) audience.

The Jon Stewart appearance on "Crossfire" made waves not only because of how bitter the discussion was (he called Tucker Carlson an inappropriate name for a portion of the male anatomy), but also because of the interesting critique he offered of some of the modern political news shows. Many of these debate shows feature partisan hacks yelling at each other, and whoever yells loudest or last generally wins the debate. This has undoubtedly hindered political dialogue by making the debate more vitriolic and polzarizing. One must remain hopeful that, in time, networks will move away from this political theater and create a more meaningful dialogue about politics

Among recent politicians, Senator John McCain (R–AZ) rediscovered a brilliant political gambit: attract copious, free, and favorable media coverage by wooing the journalists themselves. McCain was so straightforward, candid, accessible, and generous with his time during the 2000 primary season that the reporter pool collectively fell in love with him even as he out-endured them in the media game, exhausting their questions but never running short of answers. McCain named his campaign bus "The Straight Talk Express," and it soon became famous for hosting regular, intimate, on-the-road interviews. McCain had a popular issue in campaign finance reform, but only his skill in delivering that message through the media enabled him to overcome tight funding and win the New Hampshire primary over George W. Bush in a landslide upset not anticipated in the polls.

In the early months of his presidency, George W. Bush ingratiated himself with the media, as they responded well to his affable personality. Bush garnered near hero status for his leadership in response to the September 11 terrorist attacks, especially during his visits to Ground Zero and his subsequent address to Congress. The war in Afghanistan lengthened his immunity from press criticism, but by the spring of 2002, the rush of corporate scandals—some connected directly and indirectly to Bush and Cheney—removed Bush's special status. But, the Bush administration's ability to keep the media and the nation captivated by an inevitable showdown with Iraq rather than a sagging American economy aided the GOP in the 2002 midterm elections.

On some occasions, candidates and their aides will go on background to give trusted newspersons juicy morsels of negative information about rivals. **On background**—meaning that none of the news can be attributed to the source—is one of several journalistic devices used to elicit information that might otherwise never come to light. **Deep background** is another such device; whereas background talks can be attributed to unnamed senior officials, deep background news must be completely unsourced, with the reporter giving the reader no hint about the origin of the information. An even more drastic form of obtaining information is the **off-the-record** discussion, in which nothing the official says may be printed. (If a reporter can obtain the same information elsewhere, however, he or she is free to publish it.) By contrast, in an **on-the-record** session, such as a formal press conference, every word an official utters can be printed—and used against that official. It is no wonder that office holders often prefer the non-publishable alternatives!

Clearly, these rules are necessary for reporters to do their basic job—informing the public. Ironically, the same rules keep the press from fully informing their readers and viewers. Every public official knows that journalists are pledged to protect the confidentiality of their sources, and therefore the rules can sometimes be used to an official's own benefit.

GOVERNMENT REGULATION OF THE ELECTRONIC MEDIA

The U.S. government regulates the electronic component of the media. Unlike radio or television, the print media are exempt from most forms of government regulation, although even print media must not violate community standards for obscenity, for instance. There are two reasons for this unequal treatment. First, the airwaves used by the electronic media are considered public property; they are leased by the federal government to private broadcasters. Second, those airwaves are in limited supply, and without some regulation, the nation's many radio and television stations would interfere with one another's frequency signals. It was not, in fact, the federal government but rather private broadcasters, frustrated by the numerous instances in which signal jamming occurred, that initiated the call for government regulation in the early days of the electronic media. Newspapers, of course, are not subject to these technical considerations.

The first government regulation of the electronic media came in 1927, when Congress enacted the Federal Radio Act, which established the Federal Radio Commission (FRC) and declared the airwaves to be public property. In addition, the act required that all broadcasters be licensed by the FRC. In 1934, the Federal Communications Commission (FCC) replaced the FRC as the electronic media regulatory body. The FCC is composed of five members, of whom not more than three can be from the same political party. These members are selected by the president for five-year terms on an overlapping basis. Because the FCC is shielded from direct, daily control by the president or Congress—although both have influence over the FCC commissioners—it is an independent regulatory agency (see chapter 9). In addition to regulating public and commercial radio and television, the FCC oversees telephone, telegraph, satellite, and foreign communications in the United States.

In 1996, Congress passed the sweeping Telecommunications Act, deregulating whole segments of the electronic media. The goal of the legislation was to break down the barriers required by federal and state laws and by the legal settlement that broke up the AT&T/Bell monopoly in 1984, which separated local phone service, long-distance service, and cable television service. The hope was that such deregulation and increased competition would create cheaper and better programming options for consumers and increase the global competitiveness of U.S. telecommunications firms. Under the new law, consumers would be able to receive phone service from their cable provider, television programming from their local phone company, or local phone service from their long-distance service provider. Besides more flexible service options, the legislation was expected to spur the development of new products and services such as unlimited movie selections, interactive television, and advanced computer networking that would permit more people to work from their homes.

The core of the legislation was the federal preemption of state and local laws that granted monopolies to local telephone carriers. The seven "baby Bells," the regional phone companies that were allowed to monopolize local telephone service since the 1984 breakup of AT&T, were required to allow competitors to use their local networks. In return for opening their local networks to competition, the regional Bells were allowed to enter the long-distance service market, from which they had been barred since the AT&T breakup. The Telecommunications Act sought to provide an optimal balance of competing corporate interests, technological innovations, and consumer needs. Passage of the act spawned what appeared to some as limitless opportunities for entrepreneurial companies to provide enhanced services to consumers. The pooling system, for example, used to subsidize and redistribute the higher costs of providing services to rural customers, had to be revamped. In May 2002, the FCC issued a landmark ruling that cable internet services are defined as "information services", not "telecommunications" that would have subjected new providers to network sharing provisions in the 1996 act. The reality of deregulation was, in fact, a complex and convoluted evolution that has resulted in growth for industries affected by the act, but also a deluge of civil actions by corporations and consumers alike.

There have also been significant changes in the regulations for private ownership of broadcast stations. First, there is no longer a cap on how many FM and AM stations a single company can own. In the 1950s, under the 7-7-7 rule, companies were limited to seven each of television, AM, and FM stations that they could own throughout the nation. By the 1990s, however, this limit had been progressively raised to twelve television stations and twenty each of FM and AM stations. Despite eliminating the cap, there are still limits on how many stations any one firm can own in each market. The FCC examines on a case-by-case basis whether an owner should be allowed to have two television stations in the same local market.

The legislation provoked criticism by civil libertarian groups that objected to provisions designed to curb "cyberpornography" by banning the dissemination of "indecent" material on the Internet and online services. Indecency is a very broad legal standard that includes use of profanity. While it has been applied to broadcasting in a limited way, it has not been used in recent years as a standard for written material, nor for "information services" that are excluded from traditional regulation. The act also requires all large-screen televisions to include built-in "V-chips" that permit parents to block objectionable material they do not wish their family to view.

Content Regulation

content regulation
Governmental attempts to regulate the electronic media.

equal time rule
The rule that requires broadcast stations to sell campaign air time equally to all candidates if they choose to sell it to any.

fairness doctrine
Rule in effect from 1949 to 1985 requiring broadcasters to cover events adequately and to present contrasting views on important public issues.

The government subjects the electronic media to substantial **content regulation** that, again, does not apply to the print media. Charged with ensuring that the airwaves "serve the public interest, convenience, and necessity," the FCC has attempted to promote equity in broadcasting. For example, the **equal time rule** requires that broadcast stations sell campaign airtime equally to all candidates if they choose to sell it to any, which they are under no obligation to do. An exception to this rule is a political debate: Stations may exclude from this event less well-known and minor-party candidates.

Until 2000, FCC rules required broadcasters to give candidates the opportunity to respond to personal attacks and to political endorsements by the station. In October 2000, however, a federal court of appeals found these rules, long attacked by broadcasters as having a chilling effect on free speech, to be unconstitutional when the FCC was unable to justify these regulations to its satisfaction.

Perhaps the most controversial FCC regulation was the **fairness doctrine.** Implemented in 1949 and in effect until 1985, the fairness doctrine required broadcasters to be "fair" in their coverage of news events—that is, they had to cover the events adequately and present contrasting views on important public issues. Many broadcasters disliked this rule, claiming that fairness is simply too difficult to define and that the rule abridged their First Amendment freedoms. They also argued that it ultimately forced broadcasters to decrease coverage of controversial issues out of fear of a deluge of requests for air time from interest groups involved in each matter.

In a hotly debated 1985 decision, the FCC, without congressional consent, abolished the fairness doctrine, arguing that the growth of the electronic media in the United States during the preceding forty years had created enough diversity among the stations to render unnecessary the ordering of diversity within them. In 1986, a federal circuit court of appeals vindicated the FCC decision, holding that the FCC did not need congressional approval to abolish the rule. Seeking to counter the FCC's decision, Congress attempted to write the fairness doctrine into law. Although both the House and the Senate passed the bill, President Reagan vetoed it, citing his First Amendment concerns about government regulation of the news media.

The abolition of the fairness doctrine has by no means ended debate over its merit, however. Proponents, still trying to reinstate the doctrine, argue that its elimination results in a reduction of quality programming on public issues. In their view, deregulation means more advertisements, soap operas, and situation comedies wasting airtime and leaving less room for public discourse on important matters. Opponents of the fairness doctrine, on the other hand, continue to call for decreased regulation, arguing that the electronic media should be as free as the print media—especially because the electronic media are now probably more competitive than are the print media.

Censorship

The media in the United States, while not free of government regulation, enjoy considerably more liberty than do their counterparts in other countries, and even in other democracies. One of the world's oldest democracies, Great Britain nonetheless owns that nation's main electronic medium, the British Broadcasting Company (BBC). The BBC, along with the privately owned media, is subjected to unusually strict regulation on the publication of governmental secrets. For example, the sweeping Official Secrets Act of 1911 makes it a criminal offense for a Briton to publish any facts, material, or news collected in that person's capacity as a public minister or civil servant. The act was invoked when the British government banned the publication of *Spy Catcher*, a 1987 novel written by Peter Wright, a former British intelligence officer, who undoubtedly collected much of the book's information while on the job. On the other hand, the UK applies a far more liberal standard of indecency to its broadcasters, who exercise considerably more freedom than Americans with regard to explicit content.

In the United States, only government officials can be prosecuted for divulging classified information; no such law applies to journalists. Nor can the government, except under extremely rare and confined circumstances, impose prior restraints on the press—that is, the government cannot censor the press. This principle was clearly established in *New York Times Co. v. U.S.* (1971).[55] In this case, the Supreme Court ruled that the government could not prevent publication by the *New York Times* of the Pentagon Papers, classified government documents about the Vietnam War that had been stolen, photocopied, and sent to the *Times* and the *Washington Post* by Daniel Ellsberg, an antiwar activist. "Only a free and unrestrained press can effectively expose deception in the government," Justice Hugo Black wrote in a concurring opinion for the Court. "To find that the President has 'inherent power' to halt the publication of news by resort to the courts would wipe out the first Amendment."

To assist the media in determining what is and is not publishable, Great Britain provides a system called D-notice, which allows journalists to submit questionable material to a review committee before its publication. But D-notice has not quelled argument over media freedom in the United Kingdom. Indeed, the debate came to the fore during the 1982 Falkland Islands war between Great Britain and Argentina, when it centered on questions of how much information the public had a right to know and whether the media should remain neutral in covering a war in which the nation is involved. Once again, however, the British government prevailed in arguing for continued strict control of the media,

Political news coverage often involves "talking heads" in the studio and on-the-spot press conferences. Here, *Meet the Press* moderator Tim Russert (left) discusses the joint House-Senate Intelligence Committees' investigation of the September 11 attacks with members of Congress.

(Photo courtesy: Alex Wong/Getty Images)

MEDIA FREEDOM

What role the media play in politics is partly determined by how free the media are. In 2000 and 2002, Freedom House, an independent civil liberties organization, rated the degree of media freedom in 186 countries of the world. Using as criteria the degree of government ownership of the media, pressures on media, and actual violations of media freedom, the organization rated countries on a 100-point scale. The lower the score, the freer the media is from government interference. Countries rated between 0 and 30 are considered to have free media, those between 31 and 60 partly free, and those between 61 and 100 not free.

The United States in this respect is in good company. All industrial democracies are considered to have free presses, although they vary in degree. The U.S., Canadian, Japanese, and German media were rated freest among the group in the 2002 survey. State restrictions on the media are highest in Italy and France, which are close to the partly free threshold. The press in Russia, Mexico, and Indonesia are considered partly free because recent trends toward independent, competitive media institutions still must face governments that control significant media resources and that continue to try to control the content of private media.

Restrictions on the media vary. All the industrial democracies have public media outlets, most of which are more visible and influential than National Public Radio or the Public Broadcasting Service are in the United States, but the degree of government editorial control varies. In the late 1990s, Japan and the United Kingdom adopted freedom of information acts, but restrictions on the press remain. The Russian government includes a ministry, directly responsible to the president, which supervises the media. Critics charge the government with systematically eliminating independent media outlets over the last several years. Egypt's government owns stock in the major newspapers, and the president appoints the editors-in-chief.

Freedom House Scores for Media Freedom, 2001–2002		
Country	Freedom House Score	Freedom House Rating
Canada	16	Free
China	80	Not Free
Egypt	77	Not Free
France	17	Free
Germany	15	Free
India	42	Partly Free
Indonesia	53	Partly Free
Italy	27	Free
Japan	17	Free
Mexico	40	Partly Free
Russia	60	Partly Free
United Kingdom	18	Free
United States	**16**	**Free**

Note: Countries are rated on a 100-point scale; the lower the score, the freer the media.

Source: Freedom House, *Press Freedom Survey* 2002, http://freedomhouse.org/pfs2000/reports.html.

China ranks near the bottom of Freedom House's ratings, with near universal control over media outlets and routine harassment of journalists critical of the government. Media self-censorship is a problem in many countries.

Media censorship is not limited solely to authoritarian societies. The terrorist attacks on the World Trade Center and the Pentagon, followed by the war in Afghanistan, provoked government responses that were seen as potentially infringing on media freedom. Of the industrial democracies cited here, five—Canada, France, Germany, the United Kingdom, and the United States—initiated legislation or other policy measures to allow greater government and police control over media, in particular the Internet. Canada and the United States saw their media freedom ratings drop slightly from the 2000 survey in part because of issues involving censorship concerns related to government attempts to curb terrorism.

Comparative

Comparing News Media

declaring, "There can be sound military reasons for withholding the whole truth from the public domain, [or] for using the media to put out 'misinformation.'"[56]

Similar questions and arguments arose in the United States during the 1991 Persian Gulf War. Reporters were upset that the military was not forthcoming about events on and off the battlefield, while some Pentagon officials and many persons in the general public accused the press of telling the enemy too much in their dispatches. Unlike the case in Great Britain, however, the U.S. government had little recourse but to attempt to isolate offending reporters by keeping them away from the battlefield. Even this maneuver was highly controversial and very unpopular with news correspondents because it directly interfered with their job of reporting the news. Critics of the mili-

THE MEDIA'S REACTION TO SEPTEMBER 11

After terrorist attacks in the United States on September 11, 2001, a normally skeptical press became a flag-waving press, with some unpredictable consequences. American flags were everywhere on television and in the print press: on news anchors' lapels, in TV logos, and across the pages of newspapers. Dan Rather, the CBS evening news anchor and managing editor, openly cried on air and began using the first-person plural ("we Americans" and "our fighting men and women") in news reports. NBC's Tom Brokaw also choked up more than once. When his personal assistant was exposed to anthrax, he closed an evening news broadcast by disclosing he was on antibiotics, too, and saying, "In Cipro we trust." The media were personally involved in the news, much of which unfolded in their home city of New York, and they made no bones about their allegiances and their anger.

As understandable as this was, the media's lowering of the usual barriers between themselves and governmental authorities changed the tone of coverage. News organizations were remarkably uncritical of politicians, and occasionally engaged in boosterism of sorts. President George W. Bush, who once was characterized by the media as barely adequate for the job, became a new Winston Churchill. Secretary of Defense Donald Rumsfeld, once widely derided in the press as being ineffectual, became the tell-it-like-it-is media star at daily briefings. New York City Mayor Rudy Giuliani, who had been getting negative coverage for everything from his marital problems to his rude demeanor, became a national hero. Bush, Rumsfeld, and Giuliani were not as bad as the press suggested before September 11, but they also were not as perfect as depicted after the tragedy. Happy mediums are not the media's forte.

Even Congress, which hardly ever gets positive publicity as an institution, enjoyed particularly positive media for months after September 11. When members of Congress appeared on the Capitol steps to sing "God Bless America" after the attacks, Republicans and Democrats arm in arm, they effectively disarmed the media brute.

Rather than return the favor, though, the government appeared to distrust the media as much as ever. The best example came in the restrictions on news organizations as they attempted to cover the war in Afghanistan. Following the precedents set in U.S. military actions in Grenada in 1983, Panama in 1989, and the Persian Gulf War in 1991, reporters covering the war were kept away from the action in most cases, and even sequestered and isolated in some instances. In effect, the press had to rely almost entirely on the Pentagon's own analysis of what was happening and how effectively they were prosecuting the war. Obviously, there was no press check on the most far-reaching of all governmental powers—the right to wage war.

Source: Adaptation from "Sobering Up: The Media World Remade," in *American Government in a Changed World: The Effects of September 11, 2001* by Larry J. Sabato, copyright © 2002. Reprinted by permission of Pearson Education, Inc.

tary's public affairs strategy resent its emphasis on controlling information as a tool for manipulating public support. Both civilian and military officials alike have a keen awareness of and desire to avoid the "Vietnam syndrome," where popular resistance to the war, some would argue, grew out of the media's great freedom to frame events. These same questions arose once again with regard to the war on terrorism, with national security officials expressing concern about leaks that appeared in the media. Indeed, the issue took on increased controversy when it became apparent that some of the leaks may have come from members of Congress.

Such arguments are an inevitable part of the landscape in a free society. Whatever their specific quarrels with the press, most Americans would probably prefer that the media tell them too much rather than not enough. Totalitarian and authoritarian societies have a tame journalism, after all, so media excesses may be the price of unbridled freedom. Without question, a free press is of incalculable value to a nation, as the revolution in the former Soviet Union has shown. The 1991 coup against then Soviet President Mikhail Gorbachev failed in part because the coup leaders could not smother the public's continued desire for freedom, stoked by the relatively uncensored television and print journalism that existed in the final years of Gorbachev's leadership. In addition, the international media has repeatedly drawn attention to the fact that the Chinese government continues to heavily censor the Internet sites its citizens can view.

Join the Debate

IS THE BUSH ADMINISTRATION KEEPING TOO MANY SECRETS ABOUT THE WAR ON TERRORISM?

All presidential administrations worry about media leaks, which are unauthorized or deliberate disclosures of confidential information to reporters. The media relies heavily on leaks to produce interesting stories. If they are not able to get insiders to divulge accurate information, they are only able to report what the administration wants them to hear. They are therefore hindered in their ability to present the real news, and are unable to report on possible misuses of power from the administration. Some presidents, like Bill Clinton, have had major problems with leaks in their administrations. When George W. Bush moved into the White House, he made it clear that he would not tolerate leaks within his administration.

In the aftermath of September 11, 2001, the administration's reputation of being tight-lipped only grew, as the media struggled to get any more information than what was provided in White House press briefings. As the war on terrorism escalated, the administration made the case that any inside information would constitute a direct threat to national security. While most Americans supported the administration's efforts to fight terrorism, there was a certain amount of skepticism as to whether or not the U.S. government was paying too little attention to civil rights. When Abdullah al Muhajir (also known as Jose Padilla) was arrested in the spring of 2002 for allegedly planning to detonate a radioactive "dirty bomb" in the United States, the media was not alerted until more than a month after he was detained.

But the administration was not completely air-tight. In the summer of 2002, several news stories appeared that showed that the administration may have known about the September 11 attacks in advance. The FBI questioned nearly forty members of Senate and House intelligence committees, as well as sixty staff members of the CIA, Department of Defense, and the National Security Agency, as part of an investigation into leaks of the classified information. Secretary of Defense Donald Rumsfeld launched an investigation at the Pentagon into the source of a story that laid out one possible plan in a war against Iraq.

Read and think about the following article from media critic William Powers. Then, join the debate over whether or not the Bush administration is keeping too many secrets from the media and the public. Consider the debating points and questions posed at the end of this feature, and sharpen your own arguments for the position you find most viable.

The Best-Kept Secrets

By William Powers

Let's get this straight. We are in a global war that is probably the biggest news story of our lifetimes. An American citizen is arrested at a public airport in Chicago for allegedly planning terrorist attacks, then transported to New York and held in prison for more than a month, and quite a few people, including his attorney, know about it. And the media don't find out until John Ashcroft comes beaming in from Moscow to tell us the story?

How did that happen?

We know how it happened, of course. This administration keeps secrets like nobody in Washington has kept secrets for a long time—maybe ever. Unlike the previous administration, which couldn't resist telling journalists every little thing about itself down to its underwear choices, the lips of the current regime are pretty much vacuum-sealed. And when it comes to war, these people are breathtakingly good at not talking.

War secrets have always been hard to come by. Once upon a time, wartime administrations let the media feel they were in on the action by allowing reporters to tag along with the troops. Now even that privilege is gone, and for the really big stories, we're reduced to sitting in our dreary cubicles waiting for someone to read a press release on cable. As if this weren't humiliating enough, some elder journos who fondly remember ye olden wars, including Andy Rooney and Walter Cronkite, have revved up their Sopwith Camels and flown across TV screens everywhere with a dark message: This war coverage is an embarrassment, and Ernie Pyle is spinning in his grave.

The question shouldn't be how the journalism of this war measures up to the journalism of previous wars. There has never been a war like this one; everyone is working without a rule book. Basically, in this latest round of the ancient tug-of-war between government and journalists, one side decided the game was too dangerous, dropped the rope, and went off to meet in its secret clubhouse. And the other side, the media, was left standing there, wondering what to do next.

The story of Jose Padilla, the alleged dirty-bomb plotter, is an especially public reminder of this troubling situation. Many journalists today hear two different voices inside their heads. One, the professional voice, wants to condemn the government for excessive secrecy. The other voice, that of the private citizen, understands and even appreciates the secrecy because so much is at stake. Several journalists that I spoke to this week expressed various degrees of astonishment and frustration at how little they are able to learn about the war, even as they concede that secrecy is often necessary.

"I think we're in some really uncharted waters," said Christopher Isham, chief of investigative projects for ABC News. "There is a whole scope of activities that are going on that the government is trying to keep invisible, and sometimes there are good reasons for it and sometimes there are not good reasons."

Like other news organizations, ABC walks a delicate line in its war reporting and doesn't automatically run with every story. Isham said the network knows where an important U.S. detainee is being held in custody but has decided not to go with the story. "His location is not as central to the story as what he is saying and how valuable his information is. On those two points, we have been and continue to be aggressive.... It's a cost-benefit thing. They would have to move him, we'd have several bureaucracies pissed at us, ... and in the end, what would we have? We would have reported the location where he's being interrogated."

One editor at a newspaper's Washington bureau, who spoke on condition of anonymity, said not getting the Padilla story didn't bother him much.

"It wasn't like this was something that was right under everyone's noses in Washington. I don't feel like, oh my god, why didn't we have this?" But this same person said the story was a prime example of how good the Bush administration is at keeping secrets. "[This administration's] more controlled than any I've seen in my career.... In some ways it's good, and it shows discipline. But in some ways it's not good for democracy, being so closed from the world."

Steve Coll, managing editor of The Washington Post, said the Padilla story is "just one indication of a much broader pattern that I feel acutely aware of, which is that there is a hidden infrastructure to this war, not only abroad but here in the United States." He noted that among the government's allies in the war are a number of undemocratic countries where secret-police methods are common and the free press nonexistent.

"It is remarkable that you could encounter a case of this seriousness inside the United States and not get near it," Coll said. "I'm troubled as a journalist because I'd like to be able to convey a much fuller picture of what the structure of this campaign really is. It's not asking much—just a sketch of where the pressure points are, who's in detention, how they're being managed, what methods are being used."

But such a sketch will be hard to come by from this administration. Coll notes that there's a reason why it benefits those prosecuting the war to keep so many suspected terrorists in detention outside the United States.

"It's been, as I understand it, the preference of our government to operate overseas to the greatest possible extent, precisely because it's much easier to manage detainees in those systems."

And easier to keep everything secret. "It's a hidden war," says Coll. "And the formal military piece of it in Afghanistan is certainly not the most significant part of it right now."

Source: William Powers, *National Journal* (June 15, 2002). Copyright 2002 by National Journal Group Inc. All rights reserved. Reprinted by permission.

JOIN THE DEBATE!

CHECK YOUR UNDERSTANDING: Make sure you understand the following key points from the article; go back and review it if you missed any of them.

- The media is responsible for reporting news, and they are often reliant on leaks from within the administration to keep a check on the operations of our government.
- The Bush administration prides itself on not allowing leaks.
- The war on terrorism is different from most previous wars.
- Reporters and news organizations have to decide whether or not the news they reveal threatens national security.

ADDITIONAL INFORMATION: News articles don't provide all the information an informed citizen needs to know about an issue under debate. Here are some questions the article does not answer that you may need to consider in order to join the debate:

- How is the war on terrorism different from World War II and Vietnam?
- In the past, how have leaks affected national security?
- Are there other instances not related to September 11 where the Bush administration has tried to keep secrets?
- Do Americans really want to know all the details?

What other information might you want to know? Where might you gather this information? How might you evaluate the credibility of the information you gather? Is the information from a reliable source? Can you identify any potential biases?

IDENTIFYING THE ARGUMENTS: Now that you have some information on the issue, and have thought about what else you need to know, see whether you can present the arguments on both sides of the debate. Here are some ideas to get you started. We've provided one example each of "pro" and "con" arguments, but you should be able to offer others:

PRO: The Bush administration should not engage in such excessive secrecy. Here's why:

- The media has a right to report abuses of governmental power.

CON: The Bush administration should engage in excessive secrecy and work to prevent leaks. Here's why:

- Leaks can compromise national security.

TAKING A POSITION AND SUPPORTING IT: After thinking about the information in the article, what position would you take? What information supports your position? What arguments would you use to persuade others to your side of the debate? How would you counter arguments on the other side?

In the United States, freedom is secured mainly by the Constitution's basic guarantees and institutions. But, freedom is also ensured by the thousands of independently owned and operated newspapers, magazines, and broadcast stations. The cacophony of media voices may often be off key and harsh, but its very lack of orchestration enables us all to continue to sing the sweet song of freedom.

Continuity & Change

How TV Transformed Our Politics

Whether one views television as good or evil, this technological marvel of the twentieth century has transformed all aspects of American society, especially government and politics. When televisions were first mass-produced in the late 1940s and early 1950s, television news was primitive. Broadcasts were limited to fifteen minutes or less, announcers simply read headlines from the Associated Press, and few pictures or moving images were used in the broadcast. The first half-hour broadcast appeared only in the early 1960s, hosted on CBS by anchor Walter Cronkite, and television remained very stilted and entirely respectful toward public figures.

Vietnam and Watergate transformed television news coverage of politics from a positive and passive medium into an agent of change. The key broadcast in all of television's early years may have occurred in 1968, when Walter Cronkite traveled to Vietnam after the Tet Offensive, in which North Vietnamese forces launched widespread surprise military attacks in South Vietnam. Cronkite covered this crucial psychological setback and critically scrutinized President Lyndon B. Johnson's claim that there was "light at the end of the tunnel" (that is, a clear prospect of military and political success in Vietnam). Cronkite all but concluded that there was little hope for victory, and Johnson himself, sitting in the White House and watching Cronkite's report, turned to an aide and said, "We've lost the war, now that we've lost Walter Cronkite."

The phenomenal growth of cable television during the past three decades has given new competition to the major commercial television networks (ABC, CBS, NBC, and Fox). With over half of all U.S. households now wired for cable television, the networks' share of the national television audience has declined steadily. Today, fewer than six in every ten viewers are watching network stations during prime-time hours, compared with the networks' near monopoly thirty years ago. In addition to increased competition, the rise of cable television has brought with it a new breed of political talk show. Cable talk shows like *Larry King Live, The O'Reilly Factor, Hardball, Beltway Boys*, and *Capital Gang* provide almost constant media scrutiny and commentary on the latest political events. While many of the cable news shows have come and gone in this highly competitive market, the fast-moving and combative format of many of these shows appears here to stay.

As recent events remind us, TV also has a sometimes disastrous ability to interfere with political events even as they are happening. The Persian Gulf War, the Balkan conflict, and the war in Afghanistan showed us that information released to the media by the American armed forces or Congress and then broadcast to the public during a military conflict can sometimes provide the enemy with more current and accurate information than their own intelligence services. The instantaneous live reporting of election returns has long been feared to affect the decisions of voters who see election coverage from polls in other time zones before they have cast their own ballots. Some voters may be influenced to vote strategically in response to emerging poll trends, or they may be misled into thinking that the election has already been decided and that their vote could no longer make a difference. When an election runs as close as it did in 2000, such factors can make a difference in the final outcome.

One of the vital differences between television's conventional role and its role in the future will undoubtedly be the growth of interactive systems—systems that allow two-way communication between the sender and the consumer. As computer and cable technologies merge in the future, interactive systems will permit viewers to immediately voice their opinions regarding breaking news and policy issues. Potentially, such arrangements could lead to televised town meetings on issues of general interest. (Both Ross Perot and Bill Clinton talked about holding electronic "town halls.") Not only does this technological development have the potential to change the way politics is covered in this country, but it might also actually help change the role of citizenship—making television viewers more active political players in American democracy.

1. A recent trend in American media has been the concentration of commercial and cable television ownership into the hands of a relatively small number of corporate owners. Do you believe that this trend is likely to continue in the future? What are the implications for media coverage of politics?

2. Is the increase in interactive media a positive trend? What are some of the negative consequences of injecting the public voice more directly into the political process? Do the potential benefits outweigh the likely costs?

CAST YOUR VOTE   What role do you think the media should play in the political process? To cast your vote, go to **www.ablongman.com/oconnor**

SUMMARY

The simple words of the First Amendment, that "Congress shall make no law … abridging the freedom of speech, or of the press," have shaped the American republic as much as or more than any others in the Constitution. With the Constitution's sanction, as interpreted by the Supreme Court over two centuries, a vigorous and highly competitive press has emerged. In this chapter we examined the following topics:

1. **The American Press of Yesteryear**
   Journalism—the process and profession of collecting and disseminating the news—was introduced in America in 1690 with the publication of the nation's first newspaper. Until the mid- to late 1800s, when independent papers first appeared, newspapers were partisan; that is, they openly supported a particular party. In the twentieth century, first radio in the late 1920s and then television in the late 1940s revolutionized the transmission of political information, leading to more candidate-centered, entrepreneurial politics in the age of television.

2. **The Contemporary Media Scene**
   The modern media consist of print press (many thousands of daily and weekly newspapers, magazines, newsletters, and journals) and electronic media (television and radio stations and networks as well as computerized information services and the Internet). In the United States, the media are relatively uncontrolled and free to express many views, although that has not always been the case here and remains a problem in other countries.

3. **How the Media Cover Politicians and Government**
   Media coverage of politics has shifted focus from investigative journalism in the Watergate era toward the more recent attention to character issues. While there are useful aspects to both kinds of coverage, excesses have occurred, especially unnecessary invasions of privacy and the publication and broadcast of unsubstantiated rumor.

4. **The Media's Influence on the Public**
   Studies have shown that by framing issues for debate and discussion, the media have clear and recognizable effects on voters. For example, people who are relatively uninformed about a topic can be more easily swayed by media coverage about that topic. However, in most cases, the media have surprisingly little effect on people's views.

5. **The Public's Perception of the Media**
   Studies consistently show that although Americans generally believe the information that reputable media outlets provide, most dislike the sensationalism and perceived political bias presented by the media. The terrorist attacks of September 11, 2001 caused a temporary shift in the public's attitude toward the media, but within a year after the attacks, the media's popularity and support returned to the pre-September 11 levels.

6. **How Politicians Use the Media**
   Politicians constantly try to manipulate and influence media coverage. One method many officials use is passing along information on an off-the-record basis in the hopes of currying favor or producing stories favorable to their interests. However regrettable the manipulation might be at times, it is an unavoidable part of the political process.

7. **Government Regulation of the Electronic Media**
   The government has gradually loosened restrictions on the media. The Federal Communications Commission (FCC) licenses and regulates broadcasting stations but has been quite willing to grant and renew licenses, and has reduced its regulation of licensees. Content regulations have loosened, with the courts using a narrow interpretation of libel. The Telecommunications Act of 1996 further deregulated the communications landscape.

KEY TERMS

affiliates, p. 590
content regulation, p. 608
deep background, p. 606
electronic media, p. 587
equal time rule, p. 608
fairness doctrine, p. 608
media effects, p. 601
muckraking, p. 586
network, p. 590
New York Times Co. v. *Sullivan* (1964), p. 598
off the record, p. 606
on background, p. 606
on the record, p. 606
press briefing, p. 592
press conference, p. 592
press release, p. 592
print press, p. 587
wire service, p. 590
yellow journalism, p. 586

SELECTED READINGS

Arterton, F. Christopher. *Media Politics: The News Strategies of Presidential Campaigns.* Lexington, MA: Lexington Books, 1984.

Berkman, Ronald, and Laura W. Kitch. *Politics in the Media Age.* New York: McGraw-Hill, 1986.

Broder, David S. *Behind the Front Page.* New York: Simon and Schuster, 1987.

Cook, Timothy E. *Making Laws and Making News: Media Strategies in the U.S. House of Representatives.* Washington, DC: Brookings Institution, 1989.

Crouse, Timothy. *The Boys on the Bus.* New York: Ballantine, 1973.

Farnsworth, Stephen J., and S. Robert Lichter. *The Nightly News Nightmare: Network Television's Coverage of U. S. Presidential Elections, 1988–2000.* New York: Routledge, 2002.

Garment, Suzanne. *Scandal.* New York: Random House, 1991.

Graber, Doris A. *Mass Media and American Politics*, 6th ed. Washington, DC: CQ Press, 1996.

———*Media Power in Politics*, 4th ed. Washington, DC: CQ Press, 2000.

Grossman, Michael Baruch, and Martha Joynt Kumar. *Portraying the President: The White House and the News Media.* Baltimore, MD. Johns Hopkins University Press, 1981.

Hamilton, John Maxwell. *Hold the Press: The Inside Story on Newspapers.* Baton Rouge: Louisiana State University Press, 1996.

Iyengar, Shanto, and Donald R. Kinder. *News That Matters.* Chicago: University of Chicago Press, 1987.

Jamieson, Kathleen Hall and Paul Waldman. *The Press Effect: Politicians, Journalists, and the Stories That Shape the Political World.* Oxford, UK: Oxford University Press, 2002.

Kerbel, Matthew Robert. *Remote and Controlled: Media Politics in a Cynical Age.* Boulder, CO: Westview Press, 1995.

Lichter, S. Robert, Stanley Rothman, and Linda S. Lichter. *The Media Elite.* Bethesda, MD: Adler and Adler, 1986.

Linsky, Martin. *Impact: How the Press Affects Federal Policymaking.* New York: Norton, 1986.

Patterson, Thomas E. *Out of Order.* New York: Vintage, 1993.

Press, Charles, and Kenneth VerBurg. *American Politicians and Journalists.* Glenview, IL: Scott, Foresman, 1988.

Ranney, Austin. *Channels of Power: The Impact of Television on American Politics.* New York: Basic Books, 1983.

Sabato, Larry J. *Feeding Frenzy: How Attack Journalism Has Transformed American Politics*, updated ed. New York: Macmillan/Free Press, 1993.

Stephens, Mitchell. *A History of News: From the Drum to the Satellite.* New York: Viking, 1989.

West, Darrell M. *Air Wars: Television Advertising in Election Campaigns, 1952–2000.* Washington, DC: CQ Press, 2001.

Zaller, John. *The Nature and Origins of Mass Opinion.* Cambridge, UK: Cambridge University Press, 1992.

NOTES

1. See Mitchell Stephens, *A History of News: From the Drum to the Satellite* (New York: Viking, 1989).

2. Charles Press and Kenneth VerBurg, *American Politicians and Journalists* (Glenview, IL: Scott, Foresman, 1988), 8–10.

3. See Merrill D. Peterson, *Thomas Jefferson and the New Nation* (New York: Oxford University Press, 1970), 185–7.

4. For a delightful rendition of this episode, see Shelley Ross, *Fall from Grace* (New York: Ballantine, 1988), ch. 12.

5. Doris A. Graber, *Mass Media and American Politics*, 3rd ed. (Washington, DC: CQ Press, 1989), 12.

6. See Thomas C. Leonard, *The Power of the Press: The Birth of American Political Reporting* (New York: Oxford University Press, 1986), ch. 7.

7. Richard L. Rubin, *Press, Party, and Presidency* (New York: Norton, 1981), 38–9.

8. Stephen Bates, *If No News, Send Rumors* (New York: St. Martin's Press, 1989), 185.

9. Barbara Matusow, "Washington's Journalism Establishment," *Washingtonian* 23 (February 1989): 94–101, 265–70.

10. See Eleanor Randolph, "Extra! Extra! Who Cares?" *Washington Post* (April 1, 1990): C1, 4.

11. More than one hundred new Sunday papers were created in the 1980s, and Sunday circulation as a whole has increased 25 percent since 1970.

12. Harold W. Stanley and Richard G. Niemi, *Vital Statistics on American Politics* (Washington, DC: CQ Press, 1988), 58.

13. See Evans Witt, "Here, There, and Everywhere: Where Americans Get Their News," *Public Opinion* 6 (August/September 1983): 45–48; and June O. Yum and Kathleen E. Kendall, "Sources of Political Information in a Presidential Primary Campaign," *Journalism Quarterly* 65 (Spring 1988): 148–51, 177.

14. This was the fundamental conclusion of Shanto Iyengar and Donald R. Kinder, *News That Matters* (Chicago: University of Chicago Press, 1987).

15. L. Peer and B. Chestnut, "Deciphering Media Independence: The Gulf War Debate in Television and Newspaper News," *Political Communication* 12 (January 1995): 81–95.

16. Matthew Baum and Samuel Kernell, "Has Cable Ended the Golden Age of Television?" *American Political Science Review* 93 (June 1999): 99–114.

17. M. Just, T. Buhr, and A. Crigler, "Voice, Substance, and Cynicism in Presidential Campaign Media," *Political Communication* 16 (January 1999): 25–44.

18. Ben Bagdikan, *The Media Monopoly*, 4th ed. (Boston: Beacon Press, 1992).

19. Scott L. Althaus and David Tewksbury, "Patterns of Internet and Traditional News Media Use in a Networked Community," *Political Communication* 17 (2000): 21–45.

20. Ibid.

21. Dhavan V. Shah, Nojin Kwak, and R. Lance Holbert, "Connecting' and 'Disconnecting' with Civic Life: Patterns of Internet Use and the Production of Social Capital," *Political Communication* 18 (2001): 141–62.

22. Ibid.

23. Timothy E. Cook and Lyn Ragsdale, "The President and the Press: Negotiating Newsworthiness at the White House," in Michael Nelson, ed., *The Presidency and the Political System*, 5th ed. (Washington DC: CQ Press, 1998), 323.

24. Thomas Patterson, *Out of Order* (New York: Vintage, 1994).

25. Harold W. Stanley and Richard G. Niemi, *Vital Statistics on American Politics*, 4th ed. (Washington, DC: CQ Press, 1994), 28.

26. Timothy E. Cook, "Press Secretaries and Media Strategies in the House of Representatives: Deciding Whom to Pursue," *American Journal of Political Science* 32 (November 1998): 1047–69.

27. John Hibbing and Elizabeth Theiss-Morse, *Congress as Public Enemy: Political Attitudes Toward American Political Institutions* (New York: Cambridge University Press, 1995).

28. American Society of Newspaper Editors, *The Changing Face of the Newsroom* (Washington, DC: ASNE, May 1989), 29.

29. See Tom Wolfe, *The New Journalism* (New York: Harper and Row, 1973), especially 9–32.

30. The first and best in White's series was *The Making of the President 1960* (New York: Atheneum, 1961). See also Joe McGinniss, *The Selling of the President 1968* (New York: Trident, 1969).

31. See James David Barber, *The Presidential Character* (Englewood Cliffs, NJ: Prentice-Hall, 1972), 445.

32. Roderick Hart, *Seducing America: How Television Charms the Modern Voter* (New York: Oxford University Press, 1995).

33. 376 U.S. 254 (1964). See also Steven Pressman, "Libel Law: Finding the Right Balance," *Editorial Research Reports* 2 (August 18, 1989): 462–71.

34. *Curtis Publishing Co. v. Butts*, 388 U.S. 130 (1967); *Associated Press v. Walker*, 388 U.S. 130 (1967).

35. American Society of Newspaper Editors, *The Changing Face*, 33; William Schneider and I. A. Lewis, "Views on the News," *Public Opinion* 8 (August/September 1985): 6–11, 58–59; and S. Robert Lichter, Stanley Rothman, and Linda S. Lichter, *The Media Elite* (Bethesda, MD: Adler and Adler, 1986).

36. National Survey of the Role of Polls in Policymaking. Survey conducted by the Kaiser Family Foundation, http://www.kff.org/content/2001/3146/toplines.pdf.

37. See Dom Bonafede, "Crossing Over," *National Journal* 21 (January 14, 1989): 102; Richard Harwood, "Tainted Journalists," *Washington Post* (December 4, 1988): L6; Charles Trueheart, "Trading Places: The Insiders Debate," *Washington Post* (January 4, 1989): D1, 19; and Kirk Victor, "Slanted Views," *National Journal* 20 (June 4, 1988): 1512.

38. "*Roe v. Webster*," *Media Monitor* 3 (October 1989): 1–6. See also David Shaw, "Abortion and the Media" (four-part series), *Los Angeles Times* (July 1, 1990): A1, 50–51; (July 2, 1990): A1, 20; (July 3, 1990): A1, 22–23; (July 4, 1990): A1, 28–29.

39. David C. Barker, "Rushed Decisions: Political Talk Radio and Vote Choice, 1994–1996," *Journal of Politics* (May, 1999): 527–39.

40. David Domke, David P. Fan, Dhavan V. Shah, and Mark D. Watts, "The Politics of Conservative Elites and the 'Liberal Media' Argument," *Journal of Communication* 49 (Fall 1999): 35–58.

41. Eric Veblen, *The Manchester Union-Leader in New Hampshire Elections* (Hanover, NH: University of New England Press, 1975).

42. Benjamin I. Page, Robert Y. Shapiro, and Glenn R. Dempsey, "What Moves Public Opinion?" *American Political Science Review* 81 (March 1987): 23–44.

43. Iyengar and Kinder, *News That Matters*.

44. Martin P. Wattenberg, *The Decline of American Political Parties, 1952–1994* (Cambridge, MA: Harvard University Press, 1996).

45. Marc Hetherington, "The Media's Role in Forming Voters' National Economic Evaluations in 1992," *American Journal of Political Science* 40 (May 1996): 372–95.

46. For a thorough and intelligent discussion of the chain of errors in the media coverage, see Howard Kurtz, "Errors Plague Election Night Polling Service," *Washington Post* (December 22, 2000):A1.

47. Fox News/Opinion Dynamic Poll, conducted June 18–19, 2002.

48. "Internet News Takes Off: Event Driven News Audiences," June 8, 1998. The Pew Research Center for the People and the Press, http://people-press.org

49. "News Media's Improved Image Proves Short-Lived," August 4, 2002. The Pew Research Center for the People and the Press, http://people-press.org

50. "Media Seen As Fair, But Tilting to Gore," released October 15, 2000. The Pew Research Center for the People and the Press, http://people-press.org

51. "News Media's Improved Image Proves Short-Lived," August 4, 2002.

52. Ibid.

53. George C. Edwards III and Dan Wood, "Who Influences Whom? The President, Congress, and the Media," *American Political Science Review* 93 (June 1999): 327–44.

54. 403 U.S. 713 (1971).

55. House of Commons, Defense Committee, *The Handling of the Press and Public Information During the Falklands Conflict* (London: Her Majesty's Stationery Office, 1982).

Roy Hoffmann
Rear Admiral
Distinguished Service Medal, Silver Star
www.swiftvets.com

(Photo courtesy: AP/World Wide Photos)

Interest Groups

Soon after the Democratic National Convention in July 2004, an interest group calling itself Swift Boat Veterans for Truth aired a television advertisement charging that Democratic presidential nominee John Kerry was lying about his military service record. Most specifically, the ad asserted that Senator Kerry (D–MA) had exaggerated the severity of the wounds that led to his first Purple Heart. Less than a week after this ad hit the airwaves, another organized interest, MoveOn.org, countered the Swift Boat Veterans ad with a commercial attacking the many gaps in President George W. Bush's military record. "George Bush used his father to get into the National Guard," the ad charged, "and when the chips were down, went missing. Now he's allowing false advertising that attacks John Kerry, a man who served with dignity and heroism."

Although personal attacks are not unusual in modern American politics, it is important to ask who these groups are, and how they came to have such substantial influence in the 2004 presidential election. Swift Boat Veterans for Truth is a loose association of Vietnam veterans who first came together in 2000 to attack the military service record of Senator John McCain (R–AZ) during the South Carolina presidential primary. MoveOn.org is an organization founded by a group of Silicon Valley financiers in 1998 to protest the impeachment of President Bill Clinton.

Both groups became major players in American politics following the 2002 campaign finance reform law commonly know as McCain-Feingold. After that law banned all soft money donations from corporations and political action committees to political parties and candidates, political elites began to look for new ways to remain influential players in electoral politics. Groups quickly discovered a loophole in the 2002 law that allows for tax-exempt organizations—known as 527s, for the section of the Internal Revenue Code that governs them—to raise unlimited money for the purposes of voter mobilization and issue advocacy as long as they do not expressly advocate the election of a particular candidate.

This loophole allows 527s to air almost unlimited ads attacking candidates for their character, career choices, or policies, so long as the advertisements never explicitly state, for example, "Vote for John Kerry." MoveOn.org spent more than $20 million during the 2004 election cycle on print, radio, and television ads that both raised questions about members of the Bush administration and voiced support for liberal stances such as legalized same-sex marriage and opposition to outsourcing American jobs. However, even after a slow start, conservative 527s managed to spend more than $70 million on advertisements criti-cizing John Kerry. In an attempt to maximize their impact, the groups aired most of these ads in America's largest and most contentious media markets.

*T*he face of interest group politics in the United States is changing as quickly as laws, political consultants, and technology allow. The activities of big business and trade groups such as the Bankruptcy Coalition are increasing at the same time that there is conflicting evidence concerning whether ordinary citizens join political groups. In an influential essay, "Bowling Alone: America's Declining Social Capital," political scientist Robert Putnam argues that fewer Americans are joining groups,[7] while political scientist Everett Carll Ladd, executive director of the Roper Center for Public Opinion, concluded that America is in the midst of an "explosion of voluntary groups, activities and charitable donations [that] is transforming our towns and cities."[8] Although bowling leagues have withered, said Ladd, other groups such as soccer associations, health clubs, and environmental groups are flourishing. Old groups like the Elks Club and the League of Women Voters, whose membership was tracked by Putnam, no longer are attracting members, according to Ladd. That does not mean, concluded Ladd, that people aren't joining groups; they just aren't joining the ones studied by Putnam.

Why is this debate so important? Political scientists believe that involvement in these kinds of community groups and activities enhances the level of what is termed **social capital,** "the web of cooperative relationships between citizens that facilitates resolution of collective action problems.[9] The more social capital that exists in a given community, the more citizens are engaged in its governance and well-being, and the more likely they are to work for the collective good.[10] This tendency to form small-scale associations for the public good, or **civic virtue,** as Putnam calls it, creates fertile ground within communities for improved political and economic development.[11] In studying Italy, for example, Putnam found that good government was a by-product of singing groups and soccer clubs.[12] Thus, if Americans truly are joining fewer groups, we might expect the overall quality of government and its provision of services to suffer.

While the debate continues over whether America continues to be the nation of joiners that French political philosopher Alexis de Tocqueville found in the 1830s, it is clear that people are reporting more individual acts—many of them designed to pressure policy makers at all levels of government.

Today, community soccer associations may be playing the same role that bowling leagues once played in the United States. Or, as Ladd notes, political scientists, many trained in the 1960s and 1970s, may overlook the kinds of contributions most frequently made by young people today: involvement in voluntary community service work (as opposed to that often required by many school districts). Young people often don't see involvement in groups such as Habitat for Humanity or working in a soup kitchen as political, but frequently it is.

Interest groups often fill voids left by the traditional political parties and give Americans another opportunity to take their claims directly to the government (see Table 16.1). Interest groups give the unrepresented or underrepresented an opportunity to have their voices heard, thereby making the government and its policy-making process

social capital
The myriad relationships that individuals enjoy that facilitate the resolution of community problems through collective action.

civic virtue
The tendency to form small-scale associations for the public good.

TABLE 16.1   Reported Acts Designed to Influence Policy Makers (percentage)

			AGE GROUP	
Political Activity	Total	X-ers	Baby Boomers	Matures
Direct Contacting				
Written a letter to or called a public official	59	37	65	65
Signed a petition	71	55	78	72
Indirect Contacting				
Called a talk show to discuss views on a public or political issue	9	6	9	10
Joining/Attending				
Attended a community meeting about a state or local issue	60	36	67	68
Participated in a march or demonstration	20	15	27	15
Volunteered for a political campaign	24	11	25	32
Contributing				
Contributed money to a political campaign	41	22	41	54

Note: Respondents were asked: "People express their opinions about politics and current events in a number of ways besides voting. I'm going to read a list of some of these ways. Please just tell me if you have or have not ever done each. Have you ever [X]?"

Source: "Generation X-ers Show Lower Interest in Politics than Baby Boomers and Mature Generations," Quinnipiac University Polling Institute (October 26, 1999). Reprinted with permission.

more representative of diverse populations and perspectives. Additionally, interest groups offer powerful and wealthy interests even greater access to, or influence on, policy makers at all levels of government. To explore this phenomenon, in this chapter we'll look at the following issues:

- First, we will answer the question, *what are interest groups?*
- Second, we will explore the historical *roots and development of interest groups* in America.
- Third, we will discuss *what interest groups do* by looking at the various strategies and tactics used by organized interests.
- Fourth, we will analyze *what makes an interest group successful.*
- In our exploration of the theme of *continuity and change* in American politics, we will examine how the nature of interest groups in the United States has remained relatively the same over time, and whether the rise of the Internet will alter the nature of interest group formation and maintenance.

WHAT ARE INTEREST GROUPS?

Interest groups go by a variety of names. Special interests, pressure groups, organized interests, political groups, lobby groups, and public interest groups are among the most common. These various terms have produced a diverse collection of operational definitions:

- "Any association of individuals, whether formally organized or not, that attempts to influence public policy.[13]
- "An organization which seeks or claims to represent people or organizations which share one or more common interests or ideals."[14]

- "Any group that, on the basis of one or more shared attitudes, makes certain claims upon other groups in society for the establishment, maintenance, or enhancement of forms of behavior that are implied by the shared attitudes."[15]

Some definitions stress what a group does. Political scientist Robert H. Salisbury posits that:

- "An interest group is an organized association which engages in activity relative to governmental decisions."[16]

Distinguished political scientist V. O. Key Jr. tried to differentiate political parties from interest groups by arguing that:

- "[Interest groups] promote their interests by attempting to influence government rather than by nominating candidates and seeking responsibility for the management of government."[17]

disturbance theory
Political scientist David B. Truman's theory that interest groups form in part to counteract the efforts of other groups.

WEB EXPLORATION

For more on the Christian Coalition of America, NOW, and the NRA, see www.ablongman.com/oconnor

interest group
An organized group that tries to influence public policy.

David B. Truman, one of the first political scientists to study interest groups, posed what he termed **disturbance theory** to explain why interest groups form.[18] He hypothesized that groups form, in part, to counteract the activities of other groups or of organized special interests. According to Truman, the government's role is to provide a forum in which the competing demands of groups and the majority of the U.S. population can be heard and balanced. He argued that the government's role in managing competing groups is to balance their conflicting demands.

Salisbury expanded on Truman by arguing that groups are formed when resources—be they clean air, women's rights, or rights of the unborn, for example—are inadequate or scarce.[19] Unlike Truman, Salisbury stresses the role that leaders, or what he terms "entrepreneurs," play in the formation of groups.

Originally, most political scientists used the term "pressure group" because it best described what these groups do. Today, most political scientists use the terms interest group or organized interest. In this book, we use **interest group** as a generic term to describe the numerous organized groups that try to influence government policy. Thus, interest groups can be what we normally think of as organized interests as well as state and local governments, political action committees, and individual businesses and corporations. We also consider less formal groups as interest groups. Although these groups are more nebulous in form than interest groups traditionally studied by political scientists, they, too, engage in concerted action to influence government policy.

Multi-Issue Versus Single-Issue Interest Groups

Political scientists often talk of interest groups as single-issue or multi-issue. Many organizations, while founded around a single guiding principle such as the NAACP's interest in advancing the cause of civil rights, or the Christian Coalition's concern with Christian family values, are actually involved in a wide range of issue areas, including education (school vouchers, prayer in school), television ratings, and abortion. Thus, they must divide some of their energies as they lobby for

The Ununited Interests of America

varied policies in diverse forums. Similarly, the National Organization for Women (NOW) deals in issues of abortion and reproductive rights, affirmative action, economic equity, and lesbian rights, among others. Multi-issue groups often must have expertise in a wide array of areas and be prepared to work on the local, state, and national levels to advance their interests.

Single-issue groups differ from multi-issue groups in both the range and intensity of their interests. Concentration on one area generally leads to greater zeal in a group's lobbying efforts. Probably the most visible single-issue groups today are those organized on either side of the abortion and gun control debates. Right-to-life groups such as the Army of God and pro-choice groups such as Pro-Choice America NARAL are good examples of single-issue groups, as are the National Rifle Association (NRA) and the Brady Campaign to Prevent Gun Violence united with the Million Mom March. Today, people singlemindedly pursue all kinds of interests. Drug- or AIDS-awareness groups, and anti–nuclear power groups, for example, can be classified as single-issue groups. Table 16.2 categorizes a number of prominent interest groups by their issue concentration.

Before stepping down as its president in April, 2003, Charlton Heston, the legendary actor, addresses the National Rifle Association.
(Photo courtesy: Eric Gay/AP/Wide World Photos)

Kinds of Organized Interests

Political scientists also categorize organized interests by the type of interests they champion. The major types of organized interests are: (1) economic interest groups; (2) public interest groups; and, increasingly, (3) governmental units. Most of these groups lobby on behalf of their members, and many hire D.C.-based lobbying firms to lead or supplement their efforts. (For a list of top lobbying firms, see Table 16.2.)

Economic Interest Groups.   Most groups have some sort of "economic" agenda, even if it only involves acquiring enough money in donations to pay the telephone bill or to send out the next mailing. **Economic interest groups** are, however, a special type of interest group: Their primary purpose is to promote the economic interests of their members. Historically, business groups (including trade and professional groups), labor organizations (unions), and organizations representing the interests of farmers have been considered the "big three" of economic interest groups.

economic interest group
A group with the primary purpose of promoting the financial interests of its members.

Groups that mobilize to protect particular economic interests generally are the most fully and effectively organized of all the types of interest groups.[20] They exist to make profits and to obtain economic benefits for their members. To achieve these goals, however, they often find that they must resort to political means rather than trust the operation of economic markets to produce outcomes favorable for their members.

Public Interest Groups.   Political scientist Jeffrey M. Berry defines **public interest groups** as organizations "that seek a collective good, the achievement of which will not selectively and materially benefit the membership or activists of the organization."[21] Unlike economic interest groups, public interest groups do not tend to be particularly motivated by the desire to achieve goals that would benefit their members. As Berry notes, the public interest has many faces. For example, many Progressive era groups were created in the late 1800s and early 1900s to solve the varied problems of new immigrants and the poor. Today, civil and constitutional rights groups, environmental

public interest group
An organization that seeks a collective good that will not selectively and materially benefit the members of the group.

TABLE 16.2   Profiles of Selected Interest Groups

Name (Founded)	Single- or Multi-Issue	Members	PAC	2003–04 Election Cycle PAC Donation
Economic Groups				
AFL-CIO (1886)	M	13 million	AFL-CIO	$1.2 million
American Medical Association (AMA) (1847)	M	300,000	AMA PAC	$3.1 million
Association of Trial Lawyers of America (1946)	M	65,000	ATLA PAC	$2 million
National Association of Manufacturers (NAM) (1895)	M	18 million	inactive	
U.S. Chamber of Commerce (1912)	M	3 million companies	U.S. Chamber of Commerce PAC	$155,806
Public Interest Groups				
AARP (American Association of Retired Persons) (1958)	M	35,000,000	no	
Amnesty International U.S.A. (1961)	S	386,000	no	
League of United Latin American Citizens (LULAC) (1929)	M	115,000	no	
NARAL Pro-Choice America (NARAL) (1969)	S	500,000	NARAL Pro-Choice America PAC	$2.47 million
National Association for the Advancement of Colored People (NAACP) (1909)	M	500,000	no	
Human Rights Campaign (1980)	S	450,000	HRC Fund PAC	$1.37 million
National Right to Life Committee (1973)	S	400,000	National Right to Life PAC	$1.36 million
Environmental Groups				
Environmental Defense (1967)	S	300,000	no	
Greenpeace USA (1971)	S	350,000	no	
Sierra Club (1892)	S	700,000	Sierra Club Political Committee	$650,000
Good Government Groups				
Common Cause (1970)	S	200,000	no	
Public Citizen, Inc. (1971)	M	150,000	no	
Moveon.org (1998) (2004)	S	1,000,000	MOVEON PAC	20.9 million

Source: http://www.opensecrets.org

groups, good government groups such as Common Cause, peace groups, church groups, and groups that speak out for those who cannot (such as children, the mentally ill, or animals) are examples of public interest groups.

Governmental Units.   State and local governments are becoming strong organized interests as they lobby the federal government or even charitable foundations for money for a vast array of state and local programs. The Big Seven intergovernmental associations (discussed in chapter 3) and state and local governments want to make certain that they get their fair share of federal dollars in the form of block grants or pork barrel projects. Most states retain lobbyists in Washington, D.C., to advance their interests or to keep them informed about legislation that could affect them. They want to make sure that they will get their share (if not more) of the federal budget designated to go back to the states in a variety of forms, including money for roads, schools, and poverty programs.

THE ROOTS AND DEVELOPMENT OF AMERICAN INTEREST GROUPS

Political scientists long have debated how and why interest groups arise, their nature, and their role in a democratic society. Do they contribute to the betterment of society, or are they an evil best controlled by government? From his days in the Virginia Assembly, James Madison knew that factions occurred in all political systems and that the struggle for influence and power among such groups was inevitable in the political process. This knowledge led him and the other Framers to tailor a governmental system of multiple pressure points to check and balance these factions, or what today we call interest groups, in the natural course of the political process. As we discuss in chapter 2, Madison and many of the other Framers were intent on creating a government of many levels—local, state, and national—with the national government consisting of three branches. It was their belief that this division of power would prevent any one individual or group of individuals from becoming too influential. They also believed that decentralizing power would neutralize the effect of special interests, who would not be able to spread their efforts throughout so many different levels of government. Thus, the "mischief of faction" could be lessened. But, farsighted as they were, the Framers could not have envisioned the vast sums of money or technology that would be available to some interest groups.

Ironically, however, *The Federalist Papers* were a key component of one of the most skillful and successful examples of interest group activity in the history of this nation. If "the Federalists [themselves an interest group] had not been as shrewd in manipulation as they were sound in theory, their arguments could not have prevailed."[22]

National Groups Emerge (1830–1889)

Although all kinds of local groups proliferated throughout the colonies and in the new states, it was not until the 1830s, as communications networks improved, that the first groups national in scope began to emerge. Many of these first national groups were single-issue groups deeply rooted in the Christian religious revivalism that was sweeping the nation. Concern with humanitarian issues such as temperance (total abstinence from alcoholic beverages), peace, education, and most important, slavery led to the founding of numerous groups dedicated to solving these problems. Among the first of these groups was the American Anti-Slavery Society, founded in 1833 by William Lloyd Garrison.

After the Civil War, more groups were founded. For example, the Women's Christian Temperance Union (WCTU) was created in 1874 with the goal of outlawing the sale of liquor. Its members, many of them quite religious, believed that the consumption of alcohol was an evil injurious to family life because many men drank away their pay-checks, leaving no money to feed or clothe their families. The WCTU's activities took conventional and nonconventional forms including organizing prayer groups, lobbying for prohibition legislation, conducting peaceful marches, and engaging in more violent protests that included destruction of saloons. Like the WCTU, the Grange also was formed during the period following the Civil War, as an educational society for farmers to teach them about the latest agricultural developments. Although its charter formally stated that the Grange was not to become involved in "politics," in 1876, it formulated a detailed plan to pressure Congress to enact legislation favorable to farmers.

Perhaps the most effective interest group of the day was the railroad industry. In a move that couldn't take place today because of its clear impropriety, the Central Pacific Railroad sent its own **lobbyist** to Washington, D.C., in 1861, where he eventually became the clerk (staff administrator) of the committees of both houses of Congress that were charged with overseeing regulation of the railroad industry. Subsequently, the Central Pacific Railroad (later called the Southern Pacific) received vast grants of lands along its route from Congress and large subsidized loans from the national government. The railroad became so important that it later went on to have nearly total political control of the California state legislature.

After the Civil War, business interests began to play even larger roles in both state and national politics. A popular saying of the day noted that the Standard Oil Company did everything to the Pennsylvania legislature except refine it. Increasingly large

lobbyist
Interest group representative who seeks to influence legislation that will benefit his or her organization through political persuasion.

trusts, monopolies, business combinations, and corporate conglomerations in the oil, steel, and sugar industries became sufficiently powerful to control many representatives in the state and national legislatures.

The Progressive Era (1890–1920)

By the 1890s, a profound change had occurred in the nation's political and social outlook. Rapid industrialization, an influx of immigrants, and monopolistic business practices created a host of problems, including crime, poverty, squalid and unsafe working conditions, widespread political corruption, and high prices. Many Americans began to believe that new measures would be necessary to impose order on this growing chaos and to curb some of the more glaring problems. The political and social movement that grew out of these concerns was called the Progressive movement.

Not even the Progressives themselves could agree on what the term "progressive" actually meant, but their desire for reform led to an explosion of all types of interest groups including single-issue, trade, labor, and the first public interest groups. Politically, the movement took the form of the Progressive Party, which sought on many fronts to limit or end the power of the industrialists' near-total control of the steel, oil, railroad, and other key industries.

In response to the pressure applied by Progressive era groups, the national government began to regulate business. Because businesses had a vested interest in keeping wages low and costs down, more business groups organized to consolidate their strength and to counter Progressive moves. Not only did governments have to mediate Progressive and business demands, but they also had to accommodate the role of organized labor, which often allied itself with Progressive groups against big business.

Organized Labor.   Not until the creation of the American Federation of Labor (AFL) in 1886 was there any real national union activity. The AFL brought skilled workers from several trades together into one stronger national organization for the first time. Its effectiveness in mobilizing for higher wages for workers triggered more and better business organization. As business interests pushed states for "open shop" laws to outlaw unions in their factories, the AFL became increasingly political. It also was forced to react to the success of big businesses' use of legal injunctions to prohibit union organization. In 1914, massive lobbying by the AFL and its members led to passage of the Clayton Act, which the labor leader Samuel Gompers hailed as the "Magna Carta" of the labor movement. This law allowed unions to organize free from prosecution and also guaranteed their right to strike, a powerful weapon against employers.

Business Groups and Trade Associations.   The National Association of Manufacturers (NAM) was founded in 1895 by manufacturers who had suffered business reverses in the economic panic of 1893 and who believed that they were being affected adversely by the growth of organized labor. NAM first became active politically in 1913 when a major tariff bill was under congressional consideration. NAM's tactics were "so insistent and abrasive" and its expenditures of monies so lavish that President Woodrow Wilson was forced to denounce its lobbying tactics as an "unbearable situation."[23] Congress immediately called for an investigation of NAM's activities but found no member of Congress willing to testify that he had ever even encountered a member of NAM (probably because many of them had been "bought" with illegal contributions and gifts).

The second major business organization came into being in 1912, when the U.S. Chamber of Commerce was created with the assistance of the Secretary of Commerce and Labor. (This was before that Cabinet post was split into the Department of Commerce and the Department of Labor.)

NAM, the Chamber of Commerce, and other **trade associations** representing specific industries were effective spokespersons for their member companies. They were

trade associations
Groups that represent specific industries.

unable to defeat passage of the Clayton Act, but groups such as the Cotton Manufacturers planned elaborate and successful campaigns to overturn key provisions of the act
in the courts.[24] Aside from the Clayton Act, innumerable pieces of pro-business legislation were passed by Congress, whose members continued to insist that they had never
been contacted by business groups.

In 1928, the bubble burst for some business interests. At the Senate's request, the
Federal Trade Commission (FTC) undertook a massive investigation of the lobbying
tactics of the business community. The examination of Congress by the FTC revealed
extensive illegal lobbying by yet another group, the National Electric Light Association (NELA). Not only did NELA lavishly entertain members of Congress, but it also
went to great expense to educate the public on the virtues of electric lighting. Books
and pamphlets were produced and donated to schools and public libraries to sway public opinion. Needy teachers and ministers who were willing to advocate electricity were
helped with financial grants. These tactics were considered unethical by many, and business was held in public disfavor. These kinds of activities led the public to view lobbyists in a negative light.

The Rise of the Interest Group State

During the 1960s and 1970s, the Progressive spirit reappeared in the rise of public interest groups. Generally, these groups devoted themselves to representing the interests of
African Americans, women, the elderly, the poor, and consumers, or to working on
behalf of the environment. Many of their leaders and members had been active in the
civil rights and anti–Vietnam War movement of the 1960s. Other groups, like the
American Civil Liberties Union (ACLU) and the NAACP, which had survived for
nearly a century, gained renewed vigor. Many of them had as their patron the liberal
Ford Foundation, which helped to bankroll numerous groups, including the Women's
Rights Project of the ACLU, the Mexican American Legal Defense and Education
Fund, the Puerto Rican Legal Defense and Education Fund, and the Native American
Rights Fund, as discussed in chapter 6.[25] Another group that came to prominence in
this era was the American Association of Retired Persons (AARP). The elderly are the
fastest-growing group in the United States. (AARP is the largest single-interest group
in the country, with 35 million members in 2004.)

The civil rights and antiwar struggles left many Americans feeling cynical about
a government that they believed failed to respond to the will of the majority. They also
believed that if citizens banded together, they could make a difference. Thus, two
major new public interest groups—Common Cause and Public Citizen, Inc.—were
founded. Common Cause, a "good government" group similar to some of the early
Progressive movement's public interest groups, effectively has challenged aspects of
the congressional seniority system, successfully urged the passage of sweeping campaign financing reforms, and played a major role in the enactment of legislation authorizing federal financing of presidential campaigns. It continues to lobby for
accountability in government and for more efficient and responsive governmental
structures and practices.

Perhaps more well known than Common Cause is the collection of groups headed
by Ralph Nader under the name Public Citizen, Inc. In 1965, Nader, a young lawyer,
was thrust into the limelight with the publication of his book *Unsafe at Any Speed*. In it,
he charged that the Corvair, a General Motors (GM) car, was unsafe to drive; he produced voluminous evidence of how the car could flip over at average speeds on curved
roads. In 1966, he testified about auto safety before Congress and then learned that General Motors had spied on him in an effort to discredit his work. The $250,000 that GM
subsequently paid to Nader in an out-of-court settlement allowed him to establish the
Center for the Study of Responsive Law in 1969. The center analyzed the activities of
regulatory agencies and concluded that few of them enforced antitrust regulations or

WEB EXPLORATION

For more about Common
Cause and Public Citizen, Inc., see
www.ablongman.com/oconnor

cracked down on deceptive advertising practices. Nader then turned again to lobbying Congress, which led him to create Public Citizen, Inc., which would act as an umbrella organization for what was to be called the "Nader Network" of groups. In 1996, 2000, and 2004, Nader was an unsuccessful candidate for president.

Conservative Backlash: Religious and Ideological Groups.   The growth and successes that various public interest groups and the civil rights and women's rights movements had in the 1960s and 1970s (see chapter 6) ultimately led to a conservative backlash. Conservatives became very concerned about the successes liberal groups had in shaping and defining the public agenda, and religious and ideological conservatives became a potent force in U.S. politics. The first major new religious group was the Reverend Jerry Falwell's Moral Majority, founded in 1978. It was widely credited with assisting Ronald Reagan's 1980 presidential victory as well as the defeats of several liberal Democratic senators that same year. Falwell claimed to have sent from 3 million to 4 million newly registered voters to the polls.[26] In June 1989, Falwell announced that he was terminating the Moral Majority after the group suffered from a series of financial and sexual scandals involving television evangelists.

In 1990, televangelist Pat Robertson, host of the popular television program, *The 700 Club*, formed a new group, the Christian Coalition, to fill the void left by the demise of the Moral Majority. Since then, it has grown in power and influence by leaps and bounds. Its exit polls showed that religious conservatives accounted for one-third of all votes cast in 1994 and provided the margin of victory for all Republicans who won with 53 percent of the vote or less.[27]

2004 Christian Coalition
VOTER ◑ GUIDE

PRESIDENTIAL
Election

George W. Bush (R)	ISSUES	John F. Kerry (D)
Supports	Passage of a Federal Marriage Protection Amendment	Opposes
Supports	Permanent Extension of the $1,000 Per Child Tax Credit	Opposes
Supports	Educational Choice for Parents (Vouchers)	Opposes
Opposes	Unrestricted Abortion on Demand	No Response
Supports	Federal Funding for Faith-Based Charitable Organizations	No Response
Supports	Permanent Elimination of the Marriage Penalty Tax	Opposes
Supports	Permanent Elimination of the Death Tax	Opposes
Supports	Banning Partial Birth Abortions	Opposes
Opposes	Public Financing of Abortions	Supports
Opposes	Federal Firearms Registration & Licensing of Gun Owners	No Response
Opposes	Adoption of Children by Homosexuals	No Response
Supports	Prescription Drug Benefits for Medicare Recipients	Supports
Opposes	Placing US Troops Under UN Control	No Response
Opposes	Affirmative Action Programs that Provide Preferential Treatment	Supports
Supports	Allowing Younger Workers to Invest a Portion of their Social Security Tax in a Private Account	Opposes

www.georgewbush.com   www.johnkerry.com

Each candidate was sent a 2004 Federal Issue Survey by certified mail and/or facsimile machine. When possible, positions of candidates on issues were verified or determined using voting records and/or public statements.

Authorized by the Christian Coalition of America; PO Box 37030 - Washington, DC 20013

The Christian Coalition of America is a pro-family, citizen action organization. This voter guide is provided for educational purposes only and is not to be construed as an endorsement of any candidate or party.

Please visit our website at www.cc.org, and the Texas website at www.texascc.org

Vote on November 2   F

To inform voters of issues of concern during the 2004 election, the Christian Coalition of America distributed millions of voting guides in churches throughout the United States.

(Photo courtesy: Christian Coalition of America)

After the important role the Christian Coalition played in the Republicans' winning control of the Congress in 1994, some of its members became disenchanted when many of its favorite issues failed to gain support in Congress. James Dobson, leader of the fundamentalist group Focus on the Family, met with Republican House leaders in May 1998 to protest their inaction and to seek assurances that the House would act on several conservative legislative policy priorities.[28]

Concern with the outcome of the 1998 elections, steeply declining revenues, and a ruling from the Internal Revenue Service revoking its tax-exempt status led Pat Robertson to reassert his authority as the Christian Coalition's founder and to restructure the group to step up its lobbying presence in Congress. A for-profit corporation, Christian Coalition International, was created "to endorse political candidates on a state and local level [and] to make financial contributions to candidates," and a second organization, Christian Coalition of America, was created to replace the old Christian Coalition.[29] According to its Web site, its "hallmark work lies in voter education." The group distributed millions of voter guides in churches throughout the United States the weekend before the 2004 election. In 2004, it passed out 3 million voter guides in Florida; 1 million were in Spanish.[30]

The Christian Coalition of America also lobbies Congress and the White House, where it has the sympathetic ear of the president it helped to elect. In fact, one of George W. Bush's first moves as president was to create an Office of Faith-Based and Community Initiatives to work with religious groups to effect policy change. In addition, the Republican leadership introduced legislation in 2002 to amend the Internal Revenue Code of 1986 to lift some of its restrictions on the lobbying and campaign activities of churches, in a move to "resuscitate the Christian conservative movement that helped propel the party to power in the early 1990s."[31] Currently, religious institutions risk their tax exempt status if they engage in any political activities.

The Christian Coalition is not the only conservative interest group to play an important role in the policy process as well as in elections at the state and national level. The National Rifle Association (NRA) has been an active opponent of gun control legislation and of late has seen its membership rise, as well as its importance in Washington, D.C. (see Figure 16.1). Its political action committee raised $820 million to help re-elect President George W. Bush in 2004. These efforts were designed so the NRA would "have a president where we work out of their office—unbelievably friendly relations."[32] To motivate voters, the NRA spokesmen funneled millions of dollars into battleground states including Ohio, Pennsylvania and West Virginia, recognizing that the re-election of a president sympathetic to its cause would make ultimate passage of NRA-supported legislation more likely.[33]

Business Groups, Corporations, and Associations.   Conservative, religious-based groups were not the only ones organized in the 1970s to advance conservative views. Many business people, dissatisfied with the work of the National Association of Manufacturers or the Chamber of Commerce, decided to start new, more politically oriented organizations to advance their political and financial interests in Washington, D.C. The Business Roundtable, for example, was created in 1972. The Roundtable,

WEB EXPLORATION

For more on the Christian Coalition and other conservative groups, see www.ablongman.com/oconnor

FIGURE 16.1   How NRA Membership Has Increased

The National Rifle Association (NRA), a single-issue interest group, lobbies against any law that it considers a restriction on an individual's right to bear arms. NRA membership has spiked in recent years in reaction to proposed gun control legislation. Interestingly, following the Columbine High School shooting in 1999, in which twelve people were killed and several others were wounded, membership increased dramatically. Its membership also took a jump after the September 11, 2001 terrorist attacks.

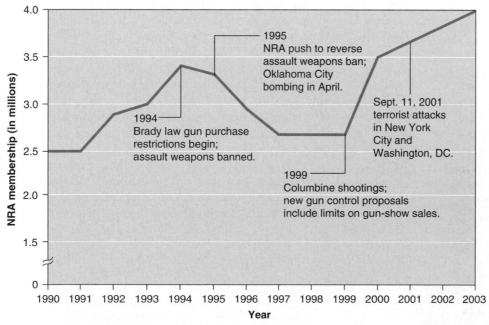

Source: Genevieve Lynn, "How the NRA Membership Has Risen," *USA Today* (May 18, 2000): 1A. © 2000, USA Today. Reprinted with permission. Updated by the authors.

whose members head about 150 large corporations, is "a fraternity of powerful and prestigious business leaders that tells 'business's side of the story' to legislators, bureaucrats, White House personnel, and other interested public officials."[34] It urges its members to engage in direct lobbying to influence the course of policy formation. In 1998, for example, the Business Roundtable's Environment Task Force lobbied hard against the Kyoto Protocol on Climate Change out of concern over its impact on American businesses. These efforts ultimately paid off when the administration of George W. Bush announced it would not support the Kyoto agreement. Another indication of the Roundtable's close ties to the federal government is the new communications network the group set up so that its member CEOs could communicate with appropriate government officials in the wake of another terrorist attack.[35]

Businesses and corporations, too, can be powerful individually or collectively as organized interests, as highlighted at the beginning of this chapter. Most large corporations, for example, employ Washington, D.C.–based lobbyists to keep them apprised of legislation that may affect them, or to lobby for the consideration of legislation that could help them. Corporations also hire D.C.–based lobbyists to lobby bureaucrats for government contracts.

Large corporations also give large sums to favored politicians or political candidates. In 1998, for example, when then Senate Majority Leader Trent Lott (R–MS) sought reelection to his Senate seat, he received $367,498 from the National Association of Realtors, $333,126 from Auto Dealers and Drivers for Free Trade (manufacturers of Japanese cars), $33,000 from Federal Express, and $58,202 from National Security PAC (defense interest advocacy). In the 2000 election, the 1,000 biggest companies gave a record $187 million to candidates for president and other national offices. Microsoft was number one. After recognizing the importance of having friends in Washington, D.C., Microsoft gave a total of $3.7 million; it gave only $237,000 to candidates in 1996. Philip Morris, the large tobacco company, contributed $3 million, with over three-quarters going to Republicans.[36]

These corporate interests have far-reaching tentacles and ties to lawmakers. Wendy Gramm, the wife of former Senator Phil Gramm (R–TX), for example, served on the board of Enron; several other spouses of House and Senate members are paid handsomely to serve on the boards of large businesses that regularly seek favors from the committees and subcommittees that their spouses serve on.[37] Although Wendy Gramm resigned after Enron's collapse, until his retirement in 2002, her husband was at the forefront of efforts to kill legislation imposing new rules on auditors and companies in the wake of the bankruptcies of Enron and WorldCom, among others.[38] A number of congressional spouses, such as Abby Blunt, the wife of House Majority Whip Roy Blunt (R–MO), are lobbyists.

Unlike public interest groups, organizations such as the Chamber of Commerce and the Business Roundtable, as well as trade and professional associations, enjoy many of the benefits other businesses do as lobbyists. They already have extensive organization, expertise, large numbers, a strong financial base, and a long-standing relationship with key actors in government. Such natural advantages have led to a huge number of business groups. One observer describes their proliferation this way:

> If you want to understand government, don't begin by reading the Constitution. It conveys precious little of today's statecraft. Instead, read selected portions of the Washington Telephone Directory, such as pages 354–58, which contain listings for all of the organizations with titles beginning with the word "National." … There are, of course, the big ones, like the National Association of Manufacturers, and the National Association of Broad-

Senator Richard Shelby (R–AL), with his wife, Annette. She resigned from defense contractor Raytheon Aerospace's board in April 2002. The senator is on the defense appropriations subcommittee, which prompted some to question his wife's service to Raytheon.

(Photo courtesy: Mickey Welsh/Montgomery Advertiser)

casters. But the pages teem with others, National Cigar Leaf Tobacco Association, National Association of Mirror Manufacturers, National Association of Miscellaneous Ornamental and Architectural Product Contractors, National Association of Margarine Manufacturers.[39]

Many of these national groups, businesses, and corporations devote tremendous resources to fighting government regulation.

Rock the Vote is an example of a quasi-trade association. While Rock the Vote is closely associated in the minds of most with MTV, it actually was founded in 1990 by several people involved in the recording industry. After court rulings finding 2 Live Crew's music obscene, Congress began debating censorship of the record industry. In response, a coalition of recording industry executives from Warner Bros., Capitol, Geffen, MCA, A & M, Virgin, and Giant Records created Rock the Vote to stir grassroots support from music listeners to make their voices heard at the ballot box. MTV pitched in with $1 million in free airtime for Rock the Vote ads. The first sixty-second MTV spot featured Madonna in a red bikini with an American flag furled around her shoulders quipping: "If you don't vote, you're going to get a spanking."[40]

Rock the Vote lobbies for legislation of interest to young people and the record industry. In 1996, it began the first program to register voters by phone and established the first Web site to offer online voter registration. Rock the Vote registered over 250,000 new voters in 1998 and an additional 500,000 in 2000. In 2004, its stepped up efforts, which even included voting kiosks at 7-11s, produced one million new voters.[41]

WEB EXPLORATION

To join Rock the Vote, go to
www.ablongman.com/oconnor

Organized Labor.   As revealed in Figure 16.2, membership in labor unions held steady throughout the early and mid-1900s and then skyrocketed toward the end of the Depression. By then, organized labor began to be a potent political force as it was able to turn out its members in support of particular political candidates.

Labor became a stronger force in U.S. politics when the American Federation of Labor merged with the Congress of Industrial Organizations in 1955. Concentrating its efforts largely on the national level, the new AFL-CIO immediately turned its energies to pressuring the government to protect concessions won from employers at the bargaining table and to other issues of concern to its members, including minimum wage laws, the environment, civil rights, medical insurance, and health care.

More recently, the once fabled political clout of organized labor has been on the wane at the national level. As Figure 16.2 shows, union membership has plummeted as the nation has changed from a land of manufacturing workers and farmers to a nation of white-collar professionals and service workers. Thus, unions and agricultural

FIGURE 16.2   Labor Union Membership, 1900–2003

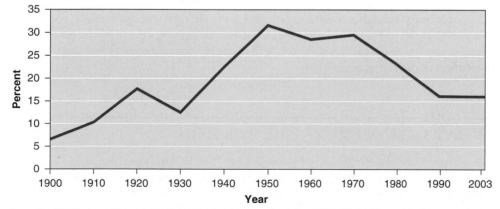

Source: Harold W. Stanley and Richard G. Niemi, eds., *Vital Statistics on American Politics, 2001–2002.* (Washington, DC: CQ Press, 2001), 402. Updated by the authors.

As part of a union, pilots can threaten a strike, as this group of Delta Airline pilots did when they were dissatisfied with the progress of their contract talks. Downturns in the economy, declining airline revenues, and industry-wide layoffs make it less likely that pilots and flight attendants will strike.

(Photo courtesy: Erik S. Lesser/AP/Wide World Photos)

organizations no longer have the large memberships or the political clout they once held in governmental circles.

By the late 1970s, it was clear that even during a Democratic administration (Carter's), organized labor lacked the impact it had during earlier decades.[42] During the Reagan administration, organized labor's influence fell to an all-time modern-day low. In spite of the tremendous resources behind the AFL-CIO and other unions, membership continues to drop.

Organized labor recognizes its troubles and has tried to recapture some of its lost political clout. In 2000, labor unions spent almost $200 million in campaign contributions and independent expenditures.[43] Not only did unions around the nation contribute substantial sums to elect pro-labor candidates, they also launched a massive effort to get fellow workers to the polls. Members also made over 100 million phone calls and distributed 32 million pieces of literature. The AFL-CIO alone had 2,000 full-time coordinators working to mobilize union households. In one successful campaign in New Jersey, for example, 73 percent of union members voted.[44] Nationwide, more than 27 million union members voted. According to a poll conducted by Hart Associates for the AFL-CIO, 65 percent of these voters supported John Kerry. However, unions still failed to deliver the election, a continued testament to their declining social and financial capital.

Although organized labor's clout on the national level continues to fall well short of what it once was, labor unions are making a visible difference in state-level policies. Recent research reveals that "labor organization profoundly affects public policy."[45] In fact, the greater the organizational strength of labor, "the more states spend on welfare, education and other activities."[46]

WEB EXPLORATION
For more on the AFL-CIO, see www.ablongman.com/oconnor

WHAT DO INTEREST GROUPS DO?

As illustrated by the discussion of groups above, "In Washington, money talks, and it is foolish for anyone to pretend it is irrelevant to this debate." So notes the director of the Center for Public Integrity, a nonprofit research center financed by foundations, corporations, and unions, in discussing the wide range of expensive policy-oriented activities engaged in by many interest groups.[47]

Not all interest groups are political, but they may become politically active when their members believe that a government policy threatens or affects group goals. Interest groups also enhance political participation by motivating like-minded individuals to work toward a common goal. Legislators often are much more likely to listen to or be concerned about the interests of a group as opposed to the interests of any one individual. Still, the congressional testimony of actor Michael J. Fox brought considerable attention to the underfunding of research for Parkinson's disease.

Just as members of Congress are assumed to represent the interests of their constituents in Washington, D.C., interest groups are assumed to represent the interests of their members to policy makers at all levels of government. In the 1950s, for example, the National Association for the Advancement of Colored People (NAACP) was able to articulate and present the interests of African Americans to national decision makers even though as a group they had little or no electoral clout, especially in the South. Without the efforts of the civil rights groups discussed in chapter 6, it is unlikely that either the courts or Congress would have acted as quickly to make discrimination illegal. All sorts of individuals—from railroad workers to women to physical therapists to campers to homosexuals to mushroom growers—have found that banding together with others who have similar interests can advance their collective interests. Getting celebrity support or hiring a lobbyist to advocate those interests in Washington, D.C., or a state capital also increases the likelihood that issues of concern to them will be addressed and acted on favorably.

There is also a downside to interest groups. Because groups make claims on society, they can increase the cost of public policies. The elderly can push for more costly health care and Social Security programs, people with disabilities for improved access to public buildings, industry for tax loopholes, and veterans for improved benefits. Many Americans believe that interest groups exist simply to advance their own selfish interests, with little regard for the rights of other groups or, more important, of people not represented by any organized group.

Whether good or bad, interest groups play an important role in U.S. politics. In addition to enhancing the democratic process by providing increased representation and participation, they increase public awareness about important issues, help frame the public agenda, and often monitor programs to guarantee effective implementation. Most often, they accomplish these things through some sort of lobbying or informational campaign.

The late actor Christopher Reeve, shown here with his wife Dana, was one of many celebrities who actively lobbied Congress to support their interests or causes.

(Photo courtesy: Richard Ellis/Corbis Sygma)

NONPROFIT ORGANIZATIONS IN COMPARATIVE CONTEXT

A survey of major interest groups in the industrial democracies would reveal a list familiar to students of American politics. Business, labor, and professional interest groups are well represented. New social movements focusing on the environment, gender equality, and other post-industrial issues have emerged across Europe, North America, and Japan in the last twenty-five years, although they often lack the political resources of the traditional lobbies.

Nonprofit organizations are quite active in the United States and the United Kingdom, countries that long have recognized the contributions that private, charitable organizations can make to the public weal. In those countries, the nonprofit sector represents a significant economic force. Nonprofit organizations (NPOs) also have begun to achieve prominence around the world in the last two decades. NPOs represent a wide array of purposes, ranging from traditional education, health, and social welfare functions to social education and advocacy. In this latter capacity, they act as a kind of interest group.

NPOs often are seen as independent, apolitical organizations that pursue public goals. Yet, they often are intimately involved in the political system. In practically all countries, they provide health and social welfare services that government cannot or will not provide. As privatization of government functions gained popularity around the world, governments became increasingly willing to let the nonprofit sector implement official welfare policies. On the other hand, as the table shows,

NPO Employment and Public Funding		
Country	Employment as % of Total Employment	% of Income from Public Funds
Mexico	0.4	n/a
Hungary	1.3	27.1
Japan	3.5	45.2
22-country average	4.8	41.3
France	4.9	57.8
Germany	4.9	64.3
United Kingdom	6.2	46.7
United States	7.8	30.5

Source: Lester Salamon and Helmut Anheier, eds., *Global Civil Society* (Baltimore, MD: The Johns Hopkins Comparative Nonprofit Sector Project, 1999).

government is a significant provider of financial support to nonprofit organizations. In the foreign aid field, for example, the largest development NPOs—Save the Children and CARE in the United States, OISCA in Japan, Misereor in Germany, to name a few—depend on public funding to carry out their work. Despite their image as voluntary, citizen-centered organizations, these NPOs cannot operate at current levels on private donations alone. The significance of public funds for the sector can be seen in Mexico. The nonprofit sector there relies overwhelming on fees and other charges from users. While this may keep NPOs from being dominated by the government, it also means that the sector remains tiny and its contribution to society limited.

Lobbying

lobbying
The activities of a group or organization that seeks to influence legislation and persuade political leaders to support the group's position.

WEB EXPLORATION
For information on interest groups that watch over lobbyists' activities, see
www.ablongman.com/oconnor

Comparative
Comparing Interest Groups

Most interest groups put lobbying at the top of their agendas. **Lobbying** is the process by which interest groups attempt to assert their influence on the policy-making process. The term lobbyist refers to any representative of a group that attempts to influence a policy maker by one or more of the tactics illustrated in Table 16.3. It is important to note that not only do large, organized interests have their own lobbyists, but other groups, including colleges, trade associations, cities, states, and even foreign nations, also hire lobbying firms (some law firms have lobbying specialists) to represent them in the halls of Congress or to get through the bureaucratic maze.

Most politically active groups use lobbying to make their interests heard and understood by those who are in a position to influence or cause change in governmental policies. (See Roots of Government: Pressure Politics of the Past.) Depending on the type of group and on the role it is looking to play, lobbying can take many forms. You probably have never thought of the Boy Scouts or Girl Scouts as political. Yet, when Congress began debating the passage of legislation dealing with discrimination in private clubs, representatives of both organizations testified in an attempt to persuade Congress to allow each one to remain a single-sex organization. Similarly, you probably don't often think of golf clubs as political. Yet, when the Augusta National Golf Course

TABLE 16.3   Percentage of Groups and Lobbyists Using Each Lobbying Technique

Technique	STATE-BASED GROUPS		WASHINGTON, DC–BASED GROUPS
	Lobbyists (n = 595)	Organizations (n = 301)	(n= 175)
1. Testifying at legislative hearings	98	99	99
2. Contacting government officials directly to present point of view	98	97	98
3. Helping to draft legislation	96	88	85
4. Alerting state legislators to the effects of a bill on their districts	96	94	75
5. Having influential constituents contact legislator's office	94	92	80
6. Consulting with government officials to plan legislative strategy	88	84	85
7. Attempting to shape implementation of policies	88	85	89
8. Mounting grassroots lobbying efforts	88	86	80
9. Helping to draft regulations, rules, or guidelines	84	81	78
10. Raising new issues and calling attention to previously ignored problems	85	83	84
11. Engaging in informal contacts with officials	83	81	95
12. Inspiring letter-writing or telegram campaigns	82	83	84
13. Entering into coalitions with other groups	79	93	90
14. Talking to media	73	74	86
15. Serving on advisory commissions and boards	58	76	76
16. Making monetary contributions to candidates	—	45	58
17. Attempting to influence appointment to public office	44	42	53
18. Doing favors for officials who need assistance	41	36	56
19. Filing suit or otherwise engaging in litigation	36	40	72
20. Working on election campaigns	—	29	24
21. Endorsing candidates	—	24	22
22. Running advertisements in media about position	18	21	31
23. Engaging in protests or demonstrations	13	21	20

Sources: State-Based Groups: Anthony J. Nownes and Patricia Freeman, "Interest Group Activity in the States," *Journal of Politics* 60 (1998): 92. Washington, DC–Based Groups: Kay Lehman Schlozman and John Tierney, "More of the Same: Washington Pressure Group Activity in a Decade of Change," *Journal of Politics* 45 (1983): 358.

refused to allow women to become members, the National Council of Women's Organizations made that decision political by contacting sponsors of the Masters Tournament and asking them to withdraw their sponsorship.

As Table 16.3 indicates, there are at least twenty-three ways for lobbyists and organizations to lobby on the state and national level. Lobbying allows interest groups to try to convince key governmental decision makers and the public of the correctness of their positions. Almost all interest groups lobby by testifying at hearings and contacting legislators. Other groups also provide information that decision makers might not have the time, opportunity, or interest to gather on their own. Of course, information these groups provide is designed to present the group's position in a favorable light, although a good lobbyist for an interest group also will note the downside to proposed legislation. Interest groups also file lawsuits to lobby the courts, and some even engage in protests or demonstrations as a form of lobbying public opinion or decision makers.

Simulation

You Are a Lobbyist

Lobbying Congress.   Members of Congress are the targets of a wide variety of lobbying activities: congressional testimony on behalf of a group, individual letters from interested constituents, campaign contributions, trips, speaking fees, or the outright payment of money for votes. Of course, the last item is illegal, but there are numerous documented instances of money changing hands for votes. Because lobbying plays such an important role in Congress, many effective lobbyists often are former members of that body, former staff aides, former White House officials or Cabinet officers, or Washington insiders. This type of lobbyist frequently drops in to visit members of Congress or their staff members and often takes them to lunch, for drinks, to play golf, or

PRESSURE POLITICS OF THE PAST

The exact origin of the term "lobbying" is disputed. In mid-seventeenth-century England, there was a room located near the floor of the House of Commons where members of Parliament would congregate and could be approached by their constituents and others who wanted to plead a particular cause. Similarly, in the United States, people often waited outside the chambers of the House and Senate to speak to members of Congress as they emerged. Because they waited in the lobbies to argue their cases, by the nineteenth century they were commonly referred to as "lobbyists." Another piece of folklore explains that when Ulysses S. Grant was president, he would frequently walk from the White House to the Willard Hotel on Pennsylvania Avenue just to relax in its comfortable and attractive lobby. Interest group representatives and those seeking favors from Grant would crowd into that lobby and try to press their claims. Soon they were nicknamed "lobbyists."

Lobbying reached an infamous peak in the late 1800s, when railroads and other big businesses openly bribed state and federal legislators to obtain favorable legislation. Congress finally got around to regulating some aspects of lobbying in 1946 with the Regulation of Lobbying Act, which required paid lobbyists to register with the House and Senate and to file quarterly financial reports, including an account of all contributions and expenditures as well as the names and addresses of those to whom they gave $500 or more. Organizations also were required to submit financial reports, although they did not have to register officially.

The purpose of the act was to publicize the activities of lobbyists and remove some of the uncertainty surrounding the

FEMALE LOBBYISTS.

(Photo courtesy: Bettmann/Corbis)

influence of lobbying on legislation. In 1954, however, a lower court ruled the act unconstitutional. Although the Supreme Court reversed the decision, it ruled that the act was applicable only to persons or organizations who solicited, collected, or received money for the principal purpose of influencing legislation by directly lobbying members of Congress. Consequently, many lobbyists did not register at all. The National Association of Manufacturers, for example, was formed in 1895 but did not register as a lobbying group until 1975.

to parties. Although much of that activity may be ethically questionable, most is not illegal. Many lobbying firms pay millions yearly to former lawmakers to lobby their old colleagues. Former Senators Robert Dole and George Mitchell earn well over a million dollars a year in a D.C. law firm specializing in lobbying for a wide array of clients.[48]

Lobbying Congress and issue advocacy are skills that many people have developed over the years. In 1869, for example, women meeting in Washington, D.C., for the second annual meeting of the National Woman Suffrage Association marched to Capitol Hill to hear one of their members (unsuccessfully) ask Congress to pass legislation to enfranchise women under the terms of the Fourteenth Amendment.

Practices such as these floor speeches are no longer permitted. Some interest groups, however, still try mass marches to Congress. For example, after the Supreme Court ruled in 1976 that discrimination against a pregnant women was not prohibited by the Civil Rights Act of 1964, hordes of lobbyists from various women's rights groups descended on Congress at one time. In response, Congress quickly enacted the Pregnancy Discrimination Act of 1978.

Today, lobbyists try to develop close relationships with senators and House members in an effort to enhance their access to the policy-making process. A symbiotic relationship between members of Congress, interest group representatives, and affected bureaucratic agencies often develops. In these iron triangles, congressional representatives and their staff members, who face an exhausting workload and legislation they know little about, frequently look to lobbyists for information. "Information is the currency on Capitol Hill, not dollars," said one lobbyist.[49] According to one aide:

> My boss demands a speech and a statement for the *Congressional Record* for every bill we introduce or co-sponsor—and we have a lot of bills. I just can't do it all myself. The better lobbyists, when they have a proposal they are pushing, bring it to me along with a couple of speeches, a *Record* insert, and a fact sheet.[50]

Not surprisingly, lobbyists work most closely with representatives who share their interests.[51] A lobbyist from the NRA, for example, would be unlikely to try to influence a liberal representative who was on record as strongly in favor of gun control. It is much more effective for a group like the NRA to provide useful information for its supporters and to those who are undecided. Good lobbyists also can encourage members to file amendments to bills favorable to their interests. They also can urge their supporters in Congress to make speeches (often written by the group) and to pressure their colleagues in the chamber.

A lobbyist's effectiveness depends largely on his or her reputation for fair play and provision of accurate information. No member of Congress wants to look uninformed. As one member noted:

> It doesn't take very long to figure out which lobbyists are straightforward, and which ones are trying to snow you. The good ones will give you the weak points as well as the strong points of their case. If anyone ever gives me false or misleading information, that's it—I'll never see him again.[52]

Attempts to Reform Congressional Lobbying. In 1946, in an effort to limit the power of lobbyists, Congress passed the Federal Regulation of Lobbying Act, which required anyone hired to lobby any member of Congress to register and file quarterly financial reports. Few lobbyists actually filed these reports. For years, numerous good government groups argued that lobbying laws should be strengthened. Civil liberties groups such as the American Civil Liberties Union (ACLU), however, argue that registration provisions violate the First Amendment's freedom of speech and the right of citizens to petition the government.

But, public opinion polls continued to reveal that many Americans believed that the votes of numerous members of Congress were often available to the highest bidder. In late 1995, after nearly fifty years of inaction, Congress passed the first effort to regulate lobbying since the 1946 act. The new act, the 1995 Lobbying Disclosure Act, was passed overwhelmingly in both houses of Congress. The new act employs a strict definition of lobbyist (one who devotes at least 20 percent of a client's or employer's time to lobbying activities), which should trigger far greater reporting of lobbyist activities. It also requires lobbyists to: (1) register with the clerk of the House and the secretary of the Senate; (2) report their clients and issues and the agency or house they lobbied; and, (3) estimate the amount they are paid by each client.

These reporting requirements make it easier for lobbying activities to be monitored by watchdog groups or the media. In fact, the first comprehensive analysis by the Center for Responsive Politics revealed that by June 1999, 20,512

★ How a bill becomes law in Congress ★

(Photo courtesy: Mike Luckovich and Creators Syndicate, Inc., by permission)

Join the Debate

CAN INTEREST GROUP COMPETITION BALANCE PUBLIC POLICY MAKING?

The pluralist theory holds that competition among interest groups in the public arena produces compromises and balanced public policy. Other democratic theorists contend that interest group competition does not necessarily result in public interest legislation or balanced policy. For instance, political party theorists suggest that parties must have a broad base of issues and people, in order to win votes, and that their desire for votes serves as an incentive for negotiation, compromise, and coalition building; however, interest groups can focus on a small group of issues and appeal to targeted audiences, and do not have as much incentive to build coalitions and negotiate compromises on public policy issues.

Given the weakness of American political parties, interest groups have become aggressive players in electoral politics as a means of pursuing the agenda of their members. Moreover, new interest groups continue to form to counter other groups and to provide vehicles for policy thrusts that the major political parties may not be able to provide. Often, interest groups raise and spend money to influence election outcomes. Recent changes to campaign finance laws will affect the campaign finance activities of both parties and interest groups, and thus may have the side effect of affecting the balance of power in struggles over public policy.

The McCain-Feingold legislation referred to in the article became law as the Bipartisan Campaign Reform Act of 2002. See Chapter 14 for more information about the effects of this legislation.

Read and think about the following news article concerning the creation of a new interest group, the competition between it and other groups, and the intertwining of interest groups, political parties, and campaign finance. Then, join the debate. Can more interest groups competing against each other increase the chances for balanced public policy, or does such interest group activity favor particular groups in society? Consider the debating points and questions posed at the end of this feature, and sharpen your own arguments for the position you find most viable.

Interest Groups' Influence Affected

By Associated Press

WASHINGTON Apr 13, 2001 (AP Online via COMTEX)—Religious leaders who tend toward the liberal or moderate side have formed a new organization in the latest effort to counter the political clout of the Christian Coalition and other Christian conservatives. The effort comes as many suggest interest groups are about to gain a more prominent role in politics because of a possible overhaul of campaign finance laws that could shift the flow of political money.

The new religious group, the Progressive Religious Partnership, will not be set up initially to join the political wars with lobbying and issue advertising. It will consider whether to take a more politically active role later. The partnership will be a nonprofit, tax-exempt organization that could take tax-deductible donations and provide an outlet for religious groups and leaders to educate and advocate their political positions. But the group has left open the possibility of adding "a political advocacy component" in the future to take a position on legislative measures before Congress.

"It's vitally important to have a counterbalance to the voice of the religious right," said Ralph Neas, president of People for the American Way, which helped form the new religious group. "We want to bring progressive voices more powerfully and effectively to the public debate."

This is not the first time moderate-to-liberal religious groups have attempted to form a counterbalance to the Christian Coalition, one of the most successful of the interest groups at political mobilization.

One of the most recent was in the mid-1990s, after Republicans gained control of Congress.

"This doesn't bother us at all," said Roberta Combs, executive director of the Christian Coalition. "Every election cycle they do this." The Christian Coalition, with about 2 million supporters, is preparing to go through states across the country this summer "to activate, educate and train people in the political process." The coalition long has published its voter guides that point out candidates' stands on issues that are of critical interest to conservatives, such as abortion.

Many believe the already powerful role that interest groups play in politics could grow if campaign finance laws are overhauled. Those with the highest stakes are the most politically active such as more narrowly focused groups such as the National

Rifle Association, the Sierra Club and groups on both sides of the abortion issue. The [McCain-Feingold] legislation … would ban millions of dollars in unregulated soft money that now goes to the political parties. Some believe at least part of that money would eventually make its way to interest groups.

"The involvement of interest groups in campaigns has gradually increased over the last 25 years," said Dwight Morris of the independent Campaign Study Group. "It's about to explode. If the law … is upheld by the court, … interest group politics has been given a gift from the heavens. People will have money that they can't give to par-

ties and they'll give to these groups or form new ones." Others are skeptical how much money now given to parties will end up with the interest groups ….

[The McCain-Feingold law] would prevent groups from taking out issue ads that mention a candidate for up to 60 days before the election. But it is uncertain whether that prohibition would hold up under a court challenge ….

"If it's held constitutional, the question everyone will have to ask themselves: Is it worth doing if we can't mention the candidate's name?" said Larry Noble, executive director of the Center for Responsive Politics. "It's a big unknown."

The influence of interest groups in educating and advocating among potential voters—or what parties refer to as the grassroots—has clearly increased over the decades. The Progressive Religious Partnership was formed as a way of balancing extensive efforts on the right.

"We're not going to demonize the religious right," said Rabbi Steven Jacobs of Temple Kol Tikvah in Los Angeles. "They raise a lot of the same questions we do."

Source: Associated Press Online, April 13, 2001. Reprinted with permission of The Associated Press.

JOIN THE DEBATE!

CHECK YOUR UNDERSTANDING: Make sure you understand the following key points from the article; go back and review it if you missed any of them:

- The Christian Coalition is a conservative interest group that has been successful in grassroots organizing and election campaigning on issues such as abortion.
- People for the American Way, a liberal interest group, is helping to create a new group, the Progressive Religious Partnership, to counter the Christian Coalition in public opinion and public policy battles.
- Campaign finance law changes designed to slow the flow of money to parties and campaigns may have the effect of increasing available money for interest groups' campaign activities.

ADDITIONAL INFORMATION: News articles don't provide all the information an informed citizen needs to know about an issue under debate. Here are some questions the article does not answer that you may need to consider in order to join the debate:

- How do the two major political parties line up with the interest groups mentioned in the article?
- How representative are members of the groups, in comparison to the American population?
- How do the financial resources of these and allied groups compare, in size and by source?
- Besides election campaigning, how do these groups attempt to influence public policy outcomes, and how successful are they?
- What are the groups doing today? Are they having any effect?

What other information might you want to know? Where might you gather this information? How might you evaluate the credibility of the information you gather? Is the information from a reliable source? Can you identify any potential biases?

IDENTIFYING THE ARGUMENTS: Now that you have some information on the issue, and have thought about what else you need to know, see whether you can present the arguments on both sides of the debate. Here are some ideas to get you started. We've provided one example each of "pro" and "con" arguments, but you should be able to offer others:

PRO: Interest group competition enhances democratic control of public policy. Here's why:

- As groups such as the Christian Coalition and the Progressive Religious Partnership compete for public opinion and victories in election campaigns, issues are debated vigorously and policy makers have a wider array of information and positions to evaluate in making policy decisions.

CON: Interest group competition diminishes democratic control of and balance in public policy. Here's why:

- Interest groups understandably stake out clear positions on issues of concern to them, and as they become the center of political and campaign finance activities, candidates and policy makers find it harder to fashion policies that respond to a wide array of interests on the issue, but must choose between one extreme position or the other.

TAKING A POSITION AND SUPPORTING IT: After thinking about the information in the article on the Christian Coalition, the Progressive Religious Partnership, and campaign finance provisions, placing it in the broader context of interest group and party influence in public policy, and articulating the arguments in the debate, what position would you take? What information supports your position? What arguments would you use to persuade others to your side of the debate? How would you counter arguments on the other side?

lobbyists were registered—a 35 percent jump from just two years earlier. The number of organizations that reported spending more than one million dollars a year on lobbying also jumped dramatically to 128. In 2000, $3.5 million was spent on lobbying for every member of Congress.[53]

As revealed in Analyzing Visuals: Top Lobbying Expenditures, health care interests not only were among the top spenders for lobbying activities but also were the source of significant campaign contributions to both Republicans and Democrats. Although contributing huge sums does not necessarily mean that votes are being bought, political scientists have found a strong correlation between a group's campaign contributions and a member's involvement in certain kinds of legislation or a representative's responsiveness to big business.[54]

Lobbying the Executive Branch. As the scope of the federal government has expanded, lobbying the executive branch has increased in importance and frequency. Groups often target one or more levels of the executive branch because there are so many potential access points including the president, White House staff, and the numerous levels of the executive branch bureaucracy. Groups try to work closely with the administration to influence policy decisions at their formulation and implementation stages. Like the situation with congressional lobbying, the effectiveness of a group often lies in its ability to provide decision makers with important information and a sense of where the public stands on the issue.

Historically, group representatives have met with presidents or their staff members to urge policy directions. In 1992, representatives of the auto industry accompanied President George Bush to lobby the Japanese for more favorable trade regulations. Most presidents have set up staff positions to provide interest groups or organizations with access to the administration. Many of these offices, such as those dealing with consumer affairs, the environment, minority affairs, or women's issues, are routinely the target of organized interests. President George W. Bush curtailed this practice and abolished the White House Office of Women's Initiatives Outreach as well as other special interest offices, much to the chagrin of liberal groups that had found a voice in the Clinton administration.

An especially strong link exists between interest groups and regulatory agencies (see chapter 8). While these agencies are ostensibly independent of Congress and the president, interest groups often have clout there. Because of the highly technical aspects of much regulatory work, many groups employ Washington attorneys and lobbying firms to deal directly with the agencies. So great is interest group influence in the decision-making process of these agencies that many people charge that the agencies have been captured by the interest groups.

Groups often monitor how the laws or policies they advocated are implemented. The National Women's Law Center, for example, has been instrumental in seeing that Title IX, which was passed by Congress to mandate educational equity for women and girls, be enforced fully. It has successfully sued several colleges and universities that have failed to provide equity in athletic funding for men and women.

Often executive branch employees leave their positions to take much more lucrative jobs in private industry, frequently in areas that they had been regulating. The Ethics in Government Act (see Table 16.4) was an attempt to curtail questionable moves by barring members of the executive branch from representing any clients before their agency for two years after leaving governmental service. Thus, someone who worked in Title IX enforcement in the Department of Education and then went to work for a university or the National Collegiate Athletic Association would have to wait two years before lobbying their old agency. Members of Congress aren't under these kinds of restrictions.

Lobbying the Courts. The courts, too, have proved a useful target for interest groups.[55] Although you might think that the courts decide cases that affect only the parties involved or that they should be immune from political pressures, interest groups for years have recognized the value of lobbying the courts, especially the Supreme

WEB EXPLORATION

To experience how the lobbying process works, go to www.ablongman.com/oconnor

TABLE 16.4	The Ethics in Government Act
In 1978, in the wake of Watergate, Congress passed the Ethics in Government Act. Its key provisions dealt with: (1) financial disclosure; and, (2) employment after government service. **(1) Financial disclosure:** The president, vice president, and top-ranking executive employees must file annual public financial disclosure reports that list: • The source and amount of all earned income; all income from stocks, bonds, and property; any investments or large debts; the source of a spouse's income, if any. • Any position or offices held in any business, labor, or nonprofit organizations.	**(2) Employment after government services:** Former executive branch employees may not: • Represent anyone before any agency for two years after leaving government service on matters that came within the former employees' sphere of responsibility (even if they were not personally involved in the matter). • Represent anyone on any matter before their former agency for one year after leaving it, even if the former employees had no connection with the matter while in the government.

Source: Congressional Quarterly Weekly Report (October 28, 1978): 3121.

Court, and many political scientists view it as a form of political participation.[56] As shown in Table 16.3, 72 percent of the Washington-based groups surveyed participated in litigation as a lobbying tool. Richard C. Cortner has noted that "Cases do not arrive on the doorstep of the Supreme Court like orphans in the night."[57] Most major cases noted in this book either have been sponsored by an interest group or one or both of the parties in the case have been supported by an *amicus curiae* (friend of the court) brief.

Generally, interest group lobbying of the courts can take two forms: direct sponsorship or the filing of *amicus curiae* briefs. When cases come to the Supreme Court that raise issues a particular organization is interested in but not actually sponsoring, often the organization will file an *amicus* brief—either alone or with other like-minded groups—to inform the justices of their policy preference, generally offered in the guise of legal arguments. Over the years, as the number of both liberal and conservative groups viewing litigation as a useful tactic has increased, so has the number of briefs submitted to the Court.

In addition to litigating, interest groups try to influence who is nominated to the federal courts. They also have played an important role of late in Senate confirmation hearings, as discussed in chapter 10. In 1991, for example, 112 groups testified or filed prepared statements for or against the nomination of Clarence Thomas to the U.S. Supreme Court.[58] Thomas's nomination was unusual in that it attracted so much opposition, including that of the NAACP. In contrast, the subsequent nominations of Justices Ruth Bader Ginsburg and Stephen Breyer attracted the attention of far fewer interest groups.

Grassroots Lobbying. As the term implies, grassroots lobbying is a form of pressure-group activity that attempts to involve those people at the bottom level of the political system.[59] Although it often involves door-to-door informational or petition drives—a tried and true method of lobbying—the term also can be used to encompass more modern forms such as fax and Internet lobbying of lawmakers. As early as the 1840s, women (who could not vote) used petition campaigns to persuade state legislators to enact Married Women's Property Acts that gave women control of their earnings and a greater legal say in the custody of their children. Petitioning has come a long way since then. In 1996, the Fund for a Feminist Majority held a weekend symposium to teach women how to use the Internet to contact lawmakers.

Interest groups regularly try to stir up their members to inspire grassroots activity, hoping that lawmakers will respond to those pressures and the attendant publicity. In essence, the goal of many organizations is to persuade ordinary voters to serve as their advocates. In the world of lobbying, there are few things more useful than a list of committed supporters. Radio talk-show hosts such as Rush Limbaugh try to stir up their

ANALYZING VISUALS

Top Lobbying Expenditures

For most interest groups, lobbying is their most important activity. Successful lobbying efforts require spending large amounts of money, as shown in the bar graph below. Based on the narrow definition of lobbying used under the Lobbying Disclosure Act, the reported expenditures account for money spent to contact Congresspersons and executive branch officials but do not include money spent for state-level lobbying, public relations work, legal work, or congressional testimony. Interest groups also supplement their lobbying efforts with campaign contributions to congressional candidates. After studying the bar graph below, answer the following critical thinking questions: What is the correlation, if any, between an interest group's expenditures for lobbying and its expenditures for campaign contributions? Which interest groups are most likely to contribute to Republican candidates? Which interest groups are most likely to contribute to Democratic candidates? What do you think explains the differences in these groups' contribution tendencies?

	Lobbying Expenditures	PAC Contributions	% to Democrats	% to Republicans
U.S. Chamber of Commerce	$20,060,000	$155,806	19	81
U.S. Chamber Institute for Legal Reform	$10,000,000	None	None	None
American Medical Association	$9,240,000	$3,125,533	19	81
General Electric	$8,440,000	$1,718,023	35	65
Pharmaceutical Research & Mnfrs. of Amer.	$8,040,000	$117,323	30	70
National Association of Realtors	$6,560,000	$6,913,071	48	52
American Hospital Association	$6,060,000	$2,376,830	43	57
Northrup Grumman	$6,000,000	$1,452,803	33	67
SBC Communications	$5,638,350	$2,406,533	32	68
American Council of Life Insurers	$5,585,567	$648,829	40	60

Lobbying Expenditures (in millions)

Source: Political MoneyLine, www.fray.com; Center for Responsive Politics, www.opensecrets.org.

listeners by urging them to contact their representatives in Washington, D.C. Some of these undefined masses, as they join together on the Internet or via faxes, may be mobilized into one or more groups.

Grassroots lobbying is a term often used by professional lobbyists for their activities "to camouflage an unpopular or unsympathetic client."[60] Typically, in these kinds of grassroots campaigns, a "large business hires a Washington firm to organize a coalition of small business, nonprofit groups, and individuals across the nation." This coalition (or better yet, arranged marriage) then draws public attention and sympathy to the proposed policy or legislation sought by the lobbyists' initial client—who, by the time the issue gets on the public agenda, has faded from the public. This kind of grassroots lobbying occurs on most major pieces of legislation.

Interest groups' use of electronic technologies for rapid mobilization of thousands of Americans at the grassroots level has caused "Congress to govern more by fear and an intense desire for simple, easy answers," said Representative Steve Gunderson (R–WI) before he left office.[61] Today, the simple grassroots campaigns of just a few years ago (fill-in-the-blank postcards and forms torn out of the newspaper) have grown much more sophisticated and much more effective.

Many interest groups and trade groups have installed banks of computerized fax machines to send faxes automatically around the country overnight, instructing each member to ask his or her employees, customers, or other people to write, call, or fax their members of Congress. Other interest groups now run carefully targeted and costly television advertisements pitching one side of an argument. Their opponents must generally respond or lose. Many of these advertisements end with a toll-free phone number that viewers can call if they find the pitch convincing. New telemarketing companies answer these calls and transfer the callers directly to the offices of the appropriate members of Congress.[62]

The Internet is the newest weapon in the arsenal of interest groups and lobbyists. E-mail is a way for groups to connect with supporters as well as to urge supporters to connect with policy makers. Digital activism can be especially effective at the local level. "Flash campaigns," as they are called, can be generated with the click of a mouse to contact hundreds or thousands of concerned citizens.[63]

Protest Activities. Most groups have few members so devoted as to put everything on the line for their cause. Some will risk jail or even death, but it is much more usual for a group's members to opt for more conventional forms of lobbying or to influence policy through the electoral process. When these forms of pressure group activities are unsuccessful or appear to be too slow to achieve results, however, some groups (or individuals within groups) resort to more forceful legal and illegal measures to attract attention to their cause. Since the Revolutionary War, violent, illegal protest has been one tactic of organized interests. The Boston Tea Party, for example, involved breaking all sorts of laws, although no one was hurt physically. Other forms of protest, such as Shays's Rebellion, ended in tragedy for some participants. Much more recently, the suicide bombers in Israel show the degree to which some protesters will go in the name of their cause.

Activists protest in April 2002, at a Capitol Hill rally calling for congressional action to stop the growing global AIDS epidemic. Participants called for immediate increases in money from Congress for affordable AIDS treatment and prevention in developing countries.

(Photo courtesy: Alex Wong/Getty Images)

During the civil rights movement, as discussed in chapter 6, Martin Luther King Jr. and his followers frequently resorted to nonviolent marches to draw attention to the plight of African Americans in the South. These forms of organized group activity were legal. Proper parade permits were obtained, and government officials notified. The protesters who tried to stop the freedom marchers, however, were engaging in illegal protest activity.

Groups on both ends of the political spectrum historically have resorted to violence in the furtherance of their objectives. Abolitionists, anti–nuclear power activists, anti-war activists, animal rights advocates, and other groups on the left have broken laws, damaged property, and even injured or killed people, as have groups on the right such as the Army of God (an anti-abortion group) and the Ku Klux Klan (KKK). From the early 1900s until the 1960s, African Americans were routinely lynched by KKK members. Today, some radical anti-abortion groups regularly block the entrances to abortion clinics; others active in the anti-abortion movement have taken credit for clinic bombings. Radical right-to-life proponents also have targeted abortion clinics with anthrax hoax letters. In 2001, clinics received over 550 hoax letters from a single individual. On one day in November 2001, alone, clinics around the nation received over 250 Federal Express envelopes that contained white powder and letters signed "Army of God."[64]

Other protest activities are less violent, sometimes tasteless, and often also illegal. After then New York City Mayor Rudy Giuliani announced that he had prostate cancer, People for the Ethical Treatment of Animals (PETA) put up controversial billboards linking prostate cancer to milk. PETA activists also have trespassed on private property to free animals from testing by humans and have thrown cans of red paint on women sporting fur coats.

Election Activities

In addition to trying to achieve their goals (or at least draw attention to them) through the conventional and unconventional forms of lobbying and protest activity, many interest groups also become involved more directly in the electoral process. The 2004 Republican and Democratic presidential nominating conventions were the targets of significant organized interest group protest concerning each party's stance on a variety of issues, including U.S. involvement in Colombian drug wars, support for Iraqi sanctions, the death penalty, abortion, and third world sweatshops.

Endorsements.   Many groups claim to be nonpartisan, that is, nonpolitical. Usually they try to have friends in both political parties to whom they can look for assistance and access. Some organizations, however, routinely endorse candidates for public office, pledging money, group support, and often campaign volunteers.

EMILY's List, a women's group (EMILY stands for "Early Money Is Like Yeast—it makes the dough rise"), not only endorses candidates but contributes heavily to races of pro-choice, Democratic women. In 1998, Planned Parenthood broke with tradition and endorsed candidates for the first time. This pro-choice group believed the change of only three senators could allow the Senate to override President Clinton's veto of anti-abortion restrictions. In 2000, the National Abortion and Reproductive Rights Action League (NARAL) was significantly involved in 110 races. It spent $7.5 million to make 3.4 million calls to pro-choice households, mailed 4.6 million pieces of mail to pro-choice households, and spent more than $1.5 million on television advertisements to encourage the election of pro-choice representatives and Al Gore.[65]

Once groups become overly political, however, their tax-exempt status is jeopardized. Federal law precludes tax-exempt organizations from taking partisan positions. The Christian Coalition for years claimed to be nonpartisan, although the FEC charged that it used money to promote specific candidates, causing it to redesign its candidate scorecards into voter guides.

THE MARCH FOR WOMEN'S LIVES

On Sunday, April 25, 2004, women and men from all over the United States gathered in Washington, D.C., to show support for abortion rights and to highlight what march organizers called the Bush administration's "war against reproductive rights and health." It was the largest women's rights march in history and came at a time when many were doubting the vitality of the women's movement. The event also marked a new effort by women's groups to place the abortion rights issue in a wider context, equating it with the need to improve access to reproductive education and health care, access to emergency contraception, and affordable prenatal care.

March organizers, who had requested a permit for at least 750,000 people, estimated that more than 1 million attended. This peaceful march was the culmination of months of planning and the concerted activity of several pro-choice organizations, including NARAL Pro-Choice America, the National Organization for Women, the Planned Parenthood Federation of America, the Feminist Majority, the American Civil Liberties Union, the Black Women's Health Imperative, and the National Latina Institute for Reproductive Health. There was a donor gathering at the home of House Minority Leader Nancy Pelosi, an afternoon tea highlighted by singer and songwriter Carole King, and a breakfast sponsored by Senator Hillary Rodham Clinton. Attracting additional media attention to the event, actresses Whoopi Goldberg, and Ashley Judd and Moby joined the marchers, along with members of Congress and former executive-branch officials such as former Secretary of State Madeleine Albright, for a day of speeches on the Mall.

As they attempted to expand the agenda from abortion rights to a wider array of reproductive rights, organizers had especially targeted young, college-age women and were heartened that busloads of students from many colleges and universities attended. In addition to student groups, more than 1,400 groups nationwide signed on to send members to Washington, D.C. Longtime abortion rights advocates are particularly conscious of the need to recruit and energize new members. Interest groups and social movements cannot maintain themselves without new recruits, and the march, while demonstrating the ability of a wide array of organized interests to come together, also attracted a new cohort of reproductive rights activists who, organizers hope, not only will spread the word around the nation, but also will become the next generation of leaders of myriad pro-choice, reproductive rights organizations.

1. How did efforts made by interest groups to engage young people translate into an energized youth vote?
2. How effective is the use of celebrity advocates as a strategy in helping an interest group achieve its goals?

Endorsements from some groups may be used by a candidate's opponent to attack a candidate. While labor union endorsements can add money to a candidate's campaign coffers, for example, the candidate risks being labeled a "tool of the labor unions" by an opponent.

Rating the Candidates or Office Holders.   Many liberal and conservative ideological groups rate candidates to help their members (and the general public) evaluate the voting records of members of Congress. The American Conservative Union (conservative) and the Americans for Democratic Action (liberal)—two groups at ideological polar extremes—routinely rate candidates and members of Congress based on their votes on key issues. (See Analyzing Visuals: Interest Group Ratings of Selected Members of Congress.) These scores help voters to know more about their representatives' votes on issues that concern them.

Creating Political Parties.   Another interest group strategy is to form a political party to publicize a cause and possibly win a few public offices. In 1848, the Free Soil

political action committee (PAC)
Federally mandated, officially registered fund-raising committee that represents interest groups in the political process.

Timeline

Interest
Groups and
Campaign
Finance

Party was formed to publicize the crusade against slavery; twenty years later, the Prohibition Party was formed to try to ban the sale of alcoholic beverages. Similarly, in the early 1970s, the now defunct National Right-to-Life Party was formed to publicize the anti-abortion position; it ran its own candidate for president in 1976.

In 1995, many in a Ross Perot–founded group, United We Stand, established the Reform Party to highlight the group's goals, including government reform (in particular, passage of new campaign finance laws) and fiscal responsibility. Consumer advocate Ralph Nader was the 1996 through 2000 nominee of the Green Party, created to bring attention to environmental issues. Groups often see forming political parties as a way to draw attention to their legislative goals and to drive one of the major political parties to give their demands serious attention.

The effectiveness of an interest group in the election arena often has been overrated by members of the news media. In general, it is very difficult to assess the effect of a particular group's impact on any one election because of the number of other factors present in any election or campaign. However, the one area in which interest groups do seem able to affect the outcome of elections directly is through a relatively new device called the political action committee, which is discussed below and in far greater detail in chapter 14.

Interest Groups and Political Action Committees.   Throughout most of history, powerful interests and individuals have used their money to buy politicians or their votes. Even if outright bribery was not involved, huge corporate or other interest group donations certainly made some politicians look as if they were in the pocket of certain special interests. Congressional passage of the Federal Election Campaign Act began to change most of that. The 1971 act required candidates to disclose all campaign contributions and limited the amount of money that they could spend on media advertising.

In 1974, in the wake of the Watergate scandal (see chapter 8), amendments to the act made it more far reaching by sharply limiting the amount of money any interest group could give to a candidate for federal office. However, the act also made it legal for corporations, labor unions, and interest groups to form what were termed **political action committees (PACs),** which could make contributions to candidates for national elections. (See chapter 14 for more on this subject.)

Technically, a PAC is a political arm of a business, labor, trade, professional, or other interest group legally authorized to raise funds on a voluntary basis from employees or members in order to contribute to a political candidate or party. PAC money changed the face of U.S. elections as corporate interests and organized interests tried to profit maximize the effect of their campaign contributions.[66]

Unlike some contributions to interest groups, contributions to PACs are not tax deductible, and PACs generally don't have members who call legislators; instead, PACs have contributors who write checks specifically for the purpose of campaign donations. PAC money plays a significant role in the campaigns of many congressional incumbents, often averaging over half a House candidate's total campaign spending. PACs generally contribute to those who have helped them before and who serve on committees or subcommittees that routinely consider legislation of concern to that group. Political scientists have found a strong relationship between committee assignments of members of the House and Senate and PAC contributions.[67] Systematic research has failed to find a significant relation between PAC contributions and floor voting, but other research shows that group expenditures are more likely to have an effect in committee votes; most often affected is the degree of a member's involvement with proposed legislation, not how the member votes.[68] Moreover, studies by economists find that "campaign contributions are made to support politicians with the 'right' beliefs … [not to] buy politicians' votes."[69]

The McCain-Feingold campaign finance reform law of 2002 dramatically altered the role of interest groups in the election process. As discussed in chapter 14, PACs can spend money in ways that political parties no longer are permitted to do. Moreover, as discussed in our opening vignette, 527s, another kind of organized interest, played a major role in the 2004 media campaign for the presidency.

ANALYZING VISUALS

Interest Group Ratings of Selected Members of Congress

Among the election activities of interest groups are the endorsement of candidates for public office and the rating of candidates and incumbents. Interest groups inform their members, as well as the public generally, of the voting records of office holders, helping voters make an informed voting decision. The table displays the ratings in 2003 of selected members of Congress by seven interest groups that vary greatly in their ideological tendencies. Each group rates the members of Congress on issues that are important to the group. For example, the AFL-CIO bases its rating on a member's votes in support of labor unions. After reviewing the table, answer the following critical thinking questions: Which members of the Senate would you consider the most liberal? Which groups' ratings did you use to reach your conclusion? Which members of the House would you consider the most conservative? Which groups' ratings did you use to reach your conclusion? Would it be important to know which of a representative's votes were used by each group to determine the rating? Explain your answer.

Member	ACU	ACLU	ADA	AFL-CIO	CC	CoC	LCV
Senate							
Dianne Feinstein (D–CA)	20	60	80	92	20	55	80
Bill Frist (R–TN)	100	20	0	15	100	100	0
Kay Bailey Hutchison (R–TX)	100	25	5	23	100	95	4
Ted Kennedy (D–MA)	0	60	100	100	0	29	84
House							
Mary Bono (R–CA)	71	27	10	11	75	95	9
John Conyers (D–MI)	0	93	100	100	14	21	91
Tom DeLay (R–TX)	92	7	0	0	100	95	0
Sheila Jackson Lee (D–TX)	4	93	100	100	0	26	68

Key

ACU = American Conservative Union   CC = Christian Coalition

ACLU = American Civil Liberties Union   CoC = Chamber of Commerce

ADA = Americans for Democratic Action   LCV = League of Conservation Voters

AFL-CIO = American Federation of Labor–Congress of Industrial Organizations

Members are rated on a scale from 1 to 100, with 1 being the lowest and 100 being the highest support of a particular group's policies.

WHAT MAKES AN INTEREST GROUP SUCCESSFUL?

Throughout our nation's history, all kinds of interests in society have organized to pressure the government for policy change. Some have been successful, and some have not. E. E. Schattschneider once wrote, "Pressure politics is essentially the politics of small groups. ... Pressure tactics are not remarkably successful in mobilizing general interests."[70] He was correct; historically, corporate interests often prevail over the concerns of public interest groups such as environmentalists.

All of the groups discussed in this chapter have one thing in common: They all want to shape the public agenda, whether by winning elections, maintaining the status quo, or obtaining favorable legislation or rulings from Congress, executive agencies, or the courts.[71] For powerful groups, simply making sure that certain issues never get discussed may be the goal. Gun manufacturers dread incidents such as the school shooting at Columbine High School in Littleton, Colorado, because it propels the issue of gun regulation out of their hands. Similarly, credit card companies profit when students and other consumers don't know about proposed changes in bankruptcy legislation that could hurt consumers. In contrast, those opposed to random stops of African American drivers or those of Middle Eastern appearance win when the issue becomes front-page news and law enforcement officials feel pressured to investigate, if not stop altogether, the discriminatory practice of racial profiling.

Groups often claim credit for "winning" legislation, court cases, or even elections individually or in coalition with other groups.[72] They also are successful when their leaders become elected officials or policy makers themselves. Each administration often is loaded with former group activists. In the Reagan administration, the secretary of the interior and the solicitor general were former leaders of a conservative public interest law firm, the Mountain States Legal Foundation. In the Clinton administration, Supreme Court appointee Ruth Bader Ginsburg was a former ACLU board member and the director of its Women's Rights Project. Senator Hillary Rodham Clinton (D–NY) was a former leader of the Children's Defense Fund and her election was hailed by its staff.

Political scientists have studied several phenomena that contribute in varying degrees—individually and collectively—to particular groups' successes. These include: (1) leaders and patrons; (2) adequate funding; and, (3) a solid membership base.

Leaders and Patrons.

Interest group theorists such as Robert H. Salisbury frequently acknowledge the key role that leaders play in the formation, viability, and success of interest groups while noting that leaders often vary from rank-and-file members on various policies. Jack L. Walker contends that without what he terms **patrons** (those who often finance a group), few organizations could begin.[73]

patrons
The persons who finance a group or individual activity.

Without the powerful pen of William Lloyd Garrison in the 1830s, who knows whether the abolitionist movement would have been as successful. Similarly, Frances Willard was the prime mover behind the WCTU, as were Marian Wright Edelman of the Children's Defense Fund in 1968, and Pat Robertson of the Christian Coalition in the 1990s. Most successful groups, especially public interest groups, are led by charismatic individuals who devote most of their energies to "the cause." The role of an interest group leader is similar to that of an entrepreneur in the business world. As in the marketing of a new product, an interest group leader must have something attractive to offer to persuade members to join. Potential members of the group must be convinced that the benefits of joining outweigh the costs. Union members, for example, must be persuaded that the cost of their union dues will be offset by the union's winning higher wages for them.

Funding.

Funding is crucial to all interest groups to build their memberships as well as to advance their policy objectives. Government, foundations, and wealthy individuals can serve as patrons providing crucial start-up funds for groups, especially public interest groups. Advertising, litigating, and lobbying are expensive.

During the 1980s, conservative groups relied on the direct-mail skills of marketing wizard Richard Viguerie to raise monies for a variety of conservative causes. In the early 1990s, pro-choice groups appealed to supporters by requesting funds to campaign for legislation in anticipation of the Supreme Court's reversal of *Roe* v. *Wade*. When the Supreme Court did not overrule *Roe* in 1992, and Ruth Bader Ginsburg was appointed to the Supreme Court, contributions to pro-choice groups such as NARAL and Planned Parenthood dropped precipitously.

Some groups, particularly political action committees (PACs), measure their successes by the number of candidates supported who won. In 1996, for example, tobacco companies contributed an estimated $11.3 million on targeted races and received $50 billion in tax breaks as a result of congressional legislation. Similarly, the airlines individually and through several trade associations contributed $3.2 million. By 1997, they had won a 2.5 percent tax reduction on each plane ticket.[74]

Members.

Alexis de Tocqueville, a French aristocrat and philosopher, toured the United States extensively during 1831 and 1832. A keen observer of American politics, he was very much impressed by the tendency of Americans to join groups in order to participate in the policy-making process. "Whenever at the head of some new undertaking you see government in France, or a man of rank in England, in the United States you will be sure to find an association," wrote Tocqueville.[75]

Despite Robert D. Putnam's qualms discussed early in this chapter, the United States is still a nation of joiners. As a college student, think of the number of interest groups or voluntary associations to which you belong. It's likely that you belong to some kind of organized religion, to a political party, or to a college or university social, civic, athletic, or academic group, at a bare minimum. You may also belong to a special interest group, such as Greenpeace, People for the Ethical Treatment of Animals, the National Right-to-Life Committee, or Amnesty International, as well as being involved in local literacy or poverty groups.

Organizations are usually composed of three kinds of members. At the top are a relatively small number of leaders who devote most of their energies to the single group. The second tier of members is generally involved psychologically as well as organizationally. They are the workers of the group—they attend meetings, pay dues, and chair committees to see that things get done. In the bottom tier are the rank and file, members who don't actively participate. They pay their dues and call themselves group members, but they do little more. Most group members fall into this last category.

Political scientist E. E. Schattschneider has noted that the interest group system in the United States has a decidedly "upper-class bias," and he concluded that 90 percent of the population does not participate in an interest group, or what he called the pressure group system.[76] Since the 1960s, survey data have revealed that group membership is drawn primarily from people with higher income and education levels. Individuals who are wealthier can afford to belong to more organizations because they have more money and, often, more leisure time. Money and education also are associated with greater confidence that one's actions will bring results, a further incentive to devote time to organizing or supporting interest groups. These elites often are more involved in politics and hold stronger opinions on many political issues.

People who do belong to groups often belong to more than one. Overlapping memberships can often affect the cohesiveness of a group. Imagine, for example, that you are an officer in the College Republicans. If you call a meeting, people may not attend because they have academic, athletic, or social obligations. Divided loyalties and multiple group memberships can often affect the success of a group, especially if any one group has too many members who simply fall into the dues-paying category.

Groups vary tremendously in their ability to enroll what are called potential members (see Table 16.5). Economist Mancur Olson Jr. notes that all groups provide some **collective good**—that is, something of value, such as money, a tax write-off, a good feeling, or a better environment, that can't be withheld from a non–group member.[77] If one union member at a factory gets a raise, for example, all other workers at that factory will, too. Therefore, those who don't join or work for the benefit of the group still

collective good
Something of value that cannot be withheld from a non–group member, for example, a tax write-off or a better environment.

TABLE 16.5 Potential Versus Actual Interest Group Members

The goal of most groups is to mobilize all potential members, but as Mancur Olson Jr. points out, the larger the group, the more difficult it is to mobilize. To illustrate the potential versus actual membership phenomenon, here are several examples of groups and their potential memberships.

Population	Group	Number of Potential Members	Number of Actual Members
Governors	National Governors Association	55 (includes territories)	55
Political Science Faculty	American Political Science Association	17,000	14,000
African Americans	National Association for the Advancement of Colored People (NAACP)	35,307,000	500,000
Physicians	American Medical Association (AMA)	707,000	300,000
Women	National Organization for Women (NOW)	140,619,000	150,000

free rider problem
Potential members fail to join a group because they can get the benefit, or collective good, sought by the group without contributing to the effort.

reap the rewards of the group's activity. The downside of this phenomenon is called the **free rider problem.** As Olson asserts, potential members may be unlikely to join a group because they realize that they will receive many of the benefits the group achieves regardless of their participation. Not only is it irrational for free riders to join any group, but the bigger the group, the greater the free rider problem. Thus, groups need to provide a variety of other incentives to convince potential members to join. These can be newsletters, discounts, or simply a good feeling.

Several scholars examining why individuals join groups have found that a group's attempt to pursue a collective good is not always a mere by-product of the group's ability to provide selective material incentives, as Olson has argued.[78] Specifically, they have found that several factors help groups overcome the free rider problem. One factor is that members representing other groups or institutions are much more likely than individuals to value efforts to obtain collective goods. Another factor is that once a policy environment appears to threaten existing rights, many individuals come to realize those threats and join groups in exchange for only collective benefits.[79] Moreover, Olson, an economist, fails to consider the fact that many political, D.C.-based groups count other groups, and not just individuals, as their members. These alliances often are considered carefully by organized interests much in the way some individuals calculate their membership in groups.[80]

These alliances have important implications.[81] While interest groups do work together in alliances, they also carve out policy niches to differentiate themselves to potential members as well as policy makers. While the National Women's Law Center, for example, vigorously pursues enforcement of Title IX through litigation, the National Organization for Women, although very supportive of Title IX, is more involved in welfare reform as it affects women. Similarly, one study of gay and lesbian groups found that they avoided direct competition by developing different issue niches.[82] Some concentrate on litigation; others lobby for domestic partnerships or inclusion of gays in the military.

Small groups often have an organizational advantage because, in a small group such as the National Governors Association, any individual's share of the collective good may be great enough to make it rational to join. Patrons, be they large foundations such as the Ford Foundation or individuals such as Jane Fonda, who donated $500,000 to the Georgia Campaign for Adolescent Pregnancy Prevention in 1995, often eliminate the free rider problem for public interest groups. They make the costs of joining minimal because they contribute much of the group's necessary financial support.[83]

Continuity & Change

A Balancing Act?

Throughout the history of the United States, interest groups have played a key role in the development of our pluralist society. Groups have arisen in response to crises, to alleviate a problem, or to maintain the status quo from attack. Government frequently has been the mediator of battles between these interest groups, and sometimes has been captured by the victors. Competition for public attention and governmental action is a recurring theme in American politics.

In the public forum, interest groups, or factions, as James Madison called them in *Federalist No. 10*, often present two opposing approaches to the same problem. When some of the colonists decided to break from Great Britain,

the colonies were split into two camps: the loyalists and the revolutionaries. Then, as the new nation became established, it was the Federalists and Anti-Federalists. During the Civil War, Americans were divided into pro-slavery and antislavery factions. Today, the dividing lines are gun control versus the right to bear arms, the right to choose versus the right to life, and the list goes on. For each of these interests, there is a group. Thus, there is the Brady Campaign to Prevent Gun Violence and the NRA. Similarly, there is the National Abortion and Reproductive Rights Action League (now NARAL Pro-Choice America) and the National Right to Life Committee.

Although the two major political parties are not per se interest groups, they represent very different approaches to solving a variety of problems, and many political interest groups are largely allied with one party or the other, highlighting the persistence, and importance, of factions in politics. While labor unions today may try to reach out to Republicans and big business to Democrats, fairly sharp lines are drawn concerning a variety of issues. In general, interest groups ally themselves with a single party and view themselves as competitors trying to capture control of the government to have an influence on its policies. It is not surprising, then, that President George W. Bush, the first president with an MBA, is pro-business and that his ties to big business and its influence on him and his administration have been questioned. A president coming out of a labor union could expect similar questions about influence.

1. As interest groups and their issues have changed over time, theories about how they form and maintain themselves have been able to explain interest groups pretty well. As Internet use increases for mobilizing potential adherents, do you see a change coming in the general nature of interest groups?
2. What role have big business interests and labor unions had as the war on terrorism has proceeded?
3. What ways have groups used to voice their support or opposition to American foreign and domestic policy? In which arena are they more successful?

CAST YOUR VOTE   In what ways will the Internet succeed as a mobilizing tool for interest groups? In what ways will it fail? To cast your vote, go to www.ablongman.com/oconnor

SUMMARY

Interest groups lie at the heart of the American social and political system. National groups first emerged in the 1830s. Since that time, the type, nature, sophistication, and tactics of groups have changed dramatically. In this chapter, we have made the following points:

1. **What Are Interest Groups?**
   Those who study interest groups have offered a variety of definitions to explain what they are. Most definitions revolve around notions of associations or groups of individuals who share some sort of common interest or attitude and who try to influence or engage in activity to affect governmental policies or the people in government. Political scientists find it helpful to categorize interest groups in several ways. They study multi-issue versus single-issue groups. They also examine economic, public interest, and governmental units as participants in the interest group process.

2. **The Roots and Development of American Interest Groups**
   Interest groups, national in scope, did not begin to emerge until around the 1830s. Later, from 1890 to 1920, the Progressive movement emerged. The 1960s saw the rise of a wide variety of liberal interest groups. By the 1970s through the 1980s, legions of conservatives were moved to form new groups to counteract those efforts. Business groups, corporations, and unions established their presence in Washington, D.C.

3. **What Do Interest Groups Do?**
   Interest groups often fill voids left by the major political parties and give Americans opportunities to make claims, as a group, on government. The most common activity of interest groups is lobbying, which takes many forms. Groups routinely pressure members of Congress and their staffs, the president and the bureaucracy, and the courts; they use a variety of techniques to educate and stimulate the public to pressure key governmental decision makers. Interest groups also attempt to influence the outcome of elections; some run their own candidates for office. Others rate elected officials to inform their members how particular legislators stand on issues of importance to them. Political action committees (PACs), a way for some groups to contribute money to candidates for office, are another method of gaining support from elected officials and ensuring that their "friends" stay in office. Reaction to public criticism of this influence led Congress to pass the first major lobbying reforms in fifty years.

4. **What Makes an Interest Group Successful?**
   Interest group success can be measured in a variety of ways, including a group's ability to get its issues on the public agenda, winning key pieces of legislation in Congress or executive branch or judicial rulings, or backing successful candidates. Several factors contribute to interest group success, including leaders and patrons, funding, and committed members.

KEY TERMS

civic virtue, p. 620
collective good, p. 649
disturbance theory, p. 622
economic interest group, p. 623
free rider problem, p. 650
interest group, p. 622
lobbying, p. 634

SELECTED READINGS

Berry, Jeffrey M. *The Interest Group Society*, 4th ed. New York: Addison Wesley, 2001.

———. *Lobbying for the People: The Political Behavior of Public Interest Groups*. Princeton, NJ: Princeton University Press, 1977.

Cigler, Allan J., and Burdett A. Loomis, eds. *Interest Group Politics*, 5th ed. Washington, DC: CQ Press, 1999.

Grossman, Gene M., and Elhanan Helpman. *Special Interest Politics*. Cambridge, MA: MIT Press, 2001.

Herrnson, Paul S., Ronald G. Shaiko, and Clyde Wilcox. *The Interest Group Connection*, 3rd ed. Chatham, NJ: Chatham House, 2002.

Kollman, Ken. *Outside Lobbying: Public Opinion and Interest Group Strategies*. Princeton, NJ: Princeton University Press, 1998.

McGlen, Nancy E., et al. *Women, Politics, and American Society*, 3rd ed. Upper Saddle River, NJ: Prentice Hall, 2002.

Olson, Mancur, Jr. *The Logic of Collective Action: Public Good and the Theory of Groups*. Cambridge, MA: Harvard University Press, 1965.

Sabato, Larry J. *PAC Power: Inside the World of Political Action Committees*. New York: Norton, 1984.

Schlozman, Kay Lehman, and John T. Tierney. *Organized Interests and American Democracy*. New York: Harper & Row, 1986.

Truman, David B. *The Governmental Process: Political Interests and Public Opinion*. New York: Knopf, 1951.

Walker, Jack L., ed. *Interest Groups in America: Patrons, Professions, and Social Movements*. Ann Arbor: University of Michigan Press, 1991.

Wilson, James Q. *Political Organizations*. Princeton, NJ: Princeton University Press, 1995.

Woliver, Laura. *From Outrage to Action: The Politics of Grassroots Dissent*. Urbana: University of Illinois Press, 1993.

Wolpe, Bruce C., and Bertram J. Levine. *Lobbying Congress: How the System Works*, 2nd ed. Washington, DC: CQ Press, 1996.

NOTES

1. Students Binge on Credit," *USA Today* (September 14, 2000): A26; and Edgar Pagaza, "Credit Card Debt Among U.S. College Students at Record High," http://horizons. Eraunews.com/Vnews/display.v/ART/2002.
2. Russ Feingold, "Lobbyists' Rush for Bankruptcy Reform," *Washington Post* (June 7, 1999): A19.
3. Ibid.
4. Ibid.
5. "Bankruptcy Reform," *Buffalo News* (May 24, 2002): C12.
6. Elaine S. Povich, "Battle over Bankruptcy Reforms," *Newsday* (May 10, 2002): A50.
7. Robert D. Putnam, "Bowling Alone: America's Declining Social Capital," *Journal of Democracy* 6(1): 650–65.
8. Quoted in Richard Morin, "Who Says We're Not Joiners," *Washington Post* (May 2, 1999): B5.
9. John Brehm and Wendy Rahn, "Individual-Level Evidence for the Causes and Consequences of Social Capital," *American Journal of Political Science* 41 (July 1997): 999.
10. Mark Schneider et al., "Institutional Arrangements and the Creation of Social Capital: The Effects of Public School Choice," *American Political Science Review* 91 (March 1997): 82–93.
11. Nicholas Lemann, "Kicking in Groups," *Atlantic Monthly* (April 1996), NEXIS.
12. Robert D. Putnam, et al. *Making Democracy Work: Civic Traditions in Modern Italy* (Princeton NJ: Princeton University Press, 1994).
13. Clive Thomas and Ronald Hrebenar, "Changing Patterns of Interest Group Activity: A Regional Perspective," in Mark Petracca, ed., *The Politics of Interests* (Boulder, CO: Westview Press, 1992), 4.
14. Graham Wilson, *Interest Groups in the United States* (New York: Oxford University Press, 1981), 4.
15. David B. Truman, *The Governmental Process: Political Interests and Public Opinion* (New York: Knopf, 1951), 33.
16. Robert H. Salisbury, "Interest Groups," in Fred I. Greenstein and Nelson W. Polsby, eds., *Handbook of Political Science*, vol. 4 (Reading, MA: Addison Wesley, 1975), 175.
17. V. O. Key Jr., *Politics, Parties, and Pressure Groups* (New York: T. J. Crowell, 1942), 23.
18. Truman, *The Governmental Process*, ch. 16.
19. Robert H. Salisbury, "An Exchange Theory of Interest Groups," *Midwest Journal of Political Science* 13 (1969): 1–32.
20. Ibid.
21. Jeffrey M. Berry, *Lobbying for the People: The Political Behavior of Public Interest Groups* (Princeton, NJ: Princeton University Press, 1977), 7.
22. Samuel Eliot Morrison and Henry Steel Commager, *The Growth of the American Republic* (New York: Oxford University Press, 1930), 163.
23. Quoted in Grant McConnell, "Lobbies and Pressure Groups," in Jack Greene, ed., *Encyclopedia of American Political History*, vol. 2 (New York: Macmillan, 1984), 768.
24. Lee Epstein, *Conservatives in Court* (Knoxville: University of Tennessee Press, 1985).
25. Jack L. Walker, "The Origins and Maintenance of Interest Groups in America," *American Political Science Review* 77 (June 1983): 390–406.
26. Peter Steinfels, "Moral Majority to Dissolve: Says Mission Accomplished," *New York Times* (June 12, 1989): A14.
27. Steve Goldstein, "The Christian Right Grows in Power," *Atlanta Journal and Constitution* (November 11, 1994): A8.
28. Richard S. Dunham, "Corporate America vs. the Religious Right?" *Business Week* (May 18, 1998): 46.
29. Thomas B. Edsall and Hanna Rosin, "Christian Coalition, Denied Tax-Exempt Status, Will Reorganize," *Washington Post* (June 11, 1999): A4.
30. Matthew Vita and Susan Schmidt, "The Interest Groups: Religious Right Mutes Voice, Not Efforts," *Washington Post* (November 2, 2000): A20.
31. Juliet Eilperin, "GOP Seeks to Ease Curbs on Churches in Politics," *Washington Post* (June 3, 2002): A4.
32. Robert Scheer, "The NRA-Friendly Candidate: Bush's Stance on Guns Proves That He is No Compassionate Conservative," *Pittsburgh Post-Gazette* (May 11, 2000): A29.

33. NRA Political Victory Fund at www.NRA.PVF.org.

34. David Mahood, *Interest Groups Participation in America: A New Intensity* (Englewood Cliffs, NJ: Prentice Hall, 1990), 23.

35. Bill Miller, "CEOs Plan Network to Link Them in Attack," *Washington Post* (March 13, 2002): E1.

36. Tom Walker, "Business Press: Microsoft Tops Political Donations," *Atlanta Journal and Constitution* (November 7, 2000): D6.

37. Ana Radelat, "Spouses Get Board Seats Forbidden to Lawmakers," *USA Today* (June 27, 2002): A7.

38. Stephen Labaton, "G.O.P. Fights Proposed Rules on Auditors," *New York Times* (May 18, 2002): C3.

39. Quoted in Ronald J. Hrebenar and Ruth K. Scott, *Interest Group Politics in America*, 2nd ed. (Englewood Cliffs, NJ: Prentice Hall, 1990), 263.

40. John Hiscock, "Madonna Rocks Censorship Vote," *Daily Telegraph* (October 22, 1990): 3.

41. Rock the Vote at www.rockthevote.com.

42. See Taylor E. Dark, *The Unions and the Democrats: An Enduring Alliance* (Ithaca, NY: ILR Press, 1999).

43. Center for Responsive Politics, www.opensecrets.org.

44. William Glanz, "Unions' All-Out Effort Comes Up Short," *Washington Times* (November 3, 2004).

45. Benjamin Radcliff and Martin Saiz, "Labor Organizations and Public Policy in the American States," *Journal of Politics* (February 1998): 121.

46. Radcliff and Saiz, "Labor Organizations and Public Policy."

47. Brenda Rios, "Big Blitz from TV to the Hill: A $100 Million Whirlwind of Spin Control," *Atlanta Journal and Constitution* (July 22, 1994): A4.

48. Sam Loewenberg, "Now, The Tricky Part: Dividing Profits," *Legal Times* (May 31, 1999): 4.

49. Michael Wines, "For New Lobbyists, It's What They Know," *New York Times* (November 3, 1993): B14.

50. Quoted in Kay Lehman Schlozman and John T. Tierney, *Organized Interests and American Democracy* (New York: Harper and Row, 1986), 85.

51. Ken Kollman, "Inviting Friends to Lobby: Interest Groups, Ideological Bias, and Congressional Committees," *American Journal of Political Science* 41 (April 1997): 519–44.

52. Quoted in Norman J. Ornstein and Shirley Elder, *Interest Groups, Lobbying and Policy Making* (Washington, DC: CQ Press, 1978), 77.

53. The Center for Responsive Politics, http://www.opensecrets.org.

54. Richard L. Hall and Frank W. Wayman, "Buying Time: Moneyed Interests and the Mobilization of Bias in Congress," *American Political Science Review* 84 (September 1990): 797–820.

55. Some political scientists speak of "iron rectangles," reflecting the growing importance of a fourth party, the courts, in the lobbying process.

56. Clement E. Vose, "Litigation as a Form of Pressure Group Activity," *Annals* 319 (September 1958): 20–31.

57. Richard C. Cortner, "Strategies and Tactics of Litigation in Constitutional Cases," *Journal of Public Law* 17 (1968): 287.

58. Karen O'Connor, "Lobbying the Justices or Lobbying for Justice?" in Paul Herrnson, Ronald G. Shaiko, and Clyde Wilcox, eds., *The Interest Group Connection* (Chatham, NJ: Chatham House, 1998), 267–88.

59. Robert A. Goldberg, *Grassroots Resistance: Social Movement in Twentieth Century America* (Belmont, CA: Wadsworth, 1991).

60. Jane Fritsch, "Sometimes, Lobbyists Strive to Keep Public in the Dark," *New York Times* (March 19, 1996): A1.

61. Joel Brinkley, "Cultivating the Grass Roots to Reap Legislative Benefits," *New York Times* (November 1, 1993): A1.

62. Ibid.

63. Marilyn J. Cohodas, "Digital Activism," *Governing Magazine* (August 2000): 70.

64. Kathryn Masterson, "Fighting Terror/Letter Campaign: Anthrax Scare Alters Fund-raiser," *Boston Globe* (December 10, 2001): A13.

65. NARAL Memorandum to Interested Parties, November 14, 2000.

66. Neil J. Mitchell, Wendy L. Hansen, and Eric M. Jepsen, "The Determinants of Domestic and Foreign Corporate Political Activity," *Journal of Politics* 59 (November 1997): 1096–1113.

67. Thomas Romer and James M. Snyder, "An Empirical Investigation of the Dynamics of PAC Contributions," *American Journal of Political Science* 38 (August 1994): 745–69.

68. Hall and Wayman, "Buying Time"; and Jack R. Wright, "Contributions, Lobbying, and Committee Voting in the U.S. House of Representatives," *American Political Science Review* 84 (June 1990): 417–38.

69. D. Bruce La Pierre, "A Little Problem of Constitutionality: … But the Court May Not Save the Day," *St. Louis Post-Dispatch* (March 27, 2002): B7.

70. E. E. Schattschneider, *The Semi-Sovereign People* (New York: Holt, Rinehart, and Winston, 1960), 51.

71. Ken Kollman, *Outside Lobbying: Public Opinion and Interest Group Strategies* (Princeton, NJ: Princeton University Press, 1998); and Karen O'Connor, *Women's Organizations' Use of the Courts* (Lexington, MA: 1980).

72. Marie Hojnacki, "Interest Groups' Decisions to Join Alliances or Work Alone," *American Journal of Political Science* 41 (January 1997): 61–87.

73. Salisbury, "Interest Groups"; and Walker, "The Origins and Maintenance of Interest Groups."

74. Ceci Connolly, "Donors to Campaigns Fared Well in Budget," *Washington Post* (August 22, 1997): A20.

75. Alexis de Tocqueville, *Democracy in America*, vol. 1, trans. Phillips Bradley (New York: Knopf, Vintage Books, 1945; orig. published in 1835), 191.

76. Schattschneider, *The Semi-Sovereign People*, 35.

77. Mancur Olson Jr. *The Logic of Collective Action: Public Goods and the Theory of Groups* (Cambridge, MA: Harvard University Press, 1965).

78. David C. King and Jack L. Walker, "The Provision of Benefits by Interest Groups in the United States," *Journal of Politics* 54 (May 1992): 394.

79. Ibid.

80. Hojnacki, "Interest Groups' Decisions."

81. William Browne, "Organized Interests and Their Issue Niches: A Search for Pluralism in a Policy Domain," *Journal of Politics* 52 (May 1990): 477.

82. Donald P. Haider-Markel, "Interest Group Survival: Shared Interests Versus Competition for Resources," *Journal of Politics* 59 (August 1997): 903–12.

83. Walker, "The Origins and Maintenance of Interest Groups," 390–406.

The Declaration of Independence

In Congress, July 4, 1776

The Unanimous Declaration of the Thirteen United States of America

When in the Course of human events it becomes necessary for one people to dissolve the political bands which have connected them with another, and to assume, among the powers of the earth, the separate and equal station to which the Laws of Nature and of Nature's God entitle them, a decent respect to the opinions of mankind requires that they should declare the causes which impel them to the separation.

We hold these truths to be self-evident, that all men are created equal, that they are endowed by their Creator with certain unalienable Rights, that among these are Life, Liberty and the pursuit of Happiness. That to secure these rights, Governments are instituted among Men, deriving their just powers from the consent of the governed. That whenever any Form of Government becomes destructive of these ends, it is the Right of the People to alter or to abolish it, and to institute new Government, laying its foundation on such principles and organizing its powers in such form, as to them shall seem most likely to effect their Safety and Happiness. Prudence, indeed, will dictate that Governments long established should not be changed for light and transient causes; and accordingly all experience hath shewn that mankind are more disposed to suffer, while evils are sufferable, than to right themselves by abolishing the forms to which they are accustomed. But when a long train of abuses and usurpations, pursuing invariably the same Object evinces a design to reduce them under absolute Despotism, it is their right, it is their duty, to throw off such Government, and to provide new Guards for their future security.—Such has been the patient sufferance of these Colonies; and such is now the necessity which constrains them to alter their former Systems of Government. The history of the present King of Great Britain is a history of repeated injuries and usurpations, all having in direct object the establishment of an absolute Tyranny over these States. To prove this, let Facts be submitted to a candid world.

He has refused his Assent to Laws, the most wholesome and necessary for the public good.

He has forbidden his Governors to pass Laws of immediate and pressing importance, unless suspended in their operation till his Assent should be obtained; and when so suspended, he has utterly neglected to attend to them.

He has refused to pass other Laws for the accommodation of large districts of people, unless those people would relinquish the right of Representation in the Legislature, a right inestimable to them and formidable to tyrants only.

He has called together legislative bodies at places unusual, uncomfortable, and distant from the depository of their Public Records, for the sole purpose of fatiguing them into compliance with his measures.

He has dissolved Representative Houses repeatedly, for opposing with manly firmness his invasions on the rights of the people.

He has refused for a long time, after such dissolutions, to cause others to be elected; whereby the Legislative Powers, incapable of Annihilation, have returned to the People at large for their exercise, the State remaining in the mean time exposed to all the dangers of invasion from without, and convulsions within.

He has endeavored to prevent the population of these States; for that purpose obstructing the Laws of Naturalization of Foreigners; refusing to pass others to encourage their migration hither, and raising the conditions of new Appropriations of Lands.

He has obstructed the Administration of Justice, by refusing his Assent to Laws for establishing Judiciary powers.

He has made Judges dependent on his Will alone, for the tenure of their offices, and the amount and payment of their salaries.

He has erected a multitude of New Offices, and sent hither swarms of Officers to harass our people, and eat out their substance.

He has kept among us, in times of peace, Standing Armies without the Consent of our legislatures.

He has affected to render the Military independent of and superior to the Civil power.

He has combined with others to subject us to a jurisdiction foreign to our constitution, and unacknowledged by our laws, giving his Assent to their Acts of pretended Legislation:

For quartering large bodies of armed troops among us:

For protecting them, by a mock Trial, from punishment for any Murders which they should commit on the Inhabitants of these States:

For cutting off our Trade with all parts of the world:

For imposing Taxes on us without our Consent:

For depriving us in many cases, of the benefits of Trial by Jury:

For transporting us beyond Seas to be tried for pretended offences:

For abolishing the free System of English Laws in a neighboring Province, establishing therein an Arbitrary government, and enlarging its Boundaries so as to render it at once an example and fit instrument for introducing the same absolute rule into these Colonies:

For taking away our Charters, abolishing our most valuable Laws, and altering fundamentally the Forms of our Governments:

For suspending our own Legislatures, and declaring themselves invested with power to legislate for us in all cases whatsoever.

He has abdicated Government here, by declaring us out of his Protection and waging War against us.

He has plundered our seas, ravaged our Coasts, burnt our towns, and destroyed the lives of our people.

He is at this time transporting large Armies of foreign Mercenaries to compleat the works of death, desolation and tyranny, already begun with circumstances of Cruelty and perfidy scarcely paralleled in the most barbarous ages, and totally unworthy the Head of a civilized nation.

He has constrained our fellow Citizens taken Captive on the high Seas to bear Arms against their Country, to become the executioners of their friends and Brethren, or to fall themselves by their Hands.

He has excited domestic insurrections amongst us, and has endeavored to bring on the inhabitants of our frontiers, the merciless Indian Savages, whose known rule of warfare, is an undistinguished destruction of all ages, sexes and conditions.

In every stage of these Oppressions We have Petitioned for Redress in the most humble terms: Our repeated Petitions have been answered only by repeated injury: A Prince, whose character is thus marked by every act which may define a Tyrant, is unfit to be the ruler of a free people.

Nor have We been wanting in attention to our British brethren. We have warned them from time to time of attempts by their legislature to extend an unwarrantable jurisdiction over us. We have reminded them of the circumstances of our emigration and settlement here. We have appealed to their native justice and magnanimity; and we have conjured them by the ties of our common kindred to disavow these usurpations, which would inevitably interrupt our connections and correspondence. They too have been deaf to the voice of justice and consanguinity. We must, therefore, acquiesce in the necessity, which denounces our Separation, and hold them, as we hold the rest of mankind, Enemies in War, in Peace Friends.

We, therefore, the Representatives of the United States of America, in General Congress, Assembled, appealing to the Supreme Judge of the world for the rectitude of our intentions, do, in the Name, and by Authority of the good People of these Colonies, solemnly publish and declare, That these United Colonies are, and of Right ought to be Free and Independent States; that they are Absolved from all Allegiance to the British Crown, and that all political connection between them and the State of Great Britain, is and ought to be totally dissolved: and that as Free and Independent States, they have full power to levy War, conclude Peace, contract Alliances, establish Commerce, and to do all other Acts and Things which Independent States may of right do. And for the support of this Declaration, with a firm reliance on the protection of Divine Providence, we mutually pledge to each other our Lives, our Fortunes and our sacred Honor.

JOHN HANCOCK

NEW HAMPSHIRE
Josiah Bartlett
William Whipple
Matthew Thornton

MASSACHUSETTS BAY
Samuel Adams
John Adams
Robert Treat Paine
Elbridge Gerry

RHODE ISLAND
Stephen Hopkins
William Ellery

CONNECTICUT
Roger Sherman
Samuel Huntington
William Williams
Oliver Wolcott

NEW YORK
William Floyd
Philip Livingston
Francis Lewis
Lewis Morris

NEW JERSEY
Richard Stockton
John Witherspoon
Francis Hopkinson
John Hart
Abraham Clark

PENNSYLVANIA
Robert Morris
Benjamin Rush
Benjamin Franklin
John Morton
George Clymer
James Smith
George Taylor
James Wilson
George Ross

DELAWARE
Caesar Rodney
George Read
Thomas McKean

MARYLAND
Samuel Chase
William Paca
Thomas Stone
Charles Carroll

VIRGINIA
George Wythe
Richard Henry Lee
Thomas Jefferson
Benjamin Harrison
Thomas Nelson, Jr.
Francis Lightfoot Lee
Carter Braxton

NORTH CAROLINA
William Hooper
Joseph Hewes
John Penn

SOUTH CAROLINA
Edward Rutledge
Thomas Heyward, Jr.
Thomas Lynch, Jr.
Arthur Middleton

GEORGIA
Button Gwinnett
Lyman Hall
George Walton

Appendix II

The Constitution of the United States of America

W e the People of the United States, in Order to form a more perfect Union, establish Justice, insure domestic Tranquility, provide for the common defence, promote the general Welfare, and secure the Blessings of Liberty to ourselves and our Posterity, do ordain and establish this Constitution for the United States of America.

ARTICLE I

SECTION 1. All legislative Powers herein granted shall be vested in a Congress of the United States, which shall consist of a Senate and House of Representatives.

SECTION 2. The House of Representatives shall be composed of Members chosen every second Year by the People of the several States, and the Electors in each State shall have the Qualifications requisite for Electors of the most numerous Branch of the State Legislature.

No person shall be a Representative who shall not have attained to the Age of twenty five Years, and been seven Years a Citizen of the United States, and who shall not, when elected, be an Inhabitant of that State in which he shall be chosen.

Representatives and direct Taxes shall be apportioned among the several States which may be included within this Union, according to their respective Numbers which shall be determined by adding to the whole Number of free Persons, including those bound to Service for a Term of Years, and excluding Indians not taxed, three fifths of all other Persons. The actual Enumeration shall be made within three Years after the first Meeting of the Congress of the United States, and within every subsequent Term ten Years, in such Manner as they shall by Law direct. The Number of Representatives shall not exceed one for every thirty Thousand, but each State shall have at Least one Representative; and until such enumerations shall be made, the State of New Hampshire shall be entitled to chuse three, Massachusetts eight, Rhode-Island and Providence Plantations one, Connecticut five, New-York six, New Jersey four, Pennsylvania eight, Delaware one, Maryland six, Virginia ten, North Carolina five, South Carolina five, and Georgia three.

When vacancies happen in the Representation from any State, the Executive Authority thereof shall issue Writs of Election to fill such Vacancies.

The House of Representatives shall chuse their speaker and other Officers; and shall have the sole Power of Impeachment.

SECTION 3. The Senate of the United States shall be composed of two Senators from each State chosen by the Legislature thereof, for six Years; and each Senator shall have one Vote.

Immediately after they shall be assembled in Consequence of the first Election, they shall be divided as equally as may be into three Classes. The Seats of the Senators of the first Class shall be vacated at the Expiration of the second year, of the second Class at the Expiration of the fourth Year, and of the third Class at the Expiration of the sixth Year, so that one third may be chosen every second Year and if Vacancies happen by Resignation, or otherwise, during the Recess of the Legislature of any State, the Executive thereof may make temporary Appointments until the next Meeting of the Legislature, which shall then fill such Vacancies.

No Person shall be a Senator who shall not have attained to the Age of thirty Years, and been nine Years a Citizen of the United States, and who shall not, when elected, be an Inhabitant of that State for which he shall be chosen.

The Vice President of the United States shall be President of the Senate, but shall have no Vote, unless they be equally divided.

The Senate shall chuse their other Officers, and also a President pro tempore, in the Absence of the Vice President, or when he shall exercise the Office of President of the United States.

The Senate shall have the sole Power to try all Impeachments. When sitting for that Purpose, they shall be on Oath or Affirmation. When the President of the United States is tried, the Chief Justice shall preside: And no Person shall be convicted without the Concurrence of two thirds of the Members present.

Judgment in Cases of Impeachment shall not extend further than to removal from Office, and disqualification to hold and enjoy any Office of honor, Trust or Profit under the United States; but the Party convicted shall nevertheless be liable and subject to Indictment, Trial, Judgment and Punishment, according to law.

SECTION 4. The Times, Places and Manner of holding Elections for Senators and Representatives, shall be prescribed in each State by the Legislature thereof; but the Congress may at any time by Law make or alter such Regulations, except as to the Places of chusing Senators.

The Congress shall assemble at least once in every Year, and such Meeting shall be on the first Monday in December, unless they shall by Law appoint a different Day.

SECTION 5. Each House shall be the Judge of the Elections, Returns and Qualifications of its own Members, and a Majority of each shall constitute a Quorum to do business; but a smaller Number may adjourn from day to day, and may be authorized to compel the Attendance of absent Members, in such Manner, and under such Penalties as each House may provide.

Each House may determine the Rules of its Proceedings, punish its Members for disorderly Behaviour, and with the Concurrence of two thirds, expel a Member.

Each House shall keep a Journal of its Proceedings, and from time to time publish the same, excepting such Parts as may in their judgment require Secrecy; and the Yeas and Nays of the Members of either House on any question shall, at the Desire of one fifth of those present, be entered on the Journal.

Neither House, during the Session of Congress, shall, without the Consent of the other, adjourn for more than three days, nor to any other Place than that in which the two Houses shall be sitting.

SECTION 6. The Senators and Representatives shall receive a Compensation for their Services, to be ascertained by Law, and paid out of the Treasury of the United States. They shall in all Cases, except Treason, Felony and Breach of the Peace, be privileged from Arrest during their Attendance at the Session of their respective Houses, and in going to and returning from the same; and for any Speech or Debate in either House, they shall not be questioned in any other Place.

No Senator or Representative shall, during the Time for which he was elected, be appointed to any civil Office under the Authority of the United States, which shall have been created, or the Emoluments whereof shall have been encreased during such time; and no Person holding any Office under the United States, shall be a Member of either House during his Continuance in Office.

SECTION 7. All Bills for raising Revenue shall originate in the House of Representatives; but the Senate may propose or concur with Amendments as on other Bills.

Every Bill which shall have passed the House of Representatives and the Senate, shall, before it become a Law, be presented to the President of the United States; If he approve he shall sign it, but if not he shall return it, with his Objections to that House in which it shall have originated, who shall enter the Objections at large on their Journal, and proceed to reconsider it. If after such Reconsideration two thirds of that House shall agree to pass the Bill, it shall be sent, together with the Objections, to the other House, by which it shall likewise be reconsidered, and if approved by two thirds of that House, it shall become a Law. But in all such Cases the Votes of both Houses shall be determined by Yeas and Nays, and the Names of the Persons voting for and against the Bill shall be entered on the Journal of each House respectively. If any Bill shall not be returned by the President within ten Days (Sundays excepted) after it shall have been presented to him, the Same shall be a Law, in like Manner as if he had signed it, unless the Congress by their Adjournment prevent its Return, in which Case it shall not be a Law.

Every Order, Resolution, or Vote to which the Concurrence of the Senate and House of Representatives may be necessary (except on a question of Adjournment) shall be presented to the President of the United States; and before the Same shall take Effect, shall be approved by him, or being disapproved by him, shall be repassed by two thirds of the Senate and House of Representatives, according to the Rules and Limitations prescribed in the Case of a Bill.

SECTION 8. The Congress shall have Power To lay and collect Taxes, Duties, Imposts and Excises, to pay the Debts and provide for the common Defence and general Welfare of the United States; but all Duties, Imposts and Excises shall be uniform throughout the United States;

To borrow Money on the credit of the United States;

To regulate Commerce with foreign Nations, and among the several States, and with the Indian Tribes;

To establish a uniform Rule of Naturalization, and uniform Laws on the subject of Bankruptcies throughout the United States;

To coin Money, regulate the Value thereof, and of foreign Coin, and fix the Standard of Weights and Measures;

To provide for the Punishment of counterfeiting the Securities and current Coin of the United States;

To establish Post Offices and post Roads;

To promote the Progress of Science and useful Arts, by securing for limited Times to Authors and Inventors exclusive Right to their respective Writings and Discoveries;

To constitute Tribunals inferior to the supreme Court;

To define and punish Piracies and Felonies committed on the high Seas, and Offences against the Law of Nations;

To declare War, grant Letters of Marque and Reprisal, and make rules concerning Captures on Land and Water;

To raise and support Armies, but no Appropriation of Money to that Use shall be for a longer Term than two Years;

To provide and maintain a Navy;

To make Rules for the Government and Regulation of the land and naval Forces;

To provide for calling forth the Militia to execute the Laws of the Union, suppress Insurrections and repel Invasions;

To provide for organizing, arming, and disciplining, the Militia, and for governing such Part of them as may be employed in the Service of the United States, reserving to the States respectively, the Appointment of the Officers, and the Authority of training the Militia according to the discipline prescribed by Congress;

To exercise exclusive Legislation in all Cases whatsoever, over such District (not exceeding ten Miles square) as may, by Cession of particular States, and the Acceptance of Congress, become the Seat of the Government of the United States, and to exercise like Authority over all Places purchased by the Consent of the Legislature of the State in which the Same shall be for the Erection of Forts, Magazines, Arsenals, dock-Yards, and other needful Buildings;—And

To make all Laws which shall be necessary and proper for carrying into Execution the foregoing Powers, and all other Powers vested by this Constitution in the Government of the United States, or in any Department or Officer thereof.

SECTION 9. The Migration or Importation of such Persons as any of the States now existing shall think proper to admit, shall not be prohibited by the Congress prior to the Year one thousand eight hundred and eight, but a Tax or duty may be imposed on such Importation, not exceeding ten dollars for each Person.

The Privilege of the Writ of Habeas Corpus shall not be suspended, unless when in Cases of Rebellion or Invasion the public Safety may require it.

No Bill of Attainder or ex post facto Law shall be passed.

No Capitation, or other direct, Tax shall be laid, unless in Proportion to the Census or Enumeration herein before directed to be taken.

No Tax or Duty shall be laid on Articles exported from any State.

No Preference shall be given by any Regulation of Commerce or Revenue to the Ports of one State over those of another: nor shall Vessels bound to, or from, one State, be obliged to enter, clear, or pay Duties in another.

No money shall be drawn from the Treasury, but in Consequence of Appropriations made by Law; and a regular Statement and Account of the Receipts and Expenditures of all public Money shall be published from time to time.

No Title of Nobility shall be granted by the United States: And no Person holding any Office of Profit or Trust under them, shall, without the Consent of the Congress, accept of any present, Emolument, Office, or Title, of any kind whatever, from any King, Prince, or foreign State.

SECTION 10. No state shall enter into any Treaty, Alliance, or Confederation; grant Letters of Marque and Reprisal; coin Money; emit Bills of Credit; make any Thing but gold and silver Coin a Tender in Payment of Debts; pass any Bill of Attainder, ex post facto Law, or Law impairing the Obligation of Contracts, or grant any Title of Nobility.

No State shall, without the Consent of the Congress, lay any Imposts or Duties on Imports or Exports, except what may be absolutely necessary for executing its inspection Laws: and the net Produce of all Duties and Imposts, laid by any State on Imports or Exports, shall be for the Use of the Treasury of the United States, and all such Laws shall be subject to the Revision and Controul of the Congress.

No State shall, without the Consent of Congress, lay any Duty of Tonnage, keep Troops, or Ships of War in time of Peace, enter into any Agreement or Compact with another State, or with a foreign Power, or engage in War, unless actually invaded, or in such imminent Danger as will not admit of delay.

ARTICLE II

SECTION 1. The executive Power shall be vested in a President of the United States of America. He shall hold his Office during the Term of four Years, and, together with the Vice President, chosen for the same Term, be elected as follows.

Each State shall appoint, in such Manner as the Legislature thereof may direct, a Number of Electors, equal to the whole Number of Senators and Representatives to which the State may be entitled in the Congress; but no Senator or Representative, or Person holding an Office of Trust of Profit under the United States, shall be appointed an Elector.

The Electors shall meet in their respective States, and vote by Ballot for two Persons, of whom one at least shall not be an Inhabitant of the same State with themselves. And they shall make a List of all the Persons voted for, and, of the Number of Votes for each; which List they shall sign and certify, and transmit sealed to the Seat of the Government of the United States, directed to the President of the Senate. The President of the Senate shall, in the Presence of the Senate and House of Representatives, open all the Certificates, and the Votes shall then be counted. The Person having the greatest Number of Votes shall be the President, if such Number be a Majority of the whole Number of Electors appointed; and if there be more than one who have such Majority, and have an equal Number of Votes, then the House of Representatives shall immediately chuse by Ballot one of them for President; and if no Person have a Majority, then from the five highest on the List the said House shall in like Manner chuse the President. But in chusing the President, the Votes shall be taken by States, the Representation from each State having one Vote; A quorum for this Purpose shall consist of a Member or Members from two thirds of the States, and a Majority of all the States shall be necessary to a Choice. In every Case, after the Choice of the President, the Person having the greatest Number of Votes of the Electors shall be the Vice President. But if there should remain two or more who have equal Votes, the Senate shall chuse from them by Ballot the Vice President.

The Congress may determine the Time of chusing the Electors, and the Day on which they shall give their Votes; which Day shall be the same throughout the United States.

No Person except a natural born Citizen, or a Citizen of the United States, at the time of the Adoption of this Constitution, shall be eligible to the Office of President; neither shall any Person be eligible to that Office who shall not have attained to the Age of thirty five Years, and been fourteen Years a Resident within the United States.

In Case of the Removal of the President from Office, or of his Death, Resignation, or Inability to discharge the Powers and Duties of the said Office, the Same shall devolve on the Vice President, and the Congress may by Law provide for the Case of Removal, Death, Resignation or Inability, both of the

President and Vice President, declaring what Officer shall then act as President, and such Officer shall act accordingly, until the Disability be removed, or a President shall be elected.

The President shall, at stated Times, receive for his Services, a Compensation, which shall neither be encreased nor diminished during the Period for which he shall have been elected, and he shall not receive within that Period any other Emolument from the United States, or any of them.

Before he enter on the Execution of his Office, he shall take the following Oath or Affirmation:—"I do solemnly swear (or affirm) that I will faithfully execute the Office of President of the United States, and will to the best of my Ability, preserve, protect and defend the Constitution of the United States."

SECTION 2. The President shall be Commander in Chief of the Army and Navy of the United States, and of the Militia of the several States, when called into the actual Service of the United States; he may require the Opinion, in writing, of the principal Officer in each of the executive Departments, upon any Subject relating to the Duties of their respective Offices, and he shall have Power to grant Reprieves and Pardons for Offences against the United States, except in Cases of Impeachment.

He shall have Power, by and with the Advice and Consent of the Senate, to make Treaties, provided two thirds of the Senators present concur; and he shall nominate, and by and with the Advice and Consent of the Senate, shall appoint Ambassadors, other public Ministers and Consuls, Judges of the supreme Court, and all other Officers of the United States, whose Appointments are not herein otherwise provided for, and which shall be established by Law: but the Congress may by Law vest the Appointment of such inferior Officers, as they think proper, in the President alone, in the Courts of Law, or in the Heads of Departments.

The President shall have Power to fill up all Vacancies that may happen during the Recess of the Senate, by granting Commissions which shall expire at the End of their next Session.

SECTION 3. He shall from time to time give to the Congress Information of the State of the Union, and recommend to their Consideration such Measures as he shall judge necessary and expedient; he may, on extraordinary Occasions, convene both Houses, or either of them, and in Case of Disagreement between them, with Respect to the Time of Adjournment, he may adjourn them to such Time as he shall think proper; he shall receive Ambassadors and other public Ministers; he shall take Care that the Laws be faithfully executed, and shall Commission all the Officers of the United States.

SECTION 4. The President, Vice President and all civil Officers of the United States, shall be removed from Office on Impeachment for, and Conviction of, Treason, Bribery, or other High Crimes and Misdemeanors.

ARTICLE III

SECTION 1. The judicial Power of the United States, shall be vested in one supreme Court, and in such inferior Courts as the Congress may from time to time ordain and establish. The Judges, both of the supreme and inferior Courts, shall hold their Offices during good Behaviour, and shall, at stated Times, receive for their Services, a Compensation, which shall not be diminished during their Continuance in Office.

SECTION 2. The judicial Power shall extend to all Cases, in Law and Equity, arising under this Constitution, the Laws of the United States, and Treaties made, or which shall be made, under their Authority;—to all Cases affecting Ambassadors, other public Ministers and Consuls;—to all Cases of admiralty and maritime Jurisdiction;—to Controversies to which the United States shall be a Party;—to Controversies between two or more States;—between a State and Citizens of another State;—between Citizens of different States;—between Citizens of the same State claiming Lands under Grants of different States,—and between a State, or the Citizens thereof, and foreign States, Citizens or Subjects.

In all Cases affecting Ambassadors, other public Ministers and Consuls, and those in which a State shall be Party, the supreme Court shall have original Jurisdiction. In all the other Cases before mentioned, the supreme Court shall have appellate Jurisdiction, both as to Law and Fact, with such Exceptions, and under such Regulations as the Congress shall make.

The Trial of all Crimes, except in Cases of Impeachment, shall be by Jury; and such Trial shall be held in the State where the said Crimes shall have been committed; but when not committed within any State, the Trial shall be at such Place or Places as the Congress may by Law have directed.

SECTION 3. Treason against the United States, shall consist only in levying War against them, or in adhering to their Enemies, giving them Aid and Comfort. No Person shall be convicted of Treason unless on the Testimony of two Witnesses to the same overt Act, or on Confession in open Court.

The Congress shall have Power to declare the Punishment of Treason, but no Attainder of Treason shall work Corruption of Blood, or Forfeiture except during the Life of the Person attainted.

ARTICLE IV

SECTION 1. Full Faith and Credit shall be given in each State to the public Acts, Records, and judicial Proceedings of every other State. And the Congress may by general Laws prescribe the Manner in which such Acts, Records and Proceedings shall be proved, and the Effect thereof.

SECTION 2. The Citizens of each State shall be entitled to all Privileges and Immunities of Citizens in the several States.

A Person charged in any State with Treason, Felony, or other Crime, who shall flee from Justice, and be found in another State, shall on Demand of the executive Authority of the State from which he fled, be delivered up, to be removed to the State having Jurisdiction of the Crime.

No Person held to Service or Labour in one State under the Laws thereof, escaping into another, shall, in Consequence of any Law or Regulation therein, be discharged from such Service or Labour, but shall be delivered up on Claim of the Party to whom such Service or Labour may be due.

SECTION 3. New States may be admitted by the Congress into this Union; but no new State shall be formed or erected within the Jurisdiction of any other State; nor any State be formed by the Junction of two or more States, or Parts of States, without the Consent of the Legislatures of the States concerned as well as of the Congress.

The Congress shall have Power to dispose of and make all needful Rules and Regulations respecting the Territory or other Property belonging to the United States; and nothing in this Constitution shall be so construed as to Prejudice any Claims of the United States, or of any particular State.

SECTION 4. The United States shall guarantee to every State in this Union a Republican Form of Government, and shall protect each of them against Invasion; and on Application of the Legislature, or of the Executive (when the Legislature cannot be convened) against domestic Violence.

ARTICLE V

The Congress, whenever two thirds of both Houses shall deem it necessary, shall propose Amendments to this Constitution, or, on the Application of the Legislatures of two thirds of the several States, shall call a Convention for proposing Amendments, which, in either Case, shall be valid to all Intents and Purposes, as Part of this Constitution, when ratified by the Legislatures of three fourths of the several States, or by Conventions in three fourths thereof, as the one or the other Mode of Ratification may be proposed by the Congress; Provided that no Amendment which may be made prior to the Year One thousand eight hundred and eight shall in any Manner affect the first and fourth Clauses in the Ninth Section of the first Article; and that no State, without its Consent, shall be deprived of its equal Suffrage in the Senate.

ARTICLE VI

All Debts contracted and Engagements entered into, before the Adoption of this Constitution, shall be as valid against the United States under this Constitution, as under the Confederation.

This Constitution, and the Laws of the United States which shall be made in Pursuance thereof; and all Treaties made, or which shall be made, under the Authority of the United States, shall be the supreme Law of the Land; and the Judges in every State shall be bound thereby, any Thing in the Constitution or Laws of any State to the Contrary notwithstanding.

The Senators and Representatives before mentioned, and the Members of the several State Legislatures, and all executive and judicial Officers, both of the United States and of the several States, shall be bound by Oath or Affirmation, to support this Constitution; but no religious Test shall ever be required as a Qualification to any Office or public Trust under the United States.

ARTICLE VII

The Ratification of the Conventions of nine States, shall be sufficient for the Establishment of this Constitution between the States so ratifying the Same.

Done in Convention by the Unanimous Consent of the States present the Seventeenth Day of September in the Year of our Lord one thousand seven hundred and Eighty seven and of the Independence of the United States of America the Twelfth. IN WITNESS whereof We have hereunto subscribed our Names,

G. WASHINGTON,
Presid't. and deputy from Virginia

Attest
WILLIAM JACKSON,
Secretary

DELAWARE
George Read
Gunning Bedford, Jr.
John Dickinson
Richard Basset
Jacob Broom

MASSACHUSETTS BAY
Nathaniel Gorham
Rufus King

CONNECTICUT
William Samuel Johnson
Roger Sherman

NEW YORK
Alexander Hamilton

NEW JERSEY
William Livingston
David Brearley
William Paterson
Jonathan Dayton

PENNSYLVANIA
Benjamin Franklin
Thomas Mifflin
Robert Morris
George Clymer
Thomas FitzSimons
Jared Ingersoll
James Wilson
Gouverneur Morris

NEW HAMPSHIRE
John Langdon
Nicholas Gilman

MARYLAND
James McHenry
Daniel of St. Thomas
* Jenifer*
Daniel Carroll

VIRGINIA
John Blair
James Madison, Jr.

NORTH CAROLINA
William Blount
Richard Dobbs Spaight
Hugh Williamson

SOUTH CAROLINA
John Rutledge
Charles Cotesworth Pinckney
Charles Pinckney
Pierce Butler

GEORGIA
William Few
Abraham Baldwin

Articles in addition to, and amendment of the Constitution of the United States of America, proposed by Congress and ratified by the Legislatures of the several states, pursuant to the Fifth Article of the original Constitution.

(*The first ten amendments were passed by Congress on September 25, 1789, and were ratified on December 15, 1791.*)

AMENDMENT I

Congress shall make no law respecting an establishment of religion, or prohibiting the free exercise thereof; or abridging the freedom of speech, or of the press; or the right of the people peaceably to assemble, and to petition the Government for a redress of grievances.

AMENDMENT II

A well regulated Militia, being necessary to the security of a free State, the right of the people to keep and bear Arms, shall not be infringed.

AMENDMENT III

No Soldier shall, in time of peace be quartered in any house, without the consent of the Owner, nor in time of war, but in a manner to be prescribed by law.

AMENDMENT IV

The right of the people to be secure in their persons, houses, papers, and effects, against unreasonable searches and seizures, shall not be violated, and no warrants shall issue, but upon probable cause, supported by Oath or affirmation, and particularly describing the place to be searched, and the persons or things to be seized.

AMENDMENT V

No person shall be held to answer for a capital, or otherwise infamous crime, unless on a presentment or indictment of a Grand Jury, except in cases arising in the land or naval forces, or in the Militia, when in actual service in time of War or public danger; nor shall any person be subject for the same offence to be twice put in jeopardy of life or limb; nor shall be compelled in any criminal case to be a witness against himself, nor be deprived of life, liberty, or property, without due process of law; nor shall private property be taken for public use, without just compensation.

AMENDMENT VI

In all criminal prosecutions, the accused shall enjoy the right to a speedy and public trial, by an impartial jury of the State and district wherein the crime shall have been committed, which district shall have been previously ascertained by law, and to be informed of the nature and cause of the accusation; to be confronted with the witnesses against him; to have com-pulsory process for obtaining witnesses in his favor, and to have the assistance of counsel for his defence.

AMENDMENT VII

In Suits at common law, where the value in controversy shall exceed twenty dollars, the right of trial by jury shall be preserved, and no fact tried by a jury, shall be otherwise re-examined in any Court of the United States, than according to the rules of the common law.

AMENDMENT VIII

Excessive bail shall not be required, nor excessive fines imposed, nor cruel and unusual punishments inflicted.

AMENDMENT IX

The enumeration in the Constitution, of certain rights, shall not be construed to deny or disparage others retained by the people.

AMENDMENT X

The powers not delegated to the United States by the Constitution, nor prohibited by it to the States, are reserved to the States respectively, or to the people.

AMENDMENT XI *(Ratified on February 7, 1795)*

The Judicial power of the United States shall not be construed to extend to any suit in law or equity, commenced or prosecuted against one of the United States by Citizens of another State, or by Citizens or Subjects of any Foreign State.

AMENDMENT XII *(Ratified on June 15, 1804)*

The Electors shall meet in their respective states, and vote by ballot for President and Vice-President, one of whom, at least, shall not be an inhabitant of the same state with themselves; they shall name in their ballots the person voted for as President, and in distinct ballots the person voted for as Vice-President, and they shall make distinct lists of all persons voted for as President, and of all persons voted for as Vice-President, and of the number of votes for each, which lists they shall sign and certify, and transmit sealed to the seat of the government of the United States, directed to the President of the Senate;—The President of the Senate shall, in the presence of the Senate and House of Representatives, open all the certificates and the votes shall then be counted;—The person having the greatest number of votes for President, shall be the President, if such number be a majority of the whole number of Electors appointed; and if no person have such majority; then from the persons having the highest numbers not exceeding three on the list of those voted for as President, the House of Representatives shall choose immediately, by ballot, the President. But in choosing the President, the votes shall be taken by states, the representation from each state having one vote; a quorum for this purpose shall consist of a member or members from two-thirds of the states, and a majority of all the states shall be necessary to a choice. And if the House of Representatives shall not choose a President whenever the right of choice shall devolve upon them, before the fourth day of March next following, then the Vice-President shall act as President, as in the case of the death or other constitutional disability of the President.—The person having the greatest number of votes as Vice-President, shall be the Vice-President, if such number be a majority of the whole number of Electors appointed, and if no person have a majority, then from the two highest numbers on the list, the Senate shall choose the Vice-President; a quorum for the purpose shall consist of two-thirds of the whole number of Senators, and a majority of the whole number shall be necessary to a choice. But no person constitutionally ineligible to the office of President shall be eligible to that of Vice-President of the United States.

AMENDMENT XIII *(Ratified on December 6, 1865)*

SECTION 1. Neither slavery nor involuntary servitude, except as a punishment for crime whereof the party shall have been duly convicted, shall exist within the United States, or any place subject to their jurisdiction.

SECTION 2. Congress shall have power to enforce this article by appropriate legislation.

AMENDMENT XIV *(Ratified on July 9, 1868)*

SECTION 1. All persons born or naturalized in the United States, and subject to the jurisdiction thereof, are citizens of the United States and of the State wherein they reside. No State shall make or enforce any law which shall abridge the privileges or immunities of citizens of the United States; nor shall any State deprive any person of life, liberty, or property, without due process of law; nor deny to any person within its jurisdiction the equal protection of the laws.

SECTION 2. Representatives shall be apportioned among the several States according to their respective numbers, counting the whole number of persons in each State, excluding Indians not taxed. But when the right to vote at any election for the choice of electors for President and Vice President of the United States, Representatives in Congress, the Executive and Judicial officers of a State, or the members of the Legislature thereof, is denied to any of the male inhabitants of such State, being twenty-one years of age, and citizens of the United States, or in any way abridged, except for participation in rebellion, or other crime, the basis of representation therein shall be reduced in the proportion which the number of such male citizens shall bear to the whole number of male citizens twenty-one years of age in such State.

SECTION 3. No person shall be a Senator or Representative in Congress, or elector of President and Vice President, or hold any office, civil or military, under the United States, or under any State, who, having previously taken an oath, as a member of Congress, or as an officer of the United States, or as a member of any State legislature, or as an executive or judicial officer of any State, to support the Constitution of the United States, shall have engaged in insurrection or rebellion against the same, or given aid or comfort to the enemies thereof. But Congress may by a vote of two-thirds of each House, remove such disability.

SECTION 4. The validity of the public debt of the United States, authorized by law, including debts incurred for payment of pensions and bounties for services in suppressing insurrection or rebellion, shall not be questioned. But neither the United States nor any State shall assume or pay any debt or obligation incurred in aid of insurrection or rebellion against the United States, or any claim for the loss or emancipation of any slave, but all such debts, obligations and claims shall be held illegal and void.

SECTION 5. The Congress shall have power to enforce, by appropriate legislation, the provisions of this article.

AMENDMENT XV *(Ratified on February 3, 1870)*

SECTION 1. The right of citizens of the United States to vote shall not be denied or abridged by the United States or by any State on account of race, color, or previous condition of servitude.

SECTION 2. The Congress shall have power to enforce this article by appropriate legislation.

AMENDMENT XVI *(Ratified on February 3, 1913)*

The Congress shall have power to lay and collect taxes on incomes, from whatever source derived, without apportionment among the several States, and without regard to any census or enumeration.

AMENDMENT XVII *(Ratified on April 8, 1913)*

The Senate of the United States shall be composed of two Senators from each State, elected by the people thereof, for six years; and each Senator shall have one vote. The electors in each State shall have the qualifications requisite for electors of the most numerous branch of the State legislatures.

When vacancies happen in the representation of any State in the Senate, the executive authority of such State shall issue writs of election to fill such vacancies: Provided, That the legislature of any State may empower the executive thereof to make temporary appointments until the people fill the vacancies by election as the legislature may direct.

This amendment shall not be so construed as to affect the election or term of any Senator chosen before it becomes valid as part of the Constitution.

AMENDMENT XVIII *(Ratified on January 16, 1919)*

SECTION 1. After one year from the ratification of this article the manufacture, sale, or transportation of intoxicating liquors within, the importation thereof into, or the exportation thereof from the United States and all territory subject to the jurisdiction thereof for beverage purposes is hereby prohibited.

SECTION 2. The Congress and the several States shall have concurrent power to enforce this article by appropriate legislation.

SECTION 3. This article shall be inoperative unless it shall have been ratified as an amendment to the Constitution by the legislatures of the several States, as provided in the Constitution, within seven years from the date of the submission hereof to the States by the Congress.

AMENDMENT XIX *(Ratified on August 18, 1920)*

The right of citizens of the United States to vote shall not be denied or abridged by the United States or by any State on account of sex.

Congress shall have power to enforce this article by appropriate legislation.

AMENDMENT XX *(Ratified on February 6, 1933)*

SECTION 1. The terms of the President and Vice President shall end at noon on the 20th day of January, and the terms of Senators and Representatives at noon on the 3d day of January, of the years in which such terms would have ended if this article had not been ratified; and the terms of their successors shall then begin.

SECTION 2. The Congress shall assemble at least once in every year, and such meeting shall begin at noon on the 3d day of January, unless they shall by law appoint a different day.

SECTION 3. If, at the time fixed for the beginning of the term of the President, the President elect shall have died, the Vice President elect shall become President. If a President shall not have been chosen before the time fixed for the beginning of his term, or if the President elect shall have failed to qualify, then the Vice President elect shall act as President until a President shall have qualified; and the Congress may by law provide for the case wherein neither a President elect nor a Vice President elect shall have qualified, declaring who shall then act as President, or the manner in which one who is to act shall be selected, and such person shall act accordingly until a President or Vice President shall have qualified.

SECTION 4. The Congress may by law provide for the case of the death of any of the persons from whom the House of Representatives may choose a President whenever the rights of choice shall have devolved upon them, and for the case of the death of any of the persons from whom the Senate may choose a Vice President whenever the right of choice shall have devolved upon them.

SECTION 5. Sections 1 and 2 shall take effect on the 15th day of October following the ratification of this article.

SECTION 6. This article shall be inoperative unless it shall have been ratified as an amendment to the Constitution by the legislatures of three-fourths of the several States within seven years from the date of its submission.

AMENDMENT XXI *(Ratified on December 5, 1933)*

SECTION 1. The eighteenth article of amendment to the Constitution of the United States is hereby repealed.

SECTION 2. The transportation or importation into any State, Territory, or possession of the United States for delivery or use therein of intoxicating liquors, in violation of the laws thereof, is hereby prohibited.

SECTION 3. This article shall be inoperative unless it shall have been ratified as an amendment to the Constitution by conventions in the several States, as provided in the Constitution, within seven years from the date of the submission hereof to the States by the Congress.

AMENDMENT XXII *(Ratified on February 27, 1951)*

SECTION 1. No person shall be elected to the office of the President more than twice, and no person who has held the office of President, or acted as President, for more than two years of a term to which some other person was elected President shall be elected to the office of the President more than once. But this Article shall not apply to any person holding the office of President when this Article was proposed by the Congress, and shall not prevent any person who may be holding the office of President, or acting as President, during the term within which this Article becomes operative from holding the office of President or acting as President during the remainder of such term.

SECTION 2. This article shall be inoperative unless it shall have been ratified as an amendment to the Constitution by the legislatures of three-fourths of the several States within seven years from the date of its submission to the States by the Congress.

AMENDMENT XXIII *(Ratified on March 29, 1961)*

SECTION 1. The District constituting the seat of Government of the United States shall appoint in such manner as the Congress may direct:

A number of electors of President and Vice President equal to the whole number of Senators and Representatives in Congress to which the District would be entitled if it were a State, but in no event more than the least populous State; they shall be in addition to those appointed by the States, but they shall be considered, for the purposes of the election of President and Vice President, to be electors appointed by a State; and they shall meet in the District and perform such duties as provided by the twelfth article of amendment.

SECTION 2. The Congress shall have power to enforce this article by appropriate legislation.

AMENDMENT XXIV *(Ratified on January 23, 1964)*

SECTION 1. The right of citizens of the United States to vote in any primary or other election for President or Vice President, for electors for President or Vice President, or for Senator or Representative in Congress, shall not be denied or abridged by the United States or any State by reason of failure to pay any poll tax or other tax.

SECTION 2. The Congress shall have power to enforce this article by appropriate legislation.

AMENDMENT XXV *(Ratified on February 10, 1967)*

SECTION 1. In case of the removal of the President from office or of his death or resignation, the Vice President shall become President.

SECTION 2. Whenever there is a vacancy in the office of the Vice President, the President shall nominate a Vice President who shall take office upon confirmation by a majority vote of both Houses of Congress.

SECTION 3. Whenever the President transmits to the President pro tempore of the Senate and the Speaker of the House of Representatives his written declaration that he is unable to discharge the powers and duties of his office, and until he transmits to them a written declaration to the contrary, such powers and duties shall be discharged by the Vice President as Acting President.

SECTION 4. Whenever the Vice President and a majority of either the principal officers of the executive departments or of such other body as Congress may by law provide, transmit to the President pro tempore of the Senate and the Speaker of the House of Representatives their written declaration that the President is unable to discharge the powers and duties of his office, the Vice President shall immediately assume the powers and duties of the office as Acting President.

Thereafter, when the President transmits to the President pro tempore of the Senate and the Speaker of the House of Representatives his written declaration that no inability exists, he shall resume the powers and duties of his office unless the Vice President and a majority of either the principal officers of the executive department or of such other body as Congress may by law provide, transmit within four days to the President pro tempore of the Senate and the Speaker of the House of Representatives their written declaration that the President is unable to discharge the powers and duties of his office. Thereupon Congress shall decide the issue, assembling within forty-eight hours for that purpose if not in session. If the Congress, within twenty-one days after receipt of the latter written declaration, or, if Congress is not in session, within twenty-one days after Congress is required to assemble, determines by two-thirds vote of both Houses that the President is unable to discharge the powers and duties of his office, the Vice President shall continue to discharge the same as Acting President; otherwise, the President shall resume the powers and duties of his office.

AMENDMENT XXVI *(Ratified on July 1, 1971)*

SECTION 1. The right of citizens of the United States, who are eighteen years of age or older, to vote shall not be denied or abridged by the United States or by any State on account of age.

SECTION 2. The Congress shall have power to enforce this article by appropriate legislation.

AMENDMENT XXVII *(Ratified on May 7, 1992)*

No law, varying the compensation for the services of the Senators and Representatives shall take effect until an election of Representatives shall have intervened.

Federalist No. 10

November 22, 1787

James Madison

TO THE PEOPLE OF THE STATE OF NEW YORK.

Among the numerous advantages promised by a well constructed Union, none deserves to be more accurately developed than its tendency to break and control the violence of faction. The friend of popular governments, never finds himself so much alarmed for their character and fate, as when he contemplates their propensity to this dangerous vice. He will not fail therefore to set a due value on any plan which, without violating the principles to which he is attached, provides a proper cure for it. The instability, injustice and confusion introduced into the public councils, have in truth been the mortal diseases under which popular governments have every where perished; as they continue to be the favorite and fruitful topics from which the adversaries to liberty derive their most specious declamations. The valuable improvements made by the American Constitutions on the popular models, both ancient and modern, cannot certainly be too much admired; but it would be an unwarrantable partiality, to contend that they have as effectually obviated the danger on this side as was wished and expected. Complaints are every where heard from our most considerate and virtuous citizens, equally the friends of public and private faith, and of public and personal liberty; that our governments are too unstable; that the public good is disregarded in the conflicts of rival parties; and that measures are too often decided, not according to the rules of justice, and the rights of the minor party; but by the superior force of an interested and over-bearing majority. However anxiously we may wish that these complaints had no foundation, the evidence of known facts will not permit us to deny that they are in some degree true. It will be found indeed, on a candid review of our situation, that some of the distresses under which we labor, have been erroneously charged on the operation of our governments; but it will be found, at the same time, that other causes will not alone account for many of our heaviest misfortunes; and particularly, for that prevailing and increasing distrust of public engagements, and alarm for private rights, which are echoed from one end of the continent to the other.

These must be chiefly, if not wholly, effects of the unsteadiness and injustice, with which a factious spirit has tainted our public administrations.

By a faction I understand a number of citizens, whether amounting to a majority or minority of the whole, who are united and actuated by some common impulse of passion, or of interest, adverse to the rights of other citizens, or to the permanent and aggregate interests of the community.

There are two methods of curing the mischiefs of faction: the one, by removing its causes; the other, by controlling its effects.

There are again two methods of removing the causes of faction: the one by destroying the liberty which is essential to its existence; the other, by giving to every citizen the same opinions, the same passions, and the same interests.

It could never be more truly said than of the first remedy, that it is worse than the disease. Liberty is to faction, what air is to fire, an aliment without which it instantly expires. But it could not be a less folly to abolish liberty, which is essential to political life, because it nourishes faction, than it would be to wish the annihilation of air, which is essential to animal life, because it imparts to fire its destructive agency.

The second expedient is as impracticable, as the first would be unwise. As long as the reason of man continues fallible, and he is at liberty to exercise it, different opinions will be formed. As long as the connection subsists between his reason and his self-love, his opinions and his passions will have a reciprocal influence on each other; and the former will be objects to which the latter will attach themselves. The diversity in the faculties of men from which the rights of property originate, is not less an insuperable obstacle to a uniformity of interests. The protection of these faculties is the first object of Government. From the protection of different and unequal faculties of acquiring property, the possession of different degrees and kinds of property immediately results: and from the influence of these on the sentiments and views of the respective proprietors, ensues a division of the society into different interests and parties.

The latent causes of faction are thus sown in the nature of man; and we see them every where brought into different degrees of activity, according to the different circumstances of civil society. A zeal for different opinions concerning religion, concerning Government and many other points, as well of speculation as of practice; an attachment to different leaders ambitiously contending for pre-eminence and power; or to persons of other descriptions whose fortunes have been interesting to the human passions, have in turn divided mankind into parties, inflamed them with mutual animosity, and rendered them much more disposed to vex and oppress each other, than to cooperate for their common good. So strong is this propensity of mankind to fall into mutual animosities, that where no substantial occasion presents itself, the most frivolous and fanciful distinctions have been sufficient to kindle their unfriendly passions, and excite their most violent conflicts. But the most common and durable source of factions, has been the various and unequal distribution of property. Those who hold, and those who are without property, have ever formed distinct interests in society. Those who are creditors, and those who are debtors, fall under a like discrimination. A landed interest, a manufacturing interest, a mercantile interest, a monied interest, with many lesser interests, grow up of necessity in civilized nations, and divide them into different classes, actuated by different sentiments and views. The regulation of these various and interfering interests forms the principal task of modern Legislation, and involves the spirit of party and faction in the necessary and ordinary operations of Government.

No man is allowed to be a judge in his own cause; because his interest would certainly bias his judgment, and, not improbably, corrupt his integrity. With equal, nay with greater reason, a body of men, are unfit to be both judges and parties, at the same time; yet, what are many of the most important acts of legislation, but so many judicial determinations, not indeed concerning the rights of single persons, but concerning the rights of large bodies of citizens, and what are the different classes of legislators, but advocates and parties to the causes which they determine? Is a law proposed concerning private debts? It is a question to which the creditors are parties on one side, and the debtors on the other. Justice ought to hold the balance between them. Yet the parties are and must be themselves the judges; and the most numerous party, or, in other words, the most powerful faction must be expected to prevail. Shall domestic manufactures be encouraged, and in what degree, by restrictions on foreign manufactures? are questions which would be differently decided by the landed and the manufacturing classes; and probably by neither, with a sole regard to justice and the public good. The apportionment of taxes on the various descriptions of property, is an act which seems to require the most exact impartiality; yet, there is perhaps no legislative act in which greater opportunity and temptation are given to a predominant party, to trample on the rules of justice. Every shilling with which they over-burden the inferior number, is a shilling saved to their own pockets.

It is in vain to say, that enlightened statesmen will be able to adjust these clashing interests, and render them all subservient to the public good. Enlightened statesmen will not always be at the helm: Nor, in many cases, can such an adjustment be made at all, without taking into view indirect and remote considerations, which will rarely prevail over the immediate interest which one party may find in disregarding the rights of another, or the good of the whole.

The inference to which we are brought, is, that the *causes* of faction cannot be removed; and that relief is only to be sought in the means of controlling its *effects*.

If a faction consists of less than a majority, relief is supplied by the republican principle, which enables the majority to defeat its sinister views by regular vote: It may clog the administration, it may convulse the society; but it will be unable to execute and mask its violence under the forms of the Constitution. When a majority is included in a faction, the form of popular government on the other hand enables it to sacrifice to its ruling passion or interest, both the public good and the rights of other citizens. To secure the public good, and private rights, against the danger of such a faction, and at the same time to preserve the spirit and the form of popular government, is then the great object to which our enquiries are directed: Let me add that it is the great desideratum, by which alone this form of government can be rescued from the opprobrium under which it has so long labored, and be recommended to the esteem and adoption of mankind.

By what means is this object attainable? Evidently by one of two only. Either the existence of the same passion or interest in a majority at the same time, must be prevented; or the majority, having such co-existent passion or interest, must be rendered, by their number and local situation, unable to concert and carry into effect schemes of oppression. If the impulse and the opportunity be suffered to coincide, we well know that neither moral nor religious motives can be relied on as an adequate control. They are not found to be such on the injustice and violence of individuals, and lose their efficacy in proportion to the number combined together; that is, in proportion as their efficacy becomes needful.

From this view of the subject, it may be concluded, that a pure Democracy, by which I mean, a Society, consisting of a small number of citizens, who assemble and administer the Government in person, can admit of no cure for the mischiefs of faction. A common passion or interest will, in almost every case, be felt by a majority of the whole; a communication and concert results from the form of Government itself; and there is nothing to check the inducements to sacrifice the weaker party, or an obnoxious individual. Hence it is, that such Democracies have ever been spectacles of turbulence and contention; have ever been found incompatible with personal security, or the rights of property; and have in general been as short in their lives, as they have been violent in their deaths. Theoretic politicians, who have patronized this species of Government, have erroneously supposed, that by reducing mankind to a perfect equality in their political rights, they would, at the same time, be perfectly equalized and assimilated in their possessions, their opinions, and their passions.

A republic, by which I mean a government in which the scheme of representation takes place, opens a different prospect, and promises the cure for which we are seeking. Let us examine the points in which it varies from pure democracy, and we shall comprehend both the nature of the cure and the efficacy which it must derive from the union.

The two great points of difference, between a democracy and a republic, are, first, the delegation of the government, in the latter, to a small number of citizens, elected by the rest; secondly, the greater number of citizens, and greater sphere of country, over which the latter may be extended.

The effect of the first difference is, on the one hand, to refine and enlarge the public views, by passing them through the medium of a chosen body of citizens, whose wisdom may best discern the true interest of their country, and whose patriotism and love of justice, will be least likely to sacrifice it to temporary or partial considerations. Under such a regulation, it may well happen, that the public voice, pronounced by the representatives of the people, will be more consonant to the public good, than if pronounced by the people themselves, convened for the purpose. On the other hand the effect may be inverted. Men of factious tempers, of local prejudices, or of sinister designs, may by intrigue, by corruption, or by other means, first obtain the suffrages, and then betray the interest of the people. The question resulting is, whether small or extensive republics are most favorable to the election of proper guardians of the public weal, and it is clearly decided in favor of the latter by two obvious considerations.

In the first place, it is to be remarked that, however small the republic may be, the representatives must be raised to a certain number, in order to guard against the cabals of a few; and that however large it may be, they must be limited to a certain number, in order to guard against the confusion of a multitude. Hence, the number of representatives in the two cases not being in proportion to that of the constituents, and being proportionally greatest in the small republic, it follows, that if the proportion of fit characters be not less in the large than in the small republic, the former will present a greater option, and consequently a greater probability of a fit choice.

In the next place, as each Representative will be chosen by a greater number of citizens in the large than in the small Republic, it will be more difficult for unworthy candidates to practise with success the vicious arts, by which elections are too often carried; and the suffrages of the people being more free, will be more likely to center on men who possess the most attractive merit, and the most diffusive and established characters.

It must be confessed, that in this, as in most other cases, there is a mean, on both sides of which inconveniences will be found to lie. By enlarging too much the number of electors, you render the representatives too little acquainted with all their local circumstances and lesser interests; as by reducing it too much, you render him unduly attached to these, and too little fit to comprehend and pursue great and national objects. The Federal Constitution forms a happy combination in this respect; the great and aggregate interests being referred to the national, the local and particular, to the state legislatures.

The other point of difference is, the greater number of citizens and extent of territory which may be brought within the compass of Republican, than of Democratic Government; and it is this circumstance principally which renders factious combinations less to be dreaded in the former, than in the latter. The smaller the society, the fewer probably will be the distinct parties and interests composing it; the fewer the distinct parties and interests, the more frequently will a majority be found of the same party; and the smaller the number of individuals composing a majority, and the smaller the compass within which they are placed, the more easily will they concert and execute their plans of oppression. Extend the sphere, and you take in a greater variety of parties and interests; you make it less probable that a majority of the whole will have a common motive to invade the rights of other citizens; or if such a common motive exists, it will be more difficult for all who feel it to discover their own strength, and to act in unison with each other. Besides other impediments, it may be remarked, that where there is a consciousness of unjust or dishonorable purposes, communication is always checked by distrust, in proportion to the number whose concurrence is necessary.

Hence it clearly appears, that the same advantage, which a Republic has over a Democracy, in controlling the effects of faction, is enjoyed by a large over a small Republic—is enjoyed by the Union over the States composing it. Does this advantage consist in the substitution of Representatives, whose enlightened views and virtuous sentiments render them superior to local prejudices, and to schemes of injustice? It will not be denied, that the Representation of the Union will be most likely to possess these requisite endowments. Does it consist in the greater security afforded by a greater variety of parties, against the event of any one party being able to outnumber and oppress the rest? In an equal degree does the increased variety of parties, comprised within the Union, increase this security? Does it, in fine, consist in the greater obstacles opposed to the concert and accomplishment of the secret wishes of an unjust and interested majority? Here, again, the extent of the Union gives it the most palpable advantage.

The influence of factious leaders may kindle a flame within their particular States, but will be unable to spread a general conflagration through the other States: a religious sect, may degenerate into a political faction in a part of the Confederacy but the variety of sects dispersed over the entire face of it, must secure the national Councils against any danger from that source: a rage for paper money, for an abolition of debts, for an equal division of property, or for any other improper or wicked project, will be less apt to pervade the whole body of the Union, than a particular member of it; in the same proportion as such a malady is more likely to taint a particular county or district, than an entire State.

In the extent and proper structure of the Union, therefore, we behold a Republican remedy for the diseases most incident to Republican Government. And according to the degree of pleasure and pride, we feel in being Republicans, ought to be our zeal in cherishing the spirit, and supporting the character of Federalists.

PUBLIUS

Federalist No. 51

February 6, 1788
James Madison

TO THE PEOPLE OF THE STATE OF NEW YORK.

To what expedient then shall we finally resort for maintaining in practice the necessary partition of power among the several departments, as laid down in the constitution? The only answer that can be given is, that as all these exterior provisions are found to be inadequate, the defect must be supplied, by so contriving the interior structure of the government, as that its several constituent parts may, by their mutual relations, be the means of keeping each other in their proper places. Without presuming to undertake a full development of this important idea, I will hazard a few general observations, which may perhaps place it in a clearer light, and enable us to form a more correct judgment of the principles and structure of the government planned by the convention.

In order to lay a due foundation for that separate and distinct exercise of the different powers of government, which to a certain extent, is admitted on all hands to be essential to the preservation of liberty, it is evident that each department should have a will of its own; and consequently should be so constituted, that the members of each should have as little agency as possible in the appointment of the members of the others. Were this principle rigorously adhered to, it would require that all the appointments for the supreme executive, legislative, and judiciary magistracies, should be drawn from the same fountain of authority, the people, through channels, having no communication whatever with one another. Perhaps such a plan of constructing the several departments would be less difficult in practice than it may in contemplation appear. Some difficulties however, and some additional expense, would attend the execution of it. Some deviations therefore from the principle must be admitted. In the constitution of the judiciary department in particular, it might be inexpedient to insist rigorously on the principle; first, because peculiar qualifications being essential in the members, the primary consideration ought to be to select that mode of choice, which best secures these qualifications; secondly, because the permanent tenure by which the appointments are held in that department, must soon destroy all sense of dependence on the authority conferring them.

It is equally evident that the members of each department should be as little dependent as possible on those of the others, for the emoluments annexed to their offices. Were the executive magistrate, or the judges, not independent of the legislature in this particular, their independence in every other would be merely nominal.

But the great security against a gradual concentration of the several powers in the same department, consists in giving to those who administer each department, the necessary constitutional means, and personal motives, to resist encroachments of the others. The provision for defense must in this, as in all other cases, be made commensurate to the danger of attack. Ambition must be made to counteract ambition. The interest of the man must be connected with the constitutional right of the place. It may be a reflection on human nature, that such devices should be necessary to control the abuses of government. But what is government itself but the greatest of all reflections on human nature? If men were angels, no government would be necessary. If angels were to govern men, neither external nor internal controls on government would be necessary. In framing a government which is to be administered by men over men, the great difficulty lies in this: You must first enable the government to control the governed; and in the next place, oblige it to control itself. A dependence on the people is no doubt the primary control on the government; but experience has taught mankind the necessity of auxiliary precautions.

This policy of supplying by opposite and rival interests, the defect of better motives, might be traced through the whole system of human affairs, private as well as public. We see it particularly displayed in all the subordinate distributions of power; where the constant aim is to divide and arrange the several offices in such a manner as that each may be a check on the other; that the private interest of every individual, may be a sentinel over the public rights. These inventions of prudence cannot be less requisite in the distribution of the supreme powers of the state.

But it is not possible to give to each department an equal power of self defense. In republican government the legislative authority, necessarily, predominates. The remedy for this inconveniency is, to divide the legislature into different branches; and to render them by different modes of election, and different principles of action, as little connected with each other, as the nature of their common functions, and their common dependence on the society, will admit. It may even be necessary to guard against dangerous encroachments by still further precautions. As the weight of the legislative authority requires that it should be thus divided, the weakness of the executive may require, on the other hand, that it should be fortified. An absolute negative, on the legislature, appears at first view to be the natural defense with which the executive magistrate should be armed. But perhaps it would be neither altogether safe, nor alone sufficient. On ordinary occasions, it might not be exerted with the requisite firmness; and on extraordinary occasions, it might be prefidiously abused. May not this defect of an absolute negative be supplied, by some qualified connection between this weaker department, and the weaker branch of the stronger department, by which the latter may be led to support the constitutional rights of the former, without being too much detached from the rights of its own department? If the principles on which these observations are founded be just, as I persuade myself they are, and they be applied as a criterion, to the several state constitutions, and to the federal constitution, it will be found, that if the latter does not perfectly correspond with them, the former are infinitely less able to bear such a test.

There are moreover two considerations particularly applicable to the federal system of America, which place that system in a very interesting point of view.

First. In a single republic, all the power surrendered by the people, is submitted to the administration of a single government; and usurpations are guarded against by a division of the government into distinct and separate departments. In the compound republic of America, the power surrendered by the people, is first divided between two distinct governments, and then the portion allotted to each, subdivided among distinct and separate departments. Hence a double security arises to the rights of the people. The different governments will control each other; at the same time that each will be controlled by itself.

Second. It is of great importance in a republic, not only to guard the society against the oppression of its rulers; but to guard one part of the society against the injustice of the other part. Different interests necessarily exist in different classes of citizens. If a majority be united by a common interest, the rights of the minority will be insecure. There are but two

methods of providing against this evil: The one by creating a will in the community independent of the majority, that is, of the society itself, the other by comprehending in the society so many separate descriptions of citizens, as will render an unjust combination of a majority of the whole, very improbable, if not impracticable. The first method prevails in all governments possessing an hereditary or self appointed authority. This at best is but a precarious security; because a power independent of the society may as well espouse the unjust views of the major, as the rightful interests, of the minor party, and may possibly be turned against both parties. The second method will be exemplified in the federal republic of the United States. While all authority in it will be derived from and dependent on the society, the society itself will be broken into so many parts, interests and classes of citizens, that the rights of individuals or of the minority, will be in little danger from interested combinations of the majority. In a free government, the security for civil rights must be the same as for religious rights. It consists in the one case in the multiplicity of interests, and in the other, in the multiplicity of sects. The degree of security in both cases will depend on the number of interests and sects; and this may be presumed to depend on the extent of country and number of people comprehended under the same government. This view of the subject must particularly recommend a proper federal system to all the sincere and considerate friends of republican government: Since it shows that in exact proportion as the territory of the union may be formed into more circumscribed confederacies or states, oppressive combinations of a majority will be facilitated, the best security under the republican form, for the rights of every class of citizens, will be diminished; and consequently, the stability and independence of some member of the government, the only other security, must be proportionally increased. Justice is the end of government. It is the end of civil society. It ever has been, and ever will be pursued, until it be obtained, or until liberty be lost in the pursuit. In a society under the forms of which the stronger faction can readily unite and oppress the weaker, anarchy may as truly be said to reign, as in a state of nature where the weaker individual is not secured against the violence of the stronger: And as in the latter state even the stronger individuals are prompted by the uncertainty of their condition, to submit to a government which may protect the weak as well as themselves: So in the former state, will the more powerful factions or parties be gradually induced by a like motive, to wish for a government which will protect all parties, the weaker as well as the more powerful. It can be little doubted, that if the state of Rhode Island was separated from the confederacy, and left to itself, the insecurity of rights under the popular form of government within such narrow limits, would be displayed by such reiterated oppressions of factious majorities, that some power altogether independent of the people would soon be called for by the voice of the very factions whose misrule had proved the necessity of it. In the extended republic of the United States, and among the great variety of interests, parties and sects which it embraces, a coalition of a majority of the whole society could seldom take place on any other principles than those of justice and the general good; and there being thus less danger to a minor from the will of the major party, there must be less pretext also, to provide for the security of the former, by introducing into the government a will not dependent on the latter; or in other words, a will independent of the society itself. It is no less certain than it is important, notwithstanding the contrary opinions which have been entertained, that the larger the society, provided it lie within a practicable sphere, the more duly capable it will be of self government. And happily for the *republican cause*, the practicable sphere may be carried to a very great extent, by a judicious modification and mixture of the *federal principle*.

PUBLIUS

Presidents, Congresses, and Chief Justices: 1789–2005

Term	President and Vice President	Party of President	Congress	Majority Party		Chief Justice of the United States
				House	Senate	
1789–1797	**George Washington** John Adams	None	1st 2nd 3rd 4th	(N/A) (N/A) (N/A) (N/A)	(N/A) (N/A) (N/A) (N/A)	John Jay (1789–1795) John Rutledge (1795) Oliver Ellsworth (1796–1800)
1797–1801	**John Adams** Thomas Jefferson	Federalist	5th 6th	(N/A) Fed	(N/A) Fed	Oliver Ellsworth (1796–1800) John Marshall (1801–1835)
1801–1809	**Thomas Jefferson** Aaron Burr (1801–1805) George Clinton (1805–1809)	Democratic-Republican	7th 8th 9th 10th	Dem-Rep Dem-Rep Dem-Rep Dem-Rep	Dem-Rep Dem-Rep Dem-Rep Dem-Rep	John Marshall (1801–1835)
1809–1817	**James Madison** George Clinton (1809–1812)[a] Elbridge Gerry (1813–1814)[a]	Democratic-Republican	11th 12th 13th 14th	Dem-Rep Dem-Rep Dem-Rep Dem-Rep	Dem-Rep Dem-Rep Dem-Rep Dem-Rep	John Marshall (1801–1835)
1817–1825	**James Monroe** Daniel D. Tompkins	Democratic-Republican	15th 16th 17th 18th	Dem-Rep Dem-Rep Dem-Rep Dem-Rep	Dem-Rep Dem-Rep Dem-Rep Dem-Rep	John Marshall (1801–1835)
1825–1829	**John Quincy Adams** John C. Calhoun	National-Republican	19th 20th	Nat'l Rep Dem	Nat'l Rep Dem	John Marshall (1801–1835)
1829–1837	**Andrew Jackson** John C. Calhoun (1829–1832)[c] Martin Van Buren (1833–1837)	Democrat	21st 22nd 23rd 24th	Dem Dem Dem Dem	Dem Dem Dem Dem	John Marshall (1801–1835) Roger B. Taney (1836–1864)
1837–1841	**Martin Van Buren** Richard M. Johnson	Democrat	25th 26th	Dem Dem	Dem Dem	Roger B. Taney (1836–1864)
1841	**William H. Harrison**[a] John Tyler (1841)	Whig				Roger B. Taney (1836–1864)
1841–1845	**John Tyler** (VP vacant)	Whig	27th 28th	Whig Dem	Whig Whig	Roger B. Taney (1836–1864)
1845–1849	**James K. Polk** George M. Dallas	Democrat	29th 30th	Dem Whig	Dem Dem	Roger B. Taney (1836–1864)
1849–1850	**Zachary Taylor**[a] Millard Fillmore	Whig	31st	Dem	Dem	Roger B. Taney (1836–1864)

Term	President and Vice President	Party of President	Congress	Majority Party House	Majority Party Senate	Chief Justice of the United States
1850–1853	**Millard Fillmore** (VP vacant)	Whig	32nd	Dem	Dem	Roger B. Taney (1836–1864)
1853–1857	**Franklin Pierce** William R. D. King (1853)[a]	Democrat	33rd 34th	Dem Rep	Dem Dem	Roger B. Taney (1836–1864)
1857–1861	**James Buchanan** John C. Breckinridge	Democrat	35th 36th	Dem Rep	Dem Dem	Roger B. Taney (1836–1864)
1861–1865	**Abraham Lincoln**[a] Hannibal Hamlin (1861–1865) Andrew Johnson (1865)	Republican	37th 38th	Rep Rep	Rep Rep	Roger B. Taney (1836–1864) Salmon P. Chase (1864–1873)
1865–1869	**Andrew Johnson** (VP vacant)	Republican	39th 40th	Union Rep	Union Rep	Salmon P. Chase (1864–1873)
1869–1877	**Ulysses S. Grant** Schuyler Colfax (1869–1873) Henry Wilson (1873–1875)[a]	Republican	41st 42nd 43rd 44th	Rep Rep Rep Dem	Rep Rep Rep Rep	Salmon P. Chase (1864–1873) Morrison R. Waite (1874–1888)
1877–1881	**Rutherford B. Hayes** William A. Wheeler	Republican	45th 46th	Dem Dem	Rep Dem	Morrison R. Waite (1874–1888)
1881	**James A. Garfield**[a] Chester A. Arthur	Republican	47th	Rep	Rep	Morrison R. Waite (1874–1888)
1881–1885	**Chester A. Arthur** (VP vacant)	Republican	48th	Dem	Rep	Morrison R. Waite (1874–1888)
1885–1889	**Grover Cleveland** Thomas A. Hendricks (1885)[a]	Democrat	49th 50th	Dem Dem	Rep Rep	Morrison R. Waite (1874–1888) Melville W. Fuller (1888–1910)
1889–1893	**Benjamin Harrison** Levi P. Morton	Republican	51st 52nd	Rep Dem	Rep Rep	Melville W. Fuller (1888–1910)
1893–1897	**Grover Cleveland** Adlai E. Stevenson	Democrat	53rd 54th	Dem Rep	Dem Rep	Melville W. Fuller (1888–1910)
1897–1901	**William McKinley**[a] Garret A. Hobart (1897–1899)[a] Theodore Roosevelt (1901)	Republican	55th 56th	Rep Rep	Rep Rep	Melville W. Fuller (1888–1910)
1901–1909	**Theodore Roosevelt** (VP vacant, 1901–1905) Charles W. Fairbanks (1905–1909)	Republican	57th 58th 59th 60th	Rep Rep Rep Rep	Rep Rep Rep Rep	Melville W. Fuller (1888–1910)
1909–1913	**William Howard Taft** James S. Sherman (1909–1912)[a]	Republican	61st 62nd	Rep Dem	Rep Rep	Melville W. Fuller (1888–1910) Edward D. White (1910–1921)
1913–1921	**Woodrow Wilson** Thomas R. Marshall	Democrat	63rd 64th 65th 66th	Dem Dem Dem Rep	Dem Dem Dem Rep	Edward D. White (1910–1921)
1921–1923	**Warren G. Harding**[a] Calvin Coolidge	Republican	67th	Rep	Rep	William Howard Taft (1921–1930)
1923–1929	**Calvin Coolidge** (VP vacant, 1923–1925) Charles G. Dawes (1925–1929)	Republican	68th 69th 70th	Rep Rep Rep	Rep Rep Rep	William Howard Taft (1921–1930)
1929–1933	**Herbert Hoover** Charles Curtis	Republican	71st 72nd	Rep Dem	Rep Rep	William Howard Taft (1921–1930) Charles Evans Hughes (1930–1941)

Term	President and Vice President	Party of President	Congress	Majority Party		Chief Justice of the United States
				House	Senate	
1933–1945	**Franklin D. Roosevelt**[a] John Nance Garner (1933–1941) Henry A. Wallace (1941–1945) Harry S Truman (1945)	Democrat	73rd 74th 75th 76th 77th 78th	Dem Dem Dem Dem Dem Dem	Dem Dem Dem Dem Dem Dem	Charles Evans Hughes (1930–1941) Harlan F. Stone (1941–1946)
1945–1953	**Harry S Truman** (VP vacant, 1945–1949) Alben W. Barkley (1949–1953)	Democrat	79th 80th 81st 82nd	Dem Rep Dem Dem	Dem Rep Dem Dem	Harlan F. Stone (1941–1946) Frederick M. Vinson (1946–1953)
1953–1961	**Dwight D. Eisenhower** Richard M. Nixon	Republican	83rd 84th 85th 86th	Rep Dem Dem Dem	Rep Dem Dem Dem	Frederick M. Vinson (1946–1953) Earl Warren (1953–1969)
1961–1963	**John F. Kennedy**[a] Lyndon B. Johnson (1961–1963)	Democrat	87th	Dem	Dem	Earl Warren (1953–1969)
1963–1969	**Lyndon B. Johnson** (VP vacant, 1963–1965) Hubert H. Humphrey (1965–1969)	Democrat	88th 89th 90th	Dem Dem Dem	Dem Dem Dem	Earl Warren (1953–1969)
1969–1974	**Richard M. Nixon**[b] Spiro Agnew (1969–1973)[c] Gerald R. Ford (1973–1974)[d]	Republican	91st 92md	Dem Dem	Dem Dem	Earl Warren (1953–1969) Warren E. Burger (1969–1986)
1974–1977	**Gerald R. Ford** Nelson A. Rockefeller	Republican	93rd 94th	Dem Dem	Dem Dem	Warren E. Burger (1969–1986)
1977–1981	**Jimmy Carter** Walter Mondale	Democrat	95th 96th	Dem Dem	Dem Dem	Warren E. Burger (1969–1986)
1981–1989	**Ronald Reagan** George Bush	Republican	97th 98th 99th 100th	Dem Dem Dem Dem	Rep Rep Rep Dem	Warren E. Burger (1969–1986) William H. Rehnquist (1986–)
1989–1993	**George Bush** Dan Quayle	Republican	101st 102nd	Dem Dem	Dem Dem	William H. Rehnquist (1986–)
1993–2001	**Bill Clinton** Al Gore	Democrat	103rd 104th 105th 106th	Dem Rep Rep Rep	Dem Rep Rep Rep	William H. Rehnquist (1986–)
2001–	**George W. Bush** Dick Cheney	Republican	107th 108th 109th	Rep Rep Rep	Dem Rep Rep	William H. Rehnquist (1986–)

[a]Died in office.
[b]Resigned from the presidency.
[c]Resigned from the vice presidency.
[d]Appointed Vice President.

Selected Supreme Court Cases

- *Agostini* v. *Felton* (1997): The Court agreed to permit public school teachers to go into parochial schools during school hours to provide remedial education to disadvantaged students because it was not an excessive entanglement of church and state.

- *Alden* v. *Maine* (1999): In another case involving sovereign immunity, the Court ruled that Congress lacks the authority to abrogate a state's immunity in its own courts.

- *Ashcroft* v. *Free Speech Coalition* (2002): The Court ruled that the Child Online Protection Act of 1998 was unconstitutional because it was too vague in its reliance on "community standards" to define what is harmful to minors.

- *Avery* v. *Midland* (1968): The Court declared that the one-person, one-vote standard applied to counties as well as congressional and state legislative districts.

- *Baker* v. *Carr* (1962): Watershed case establishing the principle of one-person, one-vote, which requires that each legislative district within a state have the same number of eligible voters so that representation is equitably based on population.

- *Barron* v. *Baltimore* (1833): Decision that limited the application of the Bill of Rights to the actions of Congress alone.

- *Benton* v. *Maryland* (1969): Incorporated the Fifth Amendment's double jeopardy clause.

- *Board of Regents* v. *Southworth* (2000): Unanimous ruling from the Supreme Court which stated that public universities could charge students a mandatory activities fee that could be used to facilitate extracurricular student political speech so long as the programs are neutral in their application.

- *Boerne* v. *Flores* (1997): The Court ruled that Congress could not force the Religious Freedom Restoration act upon the state governments.

- *Bowers* v. *Hardwick* (1986): Unsuccessful attempt to challenge Georgia's sodomy law.

- *Boy Scouts of America* v. *Dale* (2000): The Court ruled that the Boy Scouts could exclude gays from serving as scoutmasters because a private group has the right to set its own moral code.

- *Bradwell* v. *Illinois* (1873): In this case, a woman argued that Illinois's refusal to allow her to practice law despite the fact that she had passed the bar, violated her citizenship rights under the privileges and immunities clause of the Fourteenth Amendment; the justices denied her claim.

- *Bragdon* v. *Abbott* (1998): The Court ruled that individuals infected with HIV but not sick enough to qualify as having AIDS were protected from discrimination by the 1990 Americans with Disabilities Act (ADA).

- *Brandenburg* v. *Ohio* (1969): The Court fashioned the direct incitement test for deciding whether certain kinds of speech could be regulated by the government. This test holds that advocacy of illegal action is protected by the First Amendment unless imminent action is intended and likely to occur.

- *Brown* v. *Board of Education* (1954): U.S. Supreme Court decision holding that school segregation is inherently unconstitutional because it violates the Fourteenth Amendment's guarantee of equal protection; marked the end of legal segregation in the United States.

- *Brown* v. *Board of Education II* (1955): Follow-up to *Brown* v. *Board of Education*, this case laid out the process for school desegregation and established the concept of dismantling segregationist systems "with all deliberate speed."

- *Brown University* v. *Cohen* (1997): Landmark Title IX case that put all colleges and universities on notice that discrimination against women would not be tolerated, even when, as in the case of Brown University, the university had tremendously expanded sports opportunities for women.

- *Buckley* v. *Valeo* (1976): The Court ruled that money spent by an individual or political committee in support or opposition of a candidate (but independent of the candidate's campaign) was a form of symbolic speech, and therefore could not be limited under the First Amendment.

- *Bush* v. *Gore* (2000): Controversial 2000 election case that made the final decision on the Florida recounts, and thus, the result of the 2000 election. The Rehnquist Court broke from tradition in this case by refusing to defer to the state court's decision.

- *Cantwell* v. *Connecticut* (1940): The case in which the Supreme Court incorporated the freedom of religion, ruling that the freedom to believe is absolute, but the freedom to act is subject to the regulation of society.

- *Chandler* v. *Miller* (1997): The Supreme Court refused to allow Georgia to require all candidates for state office to pass a urinalysis thirty days before qualifying for nomination or election, concluding that this law violated the search-and-seizure clause.

- *Chaplinsky* v. *New Hampshire* (1942): Established the Supreme Court's rationale for distinguishing between protected and unprotected speech.

- *Chicago, B&O R.R. Co.* v. *Chicago* (1897): Incorporated the Fifth Amendment's just compensation clause.

- *Chisholm* v. *Georgia* (1793): The Court interpreted its jurisdiction under Article III, section 2, of the Constitution to include the right to hear suits brought by a citizen of one state against another state.

- *Civil Rights Cases* (1883): Name attached to five cases brought under the Civil Rights Act of 1875. In 1883, the Supreme Court decided that discrimination in a variety of public accommodations, including theaters, hotels, and railroads, could not be prohibited by the act because it was private and not state discrimination.

- *Clinton* v. *City of New York* (1998): The Court ruled that the line-item veto was unconstitutional because it gave powers to the president denied him by the U.S. Constitution.

- *Clinton* v. *Jones* (1997): The Court refused to reverse a lower court's decision that allowed Paula Jones's civil case against President Bill Clinton to proceed.

- *Cohens* v. *Virginia* (1821): The Court defined its jurisdiction to include the right to review all state criminal cases; additionally, this case built on *Martin* v. *Hunter's Lessee*, clarifying the Court's power to declare state laws unconstitutional.

- *Colorado Republican Federal Campaign Committee* v. *Federal Election Commission* (1996): The Supreme Court extended its ruling in *Buckley* v. *Valeo* to also include political parties.

- *Cooper* v. *Aaron* (1958): Case wherein the court broke with tradition and issued a unanimous decision against the Little Rock School Board ruling that the district's evasive schemes to avoid the *Brown II* decision were illegal.

- *Craig* v. *Boren* (1976): The Court ruled that keeping drunk drivers off the roads may be an important governmental objective, but allowing women aged eighteen to twenty-one to drink alcoholic beverages while prohibiting men of the same age from drinking is not substantially related to that goal.

- *Cruzan by Cruzan* v. *Director, Missouri Department of Health* (1990): The Court rejected any attempt to extend the right to privacy into the area of assisted suicide. However, the Court did note that individuals could terminate medical treatment if they were able to express, or had done so in writing, their desire to have medical treatment terminated in the event they became incompetent.

- *DeJonge* v. *Oregon* (1937): Incorporated the First Amendment's right to freedom of assembly.

- *Doe* v. *Bolton* (1973): In combination with *Roe* v. *Wade*, established a woman's right to an abortion.

- *Dred Scott* v. *Sandford* (1857): Concluded that the U.S. Congress lacked the constitutional authority to bar slavery in the territories; this decision narrowed the scope of national power while it enhanced that of the states. This case marks the first time since *Marbury* v. *Madison* that the Supreme Court found an act of Congress unconstitutional.

- *Duncan* v. *Louisiana* (1968): Incorporated the Sixth Amendment's trial by jury clause.

- *Engel* v. *Vitale* (1962): The Court ruled that the recitation in public classrooms of a nondenominational prayer was unconstitutional and a violation of the establishment clause.

- *Fletcher* v. *Peck* (1810): The Court ruled that state legislatures could not make laws that voided contracts or grants made by earlier legislative action.

- *Florida Prepaid* v. *College Savings Bank* (1999): The Court ruled that Congress does not have the authority under the commerce clause or the patent clause to change patent laws in a manner that would negatively affect a state's right to assert its immunity from suit.

- *Furman* v. *Georgia* (1972): The Supreme Court used this case to end capital punishment, at least in the short run. (The case was overturned by *Gregg* v. *Georgia* in 1976.)

- *Garcia* v. *San Antonio Metropolitan Transport Authority* (**1985**): In this case, the court ruled that Congress has the broad power to impose its will on state and local governments, even in areas that have traditionally been left to state and local discretion.
- *Gibbons* v. *Ogden* (**1824**): The Court upheld broad congressional power over interstate commerce.
- *Gideon* v. *Wainwright* (**1963**): Granted indigents the right to counsel.
- *Gitlow* v. *New York* (**1925**): Incorporated the free speech clause of the First Amendment, ruling that the states were not completely free to limit forms of political expression.
- *Gray* v. *Sanders* (**1963**): Court held that voting by unit sytems was unconstitutional.
- *Gregg* v. *Georgia* (**1976**): Overturning *Furman* v. *Georgia*, the case ruled that Georgia's rewritten death penalty statute was constitutional.
- *Griswold* v. *Connecticut* (**1965**): Supreme Court case that established the Constitution's implied right to privacy.
- *Grutter* v. *Bollinger (2003):* Upheld University of Michigan affirmative action plan.
- *Harris* v. *Forklift Systems* (**1993**): The Court ruled that a federal civil rights law created a "broad rule of workplace equality."
- *Hoyt* v. *Florida* (**1961**): The Court ruled that an all-male jury did not violate a woman's rights under the Fourteenth Amendment.
- *Hunt* v. *Cromartie* (**1999, 2001**): Continuation of redistricting litigation begun with *Shaw* v. *Reno* (1993). The Court reversed district court conclusions that the North Carolina legislature had used race-driven criteria in violation of the equal protection clause to redraw district lines.
- *Immigration and Naturalization Service* v. *Chadha* (**1983**): The Court ruled that the legislative veto as it was used in many circumstances was unconstitutional because it violated the separation of powers principle.
- *Klopfer* v. *North Carolina* (**1967**): Incorporated the Sixth Amendment's right to a speedy trial.
- *Korematsu* v. *U.S.* (**1944**): In this case, the Court ruled that the internment of Japanese Americans during World War II was not unconstitutional.
- *Lawrence* v. *Texas (2003):* Invalidated Texas law criminalizing consensual same sex sodomy.
- *Lemon* v. *Kurtzman* (**1971**): The Court determined that the direct government assistance to religious schools was unconstitutional. In the majority opinion, the Court created what has become known as the "Lemon Test" for deciding if a law is in violation of the establishment clause.
- *Lynch* v. *Donnelly* (**1984**): In a defeat for the ACLU, the Court held that a city's inclusion of a crèche in its annual Christmas display in a private park did not violate the establishment clause.
- *Malloy* v. *Hogan* (**1964**): Incorporated the Fifth Amendment's self-incrimination clause.
- *Mapp* v. *Ohio* (**1961**): Incorporated a portion of the Fourth Amendment by establishing that illegally obtained evidence cannot be used at trial.
- *Marbury* v. *Madison* (**1803**): Supreme Court case in which the Court first asserted the power of judicial review in finding that a congressional statute extending the Court's original jurisdiction was unconstitutional.
- *Martin* v. *Hunter's Lessee* (**1816**): The Court's power of judicial review in regard to state law was clarified in this case.
- *Ex parte McCardle* (**1869**): Post–Civil War case that reinforced Congress's power to determine the jurisdiction of the Supreme Court.
- *McCleskey* v. *Kemp* (**1987**): The Court ruled that the imposition of the death penalty did not violate the equal protection clause.
- *McCleskey* v. *Zant* (**1991**): On this appeal of the 1987 *McCleskey* case, the Court produced new standards designed to make it much more difficult for death-row inmates to file repeated appeals.
- *McCulloch* v. *Maryland* (**1819**): Supreme Court upheld the power of the national government and denied the right of a state to tax the bank. The Court's broad interpretation of the necessary and proper clause paved the way for later rulings upholding expansive federal powers.
- *Miller* v. *California* (**1973**): Case wherein the Supreme Court began to formulate rules designed to make it easier for states to regulate obscene materials and to return to communities a greater role in determining what is obscene.
- *Minor* v. *Happersett* (**1875**): The Supreme Court once again examined the privileges and immunities clause of the Fourteenth Amendment, ruling that voting was not a privilege of citizenship.

- *Miranda* v. *Arizona* **(1966):** The Fifth Amendment requires that individuals arrested for a crime must be advised of their right to remain silent and to have counsel present.

- *Morrison* v. *U.S.* **(2000):** The Court ruled that Congress has no authority under the commerce clause to enact a provision of the Violence Against Women Act providing a federal remedy to victims of gender-motivated violence.

- *Muller* v. *Oregon* **(1908):** Case that ruled Oregon's law barring women from working more than ten hours a day was constitutional; also an attempt to define women's unique status as mothers to justify their differential treatment.

- *Near* v. *Minnesota* **(1931):** By ruling that a state law violated the freedom of the press, the Supreme Court incorporated the free press provision of the First Amendment.

- *New York* v. *Smith* **(1992):** A section of the Low-Level Waste Act that required states to dispose of radioactive waste within their borders was found unconstitutional because it would force states into the service of the federal government.

- *New York Times Co.* v. *Sullivan* **(1964):** Supreme Court decision ruling that simply publishing a defamatory falsehood is not enough to justify a libel judgment. "Actual malice" must be proved to support a finding of libel against a public figure.

- *New York Times Co.* v. *U.S.* **(1971):** Also called the Pentagon Papers case; the Supreme Court ruled that any attempt by the government to prevent expression carried "a heavy presumption" against its constitutionality.

- *NLRB* v. *Jones and Laughlin Steel Co.* **(1937):** Case that upheld the National Labor Relations Act of 1935, marking a turning point in the Court's ideology toward the programs of President Franklin D. Roosevelt's New Deal.

- *In re Oliver* **(1948):** Incorporated the Sixth Amendment's right to a public trial.

- *Palko* v. *Connecticut* **(1937):** Set the Court's rationale of selective incorporation, a judicial doctrine whereby most but not all of the protections found in the Bill of Rights are made applicable to the states via the Fourteenth Amendment.

- *Parker* v. *Gladden* **(1966):** Incorporated the Sixth Amendment's right to an impartial trial.

- *Planned Parenthood* v. *Casey* **(1992):** An unsuccessful attempt to challenge Pennsylvania's restrictive abortion regulations.

- *Plessy* v. *Ferguson* **(1896):** *Plessy* challenged a Louisiana statute requiring that railroads provide separate accommodations for blacks and whites. The Court found that separate but equal accommodations did not violate the equal protection clause of the Fourteenth Amendment.

- *Pointer* v. *Texas* **(1965):** Incorporated the Sixth Amendment's right to confrontation of witnesses.

- *Printz* v. *U.S.* **(1997):** The Court found that Congress lacks the authority to compel state officers to execute federal laws, specifically relating to background checks on handgun purchasers.

- *Quilici* v. *Village of Morton Grove* **(1983):** The Supreme Court refused to review a lower court's ruling upholding the constitutionality of a local ordinance banning handguns against a Second Amendment challenge.

- *R.A.V.* v. *City of St. Paul* **(1992):** The Court concluded that St. Paul, Minnesota's Bias-Motivated Crime Ordinance violated the First Amendment because it regulated speech based on the content of the speech.

- *Reed* v. *Reed* **(1971):** Turned the tide in terms of constitutional litigation, ruling that the equal protection clause of the Fourteenth Amendment prohibited unreasonable classifications based on sex.

- *Regents of the University of California* v. *Bakke* **(1978):** A sharply divided Court concluded that the university's rejection of Bakke as a student had been illegal because the use of strict affirmative action quotas was inappropriate.

- *Reno* v. *American Civil Liberties Union* **(1997):** The Court ruled that the 1996 Communications Decency Act prohibiting transfer of obscene or indecent materials over the Internet to minors violated the First Amendment because it was too vague and overbroad.

- *Reynolds* v. *Sims* **(1964):** In this case, the Court decided that every person should have an equally weighted vote in electing governmental representatives.

- *Robinson* v. *California* (1962): Incorporated the Eighth Amendment's right to freedom from cruel and unusual punishment.

- *Roe* v. *Wade* (1973): The Supreme Court found that a woman's right to an abortion was protected by the right to privacy that could be implied from specific guarantees found in the Bill of Rights and the Fourteenth Amendment.

- *Roth* v. *U.S.* (1957): The Court held that in order to be obscene, material must be "utterly without redeeming social value."

- *Romer* v. *Evans* (1996): A Colorado constitutional amendment precluding any legislative, executive, or judicial action at any state or local level designed to bar discrimination based on sexual preference was ruled not rational or reasonable.

- *Santa Fe Independent School District* v. *Doe* (2000): The Court ruled that student-led, student-initiated prayer at high school football games violated the establishment clause.

- *Schenck* v. *U.S.* (1919): Case in which the Supreme Court interpreted the First Amendment to allow Congress to restrict speech that was "of such a nature as to create a clear and present danger that will bring about the substantive evils that Congress has a right to prevent."

- *Seminole Tribe* v. *Florida* (1996): Congress cannot impose a duty on states forcing them to negotiate with Indian tribes; the state's sovereign immunity protects it from a congressional directive about how to do business.

- *Shaw* v. *Reno* (1993): First in a series of redistricting cases in which the North Carolina legislature's reapportionment of congressional districts based on the 1990 Census was contested because the plan included an irregularly-shaped district in which race seemed to be a dominant consideration. The Court ruled that districts created with race as the dominant consideration violated the equal protection clause of the Fourteenth Amendment.

- *In re Sindram* (1991): The Court chastised Michael Sindram for filing his petition *in forma pauperis* to require the Maryland courts to expedite his request to expunge a $35 speeding ticket from his record.

- *The Slaughterhouse Cases* (1873): The Court upheld Louisiana's right to create a monopoly on the operation of slaughterhouses, despite the Butcher's Benevolent Association's claim that this action deprived its members of their livelihood and the privileges and immunities granted by the Fourteenth Amendment.

- *South Dakota* v. *Dole* (1987): The Court ruled that it was permissible for the federal government to require states that wanted transportation funds to pass laws setting twenty-one as the legal drinking age.

- *Stenberg* v. *Carhart* (2000): The Court ruled that a Nebraska "partial birth" abortion statute was unconstitutionally vague and unenforceable, calling into question the laws of twenty-nine other states.

- *Stromberg* v. *California* (1931): The Court overturned the conviction of a director of a Communist youth camp under a state statute prohibiting the display of a red flag.

- *Swann* v. *Charlotte-Mecklenburg School District* (1971): The Supreme Court ruled that all vestiges of *de jure* discrimination must be eliminated at once.

- *Texas* v. *Johnson* (1989): Case in which the Court overturned the conviction of a Texas man found guilty of setting fire to an American flag.

- *Tinker* v. *Des Moines Independent School District* (1969): Upheld student's rights to express themselves by wearing black armbands symbolizing protest of the Vietnam War.

- *U.S.* v. *Curtiss-Wright Export Corporation* (1936): The Court upheld the rights of Congress to grant the president authority to act in foreign affairs and to allow the president to prohibit arms shipments to participants in foreign wars.

- *U.S.* v. *Lopez* (1995): The Court invalidated a section of the Gun Free School Zones Act, ruling that regulating guns did not fall within the scope of the commerce clause, and therefore the powers of the federal government. Only states have the authority to ban guns in school zones.

- *U.S.* v. *Miller* (1939): The last time the Supreme Court addressed the constitutionality of the Second Amendment; ruled that the Amendment was only intended to protect a citizen's right to own ordinary militia weapons.

- *U.S.* v. *Nixon* (1974): In a case involving President Richard M. Nixon's refusal to turn over tape recordings of his conversations, the Court ruled that executive privilege does not grant the president an absolute right to secure all presidential documents.

- *U.S. Term Limits* v. *Thornton* (1995): The Supreme Court ruled that states do not have the authority to enact term limits for federal elected officials.

- *Washington* v. *Texas* (1967): Incorporated the Sixth Amendments right to a compulsory trial.

- *Webster* v. *Reproductive Health Services* (1989): In upholding several restrictive abortion regulations, the Court opened the door for state governments to enact new restrictions on abortion.

- *Weeks* v. *U.S.* (1914): Case wherein the Supreme Court adopted the exclusionary rule, which bars the use of illegally obtained evidence at trial.

- *Wesberry* v. *Sanders* (1964): Established the principal of one person, one vote for congressional districts.

- *Wolf* v. *Colorado* (1949): The Court ruled that illegally obtained evidence did not necessarily have to be eliminated from use during trial.

- *Youngstown Sheet & Tube Co.* v. *Sawyer* (1952): The Court invalidated President Harry S Truman's seizure of the nation's steel mills.

- *Zelman* v. *Simmons-Harris* (2002): The Court concluded that governments can give money to parents to allow them to send their children to private or religious schools.

A

administrative adjudication: A quasi-judicial process in which a bureaucratic agency settles disputes between two parties in a manner similar to the way courts resolve disputes.

administrative discretion: The ability of bureaucrats to make choices concerning the best way to implement congressional intentions.

advisory referendum: A process in which voters cast nonbinding ballots on an issue or proposal.

affiliates: Local television stations that carry the programming of a national network.

affirmative action: Policies designed to give special attention or compensatory treatment to members of a previously disadvantaged group.

amicus curiae: "Friend of the court"; a third party to a lawsuit who files a legal brief for the purpose of raising additional points of view in an attempt to influence a court's decision.

Anti-Federalists: Those who favored strong state governments and a weak national government; opposed the ratification of the U.S. Constitution.

appellate court: Court that generally reviews only findings of law made by lower courts.

appellate jurisdiction: The power vested in an appellate court to review and/or revise the decision of a lower court.

aristocracy: A system of government in which control is based on rule of the highest.

Articles of Confederation: The compact among the thirteen original states that was the basis of their government. Written in 1776, the Articles were not ratified by all the states until 1781.

articles of impeachment: The specific charges brought against a president or a federal judge by the House of Representatives.

at-large election: Election in which candidates for office must compete throughout the jurisdiction as a whole.

B

bicameral legislature: A legislature divided into two houses; the U.S. Congress and the state legislatures are bicameral except Nebraska, which is unicameral.

bill: A proposed law.

bill of attainder: A law declaring an act illegal without a judicial trial.

Bill of Rights: The first ten amendments to the U.S. Constitution.

Black Codes: Laws denying most legal rights to newly freed slaves; passed by southern states following the Civil War.

blanket primary: A primary in which voters may cast ballots in either party's primary (but not both) on an office-by-office basis.

block grant: Broad grant with few strings attached; given to states by the federal government for specified activities, such as secondary education or health services.

brief: A document containing the legal written arguments in a case filed with a court by a party prior to a hearing or trial.

Brown v. Board of Education (1954): U.S. Supreme Court decision holding that school segregation is inherently unconstitutional because it violates the Fourteenth Amendment's guarantee of equal protection; marked the end of legal segregation in the United States.

bureaucracy: A set of complex hierarchical departments, agencies, commissions, and their staffs that exist to help a chief executive officer carry out his or her duty to enforce the law.

C

Cabinet: The formal body of presidential advisers who head the fifteen executive departments. Presidents often add others to this body of formal advisers.

campaign manager: The individual who travels with the candidate and coordinates the many different aspects of the campaign.

candidate debate: Forum in which political candidates face each other to discuss their platforms, records, and character.

capitalism: The economic system that favors private control of business and minimal governmental regulation of private industry.

casework: The process of solving constituents' problems dealing with the bureaucracy.

categorical grant: Grant for which Congress appropriates funds for a specific purpose.

charter: A document that, like a constitution, specifies the basic policies, procedures, and institutions of a municipality.

charter school: Public school sanctioned by a specific agreement that allows the program to operate outside the usual rules and regulations.

checks and balances: A governmental structure that gives each of the three branches of government some degree of oversight and control over the actions of the others.

city charter: A document similar to a constitution, setting out city government structure and powers and its political processes.

city council: The legislature in a city government.

civic virtue: The tendency to form small-scale associations for the public good.

civil law: Codes of behavior related to business and contractual relationships between groups and individuals.

civil liberties: The personal rights and freedoms that the federal government cannot abridge by law, constitution, or judicial interpretation.

civil rights: Refers to the positive acts governments take to protect individuals against arbitrary or discriminatory treatment by governments or individuals based on categories such as race, sex, national origin, age, or sexual orientation.

Civil Rights Act of 1964: Legislation passed by Congress to outlaw segregation in public facilities and racial discrimination in employment, education, and voting; created the Equal Employment Opportunity Commission.

Civil Rights Cases (1883): Name attached to five cases brought under the Civil Rights Act of 1875. In 1883, the Supreme Court decided that discrimination in a variety of public accommodations, including theaters, hotels, and railroads, could not be prohibited by the act because it was private, not state, discrimination.

civil service laws: These acts removed the staffing of the bureaucracy from political parties and created a professional bureaucracy filled through competition.

civil service system: The system created by civil service laws by which many appointments to the federal bureaucracy are made.

civil society: Society created when citizens are allowed to organize and express their views publicly as they engage in an open debate about public policy.

clear and present danger test: Test articulated by the Supreme Court in *Schenck* v. *U.S.* (1919) to draw the line between protected and unprotected speech; the Court looks to see "whether the words used…" could "create a clear and present danger that they will bring about substantive evils" that Congress seeks "to prevent".

clientele agencies: Executive departments directed by law to foster and promote the interests of a specific segment or group in the U.S. population (such as the Department of Education).

closed primary: A primary election in which only a party's registered voters are eligible to vote.

cloture: Motion requiring sixty senators to cut off debate.

coalition: A group of interests or organizations that join forces for the purpose of electing public officials.

coattail effect: The tendency of lesser-known or weaker candidates lower on the ballot to profit in an election by the presence on the party's ticket of a more popular candidate.

collective good: Something of value that cannot be withheld from a non–group member, for example, a tax write-off or a better environment.

commission: Form of local government in which several officials are elected to top positions that have both legislative and executive responsibilities.

Committees of Correspondence: Organizations in each of the American colonies created to keep colonists abreast of developments with the British; served as powerful molders of public opinion against the British.

common law: Legal traditions of society that are for the most part unwritten but based on the aggregation of rulings and interpretations of judges beginning in thirteenth-century England.

communism: An economic system in which workers own the means of production and control the distribution of resources.

commute: The action of a governor when he or she cancels all or part of the sentence of someone convicted of a crime, while keeping the conviction on the record.

compact: A formal, legal agreement between a state and a tribe.

concurrent powers: Authority possessed by both the state and national governments that may be exercised concurrently as long as that power is not exclusively within the scope of national power or in conflict with national law.

confederation: Type of government in which the national government derives its powers from the states; a league of independent states.

conference committee: Joint committee created to iron out differences between Senate and House versions of a specific piece of legislation.

congressional review: The process by which Congress can nullify an executive branch regulation by a resolution jointly passed in both houses within sixty days of announcement of the regulation and accepted by the president.

congressionalist: One who believes that Article II's provision that the president should ensure "faithful execution of the laws" should be read as an injunction against substituting presidential authority for legislative intent.

conservative: One thought to believe that a government is best that governs least and that big government can only infringe on individual, personal, and economic rights.

constitutional courts: Federal courts specifically created by the U.S. Constitution or by Congress pursuant to its authority in Article III.

content regulation: Governmental attempts to regulate the electronic media.

Contract with America: Campaign pledge signed by most Republican candidates in 1994 to guide their legislative agenda.

contrast ad: Ad that compares the records and proposals of the candidates, with a bias toward the sponsor.

cooperative federalism: The relationship between the national and state governments that began with the New Deal.

county: A geographic district created within a state with a government that has general responsibilities for land, welfare, environment, and, where appropriate, rural service policies.

criminal law: Codes of behavior related to the protection of property and individual safety.

critical election: An election that signals a party realignment through voter polarization around new issues.

crossover voting: Participation in the primary of a party with which the voter is not affiliated.

D

de facto **discrimination:** Racial discrimination that results from practice (such as housing patterns or other social factors) rather than the law.

de jure **discrimination:** Racial segregation that is a direct result of law or official policy.

Declaration of Independence: Document drafted by Thomas Jefferson in 1776 that proclaimed the right of the American colonies to separate from Great Britain.

deep background: Information gathered for news stories that must be completely unsourced.

delegate: Role played by elected representatives who vote the way their constituents would want them to, regardless of their own opinions.

democracy: A system of government that gives power to the people, whether directly or through their elected representatives.

departments: Major administrative units with responsibility for a broad area of government operations. Departmental status usually indicates a permanent national interest in that particular governmental function, such as defense, commerce, or agriculture.

Dillon's Rule: A court ruling that local governments do not have any inherent sovereignty but instead must be authorized by state government.

direct democracy: A system of government in which members of the polity meet to discuss all policy decisions and then agree to abide by majority rule.

direct incitement test: A test articulated by the Supreme Court in *Brandenberg* v. *Ohio* (1969) that holds that advocacy of illegal action is protected by the First Amendment unless imminent lawless action is intended and likely to occur.

direct initiative: A process in which voters can place a proposal on a ballot and enact it into law without involving the legislature or the governor.

direct mailer: A professional who supervises a political campaign's direct-mail fund-raising strategies.

direct (popular) referendum: A process in which voters can veto a bill recently passed in the legislature by placing the issue on a ballot and expressing disapproval.

direct primary: The selection of party candidates through the ballots of qualified voters rather than at party nomination conventions.

discharge petition: Petition that gives a majority of the House of Representatives the authority to bring an issue to the floor in the face of committee inaction.

district-based election: Election in which candidates run for an office that represents only the voters of a specific district within the jurisdiction.

disturbance theory: Political scientist David B. Truman's theory that interest groups form in part to counteract the efforts of other groups.

divided government: The political condition in which different political parties control the White House and Congress.

domestic dependent nation: A type of sovereignty that makes an Indian tribe in the United States outside the authority of state governments but reliant on the federal government for the definition of tribal authority.

dual federalism: The belief that having separate and equally powerful levels of government is the best arrangement.

dualist theory: The theory that there has always been an underlying binary party nature to U.S. politics.

due process clause: Clause contained in the Fifth and Fourteenth Amendments. Over the years, it has been construed to guarantee to individuals a variety of rights ranging from economic liberty to criminal procedural rights to protection from arbitrary governmental action.

due process rights: Procedural guarantees provided by the Fourth, Fifth, Sixth, and Eighth Amendments for those accused of crimes.

E

economic interest group: A group with the primary purpose of promoting the financial interests of its members.

Eighth Amendment: Part of the Bill of Rights that states: "Excessive bail shall not be required, nor excessive fines imposed, nor cruel and unusual punishments inflicted."

elector: Member of the electoral college chosen by methods determined in each state.

electoral college: Representatives of each state who cast the final ballots that actually elect a president.

electorate: Citizens eligible to vote.

electronic media: The broadcast media, including television, radio, computerized information services, and the Internet.

enumerated powers: Seventeen specific powers granted to Congress under Article I, section 8, of the U.S. Constitution; these powers include taxation, coinage of money, regulation of commerce, and the authority to provide for a national defense.

Equal Employment Opportunity Commission: Federal agency created to enforce the Civil Rights Act of 1964, which forbids discrimination on the basis of race, creed, national origin, religion, or sex in hiring, promotion, or firing.

equal protection clause: Section of the Fourteenth Amendment that guarantees that all citizens receive "equal protection of the laws"; has been used to bar discrimination against blacks and women.

Equal Rights Amendment: Proposed amendment that would bar discrimination against women by federal or state governments.

equal time rule: The rule that requires broadcast stations to sell campaign air time equally to all candidates if they choose to sell it to any.

establishment clause: The first clause in the First Amendment. It prohibits the national government from establishing a national religion.

ex post facto law: Law passed after the fact, thereby making previously legal activity illegal and subject to current penalty; prohibited by the U.S. Constitution.

exclusionary rule: Judicially created rule that prohibits police from using illegally seized evidence at trial.

executive agreement: Formal government agreement entered into by the executive branch that does not require the advice and consent of the U.S. Senate.

Executive Office of the President (EOP): Establishment created in 1939 to help the president oversee the bureaucracy.

executive order: A rule or regulation issued by the president that has the effect of law. All executive orders must be published in the *Federal Register*.

executive privilege: An assertion of presidential power that reasons that the president can withhold information requested by the courts in matters relating to his office.

exit polls: Polls conducted at selected polling places on Election Day.

extradite: To send someone against his or her will to another state to face criminal charges.

F

fairness doctrine: Rule in effect from 1949 to 1985 requiring broadcasters to cover events adequately and to present contrasting views on important public issues.

Federal Employees Political Activities Act: 1993 liberalization of the Hatch Act. Federal employees are now allowed to run for office in nonpartisan elections and to contribute money to campaigns in partisan elections.

federal system: Plan of government created in the U.S. Constitution in which power is divided between the national government and the state governments and in which independent states are bound together under one national government.

federalism: The philosophy that describes the governmental system created by the Framers; see also **federal system**.

The Federalist Papers: A series of eighty-five political papers written by John Jay, Alexander Hamilton, and James Madison in support of ratification of the U.S. Constitution.

Federalists: Those who favored a stronger national government and supported the proposed U.S. Constitution; later became the first U.S. political party.

Fifteenth Amendment: One of the three Civil War amendments; specifically enfranchised newly freed male slaves.

Fifth Amendment: Part of the Bill of Rights that imposes a number of restrictions on the federal government with respect to the rights of persons suspected of committing a crime. It provides for indictment by a grand jury, protection against self-incrimination, and prevents the national government from denying a person life, liberty, or property without the due process of law. It also prevents the national government from taking property without fair compensation.

filibuster: A formal way of halting action on a bill by means of long speeches or unlimited debate in the Senate.

finance chair: A professional who coordinates the fund-raising efforts for the campaign.

First Amendment: Part of the Bill of Rights that imposes a number of restrictions on the federal government with respect to the civil liberties of the people, including freedom of religion, speech, press, assembly, and petition.

First Continental Congress: Meeting held in Philadelphia from September 5 to October 26, 1774, in which fifty-six delegates (from every colony except Georgia) adopted a resolution in opposition to the Coercive Acts.

Fourteenth Amendment: One of the three Civil War amendments; guarantees equal protection and due process of the laws to all U.S. citizens.

Fourth Amendment: Part of the Bill of Rights that reads: "The right of the people to be secure in their persons, houses, papers, and effects, against unreasonable searches and seizures, shall not be violated, and no

Warrants shall issue, but upon probable cause, supported by Oath or affirmation, and particularly describing the place to be searched, and the persons or things to the seized."

free exercise clause: The second clause of the First Amendment. It prohibits the U.S. government from interfering with a citizen's right to practice his or her religion.

free market economy: The economic system in which the "invisible hand" of the market regulates prices, wages, product mix, and so on.

free media: Coverage of a candidate's campaign by the news media.

free rider problem: Potential members fail to join a group because they can get the benefit, or collective good, sought by the group without contributing to the effort.

front-loading: The tendency of states to choose an early date on the primary calendar.

G

general election: Election in which voters decide which candidates will actually fill elective public offices.

general election campaign: That part of a political campaign aimed at winning a general election.

gerrymandering: The legislative process through which the majority party in each statehouse tries to assure that the maximum number of representatives from its political party can be elected to Congress through the redrawing of legislative districts.

get-out-the-vote (GOTV): A push at the end of a political campaign to encourage supporters to go to the polls.

Gibbons v. Ogden **(1824):** The Court upheld broad congressional power over interstate commerce.

government corporations: Businesses established by Congress that perform functions that could be provided by private businesses (such as the U.S. Postal Service).

governmental party: The office holders and candidates who run under a political party's banner.

governor: Chief elected executive in state government.

grandfather clause: Voting qualification provision that allowed only those whose grandfathers had voted before Reconstruction to vote unless they passed a wealth or literacy test.

Great Compromise: A decision made during the Philadelphia Convention to give each state the same number of representatives in the Senate regardless of size; representation in the House was determined by population.

H

hard money: Legally specified and limited contributions that are clearly regulated by the Federal Election Campaign Act and by the Federal Election Commission.

Hatch Act: Law enacted in 1939 to prohibit civil servants from taking activist roles in partisan campaigns. This act prohibited federal employees from making political contributions, working for a particular party, or campaigning for a particular candidate.

hold: A tactic by which a senator asks to be informed before a particular bill is brought to the floor. This stops the bill from coming to the floor until the hold is removed.

I

impeachment: The power delegated to the House of Representatives in the Constitution to charge the president, vice president, or other "civil officers," including federal judges, with "Treason, Bribery, or other High Crimes and Misdemeanors." This is the first step in the constitutional process of removing such government officials from office.

implementation: The process by which a law or policy is put into operation by the bureaucracy.

implied power: A power derived from an enumerated power and the necessary and proper clause. These powers are not stated specifically but are considered to be reasonably implied through the exercise of delegated powers.

in forma pauperis: Literally, "as a pauper"; a way for an indigent or poor person to appeal a case to the U.S. Supreme Court.

inclusion: The principle that state courts will apply federal laws when those laws directly conflict with the laws of a state.

incorporation doctrine: An interpretation of the Constitution that holds that the due process clause of the Fourteenth Amendment requires that state and local governments also guarantee those rights.

incumbency: The condition of already holding elected office.

incumbency factor: The fact that being in office helps a person stay in office because of a variety of benefits that go with the position.

independent executive agencies: Governmental units that closely resemble a Cabinet department but have a narrower area of responsibility (such as the Central Intelligence Agency) and are not part of any Cabinet department.

independent regulatory commission: An agency created by Congress that is generally concerned with a specific aspect of the economy.

indirect initiative: A process in which the legislature places a proposal on a ballot and allows voters to enact it into law, without involving the governor or further action by the legislature.

indirect (representative) democracy: A system of government that gives citizens the opportunity to vote for representatives who will work on their behalf.

inherent powers: Powers of the president that can be derived or inferred from specific powers in the Constitution.

initiative: A process that allows citizens to propose legislation and submit it to the state electorate for popular vote.

inoculation ad: Advertising that attempts to counteract an anticipated attack from the opposition before the attack is launched.

interagency councils: Working groups created to facilitate coordination of policy making and implementation across a host of governmental agencies.

interest group: An organized group that tries to influence public policy.

intergovernmental lobby: The pressure group or groups that are created when state and local governments hire lobbyists to lobby the national government.

interstate compacts: Contracts between states that carry the force of law; generally now used as a tool to address multistate policy concerns.

iron triangles: The relatively stable relationships and patterns of interaction that occur among an agency, interest groups, and congressional committees or subcommittees.

issue networks: The loose and informal relationships that exist among a large number of actors who work in broad policy areas.

issue-oriented politics: Politics that focuses on specific issues rather than on party, candidate, or other loyalties.

J

Jim Crow laws: Laws enacted by southern states that discriminated against blacks by creating "whites only" schools, theaters, hotels, and other public accommodations.

judicial activism: A philosophy of judicial decision making that argues judges should use their power broadly to further justice, especially in the areas of equality and personal liberty.

judicial implementation: Refers to how and whether judicial decisions are translated into actual public policies affecting more than the immediate parties to a lawsuit.

judicial restraint: A philosophy of judicial decision making that argues courts should allow the decisions of other branches of government to stand, even when they offend a judge's own sense of principles.

judicial review: Power of the courts to review acts of other branches of government and the states.

Judiciary Act of 1789: Established the basic three-tiered structure of the federal court system.

jurisdiction: Authority vested in a particular court to hear and decide the issues in any particular case.

L

legislative courts: Courts established by Congress for specialized purposes, such as the Court of Military Appeals.

legislative veto: A procedure by which one or both houses of Congress can disallow an act of the president or executive agency by a simple majority vote; ruled unconstitutional by the Supreme Court.

libel: False written statements or written statements tending to call someone's reputation into disrepute.

liberal: One considered to favor extensive governmental involvement in the economy and the provision of social services and to take an activist role in protecting the rights of women, the elderly, minorities, and the environment.

libertarian: One who favors a free market economy and no governmental interference in personal liberties.

line-item veto: The authority of a chief executive to delete part of a bill passed by the legislature that involves taxing and/or spending. The legislature may override a veto, usually with a two-thirds majority of each chamber.

lobbying: The activities of a group or organization that seeks to influence legislation and persuade political leaders to support the group's position.

lobbyist: Interest group representative who seeks to influence legislation that will benefit his or her organization through political persuasion.

Louisiana Purchase: The 1803 land purchase authorized by President Thomas Jefferson, which expanded the size of the United States dramatically.

M

machine: A party organization that recruits its members with tangible incentives and is characterized by a high degree of control over member activity.

majority leader: The elected leader of the party controlling the most seats in the House of Representatives or the Senate; is second in authority to the speaker of the House and in the Senate is regarded as its most powerful member.

majority party: The political party in each house of Congress with the most members.

majority rule: The central premise of direct democracy in which only policies that collectively garner the support of a majority of voters will be made into law.

manager: A professional executive hired by a city council or county board to manage daily operations and to recommend policy changes.

mandate: A command, indicated by an electorate's votes, for the elected officials to carry out their platforms.

mandates: National laws that direct states or local governments to comply with federal rules or regulations (such as clean air or water standards) under threat of civil or criminal penalties or as a condition of receipt of any federal grants.

Marbury v. Madison (1803): Supreme Court first asserted the power of judicial review in finding that the congressional statute extending the Court's original jurisdiction was unconstitutional.

margin of error: A measure of the accuracy of a public opinion poll.

matching funds: Donations to presidential campaigns from the federal government that are determined by the amount of private funds a qualifying candidate raises.

mayor: Chief elected executive of a city.

McCulloch v. Maryland (1819): The Supreme Court upheld the power of the national government and denied the right of a state to tax the bank. The Court's broad interpretation of the necessary and proper clause paved the way for later rulings upholding expansive federal powers.

media campaign: That part of a political campaign waged in the broadcast and print media.

media consultant: A professional who produces political candidates' television, radio, and print advertisements.

media effects: The influence of news sources on public opinion.

mercantile system: A system that binds trade and its administration to the national government.

merit system: The system by which federal civil service jobs are classified into grades or levels, to which appointments are made on the basis of performance on competitive examinations.

midterm election: Election that takes place in the middle of a presidential term.

minority leader: The elected leader of the party with the second highest number of elected representatives in the House of Representatives or the Senate.

minority party: The political party in each house of Congress with the second most members.

Miranda rights: Statements that must be made by the police informing a suspect of his

or her constitutional rights protected by the Fifth Amendment, including the right to an attorney provided by the court if the suspect cannot afford one.

Miranda v. Arizona (1966): A landmark Supreme Court ruling that held the Fifth Amendment requires that individuals arrested for a crime must be advised of their right to remain silent and to have counsel present.

Missouri (Merit) Plan: A method of selecting judges in which a governor must appoint someone from a list provided by an independent panel. Judges are then kept in office if they get a majority of "yes" votes in general elections.

monarchy: A form of government in which power is vested in hereditary kings and queens.

muckraking: A form of newspaper publishing, in vogue in the early twentieth century, concerned with reforming government and business conduct.

municipality: A government with general responsibilities, such as a city, town, or village government, that is created in response to the emergence of relatively densely populated areas.

N

national convention: A party conclave (meeting) held in the presidential election year for the purposes of nominating a presidential and vice presidential ticket and adopting a platform.

national party platform: A statement of the general and specific philosophy and policy goals of a political party, usually promulgated at the national convention.

natural law: A doctrine that society should be governed by certain ethical principles that are part of nature and, as such, can be understood by reason.

necessary and proper clause: The final paragraph of Article I, section 8, of the U.S. Constitution, which gives Congress the authority to pass all laws "necessary and proper" to carry out the enumerated powers specified in the Constitution; also called the "elastic" clause.

negative ad: Advertising on behalf of a candidate that attacks the opponent's platform or character.

network: An association of broadcast stations (radio or television) that share programming through a financial arrangement.

New Deal: The name given to the program of "Relief, Recovery, Reform" begun by President Franklin D. Roosevelt in 1933 designed to bring the United States out of the Great Depression.

New Jersey Plan: A framework for the Constitution proposed by a group of small states; its key points were a one-house legislature with one vote for each state, a multiperson "executive," the establishment of the acts of

Congress as the "supreme law" of the land, and a supreme judiciary with limited power.

New York Times Co. v. Sullivan (1964): The Supreme Court concluded that "actual malice" must be proved to support a finding of libel against a public figure.

Nineteenth Amendment: Amendment to the Constitution that guaranteed women the right to vote.

Ninth Amendment: Part of the Bill of Rights that reads "The enumeration in the Constitution, of certain rights, shall not be construed to deny or disparage others retained by the people."

nomination campaign: That part of a political campaign aimed at winning a primary election.

nonpartisan election: A contest in which candidates run without formal identification or association with a political party.

nonpartisan primary: A primary used to select candidates regardless of party affiliation.

O

off the record: Term applied to information gathered for a news story that cannot be used at all.

off-year election: Election that takes place in the middle of a presidential term.

oligarchy: A form of government in which the right to participate is always conditioned on the possession of wealth, social status, military position, or achievement.

on background: A term for when sources are not specifically named in a news story.

on the record: Term applied to information gathered for a news story that can be used and cited.

one-partyism: A political system in which one party dominates and wins virtually all contests.

one-person, one-vote: The principle that each legislative district within a state should have the same number of eligible voters so that representation is equitably based on population.

open primary: A primary in which party members, independents, and sometimes members of the other party are allowed to vote.

organizational campaign: That part of a political campaign involved in fund-raising, literature distribution, and all other activities not directly involving the candidate.

organizational party: The workers and activists who staff the party's formal organization.

original jurisdiction: The jurisdiction of courts that hear a case first, usually in a trial. Courts determine the facts of a case under their original jurisdiction.

oversight: Congressional review of the activities of an agency, department, or office.

P

package or general veto: The authority of a chief executive to void an entire bill that has been passed by the legislature. This veto applies to all bills, whether or not they have taxing or spending components, and the legislature may override this veto, usually with a two-thirds majority of each chamber.

paid media: Political advertisements purchased for a candidate's campaign.

pardon: An executive grant providing restoration of all rights and privileges of citizenship to a specific individual charged or convicted of a crime.

parole: The authority of a governor to release a prisoner before his or her full sentence has been completed and to specify conditions that must be met as part of the release.

party caucus or conference: A formal gathering of all party members.

party identification: A citizen's personal affinity for a political party, usually expressed by his or her tendency to vote for the candidates of that party.

party in the electorate: The voters who consider themselves allied or associated with the party.

party realignment: A shifting of party coalition groupings in the electorate that remains in place for several elections.

patrons: Persons who finance a group or individual activity.

patronage: Jobs, grants, or other special favors that are given as rewards to friends and political allies for their support.

Pendleton Act: Reform measure that created the Civil Service Commission to administer a partial merit system. The act classified the federal service by grades, to which appointments were made based on the results of a competitive examination. It made it illegal for federal political appointees to be required to contribute to a particular political party.

personal campaign: That part of a political campaign concerned with presenting the candidate's public image.

personal liberty: A key characteristic of U.S. democracy. Initially meaning freedom from governmental interference, today it includes demands for freedom to engage in a variety of practices free from governmental discrimination.

Plessy v. Ferguson (1896): Plessy challenged a Louisiana statute requiring that railroads provide separate accommodations for blacks and whites. The Court found that separate but equal accommodations did not violate the equal protection clause of the Fourteenth Amendment.

pocket veto: If Congress adjourns during the ten days the president has to consider a bill

passed by both houses of Congress, without the president's signature, the bill is considered vetoed.

political action committee (PAC): Federally mandated, officially registered fund-raising committee that represents interest groups in the political process.

political consultant: Professional who manages campaigns and political advertisements for political candidates.

political culture: Attitudes toward the political system and its various parts, and attitudes toward the role of the self in the system.

political ideology: An individual's coherent set of values and beliefs about the purpose and scope of government.

political machine: An organization designed to solicit votes from certain neighborhoods or communities for a particular political party in return for services and jobs if that party wins.

political party: A group of office holders, candidates, activists, and voters who identify with a group label and seek to elect to public office individuals who run under that label.

political socialization: The process through which an individual acquires particular political orientations; the learning process by which people acquire their political beliefs and values.

politico: Role played by elected representatives who act as trustees or as delegates, depending on the issue.

politics: The process by which policy decisions are made.

pollster: A professional who takes public opinion surveys that guide political campaigns.

popular consent: The idea that governments must draw their powers from the consent of the governed.

popular sovereignty: The right of the majority to govern themselves.

pork barrel: Legislation that allows representatives to "bring home the bacon" to their districts in the form of public works programs, military bases, or other programs designed to benefit their districts directly.

positive ad: Advertising on behalf of a candidate that stresses the candidate's qualifications, family, and issue positions, without reference to the opponent.

precedent: Prior judicial decision that serves as a rule for settling subsequent cases of a similar nature.

preemption: A concept derived from the Constitution's supremacy clause that allows the national government to override or preempt state or local actions in certain areas.

presidentialist: One who believes that Article II's grant of executive power is a broad grant of authority allowing a president wide discretionary powers.

press briefing: A relatively restricted session between a press secretary or aide and the press.

press conference: An unrestricted session between an elected official and the press.

press release: A document offering an official comment or position.

primary election: Election in which voters decide which of the candidates within a party will represent the party in the general election.

print press: The traditional form of mass media, comprising newspapers, magazines, and journals.

prior restraint: Constitutional doctrine that prevents the government from prohibiting speech or publication before the fact; generally held to be in violation of the First Amendment.

Progressive movement: Advocated measures to destroy political machines and instead have direct participation by voters in the nomination of candidates and the establishment of public policy.

progressive tax: The level of tax increases with the wealth or ability of an individual or business to pay.

proportional representation: A voting system that apportions legislative seats according to the percentage of the vote won by a particular political party.

prospective judgment: A voter's evaluation of a candidate based on what he or she pledges to do about an issue if elected.

public corporation (authority): Government organization established to provide a particular service or to run a particular facility that is independent of other city or state agencies and supposed to be operated like a business. Examples include a port authority or a mass transit system.

public funds: Donations from the general tax revenues to the campaigns of qualifying presidential candidates.

public interest group: An organization that seeks a collective good that will not selectively and materially benefit the members of the group.

public opinion: What the public thinks about a particular issue or set of issues at any point in time.

public opinion polls: Interviews or surveys with samples of citizens that are used to estimate the feelings and beliefs of the entire population.

push polls: "Polls" taken for the purpose of providing information on an opponent that would lead respondents to vote against that candidate.

R

raiding: An organized attempt by voters of one party to influence the primary results of the other party.

random sampling: A method of poll selection that gives each person in a group the same chance of being selected.

recall: Removal of an incumbent from office by popular vote.

redistricting: The redrawing of congressional districts to reflect increases or decreases in seats allotted to the states, as well as population shifts within a state.

referendum: A procedure whereby the state legislature submits proposed legislation to the state's voters for approval.

regional primary: A proposed system in which the country would be divided into five or six geographic areas and all states in each region would hold their presidential primary elections on the same day.

regressive tax: The level of tax increases as the wealth or ability of an individual or business to pay decreases.

regulations: Rules that govern the operation of a particular government program that have the force of law.

republic: A government rooted in the consent of the governed; a representative or indirect democracy.

reserve (or police) powers: Powers reserved to the states by the Tenth Amendment that lie at the foundation of a state's right to legislate for the public health and welfare of its citizens.

reservation land: Land designated in a treaty that is under the authority of an Indian nation and is exempt from most state laws and taxes.

restrictive constitution: Constitution that incorporates detailed provisions in order to limit the powers of government.

retrospective judgment: A voter's evaluation of the performance of the party in power.

right-of-rebuttal rule: A Federal Communications Commission regulation that people attacked on a radio or television broadcast be offered the opportunity to respond.

right to privacy: The right to be left alone; a judicially created doctrine encompassing an individual's decision to use birth control or secure an abortion.

***Roe v. Wade* (1973):** The Supreme Court found that a woman's right to an abortion was protected by the right to privacy that could be implied from specific guarantees found in the Bill of Rights applied to the states through the Fourteenth Amendment.

rule making: A quasi-legislative administrative process that has the characteristics of a legislative act.

Rule of Four: At least four justices of the Supreme Court must vote to consider a case before it can be heard.

runoff primary: A second primary election between the two candidates receiving the greatest number of votes in the first primary.

S

sampling error or margin of error: A measure of the accuracy of a public opinion poll.

Second Continental Congress: Meeting that convened in Philadelphia on May 10, 1775, at which it was decided that an army should be raised and George Washington of Virginia was named commander in chief.

secular realignment: The gradual rearrangement of party coalitions, based more on demographic shifts than on shocks to the political system.

segregated funds: Money that comes in from a certain tax or fee and then is restricted to a specific use, such as a gasoline tax that is used for road maintenance.

selective incorporation: A judicial doctrine whereby most but not all of the protections found in the Bill of Rights are made applicable to the states via the Fourteenth Amendment.

senatorial courtesy: A process by which presidents, when selecting district court judges, defer to the senator in whose state the vacancy occurs.

separation of powers: A way of dividing power among three branches of government in which members of the House of Representatives, members of the Senate, the president, and the federal courts are selected by and responsible to different constituencies.

Seventeenth Amendment: Made senators directly elected by the people; removed their selection from state legislatures.

Shays's Rebellion: A 1786 rebellion in which an army of 1,500 disgruntled and angry farmers led by Daniel Shays marched to Springfield, Massachusetts, and forcibly restrained the state court from foreclosing mortgages on their farms.

Sixteenth Amendment: Authorized Congress to enact a national income tax.

Sixth Amendment: Part of the Bill of Rights that sets out the basic requirements of procedural due process for federal courts to follow in criminal trials. These include speedy and public trials, impartial juries, trials in the state where crime was committed, notice of the charges, the right to confront and obtain favorable witnesses, and the right to counsel.

slander: Untrue spoken statements that defame the character of a person.

social capital: The myriad relationships that individuals enjoy that facilitate the resolution of community problems through collective action.

social contract theory: The belief that people are free and equal by God-given right and that this in turn requires that all people give their consent to be governed; espoused by John Locke and influential in the writing of the Declaration of Independence.

socialism: An economic system that advocates for collective ownership and control of the means of production.

soft money: The virtually unregulated money funneled by individuals and political committees through state and local parties.

solicitor general: The fourth-ranking member of the Department of Justice; responsible for handling all appeals on behalf of the U.S. government to the Supreme Court.

sovereign immunity: The right of a state to be free from lawsuit unless it gives permission to the suit. Under the Eleventh Amendment, all states are considered sovereign.

speaker of the House: The only officer of the House of Representatives specifically mentioned in the Constitution; elected at the beginning of each new Congress by the entire House; traditionally a member of the majority party.

special district: A local government that is responsible for a particular function, such as K–12 education, water, sewerage, or parks.

spoils system: The firing of public-office holders of a defeated political party and their replacement with loyalists of the newly elected party.

spot ad: Television advertising on behalf of a candidate that is broadcast in sixty-, thirty-, or ten-second duration.

Stamp Act Congress: Meeting of representatives of nine of the thirteen colonies held in New York City in 1765, during which representatives drafted a document to send to the king listing how their rights had been violated.

standing committee: Committee to which proposed bills are referred.

stare decisis: In court rulings, a reliance on past decisions or precedents to formulate decisions in new cases.

state constitution: The document that describes the basic policies, procedures, and institutions of the government of a specific state, much as the U.S. Constitution does for the federal government.

stewardship theory: The theory that holds that Article II confers on the president the power *and* the duty to take whatever actions are deemed necessary in the national interest, unless prohibited by the Constitution or by law.

stratified sampling: A variation of random sampling; Census data are used to divide a country into four sampling regions. Sets of counties and standard metropolitan statistical areas are then randomly selected in proportion to the total national population.

straw polls: Unscientific surveys used to gauge public opinion on a variety of issues and policies.

strict constructionist: An approach to constitutional interpretation that emphasizes the Framers' original intentions.

strict scrutiny: A heightened standard of review used by the Supreme Court to determine the constitutional validity of a challenged practice.

substantive due process: Judicial interpretation of the Fifth and Fourteenth Amendments' due process clause that protects citizens from arbitrary or unjust laws.

suffrage movement: The drive for voting rights for women that took place in the United States from 1890 to 1920.

sunset law: A law that sets a date for a program or regulation to expire unless reauthorized by the legislature.

sunshine law: Legislation that requires government meetings and records to be open to the public.

superdelegate: Delegate slot to the Democratic Party's national convention that is reserved for an elected party official.

supremacy clause: Portion of Article VI of the U.S. Constitution that mandates that national law is supreme to (that is, supercedes) all other laws passed by the states or by any other subdivision of government.

suspect classification: Category or class, such as race, that triggers the highest standard of scrutiny from the Supreme Court.

symbolic speech: Symbols, signs, and other methods of expression generally also considered to be protected by the First Amendment.

T

Taftian theory: The theory that holds that the president is limited by the specific grants of executive power found in the Constitution.

Tenth Amendment: The final part of the Bill of Rights that defines the basic principle of American federalism in stating "The powers not delegated to the United States by the Constitution, nor prohibited by it to the States, are reserved to the States respectively, or to the people".

third-partyism: The tendency of third parties to arise with some regularity in a nominally two-party system.

Thirteenth Amendment: One of the three Civil War amendments; specifically bans slavery in the United States.

Three-Fifths Compromise: Agreement reached at the Constitutional Convention stipulating that each slave was to be counted as three-fifths of a person for purposes of determining population for representation in the U.S. House of Representatives.

ticket-split: To vote for candidates of different parties for various offices in the same election.

ticket-splitting: Voting for candidates of different parties for various offices in the same election.

Title IX: Provision of the Educational Amendments of 1972 that bars educational institutions receiving federal funds from discriminating against female students.

totalitarianism: An economic system in which the government has total control over the economy.

town meeting: Form of local government in which all eligible voters are invited to attend a meeting at which budgets and ordinances are proposed and voted on.

tracking polls: Continuous surveys that enable a campaign to chart its daily rise or fall in support.

trade associations: Groups that represent specific industries.

trial court: Court of original jurisdiction where a case begins.

trust land: Land owned by an Indian nation and designated by the federal Bureau of Indian Affairs as exempt from most state laws and taxes.

trust relationship: The legal obligation of the United States federal government to protect the interests of Indian tribes.

trustee: Role played by elected representatives who listen to constituents' opinions and then use their best judgment to make final decisions.

turnout: The proportion of the voting-age public that votes.

Twenty-Fifth Amendment: Adopted in 1967 to establish procedures for filling vacancies in the office of president and vice president as well as providing for procedures to deal with the disability of a president.

Twenty-Second Amendment: Adopted in 1951, prevents a president from serving more than two terms or more than ten years in office.

U

unit rule: A traditional party practice under which the majority of a state delegation can force the minority to vote for its candidate.

U.S. v. Nixon (1974): The Supreme Court ruled that there is no constitutional absolute executive privilege that would allow a president to refuse to comply with a court order to produce information needed in a criminal trial.

V

veto power: The formal, constitutional authority of the president to reject bills passed by both houses of Congress, thus preventing their becoming law without further congressional action.

Virginia Plan: The first general plan for the Constitution, proposed by James Madison. Its key points were a bicameral legislature, an executive chosen by the legislature, and a judiciary also named by the legislature.

voter canvass: The process by which a campaign gets in touch with individual voters, either by door-to-door solicitation or by telephone.

W

War Powers Act: Passed by Congress in 1973; the president is limited in the deployment of troops overseas to a sixty-day period in peacetime (which can be extended for an extra thirty days to permit withdrawal) unless Congress explicitly gives its approval for a longer period.

whip: One of several representatives who keep close contact with all members and take "nose counts" on key votes, prepare summaries of bills, and in general act as communications links within the party.

wire service: An electronic delivery of news gathered by the news service's correspondents and sent to all member news media organizations.

writ of *certiorari*: A request for the Court to order up the records from a lower court to review the case.

Y

yellow journalism: A form of newspaper publishing in vogue in the late-nineteenth century that featured pictures, comics, color, and sensationalized, oversimplified news coverage.

HOW IT HAPPENED!

The 2004 Race for the White House as reported in *The New York Times*

Edited by Quentin Kidd, Christopher Newport University

INTRODUCTION

After the debacle of the 2000 presidential election, Americans were understandably anxious about the 2004 presidential election. Perhaps at no time in the history of the United States had so many people been so worried about the outcome of an election, so ready to fight for their candidate, and so hoping that everything would just go smoothly. And in the end, everything did go more or less smoothly. We actually knew who the next president would be within 20 hours of most polls closing.

The goal of this reader is to give students of American politics a long view on the 2004 presidential election. In particular, this reader seeks to explore one fundamental question about the election: how did it happen? We explore this question by following the coverage in *The New York Times* from the early primary contests between the Democratic hopefuls to the victory speech of President George W. Bush.

Why *The New York Times*? Because it is arguably the nation's foremost newspaper: it is the nation's newspaper of record. What does it mean to be a newspaper of record? It means that *The New York Times* is looked to as the newspaper that reports on events important to the nation, and it has been chronicling the ebbs and flows, the important stories, the tragedies and triumphs of America since 1851.

This reader is divided into three parts: The Primaries, The Conventions, and The Horse Race. Each part represents a distinct phase of the race for the White House. The primaries represent that phase of the election process where party activists and candidates' supporters battle it out over who will be their party's candidate for president. At this time the two major political parties are also sizing each other up and looking over their shoulders to see whether any third party candidates are lurking in the shadows ready to cause problems for them. The conventions are where each party officially nominates its candidate, and that candidate officially accepts the party's nomination. Rarely anymore are there any surprises at the conventions, so the parties and candidates generally start aiming their criticism at each other more forcefully around convention time. The horse race is the period from Labor Day to Election Day, when the candidates sprint across the country in a furious effort to convince voters to send them to the White House.

To help you along the way, a study question follows each article, and at the end five discussion questions will help you assess the evolution of the campaign from primaries to election day. As you read each article, keep in mind the final outcome of the election and try to develop a sense of each story in the context of the whole campaign.

THE PRIMARIES

Poll Shows Candidates Failing to Move Democratic Primary Voters

By ADAM NAGOURNEY and JANET ELDER   *Published Thursday, December 18, 2003*

Three years after one of the most disputed presidential contests in the nation's history, Americans remain polarized and divided as they approach the 2004 White House election. But most voters, including most Democrats, are largely unmoved by any of the nine Democrats who are seeking to unseat President Bush, according to the latest *New York Times*/CBS News Poll.

The poll suggests that Democrats clearly have a chance next year. Forty-five percent of voters said they would probably vote for Mr. Bush, compared with 39 percent who said they would probably vote for his Democratic opponent, no matter who that is. And 38 percent say they do not believe that Mr. Bush was legitimately elected, nearly the same number who expressed that view the month after that election.

But Mr. Bush shows broad signs of strength going into the 2004 election. Voters continue to choose the Republican Party as better able to manage national security and foreign policy.

Democrats are battling a perception that they are fighting a losing battle, particularly after Saddam Hussein's capture in Iraq. In a question asked after his capture, voters said by three to one they expected Mr. Bush to win next year.

Views of the Democratic contenders remain largely unformed. Howard Dean, the former governor of Vermont, who is seen by most Democratic Party officials as the clear leader in the nomination contest, is favorably rated by one-third of Democratic primary voters. But more than half of all Democrats say they do not know enough about Dr. Dean to offer an opinion.

In a potential sign of concern for Democrats who are contemplating the prospects of a contest between Mr. Bush and Dr. Dean, one-quarter of registered voters already have an unfavorable view of Dr. Dean.

The New York Times and CBS News conducted what were in effect back-to-back polls, before and after Mr. Hussein's capture, offering an early glimpse of how the events in Iraq might affect the primary contests.

In one very rough measure, the number of voters who said they had a favorable view of Senator Joseph I. Lieberman of Connecticut, the field's strongest supporter of the military campaign in Iraq, jumped over the weekend. Mr. Lieberman was the first pro-war Democratic contender to attack Dr. Dean's antiwar position, winning him the publicity that the candidates have been struggling for in their crowded field.

Before the capture, 25 percent of likely Democratic primary voters said they had a favorable rating of Mr. Lieberman. In the second poll, the number increased, to 37 percent.

The first nationwide telephone poll, of 1,057 adults, was conducted from Dec. 10 to Dec. 13 and had a margin of sampling error of plus or minus three percentage points. The second poll, conducted from Sunday through Tuesday, involved 857 adults, including 290 self-identified Democratic primary voters. The margin of sampling error for the entire poll is plus or minus three percentage points. For Democratic voters, it is plus or minus six points.

The poll reinforced the feeling among Democratic leaders of Dr. Dean's position. He was supported by 23 percent of Democratic primary voters, followed by Mr. Lieberman and Gen. Wesley K. Clark, each with 10 percent.

The rest of the field appears to be having more than a little difficulty making inroads with Democratic voters. Representative Richard A. Gephardt of Missouri, who is mounting his second bid for president, was chosen by 6 percent of Democratic respondents. The Rev. Al Sharpton of New York had the support of 5 percent. Senator John Kerry of Massachusetts drew 4 percent, and Senator John Edwards of North Carolina was the choice of 2 percent. Representative Dennis J. Kucinich of Ohio and former Senator Carol Moseley Braun of Illinois were each the choice of 1 percent of the Democratic respondents.

Study Question:

Why were voters not particularly excited about the Democratic candidates in December 2003?

Under Attack, Kerry Appears to Build Momentum

By DAVID M. HALBFINGER *Published Sunday, January 18, 2004*

MAQUOKETA — Under attack by his rivals at long last, Senator John Kerry could not have been happier.

After spending most of 2003 reeling from his own troubles and his rivals' successes and clamoring for attention, Mr. Kerry, once considered the leading prospect for the Democratic presidential nomination, joked that he finally seemed to be getting the breaks.

"Here it is, the strategy," he said Friday, pulling a four-leaf clover from his pocket as his motor coach cruised across northeastern Iowa in what was starting to resemble a Kerry Comeback Tour. Yet luck had little to do with Mr. Kerry's apparent surge into contention.

Interviews with dozens of new Kerry supporters and still-undecided voters this week suggest that many Iowans once enchanted by Howard Dean, but alienated by a steady diet of critical reports about him, have begun to swing Mr. Kerry's way. And Mr. Kerry, the maximally accessible Massachusetts senator, has been enjoying consistently favorable coverage for the first time.

More than anything, though, what is pushing Iowans into Mr. Kerry's corner appears to be as much the way he listens to them as what he has to say. A recurring scene has the candidate planting his duck boots or brown loafers in front of a skeptical audience and taking question after question, repeatedly asking for a show of hands to see how many are undecided, and waiting as the number drops toward zero.

Wednesday night in Des Moines, as 260 people listened in a theater and 170 more watched him on a closed-circuit TV in a spillover room, he took questions for nearly two hours.

"We're staying here till the sun rises, until we get you to agree," he said. Another few minutes, and half as many hands were in the air, and the questions kept coming, the heads kept nodding, and the candidate kept feeding off the energy in the room.

Ruth Mitchell, 42, approached Mr. Kerry afterward to say that he had won her over. "I want to see someone who could converse honestly with people," she said. "I'm tired of the stump speeches. I like his ability to do the give-and-take. His answers are concise, but concrete. I'm persuaded this is not something he came up with to run for president, this is his life."

The next morning in Council Bluffs, Mr. Kerry spoke at a pancake breakfast to 250 people jammed into a basement meeting room. Linda Snyder, 54, said she had come because she thought Dr. Dean had "a lot of flash and pizazz, but I don't know if we can trust him." Yet she said she worried about Mr. Kerry's lacked of charisma. "Before, he was just yecch," she said.

Afterward, Ms. Snyder said she was worried no more and would now push her friends and neighbors to support Mr. Kerry. "I feel much more confident in his ability to take his experience and get it across to the American people," she said.

Friday in New Hampton, Mr. Kerry gave an unremarkable speech but impressed Gladys Christoph, 51. She said she initially was drawn to Dr. Dean but not when she saw him in action. "When he's asked a question, he doesn't respond to it, he gives a pat answer," she said. "That sounds cute, but it doesn't approach what the people were asking. When Kerry answers a question, he is responding to the person."

Ms. Christoph said she was now solidly for Mr. Kerry: "There's a wonderful firm presence about him that seems he could be in command, and yet he's flexible."

For months, Mr. Kerry's advisers watched as, each time Dr. Dean encountered trouble, something occurred to change the subject. "There was a time when Howard Dean said crazier and crazier stuff, and kept getting more popular," one aide said.

But Mr. Kerry has been making his own luck this week. On Sunday, he took an unexpected phone call from Christie Vilsack, Iowa's first lady, offering her support; she is now appearing in commercials for him. On Wednesday, the state agriculture secretary endorsed him.

Those surrogates were campaigning for Mr. Kerry over the weekend, as were former Senators Bob Kerrey, Max Cleland and Gary Hart; the actor Scott Wolf and the band Blink-182, to court the youth vote; and the senator's wife, Teresa Heinz Kerry, and daughter, Vanessa, to woo women voters. Nearly every Massachusetts congressman has fanned out across the state, and Senator Edward M. Kennedy is to be in Iowa on Sunday and Monday.

While Mr. Kerry has said all along he was optimistic about his chances, he is showing it now. "I believe in this candidacy," he said Friday. "I believe in this candidate, I believe in myself, in what I can offer as leadership to the country. There's nothing made up here. This is real. This is me, 35 years of me, that I think is ready to lead."

Late Friday, after rallying about 300 students at Clarke College in Dubuque, about 30 miles north of here, he spoke to his precinct captains there. He told them to ignore the polls. "There's great capacity for people going to the caucus to surprise you," he said, unaware reporters were listening. "We have to keep on being the surprise."

Study Question:

Why did Iowans appear to be moving into Kerry's camp?

Massachusetts Senator Gets Lift for the Race in New Hampshire

By ADAM NAGOURNEY *Published Tuesday, January 20, 2004*

DES MOINES — Senator John Kerry of Massachusetts won the Iowa caucuses here tonight, brushing aside the insurgent candidacy of Howard Dean with an appeal that he would be the strongest candidate the Democrats had to beat President Bush.

Senator John Edwards of North Carolina came in second, catapulting him into the first tier of contenders in a showing that ended up pushing Dr. Dean into third place.

Representative Richard A. Gephardt of Missouri finished fourth, a devastating showing. Mr. Gephardt's aides said tonight that he was flying not to New Hampshire, where he had been scheduled to hold a "Countdown to Victory Kick Off Rally in Manchester," and was instead heading home to St. Louis.

In his remarks to supporters tonight, Mr. Gephardt indicated he would quit the race and support the eventual winner.

"My campaign to fight for working people may be ending tonight, but our fight will never end," he said, his voice quavering at points. He said he would vigorously support the Democratic nominee.

"We will reclaim the White House in 2004 because we have to," he said.

With 98 percent of the precincts reporting, Mr. Kerry had nearly 38 percent of the delegate support awarded in the caucuses, Mr. Edwards 32 percent, Dr. Dean 18 percent, Mr. Gephardt 10.5 percent and Dennis Kucinich 1 percent. More than 120,00 people participated, nearly equaling the record of 125,000 reported for the 1988 caucuses a number party officials believe was inflated. Democratic officials had hoped to produce a strong turnout above 100,000 to demonstrate that Iowa should continue to host the first presidential nominating event.

At a victory rally, Mr. Kerry was introduced by his fellow Massachusetts Democrat, Senator Edward M. Kennedy. Fighting laryngitis, Mr. Kerry told a cheering crowd, "Iowa, I love you."

He called himself "The Comeback Kerry" in reference to his recent surge in the state, and vowed to take on President Bush "and the special interests, and literally give America back its future and its soul."

The victory by Mr. Kerry would seem to validate the thoroughly unconventional campaign tack he took: to come to Iowa to replenish a candidacy that had been languishing in New Hampshire, and use an unexpected victory to power him back to life in his neighboring state. By every measure, his showing here gave him a huge lift as he headed back to New Hampshire to confront the candidacy of Gen. Wesley K. Clark, who skipped the Iowa contest.

The day also delivered a huge and unexpected victory for Mr. Edwards, who seemed delighted if a bit surprised by the outcome tonight.

"My message is finally coming through," he said. "In the end, the caucusgoers heard it. That's the reason for this momentum and this surprise."

The result was a serious setback for Dr. Dean, who had campaigned intensely across this state for more than a year. It was a clear disappointment to a candidate who just a week ago was confident of victory here and in New Hampshire. Surveys of voters entering the caucus sites suggested that what was Dr. Dean's central appeal — his opposition to the war — had done him little good tonight.

Instead, the issue that Democratic voters here and in New Hampshire repeatedly said was a top priority — finding a candidate who could beat President Bush — weighed heavily upon them, to Dr. Dean's disadvantage. Among the more than a quarter of voters who called electability their top priority, Mr. Kerry won by a ratio of almost two to one.

Trying to put the best face on his finish, Dr. Dean told a gathering of cheering supporters tonight, "If you had told us one year ago that we would finish third, we would have been delighted with that." With the sleeves rolled up on his blue shirt, Dr. Dean rattled off the names of the states he would proceed on to in his fight for the nomination.

"I have called Senator Kerry and Senator Edwards and congratulated them, and told them we would see them around the corner, starting tomorrow morning," he said.

His stance left little doubt about where this battle is about to turn: to the state with the first direct voter primary, New Hampshire, on Jan. 27.

"I'm looking forward to the primary," Dr. Dean said. "It's a new day, a new state."

Iowans who voted in the caucuses were far more likely to cite health care and the economy than the war in Iraq as their most pressing concerns in this election, even after a year in which the war in Iraq significantly shaped the Democratic presidential contest, according to a survey of voters entering caucus sites.

The survey found that the caucuses, the most competitive Democratic contest this state has had in at least 16 years, produced a spike of new interest, with about half of caucusgoers saying they were attending their first caucus. At the same time, the survey confirmed what voters here and in New Hampshire have repeatedly said from the start of the year: That defeating President Bush was a top priority for Democratic voters this year.

More than a quarter described it as the key consideration in casting their votes. Three in 10 said the decisions were based on the candidates' taking strong stands on issues.

In a sign of how the climate here has changed over the last six months, barely 15 percent said the war in Iraq had shaped their final decision, even though 75 percent said they opposed the war. Dr. Dean, the former governor of Vermont, emerged as a major contender here in large part by opposing the war in Iraq, drawing a sharp contrast with three opponents who voted for the war while in Congress: Mr. Gephardt, Mr. Kerry and Mr. Edwards.

Dr. Dean won barely half the support of voters who called the war in Iraq their top priority. And opponents of the war split almost evenly between Dr. Dean and Mr. Kerry, who voted for the Iraqi resolution in Congress, a position for which he was repeatedly lambasted here during this campaign.

The survey also suggested that the central theme of Mr. Gephardt's appeal — pledging to fight against overly liberal trade agreements — did not fare well. Barely five percent of voters named that as their top issue; and he won the support of just one-third of union households.

Among elderly voters, a key contingent in Iowa, and another target of Mr. Gephardt, Mr. Kerry won the support of about one-third, compared to about one-quarter for Mr. Gephardt. The elderly made up one-third of the electorate.

The survey also reflected the extent to which the election shifted in the final week: almost half of Mr. Kerry's supporters and half of Mr. Edwards' supporters said they decided to support them in the last week. By contrast, just a third of Dr. Dean's supporters made their decision in the final days of the campaign, suggesting the extent to which Mr. Edwards and Mr. Kerry won the undecided vote.

The survey was conducted by Edison/Mitofsky for the National Election Pool of the networks and The Associated Press with 1,064 participants as they arrived tonight for the caucuses in 50 precincts throughout the state. The margin of sampling error is plus or minus 4 percentage points.

As the caucuses opened, some of the sites were packed, with some voters saying they had not quite made up their minds about what to do, reflecting what many Democrats have said was the extraordinary volatility of this contest.

In Waukee, a Des Moines suburb, Terry Meyer, a retired computer systems analyst, said as he walked into his caucus site that he was leaning toward Mr. Kerry, that he thought Mr. Kerry had the best chance of defeating President Bush.

"Really, the man whose ideas I really like and who I was torn between is Kucinich," he said. "But now that he's not really so much of a factor, I think I might go over to Kerry."

"I just think that Kerry has more experience and the better chance," he said.

In Indianola, Larry Buttrey, 62, a retired machinist, said he was leaning toward Mr. Edwards, citing the very thing that Mr. Edwards had emphasized to differentiate himself: that he was trying to avoid attacking his opponents.

"He's the only one I heard so far who hasn't blasted the other candidates," Mr. Buttrey said. "I don't want to hear what the other guy's doing. I want to hear what you're going to do."

With the Iowa voting completed, the candidates move into an exhausting sprint of primaries and caucuses that party officials say should determine a nominee by the beginning of March. It starts with the vote in New Hampshire next Tuesday and continues the following Tuesday, when there are contests in seven states.

And the nomination battle is about to effectively gain two more contestants: General Clark and Senator Joseph I. Lieberman of Connecticut. Both men skipped the Iowa caucuses, instead spending time in New Hampshire.

General Clark, who earlier this month said that the Democratic primary was "a two-person race" between himself and Dr. Dean, responded to Mr. Kerry's victory tonight by saying, "I don't know what to call it now."

"It's up to the voters to decide how many people are in the race," General Clark said.

But General Clark immediately began to try to draw contrasts between his own campaign and that of Senator Kerry, as well as between their respective experiences in the military and since leaving the military. Mr. Kerry's campaign has been one of the most aggressive in attacking General Clark's credentials as a Democrat and his experience, something that General Clark has consistently referred to as "old-style politics."

"I'm not a politician," he added. "I'm a person who spent his life in public service and leadership. So I'm not playing old-style politics on this."

With the caucuses starting at 6:30 p.m., the campaigning went on until the last minute. The candidates traveled across the state, restating the appeals that got them here, urging voters to turn out and stopping off to attend celebrations marking Martin Luther King's Birthday.

Campaign headquarters here were bustling with energy and tension, as the campaigns began executing the plans they had put into place long ago to turn out their voters.

"Go out and get more votes, we need to win this place," Joe Trippi, Dr. Dean's campaign manager, said to a volunteer as he bounded out the door of campaign headquarters. Dr. Dean's headquarters was elbow-room-only: a blur of orange, yellow and red caps. The color of the cap signified the rank of the worker.

As the 6:30 hour approached, volunteers at Dr. Dean's headquarters, many of whom had flown in from out of the state to help out, were as-signed to work the telephones, knock once more on doors and drive voters to caucus sites.

Study Question:

Why did Senator Kerry call himself "The Comeback Kerry"?

The President Makes Danger His Campaign Theme

By ELISABETH BUMILLER   *Published Sunday, January 25, 2004*

WASHINGTON — There was something familiar in the language that President Bush used in his State of the Union speech Tuesday when he asked Americans to stay with him through the journey that began on the morning of Sept. 11, 2001. "We've not come all this way through tragedy and trial and war only to falter and leave our work unfinished," Mr. Bush said, in words that bore the strong imprint of his chief speechwriter, Michael Gerson, an evangelical Christian.

Some listeners detected an allusion to a passage in "Amazing Grace," the hymn written by a slave trader turned minister and abolitionist, John Newton, after he survived an Atlantic storm: Through many dangers, toils and snares, I have already come; 'Tis grace has brought me safe thus far, and grace will lead me home.

Newton was referring in the last two lines to his salvation by God, a sentiment often echoed by the president. But in this speech, which served as the opening shot of Mr. Bush's 2004 campaign, the real message was there if listeners substituted the name "Bush" for "grace."

In short, Mr. Bush was holding himself out as the candidate who can best protect the nation from the evils of a post-9/11 world. Many Democrats call it the politics of fear; Republicans call it reality.

Whatever the terminology, Mr. Bush has never before so bluntly told voters that the choice was between him and "the dangerous illusion" (read Democrats) that the threat had passed. Members of both parties say that running on national security may well guarantee Mr. Bush a second term. The White House is betting the election on it.

This is hardly news to the Democrats, who have never said the fear is not real. The candidacy of Gen. Wesley K. Clark, the commander of the Kosovo bombing campaign, was driven in large part by Democrats nervous about the national security credentials of the antiwar Howard Dean; John Kerry began to surge after a soldier whose life he saved in Vietnam turned up in Iowa. The Democrats tried to make the economy the issue in the 2002 midterm elections, but Mr. Bush led the Republicans to gains by vowing to hunt the killers down "one by one" and charging the Democrats with holding up the creation of the Department of Homeland Security.

The State of the Union speech took the strategy to new heights. "This was a remarkably candid acknowledgment of how much he intends to exploit the political value of his posture as the only effective warrior in the war against terror," said David M. Kennedy, a professor of history at Stanford. "It's a very strong card, and may well prove to be a trump card."

Historically, Americans have not voted out the commander in chief in the middle of war, which helps explain, Democrats say, why Mr. Bush used the grand stage of the State of the Union speech to underline the threat. ("And it is tempting to believe that the danger is behind us. That hope is understandable, comforting and false.") It is also why the president traced the two-year narrative of a war on terror and then rebutted those who questioned, as he put it, "if America is really in a war."

Historians say that Franklin D. Roosevelt would probably not have won a third term in 1940 had there not been the crisis in Europe and Hitler's invasion of France that June. "There were forces on the right who didn't like anything about the New Deal, he had not brought about economic recovery and a lot of people thought he had too much power," Mr. Kennedy said. "There's very little question he owes his third term, and his fourth as well, to the international crisis."

Similarly, in the Civil War election of 1864, Abraham Lincoln survived a challenge by George B. McClellan, the Democratic nominee and the general Lincoln had fired the year before. But it might have been otherwise had not General Sherman captured Atlanta two months before the election, turning Lincoln's fortunes around after a summer of devastating casualties. "Lincoln was elected on a tide of military success," said James

M. McPherson, the Civil War historian. "But Lincoln and everybody else acknowledged that if the election had been held in August, it would have gone the other way."

Of course, unpopular wars have driven some presidents from office, like Lyndon B. Johnson, who chose not to run for re-election in 1968 because of his vulnerabilities over Vietnam. Harry S. Truman was so unpopular in 1952 because of the stalemate in Korea that he might not have won his party's nomination.

It is no surprise that the biggest fear of the current White House, short of another terrorist attack, is that Iraq will implode before the election. Barring that, political analysts say Mr. Bush is wise to wield his most powerful advantage against the opposition. In a *New York Times*/CBS News poll conducted just before the State of the Union, 68 percent, including majorities of both Democrats and independents, gave Mr. Bush high marks for the campaign against terrorism.

So it is in Mr. Bush's interest to talk about the threat, just as it is in his interest to warn, as he did on Tuesday, that terrorists are still plotting against America. "Just think about the political calculation," said Walter Russell Mead of the Council on Foreign Relations. "You don't want to say, 'thanks to me, you're safe now,' and then tomorrow there's no Cleveland, Ohio."

People close to Mr. Bush reject the notion of a "political calculation," as Mr. Mead put it, and say the president is in fact haunted by the specter of Sept. 11 and the fears of a replay on his watch. Mr. Bush still begins each day with the daily "threat assessment," a compilation of what intelligence and law enforcement agencies pick up about potential terrorist activity. Aides say that it is a disturbing look at the nation's vulnerabilities, and that it has had a powerful effect on the president's psyche.

But no one at the White House denies that pushing the president's antiterrorism policy is good politics. Notably, none of the Democrats have accused Mr. Bush of exaggerating the vulnerability of the United States. "In all the opposition, one thing you're not hearing is, 'The boy is crying wolf,'" Mr. Mead said.

The problem for the challengers, Democrats themselves say, is no presidential candidate has effectively challenged Mr. Bush on security.

"You have to say how you're going to protect America, not just what Bush does wrong," said Senator Charles E. Schumer, the New York Democrat who has criticized the administration for not spending more on domestic security. "I don't think most Americans are totally satisfied with the Bush fight against terrorism, but they certainly prefer it to a weaker or nonexistent one."

Polls show that Mr. Bush is vulnerable to Democrats on domestic issues; 51 percent of Americans disapprove of his handling of the economy, according to *The New York Times*/CBS News poll. The economy was the No. 1 issue that people wanted to hear the candidates discuss.

But David Winston, a Republican pollster, said that running on national security made sense. During the State of the Union, he conducted a focus group of 30 independent voters, who were instructed to rate parts of the speech. The line that won the best response — aside from Mr. Bush's praise of the troops — was the president's vow that the United States will never seek "a permission slip" to defend its security.

"It was the home-run line," Mr. Winston said.

Study Question:

While President Bush was talking about fear, what did Democrats (and polls) show he was vulnerable on?

Kerry Rolling On; Edwards a Victor in South Carolina

By ADAM NAGOURNEY   *Published Wednesday, February 4, 2004*

Senator John Kerry won substantial victories in the Democratic presidential primaries in Missouri and Delaware last night, but Senator John Edwards won handily in South Carolina, allowing him to portray the contest as a two-way battle with Mr. Kerry and keep the race rolling through February.

Mr. Kerry, of Massachusetts, captured Missouri, the state with the largest number of delegates at stake yesterday, while Mr. Edwards, of North Carolina, won in South Carolina, the third-biggest state of the night. Mr. Edwards had said a victory in South Carolina, where he was born, was essential to his staying in the race for president.

Mr. Kerry also appeared to be heading for a victory in Arizona, according to surveys of voters leaving the polls.

Mr. Edwards declared victory at 8 p.m. sharp, at a rally at a restaurant in Columbia, S.C., the state where he campaigned six of the past seven days.

"Tonight you said that the politics of lifting people up beats the politics of tearing people down," he said.

Mr. Kerry learned of the results as his campaign jet touched down in Washington State, where there is a caucus on Saturday, and quickly savored his Missouri victory. That state was the biggest prize last night, with 74 delegates at stake.

"Fabulous, I'll take 50 percent anywhere, anytime," Mr. Kerry said. Asked about Mr. Edwards's victory in South Carolina, he said, "I think coming in second, given where I've been, is enormous."

Senator Joseph I. Lieberman of Connecticut, who was the Democratic candidate for vice president in 2000, and at one point the best-known Democrat in the field, abandoned his bid for the presidency last night after drawing barely 11 percent of the vote in Delaware. Mr. Lieberman said he was bowing to the realism of the moment; he came in fifth place in New Hampshire last week and had been looking to Delaware to revive his candidacy.

In Oklahoma, one of the most heavily contested states of the night, Mr. Edwards and Gen. Wesley K. Clark were locked in an extremely tight battle for first place, with nearly three-fourths of the vote counted. Mr. Kerry was in third place.

General Clark, of Arkansas, was in Oklahoma every day for the past week, and was looking for a victory there to keep his candidacy in play.

The results on what was the busiest night thus far in the Democratic nomination battle left little doubt that this show would go on, although with a smaller field. Mr. Edwards's aides announced even before the polls closed that he would take a bus trip on Friday through Virginia, which has a primary on Feb. 10, but that he would compete in the Michigan caucuses this Saturday, in an effort to erase a perception, being pressed by the Kerry campaign, that his was merely a regional candidacy.

Howard Dean, the former governor of Vermont, who had once looked to clinch the nomination with the round of contests yesterday, suffered another disappointing night. Dr. Dean spent no money on advertising in those states but had campaigned in South Carolina, Missouri and Delaware.

Dr. Dean was trailing the pack in all four states, and he moved early in the night to try to blunt the damage of the showing, with an appearance before supporters in Washington state, where Dr. Dean had turned his attention.

"Well, the votes are starting to come in, and we're going to have a tough night tonight," Dr Dean said. "But you know what? Here's why we're going to keep going and going and going and going and going and going, just like the Energizer bunny. We're going to pick up some delegates tonight, and this is all about who gets the most delegates in Boston in July, and it's going to be us."

Yesterday's vote recast the contest for the nomination, though to what extent was a matter of debate among Democrats. At the very least, it allowed Mr. Edwards to keep his foot in the door, providing an alternative for Democrats who are uncomfortable with Mr. Kerry.

Mr. Edwards posted his victory in the state where he was born, and some Democrats said the first-term senator would be under pressure to prove that his appeal went beyond the South, though his aides were pointing to a strong showing in Oklahoma as well.

His aides said he had about $1 million on hand, though he will now be under intense pressure to raise a lot of money quickly.

Mr. Kerry won states far outside his home region, including in the Midwest and the Great Plains. In South Carolina, he came in second, ahead of General Clark, who is also a Southerner and who had once looked to win in the state, and ahead of the Rev. Al Sharpton, the only black candidate in the race, who had at one point predicted he could win a state where about half the Democratic electorate was African-American.

The contests yesterday marked the first time the candidates faced competitive races in states with sizable groups of minority voters.

In South Carolina, surveys of voters leaving the polls found that Mr. Kerry and Mr. Edwards each drew about one-third of the black vote. Mr. Sharpton drew just one-fifth.

Mr. Edwards did well among black voters in South Carolina, as did Mr. Kerry among Hispanic voters in Arizona. Nearly 2 in 10 voters in Arizona said they were Hispanic, and half of them voted for Mr. Kerry.

The poll in South Carolina also found that voters looking for a candidate who stands up for what he believes were much more likely to vote for Mr. Edwards than for Mr. Kerry. But voters looking for someone who could defeat President Bush were more apt to back Mr. Kerry.

Nearly half the voters in South Carolina said the economy and jobs were the most critical issues in casting their votes; nearly half of them voted for Mr. Edwards, twice as many as voted for Mr. Kerry.

The polls were taken in Arizona, Missouri, Oklahoma and South Carolina, and were conducted by Edison Media Research and Mitofsky International for a pool of the five television networks and The Associated Press.

Democrats interviewed as they cast their votes around the nation yesterday echoed the same themes that were heard among party members in New Hampshire and Iowa: that they were looking first and foremost at who could defeat Mr. Bush.

But in St. Louis, Mike Showers, 54, who said he had been unemployed since a Norwegian company bought the food processing plant where he worked and shut it down, said he was worried about Mr. Kerry.

"I don't believe that Kerry is the strongest candidate," Mr. Showers said. "To me, he reminds me of Al Gore, who they all said could beat George Bush easily." He said that Mr. Edwards "doesn't have a lot of political experience, but he's from a middle-class family and he has middle-class values, and that's the most important thing to me."

Mr. Edwards, looking fatigued, said in a television interview last night that he would seek in the days ahead to draw contrasts with Mr. Kerry, based on differences in the two men's upbringings and some of their positions.

But pressed in an interview on CNN by Bob Dole, who was the Republican Party candidate for president in 1996, about how he would do it, Mr. Edwards acknowledged that he might be constrained by the way he had presented his candidacy as avoiding the kind of attacks that are part of politics now.

Mr. Dole, who said he was speaking from experience, suggested that it would not be enough for Mr. Edwards to try to distinguish himself from Mr. Kerry by pointing only to their difference of opinion on the North American Free Trade Agreement, which Mr. Kerry voted for in the Senate.

"The key for me, Bob, is I got to this place by running a very positive, uplifting campaign, which is something that you and your spouse know a lot about," Mr. Edwards said. "I have to be very careful not to lose that."

"That doesn't mean that I don't have to point out clear differences between myself and other candidates, between myself and Senator Kerry, that go beyond trade and background," he said. "There are significant issue differences between us, and those will become clear as we go forward."

Study Question:

While Kerry and Edwards basked in the glow of victories, who abandoned their race after suffering losses?

Gephardt to Endorse Kerry

By DAVID M. HALBFINGER

Published Friday, February 6, 2004

Senator John Kerry secured a series of high-profile endorsements yesterday, most significantly that of the former presidential contender Representative Richard A. Gephardt, as he worked to create an air of inevitability about his nomination and drive his remaining rivals from the Democratic race.

Mr. Gephardt, who dropped out of the presidential race after a fourth-place finish in Iowa, planned to put his support behind Mr. Kerry today in Warren, Mich., Democrats said, giving the senator a powerful boost with the industrial unions and blue-collar workers important in the Michigan caucuses tomorrow. Polls show that Mr. Kerry already has a commanding lead in the state.

The Gephardt endorsement was only one that the Kerry campaign rolled out as the senator flew from Maine to Manhattan to Michigan and also picked up checks from a growing cadre of fund-raisers.

Mr. Kerry, of Massachusetts, was endorsed by Gov. John Baldacci of Maine, who spoke over a loudspeaker from his office in Portland, still suffering from a broken rib and bruises from a car accident on Wednesday. Mr. Kerry also picked up the backing of former Senator George J. Mitchell of Maine, in advance of the state's caucuses on Sunday.

In Michigan, Mr. Kerry received the endorsements of Senators Carl Levin and Debbie Stabenow.

And in New York, where he raised more than $750,000 at a fund-raiser, Mr. Kerry was endorsed by Speaker Sheldon Silver of the State Assembly, Comptroller Alan Hevesi and Betsy Gotbaum, the New York City public advocate, all of whom previously supported Senator Joseph I. Lieberman of Connecticut. Mr. Kerry was also endorsed by about 15 members of the Assembly.

Before leaving Boston yesterday morning, Mr. Kerry and his deputy campaign manager, Steve Elmendorf, who had worked for Mr. Gephardt, met with representatives of 18 industrial unions, including the Teamsters. An official said an endorsement was not in hand but could come as early as next week.

As Mr. Kerry raced from the Northeast to Michigan, Senator John Edwards and Gen. Wesley K. Clark battled in the South. Howard Dean headed to Wisconsin, on which he is resting the fate of his candidacy.

General Clark slammed the voting records of both Mr. Kerry and Mr. Edwards. "The American people don't want another Washington insider who never plays it straight," he said at a rally in Lebanon, Tenn. "They don't want a follower who makes decisions by licking his finger and sticking it up in the wind and seeing which way it blows."

Senator Edwards campaigned hard on trade issues, promising to toughen trade agreements that he blamed for the loss of tens of thousands of jobs.

"Think of the devastation that creates, creates for communities, creates for families, all these jobs going overseas," Mr. Edwards said in Nashville before starting a campaign tour in Virginia and Tennessee, which hold primaries Tuesday.

Mr. Kerry took aim at President Bush, calling for an independent inquiry into the integrity of intelligence on Iraq after the C.I.A.'s director said the intelligence agency had never called weapons of mass destruction an imminent threat.

"It goes to the core of why the nation went to war," he said. "If there is that kind of failure, that kind of separation between the truth of what the C.I.A. tells the White House and what happens, then we have to separate that investigation from that White House so the American people get the truth."

At a Portland rally, a heckler interrupted Mr. Kerry's speech, shouting, "How about your vote for the war, and the Patriot Act and for John Ashcroft?"

Mr. Kerry, who voted against Mr. Ashcroft's confirmation as attorney general, shot back, "I don't run away from anything I'll never run away from those votes."

Later, he affirmed his support for civil unions but not for gay marriage, a day after Massachusetts' highest court ruled that people of the same sex must have the right to marry. He dismissed a suggestion that Republicans could try to use the ruling in against him.

"Well, big deal for the Republicans," Mr. Kerry said. "If they want to choose some kind of wedge issue and distort my position, I will fight back very clearly." He added, "I have the same position that Vice President Dick Cheney has."

Mr. Kerry also faced questions about his dealings with the insurance company the American International Group.

The Associated Press reported that Mr. Kerry and his fellow Massachusetts senator, Edward M. Kennedy, fought against a bill that would have stripped $150 million from the Big Dig, the Boston infrastructure project, after the Transportation Department found that the project had overpaid $129.8 million to the insurer for worker compensation and liability insurance, then allowed the insurer to keep the money in a trust and invest it.

Over the next two years, The A.P. said, the insurance group paid Mr. Kerry's way to Vermont and donated $18,000 to his Senate and presidential campaigns and $30,000 to Mr. Kerry's Citizen Soldier Fund, which he used to lay the groundwork for his presidential bid by helping Democrats in states like Iowa and New Hampshire.

Mr. Kerry said yesterday that the Vermont trip was a one-day round trip to give a speech and was "perfectly normal procedure in the context of the United States Senate." He said he opposed the bill affecting the insurance group, as did "every single member" of the Massachusetts Congressional delegation, because it would have stripped $150 million from the Big Dig.

And he noted he had opposed the insurance industry on bankruptcy legislation and terrorism insurance, which he said "were far more important to them than anything to do with the Big Dig."

Study Question:

What important constituency did Representative Richard Gephardt's endorsement help Senator Kerry with?

Bush States His Case Early

By ELISABETH BUMILLER

Published Monday, February 9, 2004

WASHINGTON — George W. Bush's goal in stepping down from his presidential pedestal and into the political hothouse of "Meet the Press" was to frame the election on his capacity to make the tough, unpopular decisions that he thinks are in the best interests of the national security and economic health of the United States.

Mr. Bush, who opened the window a little wider into his thinking about his decision to take the nation to war with Iraq, tried to use his unusual hourlong encounter in the Oval Office with Tim Russert of NBC to make a larger case for his presidency and, by extension, what he hopes will be seen as his sincerity.

The moment that seemed to capture that strategy came early on in the interview, when Mr. Bush said he wanted to share "my sentiment" as he marched toward his confrontation with Saddam Hussein.

"It's important for people to understand the context in which I made a decision in the Oval Office," Mr. Bush said. "I'm dealing with a world in which we have gotten struck by terrorists with airplanes, and we get intelligence saying that, you know, we want to harm America. And the worst nightmare scenario for any president is to realize that these kind of terrorist networks have the capacity to arm up with some of these deadly weapons, and they strike us."

The "most solemn responsibility" of an American president, Mr. Bush concluded, "is to keep this country secure."

It is too early to say if Mr. Bush's interview worked the magic he wanted, and the Republicans will be polling to find out. Democrats instantly criticized the president's comments during the interview as more backpedaling on his reasons for going to war.

"What we saw today was an administration with shifting rationale for a questionable war," Senator Edward M. Kennedy, Democrat of Massachusetts, said through his spokesman, Jim Manley.

But many of Mr. Bush's supporters insisted that he had made a critical connection to voters.

"He made a better connection today, period, than I'd seen before," said Michael K. Deaver, the image maker for Ronald Reagan who has on occasion advised the current administration. "I think he had his arguments down, they didn't sound like they were rehearsed, but clearly what he believed. He basically said, 'I am who I am and I'm not going to change.' And that's a great strength."

Still, the great risk for Mr. Bush, Democrats and Republicans said on Sunday, is that he could just as easily lose as win an election that turns into a referendum on his judgment and character. Mr. Bush is particularly vulnerable, they said, if the Democrats raise enough doubts about his credibility on the war and on the economy, which now faces the highest federal budget deficit in history.

The Democratic front-runner, Senator John Kerry, made clear that was his strategy early on Sunday, when he issued a statement on Mr. Bush's performance.

"This morning on 'Meet the Press,' President Bush said his decision to go to war with Iraq when he did was because Saddam Hussein had 'the ability to make weapons,'" Mr. Kerry said. "This is a far cry from what the president and his administration told the American people throughout 2002. Back then, President Bush repeatedly told the American people that Saddam Hussein 'has got chemical weapons.'"

He added, "And it was on that basis that he sent American sons and daughters off to war."

Whatever the result of the interview, it clearly showed that the White House has decided it cannot just throw $100 million in advertising at a Democratic nominee and try to turn him into George McGovern, the liberal trounced in the 1972 election by President Richard M. Nixon. If anything, the interview showed that Mr. Bush has concluded that he must make a persuasive argument not only for his presidency, but in effect his own electability.

The interview put on display what sometimes seemed an odd hybrid of Mr. Bush as both president and presidential candidate. If he seemed to descend from his commander-in-chief mountaintop by dueling with Mr. Russert — the Washington insider who usually interrogates people who seek rather than sit in the Oval Office — he also did not entirely assume the role of a candidate willing to engage in partisan combat.

When Mr. Russert baited Mr. Bush with a comment from Mr. Kerry that Mr. Kerry was "appalled" by "the president's lack of knowledge," Mr. Bush simply smiled, called it "politics" and added that "if you close your eyes and listen carefully to what you just said, it sounds like the year 2000 all over again."

If the response appeared tentative, Mr. Bush's campaign officials insisted it was all part of the plan, at least at this point in the campaign. "He didn't take that bit because he understands that people want a leader in Washington, they want somebody who is not going to lead by responding to polls and who is not going to engage in attack politics," said Gerald L. Parsky, the chairman of Mr. Bush's campaign in California.

Another Bush campaign adviser said the goal of the White House was not only to explain Mr. Bush's decision-making, but also to show him as more human and humble than his warrior image suggests.

The adviser said he was optimistic that the polling numbers — some of which show Mr. Bush trailing Mr. Kerry in a hypothetical election match-up by as much as seven percentage points — would improve for the president after the interview. (Officially, the Bush White House says it pays no attention to polls.)

"I think that will make him a little less vulnerable to charges of arrogance and hardheadedness," the adviser said, hopefully, "and that he's unwilling to ever acknowledge mistakes."

Study Question:

Why did President Bush give this interview on "Meet the Press"?

Kerry and Edwards Square Off as Dean Abandons Campaign

By ADAM NAGOURNEY and DAVID M. HALBFINGER　　　　*Published Thursday, February 19, 2004*

MILWAUKEE — Howard Dean ended his bid for the presidency on Wednesday, leaving John Kerry and John Edwards battling over free trade and jobs as the Democratic presidential contest veered into a more combative two-man struggle.

As Dr. Dean announced that he was abandoning his campaign after losing his 17th state contest with a devastating third-place finish in the Wisconsin primary, Senators Kerry and Edwards moved aggressively to fill the space. They picked the states they would compete in over the next two weeks and argued over Mr. Kerry's support of free trade agreements and his contributions from lobbyists.

"As Senator Kerry himself has pointed out many times during this campaign, records matter," Mr. Edwards said in a noisy afternoon conference call with 100 reporters, the number a clear indication of how his status has changed after a strong second-place showing in Wisconsin. "I think there is a significant difference between us on this issue."

The White House, too, was consumed with the economy. The Bush administration backed away from a forecast it made public only last week predicting average job gains of more than 300,000 a month for 2004. The administration said it remained confident of robust though unspecified job growth.

Mr. Edwards, a first-term senator from North Carolina, noted that Mr. Kerry, a four-term senator from Massachusetts, voted in the Senate for the North American Free Trade Agreement in 1993. Mr. Edwards asserted that he would have voted against it had he been in the Senate. He said he would, as president, renegotiate the treaty to provide protections for American workers.

In Ohio, one of 10 states that vote on March 2, Mr. Kerry declared that he and Mr. Edwards held indistinguishable positions on future trade agreements. Mr. Kerry was preparing to return to Washington to accept the endorsement of the A.F.L.-C.I.O., an event his aides asserted would help rebut Mr. Edwards's challenge on this issue in states like Ohio, as well as California and New York, which also vote on March 2.

"We have the same policy on trade, exactly the same policy," Mr. Kerry said, campaigning in Dayton, where he stood in front of a huge banner that read, "John Kerry: Protecting America's Jobs."

"He voted for the China trade agreement; so did I," he said, referring to legislation that granted China permanent normal trade relations.

"And we, both of us, want to have labor agreements and environment agreements as part of a trade agreement, so it's the exact same policy," Mr. Kerry said, before registering a note of skepticism about Mr. Edwards's commitment on the issue.

"Well, he wasn't in the Senate back then," Mr. Kerry said. "I don't know where he registered his vote, but it wasn't in the Senate."

In Burlington, Vt., Dr. Dean, the former governor there, said he was ending his presidential campaign but gave no indication that he would endorse any opponent. "I am no longer actively pursuing the presidency," Dr. Dean said, adding, "We will, however, continue to build a new organization using our enormous grass-roots network to continue the effort to transform the Democratic Party and to change our country."

Both Mr. Kerry and Mr. Edwards spoke to Dr. Dean on Wednesday, and Mr. Edwards said he would welcome Dr. Dean's support.

The exchanges between Mr. Edwards and Mr. Kerry began almost as soon as Dr. Dean gave his final speech as a presidential candidate for 2004. The sparring signaled that the contest had entered a new and more competitive stage. Mr. Edwards appeared to some extent constrained in his attacks, because he has spent much of this campaign criticizing other Democrats for running negative campaigns. He kept many of his challenges to Mr. Kerry carefully calibrated.

At least from the outset, the change of tone in the race appeared to pose a particular challenge for Mr. Kerry. He found himself battling on two fronts as President Bush's re-election operation also fired off attacks on many of the same issues that Mr. Edwards was raising.

The Republican broadsides came after a primary here preceded by a week of intense White House attacks on Mr. Kerry. These included an Internet advertisement that portrayed him as a tool of special interests. Aides to Mr. Kerry and Mr. Edwards say the attacks might have contributed to Mr. Kerry's unexpectedly modest defeat of Mr. Edwards, by a vote of 40 percent to 34 percent.

Republicans are allowed to vote in Wisconsin's Democratic primary, and they made up 9 percent of the voters on Tuesday, according to a survey of those leaving the polls. Mr. Edwards defeated Mr. Kerry among voters who said they were Republicans, 44 percent to 18 percent.

Aides to Mr. Kerry and some national Democratic leaders suggested that in attacking Mr. Kerry before the Wisconsin vote, Mr. Bush's re-election campaign was trying to end a stream of clear victories that appeared to be building Mr. Kerry into a formidable challenger to the president. The attacks were also intended to encourage Democratic in-fighting, they suggested.

Mr. Edwards suddenly found himself in a stronger position after placing second in Wisconsin. Although he has won only one contest so far — in South Carolina, where he was born — he moved to make the most of his moment and to put Mr. Kerry on the defensive. He had begun to sharpen his differences with Mr. Kerry on trade during the South Carolina primary and continued to do so in his conference call with reporters.

The call came as Mr. Edwards spent much of the day raising money, including in New York, to try to collect the cash that his aides said he would need to be competitive in the 14 states that hold Democratic contests on March 2 and March 9.

In the call, Mr. Edwards said that beyond trade, he would draw attention to other differences between the rivals, including "the fact that I don't take contributions from Washington lobbyists."

He also said the candidates had different policies on helping the middle class. He mentioned specifically programs he had advocated to encourage middle-class savings.

Asked about the criticism, Mr. Kerry's press secretary, Stephanie Cutter, responded, "This is an interesting line of attack from the positive campaign of John Edwards considering that his campaign is wholly funded by trial lawyers, which are widely recognized as special interests and lobbyists." Mr. Edwards himself is a former trial lawyer.

In a sign of the new fury of the contest, Mr. Kerry's aides were among the 100 people on the conference call; they e-mailed newspaper clippings to provide a running rebuttal to Mr. Edwards as he sought to contrast the views of the two men on trade agreements.

"Edwards promised to run a positive campaign," one Kerry campaign statement read, noting that Mr. Edwards had voted for the China trade agreement. "But now Edwards attacks John Kerry and runs from his own record."

Mr. Edwards's aides said he was adding to the number of states where he will try to compete on March 2. They said he would turn his sights to California, a state that he had earlier said was too expensive for him.

Mr. Edwards said in the conference call that California, with its 370 delegates, was impossible to ignore for a candidate who wanted to remain competitive.

And Mr. Edwards planned to campaign heavily in New York as well, where there are 236 delegates. Because of the way delegates are allocated under party rules — as a percentage of the vote won — Mr. Edwards is facing intense pressure to compete in as many states as he can. Mr. Kerry now has 497 delegates, compared with 188 for Mr. Edwards.

And Dr. Dean's decision to step aside means that his 119 so-called superdelegates — for the most part, public officials free to chose any candidate, regardless of the primary vote — are now back in play. Aides to Mr. Kerry and Mr. Edwards said they are moving to recruit them.

In seizing on trade treaties as an issue, Mr. Edwards's aides said they were looking particularly at Ohio, parts of California and upstate New York, parts of the country that are reeling from job losses and, they said, would be amenable to Mr. Edwards's argument that Mr. Kerry had cast a vote that cost them jobs.

In attacking Mr. Kerry for his 1993 vote, Mr. Edwards rejected Mr. Kerry's contention that there was little difference in what they would do with future job treaties as president.

"I think your record is an indication of what you'll do in the future and also shows the strength of your convictions on a particular issue," Mr. Edwards said.

But Mr. Edwards acknowledged in an interview earlier this week that there was little evidence of his having opposed Nafta before 1997 or 1998, when he first ran for the Senate. He has close ties to the Democratic Leadership Council, a group of moderate Democrats that has pushed for liberalized trade agreements, but he said he had made his views known throughout that campaign.

"What I've said is when I campaigned in '98 since I wasn't in the Congress when passed I campaigned and I was against Nafta," he said in the interview. But he said it was not a major part of his Senate campaign.

Adam Nagourney reported from Milwaukee for this article, and David M. Halbfinger from Dayton, Ohio.

Study Question:

Why did Republicans begin attacking Senator Kerry after his string of primary victories?

— ★ ★ ★ —

With Super Tuesday Behind Him, Kerry Shifts to High General-Election Gear

By **DAVID M. HALBFINGER**   *Published Thursday, March 4, 2004*

ORLANDO, Fla. — Senator John Kerry of Massachusetts began his general election campaign at a full sprint on Wednesday, flying here to rally voters in the battleground state that is his party's bloody shirt, naming a Democratic financier to oversee his search for a running mate and orchestrating a takeover of the Democratic National Committee.

A day after effectively sealing the nomination with victories in 9 of the 10 Super Tuesday states, Mr. Kerry did not pause before starting what is shaping up to be a long and hard-fought race to November, surrounding himself with off-duty police officers and firefighters and showcasing his law-and-order credentials as a former prosecutor.

As aides to President Bush introduced the first of an anticipated avalanche of television commercials for his campaign, some of which used images from the Sept. 11 attacks, Senator Kerry assailed Mr. Bush on precisely the area he is showcasing as his strength, accusing the president of "broken promises" on national and homeland security.

"Everybody remembers the poignant, very moving picture extraordinary photograph of the president on the rubble at ground zero in New York," Mr. Kerry said, "but they also remember the promise that was made to the first responders of America."

He said that fire departments were understaffed, federal money for police departments was being cut, and bipartisan recommendations on antiterror measures were being ignored.

But it was the speed with which Mr. Kerry began his selection process to select a running mate that showed how quickly he was moving after winning 27 of 30 nominating contests and driving his last serious rival, Senator John Edwards of North Carolina, from the race.

Mr. Kerry named Jim Johnson, a merchant banker, onetime chairman and chief executive of Fannie Mae and former top adviser to Vice President Walter F. Mondale, to identify and screen potential running mates during the next several weeks. Campaign officials described Mr. Johnson, a veteran of presidential politics from his service as Mr. Mondale's 1984 campaign chairman, as a frequent dinner companion and neighbor of Mr. Kerry in the resort town of Ketchum, Idaho.

Aides played down the idea that Mr. Kerry would announce a running mate too far in advance of the Democratic National Convention, which is to be held in Boston in July. They said that Mr. Kerry was acting quickly in large part because Vice President Al Gore did not in 2000 — a year when Mr. Kerry and Mr. Edwards were both considered for the job, then rejected.

"He believes Democrats in the past erred in resting on their laurels after effectively securing the nomination," an adviser said of Mr. Kerry. "And as someone who has been through the vice presidential vetting process, he's familiar with it and wants a process that's good for the party and good for the campaign."

In an interview with an Orlando television station, Mr. Kerry alluded to his experience on Mr. Gore's short list. "I believe it has to be very private," he said. "It's a very personal process. I wouldn't begin to just throw names around." He added: "I've been through it, and wouldn't do it."

But names were already flying in Democratic circles, starting with that of Mr. Edwards. Campaign officials said one consideration would certainly be whether a potential running mate could help the ticket carry a battleground state.

Those being discussed Wednesday included Representative Richard A. Gephardt of Missouri, the two Florida senators Bob Graham and Bill Nelson — who campaigned with Mr. Kerry Wednesday — and Senator Evan Bayh of Indiana.

Also in the mix were several governors: Tom Vilsack of Iowa, who was seen as a tacit supporter of Mr. Kerry in the caucuses there; Janet Napolitano of Arizona; Bill Richardson of New Mexico; and Mark Warner of Virginia, who leads a populous Southern state that leans Republican.

Back in Washington, Mr. Kerry was putting his imprint on the Democratic National Committee, as his top campaign aides negotiated with party leaders to install a Kerry loyalist, probably an elected or former elected official, as general chairman and principal spokesman. This would leave the national chairman, Terry McAuliffe, in place but with a less visible role and focused more on raising money, his signature strength.

Mr. McAuliffe had concerned the Kerry campaign, officials said, by taking the initiative in attacking Mr. Bush over his National Guard service in particular, by saying he had gone "AWOL" from Guard duty in 1972 without clearing it with Mr. Kerry.

Officials at both the Democratic National Committee and the Kerry camp said the Kerry campaign wanted to name a chief operating officer as its liaison to the party to sign checks and keep the organization moving. They said that Michael Whouley, a top Kerry adviser who in 2000 was the chief field organizer for Mr. Gore and directed party operations, had no interest in assuming that role again.

Advisers said that by taking action on several fronts, Mr. Kerry intended to convey a message to potential donors and voters alike. "This is a new cycle, a new day, a new environment," a campaign official said. "It's going to send a signal that this is a campaign that's playing to win."

The trip to Florida, which holds its primary on Tuesday, made for a fortuitous intersection of general-election calculus and the accelerated Democratic calendar. As he campaigned, Mr. Kerry did not let pass the chance to remind Democrats of the 2000 electoral nightmare they could have scarcely forgotten.

With Senators Graham and Nelson at his side, Mr. Kerry noted that they were "living testimony to what happens in Florida when you count all the votes."

The two Florida senators accompanied Mr. Kerry to Orlando from Washington, and Mr. Graham was aboard the campaign plane long before the candidate arrived, in plenty of time to fan the flames of running-mate speculation.

"I will do anything within reason — I will not sacrifice one of my grandchildren — to help John Kerry get elected," Mr. Graham said when asked if he hoped to be considered.

On the ground in Orlando, Mr. Kerry briefly tended to what may be his largest disadvantage in running against Mr. Bush, meeting behind closed doors with a group of Florida donors and business executives to get his fund-raising operation into high gear.

And in public Mr. Kerry played up the themes of domestic security and international security. He declared that Mr. Bush had failed to build a broad enough international coalition in Iraq, leaving Americans to foot too much of the bill in dollars and in casualties.

"I don't think there's a person in this room who believes this president went to war as a last resort," he said in a town-hall-style meeting. "Those are broken promises."

In the meeting, he mainly played up his law-enforcement experience 25 years ago while accepting the endorsement of the International Union of Police Associations as off-duty officers wearing blue "Cops for Kerry" T-shirts alternated with the gold-shirted firefighters who had long ago endorsed him.

"I have been to murder scenes," Mr. Kerry said. "I've prosecuted murderers, rapists, armed robbers. I've sent people to jail for the rest of their life. And I learned firsthand what happens when local police don't talk to county police don't talk to the state police don't talk to the F.B.I. We can't afford that any more in America."

Mr. Kerry said he had fought for a federal program aimed at putting 100,000 police officers on the street, and "I can't for the life of me understand why George Bush turned around on his position with respect to law enforcement" and was cutting money for that program "even as crime is rising."

"George Bush thinks it's more important to give people earning $200,000 a year a tax cut," Mr. Kerry said. "I think it's more important to keep the United States of America safe and keep these police officers on the beat."

He said the administration ignored the "fundamentals" of preparedness, noting that Israel trains its police officers to think like terrorists to anticipate attacks. "People in this country deserve more than words and empty promises," he said. "We deserve at least an honest discussion about what we can afford to do and can't afford to do and how we are truly going to make America safer."

Shortly thereafter, Mr. Kerry benefited from a show of law and order. He was whisked off to the airport again, his motorcade trailing 32 police officers on motorcycles.

Study Question:

Why did Senator Kerry move quickly to begin looking for a running mate after securing the Democratic nomination?

Nation's Direction Prompts Voters' Concern, Poll Finds

By ADAM NAGOURNEY and JANET ELDER   *Published Tuesday, March 16, 2004*

George Bush and John Kerry enter the general election at a time of growing concern among Americans that the nation is veering in the wrong direction, the latest *New York Times*/CBS News poll shows. Mr. Bush faces unrest over his management of the economy, while the public has doubts about Mr. Kerry's political convictions.

Americans do view Mr. Bush and Mr. Kerry as strong leaders who share their moral values and have a clear vision of where they want to take the country, the poll found.

But while the candidates are starting on roughly equal ground on those critical generic measures of leadership, the poll found that nearly half of respondents have not yet formed an opinion about Mr. Kerry. That result suggests that Mr. Bush has an opening to mold public opinion of his largely unknown challenger.

Already, most voters think Mr. Kerry is a politician who says what people want to hear, the poll found, rather than what he believes — the line of attack Mr. Bush has used against him in speeches.

At the same time, there is sweeping concern among Americans about the president's economic policies, including his ability to create jobs and the effectiveness of his tax cuts, according to the poll. By a margin of greater than 30 points, more people said the policies of Mr. Bush's administration had reduced the number of jobs in the country rather than increased them. Those findings could prove particularly significant if the election is fought over economic issues in hard-hit states like Ohio.

Perhaps most significant for Mr. Bush, the number of Americans who think that the nation is heading in the wrong direction is now 54 percent, as high as it has been in his presidency. The right direction/wrong direction figure is a measure that pollsters view as a highly reliable early indicator of problems for an incumbent.

"Our priorities need to be reshuffled," Darrell Griffin, 64, a Republican retired engineer from Hemphill, Tex., said in a follow-up interview. "The protection of the homeland and our allies from terrorism is important, but our economy in our own country and Social Security and things like that here at home are pretty important, too."

The *Times*/CBS News poll offered the latest evidence that the race for president was as tight as has long been predicted. Even after two weeks in which Mr. Bush has run televised advertisements promoting himself and attacking Mr. Kerry, and in which Mr. Kerry has enjoyed the glow of favorable coverage that greeted his near-sweep of Democratic primaries, the two men are effectively tied, with 46 percent of voters saying they supported Mr. Bush and 43 percent backing Mr. Kerry.

The candidacy of Ralph Nader looms as a potentially lethal threat to Democratic hopes of regaining the White House: With Mr. Nader in the race, Mr. Bush leads Mr. Kerry by 46 percent to 38 percent, with Mr. Nader drawing 7 percent of the votes. In a sign of the polarized electorate Mr. Bush and Mr. Kerry are facing, three-quarters of supporters of each candidate asserted they would not change their mind before the election.

The nationwide telephone poll of 1,206 adults, including 984 registered voters, was taken from last Wednesday through Sunday. It has a margin of sampling error of plus or minus three percentage points.

The questioning was completed before the vote in Spain on Sunday that produced in the ouster of one of Mr. Bush's principal allies in the Iraq war, the party of José María Aznar. The vote followed a terrorist bombing there that has been linked to Al Qaeda.

The *Times*/CBS News poll found that Mr. Bush continued to enjoy an advantage over Mr. Kerry in managing foreign policy, and in protecting the nation against terrorism. Indeed, fighting terrorism remains Mr. Bush's greatest area of strength.

But the poll suggested other potential obstacles as Mr. Bush moves into his re-election campaign.

After a month in which Mr. Bush called for a constitutional amendment to ban same-sex marriage, he is viewed in sharply ideological terms, with more than 50 percent of voters describing him as conservative, again as high as it has been during his presidency. The finding suggests the risks Mr. Bush faces as he tries to build up his standing with conservative members of his party, and the challenge he faces as he seeks to expand his support.

By 59 percent to 35 percent, respondents said they supported a constitutional amendment that would "allow marriage only between a man and a woman." But 56 percent said that they did not view the issue as important enough to merit changing the nation's constitution.

"It seems like a waste of time and energy when we should be thinking more about figuring out how we're going to have Social Security," said Ronald Sharp, 44, a Republican and retired mental health care aide from Detroit.

Nearly two-thirds of respondents said it was unacceptable for candidates to use images from the World Trade Center's destruction in political advertisements. Mr. Bush is running an advertisement that shows the aftermath of the attack on Sept. 11, 2001, and has refused to take it off the air in the face of criticism by Mr. Kerry's allies, firefighters and some families of victims.

"They shouldn't exploit what happened to make a political issue," said Nan McNeill, 56, a Republican ranch owner in Tonopah, Ariz. "The fact that it happened is something that no one can deny, but no political party can actually say this is what should have been done or shouldn't have been done, so I don't think that it should be an issue at all."

But the biggest difficulty for Mr. Bush is the perception of his management of the economy. The number of Americans who say they approve of his economic record is now among the lowest of his presidency, 38 percent. In addition, 57 percent of voters said they were uneasy about Mr. Bush's ability to make the right decision on the economy, compared with just 39 percent who said they had confidence in his economic-decision making. Voters were evenly split over whether they were uneasy or confident about Mr. Kerry's ability to make economic decisions.

Mr. Kerry is viewed by Americans as much more likely to succeed at creating jobs and improving the economy than Mr. Bush. He also is viewed as more likely to protect Social Security and hold down the cost of drugs, two areas that could give him an advantage with the elderly voters.

But at the start of what Mr. Bush's advisers said would be an intensive campaign to raise questions about Mr. Kerry's ideology and political convictions, the poll found that 39 percent of respondents considered Mr. Kerry a liberal — a characterization the Republicans have been encouraging.

And by 57 percent to 33 percent, respondents said that Mr. Kerry says what people want to hear, rather than what he believes in. By contrast, 45 percent said Mr. Bush says what people want to hear, while 51 percent said he says what he means.

"He seems to change his mind or his opinion about things depending on whom he's talking to," David Carpenter, 78, an independent and retired engineer from Wakefield, Mass., said of Mr. Kerry. "He just tries to appease those that are in front of him, and as a result he isn't consistent. The lack of consistency indicates to me that he's trying to appease the people that he's talking to or appeal to them rather than sticking to a straight line. He's done it with the war in Iraq."

The poll reflected the clear unease among Americans over marriages, or civil unions, by same-sex couples. Nearly two-thirds of respondents said they believed the issue did not merit being part of a presidential campaign.

And while the public supports an amendment to allow marriage between only a man and a woman, 22 percent said they supported allowing gay marriage, while another 33 percent said they supported permitting gay couples to form civil unions.

Fred Backus contributed reporting for this article.

Study Question:

What are President Bush and Senator Kerry's primary weaknesses according to the result of this poll?

THE CONVENTIONS

President Makes His Pitch, on Jobs and at Ballgame

By NEIL A. LEWIS   *Published Tuesday, April 6, 2004*

ST. LOUIS — President Bush focused his campaign Monday on job creation, celebrating employment figures for March that surpassed all but the most optimistic expectations before exercising that quintessentially presidential prerogative of throwing out the first ball on opening day at a field of his choosing.

Mr. Bush chose to do so here in Missouri, an important tossup state in the presidential race. When he sprinted out of the home-team dugout at Busch Stadium here wearing a Cardinals jacket, he drew a cheer from the stands exceeding even that given a few minutes earlier to Stan Musial, perhaps St. Louis's most revered Hall of Famer. The president then threw an arguable strike to Mike Matheny, the Cardinals' catcher.

But for most of the day, his campaign and that of his presumed Democratic challenger, Senator John Kerry, tangled over jobs and fiscal responsibility.

At a community college in Charlotte, N.C., that serves as a center for federal job training, Mr. Bush announced that he intended to double the number of workers in such training to 400,000 a year.

No new money will be committed to the effort, however. Mr. Bush told his audience that the cost of training twice as many people would be paid by trimming overhead in several jobs programs that would be consolidated into one. The president said he had discovered that jobs training was not working well because "too much money is spent on things that have little to do with job training, such as management studies or travel."

Mr. Bush also pointed to last week's employment report showing that 308,000 jobs were created in March, the largest increase in about four years.

But Mr. Kerry, in round-table discussions in Washington with reporters from regional newspapers, played down that figure, arguing that it had resulted in part from the end of a strike by grocery workers in California. And 40,000 others of the people added to payrolls, he said, "were part-time workers in the construction industry."

"So you are not looking at the kind of robust, important job creation that the country really needs to raise the standard of living in our country," Mr. Kerry added.

The senator also called attention to other figures, those showing the hundreds of thousands of jobs lost over the entire term of the Bush presidency. He noted that after the Sept. 11 attacks, the president promised to create 5.1 million jobs. Instead, Mr. Kerry said, "he's lost 1.8 million private-sector jobs since that pledge."

"He has failed in his promise," the senator said, "by seven million jobs."

Mr. Kerry said it was his hope that the economy would in fact strengthen.

"I hope we create jobs," he said. "Nothing would be better for our country or for me, because the better the country does, the more people will be open to a broader set of choices that we have in the nation about our future. And on every issue, this administration is moving in the wrong direction."

For his part, Mr. Bush portrayed the economy as recovering and said a big reason was his tax cuts.

"When I first came to office, the country was headed into a recession," he said. "Fortunately we cut taxes, which made this recession the shallowest, one of the shallowest, in American history."

He argued that it was war and corporate scandals that had slowed the economic recovery until now.

"The march to war was a difficult period for our economy," he said. "We're now marching to peace. But think what our economy has been through: a recession, an attack, corporate scandals and a march to war. And we've overcome them all."

As the two candidates stumped, the Kerry organization introduced a new Internet advertisement amplifying its accusation that Mr. Bush had approved or proposed programs carrying a 10-year cost of $6 trillion without offering a way to pay for them.

The minute-long ad focuses on a blackboard as the voice of a teacher, off camera, tells a young pupil named George, "It looks like you're having a little trouble with your math," adding, "You've overspent by $6 trillion."

"You spent another $616 billion for your prescription drug plan," the teacher says by way of example, to which the voice of a young boy responds, "I know, but the drug companies need the money." She goes on to mention other initiatives, including the president's plan to make his tax cuts permanent.

Mr. Bush's campaign aides said that the ad relied on specious figures. And in part, they said, it criticizes spending on programs that Mr. Kerry himself supports.

The Bush campaign pointed to Mr. Kerry's support for a Medicare bill that it said would have cost $625 billion over 10 years. Mr. Kerry's campaign did not dispute the assertion but said the issue at hand was Mr. Bush's spending record and its effect on the deficit.

In between the community college appearance and the ballgame, Mr. Bush attended a fund-raiser in Charlotte on Monday that Republican officials said raised more than $1.5 million.

Katharine Q. Seelye contributed reporting from Washington for this article and Jim Rutenberg from New York.

Study Questions:

What news did President Bush cite as evidence that the economy was getting better?

Kerry Struggling to Find a Theme, Democrats Fear

By ADAM NAGOURNEY   *Published Sunday, May 2, 2004*

WASHINGTON — Two months after Senator John Kerry effectively captured the Democratic presidential nomination, party officials say his campaign is being regularly outmaneuvered by the White House as it struggles to find a focus and to make the transition from the primaries to the fight with President Bush.

Even while expressing confidence about Mr. Kerry's prospects, Democratic Party officials said they were concerned about what they described as his trouble in settling on a defining theme for his candidacy, the pace of his advertising and his progress in setting up field organizations in battleground states.

"George Bush has had three of the worst months of his presidency, but they are stuck and they've got to move past this moment," said Donna Brazile, who managed Al Gore's 2000 presidential campaign.

While Ms. Brazile said she thought Mr. Kerry had the time, the political skill and the money to defeat what many Democrats described as a highly vulnerable president, she said, "This is a very crucial moment in the campaign."

Senator John Edwards of North Carolina, one of Mr. Kerry's rivals for the nomination and a potential running mate, has told aides over the past two weeks that he is concerned by signs of trouble in Mr. Kerry's campaign, advisers said. Mr. Edwards disputed that characterization of his views in an interview on Saturday, saying he thought Mr. Kerry was running a "strong campaign."

In Ohio, the state that strategists for Mr. Kerry and Mr. Bush view as perhaps the most critical battleground, Mr. Kerry has yet to hire a state director or open a campaign office. His operation is relying so far on the work of committees working independent of the Kerry campaign.

By contrast, Mr. Bush appointed an Ohio state director on Jan. 1, and opened a headquarters in Columbus, staffed by 13 people, three months ago, his aides said.

The Kerry campaign has yet to open its own full-fledged campaign "war room" staffed with researchers, tacticians and press aides to deal with Republican attacks and systematically marshal surrogates to make Mr. Kerry's case.

In one example of how this has hindered the operation, Mr. Kerry's aides fielded complaints from donors and party leaders this week when the candidate went on television to respond, in a contentious interview, to questions about his anti-Vietnam activities 30 years ago.

Mr. Bush's campaign opened its war room in early March, and it has pumped out a steady barrage of attacks and information about Mr. Kerry's record that Democrats said had blocked Mr. Kerry's attempt to make the election a referendum on Mr. Bush.

Mr. Kerry has yet to unveil a long-promised biographical advertisement highlighting his war record that Democrats urged him to broadcast as soon as possible as a rebuttal to Mr. Bush's $50 million crush of advertisements. Democrats outside the campaign blamed the ouster of a senior media adviser in March for the delay.

Mr. Kerry's advisers denied that and said the biography advertisement would start next week, saying that had always been their plan.

For many Democrats, Mr. Kerry's single biggest difficulty was what they described as his continuing search for a defining theme for his candidacy — typically one of the most urgent tasks of any presidential candidate.

Last week, after completing the most in-depth poll of his campaign, Mr. Kerry unveiled yet another theme for his candidacy: "Together, we can build a stronger America." It was, by the count of one aide, the sixth message Mr. Kerry has rolled out since he announced his candidacy nearly 18 months ago.

"We need to be honest with ourselves: Our candidate is not one who's good with a 30-second sound bite," said Representative Harold E. Ford Jr. of Tennessee, co-chairman of Mr. Kerry's campaign. "He is very thoughtful and it takes him a while to say things."

Mr. Kerry's aides and some Democrats outside the campaign described the concerns as overstated, and said that any drift that might be taking place now would have little meaning next fall. They said Mr. Kerry had used the spring to raise money and that a war room and offices in Ohio and other battleground states would open shortly. And they noted that independent organizations had picked up a lot of the slack so far with big expenditures on television advertising and get-out-the-vote operations.

"This campaign has got six months to go," said Steve Elmendorf, a deputy campaign manager. "He goes out daily and talks about his vision for the country and his vision for the future. You have to take the long view here. You're not going to win every day, and you're not going to win every week."

Mr. Elmendorf added, "I know people are feeling anxious timing-wise, but you have to build a national campaign."

Senator Joseph R. Biden Jr., Democrat of Delaware, said Mr. Kerry was "doing better than he's perceived to be doing," adding, "He's starting to get his sea legs."

"I'm not worried I really am not," Mr. Biden said. "Democrats are so, so, so hungry to defeat Bush that they get so up when things look up and get so down when things look down."

But other Democrats, even while cheered by polls showing that Mr. Bush appeared vulnerable, noted that Mr. Bush was moving aggressively to discredit Mr. Kerry now so that he would be diminished as a candidate by the fall campaign. They said that Mr. Kerry needed to fight that.

"What is the message today, where is the message discipline today?" said one senior Democratic official, who refused to speak by name about the campaign. "Why don't we have people in these 18 states?"

Gov. Edward G. Rendell of Pennsylvania, a former Democratic chairman, said that Mr. Kerry could defeat Mr. Bush if he began laying out a serious case now. He said Mr. Kerry could not wait until the fall.

"If he hasn't established himself as a plausible alternative, people will have tuned out," Mr. Rendell said.

The growing pains reflect in part an organization that, aside from the two senior media consultants Bob Shrum and Mike Donilon has little experience in running presidential campaigns. Mr. Kerry's campaign has been hindered, some aides said, by a turnover in staff members and internal bickering, albeit nowhere near the level that occurred in the campaign last fall.

At a recent meeting of senior staff members, Democrats said, Mr. Kerry's aides became entangled in a lengthy debate over what might seem to be a less than urgent issue: whether they should send a Democratic operative to Bush rallies dressed as Pinocchio, a chicken or a mule, to illustrate various lines of attacks Democrats want to use against Mr. Bush. (They say they want to portray him as a liar, a draft avoider and stubborn.)

But more fundamentally, it underlines what many Democrats have long said has been Mr. Kerry's continuing difficulty this year to present a unifying theme for his candidacy.

In the primaries, Mr. Kerry's biography was his message, as he argued that his experience as a Vietnam veteran made him the strongest opponent to Mr. Bush. That argument for his election evaporated the moment the race ended, Democrats said, and Mr. Kerry has yet to adjust to the new electoral terrain.

Mr. Kerry's advisers disputed that, saying that Mr. Kerry was laying out a clear case for his candidacy as he traveled across the country.

"Anybody who thinks that John Kerry doesn't have a message needs to get out of Washington, D.C.," said Stephanie Cutter, a senior aide, adding, "America is fully open and receptive to the message of putting jobs first and getting America back on track."

Mr. Bush began talking about himself as a "compassionate conservative" in his announcement of his candidacy 18 months before Election Day 2000. This time, Democrats said, Mr. Bush appears to have settled again on an early theme.

"Bush's message is clear," said Carter Eskew, who was a senior adviser to Mr. Gore. "His message is that he is a steady leader and Kerry's a flip-flopper."

Mr. Kerry's predicament has been complicated by the fact that there was no lull after the primary battle. Instead, he faced the twin tasks of building a general election campaign apparatus and dealing with a White House that had spent a year raising money, investigating Mr. Kerry's record and hiring staff members to prepare for this moment.

The result, some Democrats said, has often been a mismatch. In an episode this week that distressed some of Mr. Kerry's strongest supporters, Mr. Kerry was put in a position where he appeared to be defending his Vietnam War record, in a dispute over whether he had thrown away medals in an antiwar protest.

"This Vietnam thing — I'm lost at how you can lose that," said one Democratic member of Congress, who spoke on condition of anonymity. "You go to Vietnam, you're carrying around shrapnel, and you're seen as somehow not telling the truth. I am scratching my head in bewilderment."

Ms. Cutter, though, scoffed at the suggestion that the Kerry campaign was being outmaneuvered by the White House.

"Haven't we run around them too?" Ms. Cutter said. "For every story that George Bush is in, John Kerry is in it, too. When you're running against the power of the White House and all that money, where we are is a pretty impressive feat.

"And we're just starting."

Study Question:

What had Senator Kerry's campaign not done in Ohio at this time that was seen as a sign of organizational weakness?

Polls Show Bush's Job-Approval Ratings Sinking

By DAVID E. SANGER   Published Friday, May 14, 2004

WASHINGTON — As President Bush was traveling through the Midwest on his exuberant bus tour last week, his campaign aides still sounded confident that the revelations of how Iraqi prisoners were abused would do far more harm to the United States' image abroad than to the president's standing at home.

But only a week later, at the very moment Mr. Bush's aides had hoped to be basking in the glow of improving economic numbers, months of setbacks in Iraq are clearly taking their toll.

Mr. Bush's job-approval numbers have sunk to all-time lows, with a majority of Americans now saying, for the first time, that the invasion of Iraq was not worth the mounting cost. At the same time, they give the president far higher marks for his execution of the battle against terrorists, even though he has argued that they are all part of one war.

Congress, including prominent conservatives, has grown so restive about the wisdom of Mr. Bush's strategy that on Thursday the deputy secretary of defense, Paul D. Wolfowitz, had to retreat from a Senate hearing when members of both parties demanded far more specifics than he could provide about plans for spending the $25 billion the president is seeking to pursue the war in Iraq and Afghanistan.

And for the first time, even some of the most loyal administration aides, who have regularly defended every twist in the Iraq strategy, are conceding that the president and his top advisers are stuck in what one of them called "the perpetual debate" about whether to change strategy or soldier on. Mr. Bush's usually sunny campaign advisers make no effort to hide the depth of the problem.

"Look, obviously events and the coverage and what's reported are going to have an effect on how people see the direction of the country," said Matthew Dowd, the chief strategist for Bush-Cheney '04. "In the last two months or three months, there hasn't been a wealth of positive news. It was bound to have an effect, and we expected that."

But Mr. Dowd said that changing Mr. Bush's tone on the campaign trail was not an option. So with some modifications, Mr. Bush is following the script he and his chief political adviser, Karl Rove, drafted as the prisoner scandal emerged: He repeats his disgust with the abuses, then turns the subject immediately back to his broader goals in the war on terrorism,

merging it with the action in Iraq. He did so again on Thursday in a West Virginia school gymnasium.

"We're being tested," Mr. Bush said. "People are testing our mettle. And I will not yield to the whims of the few."

After vigorous applause, he added, "I won't yield because I believe so strongly in what we're doing, and I have faith in the power of freedom to spread its wings in parts of the world that desperately need freedom."

Several of Mr. Bush's advisers have said in recent weeks that they believe the bigger mistake for the president would be to show any weakness, or to yield even to those in his own party who may not want to cut and run, but may be interested in moving quickly to the exits after June 30.

And so far, he is under relatively little pressure from his Democratic opponent in the presidential race, Senator John Kerry, to make a major course correction. Mr. Kerry called months ago for greater United Nations participation; for the last few months, Mr. Bush has done the same. And while Mr. Kerry harshly criticized the president on the prison scandal on Wednesday, he has said that a withdrawal from Iraq would be disastrous, and on Thursday he even endorsed, without qualification, Mr. Bush's request for the $25 billion in additional financing.

"The situation in Iraq has deteriorated far beyond what the administration anticipated," Mr. Kerry said in a statement meant to pre-empt any questions about whether he would hedge his support for the additional money, as he did on a larger request last year. "This money is urgently needed, and it is completely focused on the needs of our troops. We must give our troops the equipment and support to carry out their missions in Iraq and Afghanistan."

Mr. Bush's advisers say they have been surprised that their own candidate's decline in the polls has not resulted in an equivalent boost for Mr. Kerry. But several members of Mr. Bush's foreign policy team noted Mr. Kerry's new line of attack on Wednesday, when he said that Mr. Bush's aides "dismiss the Geneva Conventions, starting in Afghanistan and Guantánamo, so that the status of prisoners both legal and moral becomes ambiguous at best."

Some Republicans close to Mr. Bush's campaign are concerned that Mr. Kerry's comments are the beginning of a new effort to fuel the notion that Mr. Bush's take-no-prisoners attitude created the conditions that allowed prisoner abuses to flourish.

"No one in the White House knows if that argument will stick," said one conservative who met with Mr. Bush's aides this week. "Clearly, it worries them. And it should."

Asked about the state of the presidential race on Thursday as he flew back to Washington from Little Rock, Ark., Mr. Kerry was upbeat. Saying there was much work yet to be done, he added, "I'd rather be where we are, growing, than where they are."

The polls out this week found Mr. Bush, by some measures, at the lowest point of his presidency. Only 46 percent of Americans told the Gallup Poll they approved of the way Mr. Bush was handling his job, and a majority, 51 percent, said they disapproved. Other polls had similar results. A poll by the Pew Research Center found that 44 percent of Americans approved of the president's handling of his job and 48 percent disapproved.

Those numbers alarm many of Mr. Bush's supporters, but Mr. Dowd said: "I always counsel people when we are ahead and behind that since this country is very divided, this thing is always going to be played by the 45-yard lines. And we are still in that place."

Perhaps most alarming for Mr. Bush is the public's assessment that things in the United States are not going particularly well, with only 33 percent of the respondents in the Pew poll saying they were satisfied with the way things were going in the country and 61 percent saying they were dissatisfied.

All this comes at a time when the public's support for the war in Iraq is rapidly fading. For the first time since the war began, a majority of respondents in the Gallup poll, 54 percent, said it was not worth going to war in Iraq; 44 percent said it was worth it.

Only 41 percent said they approved of the way Mr. Bush was handling the situation in Iraq, while nearly 6 in 10, or 58 percent, said they disapproved.

Still, despite the failure to find unconventional weapons and the failure to anticipate the rising insurgency, a majority said it was not a mistake to send troops to Iraq in the first place, a critical argument in Mr. Bush's stump speech.

The polls were taken before the beheading of Nicholas E. Berg was made public. The Gallup poll of 1,003 adults was conducted May 7-9; the Pew, of 1,800 adults, was conducted May 3-9. Each poll was conducted nationwide by telephone and had a margin of sampling error of plus or minus three percentage points.

Study Question:

What "perpetual debate" is it reported that the Bush administration is caught up in? Why is this damaging to the president?

Kerry Outlines Foreign Policy, Attacking Bush

By ROBIN TONER and DAVID E. SANGER   *Published Friday, May 28, 2004*

SEATTLE — Senator John Kerry mounted a broad new attack on the Bush administration's handling of national security on Thursday by accusing the president of undermining "the legacy of generations of American leadership" with a foreign policy that has abandoned the alliance-building of the post-World War II era.

Opening a two-week critique of administration foreign policy, Mr. Kerry sought to present a clear alternative to Mr. Bush's approach to Iraq and the war on terrorism, while pursuing the same central goal: destroying Al Qaeda and its allies. "Let there be no doubt," he warned the terrorist group, "this country is united in its determination to defeat terrorism."

He said that Mr. Bush, by making military pre-emption the central doctrine of a new American foreign policy and employing it too quickly in Iraq, had ignored Theodore Roosevelt's warning that if a man "lacks civility, a big stick will not save him from trouble."

"They looked to force before exhausting diplomacy," he said of the administration's national security team. "They bullied when they should have persuaded. They have gone it alone when they should have assembled a whole team. They have hoped for the best when they should have prepared for the worst. They have made America less safe than we should be in a dangerous world."

Mr. Kerry concluded, "In short, they have undermined the legacy of generations of American leadership, and that is what we must restore, and that is what I will restore."

Foreshadowing proposals that his campaign plans to announce next week, he promised to "modernize the world's most powerful military to meet the new threats" of the 21st century, and to "free America from its dangerous dependence on Mideast oil." At the same time, he vowed he would confront Saudi Arabia, one of America's key suppliers for its role in "financing and providing ideological support of Al Qaeda and other terrorist groups."

Mr. Kerry's tone was more measured than that of former Vice President Al Gore, who called Wednesday for the resignations of almost all of the top national security officials in the Bush White House, except for Secretary of State Colin L. Powell. Instead, Mr. Kerry attacked the competence of the entire administration, declaring that America's military should know he would never ask them "to fight a war without a plan to win the peace."

The speech, and the focus on foreign policy, come at a time of both political opportunity and risk for Mr. Kerry in the middle of the first wartime presidential campaign since 1972. Continued turmoil in Iraq and the prisoner abuse scandal have led to growing doubts about Mr. Bush's policies, and largely account for the president's sinking rating in the polls. Yet Mr. Kerry remains under pressure from some in his own party to present a more forceful alternative to Mr. Bush's approach, with many antiwar Democrats calling for a definite date for pulling out of Iraq.

It was unclear whether Mr. Kerry's careful balancing act on Thursday would satisfy them. "He wants us out of Iraq, but he realizes we can only do that by building a true global coalition," said Representative Sherrod Brown, Democrat of Ohio. "And while some people would like to hear an exit date, I think they understand that we need the coalition to get to that point."

In Mr. Kerry's speech, delivered in sober tones to an invited audience of about 450 people, including many veterans, he paid tribute to the "greatest generation," and then turned the lessons of World War II to current political purposes.

"Our leaders then understood that America drew its power not only from the might of weapons, but also from the trust and respect of nations around the world," he said.

Recalling his own service in Vietnam, Mr. Kerry described Mr. Bush as a man so stubborn that he was unable to rescue a flawed Iraq strategy. "One thing I learned in the Navy," he said, "is that when the course you're on is headed for the shoals, it's pretty smart to shift the rudder."

Mr. Bush, who gave an address on his Iraq strategy on Monday and is scheduled to deliver another at the Air Force Academy in Colorado next week, traveled on Thursday to Nashville, Tenn., to promote his plan to encourage doctors and hospitals to computerize health records. He stopped in a pediatric intensive care ward, drawing attacks from Democrats who said his administration had sought to cut financing for children's hospitals, and attended a fund-raiser that took in $1.7 million for the Republican party. In the 2000 election, Mr. Bush easily won Tennessee, the home state of Mr. Gore, his Democratic opponent.

On Iraq, Mr. Kerry called on Mr. Bush to make a "sustained effort" in the coming weeks to build international support, including at a summit meeting that will be held in Istanbul next month just days before the scheduled handover of Iraqi sovereignty to a transition government.

"He should start at the summit in Istanbul by persuading NATO to accept Iraq as an alliance mission, with more troops from NATO and its partners," Mr. Kerry said. Mr. Powell noted earlier this week that many NATO countries are already in Iraq, and many others do not have the capacity to provide troops.

Mr. Kerry reiterated a proposal that the Administration has dismissed: Creating a United Nations high commissioner to oversee the reconstruction of Iraq, a step that Mr. Kerry's foreign policy aides, mostly veterans of the Clinton Administration, insist would make it far more likely that other nations would contribute to the cause. One senior administration official said today that Mr. Kerry "doesn't appreciate the fact that Iraqis deeply distrust the United Nations" after it left the country last summer, after the bombing of its Baghdad headquarters.

"If President Bush doesn't secure new support from our allies, we will, once again, feel the consequences of a foreign policy that has divided the world instead of uniting it," Mr. Kerry warned. "Our troops will be in greater peril, the mission in Iraq will be harder to accomplish, and our country will be less secure."

Asked about Mr. Kerry's proposal to make greater use of NATO in Iraq, Scott McClellan, the White House press secretary, said on Thursday, "I think he needs to do a better job of explaining his own contradictions." He added that Mr. Kerry is "someone who's been on all sides of the issue when it comes to Iraq. But, you know, this President has worked to build a strong coalition in Iraq and has long called for the United Nations to play a vital role going forward."

Mr. Kerry's focus on energy independence was clearly an effort to attack what his advisers view as one of Mr. Bush's greatest vulnerabilities on the campaign trail, Mr. Kerry often draws his biggest cheers when he describes Vice President Dick Cheney's ties to the oil industry. "If we are serious about energy independence," he said, "then we can finally be serious about confronting the role of Saudi Arabia in financing and providing ideological support of Al Qaeda and other terrorist groups. We cannot continue this administration's kid-glove approach to the supply and laundering of terrorist money." He threatened to "shut out of the U.S. financial system" any country that does not comply.

Study Question:

Why does Senator Kerry think that calling for a United Nations high commissioner in Iraq would be a good step for the United States to take?

Kerry Selects a Partner With Contrasts That Complement

By ADAM NAGOURNEY   *Published Wednesday, July 7, 2004*

WASHINGTON — In John Edwards, Senator John Kerry selected a running mate who embodies the very attributes that some Democrats worry that Mr. Kerry lacks: a vigorous campaign presence, an engaging personal manner and a crisp message that stirred Democrats from Iowa to New Hampshire.

Mr. Kerry even took a risk or two in compensating for his own shortcomings, embracing a trial lawyer who has less governmental experience than any other major vice-presidential candidate in at least 20 years.

As a result, many Democrats said Tuesday, this highest-profile decision of Mr. Kerry's public life was as instructive about the party's presumed presidential candidate as it was about Mr. Edwards. It was the move of a candidate who is proving to be methodical, discreet, coolly pragmatic and exceedingly self-assured; one who is so intensely focused on victory as to be presumably unruffled by the unflattering stylistic contrasts that will surely be drawn whenever he and Mr. Edwards share a stage.

"The fact that he's big enough to accept somebody on the ticket that has that kind of impressive and shiny personality — the public will see that," said Walter F. Mondale, the former vice president. "He was looking for someone who could add strength, not just geographicality, to the ticket and help him get elected."

"Presidential candidates are always suspicious of anybody on the platform who outshines them. I remember how Lyndon used to chafe when Hubert was on the platform," Mr. Mondale continued, referring to his fellow Minnesotan Hubert H. Humphrey and President Lyndon B. Johnson. "Hubert told me he learned to trim his sails when Johnson was there."

And so it was that Mr. Kerry settled on someone whose strengths as a campaigner were often held up to highlight Mr. Kerry's own shortcomings, but whose political attributes were widely agreed upon by Democrats who pressed Mr. Kerry to choose him. In fact, even one Republican who should know, former Vice President Dan Quayle, said the selection was the "logical, natural choice."

It is not just a matter of Mr. Edwards's patching up any holes in the Kerry résumé. He is a prodigious fund-raiser, especially given his deep ties to trial lawyers. He has a strong appeal to minority voters. And he brings the skills of a courtroom lawyer to a campaign debate, as Mr. Kerry learned earlier this year, and as Dick Cheney will soon experience firsthand.

As several Democrats argued Tuesday, Mr. Edwards's selection will probably reconfigure the geographic calculus of both campaigns, putting new regions in play. As a trial lawyer and a politician, Mr. Edwards has over the years styled himself as a champion of the working class, the son of a mill worker who grew up in the rural South. It is a background that suggests that Mr. Edwards will be a strong salesman for the Kerry ticket in rural parts of the Midwest, where even a shift in a handful of votes could be critical.

"He opens up a part of rural America that has been shutting down for Democrats," said James Carville, a Democratic commentator close to Mr. Edwards. "He knows how to talk to them: his language, his speech, his mannerisms, his everything, tells them I was one of you, I understand you."

And while few Democrats believe it is likely that Mr. Edwards can win his own state, North Carolina (the betting among Democratic officials is that Mr. Edwards would have had a tough time winning re-election as senator), his presence on the ticket means that the White House may be forced to divert some resources into Southern states that it would just as soon take for granted.

Yet for all the benefits, there are decided risks to the choice of Mr. Edwards, as even some Democrats said Tuesday. While Mr. Kerry insisted that he would name a running mate whose qualifications to step in as president during a time of war were unassailable, he chose a 51-year-old who has served just five years in the Senate.

Before Mr. Kerry even alerted his supporters of his decision in a mass e-mail message on Tuesday morning, Mr. Bush's camp began pounding Mr. Edwards's qualifications, invoking the words of skepticism Mr. Kerry had voiced about Mr. Edwards during the primary. Michael Nelson, a political scientist at Rhodes College in Memphis, suggested that the selection of Mr. Edwards had the effect of guaranteeing that Mr. Bush would not push Vice President Dick Cheney off the ticket because of the contrast between the two on national security.

"To the extent that you can get voters to concentrate on another terrorist attack and who is going to be there in the cockpit if the president is on the road somewhere," Mr. Nelson said, "that's exactly the kind of frame in which Cheney looks impressive."

But if this campaign has proved anything, it is that Mr. Kerry does not take big risks unless he has to. And considering the number of Democrats who urged Mr. Kerry to take this course, and the fact that presidential candidates typically tap their closest primary competitor, this would hardly qualify as a huge risk.

"It's a very logical choice if you stand back and think about it," Mr. Quayle said. "It's a safe choice."

It was also very much an insight into the style Mr. Kerry has brought to this campaign. Mr. Mondale, remembering his own risky, and ultimately damaging decision, to choose Geraldine A. Ferraro as a running mate in 1984, said he was impressed at Mr. Kerry's success at keeping his deliberations almost entirely secret and organized. "It shows that he's very careful and organized and that he is quite aware of different traps that his predecessors have gotten into in the V.P. selection process," Mr. Mondale said.

It is hardly a secret that Mr. Kerry and Mr. Edwards were not the best of friends during the primary and were never particularly close in the Senate. Some Democrats had suggested that, given their basically cordial relationship — combined with the ego concerns of any presidential candidate that Mr. Mondale noted in recalling Johnson's view of Humphrey — Mr. Kerry would ultimately turn in this vice-presidential selection process to a comfortable friend, Representative Richard A. Gephardt of Missouri.

But James A. Johnson, who headed the search process for Mr. Kerry (and who was Mr. Mondale's campaign chairman in 1984), said that at his very first meeting with Mr. Kerry about the vice-presidential search, the senator made clear that he did not want Mr. Johnson to discount any prospective candidate with whom he quarreled during the primary, or who might eclipse him.

In the end, this might be the single most instructive thing about the choice that Mr. Kerry made on Tuesday. He is, it seems, not very different from the Democratic voters he encountered across the country this year: Ravenous for victory against Mr. Bush, and prepared to do almost whatever it takes to win.

Study Question:

What qualities did Senator Edwards have that many thought would help Senator Kerry's campaign?

— ★ ★ ★ —

Republicans Move Fast to Make Experience of Edwards an Issue

By CARL HULSE and DAVID E. SANGER   *Published Thursday, July 8, 2004*

WASHINGTON — At President Bush's first campaign stop in North Carolina on Wednesday morning, he was asked how Vice President Dick Cheney stacked up against the new Democratic vice-presidential candidate, who, the president was told, is already being described as "charming, engaging, a nimble campaigner, a populist and even sexy."

Mr. Bush was ready with a one-liner: "Dick Cheney can be president."

With that sharp retort, Mr. Bush showed how aggressively Republicans were moving to expose what party leaders view as Senator John Edwards's greatest vulnerability: his lack of experience.

Hoping to offset what they acknowledge is the fresh-faced political appeal of Mr. Edwards, Republicans are trying to make the case that in a dangerous new world, filled with marauding terrorists and nations racing to go nuclear, he is not ready to step into the Oval Office should events require. They argue that he does not even have a full Senate term under his belt, that he is responsible for no significant legislation and that his service on the Senate Intelligence Committee, which Democrats say amounts to far more experience than many candidates have had, hardly amounts to adequate preparation.

"He may have left some footprints on the beaches of North Carolina, but you couldn't find any on the floor of the Senate," said Senator Mitch McConnell of Kentucky, the No. 2 Republican, who said he could not "think of a single thing" memorable about Mr. Edwards's Senate service.

In fact, Mr. Edwards's record indicates he is neither the neophyte that the Republicans portray him to be nor the kind of deeply engaged thinker about terrorism and United States security that one might envision after listening to the conference calls of the campaign of Senator John Kerry. Mr. Edwards spent significant time on security issues before and after Sept. 11, 2001, but by that time he was already contemplating running for president, an effort that kept him away from Capitol Hill.

Before he dropped out of the race earlier this year, Mr. Edwards won praise when he gave a speech that focused on how to create a "global nuclear compact" that would deal with nations abusing provisions of the Nuclear Non-Proliferation Treaty to build nuclear weapons. It paved the way for a similar set of proposals Mr. Kerry made only recently.

What remains to be seen, however, is how well Mr. Edwards can integrate national security issues when he is away from his speechwriters, when there are no briefing books. When *The New York Times* was interviewing the Democratic hopefuls on foreign policy early this year, Mr. Edwards was the only one of the major candidates who did not sit down for a detailed discussion. He cited scheduling pressures.

On Wednesday, Democrats were ready for the critique that their candidate was a lightweight on national security, and they wasted no time opening a counteroffensive. They asserted that Mr. Edwards's five years in the Senate stacked up nicely with the amount of time Mr. Bush himself served as governor of Texas — his first public office — before moving to the Oval Office. Within hours of the announcement of Mr. Edwards's selection on Tuesday, the Kerry campaign was already offering old Democratic foreign policy hands to testify to the candidate's bona fides as a quick learner if not a longtime player.

"His proliferation speech was probably the best foreign policy speech of any candidate during the primaries," Samuel R. Berger, the national security adviser under President Bill Clinton, said Tuesday. "And when 9/11 came along, he probably knew more about the terror issues than most members of the Intelligence Committee."

On Capitol Hill, that theme was echoed with a jab at President Bush. "John Edwards has a lot more Washington experience than George Bush had four years ago," said the Senate Democratic leader, Tom Daschle of South Dakota. "But secondly, it isn't the length of experience in any case, it's the quality of the experience." Moreover, Democrats argue, Mr. Kerry's depth of experience makes it far less important that his running mate do for him what Mr. Cheney did for Mr. Bush.

Senator Edward M. Kennedy, Democrat of Massachusetts and a close ally of Mr. Kerry, noted that his brother John F. Kennedy fell just short of being chosen for the ticket in 1956 with only four years in the Senate to his credit and was elected president at age 43 in 1960.

"The most important qualities are character and judgment, and I think he has demonstrated those here in the Senate and clearly over the course of his life," said Mr. Kennedy.

But Senator Trent Lott, Republican of Mississippi and a fellow member of the Intelligence Committee, said that Democrats would be making a mistake if they were planning to use Mr. Edwards's service on the committee as evidence that he is now ready to participate in Oval Office decision-making.

"The very idea they would maintain that being on the Intelligence Committee for four years would qualify him in a national security-foreign policy sense is ridiculous," Mr. Lott said. "That is a very slim reed."

Republicans are also assailing Mr. Edwards, a former trial lawyer, for his opposition to limiting liability suits, a favorite cause of Mr. Bush and many business organizations. But it is the experience issue, they are convinced, that has the broader political impact. A senior White House official, who would not speak for attribution, said that Mr. Bush's sharp comment on Wednesday morning was an effort to remind Mr. Kerry of his own criteria for a vice president. "Kerry said the primary test is whether he is experienced enough to do the job of president," the official said. "That is the very thing that he took issue with in the case of Edwards, and Edwards fails the senator's own test."

But just in case the president's own words were not enough, on Wednesday afternoon the Bush campaign issued a roundup of quotations and commentary focusing on Mr. Edwards's experience.

"I think it is a problem," said Charlie Black, a Republican strategist, about Mr. Edwards's public service résumé. "What it shows is that Kerry picked the guy because of his campaigning ability rather than his experience and his ability to govern. That just confirms what people think, that Kerry is a political opportunist rather than a political leader."

Senator John E. Sununu, Republican of New Hampshire, said he believed the choice also put a spotlight on what he viewed as Mr. Kerry's own lackluster Senate record. "Now you have two people with a total of 25 years in the Senate with no substantial legislation," he said.

Peter Hart, a Democratic pollster, agreed with Republicans that voters would set a higher standard for competence and experience in this election, given terrorism and the war in Iraq. But he said Mr. Kerry had already cleared that hurdle on the basis of his own qualifications.

"Unlike George W. Bush, who needed a Cheney; unlike Carter, who needed a Mondale; unlike Clinton, who needed a Gore; and unlike Reagan, who needed a Bush, Kerry has the freedom to add to his ticket in terms of linkage with the voters," Mr. Hart said.

Some of Mr. Edwards's Democratic colleagues on the Intelligence Committee also rejected the assertion that he did not have the credentials for the job. Senator Ron Wyden, Democrat of Oregon, said he sat two seats away from Mr. Edwards and recalled that he was among the first to articulate flaws he saw in intelligence gathering.

Study Question:

What, according to Republicans, is Senator Edwards's primary weakness?

★ ★ ★

Invoking His Past, Kerry Vows to Command 'a Nation at War'

By ADAM NAGOURNEY

Published Friday, July 30, 2004

BOSTON — John Forbes Kerry stood before the Democratic National Convention on Thursday night, pledging to "restore trust and credibility to the White House" as he accused President Bush of misleading the nation into war and pursuing policies that he described as a threat to the environment, the economy and the Constitution.

Mr. Kerry promised to take charge of "a nation at war." He invoked his service in Vietnam 35 years ago as he vowed to protect Americans from terror in the 21st century.

"I defended this country as a young man and I will defend it as president," Mr. Kerry said, according to a text of his remarks prepared for delivery. "Let there be no mistake: I will never hesitate to use force when it is required. Any attack will be met with a swift and certain response."

Beyond reinforcing his own credentials as a wartime president, Mr. Kerry used this speech on Tuesday — to what was likely to be the largest audience he has ever faced — to offer a blistering critique of Mr. Bush's 40 months in office, going so far as to echo the very attack Mr. Bush used again Bill Clinton when he ran for president in 2000.

"We have it in our power to change the world again, but only if we're true to our ideals — and that starts by telling the truth to the American people," Mr. Kerry said. "That is my first pledge to you tonight. As president, I will restore trust and credibility to the White House."

Expanding on that theme, Mr. Kerry said, according to the text: "I will be a commander in chief who will never mislead us into war. I will have a vice president who will not conduct secret meetings with polluters to rewrite our environmental laws. I will have a secretary of defense who will listen to the best advice of our military leaders. And I will appoint an attorney general who actually upholds the Constitution of the United States."

For anyone watching the proceedings on this last night of the 44th Democratic convention, there could be little doubt about the urgent and complicated task Mr. Kerry faced: to convince the nation's voters that he could match Mr. Bush's credentials as a wartime president, that he was tough enough to use force when needed and that they should turn out a president in the middle of the war.

As Mr. Kerry came here to accept his party's nomination, he confronted polls that showed him and Mr. Bush locked in a tie, but with signs that Americans, while unhappy with Mr. Bush, were not prepared to turn the White House over to a man that Mr. Bush has sought to diminish as liberal and unprincipled.

The speech brought an end to one of the most peaceful and united Democratic conventions in 50 years and ushered in what will be an extraordinarily busy month of politicking before the Republican National Convention in New York.

It also signaled a remarkable moment for Mr. Kerry, whose hopes of winning the nomination were written off even by many of his friends as the Democratic primary voting began last winter.

Mr. Kerry heads out of Boston on Friday for a two-week cross-country bus trip that will take him from "shining sea to shining sea," as his press secretary, Stephanie Cutter, put it.

Mr. Bush, not wasting a moment, is heading out on his own campaign trip to the Midwest on Friday, and aides said he would use the trip to unveil proposals to help the nation adjust to the economic strains of this new century.

Mr. Kerry, who said on the eve of the convention that he did not want the week-long gathering to dissolve into a forum of attacks on Mr. Bush, barely mentioned Mr. Bush by name in his long speech this evening, according to the advance text of his address.

Yet with every sentence, he set out differences between the men on issues as he sought to pre-empt attacks on him by the White House, and he tried to use the opportunity provided by having the first convention to set the theme of the campaign.

In the process, Mr. Kerry borrowed the words of Vice President Dick Cheney; Ron Reagan, son of the late president; and even Mr. Bush himself.

"I want to say these next words directly to President George W. Bush: In the weeks ahead, let's be optimists, not just opponents," Mr. Kerry said.

"Let's build unity in the American family, not angry division. Let's honor this nation's diversity; let's respect one another; and let's never misuse for political purposes the most precious document in American history, the Constitution of the United States."

He added: "The high road may be harder, but it leads to a better place. And that's why Republicans and Democrats must make this election a contest of big ideas, not small-minded attacks."

Mr. Kerry borrowed from remarks Mr. Reagan made at his father's funeral in directly confronting what he suggested was Mr. Bush's attempt to draw differences between the senator and the president on values and religion.

"In this campaign, we welcome people of faith: America is not us and them," he said. "I think of what Ron Reagan said of his father a few weeks ago, and I want to say this to you tonight: I don't wear my own faith on my sleeve.

"But faith has given me values and hope to live by, from Vietnam to this day, from Sunday to Sunday," he said. "I don't want to claim that God is on our side."

He even invoked one of Mr. Cheney's favorite lines from the 2000 campaign in drawing a contrast with Mr. Bush. "America can do better: So tonight we say, help is on the way," he said.

Mr. Kerry surrounded himself on stage with symbols of military might and reminders of his own service in war. There was grainy videotape showing him, gun in hand, on the fields of Vietnam.

He was introduced by Max Cleland, a former senator from Georgia who lost three limbs as a result of his own service in Vietnam.

The nation met 14 crewmates — members of his "band of brothers" — who accompanied him as he commanded Swift boats down the bullet-ridden Mekong Delta.

"We need a strong military and we need to lead strong alliances," Mr. Kerry said, when it came time for him to speak. "And then, with confidence and determination, we will be able to tell the terrorists: You will lose and we will win. The future doesn't belong to fear; it belongs to freedom."

Mr. Kerry was not alone in challenging Mr. Bush's management of the war.

Gen. Wesley K. Clark invoked Woodrow Wilson, Franklin Roosevelt and Harry Truman to portray the Democratic Party as a political body steeped in military history and success.

"This hall and this party are filled with veterans who have served under this flag — our flag," Mr. Clark said. "We rose and stood reveille to this flag. We saluted this flag. We fought for this flag. And we've seen brave men and women buried under this flag. This flag is ours. And nobody will take it away from us."

Mr. Clark implored his audience to embrace Mr. Kerry. "America," he said, "hear this soldier."

Senator Joseph R. Biden Jr., following up on Mr. Kerry's own remarks on foreign policy, said: "Let no enemy mistake our basic decency for lack of resolve. Americans will fight with every fiber of our being to protect our country and our people. When John Kerry is commander in chief, he will not hesitate to unleash the unparalleled power of our military, on any nation or group that does us harm, without asking anyone's permission."

While foreign policy dominated much of Mr. Kerry's address, it was far from his only theme of the speech, and reflected the calculation of Mr. Kerry's advisers that he needed to at least neutralize the issue of terrorism in order to move the election debate to issues that might play better for the Democrats.

Mr. Kerry presented himself as a the candidate of "the middle class who deserve a champion, and those struggling to join it."

Even as he took pains to say he had an optimistic view of the future — again, responding to Mr. Bush's effort to portray him as dour and pessimistic — he spoke of a nation that was suffering because of Mr. Bush's policies.

"We are a nation at war — a global war on terror against an enemy unlike any we have ever known before," he said. "And here at home, wages are falling, health care costs are rising, and our great middle class is shrinking. People are working weekends; they're working two jobs, three jobs, and they're still not getting ahead."

"We can do better and we will," he said. "We're the optimists."

Again and again, Mr. Kerry used his speech to try to push back on lines of attack that the White House had launched against him, such as its portrayal of him as inconsistent.

"Now I know there are those who criticize me for seeing complexities — and I do — because some issues just aren't all that simple," he said. "Saying there are weapons of mass destruction in Iraq doesn't make it so. Saying we can fight a war on the cheap doesn't make it so.

"And proclaiming mission accomplished certainly doesn't make it so."

Study Question:

What was Senator Kerry's "urgent and complicated" task at the convention?

★ ★ ★

Upbeat Republicans Revive Bush Theme of Compassion

By TODD S. PURDUM   *Published Wednesday, September 1, 2004*

Facing perhaps three times the television audience that saw its sharp-edged speakers on Monday, the Republican National Convention circled back last night to President Bush's winning 2000 campaign theme of "compassionate conservatism," portraying him as not only hardheaded but also bighearted enough to lead "the most historic struggle my generation has ever known," as his wife, Laura, put it in a prime-time speech.

On the first night the major broadcast networks carried live coverage of the proceedings, the party offered up glowing testimonials from Arnold Schwarzenegger, the Terminator turned popular Republican governor of California; prominent black Republicans like Education Secretary Rod Paige and Lt. Gov. Michael S. Steele of Maryland; the president's telegenic nephew George P. Bush, who is Hispanic; and a variety of Republican women, chief among them Mrs. Bush herself.

"No American president ever wants to go to war," said Mrs. Bush, who was presented to the delegates via satellite by her husband from the campaign trail in Pennsylvania, after their twin 22-year-old daughters introduced him to the hall in a goofily affectionate tribute that amounted to their national political debut.

"Abraham Lincoln didn't want to go to war," Mrs. Bush said, "but he knew that saving the union required it. Franklin Roosevelt didn't want to go to war, but he knew that defeating tyranny demanded it. And my husband didn't want to go to war, but he knew the safety and security of America and the world depended on it."

Mrs. Bush, who told Mr. Bush she would marry him almost 27 years ago so long as she never had to make a political speech, proceeded last night to make a heartfelt and articulate one, describing her husband in terms he seldom if ever applies to himself as "wrestling with these agonizing decisions" about war in Iraq.

She delivered a ringing endorsement of "George's work to protect our country and defeat terror, so that all children can grow up in a more peaceful world."

Mr. Schwarzenegger, whose victory in a recall election last year upended normal partisan politics in the most populous state, offered the delegates a twist on his signature cinematic line, declaring: "Ladies and gentlemen, America is back. Back from the attack on our homeland, back from the attack on our economy and back from the attack on our way of life. We are back because of the perseverance, character and leadership of the 43rd president of the United States, George W. Bush."

And, to deafening applause and cheers, he said: "To those critics who are so pessimistic about our economy, I say, Don't be economic girlie men! The U.S. economy remains the envy of the world."

If Monday was a tribute to Mr. Bush's battle against terrorism, the second day of the convention focused more on the domestic issues Mr. Bush campaigned on in 2000. Speaker after speaker testified that he had made great headway in delivering on his promises, and had gone to war only to project the same compassionate American values overseas.

There were repeated appeals to the aspirations and dreams of immigrants and minorities, and repeated assertions that the Republicans remain the party of free enterprise and individual achievement, yet not insensitive to those in need. Lest the upbeat theme be lost on anyone, delegates waved signs proclaiming themselves "people of compassion."

George P. Bush, long one of his uncle's most popular surrogate campaigners, especially among Latinos and immigrant groups, spoke in English and Spanish, telling delegates: "Our party has always represented the interests of all people seeking opportunity. We are the home of entrepreneurs, men and women who want to know the pride of accomplishment, the honor of self-sufficiency."

But the night was not without some more passionate — and confrontational — words. Several speakers defended Mr. Bush's decision to place limits on federal stem-cell research as a sign of the party's stance regarding human life. Senator Elizabeth Dole of North Carolina, one of Mr. Bush's rivals for the nomination in 2000, offered a blunt defense of the party's stance against same-sex marriage, abortion and secularism.

"Two thousand years ago a man said, 'I have come to give life and to give it in full,'" Mrs. Dole said. "In America, I have the freedom to call that man Lord, and I do. In the United States of America, we are free to worship without discrimination, without intervention and even without activist judges trying to strip the name of God from the Pledge of Allegiance, from the money in our pockets and from the walls of our courthouses. The Constitution guarantees freedom of religion, not freedom from religion. The right to worship God isn't something Republicans invented, but it is something Republicans will defend."

Senator Bill Frist of Tennessee described the Democratic nominee, John Kerry, as "the personal injury lawyers' best friend" and promoted the Republicans' effort to expand access to health care, saying, "I'll tell you what Senator Kerry's prescription will be: Take a handful of tax increases and don't call me in the morning."

And Mr. Steele, the first African-American elected to statewide office in Maryland, styled himself as the Republican answer to the Democrats' black keynote speaker, Barack Obama of Illinois, and unleashed some tough words about Mr. Kerry, who he noted "recently said he doesn't want to use the word 'war' to describe our efforts to fight terrorism."

"Well, I don't want to use the words 'commander in chief' to describe John Kerry," Mr. Steele said.

Mr. Paige offered a tribute to Mr. Bush's education policy, declaring: "This election may be multiple choice, but there's only one correct choice. To go forward, not back. To choose compassion, not cynicism. To set high standards, not settle for second best. To elect a true reformer with proven results, not a Johnny-come-lately with more promises."

Just before 7:30 p.m., Pennsylvania, the swing state that Mr. Bush has visited more than 30 times — more often than any other as president — cast all its 75 votes for Mr. Bush, officially putting him over the top of the 1,255 votes needed for nomination.

A couple hours later, Mr. Schwarzenegger recalled his youth in Austria, which was still partly Soviet-occupied, and the fear he felt at a Soviet checkpoint. "I was a little boy; I wasn't an action-hero back then," he said. "But I remember how scared I was that the soldiers would pull my father or my uncle out of the car and I'd never see him again."

By contrast, he said, "in this country, it doesn't make any difference where you were born. It doesn't make any difference who your parents were. It doesn't make any difference if, like me, you couldn't even speak English until you were in your 20's. America gave me opportunities, and my immigrant dreams came true. I want other people to get the same chances I did, the same opportunities. And I believe they can. That's why I believe in this party and why I believe in this president."

As a large part of the California delegation donned Terminator sunglasses in tribute, he described the United States as a nation that sends Peace Corps volunteers to "teach village children," that "gives more than any other country to fight AIDS in Africa and the developing world," and that "fights not for imperialism, but for human rights and democracy."

He recalled his recent visits with wounded American troops to rebut the trademark reference of Senator John Edwards, the Democratic vice-presidential contender, to two Americas, one rich and one poor. "I tell you this: Our young men and women in uniform do not believe there are two Americas," Mr. Schwarzenegger said. "They believe there's one America, and they're fighting for it."

On the convention floor, Gov. George E. Pataki of New York summed up the crowd's response and his own: "All I can say is, 'Wow.'"

Polls show that Mr. Schwarzenegger and Mrs. Bush are far more popular with voters across the country than the president is, and it was no accident that they were chosen to head the bill on the night the convention first reached a broad national audience in prime time.

Mrs. Bush seemed eager to offer a life partner's loving explanation of a man who always seems to shrink from explaining himself.

"Tonight," she said, "I want to try and answer the question that I believe many people would ask me if we sat down for a cup of coffee or ran into each other at the store: You know him better than anyone, you've seen things no one else has, why do you think we should re-elect your husband as president?"

She answered herself by saying, "As you might imagine, I have a lot to say about that."

She went on to describe "some very quiet nights at the dinner table," nighttime phone talks with foreign leaders and "an intense weekend at Camp David" with Prime Minister Tony Blair of Britain as Mr. Bush weighed his options for confronting Saddam Hussein. "And I was there when my husband had to decide," she said. "Once again, as in our parents' generation, America had to make the tough choices, the hard decisions, and lead the world toward greater security and freedom."

As a result, she said, "50 million more men, women and children live in freedom thanks to the United States of America and our allies."

The Bush twins lent an energetic, slightly madcap air to a scene that was otherwise often serious, teasing their parents and grandparents for their taste in music, and gently mocking their father's own youthful indiscretions while describing their family's lessons about "unconditional love," as Barbara put it.

Jenna explained their approach to the delegates, saying: "All those times when you're growing up and your parents embarrass you? This is payback time on live TV."

Study Question:

Why were Governor Schwarzenegger and First Lady Laura Bush highlighted at the Republican National Convention?

THE HORSE RACE

Kerry Needs to Sharpen His Attacks, Democrats Say

By DAVID M. HALBFINGER and JODI WILGOREN   *Published Wednesday, September 1, 2004*

NANTUCKET, Mass. — Democrats say they fear that Senator John Kerry squandered the capital from the Democratic National Convention as he spent August reeling from a frontal assault on his character and Vietnam War record, with many urging him to immediately sharpen his attack on Mr. Bush and make a more persuasive case for change.

Mr. Kerry's inner circle, aware that he will probably enter the closing eight weeks of the race behind Mr. Bush, has been huddled in strategy meetings and adding staff members. At the same time, some prominent Democrats outside the campaign have been calling for a new urgency and have been chafing at Mr. Kerry's decision to remain at his vacation home here this week, mostly out of the spotlight during the Republican convention. He is, however, scheduled to speak to the American Legion on Wednesday in Nashville.

"I want him to be campaigning like his life depended on it," said Representative Charles B. Rangel, Democrat of New York. "I don't want him to be playing football or surfing or bicycling. I want him to tell people we're at war and we shouldn't be at war, to talk about all of the things we used to have and we lost in the last four years."

In Virginia, where Democrats have been viewing the presidential race as winnable for the first time in decades, the state Democratic chairman, Kerry Donley, said he, too, thought it was unwise for Mr. Kerry to have hunkered down this week. "You have to take the campaign to the people," Mr. Donley said. "I'd like to see him out there right now."

Thursday at midnight, Mr. Kerry will begin a four-day bus blitz in Springfield, Ohio, and the candidate and his running mate and their families will fan out to rallies in 22 states over the Labor Day weekend. Wednesday, the campaign plans to buy $45 million in television time to run advertisements in 20 states until Election Day.

Some of Mr. Kerry's own advisers, speaking on condition of anonymity, attributed his lost month of August to his own lackluster performance on the stump, as well as a few tactical blunders, such as his insistence, under prodding from Mr. Bush, that he would still have voted to authorize force in Iraq even if he knew all that he does now about the failure to find unconventional weapons. One of Mr. Kerry's confidants said Mr. Kerry had expressed frustration that the campaign seemed unable to gain any traction in recent weeks.

Other Democrats criticized what they see as a too-cautious campaign, relying too heavily on the election being a referendum on an unpopular president.

"They seem to be trying to figure out what to do here, and it's a little late for that, you know," said one veteran Democratic strategist, who like many others refused to be quoted by name in criticizing the campaign.

Stephanie Cutter, Mr. Kerry's communications director, insisted that the campaign remained on its long-term game plan.

"We knew we were going dark in August and that the Bush campaign was going to unleash tens of millions of dollars of negative attacks," Ms. Cutter said of Mr. Kerry's decision to conserve resources in August by run-

ning few advertisements.. "That's what they did, and much to their dismay, we're still standing."

But outside the campaign, some are even second-guessing the decision to make the Democratic convention so focused on Mr. Kerry's personal biography and war record.

"We're going to have to make a real strong case for change," said Robert T. Matsui, the Californian who heads the Democrats' Congressional Campaign Committee. "I think that's where we must begin to focus and my hope is that's where we're going to be going."

Representative Jerrold Nadler of New York said that he thought the campaign's handling of domestic issues was fine, but that Mr. Kerry needed to devise a sharper attack on Mr. Bush at the heart of his case for re-election: national security.

"We have them beaten on every issue six ways to Sunday, even on Iraq; the majority of people say it was a mistake to go in, except on the war on terrorism," Mr. Nalder said. "A lot of political campaign managers say you ignore it. I think you take him head on on it."

Mr. Kerry huddled here in recent days with Mary Beth Cahill, his campaign manager, and several key advisers. His campaign said the sessions were preparation for his debates with Mr. Bush and denied persistent speculation about a looming personnel shakeup.

Several senior Kerry aides who spoke on the condition of anonymity said the addition of two former Clinton hands, Joel Johnson and Joe Lockhart, had improved both operations and the mood inside the campaign headquarters in Washington.

Mr. Johnson's role is to keep the communications team laser-focused on Mr. Kerry's core messages rather than being distracted by each new attack from the Bush camp. Mr. Lockhart is to begin traveling with Mr. Kerry in Nashville and will work directly with reporters.

The two campaign veterans, both of whom Ms. Cutter worked with in the Clinton White House, have siphoned off some of her responsibilities, but not her title; aides said her job remained secure, if refocused.

Some inside the campaign also said the coming weeks would bring increasing influence from several longtime Kerry strategists: John Sasso, whom Mr. Kerry made general election manager of the Democratic National Committee; Michael Whouley, the ground guru who is credited with helping Mr. Kerry win the Iowa caucuses; and Tad Devine, who already is one of the team's senior media minds and public voices; as well as Doug Sosnick, another former Clinton aide.

"There's not going to be a staff shakeup," Ms. Cutter said definitively. "We are building up the team with the best and the brightest to take us through the homestretch."

Mr. Lockhart added: "Any idea that the senior leadership of this campaign is about to be changed is just not true."

The arrival of the new staff members came after several weeks in which Mr. Kerry was slow to respond to an assault on his Vietnam combat record and character, with largely unsubstantiated accusations, by the group Swift Boat Veterans for Truth.

"I wish he'd borrowed a page from Bill Clinton — when attacked, you respond quickly, that day," said Ron Oliver, the Arkansas Democratic chairman.

But Bill Carrick, a longtime Democratic strategist, said he would not have "gotten engaged in it" at all. "I think it is a distraction," he said.

Several longtime Kerry aides said that no matter how badly August had gone for Mr. Kerry, he still had the debates ahead and that he had shown again and again that he performs best when his back is against the wall.

"This is still the guy who can dig deeper than anyone when it counts," said one veteran adviser. "What I hate is that they're going to make it about his ability to do that one more time, when it didn't have to be. Imagine the pressure."

Study Question:

What are some of the reasons for Senator Kerry's being criticized as too cautious?

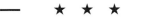

Bush's Backers Donate Heavily to Veteran Ads

By GLEN JUSTICE and ERIC LICHTBLAU

Published Saturday, September 11, 2004

WASHINGTON — Swift Boat Veterans for Truth, an advocacy group that jolted the presidential race with commercials questioning Senator John Kerry's military service, said it had raised $6.7 million in a windfall brought about by the group's high profile in recent weeks.

Several of the largest donors are longtime supporters of President Bush, according to a financial disclosure report filed on Friday with the Federal Election Commission.

The largest contributor was T. Boone Pickens, a famous Texas oilman and longtime Republican supporter who was a major political backer of Mr. Bush's father, who gave $500,000 to the Swift boat group. Aubrey McClendon, chief executive of Chesapeake Energy in Oklahoma, gave $250,000; Bob Perry, another Bush supporter from Texas, gave $200,000 to seed the group; and Albert Huddleston, a Texas energy executive who has raised money for Mr. Bush, gave $100,000, records show.

Sam Wyly, the wealthy Texas entrepreneur who financed commercials attacking Senator John McCain in the 2000 Republican primary against Mr. Bush, also made the list at $10,000, as did his brother Charles, records show. At least two Swift boat donors are also listed as Bush Pioneers, meaning they raised at least $100,000 for Mr. Bush.

"The words 'tidal wave' come to mind," said Mike Russell, a spokesman for the group, who added that "you don't often see that type of grassroots reaction."

The group's impact is one of the most visible examples of the effect that so-called 527 committees are having on the presidential race. The groups, named for the section of the tax code that created them, can collect unlimited soft money contributions not allowed for political parties and candidates.

Democrats made heavy use of these groups early in the race, raising tens of millions through organizations like the Media Fund, America Coming Together and the MoveOn.org Voter Fund, drawing complaints from Republicans who said they were illegal. Mr. Bush's campaign filed a complaint with the election commission in March alleging that the Kerry campaign and the Democratic groups were violating campaign finance laws by coordinating illegally.

Indeed, a procession of top strategists have moved back and forth between Mr. Kerry's campaign and the advocacy groups, drawing fresh rounds of Republican protests.

Swift Boat Veterans for Truth has spent more than $4.2 million since April, Mr. Russell said, with most of it spent on radio and television advertisements. It had about $2.5 million left in the bank this week, he said, leaving the group in a strong position to continue its barrage of attack ads.

The Swift boat group's disclosure listed only part of its contributions — donors who gave $1,000 or more — and was required because the group ran advertisements covered under new campaign finance laws. The group released additional information in a statement and in interviews, saying that much of its money had come in after its provocative advertisements captured media attention in recent weeks.

Among the donors from President Bush's home state was Lawrence Gelman, a doctor in McAllen, who made six contributions of $1,000 each beginning in late August. Mr. Gelman said he first heard about the group's campaign amid last month's burst of media reports and decided he wanted to support it.

"This thing about Kerry and his medal to me sounded very odd," Mr. Gelman said. "As a physician, I understand that for someone to be wounded that many times and not have to be hospitalized sounded very strange. It made me feel better to help people who had what I thought was a legitimate point of view."

Dr. Gelman, 52, described himself as conservative politically and said that while he had donated to Mr. Bush, he was not a big fan: "To me, he's the lesser of two evils. I'm not thrilled with President Bush, but I think he would be better than Kerry."

He added that the counterattacks on the Swift boat group and its veracity have spurred him to make more contributions.

"When someone comes out against them, I get riled up and give another contribution," he said. The group began attacking Mr. Kerry's record in Vietnam months ago and started its commercials in recent weeks which, though their claims have been called into question, have monopolized the presidential race at times.

The group has used only three television ads attacking Mr. Kerry, but it has received reams of national publicity in the media. A new book, "Unfit for Command: Swift Boat Veterans Speak Out Against John Kerry" by John E. O'Neill, a fellow Vietnam veteran who has been criticizing Mr. Kerry for 30 years, and Jerome R. Corsi, hit No. 1 on the best-seller list.

Mr. O'Neill, who has been the group's most visible spokesman, donated more than $35,000 to the group, records show.

The Bush-Cheney campaign has denied involvement in the attacks and Mr. Bush has called for such advocacy groups to stop spending money in the race, saying they are "bad for the system."

Friday's disclosure drew jeers from Mr. Kerry's campaign, which has filed a complaint against the group before the election commission last month, accusing the organization of violating campaign laws by coordinating its activities with the Bush campaign.

Chad Clanton, a campaign spokesman, called Swift Boat Veterans a "discredited group."

"No matter how much money they spend," Mr. Clanton said, "two facts remain: their charges have been completely discredited, and they're clearly doing the dirty work of the Bush-Cheney campaign."

A spokesman for the Bush campaign, Scott Stanzel, declined comment on the financial disclosure.

Mr. Russell said that the group's money was proof that its commercials were resonating.

"We've been successful at getting our message out," he said. "More important, we've been successful at raising questions about Mr. Kerry's character and his fitness as commander in chief."

After the commission declined to regulate 527 committees before this year's election, Republicans entered the fray with groups of their own, which have themselves begun to raise tens of millions of dollars.

Study Question:

Why were the Swift Boat Veterans for Truth ads so controversial?

★ ★ ★

CBS Apologizes for Report on Bush Guard Service

By JIM RUTENBERG and KATE ZERNIKE   *Published Tuesday, September 21, 2004*

After nearly two weeks at the center of a news media storm, Dan Rather and CBS News admitted yesterday that they could not authenticate four documents the network had used to raise new questions about President Bush's Vietnam-era National Guard service and said the news report had been a "mistake in judgment."

Network officials said a former Texas National Guard officer had misled their producers about how he obtained the documents, which came under scrutiny almost as soon as the network broadcast its report on the CBS Evening News and "60 Minutes" on Sept. 8.

While CBS stopped short of calling the memos a fraud, it said it could not now say for certain where the documents came from.

"Based on what we now know, CBS News cannot prove that the documents are authentic, which is the only acceptable journalistic standard to justify using them in the report," said Andrew Heyward, the CBS News president. "We should not have used them. That was a mistake, which we deeply regret."

The network's admission tarnishes the reputation of what was once the nation's most prestigious broadcast news division. Just two weeks ago, its 72-year-old anchor seemed to have one of the biggest stories of the campaign, in the twilight of his career.

Mr. Rather initially insisted that the wide questioning of the documents — purportedly from the personal files of Lt. Col. Jerry B. Killian, Mr. Bush's squadron commander — came in large measure from partisans, delivered his own apology yesterday during his evening broadcast. "I want to say personally and directly I'm sorry," he said, adding, "This was an error made in good faith."

The day's concessions were a sharp turnaround from more than a week ago, when CBS News officials and Mr. Rather, for decades the face of CBS News, were standing steadfastly by the report, dismissing days of accusations from document experts that the records were fakes produced on a modern computer.

Network officials yesterday admitted that the man who gave them the documents had lied about where he got them, and that inconsistencies in the cloak-and-dagger account he gave them in the past few days had left CBS unable to say definitively where they came from. Moreover, CBS was unable to reach the person the man identified as his source, Mr. Rather said.

In an interview broadcast on CBS last night, the former guardsman who gave the memos to the network, Bill Burkett, acknowledged that he had lied. Mr. Burkett told Mr. Rather that he had felt pressure from CBS to reveal his source, and so "simply threw out a name" to explain how he had come by the documents. He insisted he had not forged them.

The network said it was appointing a panel of experts to review how such a flawed report got onto the air, especially one with such potential implications for a sitting president some 50 days before an election. It said it would make the results public.

The network's admissions quickly reverberated on the campaign trail. Mr. Bush's spokesman Scott McClellan demanded that the source of the documents be found. White House officials also called on the campaign of the Democratic presidential nominee, Senator John Kerry, to explain any contact it has had with Mr. Burkett. Joe Lockhart, a senior adviser to Mr. Kerry, acknowledged today that he had talked to Mr. Burkett. He said he had done so at the behest of a CBS producer, who had promised to help Mr. Burkett, an ardent Bush opponent, relay some campaign advice. Mr. Lockhart said there was no connection between the campaign and the memos.

Terry McAuliffe, the chairman of the Democratic National Committee said attention should still be paid to questions about whether Mr. Bush fulfilled his service obligations three decades ago.

CBS News officials said yesterday "a perfect storm," of circumstances — including intense competition, faith in the reputation and judgment of a producer, and the reliance on a source with questionable integrity — had led to their journalistic lapse.

But there was dissension inside CBS News, according to a number of people interviewed, with some saying that Mr. Rather and his producer, Mary Mapes, had simply relied too much on one dubious source. "These are not standards that would ever be tolerated," said Morley Safer, a correspondent on the sister "60 Minutes" Sunday program.

By the accounts of Mr. Rather and other officials, they began to understand that their defense was unsustainable last Thursday, when Mr. Burkett confessed to CBS that he had lied about where he got the four memorandums. While he had initially said he gotten them from another former guardsman, people at CBS said, he then told them that the documents came through a convoluted process that started with a phone call from a stranger and ended with the handoff of an envelope at the boisterous Houston Livestock Show.

Mr. Rather flew to Texas to interview Mr. Burkett on Saturday. By Sunday, the tapes were back in New York, and network officials say they knew they had a serious problem.

They said they had had a brief moment of hope when they believed they had deduced the name of a woman who might have called Mr. Burkett to offer him the documents. But on Monday, they were giving up on that lead, too.

"We couldn't confirm the new story — maybe it's true — but we can't confirm it," said one official at the network who spoke on condition of anonymity. "And in the meantime we're hanging out there, we have vouched for these things and we don't have anything to stand on. We've come to the moment where there's nothing to prove his story."

Mr. Rather and Ms Mapes, a respected producer whose credits include securing the photographs of the abuse at the Abu Ghraib prison for CBS this spring, had been working on the story of Mr. Bush's National Guard Service since Mr. Bush's first presidential campaign. They knew that other reporters were working on the same story.

Mr. Bush's aides have repeatedly said that the president fulfilled his service obligations, but the official record left gaps, including questions about why Mr. Bush failed to take his pilot physical.

Mr. Rather said he and Ms. Mapes had heard that there were records that could fill that gap and, Mr. Rather said, "We worked it."

About 18 months ago, they focused on Mr. Burkett, who said he had overheard aides to Mr. Bush, when he was governor of Texas, instructing guard officials to scrub his file of anything embarrassing. Mr. Burkett went public with that account last February. "We accelerated our questioning," Mr. Rather said.

By mid-August, they did not have the documents. Around then, Gary Killian, whose father had been Mr. Bush's squadron commander, got a call from Ms. Mapes, asking if he knew where she might find memos his father had apparently written criticizing Mr. Bush's service. Gary Killian said that he and his stepmother both told Ms. Mapes they did not believe the elder Mr. Killian had kept such records, and that he had thought well of Mr. Bush.

The Friday before Labor Day, Mr. Rather said yesterday, he heard that Ms. Mapes had the documents. He was in Florida covering Hurricane Frances, and flew to Texas.

In the course of their conversations with Mr. Burkett, the team had grown increasingly confident in his story, he said. Mr. Rather said they had called his friends and neighbors to get a sense of his credibility and were satisfied.

"I knew him before by telephone," Mr. Rather said, "and otherwise had checked out what his reputation was in the community that he lived, and even people who disliked him and had arguments with him, including Republicans and supporters of Bush. They all said he's a truth teller."

Mr. Rather said that Mr. Burkett had initially refused to say who gave him the documents, and that CBS pressured him to do so. "We made it clear that the chain of possession was very important to us," Mr. Rather said.

Mr. Rather recalled that Mr. Burkett had said he had gotten the documents from a former guard member who was now overseas. Mr. Rather said producers had tried to get in touch with him, but could not. Knowing his identity bolstered the team's confidence just the same.

"It was a person who could have had direct access to Killian's files," he said. "That made it believable."

A lawyer for Mr. Burkett, Gabe Quintanilla, said Monday that his client was given the documents at the livestock show in March, and kept them to himself because he did not know whether they were authentic.

"This is a simple West Texan middle-aged gentleman going along his own way when this happens to get dumped in his lap," the lawyer said.

After months of pressure from CBS, Mr. Quintanilla said: "He said I'll give these to you on the condition that you have them subjected to the highest scrutiny. Quite frankly, it's unfortunate that their job wasn't done on that end."

In a posting on an e-mail newsletter for Texas Democrats, Mr. Burkett wrote yesterday, "Don't believe everything you read — even from CBS."

The network's executives acknowledge that its team's failure to get in contact with the supposed original source should have been a red flag. But they said they had remained confident because Ms. Mapes and Mr. Rather had such confidence in Mr. Burkett. They also believed their other reporting had affirmed the sentiments Colonel Killian supposedly expressed in the documents. The White House, moreover, did not initially raise any doubts about the memos.

"We were completely confident from what we were hearing from Mary, and there was no reason not to trust her," said Josh Howard, the executive producer of the "60 Minutes" Wednesday edition.

The papers seemed to hand the network a huge scoop, purporting to document how Colonel Killian — who died 20 years ago — had felt pressure to "sugar coat" Mr. Bush's record because the young lieutenant, whose father was the ambassador to the United Nations, was "talking to someone upstairs." They indicated that Mr. Bush had been suspended from flying because he had not met guard standards, and had failed to appear for a physical examination.

Mr. Heyward has said his confidence was first jolted when Mr. Killian's secretary, Marian Carr Knox, stepped forward to say that while she had typed similar memos about Mr. Bush for Mr. Killian, she believed that the CBS documents were fake. Around then, Mr. Burkett admitted to Ms. Mapes that he had lied about the provenance of the documents.

On Thursday, Mr. Rather and other CBS officials talked to him by telephone. "That was the first time I heard him say, 'Look, I have misled you about one thing and one thing only,'" Mr. Rather said. Mr. Rather and Ms. Mapes persuaded Mr. Burkett to speak on camera. On Mr. Heyward's orders, one of his top deputies, Betsy West, accompanied Mr. Rather to Dallas for the interview, a four-hour session.

It was there that Mr. Burkett gave the tale of how a woman phoned him and told him that she could get documents to him if he could get himself to Houston.

Mr. Burkett, officials said, was believable in his delivery. But when researchers checked his past statements against a transcript of the interview, there were inconsistencies, executives said.

Officials convened at the CBS headquarters Sunday afternoon and decided they could hang on no longer.

Study Question:

Why was CBS led to believe in the authenticity of these documents?

— ★ ★ ★ —

Poll Finds Kerry Assured Voters in Initial Debate

By RICHARD W. STEVENSON and JANET ELDER *Published Tuesday, October 5, 2004*

Senator John Kerry came out of the first presidential debate having reassured many Americans of his ability to handle an international crisis or a terrorist attack and with a generally more favorable image, but he failed to shake the perception that he panders to voters in search of support, according to the latest *New York Times*/CBS News poll.

The poll also found significant doubts about President Bush's policies toward Iraq, with a majority of the public saying that the United States invaded too soon and that the administration did a poor job thinking through the consequences of the war. But Mr. Bush maintained an advantage on personal characteristics like strong leadership and likability, as well as in the enthusiasm of his supporters.

Four weeks from Election Day, the presidential race is again a dead heat, with Mr. Bush having given up the gains he enjoyed for the last month after the Republican convention in New York, the poll found. In both a head-to-head matchup and a three-way race including Ralph Nader, the Republican and Democratic tickets each won the support of 47 percent of registered voters surveyed in the poll.

Last month, Mr. Bush led Mr. Kerry by 50-42 in a two-way race and 50-41 in a three-way race.

The results, which parallel those of several other national polls in the past few days, are likely to intensify interest in tonight's debate in Cleveland between the vice-presidential candidates, Senator John Edwards of North Carolina and Vice President Dick Cheney, as well as the two additional presidential debates, on Friday and Oct. 13.

Aides to both campaigns said yesterday that the running mates' debate, which begins at 9 p.m. Eastern time, was unlikely to have a major impact on the vote in November. That did not stop them, though, from trying once again to set high expectations for the other side, as each campaign pointed to the debating strengths of its opponents.

Some of the drop in Mr. Bush's numbers appeared to reflect the traditional cycle in which a candidate's standing surges after his nominating convention and then declines somewhat. Both the Bush and Kerry campaigns have said for months that they expect the race to be tight at the very end.

But Mr. Kerry also scored notable gains in several areas that could be vital in a campaign being largely fought over the war in Iraq and the threat of terrorism.

Forty-one percent of registered voters said they had confidence in Mr. Kerry's ability to deal wisely with an international crisis, up from 32 percent before the debate. Thirty-nine percent said they had a lot of confidence that Mr. Kerry would make the right decisions when it came to protecting against a terrorist attack, up 13 percentage points.

On both scores, however, Mr. Kerry still trailed Mr. Bush. Fifty-one percent of voters said they had confidence in Mr. Bush's ability to deal with an international crisis, unchanged from before the debate, and 52 percent said they had a lot of confidence in his ability to protect against a terrorist attack, up slightly from 50 percent last month.

Mr. Bush's strategy of portraying Mr. Kerry as an unprincipled flip-flopper appears to have stuck in the national consciousness. Sixty percent of registered voters said Mr. Kerry told people what they wanted to hear rather than what he really believed, about the same level as throughout the spring and summer. The corresponding figure for Mr. Bush was 38 percent.

It is unclear whether the race for the White House has merely reverted to a steady state in which neither candidate can establish a clear lead, whether Mr. Bush can regain the advantage with a strong performance in the next debates or whether Thursday was a turning point at which Mr. Kerry seized the initiative.

There is also considerable uncertainty over whether national polling numbers reflect the state of play in the 18 or so swing states where the election will be decided and where the relative success of get-out-the-vote efforts by both sides could prove to be the difference. In recent weeks there has been a surge of new voter registrations in many states as the two campaigns and their allies seek to ensure that every possible supporter goes to the polls on Nov. 2.

The Kerry campaign said the poll showed that the race was moving in its direction. The nationwide telephone poll of 979 adults included 851 registered voters. The margin of sampling error for the entire sample, and for registered voters, is plus or minus three percentage points.

"The public took a measure of John Kerry standing next to the president, and came to the conclusion that he had the strength, judgment and experience to be the commander in chief," said Joe Lockhart, a senior strategist for Mr. Kerry.

Mr. Bush's team said he remained ahead in the ways that would count most on Election Day.

"We always said this race would be close," said Matthew Dowd, Mr. Bush's chief campaign strategist. "When style fades quickly, leadership and policies remain, and that is where the president has the advantage."

Over all, Mr. Kerry appears to have come off well in the debate, which respondents to the poll said, 60 percent to 23 percent, that he won.

The proportion of registered voters saying they viewed Mr. Kerry favorably jumped to its highest level, 40 percent, from 31 percent in mid-September, while the number of people who said they did not view him favorably, 41 percent, did not change appreciably.

The percentage of voters who said their opinion of Mr. Bush was favorable dipped slightly, to 44 percent from 47 percent last month, while the percentage of voters who said they did not view Mr. Bush favorably increased to 44 percent from 38 percent in that period.

Mr. Kerry, who sought to emphasize during the debate how aggressive he would be in hunting down terrorists and protecting the nation from attack, made some headway in winning back women who had been drifting toward Mr. Bush. Mr. Kerry led Mr. Bush 48 percent to 46 percent among women; last month Mr. Bush led among women 48 percent to 43 percent.

The results show not only how closely divided the nation is, but also how clearly defined the differences are between the candidates, especially on foreign policy. Just under half of voters said both Mr. Bush and Mr. Kerry would bring the right balance to judgments about when to go to war. But 46 percent said Mr. Bush would not be careful enough and 31 percent said Mr. Kerry would be too careful.

The poll indicated that Americans continued to have doubts about both candidates. Mr. Bush's job approval rating, at 47 percent, was little changed from last month and close to what has traditionally been a danger zone for an incumbent seeking re-election. His approval ratings for his handling of foreign policy, Iraq and the economy were even lower, and a narrow majority of respondents, 51 percent, said the country was on the wrong track.

The poll suggested that the daily bloodshed in Iraq and Mr. Kerry's strategy of hammering away at Mr. Bush's handling of the war might be resonating among voters. Asked what kind of job Mr. Bush had done in anticipating what would happen in Iraq as a result of the war, 59 percent said he had done a poor job and 34 percent said a good job. A slight majority, 52 percent, said the United States had been too quick to go to war in Iraq, compared with 37 percent who said the timing was about right.

But Mr. Bush maintained his reputation as an effective leader in confronting terrorism, with 57 percent of respondents saying they approved of his handling of the issue and 37 percent disapproving. Asked whether they thought of Mr. Bush as someone they would like personally, even if they did not approve of his policies, 61 percent said yes, versus 48 percent for Mr.

Kerry. Asked whether both candidates have strong qualities of leadership, 62 percent said yes for Mr. Bush and 56 percent said yes for Mr. Kerry.

Mr. Kerry continued to generate increased levels of enthusiasm for his candidacy among those who said they supported him, with 48 percent saying they strongly favored him, up from 40 percent last month. But, in a race that could hinge on turnout, Mr. Bush maintained a strong advantage on that measure, with 70 percent of his backers saying they strongly favored him, up from 63 percent.

Fifty-five percent of voters said Mr. Bush had made clear what he wants to accomplish in the next four years, a five-point increase since last month, while 45 percent of voters said Mr. Kerry had a clear agenda, up seven points in the same period.

The poll found that 65 percent of voters did not think Mr. Bush had a clear plan for getting American troops out of Iraq, and that 59 percent of voters did not think Mr. Kerry had one. Half of voters said they thought Mr. Bush made the situation in Iraq sound better than it is, and 43 percent said Mr. Kerry made it sound worse.

Study Question:

In what areas did Senator Kerry's standing improve after this debate, according to these polls?

—— ★ ★ ★ ——

Arms Report Spurs Bitter Bush-Kerry Exchange

By DAVID E. SANGER and JODI WILGOREN   *Published Friday, October 8, 2004*

WAUSAU, Wis. — President Bush and Senator John Kerry engaged in a bitter long-distance debate on Thursday about a report by the C.I.A.'s top weapons inspector, with Mr. Bush arguing that it demonstrated he was "right to take action" in Iraq despite its findings that Saddam Hussein had eliminated stockpiles of illicit weapons years before the invasion.

Mr. Kerry, emboldened by the report's unraveling of the administration's main rationale for going to war, shot back with his sharpest indictment yet, telling reporters that Mr. Bush and his vice president "may well be the last two people on the planet who won't face the truth about Iraq."

Mr. Bush's statement in Washington, and a more impassioned case he made here late Thursday afternoon, were his first responses to the 918-page report by Charles A. Duelfer. Both Mr. Bush and Vice President Dick Cheney focused on sections of the report saying that Mr. Hussein had wanted to reconstitute his weapons programs at some point and that he had found his way around economic sanctions.

Unbowed and defiant in an appearance on the South Lawn of the White House, Mr. Bush said of the Iraqi dictator, "He retained the knowledge, the materials, the means and the intent to produce weapons of mass destruction." And, he added, "he could have passed that knowledge on to our terrorist enemies."

Speaking to reporters in Englewood, Colo., Mr. Kerry said that "this week has provided definitive evidence" for why Mr. Bush should not be reelected. The president, Mr. Kerry said, was "not being straight with Americans."

Both the speed and the heat of the exchanges paved the way for the second presidential debate, to be held Friday night in St. Louis. Perhaps more important, they underscored how both candidates have staked their electoral fates to how voters judge them on Iraq, even as the debates nominally turn to questions of the economy and domestic policy.

Talking to a cheering partisan crowd here in the afternoon, the president quoted at length from a statement the Massachusetts senator made on the floor of the Senate almost exactly two years ago, warning of the danger that Mr. Hussein might spread nuclear technology around the world.

After reading from Mr. Kerry's statement, the president looked up at his crowd in a park here and asked, "Just who is the one trying to mislead the American people?"

The Kerry campaign said Mr. Bush had yanked its candidate's words out of context, and noted that in the same speech, Mr. Kerry had said: "Regime change in and of itself is not sufficient justification for going to war, particularly unilaterally, unless regime change is the only way to disarm Iraq of the weapons of mass destruction pursuant to the United Nations resolution. As bad as he is, Saddam Hussein, the dictator, is not the cause of war."

On Iraq, Mr. Bush has chosen to give no ground, even after a week

that his own aides concede has brought nothing but bad news, from the C.I.A. report to a declaration by the former American administrator in Iraq, L. Paul Bremer III, that the administration committed too few troops to secure Iraq after the invasion was over.

For Mr. Kerry, who has struggled throughout his two-year quest for the presidency to defend himself against charges that his voting record on the war was one of vacillation, the Duelfer report and Mr. Bremer's comments have provided the opportunity to attempt to refocus the debate on Mr. Bush's rationale for going to war, and his competence in executing the occupation.

On Thursday Mr. Kerry described Saddam Hussein as an enemy the Bush administration had "aggrandized and fictionalized," and he warned that if Mr. Bush does not recognize the severity of problems in Iraq, the violence in the Middle East will escalate. "If the president just does more of the same every day and it continues to deteriorate, I may be handed Lebanon, figuratively speaking," Mr. Kerry said, a reference to the civil wars that racked that country for many years.

Standing on a grassy lawn with the snow-topped Rockies in the distance, he said, "My fellow Americans, you don't make up or find reasons to go to war after the fact."

"Ambassador Bremer finally said what John Edwards and I have been saying for months," Mr. Kerry continued, referring to an acknowledgment this week by the former head of the Coalition Provisional Authority about shortcomings of the American military operation in Iraq. "President Bush's decision to send in too few troops, without thinking about what would happen after the initial fighting was over, has left our troops more vulnerable, left the situation on the ground in chaos and made the mission in Iraq much more difficult to accomplish."

Mr. Bush was clearly ready for the senator's attack, and he arrived in Wisconsin armed with statements made by Mr. Kerry before the 1991 Persian Gulf war and in the debate that led up to last year's war in Iraq.

"Just a short time ago, my opponent held a little press conference and continued his pattern of overheated rhetoric," Mr. Bush said within minutes of arriving here. "He accused me of deception. He's claiming I misled American about weapons, when he himself cited the very same intelligence" in voting to authorize Mr. Bush to threaten war.

Then he quoted Mr. Kerry's statement in the Senate, where he asked, rhetorically, "Who can say that this master of miscalculation will not develop a weapon of mass destruction, even greater, a nuclear weapon, then reinvade Kuwait or push the Kurds out, attack Israel, any number of scenarios to try to further his ambitions," or "allow those weapons to slide off to one group or another."

The heart of the difference between the two candidates is how they dealt with that assessment.

Mr. Bush says he saw such intelligence as a justification for pre-emptive war — a long-established international practice that permits a nation to strike just prior to being struck itself. The Duelfer report now indicates that the intelligence was wrong in major respects.

Mr. Kerry says that the pre-war intelligence was a reason to press for further inspections and pressure on Mr. Hussein, and that the vote to authorize war was part of that pressure. But he faults Mr. Bush for acting before that process had a chance to work.

Mr. Kerry also responded Thursday to a statement by Condoleezza Rice, the national security adviser, that the Pentagon, not the White House, was responsible for determining troop deployment. He noted that Ms. Rice works in the White House, "the place that used to have a sign that said 'The Buck Stops Here.'"

"For President Bush, it's always someone else's fault — denial, and blaming someone else," he declared. "It is wrong for this administration to blame our military leaders, particularly when our military leaders gave him the advice that he didn't follow. The truth is, the responsibility lies with the commander in chief."

Mr. Kerry had spent Wednesday in seclusion, drilling with a large team of aides in a nondescript hotel ballroom transformed to resemble Friday night's debate set, leaving the response to the C.I.A. report and to a biting speech by Mr. Bush to his running mate, Senator John Edwards.

But on Thursday he did not resist the opportunity to frame the Iraq issue in advance of Friday's debate.

To underscore the broader case he is trying to make against Mr. Bush's credibility, Mr. Kerry used the word "truth" eight times in as many minutes. "You'll always get the truth from me," he vowed, "in good times and in bad."

Asked about the section of the Duelfer report that suggested Mr. Hussein would have rebuilt his weapons if sanctions waned, Mr. Kerry said it "underscores the failures of this administration's diplomacy."

Vice President Cheney, appearing in Miami, had the opposite interpretation, saying the report showed that "as soon as the sanctions were lifted he had every intention of going right back" to resuming his illicit weapons program. "To delay, defer, wait wasn't an option," he said. "The president did exactly the right thing."

Mr. Edwards similarly echoed his running mate, charging of the Bush administration in an appearance in Bayonne, N.J., that Mr. Bush and Mr. Cheney "are willing to say left is right, up is down."

Study Question:

What did the arms report say that caused so much controversy?

Bush and Kerry Trade Attacks in Their Second Presidential Debate

By ROBIN TONER and ADAM NAGOURNEY   *Published Saturday, October 9, 2004*

President Bush forcefully defended his economic record and his decision to invade Iraq in the second presidential debate on Friday, while Senator John Kerry asserted that Mr. Bush was conducting a negative, misleading campaign because he lacked the record to justify re-election.

In the opening minutes of the 90-minute forum, held at Washington University in St. Louis and featuring questions from an audience of 140 uncommitted voters, the two men immediately began a series of attacks and counterattacks.

Mr. Bush, aggressive from the start, told the audience that Mr. Kerry had consistently shifted positions on Iraq and was unsuited to lead the nation in a dangerous era. "I don't see how you can lead this country in a time of war, in a time of uncertainty," with a record of such inconsistency, Mr. Bush said.

Mr. Bush defended his handling of Iraq, asserting that he saw a "unique threat" in Mr. Hussein, "as did my opponent," adding, "We all thought there were weapons there."

Mr. Kerry asserted that Mr. Bush was attacking him to deflect attention from his record. "The president didn't find weapons of mass destruction in Iraq, so he's turned his campaign into a weapon of mass deception," Mr. Kerry said. "And the result is you've been bombarded with advertisements suggesting that I've changed my position on this, that, or the other thing"

The Democratic challenger also quickly noted that Mr. Bush was the first president since the Depression to preside over a net loss of jobs.

The first questioner asked Mr. Kerry about his reputation for being "wishy-washy." He answered by starting an attack on Mr. Bush's credibility, saying the president's campaign was a "weapon of mass deception." Mr. Kerry said he had differences with Mr. Bush over the implementation of several major pieces of legislation, including the Patriot Act and the No Child Left Behind education law, but that he had been consistent in the way he approached economic and foreign policy.

Referring to Mr. Bush's tax cuts, Mr. Kerry said his economic policy would not focus on helping the wealthy, as the president's had. "That's not wishy-washy, that's what I'm fighting for — you," Mr. Kerry said.

Mr. Bush pressed his case that Mr. Kerry had caved in to political pressure, especially over Iraq.

"I see why people in your workplace think he changes positions a lot because he does," Mr. Bush said.

Mr. Bush mentioned Mr. Kerry's position for the Iraq war, his positions on tax cuts and other matters on which the Bush campaign has tried to portray Mr. Kerry's position as ever-shifting.

"I don't see how in a time of war, in a time of uncertainty, you can change your mind because of politics," Mr. Bush said.

Asked if it was "reasonable" to attack Iraq when it had no more access to banned chemical, biological and nuclear weapons than did countries like North Korea, the president said: "I saw a unique threat in Saddam Hussein, as did my opponent, because we thought he had weapons of mass destruction. And the unique threat was that he could give them to Al Qaeda."

If Mr. Kerry's approach had been followed, Mr. Bush said, "Saddam Hussein would still be in power and the world would be more dangerous."

In his response, Mr. Kerry said Mr. Bush was trying to distract the public with the accusation that Mr. Kerry had changed his mind because the domestic situation was a mess.

"The president wishes I had changed my mind," Mr. Kerry said. "He wants you to believe that, because he can't come here and tell you he's created new jobs for Americans," Mr. Kerry said. "We've got five million Americans who've lost their health care, 96,000 of them right here in Missouri," he said.

"I've never changed my mind about Iraq," he said. He said he had always thought Mr. Hussein was a threat, and wanted to give the president authority to use force against him back in the Clinton administration.

But he criticized Mr. Bush's conduct of the war. "This president rushed to war, pushed our allies aside, and Iran now is more dangerous, and so is North Korea, with nuclear weapons," he said.

Mr. Bush "took his eye off the ball" with his focus on Iraq, Mr. Kerry said.

Responding to Mr. Bush's claim that sanctions had not been working, Mr. Kerry said the fact that Mr. Hussein did not have weapons of mass destruction demonstrated that diplomacy was indeed working. If the United States had used smart diplomacy, Mr. Kerry said, "We could have saved $200 billion and an invasion of Iraq, and Osama bin Laden could be in jail or dead."

The debate — the second of three scheduled encounters between Mr. Bush and Mr. Kerry — came at a difficult time for the president, after a week of setbacks on the domestic and foreign policy fronts and a series of polls showing the race statistically even.

Just hours before the debate began, the Labor Department reported private sector job growth of 96,000 in September, a weaker-than-expected showing that Republicans scrambled to defend. It was the last jobs report before the election, and Democrats were quick to note that Mr. Bush was the first president since Herbert Hoover to seek re-election with a net loss in jobs during his term — 585,000 in Mr. Bush's case.

Mr. Bush was also on the defensive after the chief United States weapons inspector for Iraq issued a report on Wednesday that said there was no evidence that Mr. Hussein had, or was about to acquire, prohibited unconventional weapons — undermining a central rationale for the war.

The political pressures for Mr. Bush were heightened because of his lackluster performance in the first debate, when he repeatedly showed his irritation and impatience at Mr. Kerry's criticism. Before that debate, Mr.

Bush had held a modest but significant lead in almost every poll. That lead quickly eroded; a Time Magazine poll released Friday, taken Oct. 6 and Oct. 7, found each man with 45 percent of the vote.

In the face of those challenges, Mr. Bush came back swinging this week, asserting that the Democratic challenger would purse a "policy of retreat" in Iraq and advance policies that "would weaken America" at a dangerous time.

The Kerry campaign entered the debate on a decidedly confident note, with Democrats convinced that the campaign's core message — that Mr. Bush was out of touch with reality on the economy and Iraq — was striking a powerful chord with the voters. The Kerry team handed out rose-colored glasses at the debate to underscore their point that Mr. Bush failed to see the problems confronting Americans.

The Republican Party, meanwhile, fielded volunteers in dolphin suits (one named Flipper) to highlight their assertion that Mr. Kerry's 20-year Senate career was full of flip-flops on national security, the economy, and other major issues.

The debate, which was moderated by Charles Gibson of ABC, required Mr. Kerry and Mr. Bush to answer questions from voters who were leaning toward one candidate but were still uncommitted. The voters were selected by the Gallup Organization, and submitted their questions in advance to Mr. Gibson, who picked which would be asked. The debate was intended to be evenly divided between domestic and foreign policy.

The third and final debate will be held next Wednesday at Arizona State University.

Study Question:

Why did President Bush have more pressure on him in this second debate?

★ ★ ★ ——

Group of Bishops Using Influence to Oppose Kerry

By DAVID D. KIRKPATRICK and LAURIE GOODSTEIN   *Published Tuesday, October 12, 2004*

DENVER — For Archbishop Charles J. Chaput, the highest-ranking Roman Catholic prelate in Colorado, there is only one way for a faithful Catholic to vote in this presidential election, for President Bush and against Senator John Kerry.

"The church says abortion is a foundational issue," the archbishop explained to a group of Catholic college students gathered in a sports bar here in this swing state on Friday night. He stopped short of telling them whom to vote for, but he reminded them of Mr. Kerry's support for abortion rights. And he pointed out the potential impact his re-election could have on Roe v. Wade.

"Supreme Court cases can be overturned, right?" he asked.

Archbishop Chaput, who has never explicitly endorsed a candidate, is part of a group of bishops intent on throwing the weight of the church into the elections.

Galvanized by battles against same-sex marriage and stem cell research and alarmed at the prospect of a President Kerry — who is Catholic but supports abortion rights — these bishops and like-minded Catholic groups are blanketing churches with guides identifying abortion, gay marriage and the stem cell debate as among a handful of "non-negotiable issues."

To the dismay of liberal Catholics and some other bishops, traditional church concerns about the death penalty or war are often not mentioned.

Archbishop Chaput has discussed Catholic priorities in the election in 14 of his 28 columns in the free diocesan newspaper this year. His archdiocese has organized voter registration drives in more than 40 of the largest parishes in the state and sent voter guides to churches around the state. Many have committees to help turn out voters and are distributing applications for absentee ballots.

In an interview in his residence here, Archbishop Chaput said a vote for a candidate like Mr. Kerry who supports abortion rights or embryonic stem cell research would be a sin that must be confessed before receiving Communion.

"If you vote this way, are you cooperating in evil?" he asked. "And if you know you are cooperating in evil, should you go to confession? The answer is yes."

The efforts of Archbishop Chaput and his allies are converging with a concerted drive for conservative Catholic voters by the Bush campaign. It has spent four years cultivating Catholic leaders, organizing more than 50,000 volunteers and hiring a corps of paid staff members to increase Catholic turnout. The campaign is pushing to break the traditional allegiance of Catholic voters to the Democratic Party, an affiliation that began to crumble with Ronald Reagan 24 years ago.

Catholics make up about a quarter of the electorate, and many conservative Catholics are concentrated in swing states, pollsters say. Conservatives organizers say they are working hard because the next president is quite likely to name at least one new Supreme Court justice.

Catholic prelates have publicly clashed with Catholic Democrats like former Gov. Mario M. Cuomo of New York and Geraldine A. Ferraro, the former representative and vice-presidential candidate.

But never before have so many bishops so explicitly warned Catholics so close to an election that to vote a certain way was to commit a sin.

Less than two weeks ago, Archbishop Raymond L. Burke of St. Louis issued just such a statement. Bishop Michael J. Sheridan of Colorado Springs and Archbishop John J. Myers of Newark have both recently declared that the obligation to oppose abortion outweighs any other issue.

In theological terms, these bishops and the voter guides argue that abortion and the destruction of embryos are categorically wrong under church doctrine. War and even the death penalty can in certain circumstances be justified.

But it is impossible to know how many bishops share this view, and there is resistance from a sizable wing of the church that argues that voting solely on abortion slights Catholic teaching on a range of other issues, including war, poverty, the environment and immigration.

Liberal Catholics contend that the church has traditionally left weighing the issues to the individual conscience. Late in the campaign, these Catholics have begun to mount a counterattack, belatedly and with far fewer resources.

In diocesan newspapers in Ohio, Pennsylvania and West Virginia, they are buying advertisements with the slogan "Life Does Not End at Birth." Organizers of the campaign say it is supported by 200 Catholic organizations, among them orders of nuns and brothers.

"We are looking at a broader picture, a more global picture," said Bishop Gabino Zavala, an auxiliary bishop of Los Angeles who is president of Pax Christi USA, a Catholic peace group that initiated the statement. "If you look at the totality of issues as a matter of conscience, someone could come to the decision to vote for either candidate."

In the presidential debate on Friday, Mr. Kerry discussed his religious beliefs. "I was an altar boy," he said. "But I can't take what is an article of faith for me and legislate it for someone who doesn't share that article of faith, whether they be agnostic, atheist, Jew, Protestant, whatever."

Alexia Kelley, director for religious outreach for the Democratic National Committee, said Mr. Kerry's policies reflected overall Catholic teachings.

The Republican Party is betting that many observant Catholics will disagree. The National Catholic Reporter reported that on a visit to the pope this year Mr. Bush asked Vatican officials directly for help in lining up American bishops in support of conservative cultural issues.

For four years, the party has held weekly conference calls with a representative of the White House for prominent Catholic conservatives. To ramp up the Catholic campaign last summer, the party dispatched its chairman, Ed Gillespie, and a roster of well-known Catholic Republicans on a speaking tour to Catholic groups throughout the swing states.

The party has recruited an undisclosed number of Catholic field coordinators who earn $2,500 a month, along with up to $500 a month for expenses to increase conservative Catholic turnout.

In an interview this week from Albuquerque, where he was rallying Catholic outreach workers, Leonard A. Leo, executive vice president of the Federalist Society, a conservative legal group, who has taken the role of informal adviser to Mr. Bush's campaign on Catholic issues, said Republicans hoped that Mr. Bush could draw even more of the Catholic vote than Reagan, who attracted 54 percent when he ran for re-election in 1984. Mr. Bush received just under half of the Catholic vote in 2000. In a Pew Research poll this month, 42 percent of white Catholics favored Mr. Bush, 29 percent favored Mr. Kerry, and 27 percent were undecided.

"I can't think of another time in recent political history where a political party and a campaign have paid more attention to faithful Catholics," Mr. Leo said.

How the bishops' guidance or the new voter guides are playing in the pews remains to be seen. In a poll for Time magazine in June, 76 percent of Catholics said the church's position on abortion made no difference in their decisions about voting. But in a *New York Times* poll conducted over the summer, 71 percent of Catholics favored some restrictions on abortion, compared with 64 percent of the general public.

Republican strategists say Catholics and others who attend religious services at least once a week tend to be more conservative. Fifty-three percent of those Catholics supported Mr. Bush in 2000 compared with 47 percent of all Catholics, according to exit polls. The Rev. Frank Pavone, national director of Priests for Life of Staten Island, N.Y., says priests with his group are going from church to church in swing states like Florida, giving fellow priests sample homilies for each Sunday in November, inserts for church bulletins and voter guides.

Father Pavone spoke by telephone from Aberdeen, S.D., where he said he was meeting with dozens of priests and nuns to teach them how to organize transportation to take parishioners to the polls. Addressing abortion, he said he told audiences, "One can't hold public office and say it's O.K. to kill some of the public."

In past elections, the main voter guide distributed in many Catholic churches was a questionnaire from the United States Conference of Catholic Bishops that listed candidates' stands on dozens of issues. This year, conservative Catholic groups sought to derail the questionnaire, because it appeared to give equal weight to each issue. When neither the Bush nor Kerry campaigns responded to the questions by the deadline, the bishops' conference abandoned the effort, a spokesman, Msgr. Francis Maniscalco, said.

Many parishes are having free-for-alls over what materials to use in helping Catholics think through their choices. Many bishops are using a document the bishops developed last year, "Faithful Citizenship." It tells Catholic voters to consider a range of issues and vote their consciences. Other parishes are instead using a guide from a conservative Web site, Catholic Answers, at www.catholic.com. The guide says it is a sin to vote for a candidate who supports any one of five "non-negotiable issues," abortion, euthanasia, embryonic stem cell research, human cloning and homosexual marriage.

Archbishop Chaput says he has had no contact with either campaign or political party. He says his sole contact with the White House has been his appointment to the United States Commission on International Religious Freedom. The prelate acknowledged that his communications director, Sergio Gutierrez, had worked in the Bush administration, but Archbishop Chaput said he had known Mr. Gutierrez long before that.

It was only logical for the Republicans to view the church as a "natural ally" on cultural issues, the archbishop said. He said that would end if a Republican candidate supported abortion rights.

"We are not with the Republican Party," he said. "They are with us."

Mr. Kerry's Catholicism is a special issue for the church, Archbishop Chaput said. To remain silent while a President Kerry supported stem cell research would seem cowardly, he said. The Rev. Andrew Kemberling, pastor of St. Thomas More Church in Centennial, the largest congregation in the archdiocese, said parishioners sometimes accused him of telling them how to vote. He said his reply was: "We are not telling them how to vote. We are telling them how to take Communion in good conscience."

Study Question:

What issue are Catholic Bishops so concerned about?

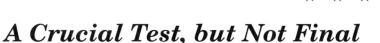

A Crucial Test, but Not Final

By TODD S. PURDUM   *Published Thursday, October 14, 2004*

George W. Bush and John Kerry ended the last of their three debates as they began them, with starkly defined differences in substance, semantics and style on almost every major question facing the American public, and they head into the campaign's homestretch amid every indication that their debates mattered — perhaps more than any such encounters in a quarter century.

They were a rough passage for Mr. Bush, who saw his September lead over Mr. Kerry slip away as the Democratic nominee established himself as a plausible presidential alternative. In a crucible where voters measure the self-confidence, authority and steadiness of the candidates, Mr. Kerry delivered a consistent set of assertive, collected performances. Mr. Bush appeared in three guises: impatient, even rattled at times during the first debate, angry and aggressive in the second, sunny and optimistic last night.

In just 13 days the debates have upended the horse race and brought Mr. Kerry back to dead-even in the polls.

But this is not 1980, when Ronald Reagan's strong performance in his sole debate against Jimmy Carter just a week before Election Day helped him gain support at an average rate of 1.2 percentage points a day, and left President Carter no time to recover.

Now, there are almost three weeks of a final free-for-all, one likely to be dominated not by set-piece face-offs or scripted conventions that the candidates themselves can control, but by forces and factors comparatively beyond the power of either. The main thing each man can control is his own message: Mr. Bush seems sure to keep accusing Mr. Kerry of a career of weak decisions on national security and tax-and-spend liberalism at home, while Mr. Kerry is all but certain to keep hammering Mr. Bush's handling of the war in Iraq and the American economy.

From the candidates' first meeting in Coral Gables, Fla., to their finale in Tempe, Ariz., last night, the debates have been the public's clearest window into just what different people Mr. Bush and Mr. Kerry are — and just what different presidents they would be. The tightly structured format minimized Mr. Kerry's penchant for prolixity and magnified Mr. Bush's instinctual impatience. Mr. Bush's certainties clashed with Mr. Kerry's subtleties, and the president's optimism was challenged by Mr. Kerry's skepticism.

As a rule, Mr. Bush summoned sweeping, time-tested labels, as he did last night, to paint Mr. Kerry as sitting "on the far left bank" of the American mainstream in an effort to appeal to core Republican supporters, while Mr. Kerry invoked the language that Bill Clinton used so successfully with swing voters, pledging to support "people working hard, playing by the rules, trying to take care of their kids."

But if both men often played to type, there were times when they played against their common caricatures last night. Mr. Kerry will never be warm and fuzzy, but television is a medium that loves a cool persona and he spoke calmly while Mr. Bush occasionally seemed agitated, as he has, to one degree or another in each debate.

Mr. Kerry has a confessed fondness for nuance, but he gave clear and direct answers last night on topics that Mr. Bush dodged, declaring his belief that people are born gay and that he would not appoint judges who would overturn Roe v. Wade. On the question of homosexuality, Mr. Bush told the moderator, "You know, Bob, I don't know," and on abortion, he twice avoided a direct answer, saying only that he would not have a "litmus test" for judges.

At one point, Mr. Bush, who prides himself on his plain-spokenness, lapsed into Washingtonese, citing the "Lewin Report," a private consultant's analysis of Mr. Kerry's health care proposal, a reference that surely mystified most viewers.

In many ways, last night's encounter was the most subdued of the three, and it will almost surely be the least watched, competing as it did against not one but two baseball playoff games.

Neither candidate made anything that would count as a major gaffe, and neither seemed to score a knockout punch. But Mr. Kerry repeatedly chastised Mr. Bush for lost jobs, the growing gulf between rich and poor, inequitable pay for women and lack of health insurance. Mr. Bush ignored the specifics of many of Mr. Kerry's complaints, instead frequently citing his efforts to improve American educational standards.

"This is one of those classic years where the debates actually did change the direction of the race," said Alan Schroeder, an associate professor at Northeastern University and author of "Presidential Debates: 40 Years of High-Risk TV." "It doesn't always happen that way. It doesn't even often happen that way. But clearly something in that first debate caused voters to take a second look at John Kerry, and take another look at George Bush."

He added: "The question is, are the debates conclusive, or are they just one more chapter in an ongoing saga that has another plot twist or two yet to come."

There is every reason to think the latter is true.

The latest polls show the race in a virtual deadlock. Both men are now fully as much at the mercy of events as they are of each other. Almost any variable — violence in Iraq or a possible terrorist attack at home, the vagaries of turnout or the verdict of the small but significant slice of voters who have yet to make up their minds — might make a difference. Each candidate has reason for hope, and ample evidence for doubt.

By many empirical measures, the race has been Mr. Kerry's to lose all year.

For months, Mr. Bush has struggled to raise his job approval ratings above 50 percent, polls have shown a clear majority of the public thinks the country is on the wrong track and events on the ground in Iraq and official inquiries in Washington have combined to raise widespread questions about the administration's rationale for war there, and widespread doubts about its conduct. All that is bad news for any incumbent, especially one who owed his ultimate victory to a single vote on the Supreme Court.

But since Sept. 11, 2001, Mr. Bush has remained buoyed by his consistently strong ratings on handling terrorism, and Mr. Kerry has never managed to open a clear, sustained lead in the horse race — even when polls showed viewers believed by lopsided margins that he had outperformed Mr. Bush in the first debate. That is bad news for any challenger, especially one in such an otherwise favorable environment.

Geoffrey Garin, a veteran Democratic pollster, said the debates were "incredibly important events" for Mr. Kerry. "I think while the debates exacerbated some of the questions people had about Bush, they were an opportunity for Kerry to address a lot of the doubts and questions people had about him," he said. "In that respect, the real general election began for him with the first debate."

Mr. Garin added: "The biggest challenge for Kerry is how voters ultimately work through their comfort level with making a change in leadership during the war on terror."

The race may yet break open either way. History suggests that incumbent presidents do not win or lose in squeakers, but decisively, as Mr. Bush's father did 12 years ago.

This President Bush's advisers make it clear that they are leaving nothing to chance. Four years ago, Mr. Bush's chief strategist expressed regret that he had given Mr. Bush a Sunday off from campaigning 10 days before an election in which he lost the popular vote. Yesterday, the White House communications director, Dan Bartlett, said that the president would campaign "just about" every day from now till Nov. 2, and added: "It'll feel like it, if it's not."

Study Question:

Did either candidate score a knockout punch in this third debate? Why or why not, according to this report?

Bush Leads. Make That Kerry. Why Can't the Pollsters Agree?

By JIM RUTENBERG
Published Tuesday, October 19, 2004

WASHINGTON — What is going to happen on Election Day? It depends on which pollster you ask.

President Bush leads Senator John Kerry by a margin of eight points among likely voters, according to the most recent poll from Gallup, USA Today and CNN. The margin of sampling error was four points.

But wait: Mr. Bush is up by only three points in the latest tracking poll from ABC News and The Washington Post, although with a margin of error of three percentage points.

Not so fast: The race is actually even, according to the latest *New York Times*/CBS News Poll. And Time magazine's new poll says much the same thing.

But while the headlines they produce may diverge, the actual findings of these polls may not be so different. The differing conclusions reflect how different pollsters use complex formulas to interpret very similar findings among self-described registered voters and try to come up with a result they think best accounts for who will actually show up at the polls.

The different interpretations have drawn a litany of complaints from partisans on both sides. Some are questioning everything about the surveys, including pollsters' political motives, their methodologies and whether accurate polling can be done in the age of cellular phones that cannot be called and caller ID systems that make screening out unfamiliar numbers easy.

But pollsters, who insist that they have the best intentions, say the differences in their surveys only highlight the difficulties this year in determining who is going to vote, no small task at a time of unusually high voter interest and many new voter registrations. And how pollsters set about figuring that out, they say, can make all of the difference in how the results are presented on television and in newspapers.

Five polls taken from Oct. 14 to Oct. 17 found similar results among registered voters. Mr. Kerry received support from 45 percent to 46 percent of those surveyed; Mr. Bush received from 45 percent to 49 percent. These polls, all with margins of error of plus or minus three or four points, showed the race as either tied among registered voters or with Mr. Bush ahead by two to three points — in each case a statistical tie.

But when Newsweek, for instance, looked not at registered voters but at "likely voters," Mr. Bush's lead grew to six points, from just two — still within the poll's margin of error, though a more impressive-sounding lead to the average voter.

Similarly, when the Gallup Organization applied its formula, Mr. Bush's three-point lead among registered voters grew to eight points among "likely voters." With a four-point margin of error on each candidate's result,

even this seemingly larger lead was at the edge of the poll's margin of error.

Pollsters say they have to look closely at likely voters because many registered voters do not show up come Election Day. In 2000, for instance, more than 30 percent of registered voters did not vote.

But pollsters acknowledge that the winnowing process calls for more art than science.

"Science is put in place and then the pollster has to exercise judgment about how to define likely voters," said Nancy Belden, president of the American Association for Public Opinion Research. "And every polling organization may define a likely voter slightly differently, or in some cases, more than slightly differently than the next polling organizations."

Ms. Belden added, "Each organization is doing its best to try to define the voters in the way that that organization thinks is closest to the truth."

Gallup, for instance, uses a mixture of questions to determine likely voting based on how seriously a respondent is planning to vote and how frequently he has voted in the past. It gauges this with seven questions, including one about whether the respondent knows where the local polling place is. After estimating what the actual turnout will be, Gallup includes the preferences of just that fraction of their respondents.

The New York Times and CBS, on the other hand, include responses from all those determined to be likely voters, but gives some of their votes more weight than others depending on how they fit on a scale rating their likelihood of voting.

Trying to divine likely voters is nothing new. And there are plenty of other factors that can affect the polls, from the way questions are asked to the dates of the poll.

Several pollsters said, for instance, that some polls seemed to give Mr. Bush a bigger edge because they were taken amid news reports about Mr. Kerry's referring in a debate to Vice President Dick Cheney's daughter's sexual orientation. The comment did not sit well with some people and was denounced by Mr. Cheney and his wife, Lynne.

But this year is presenting new, complicating factors, from the closeness of the race to the influx of new registered voters.

"There are many things about this election that may be different than past elections, and one is this phenomenon of how many people are possibly registered," Ms. Belden said. "That could make an enormous difference."

Hundreds of thousands of new voters have been added to the registration rolls in states like Florida, Pennsylvania and Ohio, by some estimates. Since many of these people have not been regular voters, polls that weigh the likelihood of voting in part based on past behavior may not be taking sufficient account of them.

The same goes for increased voting registrations among younger voters, many of whom seem excited about voting for the first time, according to pollsters. Pollsters have varying opinions about whether or not these people will show up at the polls just because they registered.

Pollsters say voters need to be cautious about putting too much stock in any single poll.

"We're basically trying to get a read on the electorate as of the day that we're polling," said Jeffrey M. Jones, managing editor of the Gallup Poll, "not necessarily trying to predict what's going to happen on Election Day itself."

Pollsters from both parties said the best thing to do was to take all of the public polls and average them together. By that count, it is Bush by a nose. For now.

Study Question:

What role do cellular phones play in the difficulty with polls?

Bush and Kerry Focus Campaigns on 11 Key States

By ADAM NAGOURNEY and KATHARINE Q. SEELYE   *Published Sunday, October 24, 2004*

FORT MYERS, Fla. — President Bush and Senator John Kerry move into the last days of the presidential contest in agreement that the race has come down to just 11 states, and have laid out plans for a barrage of visits and television advertisements across this final battleground between now and Nov. 2.

Mr. Bush and Mr. Kerry will spend virtually all their time — and most of their remaining advertising budgets — in those states, aides said, starting here in Florida, and extending as far west as Colorado and as far north as New Hampshire.

Both sides have reassigned staff out of states that once appeared competitive, like Missouri for the Democrats and Washington State for the Republicans, and scattered them across the 11 states.

Fittingly enough for this year, with polls showing the race deadlocked, five of the states were won by President Bush in 2000 and six by Al Gore, the Democratic candidate. And at least 7 of the 11 states are now considered tied in nightly polls being conducted by the campaigns, aides said.

"Where we are is where we ended in 2000: with a limited number of states that are very, very close," said Matthew Dowd, a senior adviser to Mr. Bush. "And the good news for us is more of those states are Gore states than Bush states."

Tad Devine, a senior Kerry adviser, disputed that assessment, arguing that Mr. Bush was struggling in two states that were the bedrock of his victory in 2000, Ohio and Florida. "We're in enough states to win a clear and convincing victory in the Electoral College," Mr. Devine said.

This geographical repositioning comes as Mr. Bush and Mr. Kerry have sharpened rather than blurred their differences as the race comes to a close, staking out vastly different positions on tax cuts, health care, Social Security, abortion rights and America's role in the world. In the process, the two candidates have offered one of the sharpest choices between two presidential campaigns in a generation.

Of the 11 states on this final battleground, representing 135 of the 538 electoral votes, Mr. Bush won Colorado, Florida, Nevada, New Hampshire and Ohio in 2000. Of those, analysts and aides to both campaigns say Mr. Kerry has the best chance of winning New Hampshire, Ohio and Florida, while Nevada appears least likely to turn Democratic.

The Gore states in play are Iowa, Michigan, Minnesota, New Mexico, Pennsylvania and Wisconsin. Of those, analysts and aides said Mr. Bush had the best chance of winning Wisconsin, Iowa and New Mexico.

A sudden surge by Mr. Bush in Michigan, a state that Mr. Kerry thought he had put away, caught both sides by surprise, and both men scheduled last-minute trips there for next week.

Ed Sarpolus, a pollster in Lansing, said that Mr. Kerry was paying a price for having campaigned in other parts of the country. "He hasn't been here," he said.

More than anything, Mr. Bush's aides say, his central focus over the final 10 days will be what they have always seen as his strongest suit: the fight against terrorism. Mr. Bush's advisers will attempt to command the agenda in the remaining days with an intense and grisly procession of television advertisements and attacks by Mr. Bush and Vice President Dick Cheney on the issue.

Mr. Bush returned to the theme of terrorism during a campaign stop here in Fort Myers on Saturday, roaring into a rally in a procession of machine-gun-toting helicopters escorting Marine One as it settled, in a swirl of wind, in the middle of a field. It was a display of the power of incumbency and a reminder of a dominant theme of Mr. Bush's campaign. On television stations here this week, it was all terrorism all the time: images of the smoldering World Trade Center and Republican claims that Mr. Kerry would be weak in the face of terrorist threats.

"We will basically be talking about who will win the war on terror, who will make America safer and who will lead the effort to reform our government," said Karl Rove, Mr. Bush's senior adviser.

The emphasis on terrorism is part of a calculated appeal to some female voters, who tend to be among the late deciders in a campaign, and among whom Mr. Kerry has had difficulty building the kind of support Democrats typically have.

The president plans to conclude his campaign with an advertisement in which Mr. Bush, recounting the trauma of the nation these past three years, makes a personal appeal to be returned to office.

Bob Shrum, a senior adviser to Mr. Kerry, said Mr. Bush had been "reduced to a one-note-Johnny" campaign. He said Mr. Kerry would respond by challenging Mr. Bush's management of the war in Iraq, but also promising what Mr. Kerry has called a "fresh start" for the country, with an emphasis on job creation and health care.

"John Kerry has a fundamental argument that we need a president who can defend the country and fight for the middle class," Mr. Shrum said. "Bush can only talk to one half of that equation."

In a reflection of the rapidly changing landscape, Mr. Kerry's campaign has reassigned campaign workers once stationed in Missouri and Arizona — two states that have slipped off the Democratic wish list — to Iowa, New Mexico and Nevada. Mr. Bush has moved his staff out of Washington State.

Of the 11 states, all but Nevada and Colorado were described by both sides as being effectively tied. Mr. Kerry's aides said they had a statistically significant lead in Ohio and New Hampshire as well, but Mr. Bush's advisers disputed that.

The dynamics of the endgame are varying state by state, though the fact that 39 states are now considered firmly behind Mr. Kerry or Mr. Bush has made the challenge faced by both campaigns at least somewhat less daunting.

In Ohio, for example, aides to both men said the outcome was likely to be driven by concerns about the economy and jobs. In Wisconsin, Mr. Kerry's campaign is attacking Mr. Bush on milk prices, while in Pennsylvania, Mr. Bush has emphasized his opposition to abortion and gay marriage in an attempt to undercut Mr. Kerry and appeal to the state's sizable Roman Catholic vote.

But in places like Florida — arguably the most competitive of the 11 — minds seem so made up that the outcome is almost surely going to be a function of turnout and voter registration. And for all the talk of speeches, issues and conflicting perceptions of these two men, the power of get-out-the-vote operations that both sides have spent two years putting together may well prove to be the most important factor.

"Pennsylvania remains a tight race with Kerry having a slight edge, but it's just down to turnout now," said Terry Madonna, a political scientist at Franklin and Marshall College.

Eric Rademacher, a political scientist at the University of Cincinnati, said, "Our most recent polls show a dead heat," and he added that for all of the advertising money, campaign appearances and attention poured into Ohio this year, "it will still come down to ground-force execution."

"I don't think there is anything the candidates can do at this point to try to change minds," Mr. Rademacher said. Even the arrival of Gov. Arnold Schwarzenegger of California in Ohio next week on behalf of Mr. Bush may have little effect, he said, because "we've passed the level of saturation."

Mr. Dowd argued that support for Mr. Bush among Republicans would counter what he acknowledged was intense animosity toward Mr. Bush among Democrats, a remnant of the disputed 2000 election.

"You should start seeing some movement next week because people are trying to make up their mind," Mr. Dowd said. "But a big part of this is who turns out. Are Democrats more motivated than Republicans on Election Day?"

Mr. Kerry's senior aides said that Democrats in states like Florida were showing motivation and interest in levels they had never seen. A procession of polls that show the race as deadlocked has fed that sense.

"People waking up in these battleground states and the media telling them that the race is neck-and-neck — that's the greatest motivator of all," said Michael Whouley, a longtime friend of Mr. Kerry and a seasoned operative who is working as a senior strategist at the Democratic National Committee.

The candidates began the campaign this spring looking at a much wider universe of swing states, from 18 to 21. The narrowing of states is typical late in a campaign, though it does not always happen. It would not be surprising if Mr. Bush or Mr. Kerry moved to other states in the last days should they see an opening.

The starting assumption of both campaigns is that whoever wins two of the top three — Florida, Pennsylvania and Ohio — will win the presidency.

Mr. Bush's aides noted that Mr. Kerry was now in a situation where more Gore states were at risk than Bush states, suggesting that might allow them to endure even a loss of those three states. In addition, they said they were skeptical that Mr. Kerry would continue being competitive in Nevada and Colorado, and that Mr. Kerry would come to regret a decision to fly across the country Saturday to Colorado.

That said, Mr. Bush is in a situation where he is still fighting in states that were critical to his victory in 2000, Ohio and Florida, and that have been critical to his re-election strategy. He returned to Ohio on Friday after a 19-day absence, during which Mr. Kerry appears to have made clear gains there.

Beyond that, even though Mr. Bush has visited Pennsylvania 41 times since he took office, some state polls still show Mr. Kerry with a slight lead there. And a brief flirtation with New Jersey, one of the more solidly Democratic states, has now been abandoned by the White House, Republicans said.

The campaigns' advertising dollars reflect this shrinking list. Both Mr. Kerry's and Mr. Bush's biggest advertising buys have been in Florida, where they have both saturated several markets.

In many ways, the contest has become a battle between character traits and issues, as Mr. Kerry tries to turn the campaign into a referendum on Mr. Bush's record and proposals for the future, while Mr. Bush relentlessly seeks to paint his opponent as intellectually inconsistent and too weak to protect Americans in a time of terrorism.

And so aides to both sides say the critical question is which candidate can determine what the debate in the final days is about — terrorism or the economy.

"The most important thing to watch is the struggle for control of the agenda," said Charles Black, a Republican consultant who advises the White House. "The president wants people to have their top priority to be terrorism and security. Kerry should want their priorities to be jobs and health care."

Study Question:

Why has the race for the presidency narrowed to so few states?

Bush Hits Back at Kerry Charge Over Explosives

By ELISABETH BUMILLER and JODI WILGOREN   *Published Thursday, October 28, 2004*

PONTIAC, Mich. — President Bush broke his silence on Wednesday on the disappearance of 380 tons of explosives in Iraq, accusing Senator John Kerry of making "wild charges" about the missing explosives and of "denigrating the actions" of troops in the field.

Mr. Kerry quickly responded that while "our troops are doing a heroic job, the president, the commander in chief, is not doing his job."

The president's comments, his first on the missing explosives since Mr. Kerry began accusing him on Monday of incompetence in failing to secure Iraq after the American-led invasion, reflected concern in the Bush campaign that the issue could be hurting the president only six days before what is expected to be an extraordinarily close election.

The missing explosives were first reported Monday by *The New York Times* and CBS News, and since then the issue and the possibility that American troops in Iraq let the explosives slip into terrorist hands have dominated the presidential campaign.

"Our military is now investigating a number of possible scenarios, including that the explosives may have been moved before our troops even arrived at the site," Mr. Bush told thousands of Republicans at an airport rally in Lancaster County, Pa., his first stop of a day that took him through three states.

"This investigation is important and it's ongoing," he said, "and a political candidate who jumps to conclusions without knowing the facts is not a person you want as your commander in chief."

The exact timing of the disappearance of the explosives is critical to the political arguments of each campaign. Mr. Kerry's contention that the administration did not adequately secure the country and was unprepared for the war's aftermath presumes that the explosives disappeared after the fall of Saddam Hussein on April 9, 2003, as officials of the interim Iraqi government say.

If the explosives disappeared before Mr. Hussein fell, as Mr. Bush now says is possible, that would undercut Mr. Kerry's argument and bolster Mr. Bush's contention that his opponent is making charges without all the facts.

White House officials say Condoleezza Rice, Mr. Bush's national security adviser, was told around Oct. 15 that the explosives had vanished. White House officials say she also informed the president.

Mr. Kerry, who has accused Mr. Bush of keeping Americans in the dark about the realities of Iraq, spent his day asserting that Mr. Bush had put American troops at enormous risk.

"Mr. President, you don't honor our troops or protect them better by putting them in greater danger than they ought to be," Mr. Kerry declared to 7,500 people packed in a basketball arena in Rochester, Minn. "The bottom line is your administration was warned, you were put on notice, but you didn't put these explosives on a priority list."

He added: "Mr. President, for the sake of our brave men and women in uniform, for the sake of those troops that are in danger because of your wrong decisions, you owe America real answers about what happened, not just political attacks."

But Mr. Bush, who had let his vice president and aides speak for him on the issue for two days, sharply criticized Mr. Kerry and did not let up at a single campaign stop. The president repeatedly said the senator would say "almost anything to get elected."

"Now, the senator is making wild charges about missing explosives," Mr. Bush said time and again in Pennsylvania, Ohio and Michigan.

He then seized on a remark by Richard C. Holbrooke, a Kerry adviser, who said in an appearance on Fox News on Tuesday that all of the facts about the explosives were not known.

"One of his top foreign policy advisors admits he doesn't know the facts," Mr. Bush said. "He said, 'I don't know the truth.' End quote. Well, think about that. The senator is denigrating the actions of our troops and commanders in the field without knowing the facts."

Mr. Bush also criticized Mr. Kerry as "throwing out the wild claim" that the American military passed up the chance to capture Osama bin Laden in the caves of Tora Bora, Afghanistan, in fall 2001.

"You might remember that — he kept repeating that in the debates," Mr. Bush said at the Hancock County Fairgrounds in Findlay, Ohio. "Well, this is unjustified criticism of our military commanders in the field. This is the kind of, worst kind of Monday-morning quarterbacking."

Mr. bin Laden dropped out of sight in December 2001 during the American-led assault on the Tora Bora region and is still believed to be somewhere along the Pakistani-Afghan border.

Mr. Bush asserted that Mr. Kerry had changed his views on Tora Bora with the political winds, and said that in the fall of 2001 the senator said that "I think we've been doing this pretty effectively, and we should continue to do it that way."

Mr. Kerry made the missing explosives his dominant message for the third day running, filling the first half of a 40-minute speech nominally about the economy with an expanding discourse on Iraq. He called the story "a growing scandal" and said the public deserved "a full and honest explanation of how it happened and what the president is going to do about it."

"What we're seeing is a White House that is dodging and bobbing and weaving in their usual efforts to avoid responsibility — just as they've done every step of the way in our involvement in Iraq," he said.

Mr. Kerry and his aides are seeking to use the missing explosives as

Exhibit A for their argument that Mr. Bush has shown "incompetence" as commander in chief and been unwilling to change course.

"Three hundred and eighty tons of explosives that could be in the hands of terrorists and he'd do everything exactly the same way?" he asked in a high school gym packed with perhaps 2,000 enthusiastic supporters in Sioux City.

"On Iraq, the president doesn't see it, he doesn't see it, so he can't fix it," Mr. Kerry said. "I do see it, and I will fix it."

But he softened the assertion he made the day before that the explosives had already been used in attacks against American troops, saying instead that they "could very likely be in the hands of terrorists and insurgents, who are actually attacking our forces now 80 times a day on average."

Mr. Kerry's campaign also released a new advertisement, which aides said would begin running Thursday on national cable stations. It shows images of American flags waving as a narrator intones: "As we see the deepening crisis and chaos in Iraq, as we choose a new commander in chief and a fresh start, we will always support and honor those who serve."

The last time that international inspectors saw the explosives was in early March 2003, days before the American-led invasion. It is possible, inspectors with the International Atomic Energy Agency say, that Saddam Hussein's forces may have tried to move the material out of the 10 huge bunkers at the Al Qaqaa facility where it was stored to save it if the facility was bombed.

If so, that would partly support Mr. Bush's contention that the Iraqis could have moved 380 tons of material very far without being detected.

But Mr. Bush on Thursday did not address a critical issue raised by the discovery of the missed explosives: why American forces were not alerted to the existence of a huge cache of explosives, even though the atomic energy agency and American officials had publicly discussed the threat it posed, and knew its exact location.

The commander of the troops that went into the Al Qaqaa facility on the way to Baghdad in early April, Col. Joseph Anderson, of the Second Brigade of the Army's 101st Airborne Division, has said he was never told the site was considered sensitive, or that international inspectors had visited it before the war began.

Study Question:

Why was the explosives issue so important?

Voters, Their Minds Made Up, Say bin Laden Changes Nothing

By KIRK JOHNSON　　　　　　　　　　　　　　*Published Sunday, October 31, 2004*

DENVER — If Osama bin Laden imagined, in releasing a threatening new videotape days before the presidential election, that he could sway the votes of Kerry supporters like David and Jan Hill and Bush supporters like Paul Christene, he has another thing coming.

"We're dug in," said Ms. Hill, an accountant in Denver who said she would vote for Senator John Kerry. "People I know are so polarized, it doesn't make any difference."

Her husband, a musician, added that having been subjected to a constant barrage of commercials from the candidates, and a flood of news reports about the election, the bin Laden tape was just another note in the cacophony. "I don't think people are really responding anymore," he said. "We're shellshocked."

Many supporters of President Bush seemed equally unfazed.

"It doesn't have anything to do with the election," said Mr. Christene, an aircraft supervisor from Walford, Iowa. "I will stick with Bush."

In dozens of interviews on Friday and Saturday in five hotly contested states, such steely sentiments were echoed again and again. Supporters of Mr. Bush said the bin Laden tape had strengthened their resolve to vote Republican by reminding them of the grave threats still faced by the country, while Mr. Kerry's supporters said the tape was yet another reminder that the Bush administration had failed to catch Mr. bin Laden. Even the undecided said the tape would not influence their decision.

Indeed, with passions raised to such a pitch by this election, and with many people already committed to their choices, Mr. bin Laden and his blustering postures may have achieved a strange and remarkable feat: making himself irrelevant, despite the analysis of some political operatives that his tape could affect the election, to Mr. Bush's benefit in particular.

Many people said that while Mr. bin Laden remained a potent symbol, the issues raised by the election were bigger than one man, and that Mr. bin Laden's words, at this point, would not make any difference in how things turned out on Tuesday.

The snapshot of opinion is hardly scientific and could reflect what some people thought was the proper answer. But it may alleviate concerns that voters could be driven toward the Bush camp by Mr. bin Laden's message — or to the Kerry camp by the fact that he is still free.

The voting decision, people said over and over, has already been made.

"It's more of the same, basically, about what you'd expect from this group," said Rex Reeve of Cedar Rapids, Iowa. He said the tape would not change his mind a bit: "I'll definitely be voting for Bush."

Some people, interviewed in bars and parks and downtown city streets, said they thought that in the secret cloister of the voting booth, there might be people — the undecided or the less firmly committed — who could be affected by the bin Laden message, or the candidates' response to the message. But it was hard to find anyone who thought that would happen to him or her. And for every person who concluded that Mr. bin Laden was trying to push people toward voting for Mr. Kerry, there was another who thought the intention was to help re-elect Mr. Bush.

Of the few undecided voters found by reporters roving through five cities, none said the tape had tipped the balance.

Veronica Gonzalez of St. Paul said that the tape certainly scared her, but that she did not know whether Mr. bin Laden's words might influence her vote.

"He's a bad person," she said. "It's very scary. I might vote for Bush, but I haven't decided."

Tyler Lisenbee, a property manager from Denver who was fishing with his 10-year-old daughter, Rachel, in a lake at a downtown park, said that he voted for Mr. Bush in 2000 but was leaning toward Mr. Kerry, mainly because of the war in Iraq. The bin Laden tape, he said, has not helped him make a choice.

"Bush has been in office all this time, and Osama is still running around," Mr. Lisenbee said. "I don't know if Kerry can do a better job, but maybe it's worth trying somebody new."

Mr. Lisenbee said he thought Mr. bin Laden would not affect the election at all, "unless if they catch him in the next few days — then I'd probably vote for Bush."

Some people said that how the bin Laden message filtered through the campaigns in the final days — in other words, what sort of spin was applied to it by politicians — would probably be more important than the message itself.

Cheryl Hecksler, a teacher and Kerry supporter in Las Vegas, said she had received a call from her mother in San Marcos, Calif., saying "something about bin Laden."

"I couldn't hear very well on the cellphone, and I thought he'd been captured," Ms. Hecksler said.

While she wanted Mr. bin Laden apprehended, she said she worried about what effect that might have had on Tuesday. "I was panicked," she said. "My first reaction was that Bush would win overwhelmingly.

"Then she told me about the tape, that bin Laden looked rested, like he'd been on a Caribbean vacation," Ms. Hecksler said. "Why is this coming out now?" Quite a few people said they had already voted. But none had any regrets in light of the videotape.

Brian Clark, a government worker who lives two hours south of Little Rock, Ark., said he had already voted for Mr. Bush. "That's just the party affiliation I vote for," he said. "I'm just conservative, and it's like, anybody but Kerry."

Other people said the main thing that puzzled them was not what Mr. bin Laden said, but when he said it.

"All I can say is, wow, it's perfect timing for him to come out of the woodwork," said McKinley Olds, 33, a warehouse worker in Cleveland. "It doesn't make any difference to me, I'm still voting for Kerry."

Another Kerry supporter in Ohio, Ruth Twaddell, 53, a mental health therapist in Chagrin Falls, said that she worried mainly about the fear that might play out in other voters' minds. She said the tape made no difference to her.

"This raises people's fears, and Bush preys upon their insecurities," said Ms. Twaddell. "I don't feel personally fearful, but I know there's plenty of people for whom it's in the forefront of their minds."

Other people debated Mr. bin Laden's intent. Some were convinced that he wanted four more years of Mr. Bush, others that he wanted Mr. Kerry to be elected.

"For people who are on the margin, it helps Bush, because it resurrects the fear that something might happen — and I think that was the obvious intention," said Jeff Sanders, a petroleum engineer in Denver who supports Mr. Kerry. "What bin Laden is afraid of is Kerry's ability to create an international coalition that would really deal with terrorism."

For both Bush and Kerry supporters, the undisputed fact was that Mr. bin Laden was still out there. The question, many people said, was what that fact meant to Americans.

On Friday evening on the Las Vegas Strip, Ron Blake paused and said he admired Mr. bin Laden's gall.

"They've spent all this time looking for the guy and here he pops up, none the worse for wear," said Mr. Blake, a construction worker from Crestline, Calif., who was visiting Las Vegas with his wife, Jennifer, and infant daughter, Stephanie. "After all was said and done, we didn't get him. He's very savvy. I don't think he should be underestimated. He's like a rattlesnake in a cage — be careful, he could strike."

Scott Nelson, a real estate broker from Salt Lake City, said Mr. bin Laden was "just trying to influence the election against Bush."

"He's very good at using free publicity via the media to get his point across," said Mr. Nelson, strolling on the Strip with his wife, Debbie. "He's got to do that to keep his work going. And by doing this, he also contacts his contributors in this country, his people."

Some people said that Mr. bin Laden, perhaps in keeping with his elusive nature as the most hunted man on the planet, had become a kind of cipher — a blank screen onto which people could project what they already believed about the candidates, the war against terrorism and the nation's future.

"People are so partisan and so biased — I think this is just going to reinforce what they already believe," said Frank Scardina, a pastor in Denver who said that he would vote for Mr. Bush.

Study Question:

Why did the Osama bin Laden tape not influence many voters?

Kerry Concedes Race, but 'Our Fight Goes On'

By JAMES BARRON   *Published November 3, 2004*

Ending one of the bitterest campaigns in American history, Senator John Kerry called on fellow Democrats today to remain committed to the ideals on which he campaigned.

"Our fight goes on to put America back to work and to make our economy a great engine of job growth," he told supporters in Boston, running through a host of issues that included affordable health care, the environment and equality.

And even as he called on his supporters to "bridge the partisan divide," he had a message for President Bush. "America is in need of unity and longing for a larger measure of compassion," he said. "I hope President Bush will advance those values in the coming years."

Mr. Kerry and his running mate, Senator John Edwards, made appearances at Boston's historic Faneuil Hall about two hours after Mr. Kerry telephoned Mr. Bush at the White House to say he had decided not to challenge the results in Ohio, where a slim margin and thousands of uncounted provisional ballots could have become to this election what Florida's butterfly ballots and hanging chads were to the election of 2000.

"He said, 'Congratulations, Mr. President,'" Mr. Kerry's press secretary, Stephanie Cutter said. She described the conversation as "courteous" and said that Mr. Kerry had told the president it was time to "unify this country." Mr. Bush's presidential press secretary, Scott McClellan, characterized the call as "gracious." Mr. Bush — who stayed up until 5 a.m., checking the returns and conferring with aides — is expected to deliver his victory speech shortly after 3 p.m.

Mr. Kerry, sounding hoarse after fiddling with the microphone as the crowd cheered, said his telephone conversation with the president had been conciliatory. "We talked about the danger of division in our country and the need, the desperate need, for unity, for finding the common ground, coming together," Mr. Kerry said. "Today, I hope that we can begin the healing."

But he also expressed disappointment after a long and rough campaign that featured mammoth get-out-the-vote efforts on both sides and ended with talk of a polarized nation. Referring to volunteers who took time off from their jobs or from school to work on his campaign, he said: "I wish, you don't know how much, that I could have brought this race home for you, for them. And I say to them now, don't lose faith. What you did made a difference."

Mr. Kerry's decision not to challenge the Ohio balloting headed off a potential rerun of 2000, when ballot disputes left the election in limbo for more than than a month, until the United States Supreme Court effectively declared George Bush the nation's 43rd president over Al Gore by halting further recounts in Florida.

Unlike 2000, Mr. Bush won the popular vote this time. With 98 percent of the national vote counted, Mr. Bush was leading Mr. Kerry by a margin of 51 percent to 48 percent. Over all, the president had a margin of victory of about 3.5 million votes, and was the first presidential candidate since his father, in 1988, to receive more than 50 percent of the popular vote.

Florida gave Mr. Bush solid support this time — he received 3,836,216 votes there, or 52 percent, to 3,459,293, or 47 percent — for Mr. Kerry. And the percentages from Ohio appeared to be similar. There, with 99 percent of the vote reported, Mr. Bush was ahead by a margin of 51 percent to 48.5 percent for Mr. Kerry; the president had an edge of about 130,000 votes.

Early today, after bitter court fights against Republican efforts to post election monitors in Ohio polling places — efforts the Democrats feared would intimidate minority voters and reduce turnout — Mr. Kerry's supporters homed in on the still-uncounted provisional ballots there. Ohio allows voters to cast such a ballot if election workers find some reason to question their eligibility.

Ohio officials said early today that they knew of 135,149 such ballots. But there could be more. Before Mr. Kerry conceded, a dozen counties had not totaled their provisional ballots. In past elections, about 10 percent of the provisional ballot total had come from those counties.

As strategists from both parties scrambled to review the fine points of Ohio's election laws, it became clear that not all provisional the ballots would represent legitimate votes.

Provisional ballots can be challenged and discarded for having been filed in the wrong precinct, for example, or because the voter does not meet residency or citizenship requirements. Those decisions are made by a bipartisan board of elections, and 2-to-2 ties mean a ballot is invalidated.

For Mr. Kerry to have claimed Ohio, nearly all the provisional ballots would have had to have been accepted, and he would have had to win nearly all of them. And Mr. Kerry and his supporters would have had to go through the kind of long-running ballot challenges that he said on Tuesday he hoped to avoid.

Still, many Kerry supporters pinned their hopes on making sure that every ballot that could be counted, was. And while Mr. Kerry did not go before his supporters in Boston on Tuesday night, his running mate, Senator John Edwards, did, telling a crowd that was bleary-eyed and disappointed at the way things seemed to be going, "We will fight for every vote."

The president's speechwriters had his valedictory ready, but he held off, not wanting to antagonize Democrats at a time when a second Bush administration was hoping to claim a mandate for its agenda. As the long wait turned into an all-nighter, some of the president's supporters dozed off in the sprawling Regan Building and International Trade Center in Washington that the campaign had rented.

While the morning after Election Day began in uncertainty, with high-ranking Republicans appearing on television to say Mr. Kerry could not win the presidency, the early afternoon ended the suspense. Marc Racicot, who is chairman of the Bush re-election campaign, said on the CBS News program "The Early Show," hours before Mr. Kerry conceded defeat, that there was only "a mathematical impossibility of changing the vote in Ohio."

"The truth of the matter is, the president won Ohio and won the election," he said.

The Senate majority leader, Bill Frist, agreed.

"The president, many people felt, should just have gone ahead" and declared victory, Mr. Frist said on the Fox News Channel. He said it was "graceful" of the president to give Mr. Kerry time to concede, but Mr. Frist made clear that he saw only one way to add up the numbers. "It is apparent to everybody that he is the victor in Ohio, he has the Electoral College won and he has the highest number of popular votes in the history of the country," Mr. Frist said. "He's re-elected president of the United States."

Barack Obama, who emerged as a rising star at the Democratic National Convention and who easily won a Senate seat from Illinois, said on CNN that it made sense for the Democrats to take time to decide whether to challenge the ballots in Ohio. On "Good Morning America" on ABC, he touched on something that may become an issue between now and 2008 — the Democrats' very identity.

"The Republicans have been successful in framing themselves as the defender of American traditions, religious traditions, family traditions," Mr. Obama said, adding, "I think the Democrats have to make sure that we don't cede the field."

Mr. Kerry ceded the election to Mr. Bush in what Mr. McClellan, the White House press secretary, said was a three- or four-minute conversation. Mr. Bush took Mr. Kerry's call at his desk in the Oval Office.

"I think you were an admirable, worthy opponent," Mr. Bush told Mr. Kerry. "You waged one tough campaign. I hope you are proud of the effort you put in — you should be."

Mr. Bush exchanged hugs with the others people in the room, including Karl Rove, his political strategist; Karen Hughes, his longtime communications adviser, and Dan Bartlett, the White House communications director. They were soon joined by Andrew H. Card Jr., the White House chief of staff; Blake Gottesman, Mr. Bush's personal assistant; and other members of the president's inner circle.

Mr. McClellan said that Mr. Bush then went down the hall toward Vice President Dick Cheney's office. The two men met just outside Mr. Cheney's office, and Mr. Bush passed along the news of Senator Kerry's call, Mr. McClellan said. Mr. Bush then went back to the official residence to speak to his wife. Not long after, the 58-year-old president, a fitness enthusiast, worked out.

This election is only the second that Mr. Kerry has ever lost — he was defeated in 1972 when he ran for Congress. Unlike Mr. Gore in 2000, Mr. Kerry has a job to go back to, now that he has lost the presidency. His current Senate term runs through 2008.

His concession, coming long after the last of the polls had closed, kindled comparisons to 1960, when Richard M. Nixon conceded to John F. Kennedy in midmorning, or 1916, when Woodrow Wilson went to bed believing he had lost, only to discover that 4,000 votes from California had given him the lead over Charles Evans Hughes.

Larry Sabato, the director of the University of Virginia's Center for Politics, said the victory had made Mr. Bush unique in American history. Mr. Bush is the only president who did not win a popular-vote plurality in his first term to win a second term: John Quincy Adams in 1824, Rutherford B. Hayes in 1876 and Benjamin Harrison in 1888 all lost their bids for re-election.

For his part, Mr. Kerry explained his thinking in deciding not to wait for a complete count in Ohio.

"In America," he said, "it is vital that every vote count and that every vote be counted, but the outcome should be decided by voters, not a protracted legal process. I would not give up this fight if there was a chance that we would prevail. But it is now clear that even when all the provisional ballots are counted, which they will be, there won't be enough outstanding votes for us to be able to win Ohio, and therefore we cannot win this election."

Study Question:

What, according to this article, is one way that Bush's victory makes him unique in American history?

Bush Voices Pride, Humility and Optimism

By ADAM NAGOURNEY

Published November 3, 2004

George W. Bush declared victory in the race for president Wednesday after a decisive national election that bolstered Republican strength in Congress and led the White House to proclaim that Mr. Bush had won a mandate from the American public for a second term.

Mr. Bush beamed as he stood with Vice President Dick Cheney at a rally in Washington four hours after accepting a concession call at the White House from Senator John Kerry, the Massachusetts Democrat who waged a fierce challenge to unseat him.

"We had a long night — and a great night," Mr. Bush said. "The voters turned out in record numbers and delivered an historic victory."

"America has spoken, and I'm humbled by the trust and the confidence of my fellow citizens," he said. "With that trust comes a duty to serve all Americans, and I will do my best to fulfill that duty every day as your president."

In calling the president, Mr. Kerry abandoned a threat to contest the election result in Ohio in deference to a decisive popular vote victory by a man who four years ago won the presidency with less than 50 percent of the popular vote.

"We cannot win this election," Mr. Kerry said somberly to supporters at Faneuil Hall in Boston.

The victory by Mr. Bush amounted to a striking turn in fortunes for the nation's 43rd president, who had at times this year seemed destined to repeat his father's fate of losing a second term because of a weak economy. Instead, he won more popular votes than any previous president — 58.6 million, or 3.5 million more than Mr. Kerry, though in a nation with an expanding population of voters — and positioned himself and his party to push through a conservative agenda in Washington over the next four years.

Mr. Bush became the first Republican president since Calvin Coolidge to win re-election while gaining seats in the House and in the Senate. The Republicans picked up at least two seats in the House and four in the Senate. While not enough to provide Mr. Bush a veto-proof Congress, the party's surge did result in the defeat of Senator Tom Daschle of South Dakota, the minority leader and one of the most familiar Democratic faces in Washington.

Republican leaders were promising to renew efforts to pass bills that Democrats had blocked, like one permitting drilling in the Arctic National Wildlife Refuge and another placing caps on awards in liability lawsuits.

Mr. Bush spoke only in broad terms of what he might do in a second term. But he strongly signaled that he was looking to stabilize the governments of Afghanistan and Iraq to allow American soldiers to return home.

"We will help the emerging democracies of Iraq and Afghanistan so they can grow in strength and defend their freedom, and then our servicemen and women will come home with the honor they have earned," he said. Mr. Bush's victory appeared to clear the way for a reshuffling of his Cabinet, with John Ashcroft, the attorney general, and Tom Ridge, the homeland security secretary, most likely to leave, according to administration officials.

Mr. Cheney, in introducing the president at the rally at the Ronald Reagan Building and International Trade Center less than a half-mile from the White House, left little doubt about how this White House saw the election, and what it intended to do with it. He said the president had run "forthrightly on a clear agenda for this nation's future, and the nation responded by giving him a mandate."

Mr. Bush's victory was powered in no small part by a huge turnout among evangelical Christians, who may seek a bigger voice in critical White House decisions over the next four years — in particular, Supreme Court nominations that are likely to consume parts of Mr. Bush's second term.

Mr. Bush, as he did when he won four years ago, made a point in his victory speech of reaching out to Democrats, saying he wanted to unify a country that had been divided not only by the contest with Mr. Kerry, but by the circumstances of Mr. Bush's victory four years ago.

"I want to speak to every person who voted for my opponent," he said. "To make this nation stronger and better, I will need your support and I will work to earn it. I will do all I can do to deserve your trust. A new term is a new opportunity to reach out to the whole nation. We have one country, one Constitution, and one future that binds us."

Mr. Kerry struck a similar tone in his concession speech in Boston —

which at 16 minutes, lasted six minutes longer than Mr. Bush's — though it reprised, if indirectly, some of the criticisms he made of Mr. Bush during the campaign.

"America is in need of unity and longing for a larger measure of compassion," Mr. Kerry said. "I hope President Bush will advance those values in the coming years. I pledge to do my part to try to bridge the partisan divide."

"I know this is a difficult time for my supporters, but I ask you — all of you — to join me in doing this," said Mr. Kerry, whose voice cracked at times in an uncharacteristic display of public emotion.

That said, by any measure, the Bush victory rocked the political landscape in Washington. Aides to both parties said they were doubtful — given the history of the past four years — that the capital was headed for a period of political calm, no matter what the president and Mr. Kerry said in the aftermath of their bitter competition.

"I don't think a 51-49 election is any mandate," Terry McAuliffe, the Democratic National Committee chairman, said in an interview. "George Bush won, and I congratulate him on that. They ran a very effective campaign and he won. They need to be very careful that they now need to govern from the middle in a bipartisan way. This country as we saw in the election is very evenly split."

For much of Tuesday and into Wednesday, it seemed as if the election of 2004 was turning into a reprise of the election of 2000, with a series of tight races and some confusion in counting combining to create a night of tumult and uncertainty. At 2:30 Wednesday morning, Mr. Kerry's running mate, Senator John Edwards of North Carolina, went to the stage in Boston where Mr. Kerry had hoped to declare victory to say that the Kerry campaign was contesting the result in Ohio, and would not concede until all the outstanding votes there were counted.

Mr. Bush nearly appeared at 4 a.m. Wednesday to declare victory in the face of the Kerry campaign threat.

But the situation in Ohio was nowhere near as disputed as it was in Florida four years ago, and Mr. Bush's advisers decided to instead hold off in the hopes that Mr. Kerry would, upon awakening, decide the cause was hopeless and concede.

The 2004 election turned out to be different in another way as well. For all the fears of Democrats this year, Ralph Nader, the independent candidate, drew so few votes that he had no impact on the outcome in any state.

If Republicans were ecstatic at having won a clean victory without the baggage of 2000, Democrats were bereft at what several described as a rout, and there were immediate signs that the party was facing a dark period of intramural battles.

Several Democrats questioned Mr. Kerry's decision to concede without pressing for a full count of the votes in Ohio, warning that it would discourage first-time voters, particularly minorities, in future elections. "I understand the need to put it behind him, given the math," said Donna Brazile, who managed Al Gore's 2000 campaign for president. "But he has an obligation to allow all these votes to be counted."

Tellingly, associates to Mr. Edwards made a point of informing reporters that Mr. Edwards had urged Mr. Kerry not to give up in Ohio so soon, in what some Democrats described as probably the opening shot of — yes — the 2008 campaign. Mr. Edwards is likely to seek his party's nomination and thus is eager not to do anything in the final days of this campaign that could haunt him in 2008.

"He conveyed his point of view and Kerry made his own decision," one Edwards adviser said, adding that Mr. Edwards "was disappointed but made peace with the result."

Democrats resigned themselves to having even less influence in the Senate and the House. In the Senate, Harry Reid of Nevada was moving to take over the minority leadership post being vacated by Mr. Daschle. With the four-seat gain, Republicans will have 55 senators, still short of a 60-vote filibuster-proof margin. But Republicans said they hoped that Democrats would see Mr. Daschle's defeat as a cautionary lesson that would prevent them from trying to use legislative techniques to entangle Republican initiatives.

Mr. McAuliffe and other Democrats tried to put the best face on the defeat, saying that Mr. Kerry was facing a difficult task in trying to unseat a sitting president during wartime. He argued that Mr. Bush was helped by the emergence last weekend of a videotape featuring Osama bin Laden addressing Americans, which reminded voters of the issue — fear of terrorism — that had always been central to Mr. Bush's campaign.

"You've got to remember that he went in with a tough deck of cards," Mr. McAuliffe said of Mr. Kerry.

Still, Democrats seemed as startled as Republicans were delighted by the unlikelihood of the victory. Mr. Bush prevailed despite the legacy of one of the most disputed elections in the nation's history. He overcame polls showing that voters disapproved of his job performance and the direction in which the country was heading, two measures that typically augur defeat for an incumbent.

Mr. Bush not only won Florida, but he won it by a comfortable margin. He also won the other of the two most contested states, Ohio. He also won both states in 2000. Mr. Kerry grabbed New Hampshire from the Republican column, while Mr. Bush yanked New Mexico away from the Democrats.

Mr. Bush was ahead in another state Mr. Gore barely won last time — Iowa — though officials there were recounting the vote.

Mr. Kerry, in his appearance in Boston, sought to erase any doubt about the vote in Ohio, and made clear that he did not want a protracted repeat of the 2000 battle that tore the country. "In America, it is vital that every vote count and every vote be counted," he said. "But the outcome should be decided by voters — not a protracted legal process."

As his audience listened in near-silence, Mr. Kerry, who had built a campaign around the Bruce Springsteen song "No Surrender" and promised to fight Republicans in a way Democrats never had before, said he had no reservations about abandoning this one, and returning to his post in the United States Senate.

"I would not give up this fight if there was a chance that we would prevail," he said.

Study Question:

President Bush was the first Republican president since Calvin Coolidge to do what while also winning reelection?

READER DISCUSSION QUESTIONS

1. How do you think the events of the primaries influenced the outcome of the election?

2. Is there any one circumstance you read about here that you can point to as important in understanding why Bush won the election?

3. What were the themes of the Bush and Kerry campaigns?

4. In what ways were the debates important in this election?

5. How would you characterize President Bush and Senator Kerry as candidates?